Travel Disco

C000076937

This coupon entitles y
when you book yo

TRAVEL NETWORK
RESERVATION SERVICE

Hotels ♦ Airlines ♦ Car Rentals ♦ Cruises
All Your Travel Needs

Here's what you get: *

♦ A discount of $50 USD on a booking of $1,000** or more for two or more people!

♦ A discount of $25 USD on a booking of $500** or more for one person!

♦ Free membership for three years, and 1,000 free miles on enrollment in the unique Travel Network Miles-to-Go® frequent-traveler program. Earn one mile for every dollar spent through the program. Redeem miles for free hotel stays starting at 5,000 miles. Earn free roundtrip airline tickets starting at 25,000 miles.

♦ Personal help in planning your own, customized trip.

♦ Fast, confirmed reservations at any property recommended in this guide, subject to availability.***

♦ Special discounts on bookings in the U.S. and around the world.

♦ Low-cost visa and passport service.

♦ Reduced-rate cruise packages and special car rental programs worldwide.

Visit our website at http://www.travelnetwork.com/Frommer or call us globally at 201-567-8500, ext. 55. In the U.S., call toll-free at 1-888-940-5000, or fax 201-567-1838. In Canada, call at 1-905-707-7222, or fax 905-707-8108. In Asia, call 60-3-7191044, or fax 60-3-7185415.

---

* To qualify for these travel discounts, at least a portion of your trip must include destinations covered in this guide. No more than one coupon discount may be used in any 12-month period, for destinations covered in this guide. Cannot be combined with any other discount or promotion.
**These are U.S. dollars spent on commissionable bookings.
***A $10 USD fee, plus fax and/or phone charges, will be added to the cost of bookings at each hotel not linked to the reservation service. Customers must approve these fees in advance. If only hotels of this kind are booked, the traveler(s) must also purchase roundtrip air tickets from Travel Network for the trip.

Valid until December 31, 1998. Terms and conditions of the Miles-to-Go® program are available on request by calling 201-567-8500, ext 55.

CAL234

"Amazingly easy to use. Very portable, very complete."

—Booklist

♦

"The only mainstream guide to list specific prices. The Walter Cronkite of guidebooks—with all that implies."

—Travel & Leisure

♦

"Complete, concise, and filled with useful information."

—New York Daily News

♦

"Hotel information is close to encyclopedic."

—Des Moines Sunday Register

Frommer's® 98

California

**by Erika Lenkert, Matthew R. Poole,
Stephanie Avnet & Elizabeth Hansen**

Macmillan • USA

ABOUT THE AUTHORS

Combining the only three things he's good at—eating, sleeping, and criticizing—**Matthew R. Poole** has found a surprisingly prosperous career as a freelance travel writer. A native Northern Californian and author of nearly a dozen travel guides to California and Hawaii—including *Frommer's San Francisco*, with Erika Lenkert—he's looking forward to retiring at 30 but fears he won't be able to tell the difference. He currently lives in San Francisco and has no intention of writing a novel.

A native San Franciscan, **Erika Lenkert** spends half her time traipsing around San Francisco and Northern California in search of adventure, and the other half in Los Angeles, where she intends to become rich and famous. When she's not on the road, she spends her time working off all the decadent meals she reviews in her travels, harassing Matthew, and being subservient to her owners: two Siamese cats. Erika has contributed to dozens of guides to California and is pleased that she actually gets paid to force her opinions onto others—something she'd done pro bono for years.

A native of Los Angeles and an avid traveler, antique hound, and pop history enthusiast, **Stephanie Avnet** believes that California is best seen from behind the wheel of a red convertible. Stephanie also writes *Frommer's Los Angeles,* and her brand-new getaway guide, *Wonderful Weekends from Los Angeles* (Macmillan Travel), will hit bookshelves in mid-1998.

Longtime La Jolla resident **Elizabeth Hansen** has authored *Frommer's San Diego* as well as multiple Frommer's guides to Australia and New Zealand.

MACMILLAN TRAVEL

A Simon & Schuster Macmillan Company
1633 Broadway
New York, NY 10019

Find us online at **www.frommers.com** or on America Online at Keyword: **Frommers**.

ISBN 0-02-861778-9
ISSN 1044-2146

Editor: Cheryl Farr *with thanks to Margot Weiss and Lisa Renaud*
Production Editor: Mark Enochs
Design: Michele Laseau
Digital Cartography: Roberta Stockwell and Ortelius Design

SPECIAL SALES

Bulk purchases (10+ copies) of Frommer's and selected Macmillan travel guides are available to corporations, organizations, mail-order catalogs, institutions, and charities at special discounts, and can be customized to suit individual needs. For more information write to Special Sales, Macmillan General Reference, 1633 Broadway, New York, NY 10019.

Manufactured in the United States of America

Contents

**Appendix: Useful Toll-Free Numbers &
Websites   659**

Index   664

List of Maps

AN INVITATION TO THE READER

In researching this book, we discovered many wonderful places—hotels, restaurants, shops, and more. We're sure you'll find others. Please tell us about them, so we can share the information with your fellow travelers in upcoming editions. If you were disappointed with a recommendation, we'd love to know that, too. Please write to:

Frommer's California '98
Macmillan Travel
1633 Broadway
New York, NY 10019

AN ADDITIONAL NOTE

Please be advised that travel information is subject to change at any time—and this is especially true of prices. We therefore suggest that you write or call ahead for confirmation when making your travel plans. The authors, editors, and publisher cannot be held responsible for the experiences of readers while traveling. Your safety is important to us, however, so we encourage you to stay alert and be aware of your surroundings. Keep a close eye on cameras, purses, and wallets, all favorite targets of thieves and pickpockets.

WHAT THE SYMBOLS MEAN

✪ Frommer's Favorites

Our favorite places and experiences—outstanding for quality, value, or both.

The following abbreviations are used for credit cards:

AE	American Express	EU	Eurocard
CB	Carte Blanche	JCB	Japan Credit Bank
DC	Diners Club	MC	MasterCard
DISC	Discover	V	Visa

FIND FROMMER'S ONLINE

Arthur Frommer's Outspoken Encyclopedia of Travel (**www.frommers.com**) offers more than 6,000 pages of up-to-the-minute travel information—including the latest bargains and candid, personal articles updated daily by Arthur Frommer himself. No other website offers such comprehensive and timely coverage of the world of travel.

Area Code Changes Notice

Please note that three major area-code changes are scheduled to take place in California:

- Effective June 13, 1998, portions of Monterey, Santa Cruz, San Luis Obispo, and Merced counties are in the new **831** area code. Communities affected will include Santa Cruz, Carmel, Monterey, Big Sur, and small portions of San Luis Obispo.
- Effective June 13, 1998, the region of Los Angeles serviced by area code 213 is scheduled to be split, with all portions *excluding the downtown business district* changing to **323.**
- Effective April 18, 1998, the southern portion of Orange County is scheduled to change to the **949** area code. Communities affected will include Newport Beach, Balboa, Laguna Beach, Laguna Niguel, San Juan Capistrano, Dana Point, and part of Costa Mesa.

These changes have also been noted throughout the text where appropriate.

The Best of California

by Erika Lenkert, Matthew R. Poole,
Stephanie Avnet, and Elizabeth Hansen

In my early twenties, I took the requisite college student's pilgrimage to Europe, exploring its finer train stations and sleeping on the premier park benches from London to Istanbul. I was relatively anonymous—just another tanned and skinny, blond and blue-eyed American lugging around 60 pounds of backpack. That is, until I crossed over into the former Eastern Bloc.

The reaction was dramatic, almost palpable. Like Moses parting the sea, I would wander through the crowded streets of Prague and citizens would stop, stare, and sidestep as if a scarlet "A" were emblazoned across my chest. It wasn't until a man who spoke faltering English finally approached me that I discovered the reason for my newfound celebrity status.

"Eh, you. Where you from? No, no. Let me guess." He steps back, gives a cursory examination followed by pregnant pause. "Ah. I've got it! California! You're from California, no?" A gleam in his eyes as I tell him that, yes, he's quite correct. "Wonderful! Wonderful!" A dozen or so pilsners later with my loquacious new friend and it all becomes clear to me: To him, I truly am a celebrity—a rich, convertible-driving surfer who spends most of his days lazing on the beach, fending off hordes of buxom blondes while I argue with my agent via my portable phone. The myth is complete. I *am* the Beach Boys. I *am* Baywatch. Status by association. The tentacles of Hollywood have done what no NATO pact could achieve—they've leap-frogged the staid issues of capitalism vs. communism by offering a far more potent narcotic: the alluring mystique of sun-drenched California, of movie stars strolling down Sunset Boulevard, of beautiful women in tight shorts and bikini tops roller-skating along Venice Beach. In short, they've bought what we're selling.

Of course, the allure is understandable. It really is warm and sunny most days of the year, movie stars actually do abound in Los Angeles, and you can't swing a cat by its tail without hitting a rollerblading babe in Venice Beach. This part of the California mystique—however exaggerated it may be—truly does exist, and it's not hard to find.

But there's more—a lot more—to California that isn't scripted, sanitized, and squeezed through a cathode ray tube to the world's millions of mesmerized masses. Beyond the glitter and glamour of Hollywood is an incredibly diverse state that, if it ever seceded from the Union, would be one of the most productive and powerful nations in the world. We've got it all: misty redwood forests, an incredibly verdant central valley teeming with agriculture, the mighty Sierra Nevada mountain range, eerily fascinating deserts, a host of world-renowned cities and, of course, hundreds of miles of stunning coastline.

And despite the endemic crime, pollution, traffic, and bowel-shaking earthquakes that California is famous for, we're still the Golden Child of the United States, America's spoiled rich kid whom everyone else either loves or loathes (neighboring Oregon, for example, sells lots of license plate rims that proudly state, "I hate California"). But, truth be told, we really don't care what anyone thinks of us. Californians *know* that they live in one of the most diverse and interesting places in the world, and we're proud of the state we call home.

Granted, there's no guarantee that you'll bump into Arnold Schwarzenegger or learn how to surf, but if you have a little time, a little money, and—most important—an adventurous spirit, then Erika, Stephanie, Elizabeth, and I will help guide you through one of the most fulfilling vacations of your life. The four of us travel the world for a living, but we *choose* to live in California, simply because there's no other place on earth that has so much to offer.

—*Matthew R. Poole*

1 The Best of Natural California

- **Point Reyes National Seashore:** This extraordinarily scenic stretch of coast and wetlands is one of the best bird-watching spots in California for shore birds, songbirds, and waterfowl, as well as osprey and red-shouldered hawks. There's a rainbow-hued wildflower garden, too, and you might catch a glimpse of a whale from the Point Reyes Lighthouse. See chapter 7.
- **Sonoma Coast State Beaches:** Stretching about 10 miles from Bodega Bay to Jenner, these beaches attract more than 300 species of birds. From December to September, look for osprey. Seal pups can be spotted from March to June, and the gray whale from December to April. See chapter 7.
- **Redwood National & State Parks:** A wildlife enthusiast's dream. More than 300 bird species and 100 mammals can be seen, many of them year-round. Also watch (or watch out!) for black bears in summer. See chapter 7.
- **Yosemite National Park:** You're in for the ultimate treat at Yosemite. Nothing in the state—maybe even the world—compares to this vast wilderness playground and its miles of rivers, lakes, peaks, and valleys. With 3 out of 10 of the world's tallest waterfalls, the largest single granite monolith in the world, and some of the world's largest trees, Yosemite is one of the most fantastic natural places on the planet. You'll have a sweeping 180° view of it all from high atop Glacier Point, where a majestic High Sierras panorama unfolds at 3,200 feet. See chapter 9.
- **Año Nuevo State Reserve:** Nature enthusiasts come from all over the world to this spot 22 miles north of Santa Cruz to view the elephant seal colony. Pups are born from December through March, and molting follows between April and August. You can also spot sea lions in spring and summer, whales in winter and spring, plus more than 250 bird species. See chapter 11.
- **Point Lobos State Reserve:** Take Calif. 1 about 4 miles south of Carmel to view harbor seals, sea lions, and sea otters at play. Gray whales pass by on their migration south from December to May. The area is filled with nature walks. See chapter 11.
- **The Big Sur Coast:** Rock-strewn beaches, towering cliffs, and redwood forests combine to form what may be the world's most dramatic coastal panorama.

It's Not Easy Being Green

What is it that makes California one of the most popular destinations in the world? The food? The wine? The bathing-suit weather? Well, those may add to the ambiance, but the true draw is the state's border-to-border treasure trove of natural beauty: the mountains, the shores, and everything in between.

But imagine what would happen if everything changed: fast food restaurants and condos crowded the cliffs along Big Sur, or a small city of high-rise hotels sprung up in the heart of Yosemite Valley. Where would this beloved state be then? While everyone cringes at the thought, capitalism is ever-encroaching on California's natural environments—where there are plenty of locals and tourists, there's plenty of money to be made. If you take the time to talk to residents, you'll find that these days, the hot topic in town is yet another environmental debate.

When we last visited Big Sur, for example, we sat in Deetjen's Big Sur Inn restaurant over breakfast and listened to the locals complain and plan interference: Apparently, a resident wanted to clear the redwoods from part of his land to sell to a logging company. You might think that sounds fair. It's his land, right? Maybe so, but if he clears his land, it ruins *everyone's* view; instead of a redwood forest, you and everyone else will get an eyeful of stumps. And then maybe his neighbor will decide that he wants some logging money, too. Get ready for more stumps. That's not the Big Sur we want to visit, and that's not the Big Sur that most residents migrated to. Even though the state owns and protects plenty of acres in the area, private land still makes up a portion of Big Sur's majestic landscape, and environmental locals feel collectively responsible for protecting it.

A few hours south, we arrived at the Central Coast town of Cambria, where a similar debate is going on. As the story goes, a very large piece of prime property was sold a few years back. Residents—who have roamed the property for years and consider it a very spiritual place—were concerned, but were quickly assured by new owners that development plans were modest. Soon afterward, rumor got out that there was talk of building a group of 300-plus homes on the property—a move that would render this charming small town unrecognizable. Protests ensued and more vocal residents have been banned from "walking the ranch" altogether. The debate is ongoing.

One of the most immediate and tragic threats to natural California is, unfortunately, not a debatable topic. The entire population of Monterey pine trees has been threatened by a deadly virus called pitch canker disease; it's been estimated that as much as 85% of the native stands could die within the next 10 years. While experts are working feverishly to find a cure, certified arborist Stephen Morton, a forestry crew lead worker for the city of Monterey, told us that the outlook doesn't look good. He compared the virus to AIDS; it weakens trees enough to allow other threats (like the abundant IPS beetle) to eventually kill the tree. The hope is that some trees will develop an adaptability to hosting the virus and eventually spawn a new generation of resistant trees. But currently, that's nothing but wishful thinking.

With people continually flocking west to become Californians, the state is ever-expanding, and the threats to natural California multiply. Preserving the state's unparalleled landscape will continue to be an important and complex issue for Californians—and it will be an ongoing struggle to find the perfect balance between expansion and preservation.

—*Erika Lenkert and Matthew R. Poole*

Our favorite vantage for taking it all in is Garrapata State Park, a 2,879-acre preserve that lords over 4 spectacular miles of coastline. See chapter 11.

- **Cachuma Lake:** Situated on mountainous and scenic Calif. 154, halfway between Solvang and Santa Barbara, is this stunning winter home to dozens of American bald eagles. Loons, white pelicans, and Canada geese are some of the other migratory birds that call this glassy lake home part of the year. See chapter 12.

- **Channel Islands National Park:** This is California in its most natural state. Paddle a kayak into sea caves; camp among indigenous island fox and seabirds; and swim, snorkel, or scuba dive tidepools and kelp forests teeming with wildlife. The channel waters are prime for whale watching, and May brings elephant seal mating season, when you'll see them and their sea lion cousins sunbathing on cove beaches. See chapter 12.

- **Antelope Valley Poppy Reserve:** California's state flower, the poppy, blooms between March and May, carpeting the hillsides in brilliant hues of red, orange, and gold. This reserve, in the high desert near Los Angeles, is one of the poppy's most consistent natural growing sites. The fields extend for miles around—it's not uncommon to see motorists along Calif. 14 pull to the side of the road to marvel at the breathtaking spectacle. From L.A., take I-5 north to Calif. 14; you'll know when you've arrived. For information on the annual California Poppy Festival in Lancaster, call ☎ **805/723-6077.**

- **Joshua Tree National Park:** You'll find awesome rock formations, groves of flowering cacti and stately Joshua trees, ancient Native American petroglyphs, and shifting sand dunes in this desert wonderland—and a brilliant night sky, if you choose to camp here. See chapter 15.

- **Death Valley National Park:** Its inhospitable climate makes it the state's most unlikely tourist attraction. But the same conditions that thwarted settlers create some of the most dramatic landscapes you'll ever see. Mesmerizing rock formations, ever-changing dry lake beds, and often stifling heat provide the setting for relics of hardy 19th-century borax miners and (fool) hardy dwellers from the 1930s. See chapter 15.

- **Torrey Pines State Reserve:** Poised on a majestic cliff overlooking the Pacific Ocean, this reserve is home to the rare torrey pine. Exhibits on the local ecology are housed in the visitor center, and numerous hiking trails fan out throughout the park. See chapter 16.

- **Anza-Borrego Desert State Park:** The largest state park in the lower 48 states attracts the most visitors during the spring wildflower season, when a kaleidoscopic carpet blankets the desert floor. Others come year-round to hike the more than 100 miles of designated trails. See chapter 16.

2 The Best Beaches

- **San Francisco's Ocean Beach:** At the end of Golden Gate Park, on the westernmost side of the city, Ocean Beach is gorgeous, but recommended for strolling and sunning only. Just offshore, the jagged Seal Rocks are inhabited by colonies of sea lions, among other creatures. See chapter 4.

- **Stinson Beach:** Mount Tamalpais sweeps down to the sea at a point 6 treacherous miles north of Muir Beach on Calif. 1. Chilly waters and the threat of Jaws don't keep away thousands of sun worshipers and surfers. See chapter 5.

- **Drake's Beach:** A massive stretch of white sand at Point Reyes National Seashore, west of Inverness. Winds and choppy seas make it rough for swimmers, but sun worshipers can have their Marin County tan for the day. If the rangers say it's all right, beach driftwood can make a romantic campfire in the early evening. See chapter 7.

- **Manchester State Beach:** Take Calif. 1 8 miles north of Point Arena for a breezy introduction to the beaches of the far north. There are 5 miles of sand for beachcombing and surf fishing, and huge driftwood logs along the beach. See chapter 7.

- **Sand Dollar Beach:** The best Big Sur beach lies beyond Pacific Valley—ideal for swimming and surfing, with a panoramic view of Cone Peak, one of the coast's highest mountains. See chapter 11.

- **Santa Barbara's Cabrillo Beach:** This wide swath of clean white sand hosts beach umbrellas, sand-castle builders, and spirited volleyball games. A grassy, parklike median keeps the happy beachgoers insulated from busy Cabrillo Boulevard. On Sundays, local artists display their wares beneath the elegant palm trees. See chapter 12.

- **Malibu's Legendary Beaches:** Zuma and Surfrider Beaches are the stretches of sand that were the inspiration for the 1960s surf music that embodies the Southern California beach experience. Surfrider, just up from Malibu Pier, is home to L.A.'s best waves. Zuma is loaded with amenities, including snack bars, rest rooms, and jungle gyms. In addition to some of the state's best sunbathing, you can walk in front of the Malibu Colony, a star-studded enclave of multimillion-dollar homes set in this seductively curvaceous stretch of coast. See chapter 13.

- **Hermosa City Beach:** This is one of L.A.'s top beaches for family outings. It's also popular with the volleyball set. It offers wide sands, a paved boardwalk ("The Strand") that's great for strolling and biking, and loads of amenities—including plenty of parking. See chapter 13.

- **La Jolla's Beaches:** Roughly translated, *La Jolla* means "the jewel," and the beaches of La Jolla's cliff-lined coast truly are gems. Each has a distinct personality: Surfers love Windansea's waves; Torrey Pines and La Jolla Shores are popular for swimming and sunbathing; and Black's Beach is San Diego's unofficial (and illegal) nude beach. See chapter 16.

- **Coronado Beach:** On the west side of Coronado extending to the Hotel del Coronado, this beautiful beach is uncrowded and great for watching the sunset. Marilyn Monroe romped in the surf here during the filming of *Some Like It Hot*. See chapter 16.

3 The Best Walks

- **Golden Gate Park:** Strolling this magnificent park lets you escape the bustle of San Francisco and takes you past an array of attractions, beginning with the 1878 Conservatory of Flowers, but also including museums and a Japanese Tea Garden, and even a 430-foot-high man-made island, Strawberry Hill. End your walk by renting a rowboat and taking it for a spin. See chapter 4.

- **Point Reyes National Seashore:** In Marin County, west of Inverness and a quarter-mile north of Drake's Beach, Point Reyes Lighthouse, 6 miles to the west, will be your final goal. The scenery is among the most beautiful and enticing in the Golden State—especially the hike to Chimney Rock (follow the signs on your way to the lighthouse). See chapter 7.

- **Mendocino Headlands State Park:** Between Mendocino and the Pacific is one of the most scenic nature trails in the north. From December through March, the California gray whales pass by on their migration from the Arctic Ocean and Bering Sea to Baja California. Sunset vistas are worth the detour. See chapter 7.

- **Yosemite National Park:** Relatively short and easy hikes will take you to Yosemite Falls, the highest waterfall in North America and the fifth highest in the world (upper falls at 1,430 feet), or to Bridalveil Falls, a ragged 620-foot cascade that can be wind-tossed as much as 20 feet from side to side. A third option is the more strenuous 3¹/₂-mile Yosemite Falls Trail, which rises to a height of 2,700 feet for one of the most panoramic vistas in the West. See chapter 9.

- **The Beachfront Trails at Big Sur:** Take towering cliffs, rock-strewn beaches, and a backdrop of redwood forests, and you have one of the most dramatic stretches for coastline hiking in the world. Begin your adventure about 8 miles south of Point Lobos. See chapter 11.

- **Cabrillo Peak in Morro Bay State Park:** This park offers a terrific day hike that culminates with a fantastic 360° view of surrounding hills and the distant ocean. There are hiking trails, but the best way to reach the top is by bushwacking straight up the gentle slope. See chapter 12.

- **Beverly Hills' "Golden Triangle":** Defined by Wilshire Boulevard, Crescent Drive, and Santa Monica Boulevard, this is a window-shopper's fantasyland of tony shops with picture-perfect displays and sky-high price tags. It even boasts a cluster of shops built to resemble an Italian plaza, with its own faux-cobblestone "streets." If Rodeo Drive tariffs are out of your reach, don't worry; there are plenty of down-to-earth shops and restaurants, plus an elegant Moorish-Mediterranean City Hall that's worth a look. See chapter 13.

- **The L.A. Conservancy's Guided Walking Tours of Downtown Los Angeles:** The Conservancy conducts a dozen fascinating, information-packed tours of historic downtown L.A., seed of today's sprawling metropolis. The most popular is "Broadway Theaters," a loving look at movie palaces; other intriguing ones include "Marble Masterpieces," "Art Deco," "Mecca for Merchants," and tours of the landmark Biltmore Hotel and City Hall. See chapter 13.

- **Griffith Park:** This wooded enclave linking Hollywood with the San Fernando Valley has something for everyone. Be on the lookout for golf carts crossing near the picturesque Wilson and Harding golf courses, and for horseback riders from the nearby Equestrian Center. The L.A. Zoo and the Autry Museum lie at the northeast corner near I-5; the hills are loaded with hiking trails and picnic areas, and kids love the merry-go-round and pony rides. See chapter 13.

- **From Crystal Pier (in Pacific Beach) South to the Jetty, and then North along the Bayside to the Catamaran Hotel:** During the first part of this walk, you'll share the sidewalk with joggers, cyclists, and in-line skaters, and surfers will be testing their skill on the waves to your right. After you cross over to the Mission Bay side of Mission Boulevard, you'll experience the more subdued side of things: quiet water lapping onto white-sand beaches, and the local residents tending their gardens. A lovely way to spend the day in San Diego. See chapter 16.

- **From the San Diego Convention Center to Harbor Island:** This delightful stroll takes you around the waterfront of San Diego Bay. Along the way you'll pass Seaport Village, Tuna Bay, the cruise ship terminal, the Embarcadero, and the Maritime Museum. The foot and cycle path offers a great view of Coronado and the ships plying the harbor. See chapter 16.

4 The Best Golf Courses

- **Silverado Country Club & Resort** (Napa): This 1,200-acre country club boasts not one but two championship 18-hole golf courses designed by Robert Trent

Jones Jr. They're among America's best. The weather is mild year-round, and the course is challenging but not daunting. A real R&R spot. See chapter 6.

- **Pebble Beach Golf Course:** The famous 17-Mile Drive is the site of 10 national championships and the winter telecast of the celebrity-laden AT&T Pebble Beach National Pro-Am. The raging nearby Pacific and a scenic backdrop of the Del Monte Forest justify astronomical greens fees. See chapter 11.

- **Spyglass Hill** (Pebble Beach): Five holes border the ocean, and the rest extend deep within Del Monte Forest. The holes here have been called "long and unforgiving" by golf magazines. Its slope rating of 143 makes it one of the toughest courses in California. See chapter 11.

- **Poppy Hills** (Pebble Beach): *Golf Digest* has called this Robert Trent Jones Jr.–designed course "one of the world's top 20 courses." Also used for AT&T festivities, it cuts right through the pines of Del Monte Forest. One golf pro said the course is "long and tough on short hitters." It's maintained in a state-of-the-art condition and, unlike some of its competitors, is rarely overcrowded. See chapter 11.

- **The Links at Spanish Bay:** Perched along the 17-Mile Drive, The Links were also designed by Robert Trent Jones Jr., with a little help from Tom Watson and former USGA president Frank Tatum. Their aim was to simulate the experience of playing golf on true Scottish links. Its fescue grasses and natural fairways lead to rolls and unexpected bounces for your ball. Holes 14 through 18—taking you to the sea and back again through high dunes—call for some trick shot-making, but make the whole experience worthwhile. See chapter 11.

- **Industry Hills Golf Club, Eisenhower Course** (Los Angeles): Designed by William Francis Bell in 1979, this course consistently ranks among *Golf Digest's* top 25 public courses. Often home to the U.S. Open qualifying rounds, the Eisenhower course has extra large, undulating greens and the challenge of thick kikuyu roughs. See chapter 13.

- **Westin Mission Hills Resort, Pete Dye Course** (Rancho Mirage): Since 1987, when course architect Pete Dye sculpted this links-style, par-70 challenger, players have wrangled with the pot bunkers, hidden pin placements, and carries over water that are his classic trademarks. Rolling fairways and railroad ties also characterize Dye's 6,706-yard classic. The course takes full scenic advantage of the lavender hills all around. See chapter 15.

- **PGA West TPC Stadium Course** (La Quinta): The par-3 17th has a picturesque island green where Lee Trevino made Skins Game history with a spectacular hole-in-one. The rest of Pete Dye's 7,261-yard design is flat with huge bunkers, lots of water, and severe mounding throughout. The PGA West is part of the La Quinta Resort and Club, which received *Golf Magazine's* 1994 Gold Medal Award for the total golf resort experience. Also open for semiprivate play is the Mountain Course at La Quinta, another Dye design appearing regularly on U.S. top 100 lists. It's set dramatically against rocky mountains, which thrust into fairways to create tricky doglegs. Small Bermuda greens are well-guarded by boulders and deep bunkers. See chapter 15.

- **Torrey Pines Golf Course** (La Jolla): Two gorgeous 18-hole championship courses overlook the ocean and provide players with plenty of challenge. In February, the Buick Invitational Tournament is held here; the rest of the year these popular municipal courses are open to everybody. See chapter 16.

- **Coronado Municipal Golf Course** (San Diego): This 18-hole, par-72 municipal course overlooking Glorietta Bay is located to the left of the Coronado Bay Bridge. It's the first thing you see when you arrive in Coronado—a fabulous welcome for duffers. See chapter 16.

5 The Best Offbeat Travel Experiences

- **Hot-Air Ballooning over Napa Valley:** It's all the rage, and for good reason: Northern California's temperate weather allows for ballooning year-round, and the valley is simply beautiful from on high. Flights are best right after sunrise, when the air is calm and cool. Hotels throughout the valley can arrange a trip aloft for you, or you can book one direct with **Bonaventura Balloon Company** (☎ **800/ FLY-NAPA**) or **Adventures Aloft** (☎ **800/944-4408**). Sometimes there's a catered champagne brunch at the end of the adventure. See chapter 6.
- **Taking a Mud Bath in Calistoga:** In this town's famous volcanic-ash mud— mixed with mineral water—you can get buck naked and covered in gooey mud. At a dozen or so places you can immerse yourself in the mud, followed by a mineral-water shower and a whirlpool bath, then a steam bath. It's perhaps the most relaxing experience in California. See chapter 6.
- **Discovering "The Lost Coast":** The terrain was so rugged the state of California couldn't extend Calif. 1 along the Pacific between Rockport and Eureka. As a result, this isolated region remains pristine, with redwood trees perched precariously on cliffs some 200 feet above the rock-strewn coastline. Start the 75-mile drive from U.S. 101 at Garberville—or, better yet, from the paved road from Humboldt Redwoods State Park, 3 miles north of Weott. See chapter 7.
- **Panning for Gold in the Gold Country:** In the southern Gold Country, you can dig into living history and pan for gold. Several companies, including **Gold Prospecting Expeditions** (☎ **800/596-0009** or 209/984-4653) in Jamestown, offer dredging lessons and gold-panning tours. You'll quickly learn that this adventure is back-breaking labor. But who knows? You might get lucky and launch a new Gold Rush. See chapter 10.
- **Taking a Gastronomic Road Trip Between Bakersfield and the Gold Country:** Calif. 99 passes through fertile agricultural land and a series of small towns, each with a distinct ethnic heritage. Basque sheep farmers and bakers, Dutch dairies, Swedish and Armenian enclaves near Fresno, Portuguese and Italians near Modesto, and a French sausage maker in Lodi—they all represent the delicious diversity of California's central region. See chapter 10.
- **Riding the Amtrak Rails Along the Southern California Coast:** Relive the golden age of train travel and see the natural beauty of California, avoiding the crowded highways at the same time. Spanish-style Union Station, a marble-floored Streamline Moderne masterpiece, is the Los Angeles hub. Trains run between L.A. and the romantic mission towns of San Juan Capistrano, San Diego, Santa Barbara, and San Luis Obispo. The scenery includes lush valleys, windswept coastline, and the occasional urban stretch. Call **Amtrak** (☎ **800/USA-RAIL**) for information. See chapter 2.
- **Discovering Downtown L.A.'s Public Art:** The wealth of public art on display in downtown Los Angeles is one of the city's best-kept secrets. Some works make political or social commentary (the black experience as represented by the life of former slave Biddy Mason in a multimedia exhibit between Broadway and Spring streets just south of 3rd Street, or Judd Fine's evolutionary chronicle *Spine* installed outside the Central Library). Others are abstract and open to a variety of interpretations. Pershing Square, a formerly untended eyesore bounded by 5th, 6th, Olive, and Hill streets, has been reincarnated as a modern sculpture garden. See chapter 13.
- **Exploring Forest Lawn Memorial Park:** America's most famous cemetery is a wacky 300-acre park with more stars in the ground than Hollywood's Walk of

Fame. In addition to the Silver Screen's most dearly departed, the cemetery contains 1,000 full-scale reproductions of Renaissance statuary, the enormous Great Mausoleum with its oversized stained-glass reproduction of *The Last Supper*, and the Church of the Recessional, where Ronald Reagan married his first wife, Jane Wyman. See chapter 14.

- **Strolling Venice Beach:** All of humanity—for better and worse—is represented on a boardwalk framed by broad sands, swaying palms, and the sparkling blue Pacific. The day's carnival might include well-tanned body builders, outrageous street performers, scantily clad beach bunnies (bimbos *and* himbos), roving gangs of teens, psychedelic-era hippies, and much more. Experiment with style at the cheap sunglasses stalls, grab an exotic dog at Jody Maroni's Sausage Kingdom, and make your way to the Santa Monica pier to check out the historic photo gallery and carousel. See chapter 13.
- **Skydiving over Southern California:** Enjoy a bird's-eye view of the Southland. Local schools offer instruction at all levels (including tandem jumps for first-timers). At the **California City Skydive Center** (☎ 800/2-JUMP-HI) in the Mojave Desert, you can soar through the same skies as the space shuttle, which lands at nearby Edwards Air Force Base. Hemet and Perris are home to world-renowned schools, **Skydiving Adventures** at Hemet-Ryan Airport (☎ 800/526-9682) and the **Perris Valley Skydiving School** (☎ 800/832-8818), as is Skylark Airport at Lake Elsinore, where you'll find **Jim Wallace Skydiving** (☎ 800/795-DIVE).
- **Going to the Movies, San Diego Style:** Imagine sitting on the deck of the world's oldest merchant ship, watching a film projected on the "screen-sail"; floating on a raft in a huge indoor pool while a movie is shown on the wall; watching a silent movie accompanied by the San Diego Symphony; or sitting on the beach watching a movie that's projected on a floating barge. Only in San Diego! See chapter 16.
- **Experiencing a San Diego Christmas:** Although visions of sugarplums don't dance in most people's heads when they think about San Diego, the area does offer a variety of unusual Christmas traditions. These include Christmas on the Prado in Balboa Park; the Coronado Christmas Celebration and Parade, where Santa arrives by ferry; and the Mission Bay Boat Parade of Lights and the San Diego Harbor Parade of Lights, where decorated boats of all sizes and types are the focus of attention. And it wouldn't be Christmas without the annual reading of Dr. Seuss's *The Grinch That Stole Christmas* at Loews Coronado Bay Resort. See chapters 2 and 16.

6 The Best of Small-Town California

- **St. Helena:** A small town in the heart of the Napa Valley, St. Helena is known for its Main Street, which is lined with Victorian storefronts featuring intriguing wares. In a horse and buggy, Robert Louis Stevenson and his new bride, the cantankerous Fanny, made their way down this street. Come for the old-timey, tranquil mood and the wonderful food. See chapter 6.
- **Mendocino:** An artist's colony with a New England flavor, Mendocino serves as the backdrop for *Murder, She Wrote*. Perched on the clifftops above the Pacific Ocean, it's filled with small art galleries, general stores, weathered wooden houses, and elbow-to-elbow tourists. See chapter 7.
- **Arcata:** If you're losing your faith in America, a few days spent at this Northern California coastal town will surely restore your patriotism. One of the best small

towns in America, Arcata has it all: its own redwood forest and bird marsh, a charming town square, great family-owned restaurants, and even its own minor-league baseball team, which draws the whole town together for an afternoon of pure camaraderie. See chapter 7.

- **Nevada City:** The whole town is a national historic landmark and the best place to understand Gold Rush fever. Settled in 1849, it offers fine dining and shopping, and a stock of multigabled Victorian frame houses of the Old West. Relics of the cannibalistic Donner Party are on display at the 1861 Firehouse No. 1. See chapter 10.
- **Pacific Grove:** You can escape the Monterey crowds by heading just 2 miles west to Pacific Grove, which is known for its tranquil waterfront location and quiet, unspoiled air. Thousands of Monarch butterflies flock here between October and March to make their winter home in Washington Park. See chapter 11.
- **Cambria:** Near Hearst Castle, Cambria benefits from a constant stream of visitors, who bring the right amount of sophistication to this picturesque coastal town. Moonstone Beach holds a string of seaside lodges and hosts dozens of sunbathing elephant seals, while the village itself is filled with charming B&Bs, artists' studios and galleries, and friendly shops. See chapter 12.
- **Ojai:** When Hollywood needed a Shangri-La for the movie *Lost Horizon,* they drove north to idyllic Ojai Valley, an unspoiled hideaway of eucalyptus groves and small ranches warmly nestled among soft, green hills. Ojai is the amiable village at the valley's heart. It's a mecca for artists, free spirits, and weary city folk in need of a restful weekend in the country. See chapter 12.
- **Ventura:** This charming mission town is filled with colorful Victorians. It's also home to a pleasantly eclectic old Main Street lined with thrift and antique shops, used record stores, friendly diners, and even old-time saloons operating beneath broken-down, second-story hotels. Don't miss the historic mission on its land-scaped plaza, and the deco-era Greek Revival San Buenaventura City Hall loom-ing over the town, bedecked with smiling stone faces of the founding Franciscan friars. See chapter 12.
- **Julian:** This old mining town in the Cuyamaca Mountains near San Diego is well-known today for its wildflower fields, the fall apple harvest, and tasty flavored breads from Dudley's Bakery. There's plenty of pioneer history here, too, includ-ing a local history museum, a circa-1888 schoolhouse, and mining demonstrations. A smattering of antique shops, plenty of barbecue, and an old-fashioned soda foun-tain operating since 1886 round out the experience. See chapter 16.
- **Temecula:** This charming Riverside County town is best known for its wineries and the excellent vintages they produce, as well as the annual hot-air balloon fes-tival at harvest time. Since the wineries here are smaller than their counterparts in Northern California, and are mostly family–owned and –operated, you're more likely to be able to meet and talk with the vintners here. See chapter 16.

7 The Best Family Vacation Experiences

- **San Francisco:** The City by the Bay is filled with unexpected pleasures for every member of the family. Ride the cable cars that "climb halfway to the stars" and visit the Exploratorium, the California Academy of Sciences (which includes the Steinhart Aquarium), the zoo, the ships at the maritime museum, Golden Gate Park, and much more. See chapter 4.
- **Marine World Africa USA:** One of Northern California's most popular attrac-tions is located on Marine World Parkway at Vallejo, an hour's drive northeast of

San Francisco. This 160-acre wildlife theme park features animals of the air, land, and sea—some show-stopping performers. Killer whales, elephants, dolphins, sea lions—they're all in the act and you get a close-up look. See chapter 4.

- **Lake Tahoe:** California's Disneyland of outdoor adventure, Lake Tahoe has piles of family-fun things to do. Skiing, snowboarding, hiking, tobogganing, swimming, fishing, boating, waterskiing, mountainbiking—the list is nearly endless. Even the casinos cater to kids while mom and pop play the slots. See chapter 8.

- **Yosemite National Park:** Camping or staying in a cabin in Yosemite is a premier family attraction in California. Sites are scattered over 17 different campgrounds, and the rugged beauty of the Sierra Nevada surrounds you. During the day, the family calendar is packed with hiking, bicycling, white-water trips, and even mountaineering to rugged, snowy peaks. See chapter 9.

- **Santa Cruz:** Surfing, sea kayaking, hiking, fishing, and great shopping, not to mention those fantastic beaches and the legendary amusement park on the boardwalk—this wonderfully funky bayside town has everything you need for the perfect family vacation. See chapter 11.

- **Monterey:** It's been called "Disneyland-by-the-Sea" due to its wealth of family-friendly activities, including those on Cannery Row and Fisherman's Wharf. Be sure to check out the state-of-the-art aquarium. See chapter 11.

- **Big Bear Lake:** Families flock year-round to this lake in the San Bernardino Mountains, and not just for the skiing. Horseback riding, miniature golf, water sports, and the Alpine Slide (kind of a snowless bobsled) are fun alternatives, and you can see and learn about native wildlife at the Moonridge Animal Park. The recently expanded village has a movie theater, arcade, and dozens of cutesy bear-themed businesses. Most of the local lodging consists of clusters of woodsy cabins that are perfect for families. See chapter 14.

- **Disneyland:** The "Happiest Place On Earth" is family entertainment at its best. Whether you're wowed by Disney animation come alive, thrilled by the roller-coaster rides, or interested in the history and hidden secrets of this pop-culture icon, you won't walk away disappointed. Stay at the nearby Disneyland Hotel (connected directly to the park by monorail), a wild attraction unto itself, which offers appealing packages including multiday access to the park. There's also a terrific extra bonus: On most days, guests of the hotel get to enter the park early and enjoy the major rides with no lines. Call ahead for the day's schedule. See chapter 14.

- **San Diego Zoo, Wild Animal Park, and Sea World:** San Diego boasts three of the world's best animal attractions. At the zoo, animals live in creatively designed habitats such as Tiger River and Hippo Beach. At the Wild Animal Park, 3,000 animals roam freely over 2,200 acres. And Sea World, with its ever-changing animal shows and exhibits, is an aquatic wonderland. See chapter 16.

8 The Best Architectural Landmarks

- **The Civic Center** (San Francisco): The creation of designers John Bakewell Jr. and Arthur Brown Jr., this is perhaps the most beautiful beaux arts complex in America. See chapter 4.

- **The Painted Ladies** (San Francisco): The so-called "Painted Ladies" are the city's famous, ornately decorated Victorian homes. Check out the brilliant beauties around Alamo Square. Most of the extant 14,000 structures date from the second half of the 19th century. See chapter 4.

- **Winchester Mystery House** (San Jose): The heiress to the Winchester rifle fortune, Sarah Winchester, created one of the major "Believe It or Not?" curiosities of California, a 160-room Victorian mansion. It's been called the "world's strangest monument to a woman's fear." When a fortune teller told her she wouldn't die if she'd continue to build onto her house, her mansion underwent construction day and night from 1884 to 1922. She did die eventually, and the hammers were silenced. See chapter 5.

- **The Carson House** (Eureka): A splendidly flamboyant Victorian—and one of the state's most photographed Queen Anne–style structures. It was built in 1885 by the Newsom brothers for William Carson, the local timber baron. Today it's the headquarters of a men's club. See chapter 7.

- **Mission San Carlos Borromeo del Rio Carmelo** (Carmel): The second mission founded in California in 1770 by Father Junípero Serra (who is buried there) is perhaps the most beautiful. Its stone church and tower dome have been authentically restored, and a peaceful garden of California poppies adjoins the church. Sights include an early kitchen and the founding father's spartan sleeping quarters. See chapter 11.

- **The Control Tower and Theme Building at Los Angeles International Airport:** The spacey Jetsons-style "Theme Building," which has always loomed over LAX, unmistakably signaling your arrival, has been joined by a brand-new silhouette. The main control tower, designed by local architect Kate Diamond to evoke a stylized palm tree, now dwarfs its more familiar neighbor. Only authorized personnel are allowed to make the ascent, but you can still enjoy the view from the Theme Building's observation deck or its groovy *Star Trek*–ish Encounter restaurant and bar, whose eerie purple neon floods the surrounding area after dark. See chapter 13.

- **Los Angeles's Central Library:** The city rallied to save the downtown library when an arson fire nearly destroyed it in 1986; the triumphant result has returned much of its original splendor. Working in the early 1920s, architect Bertram G. Goodhue employed the Egyptian motifs and materials popularized by the recent discovery of King Tut's tomb, combined with the more modern use of concrete block. See chapter 13.

- **Tail o' the Pup** (Los Angeles): At first glance, you might not think twice about this hot dog–shaped bit of kitsch on West Hollywood's San Vicente Boulevard, just across from the Beverly Center. But locals adored this closet-sized wiener dispensary so much that when it was threatened by the developer's bulldozer, they spoke out en masse to save it. One of the last remaining examples of 1950s representational architecture, the "little dog that could" also serves up a great Baseball Special. See chapter 13.

- **The Gamble House** (Pasadena): The Smithsonian Institution calls this Pasadena landmark, built in 1908, "one of the most important houses in the United States." Architects Charles and Henry Greene created a masterpiece of the Japanese-influenced arts and crafts movement. Tours are conducted of the spectacular interior, designed by the Greenes down to the last piece of teak furniture and coordinating Tiffany lamp, and executed with impeccable craftsmanship. After you're done, stroll the immediate neighborhood to view several more Greene and Greene creations. See chapter 13.

- **Balboa Park** (San Diego): These Spanish/Mayan–style buildings were originally built as temporary structures for the Panama-California Exposition be-tween 1915 and 1916. Although many have been rebuilt over the years, a few of the original buildings still remain, and are worth seeking out. See chapter 16.

- **Hotel Del Coronado** (Coronado): The "Hotel Del" stands in all its ornate Victorian red-tiled glory on some of the loveliest beach in Southern California. Built in 1888, it's one of the largest remaining wooden structures in the world. Even if you're not staying, stop by to take a detailed tour of the splendidly restored interiors, elegant grounds, and fascinating minimuseum of the hotel's spirited history. On your way to Coronado, you can't miss the **Coronado Bay Bridge,** an architectural landmark in its own right. Crossing the bridge by car or bus is an undeniable thrill because you can see Mexico, the San Diego skyline, Coronado, the naval station, and San Diego Bay. See chapter 16.

9 The Best Museums

- **The Exploratorium** (San Francisco): The hands-on, interactive Exploratorium boasts 650 exhibits that help to show how things work. You use all your senses and stretch them to a new dimension. Every exhibit is designed to be useful. See chapter 4.
- **The Oakland Museum:** This one might be dubbed the "Museum of California." The colorful people and history of the Golden State, and its sometimes overpowering art and culture, are here. Everything from the region's first inhabitants to today's urban violence is depicted. See chapter 5.
- **California State Railroad Museum** (Sacramento): Old Sacramento's biggest attraction, the 100,000-square-foot museum was once the terminus of the Transcontinental and Sacramento Valley railways. The largest museum of its type in the United States, it displays 21 locomotives and railroad cars, among other attractions. One sleeping car simulates travel, with all the swaying and flashing lights of lonely towns passed in the night. See chapter 10.
- **Petersen Automotive Museum** (Los Angeles): This museum is a natural for Los Angeles, a city whose personality is so entwined with the popularity of the car. Impeccably restored vintage autos are displayed in life-size dioramas accurate to the last period detail (including an authentic 1930s-era service station). Upstairs galleries house movie-star and motion-picture vehicles, car-related artwork, and visiting exhibits. See chapter 13.
- **Autry Museum of Western Heritage** (Los Angeles): This one's a treat for both young and old. Relive California's historic cowboy past and see how the period has been depicted by Hollywood through the years, from Disney cartoon re-creations to founder Gene Autry's "singing cowboy" films to popular 1960s TV series. Highlights include a life-size woolly mammoth and a glimmering vault of ornate frontier firearms. See chapter 13.
- **Norton Simon Museum of Art** (Pasadena): This Pasadena museum is seen by millions each January 1st as a picturesque backdrop for the Rose Parade. What TV viewers miss, however, are the treasures inside, carefully collected by wealthy art lover Norton Simon and his wife, actress Jennifer Jones. The collection, spanning 2,000 years, includes Asian art and works of the Renaissance Masters, but the museum's strength is its modern collection. Fine Impressionist (Cezanne, Renoir, van Gogh) and later (Kadinsky, Picasso) works are well complemented by the 19th- and 20th-century sculpture gardens, home to works by Rodin and others. See chapter 13.
- **Museum of Contemporary Art** (San Diego): MCA is actually one museum with two locations: one in La Jolla, the other downtown. The museum is known internationally for its permanent collection, focusing primarily on work produced since 1950. See chapter 16.
- **The Museums of Balboa Park** (San Diego): Located in a relaxed, verdant setting, these museums offer a unique variety of cultural experiences. Highlights include

the Aerospace Historical Center, Museum of Man, Museum of Photographic Arts, Model Railroad Museum, Natural History Museum, and the Lily Pond and Botanical Building. Check in at the House of Hospitality for a map and "Passport to Balboa Park," a low-cost pass to a combination of the museums. See chapter 16.

10   The Best Luxury Hotels & Resorts

- **Ritz-Carlton San Francisco** (San Francisco; ☎ **800/241-3333**): Two short blocks from the top of Nob Hill, San Francisco's Ritz is world renowned among discerning travelers for its superfluously accommodating staff, luxurious amenities, and top-rated restaurant. Another bonus is the most lavish brunch in town, which is served on Sundays in the Terrace Room or on the patio amidst blooming rose bushes. See chapter 4.
- **Auberge du Soleil** (Rutherford; ☎ **707/963-1211**): The "Inn of the Sun," a Relais and Châteaux in a 33-acre olive grove, stands in vineyards in the Napa Valley. This French country-style inn is the wine country's best resort. Each of the spacious villas is named after a region of France. It's very private, discreet, and romantic. See chapter 6.
- **Meadowood Resort** (St. Helena; ☎ **800/458-8080**): A retreat of towering charm and style, this 256-acre Wine Country estate was inspired by New England's grand turn-of-the-century cottages. With its plethora of sports facilities and stress-relieving treatments, it attracts such clients as megabuck novelist Danielle Steel. See chapter 6.
- **The Estate by the Elderberries** (Oakhurst; ☎ **209/683-6860**): Close to Yosemite, the Château Sureau and Erna's Elderberry House, established in 1984, evoke the best of Europe. Exquisite furnishings, individually decorated rooms, and a cuisine worthy of the stars make for a memorable lodging and dining experience at this gateway to the wilderness. See chapter 9.
- **Stonepine** (Carmel Valley; ☎ **408/659-2245**): A mile-long driveway leads to this exquisite château on a private 330-acre estate that was built by a San Francisco banking family in the 1920s. Polo fields and stables evoke an era that seems straight out of *The Great Gatsby*. You'll be suitably pampered. See chapter 11.
- **Post Ranch Inn** (Big Sur; ☎ **800/527-2200**): The freestanding, architecturally sophisticated cabins—which virtually hang over the cliffs of Big Sur—combined with first-rate amenities, hiking trails, spectacular views, a top-notch restaurant, and a celestial outdoor heated pool make this one of the most exclusive—and romantic—resorts we've ever visited. See chapter 11.
- **Ventana Big Sur Country Inn Resort** (Big Sur; ☎ **800/628-6500**): A luxurious wilderness resort on 243 mountainous oceanfront acres, this place is chic, tranquil, and hip—this pioneer sylvan retreat at Big Sur is a magnet for celebrities. Accommodations in one- and two-story buildings—each "worthy of the wild"—blend in with the dramatic Big Sur coastline. The cuisine is first-rate. See chapter 11.
- **The Four Seasons Biltmore** (Santa Barbara; ☎ **800/332-3442**): Open since 1927, the Biltmore has palm-studded formal gardens and a prime beachfront location along "America's Riviera." Meander through the elegant Spanish/Moorish arcades and walkways, all accented by exquisite Mexican tile, then play croquet on manicured lawns or relax at the Coral Casino Beach and Cabana Club. The rooms are the epitome of refined luxury, and the service couldn't be more friendly and accommodating. See chapter 12.

- **Hotel Bel-Air** (Los Angeles; ☎ **800/648-4097**): Nestled in the foothills above UCLA, this is the choice of visiting European royalty, world leaders, and top celebrities. The graceful hotel was built in the 1920s, its grounds landscaped like a fairy-tale kingdom: Stone footbridges pass over koi-filled streams, flowering trees surround a swan-filled pond, and flagstone paths lead to richly traditional rooms. See chapter 13.
- **The Inn on Mt. Ada** (Santa Catalina Island; ☎ **800/608-7669**): This former mansion of the wealthy Wrigley family is one of the most exclusive B&B experiences you'll ever have. With only six guest rooms, the hilltop inn's hefty rates include all your meals (and thoughtful snacks laid out each afternoon), plus the use of a golf cart to putter around this auto-eschewing island paradise. You'll feel like an honored guest at a friend's Mediterranean villa. See chapter 14.
- **Ritz-Carlton Laguna Niguel** (Dana Point; ☎ **800/241-3333**): This jewel in the Ritz-Carlton chain is well known for its warmth, charm, picture-perfect setting, and impeccable service. On dramatic cliffs overlooking 2 miles of prime beach, the Ritz is done in an easy yet elegant nautical/seashore decor, accented by well-chosen antiques and fine art. See chapter 14.
- **La Quinta Resort and Club** (La Quinta; ☎ **800/854-1271**): This luxury resort, set in a grove of palms at the base of the rocky Santa Rosa Mountains, is surrounded by some of the desert's best golf courses. Single-story, Spanish-style cottages are surrounded by a gardenlike setting and 24 "private" swimming pools. The tranquil lounge/library in the unaltered original hacienda hearkens back to the early days of the resort, when Clark Gable, Greta Garbo, Frank Capra, and other luminaries regularly escaped to the seclusion of La Quinta's casitas. See chapter 15.
- **Loews Coronado Bay Resort** (Coronado; ☎ **800/81-LOEWS**): This lovely hideaway occupies a secluded 15-acre peninsula, 30 minutes from the airport and 4^1/$_2$ miles from downtown Coronado. Each room is very well appointed with elegant furnishings and large marble bathrooms. See chapter 16.
- **Hyatt Regency San Diego** (San Diego; ☎ **800/233-1234**). This impressive monolith enjoys a waterfront location and features a contemporary three-story lobby of green marble and Italian limestone. Views from the rooms are spectacular. See chapter 16.

11 The Best Moderately Priced Hotels & Inns

- **Hotel Bohème** (San Francisco; ☎ **415/433-9111**): The rooms may be small and lack extra amenities, but there's no better San Francisco experience than staying at the impeccably stylish Hotel Bohème, in the heart of North Beach. You need only to step outside your door to find some of the city's best cafes, restaurants, and nightlife. See chapter 4.
- **Burgundy House Country Inn** (Yountville; ☎ **707/944-0889**): This retreat in California's wine country evokes a small country inn in France. Built in the early 1890s, it was once a brandy distillery, but now offers cozy, old-fashioned guest rooms, with lots of delightful touches such as bouquets of fresh flowers. See chapter 6.
- **St. Orres** (Gualala; ☎ **707/884-3303**): Designed in a Russian style—complete with two Kremlinesque onion-domed towers—St. Orres offers secluded accommodations constructed from century-old timbers salvaged from a nearby mill. One of the most eye-catching inns on California's north coast. See chapter 7.
- **Albion River Inn** (Albion; ☎ **707/937-1919**): Easily one of the best rooms-with-a-view on the California coast, the Albion River Inn is dripping with romance.

Perched on a cliff overlooking the rugged shoreline, most of the luxuriously appointed rooms have a Jacuzzi tub for two elevated to window level. Add champagne and you're guaranteed to have a night you won't soon forget. See chapter 7.

- **Coloma Country Inn** (Coloma; ☎ 530/622-6919): Deep in the heart of California's northern Gold Country, this 1852 farmhouse stands on 5 acres of land. Rooms are decorated with stenciling and furnished with antiques, and old-fashioned country quilts cover the beds. Fresh flowers from the surrounding gardens brighten the house. See chapter 10.

- **The Jabberwock Bed & Breakfast** (Monterey; ☎ 408/372-4777): This place, only 4 blocks from Cannery Row, was once a convent. Set in its own gardens with waterfalls, it was named after an episode from Lewis Carroll's *Through the Looking Glass*. Each room is individually decorated, one with a fireplace. See chapter 11.

- **Olallieberry Inn** (Cambria; ☎ 888/927-3222): Nestled in the charming town of Cambria, this 1873 Greek Revival house, furnished in a romantic floral-and-lace Victorian style, is a perfect base for exploring Hearst Castle. The gracious innkeepers have your comfort and convenience at heart, providing everything from directions to Moonstone Beach to restaurant recommendations—and a scrumptious breakfast in the morning, of course. See chapter 12.

- **Bath Street Inn** (Santa Barbara; ☎ 800/341-BATH): This is one of the sweetest, most immaculate B&Bs in California. The inn makes special efforts to coddle guests and also has a wonderfully peaceful back deck shaded by an enormous wisteria. See chapter 12.

- **Hollywood Roosevelt** (Los Angeles; ☎ 800/950-7667): This hotel, overlooking the Walk of Fame, is a legendary survivor from Hollywood's Golden Age. Centrally located for sightseeing, it offers terrific city views, one of the city's most elegant lobbies, and evening entertainment at the popular art deco Cinegrill. The first Academy Awards ceremony was held here in 1929, and legends claim the hotel is haunted by the ghosts of Marilyn Monroe and Montgomery Clift. See chapter 13.

- **Casa Malibu** (Malibu; ☎ 800/831-0858): This beachfront motel will fool you from the front. Its cheesy 1970s entrance, right on noisy Pacific Coast Highway, belies the quiet restful charm found within. Situated around the courtyard garden are 21 rooms, many with private decks above the Malibu sands. Rooftops and balconies are festooned with bougainvillea vines, creating an effect reminiscent of a Mexican seaside village. There's easy beach access, and one elegant suite that was Lana Turner's favorite. See chapter 13.

- **Sommerset Suites Hotel** (San Diego; ☎ 800/962-9665): This terrific bargain is also a good choice for those who find traditional hotels too impersonal. The staff is friendly and helpful, and in the late afternoon they serve complimentary snacks, soda, beer, and wine in the cozy guest lounge. See chapter 16.

- **Ocean Park Inn** (San Diego; ☎ 800/231-7735): This three-story standout, located right on Pacific Beach's lively beach path, is visually appealing both inside and out. Behind the hotel's modern Spanish-Mediterranean facade is a sharply designed marble lobby that gives way to the less splendid, but completely comfortable, guest rooms. See chapter 16.

12 The Best Alternative Accommodations

- **An Elegant Victorian Mansion** (Eureka; ☎ 707/444-3144): Yes, that's the name of the inn. Guests relive the golden age of Victoria in an authentic way here—right down to the music and entertainment. At this 1888 house the butler greets you in morning dress. Stay in the Lily Langtry room, named after the actress and king's mistress who boarded here when she performed locally. See chapter 7.

- **KOA Kamping Kabins** (Point Arena; ☎ **707/882-2375**): Once you see the adorable little log cabins at this KOA campground, you can't help but admit that, rich or poor, this is one cool way to spend the weekend on the coast. Rustic is the key word here: Mattresses, a heater, and a light bulb are the standard amenities. All you need is some bedding (or a sleeping bag), cooking and eating utensils, and a bag of charcoal for the barbecue out on the front porch. See chapter 7.

- **Camping at Yosemite's Tuolumne Meadows** (☎ **800/436-7275**): It's especially memorable in late spring when it's carpeted with wildflowers. At an elevation of 8,600 feet, this is the largest Alpine meadow in the High Sierras and a gateway to the "High Country." A large campground is operated here by park authorities, with a full-scale naturalist program. See chapter 9.

- *Delta King* **Riverboat** (Sacramento; ☎ **800/825-5464**): This paddlewheeler is the only major floating hotel in California (with the exception of the *Queen Mary* at Long Beach). In the 1930s it carried passengers between San Francisco and California's capital, but now it's permanently moored here, its former cabins turned into bedrooms and its old staterooms serving hungry diners. See chapter 10.

- **Oceanfront Camping at Big Sur:** Kirk Creek Campground, about 3 miles north of Pacific Valley, offers camping with dramatic ocean views and access to the beach. But there are dozens more—take your pick. See chapter 11.

- **Madonna Inn** (San Luis Obispo; ☎ **800/543-9666**): You can't miss this Pepto Bismol–colored San Luis Obispo landmark when you're driving down U.S. 101. Every room of this family-run Bavarian-style chateau is unique, reflecting a love of Old World motifs, uncommon building materials, and the color pink. Try the rock-lined "Caveman" room, the frilly "Victorian" room, the atmospheric "Waterfall" room, or another of the 109 different theme rooms. This is a design genre all its own—it's an experience not to be missed! See chapter 12.

- **The Venice Beach House** (Venice; ☎ **310/823-1966**): This delightful B&B, in a sprawling 1911 bungalow just 2 blocks from the beach and boardwalk, is a great alternative to the standard cookie-cutter L.A. hotels. The nine guest rooms are all furnished with antiques and period artwork. The wood-paneled living room, bright and airy alcove, cozy patio, and lush garden are captivating. The nearby Venice Pier offers bicycle and roller-skate rentals—perfect for exploring this offbeat neighborhood. See chapter 13.

- **Two Bunch Palms Resort & Spa** (Desert Hot Springs; ☎ **800/472-4334**): This spiritual sanctuary in Desert Hot Springs has been drawing weary city dwellers with its healing mineral springs since Chicago mobster Al Capone built this hideaway in the 1930s. Two Bunch Palms later became a playground for the movie community, but today it's a friendly and informal haven offering full spa services, quiet bungalows nestled amongst the palms, and trademark pools of steaming mineral water. See chapter 15.

- **Crystal Pier Hotel** (San Diego; ☎ **800/748-5894**): Occupying a historic private pier that extends into the Pacific Ocean, this property affords guests the unusual experience of actually sleeping *over* the ocean. Ideal for beach-loving families. See chapter 16.

13 The Best Restaurants for California Cuisine

- **Chez Panisse** (Berkeley; ☎ **510/548-5525**): This is the culinary domain of Alice Waters, often called "the queen of California cuisine." Her food captivates the senses and the imagination. Although originally inspired by the Mediterranean, her kitchen has found its own style. Even Bill Clinton deserted the Big Mac for some Chez Panisse delights, such as grilled fish wrapped in fig leaves with red wine sauce, and Seckel pears poached in red wine with burnt caramel. See chapter 5.

- **Terra** (St. Helena; ☎ 707/963-8931): One of the Napa Valley's premier dining rooms is the creation of Lissa Doumani and her Japanese husband, Hiro Sone. It's on every gastronome's tour of the Wine Country, a celebration of the region's bounty—sublime, flavorful, well-crafted. The wine list is a tribute to the Golden State, emphasizing sometimes almost unknown selections from the small estates. See chapter 6.

- **Erna's Elderberry House** (Oakhurst; ☎ 209/683-6800): It's like a beacon shining across the culinary wasteland of the region around Yosemite. The six-course menu—changed nightly—is an almost perfect blend of Continental and Californian. The food is bountiful and is as fully satisfying as the elegant European ambiance. Fresh, fresh, fresh—and no natural flavor is cooked beyond recognition. Ingredients are deftly and skillfully handled to bring out their natural flavors. See chapter 9.

- **Ian's** (Cambria; ☎ 805/927-8649): The menu changes daily and reflects chef Mark Sahaydak's take on the local bounty. His individual artistry is apparent in dishes like porcini mushroom ravioli with spicy Italian sausage, and sauteed scallops in a crème fraîche and Chardonnay sauce flavored with sun-dried tomatoes. Ian's wine list reflects the very best of local and regional vineyards. See chapter 12.

- **The Ranch House** (Ojai; ☎ 805/646-2360): This restaurant has been placing its emphasis on using the freshest vegetables, fruits, and herbs since it opened its doors in 1965, long before it became a national craze. If you stroll through the lush herb garden before your meal, you might later recognize the freshly snipped sprigs that will aromatically transform your simple meat, fish, or game dish into a work of art. See chapter 12.

- **Four Oaks** (Los Angeles; ☎ 310/470-2265): California cuisine with a French accent is served beneath trees festooned with twinkling lights at this canyon hideaway. The country-cottage ambiance and chef Peter Roelant's superlative blend of fresh ingredients with luxurious Continental flourishes make the Four Oaks a Frommer's favorite luxury. Appetizers like lavender-smoked salmon with crisp potatoes and horseradish crème fraîche complement mouth-watering dishes like roasted chicken with sage, Oregon forest mushrooms, artichoke hearts, and port-balsamic sauce. See chapter 13.

- **Röckenwagner** (Santa Monica; ☎ 310/399-6504): L.A.'s gossipy tongues regularly wag about handsome chef Hans Röckenwagner, but he seems more concerned with maintaining the culinary perfection that propelled him from obscurity in funky Venice to this gallerylike space on Santa Monica's trendy Main Street, where the ever-changing menu defines "California fusion." His European training is merely a starting point for Röckenwagner, who has co-opted ethnic dishes from around the world and elevated them to culinary works of multicultural art. Don't be surprised to find Scandinavian treats like spätzle, knödel, and smoked salmon sharing space with Pacific Rim elements like mangoes, wasabi, curry, and hoisin. See chapter 13.

- **George's at the Cove** (La Jolla; ☎ 619/454-4244): This popular restaurant gets raves for its seafood dishes, creative pastas, ocean view, and great sunsets in summer. If you dine here, be sure to try the smoked-chicken soup. See chapter 16.

14 The Best Culinary Experiences

- **Dungeness Crab at San Francisco's Fisherman's Wharf:** Crabs, which are best consumed as soon as possible after being cooked, emerge right from boiling pots onto your plate. You crack the shells and pick the delectable meat out. Gastronomes treasure even the edible organs (crab butter) inside the carapace. See chapter 4.

- **French Fare, San Francisco Style:** No need to head to Paris for a fancy feast. Some of the world's finest French restaurants are right in the heart of San Francisco. The most formal affairs are **Alain Rondelli** (☎ 415/387-0408), **Fleur de Lys** (☎ 415/673-7779), and **Masa's** (415/989-7154). You can feast on a more casual—but equally incredible—meal at **La Folie** (☎ 415/776-5577). We've had some of the best meals of our lives at these restaurants, and highly recommend you splurge on *at least* one. But don't forget: Reserve well in advance. See chapter 4.

- **A Decadent Meal in the Wine Country:** Have yours at the fabled **Mustards Grill** (Yountville; ☎ **707/944-2424**); it's been called "the quintessential Napa Valley wine restaurant." It's noisy and fun as you sample the fare, many platters straight from a wood-burning oven. Try the grilled Sonoma rabbit, or calf's liver with caramelized onions. Make sure to finish with the Jack Daniel's chocolate cake. See chapter 6.

- **Tomales Bay Oysters:** Both the **Point Reyes Oyster Company** (☎ 415/663-8373) and **Johnson's Oyster Farm** (☎ 415/669-1149) sell their farm-fresh oysters—by the dozen or the hundred—for a fraction of the price you'd pay at a restaurant. Our modus operandi is to: 1) buy a couple dozen; 2) head for an empty campsite along the bay; 3) fire up the barbecue pit (don't forget the charcoal); 4) split and 'cue the little guys; 5) slather them in Johnson's special sauce; then 6) slurp 'em down—yum. See chapter 7.

- **Fresh Pacific Salmon:** Plump, firm, with brightly colored flesh, salmon is best when consumed along the northern coast, especially in a restaurant at sunset overlooking the water. Memories are made of this. Although many species are available, the best known is the Chinook or king salmon. The leanest and most delicately flavored salmon appears in the late spring. The fish is caught in the Pacific just prior to its migration upstream to spawn. This salmon is in prime condition, as it's been feeding for years on rich marine bounty. See chapter 9.

- **Roadside Strawberries and Peaches in the Central Valley:** You can sail through the Golden State's rich agricultural heartland and fill your car or your mouth with some of the finest fruit (vegetables, too) grown in America. The peaches rival those of Georgia, and there are more than 150 varieties of nectarines grown in the valley. When you see baskets of strawberries, tipped so that their luscious scarlet fruit is spilling out, you'll slam on the brakes. See chapter 10.

- **The Pastry Shops of Solvang:** It's easy to dismiss Solvang as a tacky tourist trap, but, if truth be told, the town's bakeries are among California's very best. Many Santa Barbarans regularly make the 40-minute drive to this inland hamlet just to buy dessert. See chapter 12.

- **A Sunset Horseback Ride Through Griffith Park to a Mexican Feast:** This culinary/equine excursion departs Friday evenings from Beachwood Stables in the Hollywood Hills just before dusk, winding up in Burbank at the modest but tasty—especially coming off the trail!—Viva Restaurant. Tie up your steed outside and saunter in for a steaming plate of enchiladas accompanied by an ice-cold *cerveza*, just like the real *vaqueros* (cowboys). For information, call the **Sunset Ranch** at ☎ **213/464-9612**.

- **Grand Central Market** (Los Angeles; ☎ **213/624-2378**): Fresh produce stands, exotic spice and condiment vendors, butchers and fishmongers, and prepared food counters create a noisy, fragrant, vaguely comforting atmosphere in this L.A. mainstay. The gem of this airy, cavernous complex is the fresh juice bar at the southwest corner. A market fixture for many years, it dispenses dozens of fresh varieties from an elaborate system of wall spigots (just like an old-fashioned soda fountain), deftly blending unlikely but heavenly combinations. See chapter 13.
- **Sunday Champagne Brunch Aboard the *Queen Mary*** (Long Beach; ☎ **310/435-3511** or 310/432-6964): This elegant ocean liner was the largest, finest vessel when she was built in 1934, and the grandeur of those Atlantic crossing days remains. A sumptuous buffet-style feast, accompanied by harp soloist and ice sculpture, is presented in the richly wood-furnished first-class dining room. Walk off your overindulgence on the spectacular teak decks and through the art deco interiors. See chapter 14.
- **A Date with the Coachella Valley:** Some 95% of the world's dates are farmed here in the desert. While the groves of date palms make evocative scenery, it's their savory fruit that draws visitors to the National Date Festival in Indio each February. Amid the Arabian Nights parade and dusty camel races, you can feast on an exotic array of plump Medjool, amber Deglet Noor, caramel-like Halawy, and buttery Empress. The rest of the year, date farms and markets throughout the valley sell dates from the season's harvest, as well as date milkshakes, sticky date coconut rolls, and more. See chapter 15 and the "Calendar of Events" in chapter 2.
- **San Diego County Farmers' Markets:** The bountiful harvest of San Diego County is sold on various days at moveable markets throughout the area. Finds are fresh local fruits, vegetables, and flowers, as well as specialty items such as raw apple cider (in the fall), macadamia nuts, and rhubarb pies. See chapter 16.

15 The Best Destinations for Serious Shoppers

- **San Francisco:** It's been called "a boutique town on the Bay." It's filled with hundreds of small and smart specialty shops, selling unusual clothes, books, antiques, jewelry, and gifts, much of it from the Pacific Rim. Of all the great stores in San Francisco, our favorite remains Gump's, on Post Street, between Grant Avenue and Kearny Street. Founded by German immigrants in 1865, the landmark store is known worldwide for its "treasures of Asia," including jade and pearls—plus the largest selection of fine crystal and china in the United States. See chapter 4.
- **Mendocino/Fort Bragg:** Mendocino is tailor-made for art gallery hopping, antiquing, and wine tasting. And there's even better shopping just a short drive up the coast at Fort Bragg, especially along the 300 blocks of North Franklin Street, which is lined with antique stores. See chapter 7.
- **Carmel:** Some 600 buildings in this serene little town are devoted to shops and boutiques. They sell virtually everything—fashions, housewares, art, imported goods, baskets, you name it. Seek out Carmel Plaza, a multilevel complex of boutiques and craft shops, and especially the Barnyard, with its authentic early California barns, now converted into 60-plus shops, boutiques, and restaurants. See chapter 11.
- **Santa Monica:** The entire city is a shopper's paradise. In addition to the movie theater–laden Third Street Promenade and the more traditional multilevel Santa Monica Place, you can browse the shops—some funky, some down-to-earth—and trendy cafes of Main Street and the upscale stores of quaint Montana Avenue, or lose yourself in the expansive Fred Segal complex where, in addition to a string of unusual boutiques, you'll find a fantastic ladies' milliner. See chapter 13.

- **West 3rd Street,** between La Cienega Boulevard and Fairfax Avenue, in Los Angeles: The Beverly Center? Bypass that unsightly behemoth and instead stroll in its shadow along West 3rd Street. You'll enjoy an eclectic mix of new and vintage clothing boutiques, intimate cafes, and specialty shops, interspersed with 1940s-era storefronts housing drapery makers, leather workers, stationery printers, and other craftspeople. The cluttered blocks around Orlando and Sweetzer avenues hold such treasures as the Chado Tea Room, the Traveler's Bookcase and Cook's Library specialty bookstores, Janice McCarty clothing designs, and Polkadots & Moonbeams boutique. See chapter 13.
- **South Coast Plaza** (Costa Mesa): This is the suburban shopping mall taken to its grandest extreme. With more "anchor stores" than several malls put together (including Nordstrom and Saks Fifth Avenue), South Coast Plaza is also home to a branch of Tiffany & Co., a Chanel boutique, a Versace salon, and a host of unusually highbrow shops. If your budget is in a more reasonable range, never fear—all the familiar stores are here, next to some unique Southern California specialties and a mind-boggling selection of restaurants. See chapter 14.
- **Horton Plaza**: The Disneyland of shopping malls, this place is right in the heart of San Diego and covers 6^1/$_2$ city blocks. More than 140 specialty shops, a seven-screen cinema, three department stores, and a variety of sit-down and short-order restaurants sprawl over myriad levels. See chapter 16.
- **La Jolla:** "The village," as it's still referred to by long-time locals, has become sort of a cross between Rodeo Drive and a shopping mall by the sea. A few of the old-time stores remain, but these days they're outnumbered by glossy newcomers. See chapter 16.

16 The Best of the Performing Arts

- **The San Francisco Opera:** This world-class company performs at the War Memorial Opera House, which is modeled after the Opera Garnier in Paris. The opera season opens in September with a gala and runs through December. This was the first municipal opera in the United States, and its brilliant members have been acclaimed by critics throughout the world. See chapter 4.
- **The American Conservatory Theatre** (San Francisco): The ACT is one of the nation's leading regional theaters, dating from 1967. It's been called the American equivalent of the British National Theatre, the Berliner Ensemble, and the Comédie Française in Paris. Both classical and experimental works are brilliantly performed. See chapter 4.
- **Warehouse Repertory Theatre:** Living proof that poor, maligned ol' Fort Bragg is on the road to respect is its upstart new theatrical company. Determined to make Fort Bragg the Ashland of California, Warehouse Repertory Theatre is cadre of highly talented professional actors from around the country. From Shakespeare to Shepard, artistic director Meg Patterson and her crew have brought top productions to the North Coast. See chapter 7.
- **The Monterey Jazz Festival:** When the third weekend of September rolls around, the Monterey Fairgrounds hosts this fabled classic, drawing jazz fans from around the world. The three-day festival (which is usually sold out about a month in advance) is known for presenting the sweetest jazz west of the Mississippi. It even draws fans from that city of jazz, New Orleans. See chapters 2 and 11.
- **The Carmel Bach Festival:** For over 50 years, Carmel has hosted an annual three-week celebration honoring Johann Sebastian Bach and his contemporaries. It culminates in a candlelit concert in the chapel of the Carmel Mission. It starts in mid-July, and you must order tickets way in advance. See chapters 2 and 11.

- **The Hollywood Bowl:** This iconic outdoor amphitheater is the summer home of the Los Angeles Philharmonic, a stage for visiting virtuosos—including the occasional pop star—and the setting for several splendid fireworks shows throughout the summer. It's customary to gourmet picnic before the performance, either at your seat or on the grounds; at evening's end, the aisles are littered with empty wine bottles. Those lucky enough to obtain a box seat can set their own private table. See chapter 13.

- **The Viper Room:** Head to this West Hollywood closet for a glimpse of L.A.'s hippest scene. Owner Johnny Depp took this small but historic club space on the famous Sunset Strip and gave it an atmospheric art deco vibe. He hangs out here regularly with all his trendsetting friends; visiting celebrities and musicians can be found mingling and listening to live bands every night of the week. After midnight or so, don't be surprised if big-name recording artists take the stage for an impromptu jam. See chapter 13.

- **The Groundling Theater** (Hollywood): Many Groundling alumni have hit the big time, graduating to *Saturday Night Live,* TV sitcoms, and motion pictures. The ensemble is best known for split-second improvisation and off-beat, irreverent original skits, all performed in their small, intimate theater on Melrose Avenue. You're bound to bust a gut here. See chapter 13.

- **Festival of the Arts and Pageant of the Masters** (Laguna Beach): These events draw enormous crowds to the Orange County Coast every July and August. Begun in 1932 by a handful of area painters, the festival has grown to showcase hundreds of artists. In the evening, crowds marvel at the Pageant of the Masters' *tableaux vivants*, where costumed townsfolk pose convincingly inside a giant frame and depict famous works of art, accompanied by music and narration. See chapters 2 and 14.

- **Old Globe Theatre:** This Tony Award-winning theater, fashioned after Shakespeare's original stage, produced the revival of *Damn Yankees,* and has billed such notable performers as John Goodman, Marsha Mason, Cliff Robertson, Jon Voight, and Christopher Walken. See chapter 16.

- **La Jolla Playhouse:** Winner of the 1993 Tony Award for Outstanding American Regional Theater, the LJ Playhouse stages six productions each year in its 400-seat Mandell Weiss Theater and 400-seat Mandell Weiss Forum on the campus of UCSD. This is where the Tony Award–winning production of *Tommy* was launched. See chapter 14.

Planning a Trip to California

2

by Erika Lenkert and Matthew R. Poole

In the pages that follow, we've compiled everything you need to know to handle the practical details of planning your trip in advance—airlines, how to make camping reservations, a calendar of events, driving laws, and more.

1 Visitor Information & Money

VISITOR INFORMATION

For information on the state as a whole, contact the **California Office of Tourism,** 801 K St., Suite 1600, Sacramento, CA 95812 (☎ **800/862-2543;** website: gocalif.ca.gov), and ask for their free information packet. In addition, almost every city and town in the state has a dedicated tourist bureau or chamber of commerce that will be happy to send you information on its particular parcel. These are listed under the appropriate headings in the geographically organized chapters that follow.

Foreign travelers should also see chapter 3, "For Foreign Visitors," for entry requirements and other pertinent information.

INFORMATION ON CALIFORNIA'S PARKS To find out more about California's national parks, contact the **Western Region Information Center,** National Park Service, Fort Mason, Building 201, San Francisco, CA 94123 (☎ **415/556-0560**).

For state park information, contact the **Department of Parks and Recreation,** P.O. Box 942896, Sacramento, CA 94296-0001 (☎ **916/653-6995**). Ten thousand campsites are on the department's reservation system, and can be booked up to 8 weeks in advance by calling **Destinet** at ☎ **800/444-7275.** In the past, it's been practically impossible to get through to this line, and campers have complained long and loud. The Parks Department has finally heard their pleas, and in June 1995 some improvements were implemented, including additional operators. Hours for making reservations have been extended; you can now call Monday to Saturday from 8am to 8pm, and Sundays from 8am to 5pm. You can also get reservations information online at **www.destinet.com/calif/calif.**

For information on fishing and hunting licenses, contact the **California Dept. of Fish and Game,** License and Revenue Branch, 3211 S St., Sacramento, CA 95816 (☎ **916/227-2244**).

MONEY

The ubiquitous Bank of America accepts Plus, Star, and Interlink cards, while First Interstate Bank is on-line with the Cirrus system. Both banks have dozens of branches all around California. For the location of the nearest ATM, dial ☎ **800/424-7787** for the **Cirrus** network or ☎ **800/843-7587** for the **Plus** system. You can also locate Plus ATMs on the web at **www.visa.com,** and Cirrus ATMs at **www. mastercard.com.** Most ATMs will make cash advances against MasterCard and Visa. American Express cardholders can write a personal check, guaranteed against the card, for up to $1,000 in cash at an American Express office (see "Fast Facts" in the city chapters for locations).

2 When to Go

California's climate is so varied that it's impossible to generalize about the state as a whole.

San Francisco's temperate marine climate means relatively mild weather year-round. In summer, temperatures rarely top 70°F (pack sweaters, even in August), and the city's famous fog rolls in most mornings and evenings. In winter, the mercury seldom falls below freezing, and snow is almost unheard of. Because of San Francisco's fog, summer rarely sees more than a few hot days in a row. Head a few miles inland, though, and it's likely to be clear and hot.

The Central Coast shares San Francisco's climate, though it gets warmer as you get farther south. Seasonal changes are less pronounced south of San Luis Obispo, where temperatures remain relatively stable year-round. The northern coast is rainier and foggier; winters tend to be mild but wet.

Summers are refreshingly cool around Lake Tahoe and in the Shasta Cascades—a perfect climate for hiking, camping, and other outdoor activities and a popular escape for residents of California's sweltering deserts and valleys who are looking to beat the heat. Skiers flock to this area for terrific snowfall from late November through early April.

Southern California is usually much warmer than the Bay Area, and it gets significantly more sun. This is the place to hit the beach. Even in winter, daytime thermometer readings regularly reach into the 60s and warmer. Summers can be stifling inland, but Southern California's coastal communities are always comfortable. Don't bother packing an umbrella—when it rains, Southern Californians go outside to look at the novelty. It's possible to sunbathe throughout the year, but only die-hard enthusiasts and wet-suited surfers venture into the ocean in winter. The water is warmest in summer and fall, but even then, the Pacific is too chilly for many.

The Southern California desert is sizzling hot in summer; temperatures regularly top 100°F. Winter is the time to visit the desert resorts (and remember, it gets surprisingly cold at night in the desert).

San Francisco's Average Temperatures (°F)

	Jan	Feb	Mar	Apr	May	June	July	Aug	Sept	Oct	Nov	Dec
Avg. High	56	59	60	61	63	64	64	65	69	68	63	57
Avg. Low	46	48	49	49	51	53	53	54	56	55	52	47

Los Angeles's Average Temperatures (°F)

	Jan	Feb	Mar	Apr	May	June	July	Aug	Sept	Oct	Nov	Dec
Avg. High	65	66	67	69	72	75	81	81	81	77	73	69
Avg. Low	46	48	49	52	54	57	60	60	59	55	51	49

CALIFORNIA CALENDAR OF EVENTS

January

- ✪ **Tournament of Roses,** Pasadena. A spectacular parade down Colorado Boulevard, with lavish floats, music, and extraordinary equestrian entries, followed by the Rose Bowl Game. Call ☎ 818/449-4100 for details, or just stay home and watch it on TV (you'll have a better view). January 1.
- **Gold Discovery Celebration,** Coloma. A celebration of the fateful day that rocketed California to riches, with gold-panning demonstrations, musical entertainment, Gold Rush skits, and historic house tours. Call ☎ 510/622-6198. January 24.
- **AT&T Pebble Beach National Pro-Am,** Pebble Beach. A PGA-sponsored tour where pros are teamed with celebrities to compete on three world-famous golf courses. Call ☎ 408/649-1533. Lasts a week; dates vary.
- **Bob Hope Chrysler Classic,** Palm Springs Desert Resorts. 1998 marks the 39th annual charity golf tournament, which has raised more than $30 million in its lifetime. Bob Hope is the honorary chairman. For ticket and other information, call ☎ 888/MR-BHOPE or 619/346-8184.

February

- ✪ **Chinese New Year Festival and Parade.** The largest Chinese New Year Festival in the United States is San Francisco's, which includes a Golden Dragon parade with lion-dancing, marching bands, street fair, flower sale, and festive food. Call ☎ 415/982-3000.

   L.A.'s celebration is colorful as well, with dragon dancers parading through the streets of downtown's Chinatown. Chinese opera and other events are scheduled. For this year's schedule, contact the Chinese Chamber of Commerce at ☎ 213/617-0396. Late January to early February.
- **National Date Festival and Riverside County Fair,** Indio. Coachella Valley dates and produce are featured at this annual desert festival, which also includes an Arabian Nights Pageant and camel and ostrich races. Call ☎ 619/863-8247. February 13 to 22.
- ✪ **Fresno County Blossom Trail.** A 67-mile driving tour featuring the fruit and nut orchards in full bloom. Call ☎ 209/233-0836. Occurs from late February to late March.

March

- **Return of the Swallows,** San Juan Capistrano. An annual event with a parade, dances, and special programs. Call ☎ 714/248-2048 for details. Mid-March.
- **Snowfest,** Truckee. A 10-day winter carnival with parades, ski challenges, polar-bear swim, children's carnival, and fireworks. Dates vary. Call ☎ 510/583-7625.
- **Russian River Wine Road Barrel Tasting,** Healdsburg. The vintners showcase wines still in the barrel, about-to-be-released vintages, and also some old gems from their cellars. Tastings are free and food is available to enhance the wines. Each year by February 1, a list of participants is released with the featured wines. Send a SASE to RRWR, P.O. Box 46, Healdsburg, CA 95448 or call ☎ 800/723-6336. First weekend in March.
- **Ocean Beach Kite Festival,** San Diego. Kite building, decorating, and flying are all demonstrated and contested. Phone ☎ 619/224-0189 for details. First Saturday in March.
- **Redwood Coast Dixieland Jazz Festival,** Eureka. Three days of jazz featuring 12 of the best Dixieland groups, including a variety of jam sessions. Call ☎ 707/445-3378. Last weekend in March.

April

○ **San Francisco International Film Festival.** One of America's oldest film festivals, featuring more than 100 films and videos from more than 30 countries. Tickets are relatively inexpensive, and screenings are very accessible to the general public during two weeks early in the month. Call ☎ **415/931-FILM.**

• **Red Bluff Roundup Rodeo,** Red Bluff. A 3-day rodeo with saddle-bronc riding, steer wrestling, bareback riding, brahma bull riding, team roping, and calf roping. For more information, call the Red Bluff Chamber of Commerce at ☎ **510/527-6220.** Always the third weekend in April.

• **Toyota Grand Prix,** Long Beach. An exciting weekend of Indy-class auto racing and entertainment in and around downtown Long Beach, drawing world-class drivers from the United States and Europe. Contact the Grand Prix Association at ☎ **800/752-9524** or 562/981-2600. Mid-April.

• **Fisherman's Festival,** Bodega Bay. Fishing vessels, decorated with ribbons and banners, sail out for a Blessing of the Fleet, while landlubbers enjoy music, lamb, an oyster barbecue, an arts and crafts fair, and a boat parade. End of month (dates vary).

• **Asparagus Festival,** Stockton. The spring harvest festival is celebrated with food and a variety of entertainment. Call ☎ **209/943-1987.** Late April.

○ **Renaissance Pleasure Faire,** San Bernardino. One of America's largest Renaissance festivals, this annual happening, set in Glen Ellen Regional Park in L.A.'s relatively remote countryside, is a re-created Elizabethan marketplace with costumed performers and living history displays. For ticket information, phone ☎ **800/523-2473.** Weekends from April through June.

• **La Jolla Easter Hat Parade.** Prizes are awarded in several different categories. Call ☎ **619/454-2600** for more information. Easter Sunday.

○ **Ramona Pageant,** Hemet. A unique outdoor pageant that portrays the lives of the Southern California Mission Indians. The play was adapted from Helen Hunt Jackson's 1884 novel *Ramona.* Call ☎ **909/658-3111** for details. Late April to early May.

• **Del Mar National Horse Show.** Horse and rider teams compete in national championships. Held at the Del Mar Fairgrounds. Call ☎ **619/792-4288** or 619/755-1161 for more information. Late April to early May.

May

○ **Cinco de Mayo.** A week-long celebration of one of Mexico's most jubilant holidays takes place throughout the city of Los Angeles. The fiesta's Carnival-like atmosphere is created by large crowds, live music, dances, and food. The main festivities are held in El Pueblo de Los Angeles State Historic Park, downtown; with other events around the city. Phone ☎ **213/628-1274** for information.

There's also a Cinco de Mayo celebration in San Diego, featuring folkloric music, dance, food, and historical reenactments. Held in Old Town. Call ☎ **619/296-3161** or 619/220-5422 for more information.

• **Luther Burbank Rose Parade and Festival,** Santa Rosa. Marching bands, floats, food, and roses everywhere honor horticulturist Luther Burbank. Call ☎ **707/542-ROSE.** Mid-May.

• **Venice Art Walk,** Venice Beach. An annual weekend event that gives visitors a chance to take docent-guided tours, visit five artist's studios, or take a Sunday self-guided art walk through private studios and homes of more than 50 emerging and well-known artists. Call ☎ **310/392-8630,** ext. 342. Mid-May.

• **Great Monterey Bay Squid Festival.** The squid in all its glory is the focus of the celebration here, which maintains that "a day without squid is a day in hell." Squid-cleaning and squid-cooking demonstrations are followed by a taste of the squid, which—as shown here—can be used in virtually everything but ice cream. Festival fare includes arts and crafts, educational exhibits, and the usual entertainment. Contact the festival at ☎ 408/649-6547. Memorial Day weekend.

- **Avenue of the Giants Marathon.** A scenic marathon along redwood-lined Avenue of the Giants and Humboldt Redwoods State Park, starting about 40 miles south of Eureka. Call ☎ 707/443-1226. Always on the first Sunday in May.

○ **Calaveras County Fair and Jumping Frog Jubilee,** Angel's Camp. The event inspired by Mark Twain's story "The Celebrated Jumping Frog of Calaveras County." Entrants from all over the world arrive with their frog participants. Also children's parade, livestock competition, rodeo, carnival, and fireworks. Call ☎ 209/736-2561. Third weekend in May.

- **Cross-County Kinetic Sculpture Race,** Arcata. Wild and crazy human-powered amphibious vehicles in a 3-day race from Arcata to Ferndale across mud, sand, roadway, and water. Call ☎ 707/725-3851. Memorial Day.

- **Bay to Breakers Foot Race, Golden Gate Park,** San Francisco. One of the city's most popular annual events, it's really more fun than run. Thousands of entrants show up dressed in their best Halloween-style costumes for the approximately 7¹/₂-mile run across the park. Call ☎ 415/777-7770. Third Sunday of May.

○ **Carnival,** San Francisco. The Mission District's largest annual event is a 2-day series of festivities that culminates with a parade on Mission Street over Memorial Day weekend. More than a half-million spectators line the route, and the samba musicians and dancers continue to play on 14th Street, near Harrison, at the end of the march. Call the Mission Economic and Cultural Association at ☎ 415/826-1401. Memorial Day weekend.

June

- **Music in the Mountains,** Nevada City. A 3-week classical music festival. For information, call MIM at ☎ 916/265-6124. Dates vary.

- **Whale Festival,** San Pedro. Join in building a life-size whale from sand, and enjoy a family sand sculpture contest, food, crafts, children's activities, entertainment, booths on sea life and issues, and a watermelon feast. Call ☎ 310/548-7562. Early June.

- **Playboy Jazz Festival,** Los Angeles. Bill Cosby is the traditional Master of Ceremonies, presiding over top artists at the Hollywood Bowl. Call ☎ 310/246-4000. Mid-June.

- **Pony Express Celebration and Re-Ride,** Folsom. Horses and riders follow the same route that the Pony Express took, starting in Missouri and ending with a major celebration in Folsom, about 20 miles east of Sacramento. Much of the route parallels Hwy. 50 in El Dorado County. Call ☎ 510/621-5885 or 916/985-2707. Dates vary.

- **Lesbian and Gay Freedom Day Parade.** It's celebrated all over the state, but San Francisco's party draws up to half a million participants. The parade's start and finish has been moved around in recent years to accommodate road construction, but traditionally it begins and ends at Civic Center Plaza, where hundreds of food, art, and information booths are set up around several sound stages. Call ☎ 415/864-3733 for information. Usually the third or last weekend of June.

- **Mariachi USA Festival,** Los Angeles. A 2-day family-oriented celebration of Mexican culture and tradition at the Hollywood Bowl, where festival-goers pack their picnic baskets and enjoy music, ballet, folklorico, and related performances by special guests. Call ☎ 213/848-7717. Late June.

- **Hot Air Balloon Classic,** Windsor. Hundreds of brilliant silken balloons float silently across the sky above, while gawkers enjoy a food and crafts fair. Call ☎ 707/838-7285 or 707/838-1260. Usually last weekend in June.

- **Rough and Ready Secession Celebration and Chili Cookoff,** Rough and Ready. This event celebrates the town's secession from the Union in 1850 in protest against a mining tax. It soon rejoined on the 4th of July. Food, entertainment, and more. Call ☎ **510/432-4186** or 510/273-4328. Usually fourth Saturday in June.

July

- **Independence Day.** It's celebrated all over the state, of course, but it's terrific in Pasadena, which offers Southern California's most spectacular display of fireworks following an evening of live entertainment at the Rose Bowl. Call ☎ **818/577-3100** for further information.

☼ **Festival of Arts and Pageant of the Masters,** Laguna Beach. A fantastic performance-art production in which live actors re-create famous Old Masters paintings. Other festivities include live music and the Sawdust arts festival across the street. Ticket prices range from $15 to $40. Call ☎ **800/487-FEST** or 714/494-1145; there's online info at www.coolsville.com/festival. July through August.

- **Carmel Bach Festival.** A 3-week festival honoring Johann Sebastian Bach and his contemporaries. It culminates in a candlelit concert in the chapel of the Carmel Mission. Call ☎ **408/624-1521** for tickets *way* in advance. Dates vary.

- **Gilroy Garlic Festival.** A gourmet food fair with more than 85 booths serving garlicky food from almost every ethnic background, plus close to 100 arts, crafts, and entertainment booths. Call ☎ **831/842-1625.** Last full weekend in July.

- **Mammoth Lakes Jazz Jubilee.** A 4-day festival featuring 20 bands on 10 different stages, plus food, drink, and dancing—all under the pine trees and stars. Call ☎ **760/934-2478.** Second weekend in July.

- **Shakespeare at the Beach,** Lake Tahoe. A bewitching experience of the Bard at Sand Harbor on the shore beneath the stars. Call ☎ **702/832-1606.** Three weeks in late July and August.

- **International Surf Festival,** Los Angeles. Four beachside cities—Hermosa Beach, Manhattan Beach, Redondo Beach, and Torrance—collaborate in the oldest international surf festival in California. Competitions include surfing, boogie boarding, sand-castle building, and other beach-related categories. Contact the International Surf Festival Committee at ☎ **310/376-6911** for information. End of July.

August

- **Sonoma County Showcase and Wine Auction.** Four days of wine tastings and celebrations. Held at the Sonoma County Wine and Visitors Center and at different wineries. Call ☎ **707/586-3795.** Usually first weekend in August.

- **Old Spanish Days Fiesta,** Santa Barbara. The city's biggest annual event, this 5-day festival features a grand parade with horse-drawn carriages, two Spanish marketplaces, a carnival, a rodeo, and dancers. Call ☎ **805/962-8101.** Early August.

- **Nisei Week Japanese Festival,** Little Tokyo, Los Angeles. This week-long celebration of Japanese culture and heritage is held in the Japanese American Cultural and Community Center Plaza. Festivities include parades, food, music, arts, and crafts. Call ☎ **213/687-7193.** Mid-August.

- **California State Fair,** Sacramento. At the California Exposition grounds, a gala celebration, with livestock, carnival food, exhibits, entertainment on 10 different stages, plus thoroughbred racing and a 1-mile monorail for panoramic views over the scope of it all. Call ☎ **916/263-3000.** Late August to early September.

September

- **San Diego Street Scene.** The historic Gaslamp Quarter is transformed into an urban food and music festival. Call ☎ **619/557-8487** for more information. Early September.
- **Sausalito Art Festival.** A juried exhibit of more than 180 artists. It is accompanied by music provided by Bay Area jazz, rock, and blues performers and international cuisine enhanced by wines from some 50 different Napa and Sonoma producers. Parking is impossible; take the Red & White Fleet (☎ **415/546-2628**) ferry from Fisherman's Wharf to the festival site. Call ☎ **415/332-3555** for information. Labor Day weekend.
- ✪ **Monterey Jazz Festival.** Top names in traditional and modern jazz. One of the oldest annual jazz festivals in the world. Call ☎ **831/373-3366.** Mid-September.
- **San Francisco Blues Festival,** on the grounds of Fort Mason. The largest outdoor blues music event on the West Coast. Local and national musicians perform back-to-back during three marathon days. Call ☎ **415/826-6837.** Usually in mid-September.
- **Los Angeles County Fair.** Horse racing, arts, agricultural displays, celebrity entertainment, and carnival rides are among the attractions of the largest county fair in the world, held at the Los Angeles County Fair and Exposition Center, in Pomona. Call ☎ **909/623-3111** for information. Late September.
- **Cabrillo Festival,** San Diego. A week-long fair commemorating the exploration of the West Coast by Juan Rodriquez Cabrillo in 1542. A reenactment of the event takes place at the Cabrillo National Monument. Call ☎ **619/557-5450** for more information. Late September.
- **Catalina Island Jazz Trax Festival.** Great contemporary jazz artists travel to the island to play in the legendary Avalon Casino Ballroom. The festival is over two consecutive 3-day weekends. Call ☎ **800/866-TRAX** or 619/295-0396 for more information. Late September or early October.
- **Watts Towers Day of the Drum Festival,** Los Angeles. Performances from Afro-Cuban folkloricos to East Indian tabla players. Call ☎ **213/847-4646.** Late September.
- **Tuolumne County Wild West Film Festival and Rodeo,** Sonora. A gathering of Western film stars and rodeo legends, plus arts and crafts, entertainment, rodeo, and awards dinner. Call ☎ **209/533-4420.** Last weekend in September.

October

- **Gold-Panning Championships and Historic Demonstration Day,** Coloma. Gold-panning contests, foods, crafts, music, and tours. Living history demonstrations of spinning, weaving, cooking, and doll-making. Call ☎ **510/622-6198.** Dates vary.
- **Sonoma County Harvest Fair.** A 3-day celebration of the harvest with exhibitions, art shows, and annual judging of the local wines. At the Sonoma County Fairgrounds. Call ☎ **707/545-4203.** Dates vary.
- **The Half Moon Bay Art & Pumpkin Festival,** Half Moon Bay. The festival features a Great Pumpkin Parade, pie-eating contests, a pumpkin-carving competition, arts and crafts, and all manner of squash cuisine. The highlight of the event is the Giant Pumpkin weigh-in contest, won recently by an 875-pound monster. Colorful to the extreme. For exact date and details, call the Pumpkin Hotline at ☎ **650/726-9652.**
- **Western Regional Final Championship Rodeo,** Lakeside. Top cowboys from 11 western states compete in seven rodeo events including calf roping, barrel

Christmas in San Diego

Christmas in San Diego offers a number of unique activities:

- **Christmas on the Prado,** Balboa Park. Held the first Friday and Saturday in December since 1977, this weekend of evening events includes carol sing-a-longs and food booths, plus free admission to all museums. Call ☎ **619/239-0512** for more information.
- **Coronado Christmas Celebration and Parade.** On the first Friday in December, Santa's arrival by ferry is followed by a parade along Orange Avenue. Call ☎ **619/437-8788** or 619/435-8895.
- **Mission Bay Boat Parade of Lights,** from Quivira Basin in Mission Bay. Concludes with the lighting of a 320-foot tower of Christmas lights at Sea World. Held on a Saturday in mid-December; call ☎ **619/276-8200** for exact date and time.
- **San Diego Harbor Parade of Lights,** from Shelter Island to Harbor Island to Seaport Village. Decorated boats of all sizes and types participate, and spectators line the shore and cheer for their favorites. Held on a Sunday in mid-December since 1971; check the local newspaper for exact day and time.
- *How The Grinch Stole Christmas,* read by Dr. Seuss' Cat In The Hat—and accompanied by punch and cookies—is a regular holiday activity at Loews Coronado Bay Resort in Coronado. This family fun is free of charge, and happens at various times between the day after Thanksgiving through Christmas Eve; call ☎ **619/424-4000** for this year's schedule.

—Elizabeth Hansen

racing, bull riding, team roping, and steer wrestling. Held at the Lakeside Rodeo Grounds, Calif. 67 and Mapleview Avenue, Lakeside. Call ☎ **619/561-4331.** Mid-October.

- **Halloween,** San Francisco. The City by the Bay celebrates with a fantastical parade organized at Market and Castro, and a mixed gay-straight crowd revels in costumes of extraordinary imagination. October 31.

November

- **Doo Dah Parade,** Pasadena. An outrageous spoof of the Rose Parade on the Sunday before Thanksgiving, featuring participants such as the Briefcase Brigade and a kazoo band. Call ☎ **818/449-3689.**
- **Hollywood Christmas Parade.** This spectacular star-studded parade marches through the heart of Hollywood the first or second Sunday after Thanksgiving. For information, call ☎ **213/469-2337.**
- **San Diego Dixieland Jazz Festival.** More than 30 bands perform foot-stomping jazz at the Town & Country Hotel. Call ☎ **619/297-5277** for more information. Late November.

December

- **Truckers Christmas Light Convoy,** Eureka. Big rigs decorated and festooned with lights compete for cash prizes in this lumber town. Call ☎ **707/442-5744** for exact dates and time.
- **Old Town Holiday in the Park,** San Diego. Costumed park docents lead candlelight tours of historic homes in Old Town. Call ☎ **619/220-5422** or 619/469-3174 for ticket information. Early December.

3 Getting There

BY PLANE

All major U.S. carriers serve the San Francisco, Sacramento, San Jose, Los Angeles, and San Diego airports. Domestic airlines flying in and out of these cities include **Alaska Airlines** (☎ 800/426-0333), **American Airlines** (☎ 800/433-7300), **America West** (☎ 800/235-9292), **Continental Airlines** (☎ 800/525-0280), **Delta Air Lines** (☎ 800/221-1212), **Northwest Airlines** (☎ 800/225-2525), **Southwest Airlines** (☎ 800/435-9792), **TWA** (☎ 800/221-2000), **United Airlines** (☎ 800/241-6522), and **US Airways** (☎ 800/428-4322). The lowest round-trip fares to the West Coast from New York fluctuate between about $400 and $500; from Chicago they range from $300 to $400. Foreign travelers should also see "Getting to the U.S." in chapter 3 for a list of airlines offering overseas flights into California. For details on air travel within California, see "Getting Around," below.

You might be able to get a great deal on airfare by calling a consolidator, such as **Travac** (☎ **800/TRAV-800** or 212/563-3303), **1-800-FLY4-LESS, Cheap Tickets** (☎ **800/377-1000**), or **Unitravel** (☎ **800/325-2222** or 314/569-0900).

BY CAR

Here are some handy driving times if you're on one of those see-the-U.S.A. car trips. From Phoenix, it's about 6 hours (okay, seven if you drive the speed limit) to Los Angeles on I-10. Las Vegas is 265 miles northeast of Los Angeles (about a 4- or 5-hour drive).

San Francisco is 227 miles southwest of Reno, Nevada and 577 miles northwest of Las Vegas. It's a long day's drive 640 miles south from Portland, Oregon, on I-5.

Of course, if you have time on your hands, the ultimate nostalgic road trip into California is along Route 66, "America's Main Street," which runs from the shores of Lake Michigan and winds through eight states before ending at the L.A. coast.

Before you set out on a big car trip, you might want to join the **American Automobile Association (AAA)** (☎ **800/922-8228**), which has hundreds of offices nationwide. Members receive excellent maps (they'll even help you plan an exact itinerary) and emergency road service.

BY TRAIN

Amtrak (☎ **800/USA-RAIL**) connects California with about 500 American cities. Trains bound for both Northern and Southern California leave daily from New York and pass through Chicago and Denver. The journey takes about $3^1/_2$ days, and seats fill up quickly. As of this writing, the lowest round-trip fare was $266 from New York and $240 from Chicago. These heavily restricted tickets are good for 45 to 180 days and allow up to three stops along the way.

The *Sunset Limited* is Amtrak's regularly scheduled transcontinental service, originating in Florida, and making 52 stops along the way as it passes through Alabama, Mississippi, Louisiana, Texas, New Mexico, and Arizona before arriving in Los Angeles. The train, which runs three times weekly, features reclining seats, a sightseeing car with large windows, and a full-service dining car. Round-trip coach fares begin at $286; sleeping accommodations are available for an extra charge.

Ask about special family plans, tours, and other money-saving promotions the rail carrier may be offering. Call for a brochure outlining routes and prices for the entire system.

CyberDeals for Net Surfers

It's possible to get some great deals on airfare, hotels, and car rentals via the Internet. So go grab your mouse and start surfing—you could save a bundle on your trip. The websites we've highlighted below are worth checking out, especially since all services are free (but don't forget that time is money when you're on line).

Microsoft Expedia (www.expedia.com)   The best part of this multi-purpose travel site is the "Fare Tracker": You fill out a form on the screen indicating that you're interested in cheap flights to California from your hometown, and, once a week, they'll e-mail you the best airfare deals. The site's "Travel Agent" will steer you to bargains on hotels and car rentals, and you can book everything, including flights, right on line. This site is even useful once you're booked: Before you go, log on to Expedia for oodles of up-to-date travel information, including weather reports and foreign exchange rates.

Preview Travel (www.reservations.com and www.vacations.com)   Another useful travel site, "Reservations.com" has a "Best Fare Finder," which will search the Apollo computer reservations system for the three lowest fares for any route on any days of the year. Say you want to go from Chicago to L.A. and back between December 6th and 13th: Just fill out the form on the screen with times, dates, and destinations, and within minutes, Preview will show you the best deals. If you find an airfare you like, you can book your ticket right online—you can even reserve hotels and car rentals on this site. If you're in the pre-planning stage, head to Preview's "Vacations.com" site, where you can check out the latest package deals for Hawaii and other destinations around the world by clicking on "Hot Deals."

Travelocity (www.travelocity.com)   This is one of the best travel sites out there. In addition to its "Personal Fare Watcher," which notifies you via e-mail of the lowest airfares for up to five different destinations, Travelocity will track the three lowest fares for any routes on any dates in minutes. You can book a flight right then and there, and if you need a rental car or hotel, Travelocity will find you the best deal via the SABRE computer reservations system (a huge database used by travel agents worldwide).

BY BUS

Greyhound/Trailways (☎ 800/231-2222) can get you here from anywhere cheaply, if not in great comfort. Round-trip fares vary depending on your point of origin, but few, if any, ever exceed $300.

4 Getting Around

BY CAR

California's freeway signs frequently indicate direction by naming a town rather than a point on the compass. If you've never heard of Canoga Park you might be in trouble, unless you have a map. The best state road guide is the comprehensive **Thomas Bros.** *California Road Atlas,* a 300-plus-page book of maps with schematics of towns and cities statewide. It costs $20 but is a good investment if you plan to do a lot of exploring. Smaller, accordion-style maps are handy for the state as a whole or for individual cities and regions; you'll find a very useful one inserted in the back of this book.

Trip.Com (www.thetrip.com)   This site is really geared toward the business traveler, but vacationers-to-be can also use Trip.Com's valuable fare-finding engine, which will e-mail you every week with the best city-to-city airfare deals on your selected route or routes.

Discount Tickets (www.discount-tickets.com)   Operated by the European Travel Network, this site offers discounts on airfares, accommodations, car rentals, and tours. It deals in flights between the U.S. and other countries, not domestic U.S. flights, so it's most useful for travelers coming to California from abroad.

E-Savers Programs   Several major airlines, most of which service the Hawaiian islands, offer a free e-mail service known as **E-Savers,** via which they'll send you their best bargain airfares on a weekly basis. Here's how it works: Once a week (usually Wednesday), subscribers receive a list of discounted flights to and from various destinations, both international and domestic. Now here's the catch: These fares are only available if you leave the very next Saturday (or sometimes Friday night) and return on the following Monday or Tuesday. It's really a service for the spontaneously inclined and travelers looking for a quick getaway. But the fares are cheap, so it's worth taking a look. If you have a preference for certain airlines (in other words, the ones you fly most frequently), sign up with them first. Another caveat: You'll get frequent-flier miles if you purchase one of these fares, but you can't use miles to buy the ticket.

Here's a list of airlines and their websites, where you can not only get on the e-mailing lists, but also book flights directly:

- **American Airlines:** www.americanair.com
- **Continental Airlines:** www.flycontinental.com
- **TWA:** www.twa.com
- **Northwest Airlines:** www.nwa.com
- **US Airways:** www.usairways.com

Epicurious Travel (travel.epicurious.com), another good travel site, allows you to sign up for all of these airline e-mail lists at once.

For **road conditions,** call ☎ **916/445-7623** in Northern California, ☎ **213/628-7623** in Southern California.

If you're heading into the Sierras or Shasta-Cascades for a winter ski trip, top up on antifreeze and carry snow chains for your tires (chains are mandatory in certain areas).

Here are a few sample distances between key California cities:

San Francisco	
87 miles SW of Sacramento	321 miles NW of Santa Barbara
115 miles NW of Monterey	379 miles NW of Los Angeles
278 miles SE of Eureka	548 miles NW of San Diego

Sacramento	
87 miles NE of San Francisco	383 miles N of Los Angeles
185 miles NE of Monterey	391 miles NE of Santa Barbara
304 miles SE of Eureka	484 miles NW of Palm Springs

Los Angeles	
96 miles SE of Santa Barbara	379 miles SE of San Francisco
103 miles W of Palm Springs	383 miles S of Sacramento
120 miles NW of San Diego	659 miles SE of Eureka
332 miles SE of Monterey	

RENTALS   California is one of the cheapest places in America to rent a car. The best-known firms, with locations throughout the state and at most major airports, include **Alamo** (☎ 800/327-9633), **Avis** (☎ 800/331-1212), **Budget** (☎ 800/527-0700), **Dollar** (☎ 800/421-6868), **Hertz** (☎ 800/654-3131), and **National** (☎ 800/328-4567), and **Thrifty** (☎ 800/367-2277).

Most rental firms pad their profits by selling a Loss/Damage Waiver (LDW), which usually costs an extra $9 per day. Before agreeing to this, however, check with your insurance carrier and credit- and charge-card companies. Many people don't realize that they are already covered by either one or both.

For renters, the minimum age is usually 19 to 25.

Finally, think about splurging on a convertible. Few things in life can match the feeling of flying along the California coast with the sun smiling on your shoulders and the wind whipping through your hair.

DRIVING RULES   California law requires both drivers and passengers to wear seat belts. Children under 4 years or 40 pounds must be secured in an approved child safety seat. Motorcyclists must wear a helmet. Auto insurance is mandatory; the car's registration and proof of insurance must be carried in the car.

You can turn right at a red light, unless otherwise indicated—but be sure to come to a complete stop first. Pedestrians *always* have the right-of-way.

Many California freeways have designated carpool lanes, also known as High Occupancy Vehicle (HOV) lanes or "white diamond" lanes (after the large diamonds painted on the blacktop along the lane). Some require two passengers, others three. Most on-ramps are metered during even light congestion to regulate the flow of traffic onto the freeway; cars in HOV lanes can pass the signal without stopping. Although there are tales of drivers sitting life-size mannequins next to them in order to beat the system, don't consider ignoring the stoplights for any reason if you're not part of a carpool—fines begin around $200.

BY PLANE

In addition to the major carriers listed above in "Getting There," several smaller airlines provide service within the state, including **American Eagle** (☎ 800/433-7300), **Skywest** (☎ 800/453-9417), **Shuttle by United** (☎ 800/241-6522), and **USAir Express** (☎ 800/428-4322). The round-trip fare between Los Angeles and San Francisco ranges from $64 to $198, with the cheapest flights departing on Southwest Airlines from Oakland in the Bay Area and Burbank in the Southland.

BY TRAIN

Amtrak (☎ 800/USA-RAIL; www.amtrak.com) runs trains up and down the California coast, connecting Los Angeles with San Francisco and all points in between. A one-way ticket can often be had for about $85. The coastal journey, aboard Amtrak's Coast Starlight, is a fantastically beautiful trip that runs from Seattle to Oakland; crosses Salinas, the artichoke capital of the world; climbs San Luis Obispo's bucolic hills; drops into Santa Barbara; then runs down the Malibu coast into Los Angeles. You can then continue on to San Diego. It's a popular journey—make reservations well in advance.

FAST FACTS: California

AAA   If you're a member of the **American Automobile Association** and your car breaks down, call ☎ **800/AAA-HELP** for 24-hour emergency roadside service.

American Express   To report lost or stolen traveler's checks, call ☎ **800/ 221-7282**. Local office locations are listed throughout the book.

Earthquakes   In the rare event of an earthquake, you should know about a few simple precautions that every California schoolchild is taught: If you're in a tall building, don't run outside; instead, move away from windows and towards the building's center. Crouch under a desk or table, or stand against a wall or under a doorway. If you're in bed, get under the bed or stand in a doorway, or crouch under a sturdy piece of furniture. When exiting the building, use stairwells, *not* elevators.

If you're in your car, pull over to the side of the road and stop, but wait until you're away from bridges or overpasses, and telephone or power poles and lines. Stay in your car.

If you're out walking, stay outside and away from trees, power lines, and the sides of buildings. If you're in an area with tall buildings, stand in a doorway.

Emergencies   To reach the police, ambulance service, or fire department, dial ☎ **911** from any telephone. No coins are needed at pay phones.

Liquor Laws   Liquor and grocery stores, as well as some drugstores, can legally sell packaged alcoholic beverages between 6am and 2am. Most restaurants, night-clubs, and bars are licensed to serve alcoholic beverages during the same hours. The legal age for the purchase and consumption of alcoholic beverages is 21; proof of age is strictly enforced.

Maps   Local maps can usually be obtained free from area tourist offices. State and regional maps are sold at gas stations, in drugstores, and in tourist-oriented shops all around the state; the Thomas Bros. maps are the best.

Pets   Many chain hotels and motels accept dogs (although some require a deposit or impose size restrictions). Some good bets, with their toll-free reservation num-bers, include **Best Western** (☎ 800/528-1234), **Comfort Inns** (☎ 800/228-5150), **Holiday Inns** (☎ 800/HOLIDAY), **La Quinta Inns** (☎ 800/531-5900), **Red Lion Inns** (☎ 800/547-8010), and **Motel 6** (☎ 800/466-8356). But remember that managers of individual establishments are free to set or change their pet policy, so it's vital that you contact the hotel itself to confirm your dog's reservation in-stead of relying solely on these central reservation numbers.

It's not a good idea to bring your dog to any of California's national parks—for your pet's own protection. It's just not safe for dogs to wander in these areas, where they might have dangerous encounters with wildlife.

The *California Dog Lover's Companion* (Foghorn Press) is a huge and incredibly useful resource, with lodging recommendations plus ratings of hundreds of parks and beaches, plus details on where Fido is allowed to romp off-leash. You'll learn that San Francisco is an unusually dog-friendly destination, and that dogs are wel-come at Pismo Beach and on the sands at Carmel. *On the Road Again with Man's Best Friend* (Macmillan) is another great reference tool, with detailed reviews of ac-commodations where dogs are welcome.

Taxes   California's state sales tax is 8.25%. Some municipalities include an addi-tional percentage, so tax varies throughout the state. Hotel taxes are almost always higher than tariffs levied on goods and services.

Time   California and the entire West Coast are in the Pacific standard time zone, three hours earlier than the East Coast.

3 For Foreign Visitors

by Erika Lenkert and Matthew R. Poole

This chapter will provide some specifics about getting to the United States as economically and effortlessly as possible, plus some helpful information about how things are done in California—from receiving mail to making a local or long-distance telephone call.

1 Preparing for Your Trip

ENTRY REQUIREMENTS

Immigration laws are a hot political issue in the United States these days, and the following requirements may have changed somewhat by the time you plan your trip. Check at any U.S. embassy or consulate for current information and requirements.

DOCUMENT REGULATIONS   The U.S. State Department has a **Visa Waiver Pilot Program** allowing citizens of certain countries to enter the United States without a visa for stays of up to 90 days. At press time these included Andorra, Austria, Belgium, Brunei, Denmark, Finland, France, Germany, Iceland, Ireland, Italy, Japan, Liechtenstein, Luxembourg, Monaco, the Netherlands, New Zealand, Norway, San Marino, Spain, Sweden, Switzerland, and the United Kingdom. Citizens of these countries need only a valid passport and a round-trip air or cruise ticket in their possession upon arrival. If they first enter the United States, they may then visit Mexico, Canada, Bermuda, and/or the Caribbean islands and return to the United States without needing a visa. Further information is available from any U.S. embassy or consulate. Canadian citizens may enter the United States without visas; they need only proof of residence.

Citizens of all other countries, including Australia, must have (1) a valid **passport** with an expiration date at least 6 months later than the scheduled end of their visit to the United States; and (2) a **tourist visa,** which may be obtained without charge from the nearest U.S. consulate.

To obtain a visa, the traveler must submit a completed application form (either in person or by mail) with a $1^1/_2$-inch-square photo, and must demonstrate binding ties to a residence abroad. Usually you can obtain a visa at once or within 24 hours, but it may take longer during the summer rush from June to August. If you cannot go in person, contact the nearest U.S. embassy or consulate for directions on applying by mail. Your travel agent or airline office may also be able to provide you with visa applications and instructions. The U.S. consulate or embassy that issues your visa will determine whether you will be issued a multiple- or single-entry visa and any restrictions regarding the length of your stay.

British subjects can obtain up-to-date passport and visa information by calling the **U.S. Embassy Visa Information Line** (☎ **0891/200-290**) or the **London Passport Office** (☎ **0990/210-410** for recorded information).

Foreign driver's licenses are recognized in California, although you may want to get an international driver's license if your home license is not written in English.

MEDICAL REQUIREMENTS   No inoculations are needed to enter the United States unless you are coming from, or have stopped over in, areas known to be suffering from epidemics, particularly cholera or yellow fever.

If you have a disease requiring treatment with medications containing narcotics or drugs requiring a syringe, carry a valid signed generic prescription from your physician to allay any suspicions that you are smuggling drugs. The prescription brands you are accustomed to buying in your country may not be available in the United States.

CUSTOMS REQUIREMENTS   Every adult visitor may bring in, free of duty: 1 liter of wine or hard liquor, 200 cigarettes or 100 cigars (but no cigars from Cuba) or 1 pound of smoking tobacco, and $100 worth of gifts. These exemptions are offered to travelers who spend at least 72 hours in the United States and who have not claimed them within the preceding six months. It is altogether forbidden to bring foodstuffs (particularly cheese, fruit, cooked meats, and canned goods) and plants (vegetables, seeds, tropical plants, and so on) into the country. Foreign tourists may bring in or take out up to $10,000 in U.S. or foreign currency with no formalities; larger sums must be declared to Customs on entering or leaving.

INSURANCE

Unlike most other countries, the United States does not have a national health system. Because the cost of medical care is extremely high, we strongly advise all travelers to secure health coverage before setting out on their trip.

You may want to take out a comprehensive travel policy that covers (for a relatively low premium) sickness or injury costs (medical, surgical, and hospital); loss or theft of your baggage; trip-cancellation costs; guarantee of bail in case you are arrested; costs of accident, repatriation, or death. Such packages (for example, "Europe Assistance" in Europe) are sold by automobile clubs at attractive rates, as well as by insurance companies and travel agencies and at some airports.

MONEY

The U.S. monetary system has a decimal base: One American dollar ($1) = 100 cents (100¢). Dollar bills commonly come in $1 (a "buck"), $5, $10, $20, $50, and $100 denominations (the last two are usually not welcome when paying for small purchases). There are six coin denominations: 1¢ (one cent or a "penny"); 5¢ (five cents or a "nickel"); 10¢ (ten cents or a "dime"); 25¢ (twenty-five cents or a "quarter"); 50¢ (fifty cents or a "half dollar"); and the $1 pieces (both the older, large silver dollar and the newer, small Susan B. Anthony coin are relatively rare).

Traveler's checks in U.S. dollars are accepted at most hotels, motels, restaurants, and large stores. Sometimes picture identification is required. American Express, Thomas Cook, and Barclay's traveler's checks are readily accepted.

Credit cards are the method of payment most widely used: Visa (BarclayCard in Britain), MasterCard (EuroCard in Europe, Access in Britain, Diamond in Japan), American Express, Discover, Diners Club, enRoute, JCB, and Carte Blanche, in descending order of acceptance. You can save yourself trouble by using plastic rather than cash or traveler's checks in 95% of all hotels, motels, restaurants, and retail stores. A credit card can also serve as a deposit for renting a car, as proof of identity, or as a "cash card," enabling you to draw money from automated-teller machines (ATMs) that accept them.

If you plan to travel for several weeks or more in the United States, you may want to deposit enough money into your credit-card account to cover anticipated expenses and avoid finance charges in your absence. This also reduces the likelihood of your receiving an unwelcome big bill on your return.

You can telegraph money, or have it telegraphed to you very quickly using the **Western Union** system (☎ **800/325-6000**).

SAFETY

While tourist areas are generally safe, crime is on the increase everywhere, and U.S. urban areas tend to be less safe than those in Europe or Japan. Visitors should always stay alert. This is particularly true of large U.S. cities. It's wise to ask the city's or area's tourist office if you're in doubt about which neighborhoods are unsafe.

Remember also that hotels are open to the public, and in a large hotel, security may not be able to screen everyone entering. Always lock your room door—don't assume that once inside your hotel you are automatically safe and no longer need be aware of your surroundings.

DRIVING   Safety while driving is particularly important. Question your rental agency about personal safety, or ask for a brochure of traveler safety tips when you pick up your car. Obtain written directions, or a map with the route marked in red, from the agency showing how to get to your destination. And, if possible, arrive and depart during daylight hours.

Recently more and more crime has involved cars and drivers. If you drive off a highway into a doubtful neighborhood, leave the area as quickly as possible. If you have an accident, even on the highway, stay in your car with the doors locked until you assess the situation or until the police arrive. If you are bumped from behind on the street or are involved in a minor accident with no injuries and the situation appears to be suspicious, motion to the other driver to follow you to a well-lit public area or police station. Never get out of your car in such situations.

If you see someone on the road who indicates a need for help, do not stop. Take note of the location, drive on to a well-lighted area, and telephone the police by dialing ☎ 911.

Park in well-lighted, well-traveled areas if possible. Always keep your car doors locked, whether attended or unattended. Never leave any packages or valuables in sight. If someone attempts to rob you or steal your car, do not try to resist the thief/carjacker—report the incident to the police department immediately.

2 Getting to the U.S.

Travelers from overseas can take advantage of the APEX (advance purchase excursion) fares offered by all the major U.S. and European carriers. Aside from these, attractive values are offered by Virgin Atlantic from London.

A number of U.S. airlines offer service from Europe to the United States. If they do not have direct flights from Europe to California, they can book you straight through on a connecting flight. You can make reservations by calling the following numbers in London: **American** (☎ 0181/572-5555), **Continental** (☎ 4412/9377-6464), **Delta** (☎ 0800/414-767), and **United** (☎ 0181/990-9900).

And of course many international carriers serve LAX and/or San Francisco International Airport. Helpful numbers to know include **Virgin Atlantic** (☎ 0293/747-747 in London), **British Airways** (☎ 0345/222-111 in London), and **Aer Lingus** (☎ 01/844-4747 in Dublin or 061/415-556 in Shannon). **Qantas** (☎ 008/177-767 in Australia) has flights from Sydney to Los Angeles and San Francisco; you can also take **United** (☎ **02/237-8888** in Sydney, 008/230-322 in the rest of Australia) from Australia to the West Coast. **Air New Zealand** (☎ 0800/737-000 in Auckland or 64-3/379-5200 in Christchurch) also offers service to LAX. Canadian readers might book flights on **Air Canada** (☎ 800/268-7240 or 800/361-8620 in Canada), which offers direct service from Toronto, Montréal, Calgary, and Vancouver to San Francisco, Sacramento, Los Angeles, and San Diego.

The visitor arriving by air, no matter what the port of entry, should cultivate patience and resignation before setting foot on U.S. soil. Getting through immigration control may take as long as two hours on some days, especially summer weekends, so have your guidebook or something else to read handy. Add the time it takes to clear customs and you will see you should make a very generous allowance for delay in planning connections between international and domestic flights—figure on 2 to 3 hours at least.

For the traveler arriving by car or by rail from Canada, the border-crossing formalities have been streamlined to the vanishing point. And air travelers from Canada, Bermuda, and some places in the Caribbean can sometimes go through customs and immigration at the point of departure, which is much quicker.

3 Getting Around the U.S.

For information on getting around by car, see "Getting Around" in chapter 2.

BY PLANE   On their trans-Atlantic or trans-Pacific flights, some large U.S. airlines offer special discount tickets for any of their U.S. destinations (American Airlines' Visit USA program and Delta's Discover America program, for example). The tickets or coupons are not on sale in the United States and must be purchased before you leave your point of departure. This system is the best, easiest, and fastest way to see the United States at low cost. You should obtain information well in advance from your travel agent or the office of the airline concerned, since the conditions attached to these discount tickets can be changed without advance notice.

BY TRAIN   International visitors can also buy a **USA Railpass,** good for 15 or 30 days of unlimited travel on Amtrak. The pass is available through many foreign travel agents. Prices in 1998 for a 15-day pass are $260 off-peak, $375 peak (peak season is June 17 to August 20); a 30-day pass costs $350 off-peak, $480 peak. (With a foreign passport, you can also buy passes at some Amtrak offices in the United States including locations in San Francisco, Los Angeles, Chicago, New York, Miami, Boston, and Washington, D.C.) Reservations are generally required and should be made for each part of your trip as early as possible.

Visitors should also be aware of the limitations of long-distance rail travel in the United States. With a few notable exceptions, service is rarely up to European standards: delays are common, routes are limited and often infrequently served, and fares are rarely significantly lower than discount airfares. Thus, cross-country train travel should be approached with caution.

BY BUS   The cheapest way to travel the United States is by bus. **Greyhound/Trailways** (☎ 800/231-2222), the sole nationwide bus line, offers an **Ameripass** for unlimited travel for 7 days (for $179), 15 days (for $289), 30 days (for $399), and 60 days (for $599). Do note that bus travel in the United States can be both slow and uncomfortable, so this option isn't for everyone. In addition, bus stations are often located in undesirable neighborhoods.

FAST FACTS: For the Foreign Traveler

Automobile Organizations Auto clubs will supply maps, suggested routes, guidebooks, accident and bail-bond insurance, and emergency road service. The major auto club in the United States, with 955 offices nationwide, is the **American Automobile Association (AAA).** Members of some foreign auto clubs have reciprocal arrangements with the AAA and enjoy its services at no charge. If you belong to an auto club, inquire about AAA reciprocity before you leave. The AAA can provide you with an International Driving Permit validating your foreign license, although drivers with valid licenses from most home countries don't really need this permit. You may be able to join the AAA even if you are not a member of a reciprocal club. To inquire, call ☎ **619/233-1000**. In addition, some automobile rental agencies now provide these services, so you should inquire about their availability when you rent your car.

Business Hours Offices are usually open weekdays from 9am to 5pm. Banks are open weekdays from 9am to 3pm or later and sometimes Saturday morning. Shops, especially those in shopping complexes, tend to stay open late: until about 9pm weekdays and until 6pm weekends.

Climate See "When to Go" in chapter 2.

Currency See "Preparing for Your Trip," earlier in this chapter.

Currency Exchange The "foreign-exchange bureaus" so common in Europe are rare in the United States. They're at major international airports, and there are a few in most major cities, but they're nonexistent in medium-size cities and small towns. Try to avoid having to change foreign money, or traveler's checks denominated other than in U.S. dollars, at small-town banks, or even at branches in a big city; in fact leave any currency other than U.S. dollars at home (except the cash you need for the taxi or bus ride home when you return to your own country); otherwise, your own currency may prove more nuisance to you than it's worth.

Drinking Laws The legal age to drink alcohol is 21.

Electric Current The United States uses 110–115 volts, 60 cycles, compared to 220–240 volts, 50 cycles, as in most of Europe. Besides a 100-volt converter, small appliances of non-American manufacture, such as hair dryers or shavers, will require a plug adapter, with two flat, parallel pins. The easiest solution to the power struggle is to purchase dual-voltage appliances that operate on both 110 and 220 volts, and then all that is required is a U.S. adapter plug.

Embassies/Consulates All embassies are located in Washington, D.C. Listed here are the West Coast consulates of the major English-speaking countries. The **Australian Consulate** is located at Century Plaza Towers, 19th floor, 2049 Century Park East, Los Angeles, CA 90067 (☎ 310/229-4800). The **Canadian Consulate** is at 300 South Grand Ave., 10th floor, California Plaza, Los Angeles, CA 90071 (☎ 213/346-2700). The **Irish Consulate** is located at 44 Montgomery St., Suite 3830, San Francisco, CA 94104 (☎ 415/392-4214). The **New Zealand Consulate** is at 12400 Wilshire Blvd., Los Angeles, CA 90025 (☎ 310/207-1605). Contact the **U.K. Consulate** at 11766 Wilshire Blvd., Suite 400, Los Angeles, CA 90025 (☎ 310/477-3322).

Emergencies   Call ☎ **911** for fire, police, and ambulance. If you encounter such traveler's problems as sickness, accident, or lost or stolen baggage, call Traveler's Aid, an organization that specializes in helping distressed travelers. (Check local directories for the location nearest you.) U.S. hospitals have emergency rooms, with a special entrance where you will be admitted for quick attention.

Gasoline (Petrol)   One U.S. gallon equals 3.75 liters, while 1.2 U.S. gallons equals 1 Imperial gallon. A gallon of unleaded gas (short for gasoline), which most rental cars accept, costs about $1.50 if you fill your own tank (it's called "self-serve"); about 10¢ more if the station attendant does it (called "full-service").

Holidays   On the following national legal holidays, banks, government offices, post offices, and many stores, restaurants, and museums are closed: January 1 (New Year's Day), third Monday in January (Martin Luther King, Jr. Day), third Monday in February (Presidents' Day), last Monday in May (Memorial Day), July 4 (Independence Day), first Monday in September (Labor Day), second Monday in October (Columbus Day), November 11 (Veterans Day/Armistice Day), last Thursday in November (Thanksgiving Day), and December 25 (Christmas Day). The Tuesday following the first Monday in November is Election Day.

Legal Aid   If you are stopped for a minor infraction (for example, of the highway code, such as speeding), never attempt to pay the fine directly to a police officer; you may be arrested on the much more serious charge of attempted bribery. Pay fines by mail or directly into the hands of the clerk of the court. If accused of a more serious offense, it is best to say and do nothing before consulting a lawyer. Under U.S. law, an arrested person is allowed one telephone call to a party of his or her choice. Call your embassy or consulate.

Mail   You may receive mail c/o General Delivery at the main post office of the city or region where you expect to be. The addressee must pick it up in person and must produce proof of identity (driver's license, credit card, passport, and so on).

Mailboxes are blue with a blue-and-white eagle logo and carry the inscription UNITED STATES POSTAL SERVICE. Within the United States, it costs 20¢ to mail a standard-size postcard and 32¢ to send an oversize postcard (larger than $4^1/4$ by 6 inches, or 10.8 by 15.4 centimeters). Letters that weigh up to 1 ounce (that's about five pages, 8-by-11-inch or 20.5-by-28.2-centimeters) cost 32¢, plus 23¢ for each additional ounce. A postcard to Mexico costs 35¢, a $1/2$-ounce letter 66¢; a postcard to Canada costs 40¢, a 1-ounce letter 52¢. A postcard to Europe, Australia, New Zealand, the Far East, South America, and elsewhere costs 40¢, while a letter is 60¢ for each $1/2$ ounce.

Medical Emergencies   See "Emergencies," above.

Taxes   In the United States there is no VAT (value-added tax) or other indirect tax at a national level. There is a $10 Customs tax, payable on entry to the United States, and a $6 departure tax. Sales tax is levied on goods and services by state and local governments, however, and is not included in the price tags you'll see on merchandise. These taxes are not refundable.

Telephone and Fax   Pay phones can be found on street corners, as well as in bars, restaurants, public buildings, stores, and at service stations. At press time, most pay phones charge 20¢, but local calls are scheduled to increase to 35¢ by the end of 1998.

In the past few years, many American companies have installed voice-mail systems, so be prepared to deal with a machine instead of a receptionist if calling a business number.

Travel Tip

Don't mix up the toll-free *800* (or *888*) area code with the pay-per-call *900* area code, which is usually attached to a phone-sex number that charges oodles per minute.

For long-distance or international calls, it's most economical to charge the call to a telephone charge card or a credit card; or you can use a lot of change. The pay phone will instruct you how much to deposit and when to deposit it into the slot at the top of the telephone box.

For long-distance calls in the United States, dial 1 followed by the area code and number you want. For direct overseas calls, first dial 011, followed by the country code (Australia, 61; Republic of Ireland, 353; New Zealand, 64; United Kingdom, 44; and so on), and then by the city code (for example, 71 or 81 for London, 21 for Birmingham, 1 for Dublin) and the number of the person you wish to call.

Before calling from a hotel room, always ask the hotel phone operator if there are any telephone surcharges. There almost always are, and they often are as much as 75¢ or $1, even for a local call. These charges are best avoided by using a public phone, calling collect, or using a telephone charge card.

For reversed-charge or collect calls and for person-to-person calls, dial 0 (zero, not the letter "O") followed by the area code and number you want; an operator will then come on the line, and you should specify that you are calling collect, or person-to-person, or both. If your operator-assisted call is international, immediately ask to speak with an overseas operator.

For local directory assistance ("Information"), dial **411;** for long-distance information dial 1, then the appropriate area code and 555-1212.

Time   California is on Pacific time, which is three hours earlier than on the U.S. East Coast. For instance, when it is noon in San Diego, it is 3pm in New York and Miami; 2pm in Chicago, in the central part of the country; and 1pm in Denver, Colorado, in the midwestern part of the country. California, like most of the rest of the United States, observes daylight saving time during the summer; in late spring, clocks are moved ahead one hour and then are turned back again in the fall. This results in lovely long summer evenings, when the sun sets as late as 8:30 or 9pm.

Tipping   Some rules of thumb: bartenders, 10 to 15%; bellhops, at least 50¢ per bag, or $2 to $3 for a lot of luggage; cab drivers, 10% of the fare; cafeterias and fast-food restaurants, no tip; chambermaids, $1 per day; checkroom attendants, $1 per garment; theater ushers, no tip; gas-station attendants, no tip; hairdressers and barbers, 15 to 20%; waiters and waitresses, 15 to 20% of the check; valet parking attendants, $1.

San Francisco   4

by Erika Lenkert and Matthew R. Poole

Consistently rated one of the top tourist destinations in the world, San Francisco abounds in multiple dimensions. Its famous, thrilling streets go up, and they go down; its multifarious citizens—and their adopted cultures, architectures, and cuisines—hail from San Antonio to Singapore; and its politics range from hyper-liberalism to an ever-encroaching wave of conservatism. Even something as mundane as fog takes on a new dimension as it creeps from the ocean and slowly envelops San Francisco in a resplendent blanket of mist.

In a city so multifaceted, so enamored with itself, it's hard not to find what you're looking for. Feel the cool blast of salt air as you stroll across the Golden Gate. Stuff yourself on Chinatown dim sum. Browse the Haight for incense and crystals. Walk along the beach, pierce your nose, see a play, rent a Harley—the list is endless. It's all happening in San Francisco, and everyone's invited.

1 Orientation

ARRIVING
BY PLANE

Two major airports serve the Bay Area: San Francisco International and Oakland International. All the major car-rental companies have desks at the airports; see "Getting Around," below, for details on car rentals.

SAN FRANCISCO INTERNATIONAL AIRPORT   San Francisco International Airport, located 14 miles south of downtown directly on U.S. 101, is served by almost four dozen major scheduled carriers. Travel time to downtown during commuter rush hours is about 40 minutes; at other times it's about 20 to 25 minutes.

The airport offers a toll-free hotline available weekdays from 8am to 5pm (PST) for information on ground transportation (☎ 800/736-2008). The line is answered weekdays from 7:30am to 5pm by a real person who will provide you with a rundown of all your options for getting into the city from the airport. Each of the three main terminals also has a desk where you can get the same information.

A cab from the airport to downtown will cost $25 to $30, plus tip. **SFO Airporter** buses (☎ 415/495-8404) depart from outside the lower-level baggage claim area to downtown San Francisco every 15 to 30 minutes from 5am to midnight. They stop at several Union Square–area hotels, including the Grand Hyatt, San Francisco Hilton, San Francisco Marriott, Westin St. Francis, Parc Fifty Five, Hyatt Regency, and Sheraton Palace. No reservations are needed. The cost is $10 each way, and children under 2 ride for free.

Other private shuttle companies offer door-to-door airport service, in which you share a van with a few other passengers. **SuperShuttle** (☎ 415/558-8500) will take you anywhere in the city, charging $10 per person to a hotel; $12 to a residence or business, plus $8 for each additional person; and $40 to charter an entire van for up to seven passengers. **Yellow Airport Shuttle** (☎ 415/282-7433) charges $10 per person. Each shuttle stops every 20 minutes or so and picks up passengers from the marked areas outside the terminal's upper level. Reservations are required for the return trip to the airport only and should be made one day before departure. Keep in mind that these shuttles demand they pick you up 2 hours before your flight, 3 during holidays.

The San Mateo County Transit system, **SamTrans** (☎ 415/508-6200 or 800/660-4287 within Northern California) runs two buses between the airport and the Transbay Terminal at First and Mission streets. The **7B** bus costs $1 and makes the trip in about 55 minutes. The **7F** bus costs $2 and takes only 35 minutes, but permits only one carry-on bag. Both buses run daily, every half hour from about 5:30am to 7pm, then hourly until about midnight.

OAKLAND INTERNATIONAL AIRPORT   Located about 5 miles south of downtown Oakland, at the Hagenberger Road exit of Calif. 17 (U.S. 880), Oakland International Airport (☎ 510/577-4000) is used primarily by passengers with East Bay destinations. Some San Franciscans, however, prefer this less-crowded, accessible airport when flying during busy periods.

Again, taxis from the airport to downtown San Francisco are expensive, costing approximately $45, plus tip.

Bayporter Express (☎ 415/467-1800) is a shuttle service that charges $15 for the first person, $10 for each additional person to downtown San Francisco (it costs more to outer areas of town). **Easy Way Out** (☎ 510/430-9090) is another option, charging $20 per person. Both accept advance reservations. To the right of the airport exit there are usually shuttles that will take you to the city for around $20 per person. Keep in mind that they are independently owned and prices vary.

The cheapest way to downtown San Francisco is to take the shuttle bus from the airport to **BART** (Bay Area Rapid Transit; ☎ 510/464-6000). The **AirBART** shuttle bus (☎ 510/430-9440) runs about every 15 minutes Monday through Saturday from 6am to midnight, Sunday from 8:30am to midnight, stopping in front of Terminals 1 and 2 near the ground transportation signs. The cost is $2 for the 10-minute ride to BART's Coliseum terminal. BART fares vary, depending on your destination; the trip to downtown San Francisco costs $2.45 and takes 20 minutes once onboard. The entire excursion should take around 45 minutes.

BY CAR

San Francisco is accessible via several major highways: **U.S. 101** and **Calif. 1** from the north and south; and **I-80** and **I-580** from the northeast and east, respectively. If you drive from Los Angeles, you can either take the longer coastal route along Calif. 1/U.S. 101 (437 miles, or 11 hours), or the inland route along I-5 to I-580 (389 miles, or 8 hours). From Mendocino, it's a little over 3 hours along Calif. 1, and about 3¼ along U.S. 101; and from Sacramento, it's 88 miles, or 1½ hours, along I-80.

By Train

San Francisco–bound **Amtrak** (☎ **800/872-7245** or 800/USA-RAIL) trains leave from New York and cross the country via Chicago. The journey takes about 3 1/2 days, and seats sell quickly. At this writing, the lowest round-trip fare would cost anywhere from $266 to $518 from New York and from $242 to $470 from Chicago. These heavily restricted tickets are good for 45 to 180 days and allow up to three stops along the way, depending on your ticket.

Round-trip tickets from Los Angeles can be purchased for as little as $84 or as much as $154. Trains actually arrive in Emeryville, just north of Oakland, and connect with regularly scheduled buses to San Francisco's Ferry Building and CalTrain station in downtown San Francisco.

CalTrain (☎ **800/660-4287** or 415/546-4461) operates train services between San Francisco and the towns of the peninsula. The city depot is at 700 Fourth St., at Townsend Street.

By Bus

Greyhound/Trailways (☎ **800/231-2222**) operates to San Francisco from anywhere. Round-trip fares vary, depending on your point of origin, but few, if any, ever exceed $300. The main San Francisco bus station is the Transbay Terminal, 425 Mission St. at First Street. For information, call ☎ **800/231-2222**.

VISITOR INFORMATION

The **San Francisco Visitor Information Center,** Hallidie Plaza, 900 Market St. (at Powell St.), Lower Level, San Francisco, CA 94102 (☎ **415/391-2000**), is the best source for any kind of specialized information about the city. Even if you don't have a specific question, you may want to send them $2 for their 100-page magazine *The San Francisco Book*.

CITY LAYOUT

San Francisco occupies the tip of a 32-mile-long peninsula between San Francisco Bay and the Pacific Ocean. Its land area measures about 46 square miles. Twin Peaks, in the geographic center of the city, is more than 900 feet high.

San Francisco may seem confusing at first, but it quickly becomes easy to negotiate. The city's downtown streets are arranged in a simple grid pattern, with the exception of Market Street and Columbus Avenue, which cut across the grid at right angles to each other. Hills appear to distort this pattern, however, and can be disorienting. But as you learn your way around, these same hills will become your landmarks and reference points.

MAIN ARTERIES & STREETS   **Market Street** is San Francisco's main thoroughfare. Most of the city's buses travel this route on their way to the Financial District from the outer neighborhoods to the west and south. The tall office buildings clustered downtown are at the northeast end of Market; one block beyond lie the Embarcadero and the Bay.

The Embarcadero curves along San Francisco Bay from south of the Bay Bridge to the northeast perimeter of the city and terminates at Fisherman's Wharf, the famous tourist-oriented pier. Aquatic Park, Fort Mason, and the Golden Gate National Recreation area are located farther on around the Bay, occupying the northernmost point of the peninsula.

From the eastern perimeter of Fort Mason, **Van Ness Avenue** runs due south, back to Market Street. The area we have just described forms a rough triangle, with Market Street as its southeastern boundary, the waterfront as its northern boundary, and

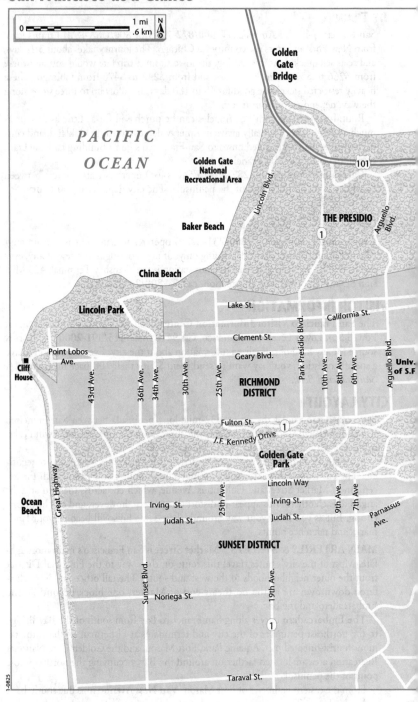

0   1 mi   N
   .6 km

Golden
Gate
Bridge

PACIFIC
OCEAN

Golden Gate
National
Recreational Area

101

Lincoln Blvd.

THE PRESIDIO

Arguello Blvd.

Baker Beach

1

China Beach

Lake St.

California St.

Lincoln Park

Clement St.

Park Presidio Blvd.

Point Lobos
Ave.

Geary Blvd.

Arguello Blvd.

Cliff
House

43rd Ave.

36th Ave.

34th Ave.

30th Ave.

25th Ave.

RICHMOND
DISTRICT

10th Ave.

8th Ave.

6th Ave.

Univ.
of S.F

Fulton St.

1

J.F. Kennedy Drive

Golden Gate
Park

Lincoln Way

Ocean
Beach

Great Highway

25th Ave.

Irving St.

Irving St.

9th Ave.

7th Ave

Judah St.

Judah St.

Parnassus
Ave.

SUNSET DISTRICT

Sunset Blvd.

19th Ave.

Noriega St.

1

Taraval St.

1-0825

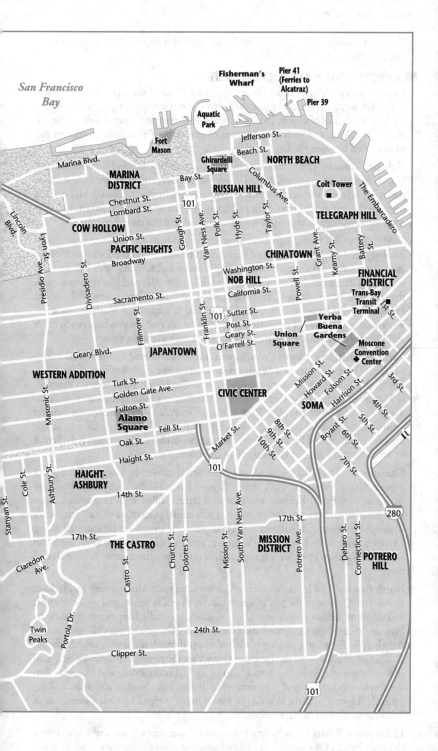

San Francisco
Bay

Fisherman's
Wharf

Pier 41
(Ferries to
Alcatraz)

Pier 39

Aquatic
Park

Jefferson St.

Fort
Mason

Beach St.

Ghirardelli
Square

NORTH BEACH

Marina Blvd.

MARINA
DISTRICT

Bay St.

Columbus Ave.

Coit Tower

RUSSIAN HILL

Chestnut St.

Lombard St.

101

COW HOLLOW

TELEGRAPH HILL

The Embarcadero

Union St.

PACIFIC HEIGHTS

Broadway

CHINATOWN

Battery St.

Washington St.

FINANCIAL
DISTRICT

NOB HILL

Sacramento St.

California St.

Trans-Bay
Transit
Terminal

1st St.

101 Sutter St.

Post St.

Yerba
Buena
Gardens

JAPANTOWN

Geary Blvd.

Geary St.

O'Farrell St.

Union
Square

Moscone
Convention
Center

3rd St.

WESTERN ADDITION

Turk St.

Golden Gate Ave.

CIVIC CENTER

Mission St.

Howard St.

Folsom St.

Harrison St.

4th St.

Fulton St.

Alamo
Square

Fell St.

SOMA

5th St.

6th St.

Oak St.

8th St.

Bryant St.

Haight St.

9th St.

7th St.

101

10th St.

Market St.

280

HAIGHT-
ASHBURY

14th St.

17th St.

17th St.

MISSION
DISTRICT

POTRERO
HILL

Claredon
Ave.

THE CASTRO

Twin
Peaks

24th St.

Clipper St.

101

47

Van Ness Avenue as its western boundary. Within this triangle lie most of the city's main tourist sights.

NEIGHBORHOODS & DISTRICTS IN BRIEF

Union Square   Union Square is the commercial hub of the city. Most major hotels and department stores are crammed into the area surrounding the actual square (named for a series of violent pro-union mass demonstrations staged here on the eve of the Civil War), and there are a plethora of upscale boutiques, restaurants, and galleries tucked between the larger buildings.

Nob Hill/Russian Hill   Bounded by Bush, Larkin, Pacific, and Stockton streets, Nob Hill is the genteel, well-heeled district of the city, still occupied by the major power brokers and the neighborhood businesses they frequent. Russian Hill extends from Pacific to Bay and from Polk to Mason. It is marked by steep streets, lush gardens, and high-rises occupied by both the monied and the more bohemian.

SoMa   In recent years, high rents have forced residents and businesses into once desolate South of Market (dubbed "SoMa"). The area is still predominantly warehouses and industrial spaces, but now many of them are brimming with life. The area is officially demarcated by the Embarcadero, Highway 101, and Market Street, with the greatest concentrations of interest around Yerba Buena Center, along Folsom and Harrison streets between Steuart and Sixth, and Brannan and Market. Along the waterfront are an array of restaurants. Farther west, around Folsom between Seventh and Eleventh streets, is where much of the city's nightclubbing occurs.

Financial District   East of Union Square, this area bordered by the Embarcadero, Market, Third, Kearny, and Washington streets is the city's business district and stomping grounds for many major corporations. The pointy TransAmerica Pyramid, at Montgomery and Clay streets, is one of the district's most conspicuous features. To its east stands the sprawling Embarcadero Center, an $8^1/_2$-acre complex housing offices, shops, and restaurants. Farther east still is the World Trade Center, standing adjacent to the old Ferry Building, the city's pre-bridge transportation hub. Ferries to Sausalito and Larkspur still leave from this point.

Chinatown   The official entrance to Chinatown is marked by a large red-and-green gate on Grant Avenue at Bush Street. Beyond lies a 24-block labyrinth, bordered by Broadway, Bush, Kearny, and Stockton streets, filled with restaurants, markets, temples, and shops—and of course, a substantial percentage of San Francisco's Chinese residents. Chinatown is a great place for urban exploration all along Stockton, Grant, and Portsmouth Square, and the alleys that lead off them like Ross and Waverly. This area is jam-packed, so don't even think about driving around here.

North Beach   The Italian quarter, which stretches from Montgomery and Jackson to Bay Street, is one of the best places in the city to grab a coffee, pull up a cafe chair, and do some serious people-watching. Nightlife is equally happening; restaurants, bars, and clubs along Columbus and Grant avenues bring folks from all over the Bay Area here to fight for a parking place and romp through the festive neighborhood. Down Columbus toward the Financial District are the remains of the city's Beat generation landmarks, including Ferlinghetti's City Lights Bookstore and Vesuvio's Bar. Broadway—a short strip of sex joints—cuts through the heart of the district. Telegraph Hill looms over the east side of North Beach, topped by Coit Tower, one of San Francisco's best vantage points.

Fisherman's Wharf   North Beach runs into Fisherman's Wharf, which was once the busy heart of the city's great harbor and waterfront industries. Today, it is a tacky-but-interesting tourist area with little if any authentic waterfront life, except for recreational boating and some friendly sea lions.

Marina District   Created on landfill for the Pan Pacific Exposition of 1915, the Marina boasts some of the best views of the Golden Gate, as well as plenty of grassy fields alongside the San Francisco Bay. Streets are lined with elegant Mediterranean-style homes and apartments, which are inhabited by the city's well-to-do singles and wealthy families. Here, too, is the Palace of Fine Arts, the Exploratorium, and Fort Mason Center. The main street is Chestnut between Franklin and Lyon, which is lined with shops, cafes, and boutiques.

Cow Hollow   Located west of Van Ness Avenue, between Russian Hill and the Presidio, this flat, grazable area supported 30 dairy farms in 1861. Today, Cow Hollow is largely residential and occupied by the city's Young and Yuppie. Its two primary commercial thoroughfares are Lombard Street, known for its many relatively inexpensive motels; and Union Street, a flourishing shopping sector filled with restaurants, pubs, cafes, and shops.

Pacific Heights   The ultra-elite, such as the Gettys and Danielle Steele—and those lucky enough to buy before the real estate boom—reside in the mansions and homes that make up Pacific Heights. When the rich meander out of their fortresses, they wander down to Union Street, a long stretch of boutiques, restaurants, cafes, and bars.

Japantown   Bounded by Octavia, Fillmore, California, and Geary Boulevard, Japantown shelters only about 4% of the city's Japanese population, but it's still a cultural experience to explore these few square blocks and the shops and restaurants within them.

Civic Center   Although millions of dollars have been expended on brick sidewalks, ornate lampposts, and elaborate street plantings, the southwestern section of Market Street remains downright dilapidated. The Civic Center, at the "bottom" of Market Street, is an exception. This large complex of buildings includes the domed City Hall, the Opera House, Davies Symphony Hall, and the city's main library. The landscaped plaza connecting the buildings is the staging area for San Francisco's frequent demonstrations for or against just about everything.

Haight-Ashbury   Part trendy, part nostalgic, part funky, the Haight, as it's most commonly known, was the soul of the psychedelic and free-loving 1960s and the center of the counterculture movement. Today, the neighborhood straddling upper Haight Street on the eastern border of Golden Gate Park is more gentrified, but the commercial area still harbors all walks of life. Leftover aged hippies mingle with grungy, begging street kids outside Ben and Jerry's ice cream (where they may still be talking about Jerry Garcia), nondescript marijuana dealers, and people with Day-Glo hair. But you don't need to be a freak or wearing tie-dye to enjoy the Haight: The food, shops, and bars cover all tastes. From Haight, walk south on Cole Street for a more peaceful and quaint neighborhood experience.

Richmond & Sunset Districts   San Francisco's suburbs of sorts, the Richmond & Sunset Districts are the city's largest and most populous districts, consisting mainly of small (though expensive) homes, shops, and neighborhood restaurants. Though both Districts border Golden Gate Park and Ocean Beach, only a small percentage of tourists venture into "The Avenues," as it's referred to by locals ("The Streets" being the South of Market District).

The Castro   One of the liveliest streets in town, Castro is practically synonymous with San Francisco's gay community, even though technically it is only a street in the Noe Valley district. Located at the very end of Market Street, between 17th and 18th streets, Castro supports dozens of shops, restaurants, and bars catering to the gay community. Open-minded straight people are welcome, too.

Mission District The Mexican and Latin American populations, along with their cuisine, traditions, and art, make the Mission District a vibrant area to visit. Because some parts of the neighborhood are poor and sprinkled with the homeless, gangs, and drug addicts, many tourists duck into Mission Dolores, cruise by a few of the 200 amazing murals, and head back downtown. But there's plenty more to see in the Mission District. There's a substantial community of lesbians around Valencia Street, several alternative arts organizations, and most recently the ultimate in young hipster nightlife. New bars, clubs, and restaurants are popping up on Mission between 18th and 24th streets and Valencia at 16th Street. Don't be afraid to visit this area, but do use caution at night.

2 Getting Around

BY PUBLIC TRANSPORTATION

The **San Francisco Municipal Railway,** better known as **Muni** (☎ 415/673-6864), operates the city's cable cars, buses, and Metro streetcars. Together, these three public transportation services crisscross the entire city, making San Francisco fully accessible to everyone. Buses and Metro streetcars cost $1 for adults, 35¢ for ages 5 to 17, and 35¢ for seniors over 65. Cable cars cost $2 ($1 for seniors from 9pm to midnight and from 6 to 7am). Needless to say, they're packed primarily with tourists. Exact change is required on all vehicles except cable cars. Fares quoted here are subject to change.

For detailed route information, phone Muni or consult the bus map at the front of the *Yellow Pages.* If you plan on making extensive use of public transportation, you may want to invest in a comprehensive route map ($2), sold at the San Francisco Visitor Information Center (see "Visitor Information" in "Orientation," above) and in many downtown retail outlets.

Muni **discount passes,** called "Passports," entitle holders to unlimited rides on buses, Metro streetcars, and cable cars. A Passport costs $6 for 1 day, and $10 or $15 for 3 or 7 consecutive days. As a bonus, your passport also entitles you to admission discounts at 24 of the city's major attractions, including the M. H. De Young Memorial Museum, the Asian Art Museum, the California Academy of Sciences, and the Japanese Tea Garden (all in Golden Gate Park); the Museum of Modern Art; Coit Tower; the Exploratorium; the zoo; and the National Maritime Museum and Historic Ships. Among the places where you can purchase a Passport are the San Francisco Visitors Information Center, the Holiday Inn Civic Center, and the TIX Bay Area booth at Union Square.

BY CABLE CAR San Francisco's cable cars may not be the most practical means of transport, but these rolling historic landmarks sure are a fun ride. There are only three lines in the city, and they're all condensed in the downtown area. The most scenic, and exciting, is the **Powell-Hyde line,** which follows a zigzag route from the corner of Powell and Market streets, over both Nob Hill and Russian Hill, to a turntable at gaslit Victorian Square in front of Aquatic Park. The **Powell-Mason line** starts at the same intersection and climbs over Nob Hill before descending to Bay Street, just 3 blocks from Fisherman's Wharf. The least scenic is the **California Street line,** which begins at the foot of Market Street and runs a straight course through Chinatown and over Nob Hill to Van Ness Avenue. All riders must exit at the last stop and wait in line for the return trip. The cable car system operates from approximately 6:30 to 12:30am.

BY BUS   Buses reach almost every corner of San Francisco, and travel over the bridges to Marin County and Oakland. All are numbered and display their destinations on the front. Stops are designated by signs, curb markings, and yellow bands on adjacent utility poles, and most bus shelters exhibit Muni's transportation map and schedule. Many buses travel along Market Street or pass near Union Square and run from about 6am to midnight, after which there is infrequent all-night "Owl" service. If you can help it, for safety purposes avoid taking buses late at night.

Popular tourist routes are nos. 5, 7, and 71, all of which run to Golden Gate Park; 41 and 45, which travel along Union Street; and 30, which runs between Union Square and Ghirardelli Square.

BY METRO STREETCAR   Five of Muni's six Metro streetcar lines, designated J, K, L, M, and N, run underground downtown and on the street in the outer neighborhoods. The sleek railcars make the same stops as BART (see below) along Market Street, including Embarcadero Station (in the Financial District), Montgomery and Powell streets (both near Union Square), and the Civic Center (near City Hall). Past the Civic Center, the routes branch off in different directions: The J line will take you to Mission Dolores; the K, L, and M lines to Castro Street; and the N line parallels Golden Gate Park. Metros run about every 15 minutes—more frequently during rush hours. Service is offered Monday through Friday from 5 to 12:30am, on Saturday from 6 to 12:20am, and on Sunday from 8 to 12:20am.

The most recent streetcar addition is not a newcomer at all, but San Francisco's beloved rejuvenated 1930s streetcars. The beautiful green-and-cream-colored F Market line runs from downtown Market Street to the Castro and back. It's a quick and charming way to get up and downtown without any hassle.

BY BART   BART, an acronym for **Bay Area Rapid Transit** (☎ **415/992-2278**), is a futuristic-looking, high-speed rail network that connects San Francisco with the East Bay—Oakland, Richmond, Concord, and Fremont. Four stations are located along Market Street (see "By Metro Streetcar," above). Fares range from $1 to $3.55, depending on how far you go. Tickets are dispensed from machines in the stations and are magnetically encoded with a dollar amount. Computerized exits automatically deduct the correct fare. Children 4 and under ride free. Trains run every 15 to 20 minutes, Monday through Friday from 4am to midnight, on Saturday from 6am to midnight, and on Sunday from 8am to midnight.

BY TAXI

If you're downtown during rush hours or leaving from a major hotel, it won't be hard to hail a cab—just look for the lighted sign on the roof that indicates if one is free. Otherwise, it's a good idea to call one of the following companies to arrange a ride: **Veteran's Cab** (☎ 415/552-1300), **Desoto Cab Co.** (☎ 415/673-1414), **Luxor Cabs** (☎ 415/282-4141), **Yellow Cab** (☎ 415/626-2345), and **Pacific** (☎ 415/986-7220). Rates are approximately $2 for the first mile and $1.80 for each mile thereafter.

BY CAR

You don't need a car to explore downtown San Francisco; in fact, in central areas, such as Chinatown, Union Square, and the Financial District, having a car can be your worst nightmare. But if you want to venture outside of the city, driving is the best way to go.

RENTALS   Among the major car-rental companies operating in the city are **Alamo** (☎ 800/327-9633); **Avis** (☎ 800/331-1212); **Budget** (☎ 800/527-0700); **Dollar** (☎ 800/800-4000); **Hertz** (☎ 800/654-3131); **National** (☎ 800/227-7368); and

San Francisco Mass Transit

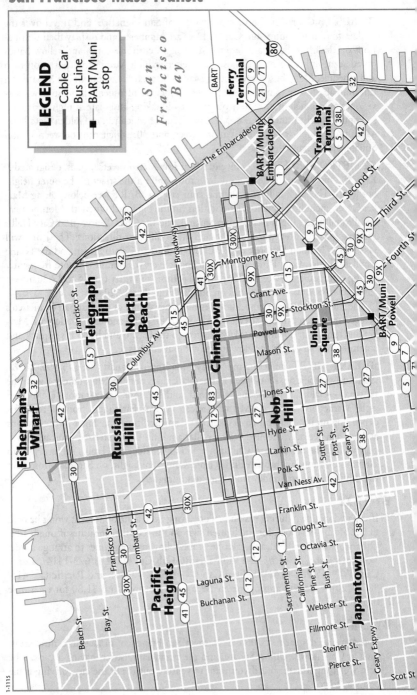

1-1115

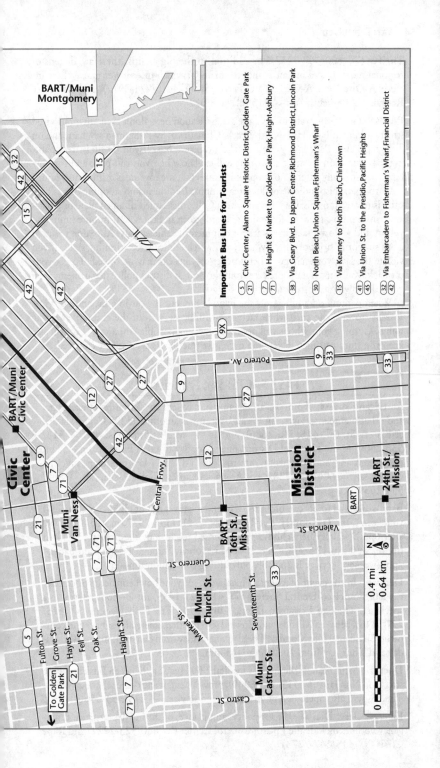

BART/Muni
Montgomery

Important Bus Lines for Tourists

5
21
Civic Center, Alamo Square Historic District, Golden Gate Park

7
71
Via Haight & Market to Golden Gate Park, Haight-Ashbury

38 Via Geary Blvd. to Japan Center, Richmond District, Lincoln Park

30 North Beach, Union Square, Fisherman's Wharf

15 Via Kearney to North Beach, Chinatown

41
45
Via Union St. to the Presidio, Pacific Heights

32
42
Via Embarcadero to Fisherman's Wharf, Financial District

Civic
Center

BART/Muni
Civic Center

Muni
Van Ness

To Golden
Gate Park

Fulton St.
Grove St.
Hayes St.
Fell St.
Oak St.
Haight St.

Market St.

Muni
Church St.

Guerrero St.

Muni
Castro St.

Castro St.

Seventeenth St.

Valencia St.

Mission
District

BART 16th St./
Mission

BART

BART 24th St./
Mission

Potrero Av.

Central Frwy.

N

0   0.4 mi
0   0.64 km

Thrifty (☎ 800/367-2277). In addition to the big chains, there are dozens of regional rental places in San Francisco, many of which offer lower rates. These include **A-One Rent-A-Car,** 434 O'Farrell St. (☎ 415/771-3977), and **Bay Area Rentals,** 229 Seventh St. (☎ 415/621-8989).

PARKING   If you want to have a relaxing vacation here, don't even attempt to find street parking in Nob Hill, North Beach, Chinatown, by Fisherman's Wharf, and on Telegraph Hill. Park in a garage or take a cab or a bus. If you do find street parking, pay attention to street signs that will explain when you can park and for how long. Be especially careful not to park in zones that are tow areas during rush hour.

Curb colors also indicate parking regulations. **Red** means no stopping or parking; **blue** is reserved for disabled drivers with a California-issued disabled plate or a placard; **white** means there's a five-minute limit; **green** indicates a 10-minute limit; and **yellow** and **yellow-black** curbs are for commercial vehicles only. Also, don't park at a bus stop or in front of a fire hydrant; and watch out for street-cleaning signs. If you violate the law, you may get a hefty ticket or your car may be towed. To get your car back, you must obtain a release from the nearest district police department, then go to the towing company to pick up the vehicle.

When parking on a hill, apply the hand brake, put the car in gear, and *curb your wheels*—toward the curb when facing downhill, away from the curb when facing uphill. Curbing your wheels will not only prevent a possible "runaway," but will also keep you from getting a ticket—an expensive fine that is aggressively enforced.

FAST FACTS: San Francisco

American Express   For travel arrangements, traveler's checks, currency exchange, and other member services, American Express has an office at 295 California St., at Battery St. (☎ **415/536-2686**), and at 455 Market St., at 1st St. (☎ **415/ 536-2600**) in the Financial District, open Monday through Friday from 8:30am to 5:30pm and Saturday from 9am to 2pm. To report lost or stolen traveler's checks, call ☎ **800/221-7282.** For American Express Global Assist, call ☎ **800/ 554-2639.**

Baby-sitters   Hotels can often recommend a baby-sitter or child-care service. If yours can't, try **Temporary Tot Tending** (☎ **415/355-7377,** or 415/871-5790 after 6pm), which offers child care by licensed teachers by the hour for children from 3 weeks to 12 years of age. It's open Monday through Friday from 6am to 7pm (weekend service is available only during convention times).

Dentist   In the event of a dental emergency, see your hotel concierge or contact the **San Francisco Dental Society** (☎ **415/421-1435**) for 24-hour referral to a specialist. The San Francisco Dental Office, 132 The Embarcadero (☎ **415/ 777-5115**), between Mission and Howard streets, offers emergency service and comprehensive dental care Monday, Tuesday, and Friday from 8am to 4:30pm, Wednesday and Thursday from 10:30am to 6:30pm.

Doctor   Saint Francis Memorial Hospital, 900 Hyde St., between Bush and Pine streets on Nob Hill (☎ **415/353-6000**), provides emergency-care service 24 hours. The hospital also operates a physician-referral service (☎ **415/353-6566**).

Emergencies   Dial ☎ **911** for police, ambulance, or the fire department. Emergency hotlines include the **Poison Control Center** (☎ **800/523-2222**) and **Rape Crisis** (☎ **415/647-7273**).

Police For emergencies, dial ☎ 911 from any phone; no coins are needed. For other matters, call ☎ **415/553-0123.**

Post Office There are dozens of post offices located all around the city. The closest office to Union Square is inside Macy's department store, 170 O'Farrell St. (☎ **415/956-3570**).

Safety Few locals would recommend that you walk alone late at night in certain areas, particularly the Tenderloin, between Union Square and the Civic Center. Compared with similar areas in other cities, however, even this section of San Francisco is relatively tranquil. Other areas where you should be particularly alert are the Mission District, around 16th and Mission streets; the lower Fillmore area, around lower Haight Street; and the SoMa area south of Market Street.

Taxes An 8.5% sales tax is added at the register for all goods and services purchased in San Francisco. The city hotel tax is a whopping 12%. There is no airport tax.

Transit Information Call Muni at ☎ **415/673-6864** during the week between 7am and 5pm and on the weekends between 9am and 5pm. At other times, recorded information is available.

Useful Telephone Numbers Tourist information (☎ 415/391-2001); **highway conditions** (☎ 415/557-3755); **KFOG Entertainment Line** (☎ 415/777-1045); **Movie Phone Line** (☎ 415/777-FILM); **Grateful Dead Hotline** (☎ 415/457-6388).

Weather Call ☎ **415/936-1212** to find out when the next fog bank is rolling in.

3 Accommodations

San Francisco is an outstanding hotel town, especially considering its relatively small size. We can't cover them all in this guide, so if you'd like a larger selection, check out *Frommer's San Francisco,* which has dozens of other options.

Most of the hotels listed below are within easy walking distance of Union Square, and accessible via cable car. Union Square is near the city's major shops, the Financial District, and all transportation. Prices listed below do not include state and city taxes, which total 12%.

The price categories below reflect the prices of double rooms during the high season, which runs approximately from April through September (in reality, rates don't vary much because the city is so popular year-round). But remember: These are rack (or published) rates; you can almost always get a better deal if you inquire about packages, weekend discounts, corporate rates, and family plans.

Bed and Breakfast California, P.O. Box 282910, San Francisco, CA 94128 (☎ **800/872-4500** or 415/696-1690; fax 415/696-1699, e-mail: info@bbintl.com, website: www.bbintl.com), offers a selection of B&Bs ranging from $60 to $140 per night (two-night minimum). Accommodations range from simple rooms in private homes to luxurious, full-service carriage houses, houseboats, and Victorian homes.

San Francisco Reservations, 22 Second St., San Francisco, CA 94105 (☎ **800/667-1500** or 415/227-1500; website www.hotelres.com), arranges reservations at more than 300 of San Francisco's hotels and often offers discounted rates. Ask about their Events and Hotel Packages that include VIP or discount admissions to various San Francisco museums.

San Francisco Accommodations

Abigail Hotel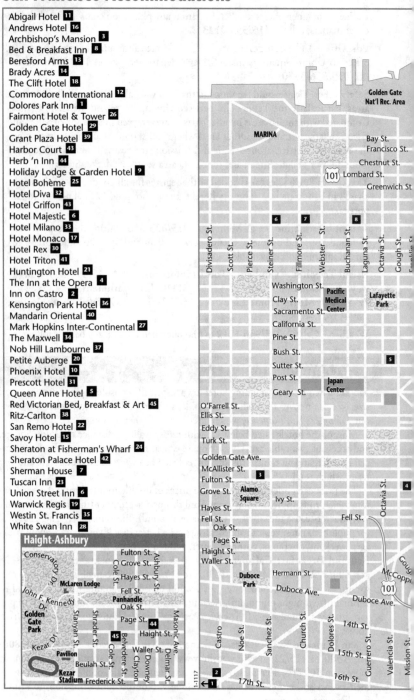
Andrews Hotel 16
Archbishop's Mansion 3
Bed & Breakfast Inn 8
Beresford Arms 13
Brady Acres 14
The Clift Hotel 18
Commodore International 12
Dolores Park Inn 1
Fairmont Hotel & Tower 26
Golden Gate Hotel 29
Grant Plaza Hotel 39
Harbor Court 43
Herb 'n Inn 44
Holiday Lodge & Garden Hotel 9
Hotel Bohème 25
Hotel Diva 32
Hotel Griffon 43
Hotel Majestic 6
Hotel Milano 33
Hotel Monaco 17
Hotel Rex 30
Hotel Triton 41
Huntington Hotel 21
The Inn at the Opera 4
Inn on Castro 2
Kensington Park Hotel 36
Mandarin Oriental 40
Mark Hopkins Inter-Continental 27
The Maxwell 34
Nob Hill Lambourne 37
Petite Auberge 20
Phoenix Hotel 10
Prescott Hotel 31
Queen Anne Hotel 5
Red Victorian Bed, Breakfast & Art 45
Ritz-Carlton 38
San Remo Hotel 22
Savoy Hotel 15
Sheraton at Fisherman's Wharf 24
Sheraton Palace Hotel 42
Sherman House 7
Tuscan Inn 23
Union Street Inn 6
Warwick Regis 19
Westin St. Francis 35
White Swan Inn 28

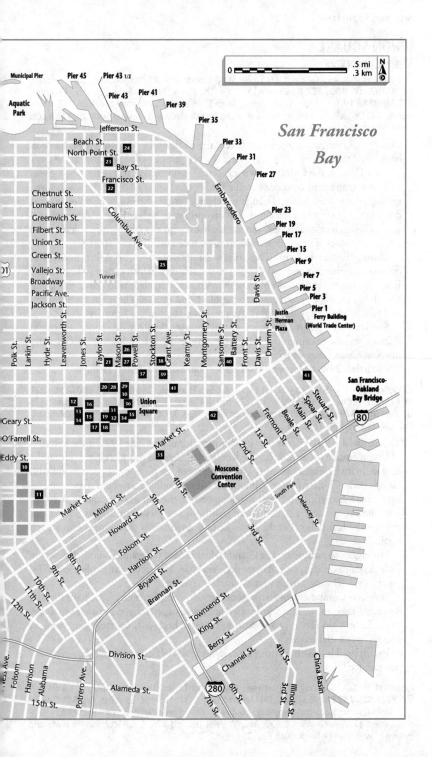

Municipal Pier · Pier 45 · Pier 43 1/2 · Pier 43 · Pier 41 · Pier 39 · Pier 35 · Pier 33 · Pier 31 · Pier 27 · Pier 23 · Pier 19 · Pier 17 · Pier 15 · Pier 9 · Pier 7 · Pier 5 · Pier 3 · Pier 1

Aquatic Park

Jefferson St.

Beach St.

North Point St.

Bay St.

Francisco St.

Chestnut St.

Lombard St.

Greenwich St.

Filbert St.

Union St.

Green St.

Vallejo St.

Broadway

Pacific Ave.

Jackson St.

Columbus Ave.

Tunnel

Embarcadero

San Francisco Bay

Davis St.

Justin Herman Plaza

Ferry Building (World Trade Center)

Polk St. · Larkin St. · Hyde St. · Leavenworth St. · Jones St. · Taylor St. · Mason St. · Powell St. · Stockton St. · Grant Ave. · Kearny St. · Montgomery St. · Sansome St. · Battery St. · Front St. · Davis St. · Drumm St.

Union Square

San Francisco-Oakland Bay Bridge

80

Geary St.

O'Farrell St.

Eddy St.

Steuart St. · Spear St. · Main St. · Beale St. · Fremont St. · 1st St. · 2nd St.

Market St.

Mission St.

Howard St.

Folsom St.

Harrison St.

Bryant St.

Brannan St.

4th St. · 5th St. · 3rd St.

Moscone Convention Center

South Park

Delancey St.

8th St. · 9th St. · 10th St. · 11th St. · 12th St.

Townsend St.

King St.

Berry St.

Channel St.

4th St. · 3rd St.

China Basin

Division St.

Alameda St.

280

Folsom · Harrison · Alabama · Potrero Ave. · 15th St. · 6th St. · 7th St. · Illinois St.

0 — .5 mi / .3 km

N

UNION SQUARE
VERY EXPENSIVE

The Clift Hotel. 495 Geary St. (at Taylor St., 2 blocks west of Union Square), San Francisco, CA 94102. ☎ **800/437-8243** or 415/775-4700. Fax 415/441-4621. 326 rms, 31 suites. A/C MINIBAR TV TEL. $255–$400 double; from $405 suite. Continental breakfast $12.50 extra. AE, CB, DC, MC, V. Parking $23. Cable car: Powell-Hyde and Powell-Mason lines (2 blocks east). Bus: 2, 3, 4, 30, 38, or 45.

One of San Francisco's top luxury hotels, the traditional and historic Clift has won both Five-Star and Five-Diamond awards for ten years in a row. Located in the city's Theater District, the Clift is known for its staff, who excel at pampering their guests and even manage to be cordial to the droves of tourists who wander slack-jawed through the palatial lobby. Though big changes are in the works, at press time the decor in the guest rooms remained old-fashioned, with high ceilings, elaborate woodwork, Georgian reproductions, and marble baths with everything from hair dryers to plush terry robes. The windows also open—a nice touch.

Dining/Entertainment: The French Room—open for breakfast, lunch, and dinner—specializes in seasonally appropriate California-French cuisine. The dramatic Redwood Room remains one of San Francisco's most opulent piano bars, with beautiful fluted redwood columns and its famous Klimt murals. The lobby lounge serves cocktails daily and a traditional English tea Monday through Saturday.

Services: 24-hour room service, concierge, twice-daily maid service, overnight laundry and shoe polishing, one-hour pressing, evening turndown, complimentary in-room fax and computers.

Facilities: 24-hour business center, gift shop, extensive fitness facility.

✪ **Hotel Monaco.** 501 Geary St. (at Taylor St.), San Francisco, CA 94102. ☎ **800/214-4220** or 415/292-0100. Fax 415/292-0111. 177 rms, 24 suites. A/C MINIBAR TV TEL. From $175 double; from $295 suite. Call for discounted rates. AE, CB, DC, DISC, JCB, MC, V. Valet parking $24. Bus: 2, 3, 4, 27, or 38.

This remodeled 1910 Beaux Arts hotel, which debuted in June 1995, is the new diva of Union Square luxury hotels. The Kimpton Group did this place right—from the cozy main lobby with a two-story French inglenook fireplace to the guest rooms with canopy beds, Chinese-inspired armoires, bamboo writing desks, bold stripes, and vibrant color. Everything is brand-spanking new, in the best of taste, and as playful as it is comfort-minded. The decor, along with the breathtaking restaurant, make this our favorite luxury hotel in the city. The only downside is that some rooms are too small.

Dining/Entertainment: The Grand Cafe is indeed the grandest room downtown, with sky-high ceilings, an elaborate deco-era style, and an amazing collection of local art. (See "Dining," below, for a complete review.)

Services: Computer, concierge, room service, complimentary wine hour nightly, overnight shoe shine, laundry/dry cleaning, newspaper delivery, in-room massage, twice-daily maid service, baby-sitting, express check-out, courtesy car, two-line phones, secretarial services.

Facilities: Health club with steam, sauna, and massage; meeting, business, and banquet facilities.

Prescott Hotel. 545 Post St. (between Mason and Taylor sts.), San Francisco, CA 94102. ☎ **800/283-7322** or 415/563-0303. Fax 415/563-6831. 165 rms, 35 suites. A/C MINIBAR TV TEL. $175 double; $235 concierge-level double (including breakfast and evening cocktail reception); from $265 suite. AE, CB, DC, MC, V. Valet parking $23. Cable car: Powell-Hyde and Powell-Mason lines (1 block east). Bus: 2, 3, 4, 30, 38, or 45.

The Prescott has always been one of our favorite hotels in San Francisco. The staff treats you like royalty, the rooms are beautiful and immaculate, the location—one block from Union Square—is perfect, and room service is provided by one of the best restaurants in the city, Postrio. Dark tones of green, plum, and burgundy blend well with the cherry-wood furnishings in the soundproofed rooms; the view, alas, isn't so pleasant. All bathrooms are supplied with terry robes and hair dryers, though only the suites have whirlpool bathtubs. "Club Level" guests are pampered with free continental breakfast, evening cocktails, and exercise bicycles or rowing machines brought up to your room on request—all for only $20 extra per night.

Dining/Entertainment: The hotel provides preferred seating for guests at Postrio; be sure to make reservations when you book your room (see "Dining," below, for complete review).

Services: Complimentary coffee and tea each morning, wine and hors d'oeuvres every evening in the living room, limousine service weekday mornings to the Financial District, concierge, twice-daily maid service, nightly turndown, newspaper delivery, same-day valet/laundry service, overnight shoe shine, room service from Postrio.

Facilities: Conference rooms, access to off-premises health club ($12), including swimming pool, free weights, and sauna.

Westin St. Francis. 335 Powell St. (between Geary and Post sts.), San Francisco, CA 94102. ☎ **800/228-3000** or 415/397-7000. Fax 415/774-0124. 1,192 rms, 83 suites. A/C MINIBAR TV TEL. Main building: $209–$290 double, from $295 suite. Tower: $300–$375 double, from $550 suite. Extra person $30. Continental breakfast $12.50 extra. AE, DC, DISC, JCB, MC, V. Valet parking $24. Cable car: Powell-Hyde and Powell-Mason lines (direct stop). Bus: 2, 3, 4, 30, 45, or 76.

Though too massive to offer the personal service you get at the smaller deluxe hotels on Nob Hill, few other hotels in San Francisco can match the majestic aura of the St. Francis. Hordes of VIPs have hung their hats and hosiery here, from Queen Elizabeth II to Mother Teresa, and all the U.S. presidents since Taft. In 1972 the 32-story Tower was added, doubling the hotel's capacity and adding the requisite banquet and conference centers (as well as a rooftop dance club). The older rooms in the main building vary in size and have more old-world charm than the newer Tower rooms, but the Tower is remarkable for its great views of the city once you rise above the 18th floor. The hotel did a massive renovation in '96, replacing the carpeting, furniture, and bedding in every guest room, gussying up the lobby, and restoring the facade.

Dining/Entertainment: Even if you stay elsewhere, it's worth a visit to partake in high tea at the Compass Rose; it's one of San Francisco's most enduring and enjoyable traditions. The Compass Rose is open daily for lunch and tea (3 to 5pm), and offers live music, dancing, champagne, cocktails, and caviar tasting in the evening. Dewey's, a sports bar, offers a do-it-yourself lunch buffet, and burgers and pizzas at night. There's also a cafe with a basic breakfast menu. Club Oz, a popular dance club with a hefty $18 cover on weekends, is open nightly.

Services: Concierge, 24-hour room service, voice mail, baby-sitting referral, Westin Kids Club (great for families), laundry, newspaper delivery, in-room massage, twice-daily maid service, secretarial services.

Facilities: Fitness center, business center, tour and car rental desks, barber/beauty salon, gift shop.

EXPENSIVE

✪ **Hotel Diva.** 440 Geary St. (between Mason and Taylor sts.), San Francisco, CA 94102. ☎ **800/553-1900** or 415/885-0200. Fax 415/346-6613. 98 rms, 12 suites. A/C TV TEL. $135 double; $155 junior suite, $300 villa suite. Rates include continental breakfast. AE, DC, DISC, JCB, MC, V. Valet parking $17. Bus: 38, 38L.

Appropriately named, the Diva is the prima donna of San Francisco's modern hotels, and one of our favorites. A showbiz darling when it opened in 1985, the Diva won "Best Hotel Design" by *Interiors* magazine for its sleek, ultramodern interiors. A stunning profusion of curvaceous glass, marble, and steel mark the Euro-tech lobby, while the rooms, each spotless and neat, are softened with fashionable Italian Modern furnishings. Nary a beat is missed with the toys and services either, which range from VCRs (with a discreet video vending machine) and Nintendo to complimentary room-delivered breakfast. *Insider tip:* Reserve one of the rooms ending in "09," which come with extra-large bathrooms with vanity mirrors and makeup tables.

Services: Limited room service, concierge, pay-per-view movies, same-day laundry.

Facilities: On-site 24-hour fitness center, business center.

✪ **Hotel Triton.** 342 Grant Ave. (at Bush St.), San Francisco, CA 94108. ☎ **800/433-6611** or 415/394-0500. Fax 415/394-0555. 140 rms, 7 suites. A/C MINIBAR TV TEL. $119–$179 double; $199–$279 suite. AE, DC, DISC, MC, V. Parking $22. Cable car: Powell-Hyde and Powell-Mason lines (2 blocks west).

Executing a bold idea that was long overdue, hotel magnate Bill Kimpton requisitioned a cadre of local artists and designers to "do their thing" to his latest acquisition. Described as vogue, chic, retro-futuristic, and even neo-Baroque, the Triton begs attention, from the Daliesque lobby to the sumptuous designer suites à la Jerry Garcia, Wyland (the ocean artist), and Joe Boxer. Two dozen environmentally sensitive "EcoRooms"—biodegradable soaps, filtered water and air, all-natural linens—were also installed to please the tree-hugger in all of us. *A mild caveat:* Don't expect perfection; many of the rooms could use a little touching up here and there, and service isn't as snappy as it could be. If you can live with this, and want to inject a little fun and style into your stay, then come join Dorothy and Toto for a trip far from Kansas.

Dining/Entertainment: Café de la Presse, a European-style newsstand and outdoor cafe, serves breakfast, lunch, and dinner. In the hotel lobby, complimentary coffee is served each morning and wine each evening.

Services: Room service, same-day laundry.

Facilities: Business center, exercise room.

Hotel Milano. 55 Fifth St. (between Market and Mission sts.), San Francisco, CA 94103. ☎ **800/398-7555** or 415/543-8555. Fax 415/543-5843. 108 rms. A/C MINIBAR TV TEL. $129–$189 double; extra person $20. AE, DC, JCB, MC, V. Valet parking $19. All Market St. buses.

Contemporary Italian design, elegantly streamlined rooms, and a central location make Hotel Milano a popular choice for vacationers and business travelers alike (there's even a film production facility and private screening room to entice the entertainment lot). The guest rooms feature everything a business exec could want, from modem hookups to a Nintendo game system. Other features include in-room safe and soundproofed windows. Some rooms have spa tub, bidet, two bathrooms, and TV with VCR.

Dining: M Point, which opened in early 1997, serves breakfast, lunch, and dinner with an American/Asian flare.

Services: Room service, concierge, laundry/valet.

Facilities: Fitness center and spa with steam and sauna, business center.

Hotel Rex. 562 Sutter St. (between Powell and Mason sts.), San Francisco, CA 94102. ☎ **800/433-4434** or 415/433-4434. Fax 415/433-3695. 92 rms, 2 suites. MINIBAR TV TEL. $145–$175 double; $375 suite. AE, CB, DC, MC, V. Parking $18. Cable car: Powell-Hyde and Powell-Mason lines (1 block east). Bus: 2, 3, 4, 30, 38, or 45.

Joie de Vivre, the most creative hotel group in the city, recently acquired this historic hotel (formerly the Orchard) situated near several fine galleries, theaters, and restaurants. It remains a European-style boutique hotel, but now sports a half-million-dollar facelift, done with the decorative flair that makes Joie de Vivre's hotels among the most popular in town. Attention to detail makes this one of the better choices in this price range in the neighborhood. The clublike lobby lounge is modeled after a 1920s library and is—like all their properties—cleverly stylish; an extra creative plus is the adjoining antiquarian bookstore. The renovated rooms, which are all above-average in size, feature telephones with voice mail and data ports. If you have one of the rooms in the back, you'll look out over a shady, peaceful courtyard.

Services: Room service (for deluxe continental breakfast only), concierge, same-day laundry/dry cleaning, complimentary newspaper, and complimentary evening wine hour.

Facilities: Access to health club across the street.

✪ **White Swan Inn.** 845 Bush St. (between Taylor and Mason sts.), San Francisco, CA 94108. ☎ **415/775-1755**. Fax 415/775-5717. 23 rms, 3 suites. MINIBAR TV TEL. $145–$160 double; $195 romance suites; $250 two-room suite. Extra person $15. Rates include full breakfast. AE, MC, V. Parking $19. Cable car: California St. line (1 block north). Bus: 1, 2, 3, 4, 27, or 45.

From the moment you're buzzed in to this well-secured inn just 2¹/₂ blocks from Union Square, you'll know you're not in any old B&B. More than 50 teddy bears grace the lobby—and if that doesn't cure homesickness, complimentary homemade cookies, tea, and coffee will. The romantically homey rooms are warm and cozy; they're also quite big, with rich wood furniture, working fireplaces, and an assortment of books tucked in nooks. The decor is English elegance at its best, if not to excess, with floral prints almost everywhere. The Romance suites aren't much better than regular rooms—just a little bigger, and outfitted with chocolates and champagne. This is a charming choice, with service and style to satisfy the most discriminating traveler. Note that there's no smoking allowed.

Dining/Entertainment: A generous breakfast is served just off a tiny garden. Afternoon tea is also served, with hors d'oeuvres, sherry, wine, and home-baked pastries. Wine and hors d'oeuvres are served every evening.

Services: Concierge, laundry, evening turndown, morning newspaper, overnight shoe shine.

Facilities: Access to off-premises health club for $15 per day.

MODERATE

Andrews Hotel. 624 Post St. (between Jones and Taylor sts.), San Francisco, CA 94109. ☎ **800/926-3739** or 415/563-6877. Fax 415/928-6919. 43 rms, 5 suites. MINIBAR TV TEL. $86–$109 double; $119 petite suite. Rates include continental breakfast and evening wine. AE, DC, JCB, MC, V. Self parking $15. Cable car: Powell-Hyde and Powell-Mason lines (3 blocks east). Bus: 2, 3, 4, 30, 38, or 45.

Two blocks west of Union Square, the Andrews was formerly a Turkish bath before its conversion in 1981. As is fitting with Euro-style hotels, the rooms are small but well maintained and comfortable; white lace curtains and fresh flowers in each room add a light touch. Some rooms have shower only, and bathrooms in general tend to be tiny; but for the location and price, the Andrews is a good, safe bet for an enjoyable stay in the city. An added bonus is the adjoining Fino Bar and Ristorante, which offers complimentary wine to hotel guests in the evening.

Beresford Arms. 701 Post St. (at Jones St.), San Francisco, CA 94109. ☎ **800/533-6533** or 415/673-2600. Fax 415/929-1535. 92 rms, 52 suites. MINIBAR TV TEL. $105 double; $125 Jacuzzi suite; $160 parlor suite. Rates include continental breakfast. Extra person $10. Children under 12 stay free in parents' room. Senior-citizen discount available. AE, CB, DC, DISC, MC, V. Parking $15. Cable car: Powell-Hyde line (3 blocks east). Bus: 2, 3, 4, 27, or 38.

Every time we visit the Beresford Arms, its lobby always seems filled with happy, chatty Europeans. Maybe it's the Jacuzzi whirlpool bathtubs and bidets that keep them smiling, or the "Manager's Social Hour" with free wine and snacks. The price is fair, too: $125 for a large, reasonably attractive (though a bit old-fashioned) suite with a choice of wet bar or fully equipped kitchen—key for families. Modest business services are available, as is valet or self-parking. Sandwiched between the Theater District and Union Square in a quieter section of San Francisco, the hotel's location is ideal for car-free visitors.

✪ **Commodore International.** 825 Sutter St. (at Jones St.), San Francisco, CA 94109. ☎ **800/338-6848** or 415/923-6800. Fax 415/923-6804. 113 rms. TV TEL. $79–$89 double or twin. AE, DC, MC, V. Parking $13. Bus: 2, 3, 4, 27, or 76.

If you're looking to pump a little fun and fantasy into your vacation, this is the place to stay. Hot hotelier Chip Conley (who transformed the Phoenix Hotel into a rocker's retreat) let his hip-hop designers do their magic on what was a dilapidated eyesore, and the result is one groovy hotel. Stealing the show is the Red Room, a Big Apple–style bar and lounge that's ruby red through and through (you gotta see this one). The stylish lobby comes in a close second, followed by the Titanic Café, a cute little diner serving buckwheat griddlecakes, Vietnamese tofu sandwiches, and dragon fire salads. Appealing to the masses, Chip left the first four floors as standard no-frills—though quite clean and comfortable—rooms, while decking out the top two floors in neo-deco overtones—well worth the extra $10 a night.

Kensington Park Hotel. 450 Post St. (between Powell and Mason sts.), San Francisco, CA 94102. ☎ **800/553-1900** or 415/788-6400. Fax 415/399-9484. 84 rms, 2 suites. TV TEL. $125 double; $350 suite. Rates include continental breakfast. Extra person $10. AE, CB, DC, MC, V. Parking $17. Cable car: Powell-Hyde and Powell-Mason lines (2 blocks east).

The Kensington caught us by surprise. We were expecting another boutique hotel with bland decor and wrinkles from age; what we found instead was a cheery, eager-to-please staff, tasteful accommodations, and extra efforts that showed that the staff really cares about its guests. The recently upgraded rooms are reminiscent of old England, with traditional mahogany furniture, beautiful damask fabrics, and enormous armoires—far more attractive than most hotel furnishings. Bathrooms may be small, but they're sweetly appointed in brass and marble. As for the views, ask for an upper corner room, and you'll be getting far beyond your money's worth. Farallon, a restaurant that opened in '97, is run by the folks from Kuleto's (see "Dining," below). Services include room service, concierge, same-day laundry, morning newspaper, and complimentary morning limo to the Financial District; fax and secretarial services also available.

The Maxwell. 386 Geary St. (at Mason St.), San Francisco, CA 94102. ☎ **800/821-5343** or 415/986-2000. Fax 415/397-2447. 150 rms, 2 suites. A/C TV TEL. $119–$145 double; $195–$350 suite. Additional person $15. Corporate discounts available. AE, CB, DC, DISC, MC, V. Parking $17. Cable car: Powell-Hyde and Powell-Mason lines (2 blocks east). Bus: 2, 3, 4, 30, 38, or 45.

What a pleasant surprise to see what Joie de Vivre (owners of the Commodore, the Phoenix, and Archbishop's Mansion) did when they acquired this hotel and reopened in 1997. What was once an old, somewhat rundown hotel in an excellent location (one block from Union Square) is now an incredibly chic boutique hotel. The designers have blended velvets and brocades with rich, rich color and patterns and hand-crafted artistic accents into what the management calls "theatre-deco-fused-with-Victoriana" decor. Rooms come with upholstered chairs, hand-painted lamps, luxurious pillows, boldly tiled sinks, and respectable prints hanging on the walls. Other pluses are writing desks, hair dryers, and two phones. Gracie's Restaurant has an oyster bar and live entertainment nightly.

☼ Petite Auberge. 863 Bush St. (between Taylor and Mason sts.), San Francisco, CA 94108. ☎ **415/928-6000**. Fax 415/775-5717. 26 rms. TV TEL. $110–$160 double; $220 petite suite. Rates include continental breakfast. AE, DC, MC, V. Parking $19. Cable car: Powell-Hyde and Powell-Mason lines. Bus: 2, 3, 4, 30, 38, or 45.

Nobody does French country like this place. We want to say that the Petite Auberge is overdone—that any hotel filled with teddy bears is absurd—but we just can't bring ourselves to do it. Bribed each year with fresh-baked cookies from a never-empty platter, we make our rounds through the rooms and ruefully admit that we're just going to have to use that word we loath to hear: adorable. Hand-crafted armoires, delicate lace curtains, cozy little fireplaces, adorable knickknacks (there's that word again)—no hotel in Provence ever had it this good. Honeymooners should splurge on the Petite suite, which has its own private entrance, deck, spa tub, fridge, and coffeemaker. The lovely muraled breakfast room opens onto a small garden where California wines and tea are served in the afternoon.

Savoy Hotel. 580 Geary St. (between Taylor and Jones sts.), San Francisco, CA 94102. ☎ **800/ 227-4223** or 415/441-2700. Fax 415/441-2700. 70 rms, 13 suites. MINIBAR TV TEL. $125–$135 double; from $195 suite. Ask about package, government, senior, and corporate rates. Rates include continental breakfast. AE, CB, DC, DISC, MC, V. Parking $18. Bus: 2, 3, 4, 27, or 38.

Both travelers and *Travel & Leisure* agree that the Savoy is a sweet and affordable small hotel a few blocks off Union Square. The rooms—which can be small—are cozily done in French provincial style, with 18th-century period furnishings, featherbeds, and goose-down pillows—plus modern conveniences such as remote-control TVs and hair dryers. Especially nice is that not all rooms are alike, and all have beautiful patterned draperies. Other perks include triple sheets, turndown service, full-length mirrors, and two-line telephones, as well as concierge service and free overnight shoe shines. Rates include complimentary late-afternoon sherry and tea and continental breakfast, served in the Brasserie Savoy, a seafood restaurant that brings even the locals downtown for dinner (see "Dining," below, for details).

Warwick Regis. 490 Geary St. (between Mason and Taylor sts.), San Francisco, CA 94102. ☎ **800/827-3447** or 415/928-7900. Fax 415/441-8788. 40 rms, 40 suites. MINIBAR TV TEL. $135–$215 double. Rates include continental breakfast. AE, CB, DC, DISC, MC, V. Parking $19. Cable car: Powell-Hyde and Powell Mason lines. Bus: 2, 3, 4, 27, or 38.

Louis XVI may have been a rotten monarch, but he certainly had taste. Fashioned in the style of pre-Revolutionary France, the Warwick is awash with pristine French and English antiques, Italian marble, chandeliers, four-poster beds, hand-carved headboards, and the like. The result is an expensive-looking hotel that, for all its pleasantries and perks, is surprisingly affordable when compared to its Union Square contemporaries (singles are as low as $105). Honeymooners should splurge on a Fireplace room, which has a canopy bed.

Dining/Entertainment: Adjoining the lobby is fashionable La Scene Café, the perfect place to start your day with a latte and end it with a nightcap.

Services: 24-hour room and concierge service, dry cleaning, laundry, twice-daily maid service, complimentary shoe shine and newspaper.

👪 Family-Friendly Hotels

The Clift *(see p. 58)*   The hotel's Young Travelers Program offers amenities from bottles and diapers to toys, games, coloring books, information about family-oriented attractions, and special treats from room service—all designed to make kids feel as pampered as their parents.

Westin St. Francis *(see p. 59)*   Kids like the St. Francis because everyone under 12 is given a Westin Kids Club hat on arrival and special sports bottles (with complimentary refills in the hotel's restaurants). Their siblings ages 3 to 7 are given dinosaur soaps, sponges, and coloring books. Parents get some extra help, too, in seeing that kids are supervised.

Holiday Lodge & Garden Hotel *(see p. 71)*   This is the best moderately priced family hotel in the city. Kids are welcomed with crayons and board games, they have free reign of the sheltered courtyard complete with outdoor heated pool. There's also free HBO, and room service from a nearby restaurant.

Facilities: VCR, hair dryer, access to nearby health club, business center, conference rooms.

INEXPENSIVE

Brady Acres. 649 Jones St. (between Geary and Post sts.), San Francisco, CA 94102. ☎ **800/627-2396** or 415/929-8033. Fax 415/441-8033. 25 rms. MINIBAR TV TEL. $60–$85 double. Available only by the week Oct–Apr; call for daily availability. MC, V. Parking in nearby garage $15. Bus: 2, 3, 4, 27, or 38.

Inside this small, four-story brick building is a budget traveler's dream come true. You'll find everything you need to keep costs to a minimum: The small but very clean rooms have a microwave oven, small refrigerator, toaster, and coffeemaker; hair dryer and alarm clock; and direct-dial phone (with free local calls) with an answering machine. Baths are newly renovated, and a coin-operated washer and dryer are in the basement, along with free laundry soap and irons. Owner Deborah Liane Brady and her staff are usually on hand to offer friendly, personal service, making this option an unbeatable deal all in all. Keep in mind that during the low season you can only rent by the week.

Golden Gate Hotel. 775 Bush St. (between Powell and Mason sts.), San Francisco, CA 94108. ☎ **800/835-1118** or 415/392-3702. Fax 415/392-6202. 23 rms (14 with bath). TV TEL. $65 double without bath, $99 double with bath. Rates include continental breakfast. AE, CB, DC, MC, V. Parking $12. Cable car: Powell-Hyde and Powell-Mason lines (1 block east). Bus: 2, 3, 4, 30, 38, or 45.

Among San Francisco's small hotels occupying historic turn-of-the-century buildings, there are some real gems—and this is one of them. It's two blocks north of Union Square and two blocks down from the crest of Nob Hill, with cable car stops at the corner for easy access to Fisherman's Wharf and Chinatown (the city's theaters and best restaurants are also within walking distance). But the best thing about the Golden Gate Hotel is that this is a family-run establishment: John and Renate Kenaston are hospitable innkeepers who take obvious pleasure in making their guests comfortable. Each individually decorated room has handsome antique furnishings from the early 1900s (including plenty of wicker), quilted bedspreads, and fresh flowers; request a room with a clawfoot tub if you enjoy a good, hot soak. Complimentary afternoon tea is served daily from 4 to 7pm.

Grant Plaza Hotel. 465 Grant Ave. (at Pine St.), San Francisco, CA 94108. ☎ **800/472-6899** or 415/434-3883. Fax 415/434-3886. 72 rms. TV TEL. $49–$75 double. AE, CB, MC, V. Nearby parking $11.50. Cable car: Powell-Hyde and Powell-Mason lines (2 blocks west).

You won't find any free little bottles of shampoo here. What you will find are cheap accommodations and basic—and we mean basic—rooms right in the middle of Union Square/Chinatown action. Many of the small, well-kept rooms in this six-story building overlook Chinatown's main street, and all of them had new bedspreads, draperies, and hair dryers added in 1997. Corner rooms on higher floors are both larger and brighter. Ask for a room on the top floor—they're the newest and are substantially nicer than the older rooms. Expect little more than a soap dispenser in the small shower (most bathrooms don't have tubs).

NOB HILL
VERY EXPENSIVE

Fairmont Hotel & Tower. 950 Mason St. (at California St.), San Francisco, CA 94108. ☎ **800/527-4727** or 415/772-5000. Fax 415/772-5013. 538 rms, 62 suites. A/C MINIBAR TV TEL. Main building: $229–$279 double; from $530 suite. Tower: $269–$359 double; from $800 suite. Extra person $30. Continental breakfast $13.50 extra. AE, CB, DC, DISC, MC, V. Parking $27. Cable car: California St. line (direct stop).

The granddaddy of Nob Hill's ritzy hotels, the Fairmont wins top honors for the most awe-inspiring lobby in San Francisco. Even if you're not staying here, it's worth a side trip to gape at its massive marble columns, vaulted ceilings, velvet chairs, gilded mirrors, and spectacular wraparound staircase. Unfortunately, such opulence doesn't carry over to the guest rooms, which are surprisingly ordinary (aside from the spectacular views from the top floors). In addition to the expected luxuries, expect such extras as goose-down pillows, electric shoe buffers, large walk-in closets, and multiline phones with voice mail in your room.

Dining/Entertainment: A variety of restaurants offers everything from contemporary California cuisine to Chinese and Polynesian specialties to deli favorites. The tropical Hurricane Bar features dancing and a generous happy hour. Afternoon tea is served daily in the lobby.

Services: 24-hour room service, 24-hour concierge, twice-daily maid service, evening turndown, laundry/valet, complimentary shoe shine, complimentary morning limousine to the Financial District.

Facilities: Health club, business center, barbershop, beauty salon, pharmacy, shopping arcade.

Huntington Hotel. 1075 California St. (between Mason and Taylor sts.), San Francisco, CA 94108. ☎ **800/227-4683** or 415/474-5400, 800/652-1539 (in CA only). Fax 415/474-6227. 110 rms, 30 suites. A/C MINIBAR TV TEL. $200–$250 double; from $295–$825 suite. Special packages available. Continental breakfast $10.75. AE, CB, DC, DISC, MC, V. Valet parking $19.50. Cable car: California St. line (direct stop). Bus: 1.

The stately Huntington has long been a favorite retreat for Hollywood stars and political VIPs who desire privacy and security. Family owned since 1924—a real rarity among large hotels—this hotel eschews pomp and circumstance; absolute privacy and unobtrusive service are its mainstay. Though the elaborate 19th-century–style lobby is rather petite, the guest rooms are quite large and feature Brunschwig and Fils fabrics, French antiques, and views of the city. Prices are steep, but special offers like the Romance Package ($215 per couple, including free champagne, sherry, and limousine service) make the Huntington worth considering for a special occasion.

Dining/Entertainment: The Big Four restaurant offers expensive seasonal continental cuisine in one of the city's most handsome dining rooms. There's live piano music nightly in the lounge.

Services: Room service, concierge, complimentary limousine to the Financial District and Union Square, overnight shoe shine, laundry, evening turndown, complimentary morning newspaper, twice-daily maid service, complimentary formal tea or sherry service upon arrival.

Facilities: Access to off-site health club and spa ($15).

Mark Hopkins Inter-Continental. 1 Nob Hill (at California and Mason sts.), San Francisco, CA 94108. ☎ **800/327-0200** or 415/392-3434. Fax 415/421-3302. 390 rms, 28 suites. A/C MINIBAR TV TEL. $200–$280 double; from $375 suite. Breakfast buffet $18 extra. AE, CB, DC, DISC, MC, V. Valet parking $23. Cable car: California St. line (direct stop). Bus: 1.

Built in 1926, this 19-story hotel caters mostly to convention-bound corporate executives who can write off the high rates. Each neoclassical room comes with all the fancy amenities you'd expect from a world-class hotel, including custom furniture, plush fabrics, sumptuous baths, and extraordinary views. (*Tip:* The even-numbered rooms on the higher floor overlook the Golden Gate.) A minor caveat is that there are only three guest elevators, making a quick trip up to your room difficult during busy periods.

Dining/Entertainment: The plush and decidedly formal Nob Hill Restaurant offers international cuisine with a California flair, plus a continental buffet breakfast; a second restaurant serves lunch, afternoon tea, cocktails, and dinner. The world-renowned Top of the Mark lounge serves cocktails and Sunday brunch, and offers dancing to live music Wednesday through Saturday.

Services: Room service, concierge, evening turndown on request, overnight shoe shine, laundry, courtesy limousine weekday mornings, complimentary newspaper delivery, in-room massage, twice-daily maid service.

Facilities: Business center, health club, Executive Club floor, car-rental desk.

✪ **Ritz-Carlton San Francisco.** 600 Stockton St. (between Pine and California sts.), San Francisco, CA 94108. ☎ **800/241-3333** or 415/296-7465. Fax 415/296-0288. 292 rms, 44 suites. A/C MINIBAR TV TEL. $300 double; $350 club-level double; from $525 suite. Weekend discounts and packages available. Continental breakfast $14.50 extra; breakfast buffet $19 extra; Sunday brunch $42. AE, CB, DC, DISC, MC, V. Parking $27. Cable car: Powell-Hyde and Powell-Mason lines (direct stop).

Ranked among the top hotels in the world (as well as the top hotel in the city) by readers of *Condé Nast Traveler*, the Ritz-Carlton has been the benchmark of San Francisco luxury hotels since it opened in 1991. A Nob Hill landmark, it's outfitted with the finest furnishings, fabrics, and artwork, and the rooms offer every possible amenity and service, from Italian-marble baths with double sinks to plush terry robes. The more expensive rooms offer good views of the city. Club rooms have a dedicated concierge, separate elevator-key access, and complimentary meals throughout the day.

Dining/Entertainment: The Ritz-Carlton Dining Room is regularly voted among the nation's top restaurants (see "Dining," below, for complete review). The less formal Terrace Restaurant offers contemporary French cuisine and courtyard dining. The lobby lounge offers afternoon tea and cocktails and sushi daily, accompanied by low-key live entertainment. Sunday brunch is easily one of the best in town.

Services: 24-hour room service, same-day valet, concierge, child care, complimentary morning newspaper, shoe shine.

Facilities: Business center, an outstanding fitness center with pool, and gift boutique.

EXPENSIVE

✪ **Nob Hill Lambourne.** 725 Pine St. (between Powell and Stockton sts.), San Francisco, CA 94108. ☎ **800/274-8466** or 415/433-2287. 9 rms, 5 executive rms, 6 suites. MINIBAR TV TEL.

$175 double; $195 executive; $275 suite. Rates include continental breakfast. AE, CB, DC, DISC, MC, V. Valet parking $22. Cable car: California St. line (1 block north).

One of San Francisco's top "business-boutique" hotels, the Lambourne bills itself as an urban health spa, offering a variety of spa treatments—from massages to yoga lessons—to ease executive-level stress. Even without this hook, the ultra-stylish Lambourne deserves a top-of-the-class rating. Top-quality, hand-sewn mattresses and goose-down comforters are complemented by such in-room extras as notebook computers with Internet access, fax machines, VCRs, stereos, kitchenettes, and coffee-makers; bathrooms have oversized tubs and hair dryers. Guests are invited to enjoy complimentary wine and hors d'ouevres at 6pm.

Services: Evening turndown, business services.

Facilities: Spa treatment room.

SOMA

EXPENSIVE

Harbor Court. 165 Steuart St. (between Mission and Howard sts.), San Francisco, CA 94105. ☎ **800/346-0555** (in the U.S.) or 415/882-1300. Fax 415/882-1313. 131 rms. A/C MINIBAR TV TEL. $160–$295 double. Continental breakfast $6.95 extra. AE, CB, DC, MC, V. Parking $19. Muni Metro: Embarcadero. Bus: 14, 32, 80x.

When the Embarcadero Freeway was torn down after the Big One in 1989, one of the major benefactors was this hotel, whose backyard view went from a wall of cement to a dazzling view of the Bay Bridge (be sure to request a bay-view room, which is only $30 extra). Located just off the Embarcadero at the edge of the Financial District, this former YMCA books a lot of corporate travelers, but anyone who prefers stylish, high-quality accommodations—half-canopy beds, large armoires, writing desks, soundproof windows—and a lively scene will be very content here.

Dining/Entertainment: In the evening, the hotel's dark, velvety restaurant, Harry Denton's, transforms into the Financial District's hot spot for hungry singles.

Services: Concierge, limited room service, dry cleaning, laundry, secretarial services, valet, courtesy car, free refreshments in lobby.

Facilities: Free use of the top-quality fitness club with Olympic-size swimming pool.

Hotel Griffon. 155 Steuart St. (between Mission and Howard sts.), San Francisco, CA 94105. ☎ **800/321-2201** or 415/495-2100. Fax 415/495-3522. 62 rms, 3 penthouse suites. A/C MINIBAR TV TEL. $185–$225 double; $295 penthouse suite. Rates include continental breakfast and newspaper. AE, CB, DC, DISC, MC, V. Parking $15. All Market St. buses, BART, and ferries.

After a complete rehab in 1989, the Hotel Griffon emerged as a top contender among San Francisco's small hotels. Ideally situated on the historic waterfront and only steps from the heart of the Financial District, the Griffon is impeccably outfitted with contemporary features such as whitewashed brick walls, lofty ceilings, marble vanities, window seats, cherry-wood furniture, and art deco–style lamps—really, this place is smooth. Be sure to request a bay view room—the added perks and Bay Bridge view make it well worth the extra $30—and inquire about the excellent weekend packages the hotel occasionally offers.

Dining/Entertainment: Rôti, which has evolved into a prime lunch spot for the nearby Financial District, offers California-style food prepared on spit roasts and wood-burning ovens in a dining room with a view of the Bay Bridge.

Services: Limited room service, laundry/valet, concierge, in-room massage, secretarial services.

Facilities: Free access to nearby health club.

FINANCIAL DISTRICT
VERY EXPENSIVE

✪ **Mandarin Oriental.** 222 Sansome St. (between Pine and California sts.), San Francisco, CA 94104. ☎ **800/622-0404** or 415/885-0999. Fax 415/433-0289. 154 rms, 4 suites. A/C MINIBAR TV TEL. $285–$375 double; from $415 junior suite. Continental breakfast $17 extra. AE, DC, JCB, MC, V. Parking $21. Muni Metro: Montgomery. All Market Street buses.

If we were seeking respite from researching this guide, we'd probably head straight here, jump into a Jacuzzi, and relax while we admire the city we love most from above. This hotel is located between the 38th and 48th floors, which allows each of the large rooms extraordinary views. Not all rooms have tub-side views, but they do have well-stocked marble bathrooms that include such luxuries as terry- and cotton-cloth robes, hair dryers, makeup mirrors, and silk slippers. The less-opulent bedrooms are done in a kind of reserved-contemporary decor with Asian accents. Additional amenities include two-line phones with fax hookups and on-command video access to more than 80 movies.

Dining: Silks has won rave reviews melding California and Asian ingredients.

Services: 24-hour room service, complimentary newspaper and shoe shine, concierge, laundry/valet.

Facilities: Business center, brand-new fitness center with cardio and Nautilus machines and free weights.

Sheraton Palace Hotel. 2 New Montgomery St. (at Market St.), San Francisco, CA 94105. ☎ **800/325-3535** or 415/392-8600. Fax 415/543-0671. 517 rms, 33 suites. A/C MINIBARS TV TEL. $300–$390 double; from $700 suite. Additional person $20. Children under 18 sharing existing bedding stay free in parents' room. Weekend rates and packages available. Continental breakfast $13.50 extra; deluxe continental breakfast $15.75 extra. AE, DC, DISC, JCB, MC, V. Parking $22. Muni Metro: All Market St. trams. All Market St. buses.

Every time you walk through these doors, you'll be reminded how incredibly majestic old luxury really is. The original 1875 Palace was rebuilt after the 1906 quake; the most spectacular attribute is still the old regal lobby and the Garden Court, a San Francisco landmark that has been restored to its original heart-stopping grandeur. Regrettably, the rooms have that standardized, chain-hotel appearance.

Dining/Entertainment: On special holidays, the Garden Court serves a $52 brunch worth indulging in, while a scaled-down version takes over on other weekends. The Pied Piper Bar is named for the Maxfield Parrish mural that dominates the room. There's also a traditional San Francisco grill with turn-of-the-century charm, and an authentic Japanese restaurant.

Services: 24-hour room service, concierge, evening turndown, laundry/valet.

Facilities: Business service center, lobby-level shops, on-site health club with skylight-covered lap pool, whirlpool, sauna, and exercise room.

NORTH BEACH
MODERATE

✪ **Hotel Bohème.** 444 Columbus St., (between Vallejo and Green sts.), San Francisco, CA 94133. ☎ **415/433-9111**. Fax 415/362-6292. 15 rms. TV TEL. $130 double. AE, CB, DISC, DC, JCB, MC, V. Parking $20 at nearby public garage. Cable car: Powell-Mason line. Bus: 12, 15, 30, 41, 45, or 83.

Although located on the busiest strip in North Beach, this recently renovated hotel's style and demeanor are more reminiscent of a prestigious home in upscale Nob Hill. Rooms are small but hopelessly romantic, with gauze-draped canopies and artistically accented walls. The staff is very hospitable, and bonuses include hair dryers and complimentary sherry in the lobby each afternoon. Some of the city's greatest cafes, restaurants, bars, and shops are just a few steps away, and Chinatown and Union Square are within walking distance.

INEXPENSIVE

✪ **San Remo Hotel.** 2237 Mason St. (at Chestnut St.), San Francisco, CA 94133. ☎ **800/ 352-REMO** or 415/776-8688. Fax 415/776-2811. E-mail: info@sanremohotel.com. 62 rms (none with bath), 1 suite. $60–$70 double; $100 suite. AE, DC, JCB, MC, V. Parking $8–$12. Cable car: Powell-Mason line. Bus: 15, 22, or 30.

Located in a quiet North Beach neighborhood and within walking distance of Fisherman's Wharf, this small European-style pension is one of the best budget hotels in San Francisco. The rooms are small and bathrooms shared, but all is forgiven when it comes time to pay the bill. Rooms are decorated in a cozy country style with brass and iron beds; oak, maple, or pine armoires; and wicker furnishings; most have ceiling fans. The shared bathrooms, each one immaculately clean, feature clawfoot tubs and brass pull-chain toilets with oak tanks and brass fixtures. If the penthouse is available, book it: You won't find a more romantic place to stay in San Francisco for so little money.

FISHERMAN'S WHARF
EXPENSIVE

The Sheraton at Fisherman's Wharf. 2500 Mason St. (between Beach and North Point sts.), San Francisco, CA 94133. ☎ **800/325-3535** or 415/362-5500. Fax 415/956-5275. 517 rms, 7 suites. A/C TV TEL. $135–$200 double; from $375 suite. Extra person $20. Continental breakfast $7.95 extra. AE, CB, DC, DISC, MC, V. Parking $12. Cable car: Powell-Mason line (1 block east, 2 blocks south). Bus: 15, 32, or 42.

Built in the mid-1970s, this modern, three-story hotel isn't the most visually appealing of hotels, but it offers the reliable comforts of a Sheraton in the heart of San Francisco's most popular tourist area. In 1995 the hotel spent $4 million renovating the rooms and adding a Corporate Floor catering exclusively to business travelers.

Dining/Entertainment: There's a Victorian-style cafe serving up breakfast, lunch, and dinner, plus live jazz several nights a week along with cocktails and assorted appetizers.

Services: Room service, concierge, evening turndown.

Facilities: Outdoor heated swimming pool, access to nearby health club, business center, hair salon, car-rental and travel desks.

Tuscan Inn. 425 North Point St. (at Mason St.), San Francisco, CA 94133. ☎ **800/648-4626** or 415/561-1100. Fax 415/561-1199. 209 rms, 12 suites. A/C MINIBAR TV TEL. $165–$198 double; $218–$258 suite. Rates include evening fireside wine reception. AE, DC, DISC, MC, V. Parking $15. Cable car: Powell-Mason line. Bus: 42, 15, or 32.

The Tuscan is the best hotel at Fisherman's Wharf. Like an island of respectability in a sea of touristy schlock, it offers a level of style and comfort far beyond its neighboring competitors. Splurge on parking—cheaper than the wharf's outrageously priced garages—then saunter your way toward the plush lobby warmed by a grand fireplace. Even the rooms, each equipped with writing desks and armchairs, are a cut above competing neighborhood hotels. The only caveat is the lack of views—a small price to pay for a good hotel in a great location.

Dining: Café Pescatore serves standard Italian fare in an airy, partial alfresco setting.

Services: Concierge, room service, laundry service, voice mail.

COW HOLLOW/PACIFIC HEIGHTS
VERY EXPENSIVE

Sherman House. 2160 Green St. (between Webster and Fillmore sts.), San Francisco, CA 94123. ☎ **800/424-5777** or 415/563-3600. Fax 415/563-1882. 8 rms, 6 suites. TV TEL. $200–$375 double; from $600 suite. Continental breakfast $14 extra. AE, CB, DC, MC, V. Valet parking $16. Cable car: Powell-Hyde line. Bus: 22, 41, or 45.

How expensive is a night at the Sherman House? Put it this way: If you have to ask, you can't afford it. This magnificent 1876 Victorian has been restored to its original splendor, and it now sets the standard in San Francisco for privacy, personal service, and all-around sumptuousness. All rooms are individually decorated with authentic antiques in French Second Empire, Biedermeier, or English Jacobean style; queen-size canopy featherbeds; and ultra-rich tapestry fabrics and down comforters. Extras include VCRs, stereos, and granite bathrooms complete with robes and whirlpools; all rooms except one have fireplaces.

Dining: The dining room has a very fine reputation, but because of a zoning dispute, it has lost its license to serve food to non-guests and is now open only to residents; this change may affect the standards.

Services: Room service, butler (who will discreetly unpack luggage), concierge, massage, personalized shopping, chauffeur, dry cleaning/laundry, complimentary newspaper delivery, twice-daily maid service, secretarial services.

Facilities: Business center.

EXPENSIVE

✪ **Union Street Inn.** 2229 Union St. (between Fillmore and Steiner sts.), San Francisco, CA 94123. ☎ **415/346-0424.** Fax 415/922-8046. Website: www.unionstreetinn.com. 5 rms, 1 cottage. TV TEL. $125–$185 standard double; $225 cottage. Rates include breakfast, hors d'oeuvres, and evening beverages. AE, MC, V. Parking $15. Bus: 22, 41, 45, or 47.

Who would've guessed that one of the most delightful B&Bs in California would be in San Francisco? This two-story Edwardian may front the perpetually busy (and trendy) Union Street, but it's quiet as a church on the inside. All individually decorated rooms are comfortably furnished, and most come with canopied or brass beds with down comforters, fresh flowers, bay windows (beg for one with a view of the garden), and private baths (a few even have Jacuzzi tubs). An extended continental breakfast is served either in the parlor, in your room, or on an outdoor terrace overlooking a lovely English garden. The ultimate honeymoon retreat is the private carriage house behind the inn, but any room at this warm, friendly inn is guaranteed to please.

MODERATE

Bed & Breakfast Inn. 4 Charlton Court (off Union St., between Buchanan and Laguna sts.), San Francisco, CA 94123. ☎ **415/921-9784.** 11 rms (4 with shared bath), 2 suites. $70–$90 double without bath, $115–$140 double with bath; $190–$275 suite. Rates include continental breakfast. No credit cards. Parking $10 a day at nearby garage. Bus: 41 or 45.

San Francisco's first B&B is composed of a trio of Victorian houses all gussied up in English country style, hidden in a cul-de-sac just off Union Street. While it doesn't have quite the casual ambiance of neighboring Union Street Inn, it's loaded with charm. Each room is uniquely decorated with family heirlooms, original art, and a profusion of fresh flowers. The Garden Suite—highly recommended for families or groups of four—comes with a fully stocked kitchen, a living room with fireplace, two bedrooms, two bathrooms (one with a Jacuzzi tub), a study, and French doors leading out into the garden. Breakfast—freshly baked croissants, fresh fruit, orange juice, and coffee, tea, or cocoa—is either brought to your room on a tray with flowers and a morning newspaper, or served in a sunny Victorian breakfast room on antique china.

Holiday Lodge & Garden Hotel. 1901 Van Ness Ave. (between Clay and Washington sts.), San Francisco, CA 94109. ☎ **415/776-4469.** Fax 415/474-7046. 75 rms (12 with kitchenettes), 2 suites. TV TEL. $99–$109 double; $119 double with kitchenette; $145–$165 suites. AE, DC, DISC, MC, V. Free parking. Cable car: Powell-Hyde line. Bus: 42, 47, or 49.

The focal point of this hotel, which is decorated in what could be called tropical contemporary style, is the outdoor heated pool and courtyard. The modern rooms were recarpeted in 1996; all have a TV with HBO. Kids are welcomed with crayons and board games. No breakfast deal is offered, but there's complimentary coffee in the lobby. Services include room service (from a local restaurant delivery service), concierge, laundry/valet, and massage.

JAPANTOWN & ENVIRONS
EXPENSIVE

The Archbishop's Mansion. 1000 Fulton St. (at Steiner St.), San Francisco, CA 94117. ☎ **800/543-5820** or 415/563-7872. 15 rms. TEL TV. $129–$285 double. Rates include continental breakfast. AE, CB, DC, MC, V. Limited free parking. Bus: 5 or 22.

One thing is for certain: The Archbishop who built this 1904 belle epoque beauty was no Puritan. Drippingly romantic, it's one of the most opulent and fabulously adorned B&Bs you could possibly hope to stay in. The Don Giovanni suite—larger than most San Francisco houses—comes with a huge, cherub-encrusted four-poster bed imported from a French castle, a palatial fireplace, elaborately embroidered linens, and a seven-head shower that you'll never want to leave. Slightly closer to earth is the deadly romantic Carmen suite, with a clawfoot tub fronting a toasty, wood-burning fireplace.

Dining: Breakfast is delivered to your room. Complimentary wine is served in the elegant parlor in the evening.

Services: Laundry/valet, concierge, limousine service, complimentary morning newspaper, limited room service.

✪ Hotel Majestic. 1500 Sutter St. (between Octavia and Gough sts.), San Francisco, CA 94109. ☎ **800/869-8966** or 415/441-1100. Fax 415/673-7331. 51 rms, 9 suites. TV TEL. $135–$170 double; from $260 suite. Group, government, corporate, and relocation rates available. Continental breakfast $8.50 extra. AE, CB, DC, DISC, MC, V. Valet parking $16.

Vacationers and business travelers alike adore the Majestic because it meets every professional need while retaining the ambiance of a luxurious old-world hotel—the lobby alone will sweep you into another era with its tapestries, brocades, Corinthian columns, and intricate, lavish detail. Rooms are furnished with French and English antiques, the centerpiece of each being a large four-poster canopy bed; you'll also find mirrored armoires and antique reproductions. All drapes, fabrics, carpet, and bedspreads were replaced in 1997, which ensures you'll rest not only in style, but in freshness as well. Extras include a well-lit full-size desk and bath robes; some rooms also have fireplaces.

Dining/Entertainment: Café Majestic and Bar, which serves California/Asian fare in a romantic setting, continues to intrigue a local clientele. Cocktails are offered from the French mahogany marble-topped bar.

Services: Room service, laundry/valet, concierge, dry cleaning, laundry service, in-room massage, secretarial service, courtesy car on weekdays, complimentary newspaper, and afternoon sherry and fresh-baked cookies 6 to 8pm nightly.

MODERATE

Queen Anne Hotel. 1590 Sutter St. (between Gough and Octavia sts.), San Francisco, CA 94109. ☎ **800/227-3970** or 415/441-2828. Fax 415/775-5212. 45 rms, 4 suites. TV TEL. $110–$170 double; $175 suite. Extra person $10. Rates include continental breakfast. AE, CB, DC, DISC, MC, V. Parking $12. Bus: 2, 3, or 4.

This majestic 1890 Victorian is a stunning hotel that remains true to its heritage and emulates San Francisco's golden days. the lavish "grand salon" greets you with English oak paneling and antiques; rooms follow suit with antique armoires, marble-top dressers, and other period pieces. Some have corner turret bay windows that look out onto tree-lined streets, plus separate parlor areas and wet bars; others have cozy reading nooks and fireplaces. All rooms have phones in the bathroom, computer hook-ups, and fridges. You can relax in the parlor, with its impressive floor-to-ceiling fireplace, or in the hotel library. Services include room service, concierge, morning newspaper, and complimentary afternoon tea and sherry. There's also access to an off-premises health club with a lap pool. If you're not partial to Union Square, this hotel comes highly recommended.

CIVIC CENTER

EXPENSIVE

The Inn at the Opera. 333 Fulton St. (at Franklin St.), San Francisco, CA 94102. ☎ **800/325-2708** or 415/863-8400. Fax 415/861-0821. 30 rms, 18 suites. MINIBAR TV TEL. $140–$190 double; from $265 suite. Extra person $15. Rates include European buffet breakfast. AE, DC, MC, V. Parking $19. Bus: 5, 21, 47, or 49.

Judging from its mild-mannered facade and offbeat location, few would ever guess that this is one of San Francisco's—if not California's—finest small hotels. From the minute you walk into a marble- and damask-filled lobby, you know you're about to be spoiled with sumptuousness. But don't take our word for it; Pavarotti, Domingo, Baryshnikov, and dozens of other stars of the stage throw their slumber parties here regularly. Queen beds with huge stuffed pillows are standard in each elegant pastel-hued guest room, along with microwaves, fridges, and bouquets of fresh flowers. The larger rooms and suites are recommended for those who need elbow room; as in most small hotels, the least expensive "standard" rooms are short on space.

Dining/Entertainment: Act IV Restaurant, the hotel's fine dining room, provides an intimate setting for dinner, while the adjacent lounge with its leather chairs, glowing fire, and soft piano music is a favorite city meeting place.

Services: 24-hour room service, concierge, laundry/valet, evening turndown, complimentary light pressing and overnight shoe shine, complimentary limousine service to the Financial District, morning newspaper.

Facilities: Business center.

MODERATE

Abigail Hotel. 246 McAllister St. (between Hyde and Larkin sts.), San Francisco, CA 94102. ☎ 800/243-6510 or 415/861-9728. Fax 415/861-5848. 59 rms, 1 suite. TV TEL. $84 double standard; $89 deluxe; $139 suite. Extra person $10. Rates include continental breakfast. AE, CB, DC, MC, V. Parking $8. Muni Metro: All Market St. trams. All Market St. buses.

Though it doesn't get much press, the Abigail is one of the better medium-priced hotels in the city; what it lacks in luxury it more than than makes up for in charm. The rooms, while on the small side, are clean, cute, and comfortably furnished with cozy antiques and down comforters. Morning coffee, pastries, and complimentary newspapers greet you in the beautiful faux-marble lobby, while lunch and dinner are served in the hot new "organic" restaurant, the Millennium. Access to a nearby health club, as well as laundry and massage services, are available upon request.

Phoenix Hotel. 601 Eddy St. (at Larkin St.), San Francisco, CA 94109. ☎ **800/248-9466** or 415/776-1380. Fax 415/885-3109. 41 rms, 3 suites. TV TEL. $99–$119 double; $149 suite. Rates include continental breakfast. AE, DC, MC, V. Free parking. Bus: 19, 31, or 38.

If you'd like to tell your friends back home that you've stayed in the same hotel as Linda Ronstadt and the Red Hot Chili Peppers, this is the place for you. Situated on the fringes of the less-than-pleasant Tenderloin District, this retro 1950s-style hotel—which has been described by *People* as the hippest hotel in town—is a gathering place for visiting rockers, writers, and filmmakers who crave a dose of Southern California on their trips to San Francisco. The focal point of the pastel-painted Palm Springs–style hotel is a heated, paisley-muraled pool set in a modern-sculpture garden. The rooms, while far from plush, are comfortably outfitted with bamboo furnishings and original local art. In addition to the usual amenities, the inn's own closed-circuit channel shows films exclusively made in or about San Francisco. Services include on-site massage, concierge, laundry/valet, and—whoo hoo!—free parking. Backflip, a super-swank cocktail lounge, serves tapas and Caribbean-style appetizers.

HAIGHT-ASHBURY
MODERATE

Red Victorian Bed, Breakfast, & Art. 1665 Haight St. (between Cole and Belvedere sts.), San Francisco, CA 94117. ☎ **415/864-1978**. Fax 415/863-3293. 18 rms (4 with bath), 1 suite. TEL. $76–$110 double without bath, $120–$126 double with bath; $200 suite. Extra person $15. Rates decrease based on length of stay, and include continental breakfast and afternoon tea. AE, MC, V. Guarded parking lot nearby. Muni Metro: N line. Bus: 7, 66, 71, or 73.

Still having flashbacks from the sixties? Or want to? No problem. A room at The Red Vic, located in the heart of Haight, will throw you right back into the Summer of Love (minus, of course, the free-flowing LSD). Owner Sami Sunchild, a confessed former flower child, has re-created this historic hotel and Peace Center as a living museum honoring the bygone era and Golden Gate Park. Rooms are inspired by San Francisco's sights and history and are decorated accordingly, psychedelic posters and all. Four guest rooms have private baths; the remaining share four bathrooms down the hall. In general, rooms and baths are clean, and the furnishings lighthearted. This hotel is not for conservatives, but if you're into it, it's pretty groovy. Rates for longer stays are a great deal. No smoking is allowed in the rooms.

INEXPENSIVE

The Herb 'n Inn. 525 Ashbury St. (between Page and Haight sts.), San Francisco, CA 94117. ☎ **415/553-8542**. Fax 415/553-8541. 4 rms. TV (upon request). $70–$85 double, 2-night minimum. MC, V. Parking with advance notice. Bus: 6,7, 33, 43, 66, or 71.

For those of you who want to immerse yourself in the sights and sounds of the legendary Haight-Ashbury District without compromising on quality (and cost), there's The Herb'n Inn. Run by sister/brother duo Pam and Bruce Brennan—who know the history and highlights of the Haight better than just about anyone—this modernized Victorian consists of four attractive guest rooms, a huge country-style kitchen, a sunny back garden, and the beginnings of Bruce's Psychedelic History Museum (a.k.a. the dining room). Top choice among the guest rooms is the Cilantro Room, which, besides being the largest, has the only private bath and a view of the garden. A hearty full breakfast is included, as well as office services (including forwarded e-mail), personal city tours à la Bruce, and plenty of free advice on how to spend your day in the city. Kids and lesbian and gay couples are welcome.

THE CASTRO

Dolores Park Inn. c/o Bernie H. Vielwerth, 3641 17th St., San Francisco, CA 94114. ☎ **415/ 621-0482.** Fax is the same; please call before faxing. 4 rms (none with bath), 1 suite (with kitchenette). TV. $89 double; $165 suite. Two-night minimum. Rates include full breakfast. MC, V. Free parking. Muni Metro: F, J, K, L, M. Bus: 22 or 24.

This conveniently located inn is within easy walking distance of many shops and clubs, and downtown is just a quick jaunt away. Each room is individually outfitted with beautiful antiques and such bonuses as coffeemakers and hair dryers. Rumor has it that high-profile celebrities (such as Tom Cruise and Robert Downey, Jr., among others) have stayed here to avoid hype. The owner takes special care in providing a warm, hospitable, and romantic environment. No smoking allowed.

Inn on Castro. 321 Castro St. (at Market St.), San Francisco, CA 94114. ☎ **415/861-0321.** 6 rms, 2 suites. TEL. $85–$135 double; suites $165. Rates include full breakfast and evening brandy. AE, MC, V. Muni Metro: F, K, L, M. Bus: 8, 22, 24, or 37.

One of the better choices in the Castro is this Edwardian-style inn, just a half block away from all the action. It's decorated with contemporary furnishings, original modern art, and fresh flowers throughout. Almost all rooms have private baths and direct-dial phones; TVs are available upon request. Most rooms share a small back patio, and the suite has its own private outdoor sitting area. There's also a two-bedroom apartment available for $140 to $200.

4 Dining

San Francisco's dining scene is one of the best in the world. Since our space is limited, we had to make tough choices, but the end result is a cross section of San Francisco's best restaurants in every price range. For a greater selection of reviews, see *Frommer's San Francisco.*

If you want a table at a top restaurant, make your reservation weeks ahead.

UNION SQUARE

EXPENSIVE

✪ **Fleur de Lys.** 777 Sutter St. (at Jones St.). ☎ **415/673-7779.** Reservations recommended. Main courses $29–$35; five-course tasting menu $65; four-course vegetarian menu $50. AE, CB, DC, MC, V. Mon–Thurs 6–10pm, Fri–Sat 5:30–10:30pm. Bus: 2, 3, 4, 27, or 38. FRENCH.

Imagine a large version of Jeannie's (as in *I Dream of Jeannie*) live-in bottle: dark, cozy, with 700 yards of rich red floor-to-ceiling hand-painted fabric enclosing the room in lavish intimacy. Throw in dimly lit French candelabras, an extraordinary sculptural floral centerpiece, and about 20 tables filled with well-dressed diners. Welcome to one of the most renowned dining rooms in San Francisco. Fleur de Lys does everything seriously, from its foie gras starter to its petit fours after dinner. And with Chef Hubert Keller (who was President Clinton's first guest chef at the White House) in the kitchen, it's hard to go wrong. You can order à la carte, from the five-course tasting menu, or from the four-course vegetarian menu. We suggest starting with the knockout blue potato chips with cauliflower purée and caviar; you might follow with herb-crusted salmon with mushrooms and spinach noodle pie, or lamb loin with black truffles. Desserts are artistic creations. A selection of 300 French and California wines makes this an all-around dining fantasy.

✪ **Masa's.** In the Hotel Vintage Court, 648 Bush St. (at Stockton St.). ☎ **415/989-7154.** Reservations required; accepted up to 21 days in advance. Fixed-price dinner $70–$75. AE, CB, DC, DISC, MC, V. Tues–Sat 6–9:30pm. Closed first week in Jan and fourth week in July. Cable car: Powell-Mason and Powell-Hyde lines. Bus: 2, 3, 4, 30, or 45. FRENCH.

Chef Julian Serrano's brilliant cuisine matched with a flawless wine list and exemplary (even unpretentious) service has solidified Masa's reputation as one of the country's great French outposts. Either fixed price or à la carte, dinner is a memorable expense-be-damned experience from start to finish. If you wish, you can simply leave the decisions up to the kitchen. Serrano's passion for using only the highest-quality ingredients accounts for the restaurant's four-star ranking—and budget-busting prices. A typical dinner may begin with the Sonoma foie gras in a Madeira truffle sauce, or poached lobster with potatoes, fried leek, and a truffle vinaigrette. Main entrees may include medaillons of New Zealand fallow deer with zinfandel sauce and caramelized green apples, or the Atlantic black bass with a saffron sauce. Dessert, as you would imagine, is heavenly.

Postrio. At the Prescott Hotel, 545 Post St. (between Mason and Taylor sts.). ☎ **415/ 776-7825.** Reservations required. Main courses $6–$15 breakfast, $14–$15 lunch, $20–$26 dinner. AE, CB, DC, DISC, MC, V. Mon–Fri 7–10am, 11:30am–2pm, and 5:30–10:30pm; Sat 9am–2pm, and 5:30–10:30pm; Sun 9am–2pm, and 5:30–10pm; bar daily 11:30am–2am. Cable car: Powell-Mason and Powell-Hyde lines. Bus: 2, 3, 4, or 38. AMERICAN.

Ever since chefs Anne and David Gingrass left to start their own enterprise, rumors have been flying that San Francisco's top restaurant isn't what it used to be. Yet it's a rare night when the kitchen doesn't perform to a full house, and Zagat's still rates it no. 1 in the city. Eating is only half the reason one comes to Postrio. After squeezing through the perpetually swinging bar—which, in its own right, dishes out excellent tapas and pizzas from a wood-burning oven in the corner—guests are forced to make a grand entrance down the antebellum staircase to the cavernous dining room below. Pure Hollywood, for sure, but fun.

The menu, prepared by brothers Mitchell and Steven Rosenthal, combines Italian, Asian, French, and California styles with mixed results. On our last visit, the sautéed salmon, for example, was a bit overcooked, but the accompanying plum glaze, wasabi mashed potatoes, and miso vinaigrette were outstanding. The grilled squab lacked flavor but, again, the accompaniment—a sweet potato foie gras spring roll— was pure genius. The artistically sculpted desserts were the highlight of the evening. Despite the prime-time rush, service was friendly and infallible, as was the presentation.

MODERATE

Brasserie Savoy. In the Savoy Hotel, 580 Geary St. (at Jones St.). ☎ **415/474-8686.** Reservations recommended. Main courses $16–$19. AE, CB, DC, DISC, MC, V. Daily 6:30–11am; Sun–Thurs and 5–10:30pm, Fri–Sat 5–11pm. Bus: 2, 3, 4, 27, or 38. CALIFORNIA/FRENCH.

If you're headed to the theater or are just looking for a good meal downtown, Brasserie Savoy is an excellent option. The atmosphere in the bright, busy dining room is charmingly French bistro, and the food is consistent, affordable, and delicious. Choices may include beef tenderloin with port sauce and green peppercorn butter, or duck breast with mille-feuille of potato and mushrooms served with a date purée and coffee sauce. On the lighter side, the crawfish risotto with red and green peppers, scallions, celery, and chive lemongrass butter is a perfect dish. Among the appetizers, the napoleon of braised rabbit with red onions, mushrooms, kalamata olives, and anise tuiles is a preferred choice, if it's offered, or any one of several freshly made salads. To finish, try the innovative crème brûlée.

Grand Cafe. In the Hotel Monaco, 501 Geary St. (at Taylor St.). ☎ **415/292-0101.** Reservations accepted. Main courses $9.25–$16. AE, CB, DC, DISC, MC, V. Daily 7am–3pm; Sun–Thurs 5–10pm (cafe menu until 1am), Fri–Sat 5–11pm (cafe menu until 2am). Valet parking $7 for 2 hours. Bus: 2, 3, 4, 27, or 38. CALIFORNIA/FRENCH.

The Grand Cafe is hands down the most amazing room in the Union Square area. The cocktail area is swank and packed with a good-looking crowd, but walk back to the enormous but cozy dining area—a restored turn-of-the-century grand ballroom with 30-foot ceilings and art nouveau and deco touches—if you really want to be impressed. From every angle you'll see playful works by local artists, including a towering bunny sculpture that you really must see for yourself. The fare has never lived up to the room, but it does offer some nice surprises and is always well-presented on colorful plates. Signature appetizers include a rich polenta soufflé served on a wild mushroom ragout with cambozola fondue, and a light and tasty house-smoked chicken salad with figs, almonds, and mobier. Skip the Dungeness crab ravioli, which lacks conviction, and choose whatever fish special chef Denis Soriano offers. He knows how to cook fish perfectly. While the food is not the best in town, the atmosphere makes a trip here worthwhile. If nothing else, stop in for a cocktail and a snack.

Kuleto's. In the Villa Florence Hotel, 221 Powell St. (between Geary and O'Farrell sts.). ☎ **415/ 397-7720.** Reservations recommended. Breakfast $3–$8; main courses $8–$18. AE, CB, DC, DISC, MC, V. Mon–Fri 7–10:30am, Sat–Sun 8–10:30am; daily 11:30am–11pm. Cable car: Powell-Mason and Powell-Hyde lines. Muni Metro: Powell. Bus: 2, 3, 4, or 38. ITALIAN.

Story has it the owners of this popular downtown bistro were so delighted with the design of their new restaurant that they named it after the architect, Pat Kuleto. Whatever the reason, Kuleto's is truly a beautiful place filled with beautiful people who are here to see and be seen. The best plan of action is to skip the wait for a table, muscle a seat at the antipasto bar, and fill up on appetizers, which are often better than the entrees. For a main course, try the penne pasta drenched in a tangy lamb sausage marinara sauce, the clam linguini (generously overloaded with fresh clams), or any of the fresh fish specials grilled over hardwoods. If you don't arrive by 6pm, expect to wait—this place fills up mucha fasta.

✪ Rumpus. 1 Tillman Place (off Grant Ave., between Sutter and Post sts.). ☎ **415/421-2300.** Reservations recommended. Main courses $11.95–$19.95. AE, DC, MC, V. Mon–Sat 11:30am– 2:30pm, Sun–Thurs 5:30–10pm, Fri–Sat 5:30–11pm. CALIFORNIA.

Tucked into a small cul-de-sac off Grant Avenue, you'll find Rumpus, a fantastic restaurant serving well-prepared California fare at reasonable prices. The perfect place for a business lunch, shopping break, or dinner with friends, Rumpus is architecturally playful, colorful, and buzzing with conversation. The menu is affordable, and offers a wealth of flavorful options, such as pan-roasted chicken whose crispy and flavorful crust is almost as delightful as the perfectly cooked chicken and mashed potatoes beneath it; and the quality cut of New York steak, which comes with savory mashed potatoes. If nothing else, make sure to stop in here for one of the best desserts we've ever had: the puddinglike chocolate brioche cake.

✪ Scala's Bistro. In the Sir Francis Drake Hotel, 432 Powell St. (at Sutter St.). ☎ **415/ 395-8555.** Reservations recommended. Breakfast $6–$9; lunch and dinner main courses $9–$17. AE, CB, DC, DISC, MC, V. Mon–Sun 6:30am–midnight. Cable car: Powell-Hyde. Bus: 2, 3, 4, 30, 45, or 76. FRENCH/ITALIAN.

This latest venture by husband and wife team Giovanni (the host) and Donna (the chef) Scala is one of the best new restaurants in the city. The Parisian-bistro/ Old-World atmosphere has just the right balance of elegance and informality, which means it's perfectly okay to have some fun here (and apparently most people do). Donna has put together a fantastic array of Italian and French dishes that are priced surprisingly low. We suggest starting with the Earth and Surf calamari appetizer (better than anything we've sampled along the Mediterranean) or the grilled portobello mushrooms. The Golden Beet salad and Anchor Steam mussels are also good bets, as is the Cipolla Pazza: hot Italian sausage spaghetti served in a roasted onion. Generous portions of the moist, rich duck leg confit will satisfy hungry appetites, but if you can only order one thing, make it Scala's signature dish: the seared salmon. Resting on a bed of creamy buttermilk mashed potatoes and ensconced with a tomato, chive, and white wine sauce, it's one of the best salmon dishes we've ever tasted. Finish with the creamy Bostini cream pie, a dreamy combo of vanilla custard and orange chiffon cake with a warm chocolate glaze.

INEXPENSIVE

Planet Hollywood. 2 Stockton St. (at Market St.). ☎ **415/421-7827.** Reservations accepted only for parties of 20 or more. $8.50–$18.95. AE, DC, DISC, MC, V. Daily 11am–1am. Muni Metro: any line. Bus: 38 or any Market St. bus. AMERICAN.

You won't find any locals here (or movie stars, for that matter), but visitors can't help but flock to Planet Hollywood. Similar to the Hard Rock, this is a themed restaurant chain that exhibits movie (instead of music) memorabilia. Expect long lines to get in, plenty of fellow out-of-towners, and a menu featuring salads, sandwiches, pastas, burgers, pizzas, and fajitas.

✪ **Tú Lan.** 8 Sixth St. (at Market St.). ☎ **415/626-0927.** $3.50–$7. No credit cards. Mon–Sat 11am–9pm. Cable cars: Powell-Mason and Powell-Hyde lines. Muni Metro: F, J, K, L, M, N. Bus: 6, 7, 27, 31, 66, or 71. VIETNAMESE.

If you can handle walking down Sixth Street past the winos, weirdoes, and street stench, you won't find better (or cheaper) Vietnamese food than at this honest-to-goodness dive. Even Julia Child has been known to pull up a chair at this shack of a restaurant to feast on such goodies as imperial rolls on a bed of rice noodles, lettuce, peanuts, and mint. Take pity on the poor waiter who never seems to bring water no matter how many times you ask; he's been working here forever, he's the only server, and the place is always packed. For the price, this has been one of our all-time favorite restaurants for more than a decade. *Take note:* Some finicky folks can't handle the down-and-dirty atmosphere.

NOB HILL
EXPENSIVE

✪ **Charles Nob Hill.** 1250 Jones St. (at Clay St.). ☎ **415/771-5400.** Main courses $25–$33. AE, MC, V. Tues–Thurs and Sun 5:30–9:30pm, Fri–Sat 5:30–10:30pm. Cable car: California and Powell-Hyde lines. Bus: 1, 12, 27, or 83. FRENCH.

We never knew beef could actually melt in your mouth until Aqua owner Charles Condy bought historic restaurant "Le Club" and introduced us to Michael Mina's culinary magic. The "classically inspired light French fare" is served in two dining rooms filled with fresh flowers and the loud buzz of an older socialite crowd. For the main course, you might choose the beef tenderloin with wild mushroom and potato torte, balsamic glazed onions, and foie gras; or a flavorful squab with veal sweet bread, lentils, and mushroom fricassee. Better yet, opt for the $65 six-course tasting menu and let the chef's preference lead you through the meal. Although the room is romantic, the atmosphere and noise level are too convivial for real intimacy—but it sure is fun to watch everyone else. Wrap up the evening with the outstanding pear and Roquefort tart. *Tip:* Don't drive here unless you valet it; you may spend over an hour looking for parking.

Ritz-Carlton Dining Room. 600 Stockton St. (at California St.). ☎ **415/296-7465.** Reservations recommended. Fixed-price menu $49–$63. AE, CB, DC, DISC, MC, V. Mon–Sat 6–10pm. Valet parking $8. Cable car: Powell-Hyde and Powell-Mason lines (direct stop). Bus: 1. CALIFORNIA/FRENCH.

Never a hotel to do anything second best, the Ritz-Carlton is renowned for pampering its guests as if they were royalty, and the Dining Room is no exception. The setting, as you would imagine, is quite regal and sumptuous, and the service keenly attentive (no half-empty water glasses in this joint). Unfortunately, celebrity chef Gary Danko—winner of the 1995 James Beard Award, the Academy Award of the food world—is no longer with the Ritz; Sylvain Portay now runs the kitchen with similar aplomb, but the loss is noticeable—dishes such as the roast Maine lobster and striped bass filet were quite good, but certainly not of the caliber Danko's fans are accustomed to. A few dishes, however, were outstanding, particularly crayfish bisque (one of the best dishes we've ever tasted) and the risotto with butternut squash and roasted squab. Dessert, alas, was also deigned for mere mortals, though the warm port-poached pear in vanilla sauce was superb.

SOMA
EXPENSIVE

Boulevard. 1 Mission St. (at Embarcadero and Steuart St.). ☎ **415/543-6084.** Reservations recommended. Main courses $19–$27. AE, CB, DC, DISC, MC, V. Mon–Fri 11:30am–2pm, bistro 2:30–5:15pm; daily 5:30–10:30pm. Valet parking $6. Bus: 15, 30, 32, 42, or 45. AMERICAN.

Master restaurant designer Pat Kuleto and chef Nancy Oaks teamed up to create one of San Francisco's most exciting restaurants more than four years ago, and Boulevard is still as popular as ever. What's the winning combination? The dramatic Belle Epoque interior combined with Oaks's well-sculpted, mouth-watering dishes. Start with the delicate crab-and-mascarpone ravioli with truffle beurre blanc and tomato cream, then embark on such wonderful concoctions as grilled wild king salmon with leek and sweet corn mashed potatoes, French beans, and herb salad; she makes a mean honey-cured pork loin, too. Vegetarian items, such as wild mushroom risotto with fresh chanterelles and Parmesan, are also available. Three levels of formality—bar, open kitchen, and main dining room—keep things from getting too snobby. Though steep prices prevent most from making Boulevard a regular gig, you'd be hard-pressed to find a better place for a special, fun-filled occasion.

Hawthorn Lane. 22 Hawthorn Lane (at Howard St. between Second and Third sts.). ☎ **415/777-9779.** Reservations recommended. Jacket appropriate but not required. Main courses $9.50–$13 lunch, $18–$25 dinner. CB, DC, JCB, MC, V. Mon–Fri 11:30am–2pm; Sun–Thurs 5:30–10pm, Fri–Sat 5:30–10:30pm. BART: Montgomery station. Muni Metro: F, J, K, L, M, N. Bus: 12, 30, 45, or 76. CALIFORNIA.

Anne and David Gingrass, now sorely missed at Postrio, are heading their own kitchen at Hawthorn Lane, strategically located a block away from the Museum of Modern Art. Menus change with the seasons and reflect the Asian and European influences that made them famous under Wolfgang Puck. The bar area is comfortable and inviting; continue on to the dining room, where earthquake reinforcement beams divide the room in a way that's not only functional but also creates an illusion of intimacy. Dishes are remarkably well balanced; in fact, accompaniments are often more exciting than the main course itself. If it's on the menu, don't pass up the black cod appetizer served with a miso glaze and spinach rolls. The light, flaky lobster tempura with a vegetable salad is another show-stopper, as is the quail glazed with maple and perched on the most delightful potato gratin. Desserts are as good to look at as they are to eat.

MODERATE

✪ **Fringale Restaurant.** 570 Fourth St. (between Brannan and Bryant sts.). ☎ **415/543-0573.** Reservations recommended. Main courses $4–$12 lunch, $9–$18 dinner. AE, MC, V. Mon–Fri 11:30am–2:30pm; Mon–Sat 5:30–10:30pm. Bus: 30 or 45. FRENCH.

One of San Francisco's best restaurants for the money, Fringale has enjoyed a week-long waiting list since the day chef/co-owner Gerald Hirigoyen first opened this small SoMa bistro. Sponged eggshell-blue walls and other muted sand and earth tones create a serene dining environment, which is all but shattered when the 18-table room fills with Hirigoyen's fans. For starters, try the steamed mussels with roasted red pepper, basil, and vinaigrette, or the sheep's milk cheese and prosciutto tureen with figs and greens. Among the dozen or so main courses on the seasonal menu you might find rack of lamb with potato gratin, or pork tenderloin confit with onion and apple marmalade. Desserts are worth savoring, too, particularly the hazelnut and roasted almond mousse cake or the signature crème brûlée with vanilla bean. The mostly French waiters provide uncharacteristically charming service, and prices are surprisingly reasonable for such high-quality cuisine.

✪ **Lulu.** 816 Folsom St. (at Fourth St.). ☎ **415/495-5775.** Reservations recommended. Main courses $7–$13 lunch, $9–$17 dinner. AE, MC, V. Sun–Thurs 11:30am–10:30pm, Fri–Sat 11:30am–11pm. Bus: 15, 30, 32, 42, or 45. CONTINENTAL.

It's hard not to love LuLu, even through there's always a long wait (reserve in advance) and the enormous converted warehouse is one of the noisier rooms in town. Locals return again and again for the roasted mussels piled high on an iron skillet; the chopped salad with lemon, anchovies, and tomatoes; the pork loin with fennel, garlic, and olive oil; and any of the other wonderful dishes. Everything is served family style and is meant to be shared. Save room for dessert—the gooey chocolate cake with ice cream is our favorite. The adjoining cafe serves the same menu plus gourmet sandwiches on a first-come, first-served basis. *Note:* The head chef recently left here to open Rose Pistola. So far the food's quality still meets expectations, and we're hoping that holds true.

Thirsty Bear Brewing Company. 661 Howard St. (1 block east of the Moscone Center). ☎ **415/974-0905.** Reservations recommended. Main courses $10–$17. AE, DC, MC, V. Mon–Sun 11:30am–1am. Bus 12, 15, 30, 45, or 76. SPANISH.

Despite the dumb name, this brewpub has quickly become a favorite of the Financial District/SoMa crowd, who come as much for the excellent house-made brews as they do for chef Daniel Olivella's outstanding Spanish food. A native of Catalunia, Spain, Olivella is a master of paella. His Paella Valenciana—a sizzling combo of chicken, shrimp, sausage, shellfish, and saffron-laden rice served in a cast iron skillet—is the best we've had outside of Barcelona. Upscale pub grub includes a variety of hot and cold tapas, a few of our favorites being the Escalivada (Olivella's mother's version of roasted vegetables served at room temperature) and the Espinacas à la Catalana (spinach sautéed with garlic, pinenuts, and raisins). Almost as impressive is the costly conversion, from a high-ceilinged brick warehouse to a two-level industrial-chic brewpub compete with pool tables, dart boards, and live music that runs the gamut from flamenco to alternative to classical.

FINANCIAL DISTRICT
EXPENSIVE

✪ **Aqua.** 252 California St. (between Battery and Front sts.). ☎ **415/956-9662.** Reservations recommended. Main courses $26–$32; six-course tasting menu $65; vegetarian tasting menu $45. AE, DC, MC, V. Mon–Fri 11:30am–2pm; Mon–Sat 5:30–10:30pm. All Market St. buses. SEAFOOD.

Without question, Aqua is San Francisco's finest seafood restaurant. Heralded Chef Michael Mina dazzles his customers with a bewildering juxtaposition of earth and sea in his seasonally changing menus. The poached steelhead salmon rests on a bed of potato and leek puree infused with Dungeness crab, beurre blanc, and oxtre caviar;

Dining with the Sun on Your Face at Belden Place

As cosmopolitan as San Francisco claims to be, it's woefully lacking in outdoor dining options compared to most European cities. One pocket of exceptions, however, is Belden Place, an adorable little brick alley in the heart of the Financial District that's closed to everything but foot traffic. When the weather is agreeable, the restaurants that line the alley break out the big umbrellas, tables, and chairs à la Boulevard Saint-Michel, and voilà—a bit of Paris just off Pine Street.

The four cafes that line Belden Place offer a wide variety of cuisine. From south to north they're **Cafe Bastille**, at no. 22 (☎ **415/986-5673**), your classic French bistro serving excellent crepes, mussels, and French onion soup along with live jazz on weekends; **Cafe Tiramisu**, at no. 28 (☎ **415/421-7044**), a superb—and stylish—Italian hotspot serving addictive risottos and gnocchi; **Plouf**, at no. 40 (☎ **415/986-6491**), one of the best new restaurants in the city, specializing in big bowls of mussels, slathered in a choice of seven sauces, as well as fresh seafood; and **Fizz Supper Club**, at 471 Pine St. (☎ **415/421-3499**), a chic American-Mediterranean bistro serving such specialties as Andouille-stuffed quail with saffron risotto cake and braised rabbit with jalapeño peach chutney. There's also live jazz nightly at Fizz, but it's a cloudless San Francisco day that draws the city's sun-starved culinary cognoscenti to all four of these wonderful cafes.

---

the miso-glazed black cod steak in vegetable jus is another work of art, perfectly paired with rock shrimp and vegetable strudel. Mina's passion for exotic mushrooms pervades most dishes, for taste as well as for show (Mina is amazingly adept at the art of presentation). Desserts are equally impressive, particularly the Aqua soufflé-of-the-day, and the chocolate tasting plate—a feast for the eyes as well as the palate. For special occasions or billable lunches, Aqua is highly recommended.

Rubicon. 558 Sacramento St. (between Sansome and Montgomery sts.). ☎ **415/434-4100.** Reservations recommended. Main courses $19–$25. AE, MC, V. Mon–Fri 11:30am–2:30pm; Mon–Sat 5:30–10:30pm. Bus 15 or 41. FRENCH CONTEMPORARY.

This place won instant publicity when it opened in 1994 thanks to the fame of its owners, Francis Ford Coppola and Robert DeNiro. Named for Coppola's Napa Valley wine, Rubicon features a contemporary and somewhat stiff dining room frequented by big-business power-lunchers and an upscale, middle-aged crowd. While the menu changes frequently, favorites among appetizers include the ahi tuna tartare with ponzu mignonette, foie gras with brandied cherries, and carpaccio of salmon with cucumber mint vinaigrette. Main courses might include a sautéed salmon with savoy cabbage, pearl onions, smoked bacon, and red wine sauce; loin of lamb with potato and celery root galette and chervil sauce; or Muscovy duck breast with braised turnips and tat soi honey coriander sauce. Finish with the pecan date tart with blood-orange sorbet or the bittersweet chocolate and peppermint gâteau.

Vertigo. At the base of the Transamerica Pyramid, 600 Montgomery St. ☎ **415/433-7250.** Reservations recommended. Main courses $17–$24. AE, DC, DISC, MC, V. Mon–Fri 11:30am–2:30pm, 5–10pm; Sat 5–10pm. Bus 15, 41, or 42. FRENCH MEDITERRANEAN.

Appropriately named Vertigo is a dizzying, dazzling spectacle of fluidity and style, made all the more vogue by its high-rent location at the base of the legendary Transamerica building. San Francisco's bigwigs adore the place, holding court at the upper terrace while proprietor extraordinaire Doug Washington woos guests with his unflappable charm and unpretentious manner. While there are a few lemons lingering on the menu, chef Jeffrey Inahara scores more hits than misses. Inahara's spectacular braised lamb shank served in a reduced jus with garlic lentils (a refreshing change from the cursed mashed potato craze) is a winner; others on the evening's menu included monkfish atop a bed of spinach with Muscat pistachio sauce, and a perfectly cooked breast of duck with red onion currant fondue. Appetizers, alas, were a minor disappointment, but all was forgiven in the end after our first bite of crème brûlée—it simply doesn't get any better than this.

MODERATE

Yank Sing. 427 Battery St. (between Clay and Washington sts.). ☎ 415/781-1111. Dim sum $2–$4.75 for 3 to 4 pieces. AE, DC, MC, V. Mon–Fri 11am–3pm. Sat–Sun 10am–4pm. Cable car: California. Bus: 1 or 42. CHINESE/DIM SUM.

Loosely translated as "a delight of the heart," Yank Sing does dim sum like no other Chinese restaurant we've visited. Poor quality of ingredients has always been the shortcoming of all but the most expensive Chinese restaurants, but Yank Sing manages to be both affordable *and* excellent. Confident, experienced servers take the nervousness out of novices—they're good at guessing your gastric threshold. Most dim sum dishes are dumplings, filled with tasty concoctions of pork, beef, fish, or vegetables. Spareribs, stuffed crab claws, scallion pancakes, pork buns, and other palate-pleasers complete the menu. Like most good dim sum meals, at Yank Sing you get to choose the small dishes from a cart that's continually wheeled around the dining room. *Tip:* Sit by the kitchen and you're guaranteed to get it while it's hot.

CHINATOWN
INEXPENSIVE

House of Nanking. 919 Kearny St. (at Columbus Ave.). ☎ **415/421-1429.** Reservations accepted for 6 or more. Main courses $4.95–$8.95. No credit cards. Mon–Fri 11am–10pm, Sat noon–10pm, Sun 4–10pm. Bus: 9, 12, 15, or 30. CHINESE.

To the unknowing passer-by, the House of Nanking has "greasy dive" written all over it. To its legion of fans, however, the wait—sometimes up to an hour—is worth what's on the plate. Located on the edge of Chinatown just off Columbus Avenue, this inconspicuous little diner is one of San Francisco's worst-kept secrets. When the line is reasonable, we drop by for a plate of pot stickers (*still* the best we've ever tasted) and chef/owner Peter Fang's signature shrimp-and-green-onion pancake served with peanut sauce. Trust the waiter when he recommends a special, or simply point to what looks good on someone else's table. Even with a new expansion that's double the elbow room, seating is tight, so prepare to be bumped around a bit, and don't expect good service—it's all part of the Nanking experience.

Sam Woh. 813 Washington St. (by Grant Ave.). ☎ **415/982-0596.** Reservations not accepted. Main courses $3.50–$6. No credit cards. Mon–Sat 11am–3am. Bus: 15, 30, 41, or 45. CHINESE.

Very handy for late-nighters, Sam's is a total dive that's well known and often packed. The restaurant's two pocket-size dining rooms are located on top of each other, on the second and third floors—take the stairs past the first-floor kitchen. You'll have to share a table, but this place is for mingling almost as much as for eating. The house specialty is *jook* (known as *congee* in its native Hong Kong)—a thick rice gruel flavored with fish, shrimp, chicken, beef, or pork; the best is Sampan, made with rice and seafood. Try sweet-and-sour pork rice, wonton soup with duck, or a roast-pork/rice-noodle roll. More traditional fried noodles and rice plates are available too. Chinese doughnuts sell for 50¢ each.

RUSSIAN HILL
INEXPENSIVE

Hard Rock Cafe. 1699 Van Ness Ave. (at Sacramento St.). ☎ **415/885-1699.** Reservations accepted for groups of 15 or more. Main courses $6–$16. AE, DC, MC, V. Sun–Thurs 11:30am–11pm, Fri–Sat 11:30am–midnight. Valet parking $4 for 2 hours. Cable car: California. Bus: 1. AMERICAN.

Like its affiliated restaurants around the world, this loud, nostalgia-laden place offers big portions of decent food at moderate prices, rock memorabilia, and plenty of blaring music to an almost exclusively out-of-town clientele. The menu offers burgers, baby back ribs, grilled fish, chicken, salads, and sandwiches. Although it's nothing unique to San Francisco, the Hard Rock is a fine place to bring the kids and grab a bite.

Swan Oyster Depot. 1517 Polk St. (between California and Sacramento sts.). ☎ **415/673-1101.** Reservations not accepted. Seafood cocktails $5–$8, clams and oysters on the half-shell $6–$7.50 per half dozen. No credit cards. Mon–Sat 8am–5:30pm. Bus: 27. SEAFOOD.

Almost 85 years old and looking even older, Swan Oyster Depot is classic San Francisco. Opened in 1912, this tiny hole-in-the-wall with the city's friendliest servers is little more than a narrow fish market that decided to slap down some stools. There are only 20 or so seats jammed cheek-by-jowl along a long marble bar. Most patrons come for a quick cup of chowder or a plate of half-shelled oysters that arrive chilling on crushed ice. The menu is limited to fresh crab, shrimp, oyster, and clam cocktails; Maine lobster; and Boston-style clam chowder. Fish is only available raw or smoked and to go. Beer and wine are available.

NORTH BEACH
EXPENSIVE

Moose's. 1652 Stockton St. (between Filbert and Union sts.). ☎ **415/989-7800.** Website: www.mooses.com. Reservations recommended. Main courses $8.50–$25. AE, CB, DC, JCB, MC, V. Mon–Thurs 11:30am–11pm, Fri–Sat 11:30am–midnight, Sun 10:30am–11pm. Valet parking $7 for 3 hrs. Bus: 15, 30, 41, or 45. MEDITERRANEAN/CALIFORNIA.

Within the last two years Moose's has brought on chef Fabrice Canelle from the Ritz-Carlton Laguna Niguel, pastry chef Heidi Steele from Santa Fe's Coyote Café, and master sommelier David O'Conner—perhaps the only one who could improve a wine list that's already received an award of excellence from *Wine Spectator.* Moose's is where Nob Hill socialites and local politicos come to dine and be seen. But it's not just an image. In fact, Nob Hill's largest dining room is rather sparse and unintimate, but everything that comes out of the kitchen is way above par. The appetizers are innovative, fresh, and well balanced (try Mediterranean fish soup with rouille and croutons cooked in the wood-fired oven), and the main courses (especially the meats) are perfectly prepared. The menu changes every few months and might include a grilled veal chop with potato galette as well as a variety of pasta, chicken, and fish dishes.

MODERATE

Enrico's. 504 Broadway (at Kearny St.). ☎ **415/982-6223.** Reservations recommended. Main courses $8–$13 lunch, $13–$19 dinner. AE, DC, DISC, MC, V. Mon–Sun noon–11pm; Fri–Sat noon–midnight; bar daily noon–2am. Bus: 12, 15, 30, or 83. MEDITERRANEAN.

Though it's taking its sweet time, North Beach's bawdy stretch of Broadway is on the road to rehabilitation. Helping things along is the newly refurbished version of Enrico's, a glitzy sidewalk restaurant and supper club that was once *the* place to hang out before Broadway took its seedy downward spiral. Families may want to skip this one, but anyone with an appreciation for live jazz (played nightly), late-night noshing, and weirdo-watching from the outdoor patio would be quite content spending an alfresco evening under the heat lamps. Chewy brick-oven pizza, zesty tapas, and thick steaks are hot items on the monthly changing menu. The best part? No cover charge, killer burgers served 'til midnight on weekends, and valet parking.

✪ **Rose Pistola.** 532 Columbus Ave. (at Union and Green sts.). ☎ **415/399-0499.** Reservations highly recommended. Main courses $6.95–$18.50 lunch, most dishes $9–$18 dinner. AE, MC, V. Sun–Thurs 11:30am–10:30pm with late-night menu until midnight, Fri–Sat 11:30am–11:30pm with late-night menu until 1am. Valet parking $4 lunch, $7 dinner. ITALIAN.

Undoubtedly the hottest new restaurant in '97, Rose Pistola is a hit for all the right reasons: It's a great place to be, the food is terrific, and the menu is varied enough for all tastes and budgets. The atmosphere—like the surrounding North Beach neighborhood—is smart, like a bustling bistro. Although the dining room is larger than most in the area, it's divided so it doesn't feel impersonal. Sidewalk seating is favored on sunny afternoons, but inside there's plenty to see as chefs crank out the eclectic food from the open kitchen. The fare is meant to be shared, so, aside from sandwiches, it all comes à la carte. Along with meats and fowl, you'll find a variety of fish choices that can be prepared one of five ways. We tried mussels in a rich tomato broth, which was so flavorful we kept it around to soak up our bread long after the shellfish had been devoured.

INEXPENSIVE

Gira Polli. 659 Union St. (at Columbus Ave.). ☎ **415/434-4472.** Reservations recommended. Main courses $7.50–$12.50. AE, MC, V. Mon–Sun 4:30–9:30pm. Bus: 15, 30, 39, 41, or 45. ITALIAN.

I (Matthew) used to live three blocks from Gira Polli, and man-oh-man do I miss it. Whenever I'd rent a video, I'd drop by here for the Gira Polli Special: a foil-lined bag filled with half a wood-fired chicken (scrumptious), Palermo potatoes (the best in the city), a fresh garden salad, perfectly cooked vegetables, and a soft roll—all for less than $10. Next, I'd nab a bottle of good, cheap wine from the liquor store next door, take my goodies home, disconnect the phone, and love life for a while. *Tip:* On sunny days, there's no better place in North Beach for a picnic lunch than Washington Square, right across the street.

✪ **Il Pollaio.** 555 Columbus Ave. (between Green and Union sts.). ☎ **415/362-7727.** $5.50–$12.50. AE, MC, V. Mon–Sat 11:30am–9pm. Cable car: Powell-Mason line. Bus: 15, 30, 39, or 41. ITALIAN/ARGENTINEAN.

Simple, affordable, and consistently delicious is the winning combination at Il Pollaio. The dining room is casual and the menu basic, but the fresh-from-the-grill chicken has lemon-tangy flavor and it's so moist it practically falls off the bone. Each meal is served with choice of salads, and if you're not in the mood for chicken, you can opt for rabbit, lamb, pork chop, or Italian sausage.

L'Osteria del Forno. 519 Columbus Ave. (between Green and Union sts.). ☎ **415/982-1124.** Sandwiches $5–$6; pizzas $10–$13; main courses $6–$8.25. No credit cards. Mon–Wed 11:30am–10pm, Fri–Sat 11:30am–10:30pm, Sun 1–10pm. Bus: 15 or 41. ITALIAN.

L'Osteria del Forno may be only slightly larger than a walk-in closet, but it's one of the top three Italian restaurants in North Beach. Peer in the window facing Columbus Avenue, and you'll probably see two Italian women with their hair up, sweating from the heat of their brick-lined oven that cranks out the best focaccia, and focaccia sandwiches, in the city. There's no pomp or circumstance involved: Locals come here strictly to eat. The menu features a variety of superb pizzas and fresh pastas, plus a few daily specials (pray for the roast pork braised in milk). Small baskets of warm focaccia bread keep you going till the entrees arrive, which should always be accompanied by a glass of house red.

Mario's Bohemian Cigar Store. 566 Columbus Ave. ☎ **415/362-0536.** Sandwiches $5–$6.25. No credit cards. Daily 10am–midnight. Closed Dec 24–Jan 1. Bus: 15, 30, 41, or 45. ITALIAN.

Across the street from Washington Square, this is one of North Beach's most popular neighborhood hangouts. The century-old bar—small, well worn, and perpetually busy—is best known for its focaccia sandwiches, including meatball or eggplant. Wash it all down with an excellent cappuccino or a house Campari as you watch the tourists stroll by. And yes, they do sell cigars. *Note:* A new, larger location has opened at 2209 Polk St., between Green and Vallejo streets (☎ 415/776-8226).

FISHERMAN'S WHARF
EXPENSIVE

Alioto's. Fisherman's Wharf (at Taylor St.). ☎ **415/673-0183.** Reservations recommended. Main courses $7–$14 lunch, $10–$50 dinner. AE, CB, DC, DISC, MC, V. Mon–Sun 11am–11pm. Cable car: Powell-Hyde. Bus: 30 or 42. SEAFOOD.

One of San Francisco's oldest restaurants, run by one of the city's most prominent families, this Fisherman's Wharf landmark has a long-standing reputation for serving the Bay's best cioppino. The curbside crab stand, **Oysteria Deli,** and the new **Steam Kettle Bar** are great for a quick, inexpensive dose of San Francisco's finest; for more formal and fancy selections, continue up the carpeted stairs to the multilevel, harbor-view dining room. Don't mess around with the menu—it's the Dungeness crab you're after. Cracked, caked, stuffed, or stewed, it's impossible to get your fill, so bring plenty of money—particularly if you intend to order from Alioto's prodigious (and pricey) wine list. If you don't care for cracked crab, the griddle-fried sand dabs and rex sole with tartar sauce are also good, though oversauced.

MODERATE

Cafe Pescatore. 2455 Mason St. (at North Point St.). ☎ **415/561-1111.** Reservations recommended. Main courses $3.95–$7.95 breakfast, $10–$16 lunch or dinner. AE, DC, DISC, MC, V. Mon–Thurs 11:30am–10pm, Fri 11:30am–11pm, Sat 5–11pm, Sun 5–10pm; Sat–Sun 7am–3pm brunch, 3–5pm cafe menu. Cable car: Powell-Mason. Bus: 42, 15, or 39. ITALIAN.

Though San Francisco locals are a rarity at Cafe Pescatore, most agree that if they had to dine at Fisherman's Wharf, this cozy trattoria would be their first choice. Two walls of sliding glass doors offer almost-alfresco seating when the weather's warm, although heavy traffic can detract from the experience. The general consensus is to order anything that's cooked in the open kitchen's wood-fired oven, such as the pizzas and roasts. A big hit is the polenta al forno—oak-roasted cheese polenta with marinara sauce and fresh pesto. The verde pizza, with pesto-flavored prawns and spinach, and the huge serving of roast chicken are also safe bets.

COW HOLLOW/PACIFIC HEIGHTS/THE MARINA DISTRICT
EXPENSIVE

✪ **La Folie.** 2316 Polk St. (between Green and Union sts.). ☎ **415/776-5577.** Reservations recommended. Main courses $24–$32; 5-course tasting menu $58.50, vegetarian tasting menu $45. AE, CB, DC, DISC, JCB, MC, V. Mon–Sat 5:30–10:30pm. Bus: 19, 41, 45, 47, 49, or 76. FRENCH.

For fantastic French food without attitude, La Folie is the place to feast. The minute you walk through the door you'll know why this is many locals' favorite restaurant. The country French decor is tasteful but not too serious; the staff is friendly, knowledgeable, and very accommodating; the atmosphere is comfortable and relaxed; and the food is truly outstanding. Unlike many renowned chefs, Roland Passot is in the kitchen nightly, and it shows. Each of his California-influenced French creations is an architectural and culinary masterpiece. We suggest starting with the roast quail and fois gras with salad, wild mushrooms, and roasted garlic—guaranteed to melt in your mouth. Main courses aren't petite as in many French restaurants, and all are accompanied by flavorful and well-balanced sauces. Try the rôti of quail and squab stuffed with wild mushrooms and wrapped in crispy potato strings, or the roast venison with vegetables, quince, and huckleberry sauce. Finish off with any of the delectable desserts.

MODERATE

Ace Wasabi's. 3339 Steiner St. (at Chestnut St.). ☎ **415/567-4903.** No reservations. Individual pieces $4–$9; main courses $10–$14. AE, DC, MC, V. Mon–Thurs 5:30–10:30pm, Fri–Sat 5:30–11pm, Sun 5–10pm. Bus: 30. JAPANESE/SUSHI.

Here's sushi with a twist. What differentiates this Marina hot spot (formerly known as Flying Kamikazes) from the usual sushi spots around town are the unique combinations, the varied menu, and the young, hip atmosphere. The innovative rolls are a nice welcome to those bored with the traditional styles, though they may be too adventuresome for some (don't worry, there's plenty of non-sea and non-raw items on the menu). Don't miss the rainbow "Three Amigos" roll, or the "Rock and Roll" with cooked eel, avocado, and cucumber. The buckwheat noodle and julienne vegetable salad is also a treat. The service could be improved—you'll wait forever for your server to pour your Sapporo—but the staff is friendly and the atmosphere is fun, so nobody seems to mind.

Betelnut. 2030 Union St. (at Buchanan St.). ☎ **415/929-8855.** Reservations recommended. Main courses $9–$16. CB, DC, DISC, MC, V. Sun–Thurs 11:30am–11pm, Fri–Sat 11:30am–midnight. Bus: 22, 41, or 45. CHINESE.

While San Francisco is teeming with Chinese restaurants, few offer the posh environment of this restaurant on upscale Union Street. As the menu explains, the theme is "Pejui Wu," a traditional Asian beer house offering local brews and savory dishes. But with the bamboo paneling, red Formica, and low-hanging lamps, the place feels more like a set out of Madonna's movie *Shanghai Surprise*. Still, the atmosphere is *en vogue*, with dimly lit booths, ringside seating overlooking the bustling stir-fry chefs, sidewalk tables, and a cramped but festive bar. Starters include sashimi and tasty salt-and-pepper whole gulf prawns; main courses include orange-glazed beef with asparagus and oyster mushrooms and Singapore chili crab. While prices seem reasonable, it's the incidentals such as white rice ($1.50 per person) and tea ($3.50 per pot) that rack up the bill. In our minds, the main reason to choose this restaurant over others is the atmosphere, and the heavenly signature dessert: mouth-watering tapioca pudding with sweet red azuki beans.

Greens Restaurant, Fort Mason. Building A, Fort Mason Center (enter Fort Mason opposite the Safeway at Buchanan and Marina sts.). ☎ **415/771-6222.** Reservations recommended 2 weeks in advance. Main courses $10–$13; fixed-priced dinner $38; brunch $7–$10. DISC, MC, V. Tues–Thurs 11:30am–2pm, Fri–Sat 11:30am–2:30pm, Sun brunch 10am–2pm; Mon–Thurs 5:30–9:30pm, Fri–Sat 6–9pm (bakery, Tues–Sat 8am–4:30pm, Sun 10am–2pm). Bus: 28 or 30. VEGETARIAN.

Knowledgeable locals swear by Greens, where executive chef Annie Somerville (author of *Fields of Greens*) cooks with the seasons, using produce from Green Gulch Farm and other local organic farms. Located in an old warehouse, with enormous windows overlooking the bridge and the bay, the restaurant is both a pioneer and a legend. A weeknight dinner might begin with tomato, white-bean, and sorrel soup, or grilled asparagus with lemon, Parmesan cheese, and watercress. What follows might be spring vegetable risotto with asparagus, peas, shiitake and crimini mushrooms, and Parmesan cheese, or Sri Lankan curry made of new potatoes, cauliflower, carrots, peppers, and snap peas stewed with tomatoes, coconut milk, ginger, and Sri Lankan spices.

Desserts are equally adventuresome—try the chocolate pave with mint crème anglaise, or the espresso ice cream with chocolate sauce.

✪ **Pane e Vino.** 3011 Steiner St. (at Union St.). ☎ **415/346-2111.** Reservations recommended. Main courses $10–$18. MC, V. Mon–Thur 11:30am–2:30pm, 5–10pm, Fri–Sat 11:30am–2:30pm, 5–10:30pm. Bus: 41 or 45. ITALIAN.

This is one of the city's top—and most authentic—Italian restaurants, as well as our personal favorite. The food is consistently excellent (try not to fill up on the outstanding breads), the prices reasonable, and the mostly Italian-accented staff always smooth and efficient under pressure. The two small dining rooms—separated by an open kitchen that emanates heavenly aromas—offer only limited seating, so expect a wait even if you have reservations. There's a wide selection of appetizers, including a fine carpaccio and the hugely popular chilled artichoke stuffed with bread and tomatoes and served with a vinaigrette. Our favorite, the antipasti of mixed grilled vegetables, always spurs a fork fight. A similarly broad selection of pastas is available, including a flavorful pennette alla boscaiola with porcini mushrooms and pancetta in a tomato cream sauce. Other specialties include a chicken breast marinated in lime juice and herbs. Top dessert picks are any of the Italian ice creams, the crème caramel, and the creamy tiramisu.

✪ **PlumpJack Café.** 3127 Fillmore St. (between Filbert and Greenwich sts.). ☎ **415/563-4755.** Reservations recommended. Main courses $14–$20. AE, MC, V. Mon–Fri 11:30am–2pm and 5:30–10:30pm, Sat 5:30–10:30pm. Bus: 41 or 45. CALIFORNIA/FRENCH/MEDITERRANEAN.

Wildly popular among San Francisco's style-setters, this small Cow Hollow restaurant is the "in" place to dine. This is partly due to the fact that it's run by one of the Getty clan (as in J. Paul), but mostly because chef Maria Helm's food is just plain good, and the whimsical decor is a veritable work of art. Though the menu changes weekly, you might find such appetizers as roasted portobello mushrooms with vegetable stuffing, reggiano, and cippolini onions, or a salad of watercress and Belgian endive with kumquats, toasted pine nuts, shaved reggiano, and champagne vinaigrette. Main dishes range from pastas (such as the cavatappi with tiger prawns, green garlic, leeks, and roast tomato sauce) to roast local halibut with grilled asparagus and blood-orange chervil vinaigrette. Top it off with an apricot soufflé or the chocolate Kahlua torte. The extensive California wine list is sold at next to retail, with many wines available by the glass.

✪ **Zinzino.** 2355 Chestnut St. (at Divisadero St.). ☎ **415/346-6623.** Reservations accepted. Main courses $9.25–$16.25. MC, V. Mon–Thurs 5:30–10pm, Fri 5:30–11pm, Sat 5–11pm, Sun 4–9:30pm. Bus: 22 or 30. ITALIAN.

Owner Ken Zankel and Spago-sired chef Andrea Rappaport have combined forces to create one of the city's top new Italian restaurants. Italian movie posters, magazines, and furnishings evoke memories of past vacations, but we rarely recall the food in Italy being this good (and certainly not this cheap). Start off with the crispy calamari with a choice of herbed aïoli or tomato sauces (second only to Scala's Earth and Turf), the roasted jumbo prawns wrapped in crisp pancetta and bathed in a tangy balsamic reduction sauce, or the peculiar-tasting shaved fennel and mint salad—or try them all. Rappaport is giving Zuni Café a run for its money with her version of roasted half chicken, the most tender bird we've ever tasted; the accompanying goat-cheese salad and potato frisee were also superb. New to the menu are Rappaport's weekly rotating specials, such as her roasted shellfish platter, oven-roasted half-lobster, or baby lamb chops.

INEXPENSIVE

Café Marimba. 2317 Chestnut St. (between Scott and Divisidero sts.). ☎ **415/776-1506.** Main courses $5–$13. AE, MC, V. Mon 5:30–10pm; Tues–Thurs 11:30am–10pm; Fri 11:30am–11pm; Sat 10:30am–11pm; Sun 10:30am–10pm. Bus: 30. MEXICAN.

As much as we hate to plug the yuppified Marina District, we have to admit that we're completely addicted to Café Marimba's grilled Yucatan-spiced snapper and grilled chicken tacos. The shrimp *mojo de ajo* is also a knockout—heck, even the chips and guac are the best in town. If you're a party of three or more, order the family-style platter of grilled meats and vegetables and prepare to do battle. We're obviously not the only ones who fancy this fun, festive cafe, so expect a long wait during peak hours (our M.O. is to sneak seats at the bar and order there). But *hasta mañana* the margaritas—*muy mál.*

✪ Doidge's. 2217 Union St. (between Fillmore and Steiner sts.). ☎ **415/921-2149.** Reservations accepted and essential on weekends. Breakfast $4.50–$10; lunch $5–$8. MC, V. Mon–Fri 8am–1:45pm, Sat–Sun 8am–2:45pm. Bus: 41 or 45. AMERICAN.

Doidge's is sweet, small, and always packed, serving up one of the better breakfasts in San Francisco since 1971. Its fame is based on eggs Benedict; eggs Florentine, prepared with thinly sliced Motherlode ham, runs a close second. Invariably the menu includes a gourmet omelet packed with luscious combinations, and to delight the kid in you, hot chocolate comes in your very own teapot. The six seats at the original mahogany counter are still the most coveted by locals.

Mel's Diner. 2165 Lombard St. (at Fillmore St.). ☎ **415/921-3039.** Reservations accepted. Main courses $4–$5.50 breakfast, $6–$8 lunch, $8–$12 dinner. No credit cards. Sun–Thurs 6am–3am, Fri–Sat 24 hrs (Lombard location only). Bus: 22, 43, or 30. AMERICAN.

Sure, it's contrived, touristy, and nowhere near healthy, but when you get that urge for a chocolate shake and banana-cream pie at the stroke of midnight, no other place in the city comes through like Mel's Diner. Modeled after a classic 1950s diner right down to the nickel jukebox at each table, Mel's harks back to the halcyon days when cholesterol and fried foods didn't stroke your guilty conscience with every greasy, wonderful bite. Too bad the prices don't reflect the fifties; a burger with fries and a Coke runs about $8, and they don't take credit.

JAPANTOWN & ENVIRONS
MODERATE

YOYO Bistro. In the Miyako Hotel, 1611 Post St. (at Laguna St.). ☎ **415/922-7788.** Reservations not needed. Main courses $15–$21; continental breakfast buffet $7.50–$18. AE, CB, DC, JCB, MC, V. Daily 6:30am–11am, 11:30am–2:30pm, and 5:30–10pm. Parking in Japan Center garage. Bus: 2, 3, 22, or 38. ASIAN/FRENCH.

You'd be wise to venture out of downtown for dinner in YOYO's dark, 50-person dining room, which is surrounded by authentic Shoji screens. Previously Elka, this restaurant changed hands in 1996 and is now run by ex-Elka employees, who have put a great deal of money and care into creating a quality dining experience. The room and the food combine contemporary and ancient, Asian and French. One of the best times to come is between 4 and 10pm for tsumami (Japanese tapas) where you can order à la carte or choose four dishes for $16 or six for $22. These scrumptious little creations are anything from fresh oysters to pork ribs, and all come with outstanding sauces. Main courses include fresh fish, duck, and chicken, all very well prepared.

INEXPENSIVE

Sanppo. 1702 Post St. (at Laguna St., across from Japan Center). ☎ **415/346-3486.** Reservations not accepted. Main courses $6–$15; combination dishes $10–$17. MC, V. Mon–Sat 11am–10pm, Sun 11:30am–10pm. Bus: 2, 3, 4, or 38. JAPANESE.

Simple and unpretentious though it is, Sanppo serves excellent, down-home Japanese food. You may be asked to share one of the few tables that surround a square counter in the small dining room. Lunches and dinners all include miso soup, rice, and pickled vegetables. At lunch you might have an order of fresh, thick-cut sashimi, teriyaki, tempura, beef donburi, or an order of gyoza (dumplings filled with savory meat and herbs) for $6 to $12. The same items are available at dinner for about $1 more. Combination dishes, including tempura, sashimi, and gyoza, or tempura and teriyaki, are also available.

CIVIC CENTER

EXPENSIVE

Stars. 150 Redwood Alley (between McAllister and Golden Gate off Van Ness). ☎ **415/861-7827.** Reservations recommended. Main courses $18–$32. AE, MC, V. Mon–Fri 11:30am–2pm; Sun–Thurs 5:30–9:30pm, Fri–Sat 5:30–10pm. Bus: 19, 31, or 38. CALIFORNIA.

San Francisco's celebrity hot spot nonpareil, Stars is the brainchild of superstar chef Jeremiah Tower. The large, loud, and vibrant restaurant features the longest bar in the city, which does little to guarantee you'll find a free stool when the place is hopping. Critics complain the quality of the food is slipping (as prices increase), but that hasn't deterred local celebs like Robin Williams and Mayor Willie Brown from making regular appearances. Though the menu changes daily, among the half-dozen main courses you might find a braised veal ragout with egg noodles, cipollini onions, and wild mushrooms; or sea scallops with braised Belgian endive, lobster cream sauce, and tarragon. If you want to treat yourself extra well, order the house-cured sturgeon with mushrooms and deviled eggs, or the foie gras with hazelnut toasts and watercress salad. *Fair warning:* Prices are high for what little you receive, and the desserts—once considered extraordinary—are not as good as they once were.

MODERATE

✪ **Hayes Street Grill.** 320 Hayes St. (near Franklin St.). ☎ **415/863-5545.** Reservations recommended. Main courses $13.50–$18.25. AE, DC, DISC, MC, V. Mon–Fri 11:30am–2pm and 5–9:30pm, Sat 6–10:30pm, Sun 5–9:30pm. Bus: 19, 31, or 38. SEAFOOD.

This small, no-nonsense seafood restaurant has built a solid reputation among San Francisco's picky epicureans for its impeccably fresh fish. Choices ranging from Hawaiian swordfish to Puget Sound salmon—cooked to perfection, naturally—are matched with your sauce of choice (Szechuan peanut, tomatillo salsa, shallot butter) and a side of their signature French fries. Fancier seafood specials are available, too, such as paella with clams, mussels, scallops, calamari, chorizo, and saffron rice, as well as an impressive selection of garden-fresh salads and local grilled meats. Finish with the outstanding crème brûlée.

✪ **Zuni Café.** 1658 Market St. (at Franklin St.). ☎ **415/552-2522.** Reservations recommended. Main courses $16–$22.50. AE, MC, V. Tues–Sat 7:30am–midnight, Sun 7:30am–11pm. Muni Metro: All Market St. trams. Valet parking $5. Bus: 6, 7, 71, or 75. MEDITERRANEAN.

Even factoring in the snotty wait staff, Zuni Café is still one of our favorite places in the city to have lunch. Its expanse of windows and prime Market Street location guarantee good people-watching—a favorite San Francisco pastime—and chef Judy

Rodgers's Mediterranean-influenced menu is wonderfully diverse and satisfying. For the full effect, sit at the bustling bar and peruse the foot-long oyster menu (a dozen or so varieties are on hand at all times); you can also sit in the stylish dining room or on the outdoor patio. Though the changing menu always includes meats and fish, the proven winners are Rodgers's brick oven–roasted chick-en for two with Tuscan-style bread salad, the polenta appetizer with mascarpone, and the hamburger on grilled rosemary focaccia (a strong contender for the city's best burger). Whatever you decide, be sure to order a side of the shoestring potatoes.

HAIGHT-ASHBURY
MODERATE

Eos. 901 Cole (at Carl St.). ☎ **415/566-3063.** Reservations recommended. Main courses $10–$16. AE, MC, V. Mon–Wed 5:30–11pm, Thurs–Sat 5:30–midnight, Sun 5–10pm. Muni Metro: N line. Bus: 6, 33, or 43. EAST-WEST FUSION.

Named after the Greek goddess of dawn, Eos is certainly basking in the spotlight thanks to chef/proprietor Arnold Wong, a master of texture and taste who perfected his craft while working at Masa's and Silks. It's not without a twinge of guilt that one mars the artistic presentation of each dish, such as the tender breast of Peking duck, smoked in ginger peach tea leaves and served with a plum kumquat chutney, or the blackened Asian catfish atop a bed of lemongrass risotto. For starters, try the almond encrusted soft shell crab dipped in spicy plum ponzu sauce if it's available. Unfortunately, the stark, industrial-deco decor does little to dampen the decibels, making a romantic outing nearly impossible unless you're into shouting. There is, however, a quiet, casual wine bar around the corner (same name) that stocks more than 400 vintages from around the globe.

INEXPENSIVE

✪ Cha Cha Cha. 1801 Haight St. (at Schrader St.). ☎ **415/386-5758.** Reservations not accepted. Tapas $4.50–$7.75; main courses $9–$13. MC, V. Mon–Sun 11:30am–4pm; Sun–Thurs 5–11pm, Fri–Sat 5–11:30pm. Muni Metro: N line. Bus: 6, 7, 66, 71, or 73. CARIBBEAN.

This is one of our all-time favorite places to come for dinner, but it's not for everybody. Cha Cha Cha is not a meal, it's an *experience.* Put your name on the mile-long list, crowd into the minuscule bar, and drink sangria while you wait. When you do finally get seated (it usually takes at least an hour), you'll dine in a loud—and we mean *loud*—dining room with banana trees and plastic tropical tablecloths. The best thing to do is order from the tapas menu and share the dishes family-style. The fried calamari, fried new potatoes, Cajun shrimp, and mussels in saffron broth are all bursting with flavor and accompanied by rich, luscious sauces; but whatever you choose, you can't go wrong. This is the kind of place where you take friends in a partying mood, let your hair down, and make an evening of it. If you want all the flavor without the festivities, come at lunch.

Zona Rosa. 1797 Haight St. (at Schrader St.). ☎ **415/668-7717.** Burritos $3.45–$4.83. No credit cards. Sun–Thurs 11am–10:30pm, Fri–Sat 10:30am–11pm. Muni Metro: N line. Bus: 6, 7, 66, 71, or 73. MEXICAN.

This is a great place to stop and get a cheap (and healthful) bite. The most popular items here are the burritos, which are made to order and include your choice of beans (refried, whole pinto, or black), meats, or vegetarian ingredients. You can sit on a stool at the window and watch all the Haight Street freaks strolling by, relax at one of five colorful interior tables, or take it to go and head to Golden Gate Park (it's just two blocks away). Zona Rosa is one of the best burrito stores around.

RICHMOND & SUNSET DISTRICTS
EXPENSIVE

✪ **Alain Rondelli.** 126 Clement St. (between Second and Third aves.). ☎ **415/387-0408.** Reservations recommended Fri and Sat. Main courses $19–$23, tasting menu from $52. MC, V. Tues–Sun 5:30–10:30pm. Valet parking $7. Bus: 2 or 38. FRENCH.

French chef Rondelli does more than simply serve exquisite and innovative French food; he dishes up a gastronomic experience you're likely to dream about for years to come. You may order à la carte, but you're better off ordering one of the 6-, 9-, 12-, or 20-course tasting menus (for the entire table only)—and completing the experience with wine ordered by the half-glass. One spoonful of the calamare—a "salad" of calamari, jalapeño, and mint floating in a heavenly tomato water, and topped off with fresh carrot juice—and you'll be inclined to jump out of your chair and proclaim *"C'est magnifique!"* Take a breather with pear and Roquefort with champagne vinegar and black pepper gastric before embarking on one of the sumptuous desserts. The grandest conjuration of all is that after such a didactic and tantalizing feast, you'll feel satiated but not overly full, and you'll float out the front doors as relaxed as if you'd just had a massage.

INEXPENSIVE

Hong Kong Flower Lounge. 5322 Geary Blvd. (between 17th and 18th aves.). ☎ **415/668-8998.** Most main dishes $5.95–$10.95; dim sum $1.20–$3.20. Mon–Fri 11am–2:30pm, Sat–Sun 10am–2:30pm; daily 5–9:30pm. Bus: 1, 2, or 38. CHINESE/DIM SUM.

You know you're at a good Chinese restaurant when most people waiting for a table are Chinese. And if you come for dim sum, be prepared to stand in line because you're not the only one who's heard this is the best in town. This has been one of our very favorite restaurants for years now. It's not the pink and green decor or the live fish swimming in the tank, or even the beautiful marble bathrooms; it's simply that every little dish that comes our way is so darn good. Don't pass up taro cake, salt-fried shrimp, shark-fin soup, and shrimp or beef crepes.

THE CASTRO
MODERATE

✪ **2223.** 2223 Market St. (between Sanchez and Noe sts.). ☎ **415/431-0692.** Reservations recommended. $12.95–$16.95. MC. V. Mon–Fri 11:30am–2:30pm, Sun 10am–2pm; Sun–Thurs 5:30–10pm, Fri–Sat 5:30–11pm. Muni Metro: F, L, K, M. Bus: 8, 22, 24, or 37. CALIFORNIA.

The decor at 2223, which is run by the owners of the renowned Cypress Club, is substantially less opulent than its counterpart, but the energy level is definitely more lively. Surrounded by hardwood floors, candles, streamlined modern light fixtures, and loud music, festive gays and straights come here to cocktail on the heavy-handed specialty drinks and dine on grilled pork chops, mustard-glazed salmon, or the ever-popular roasted chicken with garlic mashed potatoes. Along with Mecca, this is currently *the* dining and schmoozing spot in the area.

Mecca. 2029 Market St. (between Duboce and Church sts.). ☎ **415/621-7000.** Reservations recommended. Main courses $12.75–$18. AE, DC, MC, V. Mon–Sat 6–11pm, Sun 6–10pm. Muni Metro: F, K, L, or M. Bus: 8, 22, 24, or 37. MEDITERRANEAN.

In 1996, Mecca entered the scene in a decadent swirl of chocolate-brown velvet, stainless steel, cement, and brown Naugahyde, unveiling the kind of industrial-chic supper club that makes you want to order a martini just so you'll match the ambiance. And cocktail they do, that eclectic City clientele (with a heavy dash of same-sex couples) who mingle at the oval centerpiece bar. A night here promises a dose of live jazz and a tasty, though sometimes unpredictable, California meal. Menu options include such starters as pomegranate-glazed quail on endive and watercress, and herb-skewered prawns with romesco sauce and roasted potatoes. Main courses include the popular mustard seed-crusted halibut, duck breast with roasted fig and huckleberry sauce and potatoes, and a veal chop with wild mushroom potato cake. The food is good, but it's that only-in-San Francisco vibe that makes this place a smokin' hot spot in the Castro.

INEXPENSIVE

Patio Café. 531 Castro St. (at 18th St.). ☎ **415/621-4640.** Reservations not accepted. Main courses $4.75–$8.95 lunch, $6.95–$12.50 dinner. AE, MC, V. Sun–Thurs 8am–10:30pm, Fri–Sat 8am–11pm. Bus: 24 or 33. AMERICAN.

Originally established as The Baker's Café, this Castro Street bar and restaurant retains the original ovens that contributed to its early reputation, which are today purely decorative. Ringed with trellises and verdant plants, and set behind a cluster of shops, the patio features a glass roof (whose entertainment value derives from the heft and brawn of the staff, who climb skyward to manually crank it open during clement weather). Menu items include such dishes as Caesar salad, Chinese chicken salad (laced with fresh ginger), prime rib, and grilled salmon with Cajun hollandaise sauce, plus virtually any drink you can think of; the most popular drinks include the Melon Margarita and Patio Mai-Tai.

MISSION DISTRICT
EXPENSIVE

Flying Saucer. 1000 Guerrero St. (at 22nd St.). ☎ **415/641-9955.** Reservations recommended. Main courses $15–$26. AE, MC, V. Tues–Fri 6–10pm, Sat 5:30–11pm. FRENCH.

Outrageously yet artfully presented food is the hallmark of this Mission District fixture. Peering into the glass-walled kitchen, diners can catch the kitchen staff leaning over plates, carefully standing a jumbo prawn on its head atop a baked column of potato polenta. Fish, beef, and fowl dishes are competently grilled, baked, or flamed before being surrounded by a flurry of sauces and garnishes. While the pricey food is certainly intense and flavorful, the overwhelming sensation at this bistro is visual. The party extends from the plate to the decor, where plastic flying saucers mingle with colorful murals and creative lighting. The menu changes frequently, and there are almost always specials. If you ask your waiter to bring you the chef's most flamboyant-*looking* offering, chances are you won't be disappointed. Reservations are essential, as is a blind eye to the sometimes infuriatingly snotty service.

MODERATE

Bruno's. 2389 Mission St. (between 19th and 20th sts.). ☎ **415/550-7455.** Reservations recommended. Main courses $14–$19. V, MC, DC. Tues–Thurs 5:30–11pm, Fri–Sun 5:30pm–1am. Parking in back lot $5. MEDITERRANEAN.

When the new owners scraped 60 years' worth of grease and cigar smoke from the wood-paneled bar, added live music, and began serving flavorful fare in the '50s-style dining room, the hipsters came in droves. Two years later, they're still coming. The reason? Aside from people-watching, the food here is actually on par with the ambiance. House specialties include duck salad with radicchio and pancetta, grilled boneless quail, and oxtail with mashed potatoes. After dinner, meander into the bar and beyond, where bands liven the crowd. *Note:* While the dining room is closed on Monday, you can still order appetizers and dessert at the bar.

✪ **Universal Café.** 2814 19th St. (at Bryant St.). ☎ **415/821-4608.** Reservations recommended for dinner. Main courses $2–$7 breakfast, $4–$8 lunch, $8–$18 dinner. AE, MC, V.

Tues–Fri 7:30am–2:30pm and 6–10pm, Fri 9am–11:30pm, Sat 9am–2:30pm and 6–10pm, Sun 9am–2:30pm and 5:30–9:30pm. Bus: 27. AMERICAN/FRENCH.

We stumbled onto this place last year completely by accident. It was love at first sight, and first bite. Not only does it look good—suave and stylish, with thick floor-to-ceiling windows and a profusion of sculptured metal and marble—it also attracts a nightly gaggle of locals who come for the delicious focaccia sandwiches, inventive thin-crust pizzas, and gourmet salads for lunch, and superb dinner dishes such as braised duck leg on a bed of creamy polenta; sea bass served with risotto, spinach, and caramelized spinach; or hearty pot roast with lumpy mashed potatoes and fresh veggies. Granted, it's on the way to nowhere, but if you're near the Mission, it's well worth the detour.

5 The Top Attractions

✪ **Alcatraz Island.** Pier 41 (near Fisherman's Wharf). ☎ **415/773-1188.** Admission (including ferry trip) adults, $11 with audio tour, $7.75 without; seniors 62 and older, $9.25 with audio tour, $6 without; children 5–11, $5.75 with audio tour, $4.50 without. Summer, daily 9:15am–6:30pm; winter, daily 9:15–2:35pm. Advance purchase advised. Ferries depart every half hour (at 15 and 45 minutes after the hour). Arrive at least 20 minutes before sailing time.

Visible from Fisherman's Wharf, Alcatraz Island (a.k.a. "The Rock") has seen a checkered history. It was discovered in 1775 by Juan Manuel Ayala, who named it after the many pelicans that nested on the island. From the 1850s to 1933, when the army vacated the island, it served as a military post protecting the Bay shoreline. In 1934, the buildings of the military outpost were converted into a maximum security federal prison. Given the sheer cliffs, treacherous tides and currents, and frigid temperatures of the waters, it was believed to be totally escape-proof. Among the infamous gangsters who were penned in cell blocks A through D were Al Capone, Machine Gun Kelly, and Robert Stroud, who became famous as the Birdman of Alcatraz because he was an expert in ornithological diseases.

It cost a fortune to keep them imprisoned here because all supplies, including water, had to be shipped in. In 1963, after an apparent escape in which no bodies were recovered, the government closed the prison, and in 1972 it became part of the Golden Gate National Recreation Area. The wildlife that was driven away during the military and prison years has begun to return—the black-crested night heron and other sea birds are nesting here again—and a new trail has been built that passes through the island's nature areas.

We recommend buying the full fare ticket that includes the audio tour; you'll be issued a tape and a Walkman as you enter. The tape is extremely well done and includes former guards and inmates describing their experiences here. The audio tape is also nice because it tends to keep the crowds quiet and preserves an eerie atmosphere. Frequent special programs, on topics such as famous escape attempts, are given by the rangers; the day's schedule will be announced to you as you arrive.

It's a popular excursion and space is limited, so purchase tickets as far in advance as possible. The tour is operated by **Blue & Gold Fleet** (☎ **415/773-1188** for recorded ticket, schedule, and tour information or 415/705-5555 for ticket sales only) and can be charged to your American Express, MasterCard, or Visa card ($2 per ticket service charge on phone orders). Tickets may also be purchased in advance from the Blue & Gold ticket office on Pier 41, but don't count on being able to book this at the last minute. Allow about 2¹/₂ hours for the round-trip and the tour. Wear comfortable shoes and take a heavy sweater or windbreaker because even when the sun's out, it's cold. The National Parks Service also notes that there are a lot of steps to climb on the tour.

For those who want to get a closer look at Alcatraz without going ashore, two boat-tour operators offer short circumnavigations of the island. (See "Organized Tours," later in this chapter, for complete information.)

✪ **The Cable Cars.** ☎ **415/673-6864.** The Powell-Hyde and Powell-Mason lines begin at Powell and Market sts.; the California St. Line begins at the foot of Market St. Fare $3.

Designated official historic landmarks by the National Park Service in 1964, the city's beloved cable cars clank across the hills like mobile museum pieces. Each weighs about six tons and is hauled along by a steel cable, enclosed under the street in a center rail. They move at a constant $9^1/_2$ mph—never more, never less. This may strike you as slow, but it doesn't feel that way when you're cresting an almost perpendicular hill and look down at what seems like a bobsled dive straight into the ocean. But in spite of the thrills, they're perfectly safe.

✪ **Coit Tower.** Atop Telegraph Hill. ☎ **415/362-0808.** Admission to the top of the tower $3 adults, $2 seniors and students, $1 children 6–12. Daily 10am–6pm. Bus: 39 ("Coit").

In a city known for its panoramic views and vantage points, Coit Tower is "The Peak." If you're there on a clear day, it's wonderful to get here by walking up the Filbert Steps (thereby avoiding a traffic nightmare) and then taking in the panoramic views of the city and bay at the base of the tower. (In fact, we'd recommend not paying the admission and going to the top; the view is just as good from the parking area and you can see the murals for free.)

Completed in 1933, the tower is the legacy of Lillie Hitchcock Coit, a wealthy eccentric who left San Francisco a $125,000 bequest. Inside the base of the tower are the impressive WPA murals titled Life in California, 1934, which were completed during the New Deal by more than 25 artists, many of whom had studied under master muralist Diego Rivera. The individual frescoes form a unified whole, all done in traditional Mexican-style fresco, and all done with the same scale and palette.

The Exploratorium. In the Palace of Fine Arts, 3601 Lyon St. (at Marina Blvd). ☎ **415/563-7337,** or 415/561-0360 for recorded information. Admission $9 adults, $7 senior citizens, $5 children 6–17, $2.50 children 3–5, free for children under 3; free for everyone first Wed of each month. Memorial Day–Labor Day and holidays, Mon–Tues and Thurs–Sun 10am–6pm, Wed 10am–9:30pm; the rest of year Tues and Thurs–Sun 10am–5pm, Wed 10am–9:30pm. Closed Thanksgiving and Christmas Day. Bus: 30 from Stockton St. to the Marina stop.

This fun, hands-on science fair contains more than 650 permanent exhibits that explore everything from color theory to Einstein's Theory of Relativity. Optics are demonstrated in booths where you can see a bust of a statue in three dimensions—but when you try to touch it, you discover it isn't there! The same surreal experience occurs with an image of yourself: When you stretch your hand forward, a hand comes out to touch you, and the hands pass in midair. Every exhibit is designed to be used. You can whisper into a concave reflector and have a friend hear you 60 feet away, or you can design your own animated abstract art—using sound.

✪ **Golden Gate Bridge.** ☎ **415/921-5858.** Bridge-bound Golden Gate Transit buses (☎ **415/332-6600**) depart every 30–60 minutes during the day for Marin County, starting from the Transbay Terminal at Mission and First sts. and making convenient stops at Market and Seventh sts., at the Civic Center, and along Van Ness Ave. and Lombard St. Consult the route map in the Yellow Pages of the telephone directory or phone for schedule information.

With its gracefully swung single span, spidery bracing cables, and sky-high twin towers, the bridge looks more like a work of abstract art than one of the greatest practical engineering feats of the 20th century. Construction began in May 1937 and was completed at the then-colossal cost of $35 million. Contrary to pessimistic

Major San Francisco Sights

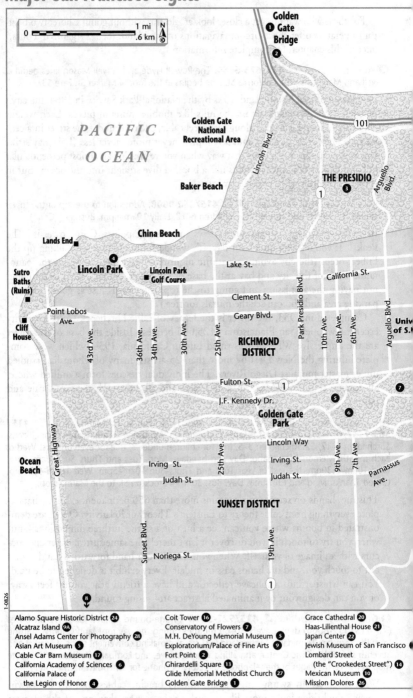

Alamo Square Historic District **24**
Alcatraz Island **9A**
Ansel Adams Center for Photography **28**
Asian Art Museum **5**
Cable Car Barn Museum **17**
California Academy of Sciences **6**
California Palace of
    the Legion of Honor **4**

Coit Tower **16**
Conservatory of Flowers **7**
M.H. DeYoung Memorial Museum **5**
Exploratorium/Palace of Fine Arts **9**
Fort Point **2**
Ghirardelli Square **13**
Glide Memorial Methodist Church **27**
Golden Gate Bridge **1**

Grace Cathedral **20**
Haas-Lilienthal House **21**
Japan Center **22**
Jewish Museum of San Francisco **?**
Lombard Street
    (the "Crookedest Street") **14**
Mexican Museum **10**
Mission Dolores **26**

1-0826

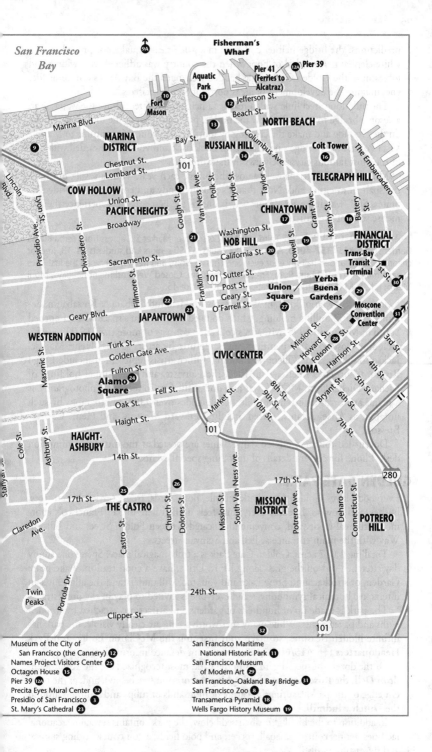

Map of San Francisco showing districts and numbered points of interest.

San Francisco Bay

Fisherman's Wharf

Pier 41 (Ferries to Alcatraz)

Pier 39 ⑫Ⓐ

Aquatic Park ⑪

Fort Mason ⑩

⑨Ⓐ

Jefferson St.

Beach St.

NORTH BEACH

⑬

Marina Blvd.

MARINA DISTRICT

Bay St.

RUSSIAN HILL

⑭

Columbus Ave.

Coit Tower ⑯

The Embarcadero

⑨

Chestnut St.

Lombard St.

101

TELEGRAPH HILL

Lincoln Blvd.

COW HOLLOW

Union St.

PACIFIC HEIGHTS

Broadway

⑮

Gough St.

Polk St.

Hyde St.

Taylor St.

CHINATOWN

⑰

Grant Ave.

Kearny St.

Battery St.

⑱

Presidio Ave.

Lyon St.

Divisadero St.

Fillmore St.

Sacramento St.

⑤

Washington St.

NOB HILL

California St.

⑳

Powell St.

⑲

FINANCIAL DISTRICT

Trans-Bay Transit Terminal

1st St.

⑳

Van Ness Ave.

Franklin St.

101

Sutter St.

Post St.

Geary St.

O'Farrell St.

Union Square ㉗

Yerba Buena Gardens

㉙

⑳

⑳

Geary Blvd.

⑳

JAPANTOWN ㉓

Moscone Convention Center

㉛

3rd St.

WESTERN ADDITION

Masonic St.

Turk St.

Golden Gate Ave.

Fulton St.

Alamo Square ㉔

Fell St.

CIVIC CENTER

Mission St.

Howard St. ㉘

Folsom St.

Harrison St.

SOMA

Bryant St.

4th St.

5th St.

6th St.

7th St.

Oak St.

Haight St.

8th St.

9th St.

10th St.

Cole St.

Ashbury St.

Stanyan St.

HAIGHT-ASHBURY

14th St.

Market St.

101

280

17th St.

⑳

⑳

Church St.

Dolores St.

17th St.

Mission St.

South Van Ness Ave.

Potrero Ave.

Deharo St.

Connecticut St.

POTRERO HILL

⑳

THE CASTRO

Castro St.

MISSION DISTRICT

Claredon Ave.

Twin Peaks

Portola Dr.

24th St.

Clipper St.

㉜

101

Museum of the City of San Francisco (the Cannery) ⑫	San Francisco Maritime National Historic Park ⑪
Names Project Visitors Center ㉕	San Francisco Museum of Modern Art ㉙
Octagon House ⑮	San Francisco–Oakland Bay Bridge ㉛
Pier 39 ⑫Ⓐ	San Francisco Zoo ⑧
Precita Eyes Mural Center ㉜	Transamerica Pyramid ⑱
Presidio of San Francisco ③	Wells Fargo History Museum ⑲
St. Mary's Cathedral ㉓	

predictions, the bridge neither collapsed in a gale or earthquake nor proved to be a white elephant. A symbol of hope when the country was afflicted with widespread joblessness, the Golden Gate single-handedly changed the Bay Area's economic life, encouraging the development of areas north of San Francisco.

The mile-long steel link, which reaches a height of 746 feet above the water, is an awesome bridge to cross. To view the bridge, park in the lot at the foot of the bridge on the city side and make the crossing by foot. Back in your car, continue to Marin's Vista Point, at the bridge's northern end. Look back and you'll be rewarded with one of the most famous cityscape views in the world.

Millions of pedestrians walk across the bridge each year. You can walk out onto the span from either end. Note that it's usually windy and cold, and the bridge vibrates. Still, walking even a short way is one of the best ways to experience the immense scale of the structure.

Museum of Modern Art. 151 Third St. (2 blocks south of Market St., across from Yerba Buena Gardens). ☎ **415/357-4000.** Admission $7 adults, $3.50 seniors and students 14–18, free for children 13 and under; half price for everyone Thurs 6–9pm, and free for everyone the first Tues of each month. Thurs 11am–9pm, Fri–Tues 11am–6pm. Closed Wed and major holidays. Muni Metro: J, K, L, M to Montgomery Station. Bus: 15, 30, or 45.

Swiss architect Mario Botta, in association with Hellmuth, Obata & Kassabaum, designed this $62 million building, which doubled the musuem's space when it opened South of Market in 1995. MOMA's collection consists of more than 15,000 works, including close to 5,000 paintings and sculptures by artists such as Henri Matisse, Jackson Pollock, and Willem de Kooning. Other artists represented include Diego Rivera, Georgia O'Keeffe, Paul Klee, the Fauvists, and exceptional holdings of Richard Diebenkorn. MOMA was also one of the first to recognize photography as a major art form; its extensive collection includes over 9,000 photographs by such notables as Ansel Adams, Alfred Steiglitz, Edward Weston, and Henri Cartier-Bresson.

Docent-led tours are offered daily. Times are posted at the museum's admission desk. Phone for current details of upcoming special events.

GOLDEN GATE PARK

Everybody loves Golden Gate Park: people, dogs, birds, frogs, turtles, bison, trees, bushes, and flowers. Literally everything feels unified here in San Francisco's enormous arboreal front yard, conveniently located between Fulton Street and Lincoln Way with the main entrance at Fell and Stanyan streets.

Totalling 1,017 acres, Golden Gate Park is a truly magical place. Spend one sunny day stretched out on the grass along J.F.K. Drive, have a good read in Shakespeare Garden, or stroll around Stow Lake and you, too, will understand the allure. It's an interactive botanical symphony—and everyone is invited to play in the orchestra.

The park is made up of hundreds of gardens and attractions attached by wooded paths and paved roads. While many sites worth seeing are clearly visible, the park has infinite hidden treasures, so make your first stop the **McClaren Lodge and Park Headquarters** (☎ 415/666-7200) if you want detailed information on the park.

Of the dozens of special gardens in the park, most recognized are the **Rhododendron Dell,** the **Rose Garden,** the **Strybing Arboretum** (see below), and, at the western edge of the park, a springtime array of thousands of tulips and daffodils around the **Dutch windmill.**

In addition to the highlights discussed below, the park contains several recreational facilities: tennis courts; baseball, soccer, and polo fields; a golf course; riding stables; and fly-casting pools.

Golden Gate Park

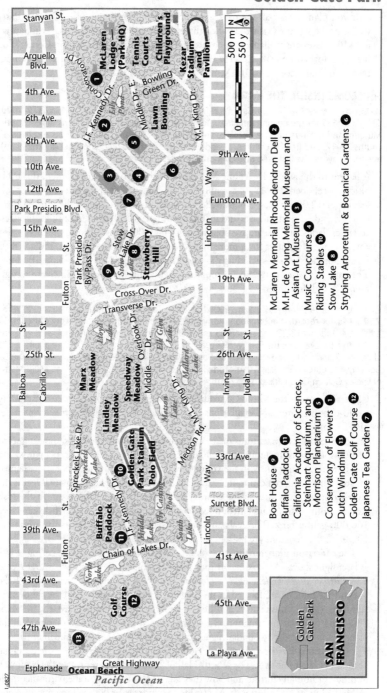

McLaren Memorial Rhododendron Dell **2**
M.H. de Young Memorial Museum and
Asian Art Museum **3**
Music Concourse **4**
Riding Stables **10**
Stow Lake **8**
Strybing Arboretum & Botanical Gardens **6**

Boat House **9**
Buffalo Paddock **11**
California Academy of Sciences,
Steinhart Aquarium, and
Morrison Planetarium **5**
Conservatory of Flowers **1**
Dutch Windmill **13**
Golden Gate Golf Course **12**
Japanese Tea Garden **7**

SAN
FRANCISCO

Golden
Gate Park

If you plan to visit all the park's attractions, consider buying the **Culture Pass,** which enables you to visit the park's three museums and the Japanese Tea Garden for $10. Passes are available at each site and at the Visitor Information Center. For further information, call ☎ **415/391-2000.** Enter the park at Kezar Drive, an extension of Fell Street. Bus: 16AX, BX, 5, 6, 7, 66, or 71.

MUSEUMS INSIDE THE PARK

Asian Art Museum. Golden Gate Park, near 10th Ave. and Fulton St. ☎ **415/379-8800,** 415/752-2635 for the hearing impaired. Admission (including the M. H. De Young Memorial Museum and California Palace of the Legion of Honor) $6 adults, $4 seniors 65 and over, $3 youths 12–17, and free for children 11 and under (fees may be higher for special exhibitions); free for everyone the first Wed of each month. Wed–Sun 10am–4:45pm. Bus: 5, 44, or 71.

Adjacent to the M. H. De Young Museum and the Japanese Tea Garden, this exhibition space, opened in 1966, can only display about 1,800 of the museum's vast collection of 12,000 pieces. About half the works on exhibit are in the ground-floor Chinese and Korean galleries and include world-class sculptures, paintings, bronzes, ceramics, jades, and decorative objects spanning 6,000 years of history. There's also a wide range of exhibits from more than 40 Asian countries—Pakistan, India, Tibet, Japan, Southeast Asia—including the world's oldest-known "dated" Chinese Buddha. The museum's free daily guided tours are highly informative and sincerely recommended. Call for times.

✪ **California Academy of Sciences.** On the Music Concourse of Golden Gate Park. ☎ **415/ 750-7145** for recorded information. Admission: Aquarium and Natural History Museum, $7 adults, $4 students 12–17 and seniors 65 and over, $1.50 children 6–11, free for children 5 and under, free for everyone the first Wed of every month; planetarium shows, $2.50 adults, $1.25 children 17 and under and seniors 65 and over. Memorial Day–Labor Day, daily 9am–6pm; Labor Day–Memorial Day, daily 10am–5pm; first Wed of every month 10am–9pm. Muni Metro: N line to Golden Gate Park. Bus: 5, 71, or 44.

Clustered around the Music Concourse in Golden Gate Park are three outstanding world-class museums and exhibitions that are guaranteed to entertain every member of the family.

The **Steinhart Aquarium** is the most diverse aquarium in the world, housing some 14,000 specimens, including amphibians, reptiles, marine mammals, penguins, and much more. A huge hit with the youngsters is the California tide pool and a hands-on area where children can touch starfish and sea urchins. The living coral reef is the largest display of its kind in the country and the only one in the West. In the Fish Roundabout, visitors are surrounded by fast-swimming schools of fish kept in a 100,000-gallon tank. The seals and dolphins are fed every 2 hours, beginning at 10:30am; the penguins are fed at 11:30am and 4pm.

The **Morrison Planetarium** projects sky shows on its 65-foot domed ceiling as well as laser light shows. Approximately four major exhibits, with titles such as *Star Death: The Birth of Black Holes* and *The Universe Unveiled,* are presented each year. Related cosmos exhibits are located in the adjacent Earth and Space Hall. Sky shows are featured at 2pm on weekdays and hourly every weekend and holiday (call ☎ **415/ 750-7141** for more information). Laserium laser light shows are also presented in the planetarium Thursday to Sunday nights (call ☎ **415/750-7138** for more information).

The **Natural History Museum** includes several halls displaying classic dioramas of fauna in their habitats. The Wattis Hall of Human Cultures traces the evolution of different human cultures and how they adapted to their natural environment; the "Wild California" exhibition in Meyer Hall includes a 14,000-gallon aquarium and seabird rookery, life-size battling elephant seals, and two larger-than-life views of microscopic life forms; in McBean-Peterson Hall visitors can walk through an exhibit tracing the course of 3¹/₂ billion years of evolution, from the earliest life forms to the present day; and in the Hohfeld Earth and Space Hall visitors can experience a simulation of two of San Francisco's biggest earthquakes, determine what their weight would be on other planets, see a real moon rock, and learn about the rotation of the planet at a replica of Foucault's Pendulum (the original one is in Paris).

M.H. De Young Memorial Museum. In Golden Gate Park near 10th Ave. and Fulton St. ☎ **415/750-3600,** or 415/863-3330 for recorded information. Admission (including the Asian Art Museum and California Palace of the Legion of Honor) $6 adults, $4 seniors 65 and over, $3 youths 12–17, free for children 11 and under (fees may be higher for special exhibitions); reduced admission for everyone the first Wed of each month. Wed–Sun 9:30am–5pm (first Wed of the month until 8:45pm). Bus: 44.

One of the city's oldest museums, the De Young is best known for its American art dating from colonial times to the 20th century, including paintings, sculptures, furniture, and decorative arts by Paul Revere, Winslow Homer, John Singer Sargent, and Georgia O'Keeffe. Special note should be taken of the American landscapes, as well as the fun trompe-l'oeil and still-life works from the turn of the century.

Named after the late 19th-century publisher of the *San Francisco Chronicle,* the museum also possesses an important textile collection, with primary emphasis on rugs from central Asia and the Near East. Other collections on view include decorative art from Africa, Oceania, and the Americas. Major traveling exhibitions are equally eclectic, including everything from ancient rugs to great Dutch paintings. Call the museum to find out what's on. Tours are offered daily; call for times.

The museum's **Café De Young** is exceptional, serving daily specials that might include Peruvian stew, Chinese chicken salad, and Italian vegetables in tomato-basil sauce. In summer, visitors can dine in the garden, among bronze statuary. The cafe is open Wednesday to Sunday from 10am to 4pm.

OTHER PARK HIGHLIGHTS

CONSERVATORY OF FLOWERS (1878)   This striking assemblage of glass and iron, modeled on the famous glass house at Kew Gardens in London, contains a rotating display of plants and shrubs at all times of the year. It's closed until further notice to visitors, but the architecture alone is worth a look.

JAPANESE TEA GARDEN (1894)   Developed for the 1894 Midwinter Exposition, this garden is a quiet place with cherry trees, shrubs, and bonsai crisscrossed by winding paths and high-arched bridges crossing over pools of water. Focal points and places for contemplation include the massive bronze Buddha that was cast in Japan in 1790 and donated by the Gump family, the Shinto wooden pagoda, and the Wishing Bridge, which reflected in the water looks as if it completes a circle. The garden is open daily: March to September from 9am to 6:30pm and October to February from 8:30am to 6pm (the tea house closes at 5:30pm). For information on admission, call ☎ 415/752-4227; for the tea house, call ☎ **415/752-1171.**

STRYBING ARBORETUM & BOTANICAL GARDENS   Some 6,000 plant species grow here, among them some very ancient plants in a special "primitive garden," rare species, and a grove of California redwoods. Docent tours are available during operating hours: Monday to Friday from 8am to 4:30pm and on Saturday and Sunday from 10am to 5pm. For more information, call ☎ 415/753-7089.

✪ STRAWBERRY HILL/STOW LAKE   Rent a paddle boat, rowboat, or motorboat here and cruise around the circular lake as painters create still-lifes and joggers pass along the grassy shoreline. Ducks waddle around waiting to be fed and turtles bathe on rocks and logs. Strawberry Hill, the 430-foot-high artificial island that lies at the center of Stow Lake, is a perfect picnic spot and boasts a bird's-eye view of San

Francisco and the bay. It also has a waterfall and peace pagoda. To reach the boathouse, call ☎ **415/752-0347.** Boat rentals are available daily from 9am to 4pm.

BEACH CHALET   First listed on the National Register of Historic places in 1981, the Spanish-Colonial Beach Chalet, at 1000 Great Hwy., at west end of Golden Gate Park near Fulton Street (☎ **415/386-8439**), was designed by the architect Willis Polk in 1925. Built with a 200-seat restaurant upstairs and a public lounge and changing rooms on the first floor, it was a popular stopover for generations of beachgoers. In the late 1930s the federal government's Works Progress Administration (WPA) commissioned Lucien Labaudt (who also painted Coit Tower's frescoes) to create incredible frescoes, mosaics, and woodcarvings of San Francisco life. After decades of use the chalet grew old and worn, forcing its closure in 1981; but in December 1996 the historic Beach Chalet reopened its doors, and through the original mosaics and new literature and displays, it continues to celebrate the city's heritage. The upstairs restaurant is far too modern to wax historical, but it's a great place to stop for a house-made brew and a glimpse of the expansive Pacific.

6 Exploring the City

Mission Dolores. 16th St. (at Dolores St.). ☎ **415/621-8203.** Admission $2 adults, $1 children 5–12. May–Oct daily 9am–4:30pm; Nov–Apr daily 9am–4pm; Good Fri 10am–noon. Closed Thanksgiving and Christmas Day. Muni Metro: J line to the corner of Church and 16th sts. Bus: 22.

This is the oldest structure in the city, built on order of Franciscan Father Junípero Serra by Father Francisco Palou. It was constructed of 36,000 sun-baked bricks and dedicated in June 1776 at the northern terminus of El Camino Real, the Spanish road from Mexico to California. It's a moving place to visit to observe the cool, serene buildings with their thick adobe walls and most of all, the cemetery-gardens where the early settlers are buried.

The NAMES Project AIDS Memorial Quilt Visitors Center. 2362-A Market St. ☎ **415/863-1966.** Thurs–Tues noon–5pm, Wed noon–10pm. Muni Metro: J, K, L, or M line to Castro Street Station; F line to Church and Market sts.

The NAMES Project began in 1987 as a memorial to those who have died of AIDS. Sewing machines and fabric were acquired, and the public was invited to make coffin-sized panels for a giant memorial quilt. More than 28,000 individual panels now commemorate the lives of those who have died. Each has been uniquely designed and sewn by the victims' friends, lovers, and family members.

The Quilt, which would cover 11 football fields if laid out end to end, was first displayed on the Capitol Mall in Washington, D.C., during a 1987 national march on Washington for Lesbian and Gay Rights. Although the Quilt is often on tour throughout the world, portions of the heart-wrenching art project are on display here. A sewing machine and fabrics are also available here, free, for your use.

Lombard Street

Known as the "crookedest street in the world," the whimsically winding block of Lombard Street, between Hyde Street and Leavenworth Street, puts smiles on the faces of thousands of visitors each year. The elevation is so steep that the road has to snake back and forth to make a descent possible.

ARCHITECTURAL HIGHLIGHTS

The **Alamo Square Historic District** contains many of the city's 14,000 Victorian "Painted Ladies," homes that have been restored and ornately painted by residents. The small area—bordered by Divisadero Street on the west, Golden Gate Avenue on the north, Webster Street on the east, and Fell Street on the south, about 10 blocks west of the Civic Center—has one of the city's largest concentrations of these. One of the most famous views of San Francisco, which you'll see on postcards and posters all around the city, depicts sharp-edged Financial District skyscrapers behind a row of Victorians. This view can be seen from Alamo Square at Fulton and Steiner streets.

Built in 1881 to a design by Brown and Bakewell, **City Hall** and the **Civic Center** are part of a City Beautiful complex done in the beaux arts style. The dome rises to a height of 308 feet on the exterior and is ornamented with occuli and topped by a lantern. The interior rotunda soars 112 feet and is finished in oak, marble, and limestone with a monumental marble staircase leading to the second floor, but you won't be able to see it; City Hall is closed for renovation for the next few years.

The Flood Mansion, 1000 California St. at Mason, was built in 1885–86 for James Clair Flood who, thanks to the Comstock Lode, rose from a bartender to one of the city's wealthiest men. The house cost $1.5 million (the fence alone carried a price tag of $30,000!). It was designed by Augustus Laver and modified by Willis Polk after the earthquake to accommodate the Pacific Union Club.

The **Octagon House,** 2645 Gough St. at Union St. (☎ **415/441-7512**), is an eight-sided, cupola-topped house dating from 1861. Its features are extraordinary, especially the circular staircase and ceiling medallion. Inside, you'll find furniture, silverware, and American pewter from the Colonial and Federal periods. There are also some historic documents, including signatures of 54 of the 56 signers of the Declaration of Independence. Even if you're not able to visit during open hours, this strange structure is worth a look. It's open on the second Sunday and second and fourth Thursdays of each month from noon to 3pm; closed January and holidays.

The **Palace of Fine Arts,** on Baker between Jefferson and Bay streets, is the only building to survive from the Pan Pacific Exhibition of 1915. Constructed by Bernard Maybeck, it was rebuilt in concrete using molds taken from the original in the 1950s. It now houses the Exploratorium (see "The Top Attractions," above).

The **Transamerica Pyramid,** 600 Montgomery St., is the tallest structure in San Francisco's skyline—48 stories tall and capped by a 212-foot spire.

Although the **San Francisco-Oakland Bay Bridge** (☎ **510/464-1148** for information) is visually less appealing than the Golden Gate Bridge (see "The Top Attractions," above), it is in many ways more spectacular. Opened in 1936, before the Golden Gate, it's 8¼ miles long, one of the world's longest steel bridges. It's not a single bridge at all, but actually a dovetailed series of spans joined in midbay—at Yerba Buena Island—by one of the world's largest (in diameter) tunnels. To the west of Yerba Buena, the bridge is really two separate suspension bridges, joined at a central anchorage. East of the island is a 1,400-foot cantilever span, followed by a succession of truss bridges.

Yerba Buena Gardens (☎ **415/978-2787**), between Mission and Howard at Third, opened in 1993 adjacent to the Moscone Convention Center. It is the city's version of New York's Lincoln Center. The center consists of a 755-seat theater designed by James Stewart Polshek and the Arts Forum designed by Fumihiko Maki, which features three galleries and a space for dance. There's also a 5-acre garden featuring several art works, the most dramatic being a mixed-media memorial to Martin Luther King Jr. created by sculptor Houston Conwill, poet Estella Majoza, and architect Joseph de Pace. It features 12 glass panels, each inscribed with quotations from King, sheltered behind a 50-foot-high waterfall.

CHURCHES

Glide Memorial United Methodist Church. 330 Ellis St. ☎ **415/771-6300.** Services held Sun 9 and 11am. Muni Metro: Powell. Bus: 37.

There would be nothing special about this plain Tenderloin-area church if it weren't for its exhilarating pastor, Cecil Williams. Williams's enthusiastic and uplifting preaching and singing with the homeless and poor people of the neighborhood has attracted nationwide fame. Go for an uplifting experience.

MUSEUMS

Also see "Golden Gate Park," above.

Ansel Adams Center for Photography. 250 Fourth St. ☎ **415/495-7000.** Admission $5 adults, $3 students, $2 seniors and children 12–17. Tues–Sun 11am–5pm; until 8pm the first Thurs of each month. Muni Metro: Powell. Bus: 30, 45, or 9X.

This popular SoMa museum features five separate galleries for changing exhibitions of contemporary and historical photography. One area is dedicated solely to displaying the works and exploring the legacy of Ansel Adams.

Cable car Barn Museum. Washington and Mason sts. ☎ **415/474-1887.** Free admission. Apr–Oct daily 10am–6pm; Nov–Mar daily 10am–5pm. Cable car: Powell Street lines stop at the museum.

If you've ever wondered how cable cars work, this nifty museum will explain (and demonstrate!) it all to you. Yes, this is a museum, but the Cable Car Barn is no stuffed shirt. It's the living powerhouse, repair shop, and storage place of the cable car system and is in full operation. The exposed machinery, which pulls the cables under San Francisco's streets, looks like a Rube Goldberg invention. Watch the massive groaning and vibrating winches as they thread the cable that hauls the cars through a huge figure eight and back into the system via slack-absorbing tension wheels. You can go through the room where you can see the cables operating underground. There's also a shop where you can buy a variety of cable-car gifts.

✪ California Palace of the Legion of Honor. In Lincoln Park (at 4th Ave. and Clement St.). ☎ **415/750-3600,** or 415/863-3330 for recorded information. Admission (including the Asian Art Museum and M. H. de Young Memorial Museum) $7 adults, $5 seniors 65 and over, $4 youths 12–17, free for children 11 and under (fees may be higher for special exhibitions); free the second Wed of each month. Tues–Sun 9:30am–5pm, first Sat of the month 9:30am–8:45pm. Bus: 38 or 18.

Designed as a memorial to California's World War I casualties, the neoclassical structure is an exact replica of the Legion of Honor Palace in Paris, right down to the inscription honneur et patrie above the portal. Reopened after a two-year, $29-million renovation and seismic upgrading project that was stalled by the discovery of almost 300 turn-of-the-century coffins, the museum's collection contains paintings, sculpture, and decorative arts from Europe, as well as international tapestries, prints, and drawings. The chronological display of more than 800 years of European art includes a fine collection of Rodin sculpture.

The Jewish Museum. 121 Steuart St. (between Mission and Howard sts.). ☎ **415/543-8880.** Admission $5 adult, $2.50 students and seniors; free the first Mon of each month. Mon–Wed noon–6pm, Thurs noon–8pm, Sun 11am–6pm.

This museum hosts a variety of shows that concentrate on immigration, assimilation, and identity of the Jewish community in the United States and around the world. They are illustrated by paintings, sculptures, photographs, and installation art. The museum is moving in 1998 to the nearby Yerba Buena Gardens area.

Mexican Museum. Building D, Fort Mason, Marina Blvd. (at Laguna St.). ☎ **415/441-0404.** Admission $3 adults; $2 children over 10. Free first Wed of the month. Wed–Fri noon–5pm, Sat–Sun 11am–5pm. Bus: 76 to 28.

The gallery, which will be relocating to the Yerba Buena Center area in 1998, maintains a collection of art covering pre-Hispanic, Colonial, folk, Mexican fine art, and Chicano/Mexican-American art. A recent show featured religious works by New Mexican women. *Note:* The museum is scheduled to relocate to the Yerba Buena Center at Third and Mission streets in 1999.

San Francisco Maritime National Historical Park and Museum. At the foot of Polk St. (near Fisherman's Wharf). ☎ **415/556-3002.** Admission to museum free; to ships $2 adults, $1 children 11–17, free for children under 11 and seniors over 62. Museum daily 10am–5pm; ships on Hyde St. Pier May 16–Sept 15 daily 10am–6pm, Sept 16–May 15 daily 9:30am–5pm. Closed Thanksgiving Day, Christmas Day, and New Year's Day. Cable car: Hyde Street line to the last stop. Bus: 19, 30, 32, 42, or 47.

Shaped like an art-deco ship and located near Fisherman's Wharf, the National Maritime Museum is filled with sailing, whaling, and fishing lore. Exhibits include intricate model craft, scrimshaw, and a collection of shipwreck photographs and historic marine scenes, including an 1851 snapshot of hundreds of abandoned ships, deserted en masse by crews dashing off to participate in the Gold Rush. The museum's walls are lined with finely carved, painted wooden figureheads from old windjammers.

Two blocks east, at Aquatic Park's Hyde Street Pier, are several historic ships that are open to the public. The *Balclutha,* one of the last surviving square-riggers, was built in Glasgow, Scotland, in 1886 and was used to carry grain from California around Cape Horn at a near-record speed of 300 miles a day; it rounded the treacherous Cape 17 times in its career. Visitors are invited to spin the wheel, squint at the compass, and imagine they're weathering a mighty storm. Kids can climb into the bunking quarters, visit the "slop chest" (galley to you, matey), and read the sea chanties (clean ones only) that decorate the walls.

The 1890 *Eureka* still carries a cargo of nostalgia for San Franciscans. It was the last of 50 paddle-wheeled ferries that regularly plied the bay; it made its final trip in 1957. Restored to its original splendor, the side-wheeler is loaded with deck cargo, including antique cars and trucks.

At the pier's small-boat shop, visitors can follow the restoration progress of historic boats from the museum's collection. It's behind the maritime bookstore on your right as you approach the ships.

Wells Fargo History Museum. 420 Montgomery St. (at California St.). ☎ **415/396-2619.** Free admission. Mon–Fri 9am–5pm. Closed bank holidays. Muni Metro: Montgomery St. Bus: Any to Market St.

Wells Fargo, one of California's largest banks, was founded on the frontier, and this museum displays hundreds of frontier relics. In the center of the main room stands a Concord stagecoach, which opened the West as surely as the Winchester rifle and the iron horse locomotive. On the mezzanine, you can take an imaginary ride in a replica stagecoach or send a telegraph message in code using a telegraph key and the codebooks, just the way the Wells Fargo agents did more than a century ago.

NEIGHBORHOODS WORTH SEEKING OUT

THE CASTRO   Castro Street around Market and 18th streets is the center of the city's gay community, anchored by the bookstore, A Different Light, and the many stores, restaurants, bars, and other institutions that cater to the community. Among the landmarks are Harvey Milk Plaza, the Quilt Project, and the Castro Theater, a 1920s movie palace. (See "Organized Tours," below, for details on a walking tour of the area.)

What a Long, Strange Trip It's Been

San Francisco's rock bands were a key element of the counterculture scene that blossomed in the city in the mid-1960s; their free-form improvisation was one of the primary expressions of the hippies' "do-your-own-thing" principle. Until 1995, you could still experience something of that scene by attending a concert by the Grateful Dead, the quintessential psychedelic rock band. Amid all the tie-dye shirts and blissful smiles remained a set of musical values that dated back to the days of Ken Kesey and his Merry Pranksters: a no-holds-barred reliance on spontaneous improvisation, even at the expense of clarity.

San Francisco was deeply saddened in August 1995 by the death of the band's leader, Jerry Garcia, one of the city's cultural icons. Jerry played in a number of Bay area bands before founding the Dead in 1965; they were soon headlining in counterculture strongholds like Bill Graham's Fillmore Theater in San Francisco. From June 1966 through the end of 1967, the Dead lived communally at 710 Ashbury St. in the Haight and played numerous free concerts there. As 1967's "Summer of Love" brought the flower children into full bloom, the Dead set the tone for one enormous citywide house party, liberally seasoned with ample doses of marijuana and acid.

The Grateful Dead played together for nearly 30 years. Over that span, they have released numerous LPs; *American Beauty, Workingman's Dead,* and *Europe '72,* all on Warner Brothers, are some of their better records. If you ever caught one of their concerts, you got a small glimpse of Haight-Ashbury in 1967. For now, Haight Street windows are full of memorials to Jerry Garcia, and you'll find Dead memorabilia readily available in small shops throughout the neighborhood if you'd like to take home a reminder of the band that meant so much to San Francisco.

—*Ian Wilker*

CHINATOWN   California Street to Broadway and Kearny to Stockton Street are the boundaries of today's Chinatown. San Francisco is home to the second-largest community of Chinese in the United States (about 33% of the city's population is Chinese), but the majority of them do not live and work in these 24 blocks, although they do return to shop and dine here on weekends.

The gateway at Grant and Bush marks the entry to Chinatown. Walk up Grant, which has become the tourist face of Chinatown, to California Street and Old St. Mary's. The square alongside it contains Bufano's monumental statue of Sun Yat Sen, founder of the Chinese Republic, who had an office in the Montgomery Block and worked toward the overthrow of the emperor from here.

The **Chinese Historical Society of America,** at 650 Commercial St. (☎ 415/ 391-1188), has a small but interesting collection relating to the Chinese in San Francisco, which can be viewed for free any time Monday through Friday from 10am to 2pm.

The heart of Chinatown is at **Portsmouth Square,** where the Chinese practice tai chi in the morning. This square was the center of early San Francisco and the spot where the American flag was first raised on July 9, 1846. From the square, Washington Street leads up to Waverly Place, where you can discover three temples.

A block north of Grant, Stockton Street is the main shopping drag of the community; it's lined with grocers, fishmongers, tea sellers, herbalists, noodle parlors, and restaurants. Here, too, is the **Kon Chow Temple** at no. 855 above the Chinatown Post Office.

Explore at your leisure, or see "Organized Tours," below, if you'd like to join a walking tour.

FISHERMAN'S WHARF & THE NORTHERN WATERFRONT   Few cities in America are as adept at wholesaling their historical sites as San Francisco, which has converted Fisherman's Wharf into one of the most popular tourist destinations in the world. Unless you come really early in the morning, you won't find any traces of the traditional waterfront life that once existed here; the only fishing going on around here is for tourist dollars. A small fleet of fewer than 30 boats still operates from here, but basically Fisherman's Wharf has been converted into one long shopping mall stretching from Ghirardelli Square at the west end to Pier 39 at the east. Some people love it, others can't get far enough away from it, but most agree that Fisherman's Wharf, for better or for worse, has to be seen at least once in a lifetime.

Ghirardelli Square, at 900 North Point, between Polk and Larkin streets (☎ **415/ 775-5500**), is best known as the former chocolate-and-spice factory of Domingo Ghirardelli. The factory has been converted into a 10-level mall containing 50-plus stores and 20 dining establishments. Scheduled street performers play regularly in the West Plaza. The stores generally stay open until 8 or 9pm in the summer and 6 or 7pm in the winter.

The Cannery, at 2801 Leavenworth St. (☎ **415/771-3112,** website: www.thecannery.com) was built in 1894 as a fruit-canning plant and converted in the 1960s into a mall containing 50-plus shops and several restaurants and galleries, including **Jacks Cannery Bar** (☎ **415/931-6400**), which features 110 beers on tap (the most anywhere in the country). Vendors' stalls and sidewalk cafes are set up in the courtyard amid a grove of century-old olive trees, and on summer weekends street performers are out in force entertaining tourists. The **Museum of the City of San Francisco** (☎ **415/928-0289**), which traces the city's development with displays and artifacts, is on the third floor. The museum is free and is open Wednesday to Sunday from 10am to 4pm.

Pier 39, on the waterfront at Embarcadero and Beach Street (☎ **415/981-8030**), is a $4^1/_2$-acre waterfront complex, a few blocks east of Fisherman's Wharf. Ostensibly a re-creation of a turn-of-the-century street scene, it features walkways of aged and weathered wood salvaged from demolished piers. But don't expect a slice of old-time maritime life. This is the busiest mall of the group, with more than 100 stores. In addition, there are 20 or so restaurants and snack outlets, some with good views of the bay. Two marinas accommodating 350 boats flank the pier and house the Blue and Gold bay sightseeing fleet.

In recent years some 600 California **sea lions** have taken up residence on the adjacent floating docks. They sun themselves and honk and bellow playfully. The latest major addition to Fisherman's Wharf is **Underwater World,** a $38-million, 707,000 gallon marine attraction filled with sharks, stingrays, and more, all witnessed via a moving footpath that transports visitors through clear acrylic tunnels.

The shops are open daily from 10:30am to 8:30pm. Cable car: Powell-Mason line to Bay Street.

THE MISSION DISTRICT   Once inhabited almost entirely by Irish immigrants, the Mission District is now the center of the city's Latino community, an oblong area stretching roughly from 14th to 30th streets between Potrero Avenue in the east and Dolores on the west. Many of the city's finest Victorians still stand in the outer areas, though many seem strangely out of place in the mostly lower-income neighborhoods. The heart of the community lies along 24th Street between

Van Ness and Potrero, where dozens of excellent ethnic restaurants, bakeries, bars, and specialty stores attract people from all over the city. Walking through the Mission District at night isn't a good idea, but it's usually quite safe during the day and highly recommended.

For an even better insight into the community, go to the **Precita Eyes Mural Arts Center** at 348 Precita Ave., at Folsom Street (☎ **415/285-2287**) and take one of the hour-long tours conducted on Saturday, which cost $4 for adults, $3 for seniors, and $1 for children under 18. You'll see 85 murals in an 8-block walk. Every year they also hold a Mural Awareness Week (usually the second week in May) when tours are given daily. Other signs of cultural life include a number of progressive theaters— Eureka, Theater Rhinoceros, and Theater Artaud, to name only a few.

At 16th and Dolores is the **Mission San Francisco de Assisi** (better known as Mission Dolores), which is the city's oldest surviving building (see the separate listing above) and the district's namesake.

NOB HILL   When the cable car was invented in 1873, this hill became the city's most exclusive residential area. The Big Four and the Comstock Bonanza kings built their mansions here, but the structures were all destroyed by the 1906 earthquake and fire. Only the Flood Mansion, which serves today as the Pacific Union Club, and the Fairmont (which was under construction when the earthquake struck) were spared. Today the area is home to some of the city's most upscale hotels and also **Grace Cathedral,** which stands on the Crocker Mansion site. Stroll around and enjoy the views, and perhaps pay a visit to Huntington Park.

NORTH BEACH   In the late 1800s, an enormous influx of Italian immigrants into North Beach firmly established this aromatic area as San Francisco's "Little Italy." Today, dozens of Italian restaurants and coffeehouses continue to flourish in what is still the center of the city's Italian community. Walk down Columbus Avenue any given morning and you're bound to be bombarded with the wonderful aromas of roasting coffee and savory pasta sauces. Though there are some interesting shops and bookstores in the area, it's the dozens of eclectic little cafes, delis, bakeries, and coffee shops that give North Beach its Italo-Bohemian character.

For a proper perspective of North Beach, sign up for a guided Javawalk with coffee-nut Elaine Sosa (see "Special-Interest Tours," below).

PARKS, GARDENS & ZOOS

In addition to Golden Gate Park (see "The Top Attractions," above), **Golden Gate National Recreation Area,** and the **Presidio** (below), San Francisco boasts more than 2,000 additional acres of parkland, most of which are perfect for picnicking.

Lincoln Park, at Clement Street and 34th Avenue, a personal favorite of ours, occupies 270 acres on the northwestern side of the city and contains the California Palace of the Legion of Honor (see "Museums," above) and a scenic 18-hole municipal golf course. But the most dramatic feature of the park are the 200-foot cliffs that overlook the Golden Gate Bridge and San Francisco Bay. Take Bus no. 38 from Union Square to 33rd and Geary streets, then transfer to bus no. 18 into the park.

✪ **San Francisco Zoo and Children's Zoo.** Sloat Blvd. and 45th Ave. ☎ **415/753-7080.** Admission to main zoo $7 adults, $3.50 seniors and youths 12–15, $1.50 for children 3–11, and free for children 2 and under if accompanied by an adult; Children's Zoo $1, free for children under 3. Carousel $2. Main zoo daily 10am–5pm; Children's Zoo daily 11am–4pm. Muni Metro: L line from downtown Market Street to the end of the line.

Located between the Pacific Ocean and Lake Merced, in the southwest corner of the city, the San Francisco Zoo is among America's highest-rated animal parks. Most of the 1,000-plus inhabitants are contained in landscaped enclosures guarded by concealed moats. The Primate Discovery Center is particularly noteworthy for its many rare and endangered species. Expansive outdoor atriums, sprawling meadows, and a midnight world for exotic nocturnal primates house such species as the ruffed-tailed lemur, black-and-white colobus monkeys, patas monkeys, and emperor tamarins, pint-size primates distinguished by their long, majestic mustaches.

Other highlights include Koala Crossing, housing kangaroos, emus, and walleroos; Gorilla World, one of the world's largest exhibits of these gentle giants; and Penguin Island, home to a large breeding colony of Magellanic penguins. The Feline Conservation Center is a wooded sanctuary and breeding facility for the zoo's endangered snow leopards, Persian leopards, and other jungle cats. And the Lion House is home to rare Sumatran and Siberian tigers, a rare white Bengal tiger, and the African lions (you can watch them being fed at 2pm Tuesday through Sunday).

At the Children's Zoo, adjacent to the main park, the barnyard is alive with strokable domestic animals such as sheep, goats, ponies, and a llama. Also of interest is the Insect Zoo, which showcases a multitude of insect species, including the hissing cockroach walking sticks.

A free, informal walking tour of the zoo is available on weekends at 11am. The Zebra Zephyr train tour takes visitors on a 30-minute "safari" daily (in winter, only on weekends). The tour is $2.50 for adults, and $1.50 for children 15 and under and seniors.

7 Organized Tours

ORIENTATION TOURS

Gray Line, Transbay Terminal, 1st and Mission streets (☎ **800/826-0202** or 415/558-9400), offers several daily itineraries with free transfers from centrally located hotels to departure points. Reservations are required for most tours.

THE 49-MILE SCENIC DRIVE

The self-guided, 49-mile drive is one easy way to orient yourself and to grasp the beauty of San Francisco and its extraordinary location. Beginning in the city, it follows a rough circle around the bay and passes virtually all the best-known sights from Chinatown to the Golden Gate Bridge, Ocean Beach, Seal Rocks, Golden Gate Park, and Twin Peaks. Originally designed for the benefit of visitors to San Francisco's 1939–40 Golden Gate International Exposition, the route is marked with blue-and-white seagull signs. Although it makes an excellent half-day tour, this mini excursion can easily take longer if you decide, for example, to stop to walk across the Golden Gate Bridge or to have tea in Golden Gate Park's Japanese Tea Garden.

The San Francisco Visitor Information Center, at Powell and Market streets, distributes free route maps. Since a few of the Scenic Drive marker signs are missing, the map will come in handy. Try to avoid the downtown area during the weekday rush hours from 7 to 9am and 4 to 6pm.

BOAT TOURS

One of the best ways to look at San Francisco is from a boat bobbing on the bay. **Blue & Gold Fleet,** at Pier 39, Fisherman's Wharf (☎ **415/773-1188**), tours the bay year-round in a sleek, 400-passenger sightseeing boat, complete with food and beverage facilities. The fully narrated, $1^1/_4$-hour cruise passes beneath the Golden Gate and Bay bridges, and comes within yards of Alcatraz Island. Frequent daily departures from Pier 39's West Marina begin at 10am during summer and 11am in winter. Tickets cost $16 for adults, $12 for kids 5 to 17 and seniors over 62; children under 5 sail free.

SPECIAL-INTEREST TOURS

A MOVING PARTY   Three Babes and a Bus (☎ 415/552-2582) is perhaps the world's hippest scheduled tour operator. This unique company runs regular night-club trips for out-of-towners and locals who want to experience the city's night scene. The Babes' ever-changing 4-hour itinerary waltzes into four different clubs per night, cutting in front of every line with priority entry. The party continues en route, when the Babes entertain. Their bus departs every Saturday night (and some Friday nights) at 9pm from a designated pick-up spot in Union Square; phone for complete information and reservations. The tour costs $30, including cover charges.

EXPLORING THE CASTRO   Cruisin' the Castro (☎ 415/550-8110) will give you a totally new insight into the gay community's contribution to the political maturity, growth, and beauty of San Francisco. Tours are personally led by Ms. Trevor Hailey, who was involved in the development of the Castro in the 1970s and knew Harvey Milk—the first openly gay politician elected to office in the United States. Tours are offered Tuesday through Saturday, from 10am to 1:45pm, and begin at Harvey Milk Plaza, atop the Castro Street Muni station. The cost includes lunch at the Lutie Pietia. Reservations are required. Prices are $30 for adults and $25 for seniors 62 and older and children 16 and under.

A HIPPIE TOUR   The Grateful Dead's crash pad, Janis Joplin's house, and other monuments to the Summer of Love—the **Haight-Ashbury Flower Power Walking Tour** will take you to the city's hippie haunts. Tours begin at 9:30am Tuesday and Saturday and cost $15 per person. For reservations, call ☎ **415/863-1621.**

NORTH BEACH CAFE SOIREE   Javawalk is a 2-hour walking tour by self-described "coffeehouse lizard" Elaine Sosa. Aside from visiting cafes, Javawalk also serves up a good share of historical and architectural trivia. Sosa keeps the tour interactive and fun, and it's obvious that she knows a dearth of tales and trivia about the history of coffee and it's North Beach roots. Tours are Tuesday to Saturday at 10am. The price is $20 for adults and $10 for kids 12 and under. For information and reservations call ☎ **415/673-9255.**

AN INSIDER'S TOUR OF CHINATOWN   Founded by author, TV personality, cooking instructor, and restaurant critic Shirley Fong-Torres, **Wok Wiz China-town Walking Tours** (☎ **800/281-9255** or 415/981-8989) takes you into nooks and crannies not usually seen by tourists. Each of her guides is intimately acquainted with all of Chinatown's backways, alleys, and small businesses. You'll learn about dim sum (a "delight of the heart") and the Chinese tea ceremony; meet a Chinese herbalist; stop at a pastry shop to observe rice noodles being made; watch artist Y. K. Lau do his delicate brush painting; learn about jook, a traditional Chinese breakfast; stop in at a fortune-cookie factory; and visit a Chinese produce market and learn to identify the vegetables used in Chinese cuisine. Tours are conducted daily from 10am to 1:30pm and include a Chinese lunch. The tour begins in the lobby of the Chinatown Holiday Inn at 750 Kearny St. (between Washington and Clay streets). Groups are generally limited to 12, and reservations are essential. Prices (including lunch) are $37 adults, $35 seniors 60 and older, and $28 children under 12.

Shirley Fong-Torres also operates an I Can't Believe I Ate My Way Through Chinatown gastronomical tour that starts with a Chinese breakfast in a noodle house, moves to a wok shop, and then makes further stops at a vegetarian restaurant, a rice-noodle factory, and a supermarket before taking a break for a dim sum luncheon (most Saturdays; $65 per person including breakfast and lunch). There is also a Walk & Wok tour which includes shopping for food in Chinatown, then cooking (and eating) it together at Shirley's Cooking Center (most Saturdays; $75 per person).

8   Golden Gate National Recreation Area & the Presidio

GOLDEN GATE NATIONAL RECREATION AREA

No urban shoreline is as stunning as San Francisco's. Golden Gate National Recreation Area, wrapping around the northern and western edge of the city and run by the National Park Service, lets visitors fully enjoy it. Along this shoreline are several landmarks. From its edge visitors have views of the Bay and the ocean. Muni provides transportation to most sites, including Aquatic Park, the Cliff House, and Ocean Beach. For more information, contact the **National Park Service** at ☎ **415/556-0560.** For additional information, see "Outdoor Activities" below.

Here is a brief rundown of the major features of the recreation area, starting at the northern section and moving westward around the coastline:

Aquatic Park, adjacent to the Hyde Street Pier, is a small swimming beach, although it's not that appealing and the water's ridiculously cold.

Fort Mason Center occupies an area from Bay Street to the shoreline and consists of several buildings and piers, which were used during World War II. Today they are occupied by a variety of museums, theaters, and cultural, educational, and community organizations, as well as by Greens vegetarian restaurant, which affords views of the Golden Gate Bridge. For information about Fort Mason events, call ☎ **415/441-5705.** Park headquarters is also at Fort Mason.

Farther west along the Bay, **Marina Green,** at the northern end of Fillmore, is a favorite spot for kite flying or watching the sailboats on the Bay and the birds gliding above. Next stop along the Bay is the St. Francis Yacht Club. From here begins the 3¹/₂-mile paved **Golden Gate Promenade,** a favorite biking and hiking path, which sweeps along Crissy Field, leading ultimately to Fort Point under the Golden Gate Bridge. This Promenade defines the outer limits of the **Presidio** (see below).

Fort Point (☎ **415/556-1373**), a National Historic Site sitting directly under the Golden Gate Bridge, was built in 1853 to protect the narrow entrance to the harbor. You might recognize it from Alfred Hitchcock's Vertigo; the master of suspense filmed some of the most important scenes here. During the Civil War, the brick Fort Point was manned by 140 men and 90 pieces of artillery to prevent a Confederate takeover of California. Rangers in Civil War regalia lead regular tours and sometimes fire the old cannons. Call ☎ **415/556-1693** for schedules and information.

Lincoln Boulevard sweeps around the western edge of the Bay to two of the most popular beaches in San Francisco. **Baker Beach,** a small and beautiful strand just outside the Golden Gate where the waves roll ashore, is a fine spot for sunbathing, walking, or fishing—it's packed on sunny days. Because of the cold water and the roaring currents that pour out of the bay twice a day, swimming is not advised here for any but the most confident. (You'll also see some nude sunbathers here.)

Here you can pick up the **Coastal Trail,** which leads through the Presidio (see below). A short distance from Baker, **China Beach** is a small cove where swimming is permitted. Changing rooms, showers, sundeck, and rest rooms are available.

Golden Gate National Recreation Area & the Presidio

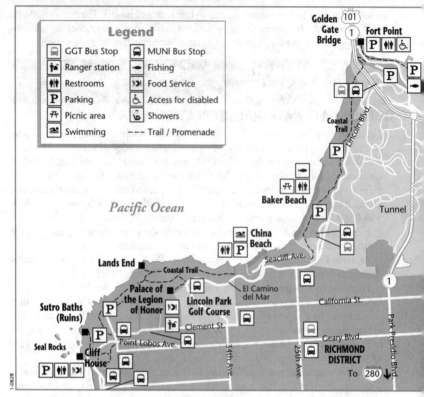

A little farther round the coast appears **Lands End,** looking out to **Pyramid Rock.** Both a lower and an upper trail provide hiking opportunities amid windswept cypress and pine on the cliffs above the Pacific.

Still farther along the coast lies **Point Lobos,** the **Sutro Baths,** and the **Cliff House.** This last has been serving refreshments to visitors since 1863. Here you can view the Seal Rocks, home to a colony of sea lions and many marine birds. There's an information center here (open daily 10am to 5pm; ☎ 415/556-8642) and the kids will enjoy the Musèe Mecanique, an authentic old-fashioned arcade with 150 coin-operated amusements. Only traces of the Sutro Baths remain today northeast of the Cliff House. This swimming facility was a major summer attraction that could accommodate 24,000 people, but it burned down in 1966. A little farther inland at the western end of California Street is Lincoln Park, which contains a golf course and the Palace of the Legion of Honor.

From the Cliff House, the Esplanade continues south along the 4-mile-long **Ocean Beach,** which is not suitable for swimming. At the southern end of Ocean Beach is another area of the park around **Fort Funston** where there's an easy loop trail across the cliffs (for information call the ranger station at ☎ 415/239-2366). Here, too, you can watch the hang gliders taking advantage of the high cliffs and strong winds.

Farther south along Route 280, **Sweeney Ridge,** which can only be reached by car, affords sweeping views of the coastline from the many trails that crisscross these 1,000 acres of land. It was from here that the expedition led by Don Gaspar de Portola first saw San Francisco Bay in 1769. It's in Pacifica and can be reached via Sneath Lane off Route 35 (Skyline Boulevard) in San Bruno.

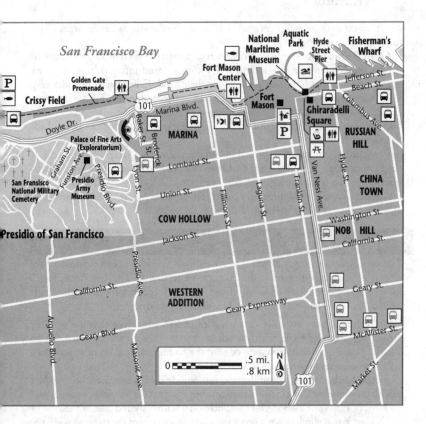

THE PRESIDIO

In 1989 the Department of Defense announced what many had long thought impossible: The U.S. Army, which had held the Presidio as a military base since before the Civil War, was pulling out and leaving the most prized piece of real estate in San Francisco to the National Park Service as an example of post–Cold War retrofitting. Now an urban national park, it combines historical, architectural, and natural aspects.

The 1,480-acre area incorporates a variety of terrain—coastal scrub, dunes, and prairie grasslands that shelter many rare plants and more than 150 species of birds, some of which nest here. There are also more than 350 historic buildings to see, a scenic golf course to play, a national cemetery to visit, and a variety of terrains and natural habitats to explore. The Park Service offers a number of walking and biking tours around the Presidio; reservations are required.

Walkers and joggers will enjoy the forests of the Presidio. It was once a bleak field of wind-blasted rock, sand, and grass, but in a strangely humanitarian gesture, 60,000 trees were planted in the 1880s to make the place more livable for the troops. Today, on the two-mile **Ecology Loop Trail,** walkers can see more than 30 different species of those trees, including redwood, spruce, cypress, and acacias. Hikers can follow the 2½-mile **Coastal Trail** from Fort Point along this part of the coastline all the way to Land's End. It follows the bluff top from Baker Beach to the southern base of the Golden Gate Bridge.

Anyone interested in the military history of the Presidio must stop at the **Presidio Army Museum,** loaded with military arcana from 200 years of base history. The museum, at the corner of Lincoln Boulevard and Funston Avenue, tells its story in dioramas, exhibitions, and photographs. It's open Wednesday to Sunday from 10am to 4pm.

Crissy Field is a former airfield that in recent years has become known as one of the see-and-be-seen proving grounds of California's windsurfing culture. Between March and October hundreds come to try their hand. Crissy beach provides easy water access and plenty of room to rig up; it's not recommended for the inexperienced. This is also a popular place for joggers en route from the Marina District to Fort Point and back. At the west end of Crissy Field is a pier that can be used for fishing and crabbing.

For schedules, maps, and general information about ongoing developments at the Presidio, the best source is the **Golden Gate National Recreation Area Headquarters** at Fort Mason, Bldg. 102, San Francisco, CA 94123 (☎ **415/556-2236**). It's on the west side of Montgomery Street, on the main parade ground (open daily 10am to 5pm; ☎ 415/556-4323). Bus: 82X, 28, or 76.

9 Staying Active

The prime places to enjoy all kinds of recreational activities in San Francisco have already been described earlier in this chapter. See section 5, "The Top Attractions," for a complete description of Golden Gate Park; and section 8 for complete details on Golden Gate National Recreation Area and the Presidio.

BEACHES   There are only two beaches in San Francisco that are safe for swimming: **Aquatic Park,** which is adjacent to the Hyde Park Pier, and **China Beach,** a small cove on the western edge of the South Bay. But dip in at your own risk—there are no lifeguards on duty.

Baker Beach, a small, beautiful strand just outside the Golden Gate, isn't the best place for swimming due to strong currents, but it's great for sunning, walking, picnicking, or fishing. It's wonderful to sit here on a sunny day and take in the view of the bridge. You'll climb down a very long flight of stairs from the street to reach the beach.

Ocean Beach, at the end of Golden Gate Park, on the westernmost side of the city, is San Francisco's largest beach (4 miles long). Just offshore, at the northern end of the beach in front of the Cliff House, are the jagged Seal Rocks, which are inhabited by various shore birds and a large colony of barking sea lions. Bring binoculars for a close-up view. Ocean Beach is for strolling or sunning, but don't swim here—tides are tricky, and each year bathers and surfers drown in the rough waters.

BICYCLING   Two city-designated bike routes are maintained by the Recreation and Parks Department. One winds for 7½ miles through Golden Gate Park to Lake Merced; the other traverses the city, starting in the south, and follows a route over the Golden Gate Bridge. A bike map is available from the San Francisco Visitor Information Center and from bicycle shops all around town.

A massive new seawall, constructed to buffer Ocean Beach from storm-driven waves, doubles as a public walk and bikeway along 5 waterfront blocks of the Great Highway between Noriega and Santiago streets. It's an easy ride from the Cliff House or Golden Gate Park.

Park Cyclery, 1749 Waller St. (☎ **415/752-8383**), is one of two shops in the Haight Street/Stanyan Street area that rent bikes. Next to Golden Gate Park, the cyclery rents mountain bikes exclusively, along with helmets, locks, and accessories. The charge is $5 per hour or $25 per day.

There's also great biking in the Presidio. From there you can venture across the Golden Gate Bridge and into the Marin hills.

CITY STAIR-CLIMBING   You don't need a Stairmaster in San Francisco. The **Filbert Street Steps,** 377 of them running between Sansome Street and Telegraph Hill, scale the eastern face of Telegraph Hill, from Sansome and Filbert past charming 19th-century cottages and lush gardens. Napier Lane, a narrow wooden plank walkway, leads to Montgomery Street. Turn right and follow the path to the end of the cul-de-sac, where another stairway continues to Telegraph's panoramic summit.

The **Lyon Street Steps,** between Green Street and Broadway, comprise another historic stairway street, containing four steep sets of stairs totaling 288 steps. Begin at Green Street and climb all the way up, past manicured hedges and flower gardens, to an iron gate that opens into the Presidio. A block east, on Baker Street, another set of 369 steps descends to Green Street.

GOLF   **Golden Gate Park Course,** 47th Avenue and Fulton Street (☎ **415/ 751-8987**), is a nine-hole course over 1,357 yards and is par 27. All holes are par 3, tightly set, and well trapped with small greens. Greens fees are very reasonable: $10 per person on Monday through Friday and $13 on Saturday and Sunday. The course is open daily from 9am to dusk.

Lincoln Park Golf Course, 34th Avenue and Clement Street (☎ **415/ 221-9911**), San Francisco's prettiest municipal course, has terrific views and fairways lined with Monterey cypress trees. Its 18 holes encompass 5,081 yards, for a par 68. Greens fees are $23 per person on Monday through Friday and $27 on Saturday and Sunday. The course is open daily from 6:30am to dusk.

SKATING   Although people skate in Golden Gate Park all week long, Sunday is best, when John F. Kennedy Drive, between Kezar Drive and Transverse Road, is closed to automobiles. A smooth "skate pad" is located on your right, just past the Conservatory. **Skates on Haight,** 1818 Haight St. (☎ **415/752-8376**), is the best place to rent either in-line or conventional skates and is located only one block from the park. Protective wrist guards and knee pads are included free. The cost is $6 per hour for in-line Rollerblades and $5 per hour for "conventionals." A major credit card and ID deposit are required.

10 Shopping

Store hours are generally Monday through Saturday from 10am to 6pm and on Sunday from noon to 5pm. Most department stores stay open later, as do shops around Fisherman's Wharf.

Sales tax in San Francisco is 8$^1/_2$%, which is added on at the register for all goods and services purchased. If you live out of state and buy an expensive item, you may want to consider having the store ship it home for you. You'll escape paying the sales tax, but will have to pay for its transport.

MAJOR SHOPPING AREAS

UNION SQUARE & ENVIRONS   San Francisco's most congested and popular shopping mecca is centered around Union Square and enclosed by Bush, Taylor, Market, and Montgomery streets. Most of the big department stores and many high-end specialty shops are in this area. Be sure to venture to Grant Avenue, Post and Sutter streets, and Maiden Lane.

CHINATOWN   When you pass under the gate to Chinatown on Grant Avenue, say good-bye to the world of fashion and hello to a swarm of cheap tourist shops selling everything from linen and jade to plastic toys and $2 slippers. The real gems are tucked on side streets or are small, one-person shops selling Chinese herbs, original art, and jewelry. Grant Avenue is the area's main thoroughfare, and side streets between Bush Street and Columbus Avenue are full of restaurants, markets, and eclectic shops. Walking is best, since traffic through this area is slow at best and parking next to impossible. Most of the stores in Chinatown are open daily from 10am to 10pm. Serviced by bus lines 9X, 15, 30, 41, and 45.

SOMA Though this area isn't suitable for strolling, you'll find almost all the discount shopping in warehouse spaces south of Market. You can pick up a discount shopping guide at most major hotels. Many bus lines pass through this area.

UNION STREET Union Street, from Fillmore to Van Ness, caters to the upper-middle-class crowd. It's a great place to stroll; window shop the plethora of boutiques, cafes, and restaurants; and watch the beautiful people parade by. Serviced by bus lines 22, 41, 42, and 45.

CHESTNUT STREET Parallel to and a few blocks north of Union Street, Chestnut is a younger Union Street, with endless shopping and dining choices, and the ever-tanned, superfit population of postgraduate singles who hang around cafes and scope each other out. Serviced by bus lines 22, 28, 30, 41, 42, 43, and 76.

FISHERMAN'S WHARF & ENVIRONS The tourist-oriented malls—Ghiradelli Square, Pier 39, the Cannery, and the Anchorage—run along Jefferson Street and include hundreds of shops, restaurants, and attractions.

FILLMORE STREET Some of the best shopping in town is packed into 5 blocks of Fillmore Street in Pacific Heights. From Jackson to Sutter streets, Fillmore is the perfect place to grab a bite and peruse the high-priced boutiques, craft shops, and incredible houseware stores. Don't miss Zinc Details and Fillamento. Serviced by bus lines 1, 2, 3, 4, 12, 22, and 24.

HAIGHT STREET Green hair, spiked hair, no hair, or mohair—even the hippies look conservative next to Haight Street's dramatic fashion freaks. The shopping in the 6 blocks of upper Haight Street, between Central Avenue and Stanyan Street, reflects its clientele and offers everything from incense and European and American street styles to furniture and antique clothing. Bus lines 7, 66, 71, and 73 run down Haight Street. The Muni Metro N line stops at Waller Street and at Cole Street.

SHOPPING A TO Z
ART

The *San Francisco Gallery Guide,* a comprehensive, bimonthly publication listing the city's current shows, is available free by mail. Send a self-addressed stamped envelope to **San Francisco Bay Area Gallery Guide,** 1369 Fulton St., San Francisco, CA 94117 (☎ **415/921-1600**), or pick one up at the **San Francisco Visitor Information Center** at 900 Market St. (at Powell Street). Most of the city's major art galleries are clustered downtown in the Union Square area.

✪ **Catherine Clark Gallery.** 49 Geary St., 2nd Floor (between Kearny and Grant sts.). ☎ **415/399-1439**.

Catherine Clark's is a different kind of gallery experience. While many galleries focus on already-established artists and out-of-this world price points, Catherine's exhibits up-and-coming contemporary artists (who are mainly from California) and nurtures beginning collectors by offering an unusual purchasing plan. Almost unheard of in the art business, you can buy a piece here on layaway and take up to a year to pay for it—interest free! Prices here make art a realistic purchase for everyone for a change, but serious collectors still frequent her shows because she has such a keen eye for talent. Shows change frequently. No credit cards are accepted.

BOOKS

Charlotte's Web. 2278 Union St. (between Steiner and Fillmore sts.). ☎ **415/441-4700.**

A first-rate children's bookstore, Charlotte's Web is notable for its particularly knowledgeable owner, who sells everything from cloth books for babies to histories and poetry for young adults.

City Lights Booksellers & Publishers. 261 Columbus Ave. (at Broadway). ☎ **415/362-8193.**

Brooding literary types browse this famous bookstore owned by Lawrence Ferlinghetti, the renowned beat generation poet. The three-level bookshop prides itself on a comprehensive collection of art, poetry, and political paperbacks, as well as more mainstream books.

A Clean, Well-Lighted Place for Books. 601 Van Ness Ave. (between Turk St. and Golden Gate Ave.). ☎ **415/441-6670.**

Voted best bookstore by the *San Francisco Bay Guardian,* this independent has good new fiction and nonfiction sections and also specializes in music, art, mystery, and cookbooks. The store is very well known for its schedule of author readings and events. For a calendar of events, call the store or check their website at **www. bookstore.com.**

Eastwind Books & Arts. 1435A Stockton St. (at Columbus Ave.). ☎ **415/772-5877** Chinese department, ☎ 415/772-5899 English department.

The emphasis here is the incredible collection of Chinese books, stationery, and stamps, as well as Asian-American and English books covering health, history, cooking, martial arts, medicine, art, and culture. If you can't make it by, but would like to get a catalog, e-mail them at **info@eastwindsf.com.**

Green Apple Books. 506 Clement St. (at 6th Ave.). ☎ **415/387-2272.**

The local favorite for used books, Green Apple is crammed with titles—more than 60,000 new and 100,000 used books. Their extended sections in psychology, cooking, art, history, collection of modern first editions, and rare graphic comics is only superseded by the staff's superlative service.

Markus Books. 1712 Fillmore St. (at Post St.). ☎ **415/346-4222.**

Markus has the Bay Area's best selection of books relating to African-American and African culture. In addition to a good collection of children's books, you'll find strong sections for fiction, history, politics, art, and biography.

McDonald's Bookshop. 48 Turk St. (at Market St.). ☎ **415/673-2235.**

San Francisco's biggest used-book shop claims to stock more than a million volumes, including out-of-print, esoteric, and hard-to-find books in all categories and languages. As a birthday novelty, they'll find a copy of *Life* magazine from the month and year in which you were born.

CHINA, SILVER & GLASS

Gump's. 135 Post St. (between Kearny St. and Grant Ave.). ☎ **415/982-1616.**

Founded almost a century ago, Gump's offers gifts and treasures ranging from Asian antiquities to contemporary art, glass, and exquisite jade and pearl jewelry. Many items are made specifically for the store. Gump's also has one of the most revered window displays each holiday season.

DISCOUNT SHOPPING

Esprit Outlet Store. 499 Illinois St. (at 16th St.). ☎ **415/957-2550.**

All the Esprit collections and Susie Tompkins merchandise are available here at 30% or more off regular prices. In addition to clothes, the store sells accessories, shoes, and assorted other items.

New West. 426 Brannan St. (between Third and Fourth sts.). ☎ **415/882-4929.**

This SoMa boutique offers top designer fashions from shoes to suits at rock-bottom prices. There are no cheap knockoffs here, just good men's and women's clothes and accessories. New West also has its own stylish clothing line.

The North Face. 1325 Howard St. (between Ninth and Tenth sts.). ☎ **415/626-6444.**

Well known for its sporting, camping, and hiking equipment, this off-price outlet carries a limited but high-quality selection of skiwear, boots, sweaters, and goods such as tents, packs, and sleeping bags. The North Face makes heavy use of Gore-Tex, down, and other durable, lightweight materials.

FASHION

One by Two. 418 Hayes St. (at Gough St.). ☎ **415/252-1460.**

If you're interested in the latest chic and wild trendy wear, browse local designer Al Abayan's boutique featuring urban sportswear with a modern twist. His style is young, clean, and colorful in thick, expensive fabrics, with lots of unisex items. "In" wear doesn't always come cheaply here, but you can bet you won't see everyone wearing your outfit in your hometown.

Three Bags Full. 2181 Union St. (at Fillmore). ☎ **415/567-5753.**

Snuggling up in a cozy sweater can be a fashionable event if you do your shopping at this pricey boutique, which carries the gamut in handmade and one-of-a-kind playful and extravagant knitwear.

Men's Fashions

Cable Car Clothiers. 246 Sutter St. (between Grant Ave. and Kearny St.). ☎ **415/397-4740.**

Dapper men head to this beautiful landmark building for traditional attire, such as three-button suits with natural shoulders, Aquascutum coats, McGeorge sweaters, and Countess Mara neckwear.

MAC. 5 Claude Lane (off Sutter St. between Grant Ave. and Kearny St.). ☎ **415/837-0615.**

The more classic than corporate man shops here for imported tailored suits in new and intriguing fabrics. Lines include London's Katherine Hamnette, Belgium's SO, Italy's Alberto Biani, New York's John Bartlett, and San Francisco's Lat Naylor. Their women's store is located at 1543 Grant Ave. (between Filbert and Union streets.; ☎ 415/837-1604).

Women's Fashions

Métier. 50 Maiden Lane (at Grant Ave. and Kearny St.). ☎ **415/989-5395.**

The classic, sophisticated, and expensive creations for women found here include European ready-to-wear lines and designers Peter Cohen, Harriet Selwyn, Alberto Biani, Victor Victoria, and local Lat Naylor, as well as a distinguished collection of antique-style, high-end jewelry.

Solo Fashion. 1599 Haight St. (at Clayton St.). ☎ **415/621-0342.**

While strolling upper Haight, stop in here for a good selection of upbeat, contemporary, English-style street wear, along with a collection of dresses designed exclusively for this shop.

In case you want to see the world.

At American Express, we're here to make your journey a smooth one. So we have over 1,700 travel service locations in over 120 countries ready to help. What else would you expect from the world's largest travel agency?

do more®

Travel

In case you want to be welcomed there.

We're here to see that you're always welcomed at establishments everywhere. That's why millions of people carry the American Express® Card—for peace of mind, confidence, and security, around the world or just around the corner.

do more®

AMERICAN EXPRESS

Cards

And just in case.

We're here with American Express® Travelers Cheques and Cheques *for Two*.® They're the safest way to carry money on your vacation and the surest way to get a refund, practically anywhere, anytime.

Another way we help you…

do more

Travelers Cheques

Vintage Clothing

Aardvark's. 1501 Haight St. (at Ashbury St.). ☎ **415/621-3141.**

One of San Francisco's largest secondhand clothing dealers, Aardvark's has seemingly endless racks of shirts, pants, dresses, skirts, and hats from the last 30 years.

Buffalo Exchange. 1555 Haight St. (between Clayton and Ashbury sts.). ☎ **415/431-7733.**

This large storefront on upper Haight Street is crammed with racks of antique and new fashions from the 1960s, 1970s, and 1990s. It stocks everything from suits and dresses to neckties, hats, handbags, and jewelry. Buffalo Exchange anticipates some of the hottest new street fashions. A second shop is located at 1800 Polk St. (at Washington Street) (☎ 415/346-5741).

La Rosa. 1711 Haight St. (at Cole St.). ☎ **415/668-3744.**

On a street packed with vintage clothing shops, this is one of the more upscale options, featuring a selection of high-quality, dry-cleaned, secondhand goods. Formal suits and dresses are its specialty, but you'll also find sport coats, slacks, and shoes. You may also want to visit its more moderately priced sister store, **Held Over,** on Haight near Ashbury.

FOOD

Farmers Market. Embarcadero, in front of the Ferry Building. ☎ **510/528-6987.**

Every Saturday from 8:30am to 1:30pm Northern California fruit, vegetable, bread, and dairy vendors join local restaurateurs in selling fresh, delicious edibles. There's no better way to enjoy a bright San Francisco morning than strolling this gourmet street market and snacking your way through breakfast. You can also pick up locally made vinegars and oils—they make wonderful gifts. From May to November the market also happens on Tuesdays.

Joseph Schmidt Confections. 3489 16th St. (at Sanchez St.). ☎ **415/861-8682.**

Chocolate takes the shape of exquisite sculptural masterpieces that are so beautiful, you'll be hesitant to bite the head off your adorable chocolate panda bear. But once you do, you'll know why this is the most popular chocolatier in town. Prices are also remarkably reasonable.

GIFTS

✪ **Dandelion.** 55 Potrero Ave. (at Alameda St.). ☎ **415/436-9500.**

There's something for every taste and budget among this wonderful collection of gifts, collectibles, and furnishings, ranging from an excellent collection of tea pots, decorative dishes, and gourmet foods, to silver, books, cards, and picture frames. Don't miss the zenlike second floor, with its variety of peaceful furnishings in Indian, Japanese, and western styles.

SFMOMA MuseumStore. 151 Third St. (2 blocks south of Market St., across from Yerba Buena Gardens). ☎ **415/357-4000.**

With an array of artistic cards, books, jewelry, housewares, knickknacks, and creative tokens of San Francisco, it's virtually impossible not to find *something* you'll consider a must-have. Aside from being one of locals' favorite shops, it also offers far more tasteful mementos than most Fisherman's Wharf options.

Quantity Postcards. 1441 Grant St. (at Green St.). ☎ **415/986-8866.**

You'll find the perfect postcard for literally everyone you know here, as well as some depictions of old San Francisco, movie stars, and Day-Glo posters featuring concert-poster artist Frank Kozik. Even if you don't need any cards, you'll enjoy browsing the eclectic collection of mailables.

HOUSEWARES

Biordi Art Imports. 412 Columbus Ave. (at Vallejo St.). ☎ **415/392-8096.**

Whether it's your intention to decorate your dinner table, color up your kitchen, or liven the living room, Biordi's Italian Majolica pottery is the most exquisite and unique way to do it. Every piece is a show-stopper. Call for a catalog if you like. They'll ship anywhere.

Fillamento. 2185 Fillmore St. (at Sacramento St.). ☎ **415/931-2224.**

The best housewares store in the city is always packed with shoppers searching for the most classic, artistic, and refined housewares. Whether you're looking to set a good table or revamp your bedroom, you'll find it all here.

○ **Zinc Details.** 1905 Fillmore St. (between Bush and Pine sts.). ☎ **415/776-2100.**

One of our favorite stores in the city, Zinc Details has received accolades from everyone from *Elle Decor Japan* to *Metropolitan Home* for its amazing collection of locally handcrafted glass vases, pendant lights, ceramics, and furniture. Each piece is a true work of art created specifically for the store (except vintage items) and these pieces are in such high demand that the store's wholesale accounts include Barney's New York and The Guggenheim Museum Store.

RECORDS & CDs

Groove Merchant Records. 687 Haight St. (at Pierce and Steiner sts.). ☎ **415/252-5766.**

Collectors of rare vinyl jazz, soul, funk, and Latin must check out Groove Merchant, whose own record label was in the forefront of the Bay Area acid jazz movement and continues to reissue old and rare groove and contemporary artists.

Recycled Records. 1377 Haight St. (between Central and Masonic sts.). ☎ **415/626-4075.**

Easily one of the best used-record stores in the city, this loud shop in the Haight has a good selection of promotional CDs and cases of used "classic" rock LPs. Sheet music, tour programs, and old *TV Guides* are also sold.

Streetlight Records. 3979 24th St. (between Noe and Sanchez sts.). ☎ **415/282-3550.**

Overstuffed with used music in all three formats, this place is best known for its records and excellent CD collection. Rock music is cheap here, and a money-back guarantee guards against defects. Their second location is at 2350 Market St. (between Castro and Noe sts.) (☎ **415/282-8000**).

Virgin Megastore. Market St. at Stockton. ☎ **415/397-4525**.

With thousands of CDs, including an impressive collection of imports, videos, laser discs, a multimedia department, a cafe, and related books, any music lover could blow his entire vacation fund in this enormous Union Square store.

11 San Francisco After Dark

For up-to-date nightlife information, turn to the *San Francisco Weekly* and the *San Francisco Bay Guardian,* both of which contain comprehensive current listings. They're available free at bars and restaurants, and from street-corner boxes all around the city. *Where,* a free tourist monthly, also has information on programs and performance times; it's available in most of the city's finer hotels. The Sunday edition of the *San Francisco Examiner and Chronicle* also features a "Datebook" section, printed on pink paper, with information and listings on the week's upcoming events. For a more complete selection of after-dark options, see *Frommer's San Francisco.*

GETTING TICKETS   **Tix Bay Area** (☎ 415/433-7827) sells advance full-price tickets for most performance halls, sporting events, concerts, and clubs. They also sell half-price tickets to theater, dance, and music performances on the day of show only; tickets for Sunday and Monday events, if available, are sold on Saturday. A service charge, ranging from $1 to $3, is levied on each ticket. Only cash or traveler's checks are accepted for half-price tickets; Visa and MasterCard are accepted for full-price tickets. Tix is located on Stockton Street, between Post and Geary streets on the east side of Union Square (opposite Maiden Lane). It's open Tuesday to Thursday from 11am to 6pm and Friday and Saturday from 11am to 7pm.

Tickets to most theater and dance events are also available through **City Box Office,** 153 Kearny St., Suite 402 (☎ **415/392-4400**).

BASS Ticketmaster (☎ **510/762-2277**) sells computer-generated tickets to concerts, sporting events, plays, and special events. Downtown BASS Ticketmaster ticketing offices include Tix Bay Area and **Warehouse** stores throughout the city; the most convenient location is at 30 Powell St.

THE PERFORMING ARTS

San Francisco Performances, 500 Sutter St., Suite 710 (☎ **415/398-6449**), has been bringing acclaimed artists to the Bay Area for more than 15 years. Shows run the gamut from classical chamber music to dance and jazz. Performances are in several venues, including the city's Performing Arts Center, Herbst Theater, and the Center for the Performing Arts at Yerba Buena Center. The season lasts from late September through May. Tickets cost $12 to $55 and are available through City Box Office (☎ **415/392-4400**). There's also a 6pm Thursday after-work concert series at the **EC Cabaret,** 3 Embarcadero Center, in fall and winter, $6 admission at the door (☎ **415/398-6449** for information).

American Conservatory Theater (A.C.T.). At the Geary Theater, 415 Geary St. (at Mason St.). ☎ **415/749-2228.** Tickets $14–$47.50.

A.C.T. made its debut in 1967 and quickly established itself as the city's premier resident theater group. The troupe is so venerated that it has been compared to the superb British National Theatre, the Berliner Ensemble, and the Comédie Française. A.C.T. recently returned to its home, the fabulous Geary Theater (1910), a national historic landmark, after the theater sustained severe damage in the 1989 earthquake. Now it's fully refurbished and modernized to such an extent that it's regarded as one of America's finest performance spaces. The season runs from October through June and features both classical and experimental works.

The Magic Theatre. At Bldg. D, Fort Mason Center, Marina Blvd. (at Buchanan St.). ☎ **415/ 441-8822.** Tickets $18–$23. Discounts for students and seniors.

Over the years the highly acclaimed Magic Theatre has nurtured such talents as Sam Shepard and Jon Robin Baitz (Shepard's Pulitzer prize–winning play *Buried Child* premiered here), and it's still dedicated to presenting the works of new playwrights. More recent productions have included works by Athol Fugard, Claire Chafee, and Nilo Cruz. The season usually runs from September through July; performances are offered Wednesday to Sunday.

San Francisco Ballet. At War Memorial Opera House, 301 Van Ness Ave. (at Grove St.), ☎ **415/865-2000** or 415/703-9400 for tickets and information. Tickets $18–$85.

Founded in 1933, the San Francisco Ballet is the oldest professional ballet company in the U.S. and regarded as one of the country's finest, performing an eclectic repertoire of full-length, neoclassical, and contemporary ballets. Even *The New York Times* proclaimed, "The San Francisco Ballet under Helgi Tomasson's leadership is one of the spectacular success stories of the arts in America." The 1998 Repertory Season runs from February through June. All performances are accompanied by the San Francisco Ballet Orchestra.

San Francisco Opera. At the War Memorial Opera House, 301 Van Ness Ave. (at Grove St.), ☎ **415/864-3330.** Tickets $10–$140.

This was the United States's first municipal opera and is one of the city's cultural icons. Brilliantly balanced casts may feature celebrated stars like Frederica VonStade and Placido Domingo, along with promising newcomers and the regular members, in productions that range from traditional to avant-garde. All productions have English supertitles. The opera season starts in September and lasts just 14 weeks. Performances are held most evenings, except Monday, with matinees on Sundays. Tickets go on sale as early as June, and the best seats quickly sell out. Unless Pavarotti or Domingo is in town, some less-coveted seats are usually available until curtain time.

San Francisco Symphony. At Davies Symphony Hall, 201 Van Ness Ave. (at Grove St.). ☎ **415/864-6000.** Tickets $10–$68.

Founded in 1911, the internationally respected San Francisco Symphony has long been an important part of this city's cultural life under such legendary conductors as Pierre Monteux and Seiji Ozawa. In 1995, Michael Tilson Thomas took over from Herbert Blomstedt and has already led the orchestra to new heights and crafted an exciting repertoire of classical and modern music. The season runs from September to May. Summer symphony activities include a Composer Festival and a Summer Pops series.

COMEDY & CABARET

Call the venues below for exact showtimes.

Bay Area Theatresports (BATS). Bayfront Theater at the Fort Mason Center, Bldg. B, 3rd Floor. ☎ **415/824-8220.** Tickets $8.

BATS operates an improvisational tournament in which four-actor teams compete against each other, taking on improvisational challenges from the audience. Judges then flash scorecards good-naturedly or honk a horn for scenes that just aren't working. Shows are staged on Mondays only. Phone for reservations.

Beach Blanket Babylon. At Club Fugazi, 678 Green St./Beach Blanket Babylon Blvd. (between Powell St. and Columbus Ave.). ☎ **415/421-4222.** Tickets $18–$45.

This comedic musical send-up is best known for its outrageous costumes and oversize headdresses. It's been playing almost 22 years now, and still almost every performance sells out. The show is updated often enough that locals still attend. Those under 21 are welcome only at the Sunday matinee, when no alcohol is served; photo ID is required for evening performances. It's wise to write for tickets at least 3 weeks in advance for weekend performance tickets or obtain them through Tix (see above). *Note:* When you purchase tickets, they will be within a specific section depending upon price; however, seating is still first-come/first-seated within that section.

Cobb's Comedy Club. In the Cannery at Fisherman's Wharf, 2801 Beach St. (between Leavenworth and Hyde sts.). ☎ **415/928-4320.** Cover $5 Mon, $8–$10 Tues–Sun (plus a 2-drink minimum nightly). Validated parking.

Cobb's features such national headliners as George Wallace, Emo Philips, and Jake Johannsen. There's comedy every night, including a 15-comedian All-Pro Monday showcase. Cobb's is open to those 18 and over and occasionally to kids aged 16 and 17 if they're accompanied by a parent or legal guardian (call ahead first).

Finocchio's. 506 Broadway (at Kearny St.). ☎ **415/982-9388.** Cover $12–15.

For more than 50 years this family-run cabaret club has showcased the best female impersonators in a funny, kitschy show. Three different revues are presented nightly (usually Thursday through Saturday), and a single cover is good for the entire evening. Guests must be 21 and over. Parking available next door at the Flying Dutchman.

Punch Line. 444 Battery St., plaza level (between Washington and Clay sts.). ☎ **415/397-4337,** or 415/397-7573 (for recorded information). Cover $5 Sun, $6–$15 Mon–Sat (plus a 2-drink minimum).

Adjacent to the Embarcadero One office building, this is the largest comedy nightclub in the city. Top national and local talent are featured Tuesday to Saturday. Showcase night is Sunday, when 15 to 20 rising stars take the mike. There's an all-star showcase or a special event on Monday nights. If you don't want to wait in line, buy tickets in advance from BASS outlets (☎ **510/762-2277**).

THE CLUB & MUSIC SCENE

The hippest dance places are located South of Market Street (SoMa) in former warehouses, while the most popular cafe culture is still centered in North Beach.

Note that the club and music scene is always changing, often outdating recommendations before the ink can dry on a page. Most of the venues below are promoted as different clubs on various nights of the week, each with its own look, sound, and style. Discount passes and club announcements are often available at hip clothing stores and other shops along upper Haight Street.

If you'd like to go club hopping with some locals in the know, consider the **Three Babes and a Bus** club tour (see p.108).

ROCK & BLUES CLUBS

In addition to the following listings, see "Dance Clubs," below, for (usually) live, danceable rock.

Blues. 2125 Lombard St. (at Fillmore St.). ☎ **415/771-BLUE**. Cover $5–$6.

This small, dark blues bar is packed most nights with an eclectic ethnic mix of mostly locals. The bands are usually pretty good and easy to dance to. Owner Max Young claims it's "the only real dark, dingy blues club in the city." Gotta love that.

The Fillmore. 1805 Geary Blvd. (at Fillmore St.). ☎ **415/346-6000.** Tickets $9–$25.

Reopened after years of neglect, The Fillmore, made famous by promoter Bill Graham in the 1960s, is once again attracting big names. Check the local listings in magazines, or call the theater for information on upcoming events.

The Saloon. 1232 Grant Ave. (at Vallejo St.). ☎ **415/989-7666.** Cover $3–$5 Fri–Sat.

An authentic Gold Rush survivor, this North Beach dive is the oldest extant bar in the city. Popular with both bikers and daytime pinstripers, there's live blues nightly.

Slim's. 333 11th St. (at Folsom St.). ☎ **415/522-0333.** Cover $5–$20 (plus a 2-drink minimum).

Co-owned by musician Boz Scaggs (who sometimes takes the stage under the name "Presidio Slim"), this big, glitzy restaurant/bar specializes in excellent American music—home-grown rock, jazz, blues, and alternative music—almost nightly.

Jazz & Latin Clubs

✪ **Cafe du Nord.** 2170 Market St. (at Sanchez St.) ☎ **415/861-5016.** Nominal cover varies.

Although it's been around since 1907, this basement-cum-jazz-supper club has finally been recognized as a respectable jazz venue. With a younger generation now appreciating the music, the place is often packed from the 40-foot mahogany bar to the back room with a pool table. Du Nord is even putting out its own compilation CDs now, which are definitely worth purchasing.

Cesar's Latin Palace. 3140 Mission St. (at Army St.). ☎ **415/648-6611.** Cover $5–$8.

Live Latin bands perform to a very mixed crowd—ethnically, economically, and generationally. There's plenty of dancing and drinking in this high-energy club.

Jazz at Pearl's. 256 Columbus Ave. (at Broadway). ☎ **415/291-8255.** No cover (2-drink minimum). Valet parking $3.

This is one of the best venues for jazz in the city. Ribs and chicken are served with the sounds, too, with prices ranging from $4 to $8.95. The live jams last until 2am nightly.

Dance Clubs

Club Ten 15. 1015 Folsom St. (at 6th St.). ☎ **415/431-1200.** Cover $5–$10.

Get decked out and plan for a late-nighter if you're headed to this enormous party warehouse. Three levels of dance floors offer a variety of dancing venues, complete with a 20- and 30-something gyrating mass who live for the DJs' pounding house, disco, and acid jazz. Each night is a different club that attracts its own crowd that ranges from yuppie to hip-hop. As this book goes to press, **Nikita** (☎ **415/267-0568**) is held on Fridays from 10pm to 6am, featuring different sounds: '70s disco, progressive house, techno, trip-hop, and acid jazz. Saturday is **Release,** a combo of hip-hop and disco, deep house, and acid jazz (☎ **415/281-0823**). Other nights are hot, too, so call ☎ **415/431-1200** for a complete schedule of events.

Coconut Grove Supper Club. 1415 Van Ness Ave. (between Bush and Pine sts.) ☎ **415/776-1616.** Cover $5 Sun–Thurs, $10 Fri–Sat after 9pm for those not eating dinner.

Reopened in '96 after being shunned for outrageous prices, the new—and far less expensive—Coconut Grove Supper Club is doing a brisk business serving a California/tropical/Cajun menu and live music to a mostly young, hip audience. Dancing and chocolate martinis are the main attractions. If you want something a little sophisticated and at the same time funky and fun, this is the place to go. The dress code is lax, but vintage is definitely the main attire.

Johnny Love's. 1500 Broadway (at Polk St.). ☎ **415/931-6053.** Cover Fri–Sat $10, $5 Wed–Thurs. Free before 9pm.

Named after the friendly owner-cum-house bartender who woos flocks of women with a canned line, boyish grin, and a kiss, Johnny Love's is the city's quintessential singles spot and one of the best bars in town to dance to live music. The crowd here is definitely out for a good time, so the scene is festive (while most bar atmospheres around town are too posed to really get down). This place is mainly a bar and restaurant, so be prepared to bump elbows with your neighbors on the small dance floor. Love's serves food, but there are better dining options within a few blocks.

181 Eddy. 181 Eddy St. (at Taylor St.). ☎ **415/673-8181.** Cover $5–$10.

Twenty-something and looking to gyrate the night away in a dark retro club crammed with glamorous hotties? With a combination of great ambiance, decent food, and throw-down funk and acid jazz, 181 has made a niche for itself. Early evening there's live entertainment and later a DJ spinning slamming old-school. The all-night pool room is packed with both players and voyeurs who recline along terraced banquettes, smoke cigarettes, and look cool. A decent dinner is served here too, and there's parking next door for $6. Dress code says no tennis shoes, torn Levi's, or baseball caps.

330 Ritch. 330 Ritch (between Third and Fourth sts. off Townsend). ☎ **415/541-9574** or 415/522-9558. Cover $3–$10.

If you can find the place, you must be cool. It's located on a 2-block alley in SoMa, and even locals have a hard time remembering how to get there. But once you do, expect happy hour cocktails (specials on a few select mixed drinks and draft brews), pool tables, and a hip, young crowd at play. Weekends, the place really livens up when bands take center stage on Fridays, and the Latin lovers salsa all night to the spicy beat. Free swing dancing lessons (with $5 cover charge) are offered every Wednesday to the Bay Area's best swing bands. A "hearty American" dinner is served Wednesday through Saturday from 6–10pm.

RETRO CLUBS

Bruno's. 2389 Mission St. (at 20th St.). ☎ **415/550-7455.** Cover $3 to $5 after 9:30pm.

Before its recognition as a destination restaurant, Mission District hipsters were already keen on this retro hotspot. Live music is played nightly in the back lounge, and the long, '50s-style full bar is almost always crowded with a mixture of wannabes, the cool, and the curious. Appetizers and dessert are served until 1am.

Club Deluxe. 1511 Haight St. (at Ashbury St.) ☎ **415/552-6949.** Cover $4.

Before the recent '40s trend hit the city, Deluxe and its fedora-wearing clientele had been celebrating the bygone era for years. And fortunately, even with all the retro-hype, the vibe here hasn't changed. Expect an eclectic mix of throw-backs and generic San Franciscans in the intimate, smoky bar and ajoining lounge, and live jazz or blues most nights. Although many regulars dress the part, there's no attitude here, so come as you like.

Harry Denton's Starlight Room. Atop the Sir Francis Drake Hotel, 450 Powell St., 21st Floor. ☎ **415/395-8595.** Cover $5 Wed–Thurs after 7pm, $10 Fri–Sat after 8pm.

Come dressed to the nines or in casual attire to this old-fashioned cocktail lounge-cum-nightclub where tourists and locals sip cocktails at sunset and boogie down to live swing and big-band tunes after dark. The room is classic 1930s San Francisco, with red-velvet banquettes, chandeliers, and fabulous views. Early evening is more relaxed, but come the weekend, this place gets loose.

High-Ball Lounge. 473 Broadway (between Kearny and Montgomery). ☎ **415/397-9464.** Cover $5–$7.

Retro-jazz is in full swing in the city, and one of the most popular places to listen and dance to it is at this North Beach joint. Harkening back to Broadway at its best, the vibe is full-on '40s–'50s, from the red banquettes and stage curtains to the small, dark, and smoky room. Live bands perform nightly to a young, swingin' crowd. There's also a swing dance class one night a week.

THE BAR SCENE

Persian Aub Zam Zam. 1633 Haight St. (at Clayton St.). ☎ **415/861-2545.**

Step through the forbidding metal doors and you'll feel as if you're in *Casablanca*. Regulars come here for the acerbic owner/bartender, Bruno, who kicks almost everyone else out. Order a Finlandia vodka martini and you'll be allowed to stay. Sit at the bar; the tables are "closed."

Spec's. 12 Saroyan Place (at 250 Columbus Ave.). ☎ **415/421-4112.**

Specs's incognito locale, down a tiny alley, makes it less of a walk-in bar and more of a lively locals' hangout. Its funky maritime decor gives it character that intrigues every visitor, and the clientele is funky enough to keep you preoccupied while you drink a beer.

BEER BARS & BREWPUBS

Gordon-Biersch Brewery. 2 Harrison St. (on the Embarcadero). ☎ **415/243-8246.**

This is San Francisco's largest brew-restaurant, serving decent food and tasty brew. There are always several beers to choose from, ranging from light to dark.

San Francisco Brewing Company. 155 Columbus Ave. (at Pacific St.). ☎ **415/434-3344.**

Surprisingly low-key for an ale house, this cozy brewpub serves its brew along with burgers, fries, and the like. It's one of the city's few remaining old saloons, aglow with stained-glass windows, beveled skylights, a mahogany bar, and a massive overhead fan running the full length of the bar—a bizarre contraption crafted from brass and palm fronds. The handmade copper brew kettle is visible from the street. There's music most evenings. The happy hour special, a buck for a 1.75-pint microbrew beer, runs daily from 4 to 6pm and midnight to 1am.

Thirsty Bear Brewing Company. 661 Howard St. (1 block east of the Moscone Center). ☎ **415/974-0905.**

Seven superb, handcrafted varieties of brew, ranging from a fruit-flavored Strawberry Ale to a steak-in-a-cup stout, are always on tap at this stylish high-ceilinged brick edifice. Excellent Spanish food, too (see "Dining," above). Pool tables and dart boards are upstairs, and live music ranging from jazz to classical can be heard most nights.

Toronado. 547 Haight St. (at Fillmore St.). ☎ **415/863-2276.**

Lower Haight isn't exactly charming, but it has plenty of nightlife catering to an artistic/grungy/skateboarding 20-something crowd. While Toronado definitely draws in the young'uns, its 40+ microbrews on tap and 60 bottled beers also entice a more eclectic clientele. The brooding atmosphere matches the surroundings: an aluminum bar, a few tall tables, dark lighting, and a back room packed with tables and chairs. A DJ picks up the pace on Friday and Saturday nights.

20 Tank Brewery. 316 11th St. (at Folsom St.). ☎ **415/255-9455.**

Right in the heart of SoMa's popular strip, this huge, come-as-you-are bar is known for serving good beer at fair prices. Pizzas, sandwiches, chilis, and assorted appetizers are also available. Pub games include darts, shuffleboard, and dice.

COCKTAILS WITH A VIEW

Also consider **Harry Denton's Starlight Room,** atop the Sir Francis Drake Hotel, 450 Powell St. (☎ **415/395-8595**); see "Retro Clubs," above, for review.

The Carnelian Room. In the Bank of America Building, 555 California St. (between Kearny and Montgomery sts.). ☎ **415/433-7500.** Jackets and ties required for men.

This 52nd-floor lounge offers uninterrupted views of the city. From a window-front table you feel as if you can reach out, pluck up the TransAmerica Pyramid, and stir your martini with it. In addition to cocktails, "Discovery Dinners" are offered for

$32.50 per person. The restaurant has the most extensive wine list in the city—1,275 selections to be exact.

Cityscape. Atop Hilton Tower I, 333 O'Farrell St. (at Mason St.), 46th Floor. ☎ **415/923-5002.**

When you sit under the glass roof and sip a drink here, it's as if you're sitting out under the stars and enjoying views of the Bay. The mirrored columns and floor-to-ceiling draperies help create an elegant and romantic ambiance. There's nightly dancing to a DJ's picks from 8pm.

Crown Room. In the Fairmont Hotel, 950 Mason St., 24th Floor. ☎ **415/772-5131.**

Of all the bars listed here, the Crown Room is definitely the plushest. Reached by an external glass elevator, the panoramic view from the top will encourage you to linger. In addition to drinks (steep at $7 to $9), dinner buffets are served for $35.

Equinox. In the Hyatt Regency Hotel, 5 Embarcadero Center. ☎ **415/788-1234.**

The sales hook of the Hyatt's rooftop Equinox is a revolving floor that gives each table a 360° panoramic view of the city every 45 minutes. In addition to cocktails, dinner is served daily.

Top of the Mark. In the Mark Hopkins Intercontinental, 1 Nob Hill (California and Mason sts.). ☎ **415/616-6916.** Cover $6–$10 when live music is offered.

This is one of the most famous cocktail lounges in the world. During World War II, it was considered de rigueur for Pacific-bound servicemen to toast their good-bye to the States here. The spectacular glass-walled room features an unparalleled view. Live entertainment is offered at 8:30 nightly. Drinks are pricey.

GAY & LESBIAN BARS & CLUBS

Check out the free weekly *Bay Area Reporter* for comprehensive gay and lesbian club listings. It's available at the corner of 18th and Castro streets, at 9th and Harrison streets, and at bars and shops around town.

The End Up. 401 6th St. (at Harrison St.). ☎ **415/357-0827.** Cover varies.

It's a different club here every night of the week, but regardless of who's throwing the party, the place is always jumping. There are two pool tables, a flaming fireplace, outdoor patio, and a mob of gyrating souls on the dance floor. Some nights are straight, so call for gay nights.

The Stud. 399 Ninth St. (at Harrison St.). ☎ **415/863-6623.** Cover $2–$6 weekends.

The Stud, which has been around for 30 years, is one of the most successful gay establishments in town, and it's mellow enough for straights as well as gays. The interior has an antique-shop look and a miniature train circling over the bar and dance floor. Music is a balanced mix of old and new; nights vary from cabaret and oldies to disco. Call in advance for the evening's venue.

The Swallow. 1750 Polk St. (between Clay and Washington sts.). ☎ **415/775-4152.** No cover.

Some consider this classy piano bar for the middle-age and up crowd the best gay bar on Polk.

12 An Easy Side Trip: Marine World Africa USA

Thirty miles northeast of San Francisco, **Marine World Africa USA,** on Marine World Parkway in Vallejo (☎ **707/643-6722**), is a kind of Disney-meets–Wild Kingdom theme park, offering aquatic and other trained animal performances, as well as a glimpse of exotic animals living in spacious, well-kept habitats.

ESSENTIALS

GETTING THERE   The **Blue & Gold Fleet** operates a high-speed ferry service from Pier 41 at Fisherman's Wharf to Vallejo and Marine World. It's a package deal that leaves at 10:35am and returns at 6pm. The scenic cruise, which takes you past Alcatraz and the Golden Gate Bridge, takes 80 minutes; in Vallejo, a brief shuttle ride gets you to the theme park. The round-trip, including park admission, is $40 for adults, $33 for seniors 62 and over and kids 13 to 18, and $24.50 for kids 5 to 12. Service is limited; call ☎ **415/773-1188** for departure times and information, ☎ **415/705-5555** to reserve tickets.

To reach the park **by car** from San Francisco, take I-80 north to Calif. 37 and follow the signs to the park; it's less than an hour's drive.

ADMISSION & OPEN HOURS   Admission is $26.95 for adults, $22.95 for seniors over 60, $18.95 for kids 4 to 12, and free for children under 4. Carte Blanche, Diners Club, MasterCard, and Visa are accepted. The park is open from Memorial Day through Labor Day, daily from 9:30am to 6pm; the rest of the year, Friday, Saturday, and Sunday from 9:30am to 5pm. The park closes for the winter months (usually November through March).

SEEING THE PARK

You can leisurely wander through the park or attend the variety of events scheduled continuously throughout the day. The best way to see the park is to get there early, plot your own itinerary from the leaflet and map given to you at the entrance, and then stick to it. Otherwise, you'll find yourself missing parts of each presentation and feeling frustrated.

At the **Killer Whale and Dolphin Show,** the front seven rows of seats are saved for guests who want a thorough drenching. **Shark Experience,** a moving walkway through a clear acrylic tunnel, brings visitors through a 300,000-gallon tropical shark-filled tank.

Cross a bridge over a waterfall, past the flamingos, and you enter **"Africa USA."** Here you'll find **Elephant Encounter,** where visitors can meet (and pet!) some of the park's 11 Asian and African elephants. In addition to shows, you can get more up close and personal at the elephant ride ($3) or the giraffe feeding (50¢). At **Tiger Island,** you can see trainers and Bengal tigers playing and swimming together. An informative show about the park's exotic and endangered animals is performed in the **Wildlife Theater.**

Hawks and other feathered friends swoop overhead and onto the stage at the **Bird Show.** There's also an enclosed **Butterfly World** where one of the many beautiful inhabitants may happen to land on you (don't touch them, though!); a **Small Animal Petting Kraal** (with llamas); **Walrus Experience,** where the adorably chubby and curious creatures splash about and look you in the eye; **Walkabout! An Australian Adventure,** where kangaroos, wallabies, and emu hop freely and koalas hang out in nearby trees; and **Gentle Jungle,** a playground that combines education, fun, and adventure. Here, inside the Prairie Crawl, children can crawl through burrows in the prairie dog village and pop up into Plexiglas domes so they can see the world from these animals' point of view.

A 55-acre lake is the stage for a **Water Ski and Boat Show** April through October. Daredevil athletes jump, spin, and even create a human pyramid while wearing water skis. In winter, kids throw on their ski clothes and spend the day sledding at **Snow World.**

A wide variety of reasonably priced fast food is available at **Lakeside Plaza.** There's also a restaurant, or you can bring your own picnic.

The San Francisco Bay Area

5

by Erika Lenkert and Matthew R. Poole

Without question, the Bay City is captivating. But don't let it ensnare you to the point of ignoring its environs, which contain a multitude of natural spectacles like Mount Tamalpais and Muir Woods; scenic communities like Tiburon, Sausalito, and Half Moon Bay; and cities like gritty Oakland and its youth-oriented next-door neighbor, Berkeley. A little farther north stretch the valleys of Napa and Sonoma, the finest wine region in the nation (see chapter 6). And to the south lies high-tech Silicon Valley and San Jose, Northern California's largest city.

1 Berkeley

10 miles NE of San Francisco

Berkeley would be little more than a quaint, sleepy town east of the big city if it weren't for the University of California at Berkeley, which is world renowned for its first-rate academic standards, 16 Nobel Prize winners, and protests that led to the most renowned student riots in U.S. history. Today, there's still hippie idealism in the air, but the radicals have aged; the '60s are only present in tie-dye and paraphernalia shops, and the students have less angst. Still, it's a charming town with all types of people, a beautiful campus, vast parks, great shopping, and some incredible restaurants.

ESSENTIALS

GETTING THERE   The Berkeley BART station is 2 blocks from the university. The fare from San Francisco is less than $3. Call **BART** at ☎ **510/793-2278.**

If you're **driving** from San Francisco, take I-80 east to the University exit. Count on walking some distance because you won't find a parking spot near the university.

VISITOR INFORMATION   The **Berkeley Convention and Visitors Bureau,** 2015 Center St., Berkeley, CA 94703 (☎ **800/ 847-4823** or 510/549-7040), can answer your questions and even find accommodations for you. Call the **Visitor Hotline** (☎ **510/ 549-8710**) for information on events and happenings in Berkeley.

EXPLORING THE UNIVERSITY & ENVIRONS

Hanging out is the preferred Berkeley pastime, and the best place to do it is on **Telegraph Avenue,** the street that leads to the campus's

The Bay Area

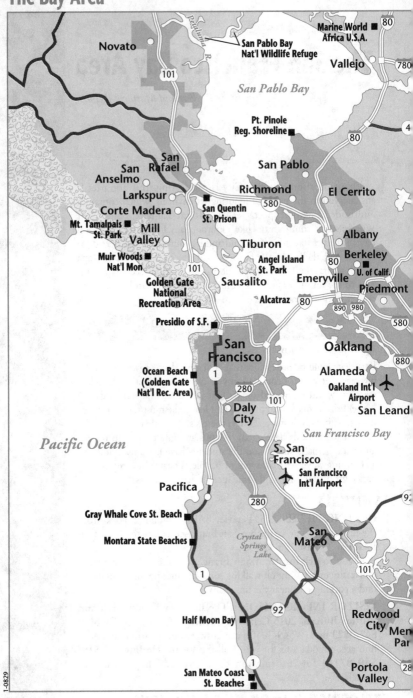

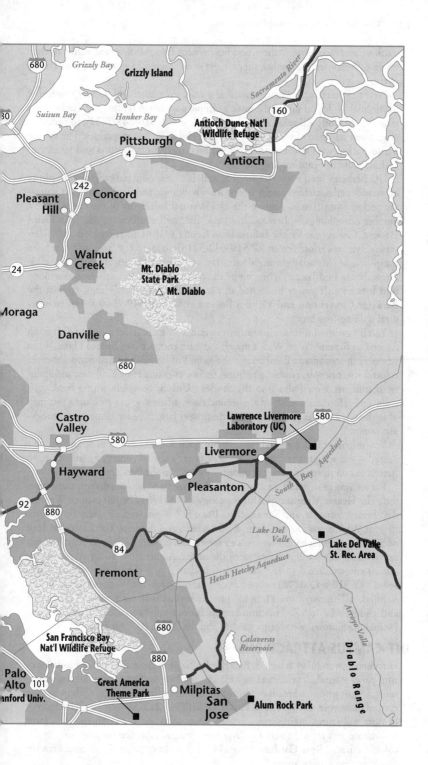

southern entrance. Most of the action lies between Bancroft Way and Ashby Avenue where coffeehouses, restaurants, shops, great book and record stores, and craft booths swarm with life.

Pretend you're local: Plant yourself at a cafe, sip a latte, and ponder something intellectual while you survey the town's unique population bustling by. Bibliophiles must stop at **Cody's Books,** 2454 Telegraph Ave. (☎ **510/845-7852**), to peruse its gargantuan selection of titles, independent press books, and magazines. The avenue is also packed with street vendors selling everything from T-shirts and jewelry to I Ching and tarot-card readings.

UC Berkeley itself is worth a stroll as well. It's a beautiful old campus with plenty of woodsy paths, architecturally noteworthy buildings, and 31,000 students scurrying to and from classes. Among the architectural highlights of the campus are a number of buildings by Bernard Maybeck, Bakewell and Brown, and John Galen Howard. Contact the **Visitor Information Center** at 101 University Hall, 2200 University Ave. (at Oxford Street; ☎ **510/642-5215**), to join a free, regularly scheduled campus tour (Monday through Saturday at 10am; no tours offered from mid-December to mid-January); or stop by the office and pick up a self-guided walking tour brochure. If you're interested in notable off-campus buildings, contact the **Berkeley Convention and Visitors Bureau** at ☎ **510/549-7040** for an architectural walking-tour brochure.

You'll find the university's southern entrance at the northern end of Telegraph Avenue, at Bancroft Way. Walk through the main entrance into **Sproul Plaza.** When school is in session you'll encounter the gamut of Berkeley's inhabitants here: the colorful street people, rambling political zealots, chanting Hare Krishnas, and ambitious students. You'll also find the **Student Union,** complete with a bookstore, cafes, and information desk on the second floor, where you can pick up a free map of Berkeley, as well as the local student newspaper (also found in dispensers throughout campus).

You might be lucky enough to stumble upon some impromptu musicians or a heated—and sometimes absurd—debate. There's always something going on, so stretch out on the grass for a few minutes and take in the Berkeley vibe.

For viewing more traditional art forms, there are some noteworthy museums here, too. The **Hearst Museum of Anthropology** (☎ **510/642-3682**) is open Wednesday, Friday, Saturday, and Sunday from 10am to 4:30pm, and Thursday from 10am to 9pm. Admission is $2 for adults, $1 for seniors and children. The **Lawrence Hall of Science,** offering hands-on science exploration, is open daily from 10am to 5pm and is also a wonderful place to watch the sunset. Admission is $6 for adults, $4 for seniors and children 7 to 18, and $2 for children 3 to 6. The **University Art Museum** (☎ **510/642-0808**) is open from 11am to 5pm, on Wednesday and Friday to Sunday, Thursday from 11am to 9pm. Admission is $6 for adults, $4 for seniors and children 12 to 17. This museum includes a substantial collection of Hans Hofmann paintings, a sculpture garden, and the Pacific Film Archive.

OFF-CAMPUS ATTRACTIONS

Unbeknownst to many travelers, Berkeley has some of the most extensive and beautiful parks around. If you want to wear out the kids or if you enjoy hiking, swimming, or just getting a breath of California air and sniffing a few roses, jump in your car and make your way to **Tilden Park** (☎ **510/843-2137**), where you'll find plenty of flora and fauna, hiking trails, an old steam train and merry-go-round, a farm and nature area for kids, and a chilly arbor-encircled lake. On the way, stop at the colorful terraced **Rose Garden,** located in north Berkeley on Euclid Avenue between Bay View and Eunice Street.

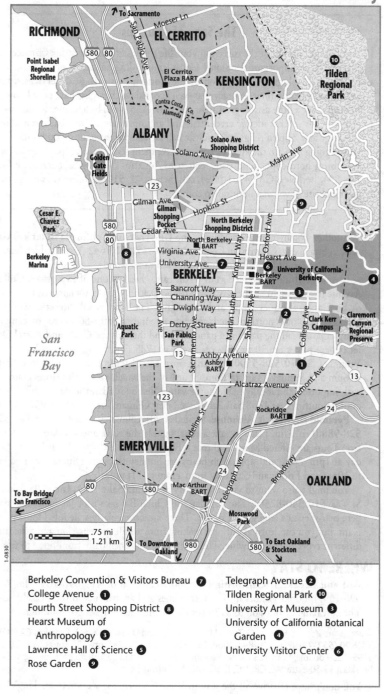

Berkeley

RICHMOND

To Sacramento

Moeser Ln

San Pablo Ave

EL CERRITO

Point Isabel
Regional
Shoreline

580 80

El Cerrito
Plaza BART

KENSINGTON

Tilden
Regional
Park ⑩

Contra Costa Co.
Alameda Co.

ALBANY

Solano Ave
Shopping District

Solano Ave

Martin Ave

Golden
Gate
Fields

123

Gilman Ave.
Gilman
Shopping
Pocket

Hopkins St

North Berkeley
Shopping District

Oxford Ave

⑨

Cesar E.
Chavez
Park

580

80

Cedar Ave.

North Berkeley
BART

Hearst Ave

⑤

Berkeley
Marina

⑧

Virginia Ave.

University Ave.

⑦

King Jr. Way

Berkeley
BART

⑥

University of California-
Berkeley

④

BERKELEY

③

Bancroft Way
Channing Way
Dwight Way

②

Martin Luther

Shattuck Ave

Clark Kerr
Campus

College Ave

Claremont
Canyon
Regional
Preserve

San
Francisco
Bay

Aquatic
Park

San Pablo Ave

Derby Street

San Pablo
Park

13

Ashby Avenue
Ashby
BART

①

Claremont Ave

13

Sacramento Ave

Alcatraz Avenue

123

Rockridge
BART

24

Adeline St

EMERYVILLE

80

580

Mac Arthur
BART

24

Telegraph Ave

Broadway

OAKLAND

To Bay Bridge/
San Francisco

0 .75 mi
1.21 km

N

Mosswood
Park

To Downtown
Oakland

980

To East Oakland
& Stockton

580

1-0830

Berkeley Convention & Visitors Bureau ⑦

College Avenue ①

Fourth Street Shopping District ⑧

Hearst Museum of
Anthropology ③

Lawrence Hall of Science ⑤

Rose Garden ⑨

Telegraph Avenue ②

Tilden Regional Park ⑩

University Art Museum ③

University of California Botanical
Garden ④

University Visitor Center ⑥

The Sage of Aquarius

Are you curious about the direction your life is taking? Need a little assistance in making those important decisions? Consider spending an afternoon in Berkeley having an astrological consultation by the **Aquarius Astrological Services**, who are so renowned for their accuracy that even licensed psychologists have been known to drop in for a little astrological assistance. The AAS is run by a former world traveler who has solid academic credentials and an impressive 30-year background in astrology and eastern religions. You can call for an appointment if you know that you're going to be in the area, or you can have them send you a 25-page report for your birth horoscope. Send your request to Aquarius Astrological Services, P.O. Box 894, Berkeley, CA 94701-0894, call them at ☎ **510/549-3345,** or plug into their website at www.aquariusastro.com.

Another worthy nature excursion is the **University of California Botanical Garden,** in Strawberry Canyon on Centennial Drive (☎ 510/642-3343), which features a vast collection of herbage ranging from cacti to redwoods.

If you're itching to exercise your credit cards, head to one of two places: **College Avenue** from Dwight all the way down to the Oakland border is crammed with eclectic boutiques, antiques shops, and restaurants. The other is **4th Street** in west Berkeley, just 2 blocks north of the University Avenue exit off I-80 where you can grab a cup of java, read the paper at a patio table, and then hit the **Crate and Barrel Outlet** (where prices are 30 to 70% off retail) at 1785 Fourth St., between Hearst and Virginia (☎ 510/528-5500), which is open Monday through Saturday from 10am to 6pm and Sunday 11am to 6pm, or any of the small, wonderful stores crammed with imported and locally made housewares. Nearby is **REI,** the Bay Area's favorite outdoor outfitters at 1338 San Pablo Ave., near Gilman Street. (☎ 510/527-4140).

Pyramid Brewery & Alehouse, located at 901 Gilman St., at 6th Street, (☎ 510/ 528-9880), is a fun place to take a tour, sample the suds, and snack on California fare. Tours are offered Monday through Friday at 2pm and 4pm, Saturday and Sunday at 1pm, 2pm, and 4pm. Pub hours are Sunday through Thursday from 11am to 10pm and Friday and Saturday from 11am to 11pm.

You might also want to visit the factory of **Takara Sake USA, Inc.,** 708 Addison St. (☎ 510/540-8250). The popular Sho Chiku Bai sake isn't Japanese: It's made here by America's largest sake maker. There are no regularly scheduled tours of the plant, but you can learn about sake making from a slide presentation and taste three different types of the rice wine. The tasting room is open daily from noon to 6pm.

WHERE TO STAY

Bed and Breakfast California (☎ 800/872-4500 or 415/696-1690; fax 415/ 696-1699), books visitors into private homes and apartments in the Berkeley area. The cost ranges from $60 to $175 per night, and there's a 2-night minimum.

Claremont Resort & Spa. 41 Tunnel Rd. (at Ashby and Domingo aves.), Berkeley, CA 94705. ☎ 800/551-7266 or 510/843-3000. Fax 510/843-6239. 245 rms, 35 suites. A/C TV TEL. $199–$259 double; from $234 suite. Packages available, including 1-night packages from $159. Breakfast $9.50 extra. AE, CB, DC, DISC, MC, V. Parking $8.

You don't have to drive all the way to Wine Country for a spa retreat. The Victorian Claremont, one of the most beautiful and elaborate mansions in the East Bay, will pamper you silly—and it's only a half-hour drive from the city. The 22-acre spread overlooks the distant San Francisco Bay and is surrounded by lush, well-tended gardens and outdoor sculpture. Rooms, though individually decorated with old-fashioned stateliness, don't contend with their surroundings; however, the 40 new guest rooms added in 1997, though more expensive, offer everything a guest could possibly wish for: cheery country decor, custom furnishings, double sinks, data ports, VCRs, CD players, Internet access lines, and private e-mail accounts.

But the reason to come here isn't to hang out in your room; the idea is to rejuvinate yourself at the elaborate spa, which offers five different types of massage, body-care treatments (including a loofah scrub, mud and herbal wrap, aromabath, and Turkish scrub), and a variety of fitness facilities. There's an exercise room, aerobics, yoga, a weight room, 2 lap pools, and 10 tennis courts. The beauty salon offers a complete range of skin and beauty treatments. The cuisine isn't up to par with that of Sonoma Mission Inn, but does offer nutritionally balanced plates of seafood, salad, and pasta.

French Hotel. 1538 Shattuck Ave., Berkeley, CA 94709. ☎ **510/548-9930.** 18 rms. TV TEL. $85–$125 single or double. Government employee, university, and group rates available. Breakfast $4.50 extra. AE, CB, DC, MC, V. Free parking. From I-80 north, take the University Ave. exit and turn left onto Shattuck Ave.; the hotel is 6 blocks down on your left. BART: Berkeley.

This small hotel is in north Berkeley, the sleepier side of town, and is within crawling distance from the renowned restaurant Chez Panisse (see "Where to Dine," below). The guest rooms are light, airy, and well decorated, and all but three have balconies. In lieu of a dresser, stacked sliding white baskets are provided for your personal items. The downstairs cafe, a casual meeting place with exposed brick walls and outdoor tables, serves espresso, pastries, and other light items. Many items can be delivered to your room.

Gramma's Rose Garden Inn. 2740 Telegraph Ave., Berkeley, CA 94705. ☎ **510/549-2145.** Fax 510/549-1085. 40 rms, all nonsmoking. TV TEL. $99–$165 double. Rates include breakfast. AE, DC, MC, V. Free parking. Take I-80 north to the Ashby exit and turn left onto Telegraph Ave.; the hotel is located 4 blocks up. BART: Ashby.

Gramma's restored Tudor-style mansion includes a main house, carriage house, garden house, and the Fay house, with guest rooms furnished in period antiques, floral-print wallpapers, and patchwork quilts. Accommodations in the restored carriage house overlook a garden and have fireplaces and king-size beds. All rooms here are nonsmoking. Guests are served a complimentary breakfast in the downstairs dining room or on the deck overlooking the garden, as well as complimentary wine and cheese in the evening. There's also a bottomless cookie jar and fresh-brewed coffee for any spontaneous sweet tooth. Dinner is served in the Greenhouse Cafe.

Hotel Durant. 2600 Durant Ave., Berkeley, CA 94704. ☎ **800/2-DURANT** or 510/845-8981. Fax 510/486-8336. 140 rms and suites. TV TEL. $99–$114 double; $142–$202 suite. Rates include continental breakfast. AE, DC, DISC, MC, V. Valet parking $5.

Smack-dab in the middle of the collegiate action, this charming hotel is 2 blocks from campus and just steps from Telegraph Avenue. Once inside, however, you're not likely to hear the bellowing fraternity brothers who may be tossing back a few at Henry's, the popular downstairs bar and restaurant. A stately plush lobby leads to basic, clean Victorian-accented accommodations. While the rooms are nothing special, the prime location and inexpensive valet parking make this hotel a popular choice.

WHERE TO DINE
EXPENSIVE

✪ **Chez Panisse.** 1517 Shattuck Ave. (between Cedar and Vine). ☎ **510/548-5525.** Fax 510/548-0140. Reservations essential for restaurant, accepted a month in advance; for cafe, accepted for lunch at 9am on the day, not accepted for dinner. Main courses $13–$18; fixed-price dinner $38–$68. AE, CB, DC, MC, V. Restaurant, dinner seatings Mon–Sat at 6–6:30, 8:30–9:15pm. Cafe, Mon–Thurs 11:30am–3pm and 5–10:30pm, Fri–Sat 11:30am–4pm and 5–11:30pm. BART: Berkeley. From I-80 north, take the University exit and turn left onto Shattuck Ave. CALIFORNIA.

It was in this kitchen, according to gourmands in the know, that Californian Cuisine was born. Indeed, California Cuisine is so much a product of chef Alice Waters's genius that all other restaurants following in her wake should be dated "AAW" (After Alice Waters). Read the menus posted outside and you'll understand why. Most of the produce and meat still come from local farms and are organically produced, and after all these years Alice still attends to her restaurant with great integrity and innovation.

Alice's creations are served in a delightful redwood and stucco cottage with a brick terrace filled with flowering potted plants. There are two separate dining areas: the cafe and the restaurant, both offering a Mediterranean-inspired cuisine.

In the upstairs cafe, a delicately smoked gravlax or a roasted eggplant soup with pesto, followed by lamb ragoût garnished with apricots, onions, and spices served with couscous, might be featured at lunch or dinner. Dinner reservations aren't taken for the cafe, but the wait is worth it.

The cozy downstairs restaurant is an appropriately warm environment to indulge in the fixed-price four-course gourmet dinner, which is served Tuesday to Thursday. Friday and Saturday it's four courses plus an apéritif, and Monday is bargain night with a three-course dinner for $38. The menu, which changes daily, is posted outside the restaurant each Saturday for the following week. Meals are complemented by an excellent wine list.

MODERATE

✪ **Cafe Rouge.** 1782 Fourth Street (between Delaware and Hearst). ☎ **510/525-1440.** Main courses $9.50–$20. MC, V. Tues–Sun 11:30am–midnight, Mon 11:30am–3pm. BISTRO.

After cooking at San Francisco's renowned Zuni Café for 10 years, chef/owner Marsha McBride launched her own restaurant, and the East Bay immediately welcomed her. Now one of the hottest spots in town, the large, loftlike dining room is softened with velvet curtains, lovely art, and bright light fixtures. There are lots of salads on the starter menu, as well as signature dishes like the rotisserie chicken with oil and thyme and the grilled lamb chops. But East Bay carnivores are especially happy with the burger; just like Zuni's, it's top-notch.

O **Chamé.** 1830 Fourth St. (near Hearst). ☎ **510/841-8783.** Reservations necessary Fri–Sat. Main courses $7–$17.50. AE, DC, MC, V. Mon–Sat 11:30am–3pm; Mon–Thurs 5:30–9pm, Fri–Sat 5:30–9:30pm. JAPANESE.

Spare and plain in its decor, this spot has a meditative air to complement the traditional and experimental Japanese-inspired cuisine. The menu, which changes daily, offers meal-in-a-bowl dishes (from $7 to $11) that allow a choice of soba or udon noodles in a clear soup with a variety of toppings (from shrimp and wakame seaweed to beef with burdock root and carrot); appetizers and salads, which include a flavorsome melding of grilled shiitake mushrooms and sweet peppers and Portobello mushrooms, watercress, and green onion pancakes; a sashimi of the day; and specials, which always include a delicious roasted salmon.

✪ **Rivoli.** 1539 Solano. ☎ **510/526-2542.** Reservations recommended. Main courses $10.25–$15.75. MC, V. Mon–Thurs 5:30–9:30pm, Fri 5:30–10pm, Sat 5–10pm, Sun 5–9pm. CALIFORNIA.

One of the favored dinner destinations in the East Bay, Rivoli's winning combination is top-notch food at very reasonable prices. The owners have created a warm, intimate dining environment that overlooks a sweet little garden. Aside from a few house favorites, the menu changes every 3 weeks in order to serve whatever's freshest and in season. While many love it, we weren't thrilled with the Portobello mushroom fritter, which in our minds was a glorified variation on the fried zucchini stick. However, we did have an absolute A+ dish here: the hearty oven-braised pork ragoût with butternut squash and dandelion greens intermingled with tender and crispy semolina gnocchi. Perfection at this price ($13.50 for the ragoût) is enough to put most high-end San Francisco restaurants to shame. Finish the evening with the Meyer lemon cheesecake; it's a decadent sour-cream–like affair with a subtle pistachio crust.

INEXPENSIVE

Bette's Oceanview Diner. 1807A 4th St. ☎ **510/644-3230.** Breakfast $5–$7.50. MC, V. Mon–Thurs 6:30am–2:30pm, Fri–Sun 6:30am–4pm. AMERICAN.

Situated in the middle of Berkeley's blooming chi-chi shopping area, Bette's may look like an old-style diner, but one glance at the menu and you'll know it's risen to match their surroundings. Sure, there are pancakes, eggs, and all the breakfast basics on the menu, but Bette's leaves out the grease and substitutes advanced culinary style. Savor any of the fresh housemade morning buns or scones and splurge on with a delightful mound of an omelet filled with fresh ingredients such as roasted red bell pepper with herb-cream cheese. Other specialties include soufflé pancakes (banana rum, apple brandy, fresh berry, and chocolate swirl), and grate-to-order potato pancakes.

Blue Nile. 2525 Telegraph Ave. ☎ **510/540-6777.** Reservations required Fri–Sat. Main courses. $6.50–$7.45. MC, V. Tues–Sat 11:30am–10pm, Sun 5–10pm. ETHIOPIAN.

Step through the beaded curtains into the Blue Nile, and the African paintings and music will summon your appetite to other parts of the world. But the journey doesn't end there—be prepared to savor the flavorful specialties such as *doro wat* (a spiced stew of beef, lamb, or chicken, served with a fluffy crepe injera) or *gomen wat* (mustard greens sautéed in cream) with no utensils other than your fingers. Sure, you *could* convince the wait staff to drum up a fork or two, but don't bother. After all, when in Africa. . . . No appetizers are served, but meals come with a small salad.

✪ **Cafe Intermezzo.** 2422 Telegraph Ave. ☎ **510/849-4592.** Most items $3.25–$5.65. No credit cards. Daily 10am–10pm. SOUPS/SANDWICHES.

Pay no heed to the line out the door. Counter persons whip up orders with such fervor, you'll be happily munching in 5 to 10 minutes on what we consider the best and most enormous salads in the Bay Area. The dressings aren't any fancier than Italian or poppy seed, but the salads are literally a trough of fresh greens with kidney and garbanzo beans, sprouts, avocado, egg, and cucumber. One salad is a meal for two and comes with thick fresh slices of bread and slabs of butter. Soups and sandwiches here are also delicious and one of the best deals around.

Cambodianas. 2156 University Ave. (between Shattuck and Oxford). ☎ **510/843-4630.** Reservations recommended, especially Fri–Sat. Main courses $7.50–$13; fixed-price dinner $10.95. AE, CB, DC, JCB, MC, V. Mon–Fri 11:30am–3pm; Mon–Thurs 5–10pm, Fri–Sat 5–10:30pm, Sun 5–9:30pm. CAMBODIAN.

For those who relish the spicy cuisine of Cambodia, this is quite a find. The decor is as colorful as the fare—amidst brilliant blue, yellow, and green walls with Breuer-style chairs set at tables where you can feast on a variety of dishes. Especially tasty is the curry or naga dish with a sauce of tamarind, turmeric, lemongrass, shrimp paste, coconut milk galinga, shallot, lemon leaf, sugar, and green chili. This sauce may smother salmon, prawns, chicken, or steak. Another tempting dish is the chicken chaktomuk prepared with pineapple, red peppers, and zucchini in soy and oyster sauce. There are plenty of vegetarian and low-cal options, and the three-course, fixed-price dinner is an excellent value.

BERKELEY AFTER DARK

Blake's, 2367 Telegraph Ave. (☎ **510/848-0886**), was recently voted the town's best bar by the student newspaper. Three floors provide a variety of entertainment ranging from a pool table to dancing. There's an unspectacular but cheap full-service restaurant and bar. The draws here are the music, affordable prices, and down-home atmosphere, not the food.

The **Triple Rock Brewery and Alehouse,** 1920 Shattuck Ave., at Hearst (☎ **510/843-2739**), is a top-notch Berkeley favorite known for its fresh brew, which is piped directly from the glass-enclosed brewery to the bar, where sandwiches and chilis are also served. Play a game of shuffleboard, or on a sunny afternoon head to the rooftop deck with your brew.

2 Oakland

10 miles E of San Francisco

Though it's less than a dozen miles from San Francisco, the city of Oakland is worlds apart from its sister city across the bay. Originally little more than a cluster of ranches and farms, Oakland's size and stature exploded practically overnight as the last mile of transcontinental railroad track was laid down. Major shipping interests soon followed, and to this day Oakland has retained its hold as one of the busiest industrial ports on the West Coast.

The price for all this economic success, however, is Oakland's lowbrow reputation for being a predominantly working-class city, forever in the shadow of San Francisco's chic spotlight. But with all its shortcomings and bad press, Oakland still manages to have a few pleasant surprises up its sleeve for those who venture this way. Rent a sailboat on Lake Merritt, stroll along the waterfront, explore the fantastic Oakland Museum—they're all great reasons to hop the bay and spend a fog-free day exploring one of California's largest and most ethnically diverse cities.

ESSENTIALS

GETTING THERE   Bay Area Rapid Transit (BART) makes the trip from San Francisco to Oakland through one of the longest underwater transit tunnels in the world. Fares range from $1 to $4, depending on your station of origin; children 4 and under ride free. BART trains operate Monday to Saturday, from 6am to midnight, and on Sunday from 9am to midnight. Exit at the 12th Street station for downtown Oakland.

By car from San Francisco, take I-80 across the San Francisco–Oakland Bay Bridge and follow the signs to downtown Oakland. Exit at Grand Avenue South for the Lake Merritt area.

CITY LAYOUT   Downtown Oakland is bordered by Grand Avenue on the north, I-980 on the west, Inner Harbor on the south, and Lake Merritt on the east. Between these landmarks are three BART stations (12th Street, 19th Street, and Lake Merritt), City Hall, the Oakland Museum, Jack London Square, and several other sights.

WHAT TO SEE & DO

Lake Merritt is Oakland's primary tourist attraction along with Jack London Square (see below). Three and a half miles in circumference, the tidal lagoon was bridged and dammed in the 1860s and is now a wildlife refuge that is home to flocks of migrating ducks, herons, and geese. It's surrounded on three sides by the 122-acre **Lakeside Park,** a popular place to picnic, feed the ducks, and escape the fog. At the **Sailboat House** (☎ 510/444-3807), in Lakeside Park along the north shore, you can rent sailboats, rowboats, pedal boats, and canoes for $6 to $12 per hour.

Another site worth visiting is Oakland's **Paramount Theatre** (☎ 510/893-2300), an outstanding example of art deco architecture and decor. Built in 1931 and authentically restored in 1973, it now functions as the city's main performing arts center. Guided tours of the 3,000-seat theater are given the first and third Saturdays of each month, excluding holidays. No reservations are necessary; just show up at 10am at the box office entrance on 21st Street at Broadway. Admission is $1.

JACK LONDON SQUARE   If you take pleasure from strolling sailboat-filled wharves or are a die-hard fan of Jack London, you might actually enjoy a visit to **Jack London Square.** Oakland's only patent tourist area, this low-key version of San Francisco's Fisherman's Wharf shamelessly plays up the fact that Jack London spent most of his youth along this waterfront. The square fronts the harbor, housing a tourist-tacky complex of boutiques and eateries that are about as far away from the "call of the wild" as you can get. Most are open from Monday to Saturday from 10am to 9pm (some restaurants stay open later). In the center of the square is a small, reconstructed Yukon cabin in which Jack London lived while prospecting in the Klondike during the Gold Rush of 1897.

In the middle of Jack London Square you'll find a more authentic memorial, **Heinold's First and Last Chance Saloon,** a funky, friendly little bar and historic landmark that's actually worth a visit. This is where London did some of his writing and most of his drinking; the corner table he used has remained exactly as it was nearly a century ago. Also in the square are the mast and nameplate from the **U.S.S. Oakland,** a ship that saw extensive action in the Pacific during World War II, and a wonderful museum filled with interesting London memorabilia.

The square is located at Broadway and Embarcadero. Take I-880 to Broadway, turn south, and go to the end. BART: 12th Street station; then walk south along Broadway (about 1/2 mile) or take bus no. 51a to the foot of Broadway.

THE U.S.S. *POTOMAC*   It took the Potomac Association's hundreds of volunteers more than 12 years—at a cost of $5 million—to restore the 165-foot presidential yacht **U.S.S. *Potomac,*** President Franklin Delano Roosevelt's beloved "Floating White House." Now a proud and permanent memorial berthed at the Port of Oakland's FDR Pier at Jack London Square, the revitalized *Potomac* is open to the public for dockside tours, as well as 2-hour public education cruises along the San Francisco waterfront and around Treasure Island.

Dockside tours are available Wednesdays and Fridays from 10am to 2pm and Sundays noon to 4pm from April through October, and Sundays from noon to 4pm from November through March. Admission is $5 for families with children under 18, $3 for adults, $2 for seniors, $1 for children ages 6 to 17; children age 5 and under free. Cruises are offered from April through October, with 10am and 1:30pm departures on the first and third Thursdays, and the second and fourth Saturdays of each month. Tickets are $30 for adults, $15 for children 6 to 17, children 5 and under free. Due to the popularity of the cruises, advance purchase is strongly recommended. Hours and days open are subject to change, so be sure to call the 24-hour information line (☎ 510/839-8256). Tickets can be purchased in advance by calling the **Potomac Association** (☎ 510/839-7533, ext. 1). The **Potomac Visitor Center** is at 540 Water St., at Clay and Water streets, adjacent to the FDR pier at the north end of Jack London Square.

Children's Fairyland. Lakeside Park (Grand Ave. and Bellevue Dr.). ☎ **510/452-2259.** Admission $3.25 adults, $2.75 children 12 and under. Summer, Sat–Sun 10am–5:30pm, Mon–Fri 10am–4:30pm; spring and fall, Wed–Sun 10am–4:30pm; winter, Fri–Sun and holidays 10am–4:30pm. BART: Exit at 19th St. and walk north along Broadway; turn right on Grand Ave. to the park. From I-580 south, exit at Grand Ave.; Children's Fairyland is at the far end of the park, on your left at Bellevue Ave.

On the north shore of Lake Merritt is one of the most imaginative children's parks in the United States, enough to inspire Walt Disney to build Disneyland. Kids can peer into old Geppetto's workshop, watch the Mad Hatter eternally pouring tea for Alice, see Noah's Ark overloaded with animal passengers, and view Beatrix Potter's village of storybook characters. Fairy tales also come alive during puppet shows at 11am, 2pm, and 4pm.

Oakland Museum of California. 1000 Oak St. ☎ **510/238-3401**, or 510/238-2200 for recorded information. Admission $5 adults, $3 students and seniors, free for children 5 and under; free for everyone Sun 4–7pm. Wed–Sat 10am–5pm, Sun noon–7pm. Closed Thanksgiving Day, Christmas Day, New Year's Day, and July 4. BART: Lake Merritt station (1 block south of the museum). From I-880 north, take the Oak St. exit; the museum is 5 blocks east at Oak and 10th sts. Or take I-580 to I-980 and exit at the Jackson St. ramp.

Located 2 blocks south of the lake, this museum includes just about everything you'd want to know about the state and its people, history, culture, geology, art, environment, and ecology. It's actually three museums in one: exhibitions of works by California artists from Bierstadt to Diebenkorn; collections of artifacts from California's history, from Pomo Indian basketry to Country Joe McDonald's guitar; and re-creations of California habitats from the coast to the White Mountains. The museum holds major shows of California artists, like the recent exhibit of the work of ceramic sculptor Peter Voulkos, or shows dedicated to major California movements, such as arts and crafts from 1890 to 1930. There are 45-minute guided tours leaving the gallery information desks on request or by appointment. There is a fine cafe, a gallery (☎ **510/834-2329**) selling works by California artists, and a book and gift shop.

WHERE TO DINE

Bay Wolf. 3853 Piedmont Ave. (off Broadway between 40th St. and MacArthur Blvd.). ☎ **510/655-6004.** Main courses $14–$18. MC, V. Mon–Fri 11:30am–2pm, 5:30–9pm; Sat–Sun 5:30–9pm. CALIFORNIA.

Bay Wolf, one of Oakland's most venerable and revered restaurants, has been going strong for nearly 2 decades. East Bay diners have been coming to this converted brown Victorian for years to let chef/owner Michael Wilds do the cooking. Though Wilds has passed his apron on to chef Lauren Lyle, Bay Wolf's reputation for simple yet sagacious preparations using only fresh ingredients remains. Main courses vary from a flavorful seafood stew seasoned with saffron and brimful of cracked Dungeness crab, prawns, rockfish, and mussels to tender braised lamb shanks with white beans, artichokes, and rosemary. Informal service means you can leave the tie at home. New additions include heat lamps on the front deck, allowing for open-air evening dining—a treat San Franciscans rarely experience.

Citron. 5484 College Ave. (off the northeastern end of Broadway between Taft and Lawton sts.) ☎ **510/653-5484.** Main courses $12–$18. MC, V. Daily 5:30–9:30pm. FRENCH/MEDITERRANEAN.

This petite, adorable French bistro was an instant smash when it first opened in 1992, and it continues to draw raves for its small yet enticingly eclectic menu. Chef Chris Rossi draws the flavors of France, Italy, and Spain together with fresh California produce for Chez Panisse–like results. Though the menu changes every few weeks, dishes range from grilled Colorado lamb sirloin with wild mushroom spoon bread and rosemary jus, to osso buco of lamb on a bed of flageolet bean and sun-dried tomato ragoût and sprinkled with a pistachio gremolata garnish. The fresh salads and citron "40 clove" chicken are also superb.

✪ **Oliveto Restaurant.** Rockridge Market Hall, 5655 College Ave. (off the northeastern end of Broadway at Keith St., across from the Rockridge BART station). ☎ **510/547-5356.** Reservations recommended. Main courses $16–$21. AE, DC, MC, V. Mon–Fri 11:30am–2pm, Mon–Sat 5:30–10pm, Sun 5–9pm. ITALIAN.

Paul Bertolli, former chef at the world-renowned Chez Panisse, jumped ship to open one of the top Italian restaurants in the Bay Area, and certainly the best in Oakland. During the week it's a madhouse at lunch, when BART commuters pile in for the wood-fired pizzas and tapas served in the restaurant's lower level. The main dining room upstairs—suavely bedecked with neo-Florentine decor and partial open kitchen—is packed nightly with fans of Bertolli's house-made pastas, sausages, and prosciutto. An assortment of pricey grills, braises, and roasts anchor the daily changing menu, but it's the reasonably priced pastas, pizzetas, and awesome salads that offer the most tang for your buck. *Tip:* There's free parking in the lot at the rear of the Market Hall building.

3 Sausalito

5 miles N of San Francisco

Just off the northern end of the Golden Gate Bridge is the eclectic little town of Sausalito, a slightly bohemian, nonchalant, and studiedly quaint adjunct to San Francisco. With approximately 7,500 residents, Sausalito feels rather like St. Tropez on the French Riviera—minus the starlets and the social rat race. It has its quota of paper millionaires, but they rub their permanently suntanned shoulders with a good number of hard-up artists, struggling authors, shipyard workers, and fishers. Next to the swank restaurants, plush bars, and antique shops and galleries, you'll see hamburger joints, beer parlors, and secondhand bookstores.

Above all, Sausalito has scenery and sunshine, for once you cross the Golden Gate Bridge you're out of the San Francisco fog patch and under blue California sky (we hope). Almost all the tourist action, which is almost singularly limited to window shopping and eating, takes place at sea level on Bridgeway.

ESSENTIALS

The **Golden Gate Ferry Service** fleet, Ferry Building (☎ **415/923-2000**), operates between the San Francisco Ferry Building, at the foot of Market Street, and downtown Sausalito. Service is frequent, departing at reasonable intervals every day of the year except New Year's Day, Thanksgiving Day, and Christmas Day. Phone for exact schedule. The ride takes a half hour and costs $4.25 for adults and $3.20 for kids 6 to 12. Senior and disabled passengers ride for $2.10; children 5 and under ride free.

Ferries of the **Blue & Gold Fleet** (☎ **415/773-1188** or 415/705-5555) leave from Pier 43½ (Fisherman's Wharf) and cost $11 round-trip, half price for kids 5 to 11. Boats run on a seasonal schedule; call for departure information.

By car from San Francisco, take U.S. 101 north, then the first right after the Golden Gate Bridge (Alexander exit). Alexander becomes Bridgeway in Sausalito.

EXPLORING THE TOWN

Sausalito's main touring strip is **Bridgeway,** which runs along the water, but those in the know make a quick detour to **Caledonia Street** 1 block inland. Not only is it less congested, there's a far better selection of cafes and shops.

Bay Model Visitors Center. 2100 Bridgeway. ☎ **415/332-3871.** Free admission. Winter, Tues–Sat 9am–4pm; summer, Tues–Fri 9am–4pm, Sat–Sun 10am–6pm.

The U.S. Army Corps of Engineers uses this high-tech, 1½-acre model of San Francisco's bay and delta to resolve problems and observe what impact any changes in water flow will have. The model reproduces (in scale) the rise and fall of tides, the flows and currents of water, the mixing of fresh and salt water, and it indicates trends in sediment movement. There's a 10-minute film that explains it all and a tour, but the most interesting time to visit is when it's actually being used, so call ahead.

SHOPPING

Sausalito is a mecca for shoppers seeking handmade, original, and offbeat clothes and footwear, as well as arts and crafts. The town's best shops are in the nooks and crannies off Bridgeway and along Caledonia Street.

Village Fair, at 777 Bridgeway, is Sausalito's closest approximation to a mall. It's a complex of 30 shops, souvenir stores, coffee bars, and gardens. Among them, **Quest Gallery** (☎ 415/332-6832), which specializes in the works of celebrated California artists (many of whom sell exclusively through this store), is worth seeking out. **Burlwood Gallery,** 721 Bridgeway (☎ 415/332-6550), sells one-of-a-kind redwood furniture plus fine jewelry, hand-blown glass, and other interesting gifts.

Pegasus Leather Company, 28 Princess St., off Bridgeway (☎ 415/332-5624), specializes in beautiful leather clothing and accessories. The **Sausalito Country Store,** 789 Bridgeway (☎ 415/332-7890), sells oodles of handmade, country-style goods for the home and garden, many by local artists and artisans.

Finally, there's **Magnet Madness,** 795 Bridgeway (☎ 415/331-9226), which features something every one of us can actually afford: refrigerator magnets. Thousands of colorful and creative little gems, from Airedales to zucchini, are backed with a magnet and stuck to the walls of this irresistible store.

WHERE TO STAY

Casa Madrona. 801 Bridgeway, Sausalito, CA 94965. ☎ **800/567-9524** or 415/332-0502. Fax 415/332-2537. Website: www.casam.com. 34 rms. MINIBAR TEL. $138–$260 double; $448 Madrona Villa suite. Extra person $25. Free breakfast 7:30–9am. Two-night minimum stay on weekends. AE, MC, V. Parking $7.

Sooner or later most visitors to Sausalito look up and wonder at the ornate mansion on the hill. It's part of this hideaway, built in 1885 by a wealthy lumber baron. The epitome of luxury in its day, the mansion had slipped into decay when it was saved by Henri Deschamps and converted into a hotel and restaurant. Successive renovations and extensions have added a rambling, New England–style building to the hillside below the main house. Now a certified historic landmark, the hotel offers rooms, suites, and cottages. The 16 newest units are each uniquely decorated by different local designers and have panoramic views of the San Francisco skyline and bay. The mansion rooms are also decorated in a variety of styles; some have Jacuzzis, while others have fireplaces.

Mikayla Restaurant (☎ 415/331-5888) serves superb America West Coast cuisine—scallopine of leg of lamb with grilled leeks, caramelized scallops with crispy onion rings—in a beautiful setting orchestrated by renowned local artist/ designer Laurel Burch overlooking the bay and San Francisco sky-line. Open for dinner nightly from 6 to 9pm and for Sunday brunch from 10am to 2pm.

✪ **Inn Above The Tide.** 30 El Portal (next to the Sausalito Ferry Landing), Sausalito, CA 94965. ☎ **800/893-8433** or 415/332-9535. Fax 415/332-6714. 28 rooms, 2 suites. A/C TV TEL.

$205–$425 double (2-night minimum stay on weekends). Rates include continental breakfast. AE, MC, V. Parking $8.

Perched directly over the bay atop well-grounded pilings, this former luxury apartment complex underwent a $4 million transformation into one of Sausalito's—if not the Bay Area's—finest accommodations. It's view that clinches it: Every room comes with an unparalleled panorama of the San Francisco Bay, including a postcard-quality vista of the city glimmering in the distance. Should you manage to tear yourself away from your private deck (we were tempted to drag our mattress outside), you'll find that your sumptuously appointed room sports a romantic little fireplace, a vast sunken Jacuzzi tub, remote-control air-conditioning, and wondrously comfortable queen- or king-size beds. Be sure to request that your breakfast and newspaper be delivered to your deck, then cancel your early appointments: On sunny mornings, nobody checks out early.

WHERE TO DINE

Feng Nian Chinese Restaurant. 2650 Bridgeway (near Harbor Dr., before downtown Sausalito). ☎ **415/331-5300.** Lunch specials $4.50–$5.95; main courses $6.55–$14. AE, DISC, MC, V. Mon and Wed–Thurs 11:30am–9:30pm, Fri–Sat 11:30am–10pm, Sun 12:30–9:30pm. CHINESE.

A pretty restaurant serving fine quality Chinese food, Feng Nian has such a wide selection of appetizers that a combination of several would make a delicious meal in itself. Choosing one of the chef's suggestions isn't easy. The crispy roast duck is a personal favorite, but if you'd like an assortment, try the flaming combination (enough for two) that includes egg roll, fried prawn, paper-wrapped chicken, barbecued ribs, fried chicken, and teriyaki. If you enjoy seafood, try the twice-sizzling seafood, with prawns, scallops, squid, and fresh vegetables in oyster sauce; it's prepared at your table. Beef dishes are prepared in a variety of ways, from Mongolian to Mandarin. There's also a number of main courses for vegetarians.

Guernica. 2009 Bridgeway. ☎ **415/332-1512.** Reservations recommended. Main courses $10–$17. AE, MC, V. Daily 5–10pm. FRENCH/BASQUE.

Established in 1976, Guernica is one of those funky old kinds of restaurants that you'd probably pass up for something more chic and modern down the street if you didn't know better. Be sure to call ahead and order Guernica's legendary paella valenciana in advance, and bring a partner 'cause it's served for two but will feed three. Other main courses range from grilled rabbit with a spicy red diablo sauce to a hearty rack of lamb Guernica and medaillons of pork loin with baked apples and calvados. Rich desserts include such in-season specialties as strawberry tart, peach Melba, and Basque-style rice pudding.

Horizons. 558 Brideway. ☎ **415/331-3232.** Reservations accepted weekdays only. Main courses $9–$19, salads and sandwiches $6–$11. AE, MC, V. Mon–Fri 11am–11pm, Sat–Sun 10am–11pm. 2 hours free valet parking. SEAFOOD/AMERICAN.

Eventually, every San Franciscan ends up at Horizons to meet a friend for Sunday Bloody Marys. It's not much to look at from the outside, but it gets better as you head past the funky dark-wood interior toward the waterside terrace. On warm days it's worth the wait for alfresco seating, if only to watch dreamy sailboats glide past San Francisco's distant skyline. The food here can't touch the view, but it's well portioned and satisfying enough. Seafood dishes are the main items, including steamed clams and mussels, freshly shucked oysters, and a variety of seafood pastas. In fine Marin tradition, Horizons has an "herb tea and espresso" bar, and is a totally nonsmoking restaurant.

WHERE TO STOCK UP FOR A PICNIC—& WHERE TO ENJOY IT

Even Sausalito's naysayers have to admit that it's hard not to enjoy eating your way down Bridgeway on a warm, sunny day. If the crowds are too much or the prices too steep at the bayside restaurants, grab a bite to go for an impromptu picnic in the park fronting the marina.

Small, clean, cute, and cheap, **Café Soleil,** 37 Caledonia St. (☎ **415/331-9355**), whips up some good soups, salads, and sandwiches along with killer smoothies. Order to go at the counter, then take your goods a block over to the marina for a dock side lunch.

Caledonia Kitchen, 400 Caledonia St. (☎ **415/331-0220**), is the sort of place you wish was just around the corner from your house—a beautiful little cafe serving a huge assortment of fresh salads, soups, chili, gourmet sandwiches, and inexpensive entrees like herbed roast chicken or vegetarian lasagna for only $4.95. Continental-style breakfast items and good coffee and espresso drinks are also on the menu.

Like the name says, the specialty at tiny, narrow **Hamburgers,** 737 Bridgeway (☎ **415/332-9471**), is juicy flame-broiled burgers, arguably Marin County's best. Look for the rotating grill in the window off Bridgeway, then stand in line and salivate with the rest. Chicken burgers are a slightly healthier option. Order a side of fries, grab a bunch of napkins, then head over to the park across the street.

You can get anything at **The Stuffed Croissant,** 43 Caledonia St. (☎ **415/332-7103**), from a snack to a meal. There are all sorts of gourmet stuffed croissants, as well as bagels, soups, and stews. Hot, cheap meals such as chicken curry with rice are also popular. For dessert there's carrot cake, fudge and peanut brownies, and more.

Classic, European-style **Venice Gourmet Delicatessen,** 625 Bridgeway (☎ **415/332-3544**), has all the makings for a superb picnic: wines, cheese, fruits, stuffed vine leaves, salads, quiche, delicious sandwiches (made to order on sourdough bread), and fresh-baked pastries.

4 Angel Island & Tiburon

8 miles N of San Francisco

A federal and state wildlife refuge, **Angel Island** is the largest of the San Francisco Bay's three islets (the others being Alcatraz and Yerba Buena). The island has been, at various times, a prison, a quarantine station for immigrants, a missile base, and even a favorite site for duels. Nowadays, though, most of the people who visit here are content with picnicking on the large green lawn that fronts the docking area. Loaded with the appropriate recreational supplies, they claim a barbecue, plop their fannies down on the lush green grass, and while away an afternoon free of phones, televisions, and traffic. Hiking, mountain biking, and guided tram tours are also popular options.

Tiburon, situated on a peninsula of the same name, looks like a cross between a fishing village and a Hollywood western set—imagine San Francisco reduced to toy dimensions. This seacoast town rambles over a series of green hills and ends up at a spindly, multicolored pier on the waterfront, like a Fisherman's Wharf in miniature. But in reality it's an extremely plush patch of yacht-club suburbia, as you'll see by both the marine craft and the homes of their owners. **Main Street** is lined with ramshackle, color-splashed old frame houses that shelter chic boutiques, souvenir stores, antique shops, and art galleries. Other roads are narrow, winding, and hilly, and lead up to dramatically situated homes that have spectacular views of San Francisco's skyline and the islands in the bay.

ESSENTIALS

Ferries of the **Blue & Gold Fleet** (☎ **415/773-1188** or 415/705-5555) leave from San Francisco's Pier 43½ (Fisherman's Wharf) and travel to both Angel Island and Tiburon. On weekdays, ferries operate from Tiburon to the Ferry Building, at the foot of Market Street. Boats run on a seasonal schedule; call for departure information. The round-trip fare is $10 to Angel Island, $11 to Tiburon; it's half-price for kids 5 to 11.

By car from San Francisco, take U.S. 101 to the Tiburon/Calif. 131 exit, then follow Tiburon Boulevard for about 5 miles into downtown Tiburon, and turn right onto Main Street. It's a 40-minute drive from San Francisco. Catch the ferry (☎ **415/435-2131** or 415/388-6770) to Angel Island from the dock located at Tiburon Boulevard and Main Street. The 15-minute round-trip, which only runs on weekends, costs $6 adult, $4 children 5 to 11, and $1 for bikes.

ANGEL ISLAND

Passengers disembark from the ferry at **Ayala Cove,** a small marina abutting a huge lawn area equipped with tables, benches, barbecue pits, and rest rooms. Also at Ayala Cove is a small store, gift shop, cafe (with surprisingly good grub), and overpriced mountain-bike rental shop (helmets included).

Among the 12 miles of Angel Island's hiking and mountain-bike trails is the **Perimeter Road,** a partly paved path that circles the island and winds its way past disused troop barracks, former gun emplacements, and other military buildings; several turnoffs lead up to the top of Mount Livermore, 776 feet above the bay. Sometimes referred to as the "Ellis Island of the West," from 1910 to 1940 Angel Island was used as a holding area for Chinese immigrants awaiting their citizenship papers. You can still see some faded Chinese characters on the walls of the barracks where the immigrants were held. During the warmer months you can camp at a limited number of sites; reservations are required.

Also offered at Angel Island are guided **sea kayak tours**. The all-day trips, which include a catered lunch, combine the thrill of paddling stable one-, two-, or three-person kayaks with an informative, naturalist-led tour that encircles the island (conditions permitting). All equipment is provided, kids are welcome, and no experience is necessary. Rates run about $100 per person. For more information, call **Sea Trek** at ☎ **415/488-1000**.

For recorded information on **Angel Island State Park,** call ☎ **415/435-1915.**

TIBURON

The main thing to do in Tiburon is stroll along the waterfront, pop into the stores, and spend an easy $50 on drinks and appetizers before heading back to the city. For a taste of the Wine Country, stop in at **Windsor Vineyards,** 72 Main St. (☎ **800/214-9463** or 415/435-3113), where 35 choices are available for a free tasting in their Victorian tasting room. Carry-packs are available (they hold six bottles). Ask about personalized labels for your own selections. The shop is open daily from 10am to 6pm (Friday and Saturday till 7pm).

WHERE TO DINE

Guaymas. 5 Main St. ☎ **415/435-6300.** Main courses $12–$18. AE, CB, DC, MC, V. Mon–Thurs 11:30am–10pm, Fri–Sat 11:30am–11pm, Sun 10:30am–10pm MEXICAN.

Guaymas offers authentic Mexican regional cuisine and a spectacular panoramic view of San Francisco and the Bay. In good weather, the two outdoor patios are almost always packed with diners soaking in the sun and scene. If it's chilly outside, a beehive-shaped adobe fireplace warms the colorful dining room.

Guaymas is named after a fishing village on Mexico's Sea of Cortez, and both the town and the restaurant are famous for their camarones (giant shrimp). In addition, the restaurant features ceviche, handmade tamales, and charcoal-grilled beef, seafood, and fowl. Save room for dessert, especially the scrumptious fritter with "drunken" bananas and ice cream. In addition to a good selection of California wines, the restaurant offers an exceptional variety of tequilas, Mexican beers, and mineral waters flavored with flowers, grains, and fruits.

Sam's Anchor Café. 27 Main St. ☎ **415/435-4527.** Main courses $8–$16. AE, MC, V. Mon–Thurs 11am–10pm, Fri 11am–10:30pm, Sat 10am–10:30pm, Sun 9:30am–10pm. SEAFOOD.

Summer Sundays are liveliest in Tiburon, when weekend boaters tie up to the docks at waterside restaurants like this one, the kind of place where you and your cronies can take off your shoes and have a fun, relaxed time eating burgers and drinking margaritas outside on the pier. The fare is pretty typical—sandwiches, salads, and seafood such as deep-fried oysters—but the quality and selection of the food is inconsequential: Beers, burgers, and a designated driver are all you really need.

Sweden House Bakery-Café. 35 Main St. ☎ **415/435-9767.** Reservations not accepted. Omelets $6.50–$7; sandwiches $6–$8. MC, V. Mon–Fri 8am–6pm, Sat–Sun 8am–7pm. SWEDISH/AMERICAN.

This small, cozy cafe with gingham-covered walls adorned with copperware and kitchen utensils is a local favorite. On sunny mornings there's no better seat in the Bay Area than on the bakery's terrace, where you can nurse an espresso and pastry while gazing out over the bay. Full breakfasts are served, too, all accompanied by toasted Swedish limpa bread; skip the eggs and bacon routine and go with the tasty Swedish pancakes: lingonberry, blueberry, and apple. At lunch, there's typical American fare plus traditional open-face sandwiches, including avocado and bacon or asparagus tips rolled in Danish ham. Beer and wine are available.

5　Muir Woods & Mount Tamalpais

12 miles N of the Golden Gate Bridge

While the rest of Marin County's redwood forests were being devoured to feed the building spree in San Francisco around the turn of the century, the trees of **Muir Woods,** in a remote ravine on the flanks of **Mount Tamalpais,** escaped destruction in favor of easier pickings.

MUIR WOODS

Although the magnificent California redwoods have been successfully transplanted to five continents, their homeland is a 500-mile strip along the mountainous coast of southwestern Oregon and northern California. The coast redwood, or *Sequoia sempervirens,* is the tallest tree in the immediate region, and the largest-known specimen towers 367.8 feet. It has an even larger relative, the *Sequoiadendron giganteum* of the California Sierra Nevada, but the coastal variety is stunning enough. Soaring toward the sky like a wooden cathedral, it's unlike any other forest in the world and an experience you won't soon forget.

Muir Woods is tiny compared to the Redwood National Forest farther north, but you can still get a good idea of what it must have been like when these redwood giants dominated the entire coastal region. What is truly amazing is that they exist a mere 6 miles (as the crow flies) from San Francisco; close enough, unfortunately, that tour buses arrive in droves on the weekends. You can, however, avoid the masses by hiking up the Ocean View Trail and returning via the Fern Creek Trail—a moderate hike that shows off the woods' best sides and leaves the lazy-butts behind.

To reach Muir Woods from San Francisco, cross the Golden Gate Bridge heading north on U.S. 101, take the Stinson Beach/Calif. 1 exit heading west, and follow the signs (and the traffic). The park is open daily from 8am to sunset, and while there's no admission, a donation box is posted out front to prompt your conscience. There's also a small gift shop, educational displays, and docent-led tours that you're welcome to stand in on. For more information, call the **Muir Woods information line** (☎ **415/388-2595**).

MOUNT TAMALPAIS

The birthplace of mountain biking, Mount Tam—as the locals call it—is Bay Area's favorite outdoor playground and the most dominant mountain in the region. Most every local has his or her secret trail and scenic overlook, as well as an opinion on the dilemma between mountain bikers and hikers (a touchy subject around here). The main trails—mostly fire roads—see a lot of foot and bicycle traffic on the weekends, particularly on clear, sunny days when you can see 100 miles in all directions, from the foothills of the Sierra to the western horizon. It's a great place to escape from the city for a leisurely hike and to soak in the breathtaking views of the bay.

To get to Mount Tamalpais by car, cross the Golden Gate Bridge heading north on U.S. 101 and take the Stinson Beach/Calif. 1 exit; follow the shoreline highway about 2¹/₂ miles and turn onto the Panoramic Highway heading west. After about 5¹/₂ miles, turn onto Pantoll Road and continue for about a mile to Ridgecrest Boulevard. Ridgecrest winds to a parking lot below East Peak. From there, it's a 15-minute hike up to the top.

6 Half Moon Bay

28 miles SW of San Francisco

A mere 45-minute drive from San Francisco is a heavenly little seaside hamlet called Half Moon Bay, one of the finest—and friendliest—small towns on the California coast. While other coastal communities take strides to make tourists unwelcome, Half Moon Bay residents are disarmingly amicable, bestowing a greeting to anyone and everyone who stops for a visit. Half Moon Bay is a peaceful, unfettered slice of textbook California: pristine beaches, redwood forests, nature preserves, rustic fishing harbors, horse ranches, organic farms, and host of superb inns and restaurants—everything you need for the perfect getaway.

ESSENTIALS

There's no public transportation to Half Moon Bay. There are two ways to get here by car: the fast way and the scenic way. To save time, take Calif. 92 West from either I-280 or Calif. 101 out of San Francisco, which will take you over a small mountain range and drop you directly into Half Moon Bay. A better—and far prettier—route is via Calif. 1, which technically starts at the south end of the Golden Gate Bridge and veers southwest to the shoreline a few miles south of Daly City. Both routes are clearly marked with numerous signs, so don't worry about getting lost.

Downtown Half Moon Bay, however, is easy to miss since it's not on Calif. 1, but a few hundred yards inland. Head 2 blocks up Calif. 92 from the Calif. 1 intersection, then turn south at the Shell gas station onto Main Street; follow it until you cross a small bridge.

For more information, call the **Half Moon Bay Coastside Chamber of Commerce** at ☎ **650/726-8380.**

Note: Temperatures rarely venture into the 70s in Half Moon Bay, so be sure to pack for cool—and often wet—weather.

EXPLORING HALF MOON BAY & ENVIRONS

The best things to do in Half Moon Bay are the same things the locals do. For example, there's a wonderful **paved beach trail** that winds 3 miles from Half Moon Bay to picturesque **Pillar Point Harbor,** where you can watch the trawlers unload their daily catch. Walking, biking, jogging, and skating are all kosher, and be sure to keep a lookout for dolphins and whales. Bicycles can be rented from the **Bicyclery,** 432 Main St. (☎ 650/726-6000). Prices range from $6 an hour to $24 all day.

Half Moon Bay is also known for its organically grown produce, and the best place to stock up on fruits and vegetables is the **Andreotti Family Farm,** a charming old-fashioned outfit that's been in business since 1926. Every Friday, Saturday, and Sunday a member of the Andreotti family slides open the door to their weathered old barn at 10am sharp to reveal a cornucopia of strawberries, artichokes, cucumbers, and such. The barn is at 227 Kelly Ave., off Calif. 1 (☎ 650/726-9461); head toward the beach and you'll see it on your right-hand side. Open 'til 6pm year-round.

A few miles up Calif. 92 is the **Obester Winery,** 12341 San Mateo Rd. (☎ 650/ 726-9463), a small wood shack filled with award-winning wines that are free for the tasting daily from 10am to 5pm.

Half Moon Bay has a spectacular second-growth redwood forest that few out-of-towners know about. Located on the western slopes of the Santa Cruz Mountains, **Purisima Creek Redwoods** (☎ 650/726-1200) is a lush preserve filled with fields of wildflowers, lush redwood forests, and fern-lined creek banks. It's accessible to hikers, mountain bikers, and equestrians, though you'll hardly see a soul on the weekdays. From the Calif. 1/Calif. 92 intersection in Half Moon Bay, drive 1 mile south on Calif. 1 to Higgins Purisima Creek Road, turn left, and continue 4¹/₂ miles to a small, unmarked gravel parking area at a sharp bend in the road and park.

BEACHES & PRESERVES   The 4-mile arc of golden-colored sand that rings Half Moon Bay is broken up into three state-run beaches—Dunes, Venice, and Francis—all a part of **Half Moon Bay State Beach.** There's a $4 per vehicle entrance fee for all three beaches. Though surfing is allowed, swimming isn't a good idea unless you happen to be cold-blooded.

When the surf's up, be sure to check out the bonzai surfers at **Maverick Beach,** located just south of the radar tracking station past Pillar Point Harbor. To get here, take Westpoint Road to the West Shoreline Access parking lot and follow the trail to the beach. While you're there, keep a lookout for sea lions basking on the offshore rocks. Also adjacent to the parking lot is tiny **Pillar Point Marsh,** a unique fresh- and saltwater marsh that's home and way station to nearly 20% of all North American bird species, from great blue herons to snowy egrets and red-winged black birds.

A few miles farther north on Calif. 1 is the **Fitzgerald Marine Reserve,** one of the most diverse tidal basins on the West Coast, as well as one of the safest, thanks to a wave-buffering rock terrace 50 yards from the beach. Call before coming to find out when it's low tide (all the sea creatures are hidden at high tide) and about the docent-led tour schedules (usually offered on Saturdays). Rubber-soled shoes are recommended. It's located at the west end of California Avenue off Calif. 1 in Moss Beach; (☎ 650/728-3584).

Sixteen miles south of Half Moon Bay on Calif. 1 (at the turnoff to Pescadero) is the **Pescadero Marsh Natural Preserve,** one of the few remaining natural marshes left on the central California coast. Part of the Pacific flyway, it's a resting stop for nearly 200 bird species, including great blue herons that nest in the northern row of eucalyptus trees. Passing through the marsh is the mile-long Sequoia Audubon Trail, accessible from the parking lot at Pescadero State Beach on Calif. 1 (the trail starts below the Pescadero Creek Bridge). Docent-led tours take place every Saturday at 10:30am and every Sunday at 1pm, weather permitting; call ☎ **650/ 879-0832.**

Starting in December and continuing through March, the **Año Nuevo State Reserve** is home to one of California's most amazing animal attractions: the hallowed breeding grounds of the northern elephant seal. Every winter people reserve tickets months in advance for a chance to witness a fearsome clash between the 2¹/₂-ton bulls over mating privileges among the harems of females. Reservations are required for the 2¹/₂-hour naturalist-led tours (held rain or shine December 15 to March 31). For tickets and tour information, call ☎ **800/444-7275.** Even if it's not mating season, you can still see the elephant seals lolling around the shore almost year-round, particularly between April and August when they come ashore to molt.

OUTDOOR ACTIVITIES   One of the most popular activities in town is horseback riding along the beach. **Sea Horse Ranch** (a.k.a. Friendly Acres Horse Ranch), on Calif. 1 a mile north of Half Moon Bay (☎ **650/726-2362** or 650/726-8550), offers guided and unguided rides along the beach or on well-worn trails for about $35. It's open daily from 8am to 6pm.

For golfers, there's **Half Moon Bay Golf Links,** 2000 Fairway Dr., at the south end of Half Moon Bay next to the Half Moon Bay Lodge (☎ **650/726-6384**). Designed by Arnold Palmer, the oceanside 18-hole course has been rated among the top 100 courses in the country, as well as no. 1 in the Bay Area. Greens fees range from $50 to $100. Reserve your tee time as far in advance as possible.

SHOPPING   Main Street is a shopper's paradise. Dozens of small stores and boutiques line the ¹/₄-mile strip, selling everything from feed and tack to custom furniture and camping gear. From north to south, must-stops include the **Buffalo Shirt Company**, 315 Main St. (☎ **650/726-3194**), which carries a fine selection of casual wear, Indian rugs, and outdoor gear; **Cartwheels,** 330 Main St. (☎ **650/726-6060**), a nifty store specializing in rustic wood furniture, rugs, and toys; and **Half Moon Bay Feed & Fuel**, 331 Main St. (☎ **650/726-4814**), a great place to pick up a treat for your pet. **Cedanna,** 421 Main St. (☎ **650/726-6776**) is loaded with colorful glassware and unusual home accessories. **Cunha's Country Store,** 448 Main St. (☎ **650/726-4071**), the town's beloved grocery and general store, is a mandatory stop for regular visitors from the Bay Area. And, of course, what would Half Moon Bay be without a good bookstore like **Coastside Books,** 521 Main St. (☎ **650/726-5889**), which also carries a fair selection of children's books and postcards.

End your shopping spree with a stop at **Cottage Industries,** 621 Main St. (☎ **650/712-8078**) to marvel at the high-quality hand-crafted furniture, as well as the western wear, jewelry, and saddlery next door at **Coyote Creek,** 641 Main St. (☎ **650/712-8731**).

WHERE TO STAY

✪ **Cypress Inn on Miramar Beach.** 407 Mirada Rd., Half Moon Bay, CA 94019. ☎ **800/ 83-BEACH** or 650/726-6002. Fax 650/712-0380. 12 rms. TV TEL (in Beach House rooms only). $150–$275. Rates include breakfast, afternoon tea, and wine and hors d'oeuvres. AE, MC, V. Go 3 miles north of the junction of Calif. 92 and Calif. 1, then turn west on Medio and take it to the end.

Easily our favorite place to stay in Half Moon Bay, the Cypress Inn is blissfully free of Victorian charm. Instead you have a modern, artistically designed building infused with colorful native folk art and rustic furniture. Each room has a billowy feather bed, private balcony, gas fireplace, private bath, and an unobstructed ocean view. Adjacent to the inn are four Beach House rooms equipped with built-in stereo systems and hidden TVs, though they lack the Santa-Fe–meets–California effect that we adore in the main house. The ace in the hole, however, is that it's the only B&B perched right on the beach.

Harbor House. 346 Princeton Ave. (3¹/₂ miles north of Half Moon Bay west of Pillar Point Harbor), Half Moon Bay, CA 94019. ☎ **650/728-1572.** Fax 650/728-8271. 6 rms, 1 penthouse. TV TEL. $125–$175 double, $200–$250 penthouse. MC, V. Rates include complimentary continental breakfast.

If all you're looking for is a clean, quiet, moderately priced inn with a clear view of the ocean, you'll be very satisfied with Chris Mickelsen's spanking new Harbor House. Each room is simply yet pleasantly decorated with natural wood and wicker furnishings, queen beds with down comforters, kitchenettes, tile floors, and fireplace. A major plus is that they also come with private decks or patios overlooking the cool blue Pacific. The "penthouse" is a barn-sized studio overlooking the ocean that could easily house and feed a Girl Scout contingent—a real bargain for families or groups. There's even access to a gym across the street.

The Zaballa House. 324 Main St. (at the north end of town), Half Moon Bay, CA 94019. ☎ **650/726-9123.** Fax 650/726-3921. 12 units. $80–$250 double. Rates include breakfast, afternoon tea, and wine and hors d'oeuvres. AE, DISC, MC, V.

The oldest building in Half Moon Bay, this pale-blue Victorian is decidedly pretty and unpretentious. Simon, the British innkeeper, is an immediately likable bloke who has a gift for making you feel like a favored guest. The nine guest rooms in the main house are pleasantly decorated with understated wallpaper and country furniture; some have fireplaces, vaulted ceilings, or Jacuzzi tubs, and all have private baths. Three new mini-suites have been added behind the main house, each equipped with a kitchenette, double Jacuzzi, fireplace, TV/VCR, and private deck (our favorite is the Casablanca room, which comes with an eponymous video). None have telephones, but guests are welcome to use the phone in the front parlor. Prices are quite reasonable considering the amenities and central location.

WHERE TO DINE

Barbara's Fish Trap. 281 Capistrano Rd., Princeton. ☎ **650/728-7049.** Main courses $10–$15. No credit cards. Daily 11am–9:30pm. SEAFOOD.

You wouldn't expect a place called Barbara's Fish Trap to be fancy, and guess what? It ain't. Perched on pillars above the Pillar Point Harbor, this down-home fish grotto—complete with checkered plastic tablecloths and fishnets on the ceilings—offers a large selection of deep-fried seafood as well as broiled items such as tangy Cajun-spiced snapper. The garlic prawns and steamed mussels are among their better dishes, as are the fish-and-chips. Be sure to check out the specials board hanging on the south wall for the day's fresh catch.

✪ **Pasta Moon.** 315 Main St, Half Moon Bay. ☎ **650/726-5125.** Reservations recommended. Main courses $12.95–$16.95. AE, DISC, MC, V. Lunch, Mon–Fri 11:30am–2:30pm, Sat noon–3pm; dinner, Sun–Thurs 5:30–9:30pm, Fri–Sat 5:30–10pm; brunch, Sun 11am–2:30pm. ITALIAN.

When visitors ask, "Where the best place to eat around here?," the inevitable answer is Pasta Moon, a handsome nouveau-Italian restaurant in downtown Half Moon Bay, where everything's prepared from scratch using only the freshest ingredients. Chef Sean Lynd's pasta dishes, always freshly made and perfectly cooked, earn the highest recommendations. We love the house-made black pepper fettuccine with spicy calabrese sausage and braised winter greens, and the hand-cut papperdelle with sweet fennel sausage, tomatoes, and creme. For dessert, try the wonderful tiramisu.

✪ **Mezza Luna.** 3048 N. Cabrillo Hwy. (Calif. 1), Half Moon Bay. ☎ **650/712-9223.** Reservations recommended. DISC, MC, V. Lunch, Mon–Sat 11:30am–3pm; dinner, Sun–Thurs 5:30–10pm, Fri–Sat 5:30–10:30pm. ITALIAN.

Though Pasta Moon serves excellent Italian food, it's not truly *authentic* Italian. For that, there's Mezza Luna. Run by a gaggle of suave, soft-spoken Italian men, the red-and-green cinder-block building looks rather cheesy from the outside, but things get better as you enter, and all is forgiven when you bite into the *antipasto della casa*, a large platter of marinated grilled vegetables doused with the perfect blend of extra-virgin olive oil and red wine vinegar. Among the entrees, the *penne del pastore*— perfectly cooked tube pasta quenched with a tangy tomato sauce, fresh eggplant, and topped with aged ricotta cheese—is delicious. Heck, even the dipping sauce for the warm focaccia bread is fantastic. The wine list and decor could use more work, but as far as the food goes there's little room for improvement.

✪ **Sushi Main Street.** 696 Mill St., Half Moon Bay. ☎ **650/726-6336.** Main courses $5–$10. MC. Mon–Sat 11:30am–2:30pm and 5–9pm, Sun 5–9pm. JAPANESE.

Who'da thunk that one of the most exquisite Japanese restaurants in California would be in tiny Half Moon Bay? Chef/owner Hirohito Shigeta started out his business 9 years ago in a tiny space on Main Street and kept the old name when he moved into larger digs down the street. His wife Karolynne—an interior designer with impeccable taste—in turn decorated the new space with her vast collection of museum-quality Balinese artifacts, and the result is astoundingly beautiful. But even if it looked like the inside of a trailer home, it would still be worth a visit for the exceptional sushi, tempura, and soba, prepared in part by Andrew, one of the few *gai-jin* (white man) sushi chefs on the West Coast. Adventurous sushi warriors will want to try the New Zealand roll (mussels, radish, sprouts, avocado, and teriyaki), the unagi papaya, and the marinated salmon roll with cream cheese and spinach. For a traditional shoeless Japanese meal, request the knee-high table perched in the corner.

7 San Jose & Environs

45 miles SE of San Francisco

Some may mourn the San Jose of yesterday, a sleepy small town of orchards, crops, and cattle, but those days are long gone. Founded in 1717 and previously dwelling in the shadows of San Francisco, San Jose is now Northern California's largest city. With surveys that declare it one of the safest and sunniest cities in the country and rank it the fifth most popular place to live in America, San Jose is a force to be reckoned with. Today the prosperity of Silicon Valley has transformed what was once an agricultural backwater into a thriving city of restaurants, shops, a state-of-the-art light rail system, a sports arena (go Sharks!), and a reputable art scene.

ESSENTIALS

GETTING THERE   BART (☎ 510/465-2278) travels from San Francisco to Fremont in 1¼ hours; you can take a bus from there. **Cal train** (☎ 800/660-4287) operates frequently from San Francisco and takes about an hour and 25 minutes.

VISITOR INFORMATION   Contact the **San Jose Visitors Information & Business Center,** located in the San Jose McEvery Convention Center at 150 W. San Carlos St., San Jose, CA 95113 (☎ **408/977-0900**).

GETTING AROUND   Light Rail (☎ **408/321-2300**) is best for getting around. A ticket is good for 2 hours, and stops include Paramount's Great America, the Convention Center, and downtown museums. Or you can use the historic trolleys, which operate in a loop around downtown (summer only). Tickets can be purchased at Light Rail stations.

MUSEUMS WORTH SEEKING OUT

Downtown San Jose has several museums worth mentioning:

The **Tech Museum of Innovation,** 145 W. San Carlos St., between Market and Almaden Boulevard (☎ **408/279-7150**), allows visitors to grapple with modern technology. You can use CAD (computer-aided design) to create a bicycle and then test it in a wind tunnel, or learn about DNA (how *do* they develop bigger and better vegetables?) by experimenting with genetic models. Admission is $6 for adults, $4 for children 6 to 18 and seniors; open Tuesday to Sunday from 10am to 5pm.

The **San Jose Museum of Art,** 110 S. Market St. (☎ **408/294-2787**), is collaborating with New York's Whitney Museum for shows that trace the development of 20th-century American art. The 1998 series will include works by Mary Marsh and Patrick Dougherty, as well as exhibits such as the History of Street Photography and Photographs from the American Civil Rights Era. The newly renovated Historic Wing now includes a cafe, bookstore, and education center. Admission is $6 for adults, $3 for children 6 to 17 and seniors. Open Tuesday to Sunday 10am to 5pm (it's open until 8pm on Thursday).

The **Children's Discovery Museum**, 180 Woz Way (☎ **408/298-5437**), offers more than 150 interactive exhibits, as well as shows and workshops for kids, which explore science, humanities, arts, and technology. "ArtWorks Too!" is an art center offering a different art project for kids to work on each month, while "Bubbalogna," an exhibit that explores the whimsical and scientifically intriguing world of bubbles, also draws rave reviews. Smaller kids enjoy dressing up in costumes and playing on the fire truck. Admission is $6 for adults, $5 for seniors, and $4 for children 2 to 18. Open Tuesday to Saturday from 10am to 5pm, Sunday from noon to 5pm.

The **San Jose Historical Museum**, 1600 Senter Rd. (☎ **408/287-2290**), occupies 25 acres in Kelley Park and features 26 original and replica buildings that have been restored to represent life in 1880s San Jose. The usual cast of characters is here—the doctor, the printer, the postmaster—with an occasional local surprise, such as the 1888 Chinese temple and the original Stevens fruit barn. Admission is $4 for adults, $3 for seniors, $2 for children 4 to 17. Open Tuedsay to Sunday from 11am to 4pm.

The **Rosicrucian Egyptian Museum & Planetarium**, 1342 Naglee Ave. (☎ **408/947-3635** or 408/947-3635), is associated with an educational organization that traces its origins back to the ancient Egyptians, who strongly believed in the afterlife and reincarnation. On display are human and animal mummies, funerary boats, and canopic jars, as well as jewelry, pottery, and bronze tools. There's also a replica of a noble Egyptian's tomb. Admission is $7 for adults, $5 for seniors, and $3.50 for children 6 to 15. Open Wednesday to Tuesday from 10am to 5pm. Call for show times at the Planetarium, which costs $4 for adults, $3 for children.

THEME PARK THRILLS

Paramount's Great America, Great America Parkway (off U.S. 101), Santa Clara (☎ **408/988-1776**), provides 100 acres of family entertainment. A pretty cool place

The Winchester Mystery House

Begun in 1884, the **Winchester Mystery House,** at 525 S. Winchester Blvd., San Jose (☎ **408/247-2101**), is a monument to one woman's paranoia. It's the legacy of Sarah L. Winchester, widow of the son of the famous rifle magnate. After the deaths of her husband and baby daughter, Mrs. Winchester consulted with a seer, who proclaimed that the family had been targeted by the evil spirits of those killed with Winchester repeaters, who would only be appeased by perpetual construction on the Winchester mansion. Convinced that she'd live as long as the building continued, the widow used much of her $20 million inheritance to finance the construction, which went on 24 hours a day, 7 days a week, 365 days a year, for 38 years. (Ricki Lake would love to have her as a guest, we're sure.)

As you can probably guess, this is no ordinary home. With 160 rooms, it sprawls across a half-dozen acres. And it's full of disturbing features: a staircase leading nowhere, a Tiffany window with a spiderweb design, and doors that open onto blank walls. There are 13 bathrooms, 13 windows and doors in the old sewing room, 13 palms lining the main driveway, 13 hooks in the seance room, and chandeliers with 13 lights. Such schemes were designed to confound the spirits that seemed to plague the heiress.

Touring the house and grounds costs $13.50 for adults, $10.50 for seniors, and $7.50 for children 6 to 12. Tours leave about every 15 minutes. The house is open daily from 9am to 8pm.

to lose your lunch, the park includes such favorites as the Top Gun suspended jet coaster, the Days of Thunder auto-racing simulator, a 3-acre Nickelodeon Center for children, "Drop Zone" (the world's tallest free-fall ride), and the new Xtreme Skyflyer, which combines skydiving with hang gliding. Be sure to check for concerts and special events. Admission is $28.99 for adults, $18.99 for seniors, and $15.99 for children 3 to 6. Open Saturdays and Sundays from 10am to 9pm from March 15 through May 29; daily from 10am to 9pm May 29 through August 25; and Saturdays and Sundays from 10am to 9pm August 30 through October 18 (the schedule is subject to change due to weather, so be sure to call ahead). From San Francisco, take U.S. 101 south for about 45 miles to the Great America Parkway exit.

WHERE TO STAY

Fairmont. 170 S. Market St., San Jose, CA 95113. ☎ **408/998-1900.** Fax 408/287-1648. 541 rms. A/C MINI BAR TV TEL. $169–$229 double; $325–$1800 suite. AE, DC, DISC, JCB, MC, V.

Ideally situated near the Convention Center and the Center of Performing Arts, this hotel is in a landmark building. A popular spot to have afternoon tea or cocktails, the lobby attracts many who are just passing through. From the lobby to the rooms—which offer many modern features including fax and high-speed modem lines—the emphasis is on comfort. Amenities include 24-hour room service, concierge, laundry/valet, and a rooftop pool on the fourth floor surrounded by tropical foliage. Three restaurants are available, including Les Saisons for fine French/continental cuisine, a Chinese restaurant, and a coffee shop that's nicely accented with a massive marble soda fountain.

Hotel De Anza. 233 W. Santa Clara St., San Jose, CA 95113. ☎ **800/843-3700** or 408/ 286-1000. Fax 408/286-0500. 100 rms. A/C TV TEL. $175–$220 double; $325 suite. Special weekend rates available. AE, DC, MC, V.

Located downtown in a landmark art deco building, this hotel is small enough to provide personal service. The room decor may reflect a 1930s style in the furnishings, but the amenities are state of the art. There are three telephones in each room, including one with data line and fax port, plus voice-mail service. Computers and fax machines are supplied on request. Additional amenities include a VCR and complimentary video rental. Bathrobes, a hair dryer, a makeup mirror, a TV, and a phone are also available in each bathroom. There's room service, laundry/valet, complimentary shoe shine, nightly turndown, and a health club with Nautilus machines. There's a club lounge as well as La Pastaia restaurant, which serves fine Italian cuisine.

WHERE TO DINE

Emile's. 545 S. 2nd St. ☎ **408/289-1960.** Reservations recommended. Main courses $20–$30. AE, CB, DC, DISC, MC, V. Fri 11:30am–2pm, Tues–Sat 6:30–9:30pm. CONTEMPORARY EUROPEAN.

Chef/proprietor Emile Mooser uses local ingredients to produce a tasty, contemporary cuisine. To start, try the seared and peppered foie gras with poached pears and arugula salad, or Mooser's interesting variation on French onion soup, made with Parmesan and gruyère cheese. Follow with a roasted pork tenderloin, served on a bed of creamy polenta, or perhaps the seared salmon served with baby artichokes, trumpet mushrooms, and a veal stock reduction. Mirrors, recessed lighting, and large, bold floral arrangements create an elegant atmosphere. For dessert, go with the warm chocolate truffle cake with raspberry sorbet.

Paolo's. 333 W. San Carlos St. ☎ **408/294-2558.** Reservations recommended. Main courses $7–$20. AE, CB, DC, MC, V. Mon–Fri 11am–2:30pm, Mon–Sat 5:30–10pm. REGIONAL/NORTHERN ITALIAN.

Paolo's attracts a business crowd at lunchtime and a rather cultured crowd in the evening. The cuisine is refined northern Italian, with innovative flourishes. Among the appetizers, for instance, the beef carpaccio is served with a piquant vegetable sauce. The main dishes might include sea scallops roasted with whole garlic, cherry tomatoes, and thyme, or a classic roasted quail with white raisins, grappa, and natural juices. Desserts also stretch beyond the typical Italian favorites to include a chocolate torte with orange-caramel sauce, or lemon-curd tart with toasted coconut and pistachio nuts. An extensive wine list features more than 600 selections.

OFF THE BEATEN TRACK: SARATOGA

Walk down Saratoga's Main Street and you're bound to get the feeling that the real world has yet to infiltrate this sprawl of expensive shops, restaurants, and homes that is not unlike a miniature Carmel. In addition to marveling at the seeming isolation of the town, be sure to check out the many small wineries in the area such as **Savanah Chanel Vineyards** (☎ **408/741-2930**).

WHERE TO STAY & DINE

The Inn at Saratoga. 20645 4th St., Saratoga, CA 95070. ☎ **800/338-5020** or 408/867-5020. Fax 408/741-0981. 45 rms, 4 suites. A/C TV TEL. $155 double; $235–$250 rm with whirlpool bath; from $430 suite. AE, DC, MC, V.

This small hotel overlooking Saratoga Creek and Wildwood Park provides a tranquil atmosphere. The rooms are spacious enough to contain sitting alcoves, with floor-to-ceiling windows that take advantage of the bucolic views. Units are pleasantly decorated in a contemporary style with floral bed covers; two suites have pencil four posters, and some offer whirlpool baths. Modern amenities include VCRs and computer-capable communications jacks. A continental breakfast that has all the trimmings, including scrumptious house made pastries, is available in the lobby or out on the attractive patio. Extra perks include complimentary newspaper, nightly turndown, tea, wine and hors d'oeuvres, and laundry/valet service.

✪ **Le Mouton Noir.** 14560 Big Basin Way, Saratoga. ☎ **408/867-7017.** Reservations required. Main courses $17.50–$26. AE, CB, DC, MC, V. Sat 11:30am–2pm; Mon–Fri 6–9pm, Sat 5:30–9pm, Sun 5–9pm. INTERNATIONAL.

The extraordinary food at Le Mouton Noir can satisfy a variety of tastes. Adventurous diners will enjoy the grilled tenderloin of farm-raised ostrich served with a blackberry cabernet sauce, while fans of classic European fare will love the oven-roasted rack of Australian lamb with Peruvian potatoes and artichoke pudding. Culinary top billing, however, goes to the tender medaillons of veal sauteed in shallot butter with prawns, white asparagus, and wild mushrooms. Among the extravagant desserts, choose the Tia Maria or the pots de crème. The decor is elegant and countryfied— a little too much so for us, but Martha Stewart would be proud. Try not to be too hungry when you arrive, as the portions are somewhat meager, in typical California-cuisine fashion.

GILROY & SAN JUAN BAUTISTA

A short drive down U.S. 101 from San Jose, **Gilroy** is famous for its garlic festival, which is held in July. Recently it has become known for its outlet shopping, too. For information, contact the **Gilroy Visitor's Bureau** at ☎ **408/842-6436.**

A little farther down, U.S. 101 brings you to **San Juan Bautista**, a historic town with a definite Spanish/Mexican flavor. **Mission San Juan Bautista** (open daily 9:30am to 5pm) is a serene outpost that looks out over meadowlands, and one can imagine how isolated it must have been when it was built in 1797. The interior walls are decorated with frescoes, while the reredos has six hand-carved painted wooden statues, including a life-size polychrome figure of San Juan Bautista. More than 4,000 Native Americans are buried in the cemetery beside the church.

A grassy plaza spreads in front of the mission; around it stand a nunnery (built in 1815), the Castro House, the Plaza Hotel (1858), and stables, which together constitute the **San Juan Bautista Historic Park** (☎ **408/623-4881**). Admission is $2 for adults and $1 for children, and it's open daily from 10am to 4:30pm.

The **Castro House** was the home of the Mexican administrator, José María Castro. In 1848 it was purchased by the Breen family, members of the Donner party who had survived 111 days stranded in the snow-bound Sierra Nevada in 1846.

The **Plaza Hotel** was a major stop on the stagecoach route in the mid-1800s when 10 or so stages passed through here daily. Once the railroad bypassed the town in 1876, it became a quiet backwater, which is why it has survived intact. The town's main street is lined with antique stores that are worth browsing and several Mexican restaurants. The big event here is the Annual Flea Market and Antique Show held in August. For additional information, contact the **San Juan Bautista Chamber of Commerce** at ☎ **408/623-2454.**

6 The Wine Country

by Erika Lenkert and Matthew R. Poole

California's Napa and Sonoma valleys are two of the most famous wine-growing regions in the world, and two of our favorite places to visit in the state. The workaday valleys that are a way of life for thousands of vintners are also the ultimate retreat for wine lovers and romantics. Hundreds of wineries are nestled among the vines, and most are open to visitors. But even if you don't want to wine-taste, the fresh country air, beautiful rolling countryside, and world-class restaurants and spas are reason enough to come. If you can, plan on spending more than a day here; you'll need a couple of days just to get to know one of the valleys. No matter how long you stay, you'll probably never get enough of the Wine Country's romantic, indulgent atmosphere.

While Napa and Sonoma are close to each other (about a half-hour drive apart), each is attraction-packed enough that your best bet is to focus on just one of the valleys, especially if your time is limited. We recommend that you read about each below, then decide which one is right for you—unless, of course, you're lucky enough to have time to explore both.

1 Napa Valley

Compared with its sister valley, Sonoma, Napa is a farther drive from San Francisco and is home to hundreds more wineries, which generally have more of a touristy, big-business-y feel to them. You'll still get plenty of rolling, mustard flower–covered hills and vast stretches of vineyards, but they come hand-in-hand with large, upscale restaurants; designer discount outlets; rows of hotels; and, in summer, plenty of traffic. But even with hordes of visitors year-round, Napa is still pretty sleepy, focusing on daytime attractions—wine tasting, outdoor activities, and spas—and fabulous food. Nightlife is very limited; but after indulging all day, most visitors are ready to turn in early anyway.

Napa Valley is relatively condensed. It's just 35 miles long, which means you can venture from one end to the other in less than a half hour (traffic permitting). Conveniently, most of the large wineries—as well as most of the hotels, shops, and restaurants—are located along a single road, Calif. 29, which starts at the mouth of the Napa River, near the north end of San Francisco Bay, and continues north

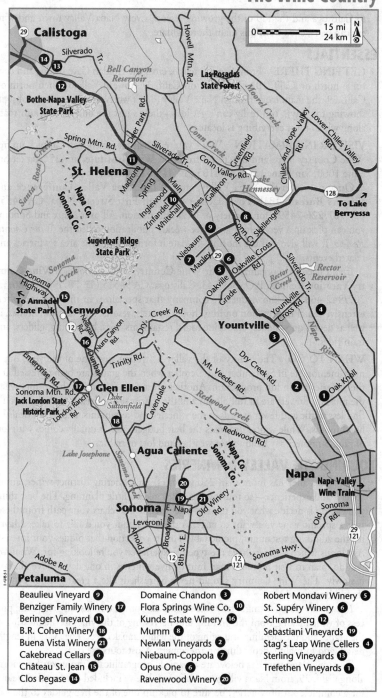

The Wine Country

0 ———— 15 mi
24 km
N

Calistoga (29)

Silverado Tr. (14) (13)

Bell Canyon Reservoir

Las Posadas State Forest

Howell Mtn. Rd.

Moore Creek

(12)

Bothe-Napa Valley State Park

Spring Mtn. Rd.

Dyer Park Rd.

Silverado Tr.

Conn Creek

Conn Valley Rd.

Greenfield Rd.

Chiles and Pope Valley Rd.

Lower Chiles Valley Rd.

St. Helena (11)

Madrona

Spring

Main

Inglewood

Zinfandel

Whitehall

Mees

Galleron

(10)

Lake Hennessey

(128)

To Lake Berryessa

Napa Co.
Sonoma Co.

Santa Rosa Creek

Sugarloaf Ridge State Park

Sonoma Creek

Niebaum (7)

Manley (9)

Conn G. Skellenger (8)

(29) (6)

(5)

Oakville Cross Rd.

Rector Creek

Rector Reservoir

Silverado Tr.

Sonoma Highway

To Annadel State Park →

Kenwood (15)

Creek Rd.

(12)

Nelligan Rd.

Adobe

Nuns Canyon Rd.

(16)

Trinity Rd.

Dry Creek Rd.

Oakville Grade

Yountville Cross Rd.

(4)

Yountville

(3)

Napa River

Oak Knoll

Enterprise Rd.

(17)

Glen Ellen

Lake Suttonfield

Mt. Veeder Rd.

Dry Creek Rd.

(2)

(1)

Sonoma Mtn. Rd.

Jack London State Historic Park

London Ranch Rd.

(18)

Cavendale Rd.

Redwood Creek

Redwood Rd.

Napa Co.
Sonoma Co.

Lake Josephine

Agua Caliente

Napa

Napa Valley Wine Train →

(20)

Sonoma Creek

(19) (21)

Old Winery Rd.

Sonoma

E. Napa

Leveroni

Old Sonoma Rd.

(29) (121)

Broadway

8th St. E.

Napa

Adobe Rd.

(12)

(12) (121)

Sonoma Hwy.

Petaluma

Beaulieu Vineyard (9)	Domaine Chandon (3)	Robert Mondavi Winery (5)
Benziger Family Winery (17)	Flora Springs Wine Co. (10)	St. Supéry Winery (6)
Beringer Vineyard (11)	Kunde Estate Winery (16)	Schramsberg (12)
B.R. Cohen Winery (18)	Mumm (8)	Sebastiani Vineyards (19)
Buena Vista Winery (21)	Newlan Vineyards (2)	Stag's Leap Wine Cellers (4)
Cakebread Cellars (6)	Niebaum-Coppola (7)	Sterling Vineyards (13)
Château St. Jean (15)	Opus One (6)	Trefethen Vineyards (1)
Clos Pegase (14)	Ravenwood Winery (20)	

to Calistoga and the top of the growing region. Every Napa Valley town and winery can be reached from this main thoroughfare.

ESSENTIALS

GETTING THERE   From San Francisco, cross the Golden Gate Bridge and continue north on Calif. 101. Turn east on Calif. 37 (toward Vallejo), then north on Calif. 29, the main road through Napa Valley (don't worry, there are plenty of signs showing the way). You really can't get lost—there's just the one north-south road, along which most everything is located.

VISITOR INFORMATION   While you're in San Francisco, you can pick up free Wine Country maps and brochures from the **Wine Institute,** at 425 Market St., Suite 1000, San Francisco, CA 94105 (☎ 415/512-0151).

Once you're in the Napa Valley, stop at the **Napa Valley Conference and Visitors Bureau,** 1310 Town Center Mall (off First Street), Napa, CA 94559 (☎ 707/226-7459), for a variety of local information. All over Napa and Sonoma you can pick up a very informative free weekly publication called the *Wine Country Review*. It will give you the most up-to-date information on the area's wineries and related events.

If you need help organizing your Wine Country vacation, contact **Wine Country Vacation Rentals,** P.O. Box 543, Calistoga, CA 94515 (☎ 707/942-2186; fax 707/942-4681), a knowledgeable company that specializes in the area and offers extensive rental information on inns, hotels, motels, resorts, and vacation homes, as well as details on wineries, limousine tours, restaurants, spas, ballooning, gliders, and train rides.

WHEN TO GO   The beauty of the valley is striking any time of the year, but is most memorable in September and October when the grapes are being pressed and the wineries are in full production. Another great time to come is the spring, when the mustard flowers are in full bloom and the tourist season hasn't yet begun; you'll find less traffic and fewer crowds at the wineries and restaurants, and better deals on hotel rooms. While winter promises the best budget rates, it usually comes with lots of rain. Summer? Say hello to hot weather and lots of traffic.

TOURING THE VALLEY & WINERIES

The Napa Valley has more than 250 wineries, each offering distinct wines, atmosphere, and experience—so touring the valley takes a little planning. The best thing you can do is decide what you're most interested in and chart your path from there. Is it a specific wine you want to taste? A particular tour you'd like to take? Maybe it's the adjoining restaurant, picnic tables, or art collection that piques your interest. Ask locals which vintners have the type of experience you're looking for. Whatever you do, plan to visit no more than four or five wineries in one day. Above all, take it slowly. The Wine Country should never be rushed; like a great glass of wine, it should be savored.

Most wineries offer tours daily from 10am to 5pm. Tours usually chart the process of wine making from the grafting and harvesting of the vines to the pressing of the grapes and the blending and aging of the wines in oak casks. They vary in length, detail, and formality, depending on the winery. Most tours are free.

The towns and wineries below are organized geographically, from south to north along Calif. 29, from Napa village to Calistoga. We've included our favorites below; for a complete list of wineries, be sure to pick up one of the free guides to the valley (see "Essentials," above). Also bear in mind that some of our most memorable Wine Country experiences haven't been on tours or in formal tasting halls, but at the mom-and-pop wineries throughout the region. These are the places where you'll make discoveries, pick up bottles that are only sold from the proprietor's front room, and talk with the colorful people who made the wine they're selling you with their own hands. The big, commercially oriented wineries are not to be missed, for sure, but don't pass up the other, more personal side of the Napa Valley experience either.

Seeing the Wine Country by Rail

You don't have to worry about drinking and driving if you visit the Wine Country aboard the Napa Valley Wine Train, a rolling restaurant that makes the 3-hour, 36-mile journey through the vineyards of Napa, Yountville, Oakville, Rutherford, and St. Helena. The vintage-style cars—finished with polished Honduran mahogany paneling and etched-glass partitions—harken back to the opulent sophistication of the 1920s and 1930s. Gourmet meals are served by an attentive staff, complete with all the appropriate details—damask linen, bone china, silver flatware, and etched crystal. The fixed menus consist of three to five courses, which might include a salmon dish or Black Angus filet mignon served with a cabernet and roquefort sauce. In addition to the dining rooms, the train pulls a Wine Tasting Car, a Deli Car, and three 50-passenger lounges.

The wine train now makes a stop at the Grgich Winery in Rutherford for a tour of the barreling, bottling, and wine-making process, followed by a tasting.

The **Napa Valley Wine Train** leaves from the McKinstry Street Depot, 1275 McKinstry St. (near 1st St. and Soscol Ave.), Napa (☎ **800/427-4124** or 707/ 253-2111). Train fare without meals is $33 for daytime rides and $22 for evening rides; it's an additional $25 for brunch, $30 for lunch, or $39.50 for dinner. Departures are Monday to Friday at 11:30am; Saturday, Sunday, and holidays at 8:30am and noon; and Tuesday to Sunday and holidays at 6pm. (The schedule is reduced in January and February.) *Tip:* Sit on the west side for the best views. *Fair warning:* Photos are taken before you board; so if you want this moment captured on film, be prepared.

Hot-Air Ballooning over the Valley

Don't feel like driving through the Napa Valley? Try a different perspective: Balloon over it. Believe it or not, Napa Valley is the most popular hot-air-balloon "flight corridor" in the *world*. Northern California's temperate weather allows for ballooning year-round, and on summer weekends it's a rare day in the valley when you don't see at least one of the colorful airships floating above the vineyards.

Trips usually depart early in the morning when the air is cooler and the balloons have better lift. Flight paths vary with the direction and speed of the changing breezes, so "chase" crews on the ground must follow the balloon to its undetermined destination. Most flights last about an hour and end with a traditional champagne celebration and breakfast. Reservations are required and should be made as far in advance as possible. Prices range from $165 to $195 per person for the basic package; wedding, wine-tasting, picnic, and lodging packages are also available. For more information or reservations, call Napa's **Bonaventura Balloon Company** (☎ **800/ FLY-NAPA** or 707/944-2882), a highly reputable organization owned and operated by pilot Joyce Bowen; or **Adventures Aloft** (☎ **800/944-4408** or 707/944-4408; www.nvaloft.com), Napa Valley's oldest hot-air-balloon company.

THE VILLAGE OF NAPA

The town of Napa serves mainly as the commercial center of the Wine Country and the gateway to Napa Valley—hence the high-speed freeway that whips you right past it and on to the "tourist" towns of St. Helena and Calistoga. However, it does have some wonderful wineries that are worth exploring to the north of town, as well as a few other attractions (see below).

Newlan Vineyards. 5225 Solano Ave., Napa. ☎ **707/257-2399.** Daily 10am–5pm.

This small, family-owned winery produces only about 10,000 cases a year. Cabernet sauvignon, pinot noir, chardonnay, zinfandel, and late harvest Johannesburg Riesling are produced. Wine tasting, which is offered anytime during open hours, costs $3 and includes a take-home wine glass.

Stag's Leap Wine Cellars. 5766 Silverado Trail, Napa. ☎ **707/944-2020.** Sales and tasting daily 10am–4pm; tours by appointment only. Silverado Trail parallels Calif. 29; from Calif. 29, go east on Trancas St. or Oak Knoll Ave., then north to the cellars.

Founded in 1972, Stag's Leap shocked the oenological world in 1976 when its 1973 cabernet won first place over French wines in a Parisian blind tasting. For $3 per person, you can be the judge of the winery's current releases, or you can fork over the big bucks for one of Stag's Leap's best-known wines, Cabernet Sauvignon Cask 23.

Trefethen Vineyards. 1160 Oak Knoll Ave., Napa. ☎ **707/255-7700.** Daily 10am–4:30pm; tours by appointment year-round. From Calif. 29, take Oak Knoll Ave. east.

Listed on the National Register of Historical Places, the vineyard's main building was built in 1886, and remains Napa's only wooden, gravity-powered winery. Although Trefethen is one of the valley's oldest wineries, it didn't produce its first chardonnay until 1973—but thank goodness it did. Its whites and reds are both award-winners and a pleasure to the palate. Tours are offered by appointment only; tastings are free.

What to See & Do Beyond the Wineries

If you have plenty of time and a penchant for Victorian architecture, the **Napa Valley Conference and Visitors Bureau,** 1310 Napa Town Center Mall, off 1st Street (☎ 707/226-7459), offers self-guided walking tours of the town's historic buildings, and there are a few other activities and attractions worth stopping for.

ANTIQUING   Looking for a trinket but don't know quite what you want? Plan to spend at least an hour strolling **Red Hen's** co-op collection of antiques. There's everything here from baseball cards to living-room sets, and prices are remarkably affordable. You can't miss this enormous red, barn-style building at 5091 St. Helena Hwy. (on Calif. 29 at Oak Knoll Ave. W.), Napa (☎ 707/257-0822). It's open daily from 10am to 5:30pm.

HITTING THE LINKS   South of downtown Napa, 1.3 miles east of Calif. 29 on Calif. 12, is **The Chardonnay Club** (☎ 707/257-8950), a challenging 36-hole land-links golf complex with first-class service. You pay just one fee, which makes you a member for the day. Privileges include the use of a golf cart, the practice range (including a bucket of balls), and services usually found only at a private club (the day we played, a snack cart came by on the course with a full complement of sandwiches and soft drinks—and at the end of the round our clubs were cleaned). The course ambles through and around 325 acres of vineyards, hills, creeks, canyons, and rock ridges. There are three nines of similar challenge, all starting at the clubhouse so that you can play the 18 of your choice. Five sets of tees provide you with a course measuring from 5,300 yards to a healthy 7,100. Starting times can be reserved up to 2 weeks in advance. Greens fees (including mandatory cart and practice balls) are $60 Monday to Friday, and $90 on Saturday, Sunday, and holidays; at 1pm, fees go down to $45 and $55 respectively.

YOUNTVILLE

Founded by George Calvert Yount, the first white American to settle in the valley, Yountville lacks the small-town charm of neighboring St. Helena and Calistoga—for better or worse, the town lacks a rambunctious main street—but it does serve as a good base for exploring the valley and has a handful of excellent wineries, restaurants, and inns (see "Where to Stay" and "Where to Dine," below).

Domaine Chandon. 1 California Dr. (at Calif. 29), Yountville. ☎ **707/944-2280.** Nov–Apr, Wed–Sun 11am–6pm; May–Oct, daily 11am–6pm.

The valley's most renowned sparkling winery was founded in 1973 by French champagne house Möet et Chandon. The grounds suit Domaine Chandon's reputation perfectly—this is the kind of place where the world's wealthy might stroll the beautifully manicured gardens under the shade of a delicate parasol, stop for sips of the winery's famous sparkling wine at the outdoor patio, then glide into the dining room for a world-class luncheon.

If you can pull yourself away from the bubbly (sold by the glass and served with complimentary hors d'oeuvres), there's a comprehensive tour of the facilities that's worth the time. In addition to a shop, there's a small gallery housing artifacts from Möet et Chandon depicting the history of champagnes. The Domaine Chandon restaurant is one of the best in the valley (see p. 171 for complete information).

What to See & Do Beyond the Wineries

At the center of the village is **Vintage 1870** (☎ 707/944-2451), once a winery (from 1871 to 1955) and now a gallery with specialty shops selling antiques, wine accessories, country collectibles, and more; it's also home to three restaurants.

OAKVILLE

Driving farther north on the St. Helena Highway (Calif. 29) brings you to the Oakville Cross Road and the ✪ **Oakville Grocery Co.,** 7856 St. Helena Hwy. (☎ 707/944-8802), one of the finest gourmet food stores this side of New York's Dean & Deluca. Here you can put together the provisions for a memorable picnic. You'll find the best breads and the choicest selection of cheeses in the northern Bay Area, as well as pâtés, fresh foie gras (domestic and French, seasonally), smoked Norwegian salmon, fresh caviar (Beluga, Sevruga, Osetra), and an exceptional selection of California wines, of course. The grocery will prepare a picnic basket for you with 24-hours' notice. Delivery service is available to some areas. The grocery is open daily from 10am to 6pm (the espresso bar opens at 7am).

Robert Mondavi Winery. 7801 St. Helena Hwy. (Calif. 29), Oakville. ☎ **800/MONDAVI** or 707/226-1395. May–Oct, daily 9:30am–5:30pm; Nov–Apr, daily 9:30am–4:30pm.

If you continue on Calif. 29 up to Oakville, you'll arrive at the ultimate high-tech Napa Valley winery, housed in a magnificent mission-style facility. Almost every processing variable in its wine making is computer controlled—and absolutely fascinating to watch. Reservations are recommended for the guided tour. It's wise to make them 1 to 2 weeks in advance, especially if you plan to go on a weekend. After the tour, you can taste the results of all this attention to detail with selected current wines. The Vineyard Room usually features an art show, and you'll find some exceptional antiques in the reception hall. In summer the winery hosts some great outdoor jazz concerts.

Opus One. 7900 St. Helena Hwy. (Calif. 29), Oakville. ☎ **707/944-9442.** Daily 10:30am–12:30pm and 1:30–3:30pm. Tours by appointment only (in high season, book 3 weeks in advance).

Unlike most other vineyard experiences, a visit to Opus One is a serious and stately affair that takes after its wine and its owners—Robert Mondavi and Baroness Phillipe de Rothschild—who, after years of discussion, embarked on this state-of-the-art collaboration. Architecture buffs in particular will appreciate the tour, which takes in both the impressive Greco-Roman–meets–20th-century building and the no-holds-barred ultra-high-tech production and aging facilities. This entire facility caters to one ultra-premium wine, which is offered here for a whopping $12 per 4-ounce taste. But wine lovers should happily fork over the cash: It's likely to be one of the most memorable reds you'll ever sample. Grab your glass and head to the redwood rooftop deck to enjoy the view.

RUTHERFORD

Beaulieu Vineyard. 1960 St. Helena Hwy. (Calif. 29), Rutherford. ☎ **707/963-2411.** Daily 10am–5pm; tours, daily 11am–4pm.

Bordeaux native Georges de Latour founded the third-oldest continuously operating winery in Napa Valley in 1900, and with the help of legendary oenologist André Tchelistcheff, produced world-class award-winning wines that have been served by every president of the United States since Roosevelt. The brick and redwood tasting room isn't much to look at, but with Beaulieu's (say bowl-you) stellar reputation, they have no need to visually impress. They do, however, offer you a complimentary glass of chardonnay the minute you walk through the door. The Private Reserve Tasting Room nearby offers tastes of reserve wines for a small fee. A free tour explains the wine-making process and the vineyard's history.

Cakebread Cellars. 8300 St. Helena Hwy. (Calif. 29), Rutherford. ☎ **707/963-5221.** Daily 10am–4pm. Tours by reservation only.

This winery's moniker is actually the winery owners' surname, but it suits the wines produced here twofold: The focus here is on making wine that pairs well with food. Apparently, they've done such a good job that 85% of their 50,000 annual cases go directly to restaurants, which means only a select few get to take home a bottle. The sauvignon blanc, chardonnay, cabernet, merlot, and zinfandel are all made from Napa Valley grapes, partially from the winery's 75 acres and the rest from local growers. The tasting room is a large barn-like space where the hospitable hosts pour freely.

Mumm. 8445 Silverado Trail, Rutherford. ☎ **800/686-6272** or 707/942-3434. Apr–Oct, daily 10:30am–6pm; Nov–Mar, daily 10am–5pm. Tours offered every hour daily 11am–4pm in summer; 11am–3pm in winter.

At first glance Mumm, housed in a big redwood barn, looks almost humble. But once you're in the front door, you'll know they mean big business. Just beyond the extensive gift shop (filled with all sorts of namesake mementos) is the tasting room, where guests can purchase sparkling wine by the glass (ranging from $3.50 to $6) and take in the breathtaking vineyard and mountain views. Unfortunately, there's no food or picnicking here, but during warm weather, with the open patio and a glass of champagne, you'll forget all about nibbling. Mumm also offers a 45-minute educational tour, and there's an art gallery that exhibits Ansel Adams photographs of the Wine Country.

Niebaum-Coppola. 1991 St. Helena Hwy. (Calif. 29), Rutherford. ☎ **707/963-9099.** Daily 10am–5pm.

In March 1995, Hollywood met Napa Valley when Francis Ford Coppola bought historic Inglenook Vineyards. Although Coppola has been dabbling in wine production for years, this is his biggest endeavor yet. He's already plunked down millions to renovate the beautiful 1880s ivy-draped stone winery, and plans are to restore the entire property to its historic dimension—but it will, of course, be combined with the glitz you'd expect from Tinsletown. On display are authentic Academy awards and memorabilia from such Coppola films as *The Godfather* and *Bram Stoker's Dracula;* the Centennial Museum chronicles the history of the estate and its wine making as well as Coppola's filmmaking. With all the Hollywood hullabaloo, wine is not forgotten, however: The goal is to produce 75,000 cases a year of quality wine made from organically grown grapes. Wine tasting is $5; if you've had enough for the day, perk yourself up at the cappuccino bar. You're welcome to picnic at any of the designated (and beautiful) garden sites.

St. Supéry Winery. 8440 St. Helena Hwy. (Calif. 29), Rutherford. ☎ **800/942-0809.** Daily 9:30am–4:30pm.

The outside may look like a modern corporate office building, but inside is a functional and welcoming winery that encourages first-time wine tasters to learn more about oenology. On the self-guided tour, you can wander through the demonstration vineyard where you'll learn about growing techniques. Inside, kids gravitate toward "SmellaVision," an interactive display that teaches you how to identify different wine ingredients. Adjoining is the Atkinson House, which houses more than 100 years of wine-making history. For $2.50 you'll get lifetime tasting privileges, and though they probably won't be pouring their ever-popular Moscato dessert wine, the sauvignon blanc and chardonnay flow freely.

What to See & Do Beyond the Wineries

Want to bring home an unusual and beautiful handcrafted decoration for your home or yard? Seek out **Napa Valley Grapevine Wreath Company,** P.O. Box 67, Rutherford, CA 94573 (☎ 707/963-8893), which weaves big and small indoor or outdoor sculptures made out of little more than cabernet grapevines. Options range from a basic wreath to a star or a full-scale reindeer and all are priced competitively. Call for directions—this tiny shack of a shop is hidden on a side road between Rutherford's vineyards. Hours vary during winter, but are generally Wednesday to Monday from 10:30am to 5:30pm.

ST. HELENA

Located 17 miles north of Napa on Calif. 29, this former Seventh Day Adventist village manages to maintain a pseudo–Old West feel while simultaneously catering to upscale shoppers with deep pockets—hence **Vanderbilt's,** purveyor of fine housewares, at 1429 Main St. It's a quiet, attractive little town hosting a slew of beautiful old homes as well as first-rate restaurants and accommodations (also see "Where to Stay" and "Where to Dine," below), and some exceptional wineries.

Beringer Vineyards. 2000 Main St., St. Helena. ☎ **707/963-7115.** Daily 9:30am–5pm (last tour at 4pm).

Follow the line of cars just north of St. Helena's business district to Beringer Vineyards, where everyone stops at the remarkable Rhine House to taste wine and view the hand-dug tunnels carved out of the mountainside. Founded in 1876 by brothers Jacob and Frederick, this is the oldest continuously operating winery in the Napa Valley, open even during Prohibition, when Beringer kept afloat by making "sacramental" wines. Tasting of current vintages is conducted in the Rhine House; reserve wines are available in the Founders' Room (upstairs). A modest fee is charged per taste.

Flora Springs Wine Co. 1978 W. Zinfandel Lane (off Calif. 29), St. Helena. ☎ **707/963-5711.** By reservation only; call ahead.

While this handsome stone winery dates from Napa Valley's early days, the Flora Springs label first appeared in 1978. It's well known for its barrel-fermented chardonnay, its cabernet sauvignon, and Trilogy, a Bordeaux-style blend.

What to See & Do Beyond the Wineries

Literary buffs and other romantics will want to visit the **Silverado Museum,** 1490 Library Lane (☎ **707/963-3757**), which is devoted to the life and works of Robert Louis Stevenson, who honeymooned here in 1880 in an abandoned Silverado Mine bunkhouse. More than 8,000 items include original manuscripts, letters, photographs, and portraits, plus the desk he used in Samoa. Open Tuesday to Sunday noon to 4pm; admission is free.

BIKING   The quieter northern end of the valley is an ideal place to rent a bicycle and ride the Silverado Trail. **St. Helena Cyclery,** at 1156 Main St. (☎ **707/ 963-7736**), rents bikes for $7 per hour or $25 a day, including rear rack and picnic bag.

SHOPPING   Don't bother forking over big bucks at a gift shop for fancy bottles of olive oil. **Napa Valley Olive Oil Manufacturing Company,** located at 835 Charter Oak Rd. (at the end of the road behind Tra Vigne restaurant), St. Helena (☎ **707/963-4173**), presses and bottles its own oils and sells them at a fraction of the price you'll pay elsewhere. They also have an extensive selection of Italian cooking ingredients, imported snacks, and the best deals on exotic mushrooms we've ever seen.

CALISTOGA

Sam Brannan, entrepreneur extraordinaire and California's first millionaire, made his first bundle by supplying miners during the Gold Rush. Flushed with success, he went on to take advantage of the natural geothermal springs at the north end of the Napa Valley by building a hotel and spa here in 1859. Flubbing up a speech comparing this natural California wonder to the Saratoga Springs resort on the East Coast, he serendipitously coined the term Calistoga and it stuck.

This small, simple resort town remains popular and uncomplicated today, particularly with city folk who come here to unwind. The vibe is more casual—and a little more groovy—than in neighboring towns to the south. Calistoga's main street is still only about 6 blocks long, and no building is higher than 2 stories. It's a great place to relax and indulge in mineral waters, mud baths, Jacuzzis, massages, and, of course, wine. But there's plenty to do in Calistoga even beyond the wineries and the world-famous mud baths (for details, see below).

✪ **Clos Pegase.** 1060 Dunaweal Lane (off Calif. 29 or the Silverado Trail), Calistoga. ☎ **707/ 942-4981.** Daily 11am–5pm. Tours daily at 11am and 2pm.

What happens when a man falls in love with art and wine making, purchases more than 450 acres of prime growing property, and sponsors a competition commissioned by the San Francisco Museum of Modern Art to create a "temple to wine"? You'll find out if you visit this magnificent winery. Renowned architect Michael Graves designed this incredible oasis, which integrates art, 20,000 square feet of aging caves, and a luxurious private hilltop home. Viewing the art here is as much the point as tasting the wine. The grounds feature an impressive sculpture garden as well as scenic picnic spots. Tasting all the current releases will cost $2.50, and reserves are $2 each.

✪ **Schramsberg.** 1400 Schramsberg Rd. (off Calif. 29), Calistoga. ☎ **707/942-4558.** Daily 9am–5pm. Tours by appointment only. From Calif. 29, go west onto Petersen Rd.

This is the label that presidents serve when toasting with dignitaries from around the globe, and there's plenty of historical memorabilia in the front room to prove it. But

Find the New You: Take a Calistoga Mud Bath

The one thing you should do while you're in Calisoga is what people have been doing here for the last 150 years: Take a mud bath. The natural baths are composed of local volcanic ash, imported peat, and naturally boiling mineral hot-springs water, all mulled together to produce a thick mud that simmers at a temperature of about 104°F.

Once you overcome the hurdle of deciding how best to place your naked body into the mushy stone tub, the rest is pure relaxation—you soak with surprising buoyancy for about 10 to 12 minutes. A warm mineral-water shower, a mineral-water whirlpool bath, and a mineral-water steam room visit follow. Afterward, a relaxing blanket-wrap will slowly cool down your delighted body. All of this takes about 1½ hours and costs about $45; with a massage, add another half hour and $20 (we recommend a full hour). The outcome is a rejuvenated, revitalized, squeaky-clean you. Mud baths aren't recommended for those who are pregnant or have high blood pressure.

The spas also offer a variety of other treatments, such as hand and foot massages, herbal wraps, acupressure face-lifts, skin rubs, and herbal facials. Prices range from $35 to $125, and appointments are necessary for all services; call at least a week in advance.

Indulge yourself at any of these Calistoga spas: **Dr. Wilkinson's Hot Springs,** 1507 Lincoln Ave. (☎ **707/942-4102**); **Lincoln Avenue Spa,** 1339 Lincoln Ave. (☎ **707/942-5296**); **Golden Haven Hot Springs Spa,** 1713 Lake St. (☎ **707/ 942-6793**); and **Calistoga Spa Hot Springs,** 1006 Washington St. (☎ **707/ 942-6269**).

Schramsberg's real mystique begins when you enter its champagne caves, which wind 2½ miles (the longest in North America, they say) and were partly hand-carved by Chinese laborers in the 1800s. They have authentic Tom Sawyer ambiance, complete with dangling cobwebs and seemingly endless passageways; you can't help but feel you're on an adventure. The tour is comprehensive and unintimidating, and ends in a charming tasting room, where you'll sit around a big table and sample several selections of bubbly (for $6). This 200-acre champagne estate, a landmark once frequented by Robert Louis Stevenson, has a wonderful Old-World feel and is well worth exploring. Note, however, that tastings are only offered to those who take the free tour (you must reserve a spot in advance).

Sterling Vineyards. 1111 Dunaweal Lane (½ mile east of Calif. 29), Calistoga. ☎ **800/ 726-6136** or 707/942-3344. Daily 10:30am–4:30pm.

No, you don't need climbing shoes to reach this Mediterranean-style winery, perched 300 feet up on a rocky knoll. Just fork over $6 and you'll arrive via aerial tram, which offers exceptional views along the way. Once on land, follow the self-guided tour, which will take you through the fermenters and into the aging cellars. The winery, currently owned by the Seagram company, produces more than 200,000 cases per year. Samples at the panoramic tasting room are included in the tram fare.

What to See & Do Beyond the Wineries

Calistoga Depot, at 1458 Lincoln Ave. (on the site of Calistoga's original 1868 railroad station), now houses a variety of shops, some of which are housed in six restored passenger cars dating from 1916.

NATURAL WONDERS **Old Faithful Geyser of California,** at 1299 Tubbs Lane (☎ 707/942-6463), is one of only three "old faithful" geysers in the world. It's been blowing off steam at regular intervals for as long as anyone can remember. The 350°F water spews out to a height of about 60 feet every 40 minutes or so, day and night (varying with natural influences such as barometric pressure, the moon, tides, and tectonic stresses). The performance lasts about 3 minutes. You'll learn a lot about the origins of geothermal steam on your visit. You can bring a picnic lunch with you and catch the show as many times as you wish. An exhibit hall, gift shop, and snack bar are open every day. Admission is $5 for adults, $4 for seniors, and $2 for children 6 to 11. Open daily from 9am to 6pm (to 5pm in winter). To get there, follow the signs from downtown Calistoga; it's between Calif. 29 and Calif. 128.

You won't see thousands of trees turned into stone, but you'll still find many interesting petrified specimens at the **Petrified Forest,** 4100 Petrified Forest Rd. (☎ 707/942-6667). Volcanic ash blanketed this area after the eruption of Mount St. Helena three million years ago. As a result, you'll find redwoods that have turned to rock through the slow infiltration of silicas and other minerals, as well as petrified seashells, clams, and marine life indicating that water covered this area even before the redwood forest. Admission is $3 for adults, $1 for children 4 to 11, and free for children under 4. Open daily from 10am to 5:30pm (to 4:30pm in winter). To get there from Calif. 128, turn right onto Petrified Forest Road, just past Lincoln Avenue.

BIKING Cycling enthusiasts can rent bikes from **Getaway Adventures BHK** (biking, hiking, and kayaking), 1117 Lincoln Ave. (☎ 800/499-BIKE or 707/942-0332). Full-day tours ($89), which include lunch and a visit to four or five wineries, are available, as are downhill cruises ($49) for people who hate to pedal. On weekdays they'll even deliver bikes to you.

GLIDER RIDES Calistoga offers a unique way of seeing its vineyard-filled valleys—from a glider. These quiet "birds" leave from the **Calistoga Gliderport,** 1546 Lincoln Ave., Calistoga, CA 94515 (☎ 707/942-5000). Twenty-minute rides are $69 for one, $110 for two (weight limits apply). Thirty-minute rides are also available.

WHERE TO STAY

Because Napa Valley is so small, it really doesn't much matter which town you base yourself in. Hotels here run the gamut—from motels and B&Bs to world-class luxury retreats—and all are easily accessible from the main highway.

When planning your trip, keep in mind that during the high season—between June and November—most hotels charge peak rates and sell out completely on weekends; many have a 2-night minimum. In the off-season, you have far better bargaining power and may be able to get a room at almost half the summer rate.

VERY EXPENSIVE

✪ **Auberge du Soleil.** 180 Rutherford Hill Rd., Rutherford, CA 94573. ☎ **707/963-1211.** Fax 707/963-8764. 50 rms and suites. A/C MINIBAR TV TEL. Weekdays $175–$750 double; Apr–Nov, weekends $350–$950 double. Rates are discounted Dec–Mar. AE, DC, DISC, MC, V. From Rutherford, turn right on Calif. 128 and go 3 miles to the Silverado Trail; turn left and head north about 200 yards to Rutherford Hill Rd.; turn right.

This is the kind of place you'd imagine movie stars would frequent for a clandestine affair or a weekend retreat. Set high above the Napa Valley in a 33-acre olive grove, it's quiet, indulgent, and luxuriously romantic. The rooms are large enough to get lost in—and you might want to once you discover all the amenities. The bathtub alone—an enormous hot tub with a skylight overhead—will entice you to grab a glass of California red and settle in for a while. A wood-burning fireplace is surrounded by oversized, cushy furniture—the ideal place to relax and listen to CDs (the stereo comes with a few selections, and there's also a VCR). Fresh flowers, original art, terra-cotta floors, and natural-wood and leather furnishings whisk you out of the Wine Country and into the Southwest. Each sun-washed private deck has views of the valley that are nothing less than spectacular. There's a celestial swimming pool and a tiny workout room with one of the grandest views around, plus an array of spa services. All in all, this is one of the best places we've ever stayed.

Dining: See "Where to Dine," below.

Services: Concierge, newspaper delivery, valet parking, 24-hour room service, twice-daily maid service, laundry/valet, complimentary shoe shine.

Facilities: Outdoor pool with sundeck, massage rooms, 3 tennis courts, exercise room, beauty salon. A sculpture and nature trail with picnic areas crisscrosses the property.

The Inn at Southbridge. 1020 Main St., St. Helena, CA 94574. ☎ **800/520-6800** or 707/ 967-9400. Fax 707/967-9486. MINIBAR TV TEL. $235–$415 double. AE, CB, DC, JCB, MC, V.

Eschewing the lace-and-latticework theme that plagues most Wine Country inns, the Inn at Southbridge takes an unswervingly modern, pragmatic approach to accommodating its guests. Instead of stuffed teddy bears in the rooms you'll find terry-cloth robes, fireplaces, bathroom skylights, down comforters, private balconies, and a host of other little luxuries. The decor is upscale Pottery Barn—trendy, and for some a welcome departure from quaintly traditional hotel-style stuff. Functional touches include voice mail and fax modems. *Notable Bummers:* The hotel is located along the highway, so it's lacking that reclusive feel many other upscale hotels offer, and its less-than-prime location makes it overpriced—but it has every possible amenity, and it's still a great place to stay.

Dining: On the premises is Tomatina, owned and run by the owners of Tra Vigne, an Italian restaurant conveniently located next door (see "Where to Dine," below).

Services: Concierge, limited room service, dry cleaning, laundry, newspaper delivery, in-room massage, twice-daily maid service, baby-sitting, secretarial services, complimentary refreshments in lobby.

Facilities: The spa offers access to gym, steam, sauna, outdoor heated pool, Jacuzzi, and spa treatments.

✪ **Meadowood Resort.** 900 Meadowood Lane, St. Helena, CA 94574. ☎ **800/458-8080** or 707/963-3646. Fax 707/963-3532. 85 rms. A/C MINIBAR TV TEL. $320–$465 double; 1-bedroom lodge from $540; 2-bedroom from $850; 3-bedroom from $1,180; 4-bedroom from $1,575. Ask about promotional offers and off-season rates. Two-night minimum on weekends. AE, DISC, DC, MC, V.

Less reclusive than Auberge du Soleil, Meadowood is the wealthy grown-ups' summer camp. The resort, tucked away on 250 acres of pristine mountainside amidst a forest of madrone and oak trees, is quiet and exclusive enough to make you forget that busy wineries are 10 minutes away. Rooms are furnished with American country classics and have beamed ceilings, private patios, stone fireplaces, and wilderness views; many are individual suite-lodges that are so far removed from the common areas that you must drive to get to them (lazier folks can opt for more centrally located accommodations). You can spend your days playing golf, tennis, or croquet; lounging around the pools or spa; or hiking the surrounding areas. Those who actually want to leave here to do some wine tasting can check in with John Thoreen, the hotel's wine tutor, whose sole purpose is to help guests better understand and enjoy Napa Valley wines.

Dining: See "Where to Dine," below.

Services: Concierge, room service, dry cleaning and laundry, full-service spa, newspaper delivery, secretarial services, and baby-sitting available through the concierge.

Facilities: Nine-hole golf course, croquet lawns, 2 outdoor pools with sundeck, massage rooms, 7 tennis courts, exercise room, hiking trails, and an executive conference center.

Silverado Country Club & Resort. 1600 Atlas Peak Rd., Napa, CA 94558. ☎ **800/ 532-0500** or 707/257-0200. Fax 707/257-2867. 275 suites. A/C MINIBAR TV TEL. $215 junior suite; $275 1-bedroom suite; $385–$485 2- or 3-bedroom suite. Golf and promotional packages available. Breakfast $8.50 extra. AE, CB, DC, DISC, MC, V. Free parking. Drive north on Calif. 29 to Trancas St.; turn east to Atlas Peak Rd.

If you long for the opulence of an East Coast country club, bring your racket and golf clubs to this 1,200-acre resort in the Napa foothills. The focus here is on the sporting life; the spacious accommodations—which range from very large studios ("junior suites") with a king-size bed, kitchenette, and a roomy, well-appointed bath to one-, two- or three-bedroom cottage suites—are up to par, and each comes with a wood-burning fireplace. Cottage suites are in private, low-rise groupings, each tucked away in shared courtyards and along peaceful walkways. All rooms are individually decorated with country home–style furnishings and manage to offer a sense of privacy despite the resort's size.

Dining: There's a quintessential steak and seafood restaurant, as well as a garden-view restaurant serving superb California and Pacific Rim cuisine, and a large indoor/outdoor bar and grill that serves breakfast, lunch, and cocktails.

Services: Limited room service, concierge, dry cleaning, laundry, baby-sitting, secretarial services, valet parking.

Facilities: Two cleverly designed golf courses by Robert Trent Jones, Jr.: The 6,500-yard South Course, with a dozen water crossings; and the 6,700-yard North Course, somewhat longer but a bit more forgiving. A staff of pros is on hand. Greens fee is $110 for 18 holes on either course, including a mandatory cart. Also tennis courts, several swimming pools, tour desk, conference rooms, and business center.

EXPENSIVE

Bartels Ranch & Country Inn. 1200 Conn Valley Rd., St. Helena, CA 94574. ☎ **707/ 963-4001.** Fax 707/963-5100. 4 rms. A/C TV TEL. $135–$365 double. AE, DC, DISC, MC, JCB, V. From downtown St. Helena, turn east on Pope St., cross Silverado Trail and continue onto Howell Mountain Rd.; bear right onto Conn Valley Rd.; the inn is 2 miles ahead on the left.

Perched on 60 acres of rolling meadows studded with fig trees, cypress, old oaks, and a recently planted vineyard, this palatial retreat is run by ebullient innkeeper Jamie Bartels, who designed the 7,000-square-foot stone ranch house and has decorated it with her own collection of butterflies and other mementos. Her four individually decorated rooms provide every comfort—fireplaces, VCRs (with video library), CD players, balconies—plus conveniences like ironing boards, hair dryers, and private baths; a couple of the rooms even have their own Jacuzzis. There's a communal sundeck and pool, as well as a book-filled game room with pool and Ping-Pong tables. The bountiful breakfasts consist of fresh fruits, breads, and egg dishes; complimentary wine, fruit, and cheese are served each afternoon. Other treats include evening dessert, and there is always coffee, tea, and cookies on hand. Forever aiming to please, Jamie can provide her guests with picnic supplies, lend bicycles, and arrange massages or tours. A bocce ball court, croquet lawns, and access to horseback riding and tennis are other outdoor options.

Brannan Cottage Inn. 109 Wapoo Ave. (at Lincoln Ave.; P.O. Box 81), Calistoga, CA 94515. ☎ **707/942-4200.** 6 rms. $140–$160 double. Rates include full breakfast. MC, V.

At the east end of town on a quiet side street stands this cute little 1860 cottage, complete with requisite white picket fence. One of Sam Brannan's original resort cottages, the inn was restored through a community effort to salvage an important piece of Calistoga's heritage; it's now on the National Register of Historic Places. The six spacious, cozy rooms are decorated with country-style antiques, down comforters, and white lace curtains; each room also has air-conditioning, ceiling fan, private bath, and its own entrance. There's a comfortable parlor and a pleasant brick terrace furnished with umbrella tables. A full buffet-style breakfast is served in the outdoor garden, weather permitting.

Burgundy House Country Inn. 6711 Washington St. (P.O. Box 3156), Yountville, CA 94599. ☎ **707/944-0889.** 5 rms, all with bath. A/C. $135 double. Rates include breakfast. MC, V. Free parking. From Calif. 29 north, take the Yountville exit and turn left onto Washington St.

This distinctly French country inn, built in the early 1890s as a brandy distillery of local fieldstone and river rock, is tiny but impressive. The interior still features thick stone walls and hand-hewn post and lintel beams, enhanced today by antique country furnishings. The five cozy guest rooms (all nonsmoking) have colorful quilted spreads and comfortable beds. Delightful touches include fresh flowers in each of the rooms and complimentary port and sherry in the common area. The full breakfast can be taken inside or outdoors in the pretty garden.

✪ **Cottage Grove Inn.** 1711 Lincoln Ave., Calistoga, CA 94515. ☎ **800/799-2284** or 707/942-8400. Fax 707/942-2653. 16 cottages (1 with access for travelers with disabilities). A/C TV TEL. $150–$175 double. Rates include continental breakfast. DC, MC, V.

Standing in two parallel rows at the end of the main strip in Calistoga are the perfect couples' retreats—brand-spanking-new cottages that, though located on a residential street, seem well-removed from the action once you've stepped across the threshold. Each compact guest house comes complete with a wood-burning fireplace, homey furnishings (perfect for curling up in front of the fire), cozy quilts, and an enormous bathroom with a skylight and a deep, two-person Jacuzzi tub, plus such niceties as gourmet coffee, a stereo with CD player, VCR (there's a video library on-site), wet bar, and fridge. *Smokers Beware:* It's not allowed inside, but you can puff all you want on the small front porch.

Harvest Inn. 1 Main St., St. Helena, CA 94574. ☎ **800/950-8466** or 707/963-9463. 54 rms. A/C TV TEL. $159–$290 double. AE, DC, DISC, MC, V.

If you like your accommodations loaded with 20th-century luxuries yet reminiscent of Olde England, you'll like the Harvest Inn. Ornate brick walkways lead through beautifully landscaped grounds to this Tudor-style inn. Each of the immaculate rooms—with names like "The Earl of Ecstasy" and "Camelot"—are furnished in dark Tudor style with oak beds and dressers, black leather chairs, and antique furnishings; most have brick fireplaces, wet bars, and refrigerators. Facilities include a wine bar, heated swimming pools, and outdoor spas.

Hotel St. Helena. 1309 Main St., St. Helena, CA 94574. ☎ **888/478-4355** or 707/963-4388. Website: www.napavalley.com/napavalley/lodging/hotels/sthelena. 17 rms, 14 with private bath; 1 suite. A/C TEL. $145 double without bath; $195 double with bath; $275 suite. Rates include continental breakfast. AE, DC, MC, V.

This downtown hotel occupies a historic 1881 building, the oldest wooden structure in St. Helena. The hotel keepers celebrated the building's 100th birthday with a much-needed renovation; now, it's more comfortable than ever. The hallways are cluttered with stuffed animals, wicker strollers, and other memorabilia. Most of the rooms have been similarly decorated, with brass beds, wall-to-wall burgundy carpeting, and oak or maple furnishings. There's a garden patio and wine bar. TVs are available upon request. Smoking is discouraged.

Mount View Hotel. 1457 Lincoln Ave. (on Calif. 29, near Fairway St.), Calistoga, CA 94515. ☎ **707/942-6877.** Fax 707/942-6904. 22 rms, 8 suites, 3 cottages. A/C TV TEL. $110–$150 double; $155–$200 suite; $205 cottage. Packages available. Two-night minimum on high-season weekends. AE, MC, V.

Located on the main highway in the middle of Calistoga, this hotel is one of the sweetest options in town. Rooms are decorated in the best of taste, in either Victorian or art deco styles, and trimmed with beautiful hand-painted accents. There are also three self-contained cottages—with queen-size bed, wet bar, private deck, and hot tub—and eight suites. Almost everything in town is within walking distance, although once you settle in, you might not want to leave the quiet, sunny swimming area (the pool is heated); there's also a European spa and Jacuzzi.

The hotel doesn't serve breakfast, but there are plenty of cafes on the block. The hotel's restaurant, Catahoula, serves tasty Cajun/Creole cuisine for lunch and dinner Wednesday to Monday (see "Where to Dine," below).

Napa Valley Lodge. 2230 Madison St., Yountville, CA 94599. ☎ **800/368-2468** or 707/944-2468. Fax 707/944-9362. 55 rms. $142–$310 double. Rates include champagne breakfast buffet. MC, V.

If you don't mind a corporate feel or a view of the highway beyond the swimming pool, the Napa Valley Lodge offers ultraclean, good-sized accommodations. Rooms are better appointed than many in the area, and many have vaulted ceilings and fireplaces. All come with king- or queen-size beds, wicker furnishings, coffeemakers, and either a private balcony or a patio. The cheapest rooms are darker, ground-level, motel-style accommodations. If you don't want to hang out in your room, you can always head to the swimming pool, garden spa, sauna, or fitness center. Extras include concierge, on-command video, afternoon tea and cookies in the lobby, and Friday evening wine tasting in the library. With all the extras, it's no wonder AAA gave the Napa Valley Lodge the four-diamond award for excellence. Ask about winter discounts—they can be as high as 30%.

Rancho Caymus. 1140 Rutherford Rd. (P.O. Box 78), Rutherford, CA 94573. ☎ **800/845-1777** or 707/963-1777. Fax 707/963-5387. 26 suites. A/C MINIBAR TV TEL. $135–$165 double; from $245 master suite; $295 2-bedroom suite. Rates include continental breakfast. AE, DC, MC, V. From Calif. 29 north, turn right onto Rutherford Rd./Calif. 128 east; the hotel is ahead on your left.

This Spanish-style hacienda, with two floors opening onto wisteria-covered balconies, was the creation of sculptor Mary Tilden Morton (of Morton Salt). Morton wanted each room in the hacienda to be a work of art, hiring the most skilled craftspeople of her day. She designed the adobe fireplaces herself and wandered through Mexico and South America purchasing artifacts for the property.

Guest rooms are situated around a whimsical garden courtyard with an enormous outdoor fireplace. Inside, the whimsical mix-and-match decor is on the funky side, with overly varnished dark-wood furnishings and braided rugs. The inn is cozy, however, and rooms are decent-sized, split-level suites with queen-size beds. Other amenities include wet bars, sofa beds in the sitting areas, and small, private patios. Most of the suites have fireplaces, and five have kitchenettes and whirlpool tubs. Breakfast, which includes fresh fruit, granola, orange juice, and breads, is served in the inn's dining room.

Vintage Inn. 6541 Washington St., Yountville, CA 94599. ☎ **800/351-1133** or 707/944-1112. Fax 707/944-1617. 72 rms, 8 minisuites. A/C TV TEL. $150–$275 double; $240–$325 minisuites and villas. Extra person $25. Rates include continental breakfast and afternoon tea. AE, CB, DC, DISC, MC, V. Free parking. From Calif. 29 north, take the Yountville exit and turn left onto Washington St.

This contemporary-style, French-country luxury inn is situated on an old 23-acre winery estate in the heart of adorable Yountville. Rooms are bright and cozy; each has a fireplace or private veranda, oversize beds, and a coffeemaker, plus a Jacuzzi tub and plush bathrobes. If you're looking for a workout, you may rent a bike, reserve one of the two tennis courts, or take a dip—the 60-foot swimming pool and outdoor whirlpool are heated year-round. A continental champagne breakfast (cereals, yogurt, pastries, egg salad, and fruit) and afternoon tea are served daily in the Vintage Club. Services include concierge and laundry/valet.

Wine Country Inn. 1152 Lodi Lane, St. Helena, CA 94574. ☎ **707/963-7077.** Fax 707/963-9018. 24 rms. A/C TEL. $130–$258 double. Rates include breakfast. MC, V.

Just off the highway behind Freemark Abbey Vineyard, this attractive wood-and-stone inn, complete with a French-style mansard roof and turret, overlooks a pastoral landscape of Napa Valley vineyards. The rooms are furnished with iron or brass beds and pine country furnishings; most have fireplaces and private terraces overlooking the valley, while others have private hot tubs. One of the inn's best features, besides the absence of televisions, is the outdoor pool, which is attractively landscaped into the hillside.

MODERATE

Cedar Gables Inn. 486 Coombs St., Napa, CA 94559. ☎ **800/309-7969** or 707/224-7969. Fax 707/224-4838. Website: www.cedargablesinn.com. 6 rms. $119–$169 double ($10 less in winter). Rates include breakfast. AE, DISC, MC, V. From Calif. 29 north, exit onto 1st St. and follow signs to downtown; turn right onto Coombs St.; the house is at the corner of Oak St.

Innkeepers Margaret and Craig Snasdell have developed quite a following with their cozy, romantic B&B in Old Town Napa. The Victorian was built in 1892, and rooms reflect the era with rich tapestries and gilded antiques. Some rooms have fireplaces; four have whirlpool tubs; and all feature queen-size brass, wood, or iron beds. Guests meet each evening in front of the roaring fireplace in the family room for complimentary wine and cheese. At other times, it's a perfect place to cuddle up and watch the large-screen TV.

Château Hotel. 4195 Solano Ave., Napa, CA 94558. ☎ **800/253-6272** (in California) or 707/253-9300. Fax 707/253-0906. 115 rms, 6 suites. A/C TV TEL. Apr–Oct, $115 double; Nov–Mar, $100 double; from $155 suite. Rates include buffet breakfast. AE, CB, DC, MC, V. From Calif. 29 north, turn left just past Trower Ave. at the entrance to the Napa Valley wine region.

This contemporary 2-story motel complex tries to evoke the aura of a French country inn, but it isn't fooling anybody—a motel's a motel. But the rooms and bathrooms are spacious and have separate vanity/dressing areas; most rooms have refrigerators. Ten rooms are specially designed for disabled guests. If you're used to a daily swim, the Château also has a heated pool and spa.

Dr. Wilkinson's Hot Springs. 1507 Lincoln Ave. (Calif. 29, between Fairway and Stevenson aves.), Calistoga, CA 94515. ☎ **707/942-4102.** 42 rms. A/C MINIBAR TV TEL. Winter, $74–$119 double; Summer, $89–$119 double. Weekly discounts and packages available. AE, MC, V.

This spa/resort was originally established by "Doc" Wilkinson, who arrived in Napa Valley just after World War II. The rooms range from Victorian-style accommodations with sundecks and garden patios to rather basic and functional motel-like rooms. All rooms have drip coffeemakers and refrigerators; some have kitchens. Facilities include three mineral-water pools (two outdoor and one indoor), a Jacuzzi, a steam room, mud baths, and a health club. Facials and all kinds of body treatments are available in the salon.

✪ **El Bonita Motel.** 195 Main St. (at El Bonita Ave.), St. Helena, CA 94574. ☎ **800/ 541-3284** or 707/963-3216. Fax 707/963-8838 41 rms. A/C MINIBAR TV TEL. $82–$145 double. AE, CB, DC, DISC, MC, V.

This 1930s art deco motel was built a bit too close to Calif. 29 for comfort, but the 2¹/₂ acres of beautifully landscaped gardens behind the hotel (away from the road) help even the score. The rooms, while small, are spotlessly clean and decorated with new furnishings; all have microwaves and coffeemakers, and some have kitchens or whirlpool baths. Families, attracted to the larger bungalows with kitchenettes, often consider El Bonita one of the best values in Napa Valley, especially considering that the motel comes with a heated outdoor pool, Jacuzzi, sauna, and a new massage facility.

Tall Timbers Chalets. 1012 Darms Lane, Napa, CA 94558. ☎ **707/252-7810.** Fax 707/ 252-1055. 8 cottages. A/C MINIBAR TV. Dec–Feb, Sun–Thurs $75 double, Fri–Sat and holidays $90–$105 double; Mar–Nov, Sun–Thurs $80–$95 double, Fri–Sat and holidays $95–$150 double. Extra person $20. AE, MC, V. Free parking. From Calif. 29 north, turn left onto Darms Lane before you reach Yountville.

While many hotels' prices skyrocket during the high season, Tall Timbers—a group of eight whitewashed, roomy cottages surrounded by pines and eucalyptus—remains a cute, centrally located, and affordable option. Each cottage is nicely decorated and includes a toaster oven and coffeemaker, as well as a basket of fresh fruit waiting for you upon your arrival. Other sweet touches include a basic breakfast of muffins and fruit drinks in the refrigerator and a complimentary bottle of champagne. Each cottage sleeps up to four (there's a bedroom plus a queen-size sofa bed in the living room) and two have sundecks (you cannot be guaranteed one).

Mary, who runs the place, requires a check in advance to reserve a room, and when the valley is booked, she may even rent out her own room adjoining the office. If you come expecting some of the cheapest simple lodgings in the area rather than the Ritz, you'll be pleased with your stay. There are no phones in the cottages, but you can use the one in the main office. Tall Timbers isn't particularly difficult to find, but to be one the safe side, ask for specific directions. Smoking is not allowed.

INEXPENSIVE

Napa Valley Budget Inn. 3380 Solano Ave., Napa, CA 94558. ☎ **707/257-6111.** 58 rms. A/C TV TEL. $56–$90 double. AE, DC, DISC, MC, V. Rates include continental breakfast. From Calif. 29 north, turn left onto the Redwood Rd. turnoff and go 1 block to Solano Ave.; then turn left and go a half block to the motel.

The location of this no-frills lodging is excellent—close to Calif. 29—and rooms are simple, clean, and comfortable. Local calls are free, and there's a small heated pool on the premises.

WHERE TO DINE
EXPENSIVE

Auberge du Soleil. 180 Rutherford Hill Rd., Rutherford. ☎ **707/963-1211.** Reservations recommended. Main courses $25–$30 dinner; fixed-price dinner $60. AE, DISC, MC, V. Daily 7–11am, 11:30am–2:30pm, and 6–9:30pm. WINE COUNTRY CUISINE.

Auberge du Soleil may be better known for its inn, but it was the restaurant that started all the fuss about this world-class resort. Alfresco dining is taken to an entirely new level here, particularly on warm summer nights when diners are rewarded with a gorgeous sunset view of the mountains. Inside, a magnificent fireplace, huge wood pillars, and fresh flowers combine to create a warm, rustic ambiance. Chef Andrew Sutton characterizes his cooking as "Wine Country cuisine," a reflection of the region's produce and international influence: Pacific Rim, Southwestern, and Mediterranean styles predominate. Signature dishes include a tasting platter of truffled deviled quail eggs, smoked sturgeon, Thai lobster salad, caviar, and more; and a grape-vine smoked salmon with walnut-wheat croutons and roasted shallot-caper relish. Regardless of what you order, be sure to arrive before sunset and beg for terrace seating.

✪ **Domaine Chandon.** 1 California Dr., Yountville. ☎ **707/944-2892.** Reservations required. Main courses $13–$17 at lunch, $24–$28 at dinner. AE, DC, MC, V. Summer, daily 11:30am–2:30pm; Wed–Sun 6–9:30pm. Winter, Wed–Sun 11:30am–2:30pm and 6–9pm. Closed first 3 weeks of Jan. From Calif. 29 north, take the Yountville exit; the restaurant is on the west side of the highway. CALIFORNIA/FRENCH.

There may be no experience more extravagant than a meal here. Before even seeing the dining room, you'll know you're in the lap of luxury when you see the magnificent grounds. Inside isn't shabby either, with a formal glass-enclosed dining area overlooking the grounds and a waitstaff so attentive you're never in need of anything. On warmer days, you can dine outdoors overlooking the vineyards. As for the menu, just listen for the "mmmmms" and "aaaaaahs" from the surrounding tables and anticipate chiming in when you savor the renowned cream of tomato soup in puff pastry; the caramelized sea scallops with carrots, white corn, and crispy onion rings; or double-cut pork chop with garlic-roasted potatoes, cipollini onions, and caramelized shallot sauce. No matter how much you love every bite of your meal, try not to fill up before dessert. End with any of the sweets, such as the hot, gooey chocolate cake with vanilla ice cream.

✪ **The French Laundry.** 6640 Washington St. (at Creek St.), Yountville. ☎ **707/944-2380.** Reservations required. Prix-fixe menu $59 (5-course), $75 (9-course). AE, MC, V. Mon–Thurs 5:30–9:30pm, Fri–Sun 11:30am–1:45pm and 5:30–9:30pm. AMERICAN/FRENCH.

If your restaurant has the chutzpah to post neither a sign nor an address, it had better be good. Fortunately, this Yountville institution *is* that good. Though it has been around since 1978, it wasn't until renowned chef/owner Thomas Keller bought the restaurant a few years back that it caught the attention of Epicureans worldwide. Dinner is an all-night affair; when it's finally over, you're ready to sit down and do it all over again. Truly, it's that wonderful.

Technically, the prix-fixe menu offers a choice of five or nine courses (including a vegetarian menu), but after a slew of cameo appearances from the kitchen, everyone starts to lose count. Signature dishes include Keller's "tongue in cheek" (a marinated and braised round of sliced lamb tongue and tender beef cheeks) and "macaroni and cheese" (sweet butter-poached Maine lobster with creamy lobster broth and orzo with marscapone cheese). Portions are small, but only because Keller wants his guests to taste as many different things as possible—nobody leaves hungry. The excellent staff is well acquainted with the wide selection of regional wines; the house charges a $20 corkage fee if you choose to bring your own wine. On warm summer nights, consider requesting a table in the flower-filled garden.

La Boucane. 1778 2nd St. (1 block east of Jefferson St.), Napa. ☎ **707/253-1177.** Reservations recommended. Main courses $14–$21. MC, V. Mon–Sat 5:30–10pm. FRENCH.

You'll be graciously welcomed into the domain of chef/owner Jacques Mokrani, who took this 1885 "Victorian lady" and refurbished her in a traditional French style with antiques and lots of chintz. The dinner-only menu is also classically French, featuring such dishes as duck à l'orange, sole meunière, and tournedos forestière. Try the poulet sauté Boucane, prepared with cognac, shallots, mushrooms, and sherry. To start, there are escargots and prawns provençal, and to finish, a traditional chocolate mousse and crème caramel. Granted, La Boucane isn't on the road to glory, but its tried-and-true French fare is better than most in the area.

✪ **Restaurant at Meadowood.** At the Meadowood Resort, 900 Meadowood Lane, St. Helena. ☎ 707/963-3646. Reservations recommended. Fixed-price $48, $75 including wine pairings; vegetarian $35. AE, DISC, DC, MC, V. Daily 6–10pm. AMERICAN/FRENCH.

One of Napa's more ambitious four-course dinners is served at Meadowood, a top-rated resort with a gazebo-style clubhouse dining room overlooking the golf course. When we dined here, dinner started with a flavorful, warm quail salad with smoky lentils and soy sauce, which was robust but not too heavy. Next came a crispy-skinned salmon trout served with exotic mushrooms and truffle oil—superb. Caramelized banana with currants and vanilla ice cream finished the evening, thank goodness, because we couldn't eat another bite. Though we didn't have room to taste it, the vegetarian four-course meal sounded just as wonderful and featured couscous layered with zucchini flavored with anise seeds, and crispy strudel with artichokes, onions, and wild mushrooms. Take a little stroll around the tranquil grounds afterward.

✪ **Terra.** 1345 Railroad Ave. (between Adams and Hunt sts.), St. Helena. ☎ **707/963-8931.** Reservations recommended. Main courses $14–$23. CB, DC, MC, V. Sun–Mon and Wed–Thur 6–9pm, Fri–Sat 6–10pm. CONTEMPORARY AMERICAN.

St. Helena's restaurant of choice, Terra, is the creation of Lissa Doumani and her husband, Hiro Sone, a master chef who hails from Japan and once worked with Wolfgang Puck at Los Angeles's Spago. Sone makes full use of the region's bounty; he seems to know how to coax every nuance of flavor from his fine local ingredients. The simple dining room is a perfect foil for Sone's extraordinary food. Among the appetizers, the terrine of foie gras with apple, walnut, and endive salad and the home-smoked salmon with beets, potatoes, and frisée are the stars of the show. The main dishes successfully fuse different cooking styles: Try the grilled salmon with Thai red-curry sauce or the sake-marinated sea bass with shrimp dumplings in shiso broth. A recommended finale? The chocolate-cognac mousse cake with sun-dried cherry ice cream.

MODERATE

All Seasons Café. 1400 Lincoln Ave. (at Washington St.), Calistoga. ☎ **707/942-9111.** Reservations recommended on weekends. Main courses $13–$19 at dinner. MC, V. Mon–Tues and Thurs–Fri 11am–3pm, Thurs–Tues 5:30–10pm (wine shop, Thurs–Tues 11am–8pm). CALIFORNIA.

Wine Country devotees often wend their way to the All Seasons Café in downtown Calistoga because of its extensive wine list and knowledgeable staff. The trick here is to buy a bottle of wine from the cafe's wine shop, then bring it to your table; the cafe adds a corkage fee of around $7.50 instead of tripling the price of the bottle (as they do at most restaurants). The menu is diverse, ranging from pizzas and pastas to such main courses as braised lamb shank "osso bucco" in an orange, madeira, and tomato sauce. Anything with the house-smoked salmon or spiced sausages is also a safe bet. Chef John Coss saves his guests from any major faux pas by matching wines to his dishes on the menu, so you know what's just right for chantrelle mushroom pizza.

Bistro Don Giovanni. 4110 St. Helena Hwy. (on Calif. 29, just north of Salvador Ave.), Napa. ☎ **707/224-3300.** Reservations recommended Sat–Sun. Main courses $11–$15. AE, DC, MC, V. Mon–Thurs 11:30am–10pm, Fri–Sun 11:30am–11pm. NORTHERN ITALIAN.

Donna and Giovanni Scala—who also run the fantastic Scala's Bistro in San Francisco (see chapter 4)—serve refined Italian fare prepared with top-quality ingredients and a California flair at this large, lively, Mediterranean-style restaurant. The menu features pastas, risottos, pizzas (baked in a wood-burning oven), and a half-dozen other main courses such as braised lamb shank and Niman Schell bistro burgers. Less traditional appetizers include a grilled pear with a frisée-and-arugula salad with bleu cheese, caramelized walnuts, and bacon; the matchstick zucchini sprinkled with Parmesan cheese has become a signature dish. Pasta lovers should go for the farfalle with asparagus, porcini, wild mushrooms, pecorino cheese, and truffle oil; the seared salmon with tomato, white wine, and chive sauce is another winner. Alfresco dining among the vineyards is available—and highly recommended on a warm, sunny day.

Brava Terrace. 3010 St. Helena Hwy. (Calif. 29), St. Helena. ☎ **707/963-9300.** Reservations recommended. Main courses $8–$19. AE, DC, DISC, MC, V. Thurs–Tues noon–9pm. CALIFORNIA/MEDITERRANEAN.

Fred Halpert earned acclaim as the head chef at the Portman Hotel in San Francisco; in 1991, he set up his own shop in the Wine Country, where he became a hit almost at once. Halpert is always searching for new taste sensations; fortunately, that experimentation is backed up by a thorough training in the flavors and zest of Provence and other locales. The food is both good and reasonably priced. You can order a simple sandwich of roasted vegetable with sun-dried tomato butter, or go whole hog for such main courses as coq au vin or a grilled pork chop with barbecue sauce. There's always a fish, a pasta, and a risotto of the day. Be sure to try the spicy fries (a heartburn special). If your stomach can handle this wild and robust mix of flavors and food, finish your meal with the chocolate chip crème brûlée. A dozen wines by the glass are available. *Beware:* Service can be slow on weekends.

Brix. 7377 St. Helena Hwy. (Calif. 29), Yountville. ☎ **707/944-2749.** Reservations recommended. Main courses $12–$22. AE, DC, DISC, MC, V. Sun–Thurs 11:30am–9:30pm, Fri–Sat 11:30am–10pm. ASIAN FUSION.

One of the largest new restaurants to open in the area in 1997, Brix is also one of the most popular. In winter, a table by the corner fireplace promises romantic dining; in summer, you can overlook the vineyards for a more pronounced Wine Country experience. Executive Chef Tod Michael Kawachi does a wonderful job integrating Asian flavors with California cuisine, and the result is a rich culinary adventure. While starters—such as a very tasty grilled Portobello mushroom salad with bleu cheese and sherry-walnut vinaigrette (ask them not to go too heavy on the dressing!)—are interesting, only the starved should indulge, as portions are large and very satisfying. We tried the Hawaiian ono with a rock shrimp and shiitake coconut-curry ragoût, and a Thai pesto smoked rack of lamb with spicy peanut sate and zinfandel glaze. Both were very good, with knockout sauces, but what really impressed us was the Chinese-style whole crispy fish with cilantro black-bean sauce—an absolute must-have.

✪ Catahoula. 1457 Lincoln Ave., Calistoga. ☎ **707/942-2275.** Reservations recommended. Main courses $11–$20. MC, V. Mon and Wed–Fri noon–2:30pm, Sat–Sun noon–3:30pm; Mon, Wed–Thurs, and Sun 5:30–10pm, Fri and Sat 5:30–10:30pm. AMERICAN/SOUTHERN.

The domain of chef Jan Birnbaum, formerly of New York's Quilted Giraffe and San Francisco's Campton Place, this restaurant is the current favorite in town. And with good reason: It's the only place in Napa where you can get a decent rooster gumbo.

You'd have to travel all over Louisiana to find another pan-fried jalapeño-pecan cat-fish like this one. Catahoula's funky and fun, and the food that comes out of the wood-burning oven—like the roast duck with chili-cilantro potatoes or the whole roasted fish with lemon broth, orzo, and escarole—is exciting. Start with the spicy gumbo ya ya with andouille sausage, and finish with what may be a first for many non-Southerners: buttermilk ice cream.

Mustards Grill. 7399 St. Helena Hwy. (Calif. 29), Yountville. ☎ **707/944-2424.** Reservations recommended. Main courses $11–$17. CB, DC, DISC, MC, V. Apr–Oct, daily 11:30am–10pm; Nov–Mar, daily 11:30am–9pm. CALIFORNIA.

It's always a pleasant surprise to find a serious restaurant with a strong sense of humor; Mustards is one of those places. The minute we sat down here and glanced at the menu, it immediately advised us: "Have a glass of wine," which we did (although it took some time to choose from the 11-page list). We were left alone long enough to notice that Mustards is a convivial, barn-style space before the jovial waiter pointed out the ambitious chalkboard list of specials. Following California's most recent trend, we started out with a wonderfully light seared ahi tuna that melted in our mouths the way ahi should. Although the hoisin quail with apricot sauce and bok choy and the lamb shank braised in syrah with fennel and onions were tempting, we opted for a moist, perfectly flavored grilled chicken breast with mashed potatoes and fresh herbs. The menu includes something for everyone, from gourmands and vegetarians to good old burger lovers.

Napa Valley Grille. 6795 Washington St. (on Calif. 29 at Madison St.), Yountville. ☎ **707/944-8686.** Reservations accepted. Main courses $12–$22; lunch $7–$14. AE, CB, DC, DISC, MC, V. Mon–Thurs 11:30am–9:30pm, Fri–Sat 11:30am–10pm, Sun 10:30am–9:30pm. CALIFORNIA/MEDITERRANEAN.

In case you've forgotten that you're in the thick of the wine-growing region, the grape motif woven into this restaurant's decor will undoubtedly remind you. The menu synchronizes with its "Wine Country cuisine" prepared with fresh, local ingredients and an extensive wine list featuring—you guessed it—Napa Valley wines. On sunny afternoons, most opt for the umbrella-shaded patio, but inside you can watch the swirl of activity in the open kitchen. The menu offers an array of dishes: smoked duck, grilled game hen, or a pasta such as black spaghetti with rock shrimp, scallops, calamari, enoki mushrooms, and a white wine sauce. Lunches feature a long list of salads to cool you off from the summer heat, and brunch always offers myriad morning munchies, including a smoked-salmon omelet with roasted peppers and herbed cream, or Dungeness crab cakes with poached eggs and Cajun hollandaise.

✪ **Tra Vigne Restaurant.** 1050 Charter Oak Ave., St. Helena. ☎ **707/963-4444.** Reservations recommended. Main courses $12.50–$18.95; Cantinetta $4–$8. CB, DC, DISC, MC, V. Daily 11:30am–10pm; Cantinetta daily 11:30am–6pm. ITALIAN.

If you can only dine at one restaurant while visiting the Wine Country, make it Tra Vigne. Sure, there are a few fancier places in town, but there's no restaurant that measures up to this near-perfect mix of atmosphere, food, and pricing. The enormous dining room packs 'em in every night—and whether diners are seated on the veranda (heated on cold nights) or in the center of the bustling scene, they're usually thrilled just to have a seat. Even though the wonderful bread served with house-made flavored olive oils is tempting, save plenty of room for the robust California dishes cooked with Italian style that's made this place everyone's favorite. The menu features about five or so pizzas, including a succulent version with caramelized onions, thyme, and gorgonzola. The dishes of the day might include a grilled Sonoma rabbit with teleme-layered potatoes, oven-dried tomatoes, and mustard pan sauce, and a dozen or so antipasti. Pastas are equally tempting, including ceppo with sausage, spinach, potatoes, sun-dried tomatoes, and pecorino. Desserts are equally delicious.

The adjoining Cantinetta offers a small selection of sandwiches, pizzas, and lighter meals (see below).

✪ **Trilogy.** 1234 Main St. (at Hunt Ave.), St. Helena. ☎ **707/963-5507.** Reservations required. Main courses $14.50–$20; lunch, 2-course fixed-price menu $15; dinner, 3-course fixed-price menu $28. MC, V. Tues–Fri noon–2pm; Tues–Sat 6–9pm. Closed 3 weeks in Dec. CALIFORNIA/FRENCH.

With a wine list that's probably second to none in the valley, this small, low-key restaurant is a favorite of Wine Country moguls. Diane Pariseau and her assistant do virtually everything themselves, turning out exceptionally fresh food prepared with a fine-honed technique. An à la carte menu is available, but the real treat here is the $28 three-course fixed-price menu, with each course accompanied by the appropriate glass of superior-quality wine for an extra $12 ("The best deal around," says Pariseau). The menu changes daily, but expect such delectable starters as salmon-potato cakes with chili aioli or seared tuna with Japanese noodle salad and wasabi dressing. Other selections may include roasted pork tenderloin with shiitake mushroom sauce (recommended with a hearty Ravenswood 1994 zinfandel), or a sautéed duck breast with sun-dried cherry sauce (best accompanied by a glass of 1992 Hanzell pinot noir).

Wappo Bar & Bistro. 1226B Washington St., Calistoga (off Lincoln Ave.). ☎ **707/942-4712.** Main courses $8.50–$14.50. AE, DC, MC, V. Wed–Mon 11:30am–2:30pm and 6–9:30pm. INTERNATIONAL.

One of the best alfresco dining experiences in the Wine Country is under Wappo's honeysuckle- and vine-covered arbor, but you'll also be comfortable inside this small bistro at one of the well-spaced, well-polished tables. The menu offers a wide range of choices, from Chilean sea bass with mint chutney to roast rabbit with potato gnocchi with mustard cream and spinach, for example. The desserts of choice are the black-bottom coconut cream pie and the strawberry-rhubarb pie.

✪ **Wine Spectator Greystone Restaurant.** 2555 Main St. (at the Culinary Institute of America at Greystone), St. Helena. ☎ **707/967-1010.** Reservations strongly recommended. Tapas $3–$6; main courses $16–$18.50 (prices same for lunch and dinner). Daily 11:30am–3pm and 5:30–10pm; 3:30–5:30pm tapas at the bar. MEDITERRANEAN.

This place offers a combination visual and culinary feast that's unparalleled in the area, if not the state. While the room itself is an enormous stone-walled former winery, the festive decor and wafts of heavenly aromas warm the space well. Cooking islands—complete with scurrying chefs, steaming pots, and rotating chicken—provide stove-side scenics and your ultimately edible entertainment. The tapas, or tasting, menu focuses on Mediterranean-influenced dishes, including a pork kebab that turned our vegetarian guest into a meat eater, and a grilled calamari that contradicts the sea-dweller's rubbery reputation with every moist and peppery bite. Tapas portions are small, but affordable. Pastas and salads are a bit heftier. Main courses, such as a Moroccan spiced braised lamb shank with dried fruit and almond couscous are well portioned and darn good, but we recommend you opt for a barrage of appetizers for your table to share. While the food is quite serious, the atmosphere is playful, and casual enough that you'll feel comfortable in jeans or shorts. If you want to ensure a meal here (which we recommend you do), reserve far in advance.

INEXPENSIVE

✪ **The Cantinetta.** 1050 Charter Oak Ave. (at Tra Vigne Restaurant) St. Helena. ☎ **707/963-8888.** Main courses $4–$8. CB, DC, DISC, MC, V. Daily 11:30am–6pm. ITALIAN.

Regardless of where we dine while we're here, we always make a point of stopping at the Cantinetta for an espresso and a snack. Part cafe, part shop, it's a casual place with a few tables and a counter. The foccacias (we've never had better in our lives!), pasta salads, and pastries are outstanding, and there's a selection of cookies and other wonderful treats. Also available are flavored oils (free tastings), wines, and an array of gourmet items, many of which were created here. You can also get great picnic grub to go.

The Diner. 6476 Washington St., Yountville. ☎ **707/944-2626.** Reservations not accepted. Breakfast $4–$8; lunch $6–$10; dinner $8–$13.25. No credit cards. Tues–Sun 8am–3pm and 5:30–9pm. From Calif. 29 north, take the Yountville exit and turn left onto Washington St. AMERICAN/MEXICAN.

Funky California meets traditional roadside eatery at this diner that features a functioning Irish Waterford wood stove, a collection of vintage-diner water pitchers, and an art exhibit that changes monthly. The Diner's fare is far from that of a regular greasy spoon—the "home-style" menu is extensive, portions are huge, and the food is very good. Breakfasts feature good old-fashioned omelets, French toast, and German potato pancakes. Lunch and dinner dishes include a host of Mexican and American dishes such as chicken picatta with veggies and rice, grilled fresh fish, giant burritos, and thick sandwiches made with house-roasted meats and homemade bread.

Smokehouse Café. 1458 Calistoga Ave., Calistoga. ☎ **707/942-6060.** Main courses $5–$15. MC, V. Daily 7:30am–10pm. REGIONAL AMERICAN.

Who would've guessed that the best spareribs and house-smoked meats in Northern California would come from this little kitchen in Calistoga? Here's the winning game plan: Start with the Sacramento delta crawfish cakes (better than any wimpy crab cakes you'll find in San Francisco) and husk-roasted Cheyenne corn, then move on to the slow pig sandwich, a half-slab of ribs, or house-made sausages—all of which take up to a week to prepare (not while you wait, luckily). The clincher, though, is the fluffy all-you-can-eat cornbread dipped in pure cane syrup, which comes with every full-plate dinner. Kids are especially catered to—a rarity in these parts—and patio dining is available during the summer for breakfast, lunch, and dinner.

2 Sonoma Valley

Sonoma is often thought of as the "other" Wine Country, forever in the shadow of Napa Valley. Truth is, even though there are far fewer wineries here (and far fewer tourists), its wines have actually won more awards than Napa's. Sonoma County stretches west to the coast, is more rural and less traveled than its neighbor to the east, and offers a more genuine "escape from it all" than a trip to Napa. Roads are less crowded, more quaint, and still devoid of back-to-back tourist attractions and hotels. Small, family-owned wineries are its mainstay, just like in the old days of wine making when everyone started with the intention of going broke and loved every minute of it. As opposed to the corporate-run tours most Napa Valley wineries run, tastings on the west side of the Mayacamas Mountains are usually free, low key, and come with plenty of friendly banter between the wine makers and their guests.

ESSENTIALS

GETTING THERE   From San Francisco, cross the Golden Gate Bridge and stay on U.S. 101 north. Exit at Calif. 37; after 10 miles, turn north onto Calif. 121. After another 10 miles, turn north onto Calif. 12 (Broadway), which will take you into town. From the town of Napa, take Calif. 121 south to Calif. 12. The roads are well marked with directional signs.

VISITOR INFORMATION   Before you begin your explorations of the area, visit the **Sonoma Valley Visitors Bureau,** 453 1st St. E., Sonoma, CA 95476 (☎ **707/ 996-1090;** fax 707/996-9212; website: www.sonomavalley.com). Located right on the plaza in the town of Sonoma, it offers free maps and brochures about lo-cal happenings. The office is open daily from 9am to 5pm in winter and 9am to 7pm in summer. An additional office has been added a few miles south of Sono-ma at 25200 Arnold Dr. (Calif. 121; ☎ **707/996-1090**); it's open daily from 9am to 5pm.

The **Sonoma County Convention and Visitors Bureau,** 5000 Roberts Lake Rd., Suite A, Rohnert Park, CA 94928 (☎ **800/326-7666** or 707/586-8100; fax 707/ 586-8111), offers a free visitors guide, with information about the whole county. They're also happy to provide lots of specialized information. Write as far in advance as possible.

WHEN TO GO   See "When to Go" in Napa section, above.

TOURING THE VALLEY & WINERIES

Like its sister valley, Napa, Sonoma Valley produces some of the finest wines in the nation. What makes a trip to Sonoma so pleasant is the intimate quality of so many of its vineyards and wineries. California's first winery, Buena Vista, was founded in Sonoma Valley in 1857, and it's still in operation today (see below). Today, Sonoma is home to about 35 wineries and 13,000 acres of vineyards. Chardonnay is the variety for which Sonoma is most noted, and it represents almost one-quarter of the valley's vine acreage.

The wineries here tend to be a little more spread out than they are in Napa, but they're still easy to find. The visitors bureaus listed above will provide you with maps to the valley's wineries. We've listed a few of our favorites below.

Biking Around the Valley

Sonoma and its neighboring towns are so small, close together, and relatively flat that it's not difficult to get around on two wheels. In fact, if you're up to it and you're not in a hurry, there may be no better way to enjoy the area than by pedaling through it.

You can rent a bike at the **Goodtime Bicycle Company,** 18503 Calif. 12, Sonoma (☎ 707/938-0453). They'll happily point you to easy bike trails. They also provide a picnic on request. Bikes, helmets, and everything else you'll need cost $25 a day, or $5 per hour (delivery is a $25 flat day rate). Bikes are also available from **Sonoma Valley Cyclery,** 20093 Broadway, Sonoma (☎ **707/935-3377**), for $20 a day, or $6 per hour. For biking information in Sonoma County, call the friendly folks at **Dave's Bikes Sport,** 353 College Ave., Santa Rosa (☎ **707/528-3283**).

SONOMA

Sonoma owes much of its appeal to Mexican General Mariano Guadalupe Vallejo, who fashioned this pleasant, slow-paced town after a typical Mexican village—right down to central plaza, Sonoma's geographical and commercial center. The Plaza sits at the top of a T formed by Broadway (Calif. 12) and Napa Street. Most of the surrounding streets form a grid pattern around this axis, making Sonoma easy to negotiate. The plaza's Bear Flag Monument marks the spot where the crude Bear Flag was raised in 1846, signaling the end of Mexican rule; the symbol was later adopted by the state of California. The 8-acre park at the center of the plaza, with two ponds frequented by ducks and geese, is perfect for an afternoon siesta in the cool shade.

Buena Vista. 18000 Old Winery Rd. (P.O. Box 1842), Sonoma, CA 95476. ☎ **707/ 938-1266.** Daily 10:30am–4:30pm.

Buena Vista, the patriarch of California wineries, is located slightly northeast of the town of Sonoma. It was founded in 1857 by Count Agoston Haraszthy, the Hungarian émigré who's called the father of the California wine industry. A close friend of General Vallejo, Haraszthy returned from Europe in 1861 with 100,000 of the finest vine cuttings, which he made available to all wine growers. Although Buena Vista's wine making now takes place in an ultramodern facility outside Sonoma, the winery still maintains a complimentary tasting room here, inside the restored 1862 Press House. There's also a self-guided tour that you can follow anytime during operating hours and a guided tour 2pm daily. After tasting, grab your favorite bottle, a selection of cheeses from the Sonoma Cheese Factory, salami, bread, and pâté (all available in the tasting room) and plant yourself at one of the 12 scenic picnic tables.

Ravenswood Winery. 18701 Gehricke Rd., Sonoma. ☎ **707/938-1960.** Fax 707/938-9459. Daily 10am–4:30pm. Reservations required for tours.

This small, traditional winery in the Sonoma Hills, built right into the hillside to keep it cool inside, crushed its first grapes in 1976 for its inaugural zinfandel. The winery is best known for its reds, especially its big, bold zinfandels, but it also produces a merlot, a cabernet sauvignon, and some whites. You'll be able to taste these as well as some younger blends, which are less expensive than the older vintages. Tours follow the wine-making process from grape to glass, and include the oak-barrel aging rooms. A "Barbecue Overlooking the Vineyards" is held each weekend from Memorial Day through the end of September (call for details and reservations), but picnic tables also beckon a bring-your-own feast.

Sebastiani Vineyards Winery. 389 4th St. E., Sonoma. ☎ **800/888-5532** or 707/938-5532. Daily 10am–5pm (last tour begins at 4pm).

Although Sebastiani doesn't occupy the most scenic setting or structures in Sonoma Valley, its place in the history and development of the region is unique, and it does offer an interesting and informative guided tour. The 25-minute tour, through aging stone cellars containing more than 300 carved casks, is well worth the time. You can see the winery's original turn-of-the-century crusher and press, as well as a large collection of oak-barrel carvings. If you don't want to take the tour, go straight to the tasting room, where you can sample an extensive selection of wines. A picnic area is adjacent to the cellars.

What to See & Do Beyond the Wineries

The best way to see the town of Sonoma is to follow the **Sonoma Walking Tour,** available from the Sonoma Valley Visitors Bureau (see "Visitor Information," above). Highlights include General Vallejo's 1852 Victorian-style home; Sonoma Barracks, erected in 1836 to house Mexican army troops; and the Blue Wing Inn, an 1840 hostelry built to accommodate tourists and new settlers while they erected homes in Sonoma—John Frémont, Kit Carson, and Ulysses S. Grant were all guests.

The **Mission San Francisco Solano de Sonoma,** on Sonoma Plaza at the corner of First Street East and Spain Street (☎ **707/938-1519**), was founded in 1823. It was the northernmost, and last, mission built in California. It was also the only one established on the northern coast by the Mexican rulers, who wished to protect their territory against expansionist Russian fur traders. It's now part of Sonoma State Historic Park. Admission is $2 for adults, $1 for children 6 to 12 and free for children under 6. Open daily 10am to 5pm except Thanksgiving, Christmas, and New Year's.

The **Arts Guild of Sonoma,** 140 E. Napa St. (☎ **707/996-3115**), showcases the works of local artists. Exhibits change frequently and include a wide variety of styles and media. Admission is free. Open Wednesday to Monday 11am to 5pm.

Most of the town's shops, which offer everything from food and wines to clothing and books, are located around the plaza, including **The Mercado,** a small shopping center at 452 1st St. E. that houses several good stores selling unusual wares. The most interesting shops cater to the kitchen.

GLEN ELLEN

This small Wine Country town about 7 miles north of Sonoma hasn't changed much since the days when Jack London settled on his Beauty Ranch, about a mile west. A trip to Glen Ellen feels like a visit to an undiscovered old town. Other than the wineries, there are few real signs of commercialism, and the shops and restaurants—located along one main winding lane—cater to a small, local clientele.

✪ **The Benziger Family Winery.** 1883 London Ranch Rd., Glen Ellen. ☎ **707/935-3000.** Tasting room daily 10am to 5pm; tram tours daily (weather permitting) at 12:30, 2, and 3:30pm.

When the Benzigers moved from New York, purchased the plot next to Jack London State Park, and started the Glen Ellen label, they had no idea they'd become the valley's second-largest wine producer. However, after their fast track to the top, they sold the rights to the label in order to create lower-volume, higher-quality wines. A visit here confirms that you are indeed visiting a "family" winery; at any given time three generations of Benzigers may be running around, and you're instantly made to feel like you're part of the clan. The property is pastoral and user friendly, with a self-guided tour, gardens, a friendly tasting room, an art gallery, and roaming peacocks. The free "tram" tour is plenty of fun as it winds through the estate and the winemaking process and makes a champagne-tasting pit stop on a scenic bluff. There are several perfect picnic spots.

B. R. Cohn Winery. 15140 Sonoma Hwy. (just north of Madrone Rd.), Glen Ellen. ☎ **707/938-4064.** Daily 10am to 5pm.

With little more than a simple tasting room perched atop a small hill, the B. R. Cohn Winery experience is casual and straightforward—a welcome departure if you've been touring larger wineries. The staff is friendly and informative; tastings of the delicious chardonnay, cabernet, and pinot noir are free; and wines and olive oil are available for purchase. There are scenic picnic tables on the cement patio, which overlooks the road and vineyards, but you'll have to bring your own feast. One nice bonus is they often sell selections that aren't available elsewhere. In 1998 they'll be moving the room to the main house, which will make for a cozier experience, and they're adding more outdoor tables around the surrounding olive trees.

What to See & Do Beyond the Wineries

Hikers, horseback riders, and picnickers enjoy ☎ **Jack London State Historic Park,** 2400 London Ranch Rd., off Arnold Dr.; (☎ **707/938-5216**). Within its 800 acres, which were once home to the renowned writer, you'll find 9 miles of trails, the remains of London's burned-down dream house as well as preserved structures, and plenty of ideal picnic spots. An on-site museum, called the House of Happy Walls, was built by Jack's wife to display a collection from the author's life. The park is open daily from 9:30am to 7pm in summer, and 9:30am to 5pm during winter. The museum is open daily from 10am to 5pm. Admission to the park is $5 per car, $4 per car for seniors 62 and over. Pick up the $1 self-guided tour map on arrival to help acquaint you with the grounds. In summer, golf-cart rides are offered daily from noon to 4pm to those who don't want to hoof it.

If you'd like to see the park on horseback, **Sonoma Cattle Company & Napa Valley Trail Rides** can saddle you up. Rides may not be offered in the off-season, so call ☎ **707/996-8566** for information on tours and rates, or write P.O. Box 877, Glen Ellen, CA 95442.

Shoppers and food lovers might find **The Olive Press,** Jack London Village, 14301 Arnold Dr. (☎ **707/939-8900**), interesting. With olive trees abounding in the area and the local's penchant for gourmet foods, it's no surprise that fresh-pressed olive oil has become a lucrative business in this neck of the woods, and The Olive Press is case in point. You can watch the olive press in action as it conveys the fruit up a belt, cleans it, and begins the pressing process. There's a nifty gift shop with decorative bottles that can be filled with the oil of your choice, and other gourmet knickknacks. Don't expect a bargain here, however. Even if you bring your own bottle, a gallon of oil can go for $100. If you're headed to Napa, you'll find a far better deal at the Napa Valley Olive Oil Manufacturing Company (see above). Next door is the Glen Ellen Winery tasting room and History Center. Open daily 10am to 5pm.

KENWOOD

Château St. Jean. 8555 Sonoma Hwy. (Calif. 12), Kenwood. ☎ **707/833-4134.** Self-guided tours, daily 10am–4pm; tasting room, daily 10am–4:30pm.

Château St. Jean (at the foot of Sugarloaf Ridge, just north of Kenwood and east of Calif. 12) is notable for its exceptionally beautiful buildings, well-landscaped grounds, and elegant tasting room. A private drive takes you to what was once a 250-acre country retreat, built in 1920. A well-manicured lawn is now a picnic area, complete with a fountain and benches. There's a self-guided tour with detailed and photographic descriptions of the wine-making process. When you're done with it, be sure to walk up to the top of the tower for a view of the valley. Back in the tasting room, you can sample several chardonnays, a cabernet, a fumé blanc, a merlot, a Riesling, and a gewürztraminer.

Kunde Estate Winery. Box 639, 10155 Sonoma Hwy. (Calif. 12), Kenwood. ☎ **707/833-5501**. Website: www.kunde.com. Tastings daily 11am–5pm.

Expect a friendly, unintimidating welcoming at this scenic winery, which also happens to be where Geena Davis and Renny Harlin tied the knot in 1993. One of the largest grape suppliers in the area, Kunde owns 2,000 acres of prime vineyards that extend around the property and beyond and provides grapes to more than 28 Sonoma and Napa wineries. Kunde makes nothing but estate wines. In addition to plenty of free tasting options, both red and white, there's a nice gift shop. A tour of the property's wine caves includes a history of the winery. Private tours are available by appointment, but most folks are happy just to stop by for some vino and relax at one of the many picnic tables strategically placed around a sweet man-made pond with fountains. Animal lovers will especially appreciate Kunde's preservation efforts; the property has a rare duck estuary with more than 50 species. Cave tours are held on the half hour Friday to Sunday from 11am to 4pm.

WHERE TO STAY
VERY EXPENSIVE

✪ **Kenwood Inn & Spa.** 10400 Sonoma Hwy., Kenwood, CA 95452. ☎ **800/353-6966** or 707/833-1293. Fax 707/833-1247. 12 rms. Apr–Oct, $215–$365 double (2-night minimum on weekends); Nov–Mar, $195–$315 double. Rates include gourmet breakfast and bottle of wine. AE, MC, V.

Inspired by the villas of Tuscany, the honey-colored, Italian-style buildings, flower-filled flagstone courtyard, and pastoral views of vineyard-covered hills are enough to make any northern Italian homesick. We were immediately impressed with the friendly staff who made us feel right at home. Every spacious room is lavishly and exquisitely decorated with imported tapestries, velvets, and antiques; each has a fireplace, balcony (unless you're on the ground floor), feather bed, CD player, and down comforter—but no phone or TV, so you can relax.

An impressive two-course gourmet breakfast is served poolside or in the Mediterranean-style dining room; ours consisted of a poached egg accompanied by light, flavorful potatoes, red bell peppers, and other roasted vegetables, all artfully arranged, followed by a delicious homemade scone with fresh berries and a small lemon tart (yum!).

While there's no gym here, the rooms are worlds better than those a few miles away at Sonoma Mission Inn; if you insist on access to a workout room, our recommendation is to stay here and buy a day pass to Sonoma Mission Inn's spa ($35 per day). A minor caveat is road noise, which you're unlikely to hear from your room, but can be slightly heard over the tranquil pumped-in music around the courtyard and pool.

Dining: Full gourmet breakfast served in dining room in winter, on terrace in summer.

Services: Concierge, dry cleaning and laundry, massage, facials, skin treatments.

Facilities: Heated pool, Jacuzzi, steam room.

Sonoma Mission Inn & Spa. 18140 Calif. 12 (P.O. Box 1447), Sonoma, CA 94576. ☎ **800/862-4945** or 707/938-9000. Fax 707/938-4250. 198 rms. A/C MINIBAR TV TEL. Nov–Apr, $120–$275 Historic Inn room; $160–$360 Wine Country room. May–Oct, $140–$285 Historic Inn room; $180–$370 Wine Country room. Year-round, from $285 suite. AE, CB, DC, MC, V. From central Sonoma, drive 3 miles north on Calif. 12.

This 1920s-era resort is housed in a three-story pink Mediterranean-style structure set on 8 well-groomed acres directly above the world-class spa's lifeblood: a 127°F natural artesian mineral water, now piped directly into the world-class spa's two pools and whirlpools. While Clara Bow or Mary Pickford would have felt at home here, you're more likely to see Barbra Streisand or Harrison Ford strolling around in their aquatic Skivvies. The rooms are furnished in a modern theme with framed watercolors, ceiling fans, and such extra amenities as bathroom scales, hair dryers, and oversize bath towels. The Wine Country rooms are in a newer building and have king-size beds, down comforters, desks, and refrigerators; some offer fireplaces and many have balconies. The older Historic Inn rooms are sweetly appointed with homey furnishings and are slightly smaller; most have queen-size beds. All rooms have VCRs and come with a complimentary bottle of wine.

Expect changes to the inn in the coming year, as it's recently been bought by a Texas company with some seriously deep pockets. A new complex of large, attractive suites has already been built, and plans to expand the spa are in the works.

Dining: The Grille, run by chef Toni Sakaguchi, is known for its low-calorie, sodium, and cholesterol California cuisine and its 200 varieties of Napa and Sonoma wines (see "Where to Dine," below). The casual cafe, serving American cuisine at lunch, is renowned for its bountiful breakfasts.

Services: Room service, concierge, laundry, dry cleaning, newspaper delivery, in-room massage, baby-sitting, secretarial services, valet parking, complimentary refreshments.

Facilities: Full spa facilities with a full range of treatments and nutritional consultation; health club; tennis courts. The tariff for individual spa and salon services ranges from $35 to $134. The use of the spa's bathhouse, which includes a sauna, steam room, whirlpool, outdoor exercise pool, and gym with weight equipment, costs $10 weekdays and Sundays, and $20 on Saturdays, but is complimentary with any spa service. Guests have use of the nearby 18-hole Sonoma Golf Club.

MODERATE

El Dorado Hotel. 405 First St. W., Sonoma, CA 95476. ☎ **800/289-3031** or 707/996-3030. Fax 707/996-3148. 27 rms. A/C TV TEL. Winter, $90–$110 double; summer, $115–$145 double. Rates include continental breakfast and a split of wine. Wheelchair-accessible rooms available. AE, MC, V.

This place may look like a 19th-century Wild West relic from the outside, but you won't be sleeping on a rickety antique bed and bathing in a cramped clawfoot tub here—inside it's all 20th-century deluxe. Each modern, handsomely appointed guest room—designed by the same folks who put together the Auberge du Soleil in Napa Valley (see above)—has French windows, a small terrace, a canopy bed, and a private bath with plush towels and hair dryers; some offer lovely views of the Plaza, while others overlook the hotel's private courtyard and heated pool.

Breakfast, served either inside or out, includes coffee, fruits, and freshly baked breads and pastries. Within the hotel is Piatti, a popular restaurant serving regional Italian cuisine (see "Where to Dine," below). Services include a concierge, laundry, in-room massage, bicycle rental, and access to a nearby health club.

✪ **Sonoma Chalet.** 18935 5th St. W., Sonoma, CA 95476. ☎ **707/938-3129.** 3 rms, 3 cottages, 1 suite. AC (some rooms). Apr–Oct $95–$145 double; Nov–Mar $85–$135 double. Rates include continental breakfast. AE, MC, V.

This is one of the few accommodations in Sonoma that is truly secluded; it's on the outskirts of town, in a peaceful country setting overlooking a 200-acre ranch. Accommodations are in a Swiss-style farmhouse and several cottages, but they're by no means rustic—all were delightfully decorated by someone with an eye for color and a concern for comfort. They have clawfoot tubs, beds covered with country quilts, oriental carpets, comfortable furnishings, and private decks; some have woodstoves. A breakfast of fruit, yogurt, pastries, and cereal is served either in the country kitchen or in your room—and the gaggles of ducks, chickens, and ornery geese will be glad to help you finish off the crumbs.

Sonoma Hotel. 110 W. Spain St., Sonoma, CA 95476. ☎ **800/468-6016** or 707/996-2996. Fax 707/996-7014. 17 rms, 5 with bath. Winter, Sun–Thur $65 double without bath, $95 double with bath; Fri–Sat $75 double without bath, $115–$125 double with bath. Summer, $75–$85 double without bath, $115–$125 double with bath. Rates include continental breakfast. AE, MC, V. Free parking.

This cute, little historic hotel on Sonoma's tree-lined Town Square still retains the same ambiance it did over a century ago when it first opened. With an emphasis on European-style elegance and comfort, each room is decorated in an early California style, with antique furnishings, fine woods, and floral-print wallpapers. Some of the rooms feature brass beds, and all are blissfully devoid of phones and TVs. Five of the third-floor rooms share immaculate baths (and significantly reduced rates), while rooms with private baths have deep clawfoot tubs with overhead showers. Perks include nightly turndown, continental breakfast, and a bottle of wine on arrival. Also within the hotel is a small restaurant and bar.

INEXPENSIVE

✪ **El Pueblo Inn.** 896 W. Napa St., Sonoma, CA 94576. ☎ **800/900-8844** or 707/996-3651. 38 rms. A/C TEL. May–Oct, $80–$94 double; Mar–Apr and Nov, $69–$80 double; Dec–Feb, $65–$80 double. AE, DISC, MC, JCB, V.

This ain't Sonoma's fanciest hotel, but it offers some of the best-priced accommodations around. Located on Sonoma's main east-west street eight blocks from the center of town, the rooms here are pleasant enough, with post-and-beam construction, exposed brick walls, light wood furniture, and geometric prints. A drip coffee machine with packets of coffee should be a comfort to early risers. An outdoor heated pool will cool you off in hot weather. If possible, reservations should be made at least a month in advance for the spring and summer months.

WHERE TO DINE
EXPENSIVE

✪ **Babette's.** 464 1st St. E. (at the Plaza), Sonoma. ☎ **707/939-8921.** Reservations recommended for dining room. Café $8.75–$14.95; dining room fixed-price $45. MC, V. Café noon–10pm; dining room, Thurs–Sat 6–10pm. FRENCH.

After being voted the "Best Best-Kept Secret" by the *San Francisco Bay Guardian*, Babette's is a secret no more—it's one of the hottest places to dine in Sonoma. Thankfully, this quaint little spot has maintained its homey atmosphere; like most of Sonoma's restaurants, this one's intimate and casual. The front-room café feels like a large living room with couches in the center of the room, a cozy wine bar to the back, and small tables lining the walls. The food is highly regarded and delightfully affordable. Along with soups, salads, and sandwiches—all less than $8—main courses include cassoulet baked with duck confit, house-made pork sausage, lamb, and white beans; and a vegetarian penne with capers and olives in a fennel-tomato sauce.

The main dining room is a small, intimate space with stage-like red curtains lining one wall and tables spaciously dispersed. The menu is a five-course fixed-price affair and might include caviar; roasted quail with garden cress, quinoa, and blood-orange vinaigrette; roasted monkfish on a sauce of smoked ham hocks, leeks, and red wine; pan-roasted veal on vegetables and black chanterelles; and fresh goat cheese on toasts with an endive and herb salad. Wines paired with each course will cost an additional $29.

✪ **Glen Ellen Inn Restaurant.** 13670 Arnold Dr., Glen Ellen. ☎ **707/996-6409.** Reservations recommended. Main courses $10.95–$23. AE, MC, V. Off-season, Thurs–Tues 5:30pm–closing (depending on reservations); summer, nightly 5:30pm–closing. CALIFORNIA.

Christian and Karen Bertrand run the favored dining option in Glen Ellen. The room is so small and cozy (there are just eight tables) that you practically feel like you're in the open kitchen, but that's exactly the place's charm. Garden seating is choice on sunny days, but the covered, heated patio is always welcoming. First courses might include a wild mushroom and sausage "purse" served in a brandy cream sauce and warm goat cheese croquettes. Main courses change with the seasons but might range from linguini with artichoke hearts and feta to a stellar late-harvest ravioli, which is stuffed with pumpkin, walnuts, and sun-dried cranberries on a bed of butternut squash. Other favorites include the marinated pork tenderloin on smoked mozzarella polenta and topped with roasted pepper onion compote and the classic filet mignon. The wine list offers by the bottle, as well as more than a dozen selections by the glass.

The Grille. At Sonoma Mission Inn, 18140 Calif. 12, P.O. Box 1447, Sonoma. ☎ **707/938-9000.** Reservations recommended. Main courses $17–$26. AE, MC, V. Lunch, Sat 11:30am–2pm, Sun 10am–2pm; dinner, nightly 6–9:30pm. CALIFORNIA/SPA.

If you're watching your weight, dinner doesn't have to consist of chicken broth and a few carrot sticks—at least not in this spa's dining room. Here you can have a savory gourmet meal with full knowledge of how many calories you're adding—or not adding—to your thighs. Try a spicy ahi tower with sesame crackers and a zingy cucumber-ginger salad—just 239 calories. Or how about a simple, fresh butternut squash soup at 64 calories? Those who prefer a more decadent meal won't be disappointed either; the hearty New York strip with sour cream mashed potatoes in a cabernet sauce, grilled sage-rubbed duck with rice-confit salad and dried cherry essence, and grilled range chicken with pilaf and a wild mushroom ragoût all come with the flavor—and calories—expected from a fine-dining experience. Even if you stick to the healthier options, you don't have to blow it on dessert. There's a spa lemon chiffon with strawberry sauce at 114 calories and a light sorbet at 95 calories. Better yet, live a little and order the classic crème brûlée—its a brûlée purist's dream come true.

✪ **Kenwood Restaurant & Bar.** 9900 Sonoma Hwy., Kenwood. ☎ **707/833-6326.** Reservations recommended. Main courses $12.50–$24.50. MC, V. Tues–Sun 11:30am–9pm. CALIFORNIA/CONTINENTAL.

This is what California Wine Country dining should be (but what it often, disappointingly, is not). From the terrace of the Kenwood you can enjoy a view of the vineyards as you dine at umbrella-covered tables. On nippy days you can retreat inside to the Sonoma-style roadhouse, with its shiny wood floors, pine ceiling, and vibrant artwork. The decor—cushioned rattan chairs set at white cloth–covered tables— is discreetly simple, with a long oak bar on one side and a painted vine on the wall behind it.

The chef, Max Schacher, serves first-rate cuisine, complemented by a reasonably priced wine list. The menu is perfectly balanced between tradition and innovation, and the finely crafted cooking is marked by the heightened, distinctive flavors of California's Wine Country. Great starters are the Dungeness crab cake with herb mayonnaise; the super-fresh sashimi with ginger, soy, and wasabi; and the wonderful Caesar salad. Main dish choices might include poached salmon in a creamy caper sauce or braised Sonoma rabbit with grilled polenta. But the Kenwood doesn't take itself too seriously: sandwiches and burgers are also available.

MODERATE

✪ **Della Santina's.** 133 E. Napa St. (just east of the Plaza), Sonoma. ☎ **707/935-0576.** Reservations recommended. Main courses $8.75–$14.50. DISC, MC, V. Daily 11:30am–9:30pm. ITALIAN.

Those of you who just can't take another expensive, chi-chi California meal should follow the locals to this friendly and traditional Italian restaurant. How traditional? Just ask father/son team Dan and Robert; when we dined here they pointed out Signora Santina's hand-embroidered linen doilies as they proudly told us about her Tuscan recipes. And their pride is merited. Every dish we had here was refreshingly authentic, in huge portions, and well-flavored—without overbearing sauces or one *hint* of California pretentiousness. Start with traditional antipasti—especially the sliced mozzarella and tomatoes or the delicious white beans. There are nine pasta dishes, again, wonderfully authentic (gnocchi lovers rejoice!). The spit-roasted meat dishes are a local favorite, and for those who can't choose between chicken, pork, turkey, rabbit, or duck, there's a selection that offers a choice of three. Don't worry about breaking your bank on a bottle of wine; most of the savory choices here go for under $25. Desserts are wonderful, too; if it's available, don't pass up the smooth-as-silk milk pudding.

Depot Hotel Restaurant and Italian Garden. 241 1st St. W. (off Spain St.), Sonoma. ☎ **707/938-2980.** Website: www.depotel.com. Reservations recommended. Main courses $7–$16 at dinner. AE, CB, DC, DISC, MC, V. Wed–Fri 11:30am–2pm; Wed–Sun 5–on. NORTHERN ITALIAN.

Michael Ghilarducci has been the chef and owner here for the past 11 years, and he's a darn good cook. Located 1 block north of the Plaza in a handsome and historic

Where to Stock Up for a Gourmet Picnic, Sonoma Style

Sonoma has plenty of restaurants, but on a sunny day, it's really the place to picnic. Sonoma's Plaza Park is a perfect place to set up a gourmet spread; there are even picnic tables available. Below are Sonoma's top spots for stocking up for such an alfresco fete:

If you want to pick up some specialty fare on your way into town, stop at **Angelo's Wine Country Deli**, 23400 Arnold Dr. (☎ **707/938-3688**). Angelo's sells all types of smoked meats, special salsas, and homemade mustards. The deli is known for its half-dozen types of homemade beef jerky. It's open Monday to Thursday from 9am to 5pm, and Friday to Sunday from 9am to 6pm; summer-month hours are daily 9am to 6pm.

The Sonoma Cheese Factory, on the Plaza at 2 Spain St. (☎ **707/996-1000**), offers award-winning house-made cheeses and an extraordinary variety of imported meats and cheeses; a few are set out for tasting every day. The factory also sells caviar, gourmet salads, pâté, and homemade Sonoma Jack cheese. Sandwiches are available, too. While you're there, you can watch a narrated slide show about cheese-making. The factory is open weekdays from 8:30am to 5:30pm and weekends from 8:30am to 6pm.

At 315 2nd St. E. (1 block north of East Spain Street) is the **Vella Cheese Company** (☎ **800/848-0505** or 707/938-3232). Established in 1931, the folks at Vella pride themselves on making cheese into an award-winning science, their most recent victory being "U.S. Cheese Championship 1995–96" for their Monterey Dry Jack. Other cheeses range from flavorful High Moisture Jack to a mild Daisy and a razor-sharp Raw Milk Cheddar. Among other cheeses for which Vella has become famous is Oregon Blue, made at Vella's southern Oregon factory—rich, buttery, and even spreadable, one of the few premier blues produced in this country. Any of these fine handmade, all-natural cheeses can be shipped directly from the store. Vella Cheese Co. is open Monday to Saturday from 9am to 6pm, and Sunday from 10am to 5pm.

Of course, you're going to need something to wash down all of this gourmet fare. Head to the **Wine Exchange,** at the Mercado, 452 1st St. E. (☎ **707/ 938-1794**), which carries more than 600 domestic wines, as well as a decent cigar selection, and has a full wine-tasting bar. The beer connoisseur who's feeling displaced in the Wine Country will be happy to find more than 280 beers from around the world here too, including a number of exceptional domestic beers. There are wine and beer tastings daily. Open Monday to Saturday from 10am to 6pm, and Sunday from 11am to 6pm.

1870 stone building, the Depot Hotel offers pleasant outdoor dining in the Italian garden complete with central reflection pool and cascading Roman fountain. The menu is unwaveringly Italian, filled with a plethora of classic dishes such as spaghetti Bolognese and veal alla parmigiana. Start with the bounteous antipasto misto and end the feast with a dish of Michael's handmade Italian ice-cream and fresh fruit sorbets. And if you simply *must* learn how to cook some of these delicacies, the restaurant holds 1-night cooking classes throughout the year.

Mes Trois Filles Restaurant. 13648 Arnold Dr., Glen Ellen. ☎ **707/938-4844**. Reservations recommended in summer. Main courses $12.50–$16.50. AE, DC, MC, V. Wed–Sun 5:30–10:30pm. Hours vary in winter. FRENCH.

Matching the intimacy of Glen Ellen, Mes Trois Filles is a sweet little restaurant with 10 classically set tables dispersed throughout a bright, peach-colored room. Locals love this place, but it's not only because of the small-town atmosphere. Chef/owner Len Moriyama cooked at Campton Place Restaurant—one of the most highly regarded dining rooms in San Francisco—before taking his talents north. Moriyama is in the kitchen nightly and prepares such dishes as the popular wild mushroom ravioli in herbed beurre blanc, roasted breast of duck in cherry sauce, and rack of lamb in merlot sauce. Ever conscious of California's healthy attitude, heavier dishes can be prepared in less caloric variations. While everything on the menu changes to follow seasonal ingredients, desserts might include cheddar cheesecake with a wild berry sauce, chocolate Grand Marnier mousse, and poached pear in phyllo with a zinfandel zambione.

Piatti. 405 1st St. W., Sonoma. ☎ **707/996-2351.** Reservations recommended. Main courses $7–$12. AE, MC, V. Mon–Thurs 11:30am–10pm, Fri–Sat 11:30am–11pm, Sun 11:30am–10pm. ITALIAN.

This local favorite is known for serving reasonably priced food in a rustic Italian-style setting with delightful patio seating. The restaurant occupies the ground floor of the rejuvenated El Dorado Hotel, a 19th-century landmark. Good-tasting pizzas emerge from a wood-burning oven. There are also satisfying pastas, such as vegetarian lasagna and cannelloni stuffed with chicken and veal. Other dishes include a wonderful roast vegetable appetizer, rotisserie chicken with garlic mashed potatoes, and a good veal scaloppini. Granted, there are far fancier—and more intimate—restaurants in the area, but not many that can fill you up at these prices.

Swiss Hotel. 18 W. Spain St., Sonoma. ☎ **707/938-2884.** Reservations recommended. Main courses $8–$16. MC, V. Daily 11:30am–2:30pm, and 5–9:30pm. Bar, daily 11am–2am. CONTINENTAL/NORTHERN ITALIAN.

The historic Swiss Hotel, located right in the town center, is a Sonoma landmark, complete with slanting floors and aged-beamed ceilings. The turn-of-the-century long oak bar at the left of the entrance is adorned with black-and-white photos of pioneering Sonomans. The bright white dining room and rear dining patio are pleasant spots to enjoy lunch specials like penne with chicken, mushrooms, and tomato cream; sandwiches; and California-style pizzas fired in a wood-burning oven. Dinner might start with a warm winter salad of radicchio and frisee lettuce with pears, walnuts, and bleu cheese. Main courses run the gamut—we like the linguine with prawns with garlic, hot pepper, tomatoes, the filet mignon wrapped in a bleu cheese crust, and the duck in an orange-honey sauce.

INEXPENSIVE

La Casa. 121 E. Spain St. (on the Sonoma Town Square across from the mission), Sonoma. ☎ **707/996-3406.** Reservations recommended on weekends and summer evenings. Main courses $6–$11. AE, CB, DC, DISC, MC, V. Daily 11:30am–10pm, bar appetizers until midnight. MEXICAN.

This no-nonsense Mexican restaurant serves great enchiladas, fajitas, and chimichangas. To start, try the black bean soup or the ceviche made of fresh snapper, marinated in lime juice with cilantro and salsa, and served on crispy tortillas. Follow that with tamales prepared with corn husks spread with corn masa, stuffed with chicken filling, and topped with a mild red chili sauce. Or, you might opt for the delicious Suiza (deep-dish chicken enchiladas) or the fresh snapper Veracruz if it's available. On a sunny afternoon or a clear night, opt to dine patio-style, where you can sip a cerveza under the warmth of heat lamps.

The Northern Coast 7

by Erika Lenkert and Matthew R. Poole

Heading north from San Francisco, you'll come upon a California that hardly resembles the southern part of the state. It's an entirely different landscape, in climate as well as flora and fauna. You can forget about California's fabled surfing-and-bikini scene this far north; instead, you'll find miles and miles of rugged coastline with broad beaches and tiny bays harboring dramatic rock formations—from chimney stacks to bridges and blowholes—carved by the ocean waves.

The best time to visit is in the spring or fall. In spring, the headlands are carpeted with wild flowers—golden poppy, iris, and sea foam—and in fall the sun shines clear and bright. Summers are typically cool and windy, with the ubiquitous fog burning off by the afternoon.

You may think you've arrived in Alaska when you hit the beaches of Northern California. Take a dip in the sea and you'll soon agree with the locals: The Arctic waters along the north coast are best left to the seals when it comes to swimming. But that doesn't mean you can't enjoy the beaches, whether by strolling along the water or taking in the panoramic views of towering cliffs and seascapes. Unlike their southern counterparts, the beaches along the north coast are not likely to be crowded, even in summer.

As you head north toward Oregon, there's an amazing string of golden beaches off Calif. 1, all clearly marked and easily accessible. Though there are lots of options, the following beaches are our favorites, going from south to north: Muir Beach (just off Calif. 1 and about 3 miles from Muir Woods); Duxbury Reef, known for its tidepools (at Bolinas, get on Mesa Road and turn left on Overlook Drive, then right on Elm Avenue, which will take you to the parking lot); Point Reyes National Seashore at Limantour Beach; Tomales Bay State Park, reached by Sir Francis Drake Boulevard, right off Calif. 1 (go along Pierce Point Road until you come to the park); Fort Ross State Park, some 9¹/₂ miles north of the town of Jenner; Sea Ranch, off Route 1 south of Gualala; Manchester State Beach, some 9¹/₂ miles north of Point Arena; and Agate Beach in Patrick's Point State Park, which is known for its tidepools and is off U.S. 101, about 25 miles north of Eureka.

The most scenic way to reach Mendocino and points north is to drive from San Francisco along the coast via Calif. 1. The larger freeway, U.S. 101, runs inland through Healdsburg and Cloverdale and

The Northern Coast

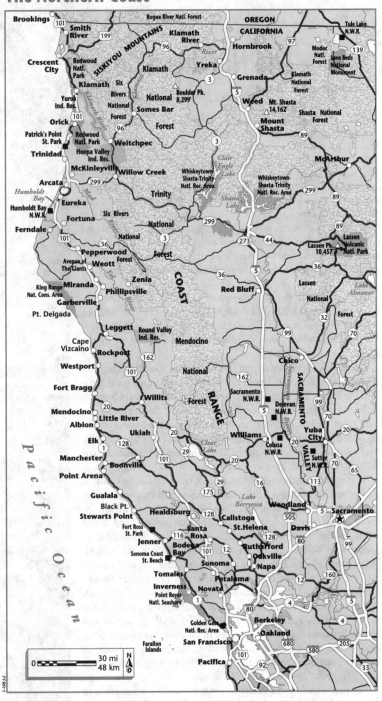

is faster, but does not provide the spectacular views of coastal cliffs and windswept beaches you will see on Calif. 1. If you decide to take the scenic route, turn toward the coast on Calif. 20 at Willits.

1 Point Reyes National Seashore

Point Reyes is a 100-square-mile peninsula of dark forests, wind-sculpted dunes, endless beaches, and plunging sea cliffs. Aside from its beautiful scenery, it also boasts historical treasures that offer a window into California's coastal past, including lighthouses, turn-of-the-century dairies and ranches, the site of Sir Francis Drake's 1579 landing, plus a complete replica of a coastal Miwok Indian village.

The national seashore system was created to protect rural and undeveloped stretches of the coast from the pressures of soaring real estate values and increasing population, preserving both the natural features and unique culture of the coast. Nowhere is the success of the system more evident than at Point Reyes. Layers of human history coexist peacefully here with one of the world's most dramatic natural settings. Residents of the surrounding towns—**Inverness, Point Reyes Station, and Olema**—have steadfastly resisted runaway development. You won't find any strip malls or fast-food joints here—just a laid-back coastal town with cafes and country inns where gentle living prevails. The park, a 71,000-acre hammer-shaped peninsula jutting 10 miles into the Pacific and backed by Tomales Bay, is loaded with wildlife ranging from tule elk, birds, and bobcats to gray whales, sea lions, and white sharks. During Audubon's annual Christmas bird count, Point Reyes, with as many as 350 different varieties, is regularly found to have the largest concentration of diverse bird species in the continental United States. The **Point Reyes Bird Observatory** (☎ **415/868-1221**), an ornithological research organization located in the park, is open to the public and offers tours and special programs.

Though the peninsula's people and wildlife live in harmony above the ground, the situation beneath the soil is much more volatile. The infamous San Andreas fault separates Point Reyes, the northernmost landmass on the Pacific Plate, from the rest of California, which rests on the North American Plate. Point Reyes is making its way toward Alaska at a rate of about 2 inches per year, but there have been times when it has moved much faster. In 1906, Point Reyes jumped north almost 20 feet in an instant, leveling San Francisco and jolting the rest of the state. The 1/2-mile **Earthquake Trail,** near the Bear Valley Visitor Center, illustrates this geological drama with a loop through an area torn by the slipping fault. Shattered fences, rifts in the ground, and a barn knocked off its foundation by the quake illustrate how alive the earth is here. If that doesn't convince you, a seismograph in the visitor center will.

The **Bear Valley Visitor Center** (☎ **415/663-1092**), just outside Olema, is the best place to begin your visit. In addition to the Earthquake Trail, you'll find great natural history and cultural displays as well as maps and information. Two features are particularly fascinating: **Kule Loklo,** a restored coastal Miwok Indian village, often hosts displays of dancing, basketmaking, Native American cooking, and indigenous art; and the Park Service's **Morgan Horse Ranch** is the only working horse-breeding farm in the national park system. The best time to visit Kule Loklo is during July, when it hosts an annual **Native American Celebration** and the whole village comes to life. Classes in Native American crafts and skills are offered intermittently throughout the year; call ☎ **415/479-3281** for more information.

Weather at Point Reyes is very fickle. The point itself is the foggiest place on the West Coast. Generally the seasons here are reversed: Summer is cold and foggy, while winter is clear and, if not exactly warm, is often at least tolerable. There are no hard-and-fast rules about the weather, though. Winter storms can rage for weeks and sometimes the summer fog stays away. The best plan is to take advantage of variations in local weather by keeping your itinerary flexible.

Keep an eye out in wooded areas for poison oak's waxy three-leaf clusters. Also be sure to check for ticks as the Lyme disease–carrying black-legged tick is common here.

Though the park is heavily visited, crowds are only a problem at a few places and only during certain times. If you visit the lighthouse on a weekend or holiday during whale season, be prepared to wait for the shuttle at Drake's Beach and to have to deal with a lot of people. Trails leaving from Bear Valley tend to be more crowded on weekends than others. Try the Five Brooks or Palomarin trailheads to avoid hordes of backcountry tourists.

Rangers lead special programs year-round, from wildlife hikes and history lessons to habitat restoration. All are free. Call the Bear Valley Visitor Center for up-to-date schedules. Other groups, such as the **Golden Gate Audubon Society** (☎ 510/843-2222) and **Oceanic Society Expeditions** (☎ 415/474-3385), run special excursions and outings to the park. During whale season the Oceanic Society takes naturalist-led whale-watching boats from the San Francisco Marina to Point Reyes every weekend, weather permitting. The 6-hour trip costs $50 for adults and $48 for kids and senior citizens. No children under 10 are allowed.

BEACHES   Beachgoers have their work cut out for them here. The **Great Beach** is one of California's longest. It is also one of the windiest and home to large and dangerous waves. You can't swim here, but the beachcombing is some of the best in the world. Tidepoolers should go to **McClure's Beach** at the end of Pierce Point Road during low tide or hike out to **Chimney Rock.** Swimmers will want to stick to **Limantour Beach** or **Drake's Beach** in the protected lee of Point Reyes. Sir Francis Drake reputedly landed the *Pelican* (later rechristened the *Golden Hind*) on the sandy shore of Drake's Bay in June 1579, to replenish supplies and make repairs before sailing home to England. Drake's Beach is now home to the **Kenneth C. Patrick Visitor Center,** which has exhibits on the area's whale fossil beds, and **Drake's Beach Cafe** (open Thursday to Monday 10am to 6pm; ☎ 415/669-1297), the only food concession in the park, and famous for its great oysters.

HIKING   There's a little of everything for hikers here. Thirty-two thousand acres, crisscrossed by 70 miles of trails, have been preserved as a wilderness that's off-limits to motor vehicles and bicycles.

The **Bear Valley Trail** leads through wooded hillsides to **Arch Rock**, where Coast Creek splashes into the ocean through a "sea tunnel." The full hike is about 8 miles round-trip.

More relaxing is the 4¹/₂-mile **Estero Trail,** a favorite with birders that meanders along the edge of Limantour Estero and Drake's Estero. (*Estero* is the Spanish word for estuary, and these brackish waters draw flocks of waterfowl and shorebirds as well as many raptors and smaller species.)

Near Wildcat Camp on the Coast Trail is **Alamere Falls,** which can also be reached via the Palomarin Trail or Five Brooks Trail in the south of the park.

Tomales Point Trail, 11 miles round-trip, gives hikers a tour of the park's rugged shoreline and passes through wilderness that is home to the park's herd of tule elk.

WHALE WATCHING   During peak season (December to March) the park service runs a shuttle from Drake's Beach to the **Point Reyes Lighthouse,** where watchers have been known to see as many as 100 whales in a single afternoon.

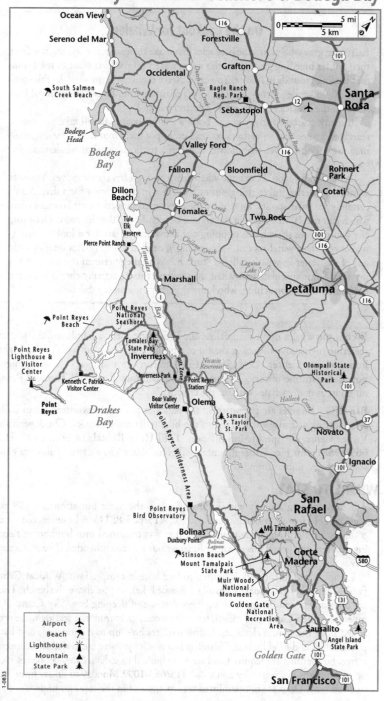

Ocean View

Sereno del Mar

116

Forestville

Occidental

Grafton

South Salmon
Creek Beach

Ragle Ranch
Reg. Park

Sebastopol

12

Santa
Rosa

101

Salmon Creek

Dutch Bill Creek

Laguna de Santa Rosa

Bodega
Head

Bodega
Bay

Valley Ford

116

Fallon

Bloomfield

Rohnert
Park

Dillon
Beach

Cotati

Tule
Elk
Reserve

Walker Creek

Tomales

Two Rock

101

116

Pierce Point Ranch

Chileno Creek

Laguna
Lake

Tomales Bay

Marshall

Petaluma

116

Point Reyes
National
Seashore

Point Reyes
Beach

Point Reyes
Lighthouse &
Visitor
Center

Tomales Bay
State Park

Inverness

Rift Zone

Nicasio
Reservoir

Olompali State
Historical
Park

101

Kenneth C. Patrick
Visitor Center

Inverness Park

Point Reyes
Station

Point
Reyes

Bear Valley
Visitor Center

Olema

Halleck Creek

Drakes
Bay

Samuel
P. Taylor
St. Park

Novato

37

101

Ignacio

Point Reyes Wilderness Area

101

Point Reyes
Bird Observatory

San
Rafael

Bolinas

Duxbury Point

Mt. Tamalpais

580

Bolinas
Lagoon

Stinson Beach
Mount Tamalpais
State Park

Corte
Madera

Muir Woods
National
Monument

Golden Gate
National
Recreation
Area

Richardson Bay

131

Sausalito

Angel Island
State Park

Golden Gate

101

San Francisco

101

Airport
Beach
Lighthouse
Mountain
State Park

1-0833

> ## On the Lookout for Whales
>
> Each year, gray whales (it's the barnacles that make them appear gray) migrate from their winter breeding grounds in the warm waters off the Baja coast to their summer feeding grounds in Alaska. You can observe them as they undertake this enormous 10,000-mile journey; the Claifornia coastline from Redwood National Park south to the Mexican border offers a perfect vantage.
>
> In many coastal towns, you can book a charter boat that will take you out in search of whales, and sometimes you can even spot them fom land. (See our information on Point Reyes Lighthouse, which is a particularly great whale-watching spot.)
>
> If you're lucky, you'll catch the whales performing a few classic moves. You may see their powerful flukes rising out of the water in preparation for a dive. You'll certainly see their spouts, formed by the condensed moisture of their exhalation, which can rise 10 to 15 feet in the air and be seen from 10 miles away. Occasionally you may see their heads popping out above the surface for a look around (a maneuver whale watchers call "spyhopping"), or their whole bodies lunging right out of the water in what's called a "breech." Why they perform the last two is a mystery. Some speculate that when they spyhop they're actually checking coastal landmarks. As for breaching, who knows? Perhaps it's sheer jubilation.

Even if the whales don't materialize, the lighthouse itself, a fabulous old structure teetering high above the sea at the tip of a promontory, is worth a visit. The **Lighthouse Visitor Center** (☎ 415/669-1534) features great displays on whale migration and maritime history. Two other spots, **Chimney Rock** and **Tomales Point,** offer just as many whales without the crowds.

BIKING   Bicycles are permitted in the park but not on the wilderness area trails, and plotting a course exclusively on the bike trails can be tricky. Check with the Visitor Center for specific information. **Trail Head Rentals** in Olema (☎ 415/663-1958) rents nice Fisher mountain bikes for about $24 a day and also is a good source of trail information.

WHERE TO STAY

The only lodging actually within Point Reyes is the rustic but affordable ($9 per night) **AYH Hostel** on Limantour Road (☎ 415/663-8811). A beautiful old ranch complex 2 miles from Limantour Beach that was converted into bunkhouse sleeping quarters, the hostel fills up early. Reservations are recommended. The maximum stay is 3 nights.

Camping within the park is limited to four hike-in camps. Two, **Wildcat Camp** (a 6¹/₂-mile hike) and **Coast Camp** (a 1.8-mile hike), sit just above the beach. They are often foggy and damp, so bring a good tent and sleeping bag. **Sky Camp** (1.7 miles) and **Glen Camp** (4.6 miles), set in the woods away from the sea, are more protected from the coastal elements. Individual sites hold up to eight people and have picnic tables and food lockers. Pit toilets and drinking water are available. Camping is free, but permits are required and stays are limited to 4 days. Sites can be reserved up to 2 months in advance by calling ☎ 415/663-1092 Monday to Friday from 9am to noon only. Dogs are not permitted on any trails or in the campgrounds.

Bear Valley Inn. 88 Bear Valley Rd., Olema, CA 94950. ☎ **415/663-1777.** 3 rms (none with private bath). $75–$135 double. Rates include breakfast. AE, MC, V.

Ron and JoAnne Nowell's venerable two-story 1899 Victorian has survived everything from a major earthquake to a recent forest fire—lucky for you, as you'll be hard pressed to find a better B&B for the price in Point Reyes. Granted, the Bear Valley Inn isn't perfect—the rooms lack private baths, and the main highway is a tad too close—but it's loaded with Victorian charm, right down to the profusion of flowers and vines outside and comfy chairs fronting a toasty-warm wood stove inside. It's in a great location, too, with three good restaurants only a block away and the entire National Seashore at your doorstep. Ron, who also runs a mountain-bike rental shop next door, can set you up wheel-wise for about $25 a day and point you in the right direction.

Blackthorne Inn. 266 Vallejo Ave. (off Sir Francis Drake Blvd., south of Inverness), P.O. Box 712, Inverness, CA 94937. ☎ **415/663-8621.** 5 rms, 3 with bath. $105–$195 double without bath; $155–$195 double with bath. Rates include buffet breakfast. MC, V.

This elaborate redwood home with its octagonal widow's walk, spiral staircase, turrets, and multiple decks looks more like a super-deluxe tree house than a B&B. Our favorite—and the most expensive—unit is the Eagle's Nest, an octagonal room enclosed by glass and topped with a private sundeck with a catwalk leading to the private outhouse. The largest room is the Forest View Studio, a virtual suite complete with deck, while the smallest room is the Hideaway with a private entrance and a sitting area facing the woods; both are furnished with wicker and decorated with floral fabrics and modern lithographs. The main sitting room in the house features a large stone fireplace, skylight, and stained-glass windows and is surrounded by a huge deck. Guests have use of the hot tub on the top deck.

✪ **Manka's Inverness Lodge.** Argyle St. (off Sir Francis Drake Blvd., 3 blocks north of downtown Inverness), P.O. Box 1110, Inverness, CA 94937. ☎ **800/58-LODGE** or 415/669-1034. 8 rms, 2 cabins. $115–$200 rm; $185–$225 cabin. MC, V.

This immediately lovable old hunting lodge is one of our favorite places to stay—and dine—on the coast. Every room resembles the sort of rustic old mountain cabin you read about in Jack London novels, and the restaurant has that perfect balance of countrified charm and polished refinement. In addition to the standard rooms in the main lodge (anything but standard with their tree-limb bedsteads, billowy down comforters, and bucolic furnishings), there are two luxuriously appointed cabins adjacent to the inn, and four smaller, less expensive rooms in the redwood annex. For the ultimate romantic splurge, inquire about the three secluded guest houses.

The lodge's reputation is built on its restaurant, which dominates the bottom floor. The specialty of the house is game and fish, including oysters from Tomales Bay. Prices range from $18 to $22. The limited menu might feature pheasant with a madeira jus, mashed potatoes, and a wild huckleberry jam, or everybody's favorite, pan-seared elk tenderloin. It's open for dinner Thursday to Monday with a brunch on Sunday.

Point Reyes Country Inn & Stables. 12050 Calif. 1, P.O. Box 501, Point Reyes Station, CA 94956. ☎ **415/663-9696.** Fax 415/663-8888. 5 rms, 2 studios. $85–$160 double. Additional human guest $25; $10–$15 per horse. Rates include breakfast. MC, V.

Are you and your horsy dreaming of a country getaway? Then book a room at Point Reyes Country Inn & Stables, a ranch-style home on 4 acres that offers pastoral accommodations for two- and four-legged guests (horses only). Each room has either a balcony or a garden, and the property has plenty of hiking and riding trails. The innkeepers have also added two new studios with kitchens above the stables, and rent out two cottages on Tomales Bay equipped with decks, stocked kitchens, fireplaces, and a shared dock.

Buy-Valves: Where to Pick Up the Northern Coast's Best Oysters

The latest addition to downtown Point Reyes Station is the **Point Reyes Oyster Company,** 11101 Calif. 1 (☎ **415/663-8373**), a new retail facility featuring fresh farm-raised Miyagi, Kumamoto, and French Belon oysters, as well as Manila clams and Bay mussels—all sold by the dozen or hundred (should you be on your honeymoon, for example). Open Monday to Friday from 10am to 6pm.

Or why not go straight to the source? **Johnson's Oyster Farm,** right on the edge of Drake's Estero in the heart of Point Reyes National Seashore, may look (and smell) like a dump, but those tasty bivalves don't come any fresher. Our modus operandi is to 1) buy a couple dozen; 2) head for an empty campsite along the bay; 3) fire up the barbecue pit (don't forget the charcoal); 4) split and 'cue the little guys; 5) slather them in Johnson's special sauce; then 6) slurp 'em down. Johnson's is located off Sir Francis Drake Boulevard, about 6 miles west(ish) of Inverness (☎ **415/669-1149**); hours are Tuesday to Sunday from 8am to 4pm.

Farther up Calif. 1, near the town of Marshall, you can gather your own clams in the bay. The **Tomales Bay Oyster Company,** 15479 Calif. 1, Tomales (☎ **415/663-1242**), sells its wares by the dozen or in sacks of 100. Open daily from 9am to 5pm.

WHERE TO DINE

The Gray Whale. 12781 Sir Francis Drake Blvd., Inverness. ☎ **415/669-1244.** Main courses $5–$10. MC, V. Daily 11am–8pm. ITALIAN.

For over a decade The Gray Whale has been a popular pit stop for Bay Areans heading to the lighthouse at Point Reyes. Why so popular? First off, it's cheap: sandwiches—such as the roasted eggplant with pesto and mozzarella—are only $5, as are most of the salads and pastas. Second, it's pretty good: Our personal favorites are the specialty pizzas, such as the Californian (artichoke hearts, fresh basil, and tomatoes) and the vegetarian (baked eggplant, roasted onions and romas, broccoli, and piles of freshly grated Parmesan cheese). Veteran hikers and mountain bikers stop by for an espresso booster, sipped on the small patio overlooking the block-long town of Inverness.

✪ **Station House Cafe.** Main St., Point Reyes Station. ☎ **415/663-1515.** Reservations recommended. Breakfast $4.45–$7.50; lunch $5.50–$9.50; dinner $6–$19. DISC, MC, V. Daily 8am–10pm. AMERICAN.

A local favorite, the Station House Cafe is known for its good food and animated atmosphere, particularly when the live music fires up on weekends. For breakfast, we recommend the fritatta with asparagus, goat cheese, and olives, which always seems to taste better while sitting outside on the shaded garden patio. Luncheon specials might include two-cheese polenta served with sautéed fresh spinach and grilled garlic-buttered tomatoes. The menu changes every week, but always features locally grown beef and a good selection of fresh fish. Rounding out the menu are homemade chili, steamed clams, fresh soup made daily, and fish-and-chips. The cafe has an extensive list of fine California wines, plus local and imported beers.

Taqueria La Quinta. 3rd and Main sts., Point Reyes Station. ☎ **415/663-8868.** Main courses $4–$6. No credit cards. Wed–Mon 11am–9pm. MEXICAN.

Fresh, good, fast, and cheap: What more could you ask for in a restaurant? Taqueria La Quinta has been one of our favorite lunch stops in downtown Point Reyes for years and years. A huge selection of Mexican-American standards is posted above the counter, but those in the know inquire about the seafood specials. Watch out for the self-serve salsa—that sucker's hot.

2   Along the Sonoma Coast

TOMALES BAY

From Point Reyes Station, Calif. 1 travels north along the eastern edge of Tomales Bay. It's a pleasant drive, with worthwhile attractions along the route. Take part in the windsurfing, kayaking, and hang gliding that are available, especially at **Dillon Beach** at the mouth of the bay. Kayak trips, including 3-hour sunset outings, $3^1/2$-hour full-moon paddles, yoga tours, day trips, and longer excursions, are organized by **Tomales Bay Kayaking** (☎ **415/663-1743**). Prices start at $45 for tours. Rentals begin at $25 for one person, $35 for two.

BODEGA BAY

Beyond the tip of the Point Reyes Peninsula the road curves around toward the coastal village of Bodega Bay, which supports a fishing fleet of 300 boats. As you drive north, Bodega Bay is a good place to stop for lunch or to stroll around town. There are several interesting shops and galleries, though the best show in town is at **Tides Whar,,** where the fishing boats come in to unload their daily catch, which is promptly gutted and packed in ice.

Bodega Head State Park is a great vantage point for whale watching during the annual migration season from January through April. At **Doran Beach** there's a large bird sanctuary (willets, curlews, godwits, and more), and the University of California Marine Biology Lab next door conducts guided tours on Friday afternoons.

The **Bodega Harbour Golf Links,** 21301 Heron Dr. (☎ **707/875-3538**), enjoys a panoramic oceanside setting. It's an 18-hole Scottish-style course designed by Robert Trent Jones, Jr. A new warm-up center and practice facility has been added; it's free of charge to registered golfers. Rates range from $50 with cart on the weekdays to $80 with cart on weekends. If golfing isn't your thing, you can go horseback riding through some spectacular local scenery by contacting **Chanslor Horse Stables** at ☎ **707/875-2721.**

One of the bay's major events is the Fisherman's Festival, in April. Local fishing boats, decorated with ribbons and banners, sail out for a Blessing of the Fleet, while landlubbers enjoy music, a lamb and oyster barbecue, and an arts and crafts fair. Another fun event is the Bodega Bay Sandcastle Building Festival at Doran Beach.

A few miles inland, the tiny town of Bodega (pop. 100) is famous as the setting of Alfred Hitchcock's *The Birds.* Fans will want to visit the Potter School House and St. Teresa's Church.

For more information, stop in at the **Bodega Bay Area Visitors Center,** 850 Calif. 1, Bodega Bay, CA 94923 (☎ **707/875-3422**). They have lots of brochures about the town and the surrounding area, including maps of the Sonoma Coast State Beaches and the best local fishing spots.

WHERE TO STAY

✪ **Bodega Bay Lodge.** 103 Calif. 1, Bodega Bay, CA 94923. ☎ **800/368-2468** or 707/875-3525. 78 rms. $175–$215 weekends, $150–$190 weekdays. Two-night minimum on weekends. AE, CB, DC, DISC, MC, V.

This is easily the best hotel in Bodega Bay. Every room has a private balcony with sweeping views of the bay and bird-filled marshes. As if that weren't enough, they even throw in a fireplace, stocked minibar, and plush furnishings and fabrics. As an added bonus, guests have complimentary access to a fitness center and sauna, as well as to a beautiful fieldstone spa and heated pool perched above the bay and surrounded by flower gardens.

Dining/Entertainment: The lodge's Duck Club Restaurant also enjoys a reputation as Bodega Bay's finest. Large picture windows take advantage of the bay view, a sublimely romantic setting for chef Jeff Reilly's Sonoma County cuisine. Entrees include farm-fresh asparagus strudel, roasted Petaluma duck, and fresh fish caught by the Bodega fleet. Breakfast and dinner are served daily.

Inn at the Tides. 800 Coast Hwy. 1, P.O. Box 640, Bodega Bay, CA 94923. ☎ **800/ 541-7788** or 707/875-2751. Fax 707/875-3023. 86 rms. TV TEL. Summer, Sun–Thurs $129– $214, Fri–Sat $149–$234. Winter rates drop about 20%. Rates include continental breakfast. Golf packages available. AE, DISC, MC, V.

The larger (and, in our opinion, the less appealing) of Bodega Bay's two upscale lodgings, the other being Bodega Bay Lodge, The Inn at the Tides consists of a cluster of condo-like wood complexes perched on the side of a gently sloping hill. The selling point here is the view; each unit is staggered just enough to guarantee a view of the bay across the highway. While all the rooms are large and comfortably furnished, the decor is rather dated and uninspiring.

Dining/Entertainment: The Bay View is open for dinner only Wednesday through Sunday. It offers sea views and has a romantic, somewhat formal ambiance, though it suffers from a so-so reputation. The owners, to their credit, have recently poured a bundle of money into revitalizing it, including hiring two new chefs.

Facilities: The amenities are first-rate, such as the heated indoor/outdoor pool, Jacuzzi, and Finnish sauna.

WHERE TO DINE

Breakers Cafe. 1400 Calif. 1, Bodega Bay. ☎ **707/875-2513.** Main courses $6–$16. MC, V. Daily 9am–9pm. CALIFORNIA.

If you're a big breakfast eater, the Breakers Cafe is your best bet in Bodega Bay. Omelets, Belgian waffles, baked polenta, house-baked muffins, and even good ol' biscuits and gravy are served in a pleasant greenhouse-style dining room filled with a profusion of healthy plants and diffused sunlight. The cafe also offers a modest lunch and dinner menu, ranging from above-average sandwiches and burgers to fresh pastas, locally caught seafood, and a small selection of vegetarian dishes. Prices run a bit steep for the seafood dishes, but most items are under $10. If the weather's warm, ask for a table on the patio.

Lucas Wharf Deli. 595 Calif. 1, Bodega Bay. ☎ **707/875-3562.** Deli items $4–$10. DISC, MC, V. Daily 10am–7pm. DELI.

We always stop here whenever we pass through Bodega Bay. Most visitors don't even give it a glance as they head into the adjacent restaurant, but that's because they don't know about the big bowls of fresh, tangy crab cioppino they dole out for only $5 a pint—a third of the restaurant price. It's a fabulously messy affair, best devoured at the nearby picnic tables. When crab season is over, the cioppino special is replaced by an equally awesome pile of fresh fish-and-chips (easily big enough for two).

Tides Wharf Restaurant. 835 Calif. 1. ☎ **707/875-3652.** Reservations recommended. Main courses $10–$24. AE, DC, MC, V. Mon–Fri 7:30am–10pm, Sat–Sun 7am–10pm. SEAFOOD.

It isn't as secluded or intimate as you might have wanted (in summer, as many as 1,000 diners a day pass through here), but it evokes all the nostalgia of the 1950s, when it served as one of the settings for Hitchcock's *The Birds.* Don't expect the weather-beaten, board-and-batten luncheonette you saw in the movie; the place has been gentrified, enlarged, and redecorated many times since, although it retains the original bar used in the film. There are views over the water, and tables are cramped but convivial (a $5-million renovation currently in progress should add extra elbow room). The bill of fare is what you might expect at a chowderhouse in Boston, with fish-and-chips, barbecued oysters, oysters Rockefeller, and all the seafood that the owners (who send their own fishing boat out into the Pacific every day) can dredge up from the cold blue waters offshore. Try the terrific open-faced crab sandwich served with melted cheese on sourdough bread.

THE SONOMA COAST STATE BEACHES, JENNER & FORT ROSS STATE HISTORIC PARK

Along 13 winding miles of Calif. 1—from Bodega Bay to Goat Rock Beach in Jenner—stretch the Sonoma Coast State Beaches. These beaches are ideal for walking, tidepooling, abalone picking, fishing, and bird-watching for such species as blue heron, cormorant, osprey, and pelicans. Each beach is clearly marked from the road, and numerous pullouts are provided for parking. Even if you don't stop at any of the beaches, the drive alone is spectacular.

At **Jenner,** the Russian River empties into the ocean. Penny Island, in the river's estuary, is home to otters and many species of birds; a colony of harbor seals lives out on the ocean rocks. **Goat Rock Beach** is a popular breeding ground for the seals; pupping season begins in March and lasts until June.

From Jenner, a 12-mile climb along some very dramatic coastline will bring you to **Fort Ross State Historic Park** (☎ **707/847-3286**), a reconstruction of the fort that was established here in 1812 by the Russians as a base for seal and otter hunting (it was abandoned in 1842). At the visitor center you can view the silver samovars and elaborate table services that the Russians used. The fenced compound contains several buildings, including the first Russian Orthodox church ever built on the North American continent outside Alaska. The park also offers beach trails and picnic grounds on more than 1,000 acres. Admission is free, but parking is a hefty $6.

North from Fort Ross the road continues to **Salt Point State Park.** This 3,500-acre expanse contains 30 campsites, 14 miles of hiking trails, dozens of tidepools, a pygmy forest, and old Pomo village sites. Your best bet is to pull off the highway any place that catches your eye and start exploring on foot. At the north end of the park head inland on Kruse Ranch Road to the 317-acre **Kruse Rhododendron Reserve** (☎ **707/847-3221**), an aesthetic miracle in April and May. Some rhododendrons grow to a height of 18 feet under the redwood and fir canopy.

WHERE TO DINE

River's End. Calif. 1., Jenner. ☎ **707/865-2484.** Reservations recommended. Main courses $13–$33 at dinner. MC, V. Mon–Sat 11am–9:30pm, Sun 10am–9:30pm. INTERNATIONAL.

Outwardly unpretentious yet deceptively urbane, this small seaside restaurant offers an artfully rustic setting, with big windows overlooking the coast (seals and sea lions might happen to be cavorting offshore). The menu is wonderfully eclectic, the product of a German-born chef who whips up versions of Indonesian bahmi goreng, a selection of Indian curries, beef saté, beef Wellington, seafood, and steaks. After dinner, take the remainder of your wine to the outside deck and enjoy the sunset.

Sizzling Tandoor. 9960 Calif. 1, at the south end of the Russian River Bridge, Jenner. ☎ **707/ 865-0625.** Main courses $8.50–$13.50. AE, DISC, MC, V. Daily 11:30am–3pm; Mon–Thurs 5–9:30pm, Fri–Sun 5–10pm. Closed Mon in winter. INDIAN.

Something of a non sequitur along a rather desolate stretch of Calif. 1 between Bodega Bay and Jenner, the Sizzling Tandoor serves huge, inexpensive plates of classic Indian cuisine. The lonely location, though peculiar, is superb. Perched high atop a windswept hill the restaurant boasts an exquisite view of the Russian River far below. The large array of curries and kabobs are accompanied by soup, vegetables, pulao rice, and the best *naan* (Indian bread) we've ever had. Even if you're not hungry, order some *naan* to go—it makes the perfect road snack.

GUALALA & POINT ARENA

Back on Calif. 1 going north you'll pass through Sea Ranch, a series of condominium beach developments, until you reach Gualala (pronounced wah-LA-la). To access the beaches along this stretch of coast you'll have to cross private property, and your entrance may therefore be restricted at any time. Still, there are about 10 or so public beaches that are ideal for walking.

The **Gualala River,** adjacent to the town of the same name, is suitable for canoeing, rafting, and kayaking since all power boats and jet skis are forbidden. Along its banks you're likely to see osprey, heron, egrets, and ducks; steelhead, salmon, and river otters make their home in the waters. Canoes, kayaks, and bicycles can be rented in Gualala for 2 hours, a half day, or a full day from **Adventure Rents** (☎ 707/884-4386), behind the Gualala Hotel on Calif. 1. A bike for 2 hours costs $15, a canoe (which seats 2 to 5 persons) costs $25 for a half day, and a double kayak for the whole day costs $60. **Gualala Kayak,** 39175 S. Calif. 1, next to the Chevron station (☎ 707/884-4705), specializes in river and sea kayaking. A single kayak costs $20 for 2 hours and $35 for a day, and a double kayak costs $65 for a day. Prices include everything from instruction to shuttle service.

Point Arena lies a few miles north of Gualala. Most folks stop here for the view at the **Point Arena Lighthouse,** which was built in 1870 after 10 ships ran aground here on a single night during a storm. A $2.50 fee covers parking, entrance to the lighthouse museum, and a surprisingly interesting tour of the 6-story, 145-step lighthouse. It's open from 11am to 2:30pm on weekdays (daily in winter), 10am to 3:30pm on weekends (☎ 707/882-2777).

WHERE TO STAY

✪ **Old Milano Hotel.** 38300 Calif. 1, Gualala, CA 95445. ☎ 707/884-3256. 6 rms (sharing 2 baths), 1 suite, 5 cottages. $80 double with garden view; $110 double with ocean view; $165 master suite; $140–$215 cottage. Rates include breakfast. MC, V.

This romantic hotel lies just north of Gualala and has a spellbinding view of Castle Rock from the front porch and sloping lawn. The inn was built in 1905 on 3 acres and is listed in the National Register of Historic Places. It has enchanting flower and herb gardens and a superbly situated hot tub, from which you look directly out to the ocean. The rooms are all decorated differently, often with rare antiques. Upstairs, six rooms share two bathrooms, each with double showers. The most alluring units are the cottages, which have sleeping alcoves, reading lofts, ocean views, and fireplaces or wood stoves; two have Jacuzzis. Our favorite is the Milano's honest-to-Betsy train caboose, a romantically private space with wood stove and two upstairs brakeman's seats.

A full breakfast is served either in your room or in the parlor. Chef Brain Knutson offers pricey California cuisine—rack of Sonoma lamb, poached salmon, roasted Peking duck—served in an intimate dining room lit by candlelight and, on cool nights, roaring fires in the stone fireplaces.

✪ **St. Orres.** 36601 Calif. 1, Box 523, Gualala, CA 95445. ☎ 707/884-3303. Fax 707/884-3903. 8 rms (sharing 3 baths), 11 cottages. $60 double without ocean view; $75 double with ocean view; $85–$180 double occupancy of cottages, depending on the size. MC, V.

An extraordinary Russian-style building—complete with two onion-domed towers—St. Orres lies 1¹/₂ miles north of Gualala. The complex was built in 1972 with century-old timbers salvaged from a nearby mill. It offers secluded cottage-style accommodations on 42 acres, as well as eight rooms in the main building (these rooms are handcrafted and share three bathrooms decorated in brilliant colors). Other accommodations are very private. Some have a full bath, wet bar, sitting area with Franklin stove, and French doors leading to a deck with a distant ocean view. Seven cottages border St. Orres Creek and have exclusive use of a spa facility that includes hot tub, sauna, and sundeck. The most luxurious is Pine Haven, with two bedrooms, two redwood decks, two baths, a tiled breakfast area, beach stone fireplace, and wet bar.

The hotel is especially well-known for its intimate restaurant (The St. Orres), a 17-seat charmer set below one of the main building's onion domes. Light filters through stained-glass windows onto strands of ivy that cascade down from the upper balcony. The only offering is a $30 three-course fixed-price meal that features game from the surrounding fields and forests. Dishes are inspired by Pacific Northwest cuisine and include wild boar, pheasant, venison, quail, and rack of lamb. Reservations are essential. It's open daily for dinner only and is closed weekdays for the first 2 weeks of December. MasterCard and Visa are accepted for hotel guests only; otherwise, no credit cards.

WHERE TO DINE

Point Arena's most cerebral hangout is a hybrid coffeehouse, bookstore, and community center called **Bookends,** 265 Main St. (☎ **707/882-2287**). We consider it a mandatory stop for a sandwich (build your own from their "Sandwich Chekov List"), double mocha, and a new read. Breakfast is served until 1pm (try the tofu scramble), and the lunch counter runs daily until closing time. Open daily in summer 7am to 9pm; winter daily 7am to 7pm.

The Food Company. 38411 Calif. 1 at Robinsons Reef Rd., Gualala. ☎ **707/884-1800.** Deli items $3–$9. MC, V. Daily 8–10:30am; Sun–Thurs 11am–8pm, Fri–Sat 11am–9pm. DELI.

If the St. Orres restaurant (see above) is out of your price range, you'll be happy to know that you can have an equally romantic lunch or dinner just down the road for a fraction of the price. Place your order at the deli counter, grab a bottle of wine from the rack, then head to the adjacent garden and plop your collective fannies at one of the picnic tables. The menu offers a dizzying array of specials from around the globe—corn tamales, Greek moussaka, lamb curry, quiche lorraine, pasta puttanesca—as well as fresh-baked breads, pastries, and sandwiches. Better yet, order it all to go and head for the beach.

NORTH FROM POINT ARENA

Driving north from Point Arena, you'll pass Elk (a cute place to stop for lunch), Manchester, Albion, and Little River on your way to Mendocino.

WHERE TO STAY

Greenwood Pier Inn. 5928 Calif. 1., Box 336, Elk, CA 95432. ☎ **707/877-9997.** Fax 707/877-3439. 5 rms, 6 cottages or duplexes. $100–$225 double. Rates include continental breakfast. AE, MC, V.

The Greenwood Pier Inn, perched on the edge of a dramatic bluff, is an eclectic, New Age kind of place. It's the unique domain of Kendrick and Isabel Petty, who operate a complex combining a cafe, country store, garden shop, and accommodations. Kendrick is an artist and passionate gardener whose collages, tiles, and marble work can be seen in the interiors of several of the buildings in the complex and also outside in the gardens. Of the accommodations, which are in various buildings in addition to the main inn, the Cliffhouse is the top choice, a seaside redwood cabin complete with a fireplace, large deck, and an upper level bathtub with ocean views. All the rooms have private decks, fireplaces or wood burners, and lie within 100 feet of the cliff edge; they have no TVs or phones, but each has access to a hot tub overlooking the ocean. A continental breakfast is delivered to your room; lunch and dinner are served daily in the cafe.

✪ Harbor House. 5600 S. Calif. 1 (Box 369), Elk, CA 95432. ☎ **707/877-3203.** 6 rms, 4 cottages. $180–$275 double. Additional person $50. Rates include full breakfast and four-course dinner. No credit cards.

While the Greenwood Pier Inn is home to New Age, the redwood-sided two-story Harbor House is very, very traditional. It was built in 1916 by the president of the Goodyear Redwood Lumber Co. as a hideaway for corporate executives and their wives. This is not a hotel, but an upscale B&B offering 3 acres of gardens, access to a private beach, and views overlooking the Pacific. None of the units has a TV or phone, and that's how guests here like it. Five of the rooms in the main building have their own fireplaces, many are furnished with antiques originally purchased by the lumber executives, and all have private baths. Cottages tend to be small, but have fireplaces and private decks.

Dining/Entertainment: The restaurant here always maintains two of its tables for nonguests, who should make reservations as far in advance as possible. Set dinners, which change nightly, cost $27 and feature both California and Pacific Northwest cuisine, making use of local herbs, freshly baked breads, and vegetables from the inn's own gardens.

KOA Kamping Kabins. On Kinney Rd. (off Calif. 1, 1.6 miles north of Point Arena). ☎ **707/882-2375.** 18 cabins. $38–$45 cabin. AE, DISC, MC, V.

What? You expect me to stay at a Kampgrounds of America?!? You bet. Once you see these adorable little log cabins, you can't help but admit that rich or poor, this is one great way to spend the weekend on the coast. The cabins have one or two bedrooms with log-frame double beds or bunk beds for the kids and sleep four to six people respectively. Rustic is the key word here: mattresses, a heater, and a light bulb are your standard amenities. After that, you're on your own, but basically all you need is some bedding or a sleeping bag, cooking and eating utensils, and a bag of charcoal for the barbecue out on the front porch (next to the log porch swing). Hot showers, bathrooms, laundry facilities, a small store, and a swimming pool are a short walk away, as is Manchester Beach.

Timber Cove Inn. 21780 Calif. 1, Jenner, CA 95450. ☎ **707/847-3231.** Fax 707/847-3704. 50 rms. $110–$140 double with pond view; $185–$225 double with ocean view; $285–$350 room with private hot tub, fireplace, and balcony. AE, MC, V.

Three miles north of Fort Ross, on a rocky promontory overlooking the ocean, this hotel was built with contemplation and meditation in mind. The massive redwood buildings blend in well with their surroundings. A stone-lined Japanese pond flanks the entrance path to the timbered lobby with its large walk-in fireplace. Adjacent is a dining room with sweeping views of the ocean. The redwood rooms are decorated with large pieces of driftwood. Throughout the complex are arrangements of wild flowers and prints by Ansel Adams, many of them scenes of Timber Cove. About half the rooms have fireplaces, and a number have sunken tiled tubs with ocean views. The most expensive are the 1,000-square-foot corner units with private hot tub, fireplace, and balcony.

WHERE TO DINE

Ledford House. 3000 N. Calif. 1, Albion. ☎ **707/937-0282.** Reservations recommended. Main courses $18–$24. AE, MC, V. Wed–Sun 5–9pm. CALIFORNIA/FRENCH.

If James Beard were alive today, he'd feel right at home at this innovative but simply decorated restaurant overlooking the pounding surf of the Pacific from a bluff above. The kitchen offers self-styled "new American cuisine," experimenting with the bounty of the Golden State to fashion rich combinations and harmonious flavors. One part of the menu is reserved primarily for the pastas and hearty stews suitable to this far northern setting, such as Antoine's cassoulet, a jumble of pork, lamb, garlic sausage, and duck confit slowly cooked with white beans. Although the menu changes monthly, for a taste of California try the salmon primavera with lemon-caper butter; or the red snapper braised with tomatoes, onions, garlic, and white wine. In the evening there's often live jazz in the lounge.

✪ **Pangaea**. 250 Main St., Point Arena. ☎ **707/882-3001.** Reservations recommended. Main courses $8–$15. Wed–Sun 6–9pm. ECLECTIC CUISINE.

North coast locals have been raving about this place since the day it opened. Chef/owner Shannon Hughes, an expatriate of St. Orres and Old Milano Hotel restaurants, decided it was time to do her own thing, and boy is she doing it well. Everything that comes out of her kitchen is wondrously fresh and inventive, such as the succulent pork confit, served on a potato tart with homemade apricot chutney. And how's this for a $3 salad: organic greens in a vinaigrette of toasted shallots, sherry vinegar, and Italian mountain gorgonzola. Even her burgers are beyond reproach, made with Niman-Schell beef, organic cheese and greens, Thai chili sauce, garlic roasted red potatoes, and homemade ketchup. Desserts—strawberry rhubarb crisp à la mode, lemon-curd tart with a blood-orange sauce—are equally impressive, as is the hip decor. Highly recommended.

3 Mendocino

Mendocino is, to our minds, *the* premier destination on California's north coast. Despite (or because of) its relative isolation, it emerged as one of Northern California's major centers for the arts in the 1950s. It's easy to see why artists were—and still are—attracted to this idyllic community, a cluster of New England–style sea captain's homes and small stores set on headlands overlooking the ocean.

At the height of the logging boom, Mendocino became an important and active port. Its population was about 3,500, and 8 hotels were built along with 17 saloons and more than a dozen bordellos. Today, it has only about 1,000 residents, most of whom reside on the north end of town. On summer weekends the population seems more like 10,000 as hordes of tourists drive up from the Bay Area, but despite the crowds Mendocino still manages to retain its small-town charm.

ESSENTIALS

GETTING THERE   The fastest route from San Francisco is via U.S. 101 north to Cloverdale. From there, take Calif. 128 west to Calif. 1, then go north along the coast. It's about a 4-hour drive. (You could also take U.S. 101 all the way to Ukiah or Willits, and cut over to the west from there.) The most scenic route from the Bay Area, if you have the time and your stomach doesn't mind the twists and turns, is to take Calif. 1 north along the coast the entire way; it's at least a 5- to 6-hour drive.

VISITOR INFORMATION   There's a small information office up the coast in Fort Bragg, stocked with lots of free brochures and maps available for purchase. Visit the **Fort Bragg/Mendocino Coast Chamber of Commerce,** 332 N. Main St. (P.O. Box 1141), Fort Bragg, CA 95437 (☎ **800/726-2780** or 707/961-6300). Pick up a copy of the center's monthly magazine, *Arts and Entertainment,* which lists upcoming events throughout Mendocino at **Mendocino Art Center,** in town at 45200 Little Lake Rd.

EXPLORING THE TOWN

Stroll through town, enjoying the architecture, and browse through the dozens of galleries and shops. Our favorites include the **Highlight Gallery,** 45052 Main St. (☎ 707/937-3132), for its handmade furniture, pottery, and other craftwork; **Old Gold,** 6 Albion St. (☎ 707/937-5005), which carries a great selection of antique and contemporary jewelry and watches; and the **Gallery Bookshop & Bookwinkle's Children's Books,** at Main and Kasten streets (☎ 707/937-2665), one of the best independent bookstores in Northern California, with a wonderful selection of books for children and adults. Another popular stop is **Mendocino Jams & Preserves,** 440 Main St. (☎ **800/708-1196** or 707/937-1037), which offers free tastings of their natural, locally made gourmet wares on little bread chips.

After exploring the town, walk out on the headlands that wrap around the town and constitute **Mendocino Headlands State Park.** (The visitor center for the park is in Ford House on Main Street.) Three miles of trails wind through the park, giving visitors panoramic views of sea arches and hidden grottoes. If you're here at the right time of year, the area will be blanketed with wild flowers, and when we last stopped by, you could pick fresh blackberries beside the trails. The headlands are home to many unique species of birds, including black oystercatchers. Behind the Mendocino Presbyterian Church on Main Street is a trail leading to stairs that take you down to the beach, a small but picturesque stretch of sand where driftwood formations have washed ashore.

On the south side of town, **Big River Beach** is accessible from Calif. 1; it's good for picnicking, walking, and sun bathing.

In town, stop by the **Mendocino Art Center,** 45200 Little Lake Rd. (☎ 707/937-5818), the town's unofficial cultural headquarters. It's also known for its gardens, three galleries, and shops that display and sell local fine arts and crafts. Admission is free; open daily from 10am to 5pm.

For a special treat, go to **Sweetwater Gardens,** 955 Ukiah St. (☎ **800/300-4140** or 707/937-4140), which offers group and private saunas and hot-tub soaks by the hour. Additional services include Swedish or deep-tissue massages. Reservations are recommended. Private tub prices are $8 per person per half hour, $11 per person per hour. Group tub prices are $7.50 per person with no time limit. Special discounts are available on Wednesdays. Open Monday to Thursday from 2 to 10pm, Friday to Sunday from noon to 11pm.

OUTDOOR PURSUITS

Explore the Big River by renting a canoe, sea cycle, kayak, or outrigger from **Catch a Canoe & Bicycles Too** (☎ 707/937-0273), located on the grounds of the Stanford Inn by the Sea (see "Where to Stay," below). If you're lucky, you'll see some osprey, blue herons, harbor seals, deer, and wood ducks. These same folks will also rent you a mountain bike (much better quality than your usual bike rental) so you can head up Calif. 1 and explore the nearby state parks on two wheels.

Horseback riding (both English and western) on the beach and into the redwoods is offered by **Ricochet Ridge Ranch,** 24201 N. Calif. 1, Fort Bragg (☎ **888/873-5777** or 707/964-PONY). Prices range from $35 for a 2-hour beach ride, to $195 for an all-day private beach/redwoods trail ride with lunch.

In addition to Mendocino Headlands State Park (see "Exploring the Town," above), there are several other state parks near Mendocino; all are within an easy drive or bike ride and make for a good day's outing. Information on all the parks' features, including maps of each one, is found in a brochure called "Mendocino Coast State Parks," available from the visitor center in Fort Bragg. These areas include **Manchester State Park,** located where the San Andreas fault sweeps to the sea; **Jug Handle State Reserve;** and **Van Damme State Park,** with a sheltered, easily accessible beach.

Our favorite of these parks, located directly on Calif. 1 just north of Mendocino, is **Russian Gulch State Park** (☎ **707/937-5804**). It's one of the region's most spectacular parks, where roaring waves crash against the cliffs that protect the park's California coastal redwoods. The most popular attraction is the Punch Bowl, a collapsed sea cave that forms a tunnel through which waves crash, creating throaty echoes. Inland, there's a scenic paved biking path, and visitors can also hike along miles of trails, including a gentle, well-marked 3-mile **Waterfall Loop** that winds past tall redwoods and damp green foliage to a 36-foot-high waterfall. Admission is $5. Thirty camping sites enjoy a beautiful setting and are available from April through mid-October ($14 to $16 per night). Phone ☎ **800/444-7275** for reservations.

Fort Bragg is just a short distance up the coast; deep-sea fishing charters are available from its harbor.

WHERE TO STAY
EXPENSIVE

✪ **Stanford Inn by the Sea.** N. Calif. 1 and Comptche Ukiah Rd. (P.O. Box 487), Mendocino, CA 95460. ☎ **800/331-8884** or 707/937-5615. Fax 707/937-0305. 23 rms, 10 suites. TV TEL. $190–$255 double; $225–$450 suites. Rates include cooked-to-order breakfast. AE, CB, DC, DISC, MC, V.

Just south of town, this rustic but ever-so-sumptuous lodge occupies 11 acres of land abutting the Big River. The grounds are captivating, with tiers of elaborate gardens, a pond for duck and geese, and fenced pastures containing horses, curious llamas, and old gnarled apple trees.

The rooms are luxuriously furnished in forest green and burgundy tones, and offer such special touches as thick terry-cloth robes and heavenly down comforters. They're made even more appealing with fresh flowers and works by local artists. All have fireplaces or stoves, stereos and VCRs (there's an extensive library of tapes available from the front desk), and private decks from which you can look out onto the Pacific. Second honeymooners should inquire about the romantic River Cottage; families will want the big ol' renovated barn. Pets are welcome here and receive the royal treatment.

Dining/Entertainment: A breakfast buffet is served every morning (you can take a tray back to your room) in the new breakfast room, and afternoon wine and hors d'oeuvres are offered as well.

Services: Concierge, laundry, in-room massage, courtesy car, and baby-sitting.

Facilities: There's a gorgeous solarium-style indoor hot tub and pool surrounded by tropical plants, as well as a new exercise room. Mountain bikes and canoes are available on the property from Catch a Canoe and Bicycles Too (bike rentals are complimentary with your stay).

MODERATE

Joshua Grindle Inn. 44800 Little Lake Rd. (P.O. Box 647), Mendocino, CA 95460. ☎ **800/GRINDLE** or 707/937-4143. 10 rms. July–Oct and Fri–Sat year-round $95–$185 double; Nov–June and Sun–Thurs $90–$155. Rates include full breakfast. AE, MC, V.

When it was built in 1879, this stately Victorian was one of the most substantial and impressive houses in Mendocino, owned by the town's wealthiest banker. This, the oldest B&B in Mendocino, features redwood siding, a wraparound porch, and large emerald lawns. From its prettily planted gardens there's a view across the village to the distant bay. There are five rooms in the main house, two in the cottage, and three in the water tower. All have well-lit, comfortably arranged sitting areas; some offer fireplaces, two have deep-soak tubs, and one has a whirlpool tub. Each is individually decorated: The library, for example, has a New England feel with its four-poster pine bed, floor-to-ceiling bookcase, and 19th-century tiles around the fireplace depicting many of the Aesop's fables. Sherry is served in the parlor in front of the fireplace and breakfast is offered in the dining room.

✪ **MacCallum House.** 45020 Albion St. (P.O. Box 206), Mendocino, CA 95460. ☎ **800/609-0492** or 707/937-0289. 18 rms. $100–$190 double. Additional person $15. DISC, MC, V. From U.S. 101, turn right onto Albion St. in downtown Mendocino.

A historic 1882 gingerbread Victorian mansion, MacCallum House is one of Mendocino's top accommodations. Originally owned by local matriarch Daisy MacCallum, the house still bears the imprint of this daughter of the town's richest lumber baron. It remained in the family until 1974, when it was turned into a B&B. Now owned by resident proprietors Melanie and Joe Redding, the home has been preserved with all of its original furnishings and contents—right down to Daisy's Christmas cards and books of pressed flowers. Boasting the occasional Tiffany lamp or authentic Persian carpet, each uniquely decorated guest room is exquisitely furnished with many original pieces—a Franklin stove, a handmade quilt, a cushioned rocking chair, or a child's cradle. The luxurious barn suite, complete with a stone fireplace, can accommodate up to six adults.

The **MacCallum House Restaurant** (☎ **707/937-5763**) has a sterling reputation. The menu changes seasonally, but a meal might start with broiled oysters bathed with garlic-basil butter and move on to a local salmon fillet or pan-broiled tenderloin with shiitake mushrooms. It's open for dinner daily from 4:30 to 9pm with brunch on the weekends; closed January through mid-February.

Mendocino Hotel & Garden Suites. 45080 Main St., Mendocino, CA 95460. ☎ **800/548-0513** or 707/937-0511. Fax 707/937-0513. 51 rms, 37 with bath; 6 suites. TEL. $65–$80 double without bath, $90–$160 double with bath; $190–$225 suite. Additional person $20. AE, MC, V.

Right in the heart of town, this 1878 hotel evokes California's Gold Rush days. Beveled-glass doors open into a Victorian-style lobby and parlor where you might expect to see Mae West. The hotel's decor combines antiques and reproductions, like the oak reception desk from a demolished Kansas bank. Remington paintings, stained-glass lamps, and Persian carpets contribute to the Wild West aura. Guest rooms feature hand-painted French porcelain sinks with floral designs, quaint wallpaper, old-fashioned beds and armoires, and photographs and memorabilia of historic Mendocino. About half the rooms are located in four handsome small buildings behind the main house. Many of the deluxe rooms have fireplaces or wood-burning stoves, as well as modern bathrooms and good views. Suites have an additional parlor, as well as a fireplace or balcony.

Breakfast and lunch are served in the Garden Room, while dinner is offered in the Victorian-style dining room. Room service is available daily from 8am to 9pm.

✪ **Rachel's Inn.** N. Calif. 1 (P. O. Box 134), Mendocino, CA 95460. ☎ **800/347-9252** or 707/937-0088. 9 rms. Mon–Thurs $96–$205 double; Fri–Sun $115–$205 double. Rates include breakfast. MC, V.

Two miles south of Mendocino, this B&B is set on an acre of land that abuts 320 acres of state park and is just a short walk from the beach. Two things make this inn special. One is Rachel herself, an attentive host who loves the Mendocino coast and who organized against the threat of offshore oil drilling in the 1980s. The second plus is that, unlike most inns in town, it is *not* decorated in Laura Ashley style. Instead, it has a refreshing contemporary look, with modern art, and an emphasis on comfort. From the house, guests can walk down to the cove, and there's also a trail from the house across the headlands. Rachel cooks a superb breakfast of huevos rancheros or something similar, plus fruit, baked goods, and cereals. The main house, built in the 1860s, contains four rooms and three suites, each equipped with a fireplace and sitting room. The South Room is a state-of-the-art unit that is specially equipped for disabled guests, with an extra large, wheelchair accessible, shower with seat.

INEXPENSIVE

✪ **Mendocino Village Inn.** 44860 Main St. (P.O. Box 626), Mendocino, CA 95460. ☎ **800/ 882-7029** or 707/937-0246. 10 rms, 8 with bath; 1 suite. $75 double without bath, $90–$175 double with bath; $175 suite. Rates include full breakfast and evening refreshments. No credit cards.

Although a street separates the Mendocino Village Inn from the ocean, it's still close to the water. A garden of flowers, plants, and frog ponds fronts the large blue-and-white guest house, which was built in 1882 by a local doctor and later occupied by famed local artist Emmy Lou Packard.

Innkeepers Bill and Kathleen Erwin have decorated each room differently. The Queen Anne Room features a four-poster canopy bed, and the sentimental Maggie's Room is named for a child who etched her name in the window glass almost a century ago (you can still see it). Except for two attic rooms, all have private baths, and four rooms have private outside entrances. Complimentary beverages are served in the evening.

IN NEARBY ALBION & LITTLE RIVER

✪ **Albion River Inn.** N. Calif. 1, (P.O. Box 100), Albion, CA 95410. ☎ **800/479-7944** or 707/937-1919. 20 rms, 6 Jacuzzi suites. TEL. $170–$200 double; $240–$260 Jacuzzi suite. Rates include full breakfast. AE, MC, V.

A quarter mile north of Albion, this modern choice overlooks the mouth of the Albion River from a bluff some 90 feet above the Pacific. The rooms are all attractively decorated in a contemporary style with comfortable furnishings and have ocean views; most have decks. You'll find wingbacks placed in front of the fireplace, down comforters on the king-size beds, well-lit desks, and earthenware lamps beside the bed. Additional amenities include a coffeemaker, refrigerator, CD stereo, and bathrobes. *Insider tip:* If you really want to impress your sweetie, reserve one of the rooms with the Jacuzzi tubs or oversized tubs for two, which have large picture windows that offer dazzling views of the coast.

The cuisine at the inn's restaurant changes daily, but the view from the tables remains the same: stellar. Fresh local produce is used whenever possible with each dish. Entree favorites include grilled sea bass, ginger-barbecued salmon, and braised Sonoma rabbit. For dessert, the homemade ice cream is smooth and loaded with flavor. On weekends, soft piano music adds to the romantic atmosphere.

✪ **Glendeven.** 8221 N. Calif. 1, Little River, CA 95456. ☎ **800/822-4536** or 707/937-0083. Fax 707/937-6108. 10 rms. Main house, $90–$105 Mon–Thurs, $100–$105 Fri–Sun and Aug; annex, $140–$160 Mon–Thurs, $125–$140 Fri–Sun and Aug. Rates include continental breakfast. MC, V.

Named one of the 12 best inns in America by *Country Inns* magazine, this 1867 farmhouse has been converted into a place of exceptional styling and comfort by its designer/owners, Jan and Janet DeVries. Accommodations are spread across 2¹/₂ acres that encompass the main house, the Barn, and an addition known as Stevenscroft. Each room is individually decorated with a well-balanced mixture of antiques and contemporary pieces. We prefer two rooms in the farmhouse (misleadingly called suites, they are really just large rooms). The king's suite includes an antique walnut bed, and the Eastlin suite is furnished with a French rosewood bed. Five rooms in the modern annex are large and spacious, but perhaps less charming. Guests are also housed in a fantastic converted Barn House Suite, which can accommodate up to five (perfect for families or groups), and in the Stevenscroft, which has high peaks, a gabled roof, and a barnlike setting. Adjacent to the inn are the numerous fern-lined canyon trails of Van Damme State Park.

Heritage House. 5200 N. Calif. 1, Little River, CA 95456. ☎ **800/235-5885** or 707/937-5885. Fax 707/937-0318. 66 rms. Summer, $105–$280 double; winter, $90–$265. Additional person $20. MC, V. Closed after Thanksgiving until Christmas, and again Jan 2 to mid-Feb.

Most of the rooms at this traditional country club–style property have views of the ocean and rugged coastline. Built in 1877 as a farmhouse and surrounded by 37 seafront acres, the main building's most infamous moment came when it served as a hideout for bandit "Baby Face" Nelson. Much of the inn as you see it dates from 1949 and has been renovated several times since. Only three guest rooms are located in the ivy-covered New England–style main building; the rest are in cottages grouped two to four under one common roof. Rooms are individually decorated with original antiques and locally made furnishings, and include such amenities as bathrobes, hair dryers, umbrellas, wine splits, and newspaper delivery (TVs and telephones are purposely missing). Most have woodburning fireplaces or stoves, private decks, sitting areas, and ocean views, and several suites have a wet bar and Jacuzzi. Wooded trails wind along the dramatic coastline, offering spectacular views.

The newly renovated Heritage House dining room offers high cuisine à la award-winning chef de cuisine Lance Dean Velasquez. The menu changes seasonally, but might include winter beef stew with smoked bacon, turnips and potatoes, or grilled Bradley Ranch New York strip with horseradish smashers and Jack Daniels sauce. Prices range from $16 to $25.

WHERE TO DINE
EXPENSIVE

✪ **Café Beaujolais.** 961 Ukiah St. ☎ **707/937-5614.** Reservations recommended. Main courses $16–$25 at dinner. DISC, MC, V. Daily 5:45–9pm. AMERICAN/FRENCH.

This is one of Mendocino's—if not Northern California's—top dining choices, owned and managed since 1977 by chef and entrepreneur Margaret Fox. The venerable French country–style tavern is set in a turn-of-the-century house; rose-colored carnival-glass chandeliers add a burnish to the oak floors and the heavy oak tables adorned with flowers. On warm summer nights, request a table at the enclosed deck overlooking the "designer" gardens.

Though Café Beaujolais started out as a breakfast and lunch place, it's strictly a dinner house now (yes, their famed weekend brunch has been discontinued). The menu changes weekly and usually lists about five main courses, such as wild sturgeon fillet pan-roasted with truffle emulsion sauce; free-range chicken stuffed with eggplant, mushrooms, cheese, garlic, and fresh herbs from local organic farms; or broiled Wildwood Ranch pork loin chop with yam puree. Tuesday to Thursday the cafe offers a prix-fixe country menu for $20 to $25 that's a pretty good deal.

The 955 Ukiah Street Restaurant. 955 Ukiah St. ☎ **707/937-1955.** Reservations recommended. Main courses $11–$18. MC, V. Thur–Sun 6–10pm. Closed after Thanksgiving weekend through Christmas and 1 week in June. CALIFORNIA/FRENCH.

Shortly after this building's construction in the 1960s, the region's most famous painter, Emmy Lou Packard, commandeered its premises as an art studio for the creation of a series of giant murals. Today, it's a large but surprisingly cozy restaurant, accented with massive railway ties and vaulted ceilings. The tables on the mezzanine level can get a little cramped; ask for a window table overlooking the gardens. The cuisine is creative and reasonably priced, a worthy alternative to the perpetually booked Café Beaujolais next door. It's hard to recommend a particular main dish, although the phyllo-wrapped red snapper with pesto and lime has a zesty tang, and the crispy duck with ginger, apples, and a Calvados sauce would earn enthusiastic friends in Normandy.

MODERATE

Bay View Café. 45040 Main St. ☎ **707/937-4197.** Reservations not accepted. Dinner $6–$15. No credit cards. Summer daily 8am–9pm; winter, daily 8am–3pm, Fri–Sun 5–9pm. AMERICAN.

This reasonably priced cafe is one of the most popular in town and the only place around besides the Mendocino Hotel that serves breakfast ("And we're *way* better," says the owner). From the second-floor dining area of the cafe there's a sweeping view of the Pacific and faraway headlands; to reach it, climb a flight of stairs running up the outside of the town's antique water tower, then detour sideways. Surrounded by dozens of ferns suspended from the ceiling, you'll find a menu with southwestern selections (the marinated chicken breast is very popular), a good array of sandwiches (our favorite is the hot crabmeat with avocado slices), fish-and-chips, and the fresh catch of the day. Breakfast ranges from the basic bacon 'n' eggs to eggs Florentine and honey-wheat pancakes.

The Mousse Cafe. 390 Kasten St. (at Albion St.). ☎ **707/937-4323.** Reservations required for dinner. Main courses $11–$17. No credit cards. Mon–Thurs 11:30am–9pm, Fri 11:30am–10:30pm, Sat 11:30am–10:30pm, Sun 9am–9pm. CONTINENTAL/CALIFORNIA.

The setting is a turn-of-the-century clapboard-sided house inspired by New England architecture and set in a pleasant garden. In 1995 the place was gutted and re-done, resulting in a brand-new, bright, streamlined interior. The menu includes many local items such as organic herbs and vegetables—try the Caesar salad. We enjoyed roast chicken with garlic mashed potatoes and a swordfish special with fresh vegetables. The Blackout cake is a chocoholic's fantasy. The food is good, the service is friendly; our only complaint is that the tables are a bit too close together, especially if it's crowded.

INEXPENSIVE

You'd be surprised what $5 will get you for lunch if you know where to go. **Tote Fete Bakery** (☎ 707/937-3383) has a wonderful little carry-out booth at the corner of Albion and Lansing streets. We like the foil-wrapped barbecue chicken sandwiches, but the pizza, foccacia bread, and twice-baked potatoes are also good choices. Dine at the stand-up counter, or opt for a picnic at the headlands down the street.

Regardless of preference—beef, chicken, turkey, or veggie—burger lovers won't be let down at **Mendo Burgers** (☎ 707/937-1111), arguably the best burger joint on the north coast. A side of thick fresh-cut fries is mandatory, as is a pile of napkins. Hidden behind the Mendocino Bakery and Café at 10483 Lansing St., it's a little hard to find, but well worth searching out.

Vegetarians should check out **Lu's Kitchen** at 45013 Ukiah St., between Lansing and Ford streets (☎ **707/937-4939**), which uses only organically grown produce for their burritos, salads, tacos, and quesadillas. It's little more than a small shack—look for the white plastic tables and chairs on the south side of the street.

In the back of the **Little River Market** (☎ **707/937-5133**), located directly across from the Little River Inn on Calif. 1, is a trio of small tables overlooking the Mendocino coastline. Order a tamale, sandwich, or whatever else is on the menu at the tiny deli inside the market, or buy a loaf of legendary Café Beaujolais bread sold at the front counter.

IN NEARBY LITTLE RIVER

Little River Restaurant. 7750 N. Calif. 1, Little River. ☎ **707/937-4945.** Reservations required. Main courses $16.50–$21.50. No credit cards. July 11–Oct 15, Fri–Tues dinner seatings at 6 and 8:30pm; rest of the year, Fri–Mon dinner seatings at 6 and 8:30pm. PACIFIC/NORTHWESTERN.

Charming, small-scale and personal, this restaurant is part of a complex that contains a general market and the village's only post office. (Don't get it confused with the larger Little River Inn across the road.) The Little River Restaurant is the personal culinary statement of Jeri Barrett (now joined by her son), who might be the only chef in the neighborhood who routinely quotes Elizabeth Barrett Browning. It enjoys a winning reputation for dishes like tenderloin of pork with a ginger-flavored scallion sauce and red snapper sautéed with lemon-dill butter and shallots. Beer and wine are served, but no hard liquor. Because there are only seven tables, making and keeping your reservations here is extremely important.

4 Fort Bragg

Mendocino County's commercial center—hence the site of most of the area's fast-food restaurants and supermarkets—Fort Bragg is far more down to earth than Mendocino. Inexpensive motels and cheap eats used to be its only attraction, but over the past few years gentrification has quickly spread throughout the town as the logging and fishing industries have continued to decline. With no room left to open new shops in Mendocino, many gallery, boutique, and restaurant owners have moved up the road. The result is a huge increase in Fort Bragg's tourist trade, particularly during the annual Whale Festival in March, and Paul Bunyan Days over Labor Day weekend.

To explore the town properly, make your first stop at the **Fort Bragg/Mendocino Coast Chamber of Commerce,** 332 N. Main St. (P.O. Box 1141), Fort Bragg, CA 95437 (☎ **800/726-2780** or 707/961-6300), and pick up a free walking map. The friendly staff will answer any questions about Mendocino, Fort Bragg, and the surrounding region.

SHOPPING & EXPLORING

The town doesn't boast as many well-coiffed stores and galleries as its dainty cousin to the south, but it does have some worthwhile shopping spots. Antique shops line the 300 block of North Franklin Street, 1 block east of Main Street, while the **old train depot,** at 401 N. Main St. (☎ **707/964-8324**), has been turned into a shopping center and historical museum with logging equipment and restored steam trains.

For the Shell of It, 344 N. Main St. (☎ **707/961-0461**), stocks handmade jewelry, baskets, and collectibles made of shells or designed around a nautical theme, as well as rocks, gems, minerals, and fossils. **The Hot Pepper Jelly Company,** 330 N. Main St. (☎ **707/961-1422**), is famous for its assortment of Mendocino food products—dozens of varieties of pepper jelly, plus local mustards, syrups, and biscotti along with hand-painted porcelain bowls, unusual baskets, and more. The **Mendocino Chocolate Company,** 542 N. Main St. (☎ **707/964-8800**), makes and sells homemade chocolates and truffles, which it ships all over the world. Painters, jewelers, sculptors, weavers, potters, and other local artists display their works at **Northcoast Artists,** 362 North Main St. (☎ **707/964-8266**). At **Windsong,** 324 N. Main St. (☎ **707/964-2050**), you'll find a clutter of colorful kites, cards, candles, and other gifts.

Fort Bragg is also the home of the **Mendocino Coast Botanical Gardens,** 18220 N. Calif. 1 (☎ **707/964-4352**), about 8 miles north of Mendocino. This cliff-top public garden, set among the pines along the rugged coast, nurtures rhododendrons, fuchsias, azaleas, and a multitude of flowering shrubs. The area contains bridges, streams, canyons, dells, picnic areas, and trails for easy walking. Children under 12 must be accompanied by their parents. Admission is $5 for adults, $4 for seniors age 60 and over, $3 for children ages 13 to 17, $1 for children ages 12 to 6, and free for children 5 and under. (Children under 18 must be accompanied by an adult.) Open April 1 through September 30 daily from 9am to 5pm, October 1 through March 31 daily from 9am to 4pm.

From Fort Bragg, the **Skunk Train** (☎ **707/964-6371**) gives riders a fine tour of the area's redwoods. Locals have always said of the logging trains that, "You can smell 'em before you can see 'em," which explains the nickname. The trains, which can be boarded at the Fort Bragg Depot at the foot of Laurel Avenue in Fort Bragg (2 blocks from the Grey Whale Inn), travel 40 miles inland along the Redwood Highway (U.S. 101) to Willits. It's a scenic route through the redwood forest, crossing 31 bridges and trestles and cutting through 2 deep tunnels. The round-trip takes 6 to 7 hours, allowing plenty of time for lunch in Willits before you return on the afternoon train. Half-day trips are offered on weekends throughout the year, and daily in summer from mid-June to early September. In summer call for reservations. The trains run year-round, but schedules vary so call for exact times. Tickets cost $26 round-trip, $21 one-way; children ages 5 to 11 board for half price.

OUTDOOR PURSUITS

Fort Bragg is the county's sportfishing center. Just south of town, **Noyo's Fishing Center,** 3245 N. Harbor, Noyo (☎ **707/964-7609**), is a good place to buy or rent tackle and the best source of information on local fishing boats. Lots of party boats leave from the town's harbor, as do whale-watching tours.

Lost Coast Adventures, North Coast Divers Supply, 19275 S. Harbor Dr. (☎ **800/961-1143** or 707/961-1143), offers scuba diving, fishing, and whale-watching expeditions, as well as kayak tours of the coastline and coastal rivers.

Three miles north of Fort Bragg off Calif. 1 lies **Mackerricher State Park** (☎ **707/937-5804**), a popular place for biking, hiking, and horseback riding. This enormous 1,700-acre park has 142 campsites and 8 miles of shoreline. For a true biking or hiking venture, travel the 8-mile-long "Haul Road," an old logging road that provides fine ocean vistas all the way to Ten Mile River. Harbor seals make their home at the park's Laguna Point Seal Watching Station, reached via an elevated wooden gangway (truly a pleasant walk).

CUTTING-EDGE THEATER

Living proof that poor, maligned ol' Fort Bragg is on the road to respect is its up-start new theatrical company, ✪ **Warehouse Repertory Theatre,** 18791 N. Calif. 1. Determined to make Fort Bragg the Ashland of California, this cadre of highly talented professional actors from around the country has finally answered the age-old Mendocino County question of "So, what is there to do around here at night?" From Shakespeare to Shepard, no play is too shocking or sultry for artistic director Meg Patterson and her crew, who have received kudos for the fresh, significant interpretations they have brought to the north coast. The Warehouse's season runs from late February through December, Thursday to Saturday (and the occasional Monday) at 8pm, with Sunday matinees at 2pm. For information about current shows and future plays, or to reserve tickets (which range from $10 to $15) call the box office at ☎ 707/961-2940 or visit their website at www.theatre@warerep.org.

WHERE TO STAY

Grey Whale Inn. 615 N. Main St., Fort Bragg, CA 95437. ☎ **800/382-7244** or 707/964-0640. Fax 707/964-4408. 14 rms. TV TEL. $100–$180 double. Discounted winter rates available midweek Nov–Mar. Rates include buffet breakfast. AE, DISC, MC, V.

A comfortable B&B 6 blocks from the beach and 2 from the Skunk Train depot, this 1915 landmark was originally built as a hospital. The spacious and airy redwood building has become a well-run, relaxed inn, furnished partly with antiques and plenty of local art. Each guest room is unique: Two have ocean views, three have fireplaces, one has a whirlpool tub, two have private decks, and one offers a shower with wheelchair access. The buffet breakfast includes homemade bread or coffee cake and fresh fruit. No smoking.

WHERE TO DINE

North Coast Brewing Company. 444 N. Main St. ☎ **707/964-3400.** Reservations accepted for large parties only. Main courses $6–$17. DISC, MC, V. Tues–Fri 2–11pm, Sat–Sun noon–11pm. AMERICAN.

This homey brewpub is the most happening place in town, especially during happy hour, when the bar and dark wood tables are occupied by boisterous locals. The building that houses the pub is a dignified, century-old redwood structure, which in previous lives has functioned as a mortuary, an annex to the local Presbyterian church, an art studio, and administration offices for the College of the Redwoods. Beer is brewed on the premises in large copper vats that are displayed behind plate glass. A pale ale, a pilsner, a stout, and a fourth seasonal brew are always available. Standard fare such as burgers and barbecued chicken sandwiches are supplemented by more substantial dishes, ranging from linguini with smoked mushrooms to a hefty pile of country-style Carolina barbecued pork. After lunch, browse the retail shop or take a free tour of the brewery.

The Restaurant. 418 Main St. ☎ **707/964-9800.** Reservations recommended. Lunch $6.50–$8.50; dinner $12.50–$19.50. MC, V. Thurs–Fri 11:30am–2pm, Sun brunch 9am–1pm; Thurs–Tues 5–9pm. PACIFIC NORTHWESTERN/CALIFORNIA.

One of the oldest family-run restaurants on the coast, this small, unpretentious Fort Bragg landmark is known for its good dinners and Sunday brunches. The eclectic menu offers dishes from just about every corner of the planet: blackened New York strip steak, sweet-and-sour stir-fry, Livorno-style shellfish stew, and even shrimp rellenos. There are also a few vegetarian specialties, including grilled polenta with melted mozzarella and sautéed mushrooms, topped with tomato-herb sauce and Parmesan cheese. The comfortable booth section is the best place to sit if you want to keep an eye on the entertainment—courtesy of ebullient chef Jim Larsen—in the kitchen. On weekends, additional entertainment comes in the form of live music.

5 The Avenue of the Giants & Ferndale

From Fort Bragg, Calif. 1 continues north along the shoreline for about 30 miles before turning inland to Leggett and U.S. 101, a.k.a. the "Redwood Highway," which runs north to Garberville. Six miles beyond Garberville, the Avenue of the Giants begins around Phillipsville; it's an alternative route that roughly parallels U.S. 101, and there are about a half-dozen interchanges between U.S. 101 and the Avenue of the Giants if you don't want to drive the whole thing. It's one of the most spectacular scenic routes in the west (Route 254), cutting along the Eel River through the 51,000-acre Humboldt Redwoods State Park. The Avenue ends just south of Scotia; from here, it's only about 10 miles to the turnoff to Ferndale, about 5 miles west of Calif. 101.

For more information or a detailed map of the area, go to the **Humboldt Redwood State Park Visitor Center,** P.O. Box 276, Weott, CA 95571 (☎ **707/ 946-2263**), just north of Hidden Springs State Campground, 2 miles south of Weott.

Thirty-three miles long, the Avenue of the Giants was left intact for sightseers when the freeway was built. The giants, of course, are the majestic coast redwoods (*Sequoia sempervirens*); more than 50,000 acres of them make up the most outstanding display in the redwood belt. Their rough-bark columns climb 100 feet or more without a branch and soar to a total height of more than 340 feet. With their immunity to insects and fire-resistant bark, they have survived for thousands of years. The oldest dated coast redwood is more than 2,200 years old.

The state park has three **campgrounds** with 248 campsites: Hidden Springs, half a mile south of Myers Flat; Burlington, 2 miles south of Weott, near park headquarters; and Albee Creek State Campground, 5 miles west of U.S. 101 on the Mattole Road north of Weott. You'll also come across picnic and swimming facilities, motels, resorts, restaurants, and numerous resting and parking areas.

Sadly, the route has several tacky attractions that attempt to turn the trees into some kind of freak show. Our suggestion is to skip these and appreciate the trees by taking advantage of the trails and the campgrounds off the beaten path. As you drive along, you'll see numerous parking areas with short loop trails leading into the forest. From south to north the first of these "attractions" is the **Chimney Tree** (☎ **707/923-2265**), where J.R.R. Tolkien's Hobbit is rumored to reside. This living, hollow redwood is more than 1,500 years old. Nearby is a gift shop and a burger place. Then there's the **One-Log House,** a small apartment-like house built inside a log. At Myers Flat midway along the Avenue, you can also drive your car through a living redwood at the **Shrine Drive Thru Tree.**

A few miles north of Weott is **Founders Grove,** named in honor of those who established the Save the Redwoods League in 1918. Farther north, close to the end of the Avenue, stands the 950-year-old **Immortal Tree,** just north of Redcrest. Near Pepperwood at the end of the Avenue, the **Drury trail** and the **Percy French trail** are two good short hikes. The park itself is also good for mountain biking. Ask the rangers for details. For more information, contact **Humboldt Redwoods State Park,** P.O. Box 100, Weott, CA 95571 (☎ **707/946-2409**).

WHERE TO STAY & DINE NEAR THE SOUTHERN ENTRANCE TO THE AVENUE OF THE GIANTS

Benbow Inn. 445 Lake Benbow Dr., Garberville, CA 95542. ☎ **800/355-3301** or 707/ 923-2124. Fax 707/923-2897. 55 rms, 1 cottage. A/C TEL. $120–$220 double; $295 cottage. AE, CB, DC, DISC, MC, V.

This national historic landmark overlooking the Eel River off U.S. 101, was designed by Albert Farr in 1925. Pretty Benbow Lake State Park is right out the front door. It's built in a mock Tudor style, and guests enter through a grand hall with cherrywood wainscoting. Rooms in the main building have fireplaces, TVs, private entrances and patios; some have VCRs. A comfortable annex with elegant woodwork was added in the 1980s. Bicycles are available.

Complimentary afternoon tea and scones are served in the lobby at 3pm (there's mulled wine in winter), and there are complimentary hors d'oeuvres in the lounge. The dramatic high-ceilinged dining room opens onto a spacious terrace and offers internationally inspired main courses ($12 to $20).

FERNDALE

The village of Ferndale, beyond the Avenue of the Giants and west of U.S. 101, has been declared a historic landmark because of its many Victorian homes and storefronts. These include a smithy and a saddlery. About 5 miles inland from the coast and close to the redwood belt, Ferndale is one of the best-preserved Victorian hamlets in Northern California. Despite its unbearably cute shops, it is nonetheless a vital part of the northern coastal tourist circuit. The small town has a number of artists in residence and is also home to one of California's oddest events, the **World Championship Great Arcata to Ferndale Cross-Country Kinetic Sculpture Race,** a bizarre 3-day event run every Memorial Day weekend. The race, which draws more than 10,000 spectators, is run over land and water in whimsically designed human-powered vehicles. Stop in at the museum at 780 Main St. if you want to see some recent race entries.

WHERE TO STAY

✪ **Gingerbread Mansion.** 400 Berding St. (P.O. Box 40), Ferndale, CA 95536. ☎ **800/ 952-4136** or 707/786-4000. Fax 707/786-4381. 5 rms, 5 suites. $140–$180 double; $150–$350 suite. Additional person $40. Rates include full breakfast and afternoon tea. AE, MC, V.

This peach-and-yellow structure with stained glass and other fine architectural details is one of Ferndale's most photographed Victorians; it was built in 1899 as the home of a local doctor and his family. Run by Ken and Sandie Torbert, it's beautifully furnished with antiques. Some of the large guest rooms have two old-fashioned clawfoot tubs for bubble baths for two, and others offer fireplaces. The latest addition is the attic-level Empire Suite, a lavish spare-no-expense blowout with Ionic columns, massage-jet shower, two fireplaces, and a king-size bed draped with Royal Sateen linens. Bathrobes and extra-large thick towels are provided. Beds are turned down for the night, and you will find hand-dipped chocolates on the nightstand. The mansion has bicycles and umbrellas for guests to use. Smoking is only permitted on the verandas.

When you rise, there's morning coffee or tea outside your door, enough to sustain you until your breakfast of fruit, cheese, muffins, breads, cakes, and a baked egg dish. Afternoon tea with sandwiches, pastries, fresh fruit, and Devonshire cream is also served.

WHERE TO DINE

Curley's Grill. 460 Main St. ☎ **707/786-9696.** Main courses $9–$18. DISC, MC, V. Daily 11:30am–9pm (last order). CALIFORNIA GRILL.

Set within what looks like a clapboard-sided Victorian farmhouse, across the street from Ferndale's Repertory Theater, this is a bright and lively restaurant that specializes exclusively in California-inspired grilled foods. Don't think for a moment that the menu is limited to steaks, however. Owner Curley Tait also grills up such items as polenta with a sausage-tomato sauce, a medley of Pacific seafish, crab cakes, and some of the freshest vegetables on the California coast. Curley has added house-made breads and desserts to the menu as well. The interior decor is vaguely art deco and showcases local artists' works, but the best seating is behind the kitchen in the secluded back patio. Curley's also offers a small but interesting selection of California wines.

6 Eureka & Environs

EUREKA

On first glance, Eureka (pop. 27,000) doesn't look very appealing; fast-food restaurants, cheap motels, and shopping malls predominate on the main thoroughfare. But if you turn west off U.S. 101 anywhere between A and M streets, you'll discover Old Town Eureka along the waterfront, which is worth exploring. It has a large number of Victorian buildings, a museum, and some good-quality stores and restaurants.

The **Clarke Memorial Museum,** 240 E St. (☎ **707/443-1947**), has a fine collection of Native American baskets and other historic artifacts. The other popular attraction is the extraordinary architectural gem, the **Carson House,** built in 1884–86 for lumber baron William Carson. A 3-story conglomeration of ornamentation, it's designed in a mélange of styles—Queen Anne, Italianate, Stick, and Eastlake. It took 100 men more than 2 years to build. Today it's a private club, so you can only marvel at the exterior of this 18-room mansion—said to be the most photographed Victorian home in America—from the sidewalk. Across the street stands the **"Pink Lady,"** designed for William Carson as a wedding present for his son. Both testify to the wealth that was once made in Eureka's lumber trade. As early as 1856, there were already seven sawmills producing 2 million board feet of lumber every month.

Humboldt Bay, where the town stands, was discovered by whites in 1850. In 1853 Fort Humboldt was established to protect settlers from local Native American tribes. Ulysses S. Grant was stationed here for 5 months until he resigned after serious disputes with his commanding officer about his drinking. The fort was abandoned in 1870. Today the fort offers a self-guided trail past a series of logging exhibits, plus a reconstructed surgeon's quarters and a restored fort hospital, used today as a museum housing Native American artifacts and military and pioneer paraphernalia. **Fort Humboldt State Historic Park** is at 3431 Fort Ave. (☎ **707/445-6567**). Admission is free; open daily from 9am to 5pm.

Humboldt Bay supplies a large portion of California's fish, and Eureka has a fishing fleet of about 200 boats. To get a better view (and perspective) of the bay and surrounding waters, you can board skipper Leroy Zerlang's *Madaket*—said to be the oldest passenger-carrying vessel in operation in the U.S.—for a 75-minute **Humboldt Bay Harbor Cruise** (☎ 707/445-1910), departing daily from the foot of C Street in downtown Eureka.

More active water recreation includes fishing for halibut, king salmon, steelhead, and even shark, depending on the season. A license is required and can be secured for 1 day. For information, contact **Larry's Guide Service,** 3380 Utah St. (☎ **707/444-0250**). Fishing information can also be obtained from the **Eureka Fly Shop,** 505 H St. (☎ **707/444-2000**), and kayaks and sailboats can be rented from **Hum Boats,** on F Street (☎ **707/443-5157**), which also provides tours and lessons.

Humboldt County is also suitable for biking because it's relatively uncongested. Bikes can be rented from **Pro Sport Center,** 508 Myrtle Ave. (☎ **707/443-6328**). Fishing, diving, biking, and hiking information are also available.

Humboldt Bay is an important stopover point along the Pacific Flyway and is the winter home for thousands of migratory birds. South of town, the Humboldt Bay National Wildlife Refuge, 1020 Ranch Rd., Loleta (☎ 707/733-5406), provides an opportunity to see many of the 200 or so species that live in the marshes and willow groves—Pacific black brant, western sandpiper, northern harrier, great blue heron, and green-winged teal. The egret rookery on the bay, best viewed from Woodley Island Marina across the bay en route to Samoa, is spectacular. Peak viewing for most species of waterbirds and raptors is between September and March. The refuge's entrance is off U.S. 101 north at the Hookton Road exit. Cross the overpass and turn right onto Ranch Road.

For information, contact the **Eureka/Humboldt County Convention and Visitors Bureau,** 1034 2nd St., Eureka, CA 95501 (☎ **800/346-3482** or 707/443-5097; fax 707/443-5115), or the **Eureka Chamber of Commerce,** 2112 Broadway, Eureka, CA 95501 (☎ **800/356-6381** or 707/442-3738).

WHERE TO STAY

✪ **An Elegant Victorian Mansion Bed & Breakfast Experience.** 14th and C sts., Eureka, CA 95501. ☎ **707/444-3144.** Fax 707/442-5594. 5 rms. $95–$185 double. Rates include breakfast. MC, V.

For anyone interested in social history and design, this is a special experience. Those who just want comfort, service, a true gourmet breakfast, and a lovely garden will also find this lodging ideal. The 1888 house is the labor of love of owners Doug and Lily Vieyra, who have combed the country for the fabrics and designs that now provide the most authentic Victorian atmosphere we have ever encountered in the United States. The wallpapers are extraordinary—brilliant blues, golds, jades, and reds in intricate patterns that feature peacocks and mythological figures. Doug has paid attention to every detail, from the butler who greets you in morning dress to the silent movies and period music on the phonograph. The rooms are individually furnished. The Van Gogh room contains the Belgian bedroom suite of Lily's mother. The Lily Langtry room, named after the actress and king's mistress who stayed here when she performed locally, features a four-poster bed and Langtry memorabilia. There's laundry service, and Swedish massage is offered. Bikes and a sauna are available, and croquet is played on the manicured lawn, where ice-cream sodas and lemonade are served in the afternoon. No smoking.

✪ **Hotel Carter.** Carter House and Bell Cottage, 301 L St., Eureka, CA 95501. ☎ **800/404-1390** or 707/445-1390. Fax 707/444-8067. 31 rms, 11 suites. TV TEL. $79–$225 double; $95–$225 suite. AE, CB, DC, DISC, MC, V. From U.S. 101 north turn left onto L St. and go to 3rd.

At the north end of Eureka's Old Town is the original building that launched Carter's renowned hostelry empire: the Carter House. Copied from a famous 1884 San Francisco Victorian, it was constructed by Mark Carter as a family home in 1982. Soon afterwards, Mark and his wife Christi Carter began taking guests, and before long they built another 20-room hotel across the street. Later, the pretty Victorian Bell Cottage was acquired. The 20 rooms in the large full-service hotel have modern furnishings and pine four-posters. The suites have such luxury appointments as VCRs, fireplaces, and Jacuzzis, and distant views of the waterfront from the Jacuzzi tubs. There are seven rooms in the original house, which is furnished with antiques, Oriental rugs, and modern artwork. The Bell Cottage's rooms are also individually decorated. On ground level is one of Eureka's finest restaurants (see below).

WHERE TO DINE

Ramone's Bakery & Cafe. 209 E St. (in Old Town). ☎ **707/445-2923.** Main courses $4–$6. No credit cards. Cafe Mon–Sat 7am–6pm, Sun 8am–5pm. BAKERY.

Ramone's combines a bakery on one side with a small cafe on the other. The baked items are extraordinary—try any one of the croissants, danish, or muffins, and you won't be disappointed. Alas, the once-popular restaurant has closed down, but you can still find a few lunch specials to choose from among the breads and pastries, such as soups, salads, burgers, and more. At any time of the day, it's a great place to stop in for a light, inexpensive meal and cup of coffee. There's a second bakery location at 2223 Harrison St. in Eureka, as well as two more in Arcata: 600 F St., and 747 13th St. at Wildberries Marketplace.

✪ **Restaurant 301.** In the Hotel Carter, 301 L St. ☎ **707/444-8062.** Reservations required in summer. Main courses $10–$18. AE, CB, DISC, DC, MC, V. Daily 6–9pm. CALIFORNIA.

The large, light, and airy dining room adjacent to the hotel's lobby has tall windows looking out on the waterfront. It's one of the best restaurants in the area, with most of the herbs and many of the vegetables picked fresh from the hotel's organic gardens across the street. The cuisine also displays Asian accents, for example, the tiger prawns with sesame, ginger, and soy, and the chicken with spicy peanut sauce. If you're an oyster lover, start with a few Humboldt Bay oysters roasted with barbecue sauce. There's an excellent and extensive wine list, courtesy of the 301 Wine Shop within the hotel.

Samoa Cookhouse. Cookhouse Rd., Samoa. ☎ **707/442-1659.** Reservations taken for large groups only. Main courses $11.95. AE, DISC, MC, V. Mon–Sat 6am–3:30pm and 5–10pm, Sun 6am–10pm (closes an hour earlier in winter). From U.S. 101, take Samoa Bridge to the end and turn left on Samoa Rd.; then take the first left. AMERICAN.

When lumber was king, cookhouses (like this one dating from 1885) were common and were community hubs. Here the millmen and longshoremen at the Hammond Lumber Company came to chow down three hot meals before, during, and after their 12-hour work day. The food is still hearty—though not particularly healthy—and served family style at long red-checkered cloth-covered tables. Nobody leaves hungry. The price includes soup, salad, fresh-baked bread, the main course, and dessert (usually pie). The lunch and dinner menu still features a different dish each day—roast beef, fried chicken, or pork chops. Breakfast typically includes eggs, sausages, bacon, pancakes, and all the orange juice and coffee you can drink. Adjacent to the dining room is a small museum featuring memorabilia from the lumbering era.

ARCATA

From Eureka it's only 7 miles to Arcata, one of our favorite towns on the Northern Coast. Sort of a cross between Mayberry and Berkeley, it has an undeniable small-town flavor—right down to the bucolic town square—yet possesses that intellectual and environmentally conscious esprit de corps so characteristic of university towns (Arcata is the home of Humboldt State University).

There are loads of things to do here. On Wednesday, Friday, and Saturday evenings between June and July, Arcata's semipro baseball team, the **Humboldt Crabs,** partake in America's favorite pastime at Arcata Ballpark at 9th and F streets. Also worth a stop: the **Humboldt State University Natural History Museum, at** 1315 G St. (☎ 707/826-4479), which is open Tuesday to Saturday; **Tin Can Mailman,** at 10th and H streets (☎ 707/822-1307), a wonderful used bookstore with more than 130,000 titles; **Redwood Park** (east end of 11th St.), which has an outstanding playground for kids and miles of forested hiking trails; and the **Humboldt Brewing Company,** 10th and I streets (☎ 707/826-BREW), creators of the heavenly Red Nectar Ale (call for tour information).

The **Arcata Marsh and Wildlife Sanctuary,** at the foot of South I St. (☎ 707/ 826-2359), is another worthwhile excursion. The 154-acre sanctuary—which doubles as Arcata's integrated wetland wastewater treatment plant—is a popular stopover for march wrens, egrets, and other waterfowl, including the rare Arctic loon. Each Saturday at 8:30am (rain or shine) the Audubon Society gives free 1-hour guided tours at the cul-de-sac at the foot of South I Street.

Heading east from Arcata, Route 299 leads to the **Trinity River** in the heart of Six Rivers National Forest. Willow Creek and Somes Bar are the prime recreational centers for the area. Here visitors can sign up for canoeing, rafting, and kayaking trips with such outfitters as **Aurora River Adventures,** in Willow Creek (☎ **800/ 562-8475** or 916/629-3843), which offers some offbeat, educationally oriented adventures that are great for kids, as well as gnarly Class V trips for the more daring. Other outfitters include **Laughing Heart Adventures/Trinity Outdoor Center,** Willow Creek (☎ **916/629-3516**); **Big Foot Rafting Company,** Willow Creek (☎ **800/722-2223** or 916/629-2263); and **Klamath River Outfitters,** 3 Sandy Bar Rd., Somes Bar (☎ **916/469-3349**).

A few miles north of Willow Creek lies the Hoopa Indian Reservation. In the Hoopa Shopping Center, the **Hoopa Tribal Museum** (☎ **916/625-4110**) archives the culture and history of the native people of Northern California—their ceremonial regalia, basketry, canoes, and tools. Hours are Monday to Friday from 8am to 5pm.

WHERE TO STAY

Hotel Arcata. 708 9th St., Arcata, CA 95521. ☎ **800/344-1221** or 707/826-0217. Fax 707/ 826-1737. 32 rms. TV TEL. $60–$110 double. Rates include continental breakfast. AE, CB, DC, DISC, MC, V.

This is the town's most prominent hotel, and many guests are parents visiting their ungrateful offspring at Humboldt State University. Located at the northeast corner of the town plaza, its handsome turn-of-the-century brick facade belies a rather bland, modern interior; few of its original furnishings remain. The bedrooms have a rather characterless decor, but they're safe and comfortable lodgings nonetheless. On the premises, under different management, is a Japanese restaurant, Tomo.

✪ **The Lady Anne.** 902 14th St., Arcata, CA 95521. ☎ **707/822-2797.** 5 rms. $90–$110 double. Rates include breakfast. MC, V.

Easily Arcata's finest lodging, this Queen Anne–style bed-and-breakfast is kept in top-notch condition by innkeepers Sharon Ferrett and Sam Pennisi, who also served a term as Arcata's mayor. The large, cozy guest rooms are individually decorated with period antiques, lace curtains, Oriental rugs, and English stained glass. For second honeymooners there's the Lady Sarah Angela Room with its four-poster bed and pleasant bay view. The Cinnamon Bear Room sleeps up to four on its king-size trundle beds, which makes it an obvious choice for parents with kids in tow. Breakfast is served in the grand dining room, warmed on winter mornings by a toasty fire. On summer afternoons, you can lounge on the veranda with a book or play a game of croquet on the front lawn. Several good dining options are only a few blocks away at Arcata Plaza.

WHERE TO DINE

The best way to review your dining options in Arcata is to stroll to the downtown area's most distinctive minimall, the Jacoby Storehouse (a deftly converted mid-19th-century warehouse), and peer into both Abruzzi and Plaza Grill.

Abruzzi. Jacoby Storehouse (at the corner of 8th and H sts.). ☎ **707/826-2345.** Reservations recommended. Main courses $8–$18. AE, DISC, MC, V. Mon–Fri 11:30am–1:30pm; Sun–Thurs 5–8:30pm, Fri–Sat 5–9pm. ITALIAN.

Abruzzi, on the street level, is the more formal and substantial of the two, and is generally acknowledged as the best restaurant in town. Menu items include chicken Frascati (with artichoke hearts, mushrooms, and Marsala), pastas, veal dishes, and well-seasoned fillet steaks.

Plaza Grill. Jacoby Storehouse (at the corner of 8th and H sts.). ☎ **707/826-0860.** Appetizers and dinners $5–$15. AE, DISC, MC, V. Sun–Thurs 5–10pm, Fri–Sat 5–11pm. AMERICAN.

The Plaza Grill is on the third floor. Despite efforts to make it more upscale, it can't seem to shake its image as a college student burger joint. The menu, however, is more substantial than you'd think, with a choice of salads, sandwiches, fish platters, and burgers.

TRINIDAD & PATRICK'S POINT STATE PARK

Back on U.S. 101 north of Arcata, you'll come to Trinidad, a tiny coastal fishing village of some 400 people. One of the smallest incorporated cities in California, it occupies a peninsula 25 miles north of Eureka. If you're not into fishing, there's little to do in town expect poke around at the handful of shops, walk along the busy pier, and wish you owned a house here.

Five miles north of Trinidad takes you to the 640-acre **Patrick's Point State Park,** 4150 Patrick's Point Dr. (☎ **707/677-3570**), which has one of the finest ocean access points in the north at sandy **Agate Beach.** It's suitable for driftwood picking, rock hounding, and camping on a sheltered bluff. The park contains a re-creation of a Sumeg Village, which is actively used by the Yurok people and neighboring tribes. A self-guided tour takes you to replicas of family homes and sweat houses.

WHERE TO STAY

✪ **The Lost Whale Inn.** 3452 Patrick's Point Dr., Trinidad, CA 95570. ☎ **800/677-7859** or 707/677-3425. Fax 707/677-0284. 8 rms. Summer, $125–$155 double; winter, $100–$130 double. Rates include country breakfast. AE, DISC, MC, V.

This modern version of a blue-and-gray Cape Cod–style house is set on 4 acres of seafront land studded with firs, alders, spruces, and redwoods. Its owners cater to children (there's a playground on the premises and mini-zoo up the street) and adults (there's also a Jacuzzi with a view of the sea), and claim (arguably) that it's the only hotel in the state of California with its own private beach. Afternoon tea and an artfully prepared and presented breakfast are included in the rates.

The decor is eclectic, with lots of statuary and paintings, and an outdoor deck facing the surf. Part of the grounds is devoted to a kitchen garden with fresh herbs and vegetables. Rooms are comfortable and don't have phones or TVs, so you can escape from the rest of the world. Families should inquire about the furnished homes—including a wonderful farmhouse—that the innkeepers also rent out. New additions include a rebuilt beach trail with stairs and handrails, and a six-person outdoor spa overlooking the ocean.

Trinidad Bay Bed & Breakfast. 560 Edwards St. (P.O. Box 849), Trinidad, CA 95570. ☎ **707/677-0840.** 2 rms, 2 suites. $125 double; $155 suite. Rates include breakfast. MC, V. Closed Dec–Jan.

Set 175 feet above the ocean, all rooms at this picturesque Cape Cod–style home have sweeping views of Trinidad Bay. On a clear day, you can see up to 65 miles of the rugged coastline. Your hosts are Paul and Carol Kirk, two seasoned innkeepers who have created what many visitors think is the most charming inn around. Rare for an older B&B, both the rooms and suites have private bathrooms. Decor throughout is an eclectic mix of New England–style antiques and more recent reproductions. If it's available, opt for the Mauve Fireplace Suite, with its wraparound window, large wood-burning fireplace, king-size bed, and private entrance.

WHERE TO DINE

✪ **Larrupin Café.** 1658 Patrick's Point Dr. ☎ **707/677-0230.** Reservations recommended. Main courses $10–$20. No credit cards. Summer, Wed–Mon 5–9pm; winter, Thurs–Sun 5–9pm. AMERICAN.

On a quiet country road 2 miles north of Trinidad, this highly praised and wondrously decorated restaurant sports an eclectic blend of Indonesian and African artifacts mingled with paintings by Northern California artists and massive bouquets of flowers. Many items are barbecued over mesquite fires, such as fish (halibut and ahi tuna, among others) that's been basted with lemon-butter and is served with mustard-flavored dill sauce. Other items include barbecued Cornish game hen served with an orange-and-brandy glaze. For appetizers, the barbecued oysters are perfectly delightful, especially in winter, when a fireplace casts a welcome warmth.

The Seascape Restaurant. Beside the Pier at the foot of Bay Street. ☎ **707/677-3762.** Reservations accepted. Full dinners $9–$20. MC, V. Daily 7am–8:30pm. CALIFORNIA.

Established in the 1940s, this is an unpretentious cross between a cafe and a diner, with three dining rooms, overworked but cheerful waitresses, and a nostalgic aura. Folks pop in for coffee or snacks from early morning till after sundown, but by far the biggest seller here is the Trinidad bay platter ($17.95). Heaped with halibut, scallops, shrimp, and accompanied by salad and rice pilaf, it's even more popular than the prawn brochette, which draws a close second.

ORICK

From Trinidad it's about another 15 miles to Orick. You can't miss it: Just look for the dozens of burl stands alongside the road. Carved with chisels and chain saws, these former redwood logs have been transformed into just about every creature you can imagine—perhaps a gift for your mother-in-law?

At the south end of Orick is the town's only saving grace, the sleek **Redwood National Park Information Center** (☎ 707/464-6101). If you plan to spend any amount of time exploring the park, stop here first and pick up a free map; the displays of fauna and wildlife aren't too bad, either. It's open daily from 8am to 5pm.

The first of the parks that make up Redwood National Park, **Prairie Creek,** is 6 miles north of Orick. About 14 miles farther on is the mouth of the **Klamath River,** famous for its salmon, trout, and steelhead. Tours aboard a jet boat take visitors upriver from the estuary to view bear, deer, elk, osprey hawks, otters, and more along the river banks. It's about $20 for a 30-mile trip. For information, contact **Klamath River Jet Boat Tours,** Klamath (☎ 800/887-JETS or 707/482-7775).

A more serene alternative to exloring the Klamath is to take a ranger-led **kayak tour.** Offered only during the summer months, the $1/2$-day trip costs only $20 and includes all the requisite kayak gear. For more information, call the **Redwood National Park Information Center** at ☎ 707/464-6101.

From Klamath it's another 20 miles to Crescent City, gateway to the other parks that make up Redwood National Park.

7 Crescent City, Gateway to Redwood National Park

Crescent City itself has little to offer, but it makes a good base for exploring Redwood National Park and the Smith River, one of the great recreational rivers of the

West. **The Battery Point Lighthouse,** at the foot of A Street (☎ 707/464-3089), which is accessible on foot only at low tide, houses a museum with exhibits on the coast's history. Tours of the lighthouse ($2 for adults, 50¢ for children) are offered Wednesday through Sunday from 10am to 4pm, tides and weather permitting, April through September.

Another draw is the **Smith River National Recreation Area,** east of Jedediah Smith State Park and part of Six Rivers National Forest. The Area Headquarters is at 10600 Calif. 199, Gasquet, CA 95543 (☎ 707/457-3131), which is reached via Route 199 from Crescent City (19 miles, about a 30-minute drive). Maps of the forest can be obtained here, at the Supervisor's Office in Eureka or at the Redwood National Park centers in Orick and Crescent City.

The 300,000-plus acres of wilderness offer camping at 5 modest-sized campgrounds (all with fewer than 50 sites), along the Smith River. Sixteen trails attract hikers from across the country. The easiest short trail is the **McClendon Ford,** which is 2 miles long and drops from 1,000 to 800 feet in elevation to the south fork of the river. Other activities include mountain biking, white-water rafting, kayaking, and fishing for salmon and trout.

For information, contact the **Crescent City–Del Norte County Chamber of Commerce,** 1001 Front St., Crescent City, CA 95531 (☎ 800/343-8300 or 707/464-3174).

WHERE TO STAY

Crescent Beach Motel. 1455 Redwood Hwy. S. (U.S. 101), Crescent City, CA 95531. ☎ 707/464-5436. 27 rms. TV. Summer, $64–$68 double; winter, $49–$52 double. AE, DISC, MC, V.

Crescent City has the dubious distinction of being the only city along the coast without a fancy hotel or bed-and-breakfast. There is, however, an armada of cheap motels, the best of which is the Crescent Beach Motel. Near the highway, about 1 mile south of town, this single-story structure is the only local motel set directly on the beach. The newly remodeled and refurbished rooms are clean and simple. Four of the units face the highway; try to get one of the others, all of which have sliding-glass doors to decks and a small lawn area overlooking the bay. There's no restaurant or bar on the premises, but one of the city's most popular restaurants, the Beachcomber (☎ 707/464-2205), is located next door.

Curly Redwood Lodge. 701 Redwood Hwy. S. (U.S. 101), Crescent City, CA 95531. ☎ 707/464-2137. 36 rms. TV TEL. Summer, $60–$65 double; winter, $37–$39 double. AE, CB, DC, MC, V.

This is a blast from the past, the kind of place where you might have stayed as a kid during one of those cross-country vacations in the family station wagon. It was built in 1959 on grasslands across from the town's harbor and completely trimmed with lumber from a single ancient redwood. Although they're not full of the latest high-tech gadgets, the bedrooms are among the largest and best-soundproofed in town, and certainly the most evocative of a bygone, more innocent age. In winter, about a third of the bedrooms (the ones upstairs) are locked and sealed. Overall, the aura is more akin to Oregon than anything you might imagine in California.

WHERE TO DINE

Beachcomber. 1400 U.S. 101. ☎ 707/464-2205. Reservations recommended. Main courses $6–$15. MC, V. Thurs–Tues 5–9pm. SEAFOOD.

The decor is as predictably nautical as the name implies: rough-cut planking, a scattering of artfully arranged driftwood, fishnets, and buoys dangling above a dimly lit space. The restaurant lies beside the beach, 2 miles south of Crescent City's center. The cuisine is a joy to fish lovers who prefer not to mask the flavor of their seafood with complicated sauces. Most of the dishes are grilled over madrone-wood barbecue pits, a technique perfected since this place was established in 1975. Pacific salmon, halibut, lincod, Pacific snapper, oysters, and steamer clams are house specialties, dishes that have visitors lining up, especially on Friday and Saturday nights.

Harbor View Grotto Restaurant & Lounge. 150 Starfish Way. ☎ **707/464-3815.** Reservations recommended. Main courses $6–$9 lunch; $8–$35 dinner. MC, V. Daily 11:30am–l0pm. SEAFOOD/STEAKS.

This is the best-established non-chain restaurant in town, specializing in fresh seafood at market prices since 1961. Completely renovated in December '95, it has pleasant views of the ocean and harbor from both the dining room and lounge. It's capped with a miniature lighthouse inspired by Crescent City's Battery Point Lighthouse. The "light eaters" menu includes a cup of white chowder (made fresh daily), salad, a main course, and vegetables; heartier appetites can choose among three different cuts of prime rib. Menu items include fresh, locally caught fish like Pacific snapper or salmon. Crab or shrimp Louis, as well as crabmeat or shrimp sandwiches, are popular.

8 Redwood National & State Parks

by Andrew Rice

When he was governor of California, Ronald Reagan once said that if you've seen one redwood, you've seen them all. He couldn't have been more wrong. Redwood National and State Parks are living proof. While he was right that one 367-foot-tall coast redwood (the world's tallest, located in the Tall Trees Grove) does in fact look pretty much like the next, Reagan was guilty of not seeing the forest for the trees.

It's impossible to explain the feeling you get in the old-growth forests of Redwood National and State Parks without resorting to Alice-in-Wonderland comparisons. Like a tropical rain forest, the redwood forest is a multistoried affair, the tall trees being only the top layer. Everything is big, misty, primeval—flowering bushes cover the ground, 10-foot-tall ferns line the creeks, and the smells are rich and musty. It's so *Jurassic Park* that you can't help but half expect to turn the corner and see a dinosaur.

When Archibald Menzies first noted the botanical existence of the coast redwood in 1794, more than 2 million acres of redwood forest carpeted the north coast. By 1965 heavy logging had reduced that to 300,000 acres, and it was obvious something had to be done if any redwoods were to survive. The state created several parks around individual groves in the 1920s, and in 1968 the federal government created Redwood National Park.

The 110,000-acre park offers a lesson in bioregionalism. When the park was first created to protect the biggest coast redwoods, the federal government allowed loggers to clear much of the surrounding area. Redwoods in the park began to suffer as the quality of the Redwood Creek drainage declined from upstream logging. In 1978 the government purchased the entire watershed, having learned that you can't preserve individual trees without preserving the ecosystem they depend on. In April 1994, the National Park Service and California Department of Parks and Recreation signed an agreement to manage the four Redwood parks cooperatively.

Redwood National & State Parks

Crescent Beach
Education Center **5**

Hiouchi Information
Education Center **1**

Humboldt Lagoons
Education Center **9**

Lady Bird Johnson
Grove **7**

Prairie Creek Visitor
Center **6**

Redwood Information
Center **8**

Redwood National
and State Parks
Headquarters and
Information Center **4**

Simpson-Reed
Grove **2**

Stout Grove **3**

Tall Trees Grove **10**

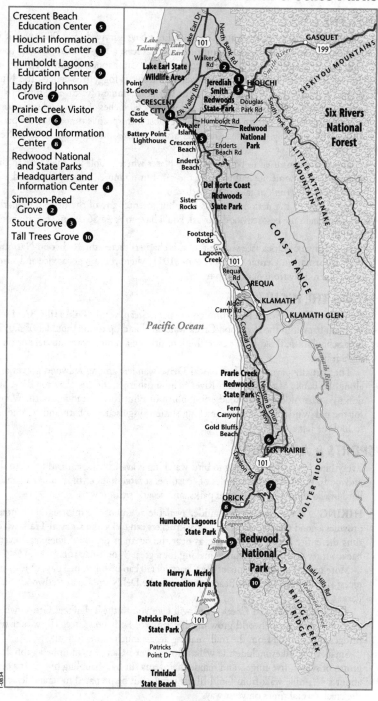

JUST THE FACTS

Frankly, all those huge trees and ferns wouldn't have survived for 1,000 years if it didn't rain one heck of a lot. Count on rain or at least a heavy drizzle during your visit, then get ecstatic when the sun comes out. It can happen anytime. Spring, of course, is the best season for wildflowers. Summer is foggy (it's called "the June gloom" but often includes July). Fall is the warmest, sunniest (relatively!) time of all, and winter isn't bad, though it is cold and wet (try 60 inches of rain), and some park facilities are closed. A storm can provide the most introspective time to see the park, since you'll probably be alone. And after a storm passes through, sunny days often follow.

The north coast used to be one of those places where people left their keys in the ignition in case someone had to move the car. But no more. Lock your car and put valuables in the trunk or take them with you.

Admission to the national park is free, but to enter any of the three state parks (which contain the best redwood groves), you'll have to pay a $6 day-use fee. It's good at all three.

In the town of Orick (see section 6 of this chapter) there's the **Redwood National Park Information Center** (☎ **707/464-6101**), where you can get advice and a free map. Open daily from 8am to 5pm.

SEEING THE HIGHLIGHTS

A number of scenic drives cut through the park. Steep, windy **Bald Hills Road** will take you back into the Redwood Creek watershed and up to the shoulder of 3,097-foot Schoolhouse Peak. Don't even think of driving a motor home up here or pulling a trailer.

The partially paved, 8-mile **Coastal Drive** wanders among redwood groves and along the banks of the Klamath River. The southern section is okay for RVs, but don't go past Alder Camp Road going north or Flint Ridge heading south. Watch for the old World War II radar tracking station disguised as a barn and farmhouse to fool the Japanese.

SPORTS & ACTIVITIES

Everything from river kayaking to bird-watching is available here. In addition to the redwoods, the park includes miles of coastline, several miles of rivers and streams, a herd of elk, three California state parks, and several small towns.

HIKING   The park map and guide, available at any of the information centers, provides a good map of hiking trails. Backpackers can tackle the **Coastal Trail,** which runs the entire length of the park, as near the ocean as possible. There are several backcountry camps on the route, making for a great 3- or 4-day trip.

More manageable segments of the Coastal Trail can be hiked in a day. One of the nicest runs is from Crescent Beach south into the Del Norte Coast Redwoods State Park.

The 8-mile **Redwood Creek Trail** will take you to the Tall Trees Grove, where the tallest trees in the world grow on the banks of Redwood Creek. In winter two bridges are removed from the trail, making access much more difficult.

Smaller day hikes include the walk through **Fern Canyon,** an unbelievably lush grotto of sword, five-finger, and maidenhair ferns cut by a babbling brook. It's only about a 1¹/₂-mile walk from Gold Bluffs beach, but be prepared to scramble across the creek several times on your way.

Ladybird Johnson Grove Loop is a short stroll through one of the park's lushest groves of redwoods.

Pets are prohibited on all of the park's trails.

WILDLIFE VIEWING   One of the most striking aspects of the park is its herd of Roosevelt elk, usually found in the appropriately named Elk Prairie in the southern end of the park. These gigantic deer can weigh 1,000 pounds, and the bulls carry huge antlers from spring to fall. Elk are also sometimes found at Gold Bluffs Beach—it's an incredible rush to suddenly come upon them out of the fog or after a turn in the trail. Nearly a hundred black bears also call the park home but are seldom seen. Unlike those at Yosemite and Yellowstone, these bears are still afraid of people. Keep them that way by observing food storage etiquette while camping and by disposing of garbage properly.

BEACHES & WHALE WATCHING   The park's beaches vary from long white sand strands to cobblestone pocket coves. The water temperature is in the high 40s to low 50s year-round, and it's often rough out there, so swimmers and surfers should be prepared for adverse conditions.

Crescent Beach is a long sandy beach just 2 miles south of Crescent City that's popular with beachcombers, surf fishermen, and surfers.

Just south of Crescent Beach is **Endert's Beach,** a protected spot with a hike-in campground and tide pools at the southern end of the beach.

High coastal overlooks (like Klamath overlook and Crescent Beach overlook) make great whale-watching outposts during the December and January southern migration and the March/April return migration. The northern sea cliffs also provide valuable nesting sites for marine birds like auklets, puffins, murres, and cormorants. Birders will also thrill at the park's freshwater lagoons. These coastal lagoons are some of the most pristine shorebird and waterfowl habitat left and are chock-full of hundreds of different species.

FISHING   The area streams are some of the best steelhead trout and salmon breeding habitat in California. Park beaches are good for surf casting, but be prepared for heavy wave action. A California fishing license is required, and you should check with rangers about any special closures before wetting a line.

RANGER PROGRAMS   The park service runs interpretive programs at the Hiouchi, Crescent Beach, and Redwood information centers during summer months, year-round at the park headquarters in Crescent City. State rangers lead campfire programs and numerous other activities throughout the year. Call the Parks Information service for both the national and state parks (☎ **707/464-6101**) to get current schedules and events.

CAMPING & ACCOMMODATIONS

Five small campgrounds are located in the national park proper. Four are walk-in camps and are free, but to use them you must get a permit from the visitor center in advance. The fifth, a car-camping strip along the freeway at Freshwater Lagoon, requests an $8 donation.

Most car campsites are in the **Prairie Creek and Jedediah Smith State Parks,** which lie entirely inside the national park. Sites there are $14 per night and can be reserved by calling the state's infuriating Destinet reservation system (☎ **800/444-7275**), which requires an additional $6.75 reservation fee. Be prepared to deal with a truly annoying computer before you call and know exactly what campground and, if possible, which site you would like. (The state park service has promised improvements in this system, but we'll see.)

An interesting option is the **boat-in campground** at Stone Lagoon in Humboldt Lagoons state park. Reachable only by canoe, kayak, or rowboat, it is on the bank of the lagoon and a short walk to the ocean beach.

Farther from the park attractions but also farther from the crowds are four **National Forest Campgrounds** in the mountains above the park. Sites are $8 to $12 per night and can be reserved by calling ☎ 800/280-2267—where an actual person can help you make decisions.

The **Redwood AYH Hostel** is the only lodging actually within the park. This very inexpensive turn-of-the-century inn has kitchen facilities, 3 showers, and 30 beds in shared rooms. The staff leads nature walks and is well versed in local history. It's located at 14480 U.S. 101, near Klamath (☎ 707/482-8265).

A number of bed-and-breakfasts and funky roadside motels are available in the surrounding communities of Crescent City, Orick, and Klamath. The **Crescent City/ Del Norte Chamber of Commerce** (☎ 800/343-8300) can steer you toward a proper match (and see the preceding two sections of this chapter for our favorite recommendations).

The Far North: The Shasta Cascades & Lake Tahoe

by Erika Lenkert and Matthew R. Poole

Dominated by snowcapped Mt. Shasta—visible for 100 miles around—California's northern mountains are largely remote and uncrowded. This vast region, often called "The Far North," stretches from the valleys east of the coastal range all the way west to the gambling casinos at the border of Nevada. It begins at the olive orchards north of Sacramento and reaches northward to the Oregon border. An outdoor playground for Californians, the area is so vast that the state of Ohio would fit comfortably within its borders.

This beautiful region offers myriad opportunities for hiking, climbing, skiing, white-water rafting, and cycling. The Far North is also filled with attractions, both man-made and natural, ranging from the Shasta Dam to Lava Beds National Monument, with dozens of caves to explore. Lassen Volcanic National Park will give you a look at three sides of a volcano, and there's even a ski area here.

One of the most celebrated natural attractions in the Golden State is Lake Tahoe. At 6,225 feet above sea level in the Sierra Nevada mountains, the lake straddles the border between Nevada and California, with gambling on the Nevada side. Although Lake Tahoe has been marred by overdevelopment, especially along the southern and eastern shores, the western coastline still provides quiet havens for hiking and biking, and the surrounding mountains offer some of the best skiing in the United States (with 15 downhill skiing resorts and 11 cross-country centers).

1 Lava Beds National Monument

by Andrew Rice

Lava Beds takes a while to grow on you. It's a windy, seemingly desolate place with high plateaus, cinder cones, and rolling hills covered with lava cinders, sagebrush, and tortured-looking junipers. Mile upon mile of this landscape covers most of this corner of California. So why, asks the first-time visitor, is this a national monument? The answer lies underground.

The earth here is like Swiss cheese, so porous in places that it actually makes a hollow sound. When lava pours from a shield volcano it doesn't cool all at once; the outer edges cool first and the core keeps flowing, forming underground tunnels like a giant pipeline system.

More than 330 lava-tube caves lace the earth at Lava Beds. These caves are open to the public to explore alone or with park rangers. And while most caves lend themselves to a fear of getting lost with their huge chambers, multiple entrances, and bizarre topography, these are simple, relatively easy-to-follow tunnels with little room to go wrong. Inside it feels like a great place for a game of hide and seek.

In the winter of 1872–73, a band of 155 Modoc Indians held off a siege by more than 500 well-armed U.S. cavalrymen using the lava flows as hideouts in a deadly game of cat and mouse. By May, weakened by starvation and exhausted, almost all the Modocs had been captured or killed. On June 1, 1873, their leader, "Captain Jack," surrendered with the last of his tribe. He and three other Modoc leaders were hanged. The surviving members of his band were banished to a reservation in Oklahoma.

JUST THE FACTS

Park elevations range from 4,000 to 5,700 feet, and this part of California can get cold at any time of year. Summer is the best time to visit, with average temperatures in the 70°s F; winter temperatures plunge down to about 40°F in the day and as low as 20°F by night. Summer is also the best time to participate in ranger-led hikes, cave trips, and campfire programs. Check at the visitor center for schedules.

SEEING THE HIGHLIGHTS

Other than a white cross, there's very little of historical note remaining above ground here. The cross marks the spot where General E. R. S. Canby, was killed during "peace" meetings with the Modocs, an act that led to the final bloodbath. He was charged with returning the Modocs to a reservation in Oregon where they were to be housed with a rival tribe.

A hike to **Schonchin Butte** (3/4 mile, one-way) will give you a good perspective on the wildly stark beauty of the monument and nearby Tule Lake Valley. Wildlife lovers should keep their eyes peeled for terrestrial animals like mule deer, coyotes, marmots, and squirrels, while watching overhead for bald eagles, 24 species of hawks, as well as enormous flocks of ducks and geese headed to the Klamath Basin, one of the largest waterfowl wintering grounds in the Lower 48. Sometimes ducks and geese darken the sky during the peak migrations.

CAVES & HIKES

The caves at **Lava Beds** are accessible to the public with very little restriction or hassle. All you need to see most of them is a good flashlight or head lamp, sturdy walking shoes, and a sense of adventure. Many of the caves are entered by ladders or stairs, others by holes in the side of a hill. Once inside, walk far enough to round a corner then shut off your light—a chilling experience, to say the least.

One-way **Cave Loop Road,** just southwest of the visitor center, is where you'll find many of the best cave hikes. About 15 lava tubes have been marked and made accessible. Two are ice caves, where the air temperature remains below freezing all year and ice crystals form on the walls. If exploring on your own gives you the creeps, check out **Mushpot Cave.** Almost adjacent to the visitor center, this cave has been outfitted with lights and a smooth walkway; you'll have plenty of company.

Hardened spelunkers will find enough remote and relatively unexplored caves in the monument, many requiring specialized climbing gear, to keep themselves busy.

Above ground, several trails crisscross the monument. The longest of these, the 8.2-mile (one-way) **Lyons Trail** spans the wildest part of the monument, where you are likely to see plenty of animals. The **Whitney Butte Trail,** 3.4 miles (one-way), leads from Merill Cave along the shoulder of 5,000-foot Whitney Butte to the edge of the Callahan Lava Flow and monument boundary.

PICNICKING, CAMPING & ACCOMMODATIONS

The 40-unit **Indian Well Campground** near the visitor center has spaces for tents and small RVs year-round, with water available only during the summer. The rest of the year you'll have to carry water from the nearby visitor center.

Two **picnic grounds,** Fleener Chimneys and Captain Jacks Stronghold, have tables but no water; open fires are prohibited.

There are no hotels or lodges in the monument, but services are available in nearby Tulelake and Klamath Falls. For more information, contact **Lava Beds National Monument,** P.O. Box 867, Tulelake, CA 96134 (☎ **530/667-2282**).

2 Mt. Shasta & the Cascades

In this section, we'll take I-5 north through the Sacramento Valley and up into the Cascades. Chances are, your first glimpse of Mt. Shasta's majestic, snowcapped peak will be a memorable one. A dormant volcano with a 17-mile-diameter base, it stands in virtual isolation and can be seen from more than 100 miles away. When John Muir first saw Shasta from 50 miles away in 1874, he wrote: "I was alone and weary. Yet my blood turned to wine, and I have not been weary since." He went on to describe it as "the pole star of the landscape," which indeed it is.

ESSENTIALS

GETTING THERE   From San Francisco, take I-80 to I-505 to I-5 to Red-ding. From the coast, pick up Calif. 299 east a few miles north of Arcata to Redding.

Redding Municipal Airport, 6751 Woodrum Circle (☎ 530/224-4320), is serviced by United Express and Horizon Air. Amtrak stops in Dunsmuir and Redding.

VISITOR INFORMATION   Regional information can be obtained from the following: **Shasta Cascade Wonderland Association,** 14250 Holiday Rd., Redding, CA 96003 (☎ 800/474-2782 or 530/275-5555); **Mt. Shasta Visitors Bureau,** 300 Pine St., Mt. Shasta, CA 96067 (☎ 800/926-4865 or 530/926-4865); **Redding Convention and Visitors Bureau,** 777 Auditorium Dr., Redding, CA 96001 (☎ 800/874-7562 or 530/225-4100); **Trinity County Chamber of Commerce,** 210 Main St., P.O. Box 517, Weaverville, CA 96093 (☎ 800/487-4648 or 530/623-6101).

WILLIAM B. IDE ADOBE STATE HISTORIC PARK

En route to Mt. Shasta from the south, you may want to stop near Red Bluff at **William B. Ide Adobe State Historic Park,** 21659 Adobe Rd. (☎ 530/529-8599), for a picnic along the Sacramento River. The 4-acre park commemorates William B. Ide, the Republic of California's first and only president, proclaimed on June 14, 1846, by those who led the Bear Flag Rebellion against the Mexicans who were excluding the Americans from California. The republic lasted only three weeks before the American victory in the Mexican–American War made California a state in the Union. The adobe home dates from 1852. Some historians claim it was not Mr. Ide's home, but it does give visitors an idea of frontier life. In the summer the park is open from 8am to sunset, and the house is open noon to 4pm; call ahead in winter. Parking is $3 per vehicle.

REDDING & SHASTA

The major town and gateway to the panoramic Shasta–Cascade region is Redding, lying at the top of the Sacramento Valley. From here you can either turn westward into the wilderness-forest of Trinity and the Klamath Mountains, or north and east into the Cascades and Shasta Trinity National Forest.

In Redding, with its fast-food joints, gas stations, and cheap motels, summer heat generally hovers at 100°F or above all summer. A city of some 60,000, Redding is the transportation hub of Northern California. The city itself has little of interest; mainly it is used as a base for exploring the natural wonders nearby.

Information is available from the **Redding Convention and Visitors Bureau,** 777 Auditorium Dr., Redding, CA 96001 (☎ **800/874-7562** or 530/225-4100), west of I-5 on Calif. 299. It is open Monday to Friday from 8am to 5pm and on Saturday and Sunday from 9am to 5pm.

Horse lovers will want to know about the **Wild Horse Sanctuary,** which can be reached via either Hwy. 36 from Red Bluff or Calif. 44 from Redding. The sanctuary was established by Jim Clapp, who saved 80 horses that were scheduled to be destroyed. The sanctuary is only 23 miles from Mt. Lassen, and visitors can view the horses and also take 2- and 3-day pack trips through the ruggedly beautiful foothills of Mt. Lassen. Two-day trips cost $235 per person. For information, call ☎ **530/ 474-5770**.

Ahead and northeast, Mt. Shasta rises to a height of more than 14,000 feet. From Redding, I-5 cuts north over the Pit River Bridge, crossing Lake Shasta and leading eventually to the mount itself. Before striking north, however, you may want to explore Lake Shasta and see **Shasta Dam.** Another option is to take a detour west of Redding to Weaverville, Whiskeytown–Shasta Trinity National Recreation Area, and **Lake Trinity** (see below).

About 3 miles west, stop at the old mining town of **Shasta,** which has been converted into a State Historic Park (☎ **530/243-8194**). Shasta was founded on gold and was the "Queen City" of the northern mines in the Klamath range. Its life was short, and it expired in 1872 when the Central Pacific Railroad bypassed it in favor of Redding. Today the business district is a ghost town, complete with a restored general store and a Masonic hall. The 1861 courthouse has been converted into a museum where you can view the jail and a gallows out back, as well as a remarkable collection of Californian art assembled by Mae Helen Bacon Boggs. The collection includes works by Maynard Dixon, Grace Hudson, and many others. Open Wednesday to Sunday from 10am to 5pm. Admission is $2 adults, $1 children 6 to 12, and free for children 5 and under.

Continue along Calif. 299 west to Calif. 3 north, which will take you to Weaverville and then to the west side of the lake and Trinity Center.

WHERE TO STAY

In addition to the choices below, Redding has a **Red Lion Motor Inn** (☎ **530/ 221-8700**) and a **La Quinta Inn** (☎ **800/531-5900** or 530/221-8200). Both are fine choices.

Tiffany House Bed and Breakfast Inn. 1510 Barbara Rd., Redding, CA 96003. ☎ **530/ 244-3225.** 3 rms, 1 cottage. $75–$95 double; $125 cottage. Rates include breakfast. AE, DISC, MC, V.

Despite the fact that this two-story gray-and-white house wasn't built until 1939, everyone in town refers to it as a Victorian. A sweeping view of the Lassen Mountain Range is visible from every guest room and cottage, as well as from the oversize deck, which seems to float above a garden in back. There's also a Music Room with piano, Victorian Parlor with fireplace, games, and puzzles, and even a swimming pool. Each guest room is furnished with a queen-size bed and antique furnishings, and all have private baths equipped with soft robes. Top choice is the

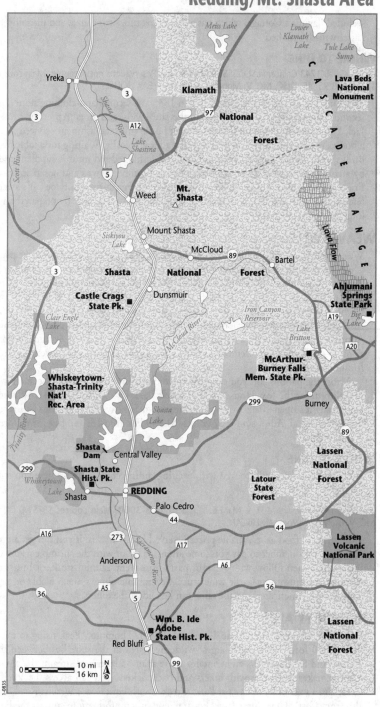

Redding/Mt. Shasta Area

Yreka

Klamath

National

Forest

Lava Beds National Monument

Meiss Lake

Lower Klamath Lake

Tule Lake Sump

CASCADE RANGE

Shasta River

Lake Shastina

Scott River

Weed

Mt. Shasta

Mount Shasta

Siskiyou Lake

Shasta

National

Forest

McCloud

Bartel

Lava Flow

Ahjumani Springs State Park

Big Lake

Dunsmuir

Castle Crags State Pk.

Clair Engle Lake

McCloud River

Iron Canyon Reservoir

Lake Britton

McArthur-Burney Falls Mem. State Pk.

Whiskeytown-Shasta-Trinity Nat'l Rec. Area

Trinity River

Shasta Lake

Burney

Shasta Dam

Central Valley

Shasta State Hist. Pk.

Whiskeytown Lake

Shasta

REDDING

Palo Cedro

Sacramento River

Latour State Forest

Lassen National Forest

Lassen Volcanic National Park

Anderson

Wm. B. Ide Adobe State Hist. Pk.

Red Bluff

Lassen National Forest

0   10 mi
    16 km

N

secluded Lavinia's Cottage, which has a 7-foot spa tub, sitting area, and magnificent laurel-wreath iron bed.

WHERE TO DINE

Jack's Grill. 1743 California St. ☎ **530/241-9705.** Reservations not accepted. Main courses $8.25–$18.95. AE, DISC, MC, V. Mon–Sat 4–11pm. STEAK HOUSE.

This building was originally constructed in 1835 as a secondhand-clothing store. The second floor served as a whorehouse in the late 1930s, and an entrepreneur named Jack Young set up the main floor as a steak house (his establishment serviced all of a body's needs, you might say). Today, it's a local favorite. Waiting for a table over drinks in the bar is part of the fun. Good old-fashioned red meat is supplemented by a couple of seafood dishes such as deep-fried jumbo prawns and ocean scallops. Prices include salad, hot garlic bread, and baked or french-fried potatoes. It's a very fetching spot, with good, honest tavern food and a jovial crowd. Be prepared for a long wait on weekends.

WEAVERVILLE

Weaverville was a gold-mining town in the 1850s, and part of the history of the place is captured at the **Jake Jackson Memorial Museum–Trinity County Historical Park,** 508 Main St. (☎ **530/623-5211**). The collection of memorabilia, from firearms to household items, is interesting for what it tells about the residents of the town—Native Americans, miners, pioneers, and especially the Chinese. In the gold rush era, the town was half Chinese, with a Chinatown of about 2,500 residents. Admission is free, though a $1 donation is suggested. It's open in April daily from noon to 4pm, May 1 to October 31 daily from 10am to 5pm, and November daily from noon to 4pm.

Across the parking lot, you can view the oldest continuously used Taoist temple in California at the **Joss House State Historic Park** (☎ **530/623-5284**). Although technically it's open 10am to 5pm Wednesday to Sunday, hours tend to be irregular, so call ahead. Admission is $2 adults, $1 children 6 to 13, and free for children 5 and under.

WHERE TO DINE

Weaverville isn't exactly packed with exciting dining choices, so up here you take what you can get.

The Pacific Brewery. 401 S. Main St. ☎ **530/623-3000.** Main courses $8–$14. DISC, MC, V. Daily 6am–9pm. AMERICAN.

Honest, good food at reasonable prices is served here—that is, if you can get a preoccupied staff member to pay you some attention. Start with the shrimp cocktail or the nachos, then follow with steak or pasta primavera, salmon steak, or breast of chicken in a mushroom-garlic wine sauce. Several microbrews are available on tap. The decor is Americana, and the same can be said of the diners.

THE TRINITY ALPS

West of Weaverville stretch the Trinity Alps, with Thompson Peak rising to more than 9,000 feet. The second-largest wilderness area in the state lies between the Trinity and Salmon rivers and contains more than 55 lakes and streams. Its alpine scenery makes it popular with hikers and backpackers. You can access the **Pacific Crest Trail** west of Mt. Shasta at Parks Creek, South Fork Road, Whalen Road, and also from Castle Crags State Park. For trail and other information, contact the Forest Service at Weaverville (☎ **530/623-2121**).

The Fifth Season, 300 N. Mt. Shasta Blvd. (☎ **530/926-3606**), offers mountaineering and backpack rentals and will provide trail maps and other information concerning Shasta's outdoor activities.

Living Waters Recreation (☎ **530/926-5446**), offers half-day to 2-day rafting trips on the Upper Sacramento, Klamath, Trinity, and Salmon rivers. **Trinity River Rafting Company** on Calif. 299W in Big Flat (☎ **800/30-RIVER** or 530/623-3033) also operates local white-water trips.

For additional outfitters and information, contact the **Trinity County Chamber of Commerce,** 210 Main St., Weaverville, CA 96093 (☎ **800/487-4648** or 530/623-6101).

WHISKEYTOWN NATIONAL RECREATION AREA

In adjacent Shasta County, Whiskeytown National Recreation Area is on the eastern shore of Trinity Lake, a quiet and relatively uncrowded lake with 157 miles of shoreline. When this reservoir was created, it was officially named Clair Engle, after the politician who created it. But locals insist on calling it Trinity after the name of the river that used to rush through the region past the towns of Minersville, Stringtown, and an earlier Whiskeytown. All of these were destroyed when the river was dammed. They now lie submerged under the lake's glassy surface.

Both Trinity Lake and the Whiskeytown National Recreation Area are in the Shasta Trinity National Forest, 1.3 million acres of wilderness with 1,269 miles of hiking trails. For information on trails, contact **Shasta Trinity National Forest** (☎ **530/246-5222**).

LAKE SHASTA

Heading north on I-5 from Redding, travel about 12 miles and take the Shasta Dam Boulevard exit to the ✪ **Shasta Dam and Power Plant** (☎ **530/275-4463**), which has an overflow spillway that is 3 times higher than Niagara Falls. The huge dam—3,460 feet long, 602 feet high, and 883 feet thick at its base—holds back the waters of the Sacramento, Pit, and McCloud rivers. A dramatic sight indeed, it is a vital component of the Central Valley water project. At the visitor center is a series of photographs and displays covering the dam's construction period. You can either walk or drive over the dam, but far more interesting are the free 1 hour tours given daily 9am to 5pm on the hour in the summer, and at 10am, noon, and 2pm from Labor Day to Memorial Day. The guided tour takes you deep within the dam's many chilly corridors (not a good place for claustrophobes) and below the spillway. It's an entertaining way to beat the summer heat.

Lake Shasta has 370 miles of shoreline and attracts anglers (bass, trout, and king salmon), water-skiers, and other boating enthusiasts—two million, in fact, in summer. The best way to enjoy the lake is aboard a houseboat; they can be rented from several companies: **Antlers Resort & Marina,** P.O. Box 140, Antlers Rd., Lakehead, CA 96051 (☎ **800/238-3924**); **Packers Bay Marina,** 16814 Packers Bay Rd., Lakehead, CA 96051 (☎ **800/331-3137** or 530/275-5570); and **Lakeshore Marina,** 20479 Lakeshore Dr., Lakehead, CA 96051 (☎ **530/238-2303**).

For information and additional houseboat rentals, contact the **Redding Convention and Visitors Bureau,** 777 Auditorium Dr., Redding, CA 96001 (☎ **800/874-7562** or 530/225-4100).

While you're here, you can visit **Lake Shasta Caverns** (☎ **530/238-2341**). These caves contain 20-foot-high stalactite and stalagmite formations—60-foot-wide curtains of them in the great Cathedral Room. To see the caves, drive about 15 miles north of Redding on I-5 to the O'Brien/Shasta Caverns exit. A ferry will take you across the lake and a short bus ride will follow to the cave entrance for a 2-hour-long tour. Admission is $14 for adults, $7 for children. The caverns are open daily year-round, with tours every half hour in summer from 9am to 4pm, and every hour in winter from 9am to 3pm.

Farther north, off I-5 about 50 miles north of Redding, you'll reach **Castle Crags State Park** (☎ **530/235-2684**), a 4,300-acre park with 64 campsites and 28 miles of hiking trails. Here granite crags that were formed 225 million years ago tower more than 6,500 feet above the Sacramento River. The park is filled with dogwood, oak, cedar, and pine as well as tiger lilies, azaleas, and orchids in summer. You can walk the 1-mile Indian Creek nature trail or take the easy 1-mile Root Creek Trail. Entrance fee is $5 per vehicle per day.

Back on I-5 the road curves around past the old railroad town of Dunsmuir and on into Mt. Shasta.

MT. SHASTA

A volcanic mountain with eight glaciers, ✪ **Mt. Shasta** is a towering peak of legend and lore. It stands alone, always snowcapped, unshadowed by other mountains—visible from 125 miles away. Although it's been dormant since 1786, eruptions cannot be ruled out, and indeed, hot sulfur springs bubble at the summit. The springs saved John Muir on his third ascent of the mountain in 1875. Caught in a severe snowstorm, he and his partner took turns submersing themselves in the hot mud to survive.

Many New Agers are convinced that Mt. Shasta is the center of an incredible energy vortex. These devotees flock to the foot of the mountain. In 1987 the foothills were host to the worldwide Harmonic Convergence, calling for a planetary union and a new phase of universal harmony. Yoga, massage, meditation, and metaphysics are all the rage here. These New Agers seem to coexist harmoniously with those whose metaphysical leanings begin and end with Dolly Parton song lyrics.

Those who don't want to climb can drive up to about 8,000 feet. From Mt. Shasta City, drive 14 miles up the Everitt Memorial Highway to the end of the road near Panther Meadow. Along the way you'll be able to stop and see the Sacramento River Canyon, the Eddy Mountains to the west, and glimpses of Mt. Lassen to the south. At the **Everitt Vista Turnout,** you can take the short hike through the forests to a lava outcrop overlooking the McCloud area.

Continue on to **Bunny Flat,** a major access point for climbing in the summer and also for cross-country skiing and sledding in winter. The highway ends at the Old Ski Bowl Vista, providing panoramic views of Mt. Lassen, Castle Crags, and the Trinity Mountains.

While in Mt. Shasta, visit the **Fish Hatchery** at 3 N. Old State Rd. (☎ **530/926-2215**), which was built in 1888. Here you can observe rainbow and brown trout being hatched to stock rivers and streams statewide—millions are born here annually. You can feed them via coin-operated food dispensers, and observe the spawning process on certain Tuesdays during the fall and winter. Admission is free, and it's open daily from 8am to sunset. Adjacent to the hatchery is the **Sisson Museum** (☎ **530/926-5508**), which displays a smattering of local history exhibits. It's open daily 10am to 4pm in summer, daily 1 to 4pm in winter, and admission is free.

SKIING   In winter, visitors can ski at **Mt. Shasta Ski Park,** 104 Siskiyou Ave., Mt. Shasta (☎ **530/926-8600**), which has 25 runs with 80% snowmaking, three triple-seat chairlifts, and a surface lift. A day pass costs less than $30. There's also a Nordic Ski center with 15$\frac{1}{2}$ miles of groomed trails, as well as a Terrain Park that's geared toward snowboarders. In summer you can ride the chairlifts to scenic views, mountain bike down the trails (all-day pass $10), or practice on the two-story climbing wall. Access to the chairlifts is 10 miles east on Mt. Shasta on its southern slopes via Calif. 89 from McCloud. For information, call ☎ **530/926-8600.** The ski lodge's number is ☎ **530/926-8612.**

WATER SPORTS   Although the source of the headwaters of the Sacramento River is found here, water doesn't gush down the mountain, but accumulates at the base. **Lake Siskiyou,** at Shasta's base, is a popular spot for boating, swimming, and fishing, and is a great vantage point for photographs of Mt. Shasta and its reflection. Waterskiing and jetskiing are not allowed, but windsurfing is, and boat rentals are offered at **Lake Siskiyou Camp Resort,** 4239 W. A. Barr Rd., Mt. Shasta (☎ **530/926-2618**).

GOLF & TENNIS   Golfers should head for the 27-hole Robert Trent Jones, Jr., golf course at **Lake Shastina Golf Resort,** 5925 Country Club Dr., Weed (☎ **530/938-3201**), or the 18-hole course at **Mount Shasta Resort,** 1000 Siskiyou Lake Blvd., Mt. Shasta (☎ **530/926-3030**); the resort also has tennis courts.

OTHER WARM-WEATHER ACTIVITIES   Mt. Shasta offers some excellent mountain biking. In the summer ride the chairlifts to the top of **Mt. Shasta Ski Park** and mountain bike down the trails. An all-day chairlift pass is only $10 (☎ **530/926-8610**).

For fishing information, go to **Hart's Guide Service,** 965 Lassen Lane (☎ **530/926-2431**), or contact Mt. Shasta Fly Fishing (☎ 530/926-6648).

For an offbeat trip, contact **Rainbow Ridge Ranch** (☎ **530/926-5794**) and join one of their llama-trekking trips. Trips last from 3 to 5 days and cost from $400.

WHERE TO STAY

Best Western Tree House. I-5 and Lake St. (P.O. Box 236), Mt. Shasta, CA 96067. ☎ **800/545-7164** or 530/926-3101. Fax 530/926-3542. 95 rms. A/C TV TEL. $79–$160 double. AE, CB, DC, MC, V.

Just off the main highway, this motor inn offers rooms with standard Scandinavian-style furnishings. Some accommodations have decks and refrigerators, making them family favorites. Facilities include a rustic dining room and lounge with a stone fireplace. There's also a huge indoor pool that's usually deserted, as well as an exercise room. This is the best place to stay in the town of Mt. Shasta, and it keeps its prices low. Downhill and cross-country ski areas are 10 miles away.

۞ McCloud Guest House. 606 W. Colombero Dr. (P.O. Box 1510), McCloud, CA 96057. ☎ **530/964-3160.** 5 rms. $80–$95 double. Rates include continental breakfast. MC, V.

Off Calif. 89, west of McCloud, and set among the oak and pine trees of Mt. Shasta's lower slopes, this bungalow-style house has a wraparound veranda and dormer windows. Built in 1907 as a residence for the president of the McCloud River Lumber Company, the house was nicely restored in 1984 by innkeepers Bill and Patti Leigh and Dennis and Pat Abreu. Upstairs there's a large comfortable parlor with a pool table for guests. Off the parlor are five individually decorated rooms with white iron beds. Three of the rooms have clawfoot tubs and two have shower only.

On the ground floor there's an atmospheric dining room with leaded- and stained-glass interior decoration. The menu offers a fine selection of Italian chicken, veal, pasta, and seafood dishes.

Mt. Shasta Ranch B&B. 1008 W. A. Barr Rd., Mt. Shasta, CA 96067. ☎ **530/926-3870.** Fax 530/926-6882. 9 rms, 4 with private bath; 1 cottage. TV. $50–$65 double without bath; $85 double with bath; $95 cottage for 2. Rates include breakfast. AE, DISC, MC, V. Take Central Mt. Shasta exit off I-5 to W. A. Barr Rd.

Mt. Shasta Ranch was conceived and built in 1923 by one of the country's most famous horse trainers and racing tycoons, H.D. ("Curley") Brown, as the centerpiece of a private retreat and thoroughbred horse ranch. Despite the encroachment of nearby buildings, the main house and its annex are still available as a cozy B&B with touches of nostalgia, the occasional antique, and spectacular views of Mt. Shasta. Four bedrooms (the ones with private bath) lie in the main house; the remaining five share two bathrooms in the carriage house. It's a 3-minute trek to the shores of nearby Lake Siskiyou (15 minutes to the ski slopes), or you could stay here to enjoy the hot tub, Ping-Pong tables, pool table, darts, and horseshoes.

Railroad Park Resort. 100 Railroad Park Rd., Dunsmuir, CA 96025. ☎ **800/974-RAIL** or 530/235-4440. Fax 530/235-4470. 23 rms, 4 cabins. A/C TV TEL. $60–$85 double. Additional person/pets $7.50. AE, DISC, MC, V. Take Railroad Park Exit off I-5, 1 mile south of Dunsmuir.

Lying a quarter of a mile from the Sacramento River, this is an offbeat place that kids enjoy. It's located at the foot of Castle Crags and contains several facilities—a restaurant and lounge, campground and RV park, rustic cabins, and the Caboose Motel. The railroad cabooses have been converted into rooms, leaving their pipes, ladders, and lofts in place. They're furnished with modern brass beds, table and chairs, dressers, and TV; and they're located around the fenced-in kidney-shaped pool and whirlpool. The restaurant and lounge are also in vintage railroad cars.

Stewart Mineral Springs Resort. 4617 Stewart Springs Rd., Weed, CA 96094. ☎ **530/ 938-2222.** 2 teepees suitable for 1–4 persons; 4 dorm rooms suitable for 1–5; 2 motel rooms suitable for 1–6; 4 cabins with kitchens for 1–2; 1 large A-frame house suitable for 10–15 persons. $15 teepee for 1, $5 for additional persons up to 4; $30 dorm room for 1, $10 for additional persons up to 4; $40 motel room for 2; $45 cabin with kitchen for 2; $300 A-frame house for up to 15. MC, V. Closed Dec 1–Mar 1 or even later depending on snow.

Stewart Mineral Springs is one of the most unusual health spas in California, loaded with lore and legends. It lies above cold-water springs that Native Americans valued for their healing powers. Don't expect anything approaching a European spa or big-city luxury here. Everything is deliberately rustic, with as few intrusions from the urban world as possible (no phones or TVs). Designed in a somewhat haphazard compound of about a dozen buildings, 4 miles west of the town of Weed, it occupies a 37-acre site of sloping, forested land accented with ponds, gazebos, and decorative bridges and riddled with hiking and nature trails, freshwater streams, and a swimming hole. There are no restaurants on-site, and the spa facilities are often beside campers and RVs that hook up to facilities at a nearby campsite.

Activities revolve around hiking, nature-watching, and taking the healing waters of the legendary springs. The bathhouse is the curative headquarters of the resort and contains 13 private rooms where water from the springs is heated and run into tubs for soaking. A staff member will describe the rituals for you: A 20-minute soak is followed with a visit to a nearby sauna and an immersion in the chilly waters of Parks Creek, just outside the bathhouse. Other feel-good options include massages ($30 per half-hour session), herbal body wraps ($65 for a 90-minute experience), and facials ($15). On Saturdays, medicine man Walking Eagle guides guests on a spiritual journey within the Native American Purification Sweat Lodge.

If you opt for treatment and R&R here, you won't be alone. Despite its rusticity, young Hollywood has discovered the place, including many soap actors, San Francisco 49ers football players, and local newscasters.

Wagon Creek Inn. 1239 Woodland Park Dr., Mt. Shasta, CA 96067. ☎ **530/926-0838.** 3 rms (1 with bath). $65 double without bath; $75 double with bath. Rates include continental breakfast. MC, V. From I-5 take the Central Mt. Shasta exit to Old Stage Road. Turn right to Woodland Park Drive.

Loretta Lynn would feel at home in one of these rustic southwest-style rooms within this log cabin home, located about 2¹/₂ miles from Mt. Shasta. The King Room has its own bath; the other two share. Guests can use the living room with fireplace, TV, and VCR. It's a homey, inexpensive place where pets and kids are welcome.

WHERE TO DINE

Lily's. 1013 S. Mt. Shasta Blvd., Mt. Shasta. ☎ **530/926-3372.** Reservations recommended. Main courses $9.50–$16. AE, DISC, MC, V. Mon–Fri 7am–9pm, Sat–Sun 7am–9:30pm. AMERICAN.

Set within a white-clapboard, turn-of-the-century house in a residential neighborhood south of the town center, this friendly little restaurant has a front porch, a picket fence, a back garden, and tables scattered randomly in both front and back. It's popular for breakfast, when chunky breads and omelets ($5 to $6) start the morning off right. Lunch and dinner dishes—polenta, enchiladas, scampi al roma, kung pao shrimp salad—span the globe.

Michael's. 313 N. Mt. Shasta Blvd., Mt. Shasta. ☎ **530/926-5288.** Main courses $13–$17. AE, DISC, MC, V. Tues–Fri 11am–2:30pm and 5–9pm, Sat noon–9pm. ITALIAN/AMERICAN.

Michael and Lynn Kobseff draw a devoted local following to their small but venerable restaurant. The menu offers a variety of worthy Italian dishes along with steaks. Among the pasta dishes, opt for the manicotti or the cannelloni alla romana, with veal, chicken, spinach, and cheese in a marinara sauce. Dinners include soup or salad, garlic bread, and coffee. Friday and Saturday are prime rib nights.

MCARTHUR–BURNEY FALLS MEMORIAL STATE PARK

On its way to Lassen Volcanic National Park (see below) from Mt. Shasta, Calif. 89 east loops back south to ○ **McArthur–Burney Falls Memorial State Park** (☎ **530/335-2777**). One of the spectacular features of this 875-acre park is a waterfall that cascades over a 129-foot cliff. Theodore Roosevelt once called the falls "the eighth wonder of the world." Giant springs lying a few hundred yards upstream feed the falls and keep them flowing, even during California's legendary dry spells.

The half-mile **Headwater Trail** will take you to a good vantage point above the falls. If you're lucky you can observe the black swift that nest in the mossy crevices behind the cascade. Other birds to look for include barn and great horned owls, the belted kingfisher, the common flicker, and even the Oregon junco. The year-round park also has a mile-long nature trail, 128 campsites, picnicking grounds, and good fishing for bass, brown trout, rainbow trout, and brook trout. For **camping reservations,** call ☎ **800/444-7275.**

From here, Lassen Volcanic National park lies about 40 miles south.

3 Lassen Volcanic National Park

by Andrew Rice

Lassen Volcanic National Park is a remarkable reminder that North America is still forming and that the ground below is alive with the forces of creation—and destruction. Lassen Peak is the southernmost peak in a chain of volcanoes (including Mount Saint Helens) that stretches all the way from British Columbia.

Though dormant, Lassen Peak is still very much alive. It last awakened in May 1914, beginning a cycle of eruptions that spit lava, steam, and ash until 1921. The eruption climaxed in 1915 when Lassen blew its top, sending a mushroom cloud of ash 7 miles high that was seen from hundreds of miles away. The peak itself has been dormant for nearly a century now, but the area still boils with a ferocious intensity:

Hot springs, fumaroles, and mud pots are all indicators that Lassen hasn't had its last word. Monitoring of geothermal features in the park shows that they are getting hotter, not cooler, and some scientists take this as a sign that the next big eruption in the Cascades is likely to happen here.

Until then, the park gives visitors an interesting chance to watch a landscape recover from the massive destruction brought on by an eruption. To the northeast of Lassen Peak is the aptly named Devastated Area, a huge swath of volcanic destruction steadily repopulating with conifer forests. After watching this area immediately revegetate with a diverse mix of conifer species, botanists have revised earlier theories that forests must be preceded by herbaceous growth.

The 106,000-acre park is a place of great beauty. The flora and fauna here is an interesting mix of species from the Cascade Range, stretching north from Lassen, and species from the Sierra Nevada, which stretches south. The resulting blend accounts for an enormous diversity of plants; 715 distinct species have been identified in the park. Though snowbound in winter, Lassen is an important summer feeding ground for transient herds of mule deer and numerous black bears.

In addition to the volcano and all its geothermal features, Lassen Volcanic National Park includes miles of hiking trails, huge alpine lakes, large meadows, cinder cones, lush forests, cross-country skiing, and great camping. Only one major road, Calif. 89 (the Park Road), crosses the park in a 39-mile half circle with entrances and visitor centers at either end. Three-quarters of the park is designated wilderness.

JUST THE FACTS

Most visitors enter the park at the Southwest Entrance Station, drive through the park, and leave through the Northwest Entrance, or vice versa. Two other entrances lead to remote portions of the park. Warner Valley is reached from the south on the road from Chester. Butte Lake entrance is reached by a cut-off road from Calif. 44 between Calif. 89 and Susanville.

Ranger stations are clustered near each entrance and provide the full spectrum of interpretive displays, ranger-led walks, informational leaflets, and emergency help. The largest **visitor center** is located just outside the northwest entrance station before Manzanita Lake. The park information number for all requests is ☎ **530/595-4444,** or write **Lassen Volcanic National Park,** P.O. Box 100, Mineral, CA 96063-0100.

Because of the dangers posed by the park's thermal features, rangers ask that you remain on trails at all times. Fires are allowed in campgrounds only; please make sure they are dead before leaving them. Mountain bikes are prohibited on all trails.

Lassen is one of the least-visited parks in the lower 48 states, so crowd control isn't as big a consideration here as in other places. Unless you're here on the Fourth of July or Labor Day weekend, you won't encounter anything that could rightly be called a crowd. Even then you can escape the hordes simply by skipping the popular sites like Bumpass Hell or the Sulphur Works and heading a few miles down any of the backcountry trails.

Modoc County (Lassen National Park does not lie in Lassen County) is one of the coldest places in California. Winter begins in late October and doesn't release its grip until June. Even in the summer you should plan for possible rain and snow. Temperatures at night can drop below freezing at any time. Winter, however, shows a different and beautiful side of Lassen that more people are starting to appreciate. Since most of the park is over a mile high and the highest point is 10,457 feet, snow accumulates in incredible quantities. Don't be surprised to find snowbanks lining the Park Road into July.

Lassen Volcanic National Park

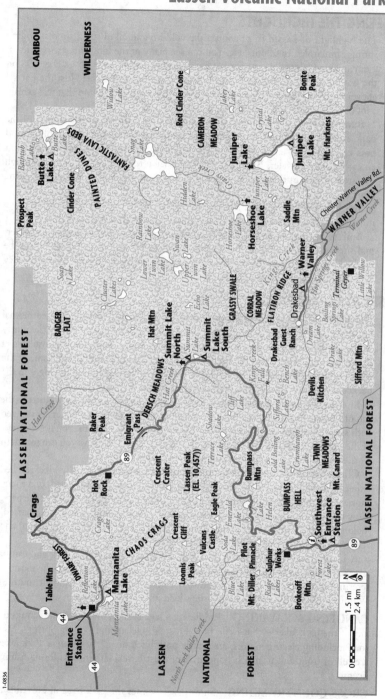

SEEING THE HIGHLIGHTS

The highlight of Lassen is, of course, the volcano and all of its offshoots: boiling springs, fumaroles, mud pots, etc. You can see many of the most interesting sites in a day, making it possible to visit Lassen as a short detour from I-5 or U.S. 395 on the way to or from Oregon. Available at park visitor centers (see "Just the Facts," above), the *Road Guide to Lassen Park* is a great traveling companion that will explain a lot of the features you'll see as you traverse the park.

Bumpass Hell, a 1¹/₂-mile walk off the Park Road in the southern part of the park, is the largest single geothermal site in the park—16 acres of bubbling mud pots cloaked in a stench of rotten-egg–smelling sulfur. The name comes from an early Lassen traveler, Bumpass, who lost a leg after he took a shortcut through the area while hunting and plunged into a boiling pool. Don't make the same error.

Sulphur Works is another stinky, steamy example of Lassen's residual heat. Two miles from the southwest park exit, the ground roars with seething gases.

Boiling Springs Lake and **Devil's Kitchen** are two of the more remote geothermal sites; they're located in the Warner Valley section of the park, which can be reached by hiking from the main road or entering the park through Warner Valley Road from the small town of Chester.

SPORTS & ACTIVITIES

HIKING   Most Lassen visitors drive through in a day or two, see the geothermal hot spots, and move on. That leaves 150 miles of trails and expanses of backcountry to the few who take the time to get off-road. The *Lassen Trails* booklet available at the visitor centers (see "Just the Facts," above) gives good descriptions of some of the most popular hikes and backpacking destinations. Anyone spending the night in the backcountry must have a wilderness permit issued at the ranger stations.

Probably the most popular hike is the 2¹/₂-mile climb from the Park Road to the top of **Lassen Peak.** The trail may sound short, but it's steep and generally covered with snow until late summer. At 10,457 feet in elevation, though, you'll get a view of the surrounding wilderness that's worth every step. On clear days you can see south all the way to the Sierra and north into the Cascades.

Cinder Cone in the northeast corner of the park is another worthy hike, reached either by walking in about 8 miles from Summit Lake on the Park Road, or a much shorter hike (but long drive) from Butte Lake at the far northeast corner of the park. Now dormant, Cinder Cone is approximately 250 years old. Black and charred-looking, Cinder Cone is bare of any sort of life (aside from very little vegetation) and surrounded by dunes of multihued volcanic ash.

A 17-mile segment of the **Pacific Crest Trail** cuts through the park and can be accessed via the Warner Valley Road or by a long hike from Hat Lake. The most interesting section of the trail for nonthrough hikers is the 5-mile segment south of Warner Valley leading to Boiling Springs Lake and Terminal Geyser.

CANOEING & KAYAKING   Paddlers can take canoes, rowboats, and kayaks on any of the park lakes except Reflection, Emerald, Helen, and Boiling Springs. Motors, including electric motors, are strictly prohibited on all park waters. Park lakes are full of trout and fishing is popular. You must have a current California fishing license.

CROSS-COUNTRY SKIING   Snow usually closes the park road in November, and most years it doesn't open until June, so cross-country skiers have their run of the park. Marked trails of all skill levels leave from Manzanita Lake at the north end of the park and Lassen Chalet at the south. You can ski the 30-mile course in a long day or easy overnight. For safety reasons the park requires all skiers to register at the ranger stations before heading into the backcountry, whether for an overnight or just the day.

Park staff also lead snowshoe hikes into the park emphasizing ecology and winter survival.

CAMPING

Backcountry camping is allowed almost everywhere, and traffic is light. Ask about closed areas when you get your wilderness permit.

Car campers have their choice of seven park campgrounds, more than enough to handle the half-million visitors who come to Lassen every summer. So few people camp in Lassen that there is no reservation system except for the **Lost Creek Group Campground,** and campers are granted a generous 14-day limit. Fees are $45 per night per group. Sites do fill up on weekends, so your best bet is to get to the park early Friday to secure a spot. If the park is packed, there are 43 campgrounds in surrounding Lassen National Forest, so you'll find a site somewhere.

By far the most "civilized" campground in the park is at **Manzanita Lake,** where you can find hot showers, flush toilets, and a camper store. When Manzanita fills up, rangers open the **Crags Campground** overflow camp about 5 miles away. It is much more basic. On the southern end of the park you'll find **Southwest Campground,** a walk-in camp directly adjacent to the Lassen Chalet parking lot.

ACCOMMODATIONS

Only one lodge operates within Lassen Park: **Drakesbad Guest Ranch.** Famous for its rustic cabins, lodge, and steaming hot-spring pool, Drakesbad is deluxe as only a place with no electricity or phones can be, with handmade quilts on every bed and kerosene lamps to read by. Full meal service is available and very good. Rates range from $100 to $110 per guest, per night, double occupancy (kids are about half price). Since the lodge is extremely popular and only open from June to September, reservations are booked as far as 2 years in advance. The spa is only for guests, but horseback riding trips are available for day visitors as well as overnight guests. You can also arrange meals for a day visit. For prices and reservation information contact the **California Parks Co.,** 2150 N. Main St., No.5, Red Bluff, CA 96080 (☎ 530/529-1512).

JUST OUTSIDE THE PARK

✪ **The Bidwell House.** 1 Main St. (P.O. Box 1790), Chester, CA 96020. ☎ **530/258-3338.** 14 rms, 12 with private bath; 1 cottage with kitchenette. $60–$65 double without bath, $78–$115 double with bath; cottage $153 for 6. Rates include full breakfast. MC, V.

In 1901, General John Bidwell, a California senator who made three unsuccessful bids for the U.S. presidency, built a country retreat and summer home for his beloved young wife, Annie. Although he died before ever living in the house, Annie eventually moved here and used it as a base for missionary work, converting scores of local Native Americans to Christianity. After her death, when Chester had developed into a prosperous logging hamlet, the building, with its farmhouse-style design and spacious veranda, was converted into the headquarters for a local ranch.

Today, the house sits at the extreme eastern end of Chester, adjacent to a rolling meadow. The lake is visible across the road, and inside, Ian and Kim James maintain one of the most charming B&B inns in the region. Seven of the rooms have

Jacuzzi tubs, and three offer wood-burning stoves. Breakfast is presented with fanfare and incorporates many gourmet touches, including home-baked breads and scrumptious omelets. The Jameses also serve dinner Thursday through Saturday.

4 Lake Tahoe

Lake Tahoe has long been California's most popular recreational playground. In summer you can enjoy boating and water sports, plus in-line skating, bungee jumping, camping, ballooning, horseback riding, bicycling, parasailing—the list is endless. In winter Lake Tahoe becomes one of the nation's premier ski destinations with its 13 downhill resorts and 15 cross-country skiing centers. There's also sleigh riding, ice-skating, snowmobiling, and snowshoeing. Year-round activities include tennis, fishing, Vegas-style gambling, and big-name entertainment on the Nevada border.

And that's not the half of it; there's also the lake.

It's disputable whether Lake Tahoe is the most beautiful lake in the world, but it's certainly near the top of the list. It's famous for its 99.997% pure water (a white dinner plate at a depth of 75 feet would be clearly visible from the surface!), and its size: The lake is so immense that the water it contains—close to 40 trillion gallons—could cover the entire state of California to a depth of $14^{1}/_{2}$ inches. Its average depth is 989 feet, although it reaches 1,645 feet in places, making it the second deepest lake in the U.S. (after Crater Lake, Oregon) and the eighth deepest in the world.

More important to the visitor, however, is this region's pristine beauty: the play of light during the day, which transforms the color of the lake from a dazzling emerald to blues and rich purples; the snowy mountain tops reflecting off the water; the fresh, crisp air; and the deep green of the trees carpeting the expanse of the valley. It's a sight that no one should miss, and that nobody ever forgets.

ESSENTIALS

GETTING THERE   It's a 4-hour drive from San Francisco; take I-80 east to Sacramento, then U.S. 50 to the lake's south shore, or I-80 east to Calif. 89 south to reach the lake's north shore.

From Los Angeles, it's a grueling 9-hour drive; take I-5 through the Central Valley to I-80 east at Sacramento, then U.S. 50 east. If the weather's good and you can spare a few additional hours, it's really worth avoiding the interstate for the scenic drive on U.S. 395 and U.S. 50, which lie along the corridor between the towering peaks of the eastern Sierras and the Inyo Mountain Range.

Reno/Tahoe International Airport, 40 miles northeast of Lake Tahoe (about a 50-minute drive), offers regularly scheduled service from 13 national airlines, including American (☎ **800/433-7300**), Delta (☎ **800/221-1212**), and United/United Express (☎ **800/241-6522**).

Amtrak (☎ **800/USA-RAIL**) services Truckee, 10 miles north of the lake; shuttle service is available to North Lake Tahoe from the station. Trains connect with the rest of the state through Sacramento.

VISITOR INFORMATION   Call the **North Lake Tahoe Resort Association** in Tahoe City (☎ **800/824-6348** or 530/583-3494), or stop by the Resort Association's **Visitor Service Center** at 245 North Lake Blvd., Tahoe City (☎ **800/ 824-6348**). It's open Monday to Friday from 8:30am to 5pm, Saturday and Sunday from 9am to 4pm.

In South Lake Tahoe, there's the **Lake Tahoe Visitors Authority,** 1156 Ski Run Blvd. (☎ **800/367-7366** or 530/544-5050), and the **South Lake Tahoe**

A Tale of Two Shores

You wouldn't think the people and places on one end of Lake Tahoe would be much different from the other, but ask any local: North Lake and South Lake—Tahoe's two main destinations—have about as much in common as snowcones and sandcastles.

Don't let the "City" in North Shore's "Tahoe City" fool you: The entire town can be driven through in about 40 seconds, whereas South Lake Tahoe is brimming with high-rise casinos, condominiums, and mini-malls.

Which side you choose to stay on is important because driving from one end of the lake to the other is a 3-hour affair on summer weekends and downright treacherous during snowstorms—so don't make the common mistake of thinking you can sleep for cheap on the South Shore and party all day on the North.

So which side is for you? If you're here to gamble, stay south: The selection of casinos is better and the lodging more abundant. If it's the great outdoors you're after, or simply a little R&R under the shade of a Douglas Fir, head north. The North Shore offers a far better selection of quality lodgings, restaurants, and scenery, whereas the South Shore shoots for quantity, offering three times as many lodgings and restaurants at better rates.

Chamber of Commerce, 3066 Lake Tahoe Blvd. (☎ **530/541-5255**), which is open Monday to Friday from 8:30am to 5pm and Saturday from 9am to 4pm (it's closed on major holidays).

SKIING

Tahoe offers California's best skiing, with 13 downhill ski resorts and 15 cross-country centers. The ski season usually lasts from November through May, but frequently extends into summer (in 1995 there was skiing until July 4th!). Lift tickets usually cost about $42 per day, $30 per half day, and $6 for children under 13. Five of the top areas—Alpine Meadows, Heavenly Resort, Kirkwood, Northstar-at-Tahoe, Sierra-at-Tahoe, and Squaw Valley—offer an interchangeable Ski Lake Tahoe lift ticket at $220 for 5 days.

If you've come to ski, contact both visitor offices (see above) for information about the ski packages offered by almost every hotel and resort on the lake—you're likely to save a bundle. The following are some of Tahoe's most popular resorts.

Alpine Meadows. P.O. Box 5279, Tahoe City, CA 96145. ☎ **800/441-4423** or 530/583-4232.

Six miles from Tahoe City, Alpine has a high elevation (8,637 feet) that gives it a long skiing season that often lasts until Memorial Day. The mid-sized resort—ranked by readers of *Snow Country* magazine as their favorite resort in California—is a great all-around performer, with 40% groomed for intermediate skiers, 35% for advanced, and 25% for beginners. A new addition this year is Tahoe's only six-passenger high-speed chair, as well as a lifted ban on snowboarding.

Diamond Peak. 1210 Ski Way, Incline Village, NV 89451. ☎ **702/832-1177** or 702/831-3249.

One of Tahoe's smaller—and less crowded and less expensive—ski resorts, Diamond Peak plugs itself as the "premier family ski resort." It's primarily a mountain for

Lake Tahoe & Environs

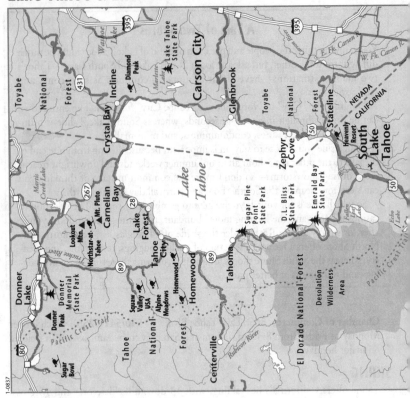

1-0837

intermediates (49%), with 36% of the mountain groomed for advanced, and 18% for beginners. Kids love the new snowboard park and sledding area. There's also cross-country skiing and snowshoeing, as well as dining and lodging in nearby Incline Village.

Heavenly Resort. P.O. Box 2180, Stateline, NV 89449. ☎ **702/586-7000.**

Celebrating its 40th anniversary, this South Lake Tahoe legend is one of the area's largest ski resorts, with 4,800 acres of ski terrain and snowmaking on 66% of the trails. The vertical drop is 3,500 feet, the steepest in the region. The terrain is 45% intermediate, 35% advanced, and 20% beginner. There are 25 lifts, including a 50-passenger aerial tram and 3 high-speed detachable quads. The resort straddles the state borders; Heavenly West on the California side has easier trails than Heavenly North, which is predominantly intermediate territory. It's less crowded, however, on the Nevada side.

Kirkwood. Off Calif. 88, P.O. Box 1, Kirkwood CA 95646. ☎ **209/258-6000.**

Kirkwood's only drawback is that it's 30 miles (45 minutes) from South Lake Tahoe on Calif. 88; otherwise, this is one of the top ski areas in Tahoe, with one of the highest average snowfalls after Squaw Valley (Alpine Meadows is third) and excellent spring skiing often running into June. The 2,300 acres of skiable terrain is 50% intermediate, 35% advanced/expert, and 15% beginner. There are 12 lifts—including 3 triple chairs—accessing 65 trails.

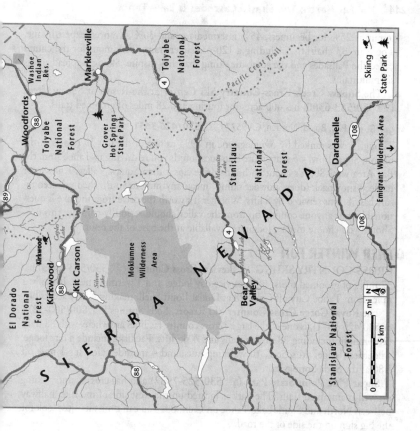

Northstar-at-Tahoe. P.O. Box 129, Truckee, CA 96160. ☎ **800/466-6784** or 530/562-1010.

More than 50% snowmaking coverage and a full-time kids' program make Northstar a top choice in Tahoe for families. It offers 2,000 acres of downhill skiing with 60 runs, 37 miles of cross-country trails, plus sleigh rides and snowmobiling. There are 12 lifts, including a 6-passenger express gondola and 4 express quad chairs. Facilities include on-site lodging and five restaurants. It's only 45 minutes from the Reno–Tahoe airport.

Ski Homewood. P.O. Box 165, 5145 West Lake Blvd., Homewood, CA 96141. ☎ **530/525-2992.**

Homewood is one of our favorite small ski areas, a homey little resort with lean lift lines and gorgeous views of the lake. The ski area covers 1,260 acres and offers 57 trails and 18 lifts. It's a good family resort, with child care for 2- to 6-year-olds and a special Snow Stars program for kids 6 to 12. It's 6 miles south of Tahoe City and 19 miles north of South Lake Tahoe. *Hot Tip:* The best ski deal in Tahoe is the 2-for-1 special on Wild Wednesdays, which usually start in January—buy one all-day adult lift ticket and receive one free.

✪ **Squaw Valley USA.** Squaw Valley, CA 96146. ☎ **800/545-4350** or 530/583-6985.

Site of the 1960 Olympic Winter Games, Squaw is almost every serious skier's favorite resort, simply because it offers the most challenging array of runs. Squaw's terrain is 25% for beginners, 45% intermediate, and 30% advanced/expert/insane. There are 33 chairlifts, including a 120-passenger tram. It's famous for the chutes called the Palisades and the acrobatic skiing that they inspire. Skiing is spread across six mountains.

The **Squaw Creek Cross-Country Ski Center** at the Resort at Squaw Creek (☎ **530/583-6300**) has 400 acres for touring and 28 miles of groomed trails.

Sugar Bowl. P.O. Box 5, Norden, CA 95724. ☎ **530/426-3651.**

Though it was ranked by *Ski* magazine in 1994 as one of the top 30 resorts in the nation, Sugar Bowl's *best* attribute is its location: If you're driving to Tahoe from the Bay Area via I-80, it's about an hour's drive closer than Squaw Valley. Known for its deep snowpack (does "powder skiing" mean anything to you?), the mid-sized resort has 58 runs serviced by 8 lifts. Whether it's worth the drive from the lake is questionable, but anyone coming up from the valley should seriously consider this one. Should you choose to stay, lodging is available at the base of the resort.

OTHER WINTER FUN

CROSS-COUNTRY SKIING   **Lakeview Cross Country** (☎ **530/583-9353**) has 37 miles of groomed trails, a full-service day lodge, and 3 warming huts. It's only 2 miles from Tahoe City off Calif. 28 at Dollar Point Shell, making it very accessible.

The **Royal Gorge Cross-Country Ski Resort,** Soda Springs (☎ **800/500-3871** or 530/426-3871), is one of the largest cross-country facilities anywhere, with 88 trails (203 miles), including 28 novice trails and 4 ski lifts. Facilities include a day lodge, wilderness lodge, ski school, 10 warming huts, and 4 trailside cafes. It's 1 mile off I-80 at the Soda Springs exit.

Sugar Pine Point State Park (☎ **530/525-7982**) also has cross-country skiing on well-maintained trails. The park is located on the west side of the lake, halfway between North and South Lake Tahoe on Calif. 89. You can't miss it—just look for the big sign on the side of the road.

ICE-SKATING   One of the world's most unusual ice rinks is at Squaw Valley's **High Camp** (☎ **530/583-6985**). The ice is accessible only by tram—a scenic ride that's included with admission. Skating costs $19 for adults and $10 for children, including cable-car ride and skate rentals. After 4pm the prices drop to $11 for adults and $6.50 for children. The rink is open year-round, daily from 11am to 9pm. Call first, as the rink closes a few days in the spring and fall for maintenance.

SNOWMOBILING   Snowmobiles are available for rent at several locations in the Lake Tahoe area. The **Zephyr Cove Snowmobile Center** (☎ **702/882-0788**) is about 4 miles north of Stateline, Nevada, on the lake's east side. It offers 2-hour guided snowmobile tours from November 26 through April 15 (weather permitting). Tours are scheduled usually thrice daily—at 10am, 12:15pm, and 2:30pm—and cost $74 for a single rider and $99 for two people on one snowmobile (limit 400 lbs.). Special moonlight tours are also offered.

High Sierra Snowmobiling, Calif. 267 and Calif. 28, Kings Beach (☎ **530/ 546-9909**), is open from November 15 through April 1 (again, weather permitting). It offers no trail tours, just a manicured track, for which it charges $30 per half hour. High Sierra is open daily from 9am to 5pm.

SUMMER ACTIVITIES

BALLOONING   View the lake and the Sierra from 10,000 to 12,000 feet above. **Lake Tahoe Balloons,** South Lake Tahoe (☎ **530/544-1221**), offers 1- to 1 1/2-hour flights followed by a champagne brunch at Café Roma at Caesars.

BIKING   There are miles of excellent paved bike paths around the lake. The 3.4-mile **Pope-Baldwin Bike Path** on the south shore runs parallel to Calif. 89 and through Camp Richardson and the Tallac Historic Site. In South Lake Tahoe another paved path runs from El Dorado Beach along the lake paralleling Calif. 50. Along the west shore there are 15 miles of paved pathways, extending from Tahoe City in three directions. On the northeast shore, Incline Village has a 2 1/2-mile trail from Gateway Park on Calif. 28.

You can rent bikes in Tahoe City at **Porter's Ski and Sport,** 501 N. Lake Blvd. (☎ 530/583-2314), and in Incline Village also at **Porter's,** 885 Tahoe Blvd. (☎ 702/831-3500). In South Lake Tahoe, go to **Anderson's Bike Rental** on the lake side of Calif. 89 at 13th Street (☎ 530/541-0500). Bike rentals usually cost $7 per hour, $20 for 4 hours, and $25 per day.

BOAT RENTALS   Several companies rent a variety of boats—canoes, power boats, and pedal boats. Among them are: **Zephyr Cove Resort Marina** (☎ 702/588-3833), which rents all three; **Paradise Watercraft** at Camp Richardson Resort (☎ 530/541-1801); **Tahoe Keys Boat Rentals** at Tahoe Keys Marina (☎ 530/544-8888 or 530/541-8405), which only rents power boats, and **North Tahoe Marina,** Calif. 28, 1 mile west of Calif. 267, Tahoe Vista (☎ 530/546-8248), which rents skis and tow lines along with 18- to 21-foot motor boats. Canoes and kayaks can be rented from **Tahoe Paddle & Oar** in Tahoe City (☎ 530/581-3029).

FISHING   Fishing in the crystal-clear waters of the lake presents a special challenge to anglers. Deep-water fishing for mackinaw trout is good year-round. Surface fishing for Kokanee salmon is best in May and June, whereas fishing for rainbow trout is ideal in the fall and winter months.

There are dozens of charter companies offering daily excursions on Lake Tahoe year-round. **Mickey's Big Mack Charters,** Tahoe City (☎ 530/546-4444, or after 6pm, 800/877-1462), is a well-respected outfit, led by experienced guide Mickey Daniels. All the fishing gear is provided, but you'll need a license, which can be purchased on the boat. Call for requirements and reservations. Mickey's boats depart from Sierra Boat Co., in Carnelian Bay, about 5 miles north of Tahoe City. Five-hour trips cost $65 per person (or 3 hours for $45) and depart daily year-round, in the early morning and late afternoon; exact times vary according to season. Other fishing specialists include: **Blue Ribbon Fishing Charters,** South Lake Tahoe (☎ 530/541-8801), and **Tahoe Sportfishing,** Ski Run Marina, 900 Ski Run Blvd., South Lake Tahoe (☎ 530/541-5448).

FITNESS CENTERS/SPAS   At the end of the day, soak your sore bones at the **North Tahoe Beach Center,** 7860 North Lake Blvd., at Kings Beach (☎ 530/546-2566). Besides offering a full line of exercise equipment, the center also boasts the largest spa on the lake, some 26 feet in diameter. It's all yours for $7 for adults and $3.50 for kids under 12. It's open daily from 10am to 10pm (on Mondays, Wednesdays, and Fridays it opens at 7am). Another spa that's popular with the locals is **Walley's Hot Springs Resort** (☎ 702/782-8155), located 2 miles north of the east end of Kingsbury Grade at 2001 Foothill Rd. in Nevada. It's worth the drive to indulge in their 6 open-air pools (each a bit warmer than the next) and massage center. Admission is $12.

GOLF   There are two Robert Trent Jones Jr. championship courses in the area: **Incline Village Championship Course,** 955 Fairway Blvd. (☎ 702/832-1144), and **Squaw Creek Golf Course,** at the Resort at Squaw Creek (☎ 530/583-6300), which is the most expensive course ($110 on weekends, $60 in the off season) at Tahoe. Other challenging courses include the **Northstar Golf Course,** Basque Drive

(☎ **530/562-2490**), which has water hazards on 14 holes and was designed by Robert Muir Graves, and South Lake's **Edgewood Tahoe,** site of the Isuzu Celebrity Gold Championship, with 18 holes and a driving range (☎ **702/588-3566**).

HIKING   The mountains surrounding Lake Tahoe are crisscrossed with hiking trails graded for all levels of experience. Before setting out, you may wish to contact the local visitors bureau for a map and more in-depth information on particular trails, or hire a guide through **Tahoe Trips & Trails** (☎ **800/581-HIKE** or 530/583-4506). Some of the most popular trails are:

Eagle Falls/Eagle Lake: One of the best trails for novice hikers, the Eagle Falls walk offers a cascading reward. The trail begins at Eagle Picnic Area, directly on Calif. 89 across from Emerald Bay.

Emerald Bay/Vikingsholm: From the parking area, 1¹/₂ miles above Tahoe's prettiest inlet, you can hike down to Vikingsholm, a 38-room replica of a medieval Scandinavian castle. The trail begins at the parking area on the north side of Emerald Bay, on Calif. 89.

Loch Levon Lakes: An easy but beautiful walk to three lakes, the Loch Levon trail is perfect for hikers who wish to stay on the beaten path. To reach the trailhead, take I-80 to the Big Bend exit and look for the sign PRIVATE ROAD PUBLIC TRAIL across from the Big Bend ranger station.

Shirley Lake: In Squaw Valley, near the tram line, this excellent hike has the advantage of a one-way adventure; you can take the tram up and hike down or vice versa. The trail begins at the end of Squaw Peak Road, next to the cable car building.

Another great option is a guided hike through the Tahoe wilderness. From $25 to $60 per person—depending on the hike, group size, and transportation—an experienced mountaineer from **Tahoe Trips & Trails** (☎ **800/581-HIKE** or 530/583-4506) will take anyone—from Grandpa to Rambo—on a guided hike specifically suited to each person's ability, from super-easy to hard-core hoofin' it. Everything is provided, including a gourmet vegetarian-friendly lunch, drinks, transportation, and answers to any question you have about the history and geology of Lake Tahoe. It's truly a great outfit that guarantees a good time at a fair price.

HORSEBACK RIDING   Camp Richardson Corral, South Lake Tahoe (☎ **530/541-3113**), offers a variety of trail rides and pack trips. A 2-hour trail ride is $35, whereas pack trips cost $150 per day, including packer, livestock, food, boat, and tackle. From December to March, sleigh rides are offered.

Northstar Stables, 2499 Northstar Dr. and Calif. 267 (☎ **530/562-2267**), at the resort of the same name, offers a variety of trail rides, lessons, and pack trips. Special breakfast and dinner rides are also available. Children under the age of 7 are not allowed on trail rides. Northstar is on the north side of Lake Tahoe, between Kings Beach and Truckee. Prices range from $5 for pony rides to $28 for 1¹/₂ hours, $50 for half-day rides, and $100 for a full day. Call for pack-trip information. Open year-round, daily 9am to 5pm; when winter prohibits trail rides, sleigh rides are available.

Squaw Valley Stables, 1525 Squaw Valley Rd. (☎ **530/583-7433**), offers trail rides and lessons for all ages and riding levels. Squaw Valley is about 5 miles north of Tahoe City. Prices range from $19 for a 1-hour guided ride to $55 per person for a half-day ride. Pony rides are $6 per half hour. Open mid-May to early September, daily from 8:30am to 4:30pm.

Sunset Ranch, Calif. 50, South Lake Tahoe (☎ **530/541-9001**), is the only stable to allow unescorted riding. A quarter of a mile west of the Lake Tahoe Airport, Sunset Ranch offers rides to both children and adults along the open meadows that abut the

Truckee River. Prices are $21 per hour, or $31 per hour for two people on a single horse; children 12 and under are $16. Open year-round, daily 9am to 6pm.

IN-LINE SKATING   Although there are trails all around Lake Tahoe, the best ones for blading are the well-paved BICYCLE AND PEDESTRIANS ONLY paths that hug the Truckee River and Calif. 89, between Tahoe City and Squaw Valley. Rollerblades and other in-line skates can be rented from the nearby **Squaw Valley Sport Shop,** Tahoe City (☎ **530/583-6278**). The shop charges $12 for a half day, $18 all day (the price covers wrist guards and other protective gear). Squaw Valley is open Sunday to Thursday from 9am to 6pm, Friday and Saturday from 9am to 7pm.

JET-SKIING   The **Lighthouse Watersports Center,** 950 N. Lake Blvd., Tahoe City (☎ **530/583-7245**), rents jet skis, paddle boats, and canoes during summer months only. Reservations are recommended for jet-ski rentals. Jet skis cost $35 per half hour and $60 per hour; paddle boats and canoes go for $15 per half hour and $20 for 2 hours. The water-sports center is open June through September, daily from 9am to 6pm.

In South Lake Tahoe, the place to rent is **Lakeview Sports,** 3131 Calif. 50, across from the El Dorado Campground (☎**530/544-0183** or 530/541-8405). They also rent mountain bikes, in-line skates, and boats.

MOUNTAIN BIKING   At both **Northstar** (☎ **530/562-1010**) and **Squaw Valley** (☎ **530/583-6985**), you can ride the cable car with your bike and cycle the trails all the way down. Call for complete information.

PARASAILING   **Lake Tahoe Parasailing,** Tahoe City (☎ **530/583-7245**), charges $40 to $50 (depending on your time aloft) and $70 for tandem flight. Rides are offered from Memorial Day to September 20th, daily from 8am to 3pm. Boats operate from Tahoe City Marina. Boat and Waverunner rentals are also available, as are waterskiing and sailboat charters.

RIVER RAFTING   The Truckee River—Lake Tahoe's only outlet—dumps plenty of water for a swift, but gentle, ride. Rafts seat anywhere between 2 to 14 people and cost about $25 for adults and $20 for kids (no kids under 5); the season runs from Memorial Day weekend to Labor Day. Rafting outfits include **Truckee River Raft Rental** (☎ **530/583-0123**), **Fanny Bridge Rafts** (☎ **530/581-0123**), and **Truckee River Rafting/Mountain Air Sports** (☎ **530/583-7238**).

TENNIS   All the major resorts have tennis courts open to the public on a fee basis. Call the **Resort at Squaw Creek** (☎ **530/583-6300**) and **Northstar** (☎ **530/562-0321**) for information and reservations.

Budget-minded players looking for good local courts should visit **Tahoe Lake School,** Grove Street, Tahoe City, where two lighted courts are available free on a first-come, first-served basis. **South Tahoe Intermediate School,** Lyons Avenue, off U.S. 50, has eight lighted courts. It charges a manageable $3 per hour.

WATERSKIING   **North Tahoe Marina,** Calif. 28, 1 mile west of Calif. 267, Tahoe Vista (☎ **530/546-8248**), rents skis and tow lines along with 18- to 24-foot motorboats. Other powerboat toys, including tubes, kneeboards, and wet suits, are also available. Rates are $65 to $110 per hour. Open May 1 through October 1, daily from 8am to 6pm.

WINDSURFING   Easy winds and relatively calm conditions make Lake Tahoe an ideal place to learn. **Lakeside Chalets,** 5240 N. Lake Blvd., Carnelian Bay (☎ **530/546-5857**), rents boards and offers lessons by appointment June through September. Windsurfers cost $20 per initial hour and $10 per hour thereafter ($50 to $60 a day).

LAKE CRUISES

The best way to experience the lake is to get out on it. *M.S. Dixie II,* Zephyr Cove Marina, Nevada (☎ **702/588-3508**), a 570-passenger vessel with bars, a dance floor, and a full dining room, offers daily cruises year-round, which may include breakfast, champagne brunch, and dinner. Zephyr Cove Marina is on U.S. 50, 4 miles north of Stateline in South Lake Tahoe. Bay cruises cost $16 for adults and $5 for children 11 and under; breakfast and brunch cruises, $18 for adults and $9 for children 11 and under; dinner cruises, $28 to $38 for adults and $12 for children 11 and under. Call for schedules.

The *Tahoe Queen* (☎ **800/238-2463** or 530/541-3364), a 500-passenger stern-wheeler, operates year-round, offering daily Emerald Bay cruises, sunset dinner-dance cruises, and shuttle service between the lake's north and south shores during the ski season. There are large outdoor and indoor viewing decks and a glass bottom for peering deep into the lake. The Emerald Bay Cruise costs $14 for adults and $5 for children 11 and under; dinner cruise, $18 for adults and $9.50 for children 11 and under (dinner optional, menu selections from $15); round-trip North/South Shore Ski Shuttle $18 for adults and $9 for children 11 and under. The *Tahoe Queen* departs from Ski Run Marina, just west of Stateline. Call to confirm rates and schedules.

The North Shore version of *Tahoe Queen* is the *Tahoe Gal* (☎ **800/218-2464** or 530/583-0141), a Mississippi River paddlewheeler that departs from the Lighthouse Marina in Tahoe City (behind Safeway). Cruises include Emerald Bay ($20 for adult and $8 for child) and Scenic Shoreline ($15 for adult and $5 for child). Dinner is available for an additional $15 for adults and $5 for children.

Woodwind **Sailing Cruises,** in the Zephyr Cove Resort, on U.S. 50, Zephyr Cove, Nevada (☎ **702/588-3000**), offers daily sailing trips aboard a 41-foot trihull craft that takes up to 30 passengers, as well as a new 55-foot catamaran. Both boats have glass bottoms that allow for good underwater viewing. Reservations are recommended. Trips cost $18 for adults and $9 for children under 12, and free for children under 2. Trips start daily at 11:30am, 1pm, 2:30pm, and 4pm from April through October. There's also a sunset champagne cruise for $26 (adults only).

A DRIVE AROUND THE LAKE

Other than cruising over it, the next best way to contemplate the lake is to drive the 72 miles around it, though at times the route can be completely clogged with traffic. And while the lake has never frozen over, the roads that surround it do; many are closed in winter, making this trip possible during summer only. If your car sports a tape player, consider buying *Drive Around the Lake*, a drive-along audio cassette that contains facts, tales and legends, places of interest, and just about everything else you could possibly want to know about the lake. It's available at numerous gift shops or at the **South Lake Tahoe Chamber of Commerce,** 3066 Lake Tahoe Blvd. (☎ **530/541-5255**), which is open Monday to Friday from 8:30am to 5pm and Saturday from 9am to 4pm (it's closed on major holidays).

We'll start at the California/Nevada border in South Lake Tahoe and loop around the western shore on Calif. 89 to Tahoe City and beyond. U.S. 50, which runs along the south shore, is an ugly, overdeveloped strip that obliterates any view of the lake unless you're staying at one of these motels. Keep heading west and you'll soon be free of this ugly zone.

First stop is the **Tallac Historic Site,** a cluster of rustic mansions that were built 100 years ago and are currently being restored by the Forest Service. A little farther on you'll find the Forest Services' **Lake Tahoe Visitors Center** located along

Taylor Creek, which offers nature trails and also an opportunity to view Kokanee salmon making their way upstream to spawn.

From here Calif. 89 climbs northward. Soon you'll be peering down into beautiful **Emerald Bay,** a 3-mile-long inlet containing tiny Fanette Island, which has an old stone teahouse clearly situated at its peak. It was built by Ms. Lora Knight, who also built Vikingsholm (see below).

Across Calif. 89 from Emerald Bay, there's another parking area. From here it's a short steep quarter-mile hike to a footbridge above Eagle Falls. Then it's about 1 mile to Eagle Lake. Register at the trailhead. **Emerald Bay State Park** (☎ **530/988-0205**) offers 100 camping sites on the south side of the bay.

It's not surprising that someone chose to build a mansion right here overlooking the bay—**Vikingsholm,** Emerald Bay, Calif. 89 (☎ **530/525-7277** or 530/525-7232). Built in 1929, this 38-room mansion is a replica of a medieval Viking castle. It is so striking that a paved parking area on the highway had to be built for all the gawkers. Tree branches shaped like spears jut out from the gutters to ward off evil spirits. Inside, carved dragon heads decorate the ceiling beams. A layer of sod blankets the roof, which sprouts wild flowers in the spring. You can visit Vikingsholm by hiking down a steep 1-mile trail (but remember, you have to come back up, too). The mansion is open for tours, every half hour on the hour and half hour, during summer only. Admission is $3 for adults and $2 for children 6 to 12, and free for kids 6 and under. It's open June 3 to Labor Day, daily 10am to 4pm.

From here it's only about 2 miles to **D. L. Bliss State Park** (☎ **530/525-7277**), where you'll find one of the lake's best beaches. It gets very crowded in summer, so get there early before all the parking places are occupied. The park also contains 168 campsites and several trails, including one along the shoreline.

About 7 miles farther on, **Sugar Pine Point State Park** (☎ **530/525-7982**) is the largest (2,000 acres) of the lake's parks and also the only one that has year-round camping. In summer there are several beaches in the park plus a nature trail; in winter there's cross-country skiing on well-maintained trails.

It's a clear drive through the small town of Homewood (site of the ski resort of the same name) to **Tahoe City,** which is smaller and much more appealing than South Lake Tahoe, although it, too, has its share of strip development.

At Tahoe City, Calif. 89 turns off to **Truckee** and to Alpine Meadows and Squaw Valley ski resorts. **Squaw Valley** is only 5 miles out, and a ride on the Squaw Valley cable car (☎ **530/583-6985**) rewards visitors with incredible vistas in summer or winter from 2,000 feet above the valley floor. The cable car operates year-round daily from 8am to 4pm. A ticket costs $12 for adults and $5 for children 4 to 12, $9 for seniors 65 and older, and free for children under 3. From Squaw Valley, it's another 5 or so miles to the railroad town of Truckee and **Donner State Park,** with its museum and monument to the Donner Party Expedition of 1846.

If you continue around the lake on Calif. 28, you'll reach Carnelian Bay, Tahoe Vista, and Kings Beach before crossing the state line into Nevada to Crystal Bay, Incline Village, the Ponderosa Ranch, and Sand Harbor Beach. **Kings Beach State Recreation Area** (☎ **530/546-7248**) is 12 miles east of Tahoe City and in summer is jammed with sunbathers and swimmers. From Incline Village, a 4-mile side trip up the Mt. Rose Highway leads to an overlook of the entire Tahoe Basin.

Remember Hoss and Little Joe Cartwright? The **Ponderosa Ranch,** Calif. 28, Incline Village (☎ **702/831-0691**), is a theme park inspired by the popular 1960s television show *Bonanza.* The original 1959 Cartwright Ranch House can be visited along with a western township complete with blacksmith's shop and staged gun

battles. There are also such activities as pony rides and a petting farm. The barbecue grill is almost always fired up, and breakfast hayrides on tractor-pulled wagons
are offered for an extra $2. Admission is $9.50 for adults, $5.50 for children 5 to 11,
and free for children under 5. It's open mid-April to October only, daily from 9:30am
to 5pm.

Also at Incline Village is **Sand Harbor**, one of the best beaches on the lake (though
it can get incredibly crowded in summer).

South of Sand Harbor, if you wish, you can then turn inland to Spooner Lake and
Carson City, capital of Nevada, or continue south along Calif. 28 to an outcropping
called **Cave Rock,** where the highway passes through 25 yards of solid stone.
Farther along is **Zephyr Cove,** from which the tour boats depart. You'll then return
to Stateline and South Lake Tahoe, your original starting point.

WHERE TO STAY
SOUTH SHORE/SOUTH LAKE TAHOE
Very Expensive

✪ **Embassy Suites Resort Lake Tahoe.** 4130 Lake Tahoe Blvd., South Lake Tahoe, CA
96150. ☎ **800/988-9850** or 530/544-5400. Fax 530/544-4900. 400 suites. A/C MINIBAR
TV TEL. $150–$240 double. Additional person $20. Rates include cooked-to-order breakfast.
Packages available. AE, DC, MC, V.

Standing near the state line, this is the only real hotel on California's south shore,
and it's in a class by itself, competing for the upscale gambling crowd and the convention business with Nevada's glittering casino hotels across the way. Family skiers
fill up the place in winter. A Bavarian-style hotel of character, it rises 9 floors, the
roofline pierced with a double layer of dormers. Accommodations are nothing unusual for those who've stayed at Embassy Suites before: dark hardwood furniture,
tasteful fabrics, well-chosen carpets, microwaves, VCR, and Nintendo.

Dining/Entertainment: Zackary's restaurant serves American and international
dishes around the clock. Turtles sport bar opens onto an outdoor deck; it keeps its
wood-fired pizza oven busy at night and turns into a disco later in the evening.

Facilities: Whirlpool, indoor pool, a basic gym.

Tahoe Seasons Resort. 3901 Saddle Rd. (off Ski Run Blvd.; P.O. Box 5656), South Lake Tahoe,
CA 96157. ☎ **800/540-4874** or 530/541-6700. Fax 530/541-0653. 183 suites. A/C TV TEL.
Summer, $150–$215 double; spring/fall, $110–$180 double. Seasonal "Romance" packages
available. AE, CB, DC, MC, V.

Big, modern, and loaded with luxuries, the Tahoe Seasons lies in a relatively
uncongested residential neighborhood at the base of the Heavenly Valley Ski Resort,
2 miles from Tahoe's casinos. Every unit here is a suite; all but 10 have gas fireplaces,
and all have huge whirlpool spas, VCRs, refrigerators, microwaves, and coffeemakers.
Skiing isn't the only activity around here: Play a round of tennis on the roof, swim
in the heated outdoor pool, or hop aboard the free casino shuttles. The ambiance is
rustic Californian, a style appreciated by the droves of second honeymooners who
come here to lose their shirts, in more ways than one. An on-site restaurant and cocktail lounge provides, among other things, room service.

Expensive

Caesar's Tahoe. 55 Calif. 50, P.O. Box 5800, Lake Tahoe, NV 89449. ☎ **800/648-3353** or
702/588-3515. 448 units. A/C TV TEL. $110–$195 double; $375 minisuite; $650 executive suite.
Additional person $10. AE, DC, MC, V.

This 16-story hotel, built in the early 1980s, has the glitter, the glitz, and the campy
references to Roman mythology that Caesar's Palace in Las Vegas has perfected for

decades. It's a more intimate version of its Las Vegas counterpart, recently spruced up with a mere $16 million renovation. We think the plastic Roman theme is a hoot—mythological figures even cavort across the elevators that take you up to your oversized room, where views of the lake stretch out across the highway.

Guest rooms are furnished with contemporary hardwood pieces and fully equipped with extra-large tubs (Roman-style, of course) and two phones. King- or queen-size beds await you, often with padded scalloped headboards à la Mae West. Suites have unique themes, such as the Hollywood Suite, which comes complete with faux palm trees. Suites can only be guaranteed at check-in, presumably because high rollers are difficult to evict on schedule.

Dining/Entertainment: There are six in-house restaurants, the most popular being the Broiler Room. It's all here: grill, yogurt shop, buffets, an Asian dining room, and even an Italian restaurant by the pool. But Planet Hollywood is the venue that packs them in—everyone from tourists to the occasional visiting pop star.

Services: 24-hour room service, concierge, laundry/valet, baby-sitting.

Facilities: A 24-hour casino plus showrooms with major entertainment. Indoor lagoon-style swimming pool, tennis courts, fitness room with Universal machines plus massage therapists.

✪ **Fantasy Inn.** 3696 Lake Tahoe Blvd., South Lake Tahoe, CA 96150. ☎ **800/367-7736** or 530/541-4200. Fax 530/541-4200. 53 rms. A/C TV TEL. Sun–Thurs, $110–$270 double; Fri–Sat, $170–$270 double. Packages available. AE, CB, DISC, DC, MC, V.

Even the "fantasy" industry is downsizing: At one time, there where five Fantasy Inns around Lake Tahoe and Reno, but, alas, now there is only one hotel left in Tahoe that caters exclusively to the adults-only, all-romance market. Despite a theme that in less skilled hands would be tacky and leering, this place actually is outfitted in relatively good taste with goodly amounts of fun. Its erotic undercurrent isn't particularly discreet, thanks to sexually provocative art and a choice of porno flicks coming over the VCR whenever they're called for. Nonetheless, the place has provided love nests for hundreds of couples (including an occasional scattering of same-sex couples).

Set on the California side, about 1 1/2 miles from the state line, it offers little in the way of outside diversions (presumably, you'll bring your own). There's no restaurant, no breakfast served, and no casino on-site.

The decor mingles camp with a sense of fun and (usually) taste. All units have one king-size or round bed, lots of mirrors (on both walls and ceilings), surround-sound stereo systems, cable TV with in-house adult-movie rentals, twin showerheads, whirlpool spa, provocative art, and accoutrements designed for two. Theme suites (Antony and Cleopatra, Romeo and Juliet, Caesar's Indulgence, and the Sultan's Tent, for example) might have round beds or "waveless waterbeds." Our favorite of all, Graceland, has a bed shaped like a heart and enough Elvis memorabilia to give you something to talk about after your passions have been satiated.

Harrah's Casino Hotel. U.S. 50 at Stateline Ave. (P.O. Box 8), Lake Tahoe, NV 89449. ☎ **800/427-7247** or 702/588-6611. Fax 702/586-6607. 540 rms, 40 junior suites and suites. TV TEL. $119–$180 double; $179–$280 junior suite; $486–$918 suite. AE, CB, DC, DISC, MC, V.

In hot competition with Caesar's, this modern Vegas-style palace in an 18-story concrete-and-glass tower is deliberately glitzy and flashy. It stands astride the California–Nevada state line, and for legal reasons, all the gambling facilities are on the Nevada side. Connected to Harvey's Resort Casino (see below) by tunnel, it's a consistently high-rated hotel, an impressive achievement for such a sprawling complex.

Rooms are among the largest in Tahoe—each with two bathrooms and those thick, fluffy, white towels Sinatra was always demanding. Most have a bay window overlooking the lake or the Sierra mountain range. Key-card locks, soundproofing, and walk-in closets are additional room features. Recent additions include full no-smoking floors, as well as an enormous Family Fun Center designed to keep the kids busy while mom and dad work the slots.

Dining/Entertainment: There are seven restaurants, the most glamorous of which are on the upper floors. Big names in show biz headline at the casino's South Shore Room. The dinner-only Summit Restaurant on the 16th floor offers panoramic views of the lake and mountains, which are often better than the food. Other choices include a 24-hour coffeeshop, an Italian cafe, and a split-level rooftop steak house. Buffets are also served on the rooftop. A sports bar is just one of many drinking meccas.

Services: Round-the-clock room service, concierge, valet, overnight laundry, shoe shine, ski shuttle, baby-sitting, car rental desk.

Facilities: Casino, glass-enclosed swimming pool, health club, and arcade.

Harvey's Casino Resort, Lake Tahoe. U.S. Hwy. 50 at Stateline Ave., Stateline, NV 89449. ☎ **800/HARVEYS** or 702/588-2411. Fax 702/588-6643. 704 rms, 36 suites. TV TEL. July 1– Labor Day $115–$195 double; rest of the year $99–$190 double. Suites $275–$500 year-round. Rates include continental breakfast. AE, CB, DC, DISC, MC, V.

Harvey's was born in Lake Tahoe in the l940s, during the great expansion of Las Vegas, and its design reflects a Vegas sensibility. Originally, the resort contained only a 12-story tower, referred to today as the Mountain Tower, but in l986, the hotel's size more than doubled with the addition of a 19-story Lake Tower. Today it's the largest hotel in Tahoe, boasting an 88,000-square-foot casino (Tahoe's largest), eight restaurants, and a cabaret with some of the most glittering, bespangled entertainment in town. More than a hotel, Harvey's is like a city unto itself, with a connecting tunnel to the neighboring Harrah's. Try to get a room between the 15th and 19th floors in the newer tower, where every room has a view of both Lake Tahoe and the surrounding Sierra.

Dining/Entertainment: There are eight restaurants, often filled with convention revelers. Llewellyn's, on the 19th floor with panoramic views of the lake, is the premier restaurant and serves contemporary cuisine. There's also the Sage Room, a traditional western steakhouse (rib eye to venison), a buffet restaurant, a seafood grotto, a pizzeria, a burger pit stop, and the very popular Mexican venue, El Vaquero. The Emerald Theater cabaret showroom features live revues, and the adjacent Emerald Lounge has live entertainment Thursday through Tuesday.

Services: 24-hour room service, concierge, laundry/valet, shoe shine, ski shuttle, car rental desk.

Facilities: Casino, swimming pool, arcade, health club and spa, children's day camp, and family fun center. The hotel also has its own wedding chapel, whose view of the lake has been the backdrop for thousands of marriages.

Moderate

Best Western Station House Inn. 901 Park Ave., South Lake Tahoe, CA 96150. ☎ **800/ 822-5953** or 530/542-1101. Fax 530/542-1714. 96 rms, 2 suites, 2 chalets. A/C TV TEL. $98– $118 double; $125–$150 suite; $175–$200 chalet. AE, DC, DISC, MC, V.

Trimmed with redwood, the Best Western Station House Inn was built in the late 1970s, nestling amid pines 2 blocks off U.S. 50. It's one of the few hotels in town that has its own private "gated" beach on the lake, and it has an in-house restaurant, Lew MarNell's. It's not a particularly exciting hotel, but it's clean and very acceptable. Bedrooms are done in a modern style with oak furnishings. The staff is friendly and competent, but not particularly polished. There's a free shuttle to the casinos and most ski resorts.

Horizon Casino Resort. Calif. 50 (P.O. Box C), Lake Tahoe, NV 89449. ☎ **800/648-3322** or 702/588-6211. Fax 702/588-0349. 509 rooms, 30 suites. A/C TV TEL. Summer $99–$149 double; winter $69–$119 double; suites from $325 year-round. Additional person and lakeview rooms $10; kids under 12 free. AE, DC, MC, V.

This massive hotel stands next to the even larger and better known Harvey's; it's definitely a runner-up in the hotel sweepstakes, but it charges a lot less for basically the same facilities. Rising in a pair of towers (with 9 and 15 floors, respectively), the Horizon was radically renovated in 1994. Its original core, built in the 1960s, was the High Sierra Hotel, whose trademark Old West trappings were ripped out in favor of a glitzy yet bland modern decor. The lobby is now a sea of white marble and mirrors. The rooms are smoother and more tasteful (and for lovers of kitsch, less amusing). The upper floors, naturally, open onto the best views of mountains and lake. The place is so big that if you've had too much to drink, you may never find your way to the room with your number on it.

The 24-hour coffeeshop often attracts hard-core gamblers in the wee hours. There's also a buffet room and a run-of-the-mill steakhouse (many guests head over to the new Planet Hollywood across the way at Caesar's). The lounge features karaoke but turns up few promising Sinatras. Second-string performers, often from Los Angeles, perform in the cabaret room, which charges a one-drink minimum. Amenities include valet parking, 24-hour room service, a fitness center, an outdoor swimming pool and hot tubs, a ski rental shop, an arcade, and a wedding chapel.

Lakeland Village Beach & Ski Resort. 3535 Lake Tahoe Blvd., South Lake Tahoe, CA 96150. ☎ **800/822-5969** or 530/544-1685. Fax 530/541-6278. 212 condo units. A/C (except in town house) TV TEL. $75–$495 for 2–10 people. AE, MC, V.

Between Ski Run Boulevard and Fairway Avenue off U.S. 50—that's a mile northeast of the casino district and a mile from Heavenly Valley—this complex, built in the 1970s, is clustered on 19 lightly forested acres. It's half residential apartment complex, half holiday resort.

Don't expect any particular sense of community here; everything about the design seems focused on privacy and anonymity. The layout is a complicated labyrinth of buildings whose wood sides blend into the surrounding landscape. The only drawback is the proximity to traffic headed into Lake Tahoe, although some units, placed out among the grounds, are quieter than those in the main lodge, which lies adjacent to the road. The only hotel service is daily maid service. When you check in, be prepared for a baffling choice of layouts; the staff will present an array of floor plans. The units, ranging from studios to four-bedroom lakeside apartments, are streamlined California architecture, and many units have upstairs sleeping lofts.

There are no restaurants on the premises, although complimentary shuttle buses carry gamblers to the nearby casinos, a grocery store is within walking distance, and all suites have fully equipped kitchens. Perks include two outdoor pools, three saunas, tennis and volleyball courts, a large private beach opening directly onto the lake, and access to a boat dock.

NORTH SHORE/TAHOE CITY

Expensive

Chinquapin Resort. 3600 N. Lake Blvd., P.O. Box 1923, Tahoe City, CA 96145. ☎ **800/732-6721** or 530/583-6991. Fax 530/583-0937. 172 town houses/condos. TV TEL. $140–$260 1-bedroom; $165–$260 2-bedroom; $210–$435 3-bedroom; $190–$550 4-bedroom. DISC, MC, V.

Built in the 1970s on 95 acres of land on the north shore of Lake Tahoe, this complex lies 3 miles east of Tahoe City and is convenient for easy access to the area's ski resorts, golf courses, restaurants, and shopping. It consists of a series of town houses and condos on forested lakefront land, including 1 mile of shoreline. One- to four-bedroom units range in size from 950 to 2,800 square feet. The development offers some 20 different floor plans, and redwood trim and fireplaces are featured in every accommodation, some of which have their own saunas. All are fully furnished, containing a kitchen (with all the equipment), fireplace, washer, and dryer, and the rooms are attractively decorated. Some one-bedroom units are more expensive than two-bedrooms because of their lakefront location. At all times, about a third of the units are available to rent; the rest are in use by their owners.

Facilities: Two sandy beaches, 7 tennis courts, a newly remodeled pool area, a pier, saunas, a sand volleyball court, and all the jogging, walking, and hiking trails an aspiring Bill Clinton would ever need.

Hyatt Regency Lake Tahoe. Country Club at Lakeshore, (P.O. Box 3239), Incline Village, NV 89450. ☎ **800/233-1234** or 702/832-1234. Fax 702/831-7508. 446 rms, 22 suites, 24 cottages. A/C TV TEL. $135–$205 double. AE, DC, DISC, MC, V.

If you like to gamble but hate those gauche, racy casinos that line the California–Nevada border, you might want to consider this Hyatt in Incline Village. Far, far classier and quieter than the casino/hotels you'll find along Stateline, the Hyatt is a resort hotel first and casino second. Far more inviting than the Baccarat tables is the resort's exquisite private beach, loaded with water toys—catamaran cruises, jet skis, parasailing—available to guests.

While the hotel itself isn't exactly an architectural masterpiece inside or out, the adjoining Lakeside Cottages are a wee bit o' heaven for families—or honeymooners—who want beachfront access and large, comfortable rooms with unobstructed panoramas of the lake. A bonus for families is the popular Camp Hyatt, which lets kids ages 3 to 12 get a break from their parents for the day.

Dining/Entertainment: The Hyatt's Lone Eagle Grill offers fine American cuisine and lakefront dining in a rustic "lodge" atmosphere with large wooden beams and an enormous 20-foot fireplace. There's also the intimate Ciao Mein Trattoria, which mixes Pacific Rim and Italian styles, and Sierra Café, which serves inexpensive burgers, soups, fajitas, buffets, and breakfasts. The small casino runs 24 hours and includes an arcade and cabaret entertainment.

Services: 24-hour room service, Camp Hyatt for kids, business services, valet.

Facilities: Outdoor heated pool and spa, health club, tennis courts, 55-foot catamaran, ski-rental shop.

✪ **Plumpjacks Squaw Valley Inn.** 1920 Squaw Valley Rd (off Calif. 89; P.O. Box 2407), Squaw Valley, CA 96146. ☎ **800/323-7666** or 530/583-1576. 60 rooms. A/C TV TEL. Summer, $130–$510; winter, $160–$925. Rates include continental breakfast. AE, DC, DISC, MC, V. Free parking.

Part ski chalet, part boutique hotel, Plumpjacks Squaw Valley Inn is easily Tahoe's most stylish and suave hotel and restaurant. Granted, it lacks the fancy toys offered by its competitor across the valley, the Resort at Squaw Creek (see below), but the Plumpjack Squaw Valley Inn is unquestionably more suave, a tribute to melding of artistry and hostelry. The entire hotel is draped in muted, earthy tones; swirling sconces and sculpted metal accents are brain-candy for the eyes, while the rest of our body parts are soothingly enveloped in thick hooded robes, terry-cloth slippers, and thick down comforters atop expensive mattresses. Each room has mountain views.

Dining/Entertainment: See "Where to Dine," below, for a complete review of the hotel's highly regarded restaurant.

Services: Room service via the restaurant from 7am to 10pm; ski rentals and storage.

Facilities: Swimming pool, two spas, retail sports shop.

✪ **The Resort at Squaw Creek.** 400 Squaw Creek Rd. (P.O. Box 3333), Olympic Valley, CA 96146. ☎ **800/327-3353** or 530/583-6300. Fax 530/581-6632. 200 rms, 205 suites. A/C MINIBAR TV TEL. $180–$250 double; $280–$395 suite. AE, CB, DC, DISC, MC, V. Valet parking $10, free self-parking.

The only deluxe resort on the California side of the lake, the $130-million Resort at Squaw Creek opened in 1990 amidst controversy about its environmental impact. It's located in an inconspicuous corner of the valley at the base of Snow King mountain, and you can't beat the resort's ski-in/ski-out access to Squaw Valley skiing. In fact, a chairlift lands just outside the door. Don't ski? Don't worry. There are lots of other sports facilities to keep active travelers happy.

The resort, 6 miles northwest of Tahoe City, encompasses two buildings connected by a shopping promenade, evocative of a luxurious Sierra lodge. One, of a harmonious design inspired by Frank Lloyd Wright, houses public areas, restaurants, and meeting areas. In jarring contrast, the other multistory building is made of black glass and steel, and contains the guest rooms, often filled with well-heeled skiers or business types on expense accounts. A waterfall cascades from the lobby to the pool area.

The accommodations are not particularly spacious, but they're well equipped with ample closets, good lighting, ironing board, hair dryer, and a speakerphone. (If only they had desks.) Suites, with spacious entertaining areas and additional TVs and telephones, come in a baffling array of sizes, each with a name the staff expects everyone to understand instantly (executive suites, panorama suites, vista suites, junior suites).

Dining/Entertainment: Glissandi, the resort's top restaurant, serves haute cuisine in a window-wrapped dining room. Cascades is open for all-day buffet-style casual dining. Ristorante Montagna has tables both indoors and out. Sweet Potatoes Deli is open early for coffee, light bites, and picnic-style lunches. Bullwhackers Pub is a combination steak house and sports bar with pool table, regular live entertainment, and happy-hour specials.

Services: Room service, concierge, overnight laundry, supervised children's activities.

Facilities: 18-hole golf course, 3 heated swimming pools, 3 outdoor whirlpools, 8 tennis courts, fitness center, shopping arcade, 18 1/2 miles of groomed cross-country skiing trails (marked for hiking and biking in the summer), an ice-skating rink (in the winter only), and an equestrian center with riding stables.

✪ **The Shore House.** 7170 N. Lake Blvd., Tahoe Vista, CA 96148. ☎ **800/207-5160** or 530/546-7270. Fax 530/546-7130. 9 rms. $125–$165 double. Rates include breakfast. DISC, MC, V.

If you're looking for a cozy, romantic bed-and-breakfast right on Lake Tahoe's shoreline, you'll be hard pressed to find a better one than The Shore House. Hosts Marty and Barb are an immediately likable pair who have made pampering an art form, whether they're personally cooking your breakfast—Marty's an ex-chef—or planning a foolproof itinerary for your day.

Each individually decorated room has its own entrance, fabulous rough-hewn log furniture (handmade in Idaho), a minifridge, and a blissfully comfortable featherbed. All guests have access to a private and pristine patch of lakeside beach and landscaped lawn that overlook the entire lake. Boat owners can even make use of their six buoys and private dock. Planning on tying the knot? No problem: Marty's a minister of the Universal Life Church, Barb can provide the marriage license, and they even have a pretty area for small, romantic weddings (talk about a full-service B&B). Sure, prices are a bit steep, but if you are looking for a romantic weekend you won't soon forget, it's worth every penny.

Moderate

Meeks Bay Resort. P.O. Box 411, Tahoma, CA 96142 (summer); P.O. Box 70248, Reno, NV 89570 (winter). ☎ **530/525-7242** (summer) or 702/829-1977 (winter). 21 units. $75 double per night, $600–$3,000 per week. No credit cards. Closed Sept 16–June 14.

Lying 10 miles south of Tahoe City on Calif. 89, Meeks Bay Resort is one of the oldest hostelries on the lake and something of a historical landmark. This wide, sweeping lakefront fronts the best fine-sand beach in Tahoe. Known centuries ago to the Washoe Indians, Meeks Bay was opened as a public campground in 1920. During the next 50 years the resort grew to include cabins and other improvements, and attracted many celebrities from Southern California. Acquired by the U.S. Forest Service in 1974 under a special-use year-round permit, the property is open from June 15 to September 15 only. Most rentals are on a weekly basis and consist of cabins perched near the lake. Units vary in size, sleeping 2 to 12, and are modest without being austere. Each has a full kitchen, and some have fireplaces. Facilities include a beachfront cafe.

On the grounds, the Kehlet Mansion is the resort's first-rate accommodation. Owned at one time by William Hewlett, cofounder of the Hewlett-Packard Corporation, and later the summer residence of billionaire Gordon Getty, this pretty little house, on a rock that juts out into the lake, is one of the best places to stay in all of Tahoe. The mansion has seven bedrooms, three bathrooms, a large kitchen, living room, and water on three sides. The entire house is rented by the week, sleeps a dozen, and costs $3,000 for Wednesday-to-Wednesday bookings.

✪ **River Ranch Lodge & Restaurant.** On Calif. 89 (at Alpine Meadows Rd; P.O. Box 197), Tahoe City, CA 96145, Alpine Meadows. ☎ **800/535-9900** or 530/583-4264. 19 rms. TV TEL. Winter, $55–$125 double; spring/fall, $39–$75 double; summer, $55–$110 double. Rates include continental breakfast. AE, MC, V.

The River Ranch Lodge has long been one of our favorite places to stay in Lake Tahoe. Situated alongside the Truckee River, the lodge is mere minutes away from Alpine Meadows and Squaw Valley ski resorts, and a short drive (or ride along the bike path) into Tahoe City. The best rooms in this rustic lodge feature private balconies that overlook the river. All have antique furnishings. Rooms 9 and 10, the farthest from the road, are the top choices.

In the summer, guests relax under umbrellas on the huge patio overlooking the river, munching on barbecued chicken while watching the rafters float by. During the ski season, the River Ranch's spectacular circular cocktail lounge, which cantilevers over the river, is an immensely popular après-ski hangout. Also a big hit is the handsome River Ranch Lodge Restaurant, which serves fresh seafood, steaks, rack of lamb, and more exotic meats such as wood-oven-roasted Montana elk loin with a dried cherry-port sauce.

Sunnyside Lodge. 1850 W. Lake Blvd. (off Calif. 89; P.O. Box 5969), Tahoe City, CA 96145. ☎ **800/822-2754** or 530/583-7200. 23 rms. Apr 6–May 22, $90–$155 double; May 23–Oct 11, $160–$200 double; Dec 12–Apr 4, $110–$175 double. Rates include continental breakfast. AE, MC, V.

Built as a private home in 1908, this hotel and restaurant stands 2 miles south of Tahoe City. It's one of the grand old lodges still left on the lake and looks very much like a giant wooden cabin, with its typical Northern California architecture, complete with dormers, steep pitched roofs, and natural-wood siding. Stretching across the building, a large deck fronts a tiny marina. Directly on the lake, the place is rustic, but fairly sophisticated, with about two dozen individually decorated bedrooms with homey bark-covered timber tables and chairs as well as both contemporary and antique-style prints. Lakefront rooms, the most desirable, go for $15 more than the others. Only four have no views at all (unless you find parked cars attractive). Five units have rock fireplaces, and two have wet bars; ten are nonsmoking. Most of the lodge's ground floor is dominated by the popular Sunnyside Restaurant (see "Where to Dine," below).

✪ **Tahoma Meadows Bed & Breakfast.** 6821 W. Lake Blvd. (on Calif. 89, 8.5 miles from Tahoe City; P.O. Box 810), Homewood, CA 96141. ☎ **800/355-1596** or 530/525-1553. 11 rms. TV. $75–$145 double. Rates include breakfast. AE, DISC, MC, V.

Owners/innkeepers Bill and Missy Sanderman—two of the friendliest folks you'll ever meet—offer one of Tahoe's best B&B bargains: 11 private cabins perched on a gentle forest slope amongst a cadre of sugar pines and flowers. Missy, a talented water-colorist, has individually decorated each cabin in a decidedly warm and cozy style that is enhanced by her framed paintings of bucolic settings (many are bought by guests). All rooms have comfy king-, queen-, or twin-size beds; most have gas log fireplaces. Favorites are the cheery Sunflower and Fox Glove cabins, both equipped with clawfoot tubs. The largest cabin, Columbine, sleeps six and is ideal for families.

A full breakfast is served at the main lodge upstairs from the independently owned (and highly recommended) Stoneyridge Cafe. Nearby activities include skiing at Ski Homewood (including shuttle service), fly fishing at the Sanderman's friend's private trout-stocked lake, and sunbathing at the lakeshore just across the street.

Inexpensive

Lake of the Sky Motor Inn. 955 N. Lake Blvd. (P.O. Box 227), Tahoe City, CA 96145. ☎ **530/583-3305.** 23 rms. Apr 30–June 13, $50–$65 double; June 14–Sept 21, $81–$89 double; winter, $50–$89 double; holidays, $99–$105 double. AE, DC, DISC, MC, V.

Not much more than a 1960s-style A-frame motel in the heart of Tahoe City, the Lake of the Sky Motor Inn offers decent accommodations in a central location, only steps away from shops and restaurants. The place is popular with budget travelers and skiers, some of whom can be seen grabbing a very early morning cup of coffee and obviously itching to get out and tackle the wilderness. Rooms throughout have almost no style, but the housekeeping is good and the comfort level in tiptop motor-inn tradition. There's a heated swimming pool as well as a barbecue area.

WHERE TO DINE
SOUTH SHORE/SOUTH LAKE TAHOE
Expensive

Nepheles. 1169 Ski Run Blvd. ☎ **530/544-8130.** Main courses $15–$22. AE, CB, DC, DISC, MC, V. Daily 5–10pm. CALIFORNIA.

En route to the Heavenly Ski Resort, this old home with its stained-glass windows stops passing drivers, some of whom come in to sample the wares. Although the cuisine draws inspiration from all over the world, it is basically Californian, with market-fresh ingredients deftly handled by the kitchen. For a real taste of the north woods, nightly menu items feature whatever game is in season—venison, elk, or wild boar.

The menu offers the usual steaks for the ol' boys, but more exciting dishes as well, including swordfish in pineapple and a garlic-cilantro salsa (how California can you get?), or perhaps duck in the classic orange sauce enlivened with a healthy dash of bourbon. If you demand ketchup with your meal, it's likely to be a bottle from Indonesia. For dessert, consider their popular "decadence," then whip up your own dessert at the ultraprivate hot tubs adjoining the restaurant.

Moderate

Cantina Los Tres Hombres. 765 Emerald Bay Rd. ☎ **530/544-1233.** Main courses $7–$13. MC, V. Daily 11:30am–10:30pm. MEXICAN.

While this restaurant's cavernous tiki-bar interior can easily be mistaken to represent the South Seas, the food is unmistakably south-of-the-border. The bar and adjacent dining area are two of the busiest rooms in South Lake Tahoe. The menu is well priced and extensive, although it sticks to the tried-and-true Cal-Mex specialties such as tacos, burritos, and enchiladas. The chilies rellenos (cheese-stuffed peppers, battered and fried) get a thumbs-up, as does the crabmeat- and mushroom-stuffed enchiladas. The dishes are unimaginative but the portions are mountainous. Service is brisk but not unfriendly, and some patrons may have had more than their share of tequila.

Scusa! 1142 Ski Run Blvd. ☎ **530/542-0100.** Main courses $9–$18. MC, V. Daily 5–10pm. ITALIAN.

Also on the trail to the Heavenly Ski Resort, this cozy Italian spot may have a decor that errs a little garishly on the neon side, but the food more than compensates. Dishes are interspersed with enough surprises to keep the locals happy. The place is civilized, basic but clean, and the staff is usually cheerful and knowledgeable unless they're rushed or having bad hair days. Among the specialties are a smoked chicken and ravioli made with cheese ravioli, sun-dried tomatoes, capers, black olives, and sage butter, and a savory baked penne with smoked mozzarella, prosciutto, roasted garlic, and foccacia crust.

The Swiss House. 787 Emerald Bay Rd. ☎ **530/542-1717.** Main courses $10–$17. AE, MC, V. Daily 11:30am–2pm and 5–9pm. SWISS/CONTINENTAL.

The ambiance of this South Lake Tahoe spot is genuine enough and warmly appreciated by diners, especially those arriving from the ski slopes in winter to find a fire blazing away. Despite its name, the place is not exactly into yodeling and cowbells, but the dishes are often alpine. The operation seems to run like Swiss clockwork, and, although we've had better Wiener schnitzels than this, the one served here is perfectly adequate. There's also cheese fondue and raclette to take you back to the old country; it's warmly flavored but so filling you might not be able to finish.

Inexpensive

✪ **Sprouts Natural Foods Cafe.** 3125 Harrison St. (at Calif. 50 and Alameda St. next to the Yellow Sub). ☎ **530/541-6969.** Meals $3.75–$6.50. No credit cards. Daily 8am–10pm. HEALTHY FOOD.

Sprouts owner Tyler Cannon has filled a much-needed niche in South Lake, serving wholesome food that looks good, tastes good, and *is* good. Most everything is made in-house, including the soups, smoothies, and fresh-squeezed juices. Menu items range from rice bowls to sandwiches (try the Real Tahoe Turkey), huge burritos, coffee drinks, muffins, fresh-fruit smoothies, and a marvelous mayo-free tuna sandwich made with yogurt and packed with fresh veggies. Order from the counter, then scramble for a vacant seat (outdoor tables are coveted) and listen for your name as Tyler's buff and beautiful servers bring out your tray of earthy delights. This is also an excellent place to pack a picnic lunch, whether skiing, hiking, or mountain biking.

Yellow Sub. U.S. 50 and 983 Tallac Ave. ☎ **530/541-8808.** Sandwiches $3–$6. No credit cards. Daily 10:30am–10pm. SANDWICHES.

When it comes to picnic supplies, there's stiff competition in South Lake Tahoe: three sandwich shops on this single block alone. Still, our favorite is Yellow Sub, with its 21 kinds of overstuffed subs, made in 6-inch and 12-inch varieties. The shop is hidden in a small shopping center across from the El Dorado Campground.

NORTH SHORE/TAHOE CITY
Expensive
✪ **Plumpjack Cafe.** In the Plumpjacks Squaw Valley Inn, 1920 Squaw Valley Rd., Squaw Valley. ☎ **530/583-1576.** Reservations recommended. Main courses $17–$20. AE, DC, DISC, MC, V. Summer, Thurs– Mon 6–9:30pm; winter, daily 7–10:30am, 11am–3pm, and 5:30–10pm. MODERN AMERICAN.

This is the latest showcase for award-winning chef Maria Helm. Though dinner prices have dropped to slightly under $20 an entree (guests balked at the original outrageous prices), none of Plumpjack's high standards have diminished. Expect impeccable service regardless of your attire (this is, after all, a ski resort), and heady menu choices ranging from risotto with shiitake mushrooms and fava beans to roasted rabbit atop a golden potato puree and a fabulous dish of braised ox tails paired with horseradish mashed potatoes and carrots. Those already familiar with Plumpjack in San Francisco know that the reasonably priced wine list is among the nation's best.

✪ **Sunsets on the Lake.** 7320 N. Lake Blvd. (on Calif. 28 at the west end of Tahoe Vista), Tahoe Vista. ☎ **530/546-3640.** Reservations recommended. Main courses $12–$21.50. AE, DC, MC, V. Winter, daily 5–10pm; June 15–Sept 10, daily 11:30am–2:30pm and 5–10pm. NORTHERN ITALIAN/CALIFORNIA.

Here's something new: a lakeside restaurant in Tahoe where the food is as spectacular as the view. Chef Lew Orlady works wonders in the kitchen of this hugely popular restaurant built of gleaming pine. The rustic, romantic ambiance is helped along by a large fireplace, white-clothed tables, and—of course—a panoramic lake view. Recommended dishes include Orlady's fantastic braised lamb shank, a hefty hunk of tender lamb perfectly complemented with shiitake mushrooms, caramelized vegetables, and garlic mashed potatoes. If the duck is among the daily specials, order it: Each tender slice explodes with flavor. So does the Portobello mushroom entree, an enormous serving of house-baked foccacia stuffed with succulent wood-fried mushrooms, roasted chilies, goat cheese, glazed red onions, and sun-dried tomato aïoli. Pretty much everything on the large Northern Italian/Californian menu is a winner, which explains the large crowds that arrive via car or boat. When the snow melts, the heated outdoor deck is open for dining and drinks. Heck, they even provide blankets for an especially cozy sunset cocktail hour.

Wolfdale's. 640 N. Lake Blvd., Tahoe City. ☎ **530/583-5700.** Reservations recommended. Main courses $16–$21. MC, V. Wed–Mon 6–10pm (July–Aug open daily). CALIFORNIA/ JAPANESE.

Although it's one of Tahoe's top restaurants, situated in an idyllic lakeside setting, Wolfdale's is visually low key. Behind a rather unassuming wood-shingle exterior is a simple, clean interior that combines country-style American furnishings with Japanese-style blond woods and screens.

Though the menu changes frequently, meals here might begin with tea-smoked duck with peanut noodles and mango chutney or sashimi with ginger and wasabi. Spinach salad tossed with smoked local trout, olives, and grated eggs is particularly memorable. Main courses are equally inventive and include grilled game hen with

Thai dipping sauce or Alaskan halibut and sea scallops wrapped in Swiss chard with leek sauce. The chefs are capable and they know how to put a personal spin on regional ingredients. They also dare to be innovative and aren't afraid of fusing flavors and textures of the East and the West.

Moderate

Sunnyside Restaurant. At the Sunnyside Lodge, 1850 W. Lake Blvd., Tahoe City. ☎ **530/583-7200.** Main courses $13–$19. AE, MC, V. Oct–June, daily 5:30–9:30pm; July–Sept, daily 10am–10pm; Sun brunch, 9am–2pm. SEAFOOD/AMERICAN.

Located about 2 miles south of Tahoe City, on Calif. 89, the Sunnyside Restaurant is worth a detour. In summer, when the sun is shining, there's no more highly coveted table in Tahoe than one on Sunnyside's lakeside veranda. Guests can also dine in the lodge's more traditional dining room with its 1930s aura.

Nothing out of the ordinary here. At lunch the menu has fresh pastas, burgers, chicken, and fish sandwiches, together with a variety of soups and salads. Dinners are fancier, with such main courses as Australian lobster tail, lamb chops with roasted-garlic chutney butter, and fresh salmon oven-baked on a cedar plank. All dinners come with San Francisco–style sourdough bread, the chef's starch of the day, and a Caesar salad or cup of creamy chowder.

Tahoe House Restaurant and Bäckerei. 625 W. Lake Blvd., Tahoe City. ☎ **530/583-1377.** Main courses $9–$18. AE, DISC, MC, V. Bakery, daily 6am–10pm; deli lunch from 11am; dinner 5–10pm. SWISS/CALIFORNIA.

Serving Tahoe's skiers, boaters, and sunbathers for nearly two decades, Tahoe House is one of the oldest Swiss restaurants on the lake, located at the "Y" in Tahoe City. Though not a trendsetter, it is known locally as a reliable venue for good food at reasonable prices. Chef/owner Barbara Vogt's menu features some Swiss-German dishes such as Wiener schnitzel, Rahmschnitzel (veal with creamy mushroom sauce), grilled Bratwurst and pork Cordon Bleu. Steaks and seafood also satisfy, as do several pastas. The full-service European-style bakery items and desserts are wonderful, as exemplified by homebaked tortes, truffles, and chocolates. Dishes are based on the seasonal availability of ingredients, and usually only the freshest and best are used. Vogt has added a selection of lighter choices, including vegetarian dishes straight from the family farm.

Inexpensive

Bridgetender Tavern and Grill. 30 W. Lake Blvd. (at Fanny Bridge), Tahoe City. ☎ **530/583-3342.** Burgers, salads, and ribs $5–$7. MC, V. Daily 11am–2am. PUB FARE.

Though it's located in one most popular tourist areas in North Lake, the Bridgetender is a local's hangout through and through. Still, they're surprisingly tolerant of out-of-towners, who come for the cheap grub and huge selection of draft beers. The tavern is built around a trio of Ponderosa pines that meld in with the decor so well you hardly notice. Big burly burgers, salads, pork ribs, and such round out the menu, and the daily beer specials—posted on the wall in Day-Glo colors—are definitely worth going over. During the summer months, dine outside among the pines.

✪ Fire Sign Café. 1785 W. Lake Blvd., Tahoe City. ☎ **530/583-0871.** Breakfast and lunches $4–$9. MC, V. Daily 7am–3pm. AMERICAN.

Choosing a place to have breakfast in North Tahoe is a no-brainer: Since the late '70s the Fire Sign Café has been the local's choice—which explains the lines out the door on weekends. Just about everything is made from scratch, such as the delicious coffee cake that accompanies the big ol' plates of bacon and eggs or blackberry-buckwheat pancakes. Even the salmon for the chef/owner Bob Young's legendary salmon omelet is smoked in-house. Lunch—burgers, salads, sandwiches, burritos, etc.—is also quite popular, particularly when the outdoor patio is open.

Izzy's Burger Spa. 100 W. Lake Blvd. (at Fanny Bridge), Tahoe City. ☎ **530/583-4111.** Burgers $3.50–$6. No credit cards. Daily 11am–7pm. BURGERS.

It's just a simple, wooden A-frame building containing a small short-order grill, but Izzy's Burger Spa flips an unusually hefty and tasty burger and an equally enticing grilled chicken-breast sandwich. On a sunny day the best seats are at the picnic tables set out front. The restaurant is directly across from the Tahoe Yogurt Factory.

Tahoe Yogurt Factory. 125 W. Lake Blvd., Tahoe City. ☎ **530/581-5253.** Coffee $1; espresso $1.30–$2.60; yogurt $1.50–$3.25; sandwiches $2–$4. No credit cards. Daily 6am–6pm (summer, daily until 10pm). YOGURT/SANDWICHES.

This small coffee shack, located at the "Y" in Tahoe City, is frequently mentioned as "the best little cafe in Tahoe"—perhaps an overstatement—but it does have its fans. There's not much more to it than basic croissants, bagels, muffins, sandwiches, smoothies, and excellent java. Small tables are placed outdoors in the summer.

✪ **Za's.** 395 N. Lake Blvd. (across from the fire station), Tahoe City. ☎ **530/583-1812.** Main courses $6–$10. MC, V. Daily 4:30–9:30pm. ITALIAN.

The sign used to say PIZZA'S until half of it fell off, which is just as well because there's a whole lot more to Za's than just pizza. One of the most popular restaurants in North Tahoe, this little gem serves great Italian food at bargain prices. Example: A hefty plate of smoked chicken fettucini in a garlic-cream sauce with roasted bell peppers, fresh artichoke hearts, and mushrooms is under $10. Start with Pudge's Plate—a pleasing platter of fresh-roasted veggies doused in a balsamic vinaigrette—and a tumbler or two of chianti, then pick from the wide range of pastas, calzone, and pizza. Za's is a bit hard to find (look behind Pete-n-Peter's Saloon), but *mama-mia,* is it worth the search.

TAHOE AFTER DARK

Tahoe is not known particularly for its nightlife, although there's always something going on in the showrooms of the major casino hotels located in Stateline, just east of South Lake Tahoe. Call **Harrah's** (☎ 702/588-6611), **Harvey's** (☎ 702/588-2411), **Caesar's** (☎ 702/588-3515), and the **Lake Tahoe Horizon** (☎ 702/588-6211) for current show schedules and prices. Most cocktail shows cost $12 to $40, and headliners are likely to include the likes of Jay Leno or Johnny Mathis.

There's usually live music nightly in **Bullwhackers Pub,** at the Resort at Squaw Creek (☎ 530/583-6300), 5 miles west of Tahoe City. The **Pierce Street Annex,** 850 N. Lake Blvd. (☎ 530/583-5800), behind the Safeway in Tahoe City, has pool tables, shuffleboard, and DJ dancing every night. It's one of the livelier places around.

The college crowd will feel at home at **Humpty's,** 877 N. Lake Blvd., across from Safeway (☎ 530/583-4867), which has the cheapest drinks in town—particularly during happy hour from 4 to 9pm—and live rock music most nights.

If it's just a casual cocktail you're after, our favorite spot is the handsome fireside lounge at **River Ranch Lodge,** which cantilevers over a turbulent stretch of the Truckee River (on Calif. 89 at the entrance to Alpine Meadows, about 10 miles northwest of Tahoe City; ☎ 530/583-4264).

9

The High Sierra: Yosemite, Mammoth Lakes & Sequoia & Kings Canyon

by Erika Lenkert and Matthew R. Poole

The national parks of California's Sierra are a mecca for travelers from across the globe. The big attraction is Yosemite, of course, but the entire region is packed with natural wonders and adventures.

It was in Yosemite that naturalist John Muir found "the most songful streams in the world . . . the noblest forests, the loftiest granite domes, the deepest ice sculptured canyons." Even today few visitors would disagree with Muir's early impressions as they explore this land of waterfalls, towering cliffs, wilderness, snow fields, alpine lakes, river beaches, and waterfalls. Yosemite Valley is riddled with dramatic waterfalls, sheer walls, and domes and peaks reaching toward the sky. The valley is the most central and accessible part of the park, stretching for some 20 miles, all the way from Wawona Tunnel in the west to Curry Village in the east. If you visit during spring or early fall, you'll encounter fewer problems with crowds.

Across the heart of the Sierra Nevada, in east-central California, sprawl Sequoia and Kings Canyon national parks, which are administered as one entity. Their peaks stretch across some 1,300 square miles, taking in the giant sequoias for which they're fabled. This is a land of alpine lakes, granite peaks, and deep canyons. At 14,495 feet, Mount Whitney is the highest point in the lower 48 states.

Another big attraction in the area is Mammoth Lakes, one of the major playgrounds of California, where you can enjoy dozens of recreational activities in a setting of lakes, streams, waterfalls, and rugged meadows that bring the Austrian countryside to mind.

Because of the vast popularity of the parks and natural areas, facilities can be strained at peak visiting times. Always make your reservations as far in advance as possible (and that definitely includes camping). You'll be glad you did.

1 Merced: Gateway to Yosemite

Merced is an ideal overnight stop en route to Yosemite.

ESSENTIALS

GETTING THERE   If you're driving from San Francisco, take I-580 east to I-5 south to Calif. 140 east.

Merced Municipal Airport, 20 Macready Dr. (☎ 209/385-6873), is served by **Shuttle by United** (☎ 800/241-6522).

Amtrak (☎ **800/USA-RAIL**), which operates along the Central Valley from Sacramento to Bakersfield, stops at Merced.

VISITOR INFORMATION   For information, contact the **Merced Convention & Visitors Bureau,** 690 W. 16th St., Merced, CA 95340 (☎ **800/446-5353** or 209/384-3333).

WHERE TO STAY

Best Western Sequoia Inn. 1213 V St. (at West 13th St.), Merced, CA 95340. ☎ **800/ 528-1234** or 209/723-3711. Fax 209/722-8551. 98 rms. A/C TV TEL. $62 double, $72 double with refrigerator/microwave. Additional person $5 extra. AE, CB, DC, DISC, MC, V.

Set about a mile north of Merced's center, relatively isolated from its neighbors, the two-story Sequoia Inn was built in the 1960s and renovated in 1995, and is probably your best option in Merced. The bedrooms are cozy if bland and contain two phones and a coffeemaker. There's a run-of-the-mill restaurant on the premises and a swimming pool.

Holiday Inn Express. 730 Motel Dr., Merced, CA 95340. ☎ **800/HOLIDAY** or 209/ 383-0333. Fax 209/383-0643. 65 rms. A/C TV TEL. $75 double. Rates include continental breakfast. 10% discounts for AAA or AARP members. AE, DC, MC, V.

Built in 1992, this is one of the newest hotels in Merced and was designed in the standard Holiday Inn format. Its 3 stories rise about a mile south of the town center. It's a good choice for families. The bedrooms are nothing out of the ordinary, but they're clean and comfortable, with modern amenities. It may be so hot outside you'll literally worship the hotel's outdoor pool and the air-conditioning in your room. Several fast-food joints lie within walking distance.

Ramada Inn. Calif. 99 and Childs Ave., Merced, CA 95340. ☎ **800/2-RAMADA** or 209/ 723-3121. Fax 209/723-0127. 112 rms. A/C TV TEL. $69 double Sun–Thurs; $79 double Fri–Sat. AE, DISC, MC, V.

New owners are working hard to make this more than merely a safe and inexpensive stopover en route to Yosemite. The rather unremarkable building lies 3 miles south of the center of Merced, and though some of the decor may be motel-bland, new textiles have recently been added and a few larger rooms now have marble bathrooms. On the premises is a swimming pool, which comes as a blessed relief during the real summer scorchers. There's also a fairly basic restaurant.

WHERE TO DINE

The Branding Iron. 640 W. 16th St. ☎ **209/722-1822.** Main courses $13–$20. AE, MC, V. Mon–Fri 11:30am–2pm; daily 5:30–9pm. STEAK/SEAFOOD.

This is by far the most animated, most popular, and most frenetic steak and seafood house in Merced. Set in the heart of town, behind trademark green awnings, it has plank-sided walls accented with burned-in marks from branding irons. The portions are massive. Prime rib is the most consistently popular, although seafood, chicken, and lobster (the most expensive item) are close seconds. Soup, salad, potato, and vegetables all accompany the main course.

Lenny's. 1052 W. Main St. (at R St.). ☎ **209/722-0350.** Dinner platters $10–$16. AE, MC, V. Mon–Sat 7am–10pm, Sun 9am–9pm. ITALIAN.

This is one of the two most prominent restaurants in Merced, feeding a stream of newcomers who tend to return after they've explored Yosemite. The menu proudly offers old-world recipes handed down in the owner's family for several generations, with lots of all-American twists. Lunch is loaded with pastas and at least 15 other dishes. Dinners are more elaborate, usually featuring chicken, veal, pasta, and vegetarian selections. All sauces, as well as all the sausages, are made on the premises in the style of long-ago Italy.

You won't lack for visual distraction here. Glass-fronted refrigerators, set end-to-end, display more than 150 kinds of beers, and one corner of the place is devoted to an espresso bar.

2 Yosemite National Park

by Andrew Rice; updated by Stacey Wells

This area first became widely known to white men when a troop of U.S. soldiers in the Mariposa Battalion, sent to chase down a band of Native Americans, stumbled upon this natural wonder and were awestruck by its beauty. They regaled their friends with tales of its impossible geography when they got home, and Yosemite's popularity has been steadily increasing ever since.

It's a place of record-setting statistics: the highest waterfall in North America and 3 of the world's 10 tallest (Upper Yosemite Falls, Ribbon Falls, and Sentinel Falls); the tallest and largest single granite monolith in the world (El Capitan); the most recognizable mountain (Half Dome); one of the world's largest trees (the Grizzly Giant in the Mariposa Grove); and literally thousands of rare plant and animal species.

What most sets the valley apart is its incredible geology. The Sierra Nevada were formed between 10 and 80 million years ago when a tremendous geological uplift pushed layers of granite lying under the ocean up into an incredible mountain range. Cracks and rifts in the rock gave erosion a start at carving canyons and valleys. Then, during the last ice age, at least three glaciers flowed through the valley, sheering vertical faces of stone and hauling away the rubble. The last glacier retreated 10,000 to 15,000 years ago, but left its legacy in the incredible number and size of the waterfalls pouring into the valley from hanging side canyons. From the 4,000-foot-high valley floor, the 8,000-foot tops of El Capitan, Half Dome, and Glacier Point look like the top of the world, but they're small in comparison to the highest mountains in the park, some of which reach almost 14,000 feet. The 7-square-mile valley is really a huge bathtub drain for the combined runoff of hundreds of square miles of snow-covered peaks.

High-country creeks flush with snowmelt catapult over the abyss left by the glaciers and form an outrageous variety of falls, from tiny ribbons that never reach the ground to the torrents of Nevada and Vernal falls. Combined with the shadows and lighting of the deep valley, the effect of all this falling water is mesmerizing. On a clear spring morning you'll see more rainbows than you can count, and a base note of roaring water echoes through the entire valley.

All that vertical stone gets put to use by hundreds who flock to the park for some of the finest climbing anywhere. Sharp-eyed visitors will spot a lot of climbers hanging off the sheer faces of Yosemite's famous walls, such as El Capitan and Half Dome. Sometimes spending as long as 10 days slung from the rock, the world's best climbers are here to see and be seen proving their mettle. At the base of the big walls you'll find climbers of all abilities practicing moves and belaying techniques on smaller pitches.

The valley is also home to beautiful meadows and the Merced River. When the last glacier retreated, its debris dammed the Merced and formed a lake. Eventually sediment from the river filled the lake and created the rich and level valley floor we see today. Tiny Mirror Lake was created later by rockfall that dammed up Tenya Creek; the addition of a man-made dam in 1890 made it more of a lake than a pond. Rafters and inner-tubers enjoy the slow-moving Merced during the heat of summer.

Yosemite National Park

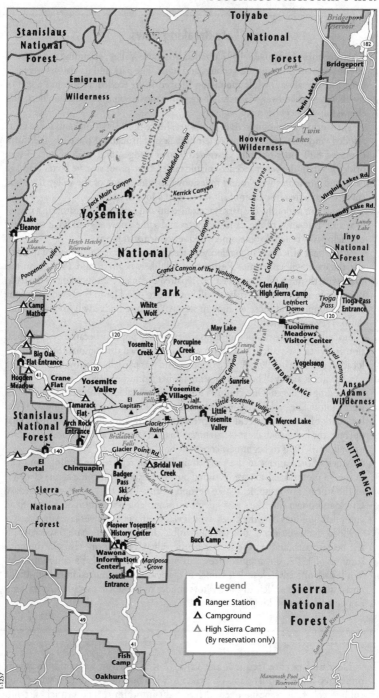

Stanislaus
National
Forest

Emigrant
Wilderness

Toiyabe

National

Forest

Bridgeport

Buckeye Creek

Bridgeport
Reservoir

182

Twin Lakes Rd

Twin
Lakes

Hoover
Wilderness

Virginia Lakes Rd.

Lundy Lake Rd.

Lundy
Lake

Pacific Crest Trail

Stubblefield Canyon

Jack Main Canyon

Kerrick Canyon

Yosemite

Lake
Eleanor

Lake
Eleanor

National

Hetch Hetchy
Reservoir

Poopenaut Valley

Tuolumne River

Rodgers Canyon

Matterhorn Canyon

Cold Canyon

Grand Canyon of the Tuolumne River

Tuolumne River

Pacific Crest Trail

Inyo

National

Forest

Park

Glen Aulin
High Sierra Camp

Lembert
Dome

Tioga
Pass

Tioga Pass
Entrance

120

Camp
Mather

White
Wolf

May Lake

Tuolumne
Meadows
Visitor Center

Lyell Canyon

Big Oak
Flat Entrance

Yosemite
Creek

Porcupine
Creek

Tenaya
Lake

Vogelsang

120

Hodgden
Meadow

Crane
Flat

41

120

Yosemite
Valley

Yosemite
Falls

El Capitan

Tenaya Canyon

John Muir Trail

Sunrise

CATHEDRAL RANGE

Ansel
Adams
Wilderness

Tamarack
Flat

Yosemite
Village

Half
Dome

Little
Yosemite
Valley

Little Yosemite Valley

Merced River

Merced Lake

Stanislaus

National

Forest

Arch Rock
Entrance

Glacier
Point

140

El
Portal

Bridalveil
Falls

Glacier Point Rd.

RITTER RANGE

Chinquapin

Badger
Pass
Ski
Area

Bridal Veil
Creek

Bridalveil Creek

Sierra

National

Forest

S. Fork Merced River

41

Pioneer Yosemite
History Center

Wawona

Buck Camp

Wawona
Information
Center

Mariposa
Grove

South
Entrance

Sierra

National

Forest

49

41

Fish
Camp

Oakhurst

San Joaquin River

Mammoth Pool
Reservoir

Legend

🏠 Ranger Station

▲ Campground

▲ High Sierra Camp
(By reservation only)

1-1257

265

Late-Breaking News

A severe storm in January 1997 flooded Yosemite Valley, stranding visitors and wreaking havoc on campsites, cabins, and trails. The park and its visitors were isolated for several days while the raging Merced River eroded a mile and a half of riverbank, washed over 550 acres of meadow, moved building-size boulders, and chewed up huge portions of highway.

The storm ruined hundreds of campsites. More than 350 motel and lodge units flooded, and 440 employees were left homeless. Throughout the park, the storm damaged 800 miles of trails, destroyed 9 road bridges, and washed out 33 trail bridges. When the water receded, picnic tables, bear-proof storage boxes, garbage cans, and fire grates were found miles downstream. Much of the valley floor was covered beneath a fine layer of silt more than a foot deep.

Almost miraculously, the park was cleaned up and reopened to visitors in a matter of weeks. But some of the damage lingers and some knowledge of what to expect can help visitors avoid some otherwise inevitable frustration.

While park officials plan to relocate or restore many of the amenities lost in January, the work will take time. Restoration will likely begin in mid-1998. Nonstop road work through the spring of 1997 repaired the main thoroughfare to the park, but once inside the valley, visitors will not have to travel far to find evidence of the flood. Campers and those wishing to stay at Yosemite Lodge will find accommodations severely limited.

Several riverfront campgrounds, once extremely popular because of their location and vistas, were destroyed. Two will remain closed throughout 1997, with relocation pending in 1998. A third campground was partially destroyed. Remaining campgrounds survived because they are farther from the river.

Flooding damaged 246 of the 495 rooms once available at Yosemite Lodge. Most were cabins. The park's long-term plan calls for relocating and rebuilding what was lost. Park officials were deciding at press time whether to allow the company that operates the lodge to make minor renovations and reopen the much-needed rooms, or wait until 1998 to begin new construction.

Much of the damage to the park's trails has been repaired, including almost all of the 33 footbridges that were washed out. Hikers will still come across evidence of the storm. For example, a hike beyond Mirror Lake that loops across Tenaya Creek and down the lake's east side now resembles a beautiful moonscape. Sand and piled boulders clog the creek, which was itself a raging river last January.

Flood damage such as this remains visible throughout the park, especially off the beaten path and on the fringes of the valley. During my visits in the midsummer of 1997, silt, toppled trees, and broken branches were a common sight. While park officials have ordered much of the devastation removed from high-traffic areas, some has been left to give visitors an idea of the storm's wrath. Observing it can be both breathtaking and ominous.

—Stacey Wells

Deer and coyote frequent the valley, often causing vehicular mayhem as one heavy-footed tourist slams on brakes to whip out the Handi-cam while another rubbernecker, also mesmerized, drives right into him. Metal crunches, tempers flare, and the deer daintily hops away, doubtlessly amused at the stupidity it just witnessed.

Bears, too, are at home in the valley. The name "Yosemite" derives from the Native American word *Yohamite,* "killer among us." Grizzlies are gone from the park now, but black bears are plentiful. Rather than posing pretty for the cameras in broad daylight, they make their presence known through late-night plundering of ice chests and food in the campgrounds.

Right in the middle of the valley's thickest urban cluster is the **Valley Visitor Center** (☎ 209/372-0299), with exhibits that will teach you about glacial geology, history, and the park's flora and fauna. Check out the **Indian Cultural Museum** next door for insight into what life in the park was once like. Excellent exhibits highlight the Miwok and Paiute cultures that thrived here; the museum has a great collection of baskets and other artifacts. Behind the center is a re-creation of an Ahwahneechee village, a Native American settlement like those that once existed here. The Museum Gallery houses a number of fine Ansel Adams prints as well as other artists' works.

You'll also find much history and memorabilia from the career of nature writer John Muir, one of the founders of the conservation movement. Muir's name is virtually synonymous with Yosemite.

While it's easy to let the tremendous beauty of the valley monopolize your attention, remember that 95% of Yosemite is wilderness. Of the four million visitors who come to the park each year, very few ever venture more than a mile from their cars. That leaves most of Yosemite's 750,000 acres open for anyone adventurous enough to hike a few miles. Even though the valley is a hands-down winner for dramatic freak-of-nature displays, the high country offers a more subtle kind of beauty: glacial lakes, roaring rivers, and miles of granite spires and domes. In the park's southwest corner, the Mariposa Grove is a striking forest of rare sequoias, the world's largest trees, as well as several meadows and the rushing south fork of the Merced River.

Tenaya Lake and Tuolumne Meadows are two of the most popular high-country destinations, as well as starting points for many great trails to the backcountry. Whether you're here for a week or just a day, both are ideal places to spend the day fishing, climbing, or hiking among the spectacular granite of the high country. Since this area of the park is under snow from November to June, the short season we call summer is really more like spring. From snowmelt to the first snowfall, the high country explodes with wildflowers and long-dormant wildlife trying to make the most of the short season.

JUST THE FACTS

ENTRY POINTS There are four main entrances to the park. Most valley visitors enter through the **Arch Rock Entrance Station** on Calif. 140. The best entrance for the Mariposa Grove and Wawona is the **South Entrance** on Calif. 41 from Mariposa. If you're going to the high country, you'll save a lot of time by coming in through the **Big Oak Flat Entrance,** which puts you straight onto Tioga Road without forcing you to deal with the congested valley. The **Tioga Pass Entrance** is only open in summer and is only really relevant if you're coming from the east side of the Sierra (in which case it's your only choice). A fifth, little-used entrance is the **Hetch Hetchy Entrance** in the euphonious Poopenaut Valley, on a dead-end road.

FEES It's $20 per car per week to enter the park or $10 per person per week. Annual Yosemite Passes are a steal at only $40. Wilderness permits are free, but reserving them requires a $3 fee per person. If you're driving across the Sierra without stopping to enjoy the park's natural wonders, you'll only be charged $5 at the park entrance.

VISITOR CENTERS & INFORMATION There's a central, 24-hour recorded information line for the park (☎ 209/372-0200). All visitor-related service lines, including hotels and information, can be accessed by touch-tone phone at ☎ **209/372-1000.**

By far the biggest visitor center is the **Valley Visitor Center** (☎ 209/372-0299). The **Wawona Ranger Station** (☎ **209/372-0564**) and **Big Oak Flat Information Center** (☎ **209/372-0615**) give general park information. For interesting biological and geological displays about the high Sierra, as well as trail advice, the **Tuolumne Meadows Visitor Center** (☎ **209/372-0263**) is great. All three can provide you with maps plus more newspapers, books, and photocopied leaflets than you'll ever read.

REGULATIONS Rangers in the Yosemite Valley spend more time being cops than being rangers. They even have their own jail, so don't do anything here you wouldn't do in your hometown—this isn't the Wild West. Despite the pressure, park regulations are pretty simple. Wilderness permits are required for all overnight backpacking trips. Fishing licenses are required. Utilize proper food-storage methods in bear country. Don't collect firewood around campgrounds. No off-road bicycle riding. Dogs are allowed in the park but must be leashed and are forbidden from trails. Don't feed the animals.

SEASONS Winter is one of the nicest times to visit the valley. It isn't crowded, as it is during summer, and a dusting of snow provides a stark contrast to all that granite. To see the waterfalls at their best, come in spring when snowmelt is at its peak. Fall can be cool, but it's beautiful and much less crowded than summer.

The high country is under about 20 feet of snow from November to May, so unless you're snow camping, summer is pretty much the only camping season. Even in summer, thundershowers are an almost-daily occurrence, and snow is not uncommon. Mosquitoes can be a plague during the peak of summer but get better after the first freeze.

RANGER PROGRAMS Even though they're overworked just trying to keep the peace, Yosemite's wonderful rangers also take time to lead a number of educational and interpretive programs ranging from backcountry hikes to fireside talks to snow-country survival clinics. Call the main park-information number with specific requests for the season and park area you'll be visiting. Also a great service are the free painting, drawing, and photography classes offered spring to fall and on holiday weekends in winter at the Art Activity Center next to the Museum Gallery.

AVOIDING THE CROWDS Unfortunately, popularity isn't always the greatest thing for wild places. Over the last 20 years, tourist-magnet Yosemite Valley has set records for the worst crowding, noise, crime, and traffic in any California national park. More than 4.1 million visitors came in 1996.

The park covers more than 1,000 square miles, but most visitors flock to the floor of Yosemite Valley, a 1-mile-wide, 7-mile-long freak of glacial scouring that tore a deep and steep valley from the solid granite of the Sierra Nevada. It's still one of the most beautiful places on earth, but the Yosemite Valley becomes a total zoo anytime between Memorial Day and Labor Day. To make it worse, the National Park Service, which once called for eliminating auto traffic in the valley and reducing infrastructure inside the park, has done the opposite. They continue to allow kitschy concession signs, rinky-dink curio shops, an auto-repair garage, several hotels, a post office, a small hospital, and last but certainly not least, a jail, turning Yosemite Valley into an urban mess, albeit a pretty one.

Cars line up bumper to bumper on almost any busy weekend. Until now, federal authorities did not show enough courage to implement one of several plans that would reduce traffic. But in 1995, Yosemite's new superintendent closed the entrances to the park 11 times between Memorial Day and mid-August when the number of visitors reached the park's quota; she turned away 10,000 vehicles.

The park's latest plan to streamline the traffic flow is a day-use reservation system, scheduled to launch in mid-1998. Currently it's anyone's guess whether or not the measures implemented to control crowds will be successful.

In the meantime, to enjoy the reasons all those people flock to the valley without having to deal with the hordes themselves, our best advice is to try to come before Memorial Day or after Labor Day.

If you must go in summer, try to do your part to help out. It's not so much the numbers of people that are ruining the valley, but their insistence on driving from attraction to attraction within the valley. Once you're here, park your car and bike, hike, or ride the shuttle buses. Curry Village and Yosemite Lodge both rent bikes in the summer (☎ **209/372-8367**). It may take longer to get from point A to point B, but you're in one of the most gorgeous places on earth—so why hurry?

SEEING THE HIGHLIGHTS
The Valley

First-time visitors are often completely dumbstruck as they enter the valley from the west. The first two things you'll see are the delicate and beautiful **Bridal Veil Falls** and the immense face of **El Capitan,** a beautiful and anything-but-delicate 3,593-foot-tall solid-granite rock. A short trail leads to the base of Bridal Veil, which at 620 feet tall is only a medium-size fall by park standards, but one of the prettiest.

This is a perfect chance to get those knee-jerk tourist impulses under control early: Resist the temptation to rush around bagging sights like they're feathers for your cap. Instead, take your time and look around. One of the best things about the valley is that many of its most famous features are visible from all over. Instead of rushing to the base of every waterfall or famous rock face and getting a crick in your neck from staring straight up, go to the visitor center and spend a half hour learning something about the features of the valley. Buy the excellent "Map and Guide to Yosemite Valley" for $2.50; it describes many excellent hikes and short nature walks. Then go take a look. Walking and biking are the best way to get around. To cover longer distances, the park shuttles run frequently and everywhere.

If you absolutely must see it all and want to have someone tell you what you're seeing, the **Valley Floor Tour** is a 2-hour narrated bus or open-air tram tour (depending on season) that provides an introduction to the valley's natural history, geology, and human culture for $16. Purchase tickets at valley hotels or call ☎ **209/372-1240** for advance reservations.

Three-quarters of a mile from the visitor center is the **Ahwahnee Hotel.** Unlike the rest of the hotel accommodations in the park (see "Accomodations," below), the Ahwahnee actually lives up to its surroundings. The native granite-and-timber lodge was built in 1927 and reflects an era when grand hotels were, well, grand. Fireplaces bigger than most Manhattan studio apartments warm the immense common rooms. Parlors and halls are filled with antique Native American rugs. Don't worry about what you're wearing unless you're going to dinner—this is Yosemite, after all.

The best single view in the valley is from **Sentinel Bridge** over the Merced River. At sunset, Half Dome's face functions as a projection screen for all the sinking sun's hues from yellow to pink to dark purple, and the river reflects it all. Ansel Adams took one of his most famous photographs from this very spot.

VALLEY WALKS & HIKES   Yosemite Falls is within a short stroll of the visitor center. You can actually see it better elsewhere in the valley, but it's really impressive to stand at the base of all that falling water. The wind, noise, and blowing spray generated when millions of gallons catapult 2,425 feet through space onto the rocks below are sometimes so overwhelming you can barely stand on the bridge below.

If you want more, the **Yosemite Falls Trail** zigzags 3¹/₂ miles from Sunnyside Campground to the top of Upper Yosemite Fall. This trail gives you an inkling of the weird, vertically oriented world climbers enter when they head up Yosemite's sheer walls. As you climb this narrow switchback trail, the valley floor drops away until people below look like ants, but the top doesn't appear any closer. It's a little unnerving at first. Plan on spending all day on this 7-mile round-trip because of the incredibly steep climb.

A mile-long trail leads from the Valley Stables (shuttle bus stop 17; no car parking) to **Mirror Lake.** The already-tiny lake is gradually becoming a meadow as it fills with silt, but the reflections of the valley walls and sky on its surface remain one of the park's most introspective sights.

Also accessible from the Valley Stables or nearby Happy Isles is the best valley hike of all—the **John Muir Trail** to Vernal and Nevada falls. It follows the Sierra crest 200 miles south to Mt. Whitney, but you only need go 1¹/₂ miles round-trip to get a great view of 317-foot Vernal Fall. Add another 1¹/₂ miles and 1,000 vertical feet for the climb to the top of Vernal Fall on the **Mist Trail,** where you'll get wet as you climb directly alongside the falls. On top of Vernal and before the base of Nevada Fall is a beautiful little valley and deep pool. For a truly outrageous view of the valley and one heck of a workout, continue on up the Mist Trail to the top of Nevada Fall. From 2,000 feet above Happy Isles where you began, it's a dizzying view straight down the face of the fall. To the east is an interesting profile perspective on Half Dome. Return either by the Mist Trail or the slightly easier John Muir Trail for a total 7-mile round-trip hike.

Half Dome may look insurmountable to anyone but an expert rock climber, but thousands every year take the popular cable route up the backside. It's almost 17 miles round-trip and a 4,900-foot elevation gain from Happy Isle on the John Muir Trail. Many do it in a day, starting at first light and rushing home to beat nightfall. A more relaxed strategy is to camp in the backpacking campground in Little Yosemite Valley just past Nevada Fall. From here the summit is an easy striking distance to the base of Half Dome. You must climb up a very steep granite face using steel cables installed by the park service. During summer, boards are installed as crossbeams, but they're still far apart. Wear shoes with lots of traction and bring your own leather gloves for the cables (your hands will thank you). The view from the top is an unbeatable vista of the high country, Tenaya Canyon, Glacier Point, and the awe-inspiring abyss of the valley below. When you shuffle up to the overhanging lip for a look down the face, be extremely careful not to kick rocks or anything else onto the climbers below who are earning this view the hard way.

THE SOUTHWEST CORNER

This corner of the park is densely forested and gently sculpted in comparison to the stark granite that makes up so much of the park. Coming from the valley, Calif. 41 passes through a long tunnel. Just prior to the entrance is **Tunnel View,** site of another famous Ansel Adams photograph, and the best scenic outlook of the valley accessible by automobile. Virtually the whole valley is laid out below: Half Dome and Yosemite Falls straight ahead in the distance, Bridal Veil to the right, and El Capitan to the left.

A few miles past the tunnel, Glacier Point Road turns off to the east. Closed in winter, this winding road leads to a picnic area at **Glacier Point,** site of another fabulous view of the valley, this time 3,000 feet below. Schedule at least an hour to drive here from the valley and an hour or two to absorb the view. This is a good place to study the glacial scouring of the valley below; the Glacier Point perspective makes it easy to picture the valley below filled with sheets of ice.

Some 30 miles south of the valley on Calif. 41 is the **Wawona Hotel** and the **Pioneer Yosemite History Center.** In 1879 the Wawona was the first lodge built in the state reserve that would later become the national park. Its Victorian architecture evokes a time when travelers spent several days in horse-drawn wagons to get to the park. What a welcome stop it must have been. The Pioneer center is a collection of early homesteading log buildings across the river from the Wawona.

One of the primary reasons Yosemite was first set aside as a park was the **Mariposa Grove** of sequoias. (Many good trails lead through the grove.) These huge trees have personalities that match their gargantuan size. Single limbs on the biggest tree in the grove, the Grizzly Giant, are 10 feet thick. The tree itself is 209 feet tall, 32 feet in diameter, and more than 2,700 years old. Totally out of proportion with the size of the trees are the tiny cones of the sequoia. Smaller than a baseball and tightly closed, the cones won't release their cargo of seeds until opened by fire.

THE HIGH COUNTRY

The high country of Yosemite has the most grandiose landscape in the entire Sierra Nevada. Dome after dome of beautifully crystalline granite reflects the sunlight above deep-green meadows and icy-cold rivers.

Tioga Pass is the gateway to the high country. At times it clings to the side of steep rock faces; in other places it weaves through canyon bottoms. Several good campgrounds make it a pleasing overnight alternative to fighting summertime crowds in the valley, though use is increasing here, too. Unlike the valley, a car is vital to getting around as the only public transportation is the once-a-day bus to Tuolumne Meadows. Leaving the valley at 8am, the bus will let you off anywhere along the way. The driver waits 2 hours at Tuolumne Meadows, which isn't much time to see anything, then heads back down to the valley, returning around 4pm. The one-way fare is $13, slightly less to intermediate destinations.

Tenaya Lake is a popular windsurfing, fishing, canoeing, sailing, and swimming spot. The water is very chilly. Many good hikes lead into the high country from here, and the granite domes surrounding the lake are popular with climbers. Fishing here varies greatly from year to year.

Near the top of Tioga Pass is stunning **Tuolumne Meadows.** This enormous meadow covering several square miles is bordered by the Tuolumne River on one side and spectacular granite peaks on the other. The meadow is cut by many stream channels full of trout, and herds of mule deer are almost always present. The **Tuolumne Meadows Lodge** and store is a welcome counterpoint to the overdeveloped valley. In winter the canvas roofs are removed and the buildings fill with snow. You can buy last-minute backpacking supplies here, and there's a basic burgers-and-fries cafe.

TUOLUMNE MEADOWS HIKES & WALKS   So many hikes lead from here into the backcountry that it's impossible to do them justice. A good trail passes an icy-cold spring and traverses several meadows.

On the far bank of the Tuolumne from the meadow, a trail leads downriver, eventually passing through the grand canyon of the Tuolumne and exiting at Hetch Hetchy. Shorter hikes will take you downriver past rapids and cascades.

An interesting geological quirk is the **Soda Spring** on the far side of Tuolumne Meadow from the road. This bubbling spring gushes carbonated water from a hole in the ground. A small log cabin marks its site.

For a great selection of Yosemite high-country hikes and backpacking trips, consult some of the specialized guidebooks to the area. *Tuolumne Meadows,* a hiking guide by Jeffrey B. Shaffer and Thomas Winnett, and *Yosemite National Park* by Thomas Winnett and Jason Winnett, both published by Wilderness Press, are two of the best.

YOSEMITE SPORTS & ACTIVITIES

BIKING　Biking is the perfect way to see the valley. Eight miles of bike paths in addition to the valley roads make this an even better option. You can rent one-speeds at the Yosemite Lodge or Curry Village for $5.25 per hour or $20 per day. If you want a fancier bike, you'll have to bring it from home. All trails in the park are closed to mountain bikes.

FISHING　The Merced River in the valley is catch and release only, and barbless hooks are required. High-country lakes and streams are literally leaping with trout. A California license is required and available in the park at the Yosemite Village Sportshop.

HORSEBACK RIDING　Three stables offer scenic day rides and multiday pack excursions in the park. **Yosemite Valley Stables** (☎ **209/372-8348**) is open spring to fall. The other two—**Wawona** (☎ **209/375-6502**) and **Tuolumne Stables** (☎ **209/372-8427**)—only operate in summer. Day rides vary from $30 to $60, depending on length. Multiday backcountry trips cost roughly $100 per day and must be booked almost a year in advance. The park wranglers can also be hired to make resupply drops at any of the backcountry High Sierra camps if you want to arrange for a food drop while on an extended trip.

ICE-SKATING　In winter the **Curry Village Ice Rink** is a lot of fun. It's outdoors and melts quickly when the weather warms up. Rates are $5 for adults and $4.50 for children. Skate rentals are available.

ROCK CLIMBING　Much of the most important technical advancement in rock climbing came out of the highly competitive Yosemite Valley climbing scene of the 1970s and 1980s. Though other places have taken some of the limelight, Yosemite is still one of the most desirable climbing destinations in the world.

The **Yosemite Mountaineering School** runs classes for beginners through advanced climbers (☎ **209/372-8444** in the valley, or 209/372-8435 at Tuolumne Meadows). Considered one of the best climbing schools in the world, it offers a basic lesson for $100 per person per day that will teach you basic body moves and rappelling, and will take you on a single pitch climb. Classes run from early spring to early October in the valley, less often in Tuolumne Meadows.

SKIING　Yes, there is an alpine ski area in Yosemite, but it isn't much of one. Opened in 1935, **Badger Pass** (☎ **209/372-8430**) is the oldest operating ski area in California. Four chairs and two T-bars cover a compact mountain of beginner and intermediate runs. At $28 per day for adults and $13 for children on weekends (about 20% cheaper midweek), it's a great place to learn how to ski or snowboard. If you're a good skier or boarder already, don't bother.

Yosemite is a better destination for cross-country skiers and snowshoers. Both the Badger Pass ski school and the mountaineering school run trips and lessons for all abilities, ranging from basic technique to trans-Sierra crossings. If you're on your own, Crane Flat is a good place to go, as is the groomed track up to Glacier Point, a 20-mile round-trip.

CAMPING

Campgrounds in Yosemite can be reserved up to 4 months in advance through **Destinet** (☎ 800/436-7275). During the busy season all valley campsites sell out within hours of becoming available on the service.

VALLEY CAMPGROUNDS

Until January 1997, the park had five car campgrounds that were always full except in the dead of winter. Now the park has half the number of campsites available, and getting a reservation on short notice takes a minor miracle. Tosemit Valley lost almost half of its 900 camping spaces in a freak winter storm that washed several campsites downstream and buried hundreds more beneath a foot of silt.

The two and a half campgrounds that remain—**North Pines, Upper Pines,** and half of **Lower Pines**—charge $15 per night. All have drinking water, flush toilets, pay phones, fire pits, and a heavy ranger presence. Showers are available for a small fee at Curry Village. Upper Pines and North Pines allow small RVs (less than 35 feet long). If you're expecting a real nature experience, skip camping in the valley unless you like doing so with 4,000 strangers.

Sunnyside Campground is the only walk-in campground in the valley and fills up with climbers since it's only $3 per night. Hard-core climbers used to live here for months at a time, but the park service has cracked down on that. It still has a much more bohemian atmosphere than at any of the other campgrounds.

ELSEWHERE IN THE PARK

Outside the valley things start looking up for campers. Two campgrounds near the south entrance of the park, **Wawona** and **Bridalveil Creek,** offer a total of 210 sites with all the amenities. Wawona is open year-round, and reservations are required (call **Destinet** at ☎ 800/436-7275). Because it sits well above snow line at more than 7,000 feet, Bridalveil is open in summer only. Both cost $10 per night.

Crane Flat, Hodgdon Meadow, and Tamarack Flat are all in the western corner of the park near the Big Oak Flat Entrance.

Crane Flat is the nearest to the valley, about a half-hour drive, with 166 sites, water, flush toilets, and fire pits. Its rates are $12 per night, and it's open from May to October. **Hodgdon Meadow** is directly adjacent to the Big Oak Flat entrance at 4,800 feet elevation. It's open year-round, charges $12 per night, and requires reservations through **Destinet** (☎ 800/436-7275). Facilities include flush toilets, running water, a ranger station, and pay phones. It's one of the least crowded low-elevation car campgrounds, but there's not a lot to do here.

Tamarack Flat is a waterless, 52-site campground with pit toilets, open June to October. It's a bargain at $6 per night.

Meadows, White Wolf, Yosemite Creek, or Porcupine Flat. All are above 8,000 feet and open in summer only.

Tuolumne Meadows is the largest campground in the park, with more than 300 spaces, but it absorbs the crowd well and has all the amenities, including campfire programs and slide shows in the outdoor amphitheater. Half the sites are reserved in advance. The rest are set aside on a first-come, first-served basis. Rates are $12 per night.

White Wolf, west of Tuolumne Meadows, is the other full-service campground in the high country, with 87 sites available for $10 per night. It offers a drier climate than the meadow and doesn't fill up as quickly.

Two primitive camps, **Porcupine Flat** and **Yosemite Creek,** are the last to fill up in the park. Both have pit toilets and no running water, and charge $6 per night.

ACCOMMODATIONS
IN THE PARK

The grand **Ahwahnee Hotel** (☎ 209/252-4848) is one of the most romantic and beautiful hotels in California. With its ballroom, pool, tennis courts, gourmet dining, outstanding views, and high-digit price tag, it's a special-occasion sort of affair. Rooms are booked a year in advance. Try to reserve one of the cottages, which cost the same as rooms in the main hotel but are more spacious.

The next best thing (and much more moderately priced) is the **Wawona Hotel** (☎ 209/252-4848), near the south entrance. Now a National Historical Landmark, the Wawona is a romantic throwback to another century. That has its ups and downs. Private bathrooms were not a big hit in the 19th century, and rooms were small to hold in heat. Still, the Wawona is a great place to play make-believe. It offers a restaurant, pool, stables, and a lounge.

Yosemite Lodge (☎ 209/252-4848) is the next step down in Yosemite Valley accommodations. It's actually a huge complex, not a lodge, with an array of accommodations ranging from luxurious suites with outdoor balconies and striking views of Yosemite Falls, to one-room cabins with shared baths in a separate building. The lodge also lost slightly more than half of its original 495 rooms in the January 1997 flood. It's down to 249 rooms, and as this book went to press, the National Park Service was debating whether to renovate the damaged accommodations or rebuild them in the summer of 1998. The lodge has a pool. Two restaurants and a cafeteria serve mediocre meals. Rates are moderate.

Curry Village (☎ 209/252-4848) is the valley's low-rent district. This compound of almost 200 cabins and 400 tent cabins varies widely in quality. Some have private baths; others share campground-style bathrooms. Ironically, the oldest cabins are the nicest. Shoddy construction gives the others a slapped-together appearance, not to mention making them cold and drafty in winter. The tent cabins have wood floors and canvas walls; without real walls to stop noise, they lack any sort of privacy, but they're fun in that summer-camp way. You'll have to sustain yourself with fast food from the Curry Village shopping center, as no cooking is allowed in the rooms. Rates are inexpensive to moderate.

An intriguing option bridging the gap between backpacking and staying in a hotel are Yosemite's five backcountry **High Sierra Camps.** These wilderness lodges are simple tent cabins and cafeteria tents located in some of the most beautiful, remote parts of the park. The five camps—Glen Aulin, May Lake, Sunrise, Merced Lake, and Vogelsang—make for good individual destinations. Or you can link several together, since they're arranged in a loose loop about a 10-mile hike from each other—a nice wilderness circuit. Overnight rates include a tent cabin, breakfast, dinner, bathrooms, and showers. High Sierra camp reservations are accepted beginning in December for the following summer; they are usually booked solid by January. Contact **High Sierra Reservations,** Yosemite Park and Curry Co., 5410 E. Home Ave., Fresno, CA 93727 (☎ 209/454-2002).

OUTSIDE THE PARK

✪ **The Estate by the Elderberries.** 48688 Victoria Lane (P.O. Box 577), Oakhurst, CA 93644. ☎ **209/683-6860** (Château du Sureau), or 209/683-6800 (Erna's Elderberry House restaurant). Fax 209/683-0800. 9 rms. A/C TEL. $350–$450 double. Rates include full breakfast. Additional person $65 extra. AE, MC, V.

If you're in search of the perfect marriage of luxurious lodging and decadent dining, the Château du Sureau and Erna's Elderberry House in Oakhurst, a 20-minute drive from the southern entrance to Yosemite along Calif. 41, give even Wine Country retreats a run for their money. The restaurant was established in 1984 and has been hailed as one of the best places to dine in the state. The château—"built to look old"—dates only from 1991 and is set back off the road on the crest of a hill. From the restaurant at the front of the property, a pathway leads through fragrant gardens past fountains to the house, which resembles a French château, complete with turret and terra-cotta–tile roof.

The interior is exquisitely furnished with fine antiques, rugs, and fabrics. Each room is decorated differently, one with a large French canopy bed decked out in French toile, another with a mother-of-pearl inlay Victorian-style bed. All have king-size beds with the finest Italian linens, goose-down comforters, wood-burning fireplaces, wrought-iron balconies, and CD sound systems with a selection of discs. TVs are available on request. The bathrooms are finished with hand-painted French tiles, and some rooms have whirlpool tubs.

Dining/Entertainment: The restaurant offers impeccable food, ambiance, and service without being stuffy. The six-course $58–$62 prix-fixe menu changes daily. A smaller three-course menu is available for $42. You might find a salmon en croûte to start, followed by quail filled with sausage spoonbread and served with huckleberry sauce and six seasonal vegetables. After a salad, a dessert such as cranberry-walnut cake with pumpkin ice cream could finish the repast.

Services: Room service (24 hours), twice-daily maid service, coffee and refreshments in the lobby.

Facilities: Outdoor pool and sundeck.

✪ **Tenaya Lodge.** 1122 Calif. 41, Fish Camp, CA 93623. ☎ **800/635-5807** or 209/683-6555. Fax 209/683-8684. 224 rms, 20 suites. A/C MINIBAR TV TEL. Winter, $89 double Sun–Thurs, $129 double Fri–Sat. Summer, $199 double Sun–Thurs, $219 double Fri–Sat. Add $20–$80 for suites. Buffet breakfast $10 per couple. Children stay free in parents' room. AE, DC, DISC, MC, V.

This three- and four-story resort opened in 1990 on a 35-acre tract of forested land loaded with hiking trails. It's the centerpiece of Fish Camp, a village whose only other attraction is a gas station and a general store. Inside, the decorative theme is a cross between an Adirondack hunting lodge and a southwestern pueblo. The lobby is dominated by a massive river-rock fireplace rising three stories. This is probably the best resort outside the southern entrance to Yosemite, with a likable staff well seasoned by the training methods of the Marriott chain. The rooms are ultramodern, with three phones and other amenities, including in-room safes.

Dining/Entertainment: Since there aren't lots of other options in town, the hotel's three restaurants draw huge crowds.

Services: Room service.

Facilities: Indoor and outdoor swimming pools, health club, on-site massage specialists, games room, sleigh and hay rides (depending on the season).

3 Mammoth Lakes

High in the Sierras, just southeast of Yosemite, Mammoth Lakes is surrounded by glacier-carved, pine-covered peaks that soar up from flower-filled meadows. It's an alpine region of sweeping beauty and one of Californians' favorite playgrounds for hiking, biking, horseback riding, skiing, and more. It's also home to one of the top-rated ski resorts in the world, which makes it a great place to frolic any time of year.

ESSENTIALS

GETTING THERE It's a 6-hour drive from San Francisco via Calif. 120 over the Tioga Pass in Yosemite (closed in winter), 5 hours north of Los Angeles via Calif. 14

and U.S. 395, and 3 hours south of Reno, Nevada, via U.S. 395. In winter, Mammoth is accessible via U.S. 395 from the north or the south.

Sierra Mountain Airways (☎ 800/22-GO-FLY) offers charter flights to the area, and **Mountain Air Express** (☎ 800/788-4247) has regularly scheduled flights. Both service **Mammoth Lakes Airport** on U.S. 395.

VISITOR INFORMATION   For information, contact the **Mammoth Lakes Visitors Bureau,** Calif. 203 (P.O. Box 48), Mammoth Lakes, CA 93546 (☎ 800/367-6572 or 760/934-2712).

ENJOYING THE OUTDOORS

Mammoth Lakes is at the heart of several wilderness areas and is cut through by the San Joaquin and Owens rivers. Mammoth Mountain overlooks the Ansel Adams Wilderness Area to the west and the John Muir Wilderness Area to the southeast, and beyond to the Inyo National Forest and the Sierra National Forest.

The **Mammoth Mountain Ski Area** (☎ 888/462-6668 or 760/934-2571) is the central focus for both summer and winter activities. Visitors can ride the lifts to see panoramic vistas; those who want an active adventure have a world of options.

DOWNHILL SKIING, CROSS-COUNTRY SKIING & SNOW-BOARDING
In winter Mammoth Mountain has more than 3,500 skiable acres, a 3,100-foot vertical drop, 150 trails (22 with snowmaking), and 31 lifts, including 2 high-speed quads. The terrain is 30% beginner, 40% intermediate, and 30% advanced. It's known for power sun, ideal spring skiing conditions, and anywhere from 8 to 12 feet of snow.

Cross-country ski centers are at **Tamarack Lodge** (☎ 760/934-2442) and **Sierra Meadows Ski Touring Center** (☎ 760/934-6161). There's also snowmobiling, dog sledding, snowshoeing, and sleigh rides.

If you're renting equipment, you'll save money if you do it in town instead of at the resort. Try **Sandy's Ski & Sports** (☎ 760/934-7518) at Calif. 203 next to Schat's Bakery for all types of winter equipment, and **Wave Rave Snowboard Shop,** on Main Street (Calif. 203; ☎ 760/934-2471), for snowboards and accessories.

The **June Mountain Ski Area** (☎ 760/648-7733), 20 minutes north of Mammoth, is smaller and offers many summer activities. It has 500 skiable acres, a 2,590-foot vertical drop, 35 trails, and 8 lifts, including 2 high-speed quads. The terrain is 35% beginner, 45% intermediate, and 20% advanced. It's at the center of a chain of lakes—Grant, Silver, Gull, and June—which can be viewed on a scenic driving loop around Calif. 158. It's especially beautiful in the fall when the aspens are ablaze with gold.

MOUNTAIN BIKING   In summer the mountain becomes one huge bike park and climbing playground. The **Bike Center** at the base of the mountain has rentals and accessories. The bike park is famous for its Kamikaze Downhill Trail, an obstacle arena where riders can test their balance and skill and the slalom course. There's also an area designed for kids. A pass granting unlimited access to the gondola and trail systems is $23 for adults, and $12 for children 12 and under; to the trails only, it's $12 for adults, and $6 for children. The park operates daily from 9am to 6pm, from about July 1 to September 29 and then weekends only to October 13.

In town, mountain bikes can also be rented from the **Footloose Sports Center** at the corner of Canyon and Minaret (☎ 760/934-2400). The **NORBA National Mountain Bike Championships** are held here in the summer.

CLIMBING   Climbing and orienteering courses are offered by **Mammoth Mountain Adventure Connection** (☎ 760/934-0606).

Mammoth Lakes Region

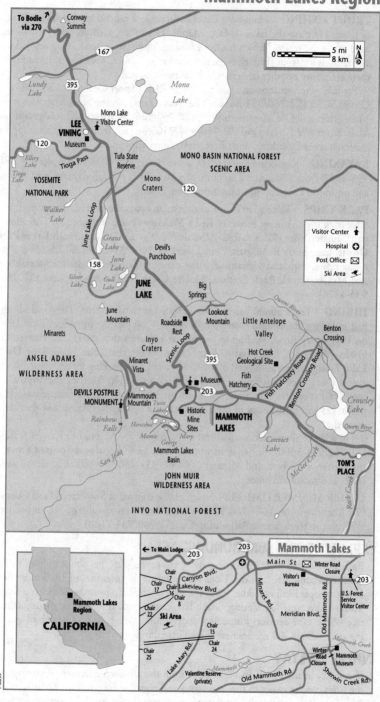

To Bodie via 270
Conway Summit
167
Lundy Lake
395
Mono Lake
Mono Lake Visitor Center
LEE VINING
120
Museum
Ellery Lake
Tioga Lake
Tioga Pass
Tufa State Reserve
YOSEMITE NATIONAL PARK
Mono Craters
120
Walker Lake
MONO BASIN NATIONAL FOREST SCENIC AREA

| | 0 | 5 mi |
| | | 8 km |

Visitor Center
Hospital
Post Office
Ski Area

June Lake Loop
Grant Lake
158
June Lake
Silver Lake
Gull Lake
JUNE LAKE
June Mountain
Devil's Punchbowl
Big Springs
Minarets
Roadside Rest
Inyo Craters
Lookout Mountain
Little Antelope Valley
Owens River
Benton Crossing
ANSEL ADAMS WILDERNESS AREA
Minaret Vista
Scenic Loop
395
Hot Creek Geological Site
Fish Hatchery
Fish Hatchery Road
Benton Crossing Road
Museum
203
DEVILS POSTPILE MONUMENT
Mammoth Mountain
Twin Lakes
Historic Mine Sites
MAMMOTH LAKES
Crowley Lake
Rainbow Falls
Horseshoe
Mamie
George
Mary
Convict Lake
Owens River
San Joaqin
Mammoth Lakes Basin
JOHN MUIR WILDERNESS AREA
McGee Creek
TOM'S PLACE
INYO NATIONAL FOREST
Rock Creek

Mammoth Lakes Region
CALIFORNIA

Mammoth Lakes

To Main Lodge
203
203
Main St
Winter Road Closure
203
Chair 7
Canyon Blvd.
Visitor's Bureau
U.S. Forest Service Visitor Center
Chair 17
Chair 16
Lakeview Blvd
Minaret Rd.
Old Mammoth Rd
Chair 8
Meridian Blvd.
Chair 22
Ski Area
Chair 15
Chair 24
Mammoth Creek
Chair 25
Lake Mary Rd.
Winter Road Closure
Mammoth Museum
Valentine Reserve (private)
Old Mammoth Rd.
Mammoth Creek
Sherwin Creek Rd.

1-0839

TROUT FISHING   Mammoth Lakes Basin sits in a canyon a couple of miles west of town. Here are the lakes—Mary, Mamie, Horseshoe, George, and Twin—that have made the region known for trout fishing. Southeast of town, Crowley Lake is also famous for trout fishing, as are the San Joaquin and Owens rivers. In addition, there are plenty of other lakes in which to spin your reel.

For fishing information and guides, contact **Rick's Sport Center,** at Calif. 203 and Center Street (☎ **760/934-3416**); **The Trout Fitter,** in the Shell Mart Center at Main Street and Old Mammoth Road (☎ **760/924-3676**); and **Kittredge Sports,** Main Street and Forest Trail (☎ **760/934-7566**), which rents equipment, supplies guides, teaches fly-fishing, and offers backcountry trips and packages.

KAYAKING   Kayaks are available at Crowley Lake from **Caldera Kayaks** (☎ **760/ 935-4942**) from $30 a day. This outfit also offers half- and full-day trips on Crowley and on Mono Lake and provides instruction, as well.

PACK TRIPS   The region is also an equestrian's paradise, and numerous outfitters offer pack trips. Among them are **Red's Meadows Pack Station,** Red's Meadows, past Minaret Vista (☎ **800/292-7758** or 760/934-2345); **Mammoth Lakes Pack Outfit,** Lake Mary Road, past Twin Lakes (☎ **760/934-2434**), which offers 1- to 6-day riding trips and semiannual horse drives, plus other wilderness workshops; and **McGee Creek Pack Station,** McGee Creek Road, Crowley Lake (☎ **760/ 935-4324**).

HIKING   Trails abound in the Mammoth Lakes Basin area. They include the half-mile-long **Panorama Dome Trail,** which is just past the turnoff to Twin Lakes on Lake Mary Road, leading to the top of a plateau that provides a view of the Owens Valley and Lakes Basin. Another trail of interest is the 5-mile-long **Duck Lake Trail,** starting at the end of the Coldwater Creek parking lot with switchbacks across Duck Pass past several lakes to Duck Lake. The head of the **Inyo Craters Trail** is reached via gravel road, off the Mammoth Scenic Loop Road. This trail takes you to the edge of these craters and a sign that explains how they were created.

For additional trail information and maps, contact the **Mammoth Ranger Station** (☎ **760/924-5500**). For equipment and maps, go to **Footloose Sports Center** at the corner of Canyon and Minaret (☎ **760/934-2400**), which also rents in-line skates and mountain bikes.

OTHER SUMMERTIME FUN   Golf can be enjoyed at **Snowcreek Golf Course,** Old Mammoth Road (☎ **760/934-6633**). Adventurers can also go hot-air ballooning with the **High Sierra Ballooning Co.** (☎ **760/934-7188**).

EXPLORING THE SURROUNDING AREA

Bodie, one of the most authentic ghost towns in the West, lies about an hour's drive north of Mammoth, past the Tioga Pass entrance to Yosemite. In 1870 more than 10,000 people lived in Bodie; today it's an eerie shell. En route to Bodie, you'll pass **Mono Lake,** near Lee Vining, which has startling tufa towers arising from its surface—limestone deposits formed by underground springs. It's a major bird-watching area—about 300 species nest or stop here during their migrations.

WHERE TO STAY

If you stay at the resort, you'll be steps from the lifts each morning. If you opt for the town, you're closer to the restaurants and nightlife. Regardless, they're within a 5-minute drive from each other, so whatever you choose, you're never too far from the action.

There are more than 700 **campsites** available in the area. These sites open on varying dates in June, depending on the weather. The largest campgrounds are at Convict Lake, Twin Lakes and Cold Water (both in the Mammoth Lakes Basin), and Red's Meadow. For additional information, call the **Mammoth Ranger Station** at ☎ 760/924-5500.

Mammoth Mountain Inn. Minaret Rd. (P.O. Box 353), Mammoth Lakes, CA 93546. ☎ **800/228-4947** or 760/934-2581. Fax 760/934-0701. 173 rms, 40 condos (some suitable for up to 13 people). TV TEL. Winter, $110–$210 double, from $225 condo; summer, $99–$130 double, from $145 condo. Special ski and mountain-biking packages available. AE, MC, V.

Located opposite the ski lodge at the base of the ski resort, the inn started out in 1954 as only one building, but was expanded a decade later into a larger, glossier complex. Though it was remodeled in the early 1990s, it still retains the rustic charm you'd expect from a mountain resort, and rooms here are well equipped and pleasantly furnished, but not exactly inspired. Families love this place because of its daycare activities, cribs ($10 one-time charge), a playground, box lunches for picnics, a games room, and even picnic tables. There's also an array of sports facilities, including bicycles, fishing or hiking guides, downhill or cross-country skiing, sleighing, horseback riding, and hay-wagon rides. The hotel has a snack bar and offers barbecues and room service. The rather standard restaurant serves breakfast, lunch, and dinner. Extras include free airport transportation and occasional entertainment. A whirlpool spa is also on-site.

Motel 6. 3372 Main St. (P.O. Box 1260), Mammoth Lakes, CA 93546. ☎ **800/4-MOTEL-6** or 760/934-6660. Fax 760/934-6989. 151 rms. AC, TV, TEL. $42–$48 double during winter; from $56 double during summer. Extra person $5. AARP discounts. AE, DC, DISC, MC, V.

The rooms may be small, but after a $1.5 million renovation in 1997, accommodations here are the newest—and nicest—around in this price range. Though quarters are a bit more cramped than some other options, factor in the heated pool (summer only), vending machines, and free coffee in the lobby, and you've got all you really need to set up camp.

Sherwin Villas. P.O. Box 2249, Mammoth Lakes, CA 93546. ☎ **800/228-5291** or 760/934-4773. 70 condos. TV. One-bedroom unit for up to 4 people, $95–$110 in winter, $70 in summer. Two-bedroom loft for up to 6 people, $130–$180 in winter, $85 in summer. Extra person $10. MC, V.

Just outside the center of town on Old Mammoth Road is the cluster of woodsy condos that make up Sherwin Villas, perfect for larger families or groups of friends traveling together. Here you'll find one-, two-, three-, and four-bedroom accommodations, each with a full kitchen (with utensils), fireplace, linens, and access to the sauna, Jacuzzi, swimming pool, tennis courts, and free ski shuttle that will take you to the slopes, which are a 5-minute drive. Considering how many people you can pack into these apartments—and that if you stay 4 weekday nights, the 5th night is free—it's a good deal. When making reservations, make sure you tell the reservationist exactly what you're looking for; each condo is independently owned and varies dramatically in both decor and quality.

✪ Sierra Lodge. 3540 Main St. (Calif. 203), Mammoth Lakes, CA 93546. ☎ **800/356-5711** or 760/934-8881. Fax 760/934-7231. TV TEL. Winter, $95–$110 double Sun–Thurs, $110–$130 double Fri–Sat. Summer, $75 double Sun–Thurs, $85 double Fri–Sat. MC, V.

In the heart of the resort town near the ski shuttle, this 2-story inn offers clean, modern surroundings, rock-built fireplaces in the public areas, and a sincere effort to please its guests. Rooms are large and equipped with a kitchenette and utensils, but

Winter Driving in the Sierras

Winter driving in the Sierra Nevada range can be dangerous. While the most hazardous roads are often closed, others are negotiable by four-wheel-drives or with tire chains. Be prepared for sudden blizzards, and protect yourself by taking these important pretrip precautions:

- Check road conditions before setting out by calling ☎ **800/427-7623.**
- If you're driving a rental car, let the rental company know you're planning to drive in snow, and ask whether the antifreeze is prepared for cold climates.
- Make sure your heater and defroster work.
- Always carry chains. If there's a blizzard, the police will not allow vehicles without chains on certain highways. You'll have to pay about $40 to "chain up" at the side of the road.
- Recommended items include an ice scraper, a small shovel, sand or burlap for traction if you get stuck, warm blankets—and an extra car key (it's surprisingly common for motorists to lock their keys in the car while putting on tire chains).

are unfortunately decorated in upscale motel-style. Still, everything is spotless, rooms have small patios or balconies, and though there's no proper closet, there is a nook to hang your things, and a few drawers. Facilities include an outdoor Jacuzzi and a fireside room for relaxing. No smoking. Breakfast is the only meal served, but many restaurants are nearby.

Snow Goose Inn. 57 Forest Trail (P.O. Box 387), Mammoth Lakes, CA 93546. ☎ **800/ 874-7368** or 760/934-2660. Fax 760/934-5655. Website: www.mammothweb.com/ snowgoose/snowgoose.html. 15 rms, 4 suites. TV TEL. Winter, Sun–Thurs $78 double, $148 suite; Fri–Sat $98 double, $168 suite. Summer, $68 double; $98 suite. Rates include breakfast, evening wine, and appetizers. Doubles with kitchens $10 extra. Special packages available. AE, MC, V.

This place is managed by owners who run it as if it were a B&B rather than a traditional hotel. Set half a block off the main street, near a number of restaurants, the Snow Goose was built in two separate 2-story buildings in 1967. The bedrooms are comfortably and attractively furnished, and two offer kitchens. The two-bedroom suites can accommodate four in a 2-story space with dinette, kitchen, and living room complete with a fireplace. Antiques add a graceful note to some of the public rooms, and the staff is helpful and will direct you to cross-country and downhill skiing possibilities 3 miles away.

Tamarack Lodge. Twin Lakes Rd. (off Lake Mary Rd.; P.O. Box 69), Mammoth Lakes, CA 93546. ☎ **800/237-6879** or 760/934-2442. Fax 760/934-2281. 10 rms, 5 with bath; 25 cabins. TEL. Winter, $80 double without bath, $95–$140 double with bath; $110–$300 cabin. Summer, $70 double without bath, $85–$105 double with bath; $85–$260 cabin. Special packages available. DISC, MC, V.

The lodge and cabin accommodations at this rustic lakeside retreat are nothing fancy, but that's exactly what's kept guests coming here since the 1920s. Folks relax in front of a fire burning in the stone hearth in the sitting room or hang out in their rooms, which are intentionally rustic with knotty-pine walls and modern furnishings. The cabins, which can accommodate two to nine people, are dotted around the property and offer a variety of configurations, from studios with wood-burning stove and shower, to two-bedroom/two-bath accommodations with fireplace. Each cabin has a fully equipped kitchen, but there's no daily maid service (fresh towels are provided at the front desk). In the main lodge there are rooms with private baths and with shared bath.

The lodge has a very popular cross-country ski center with more than 25 miles of trails and skating lanes, ski rentals, and a ski school. Boat and canoe rentals are also available. The dining room, overlooking Twin Lakes, offers Californian and continental fare.

White Horse Inn. 2180 Old Mammoth Rd. (P.O. Box 2326), Mammoth Lakes, CA 93456. ☎ **800/982-5657** or 760/924-3656. 5 rms. Winter, $105–$135 double; summer, $75–$95 double. Rates include breakfast. DISC, MC, V.

Set about a mile southwest of the resort's center, this gray-and-white gabled house was built in the 1950s. Unlike its competitors, there's no flowery Laura Ashley decor here. Each accommodation is furnished eclectically and wittily, each with a distinct theme carried out by, say, all Chinese antiques or a furniture ensemble from Austria and Mexico. A country breakfast is included as part of the price, and in nice weather you'll enjoy it on an outdoor deck. Wine and cheese are served near a billiard table during the early evening. There's a hot tub on the premises and a communal kitchen reserved for the use of guests.

WHERE TO DINE

✪ **Anything Goes Café.** 645 Old Mammoth Rd. ☎ **760/934-2424.** Reservations strongly recommended for dinner. Main courses $10–$16. MC, V. Tues 7am–3pm, Thurs–Mon 7am–3pm and 5:30–9:30pm. CALIFORNIA.

This cafe is about $1/2$ mile outside town, near the golf course, in an old, though not antique, building. Customers order lunch directly at the counter, which helps retain the low noontime prices. Overstuffed deli sandwiches, salads, and platters of California-inspired pastas are all the rage. Despite the informality of the lunch hour, it's obvious that the hardworking owners are directing the seasonings from their perch in the kitchens.

Dinners, on the other hand, are more formal, with table service, tablecloths, candlelight, and more attention to the nuances of the cuisine. The menu changes weekly, but the dinner menu will feature about six or so main courses. You might find "very French chicken," which is boned and stuffed with leeks, prosciutto, and sun-dried tomatoes with a wild-mushroom sauce and veggies; or lamb shanks braised in East Indian curry sauce over minted rice with house-made chutney and vegetables. The delicious desserts range from chocolate mousse to an array of fresh pies, tarts, and cakes.

✪ **Nevados.** Main St. (at Minaret Rd.) ☎ **760/934-4466.** Reservations recommended. Main courses $14–$23; fixed-price meal $27. AE, DC, DISC, MC, V. Daily 5:30–9:30pm. EUROPEAN/CALIFORNIA.

What makes this restaurant a favorite with the locals? Well, owner/host Tim Dawson is on hand nightly to ensure that their every need is met; the innovative cuisine is fresh and homemade; and the moist and tasty bread is house-baked. The clincher, though, is the fixed-price meal, which consists of a first course such as potato-crusted crab cake, salad of duck confit and baby lettuces, or seared tuna sashimi; a main course featuring the likes of rosemary rack of lamb or grilled New York steak; and dessert (love that warm pear and almond tart). Throw in the casual-but-sweet ambiance (white tablecloths, candles, and French country murals) and the extensive selection of wines, single-malt scotches, and single-batch bourbons, and it's no wonder this is the hangout for ski instructors and race coaches.

🟢 **The Restaurant at Convict Lake.** Convict Lake Rd. ☎ 760/934-3803. Reservations recommended. Main courses $14–$28. AE, MC, V. Summer, daily 11am–3pm and 5:30–9:30pm; winter, daily 5:30–9:30pm. CONTINENTAL/FRENCH.

The word's finally out. After years of remaining a local secret, this place was awarded four-star status by the AAA. With only 20 others in the state enjoying similar recognition, you can bet you'd better make reservations from now on. Some might argue that while the food's great, it's not exactly worthy. But throw in the rustic-but-elegant dining room's ambiance—surrounded by mountains amidst tiny wood cabins and a lake—and you've got yourself one heck of a special place.

Five miles south of the town of Mammoth Lakes, you'll find this romantic dining diversion. Amidst a woodsy, plank-sided, oversized cabin with tables placed around a copper-hooded, freestanding fireplace, and windows overlooking a forest of aspen, you can try such classic dishes as duck breast with Grand Marnier and sun-dried cherry sauce, garnished with candied-orange zest. In season, the venison, pan-seared with kalamata olives, toasted cumin, and oven-dried tomatoes and served with a fine herb glaze, is worth the trip here.

🟢 **Skadi.** 587 Old Mammoth Rd. (in the Sherwin Plaza III Shopping Mall), ☎ **760/934-3902.** Reservations recommended. Main courses $9.50–$20. AE, MC, V. Wed–Mon 5:30–10pm. ECLECTIC.

The minimall where this restaurant is located (½ mile south of Mammoth Lake's center) may not be the home of the Viking goddess of skiing and hunting whose name this restaurant bears, but she wouldn't have cared once she saw the view—it encompasses most of the mountains for miles around. This universal favorite is perfect for an après-ski cocktail at the 14-seat bar, a snack from the substantial selection of appetizers and desserts, or a full-blown dinner on the town.

The decor evokes a big-city postmodern aura that's a welcome change after all that local alpine rusticity. Main courses are self-proclaimed "Alpine cuisine" and include such dishes as smoked trout Napoleon or grilled venison with lingonberries and a game sauce. Finish the evening with crème brûlée or the frozen macadamia-nut parfait.

Whiskey Creek. 18 Main St. (at Minaret Rd.), Mammoth Lakes. ☎ 760/934-2555. Reservations recommended. Main courses $11–$22. AE, DC, MC, V. Daily 5:30–10pm. AMERICAN.

If you favor upscale surf-and-turf fare combined with alpine atmosphere, you've found your dining spot. The building's wraparound windows encompass a view of the snow-clad mountains, and the menu is known for its beef, as well as rack of lamb, meatloaf, and tasty smashed potatoes.

Though the dining room may offer a peaceful experience, the upstairs brewpub is a whole different world. The recently added Mammoth Brewing Company and its live music (every night at 9pm until at least 1am) make this place the number-one spot to mingle, slam suds, and get happy. (Think very crowded, post-collegiate frat party.) The cover charge ranges from free to $5.

4 Devils Postpile National Monument

by Andrew Rice

Just a few miles outside the town of Mammoth Lakes, Devils Postpile National Monument is home to one of nature's most curious geological spectacles. Formed when molten lava cracked as it cooled, the 60-foot-high blue-gray basalt columns that form the postpile look more like some sort of enormous eerie pipe organ or a jumble of giant pencil leads than anything you'd expect to see made from stone. The three-to seven-sided columns formed underground and were exposed when glaciers scoured this valley in the last ice age some 10,000 years ago. Similar examples of columnar basalt are found in Ireland and Scotland.

Because of its high elevation (7,900 feet) and heavy snowfall, the monument is open only from summer until early fall. The weather in the summer is usually clear and warm, but afternoon thundershowers can soak the unprepared. Nights are still cold, so bring good tents and sleeping bags if you'll be camping. The Mammoth Lakes region is famous for its beautiful lakes—but unfortunately all that water also means lots of mosquitoes. Plan for them.

From late June until early September cars are prohibited in the monument between 7:30am and 5:30pm because of the small roads' inability to handle the traffic. Visitors must take a shuttle bus from the Mammoth Mountain Inn to and from locations in the monument. While it takes some planning, the resulting peace and quiet is well worth the trouble and makes you wonder why the park service hasn't implemented similar programs at Yosemite Valley and other traffic hot spots.

HIKING   There's more to Devils Postpile than a bunch of rocks, no matter how impressive they might be. Located on the banks of the San Joaquin River in the heart of a landscape of granite peaks and crystalline mountain lakes, the 800-acre park is a gateway to a hiker's paradise. Short paths lead from here to the top of the postpile, and to Soda Springs, a spring of cold carbonated water.

A longer hike (about 1¼ miles) from the separate Rainbow Falls trailhead will take you to spectacular **Rainbow Falls,** where the entire middle fork of the San Joaquin plunges 101 feet off a lava cliff. From the trail, a stairway and short trail lead to the base of the falls and swimming holes below.

The **John Muir Trail,** which connects Yosemite National Park with Kings Canyon and Sequoia national parks, and the **Pacific Crest Trail** both run through here. Named after the famous conservationist and author who's largely credited with saving Yosemite and popularizing the Sierra Nevada as a place worth preserving, the 211-mile John Muir Trail traverses some of the most rugged and remote parts of the Sierra. There are two accesses to it in Devils Postpile, one via the ranger station, and the other from Rainbow Falls Trailhead. From here you can hike as far as your feet will take you north or south.

Note that mountain bikes are not permitted on trails.

CAMPING   While most visitors stay in or around Mammoth Lakes, the monument does maintain a 21-site campground with piped water, flush toilets, fire pits, and picnic tables on a first-come, first-served basis. Rates are $8 per night. Bears are common in the park, so proper food-storage measures must be taken. Leashed pets are permitted on trails and in camp. Call the **National Park Service** (☎ **760/934-2289**) for details. There are several other U.S. Forest Service campgrounds nearby, including **Red's Meadow** and **Upper Soda Springs** (☎ **760/924-5500**).

5 Visalia: Gateway to Sequoia & Kings Canyon

Visalia is the gateway to Sequoia and Kings Canyon national parks. It's on Calif. 198 east of Calif. 99, halfway between the coast and the Sierras and halfway between Los Angeles and Sacramento. The town is pleasant enough, with some very fine Victorian and Colonial Revival homes. Pick up a walking-tour pamphlet at the convention and visitors bureau if you're interested in strolling (see "Essentials," below).

In stride with its surroundings, Visalia has consciously preserved its natural wilderness in the form of 18 public parks, which cover almost 400 acres. Especially popular is the **Mooney Grove Park,** at 2700 S. Mooney Blvd., which is filled with the remainder of a great oak forest that once reigned here. There's also a lagoon with islands, a boathouse, and fish ponds. Another of the park's monuments to the past is the famous and moving statue *The End of the Trail* by James Earle Fraser. It depicts a battle-weary brave, head dropped to his chest, spear tip down, astride an exhausted pony. In 1968 the original was removed to the National Cowboy Hall of Fame in Oklahoma City and replaced by this copy cast in bronze.

Also in the park, the **Tulare County Museum,** at 2700 S. Mooney Blvd. (☎ **209/ 733-6616**), has some fine collections and several restored historic buildings, including the Visalia Jail and Witt's Blacksmith Shop, where C. V. Witt designed his world-famous cattle brands. Admission is $2 for adults, $1 for seniors and children 6 to 12, free for children 5 and under. It's open Wednesday to Monday from 10am to 4pm in spring, summer, and fall; Thursday to Monday in winter.

At the **Central California Chinese Cultural Center,** 500 S. Akers (☎ **209/ 625-4545**), a temple complex and museum, the Chinese in the valley gather to preserve their traditions and cultural heritage. At the center, visitors can view Chinese artifacts, archaeological objects, and paintings inside, and contemplate the 8-foot bronze statue of Confucius in the courtyard. Admission is free, and it's open year-round. Call in advance for visiting hours.

In nearby Hanford, **China Alley** is all that remains of a Chinese community that once numbered 600 in the late 19th century. Here you can see the Taoist Temple (1893) and the L. T. Sue Herb Company. Also in Hanford and worth visiting is the **Fox Theatre,** dating from the 1920s. It seats more than 1,000 and has an original Wurlitzer organ. **Courthouse Square** is a shopping complex; in the square an old 1930s carousel has been restored to its former brilliance.

ESSENTIALS

GETTING THERE   If you're driving from San Francisco, take I-580 east to I-5 south to Calif. 198 east.

The **Visalia Municipal Airport,** 9500 Airport Dr. No. 1 (☎ **209/651-1131**), is served by **Shuttle by United** (☎ **800/241-6522** or 209/651-2202). **Amtrak** (☎ **800/USA-RAIL**) stops at nearby Hanford, and there's a shuttle from there to Visalia.

VISITOR INFORMATION   For information, contact the **Visalia Convention and Visitors Bureau,** 301 E. Acequia St., Visalia, CA 93291 (☎ **800/524-0303** or 209/738-3435), or check out their website at www.cvbvasilia.com.

WHERE TO STAY

Ben Maddox House. 601 N. Encina St., Visalia, CA 93291. ☎ **800/401-9800** or 209/ 739-0721. Fax 209/625-0420. Website: www.placetostay.com/visalia-benmaddox/. 4 rms. TV TEL. $75–$90 double. Rates include breakfast. AE, DISC, MC, V.

Set in a residential street of Victorian homes, 4 blocks from the town's main street, the Ben Maddox House is an impressive sight. Its triangular gable is punctuated with a round window and two extremely tall palm trees looming over the front yard. The house, built in 1876, is constructed of redwood, and its rooms retain their original dark-oak trim and white-oak floors. The guest rooms are decorated with late-18th- and 19th-century furnishings, and the two front rooms have French doors leading to two small porch sitting areas. A swimming pool and hot tub are open to guests in the back, and a full breakfast is served.

Radisson Hotel. 300 S. Court St., Visalia, CA 93291. ☎ **800/333-3333** or 209/636-1111. Fax 209/636-8224. 201 rms, 7 suites. A/C MINIBAR TV TEL. $100–$138 double; $225–$450 suite. Additional person $15 extra. Cribs provided free. AE, CB, DC, MC, V.

Lying 7 blocks from the town center, this eight-story chain hotel is the finest in Visalia. It's a family favorite and is often visited by those en route to Sequoia and Kings Canyon national parks. Some of the attractively furnished rooms open onto balconies. This is certainly not the most glamorous Radisson in California, but it's serviceable in every way, and offers a whirlpool and room service until 2am. Free airport transfers are arranged as well. There is exercise equipment, and the hotel maintains a fleet of bikes. The restaurant serves breakfast, lunch, and dinner, with last seating at 10pm. You can also patronize the local bar, and entertainment is provided on Friday and Saturday nights. The hotel has a pool with poolside service.

The Spalding House. 631 N. Encina St., Visalia, CA 93291. ☎ **209/739-7877.** Fax 209/625-0902. 3 suites. $85 suite for 2. Rates include breakfast. MC, V.

This Colonial Revival house built in 1901 has been carefully restored by owners Wayne and Peggy Davidson. Handcrafted beveled-glass doors lead into the entry hall and the music room, with its 1923 Steinway player grand piano. Readers will particularly enjoy the library, which is lined with more than 1,500 books. There's a TV in the living room, and Oriental rugs and antiques are combined with classic reproductions throughout the house. All the rooms are suites with a sitting room, bedroom, and private bath, but no phone. No smoking.

WHERE TO DINE

Michael's on Main. 123 W. Main St. ☎ **209/635-2686.** Reservations required. Main courses $15–$22. AE, DC, MC, V. Mon–Fri 11am–3pm; Mon–Thurs 5–10pm; Fri–Sat 5–11pm. CALIFORNIA.

Along with the Vintage Press, this is the favored dining option in the area. Main courses range from fresh seafood such as blackened ahi tuna to grilled items including pork tenderloin with port/wild-mushroom sauce or grilled fillet of rabbit. In season, game is available. There are also several luscious pastas—a favorite is the rigatoni Bellini, tossed with wild mushrooms, sun-dried tomatoes, smoked duck, and quattro formaggi (four cheese) sauce.

✪ **The Vintage Press.** 216 N. Willis St. ☎ **209/733-3033.** Reservations recommended. Main courses $12–$25. AE, CB, DC, MC, V. Mon–Thurs 11:30am–2pm and 6–10:30pm, Fri–Sat 6–11pm, Sun 10am–2pm and 5–9pm. AMERICAN/CONTINENTAL.

This is the best restaurant within a surrounding 100-mile radius, a culinary stopover of widely acknowledged merit in the gastronomic wasteland between Los Angeles and San Francisco. The design is reminiscent of a fin-de-siècle gin mill in Gold-Rush San Francisco, with a bar imported from that city manufactured by the Brunswick Company (of bowling-alley fame), lots of antiques bought at local auctions, and glittering panels of leaded glass and mirrors. The place is big enough (250 seats) to feed a boatload of Gold-Rush hopefuls, and has a bustling bar/lounge where live music by a piano player is presented Thursday to Saturday from 5:30 to 9pm.

The menu is supplemented by daily specials—a zesty rack of lamb roasted in a cabernet sauce with rosemary and pistachios, for example. The regular menu offers about a dozen meat and fish dishes, with steaks supplemented by such dishes as red snapper with lemon, almonds, and capers, or pork tenderloin with Dijon mustard, red chili, and honey. To start, we recommend farm-raised fresh oysters on the half shell or the wild mushrooms with cognac in puff pastry.

6 Sequoia & Kings Canyon National Parks

by Andrew Rice

Only 200 road miles separate Yosemite from Sequoia and Kings Canyon national parks, but they're worlds apart. Where the National Park Service has taken every opportunity to modernize, accessorize, and urbanize Yosemite, leading to a frenetic tourist scene much like the cities so many of us strive to escape, at Sequoia and Kings Canyon they've treated the wilderness beauty of the park with respect and care. Only one road loops through the park, the Generals Highway, and no road traverses the Sierra here. The park service doesn't recommend that vehicles over 22 feet long use the steep and windy stretch between Potwisha Campground and the Giant Forest in Sequoia National Park. As a result, the park is much less accessible by car than most, but spectacular for those willing to head out on foot.

The Sierra Nevada tilts upward as it runs south. **Mt. Whitney,** at 14,495 feet the highest point in the lower 48 states, is just one of many high peaks in Sequoia and Kings Canyon. The Pacific Crest Trail also reaches its highest point here, crossing north to south through both parks. In addition to rocky, snow-covered peaks, Sequoia and Kings Canyon are home to the largest groves of giant sequoias in the Sierra Nevada, as well as the headwaters of the Kern, Kaweah, and Kings rivers. A few small, high-country lakes are home to some of the only remaining pure-strain golden trout. Bear, deer, and numerous smaller animals and birds depend on the park's miles of wild habitat for summer breeding and feeding grounds.

Technically two separate parks, Sequoia and Kings Canyon are contiguous and managed jointly from the park headquarters at Ash Mountain just after the entrance on Calif. 198 east of Visalia.

JUST THE FACTS

Most visitors make a loop through the parks by entering at Grant Grove and leaving through Ash Mountain, or vice versa.

ENTRANCE FEES   A $10-per-car fee is good for 1 week's worth of entry at any park entrance. An annual pass is $20.

VISITOR CENTERS & INFORMATION   The **Lodgepole** and **Grant Grove** visitor centers are the largest, with a full selection of park information and displays about the history, biology, and geology of this incredible place. Some time spent here will pay off by letting you decide which parts of the park you most want to concentrate on. For visitor information before you go, call ☎ **209/565-3341.**

AVOIDING THE CROWDS   To escape the crowds and see less-used areas of the park, enter on one of the dead-end roads to Mineral King or Cedar Grove (only open in summer), or South Fork. The lack of through traffic makes these parts of the park incredibly peaceful even at full capacity, and they're gateways to the best hiking.

RANGER PROGRAMS   Park rangers lead hikes, campfire talks, and slide shows at several campgrounds and visitor centers during the summer.

REGULATIONS   Wilderness permits are required for all backpacking trips. You can reserve permits in advance by writing the park headquarters (Superintendent, Sequoia and Kings Canyon National Parks, Three Rivers, CA 93271).

Mountain bikes and dogs are forbidden on all park trails (dogs are only permitted in developed areas, but must be leashed). The park service allows firewood gathering at campgrounds, but removing wood from living or standing trees is forbidden.

Sequoia & Kings Canyon National Parks

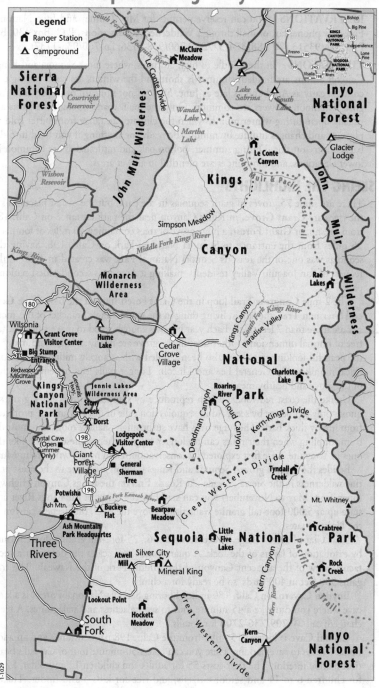

Legend
- 🏠 Ranger Station
- △ Campground

Sierra National Forest

Inyo National Forest

John Muir Wilderness

Courtright Reservoir

South Fork San Joaquin River

Le Conte Divide

McClure Meadow

Lake Sabrina

South Lake

Bishop

Big Pine

Independence

Lone Pine

Fresno

Visalia

Three Rivers

KINGS CANYON NATIONAL PARK

SEQUOIA NATIONAL PARK

Wishon Reservoir

Wanda Lake

Martha Lake

Le Conte Canyon

Glacier Lodge

Kings

John Muir & Pacific Crest Trail

Kings River

Simpson Meadow

Middle Fork Kings River

Canyon

Rae Lakes

Monarch Wilderness Area

Kings Canyon

South Fork Kings River

Paradise Valley

National

Wilsonia

Grant Grove Visitor Center

Hume Lake

Cedar Grove Village

Charlotte Lake

Big Stump Entrance

Redwood Mountain Grove

Kings Canyon National Park

Generals Hwy.

Jennie Lakes Wilderness Area

Stony Creek

Dorst

Roaring River

Deadman Canyon

Cloud Canyon

Kern-Kings Divide

Park

Crystal Cave (Open Summer Only)

Giant Forest Village

Lodgepole Visitor Center

General Sherman Tree

Great Western Divide

Tyndall Creek

Potwisha

Ash Mtn.

Middle Fork Kaweah River

Buckeye Flat

Bearpaw Meadow

Mt. Whitney

Ash Mountain Park Headquartes

Sequoia

Little Five Lakes

National

Crabtree

Three Rivers

Atwell Mill

Silver City

Mineral King

Kern Canyon

Kern River

Rock Creek

Park

Lookout Point

Hockett Meadow

Great Western Divide

Pacific Crest Trail

South Fork

Kern Canyon

Inyo National Forest

Great Western Divide

1-1029

RESERVATIONS   You can reserve permits for Mt. Whitney and Inyo National Forest by phone, fax, or mail through **Wilderness Reservations,** P.O. Box 430, Big Pine, CA 93513 (☎ **888/374-3773** or 760/938-1136; fax 760/938-1137).

THE SEASONS   In the middle to high altitudes, where most Sequoia and Kings Canyon visitors are headed, summer is short and the winters are cold. Spring can come as early as April and as late as June. Snow is not unheard of in July and August. Afternoon showers are common. Only the main roads through the parks are usually open during winter months when the climate can range from bitter cold to pleasant and changes minute by minute. Be ready for anything if you head into the backcountry on skis. During summer, poison oak and rattlesnakes are common in lower elevations, and mosquitoes are plentiful in all wet areas.

SEEING THE HIGHLIGHTS

There are some 75 groves of giant sequoias in the park, but the easiest places to see the trees are **Grant Grove,** in Kings Canyon near the park entrance on Calif. 180 from Fresno, or **Giant Forest,** a huge grove of trees containing 40 miles of footpaths 16 miles from the entrance to Sequoia National Park on Calif. 198. Saving the sequoias was one of the reasons Sequoia National Park was created in 1890 at the request of San Joaquin Valley residents, making it America's second-oldest national park.

The 2-mile **Congress Trail** loop in the Giant Forest starts at the base of the **General Sherman Tree,** the largest living thing in the world. Single branches of this monster are more than 7 feet thick. Each year it grows enough wood to make a 60-foot-tall tree of normal dimensions. Other trees in the grove are nearly as large, and many of the peaceful-looking trees have also been saddled with strangely militaristic and political monikers like General Lee and Lincoln. Longer trails lead to remote reaches of the grove and nearby meadows.

Unlike the coast redwoods, which reproduce by sprouting or by seeds, giant sequoias only reproduce by seed. Adult sequoias don't die of diseases and are protected from fire by thick bark. The huge trees have surprisingly shallow roots, and most die from toppling when their roots can no longer support them. These groves, like the ones in Yosemite, were first explored by conservationist and nature writer John Muir.

Besides the sequoia groves, Sequoia and Kings Canyon are home to the most pristine wilderness in the Sierra Nevada. At **Roads End** on the Kings Canyon Highway (open from May to November) you can stand by the banks of the Kings River and stare up at 5,000-foot-tall granite walls rising above the river, the deepest canyon in the United States.

Near Giant Forest Village, **Moro Rock** is a 6,725-foot-tall granite dome formed by exfoliation of layers of the rock. A quarter-mile trail scales the dome for a spectacular view of the adjacent Canyon of the Middle Fork of the Kaweah. The trail gains 300 feet in 400 yards, so be ready for a climb.

Boyden Cavern, on Calif. 180 in neighboring Sequoia National Forest, is a large cave where you can take a 45-minute tour to see stalactites and stalagmites. A fee is charged; call ☎ **209/736-2708** for details.

Crystal Cave is located 15 miles from the Calif. 198 park entrance and an additional 7 miles to cave parking. Here you can take a 50-minute tour of Crystal's beautiful marble interior. The tour costs $5 for adults and children 12 and older, $2.50 for children 6 to 11 and senior citizens, and free for kids 5 and under. Tickets are not sold at the cave and must be purchased at the Lodgepole or Foothills visitor centers at least 1 1/2 hours in advance. Be sure to wear sturdy shoes and bring a jacket.

HIKING THE PARK

Hiking and backpacking are what this park is really all about. Some 700 miles of trails connect canyons, lakes, and high alpine meadows and snow fields.

When hiking inside the parks' boundaries, overnight- and/or day-use permits are required. They're limited and available by writing to Wilderness Office, Sequoia and Kings Canyon National Parks, Three Rivers, CA 93271. Permits are required for all overnight trips to the backcountry; call ☎ 209/565-3708 for information.

Some of the park's most impressive hikes start in the **Mineral King** section in the southern end of Sequoia. Beginning at 7,800 feet, trails lead onward and upward to destinations like Sawtooth Pass, Crystal Lake, and the old White Chief Trail to the now-defunct White Chief Mine. Once an unsuccessful silver-mining town in the 1870s, Mineral King was the center of a pitched battle in the late 1970s when developers sought to build a huge ski resort here. They were defeated when Congress added Mineral King to the park, and the wilderness remains unspoiled.

The **John Muir Trail,** which begins in Yosemite Valley, ends here just below Mount Whitney. For many miles it coincides with the **Pacific Crest Trail** as it skirts the highest peaks in the park. This is the most difficult part of the Pacific Crest, remaining above 10,000 feet most of the time and crossing 12,000-foot-tall passes.

Other hikers like to explore the end of the park from **Cedar Grove** and **Roads End.** The **Paradise Valley Trail** is a fairly easy day trip by park standards leading to beautiful Mist Falls. The **Copper Creek Trail** immediately rises into the high wilderness around Granite Pass at 10,673 feet, one of the most strenuous day hikes in the park.

If the altitude and steepness are too much for you at these trailheads, try some of the longer hikes in the **Giant Forest** or **Grant Grove.** These forests are woven with interlocking loops that allow you to take as short or as long a hike as you want. The 6-mile **Trail of the Sequoias** in Giant Forest will take you to the grove's far-eastern end where some of the finest trees are. In Grant Grove, a 100-foot walk through the hollow trunk of the **Fallen Monarch** is a fascinating side trip. The tree has been used for shelter for more than 100 years and is tall enough inside that you can walk through without bending over.

Perhaps the most traversed trail to the park is the **Whitney Portal Trail.** It runs from east of the park near Lone Pine, through Inyo National Forest, to the summit of Mt. Whitney. Though it's a straightforward walk to the summit and it's possible to bag it in a very long day hike, you'd better be in really good shape before attempting it. Almost half the people who attempt Whitney, including those who camp partway up, don't reach the summit. Weather, altitude, and fatigue can conspire to stop even the most prepared party. Contact Whitney Portal reservations (☎ **888/ 374-3730)** 6 months in advance to make wilderness reservations if you're interested in an overnight trip into the backcountry.

The official park map and guide has good road maps for the parks, but for serious hiking you'll want to check out *Sierra South: 100 Back-Country Trips* by Thomas Winnett and Jason Winnett (Wilderness Press). Another good guide is *Kings Canyon Country,* a hiking handbook by Ginny and Lew Clark. The Grant Grove, Lodgepole, Cedar Grove, Foothills, and Mineral King visitor centers all sell a complete selection of maps and guidebooks to the park.

OTHER OUTDOOR ACTIVITIES

FISHING   Trout fishing in the lower altitudes is fairly limited; most is along the banks of the Kings and Kaweah rivers. A few high-country lakes are refuges for trout and are not stocked with hatchery fish. Before venturing into the high country, inquire at a ranger station about the area you'll be visiting to find out about closures or specific regulations. A California fishing license is required for everyone over 16 years old. Tackle and licenses are available at several park stores.

RAFTING & KAYAKING   Only recently have professional outfitters begun taking experienced rafters and kayakers down the Class IV and V Kaweah and Upper Kings rivers outside the parks. Contact Sequoia National Forest at ☎ 209/784-1500 for a current listing of companies running trips. This is only for the very adventurous.

SKIING & SNOWSHOEING   **Sequoia Ski Touring,** near Giant Forest Village (☎ 209/565-3381), offers complete rentals and trail maps for 35 miles of Sequoia backcountry trails. In Kings Canyon, Sequoia Ski Touring in Grant Grove (☎ 209/335-2314) provides the same services and an even-wider selection of trails. People with their own equipment are welcome on all trails in the park at no cost. Trail maps are available at the visitor centers. On winter weekends park rangers lead introductory snowshoe hikes at Grant Grove. The roads to Cedar Grove and Mineral King are closed in winter.

CAMPING & ACCOMMODATIONS

There are 13 campgrounds in the park, offering the most convenient and economical accommodations here, although none have hookups. Only two accept reservations: **Lodgepole Campground** and **Dorst Campground** in Sequoia (☎ 800/365-2267). Others are first-come, first-served and often fill up on weekends. Three campgrounds—Azalea, Lodgepole, and Potwisha—are open year-round. The rest are open from snowmelt to September. Call ☎ 209/565-3341 for camping information. Even in summer campers should prepare for rain and cold temperatures. Bring a good tent and warm sleeping bags.

Two large campgrounds in Sequoia are **Dorst** and **Lodgepole.** Both are close to the Giant Forest. Lodgepole is within a short stroll of a restaurant, gas station, and a visitor center. With more than 200 sites each, they tend to be the noisiest campgrounds in Sequoia. Lodgepole and Dorst charge $14 per night.

Smaller and more peaceful are **South Fork, Potwisha, Buckeye Flats, Atwell Mill,** and **Cold Springs.** South Fork, Atwell Mill, and Cold Springs have pit toilets and are $6 per night. The others, with flush toilets, running water, and public phones, charge $12.

Campers in the remote Cedar Grove area of Kings Canyon National Park in the Kings River gorge can choose from **Moraine, Sentinel, Sheep Creek,** and **Canyon View,** a group camp. All four have flush toilets and are convenient to some of the park's best hiking. The small **Cedar Grove Village** offers a restaurant and store. Sites are $12.

Three campgrounds in the Grant Grove area will put you near the sequoias without the noise and crowds of Giant Forest Village. All three—**Sunset, Azalea,** and **Crystal Springs**—have flush toilets and phones. Azalea has an RV disposal site, a ranger station, and showers nearby. The charge is $12 per site.

Lodging in the parks ranges from rustic one-room cabins with no bath or heat to a luxury motel. None of the complexes is very big. All lodging in the park is operated by the park concessionaire, **Kings Canyon National Park Services Co.,** P.O. Box 909, Kings Canyon National Park, CA 93633 (☎ 209/335-5500 for information and reservations).

Grant Grove offers a variety of cabins with private or shared baths. Cedar Grove is the site of an 18-room motel. Each room has its own bath and two queen-size beds.

10

The Gold Country & the Central Valley

by Erika Lenkert and Matthew R. Poole

On the morning of January 24, 1848, a carpenter named James Marshall was working on John Sutter's mill in Coloma when he made an exciting discovery: He stumbled on a gold nugget on the south fork of the American River. Despite Sutter's wishes to keep the find a secret, word leaked out—a word that would change the fate of California almost overnight: *Gold!*

The news spread like wildfire, and a frenzy seized the nation; the Gold Rush was on. Within 3 years, the population of the state grew from a meager 15,000 to more than 265,000. Most of these newcomers were single men under the age of 40, and not far behind were the thousands of merchants, bankers, and women who made their fortunes catering to the miners.

Sacramento grew quickly as a supply town at the base of the surrounding goldfields. The Gold Country boom lasted less than a decade; the gold supply was quickly exhausted and many towns shrank or disappeared. Sacramento, however, continued to grow as the fertile Central Valley south of it exploited another source of wealth, becoming the vegetable and fruit garden of the nation.

A trip along Calif. 49 from the northern mines to the southern mines will give visitors a sense of what life might have been like on the rough mining frontier. The towns along this route seem frozen in time, with the main streets boasting raised wooden sidewalks, double-porched buildings, ornate saloons, and Victorian storefronts. Each town tells a similar story of sudden wealth and explosive growth, yet each has left behind a different imprint. Any fan of movie westerns will recognize the setting—hundreds, perhaps even thousands, of movies have been shot in these towns.

The sprawling Central Valley, 240 miles long and 50 miles wide, is California's bread basket, the source of much of the bounty that is shipped across the nation and overseas. Much of the history of California has revolved around the struggle for control of the water used to irrigate the valley (it receives less than 10 inches of rainfall per year) and make this inland desert bloom. Despite the scarcity of water, a breathtaking panorama of orange and pistachio groves, grape vines, and strawberry fields stretches uninterrupted for miles.

1 Sacramento

Sacramento, with a population of 395,000, is one of the state's fastest growing cities. In addition to being the state capital, it is a thriving shipping and processing center for the fruit, vegetables, rice, wheat, and dairy goods that are produced in the fertile Central Valley. It's a prosperous and politically charged city, with broad tree-shaded streets lined with some impressive Victorians and well-crafted bungalows. At its heart sits the Capitol building—Sacramento's main attraction—in a well-maintained park replete with flower gardens and curious squirrels. It's far from a tourist town, but it has its share of touristy activities. Visitors and locals alike enjoy spending the day walking through Old Sacramento or floating down the American River.

ESSENTIALS

GETTING THERE   If you're driving from San Francisco, Sacramento is located about 90 miles east on I-80. From Los Angeles, take I-5 through the Central Valley directly into Sacramento. From North Lake Tahoe, get on I-80 west, and from South Lake Tahoe take U.S. 50.

Sacramento Metropolitan Airport (☎ 916/929-5411), 12 miles northwest of downtown Sacramento, is served by about a dozen airlines, including **American** (☎ 800/433-7300), **Continental** (☎ 800/525-0280), **Delta** (☎ 800/221-1212), **Northwest** (☎ 800/225-2525), and **United** (☎ 800/241-6522).

AAA Taxi and Shuttle Service (☎ 916/334-5555) will get you from the airport to downtown; they charge a flat rate of $15 to the capital, a bargain compared to the $30 a conventional taxi would cost.

Amtrak (☎ 800/USA-RAIL) trains serve Sacramento daily.

VISITOR INFORMATION   The **Sacramento Convention and Visitors Bureau,** 1421 K St., Sacramento, CA 95814 (☎ **916/264-7777;** fax 916/264-7788), provides plenty of helpful information for tourists. Once in the city, visitors can also stop by the **Sacramento Visitor Center,** 1101 2nd St. (☎ **916/442-7644**), in Old Sacramento. It's usually open daily from 8am to 5pm.

ORIENTATION   Suburbia sprawls around Sacramento, but its downtown area is relatively compact. Getting around the city is made easy by a gridlike pattern of streets that are designated by numbers or letters. The state capitol, on 10th Street between N and L streets, is the key landmark. From the front of the capitol, M Street—which is at this point called Capitol Mall—runs 10 straight blocks to Old Sacramento, one of the city's oldest sections.

EXPLORING THE CAPITAL & ENVIRONS

In town, you'll want to stroll around **Old Sacramento,** 4 square blocks at the foot of the downtown area that have become a major attraction. The blocks contain more than 100 restored buildings, including restaurants and shops. Although the area has cobblestoned streets, wooden sidewalks, and Gold Rush-era architecture, the high concentration of T-shirt shops and other gimmicky stores has turned it into a sort of historical Disneyland. While you're there, be sure to stop at the new **Discovery Museum** at 101 I Street (☎ **916/264-7057**), which houses hands-on exhibits and demonstrations on California's history, as well as plenty of fascinating scientific and technological gizmos and doodads. It's open Tuesday through Friday noon to 4:30pm and Saturday and Sunday from 10am to 4:30pm. Admission is $4 for adults, $2 for kids 6 to 12, and free for kids 5 and under.

BIKING   One good thing about a town that's as flat as a tortilla: It's perfect for exploring on a bicycle. One of the best places to ride is through Old Sacramento and along the 22-mile American River Parkway, which runs right though it. If you didn't

Downtown Sacramento

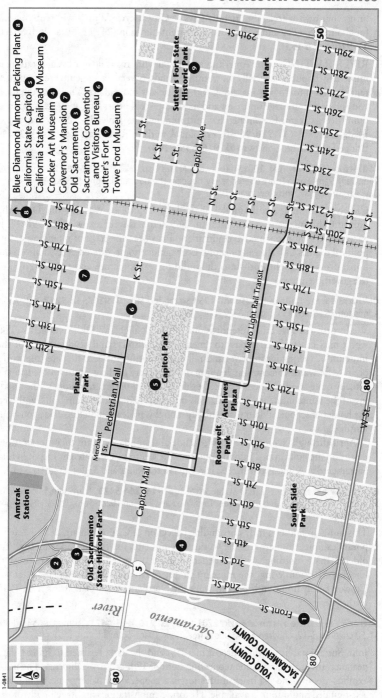

Blue Diamond Almond Packing Plant 8
California State Capitol 5
California State Railroad Museum 2
Crocker Art Museum 4
Governor's Mansion 7
Old Sacramento 3
Sacramento Convention and Visitors Bureau 6
Sutter's Fort 9
Towe Ford Museum 1

Sutter's Fort State Historic Park

Winn Park

J St.
K St.
L St.
Capitol Ave.
N St.
O St.
P St.
Q St.
R St.
S St.
T St.
U St.
V St.

50

29th St.
28th St.
27th St.
26th St.
25th St.
24th St.
23rd St.
22nd St.
21st St.
20th St.
19th St.
18th St.
17th St.
16th St.
15th St.
14th St.
13th St.
12th St.

Metro Light Rail Transit

Plaza Park
Pedestrian Mall
Merchant St.
Capitol Park
Capitol Mall
K St.

Roosevelt Park
Archives Plaza

South Side Park

Amtrak Station

Old Sacramento State Historic Park

River
Sacramento

11th St.
10th St.
9th St.
8th St.
7th St.
6th St.
5th St.
4th St.
3rd St.
2nd St.
Front St.

YOLO COUNTY
SACRAMENTO COUNTY

80
W St.

80

N

1-0841

293

bring your own wheels, the friendly guys at **City Bicycle Works** will rent you one for about $15 a day and point you in the right direction (2419 K St. at 24th Street; ☎ **916/447-2453**).

RIVER RAFTING   The American and Sacramento rivers lie nearby, and rafting is immensely popular, especially on warm weekends. Several Sacramento area outfitters rent rafts for 4 to 15 persons, along with life jackets and paddles. Their shuttles drop you and your entourage upstream and meet you 3 to 4 hours later at a predetermined point downstream. Recommended outfitters include **River Rat,** 9849 Fair Oaks Blvd., Fair Oaks (☎ **916/966-6777**), and **American River Raft Rentals,** 11257 S. Bridge St., Rancho Cordova (☎ **916/635-6400**).

California State Capitol. 10th St. (between N and L sts.). ☎ **916/324-0333**. Free admission. Daily 9am–5pm. Tours offered every hour on the hour until 4pm. Closed Thanksgiving Day, Christmas Day, and New Year's Day.

Closely resembling a scale model of the U.S. Capitol in Washington, D.C., the domed California state capitol built in 1869 and massively renovated in 1976. It is Sacramento's most distinctive landmark and has been the stage of many important political dramas in California history. Daily guided tours, offered every hour on the hour, provide insight both into the building's architecture and the workings of the government it houses.

California State Railroad Museum. 125 I St. (at 2nd St.). ☎ **916/552-5252**, ext. 7245. Admission $6 adults, $3 children 6–12. Daily 10am–5pm.

Well worth visiting, this museum is one of the highlights of Old Sacramento. You won't miss much if you bypass the memorabilia displays and head straight for the museum's 21 shiny locomotives and rail cars, beautiful antiques that are true works of art. Afterward, you can watch a film on the history of the western railroads that's actually quite good and peruse related exhibits that tell the amazing story of the building of the transcontinental railroad. This museum is not just for train buffs, and even the hordes of schoolchildren that typically mob this place shouldn't dissuade you from visiting.

April through September, on weekends and holidays, steam locomotive rides depart on the hour from 11am to 5pm from the Central Pacific Freight Depot in Old Sacramento at K and Front streets. Fares are $6 for adults and $3 for children 6 to 12.

✪ **Crocker Art Museum.** 216 O St. (at 3rd St.) ☎ **916/264-5423.** Admission $4.50 adults, $2 ages 7–17; children 6 and under free. Tues, Wed and Fri–Sun 10am–5pm, Thurs 10am–9pm. Closed major holidays.

This museum houses a truly outstanding collection of Californian art, as well as temporary exhibits from around the world. The museum itself is an imposing century-old Italianate building, with an ornate interior of carved and inlaid woods. The Crocker Mansion Wing, the museum's most recent addition, is modeled after the Crocker family home and contains works by Northern Californian artists from 1945 to the present.

Sutter's Fort State Historic Park. 2701 L St. ☎ **916/445-4422.** Admission $3 adults, $1.50 children 6–12; children 5 and under free. Daily 10am–5pm.

John Sutter established this outpost in 1839, and the park, restored to its 1846 appearance, tries to recapture the pioneering spirit of 19th-century California. The usual exhibits are on hand—a blacksmith's forge, a cooperage, a bakery, and a jail—and a self-guided audio tour is available. Historic demonstrations are staged daily in the summer.

FOR KIDS: WHERE THE WILD THINGS ARE

The best place to take your kid on a sunny afternoon in Sacramento is **Humpty Dumpty's Fairytale Town,** at William Land Park, Land Park Drive and Sutterville Road (☎ **916/264-5885**). I can still remember dragging my poor parents through the stone archway, guarded by a perilously perched Humpty Dumpty. After riding *all* the rides and climbing everything in sight, we would cross the street to the **Sacramento Zoo,** buy a big spool of cotton candy, and see *all* the animals.

WHERE TO STAY
EXPENSIVE

Hyatt Regency Sacramento. 1209 L St., Sacramento, CA 95814. ☎ **800/233-1234** or 916/443-1234. Fax 916/321-6699. 500 rms, 30 suites. A/C MINIBAR TV TEL. $169–$184 double; $205 club level rm; from $300 suite. AE, CB, DC, DISC, MC, V. Parking $6 self, $10 valet.

Sacramento's top hotel stands right in the heart of downtown, directly across from the California state capitol and near the convention center. It's *the* high-status address for visiting politicos and is popular with conventioneers as well. Its facilities and services are unmatched in the city, leaving first-class independent travelers with little choice but to stay here. While the rooms themselves are not spectacular, they conform to a very high standard and come with all the amenities you expect from Hyatt. The best are the corner units with views facing the state capitol.

Dining: Dawson's, the hotel's top restaurant, serves lunch and dinner and is worth a visit even if you're not staying at the Hyatt. Ciao Yama serves Italian/Japanese cuisine.

Services: Room service, concierge, evening turndown, car rental desk, overnight laundry, lobby shoe shines.

Facilities: Swimming pool, Jacuzzi, exercise room, gift shop.

MODERATE

Abigail's Bed-and-Breakfast. 2120 G St., Sacramento, CA 95816. ☎ **800/858-1568** or 916/441-5007. Fax 916/441-0621. 5 rms. A/C TV TEL. $100–$165 double. Rates include breakfast. AE, DISC, MC, V.

A boarding house for women during World War II, this 1912 Colonial Revival mansion has since been converted into a quaint and comfortable B&B with several pretty sitting areas, an outdoor spa in the rear garden, and Fiona, the resident cat. The home's five rooms—all with private baths—are furnished with queen-size wood or brass beds and an assortment of antiques, including a chair or small settee. Anne's Room, the B&B's best, contains an enormous mahogany four-poster bed. Every room comes with terry robes and reproductions of antique radios. Unusual for most B&Bs, a telephone and TV are available in all rooms.

✪ **Amber House Bed-and-Breakfast.** 1315 22nd St., Sacramento, CA 95816. ☎ **800/755-6526** or 916/444-8085. Fax 916/552-6529. 14 rms. A/C TV TEL. $99–$219 double. Rates include breakfast. AE, CB, DC, DISC, MC, V.

Just 8 blocks from the capitol, Amber House, a bucolic old home built in 1905 and currently owned and run by Michael and Jane Richardson, offers individually decorated rooms named for famous artists and writers. Accommodations are located in two adjacent historic houses: the Poet's Refuge, a well-crafted 1905 home with five rooms, and the Artist's Retreat, a Mediterranean-style house built in 1913; a third addition—an Old Colonial Revival home called the Amber House—is scheduled to open this summer. The Renoir Room is the B&B's best, containing a canopied, king-size bed and a Jacuzzi big enough for three. All rooms have hair dryers, VCRs, phones with computer jacks and voice mail, and marble bathrooms—11 with Jacuzzi bathtubs for two.

Amber House effectively combines elegant surroundings with impeccable service. A beautiful living room and intimate library are available for guests' use. A full breakfast is served at the time and location you request—either in your room, in the large dining room, or outside on the veranda. Coffee and a newspaper are brought to your door early every morning. And additional perks include room, concierge, and laundry service, as well as free use of bicycles kept on the B&B's premises.

Best Western Ponderosa Inn. 1100 H St., Sacramento, CA 95814. ☎ **800/528-1234** or 916/441-1314. Fax 916/441-5961. 98 rms. A/C TV TEL. $75–$135 double. Rates include continental breakfast. AE, CB, DC, DISC, MC, V.

You'd never know from the plain motel-like exterior that this is one of the best values in Sacramento. Rooms here are as up-to-date as any offered by upscale hotels such as the Hilton or the Sheraton and include well-coordinated furnishings, cable TV, a telephone with voice mail, and valet and laundry service. There's also a swimming pool in the courtyard, and complimentary coffee and pastries are served each morning in the lobby.

Delta King Riverboat. 1000 Front St., Old Sacramento, CA 95814. ☎ **800/825-5464** or 916/444-5464. 44 rms, 1 suite. A/C TV TEL. Sun–Thurs $109 double, $400 captain's quarters; Fri–Sat $139 double, $400 captain's quarters. Rates include continental breakfast. AE, DC, DISC, MC, V.

The *Delta King* carried passengers between San Francisco and Sacramento in the 1930s. Permanently moored in Sacramento since 1984, the riverboat is now a gimmicky but nonetheless charming hotel. Staying here can be quite a novelty, but the boat's cramped quarters can wear thin, especially if you're planning to spend a lot of time in your room. All rooms are nearly identical and have private baths and low ceilings. The captain's quarters, a particularly pricey suite, is a unique, mahogany-paneled stateroom, complete with an observation platform and private deck.

The Pilothouse Restaurant is popular for local office parties. When the weather is nice, there's dining on outside decks with views of Old Sacramento. The Paddlewheel Saloon, which overlooks the boat's 17-ton paddle-wheel, features regular live entertainment. On Friday and Saturday nights, the *Delta King* hosts "Suspect's Murder Mystery," an interactive whodunnit that challenges the audience to reveal the true murderer, played by period actors. It's $35 per person to attend, but that includes dinner, tax, and gratuity. Drinks, of course, are extra.

✪ Sterling Hotel. 1300 H St., Sacramento, CA 95814. ☎ **800/365-7660** or 916/448-1300. Fax 916/448-8066. 13 rms, 3 suites. A/C TV TEL. Sun–Thurs $149–$179 double, $325 suite; Fri–Sat $179–$229 double, $325 suite. Rates include continental breakfast. AE, DC, MC, V.

Set in the heart of Sacramento, 3 blocks from the capitol, this inn occupies a white-fronted Victorian mansion originally built in the 1890s and heavily renovated in 1995. The Sterling has all the charm of a small, well-managed, sophisticated inn, with a carefully tended flowering yard, tasteful decor, a scattering of antiques—and a Jacuzzi in every room.

The Chanterelle, which serves well-prepared California regional cuisine in a dignified setting is known as one of Sacramento's better restaurants. Main courses range from $13 to $19, and reservations are recommended.

INEXPENSIVE

The Sacramento Vagabond Inn. 909 Third St., Sacramento, CA 95814. ☎ **800/522-1555** or 916/446-1481. Fax 916/448-0364. 108 rms. A/C TV TEL. $83 double. Extra person $5.

Children under 19 stay free in parents' room. Rates include continental breakfast. AE, DC, DISC, MC, V.

A reliable choice within walking distance of the state capitol, the Vagabond Inn has a heated swimming pool and a host of free features, including local phone calls, weekday newspapers, and continental breakfast. Bedrooms are clean and comfortable, but not exceptional—it's the economical rates and the convenient location that make it worth your while. There's an adjoining 24-hour coffee shop as well.

WHERE TO DINE
EXPENSIVE

✪ **Biba.** 2801 Capitol Ave. ☎ **916/455-2422.** Main courses $16–$20. AE, MC, V. Mon–Fri 11:30am–2:30pm; Mon–Thurs 5:30–9:30pm, Fri–Sat 5:30–10:30pm. ITALIAN.

Locals flock to this sleek neo–art deco restaurant to sample the classical Italian cuisine of Bologna-born owner Biba Caggiano. Although the menu changes seasonally, you can expect to find about 10 or so pastas and 10 or so main courses. There might be a delicate pappardelle with a fresh seafood sauce, or a more pungent spaghetti alla Siciliana, which combines eggplant, fresh tomatoes, capers, garlic, and anchovies. For a main course, the osso bucco with Madeira wine is excellent, but save room for the double-chocolate trifle made with dark and white chocolate, Grand Marnier–soaked pound cake, and raspberry purée.

MODERATE

Capitol Grill. 2730 N St. ☎ **916/736-0744.** Reservations recommended. Main courses $6.50–$21. AE, DISC, MC, V. Mon 11am–10pm, Tue–Fri 11am–11pm, Sat 5–11pm, Sun 5–10pm. AMERICAN/SEAFOOD.

One of the liveliest restaurants in the city, Capitol Grill is popular with Sacramento's see-and-be-seen crowd, a good-looking throng of 20- and 30-somethings without any Los Angeles–style attitude (they're looking for dates, not producers) as well as politicos, lawyers, and lobbyists. An excellent selection of well-prepared dishes includes lamb osso bucco with saffron risotto, grille pork tenderloin with mashed sweet potatoes, and pan-roasted salmon wrapped in applewood-smoked bacon. We recommend the salmon pot stickers or chicken quesadilla as starters.

✪ **Harlow's.** 2708 J St. ☎ **916/441-4693.** Main courses $10–$17. AE, DC, MC, V. Tue–Sat 6–10pm. MODERN AMERICAN.

This comfortable, casual, and very popular spot has a 1930s air that might have pleased Jean Harlow herself. If you've got a hot date for the night, suggest meeting at the bar: It's Sacramento's most fashionable place to see and be seen. The pastas are superb here—ranging from the simple cannelloni in a rich meat sauce to the elaborate gnocchi in gorgonzola cream sauce. The main dishes, such as the scampi diavola with a piquant horseradish mustard cream sauce, are equally well prepared. Top it all off with the chocolate pâté, then whip out your Macanudo and join the party upstairs at the Cigar Room, where you can often find some of Sacramento's best jazz bands.

Paragary's Bar and Oven. 1401 28th St. ☎ **916/452-3335.** Reservations recommended for six or more. Main courses $10–$17. AE, DC, DISC, MC, V. Mon–Thurs 11:30am–11pm, Fri 11:30am–midnight, Sat 5pm–midnight, Sun 5–10pm. ITALIAN.

Occupying two distinct dining rooms just across the street from Capitol Grill, Paragary's vies with its neighbor for best moderately priced restaurant status in Sacramento's downtown. The fireplace room is more formal than the brighter cafe, which is outfitted with bentwood chairs and white Formica tables. During good weather, the best seats are on the sidewalk. The same menu is served no matter where you sit, with the best dishes coming from the kitchen's wood-burning pizza oven. Some of the more unusual gourmet pizza toppings are prosciutto, new potatoes, goat cheese, roasted garlic, artichokes, smoked salmon, and grilled eggplant.

The Rusty Duck. 500 Bercut Dr. ☎ **916/441-1191.** Reservations recommended. Main courses $13.95–$21.95. AE, DC, DISC, MC, V. Sun 10am–10pm; Mon–Thurs 11am–10pm; Fri 11am–11pm; Sat 4–11pm. Exit from I-5 at Richards Blvd. SEAFOOD/CALIFORNIA.

Set about 2 miles northwest of Sacramento's commercial core beside the American River, this building was inspired by a hunting lodge in Massachusetts. Rough-hewn cedar planks, river rocks, and concrete, all entwined with strands of ivy, create a kind of bucolic charm, despite the nearby roar of the I-5.

At the Duck, politicos mingle with TV stars (Alan Alda dined here the night I did, but not with me) over one of the most diverse menus in the area. A perpetual favorite is salmon rolled in mustard seed and thyme, and served with citrus-flavored watercress sauce. Also popular is the charbroiled swordfish with a brandy, white wine, oyster, and herb sauce accompanied with a dollop of red Cajun butter.

INEXPENSIVE

Aïoli. 1800 L St. ☎ **916/447-9440.** Reservations recommended. Main courses $6–$26. MC, V. Mon–Fri 10am–midnight, Sat 5–11pm, Sun 5–10pm. SPANISH.

Its fans, of whom there are many, call this the most authentic and charming Spanish restaurant in California, and they may be right. Set about 4 blocks south of the capitol, on the street level of a high-rise apartment building, it's outfitted like a bistro you might find in Andalusía, with a large folkloric dining room and a back garden. Your fellow diners might include local media figures who are regulars here and friends of the cosmopolitan staff, some of whom were born of multilingual families in Algiers. Menu items include a saffron-laden paella (prepared only for two or more), a *zarzuela* of shellfish, gazpacho, and grilled shrimp basted with herbs and olive oil.

Fox & Goose Public House. 1001 R St. (at 10th St.) ☎ **916/443-8825.** Main courses $4–$7. MC, V. Daily 7am–2pm, Mon–Fri 11am–2pm. BREAKFAST/AMERICAN-STYLE LUNCH.

The Fox is basically a giant beer hall that caters to the city's politicians, but we mention it here for its locally famous breakfasts, which include golden-brown waffles, classic bangers and crumpets, and a amazing variety of omelets, including one that's stuffed with Welsh Rarebit cheese. They offer a pretty good lunch, too—Cornish pasties, hamburgers, sandwiches, salads and such—as well as serve-yourself pub grub Monday through Friday from 5:30 to 9:30pm.

Tower Café. 1518 Broadway. ☎ **916/441-0222.** Main courses $7–$12. AE, MC, V. Mon–Fri 7–11am and 11:30am–4pm; Sun–Thurs 4:30–10pm, Fri–Sat 4:30–11pm; Sat 8am–4pm, Sun 8am–2pm. Open later for dessert and drinks only. INTERNATIONAL.

The Tower Café gets its name from the building in which it's located: a grand old 1939 movie house with a tall art deco spire. The restaurant occupies the same space in which a small mom-and-pop music store once stood. This former resident, Tower Records, has since grown into America's second-largest record retailer. While it's unlikely that Tower Café will share the phenomenal success of its predecessor, it's not because of the food or surroundings. Both are good, and even with its perpetually sluggish service, this restaurant remains our favorite Sacramento lunch spot. On warm days it seems as if everyone in the city is lunching here (in fact, recent patrons include the President and his staff), and crowd watching can be a real treat. Dishes reflect a variety of international flavors, from the Jamaican jerk chicken to Brazilian chicken salad.

2 The Gold Country

Cutting a swath for 350 miles along Calif. 49, the Gold Country stretches from Sierra City almost to the foothills of Yosemite. It still looks like a western movie set, with its mine sites, caverns, and Wild West saloons, along with ghost towns and architecture that would make Gene Autry or Roy Rogers feel right at home.

Drive along Calif. 49 and stop wherever your mood dictates. Motels, fast-food joints, and various convenience stores await you all along the route. We find the drive best in April when most of the wildflowers burst into bloom.

Placerville, east of Sacramento along Calif. 50, is in the approximate middle of the Gold Country. The northern Gold Country incorporates Placerville itself and other towns in the north, while the southern Gold Country along Calif. 49 includes such towns as Amador City, Sutter Creek, and Jackson.

THE NORTHERN GOLD COUNTRY: NEVADA CITY & GRASS VALLEY

Lying about 60 miles northeast of Sacramento, Nevada City and Grass Valley are far and away the top tourist destinations of the Northern Gold Country.

These two historic towns were at the center of the hard-rock mining fields of Northern California. Grass Valley, in fact, was California's richest mining town, producing more than $400 million worth of gold in a century. Both are attractive, although we usually spend most of our time traipsing through Nevada City. Its wealth of Victorian homes and storefronts makes it one of the most appealing small towns in California (in fact, its entire downtown has been designated a National Historic Landmark). It also has a far better selection of lodgings, although the majority of the region's best restaurants are in Grass Valley. So there you have it: Stay in Nevada City, dine in Grass Valley, and enjoy both.

It's easy to get here. If you're driving from San Francisco, take I-80 to the Calif. 49 turnoff in Auburn and follow the signs. For information about the area, go to—or call in advance—the **Grass Valley/Nevada County Chamber of Commerce,** 248 Mill St., Grass Valley, CA 95945 (☎ **530/273-4667**), or the **Nevada City Chamber of Commerce,** 132 Main St., Nevada City, CA 95959 (☎ **800/ 655-NJOY** or 530/265-2692).

NEVADA CITY Rumors of miner pulling a pound of gold a day out of Deer Creek brought hundreds of fortune seekers to the area in 1849. Within a year, it was a boisterous town of 10,000. Initially named Deer Creek Dry Diggins, it was renamed in 1850. In its heyday, everyone who was anyone visited this rollicking western outpost with its busy red-light district. Mark Twain lectured here in 1866, telling the audience about his trips to the Sandwich Islands (Hawaii). Former President Herbert Hoover also lived and worked here as a gold miner.

Pick up a walking tour map at the **Chamber of Commerce,** 132 Main St., and stroll the streets lined with impressive Victorian buildings, including the **Firehouse,** complete with bell tower, gingerbread decoration, a small museum that displays mementos from the Donner Party, a Maidu Indian basket collection, and an altar from a temple originally located in the Chinese section of Grass Valley. It's open in summer daily from 11am to 4pm; in winter it opens a half hour later and is closed on Wednesdays (☎ **530/265-5468**). The **National Hotel** (1854–56) is here, as is the **Nevada Theatre** (1865), one of the oldest theaters in the nation and still operating as such, today home to the Foothill Theatre Company.

If you want to see the source of much of the city's wealth, visit **Malakoff Diggins State Historic Park,** 23579 N. Bloomfield Rd. (☎ **530/265-2740**), 26 miles northeast of Nevada City. In the 1870s, North Bloomfield, then located in the middle of this park, had a population of 1,500. Some of the buildings have been reconstructed and refurnished to show what life was like then. The 3,000-acre park also offers several hiking trails, swimming at Blair Lake, and 30 campsites that can be reserved through Destinet by calling ☎ **800/444-7275.** The museum is open daily in summer from 10am to 5pm, but only on weekends from 10am to 4pm in the winter. To reach the park, take Calif. 49 toward Downieville for 11 miles. Turn right onto Tyler-Foote Crossing Road for 17 miles. The name will change to Curzon Grade and then to Backbone. Turn right onto Derbec Road and into the park.

Another 6 miles up Calif. 49 from the Malakoff Diggins turnoff will bring you to Pleasant Valley Road, the exit that will take you (in about 7 miles) to one of the most impressive covered bridges in the country. Built in 1862, it's 225 feet long and was crossed by many a stagecoach.

GRASS VALLEY In contrast to Nevada City's "tourist town" image, Grass Valley is the commercial/retail center of the region. The **Empire Mine State Historic Park,** 10791 E. Empire St., Grass Valley (☎ **530/273-8522**), is just outside of town. This mine, which once had 367 miles of underground shafts, produced an estimated 5.8 million ounces of gold between 1850 and 1956, when it closed. Here you can look down the shaft of the mine, walk around the mine yard, and stroll through the gardens of the mine owner. From March through November, tours are given daily and a mining movie is shown. You can also enjoy picnicking, cycling, mountain biking, or hiking in the 784-acre park. It's open year-round except for Thanksgiving Day, Christmas Day, and New Year's Day. Admission to the museum is $3 for adults and $1 for children.

In town, visitors can pick up a walking tour map at the Chamber of Commerce and explore the historic downtown area along Mill and Main streets. There are also a couple of museums that history buffs will want to visit: the Grass Valley Museum, in Mount Saint Mary's Convent and Chapel on South Church Street (☎ **530/ 273-5509**), the North Star Mining Museum (☎ **530/273-4255**), and the new Video History Museum, which houses a collection of old films of the region from the 1920s. It's located in Memorial Park off Calif. 47 (☎ **530/274-1126**).

Grass Valley was, for a time, the home of Lola Montez, singer, dancer, and paramour of the rich and famous. A fully restored home that she bought and occupied in 1853 can be viewed at 248 Mill St. (☎ **530/273-4667**), now the site of Grass Valley's Chamber of Commerce. Down the street Lotta Crabtree, Montez's famous protegée, lived at 238 Mill St., now an apartment house. Also pop into the Holbrooke Hotel at 212 Main St. to see the signature of Mark Twain, who stayed here along with five U.S. presidents. The saloon has been in continuous use since 1852, and it's the place to meet the locals and have a tall cold one.

The surrounding region offers many recreational opportunities on its rivers and lakes and in the Tahoe National Forest. You can enjoy fishing, swimming, and boating at **Scotts Flat Lake** near Nevada City (east on Calif. 20) and at **Rollins Lake** on Calif. 174, between Grass Valley and Colfax. White-water rafting is available on several rivers. **Tributary Whitewater Tours,** 20480 Woodbury Dr., Grass Valley, CA 95949 (☎ **800/672-3846** or 530/346-6812), offers half- to three-day trips from March to October. In winter you can ski at Sugar Bowl Ski resort and Royal Gorge (only 45 minutes away) or at Squaw Valley, Alpine Meadows, and Northstar, a little more than an hour away over the Donner Pass (see chapter 8). The region is also ideal for mountain biking. The Chambers of Commerce publish a trail guide, but there's

The Gold Country

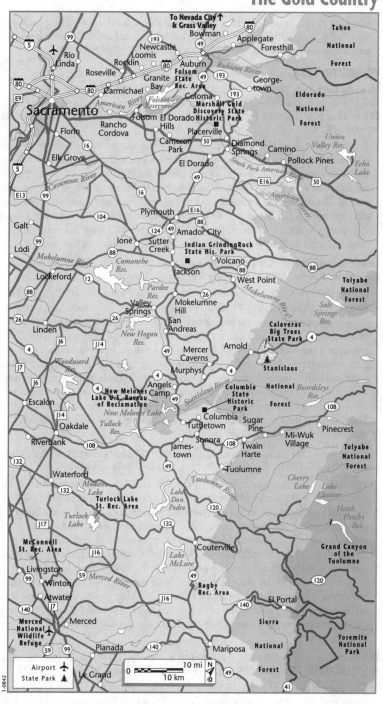

To Nevada City ↑
& Grass Valley

Bowman

Tahoe

National

Forest

Applegate
Foresthill

Newcastle
Loomis

Rocklin

Rio
Linda

Roseville

Auburn
Folsom
State
Rec. Area

Rubicon River

George-
town

Eldorado

National

Forest

Carmichael

Granite
Bay

American River

Folsom
Reservoir

Coloma
Marshall Gold
Discovery State
Park

Sacramento

Folsom

El Dorado
Hills

Florin

Rancho
Cordova

Cameron
Park

Placerville

Diamond
Springs

Camino

Union
Valley Res.

Echo
Lake

Elk Grove

El Dorado

Pollock Pines

South Fork American

American River

Cosumnes River

Galt

Plymouth

E16

Lodi

Ione

Sutter
Creek

Amador City

Indian GrindingRock
State His. Park

Lockeford

Mokelumne River

Comanche
Res.

Jackson

Volcano

West Point

Toiyabe

National

Forest

Salt
Springs
Res.

Linden

Valley
Springs

Pardee
Res.

Mokelumne River

Mokelumne
Hill

San
Andreas

New Hogan
Res.

Calaveras
Big Trees
State Park

Arnold

Woodward Res.

Mercer
Caverns

Murphys

Stanislaus

Escalon

New Melones
Lake U.S. Bureau
of Reclamation

Angels
Camp

New Melones Lake

Stanislaus River

Columbia
State
Historic
Park

National

Beardsleys
Res.

Oakdale

Tulloch
Res.

Columbia

Sugar
Pine

Riverbank

Tuttletown

Sonora

Mi-Wuk
Village

Pinecrest

Waterford

Jamestown

Twain
Harte

Toiyabe

National

Forest

Modesto
Lake

Tuolumne

Turlock Lake
St. Rec. Area

Lake
Don
Pedro

Tuolumne River

Cherry
Lake

Lake
Eleanor

Turlock
Lake

Hetch
Hetchy
Res.

McConnell
St. Rec. Area

Couterville

Lake
McLure

Grand Canyon
of the
Tuolumne

Livingston

Winton

Merced River

Atwater

Bagby
Rec. Area

El Portal

Merced
National
Wildlife
Refuge

Merced

Sierra

Planada

Mariposa

National

Yosemite
National
Park

Le Grand

Airport ✈
State Park ✦

0   10 mi
0   10 km

Forest

nowhere to rent a bike in either Nevada City or Grass Valley—bring your own wheels. For regional **hiking** information, contact **Tahoe National Forest** headquarters at Coyote Street and Calif. 49 in Nevada City (☎ **530/265-4531**).

WHERE TO STAY

Nevada City

Deer Creek Inn Bed & Breakfast. 116 Nevada St., Nevada City, CA 95959. ☎ **800/ 655-0363** or 530/265-0363. Fax 530/265-0980. 5 rms. A/C. $90–$145 double. Rates include breakfast. MC, V.

An 1860 three-floor Victorian overlooking Deer Creek and within walking distance of downtown Nevada City, this inn feels like a warm home-away-from-home. The individually decorated rooms, most with private verandas facing the creek or town, are furnished with assorted antiques and four-poster or canopy beds with down comforters. The ceiling fans provide adequate cooling in summer; most bathrooms have clawfoot tubs. A full breakfast is served either out on the deck or in the formal dining room. Guests are invited to try a little panning of their own, fish, play croquet, or simply relax and enjoy the lawn and landscaped gardens along the creek.

Emma Nevada House. 528 E. Broad St., Nevada City, CA 95959. ☎ **800/991-EMMA** or 530/265-4415. 6 rms. $100–$150 double. Rates include breakfast. AE, DC, MC, V.

Innkeeper Ruth Ann Riese runs one of the finest—and prettiest—B&Bs in the Gold Country, a picture perfect Victorian that was once the childhood home of 19th-century opera star Emma Nevada. You'll like everything about this place: its quiet location, sun-drenched decks, and wraparound porch, the understated decor, and particularly the breakfast, which is served in the beautiful hexagonal Sun Room. The guest rooms range from small and intimate to large and luxurious; all have private baths and queen-size beds, and most are available with phone and TV upon request. Top choice for honeymooners is the Empress's Chamber with its large wall of windows, soothing ivory and burgundy tones, and—of course—the Jacuzzi tub for two. You'll also like the fact that the shops and restaurants of Nevada City's Historic District are only a short walk away.

National Hotel. 211 Broad St., Nevada City, CA 95959. ☎ **530/265-4551**. 42 rms (30 with private bath). A/C TV TEL. $68 double with bath, from $113 suite with bath. AE, MC, V.

You can't miss this classic three-story Victorian, the oldest hotel in continuous operation west of the Rocky Mountains. It's located near what was once the center of the town's red-light district. The lobby is full of mementos from that era, hence the grandfather clock and early square piano. The suites are replete with Gold Rush–era antiques and large, cozy beds. Most rooms have private baths, and some come with canopy beds and romantic love seats. A definite bonus during typically sweltering summers is the secluded swimming pool filled with cool mountain water.

The hotel's Victorian dining room, which serves traditional items such as prime rib, steaks, lobster tail, and homemade desserts, also has a Gold Rush atmosphere; tables, for example, are lit with coal oil lamps. The hotel provides live entertainment on Friday and Saturday nights. There's also a popular Sunday brunch, one of the best in the county.

Red Castle Historic Lodgings. 109 Prospect St., Nevada City, CA 95959. ☎ **800/761-4766** or 530/265-5135. 7 rms. $70–$140 double. Rates include breakfast. MC, V.

This elegant but comfortable hillside inn occupies a four-story Gothic Revival brick house built in 1860; it's situated in a secluded spot with a panoramic view of the town. The highlight of the week is the Sunday afternoon "Conversations with Mark

Twain" in which guests can engage the great author (or at least a reasonable facsimile thereof—a costumed actor) in conversation while enjoying such specialties as lemon tarts and a choice cup of tea. The house has retained its original woodwork, plaster moldings, ceiling medallions, and much of the handmade glass; it lacks any modern intrusions, such as TVs and telephones. Guests enjoy bountiful five-course buffet breakfasts, and can relax on the verandas that encircle the first two floors of the house. Our favorite rooms are the Garden Room with a canopy bed and French doors leading into the gardens, and the air-conditioned three-room garret suite tucked under the eaves, furnished with sleigh beds and featuring Gothic arched windows.

Grass Valley

Holbrooke Hotel. 212 West Main St., Grass Valley, CA 95945. ☎ **800/933-7077** or 530/ 273-1353. Fax 530/273-0434. 28 rms, 2 suites. A/C TV TEL. $55–$145 double; $95–$145 suite. AE, DC, DISC, MC, V.

This Victorian-era white clapboard building was a rollicking saloon during the Gold Rush days, and then evolved into a place for exhausted miners to "rack out." The oldest and most historic hotel in town, it has hosted a number of legendary figures since opening its doors: Ulysses Grant, Benjamin Harrison, Grover Cleveland, and Gentleman Jim Corbett, among others. Seventeen of the rooms lie within the main building. The remainder are within an adjacent annex, a house occupied long ago by the hotel's owner. The rooms have high ceilings; the front rooms are large and have access to the balconies. Each is decorated with an eclectic collection of Gold Rush–era furniture.

Murphy's Inn. 318 Neal St., Grass Valley, CA. 95945. ☎ **800/895-2488** or 530/273-6873. 8 rms. A/C TV. $95–$150 double. Rates include breakfast. AE, MC, V.

This 1866 Colonial Revival house that was built for Edward Coleman, owner of the North Star mine, has been turned into a crackerjack B&B. Today it stands at the center of well-tended gardens complete with fountains, a fish pond, and a tall sequoia. Guests can relax in the gardens; on the porch, where trimmed ivy baskets hang decoratively; or in two very well-furnished and comfortable living rooms with fireplaces. The rooms are equally alluring, all decorated in a chintzy Victorian style, but each with its own unique charm. Some have fireplaces, others, such as the Sequoia Room and Karin's Room, have a skylight. Two of the most spacious units, both with fireplaces and one with a full kitchen, are in the Donation Day House.

WHERE TO DINE

Nevada City

✪ **Country Rose Cafe.** 300 Commercial St. ☎ **530/265-6252.** Reservations recommended. Main courses $14–$22. Sun–Thurs 11am–2:30pm, 5–9pm; Fri–Sat 11am–2:30pm, 5–9:30pm. AE, MC, V. COUNTRY FRENCH.

The flowery country-French atmosphere of this popular Nevada City restaurant belies a serious (and seriously priced) menu put together by owner/chef Michael Johns. Dinner selections, written on a huge feltboard that's lugged over to your table soon after you've been seated, are mostly French with a dash of Italian, Mexican and American dishes. Skip the lifeless pastas and head straight for John's specialty—fresh fish prepared in a myriad of classic styles such as filet of sole dore, swordfish oskar, and sea bass with garlic basil sauce. Other regular menu items include filet mignon, lobster, rack of lamb, and roast game hen, all served with soup and salad. Both lunch (handled by Michael's son Dave) and dinner are served on the pretty walled-in patio during the summer months, so be sure to request alfresco seating when making a reservation.

Friar Tucks. 111 N. Pine St. ☎ **530/265-9093.** Main courses $14–$20. AE, MC, V. Daily 5–9:30pm, weekends until 10pm. INTERNATIONAL.

A local favorite for nearly a quarter of a century, this restaurant consists of a series of rustic, dimly lit rooms furnished with high-backed oak booths. The weekly changing menu is eclectic, offering everything from cheese fondues and Swiss meatballs to teriyaki steak, Tuck's bouillabaisse, or duck with raspberry sauce. The accompanying wine list is surprisingly impressive. With the flavor and ambiance of a British pub, the bar is a popular local hangout, and has a guitar player who entertains nightly from 7pm. A recent expansion has added a new dining room overlooking Nevada City's historic district.

Kirby's Creekside Restaurant & Bar. 101 Broad St. ☎ **530/273-3445.** Reservations suggested. Mon–Thurs 11:30am–2:30pm, 5–9:30pm; Fri–Sat 11:30am–2:30pm, 5–10pm; Sun brunch 10am–2:30pm, dinner 5–8:30pm. INTERNATIONAL.

After being royally thumped by the floods of '97, Kirby's Creekside is back in business serving a wide variety of steak, seafood, pasta, and chicken to the sights and sounds of Deer Creek, which literally flows underneath the restaurant's large wood deck. If possible, forego the low-ceiling, low-budget dining room for a far more romantic table outdoors. For starters, try the fresh pumpkin ravioli in sage cream sauce or steamed mussels with chive sauce and sherry aïoli. Recommend dinner choices include the oven-roasted leg of lamb with honey thyme sauce, the stuffed pork chop with orange port sauce, or take a chance with the "Chef's Grand Creation: unique & exotic creations supremely chosen by the chef." Lunch is more modest—sandwiches, burgers, salads, and a half-dozen hot entrees, all surprisingly inexpensive.

Grass Valley

The Dining Room at the Holbrooke Hotel. 212 West Main St. ☎ **530/273-1353.** Reservations recommended on Fri–Sat nights. Main courses $11–$19. Daily 11:30am–2pm and 5–8:30pm; Sun brunch 10am–2pm. AE, DC, DISC, MC, V. AMERICAN.

This hotel dining room is the most formal place in town—an ironic twist, given its past life as a Gold Rush saloon and a flophouse for drunken miners. In its way, it's the most authentic and nostalgic restaurant in a town filled with worthy hardworking competitors. Items on the daily changing menu include free-range chicken topped with citrus honey glaze, oakwood smoked beef medaillons with port sauce, and a changing assortment of dishes inspired by the whimsy of chef Peter Jackson. Should your arteries need further hardening, Saturday and Sunday is "prime rib" night.

The Old California. 341 East Main St. ☎ **530/273-7341.** Main courses $5–$14. MC, V. Mon–Fri 11:30am–2pm; Sun–Thurs 5–9:30pm, Fri–Sat 5–10pm. PRIME RIB/AMERICAN.

Located about a half mile east of the commercial center of town, this restaurant has a very loyal clientele who swear by its prime rib. It occupies a sprawling, turn-of-the-century building that around 1901 housed a thriving bordello. Inside, you'll find lots of memorabilia and photos of earlier and lustier eras. A platter of prime rib, with salad and vegetables, is a bargain at $8.95; other choices include boneless breast of chicken, vegetarian pastas, prawns, calamari steak, and such fish platters of the day as grilled fillets of red snapper seasoned with herbs. The most expensive item on the menu, priced at $13.95, is a heaping platter with 16 ounces of prime rib cooked any way you like it.

The Stewart House. 124 Bank St. ☎ **530/477-1559.** Reservations recommended. Main courses $17–$23. AE, MC, V. Tues–Fri 11am–2pm, Tues–Sun 5–9pm (weekends till 10pm). FRENCH CARRIBEAN.

Owner James Harte and Executive Chef Greg Stage have teamed up to create the crème de la crème of Northern Gold Country restaurants, a high-fashion affair set within a stately 1891 Victorian that's gilded with chandeliers, gallery-quality artwork, high ceilings, lace curtains, silver settings atop white table cloths, and a gorgeous grand piano whose keys are tickled on the weekends. Along with an extensive wine list is a wide assortment of entrees and appetizers ranging from escargot and Caribbean crab cakes to seared rack of lamb encrusted with peppercorns, oven-baked lobster, seared sea scallops atop linguini, and our favorite—range quail filled with herbed goat cheese and topped with a currant brandy sauce. On warm summer nights, request a table on the walled-in back patio, and consider arriving a bit early for a pre-dinner glass of merlot at the elegant wine bar.

Tofanelli's. 302 W. Main St. ☎ **530/272-1468.** Main courses $7–$12. AE, MC, V. Mon–Fri 11am–8:30pm, Sat brunch 9am–3pm, dinner 5–9pm, Sun brunch 9am–3pm, dinner 5–8:30pm. INTERNATIONAL.

If a diet of meat and potatoes isn't your cup of tea, head to Tofanelli's, which specializes in good—and good for you—entrees for brunch, lunch, and dinner. You'll like the setting, a bright, cheery trio of dining areas (outdoor patio, atrium room, and dining room) separated by exposed brick walls and decorated with beautiful prints and paintings. Specials on the menu, such as gorgonzola ravioli topped with garlic cream sauce or mu shu vegetables with baked tofu, change weekly, but you can always rely on Tofanelli classics like Linda's famous vegetarian lasagna and the popular veggie burger. And yes, they serve good ol' New York steak, too. Don't you dare depart without a slice of Katherine's chocolate cake.

AUBURN, COLOMA & PLACERVILLE

From Grass Valley it's a short drive along Calif. 49 south to Auburn. If you're driving straight from San Francisco, take I-80 to Calif. 50 and follow the signs from there.

For information, contact the **Auburn Area Chamber of Commerce,** 601 Lincoln Way, Auburn (☎ 530/885-5616); **Placer County Tourism,** 13464 Lincoln Way, Auburn (☎ 530/887-2111); or the **El Dorado County Chamber of Commerce,** 542 Main St., Placerville (☎ 530/621-5885).

AUBURN   In Auburn you might want to linger in the **Old Town** and browse the stores. Auburn also has the **Placer County Museum** 101 Maple St. (☎ **530/ 889-6500**), a state-of-the-art exhibit on the history of Placer County, including a remarkable Native American collection, a restored sheriff's office, and mining displays. The museum is open Tuesday through Sunday from 10am to 4pm. Admission is free.

COLOMA   Auburn is en route to the site of the original discovery that started it all: Coloma, where gold was discovered in 1848. Over the next 50 years, 125 million ounces of gold were taken from the Sierra foothills (worth $50 billion today), fueling the rapid development of California and the nation. Coloma was quickly mined out, but its boom brought 10,000 people to the settlement and lasted long enough for residents to build a schoolhouse, a gunsmith, a general store, and a tiny, tin-roofed post office. The miners also planted oak and mimosa trees that shade the street during hot summers. About 70% of this quiet, pretty town lies in **The Marshall Gold Discovery State Historic Park** (☎ 530/622-3470), which preserves the spot where James Wilson Marshall discovered gold along the banks of the south fork of the American River. Although Marshall and his partner, John Sutter, tried to keep the discovery secret, the word soon leaked out. Sam Brannan, who ran a general store at Fort Sutter, secured some gold samples himself (as well as significant amounts of choice Coloma real estate), and then headed for San Francisco, where he ran through the streets shouting, "Gold! Gold! Gold! From the American River!" San Francisco rapidly emptied as men rushed off to seek their fortunes at the mines—and make Sam Brannan's.

How to Pan for Gold

Find a gold pan—ideally a 12- to 15-inch steel pan. Place the pan over an oven burner, or better yet, in a camp fire. This will darken the pan, making it easier to see any flakes of placer gold. Find some gravel, sand, or dirt in a stream that looks promising or feels lucky. Scoop dirt into the pan until it's nearly full and then place it under water and keep it there while you break up the clumps of mud and clay and toss out any stones. Then grasp the pan with both hands. Holding it level, rotate it in swirling motions. This will cause the heavier gold to loosen and settle to the bottom of the pan. Drain off the dirty water and loose stuff. Keep doing this until gold and heavier minerals called "black sand" are left in the pan. Carefully inspect the "black sand" for nuggets or speck traces of gold. You just might be lucky.

You can dredge for gold from June 1 to October 15, but you need a dredging permit. Apply for one at Regional 2 Headquarters, **CA Dept. of Fish & Game,** 1701 Nimbus Rd., Rancho Cordova, CA 95670 (☎ **530/358-2900**). Or you can sign up for one of the gold-panning tours offered in the Gold Country towns. Try calling **Gold Prospecting Expeditions** (☎ **800/596-0009** or 209/984-4653), which also runs a free gold mining camp called "Gemtown." Here you'll find over 25 Gold Country attractions such as Mark Twain's old cabin, as well as picnic areas and panning sites.

Farther up Main Street is a huge replica of the mill Marshall was building when he made his discovery. The largest building in town, the mill is powered by electricity during the summer months. Other attractions in the park include the **Gold Discovery Museum,** which relates the story of the Gold Rush, and a number of Chinese stores, all that remain of the once sizable local Chinese community. The park also has three picnic areas, four trails, recreational gold panning, and a number of buildings and exhibits relating the way of life that prevailed here in the 19th century. Admission is $5 per vehicle, and it's open daily from 10am to 5pm, except on major holidays.

Also worth a stop is the **James Marshall Monument and Gravesite,** just north of Coloma on Calif. 153 (California's shortest highway at three-tenths of a mile). At its end you'll find the huge bronze statue of James Wilson Marshall on a knoll beyond the parking lot stands. It doubles as his gravestone and points to the spot where he discovered gold on January 24, 1848, while building a sawmill. Although word of his find spread to as far away as Mexico and China, Marshall never ended up making a dime from his discovery. He ended his days as a carpenter and blacksmith in nearby Kelsey, unrecognized for his contribution.

The view from the monument is beautiful, especially in spring, when the green hills sprout wildflowers. Nearby picnic tables are scattered beneath huge oak trees. The site and its public rest rooms are kept tidy by a resident park ranger, who will request a $5 parking fee that's good for all of the park's attractions.

Folks also come here for white-water thrills on the American River (Coloma is a popular launching point). **White Water Connection,** Coloma (☎ 530/622-6446), offers half- to two-day trips down the frothy forks of the American River. It's great fun and one of the Gold Country's best outdoor attractions.

PLACERVILLE Eight miles south of Coloma is Placerville. Although its main street has a string of historic Victorian buildings, don't come here expecting a cute mining town—it's a modern commercial center. But there is the **El Dorado County**

Historical Museum, 104 Placerville Dr. (☎ **530/621-5865**), which features a large collection of Native American baskets, plus some remarkable examples of Old West–style transportation. Admission is free and it's open Wednesday to Saturday from 10am to 4pm, Sunday from noon to 4pm. The other attraction is **Hangtown's Gold Bug Park,** located 1 mile north of downtown Placerville via Bedford Ave. and Calif. 50 (☎ **530/642-5238**). Self-guided tours through the nation's only municipally owned gold mine are offered daily May through October from 10am to 4pm, and on Saturdays and Sundays November through April from noon to 4pm (weather permitting). Admission is $2 (12 and under free), and $1 for a tour cassette rental. There's also a museum, picnic facilities, and 7 miles of walking trails.

WHERE TO STAY
Auburn

Also consider the well-maintained and -equipped motel-style **Auburn Inn,** 1875 Auburn Ravine Rd., Auburn, CA 95603 (☎ **800/272-1444** or 530/885-1800), where rooms go for $60 to $66 double, including a buffet continental breakfast.

Power's Mansion Inn. 164 Cleveland Ave., Auburn, CA 95603. ☎ **530/885-1166.** 11 rms. $75–$160 double. AE, MC, V.

This century-old mansion in the heart of downtown Auburn was built by a state assemblyman who obviously felt he deserved nothing but the finest. And while the pink paint job boggles one's sensibilities, the interior's rich, dark woods and classic Victorian furnishings have been left unmarred—it's quite easy to imagine you've been transported into the past. Each of the guest rooms is decorated with period antiques and big brass beds, and all have private baths (a rarity among Gold Country classics). The not-so-subtly named Anniversary Room and the Honeymoon Suite are the best of the lot: Both have fireplaces, and the latter has a sunken heart-shaped Jacuzzi for two. Innkeeper Tony Verhaart serves a bountiful breakfast in the handsome dining room.

Coloma

✪ **Coloma Country Inn.** 345 High St., Coloma, CA 95613. ☎ **530/622-6919.** 5 rms (3 with private bath), 2 suites. $88–$99 double; $120–$170 suite. No credit cards.

In the middle of the state park, this restored 1852 country farmhouse situated on 5 landscaped acres is a very romantic place to stay. It's made even more inviting by the warmth of innkeepers Alan and Cindi Ehrgott. Alan doubles as a veteran balloon pilot, and you can sign up for an hour-long flight launched from a balloon field just a short walk away from the B&B when you book your room (the B&B/Balloon package is $215 per person). You can also make arrangements for white-water rafting trips. The rooms are very prettily decorated with stenciling, antiques, and plenty of fresh flowers from the surrounding gardens. The two suites in a separate cottage, one of which has a full kitchen, are exceptionally appealing. Afternoon tea and lemonade are served in the garden gazebo, and guests have full access to the comfortable parlor and front porch. There's an old pond on the property where kids can feed the ducks. A full breakfast is served in the formal dining room. If you're bringing children, advance notice is needed. Smoking is not permitted.

Placerville

Chichester-McKee House. 800 Spring St., Placerville, CA 95667. ☎ **800/831-4008** or 530/626-1882. 4 rms. A/C. $85–$125 double. AE, DISC, MC, V. Turn off Calif. 49 at Coloma St.; turn right on High St., then right again on Wood St. to the parking area behind the house.

A handsome Victorian featuring fretwork and stained glass, this home—the first in Placerville to have indoor plumbing—was built in 1892 for a lumber baron. Today it is furnished with the doll collection and other personal effects of innkeepers Bill and Doreen Thornhill, who are happy to give sightseeing advice. Each room contains Oriental rugs, a crocheted bedspread or quilt, and country-oak furnishings; two have a sink and toilet, and bathrobes for the shared bath down the hallway. The new Thornhill room, with fireplace, balcony, and full bath, is our favorite. Guests can relax in the parlor or the library. An elaborate breakfast of crêpes, quiches, eggs Benedict, and "Bill's Special Blend" coffee is served in the dining room.

WHERE TO DINE
Auburn

✪ **The Headquarter House.** 14500 Musso Rd. ☎ **530/878-1906.** Reservations recommended. Main courses $9–$20. AE, DC, MC, V. Daily 11am–9:30 or 10pm. Drive northeast from Auburn's center along I-80, take the Bell exit. AMERICAN/INTERNATIONAL.

Three miles east of Auburn's center is one of the area's most popular and consistently reliable restaurants. Many of its windows overlook the eighth hole of a nine-hole golf course; it's the unofficial watering hole and celebration (or commiseration) site of anyone playing on the nearby course. A pianist performs every Thursday to Sunday from 6 to around 10pm. If you prefer to dine outside, there's a deck with a half-dozen individual gazebos, each suitable for up to six diners. Menu items include steaks, prime rib, and such seafood dishes as salmon from the nearby Middlefork River, served in a lobster/pink peppercorn sauce. No smoking is allowed inside.

Latitudes. 130 Maple St. (across from the County Courthouse) ☎ **530/885-9535.** Main courses $10–$17. AE, MC, V. Mon–Fri 11:30am–3pm, Wed–Sun 5–9pm (Fri–Sat till 10pm), Sun brunch 10am–3pm. INTERNATIONAL.

Owners/chefs Pat and Pete Enoch have brought the cuisines of the world to this handsome Victorian manor in little ol' Auburn. Each month, Pat and Pete select a special regional cuisine from a chosen latitude, including select beers and wines from that country. June, for example, is Greek month; May is African, and September, Spanish. The result is a widely varied menu focusing on light, healthy dishes served at reasonable prices, such as falafel wraps and spinach crepes for lunch, curried tofu and teriyaki tempeh for dinner, and oatmeal pancakes and Spanish omelets for brunch. If all this sounds entirely too healthy, fret not: they also make a killer burger.

Placerville

Lil' Mama D. Carlo's. 482 Main St. ☎ **530/626-1612.** Reservations recommended. Main courses $8–$15. MC, V. Sun–Thurs 3pm–9pm, Fri–Sat 3pm–10pm. ITALIAN.

If you're in the mood for Italian food, there's a little *ristorante* on Placerville's Main Street that's been pleasing hungry locals for the past 17 years. Just about everything from Lil' Mama D. Carlo's kitchen is made from scratch, such as their giant ravioli hand-stuffed with ricotta, Parmesan, and spinach, or their tangy lasagna with seasoned pork sausage and thick layers of fresh Parmesan and mozzarella cheese. All entrees come with a choice of salad or minestrone soup—made fresh daily—and garlic bread. The best part, however, is the price: Most pastas are under $10, and the entire selection of El Dorado County wines is under $15.

Smith Flat House. 2021 Smith Flat Rd. ☎ **530/621-0667.** Main courses $11–$16. AE, DC, MC, V. Mon 11:30am–2pm, Tues–Sat 11:30am–2pm and 5–9pm, Sun 4:30–8:30pm. Saloon Mon–Thurs 10:30am–midnight, Fri–Sat 10:30am–2am, Sun 11am–midnight. AMERICAN.

Set at the western end of Placerville's historic center, behind a balcony where desperado shoot-outs might have taken place, this is probably the first building you see as you drive east into town from Sacramento. If there's a standard local favorite in Placerville, this is it. Fabled as the final milepost on the Lake Tahoe Wagon Trail, this place has lived through many incarnations—everything from a Pony Express depot drop-off to a dance hall with "wicked" show girls. Beginning in 1853, it fed whiskey and (probably unpalatable) food to miners and cattle farmers streaming in from the surrounding fields. Today it revels in nostalgia for the Old West. There's a saloon in the cellar with a circular mine shaft that's said to lead to the heart of the Mother Lode. Reasonably well-prepared meals are served in the street-level restaurant. The food is hearty and very American, and no one leaves hungry. The limited dinner menu focuses on steaks, chicken, and grilled or deep-fried seafood.

Zachary Jacques. 1821 Pleasant Valley Rd. ☎ **530/626-8045.** Reservations recommended. Main courses $15–$22. AE, MC, V. Wed–Sat 5:30–9:30pm, Sun 5–8:30pm. FRENCH.

Zachary Jacques is easily the best restaurant in town. The French cuisine, which changes with the seasons, is well prepared and carefully presented, with an emphasis on fresh produce and meats. Start with the *champignons farcis en croûte,* mushroom caps stuffed with spinach, Brie, sun-dried tomatoes, and basil, then baked in puff pastry. Specialties include Rack of Lamb *Valréas,* with Dijon mustard, rosemary and garlic, and *Lapin Ardèchoise,* fresh rabbit sautéed with leeks and served with whole-grain mustard sauce. Wednesday diners have a bonus option: Cassoulet Maison, a classic country dish with white beans, duck, sausages, and lamb. The Sunday "country dinners" are a real bargain—five courses for $18.

THE SOUTHERN GOLD COUNTRY

From Placerville, continue south along Calif. 49 via Plymouth and Drytown. If you're coming straight here from San Francisco, take I-80 to Route 4. You can either follow Route 4 all the way to Angels Camp to pick up Calif. 49 north, or you can turn off Route 4 to Route 99 and pick up Route 88 to Jackson.

For information, contact the **Amador County Chamber of Commerce,** 125 Peek St., Jackson (☎ **209/223-0350**).

Before you reach the southern Gold Country's appealing mining towns, you may want to turn off Calif. 49 to explore the Shenandoah Valley around Plymouth. Take Shenandoah Road east to explore the **Amador County Wine Country,** which is known for its zinfandel and, more recently, for sauvignon blanc and chenin blanc. The wineries are small and family-owned; any tour or tasting will most likely be given by the owner. There are several wineries on Shenandoah Road (Sonny Grace, Sobon Estate, and Vino Noceto); Bell Road (Karly and Story); and Steiner Road (with at least six). Bell and Steiner both branch off from Shenandoah.

AMADOR CITY & SUTTER CREEK   Once bustling mining towns, Amador City and Sutter Creek are now devoted to dredging up tourist dollars. Although Amador City sounds large and impressive, it is in fact tiny. Local merchants have made the most of a refurbished boardwalk and a few historic buildings; both villages are a shopper's paradise, with everything from turn-of-the-century antiques and folk art to handcrafted furniture, Gold Rush–memorabilia, rare books, and Native American craftwork for sale. However, parking can be difficult, especially during the summer months.

JACKSON   Jackson, the county seat of Amador County, is livelier. Be sure to take time to stroll through the town, browsing in the stores and noting the Victorian buildings. Although the Kennedy and Argonaut mines ultimately produced more than $140 million in gold, Jackson initially earned its place in the Gold Rush as a supply center. That history is apparent in the town's wide Main Street, lined by tall buildings adorned with intricate iron railings. Make no mistake: This is not a ghost town, but rather a modern minicity that has worked to preserve its pre-Victorian influence. At the southern end of the street is the famous **National Hotel,** rumored to be California's oldest continuously operating hotel since it opened its doors in 1862. Today, the hotel's **Louisiana House Bar,** a cool, dark establishment where weary travelers can rest while a honky-tonk pianist beats out ragtime, does plenty of business.

Take a good look at the **Wells Fargo Club and Charcoal Broiler,** located diagonally across the street from the hotel. This 2-story brick structure with its wooden balcony and awning is an original 1851 Wells Fargo building. Also worth a gander is the **Amador County Museum,** a huge brick building at 225 Church Street, where Will Rogers filmed *Boys will be Boys* in 1920. Today the former home of Armstead Calvin Brown and his 11 children is filled with mining memorabilia and information on two local mines, the Kennedy and the Argonaut, that were among the deepest and richest in the nation. Within the museum is a working large-scale model of the Kennedy. The museum (☎ 209/223-6386) is open Wednesday to Sunday from 10am to 4pm; admission is $2.

VOLCANO   Upon leaving Jackson, follow signs back to Calif. 49 south. Once back on the highway, begin looking immediately for Calif. 88 east. Turn left onto Calif. 88 and travel 12 miles to the beautiful and mostly unrestored town of **Volcano**— one of the most authentic ghost towns in the central Sierra. The town got its name in 1848, after miners mistook the origin of the enormous craggy boulders that lie in the center of the village. The dark rock and blind window frames of a few backless, ivy-covered buildings give the town's main throughfare a haunted look. Sprinkled between boarded-up buildings, about a hundred residents do business in the same sagging storefronts that a population of 8,000 frequented nearly 150 years ago.

The overwhelming thing you'll notice about Volcano is the silence of its streets. But the tiny, now-quiet burg has a rich history: Not only was this boomtown once home to 17 hotels, courts of quick justice, and the state's first lending library, but Volcano gold supported the Union during the Civil War. Residents even smuggled a huge cannon to the front line in a hearse (it was never used). The story goes that had the enthusiastic blues fired it, **"Old Abe"** would have exploded, it was so overcharged. The cannon sits in the town center today, under a rusting weathervane.

Looming over the small buildings is the stately **St. George Hotel** (☎ 209/ 296-4458), a 3-story, balconied building that testifies to the $90 million in gold mined in and around the town. Its ivy-covered brick and shuttered windows will remind you of colonial New England. The 20-room hotel is still in operation (though not particularly recommended) as is the restaurant, which serves breakfast Saturday and Sunday mornings and dinner Wednesday through Sunday. Even if you're not hungry, stop in for a libation at the classic old bar.

MOKELUMNE HILL   South of Jackson on Calif. 49 is one of the most evocative mining towns of the region. The town basically consists of one street overlooking a valley with a few old buildings, and somehow its sad, abandoned air has the mark of authenticity. It's not gussied up; it's just the unvarnished way it has remained for decades. At one time the hill was dotted with tents and wood and tar-paper shacks, and the town boasted a population of 15,000, including an old French quarter and a Chinatown. But now many of its former residents are merely memorialized in the town's Protestant, Jewish, and Catholic cemeteries.

WHERE TO STAY

Amador City

Imperial Hotel. Main St. (P.O. Box 195), Amador City, CA 95601. ☎ **800/242-5594** or 209/ 267-9172. 6 rms. A/C. $80–$100 double. AE, DISC, MC, V.

Right on Calif. 49, this hotel occupies a brick Victorian that was built in 1879. The individually decorated rooms—all with private baths—are upstairs above the dining room and are furnished with brass, iron, or pine beds; two come with private balconies. Our favorite room features hand-painted furnishings by local artist John Johannsen. Amenities include hair dryers and heated towel bars, as well as newspaper delivery and in-room massage upon request. The restaurant, serving Mediterranean/California cuisine, has a sterling reputation, and hotel guests can take advantage of room service when it's open (see restaurant hours below).

Sutter Creek

✪ **The Foxes.** 77 Main St. (P.O. Box 159), Sutter Creek, CA 95685. ☎ **209/267-5882.** Fax 209/267-0712. 7 rms. A/C. $110–$165 double. Rates include breakfast. DISC, MC, V.

This clapboard house with a decorous front porch was built in 1857 and is the town's most elegant hostelry. The seven rooms are all uniquely decorated, each with a queen-size bed and down comforters. Four rooms, including the Garden Room and the Fox Den, have wood-burning fireplaces. The Fox Den also has a little library of its own, while the Victorian suite features a 9-foot-tall Renaissance Revival bed and a separate sitting room. Three of the rooms have TVs tucked in armoires, and all have private baths. Breakfast, cooked to order and delivered on silver service along with the morning paper, can be served in your room or in the gazebo in the garden.

Gold Quartz Inn. 15 Bryson Dr., Sutter Creek, CA 95685. ☎ **800/752-8738** or 209/267-9155. Fax 209/267-9170. 24 rms. A/C TV TEL. $80–$150 double. AE, DISC, MC, V.

Just off Calif. 49 outside Sutter Creek, the Gold Quartz Inn is one of the town's premier B&Bs, a modern (and immaculate) establishment designed in Queen Anne style. Its amenities and first-class bedrooms make it comparable to a deluxe small hotel. The rooms are decorated with antique reproductions and furnished with iron or brass beds. All have private baths. Some units have their own porches; the only place in the hotel where smoking is allowed. Afternoon tea and a full breakfast are served daily in the dining rooms, and the adjacent parlor offers an array of sofas and a VCR with a movie library. Free laundry service is also available.

Grey Gables Inn. 161 Hanford St., Sutter Creek, CA 95685. ☎ **800/GREY-GABLES** or 209/267-1039. A/C. $105–$135 double. AE, DISC, MC, V.

A newcomer to Sutter Creek is the Grey Gables Inn, a postcard-perfect replica of a Victorian manor made all the more English by Roger and Sue Garlick, two amicable British expatriates who relish being innkeepers. The two-story B&B is surrounded by terraces of colorful gardens embellished with fountains and vine-covered arbors ("A touch of the English countryside," says Sue.). Each of the plushly carpeted guest rooms is named after a British poet such as the Byron Room, where hues of deep green and burgundy pair well with the dark wood furnishings and a Renaissance Revival bed. Aside from the king-size bed in the Bronte Room, all rooms have queen-size beds, gas-log fireplaces, large armoires, and private baths (a few with clawfoot tubs). Breakfast, delivered on fine English bone china, is served either in the formal dining room adjacent to the Victorian parlor or in your room. The only flaw in an otherwise perfect B&B is the bit-too-close proximity to heavily traveled Calif. 49, but once inside you'll hardly notice. *Note:* The shops and restaurants of Sutter Creek are within walking distance.

Jackson

Court Street Inn. 215 Court St., Jackson, CA 95642. ☎ **800/200-0416** or 209/223-0416. 7 rms. A/C. $95–$195 double. Rates include breakfast. AE, DISC, MC, V.

Two blocks from Main Street, this Victorian home—listed on the National Register of Historic Places—was built in 1870 and sports elegant details such as eyelash shutters, embossed ceilings, and a Carerra marble fireplace. Our favorite unit is the Muldoon Room, with its oak-manteled fireplace and handsome four-poster king-size bed. Romantics should like the Peiser Room's wicker bed. All of the rooms are very nicely decorated, and some have fireplaces and whirlpool or clawfoot tubs. There's a porch where guests can relax on the swing, and a hot tub is also available for stargazing. Complimentary evening refreshments are served. TVs are available on request. No smoking is allowed inside.

WHERE TO DINE

Amador City

✪ **Imperial Hotel.** Main St. (Calif. 49). ☎ **209/267-9172.** Reservations recommended. Main courses $14–$21. AE, MC, V. Daily 5–9pm. MEDITERRANEAN/CALIFORNIA.

This restored 1879 hotel has been recommended already, but even if you aren't staying here, its restaurant is worth a detour. There are only about seven main dishes offered on Executive Chef Rhonda Uhlmann's seasonally changing menu, but whatever you choose will undoubtedly be good. To start, try the oven-baked polenta, topped with tomato fondue, wild mushrooms, and Sonoma jack cheese. To follow, you might select the local version of cioppino, a tomato-based fresh seafood stew accented with Remesco pepper sauce. If you put your name on the waiting list for their New Year's celebration, you might get a seat by the year 2002—it's that popular.

Sutter Creek

Ron and Nancy's Palace. 76 Main St. ☎ **209/267-1355.** Reservations recommended on weekends. Main courses $9–$16. AE, DC, MC, V. Daily 11:30am–3pm and 5–9pm (last order). AMERICAN/CONTINENTAL.

Set within a rustic building originally built in 1853 as a stable, this place is not run by the former first couple, but is the palace of Ron and Nancy Gottheiner, experienced San Francisco restaurateurs. Many visitors come just for the two-fisted drinks served in the bar/lounge, where a battle for your attention will rage between the Elvis memorabilia favored by Nancy and the Oakland Raiders memorabilia prized by Ron. (The bar, incidentally, remains open through the afternoon, even when the restaurant area is closed.) In the three dining rooms, light from the windows is filtered through panels of stained glass.

Most dishes are enhanced with a dash of vermouth, Marsala, or California wines. One of the most popular lunchtime dishes is a steak croissant sautéed in Marsala and flavored with onions and herbs. Dinner items include linguines, prime rib, and a wildly popular pan-fried scampi with veal strips.

✪ **Zinfandels.** 51 Hanford St. ☎ **209/267-5008.** Reservations recommended. Main courses $12.25–$13.25. MC, V. Tues–Sun 5:30–9:30pm. ITALIAN/FRENCH.

Greg and Kelley West's Zinfandels is a recent Sutter Creek dining addition that has received nothing but kudos since it first opened in July '96. Greg, a six-year veteran of Greens (a highly respected vegetarian restaurant in San Francisco), is responsible for the entrees, while his wife Kelley bakes the breads and pastries. Though the emphasis is on low-fat vegetarian fare such as butternut squash risotto with pancetta, leeks, crimini mushrooms, and spinach, West also offers a trio of fresh fish, chicken, and beef dishes ranging from cannelloni filled with lamb sausage, chard, and smoked mozzarella to Patrale sole with a citrus ginger beurre blanc. The menu changes weekly to take advantage of seasonal produce from local farms, and even the wines—paired with each dish—are provided by local wineries such as Stevenot and Ironstone. Okay, so we're not exactly crazy about the tired country theme decor, but otherwise Zinfandels is highly recommended—particularly if you love good wine.

Jackson

Upstairs Restaurant & Streetside Bistro. 164 Main St. ☎ **209/223-3342.** Reservations recommended. Main courses $12–$20. DISC, MC, V. Tues–Fri 11:30am–2:30pm and 5:30–9pm, Sat–Sun 11:30am–3:30pm and 5:30–9pm. INTERNATIONAL.

This adorable little restaurant offers a limited, often changing menu, but you might stumble on some true culinary gems, such as pasta puttanesca with tomato-basil fettucine and fresh Roma tomatoes, or duck julienned and served with a blackberry/ginger port sauce. Layne McCollum, a graduate of California's Culinary Institute, is known as the town's finest and most sophisticated chef, with a reputation for imaginative and innovative cuisine. Crisp white linens, bowls of fresh flowers, and background music provide a romantic backdrop to the restaurant's 12 tables. Lunch—quiche, soups, salads and gourmet sandwiches such as smoked pork loin with red chili pesto on chipotle—is served until about 3pm in the bright, cheery Streetside Bistro. Tastefully furnished with wrought-iron furniture, tile flooring, and colorful oil paintings, the Bistro remains open after lunch for wine, house-roasted espresso drinks, and appetizers.

CONTINUING SOUTH TOWARD JAMESTOWN

ANGEL'S CAMP   From Mokelumne Hill, Calif. 49 continues south, via San Andreas, 20 miles to Angel's Camp. This is where Mark Twain heard the story that inspired his "The Celebrated Jumping Frog of Calaveras County." The frog-jumping contest started in 1928 to mark the paving of the town's streets, and to this day the ribiting competition takes place every third weekend in May. The record, 21 feet, 5³/₄ inches, was jumped in 1986 by "Rosie the Ribiter," beating the old world record by 4¹/₂ inches. Livestock exhibitions, pageants, cook-offs, arm-wrestling tournaments, carnival rides, and plenty of beer and wine keep the spectators entertained between jump-offs. For more information and entry forms ($3 per frog), call the **Jumping Frog Jubilee** headquarters at ☎ **209/736-2561.**

   Angel's Camp is built on hills that are honeycombed with mine tunnels. In the 1880s and 1890s, five mines were located along Main Street—Sultana, Angel's, Lightner, Utica, and Stickle—and the town echoed with noise, as more than 200 stamps crushed the ore. Between 1886 and 1910 the five mines generated close to $20 million.

MURPHYS & ENVIRONS   From Angel's Camp, take a 20-minute detour east along Route 4 to Murphys, one of our favorite Gold Country towns. Legend has it Murphys started as a former trading post set up by brothers Dan and John Murphy in cooperation with local Indians (John married the chief's daughter). These days its peaceful community is made up of gingerbread Victorians shaded by tall locust trees bordering narrow streets. Be sure to take a stroll down Main Street, stopping in Grounds for a bite to eat (see "Where to Dine," below) and perhaps a cool draft of Murphys Red—direct from Murphys Brewing Company—at the rustic saloon within Murphys Historic Hotel and Lodge on Main Street.

   While you're here, you might also want to check out the new **Ironstone Vineyards,** a veritable wine theme park built by the Kautz family that boasts a enormous tasting room, gallery, park, amphitheater, music room, caverns, flower shop, and even a demonstration cooking kitchen (1894 Six Mile Rd., 1 mile south of downtown Murphys; ☎ **209/728-1251**).

Also in the vicinity—just off Calif. 4, 1 mile north of Murphys off Sheep Ranch Road—are the **Mercer Caverns** (☎ **209/728-2101**). These caverns were discovered in 1885 by Walter Mercer and contain a variety of geological formations. Tours take 55 minutes; the caverns are open daily from Memorial Day through September from 10am to 8:30pm and October through May from 10am to 5pm (open until 8pm on Friday and Saturday). Admission is $6 for adults and $3 for children 5 to 11; free for children 4 and under.

Fifteen miles beyond Murphys on Route 4 is **Calaveras Big Trees State Park,** where you can witness giant sequoias that are among the biggest and oldest living things on earth. It's a popular summer retreat that offers camping, swimming, hiking, and fishing along the Stanislaus River. (It's open daily and admission is $5 per car for day use; ☎ **209/795-2334**.)

COLUMBIA   From Murphys, get back on Calif. 49, crossing the Stanislaus River bridge over the New Melones Reservoir to the most remarkable attraction in the area, ✪ **Columbia State Historic Park** (☎ **209/532-4301**), which, though somewhat hokey, is one of the best maintained Gold Rush towns in the Mother Lode (as well as one of the most popular, so expect crowds in the summer). The whole town has been preserved and functions as it did in the 1850s, with stagecoach rides, Western-style Victorian hotels and saloons, a newspaper office, a working blacksmith's forge, a Wells Fargo express office, and numerous other relics of California's early mining days. Today, cars are banned from its dusty streets, giving the shady town an authentic and uncommercial feel. Merchants still do business behind some storefronts, as horse, stagecoach, and pedestrian traffic wanders by.

If the heat and dust are getting to you, pull up a stool at the **Douglass Saloon** (open 10am to 5pm daily; ☎ **209/533-2355**) on Columbia's Main Street. Inside the swinging doors of the classic Western bar you can sample homemade sarsparilla and wild cherry, drinks the saloon has been serving since 1857. The storefront's large shuttered windows open onto a dusty main street, so put up your boots, relax awhile, and watch the stagecoach go by.

SONORA, JAMESTOWN & MARIPOSA   Only a few miles south, the county seat, Sonora, nestles in ravines and on hillsides. Here you can visit the **Tuolumne County Museum and History Center,** 158 W. Bradford Ave. (☎ **209/532-1317**), located in the 1857 county jail. Admission is free, and it's open daily year-round from 10am to 4pm.

About 4 miles down Calif. 49, **Jamestown** was the home of the Sierra Railroad Company. It's famous for its **Railtown 1897 State Historic Park** (☎ **209/984-3953**), which features three original Sierra steam locomotives. These great machines were used in many a movie, including *High Noon* and *My Little Chickadee*. Rides are given on weekends from April to October. It's open daily year-round.

From Jamestown, Calif. 49 continues south across the huge Don Pedro Reservoir and through Coulterville and Bear Valley to **Mariposa,** on the fringes of Yosemite. It's another attractive hilly mining town with plenty of atmosphere.

WHERE TO STAY

Angels Camp

Cooper House Bed & Breakfast Inn. 1184 Church St. (P.O. Box 1388), Angels Camp, CA 95222. ☎ **800/225-3764**, ext. 326 or 209/736-2145. 3 rms. A/C. $90 double. Rates include breakfast. AE, DISC, MC, V.

Once the home and office of prominent community physician, Dr. George P. Cooper, the Cooper House is now Angel Camp's only B&B. This small Arts and

Crafts home is mercifully positioned well away from the hustle and bustle of the town's Main Street. Owner/Innkeeper Kathy Reese maintains three guest rooms, all with private baths. The Zinfandel Suite has its own private entrance and deck, and the Chardonnay Suite has a king-size bed, antique clawfoot bathtub, and a private deck. The third bedroom, the Cabernet Suite, is mid-sized, with a queen-size bed, an adjoining sunroom, and a splendid garden view.

Murphys

Dunbar House, 1880. 271 Jones St. (P.O. Box 1375), Murphys, CA 95247. ☎ **800/692-6006** or 209/728-2897. 3 rms, 1 suite. A/C TV TEL. $125 double; $175 suite. Rates include breakfast. AE, MC, V.

This pretty Italianate home, built in 1880 for the bride of a local businessman, is one of the finest in the Gold Country. The inviting front porch, which overlooks the exquisite gardens, is decorated with wicker furniture and hanging baskets of ivy. Inside, the emphasis is on comfort and elegance. The rooms are furnished with quality antiques and equipped with every possible amenity. Beds have lace-trimmed linens and down comforters, and each room has a wood-burning stove and personal refrigerator stocked with mineral water and a complimentary bottle of wine. Other extras include a TV/VCR (well hidden), makeup mirror, and hair dryer, plus his-and-her reading lamps. The most expensive room, the Cedar, is a two-room suite with a private sun porch, a whirlpool bath, and complimentary champagne. Lemonade and cookies are offered in the afternoon, appetizers and wine in the early evening. Breakfast is served either in your room, the dining room, or the garden.

Columbia

City Hotel. Main St., Columbia State Park (P.O. Box 1870), CA 95310. ☎ **209/532-1479.** Fax 209/532-7027. 10 rms (all with shared bath). A/C. $75–$100 double. Rates include breakfast. AE, DISC, MC, V.

This pleasant hostelry has been operating since 1856 and offers guests access to a large parlor furnished with Victorian sofas, antiques, and Oriental rugs. The largest units are the two balcony rooms overlooking Main Street; the rooms off the parlor are also spacious. The hallway rooms are smaller but still nicely furnished with Renaissance Revival beds and antique pieces. Each room has a sink and toilet. A large buffet breakfast is served in the dining room. The hotel has a full restaurant serving fancy four-course dinners for $31.50 per person, as well as the What Cheer saloon, which boasts its original cherrywood bar, shipped around the Horn from New England.

Fallon Hotel. Washington St. (P.O. Box 1870), Columbia State Park, CA 95310. ☎ **209/532-1470.** 14 rms. A/C. $55–$95 double. Rates include breakfast. AE, DISC, MC, V.

This hotel, which opened in 1857, has been restored and decorated to evoke the 1890s. A classic two-story building with an upper balcony, the hotel has retained many of its original antiques and furniture. The largest rooms are the front balcony rooms. Only one room has a full bath; the rest have a private sink and toilet, and showers are nearby down the hall. The rooms are furnished with high-backed Victorian beds, marble-topped dressers, rockers, and similar oak pieces. A full breakfast is served in the downstairs parlor.

Sonora

Serenity. 15305 Bear Cub Dr., Sonora, CA 95370. ☎ **800/426-1441** or 209/533-1441. 4 rms. A/C. $90–$135 double. Rates include breakfast. AE, CB, DC, DISC, MC, V. From Sonora take Business 108 east to Calif. 108 to Phoenix Lake Rd. Turn left and proceed for 3 miles to Bear Cub Dr.; turn right.

This B&B set on 6 acres outside of town affords an opportunity to enjoy the beauty, peace and quiet of the area's deer-filled oak and pine forest. A traditional, modern wood house with a wraparound porch, it has all the comforts of home and then some. Beds are made with lace-trimmed linens, and each room has a sitting area and private bath; two have remote-control gas-log fireplaces. One unit has a four-poster; another a white-iron bed. Breakfast, served in the formal dining room, is a veritable feast.

Jamestown

Jamestown Hotel. Main St. (P.O. Box 539), Jamestown, CA 95327. ☎ **800/205-4901** or 209/984-3902. Fax 209/984-4149. 5 rms, 3 suites. A/C. $65–$95 double; $125 suite. Rates include continental breakfast. AE, DC, DISC, MC, V.

The most worked-over building in town, the Jamestown was originally built in 1858, and had burned down and been rebuilt twice before 1915. To achieve the old-fashioned, brick-fronted Victorian look it sports today, its current owners ripped out a lot of stucco and Spanish revival paraphernalia.

Much of the interior is devoted to the restaurant, (see "Where to Dine," below). The second floor, however, contains cozy bedrooms outfitted with antiques acquired along both coasts of North America. Each room is large, with lots of nostalgic charm, and a private bath containing a clawfoot tub.

National Hotel. 77 Main St. (P.O. Box 502), Jamestown, CA 95327. ☎ **800/894-3446** or 209/984-3446. Fax 209/984-5620. 9 rms. A/C. $80 double. Rates include continental breakfast. AE, CB, DC, DISC, MC, V.

Located in the center of town, this two-story classic Western hotel has been operating since 1859, making it one of the 10 oldest continuously operating hotels in the state. The saloon has its original 19th-century redwood bar, and you can imagine what it must have been like when miners traded gold dust for drinks. The rooms above are furnished with oak pieces and brass beds made up with quilts. All rooms have private baths. The restaurant on the main floor serves traditional American, Mediterranean, and continental cuisine such as brandy-apple pork, ruby trout amandine, and prime rib on the weekends.

WHERE TO DINE

Angels Camp

B of A Cafe. 1262 South Main St. ☎ **209/736-0765.** Main courses $9–$13. MC, V. Lunch Wed–Mon 11am–3pm, dinner Thurs 5:30–8pm, Fri–Sat 5:30–9pm, Sun 5:30–8pm. Cafe opens Wed–Mon at 8am. AMERICAN.

Katherine Reese, who also runs the Cooper House Bed and Breakfast Inn, has done a marvelous job restoring and converting this 1936 Bank of America building into a bright, cheerful cafe. Using leftover banking curios, she decorated the walls with polished teller windows, partially removed the second floor to add balcony seating, and converted the vault into a wine-tasting room. Lunch items range from country-style quiche du jour to roasted eggplant sandwiches on multigrain bread and gourmet baby green salad. Dinners include sliced pork loin marinated with Australian maplewood, lemon rosemary chicken, and mesquite-marinated baby back ribs. Daily specials include fresh fish, pasta, and vegetables, and all entrees come with fresh bread, soup or salad, and Kathy's Famous Herbed Roasted Red Potatoes. Basque-style dinners (steak, chicken, or lamb with tureens of soup, salad, and pasta for $15 per person) are served Sundays between 5 and 8pm, but be sure to make a reservation because tables fill up fast.

Camps. 676 McCauley Ranch Rd. (¹/₂ mile west of Calif. 4/Calif. 49 junction off Angel Oaks Dr.) ☎ **209/736-8181.** Reservations recommended. Main courses $9.50–$16. MC, V. Breakfast

Fri–Sun 7:30–10:30am, lunch Mon–Sat 11:30am–2:30pm, dinner Wed–Sun 5:30–10:30pm, brunch Sun 11am–2:30pm. FUSION.

Located on the edge of a sprawling golf resort on the western fringes of Angels Camp is Camps, the culinary feather in the cap of Greenhorn Creek, one of Northern California's newest destination retreats. The restaurant's architects have successfully integrated the building with its natural surroundings by constructing the outer walls with locally mined ryolite and painting it in natural earth tones. The interior is furnished with natural leather armchairs, wicker, and antique woods. The best seats in the house are on the spacious veranda overlooking the golf course, the perfect setting for Executive Chef Jean Paul Lucy's fusion cuisine, a culinary artistry that pairs local produce with European, Asian, and Caribbean influences. For example, there's the roti of duck with kumquat and sun-dried cherries, cooked crisp and basted with rosemary jus. The wildflower salad with American field greens, toasted pine nuts, and a raspberry hazelnut vinaigrette is marvelous, as is the marinated demi-rack of lamb, grilled with an essence of sweet bay and fresh thyme and served with a vegetable couscous.

Murphys

Grounds. 402 Main St. ☎ **209/728-8663.** Reservations recommended on weekends. Main courses $7.50–$13.25. DISC, MC, V. Wed–Mon 11am–3pm, 5:30–9pm. ECLECTIC.

When River Klass moved here from the East Coast to open his own restaurant, Murphys' restaurant-challenged residents heaved a collective sigh of relief. Its nickname is the "Rude Boy Cafe," but you'll find only happy smiles and friendly service from the energetic staff. The majority of Klass's business is with the locals, who have become addicted to Ground's potato pancakes that come with every made-to-order omelet. For lunch, try the sausage sandwich on house-baked bread or the grilled eggplant sandwich stuffed with smoked mozzarella and fresh basil. Although the menus change twice a week, typical dinner choices range from fettucine topped with sautéed shrimp, halibut, and mussels in a garlic cream sauce to oven-roasted sweetheart ham with glazed yams, pot roast with steamed red potatoes, and a New York steak with caramelized onions and half-mashed red potatoes. Monday is Mexican night. The long, narrow dining rooms are bright and airy with pinewood furnishings, wood floors, and an open kitchen. On sunny days, request a table on the back patio.

Sonora

Good Heavens. 49 N. Washington St. ☎ **209/532-3663.** Main courses $5–$9. No credit cards. Tues–Sun 11am–2:30pm. AMERICAN.

This lunch cafe serves only homemade items. The menu features a variety of unique sandwiches—such as cucumber and pesto cream, turkey and cranberry orange—plus an array of delicious soups, salads, and desserts. There are several daily specials—everything from chile rellenos to crepes and pastas. Each meal starts with fresh herb-and-cheese biscuits and a choice of freshly made jams, such as the decadent raspberry-chocolate or the tart orange marmalade. Don't leave without purchasing a jar or two; they're sold at the counter.

North Beach Cafe. 14317 Mono Way/Calif. 108 (from central Sonora, go 3 miles east on Calif. 108 to John's Sierra Market, turn right into parking lot). ☎ **209/536-1852.** Main courses $7.50–$12.50. Daily 11am–9pm (weekends until 10pm). No credit cards. ITALIAN.

Chef/owner Terry La Torre has turned this former auto parts store into one of the most popular restaurants in Sonora. A longtime local and progeny of a legacy of San Francisco restaurateurs, the well-rounded, mustachioed La Torre can usually be found draped in chef's whites, shouting orders to his staff as he deftly flips a New York on his blazing mesquite grill. The place is almost always abuzz with customers who come for La Torre's cooking and to bask in his infectious pomposity. The menu is predominantly Italian, including a dozen or so pastas, fresh fish, veal, chicken, and steaks. The lunch menu is less complex, ranging from chicken or steak sandwiches to burgers, soups, and salads. La Torre tends to be a bit heavy-handed with the sauces; we usually request that he halves the regular amount. Otherwise, the combination of fair prices, good food, and classic La Torre histrionics makes North Beach Cafe worth searching out.

Jamestown

Jenny Lind Room at the Jamestown Hotel. Main St. ☎ **800/205-4901** or 209/984-3902. Reservations recommended. Main courses $10–$17. AE, DC, DISC, MC, V. Mon–Sat 11am–3pm; Sun brunch 10am–3pm; daily 4:30–9pm. AMERICAN/INTERNATIONAL.

The Jenny Lind Room may not be the top restaurant in the Gold Country, but it's certainly the most authentic looking, a dark-wood affair with stuffed wingback chairs, a fireplace, and dozens of old photos. There are about 15 tables inside, plus another 13 on an outdoor deck. Menu items from chef Brian Johnson's menu include escargot in mushroom caps cooked in garlic butter, breast of chicken "Jerusalem," with artichokes, mushrooms, and lemon-scented cream sauce, and a hugely popular filet mignon stuffed with gorgonzola cheese and topped with a Portobello mushroom wine sauce. There's also a Sunday champagne brunch served until 3pm.

3 The Central Valley & Sierra National Forest

The Central Valley (also known as the San Joaquin Valley) is about as far as you can get from California's glamorous movie-stars-in-stretch-limos image. This hot, flat strip of tract homes, fast-food joints, cheap motels, and mini-malls stretches for some 225 miles, separating Los Angeles and San Francisco from the Sierra Nevada. This 18,000-square-mile valley is central to the economy of the Golden State, in part because of its cultivated and irrigated fields, orchards, pastures, and vineyards.

The major traffic arteries through the valley are Calif. 99 and I-5. Calif. 99 links the agricultural communities while I-5 provides access routes to the roadside attractions in the valley. Rivers cutting through the valley offer recreation, fishing, boating, houseboating on the delta, and white-water rafting on the rapids. And the valley's spectacular landscapes provide unrivaled natural beauty; many visitors drive through in spring just to view the orchards in bloom.

The Central Valley stands on the doorstep of some of America's greatest attractions, including Yosemite. See chapter 9 for coverage of two Central Valley towns, Merced and Visalia, which are good gateways to Yosemite, Sequoia, and Kings Canyon, respectively.

Fresno, although not much in itself, is on the doorstep of the Sierra National Forest and nearby natural attractions like the Millerton Lake State Recreation Area.

FRESNO

The running joke in California is that Fresno is the "gateway to Bakersfield." Although for most visitors Fresno is just a place to pass through en route to the state parks, it can be a good place to stop for food and lodging, and it makes a good base for exploring the Sierra National Forest (see below). However, be careful if you're looking for a bargain and plan to check into one of the cheap motels along the highway. Security may be questionable.

Founded in 1874, in the geographic center of the state, Fresno lies in the heart of the Central Valley and has experienced incredible growth in recent years. Like most growing cities, it has been plagued by an increase in crime, drugs, and urban sprawl.

As the seat of Fresno County, the city handles more than $3 billion annually in agricultural production. It also contains the world's largest dried fruit packing plant, Sun Maid, and Guild, one of the country's largest wineries.

If you have any reason at all to be in Fresno, try to visit between late February and late March so you can drive the **Fresno County Blossom Trail.** This 62-mile tour is self-guided and takes in the beauty of California's agarian bounty at its peak. The trail courses through fruit orchards in full bloom and citrus groves with lovely orange blossoms and a heady natural perfume. The **Fresno Convention and Visitor's Bureau,** 808 M St. in Fresno (☎ **800/788-0836** or 209/233-0836), supplies full details, including a map.

WHERE TO STAY

San Joaquin. 1309 W. Shaw Ave., Fresno, CA 93711. ☎ **800/775-1309** or 209/225-1309. Fax 209/225-6021. 68 suites. A/C TV TEL. $82–$89 junior suite; $125 1-bedroom suite with kitchen; $165 2-bedroom suite with kitchen; $185 3-bedroom suite with kitchen. Rates include breakfast. AE, CB, DC, DISC, MC, V.

Set on the northern edge of Fresno, this hotel was conceived as an apartment complex in the 1970s. Around 1985, a lobby was added, the floor plans were adjusted, and the place was reconfigured as an all-suite hotel. Each suite is outfitted in a slightly different style, with light, contemporary colors and furniture. Room service is available from an independently managed restaurant down the street.

WHERE TO DINE

Nicola's. 3075 N. Maroa Ave. ☎ **209/224-1660.** Reservations recommended. Main courses $10.25–$33.95. AE, DC, DISC, MC, V. Mon–Fri 11:30am–4pm; Mon–Thurs 5–10pm, Fri–Sat 5–11pm, Sun 4–10pm. ITALIAN/AMERICAN.

Restaurants come and go in Fresno, but Nicola's remains the enduring favorite of many a discriminating diner. It's also evidence that not everything in Fresno is fast food. Inside the well-upholstered, masculine setting where you can indulge in a stiff cocktail before dinner, you're likely to meet the town's district attorney and a judge or two. The place prides itself on its stuffed steak: a hearty slab of beef layered with ham and cheese, and drizzled with a white wine and mushroom *au jus* sauce. Other choices include veal scallopine, cioppino, *capellini pescatore* (angel-hair pasta with shellfish), and beefsteak with gorgonzola.

✪ **Veni, Vidi, Vici.** 1116 N. Fulton. ☎ **209/266-5510.** Reservations recommended. Main courses $16–$23. AE, CB, MC, V. Wed–Sun 5:30–10pm (late night menu from 10pm–midnight). Closed 2 weeks in early Jan. NORTHERN CALIFORNIA.

The most innovative and creative restaurant in Fresno occupies a prominent position about 6 miles south of the commercial center, in a funky neighborhood known as the Tower District. The place's rustic exterior strikes an interesting contrast to the polished and artful interior on the other side of the 15-foot doors, where the decor is accented with exposed brick walls, hanging mirrors, and chandeliers fashioned from twisted wire and metal leaves.

The menu changes, but might include roasted loin of pork with Chinese black bean and citrus-flavored glaze, served with grilled Portobello mushrooms, sun-dried tomatoes, risotto, and red-pepper coulis; or a wild mushroom lasagna with preserved tomato sauce. There are also fresh fish specials nightly. This is the only restaurant in Fresno that makes its own ice cream (the flavor of the day when we arrived was

Technicolor lime sorbet). Have a scoop or two with the restaurant's perennial dessert favorite: bittersweet chocolate cake.

SIERRA NATIONAL FOREST

Leaving Fresno's taco joints, used-car lots, and tract houses behind, an hour's drive east gets you to the Sierra National Forest, a land of lakes and coniferous forests lying between Yosemite and Sequoia and Kings Canyon national parks. The entire eastern portion of the park is still unspoiled wilderness protected by the government. Development—some of it, unfortunately, beside the bigger lakes and reservoirs—is confined to the western side.

The 1.3 million-acre forest contains 528,000 acres of wilderness. The Sierra's five wilderness areas include Ansel Adams, Dinkey Lakes, John Muir, Kaiser, and Monarch (see below). The forest offers plenty of opportunities for fishing, swimming, sailing, boating, camping, waterskiing, white-water rafting, kayaking, and horseback riding, all regulated by certain guidelines. Downhill and cross-country skiing, as well as hunting, are also available, depending on the season. Backpackers looking to retreat to the wilderness will find solace here, as the park is traversed by some 1,100 miles of forest hiking trails.

In the lower elevations, summer temperatures can frequently reach 100° F, but in the higher elevations, more comfortable temperatures in the 70s and 80s are the norm.

After visiting the ranger station at Oakhurst (see below), take Route 41 to Calif. 49, the major road into the northern part of the national forest. This is more convenient for visitors approaching the park from Northern California. Route 168 via Clovis is the primary route from Fresno if you're headed for Shaver Lake. There is no approach road from the eastern Sierras, only from the west.

To learn about hiking, camping, or other activities, or to obtain the fire and wilderness permits needed for backcountry jaunts, visit one of the ranger stations in the park's western section. These include: **Mariposa Ranger District,** 43060 Calif. 41, Oakhurst (☎ 209/683-4665); **Minarets Ranger Station,** 57003 North Fork (☎ 209/877-2218); **Kings River District,** 34849 Maxon Road, Sanger, near the Pine Flat Reservoir (☎ 209/855-8321); or the **Pineridge Ranger Station,** 29688 Auberry Road, Prather (☎ 209/855-5360).

Shaver Lake is one place where you can stock up on goods and supplies if you're going into the wilderness, but stores in Fresno carry much of the same stuff at lower prices. Cheaper supplies are also available in the town of Clovis outside Fresno (which you must pass through en route to the forest), especially at its Peacock Market, at Tollhouse Road (3rd Street), and Sunnyside Avenue (☎ **209/299-6627**).

THE MAJOR WILDERNESS & RECREATION AREAS

THE ANSEL ADAMS WILDERNESS   Divided between the Sierra and Inyo National Forests, this wilderness area covers 228,500 acres. Elevations range from 3,500 to 13,157 feet. The frost-free period extends from mid-July through August, the best time for a visit to the park's upper altitudes.

Ansel Adams is dotted with scenic alpine vistas, including steep-walled gorges and barren granite peaks. There are several small glaciers in the north and some fairly large lakes on the eastern slope of the precipitous Ritter Range. This vast wilderness has excellent stream and lake fishing, especially for rainbow, golden, and brook trout, and offers challenging mountain climbing on the Minarets Range. The wilderness is accessed by the Tioga Pass Road in the north, Route 395 and Reds Meadow Road in the east, the Minarets Highway in the west, and Route 168 to High Sierra in the south.

DINKEY LAKES WILDERNESS   The 30,000-acre Dinkey Lakes area was created in 1984 and occupies the western slope of the Sierra Nevada, southeast of Huntington Lake and just northwest of Courtright Reservoir. Most of the wilderness, timbered, rolling terrain, is 8,000 feet above sea level, reaching its highest point (10,619 feet) at Three Sisters Peak. Sixteen lakes are clustered in the west central region. You can reach the area on Kaiser Pass Road (north), Red/Coyote Jeep Road (west), Rock Creek Road (southwest), or Courtright Reservoir (southeast), generally from mid-June to late October.

JOHN MUIR WILDERNESS   Occupying 584,000 acres in the Sierra and Inyo National Forests, John Muir Wilderness—named after the turn-of-the-century naturalist—extends southeast from Mammoth Lakes along the crest of the Sierra Nevada for 30 miles before forking around the boundary of Kings Canyon National Park to Crown Valley and Mt. Whitney. Elevations range from 4,000 to 14,496 feet at Mt. Whitney, with many of the area's peaks surpassing 12,000 feet.

Split by deep canyons, the wilderness is also a land of meadows (especially beautiful when wildflowers bloom), lakes, and streams. The South and Middle Forks of the San Joaquin River, the North Fork of Kings River, and many creeks draining into Owens Valley originate in the John Muir Wilderness. Mountain hemlock, red and white fir, whitebark, and western pine dot the park's landscape. Temperatures vary wildly throughout any 24-hour period: Summer temperatures range from 25° to 85° F, and the only really frost-free period is between mid-July and August. The higher elevations are marked by barren expanses of granite splashed with many glacially carved lakes.

KAISER WILDERNESS   Immediately north of Huntington Lake and some 70 miles northeast of Fresno, Kaiser is a 22,700-acre forest tract commanding a view of the central Sierra Nevada. It was named after Kaiser Ridge, which divides the area into two different regions. Four trailheads provide easy access to the wilderness, but the northern half is much more open than the forested southern half; the primary point of entry is the Sample Meadow Campground. All other lakes are approached cross-country. Winter storms begin to blow in late October, and the grounds are generally snow covered until early June.

MONARCH WILDERNESS   This area extends across 45,000 acres in the Sierra and Sequoia National Forests. The Sierra National portion of the region—about 21,000 acres—is very rugged and hard to traverse. Steep slopes climb from the Middle and Main Forks of Kings River, with elevations increasing from 2,400 to more than 10,000 feet. Rock outcroppings are found throughout Monarch, and most of the lower elevations are mainly chaparral covered with pine stands near the tops of the higher peaks.

HUNTINGTON LAKE RECREATION AREA   At 7,000 feet, this area is a 2-hour drive east of Fresno via Route 168. The lake is one of the reservoirs in the Big Creek Hydroelectric System and has 14 miles of shoreline. It's a popular recreational area, offering camping, hiking, picnicking, sailing, swimming, windsurfing, fishing, and horseback riding. Or you can just appreciate the beauty. The main summer season stretches from Memorial Day to Labor Day. There are seven campgrounds and four picnic areas in the Huntington Lake Basin, plus numerous hiking and riding trails. For information, stop in at the **Easterwood Visitor Center** (☎ **209/ 893-6611**), open from May through September.

✪ **NEIDER GROVE OF GIANT SEQUOIAS**   This 1,540-acre tract in the Sierra National Forest contains 101 mature giant sequoias in the center of the Sequoia range, south of Yosemite National Park. A visitor center stands near the Nelder Grove

Campground, with historical relics and displays, including two restored log cabins. The Bull Buck Tree—at one time thought to be the largest in the world—is 246 feet high and has a circumference at ground level of 99 feet. There's a mile-long, self-guided walk along the "Shadow of the Giants" National Recreational Trail in the southwest corner of the grove.

OUTDOOR ACTIVITIES

CAMPING   The Sierra National Forest seems like one vast campsite. Options range from unembellished, primitive wilderness camps to developed and often crowded campgrounds with snack bars, flush toilets, bath houses, and hookups for RVs. For information and reservations, call the National Forest Reservation Center at ☎ 800/280-CAMP.

The major campgrounds are the Shaver Lake area; the Huntington Lake area (which has seven family campgrounds open from the end of June through Labor Day that must be reserved in advance); the Florence and Edison Lake area (first-come, first-served); the Dinkey Creek area (family and group camping); the Wishon and Courtright area (four campgrounds, first-come, first-served); the Pine Flat Reservoir (in the Sierra foothills, with two first-come, first served campgrounds); and Upper Kings River, east of Pine Flat Reservoir (family campgrounds, first-come basis).

FISHING   The many streams of the Sierra are home to rainbow, golden, brown, and brook trout. The best freshwater angling is in the Pineridge and Kings River Rangers District. Lower elevation reservoirs such as Shaver Lake, Bass Lake, and Pine Flat Reservoirs are known for their black bass fishing. Questions about fishing in the national forest can be directed to the **California Department of Fish and Game,** 1234 E. Shaw Ave., Fresno, CA 93710 (☎ 209/222-3761).

SKIING   Lying 65 miles northeast of Fresno on CA 168, in the Sierra National Forest, the **Sierra Summit Ski Area** is known for its alpine skiing. It also offers marked trails for cross-country skiing and snowmobiling. Information about the district is available from the Pineridge Ranger Station, 29688 Auberry Road, Prather (☎ 209/855-5355).

The resort area has 2 triple and 3 double chairlifts, plus 4 surface lifts and 30 runs, the longest of which extends for 2¹/₄ miles. There's a vertical drop-off at 1,600 feet. Other facilities include a lodge, snack bar, cafeteria, restaurant, and bar, all open daily from mid-November until mid-April. For a ski report, call ☎ 209/893-3311.

The ranger district has developed several marked cross-country trails along Route 168, ranging from a 1-mile tour for beginners to a 6-mile trail for more advanced skiers.

WHITE-WATER RAFTING   The Upper Kings River, east of Pine Flat Reservoir, offers a 10-mile rafting run through Garnet Dike to Kirch Flat Campground. Rafting season is from late April to mid-July, with the highest waters in late May and early June. To get there, take Belmont Avenue in Fresno east (toward Pine Flat Reservoir) for about 63 miles.

Two commercial rafting companies that offer guided rafting trips on the Kings River are **Kings River Expeditions** at ☎ 209/233-4881, and **Zephyr River Expeditions** at ☎ 209/532-6249.

The Monterey Peninsula & the Big Sur Coast

by Erika Lenkert and Matthew R. Poole

Located about 120 miles south of San Francisco, the Monterey Peninsula and the Big Sur coast comprise one of the world's most spectacular shorelines, skirted with cypress, rugged shores, and crescent-shaped bays. Monterey reels in visitors with its world-class aquarium and array of outdoor activities. Pacific Grove is so peaceful and quaint that the butterflies choose it as their yearly mating ground. Pebble Beach attracts the world's golfing elite. Though packed with tourists who come for the beaches, shops, and restaurants, tiny Carmel-by-the-Sea somehow remains romantic and sweet. And Big Sur's dramatic and majestic coast, backed by pristine redwood forests and rolling hills, is one of the most breathtaking and tranquil environments on earth.

Though Santa Cruz isn't really part of the Monterey Peninsula, we've included it at the beginning of this chapter since you'll pass it on the drive down from San Francisco (or up from L.A. on your way to San Francisco).

Monterey and Pacific Grove occupy the northern half of the peninsula overlooking Monterey Bay, while Pebble Beach and Carmel-by-the-Sea look out over Carmel Bay and hug the peninsula's south coast. Between the north and south coasts, which are only about 5 miles apart, are at least eight golf courses, some of the state's most stunning homes and hotels, and 17-Mile Drive, one of the most scenic coastal roads in the world. Inland lies Carmel Valley, with its elegant inns and resorts, golf courses, and guaranteed sunshine, even when the coast is socked in with fog.

Farther down the coast is Big Sur, a stunning 90-mile stretch of coast south of the Monterey Peninsula and west of the Santa Lucia Mountains.

1 Santa Cruz

For a small bayside city, Santa Cruz has a lot to offer. The main show, of course, is the Beach Boardwalk, the West Coast's only seaside amusement park, which attracts millions of visitors each year. But past the arcades and cotton candy is a surprisingly diverse and energetic city that has a little something for everyone. Shopping, hiking, mountain biking, sailing, fishing, kayaking, surfing, wine tasting, golfing, whale watching—the list of things to do here is almost endless, making Santa Cruz one of the premier family destinations on the California coast.

Area Code Change Notice

Please note that, effective June 13, 1998, portions of Monterey, Santa Cruz, San Luis Obispo, and Merced counties are scheduled to change to the **831** area code. Communities affected will include Santa Cruz, Carmel, Monterey, Big Sur, and small portions of San Luis Obispo. You will be able to dial 408 until February 20, 1999, after which you will be required to use 831 for affected numbers.

ESSENTIALS

GETTING THERE   Santa Cruz is 77 miles southeast of San Francisco. The most scenic route to Santa Cruz is along Calif. 1 from San Francisco, which, aside from the "you fall, you die" stretch called Devil's Slide, allows you to cruise at a steady 50 m.p.h. along the coast. Faster but far less romantic is Calif. 17, which is accessed near San Jose from I-280, I-880, or U.S. 101, and literally ends at the foot of the boardwalk. The exception to this rule is on weekend mornings, when Calif. 17 tends to logjam with Bay Area beachgoers while Calif. 1 remains relatively uncrowded.

VISITOR INFORMATION   For information, contact the **Santa Cruz County Conference and Visitors Council,** 701 Front St., Santa Cruz, CA 95060 (☎ **800/ 833-3494** or 408/425-1234). It's open Monday to Saturday from 9am to 5pm, Sundays from 10am to 4pm.

SPECIAL EVENTS   Special events include the **Santa Cruz Hot and Cool Jazz Festival** (☎ 408/662-1912; July); **Shakespeare Santa Cruz** (☎ 408/459-2121; July/August); and the **Cabrillo Music Festival** (☎ 408/426-6966; August).

WHAT TO SEE & DO: BEACHES, HIKING, FISHING & MORE

One of the top amusement parks in the nation, the privately owned **Santa Cruz Beach Boardwalk** draws more than 3 million visitors a year to its 28 rides and multitudes of arcades, shops, and restaurants. The park has two national landmarks—a 1924 wooden Giant Dipper roller coaster and a 1911 carousel complete with hand-carved wooden horses and a 342-pipe band organ. It's open daily in the summer from Memorial Day weekend through Labor Day and on weekends and holidays throughout the spring and fall, from 11am on (noon sometimes in winter). Admission to the boardwalk is free, but an all-day "unlimited rides" pass will set you back about $19. For more information, call ☎ **408/426-7433.**

Here, too, at 400 Beach St. is **Neptune's Kingdom** (☎ 408/426-7433), an enormous indoor family recreation center where the main feature is a two-story miniature golf course. Also on Beach Street is the **Municipal Wharf** (☎ 408/429-3628) and pier, lined with shops and restaurants—a beachfront strip that is serenaded by the sea lions below. You can also crab and fish from here. Most shops are open daily 7am to 9am, the wharf daily 5am to 2am. **Stagnaro's** (☎ 408/427-2334), also operates fishing and whale-watching trips from the pier from November through April.

Farther down on West Cliff Drive, you'll come to a favorite surfing spot, **Steamers Lane,** where you can watch the surfers coasting onto the beach. If you want to find out more about this local sport that's been practiced here for 100 years, then go to the memorial lighthouse, which contains the **Santa Cruz Surfing Museum** (☎ 408/429-3429), open Thursday to Monday from noon to 4pm in winter, and Wednesday to Monday from noon to 5pm in summer.

Continue along West Cliff and you'll eventually reach **Natural Bridges State Beach,** 2531 W. Cliff Dr. (☎ 408/423-4609), a large sandy beach with nearby tide pools and hiking trails. It's also home to a large colony of monarch butterflies that roost and mate in the nearby eucalyptus grove.

Other Santa Cruz beaches worth noting are: **Bonny Doon,** at Bonny Doon Road and Highway 1, an uncrowded sandy beach and a major surfing spot accessible by a steep walkway; **Pleasure Point Beach,** East Cliff Drive at Pleasure Point Drive; and **Twin Lakes State Beach,** which is ideal for sunning and also provides access to Schwann Lagoon, a bird sanctuary.

In addition to many cultural and sporting events, the University of California at Santa Cruz also has the **Long Marine Laboratory and Aquarium,** 100 Shaffer Rd. at the northwest end of Delaware Ave. (☎ **408/459-4308**), where you can observe the activities of marine scientists and the species kept in tide pool touch tanks and aquariums. Open Tuesday to Sunday from 1 to 4pm.

The **Santa Cruz Harbor,** 135 5th Ave. (☎ **408/475-6161**), is the place to head for boat rentals, open boat fishing (cod, shark, and salmon), and whale-watching trips. Operators include **Santa Cruz Sportfishing Inc.** (☎ **408/426-4690**) and **Shamrock Charters,** 2210 E. Cliff Dr. (☎ **408/476-2648**).

There's a great bike route along the 2-mile cliff walk. Bikes—mountain, kids', tandem, hybrid—are available by the hour, day, or week from the **Bicycle Rental and Tour Center,** 131 Center St., 2 blocks from the Municipal Wharf (☎ **408/426-8687**; open 10am to 6pm in summer). Figure on paying $25 a day, which includes helmets, locks, and packs.

There are several public golf courses, the best being the **Pasatiempo Golf Club,** at 18 Clubhouse Rd. (☎ **408/459-9155**), which is rated among the top 100 courses in the United States.

Hikers, bikers, and birders in need of some direction can call **The Tour Center,** where experienced local guides specialize in hiking, biking, and birding, as well as water-sport tours. Contact them at ☎ **408/426-8687.**

Sea kayaking is also available. Outfitters include **Kayak Connection,** 413 Lake Ave. No.4 (☎ **408/479-1121**), and **Venture Quest Kayaking** (☎ **408/425-8445** or 408/427-2267), which rents single, double, and triple kayaks at Building No.2 on the wharf and at 125 Beach St. across from the wharf. Classes, wildlife tours, and moonlight paddles are also available.

Surfing equipment can be rented at the **Cowell's Beach 'n' Bikini Surf Shop,** 109 Beach St. (☎ **408/427-2355**), and also from the **Club Ed Surf School,** on Cowell Beach in front of the Dream Inn (☎ **408/459-9283**).

In Nearby Capitola

South along the coast lies the small, attractive community of **Capitola** at the mouth of the Soquel Creek, which is a spawning ground for steelhead and salmon. You can fish without a license from the **Capitola Wharf,** 1400 Wharf Rd. (☎ **408/462-2208**), or you can rent a fishing boat from **Capitola Boat and Bait** at ☎ **408/462-2208.**

Capitola Beach fronts the Esplanade. Surf-fishing and clamming are popular pastimes at Capitola's **New Brighton State Beach,** 1500 State Park Dr. (☎ **408/475-4850**), where camping is also allowed.

Other Capitola pastimes? Antiquing! Explore the many stores along Soquel Drive between 41st and Capitola avenues.

Still farther south around the bay is **Aptos,** home to the 10,000-acre **Forest of Nisene Marks State Park** (☎ **408/763-7062**), which has hiking trails that wind through redwoods and past abandoned mining camps. This was also the epicenter of the 1989 earthquake.

About 25 miles north of Santa Cruz the **Año Nuevo State Reserve,** New Years Creek Road, off Calif. 1 in Pescadero (☎ **800/444-7275**), offers guided walks into the Northern Elephant Seal rookery from December through March. The walks take 2¹/₂ hours and cover 3 miles. Reservations are necessary. Self-guided walks are possible with a permit in summer.

In the redwood-forested mountains behind Santa Cruz, there are quite a few wineries, although visitors may not be familiar with the labels because the output is small and consumed locally. Most wineries are clustered around Boulder Creek and Felton or around Capitola. All offer tours by appointment; some feature regular tasting, including the **Bargetto Winery,** 3535 North Main, Soquel (☎ **408/475-2258**), which has a courtyard wine-tasting area overlooking the creek. For additional information, contact the **Santa Cruz Mountains Winegrowers Association** at ☎ **408/479-WINE.**

WHERE TO STAY

Two **Travelodges** (☎ **800/578-7878**), two **Best Westerns** (☎ **800/528-1234**), two **Super 8s** (☎ **800/800-8000**), and an **Econolodge** (☎ **800/553-2666**) provide moderate- and budget-priced accommodations in addition to the more inspiring choices below.

Casa Blanca Inn. 101 Main St. (at the corner of Beach), Santa Cruz, CA 95060. ☎ **408/423-1570.** Fax 408/423-0235. 34 rms. TV TEL. High season (summer) $105–$300 double; low season $68–$195 double. AE, CB, DC, MC, V.

Across from the wharf in a heavily trafficked area, this motel along the waterfront was once the Mediterranean-style Cerf Mansion, dating from 1918. Other motel-style accommodations have grown up around the main building. Originally the home of a federal judge, it offers individually decorated bedrooms, some with brass beds and velvet draperies. Some units contain fireplaces and terraces, and all are equipped with microwaves and coffeemakers. Most of the rooms have views of the water. There's a restaurant on the premises (see "Where to Dine" below) that serves good seafood in a romantic ocean-view setting.

✪ **Darling House.** 314 W. Cliff Dr., Santa Cruz, CA 95060. ☎ **408/458-1958.** 8 rms, 2 with private bath. $95 double without bath; $225 double with bath. AE, DISC, MC, V.

This lovely Spanish-style house, designed in 1910 by William Weeks, architect of Santa Cruz's Coconut Grove, has a panoramic view of the Pacific Ocean and is situated in a quiet residential area within walking distance of the Boardwalk and Lighthouse. The gardens are fragrant with citrus and orchids, and contain some stately palms, too. From the tiled front veranda, guests enter an elegant interior, the focal point of which is the dining room hand-crafted from tiger oak. The house boasts fine architectural features throughout, such as beveled glass, antiques, and handsome fireplaces. Each of the eight rooms is individually decorated, and though all have sinks, only two come with private baths. The Pacific Ocean room, decorated like a sea captain's quarters, features a fireplace, telescope, and one of the finest ocean views in Santa Cruz. A backyard hot tub is available for guests. Breakfast includes oven-fresh breads and pastries, fruit, and homemade granola made with walnuts from Darlings' own farm.

Edgewater Beach Motel. 525 Second St., Santa Cruz, CA 95060. ☎ **408/423-0440.** 17 rms. TV TEL. $105–$185 double. AE, DC, DISC, MC, V.

If the other two inns listed here are booked, consider the Edgewater Beach Motel. It looks like a time capsule from the '60s, which, oddly enough, makes it all the more appealing (how they kept the furnishings in such prime condition is a mystery).

The motel offers a range of accommodations, from family suites with kitchens to nonsmoking rooms and rooms with fireplaces; most have microwaves and all have refrigerators. The Edgewater also sports a heated pool, sundeck, and barbecue area, but the real bonus is the location—the Santa Cruz Beach Boardwalk is only a block away. *Tip:* Inquire about the Edgewater's off-season mini-vacation packages, which can save you a bundle on room rates.

IN NEARBY CAPITOLA

✪ **The Inn at Depot Hill.** 250 Monterey Ave. (near Park Ave.), Capitola, CA 95010. ☎ **800/ 57-B-AND-B** or 408/462-3376. Fax 408/462-3697. 6 rms, 6 suites. TV TEL. $165–$250 double. Rates include breakfast, afternoon tea or wine, and hors d'oeuvres, and after-dinner dessert. AE, MC, V.

Located a few blocks from the bay front, this converted railroad station has been beautifully designed and decorated with great attention to detail and to every aspect of comfort, thanks to innkeeper Suzanne Lankes. Sporting fine fabrics and linens, all rooms have wood-burning fireplaces, VCRs and stereos, telephones with fax/modem capability, bathrobes, hair dryers, two-person showers, and full baths. Most have private patios with private hot tubs (the other rooms share a common hot tub, and sign up for times). Perhaps you'll check into the Portofino Room, patterned after an Italian villa right down to the frescoes and stone cherub, or the Stratford-on-Avon, a replica of an English cottage.

The evening wine and hors d'oeuvres and the breakfast are of similar prime quality, and they can be enjoyed either in your room or out back in the garden courtyard on wrought-iron tables shaded by market umbrellas.

WHERE TO DINE

✪ **Cafe Bittersweet.** 787 Rio Del Mar Blvd. (about 10 miles SE of Santa Cruz on Hwy. 1), Rio Del Mar. ☎ **408/662-9799.** Reservations recommended. Main courses $15–$18. AE, MC, V. Tues–Sun 5–10pm. MEDITERRANEAN.

What started out as a tiny operation within a small strip development has grown into one of the most popular restaurants in the Santa Cruz region. The relocation to bigger digs in Rio Del Mar hasn't tarnished chef/owner Thomas Vinolus' reputation for serving exceptional cuisine. The menu features only five main dishes, which ensures quality. Start with the grilled shrimp over greens with garlic, sage, and white beans, or one of the fresh salads. Follow with the richly flavored veal medaillons with a brandied wild mushroom sauce. We also enjoyed the old-fashioned lasagna with three cheeses, basil, spinach, and marinara sauce.

Casablanca Restaurant. 101 Main St. (at Beach). ☎ **408/426-9063.** Reservations recommended. Main courses $14–$23. AE, DC, MC, V. Sun–Thurs 5–9pm, Fri–Sat 5–10pm, Sun brunch 9:30am–2pm. CONTINENTAL.

The candlelit dining room at the Casa Blanca Inn was obviously built for romance, right down to the stellar views of the shimmering bay. For a stimulating start, try the Sicilian red clam chowder or the fire-roasted Anaheim chili stuffed with herbed chevre and served with tomatillo salsa. Among the 10 or so main courses, we'd recommend any of the fresh seafood dishes, perhaps the red snapper sautéed with capers, scallions, and lemon butter sauce. The award-winning book-length wine list is excellent.

✪ **O'Mei.** 2316 Mission St. ☎ **408/425-8458.** Reservations suggested on Fri–Sat. Main courses $7–$12. AE, MC, V. Mon–Fri 11:30am–2pm; Mon–Thurs 5–9:30pm, Fri–Sun 5–10pm. SZECHUAN.

O'Mei's (pronounced oh-may) minimall location may not be very inviting, but the fantastic food served here more than makes up for it. The menu features some unusual specialties such as apricot-almond chicken and wine-braised chicken livers, along with more familiar dishes such as chicken with cashews or Szechuan shrimp. Dinner starts with a dim sum–style tray of exotic offerings such as sesame-cilantro-eggplant salad or pan-roasted peppers with feta cheese. A recommended dish is the sliced rock cod in black bean–sweet pepper sauce.

IN NEARBY CAPITOLA

Shadowbrook. 1750 Wharf Rd., Capitola. ☎ **408/475-1511.** Main courses $13–$22. AE, CB, DC, DISC, MC, V. Mon–Thurs 5:30–9:30pm, Fri 5:30–10pm, Sat 4:30–10:30pm, Sun 10am–2:15pm and 4:30–9pm. AMERICAN/CONTINENTAL.

Shadowbrook, one of Capitola's most venerable and romantic restaurants, occupies a serene setting above the Soquel Creek. To reach the restaurant, diners either have to take the cable-driven "hillavator" down or walk the long, steep bank of steps beside a running waterfall. At the bottom is a log cabin built in the 1920s, which has been enlarged and now contains a series of dining rooms on different levels: the wood-paneled Wine Cellar, the airy Garden Room, the Fireplace Room, and the creekside Greenhouse.

The menu doesn't hold many surprises, featuring thick-cut prime rib and steaks along with seafood such as scampi and grilled trout, plus pasta dishes including shellfish linguine and porcini ravioli. Prawn cocktail, deep-fried artichoke hearts, and baked brie are among the appetizers. Standout desserts are the mud pie and chocolate torte with raspberry sauce.

A SIDE TRIP TO MISSION SAN JUAN BAUTISTA

On U.S. 101, San Juan Bautista is a charming mission town that works hard to honor its pioneer heritage by retaining the flavor of a 19th-century village. The mission complex is perched in a picturesque farming valley, surrounded by the restored buildings of the original city plaza.

From U.S. 101, take Calif. 156 east (south) to the center of town to the mission itself, which was founded in 1797. Here you'll see the largest church in the mission chain and the only one in unbroken service since its founding. The padres here inspired many Native Americans to convert, creating one of the largest congregations in all of California. The small museum contains many musical instruments and transcriptions, evidence of the mission's musical focus—it once boasted a formidable Native American boys' choir.

Mission San Juan Bautista is open daily from 9:30am to 5pm from May to October; it closes at 4:30pm the rest of the year. Admission is $2 per person. For further information, call ☎ **408/623-4528.**

East of the church, perched at the edge of an abrupt drop created by the movement of the San Andreas Fault, is a marker pointing out the path of the old El Camino Real. Accompanying the marker are seismographic measuring equipment and an earthquake science exhibit.

There's much to see on the restored city plaza in addition to the mission. Be sure to visit the **San Juan Bautista State Historic Park.** The park is comprised of not only the old Plaza Hotel with its classic frontier barroom and furnished rooms, but also the Plaza Hall, its adjoining stables and blacksmith shop, and the Castro House, where the Breen family lived after traveling here with the ill-fated Donner Party in 1846.

Allow 1¹/₂ to 2 hours to see the entire plaza. Admission to the park buildings is $2 per person (separate from your charge to the mission).

For further information (including events schedules), call ☎ **408/623-4881.**

2 Monterey

While its neighbors are romantic coastal hideaways, Monterey is the antithesis. A harbor-town-cum-tourist-trap, it's big enough that you have to drive from downtown to Cannery Row, and affected enough that chain hotels and restaurants have put the squeeze on boutique establishments. Plenty of history and heritage remains, but you'll have to weed though minimalls to find them. Its saving grace is the fantastic aquarium and beautiful Monterey Bay, where sea lions and otters still frolic in abundance.

You can save money by staying in an inexpensive motel in Monterey and easily driving into pricier Carmel-by-the-Sea to shop and go to the beach. But if you can afford the full charm of the area, set up camp in Pacific Grove or Carmel-by-the-Sea and make Monterey a day trip.

Originally settled in 1770, Monterey was one of the West Coast's first European settlements. The town was the capital of California under the Spanish, Mexican, and American flags. California's state constitution was drafted here in 1849, paving the way for admission to the Union a year later. Many architectural buildings from the early colonial era still stand. A major whaling center in the 1800s, it also became a sardine center when the first packing plant was built in 1900. By 1913 the boats were bringing in 25 tons of sardines a night. The lives of the residents, who thronged down to the 18 canneries, were captured by John Steinbeck in his 1945 novel *Cannery Row.* After the sardines disappeared, the town and the peninsula went after tourist dollars instead.

ESSENTIALS

GETTING THERE   The region's most convenient runway, at the **Monterey Peninsula Airport** (☎ **408/373-1704**), is 3 miles east of Monterey on Calif. 68. **American Eagle** (☎ 800/433-7300), **Northwest** (☎ 800/225-2525), **Skywest** (☎ 800/453-9417), **United** (☎ 800/241 6522), and **US Air** (☎ 800/428-4322) have daily flights in and out of Monterey.

Many area hotels offer free airport shuttle service. If you take a taxi, it will cost about $20 to $25 to get to a peninsula hotel. Several national car-rental companies have airport locations, including **Dollar** (☎ 800/800-4000) and **Hertz** (☎ 800/654-3131).

VISITOR INFORMATION   The **Monterey Peninsula Visitors and Convention Bureau,** 380 Alvarado St. (near the intersection of Pacific St. and Del Monte Ave.; ☎ **408/649-1770**), has good maps and free pamphlets and publications, including an excellent visitors' guide and the magazine *Coast Weekly.*

GETTING AROUND   The **Waterfront Area Visitor Express (WAVE)** operates each year from Memorial Day weekend through Labor Day and takes passengers to and from the aquarium and other waterfront attractions. Stops are located at many hotels and motels in Monterey and Pacific Grove. At a cost of $1 for adults and 50¢ for kids and seniors, you can have unlimited rides all day between 9am and 6:30pm and eliminate the stress of parking in crowded downtown. Call Monterey Salinas Transit for further information at ☎ **408/899-2555.**

SEEING THE SIGHTS

The **Steinbeck Center Foundation,** 371 Main St., Salinas (☎ **408/753-6411**), offers a self-guided tour or information on docent-led tours of "Steinbeck Country," which show visitors sites once frequented by renowned American author and local legend John Steinbeck.

The Monterey Peninsula

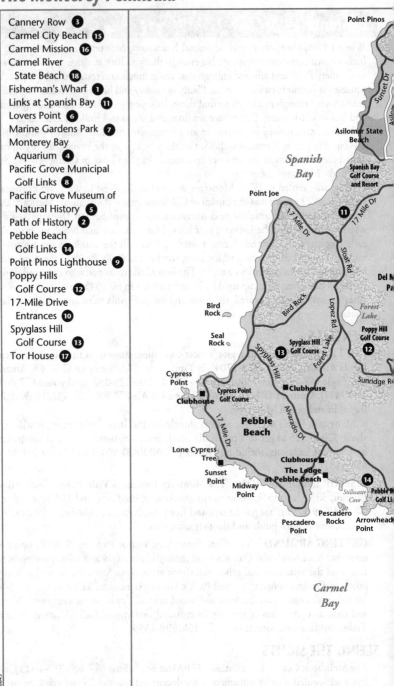

1-0843

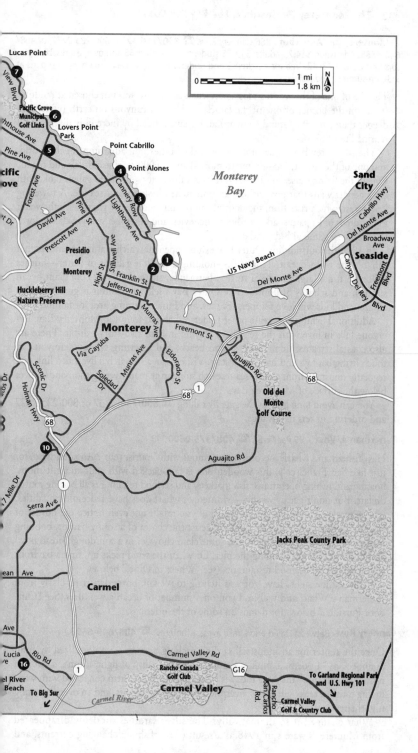

Lucas Point

⑦

View Blvd

Pacific Grove
Municipal
Golf Links   ⑥

Lighthouse Ave   Lovers Point
                   Park

Pine Ave   ⑤   Point Cabrillo

Pacific   ④ Point Alones
Grove   ③   Monterey   Sand
                                         Bay   City

        Forest Ave   Cannery Row   Cabrillo Hwy

ot Dr   David Ave   Pine St   Del Monte Ave
                                                                        Broadway
          Prescott Ave   Lighthouse Ave   Ave
                                                                    Seaside
          Presidio   US Navy Beach
          of   Canyon Del Rey
          Monterey   Franklin St   ② ①   Freemont
                  High St   Jefferson St   Del Monte Ave   Blvd
Huckleberry Hill   ①
Nature Preserve   Munras Ave

                Monterey   Freemont St

          Via Gayuba   Aguajito Rd
                        Munras Ave   68
          Soledad   Eldorado St
Scenic Dr Dr   68 ①   Old del
                                        Monte
Holman Hwy   Golf Course
     68
⑩
                        Aguajito Rd

7 Mile Dr

     ①
     Serra Ave
                                                Jacks Peak County Park

ean Ave
                Carmel

Ave

Lucia   Rio Rd   ⑯
                                    Carmel Valley Rd
el River   ①   G16   To Garland Regional Park
Beach   To Big Sur   Rancho Canada   and U.S. Hwy 101
                        Golf Club   Carmel Valley
              Carmel River   Carmel Valley   Rancho   Carmel Valley
                                              San Carlos Golf & Country Club
                                              Rd.

0 ▭▭▭ 1 mi
        1.8 km   N

331

✪ **Monterey Bay Aquarium.** 886 Cannery Row. ☎ **800/756-3737**, 800/225-2277, or 408/648-4888. Admission $14.75 adults, $11.75 students and seniors 65 and over, $6 disabled visitors and children 3–12, free for children 2 and under. AE, MC, V. Daily 10am–6pm (opens at 9:30am summer and holidays).

The site of one of the world's most spectacular aquariums was not chosen at random. It sits on the border of one of the largest underwater canyons on earth (wider and deeper than even the Grand Canyon) and is surrounded by incredibly diverse local marine life.

The Monterey Bay Aquarium is one of the best exhibit aquariums in the world, and one of the largest, too—home to more than 350,000 marine animals and plants. One of the living museum's main exhibits is a three-story, 335,000-gallon tank, with clear acrylic walls that give visitors an unmatched look at local sea life. A towering kelp forest, which rises from the floor of this oceanic zoo, gently waves with the water as hundreds of leopard sharks, sardines, anchovies, and other fish swim back and forth in an endless game of hide-and-seek.

In 1996 the outstanding Outer Bay exhibit opened, which features creatures that inhabit the open ocean. This tank—holding a million gallons of water—houses yellowfin tuna, large green sea turtles, barracuda, sharks, the very-cool giant ocean sunfish, and schools of bonito. The Outer Bay's jellyfish exhibit is guaranteed to amaze, and kids will love Flippers, Flukes, and Fun, a learning area for families.

Additional exhibits re-create other undersea habitats found in Monterey Bay. Everyone falls in love with the sea otters playing in their two-story exhibit. There are also coastal streams, tidal pools, a sand beach, and a petting pool, where you can touch living bat rays and handle sea stars. Visitors can also watch a live video link that regularly transmits from a deep-sea research submarine maneuvering thousands of feet below the surface of Monterey Bay.

You can avoid long lines at the gate by calling ☎ **800/756-3737** or 800/225-2277 and ordering tickets in advance.

Fisherman's Wharf. 99 Pacific St. ☎ **408/373-0600.**

Has "fisherman's wharf" become synonymous with "tourist trap"? Apparently so, for just like San Francisco's, this wooden pier is jam-packed with craft and gift shops, boating and fishing operations, fish markets, and seafood restaurants all baiting tourist dollars. But don't get us wrong—Monterey's wharf does have redeeming qualities. The natural surroundings are so beautiful you might not even notice the hordes of tourists around you. After all, who can resist the charm of a sunny harbor, bobbing boats, and surfacing sea lions? Grab some clam chowder in a sourdough bread bowl and find a seaside perch along the pier. Or when the wind picks up, find a bayfront seat at one of the seafood restaurants (see "Where to Dine," below).

If the seaside sights have got you itching to set sail, boats depart regularly from Fisherman's Wharf and will lead you on a number of ocean adventures. See "Outdoor Pursuits," below, for details on some of the offerings.

Cannery Row. Between David and Drake aves., Monterey. ☎ **408/649-6690.**

Once the center for an industrial sardine-packing operation immortalized by John Steinbeck as "a poem, a stink, a grating noise, a quality of light, a tone, a habit, a nostalgia, a dream," this area today is better described as a strip congested with wandering tourists, tacky gift shops, overpriced seafood restaurants, and an overall parking nightmare.

What changed it so dramatically? The silver sardines suddenly disappeared from Monterey's waters in 1948 as a result of overfishing, changing currents, and pollution. Fishermen left, canneries closed, and the Row fell into disrepair. But curious tourists continued to visit Steinbeck's fabled area, and where there are tourists, there are capitalists.

After visiting Cannery Row in the 1960s, Steinbeck wrote, "The beaches are clean where they once festered with fish guts and flies. The canneries which once put up a sickening stench are gone, their places filled with restaurants, antique shops, and the like. They fish for tourists now, not pilchards, and that species they are not likely to wipe out."

The Row is even more touristy today. The seaside strip's canneries and warehouses have been renovated and converted to restaurants, art galleries, hotels, factory outlets, and gift shops. Many of the larger buildings have become self-contained minimalls, stocked with a myriad of tacky tourist shops and eateries.

FOLLOWING THE PATH OF HISTORY

About a dozen antique buildings are clustered around Fisherman's Wharf and the adjacent town. Collectively, they comprise the Path of History, and many are a part of the **Monterey State Historic Park,** 20 Custom House Plaza (☎ **408/649-7118**). A self-guided walking tour booklet is available that describes the route. You can pick up a copy at clearly marked points along the path, including the Cooper-Molera Adobe and Colton Hall (see below). Note that the four house museums (Stevenson House, Cooper-Molera Adobe, Larkin House, and Casa Soberanes) are only accessible through a guided tour.

The path's best buildings are featured below; many don't have formal addresses, so they're listed according to the streets or street corners they fill. Path of History building hours vary from each other and change frequently, although in most cases they're open daily from 10am to 4pm in winter, and 10am to 5pm in summer. Call the Monterey State Historic Park for the latest information or go to the **State Park Visitor Center** at Stanton Center, 5 Custom House Plaza. A film on the history of Monterey is shown here free every 20 minutes, and guided walking tours of the Path leave from here daily; call for tour schedules. The price is $5 for adults, $3 for youths 13 to 18, and $2 for children 6 to 12.

MONTEREY MARITIME MUSEUM AND HISTORY CENTER   This museum, at 5 Custom House Plaza (☎ **408/373-2469**), lets you view ship models and other collections that relate the area's seafaring history. Admission is $5 for adults, $4 for seniors and military, $3 for youths 13 to 18, $2 for children 6 to 12, and free for kids 5 and under. Open daily from 10am to 5pm.

THE CUSTOM HOUSE   Dating from about 1827, this is the oldest government building in California, used by Mexican officials to inspect and tax ships trading on the California coast. It was here that Commodore John Sloat raised the stars and stripes to claim California for the United States.

CALIFORNIA'S FIRST THEATRE/JACK SWAN'S TAVERN   In 1847 Jack Swan built a lodging house and tavern at Scott and Pacific streets. Three years later several U.S. soldiers decided to produce plays as a business venture. They used blankets as curtains, barrels and boards as benches, and turned a healthy profit on their very first night. Today the troupers of the **Gold Coast Theater Company** stage authentic 19th-century melodramas here. Call for reservations after 1pm Wednesday to Saturday at ☎ **408/375-4916.** Tickets cost $9 for adults, $7 for children 13 to 19 and seniors 60 and over, and $5 for kids 12 and under. Show times are Wednesday to Saturday at 8pm in July and August, and on Friday and Saturday at 8pm the rest of the year.

COOPER-MOLERA ADOBE   At the corner of Polk and Munras streets was the home of Capt. John Rogers Cooper, a successful merchant. It was built in the 1820s and 1830s, but was expanded and improved upon as he became wealthier. Today it's furnished with antiques that reveal much about his lifestyle.

CASA SOBERANES   This colonial-era adobe house at 336 Pacific St., at Scott Street, was built during the 1840s. The home's cantilevered balcony and tile roof are of particular interest, as is the well-maintained interior, decorated with early New England furnishings and modern Mexican folk art.

LARKIN HOUSE   Built in 1835, this balconied two-story adobe house at 510 Calle Principal, at Jefferson Street, was the home of Thomas Oliver Larkin, the U.S. consul to Mexico from 1843 to 1846. The house doubled as the consular office and is furnished with many fine antiques, including some original pieces. Next door is the house that was used by William Tecumseh Sherman; it now contains a museum depicting the roles of the two men in California history.

STEVENSON HOUSE   Robert Louis Stevenson rented a second-floor room here during the autumn of 1879, and during his stay he wrote *The Old Pacific Capital*, an account of Monterey in the 1870s. Today the building has been restored, and several rooms are devoted to Stevenson memorabilia.

PACIFIC HOUSE   Built in 1847, Pacific House, at 10 Custom House Plaza, was first used for military offices and supplies. Horses were corralled behind the building, which was also a popular spot for Sunday bull and bear fights. Pacific House later sheltered several small stores and served successively as a public tavern, a courtroom, county clerk's office, newspaper office, law offices, a church, and a ballroom. The first floor now houses a museum of California history; the second floor has an extensive collection of Native American artifacts.

COLTON HALL   This structure, at 522 Pacific St., was originally built as Monterey's town hall and public school. California's constitutional congress convened here in 1849. The Old Monterey Jail adjoins the property, its grim cell walls still marked with prisoners' scribblings.

CASA DEL ORO   Built by Thomas Oliver Larkin and used as a store by Joesph Bosta, this two-story adobe stands at the corner of Scott and Oliver streets. Today Casa del Oro is again a general store, which is operated by the volunteers of Historic Gardens of Monterey.

FARMER'S MARKET   If you're in town on Tuesday afternoon, check out the street market on Alvarado Street (from Pearl to Del Monte streets) from 4 to 7pm. More than 100 vendors participate, bringing food, music, crafts, and entertainment together for an afternoon of flavorful festivities.

OUTDOOR PURSUITS

Cast your hook on a deep sea–fishing expedition. Among the operators are **Chris' Fishing Trips,** 48 Fisherman's Wharf (☎ 408/375-5951), which offers large party boats. Cod and salmon are the main catches, with separate boats leaving daily. Call for a complete price list and sailing schedule. Full-day excursions cost $32 to $40 per person.

   Sam's Fishing Fleet, 84 Fisherman's Wharf (☎ 408/372-0577), offers fishing excursions for cod, salmon, and whatever else is running, as well as seasonal whale-watching tours. Make reservations and bring lunch. Departures are at 7:30am Monday to Friday (salmon-fishing boats leave earlier) and at 6:30am on Saturday and Sunday. Check-in is 45 minutes prior to departure. Weekday prices are $28 for adults, $15 for children 11 and under; weekend and holidays cost $32 for adults, $20 for children. Equipment rental will cost a bit extra.

Kayaks can be rented from several outfitters for a spin around the bay. Contact **Monterey Bay Kayaks,** 693 Del Monte Ave. (☎ **800/649-5357** or 408/373-5357), on Del Monte Beach north of Fisherman's Wharf, which offers instruction, plus natural history tours that introduce visitors to the Monterey Bay National Marine Sanctuary. Prices start at $45 for the tours, $25 for rentals. To find out more, check them out on the Internet at **montereykayaks.com/tour.**

For bikes and in-line skates as well as kayak tours and rentals, contact **Adventures by the Sea,** at 299 Cannery Row (☎ **408/372-1807**). Bikes cost $6 per hour or $24 a day; kayaks are $25 per person; and skates are $12 for 2 hours, $24 for a day. Adventures also has other locations at 201 Alvarado Mall (☎ **408/648-7235**) at the Doubletree Hotel, and on the beach at Lovers Point in Pacific Grove.

Experienced scuba divers with their own equipment and one tank can contact **Twin Otters** (☎ **408/394-4235**), which specializes in scuba-diving trips along the reefs of Monterey and Carmel bays.

A popular—and exhilarating—way to view Monterey Bay's spectacular scenery is via hot-air balloon. Sunrise flights are offered daily by appointment, and sunset flights in fall and winter only. For information, contact **Balloons-by-the-Sea** (☎ **408/424-0111**).

North of Monterey at Marina State Beach, you can learn to hang-glide during a 3-hour course that includes five flights with **Western Hang Gliders,** Calif. 1 at Reservation Road, Marina (☎ **408/384-2622**). The cost is $89. Tandem flights are available, too.

Need to keep the kids busy or feeling playful yourself? The **Dennis the Menace Playground** at Camino El Estero and Del Monte Avenue, near Lake Estero, is an old-fashioned playground created by Pacific Grove resident and famous cartoonist Hank Ketcham. It has bridges to cross, tunnels to climb through, and an authentic Southern Pacific Railroad engine teeming with wanna-be conductors. There's also a hot dog and burger stand, and a big lake where you can rent paddleboats or feed the ducks. The park is open daily from 10am to sunset.

WHERE TO STAY

It seems there are only three types of choices for accommodations in Monterey: lace-and-flowery B&Bs, large corporate hotels with only a slight beachy feel, or run-of-the-mill motel digs. Consider which area you'd like to be in: beach, Cannery Row, wharf, secluded, central, etc.—as well as how much you want to spend.

EXPENSIVE

In addition to choices below, there are two chain hotels conveniently located near Fisherman's Wharf. The **Monterey Marriott,** 350 Calle Principal, at Del Monte Blvd. (☎ **800/228-9290** or 408/649-4234), offers some rooms with bay views and has a good rooftop restaurant serving California/Italian cuisine. It has an outdoor pool, health club, whirlpool, and saunas. There's also the **Doubletree Hotel at Fisherman's Wharf,** at 2 Portola Plaza (☎ **800/222-8733** or 408/649-4511). Both hotels are popular with business travelers and conventioneers.

✪ **Hotel Pacific.** 300 Pacific St., Monterey, CA 93940. ☎ **800/554-5542** or 408/373-5700. Fax 408/373-6921. 105 suites. A/C TV TEL. $199–$349 suite for two. Rates include continental breakfast and afternoon tea. AE, CB, DC, DISC, MC, V. Free parking.

If it's good enough for Martha Stewart, it's good enough for you. The day we arrived here, we previewed the Grande Dame of Hospitality's room before she checked in.

Area Code Change Notice

Please note that, effective June 13, 1998, portions of Monterey, Santa Cruz, San Luis Obispo, and Merced counties are scheduled to change to the **831** area code. Communities affected will include Santa Cruz, Carmel, Monterey, Big Sur, and small portions of San Luis Obispo. You will be able to dial 408 until February 20, 1999, after which you will be required to use 831 for affected numbers.

We were surprised she chose a hotel that's not on the water (it's close to the wharf and across the street from the Monterey Conference Center), but once we saw the rooms, we understood why. Beyond the elegant Spanish/Mediterranean architecture of the common areas, each accommodation is situated in one of 16 buildings clustered around courtyards and gardens complete with spas and fountains. The guest rooms are cozy Southwestern/adobe–style junior suites with overly fluffy soufflélike down comforters puffed atop four-poster feather beds (for the full effect, request a canopied bed). Rustically stylish decor, terra-cotta–tiled floors, a fireplace surrounded by a cushy couch and seats—plus two TVs, three phones, gourmet coffee and tea—all make this a place where you'll want to hibernate awhile. Tiny closets are one of the few downsides.

Services/Facilities: Room service (evenings only), laundry/valet, two Jacuzzis.

Monterey Bay Inn. 242 Cannery Row, Monterey, CA 93940. ☎ **800/424-6242** or 408/373-6242. Fax 408/373-7603. 47 rms. MINIBAR TV TEL. $119–$329 double. Rates include continental breakfast delivered to your room. AE, CB, DC, DISC, MC, V. Free parking. From Calif. 1, take the Pacific Grove/Del Monte Ave. exit and follow the signs to Cannery Row; the hotel is near the aquarium.

We once thought that aside from its central location a short walk from the aquarium, there was no reason to stay on noisy, expensive Cannery Row. But when we stepped out onto our private patio at the Monterey Bay Inn and saw otters splashing around below us, our criticism melted. If you don't spend all your time on the balcony, you'll be pleased to discover that the spacious rooms don't have that corporate chain-hotel look; they have light, beachy decor and old Monterey photos on the walls. Most have king-size beds and convertible sofas, as well as dressing areas and combination baths stocked with terry-cloth robes. Amenities include a refrigerator, VCR, and binoculars. Not surprisingly, oceanview rooms cost substantially more than those that look onto a park, harbor, or Cannery Row. Parents with small children should take precautions with the sliding glass doors, which open to minimal balustrades.

Services: Room service (5 to 10pm), dry cleaning, laundry.

Facilities: Sauna, fitness room, scuba facilities, beach and dive access, two hot tubs (one open 24 hours and the other boasts romantic bay views), conference rooms.

Monterey Plaza Hotel. 400 Cannery Row, Monterey, CA 93940. ☎ **800/631-1339**, 800/334-3999 in California or 408/646-1700. Fax 408/646-5937. 285 rms, 7 suites. MINIBAR TV TEL. $185–$245 double; $435–$785 suite. Children 17 and under stay free in parents' room. Package plans available. AE, CB, DC, MC, V. Parking $10. From Calif. 1 take the Soledad Dr. exit and follow the signs to Cannery Row.

One of the most formal hotels in town, the Monterey Plaza encompasses three buildings, two on the water and one across the street, that are connected by a second-story "bridge." The public areas are elegantly decorated with imported marble, Brazilian teak, and attractive artwork. The stately bedrooms, which were renovated in 1996, are more upscale-corporate than most around town and have double or king-size beds, decor hinting at 17th-century Ming or 19th-century Biedermeier, and baths covered with Italian marble. Many units have balconies overlooking the water (sea otters included in the view). The least desirable rooms are across the street from the ocean. Extra bonuses include terry-cloth robes and an attentive and professional staff.

Dining/Entertainment: The Duck Club, the hotel's flagship dining room, has splendid views of the bay and serves an à la carte, primarily Italian menu prepared in an open Genovese exhibition kitchen. Schooners Bistro on the Bay, with an outdoor terrace, is the new yacht-themed lounge/restaurant.

Services: Concierge, dry cleaning, room service, newspaper delivery, twice-daily maid service.

Facilities: Fitness room, beach, conference rooms.

✪ **Old Monterey Inn.** 500 Martin St. (off Pacific Ave.), Monterey, CA 93940. ☎ **800/350-2344** or 408/375-8284. Fax 408/375-6730. 9 rms, 1 cottage. $210–$290 double; from $240 cottage. Rates include American breakfast. MC, V. Free parking. From Calif. 1, take the Soledad Dr. exit and turn right onto Pacific Ave., then left onto Martin St.

Ann and Gene Swett have done a masterful job of converting their comfortable three-story family home into a half-timbered, vine-clad Tudor-style country inn. Though it's away from the surf, it's a perfect choice for romantics, with rose gardens, a bubbling brook, and brick and flagstone walkways shaded by a panoply of oaks. Each guest room enjoys peaceful garden views and cozy beds with goose-down comforters and pillows. Most rooms also have feather beds and wood-burning fireplaces, and two open onto private patios. Charmingly furnished and unique in character, they all owe a debt to Laura Ashley or Ralph Lauren. Special touches are evident throughout, including fresh fruit, flowers, and candies; sachets by the pillow; and books and magazines to read. The bathrooms come with hair dryers and complete toiletry packages. The cottage unit out back has antique wicker furniture, a fireplace, a sitting area, and an oversize bedroom with a king-size bed and a private patio.

Breakfast is also stellar, consisting of perhaps a soufflé or Belgian waffles. It's served either in your room, the dining room, or the rose garden. If you want to lunch on the beach, the Swetts will provide a picnic basket and towels. At 5pm guests are invited to have wine and hors d'oeuvres in front of a blazing fireplace.

Spindrift Inn. 652 Cannery Row, Monterey, CA 93940. ☎ **800/841-1879** or 408/646-8900. Fax 408/646-5342. 42 rms. MINIBAR TV TEL. $189–$289 double; $329–$409 double with ocean view. Rates include continental breakfast delivered to your room and afternoon tea. Parking $6. AE, CB, DC, DISC, MC, V.

Down in the middle of honky-tonk Cannery Row, but right on a narrow stretch of beach, this four-story hotel is an island of continental style and grace in a sea of commercialism. It's elegant and well maintained, and the rooms are sweetly decorated with feather beds (a few with canopies), hardwood floors, wood-burning fireplaces, and either cushioned window seats or private balconies. The luxurious bathrooms are adorned with marble and brass fixtures. Extras include terry-cloth robes and two telephones. The ocean views are definitely worth the extra cost.

Services: Nightly turndown, daily newspaper, and room service from an Italian restaurant next door.

MODERATE

Munras Avenue and northern Fremont Avenue are lined with moderate and inexpensive family-style motels, some independently owned and some chains. They're not as central as the downtown options, but if transportation's not an issue, you can save a bundle by staying in one of these areas. If the selections below are full, try calling

Best Western (☎ 800/528-1234) for several other options. There's also the **Cypress Gardens Inn,** 1150 Munras Ave. (☎ 408/373-2761), with a pool, hot tub, free movie channel, and continental breakfast; dogs are welcome.

Fireside Lodge. 1131 10th St., Monterey, CA 93940. ☎ **408/373-4172.** Fax 408/655-5640. 24 rms. TV TEL. $69–$149 double. Rates include continental breakfast. AE, CB, DC, DISC, MC, V.

Location is the primary advantage of this hotel near Fisherman's Wharf and downtown. The room furnishings are relatively standard but make an attempt at coziness with wicker chairs set around the gas-heated brick fireplace. Amenities include an in-room tea/coffeemaker, a hot tub on the premises, and a continental breakfast served daily in the hotel's lobby.

✪ **The Jabberwock Bed & Breakfast.** 598 Laine St., Monterey, CA 93940. ☎ **408/372-4777.** Fax 408/655-2946. 7 rms, 3 with bath. $110 double without bath, $200 double with bath. Rates include full breakfast, afternoon appetizers, and bedtime cookies. MC, V.

One of the best B&Bs in the area, the Jabberwock (named after an episode in Lewis Carroll's *Through the Looking Glass*) is 4 short blocks back from Cannery Row. Although centrally located, the property is tranquil, and its half-acre garden with waterfalls is a welcome respite from the downtown crowds. The seven rooms are all furnished differently, some more elegantly than others, but all with goose-down comforters and pillows. The Toves Room has a huge walnut Victorian bed; the Borogrove has a fireplace and a view of Monterey Bay; the Mimsey has a fine ocean view from its window seat; and the Wabe has an Austrian carved bed. A full breakfast is served in the dining room or in your own room. Evening hors d'oeuvres are also offered on the veranda, and a Vorpal rabbit tucks each guest in with cookies and milk.

INEXPENSIVE

Opt for a motel to get the best rates in this town. Some reliable options are **Motel 6** (☎ 800/4-MOTEL6), **Super 8** (☎ 800/800-8000), or **Best Western** (☎ 800/528-1234).

Cypress Tree Inn. 2227 N. Fremont St., Monterey, CA 93940. ☎ **408/372-7586.** Fax 408/372-2940. 55 rms. TV TEL. $58–$92 double. MC, V.

Although it's not centrally located (2 miles from downtown), if you're on a budget and have transportation, you won't be sorry if you stay here. The large rooms are spotless, and all but one has a combination tub-shower. Nine also have hot tubs. There's no shampoo, hair dryer, or in-room treats other than the taffy left by the maid, but the hostelry does have a hot tub, sauna, and guest coin-op laundry. Our only complaint: Our room was a bit chilly.

WHERE TO DINE

Bubba Gump Shrimp Co. Restaurant & Market. 720 Cannery Row (at Prescott). ☎408/373-1884. Main courses at lunch and dinner $8.95–$18.95. AE, DC, DISC, MC, V. Sun–Thurs 11am–10pm, Fri–Sat 11am–11pm. AMERICAN.

Foodies will flee at the sight of this tourist haven, but the fact is, lots of folks love this place. It could be the location—near the aquarium and offering a million-dollar unobstructed bay-front view—or the old boatyard decor that attracts visitors in droves. But it's more likely the entertainment value: Gump's (as in *Forrest Gump*) is packed with movie gimmicks and memorabilia.

The food is less exciting. As the roll of paper towels at each table suggests, you're guaranteed a go with grease, which is likely to arrive in the form of fried and buttered-up seafood. The "Bucket of Boat Trash," for example, is shrimp and lobster tails cooked and served in a bucket with a side of fries and coleslaw. There are also pork chops, a veggie dish, salads, and burgers. The "market" referred to in the moniker is a gift shop packed with T-shirts, caps, and, of course, boxes of chocolate.

Cafe Fina. 47 Fisherman's Wharf. ☎ **408/372-5200.** Reservations recommended. Main courses $13–$17. AE, CB, DC, DISC, MC, V. Mon–Fri 11:30–2:30pm, Sat–Sun 11:30am–3pm; daily 5–10pm. Free parking at Heritage Harbor (at Scott and Pacific). ITALIAN/SEAFOOD.

While other pierside restaurants lure in tourists with little more than an outstanding view, Cafe Fina's mesquite-grilled meats, well-prepared fresh fish, brick-oven pizzas, and array of delicious salads and pastas give even locals a reason to head to the wharf. Combine the food with a million-dollar vista and a casual atmosphere, and Cafe Fina ranks hands down as the best choice on the pier.

✪ **Fresh Cream.** Heritage Harbor, 99 Pacific St. ☎ **408/375-9798.** Reservations recommended. Main courses $23–$31. AE, DC, MC, V. Daily 6–10pm. FRENCH/CALIFORNIA.

Consistently rated one of the best places in California for fresh and innovative cuisine, Fresh Cream is a sure thing if you're looking for a memorable meal. The decor in the five dining rooms is elegantly understated to play up the emphasis on the food, though fresh flowers, oil lamps, and some tables with wharf views can't help but create ambiance. But once the food comes out of the kitchen, you're likely to forget your surroundings entirely and become entranced by every well-presented and perfectly prepared plate. Start with the ravioli of lobster with lobster butter and black and gold caviar or the broiled prawns with housemade dill fettucini and artichokes, mushrooms, sweet fennel, and lemon-caper beurre blanc. Venture on to a main dish such as the pan-seared ahi tuna sweetened with a pineapple-rum sauce, duck richly flavored with black-currant sauce, or veal loin with wild mushrooms and white-wine butter. Save room for a fluffy Grand Marnier soufflé or the sinful sac au chocolat.

✪ **Montrio.** 414 Calle Principal (at Franklin). ☎ **408/648-8880.** Reservations recommended. Main courses $14–$19. AE, DISC, MC, V. Mon–Thurs 11:30am–10pm, Fri–Sat 11:30am–11pm, Sun 11am–10pm. AMERICAN BISTRO.

Big-city sophistication met old Monterey when Montrio hit the ground running here in March 1995. The enormous dining room is definitely the sharpest in town, mixing chic style with a playful canopied vineyard of modern light fixtures, clouds hanging from the ceiling, and the buzz of well-dressed diners. You can watch chefs scurry around in the open kitchen, but you're more likely to keep your eyes on the tasty dishes, such as the crispy Dungeness crab cakes with spicy rémoulade, beet salad with feta cheese, sliced green apples, and candied walnuts; a succulent grilled pork T-bone with apple, pear, and currant compôte; or an oven-roasted Portobello mushroom with polenta and ragoût of vegetables. Finish the evening with chocolate mousse with crispy chocolate phyllo cookies and tangerine sauce.

Whaling Station. 763 Wave St. (between Prescott and Irving aves.). ☎ **408/373-3778.** Reservations recommended on weekends. Main courses $15–$30. AE, CB, DC, DISC, MC, V. Daily 5–10pm. From Calif. 1, take the Soledad Dr. exit and follow the signs toward Cannery Row; turn left on Wave St. 1 block before Cannery Row. AMERICAN.

If you insist on eating on Cannery Row, come to this touristy, old-fashioned dining house known for its New York, porterhouse, and other steaks grilled over oak and mesquite. A 25-year tradition guarantees you an artichoke vinaigrette appetizer before your main course, which ranges from salad to pasta and the inevitable seafood dish.

Wharfside Restaurant & Lounge. 60 Fisherman's Wharf. ☎ **408/375-3956.** Reservations recommended. Main courses $11–$20. AE, DISC, MC, V. Daily 11am–9:30pm. Closed the first 2 weeks of Dec. SEAFOOD.

A banner out front promises a "taste of Monterey," which translates into a decent helping of fresh seafood served à la tourist trap. While the fare is okay, the real flavor is the Wharfside's casual upstairs nautically themed dining room where you'll get a great view from the end of Fisherman's Wharf. There's also downstairs and upper-deck outdoor seating where you can choose from six different varieties of ravioli (made on the premises), such specialties as a combination bouillabaisse or any of the house-made desserts. Daily specials usually include fresh seasonal fish, beef, and pasta. Clam chowder, sandwiches (including hot crab), and pizzas are on the regular menu.

3 Pacific Grove

Some compare 2.6-square-mile Pacific Grove—the locals call it "P.G."—to Carmel as it was 20 years ago. Although tourists wind their way through here on oceanfront trails and dining excursions, the town remains quaint and peaceful—amazing considering that Monterey is a stone's throw away (a quarter of the Monterey Bay Aquarium is actually in Pacific Grove). While neighboring Monterey is comparatively congested and cosmopolitan, Pacific Grove is a community sprinkled with historic homes, blooming flowers, and the kind of tranquillity that inspires butterflies to flutter and deer to meander fearlessly across the road in search of another garden to graze.

ESSENTIALS

VISITOR INFORMATION Although the town is small, there is the **Pacific Grove Chamber of Commerce,** at the corner of Forest and Central avenues (☎ **408/ 373-3304**).

ORIENTATION Lighthouse Avenue is the Grove's principal thoroughfare, running from Monterey to the lighthouse at the very point of the peninsula. Lighthouse Avenue is bisected by Forest Avenue, which runs from Calif. 1 (where it's called Holman Highway, or Calif. 68) to Lover's Point, an extension of land that sticks out into the bay in the middle of Pacific Grove.

EXPLORING THE TOWN

Pacific Grove is a town to be strolled, so park the car, put on your walking shoes, and make an afternoon of it. Meander around George Washington Park and along the waterfront around the point.

The **Point Pinos Lighthouse,** at the tip of the peninsula on Ocean View Boulevard (☎ **408/648-3116**), is the oldest working lighthouse on the West Coast. It dates from 1855 when Pacific Grove was little more than a pine forest. The museum and grounds are open free to visitors Thursday to Sunday from 1 to 4pm.

Marine Gardens Park, a stretch of shoreline along Ocean View Boulevard on Monterey Bay and the Pacific, is renowned not only for its ocean views and colorful flowers, but also for its fascinating tidepool seaweed beds. Walk out to **Lover's Point** (named after Lovers of Jesus, not groping teenagers) and watch the sea otters playing in the kelp beds and cracking open an occasional abalone for lunch.

An excellent, shorter alternative, or complement, to the 17-Mile Drive (see section 4 on Pebble Beach, later in this chapter) is the scenic drive or bike ride along Pacific Grove's **Ocean View Boulevard.** This coastal stretch starts near Monterey's Cannery Row and follows the Pacific around to the lighthouse point. There it turns into Sunset Drive, which runs along secluded **Asilomar State Beach.** Park on Sunset and explore the trails, dunes, and tide pools of this sandy stretch of shore. You might find purple shore crabs, green anemone, sea bats, starfish, and limpets, as well as all kinds of kelp and algae. The 11 buildings of the conference center established here by the YWCA in 1913 are historic landmarks that were designed by noted architect Julia Morgan. If you follow this route during winter months, a furious sea rages and crashes against the rocks.

To learn more about the marine and other natural life of the region, stop in at the **Pacific Grove Museum of Natural History,** 165 Forest Ave. (☎ **408/648-3116**). It has displays about the monarch butterflies and their migration, and also stuffed examples of the local birds and mammals. Admission is free and it's open Tuesday to Sunday from 10am to 5pm.

Pacific Grove is widely known as "Butterfly Town, U.S.A.," a reference to the thousands of **monarch butterflies** that migrate here from November to February, traveling from as far away as Alaska. Many settle in the Monarch Grove sanctuary, a eucalyptus stand on Grove Acre Avenue off Lighthouse Avenue. George Washington Park, at Pine Avenue and Alder Street, is also famous for its "butterfly trees." To reach these sites, they may travel as far as 2,000 miles, covering 100 miles a day at an altitude of 10,000 feet. *Collectors beware:* The town imposes strict fines for molesting butterflies.

Just as Ocean View Boulevard serves as an alternative to the 17-Mile Drive, the **Pacific Grove Municipal Golf Course,** 77 Asilomar Ave. (☎ **408/648-3177**), serves as a reasonably priced alternative to the high-priced courses at Pebble Beach. The back nine holes of this 5,500-yard, par-70 course overlook the sea and offer the added challenge of coping with the winds. Views are panoramic, and the fairways and greens are better maintained than most semiprivate courses. There's a restaurant, pro shop, and driving range. Greens fees are $25 Monday to Thursday and $30 Friday to Sunday; optional carts cost $25. Visa and MasterCard are accepted for greens fees and equipment rental.

The **American Tin Cannery Factory Premium Outlets,** 125 Ocean View Blvd. (☎ **408/372-1442**), is a warehouse of 40 factory outlet shops. Labels represented here include Anne Klein, Joan & David, Bass Shoes, Reeboks, Carter's children's wear, Royal Doulton, Maidenform, London Fog, and Carole Little.

WHERE TO STAY

Hate making decisions? **Resort II Me** (☎ **800/449-1499**) will help you choose a hotel and make a reservation.

EXPENSIVE/MODERATE

Centrella Inn. 612 Central Ave., Pacific Grove, CA 93950. ☎ **800/233-3372** or 408/372-3372. Fax 408/372-2036. 19 rms, 4 suites, 5 cottages. $95–$159 double; $180–$195 cottage and suite. Rates include buffet breakfast. MC, V.

A couple of blocks from the waterfront, and 2 blocks from Lover's Point Beach, the two-story Centrella is an old turreted Victorian that was built as a boardinghouse in 1889. Today the rooms are decorated in a Victorian style, but they're somewhat plain—iron beds, plus side table, floor lamp, and armoire—although the bathrooms do have clawfoot tubs. In the back, connected to the house by brick walkways, are several private cottages and suites with living rooms with fireplaces, wet bars, TVs, and separate bedrooms and baths. Two have private decks; the others offer decks facing the rose garden and patio, which is set with umbrella tables and chairs. Cheese and hors d'oeuvres are served in the evening.

Gosby House. 643 Lighthouse Ave., Pacific Grove, CA 93950. ☎ **800/527-8828** or 408/375-1287. Fax 408/655-9621. 22 rms, 20 with bath. $90–$105 double without bath, $90–$150 double with bath. Rates include full breakfast. AE, MC, V. From Calif. 1, take Calif. 68 to Pacific

Grove, where it turns into Forest Ave.; continue on Forest to Lighthouse Ave., turn left, and go 3 blocks.

Originally a boardinghouse for Methodist ministers, this Victorian was built in 1887, 3 blocks from the bay. It's still one of the most charming Victorians on the Monterey Peninsula. Each room is uniquely decorated, with floral-print wallpapers, lacy pillows, and antique furnishings. Twelve guest rooms have fireplaces, and all come with the inn's trademark teddy bears. The two Carriage House rooms merit special consideration. Each has a fireplace, deck, and extra large bathroom with spa tub.

The house has a separate dining room and parlor, where guests gather for breakfast and complimentary wine and snacks in the afternoon. Other amenities include complimentary newspaper, twice-daily maid service, and bicycles. No smoking.

Green Gables Inn. 104 5th St., Pacific Grove, CA 93950. ☎ **800/722-1774** or 408/ 375-2095. Fax 408/375-5437. 11 rms, 7 with bath; 1 suite. $110–$135 double without bath, $145–$160 double with bath; $170 suite. Rates include buffet breakfast. AE, MC, V. From Calif. 1, take the Pacific Grove exit (Calif. 68) and continue to the Pacific Ocean; turn right on Ocean View Blvd. and drive half a mile to 5th St.

A Queen Anne–style mansion, looking like an English country inn, this hotel dates from 1888 when a judge from Pasadena built it to shelter his mistress from the prying eyes of his hometown. Managed by hospitable innkeepers, this little gem may not be fancy, but it's comfortable. The rooms are divided between the main building and the carriage houses behind it. The less atmospheric carriage house rooms are better for families; they have large, newly remodeled private baths with Jacuzzi tubs and more elbow room. All accommodations are individually decorated with dainty furnishings, including some antiques and an occasional poster bed. Most rooms in the original home share two immaculate bathrooms, and have an ocean view. There's an antique carousel horse in the comfortable parlor, where complimentary wine, tea, and hors d'oeuvres are served each afternoon. Teddy bears populate every nook and cranny. No smoking.

Martine Inn. 255 Ocean View Blvd., Pacific Grove, CA 93950. ☎ **800/852-5588** or 408/ 373-3388. Fax 408/373-3896. 20 rms. $135–$245 double. Rates include full breakfast. AE, DISC, MC, V.

One glance at the lavish Victorian interior and the incredible bay views and you'll know why this Mediterranean-style hotel is one of the best B&Bs in the area. Enjoy the vista via binoculars the management leaves out for guests, or stroll the bayfront promenade. Always above par, the rooms have been recently redecorated but still maintain Victorian style. You'll pay more if you want a fireplace and ocean view. And be sure to request a room with a bathtub if it matters to you (some only have a shower). A full breakfast is served at lace-covered tables in the large front room; hors d'oeuvres are served in the evening. Guests also have access to two additional sitting quarters: a small room downstairs overlooking the ocean and a larger room with shelves of books. Amenities include newspaper delivery, free coffee and refreshments, Jacuzzi, and a billiards table.

Pacific Grove Inn. 581 Pine Ave., Pacific Grove, CA 93950, ☎ **800/732-2825** or 408/ 375-2825. 13 rms, 3 suites. TV TEL. $98–$138 double; $110–$170 suite. Rates include buffet breakfast. AE, CB, DC, DISC, MC, V. From Calif. 1, take the Pacific Grove exit (Calif. 68) to the corner of Pine and Forest aves.

Five blocks from the beach, this stately, renovated 1904 Queen Anne–style mansion is one of the town's architectural gems. Despite heavy Victorian embellishments, the elegant accommodations feel light, airy, and spacious. They come with queen- or king-size beds, refrigerators, safes, and fireplaces. Afternoon tea is served in the parlor. No smoking.

✪ **Seven Gables Inn.** 555 Ocean View Blvd., Pacific Grove, CA. 93950. ☎ **408/372-4341.** 14 rms. $135–$225 double. Rates include breakfast and afternoon tea. 2-night minimum stay on weekends. MC, V.

Named after the seven gables that cap the hotel, this compound of Victorian buildings was constructed in 1886 by the Chase family (as in Chase Manhattan Bank). Outside is the coast road overlooking the sea; inside is a valuable collection of mostly European antiques. Everything here is opulent and gilded, including the rooms, which are scattered among the main house, cottages, and the guest house and offer ocean views. The accommodations are linked with verdant gardens filled with roses and marble sculpture. Afternoon tea is accompanied by an array of pastries and homemade chocolates. If the hotel's booked, ask about the Grand View Inn, a newer, comparable B&B next door that's run by the same owners.

INEXPENSIVE

The Wilkies Inn. 1038 Lighthouse Ave., Pacific Grove, CA, 93950. ☎ **408/372-5960.** Fax 408/655-1681. 24 rms. $55–$105 double. Additional person $8 extra. 2-night minimum stay on weekends. AE, DISC, MC, V.

The decor here is basic motel style, but the owners did splurge on stylish bedspreads and special amenities for divers. All the squeaky-clean rooms come with coffeemakers and free movies and local calls. Some have microwaves or partial ocean views, two have a full kitchen, and you can have a refrigerator for a few extra dollars. Considering that this place consistently charges less than the other hotels in town, gets an "A+" for service, and is located on a quiet tree-lined street, it's a great value.

WHERE TO DINE
EXPENSIVE

✪ **Fandango.** 223 17th St. ☎ **408/372-3456.** Reservations recommended. Main courses $11–$19. AE, CB, DC, DISC, MC, V. Mon–Sat 11am–3:30pm, Sun 10am–2:30pm; daily 5–9:30pm. From Calif. 1, take the Pacific Grove exit (Calif. 68), turn left on Lighthouse Ave., and continue a block to 17th St. MEDITERRANEAN.

Provincial Mediterranean specialties from Spain to Greece to North Africa spice up the menu with such offerings as seafood paella with North African couscous (the recipe has been in the owner's family for almost 200 years), cassoulet maison, cannelloni niçoise, and a Greek-style lamb shank. The atmosphere takes you straight to Europe in a fiesta of five upstairs and downstairs dining rooms cozied by roaring fires, wood tables, and antiqued walls. There's a very good international wine list and a dessert menu that includes a Grand Marnier soufflé with fresh raspberry purée sauce and profiteroles. In winter, ask to be seated in the fireplace dining room, and in summer, request the terrace room—but whenever you come, expect everything here to be lively and colorful, from the regional decor to the owner himself.

Joe Rombi's. 208 17th St. (at Lighthouse Ave.). ☎ **408/373-2416.** Reservations recommended. Main courses $12–$19. MC, V. Wed–Sun 5–10pm. ITALIAN.

Expect a fun night out at Joe Rombi's, where enormous French antique posters line the walls, lighting is perfectly dimmed, and the food is very fresh (lasagnas and pastas are made that day by the owner himself). Joe will seat you at one of the 11 intimate tables, and you'll immediately be served a basket of fresh housemade focaccia to munch while you peruse the limited menu of appetizers, soups, salads, pizzas, pastas, and four main courses (some of which come with soup and salad). Go with the fish of the day—we had a halibut dish that any upscale San Francisco restaurant would be proud to present. The food here is good, but what really makes the place pop is the aura of Joe Rombi, who's always on hand to make sure that his customers' every need is fulfilled.

✪ **Melac's.** 663 Lighthouse Ave. ☎ **408/375-1743.** Reservations required. Main courses $19–$25; fixed-price dinners $32 and $48. AE, DC, MC, V. Tues–Fri 11:30am–2pm; daily 5:30–9:30pm. FRENCH.

Take an intimate dining room with brick walls, hand-painted French-country murals, and formally set tables, combine it with a husband-and-wife team (she's a graduate of Paris's Cordon Bleu; he's the friendly French host), and you've got Pacific Grove's favorite French restaurant. Elegant yet unpretentious, this is the place to romance in front of the fireplace, while enjoying a limited menu of finely prepared classic dishes—without the stuffiness often associated with fancy French restaurants. Expect such choices as a delicious lobster ravioli appetizer with a tarragon-lobster sauce or gratin of baby leeks and chanterelles with reggiano Parmesan and Dijon mustard. Then choose from main courses of Atlantic salmon poached on a bed of dilled vegetables julienne and lemon-caper basmati rice pilaf, or veal sweetbreads roasted between layers of puff pastry with minced wild mushrooms and cognac cream (each entree is served with a dinner salad). If you want to go all out, opt for the "Petit" or "Grande Aventure," four- or six-course fixed-price dinners.

✪ **The Old Bath House.** 620 Ocean View Blvd. ☎ **408/375-5195.** Reservations required. Main courses $14–$27.50. AE, DC, DISC, MC, V. Mon–Fri 5–10:30pm, Sat 4–11pm, Sun 4–10:30pm. CONTINENTAL.

This restored Victorian restaurant with etched glass and leather furniture is perched on the edge of the earth overlooking Lover's Point. It may be pricy and frequented by tourists, but dinner here is a stately affair with knockout bay views and lovingly prepared cuisine, which makes it the perfect place for a romantic night out. You may find cream of lobster and wild-boar sausage on the starters menu. Although main courses vary, signature dishes include Dungeness crabs and duck merlot served with apples and a raspberry-merlot sauce. Complete your meal with hot pecan ice cream fritters.

MODERATE

First Awakenings. In the American Tin Cannery, 125 Ocean View Blvd. ☎ **408/372-1125.** Reservations not accepted. Breakfast $4–$7; lunch $5–$8. AE, DISC, MC, V. Daily 7am–2:30pm. From Calif. 1, take the Pacific Grove exit (Calif. 68) and turn right onto Lighthouse Ave.; after a mile turn left onto Eardley Ave. and take it to the corner of Ocean View. AMERICAN.

What was once a dank canning factory is now a bright, huge, open restaurant, flooded with light from an entire wall of windows. Ceilings don't get much taller than these, and they're topped with an enormous skylight and hung with plants and industrial overhead fans. Breakfast, the most important meal of the day here, includes eight varieties of omelets; granola with nuts, fruit, and yogurt; walnut and wheat pancakes; and raisin French toast. At lunch there's a fine choice of salads and a foot-long list of sandwiches that encompasses everything from albacore to zucchini.

✪ **The Fishwife at Asilomar Beach.** 1996¹/₂ Sunset Dr. (at Asilomar Beach). ☎ **408/375-7107.** Main courses $8.75–$13. AE, DISC, MC, V. Mon and Wed–Sat 11am–10pm, Sun 10am–10pm. From Calif. 1, take the Pacific Grove exit (Calif. 68) and stay left until it becomes Sunset Dr.; the restaurant will be on your left about 1 mile ahead, as you approach Asilomar Beach. SEAFOOD.

This restaurant dates from the 1830s, when an enterprising sailor's wife started a small food market that became famous for its Boston clam chowder. Today locals still

Red House Café, 662 Lighthouse Ave. (at 19th), Pacific Grove. ☎ 408/643-1060. There is no sign, no business cards, and no menus. This restaurant is a rustic turn-of-the-century cottage painted a delightful shade of red. In the backyard and in the carriage house is Mrs. Trawick's Garden Shop, a wonderful collection of garden ornaments, tools, and whimsies. The neighborhood birds seem very pleased to stay and add a bit of local color. Inside the restaurant an eclectic mix of clients are served a wonderful changing menu for breakfast, lunch, or pastries. We sampled a pork loin sandwich on focaccia bread, café au lait served in its traditional bowl, and an exquisite pear tart. The young couple, Laura and Chris, opened this jewel in 1997, but you can tell from the crowd that they have won over the hearts and tummies of the town. (*Authors' note:* Main courses are $4.95 to $8.95; hours are Tuesday to Sunday from 7:30am to 3pm.)

—Karla Baer Cohen and Jim Cohen, Huntington Beach, CA.

return for the savory soup as well as some of the finest seafood in Pacific Grove. Two best-sellers at dinner are calamari steak sautéed with shallots, garlic, tomatoes, and white wine; and prawns Belize, presented sizzling with red onions, tomatoes, fresh serrano chiles, jicama, lime juice, and cashews. There are also steak and pasta dishes on the menu, and all main courses come with fresh vegetables, bread, black beans, and rice or potatoes. Kids get their own color-in menu, which has smaller portions for less than $6.

Peppers Mexicali Cafe. 170 Forest Ave. ☎ **408/373-6892.** Reservations recommended. Main courses $6–$13. AE, CB, DC, DISC, MC, V. Mon and Wed–Thurs 11:30am–10pm, Fri–Sat 11:30am–10:30pm, Sun 4–10pm. MEXICAN/LATIN AMERICAN.

Peppers is the kind of place where you can't help but feel at home. The dining room is casual and inviting, with wooden floors and tables, pepper art visible from every viewpoint, and a perpetual crowd of diners who come to suck up beers and savor spicy specialties such as well-balanced seafood tacos and fajitas or house-made tamales and chile rellenos. Other fire-starters include the snapper Yucatán, which is cooked with chiles, citrus cilantro, and tomatoes; and grilled prawns with lime-cilantro dressing. Add a substantial selection of suds, an addicting compilation of chips and salsa, and a friendly service staff, and your taste buds are bound to bellow "Ole!"

4 Pebble Beach & the 17-Mile Drive

Pebble Beach is a world unto itself. Polo shirts, golf shoes, and big bankrolls are standard here, and if you have to ask how much accommodations and greens fees are, you definitely can't afford them. In this elite golfers paradise, endless grassy fairways are only interrupted by a few luxury resorts and cliffs where the ocean meets the land. It's also the site in winter of the **AT&T Pebble Beach National Pro-Am,** a celebrity tournament originally launched in 1937 by crooner Bing Crosby.

In 1980 tycoon Marvin Davis, czar of the real estate partnership that owned the links, sold the 5,300-acre resort to Japanese developer Minoru Isutani for a whopping $840 million. Isutani outraged golfers worldwide when he turned around and tried to peddle 2,000 memberships in the proposed Pebble Beach National Golf Club, at $740,000 a membership.

Scandals, investigations, and even the recession in Japan caused Pebble Beach and its neighboring courses to hit bottom in 1992. Claims circulated that wealthy Japanese tourists were given preferential treatment over American golfers who showed up.

In 1992 the Lone Cypress Company, with Japanese backing, acquired the Pebble Beach Resorts for $500 million (and considered it a bargain). In the last few years they've invested more than $24 million in the resort, and golfing magazines have cited notable improvements. Golfing critics now report that the links have never looked better, thanks in large part to the Jack Nicklaus design team who went to work to upgrade them.

THE 17-MILE DRIVE

The beautiful 17-Mile Drive demands a leisurely afternoon. Pack a picnic or make lunch reservations at Roy's in the Inn at Spanish Bay (see "Where to Stay & Dine," below), fork over $7.25 to enter the drive, and prepare to see some of the most exclusive coastal real estate in California.

The drive can be entered from any of five gates: two from Pacific Grove to the north, one from Carmel to the south, or two from Monterey to the east. The most convenient entrance from Calif. 1 is just off the main road at the Holman Highway exit. You may beat traffic by entering at the Carmel Gate and doing the tour backward.

Admission to the drive includes an informative map that lists 26 points of interest along the way. Aside from homes of the ultra-rich, highlights include Seal and Bird Rocks, where you can see countless gulls, cormorants, and other offshore birds as well as seals and sea lions; and Cypress Point Lookout, which affords a 20-mile view all the way to the Big Sur Lighthouse on a clear day. Also visible is the famous Lone Cypress tree, inspiration to so many artists and photographers, which you can admire from afar but to which you can no longer walk. The drive also traverses the Del Monte Forest, thick with tame blacktail deer, and often compared to some "billionaire's private game preserve."

One of the best ways to see 17-Mile Drive is by bike, but the ride toward Carmel is all downhill, so unless you're in great shape, arrange for a ride back or simply do it by car.

GREAT GOLF COURSES

Locals tell us it's almost impossible to get a tee time unless you're staying at the resort. If you're one of the lucky few, you can choose from several famous courses along the 17-Mile Drive.

✪ **PEBBLE BEACH GOLF LINKS**   The most famous course is Pebble Beach Golf Links (☎ 800/654-9300), at the Lodge at Pebble Beach (see "Where to Stay & Dine," below). It's home in winter to the AT&T Pebble Beach National Pro-Am, a celebrity-laden tournament televised around the world. Jack Nicklaus has claimed, "If I could play only one course for the rest of my life, this would be it." He should know; he won both the 1961 U.S. Amateur and the 1972 U.S. Open here. Indeed, 10 national championships have been decided here. Herbert Warren Wind, dean of this century's golf writers, said, "There is no finer seaside golf course in creation"— and that includes the legendary Old Course at St. Andrews in Scotland. Built in 1919, this 18-hole course is 6,799 yards and par 72. It's precariously perched over a rugged ocean. Greens fees are a staggering $225 for resort guests—if they can get a slot (it's almost impossible for anyone else to play here), $275 for non-resort guests.

✪ **SPYGLASS HILL GOLF COURSE**   Also frequented by celebrities is this course at Stevenson Drive and Spyglass Hill Road (☎ 800/654-9300). Its slope rating of 143 means that it's one of the toughest courses in California. It's a justifiably famous links: 6,859 yards and par 72 with five oceanfront holes. The rest reach deep into the

Del Monte Forest. Greens fees are $200, $175 for guests of the lodge or inn (see "Where to Stay & Dine," below). Reservations should be made a month in advance. There's an excellent Grill Room on the grounds.

✪ **POPPY HILLS**   This course, on 17-Mile Drive (☎ **408/625-1513**), was named one of the world's top 20 by *Golf Digest*. It was designed by Robert Trent Jones, Jr. in 1986. Greens fees are $105, plus $30 cart rental. You can make reservations 30 days in advance.

✪ **THE LINKS AT SPANISH BAY**   Lying on the north end of 17-Mile Drive at the Pebble Beach Resort/Inn at Spanish Bay (☎ **800/654-9300**), this is the most easily booked course. Serious golfers say it's the most challenging of the Pebble Beach links. Robert Trent Jones, Jr., Tom Watson, and Frank Tatum (former USGA president) designed the course to duplicate a Scottish links course. Greens fees are $150 for resort guests, $165 for nonguests. Required cart rental is an additional $25. Reservations can be made 60 days in advance.

DEL MONTE GOLF COURSE   At 1300 Sylvan Rd. (☎ **408/373-2700**) lies the oldest course west of the Mississippi, charging some of the most "reasonable" greens fees in the Pebble Beach area: $75 per player ($60 for resort guests), plus a cart rental of $18. The course, often cited in magazines for its "grace and charm," is relatively short, only 6,339 yards. This seldom-advertised course is actually part of the Pebble Beach complex.

WHERE TO STAY & DINE

✪ **Inn at Spanish Bay.** 2700 17-Mile Dr., Pebble Beach, CA 93953. ☎ **800/654-9300** or 408/647-7500. Fax 408/644-7960. 270 rms, 17 suites. MINIBAR TV TEL. $305–$425 double; from $625 suite. $17 gratuity added. AE, CB, DC, MC, V. From Calif. 1 south, turn west onto Calif. 68 and south onto 17-Mile Dr.; the hotel is located on your right, just past the toll plaza.

Surrounded by the renowned Links at Spanish Bay golf course, the Inn at Spanish Bay is a plush 3- and 4-story low-rise, lying 10 miles north of the Lodge at Pebble Beach and set on 236 manicured acres. Approximately half the rooms face the ocean and are more expensive than their counterparts overlooking the forest. Each accommodation contains about 600 square feet of floor space and has a private fireplace and either an outdoor deck or a patio. The baths are finished in Italian marble and the furnishings, all of which are custom made; rooms include four-poster beds with down comforters.

Dining/Entertainment: Roy Yamaguchi, Hawaii's celebrity chef, opened Roy's, his only mainland outpost, in April 1995. The menu features Euro-Asian cuisine and many of his signature dishes, plus some new ones inspired by California's regional ingredients. Roy has a way with sauces, and although he's probably not in the kitchen, his protégés whip up some great cilantro rock-shrimp cake with lobster miso sauce and Asian veggie confetti, crab pot stickers, and ravioli of shiitake, spinach, and ricotta. Main courses include slow-roasted Sonoma valley chicken with mashed potato cake and porcini mushroom gravy, grilled filet mignon with caramelized onion balsamic ragoût and potato gratin, and wood-fired pizzas from the exhibition kitchen. Traps and the adjacent Lobby Lounge serve light meals; the Bay Club serves a gourmet Mediterranean menu. You can also have breakfast or lunch at the nearby Clubhouse Bar and Grill, overlooking the first fairway. A jazz band performs in the Lobby Lounge Thursday through Sunday, but our favorite time is at dusk, when a bagpiper strolls the terrace with a skirling tribute to Scotland.

Services: Concierge, 24-hour room service, massages, evening turndown, overnight shoe shine, laundry/valet.

Facilities: World-class golf course, eight tennis courts (two lighted), a first-rate Ansel Adams gallery, pro shops, award-winning fitness center, equestrian center, bicycles, heated swimming pool.

The Lodge at Pebble Beach. 17-Mile Dr., Pebble Beach, CA 93953. ☎ **800/654-9300** or 408/624-3811. Fax 408/644-7960. 161 rms, 12 suites. MINIBAR TV TEL. $350–$475 double; from $875 suite. $15 gratuity added. AE, CB, DC, DISC, MC, V. From Calif. 1 south, turn west on Calif. 68, south onto 17-Mile Dr., and follow the coastal road to the hotel.

For the combined cost of greens fees and a room here, you could easily create a professional putting green in your own backyard—and still have some money left over. But if you're a dedicated hacker, you've got to play here at least once. Look on the bright side—at least you can expect ultra plush, recently revamped rooms, which are equipped with every conceivable amenity, including refrigerators and wood-burning fireplaces. Most are in two-story cottage clusters, with anywhere from eight to a dozen units in each. Those opening onto the ocean carry the highest price tags.

Dining/Entertainment: The Cypress Room, which overlooks the 18th green and the bay, is a seafood grill. The Tap Room, patterned after an English pub and decorated with golfing memorabilia, offers everything from prime rib to thick-crust pizza. The Gallery, overlooking the first tee, is open only for breakfast and lunch. Club XIX, an opulent and pricey classical French dining room, offers extravagant dishes such as foie gras and truffles, and stuffed quail.

Services: Concierge, 24-hour room service, priority golf tee times, supervised children's facilities, barber, evening turndown, complimentary airport transportation, massage, laundry/valet.

Facilities: Outstanding golf course, 12 tennis courts, fitness room, horseback riding, beach, bicycles for rent, heated swimming pool, sauna, hiking trails, shopping arcade.

5 Carmel

If you visited the town officially known as Carmel-by-the-Sea dozens of years ago, you're likely to be of the school that criticizes its present-day overcommercialization. Carmel began as an artists' colony that attracted such luminaries as Robinson Jeffers, Sinclair Lewis, Robert Louis Stevenson, Ansel Adams, William Rose Benet, and Mary Austin. It was a nonconformist enclave where residents resisted assigning street numbers and lighting (they carried lanterns, which they considered more romantic).

Today Carmel may not be the bohemian artists' village seasoned travelers remember, but it's still an adorable (albeit touristy) town that knows how to celebrate its surroundings. Vibrant wildflower gardens flourish along each residential street, gnarled cypress trees reach up from white sandy beaches, and at the end of each day tourists magically disappear and the town for a split second seems undiscovered.

It's still intimate enough that there's no need for street numbers. Its inns, restaurants, boutiques, and art galleries all identify their locations only by cross streets. A few hints such as Saks Fifth Avenue, convertible roadsters cruising through town, intolerable traffic, and the price tags on B&Bs indicate we're not in Kansas anymore, but rather a well-preserved upscale tourist haven.

ESSENTIALS

The **Carmel Business Association,** P.O. Box 4444, Carmel, CA 93921 (☎ **408/ 624-2522**), is above the Hog's Breath Inn on San Carlos between 5th and 6th streets. It distributes local maps, brochures, and publications. It's open Monday to Friday from 9am to 5pm. Pick up a copy of the *Carmel Gallery Guide* and a schedule of local

---

Area Code Change Notice

Please note that, effective June 13, 1998, portions of Monterey, Santa Cruz, San Luis Obispo, and Merced counties are scheduled to change to the **831** area code. Communities affected will include Santa Cruz, Carmel, Monterey, Big Sur, and small portions of San Luis Obispo. You will be able to dial 408 until February 20, 1999, after which you will be required to use 831 for affected numbers.

---

events. On weekends they have a booth set up from 11am to 3pm at Carmel Plaza on Ocean Avenue between Junipero and San Carlos streets.

EXPLORING THE TOWN

A wonderful stretch of white sand backed by cypress trees, **Carmel Beach City Park** is a wee bit o' heaven on earth (though the jammed parking lot can be closer to a visit to hell). There's plenty of room for families, surfers, and dogs with their owners (yes, pooches are allowed to run off-leash here). If the parking lot is full, there are some spaces on Ocean Avenue.

Farther south around the promontory, **Carmel River State Beach** is a less-crowded option, with white sand and dunes, plus a bird sanctuary where brown pelicans, black oystercatchers, cormorants, gulls, curlews, godwits, and sanderlings make their home.

The ✪ **Mission San Carlos Borromeo del Rio Carmelo,** on Basilica Rio Road at Lasuen Drive, off Calif. 1 (☎ **408/624-3600**), is the burial ground of Father Junípero Serra and the second-oldest of the 21 Spanish missions he launched. Founded in 1771 on a scenic site overlooking the Carmel River, it remains one of the largest and most interesting of California's missions. The present stone church, with its gracefully curving walls and Moorish bell tower, was begun in 1793. Its walls are covered with a lime plaster made of burnt seashells. The old mission kitchen, the first library in California, the high altar, and the flower gardens are all worth visiting. More than 3,000 Native Americans are buried in the adjacent cemetery; their graves are decorated with seashells. A $2 donation is requested. The mission is open June to August, Monday to Saturday from 9:30am to 7:30pm, Sunday 10:30am to 7:30pm; in other months, Monday to Saturday from 9:30am to 4:30pm and on Sunday from 10:30am to 4:30pm.

One of Carmel's prettiest homes and gardens is **Tor House,** 26304 Oceanview Ave. (☎ **408/624-1813,** or 408/624-1840 on Friday and Saturday only), built by California poet Robinson Jeffers. On Carmel Point, the house dates from 1918 and includes a 40-foot tower containing stones from around the world, which are embedded in the walls (there's even one from the Great Wall of China). Inside, an old porthole is reputed to have come from the ship on which Napoléon escaped from Elba in 1815. Admission is by guided tour only, and reservations are required. It's $7 for adults, $4 for college students, and $2 for high school students (no children under 12). Open on Friday and Saturday from 10am to 3pm.

If shopping is more your bag, leave the car at the hotel or park and check out the town on foot. You'll be surprised at the number of shops packed into this small town—more than 500 boutiques offering unique fashions, baskets, housewares, imported goods, and a veritable cornucopia of art galleries. All the commercial action is packed along the small stretch of Ocean Avenue between Junipero and San Antonio avenues.

If you want to tour the galleries, pick up a copy of the *Carmel Gallery Guide* from the Carmel Business Association (see "Essentials," above).

Shoppers will enjoy **Carmel Plaza,** a multilevel complex of boutiques, craft stores, restaurants, and gourmet food outlets on Ocean Avenue at Junipero Street, or **The Barnyard,** on Calif. 1 at Carmel Valley Road (you'll have to take the car to this authentic early-Californian barn housing 60-plus shops and restaurants).

WHERE TO STAY
EXPENSIVE

Carriage House Inn. Junipero St., between 7th and 8th aves. (P.O. Box 1900), Carmel, CA 93921. ☎ **800/433-4732** or 408/625-2585. Fax 408/624-2967. 13 rms, 2 suites. MINIBAR, TV, TEL. $205–$225 double; $275 suite. Rates include continental breakfast. Additional person $15 extra. AE, DISC, MC, V. From Calif. 1, exit onto Ocean Ave. and turn left onto Junipero St.

What is it that makes us love this place? It's not that each room comes with a VCR (and free videos from the video library), wood-burning fireplaces, small refrigerators, and king-size beds with down comforters, or that most of the second-floor rooms have sunken tubs and vaulted beam ceilings and bottom-floor rooms have single whirlpool tubs. It's the luxurious atmosphere and superfluous pampering that comes with the cost of the room. Not only do guests receive breakfast delivered to their room, but there's also wine and hors d'oeuvres served in the afternoon and cappuccino in the evening. Plus, while almost all choices in the area are frill-and-lace, the Carriage House is a more mature, formal but cozy environment.

Cobblestone Inn. Junipero St. (between 7th and 8th aves., 1^1/$_2$ blocks from Ocean Ave.; P.O. Box 3185), Carmel, CA 93921. ☎ **800/841-5252** or 408/625-5222. Fax 408/625-0478. 21 rms, 3 suites. TV TEL. $125–$165 double; $175 suite. Rates include buffet breakfast. AE, MC, V.

The Cobblestone may not be Victorian like other properties owned by the Four Sisters Inns, but it's just as flowery, well kept, and cute, with hand-stenciled wall decorations, fireplaces, and a trademark abundance of teddy bears. The first floor is completely constructed of stones taken from the Carmel River (hence the name), and the rooms encircle a slate courtyard; some look out onto the brick patio where breakfast is sometimes served. The guest rooms vary in size; some can be small and none come with bathtubs, but the largest units include wet bars, sofas, and a separate bedroom. Guests have the use of a comfortable living room with large stone fireplace and enjoy complimentary wine and hors d'oeuvres, and coffee and cookies. No smoking.

Services: Twice-daily maid service, morning newspaper, bicycle rental.

✪ **Highlands Inn.** Calif. 1 (P.O. Box 1700), Carmel, CA 93921. ☎ **800/538-9525** or 408/624-3801. Fax 408/626-1574. 42 rms, 100 spa suites. TV TEL. $295 double; $375–$450 spa suite; $900 2-bedroom, full oceanview spa suite. AE, DC, MC, V.

Four miles south of Carmel on a 12-acre cliff overlooking Point Lobos, this one- and two-story inn attracts everyone from celebrities honeymooners to business executives. It's rustic but luxurious, with plenty of character. The old-style main lounge dates from 1916 and has panoramic coastal vistas and an assortment of comfortable furnishings to cuddle up on. The rooms are distributed throughout a cluster of buildings terraced into the hillside. Since they were renovated in 1996, expect brand-new digs adorned with modern natural-wood furnishings and equipped with VCRs, coffeemakers, and hair dryers. Most have decks or balconies and wood-burning fireplaces. The suites have Jacuzzi tubs and completely equipped kitchens; four rooms have showers but no tubs.

Dining: The two restaurants are well known for their fine cuisine. The Pacific's Edge Restaurant, which hosts an annual Masters of Food and Wine event, offers dramatic views and memorable cuisine. The California Market is more casual, and you can dine inside by the potbelly stove or on the alfresco redwood deck.

Services: Concierge, room service (limited), valet, newspaper delivery, in-room massage, twice-daily maid service, free shuttle.

Facilities: A well-landscaped kidney-shaped pool fringed by pine and cypress and reached via stairways cut into the hillside, rental bicycles, three outdoor hot tubs, health club, sundeck.

✪ **La Playa.** Camino Real and 8th Ave. (P.O. Box 900), Carmel, CA 93921. ☎ **800/582-8900** or 408/624-6476. Fax 408/624-7966. 72 rms, 3 suites, 5 cottages. MINIBAR TV TEL. $125–$230 double; $230–$395 suite; $230–$495 cottage. AE, DC, MC, V.

Only 2 blocks from the beach and yet within walking distance of town, the 4-story La Playa is a romantic Mediterranean-style villa built in 1904 with a Bermudan-pink facade. Norwegian artist Christopher Jorgensen ordered its construction for his bride, an heiress of the Ghirardelli chocolate dynasty. The stylish lobby, with a white marble fireplace, sets the elegant tone with its terra-cotta floors enhanced with Oriental rugs. The rooms, which were renovated in 1997 and are arranged around a lawn and garden with a pool at the center, have Spanish-style furnishings. Beds have carved headboards; windows are shielded with white shutters. The cottages have full kitchens, wet bars, garden patios, and wood-burning fireplaces.

Dining: The Terrace Grill, a riot of color, serves California cuisine; it's very relaxing in summer dining out on the alfresco terrace overlooking the gardens.

Services: Room service and nightly turndown (excluding cottages).

✪ **Mission Ranch.** 26270 Dolores St., Carmel, CA 93923. ☎ **800/538-8221** or 408/624-6436. Fax 408/626-4163. 31 rms. TV TEL. $85–$225 double. Rates include continental breakfast. AE, MC, V.

This venerable inn, constructed in the 1850s as a dairy farm, was purchased and restored by Clint Eastwood, Carmel's former celebrity-mayor, who wanted to preserve the vista of the nearby wetlands stretching out to the bay.

Millions of dollars went into the historic property, and today the accommodations are spaciously scattered amid different structures, both old and new, and surrounded by nature, wetlands, and grazing sheep. As befits a ranch, rooms are decorated in a provincial style, with high-carved wooden beds dressed with handmade quilts.

Accommodations range from "regulars" (and less desirable) in the main barn to meadow-view units, each with a vista across the fields to the bay. All are equipped with whirlpool baths, fireplaces, and decks or patios. The Martin Family farmhouse contains six of the units, all arranged around a central parlor; while the Bunkhouse, the oldest structure on the property, contains separate living and dining areas, bedrooms, and a full kitchen.

Dining: Even if you're not staying here, call for a table at the Restaurant at Mission Ranch, where zest and flavor are put into essentially American cuisine; see "Where to Dine," below.

Facilities: Tennis courts, exercise room, putting green, pro shop.

MODERATE

Carmel Village Inn. Ocean Ave. and Junipero St. (P.O. Box 5275), Carmel, CA 93921. ☎ **408/624-3864** or 800/346-3864 in CA. Fax 408/626-6763. 34 rms, 2 suites. TV TEL. $69–$145 double; from $89 suite. Rates include continental breakfast. AE, MC, V. From Calif. 1, exit onto Ocean Ave. and continue straight to Junipero St.

Well run and centrally located, the Village Inn is nothing more than a motor lodge. The rooms, arranged around a courtyard/parking lot lined with potted geraniums, are outfitted with bland but functional decor. In addition to French country–style furniture, the guest rooms come equipped with refrigerators. Breakfast, accompanied by the morning newspaper, is served in the downstairs lounge.

The Cypress Inn. Lincoln and 7th (P.O. Box Y), Carmel-By-The-Sea, CA 93921. ☎ **800/443-7443** or 408/624-3871. Fax 408/624-8216. 34 rms. TV TEL. $95–$285 double. Rates include continental breakfast. Extra person $15. Pet $17, additional pet $10. Two-pet maximum. AE, MC. V.

Owner/actress Doris Day welcomes not only humans but also their pets to her 1921 Moorish/Mediterranean–style inn. Accommodations surround a flower-laden brick patio complete with an outdoor fireplace, and each room comes with a sitting area, wet bar, veranda, ocean view, and warm, cheery decor. The staff is exceptionally friendly and helpful, and offer such daily extras as an in-room decanter of sherry, fresh fruit, and a newspaper. Tea is served in the library bar each weekday afternoon.

Normandy Inn. Ocean Ave. (between Monte Verde and Casanova sts.; P.O. Box 1706), Carmel, CA 93921. ☎ **408/624-3825** or 800/343-3825 in CA. Fax 408/624-4614. 41 rms, 4 suites, 3 cottages. TV TEL. $100–$160 double; $180–$200 suite; $250–$350 cottage. Rates include continental breakfast. Additional person $10 extra. AE, MC, V. From Calif. 1, exit onto Ocean Ave. and continue straight for 5 blocks past Junipero St.

Three blocks from the beach, this Tudor-style hotel is like something out of a storybook, especially with an array of colorful flowers that brighten up the property. The guest rooms have French country decor, down comforters, and coffeemakers, while some also have fireplaces and/or kitchenettes. The small heated pool is banked by a sweet flower garden. Other perks include a self-service laundry and newspapers delivered to your room daily.

The three large family-style units are an especially good deal and accommodate up to eight; each one has three bedrooms, two bathrooms, a fully equipped kitchen, a dining room, a living room with a fireplace, and a back porch. Be sure to reserve far in advance, especially in summer.

Sandpiper Inn at the Beach. 2408 Bay View Ave., Carmel, CA 93923. ☎ **800/633-6433** or 408/624-6433. Fax 408/624-5964. 16 rms. $120–$190 double. Value season rates are available in off-season. Rates include extended continental breakfast. AE, MC, V.

A garden of flowers welcomes visitors to this quiet, midscale Carmel standby that's been in business for more than 60 years. The inn's rooms, which are within both sight and sound of the surf, offer an array of well-kept accommodations. The highest priced are corner rooms with four-poster beds and plenty of windows framing the ocean view. All are decorated with handsome country antiques and fresh flowers that are changed daily. Three have fireplaces.

WHERE TO DINE
EXPENSIVE

✪ **Anton & Michel.** At Court of the Fountain, Mission St. (between Ocean and 7th aves.). ☎ **408/624-2406.** Reservations recommended. Main courses $17.75–$27.50. AE, DC, MC, V. Daily 11:30am–3pm and 5:30–9:30pm. FRENCH/CONTINENTAL.

This elegant restaurant, just across from Carmel Plaza, serves traditional French cuisine in one of the most formal rooms in town. During the day it's best to dine fountainside on the patio or encased in the glass-wrapped terrace. The view is still charming in the evening when the courtyard is lit, and the fountain's water sparkles with reflections. Decorated with French chandelier lamps and original oil paintings, the main dining room is a formal affair; though, as in most restaurants in town, patrons' attire does not need to match it. Appetizers include crab cakes with cilantro-pesto aioli, or the delicate ravioli filled with goat cheese, sun-dried tomato, and shiitake mushroom mousse and served with a curry-cream sauce. French-inspired menu items include such entrees as a tender lamb Wellington in a pastry crust plus eclectic items such as a flavorful chicken breast Jerusalem, sautéed with olive oil, white wine, cream, mushrooms, and artichoke hearts.

Casanova. 5th Ave. (between San Carlos and Mission sts.). ☎ **408/625-0501.** Reservations recommended. Main courses $19–$33. MC, V. Mon–Fri 11:30am–3pm, Sat–Sun 8am–3pm; Sun–Thurs 5–10pm, Fri–Sat 5–10:30pm. From Calif. 1, take the Ocean Ave. exit and turn right on Mission, then left onto 5th Ave. NORTHERN ITALIAN/SOUTHERN FRENCH.

Sure, Casanova serves up good food, but so do plenty of other places in town—at half the price. But the European ambiance here *is* something special. The building, which once belonged to Charlie Chaplin's cook, is divided into two intimate Belgian chalet–style dining rooms perfect for leaning over a bottle of red wine and creating vacation memories. More festive folk step back to the Old World–style covered patio where it's bustling and crowded. Since all dinner entrees include antipasto and a choice of appetizers (such as baked stuffed eggplant with rice, herbs, cheese, and tomatoes), $30 is not such a bad deal. The menu features typical Mediterranean cuisine: paella, homemade pastas, meats, and fish. Casanova also boasts an award-winning wine cellar featuring more than 1,600 French, California, German, and Italian wines.

✪ **Crème Carmel.** San Carlos St. and 7th Ave. ☎ **408/624-0444.** Reservations recommended. Main courses $16.75–$21.75. AE, DC, MC, V. Mon–Sat 5:30–9pm. CALIFORNIA/FRENCH.

The discreet location of Crème Carmel (tucked away in a courtyard) hasn't hurt its business at all—it's one of the most popular upscale dining spots in town for both tourists and locals. Art, fresh flowers, and a soaring tongue-and-groove ceiling provide a sweet setting for an evening of robust flavors. The menu lists an array of decadently wonderful starters, such as prawn and goat-cheese tart with a jalapeño-and-shallot sauce, lobster with Maui onion pancakes and lobster sauce, or melt-in-your-mouth Sonoma foie gras. The main courses are equally special and might include Pacific salmon with roasted leeks and fresh basil sauce; or beef tenderloin with a cabernet sauce, fresh horseradish, and potato cake.

✪ **The Restaurant at Mission Ranch.** At Mission Ranch. 26270 Dolores St. ☎408/625-9040. Reservations recommended. Most main courses $13–$23.75. AE, DC, MC, V. Mon–Fri 4pm–midnight, Sat 11am–midnight, Sun 9am–midnight. AMERICAN.

One of California's first dairies is now the site of one of Carmel's favorite restaurants. Clint Eastwood bought the property in 1986 and renovated the ranch-style building to its original integrity, and though the chance of seeing him brings in some folks, the views, quality food, and merry atmosphere are what really make the place pop. The wooden building is encased with large windows, which accentuate the wonderful view of the marshlands, grazing sheep, and bay beyond. Warm days make patio dining the prime choice, but the key time to come is at sunset, when the sky is transforming, happy hour is in full swing (you'll find some of the cheapest drinks around, and Clint often stops by when he's in town), and the dining room begins to liven. As you'd expect from the ranch motif, meat is king here: Burgers are freshly ground on-site, and prime rib with twice-baked potato and vegetables is the favored dish. There are, of course, wonderful seafood and vegetarian options as well, and all dinners include soup or salad. Entertainment is provided at the piano bar, where locals and tourists join together to sing their favorites.

MODERATE

✪ **Flying Fish Grill.** In Carmel Plaza, Mission St. (between Ocean and 7th aves.). ☎ **408/625-1962.** Reservations recommended. Main courses $12.75–$19. AE, DISC, MC, V. Daily 5–10pm. Closed Tues during winter. PACIFIC RIM/SEAFOOD.

We always feel more confident when a restaurant's kitchen is actually run by its owner—and a dinner experience here will confirm that chef/proprietor Kenny Fukumoto is in the house. Dark, romantic, and Asian-influenced, the dining room has an intimate atmosphere with redwood booths (built by Kenny) and fish hanging (flying?) from the ceiling. The cuisine features fresh seafood with exquisite Japanese accents. Start with some sushi, tempura, or any of the other exotic and tantalizing taste teasers. Then prepare your tongue for seriously sensational main courses. House favorites include a savory rare peppered ahi, which is blackened and served with mustard/sesame-soy vinaigrette and angel-hair pasta, and a pan-fried almond sea bass with whipped potatoes, Chinese cabbage, and rock shrimp stir-fry.

The Hog's Breath Inn. San Carlos St. (between 5th and 6th aves.). ☎ **408/625-1044.** Reservations not accepted. Main courses $9.50–$23. AE, DC, MC, V. Mon–Sat 11:30am–3pm and 5–10pm, Sun 11am–3pm and 5–10pm. From Calif. 1, take the Ocean Ave. exit and turn right onto San Carlos St. AMERICAN.

What's in a name? Well, if Clint Eastwood didn't own this place, we don't know what would inspire tourists to eat at a joint named after a pig's exhalation (how very Clint!). But clamor they do for one of the tree-trunk tables with plastic chairs along a brick patio. Tables in the wood-paneled dark-and-rustic dining room decorated with farm implements fill up, too, though they're not as lively as outdoor seats. The fare here isn't remotely as legendary as the owner (whom you're not likely to see), but it's the perfect place to nosh on afternoon snacks (burgers, nachos, etc.). The small dark bar with sports on the tube is the best place to pull up a stool and throw back a few brews on a rainy day (or a sunny one for that matter).

Il Fornaio. Ocean Ave. (at Monte Verde). ☎ **408/622-5100,** or 408/622-5115 for the bakery. Main courses $8–$15. AE, DC, MC, V. Mon–Fri 7am–10pm, Sat 8am–11pm, Sun 8am–10pm. ITALIAN.

We don't care if it is a chain—Il Fornaio is still one of our favorite restaurants because we know we're guaranteed a well-prepared mocha and thick chocolate-dipped biscotti at every outpost. There's also a great selection of salads (go with the simple house salad with shaved Parmesan, croutons, and a tangy light dressing), pastas, pizzas, and rotisserie chicken, duck, and rabbit fresh from the brick oven. The housemade breads and seeded breadsticks alone are reason enough to come. We must admit that we were disappointed with tasty-but-measly $11 lasagna, so skip it and start with the seared swordfish antipasto with roast pepper and Dijon mustard; or decadent grilled polenta with sautéed wild mushrooms, provolone cheese, and Italian truffle oil. Move on to a gourmet pizza, or a pasta such as the lobster-filled ravioli with ricotta cheese, leeks, and a lemon-cream sauce. The large airy dining room and sunny terrace offer charming and diverse atmospheres. The Panetteria, a retail bakery, is the perfect place to pick up a gourmet picnic.

✪ La Bohème. Dolores St. and 7th Ave. ☎ **408/624-7500.** Reservations not accepted. Fixed-price, 3-course dinner $21.75. AE, MC, V. Daily 5:30–10pm. Closed 2 weeks before Christmas. From Calif. 1, exit onto Ocean Ave. and turn left onto Dolores St. FRENCH COUNTRY.

Like a set from Disney's "It's a Small World," La Bohème mimics a French street with cartoony asymmetrical shingled house facades and a painted blue sky overhead. Thankfully, the similarity stops with the decor, and there are no dolls singing anywhere—in French or English. Dinner here is utterly romantic French, served at cramped tables set with floral-print cloths in bright colors, hand-painted dinnerware, and vibrant floral bouquets. Dinner is a three-course, fixed-price feast consisting of a large salad, a tureen of soup, and a main dish (perhaps roast breast of duckling with green peppercorn, plumb, and red wine sauce or filet mignon with cognac-cream sauce). Vegetarian specials are available nightly. Homemade desserts and fresh coffee are sold separately, and are usually worth the extra expense. Dress is casual. Curious on-line folks can learn more at **www.laboheme.com.**

INEXPENSIVE

Caffè Napoli. Ocean Ave. (between Dolores and Lincoln). ☎ **408/625-4033.** Reservations recommended. Main courses $8–$15. MC, V. Daily 11:30am–10pm. ITALIAN.

The decor here is so quintessentially Italiana, with flags, gingham tablecloths, garlic, and baskets overhead, that we expected a flour-coated pot-bellied Padrino Napoli to emerge from the kitchen, embrace us wholeheartedly, and exclaim "Mangia! Mangia!" as he slapped down a bowl overflowing with sauce-drenched pasta. Of course there is no Padrino here, and we received no welcoming hug, but we did indulge in the fine Italian fare that keeps locals coming back for more. If the wait is too long, the host will direct you around the corner to a sibling restaurant, Little Napoli, which serves the same food but in a slightly more upscale setting. The menu is straight Italian and includes seven salad choices, antipasti, pizza, and pasta.

Little Swiss Cafe. 6th Ave. (between Lincoln and Mission). ☎ **408/624-5007.** Reservations not accepted. Menu items $4.75–$7.50. No credit cards. Mon–Sat 7:30am–3pm, Sun 8am–2pm. CONTINENTAL.

Locals led us to this quirky little spot designed to look like a Swiss cottage. Kids may love the old-fashioned, grandma-cute decor, but the grownups come for what they consider the best homemade blintzes and pancakes in town. Late risers rejoice—breakfast is served all day.

6 Carmel Valley

Inland from Carmel stretches Carmel Valley, where wealthy folks retreat beyond the reach of the coastal fog and mist. It's a scenic and perpetually sunny valley of rolling hills dotted with manicured golf courses and many a horse ranch.

Hike the trails in **Garland Regional Park,** 8 miles east of Carmel on Carmel Valley Road (dogs are welcome off-leash). The sun really bakes you out here, so bring lots of water. You could also sign up for a trail ride at the **Holman Ranch,** 60 Holman Rd. (☎ 408/659-2640), 12 miles east of Calif. 1.

Golf is offered at several resorts and courses in the valley, notably at **Quail Lodge,** 8000 Valley Green Dr. (☎ 408/624-2770), and **Rancho Canada Golf Club,** Carmel Valley Rd. (☎ 408/624-0111).

While you're in the valley, taste the wines at the **Château Julien Winery,** 8940 Carmel Valley Rd. (☎ 408/624-2600), which is open daily.

WHERE TO STAY

✪ **Quail Lodge Resort and Golf Club.** 8205 Valley Greens Dr., Carmel, CA 93923. ☎ **800/538-9516** or 408/624-1581. Fax 408/624-3726. 86 rms, 14 suites. MINIBAR TV TEL. Mar–Nov $225–$275 double; $325–$1,200 suite. Dec–Feb $188–$225 double; $255–$1,200 suite. Additional person $25 extra. AE, CB, DC, MC, V. From Calif. 1 north, past the Carmel exits, after which the highway narrows to 2 lanes, turn left on Carmel Valley Rd. and continue 3 miles to Valley Greens Dr.

The ultra elite Peninsula Hotel Group, which acquired the Quail Lodge in 1997, is currently executing a 5-year renovation plan. However, considering this resort's reputation as an executive golf haven—and one of the most highly regarded resort hotels in the country—the upgrades can only mean one thing: superfluous luxury. Lying in the foothills of the Santa Lucia Range, Quail Lodge has already received five-star ratings for 20 years running. Its pastoral setting encompasses more than 850 acres of sparkling lakes, secluded woodlands, and rolling meadows. The guest rooms are in two-story balconied wings with terraces overlooking the pool or one of the 10 man-made lakes, or in cottages holding five accommodations each. Executive villas are the most expensive and luxurious units.

Remodeled in 1996, the guest rooms are decorated in warm earth tones jazzed up with floral and striped patterns. Higher-priced accommodations, on the upper floors, have cathedral ceilings. Every room has a separate dressing area and an ample balcony; some have fireplaces and wet bars. There's a coffeemaker in every room, supplied with freshly ground beans. Afternoon tea is served in the lobby from 3 to 5pm.

Dining: The renowned Covey Restaurant serves European fare in warmly elegant surroundings. Tables are covered with Belgian linens, set with Sienna china, and adorned with fresh flowers. The Caesar salad is exceptional. Main courses include Santa Barbara abalone and the renowned rack of lamb. Jackets are requested for men, and reservations are essential.

Services: Concierge, room service, evening turndown, complimentary morning newspaper.

Facilities: 18-hole golf course designed by Robert Muir Graves, 4 tennis courts, 2 swimming pools, sauna, hot tub, hiking and jogging trails, gift shops, nearby beauty salon.

Robles del Rio. 200 Punta del Monte, Carmel Valley, CA 93924. ☎ **800/833-0843** or 408/659-3705. 26 rms, 2 suites, 5 cottages. TV. $89–$145 double; from $200 suite; from $170 cottage. Rates include continental breakfast. AE, MC, V.

Set among oak trees on a mountain top, this rustic resort has beckoned many a luminary since its 1928 opening (Arthur Murray, Red Skelton, and Alistair Cook, for example). Whether the rooms are in the main lodge or in the cottages, the furnishings have a simple, rustic style with iron or wicker beds and either feature knotty-pine walls or a Southern colonial look. The cottages have fireplaces, plus a kitchen or kitchenette. The restaurant opens onto panoramic views of the Carmel Valley. Major renovations are scheduled for 1998.

Facilities: A well-landscaped pool, outdoor hot tub, tennis, horseback riding, hiking and jogging trails.

✪ **Stonepine.** 150 E. Carmel Valley Rd., Carmel Valley, CA 93924. ☎ **408/659-2245.** Fax 408/659-5160. 3 rms, 9 suites, 1 cottage. $225–$500 double; $225–$750 suite; $750 cottage. AE, MC, V.

Once through the electronically controlled gate, guests follow a mile-long winding driveway past the polo field and stables up to this hilltop château. The wisteria-clad mansion was built in the 1920s and was once part of the private estate of Henry Potter and Helen Crocker Russel of the San Francisco banking family, who raised thoroughbreds here. Framed by box hedges, the surrounding formal English gardens are laid out into separate rose, perennial, and fruit gardens.

The very comfortable accommodations in the château are each decorated and equipped differently. The most expensive boasts a fireplace and marble Roman bath with Jacuzzi, as well as his-and-hers bathrooms and dressing rooms, plus a sitting room. The Don Quixote Suite has French doors leading out to a garden patio, while the Venetian Suite contains a canopied bed and has a separate entrance. All are furnished with fine antiques and fabrics. The rooms in the Paddock House have access to a complete country kitchen and dining room. They all have Jacuzzi tubs, too. No children under 12 are allowed in the château accommodations, but they are welcome in the Paddock and the cottage.

Dining/Entertainment: A five-course dinner is served in the very formal dining room in the château—perhaps curry-mussel soup with cilantro, a salad, hazelnut-crusted salmon with tomato-ginger sauce, and a chocolate Grand Marnier cake.

Facilities: Beyond the gardens lie the Renaissance-inspired swimming pool, tennis court, and a soccer field. Other recreational facilities include the croquet lawn, archery range, and the equestrian center. The last offers four regimens in horsemanship, all available to guests.

WHERE TO DINE

✪ **Rio Grill.** 101 Crossroads Blvd. ☎ **408/625-5436.** Reservations recommended. Main courses $10–$25. AE, DISC, MC, V. Sun–Thurs 11:30am–10pm, Fri–Sat 11:30am–11pm. From Calif. 1, take the Rio Rd. exit west for 1 block and turn right onto Crossroads Blvd. AMERICAN.

You won't mind waiting to be seated here—the lively lounge is one of the best in Carmel, attracting an interesting crowd. It's decorated with a cartoon mural of famous locals such as Clint Eastwood and the late Bing Crosby, as well as playful sculpture, cactus, and other vibrant art. The whimsical nature of the modern Santa Fe–style dining room belies the kitchen's serious preparations, which include homemade soups; a rich quesadilla with almonds, cheeses, and smoked-tomato salsa; barbecued baby back ribs from a wood-burning oven; and fresh fish from an open oak grill. The restaurant's good selection of wines includes some rare Californian vintages and covers a broad price range. As usual in this town, dress is casual.

7 The Big Sur Coast

Big Sur is more than a drive along one of the most dramatic coastlines on earth or a peaceful evening amid a forest of towering California redwoods. It's a stretch of vast wilderness so overwhelmingly beautiful—especially when the fog glows in the moonlight—that it inspires all who walk its majestic paths.

Although there is an actual Big Sur Village approximately 25 miles south of Carmel, "Big Sur" refers to the entire 90-mile stretch of coastline between Carmel and San Simeon, blessed on one side by the majestic Santa Lucia Range and on the other by the rocky Pacific coastline. It's one of the most romantic and relaxing places on earth, and if you need respite from the rat race, we can recommend no better place to find it. There's little more to do than explore the mountains and beaches, or just perch yourself atop the cliffs and take in the California sea air, but spend a few days here and you will find that you need nothing else.

ESSENTIALS

VISITOR INFORMATION The **Monterey Peninsula Visitors and Convention Bureau,** 380 Alvarado St., Monterey (☎ **408/649-1770**), also has specialized information on places and events in Big Sur.

ORIENTATION Most of this stretch is state park, and Calif. 1 runs its entire length, hugging the ocean the whole way. Restaurants, hotels, and sights are easy to spot—most are situated directly on the highway—but without major towns as reference points, their addresses can be obscure. For the purposes of orientation, we'll use the River Inn as our mileage guide. Located 29 miles south of Monterey on Calif. 1, the inn is generally considered to mark the northern end of Big Sur.

SPECIAL EVENTS If you're in the area in mid-April, check out the **Big Sur JazzFest.** After its launch in 1996, the locals have made it into an annual fundraising event, with performances at various establishments throughout the designated weekend, and a grand finale concert. Call ☎ **408/667-2654** for information.

EXPLORING THE BIG SUR COAST

Big Sur offers visitors tranquillity and wild natural beauty—ideal for hiking, picnicking, camping, fishing, and beach combing.

The first settlers arrived here only a century ago, and the present highway was built here in 1937, making the area accessible. (Electricity only arrived in the 1950s, and it's still not available in the remote inland mountains.) Big Sur's mysterious, misty beauty has inspired several modern spiritual movements, the most famous being Esalen, the birthplace of the human potential movement. Even the tourist bureau bills the area as a place in which "to slow down . . . to meditate . . . to catch up with your soul." Take the board's advice and take your time—nothing better lies ahead.

The region affords a bounty of wilderness adventure opportunities. The inland **Ventana Wilderness,** which is maintained by the U.S. Forest Service, contains 167,323 acres straddling the Santa Lucia mountains and is characterized by steep-sided ridges separated by V-shaped valleys. The streams that cascade through the area are marked by waterfalls, deep pools, and thermal springs. The wilderness offers 237 miles of **hiking trails** that lead to 55 designated trail camps—a backpacker's paradise. One of the easiest trails to access is the **Pine Ridge Trail** at Big Sur station (☎ **408/667-2315**).

From Carmel, the first stop along Calif. 1 is ✪ **Point Lobos State Reserve** (☎ **408/624-4909**), 3 miles south of Carmel. Sea lions, harbor seals, sea otters, and thousands of seabirds reside in this 550-acre reserve. You can see whales in season, too. Trails follow the shoreline and lead to hidden coves. Note that parking is limited; on weekends especially, you need to arrive early to secure a place.

From here, cross the Soberanes Creek, passing **Garrapata State Park,** a 2,879-acre preserve with 4 miles of coastline. It's unmarked and undeveloped. To explore the trails, you'll need to park at one of the turnouts on Calif. 1 near Soberanes Point and hike in.

Ten miles south of Carmel, you'll arrive at North Abalone Cove. From here, Palo Colorado Road leads back into the wilderness to the first of the **Forest Service camping areas at Bottchers Gap** ($10 to camp, $5 to park overnight).

Continuing south, you'll cross two dramatic bridges at Rocky Creek and Bixby Creek, which will bring you to the **Point Sur Lighthouse,** at the 18¹/₂-mile marker. The **Bixby Bridge,** 13 miles south of Carmel, towers nearly 260 feet above Bixby Creek Canyon. It offers canyon and ocean views and several observation alcoves at regular intervals along the bridge. The lighthouse, which sits 361 feet above the surf on a volcanic rock promontory, was built in 1887–89, when only a horse trail provided access to this part of the world. Tours, which take 2 to 3 hours and involve a steep half-mile hike each way, are scheduled on most weekends. For information call ☎ **408/625-4419.** Admission is $5 for adults, $3 for youths 13 to 17, $2 for children 5 to 12, and free for kids 4 and under.

About 3 miles south of the lighthouse is **Andrew Molera State Park** (☎ **408/667-2315**), the largest state park on the Big Sur Coast (4,800 acres). It's much less crowded than Pfeiffer–Big Sur (see below). Miles of trails meander through meadows and along beaches and bluffs. Hikers and cyclists use the primitive trail camp about ¹/₃ of a mile from the parking area. **Molera Big Sur Trail Rides** (☎ **408/625-5486**) offers coastal trail rides for riders of all levels of experience. The 2¹/₂-mile-long beach, which is sheltered from the wind by a bluff, is accessible via a mile-long path flanked in spring by wildflowers. You can walk the entire length of the beach at low tide; otherwise take the bluff trail above the beach. The park also has campgrounds.

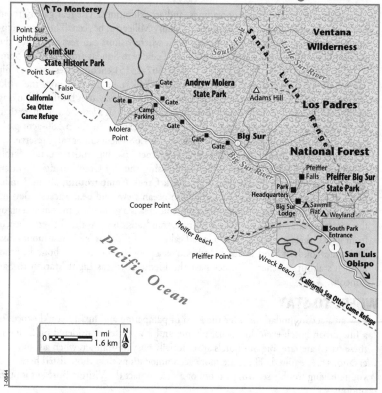

The Big Sur Coast

↑ To Monterey

Point Sur Lighthouse

Point Sur State Historic Park

Point Sur

False Sur

California Sea Otter Game Refuge

Molera Point

Gate

Gate

Camp Parking

Gate

Andrew Molera State Park

△ Adams Hill

Gate

Gate

Big Sur

South Fork Santa

Little Sur River

Lucia

Ventana Wilderness

Los Padres

Range

National Forest

Big Sur River

Pfeiffer Falls

Park Headquarters

Pfeiffer Big Sur State Park

Big Sur Lodge

△ Sawmill Flat

△ Weyland

Cooper Point

Pfeiffer Beach

Pfeiffer Point

Wreck Beach

South Park Entrance

To San Luis Obispo ↓

California Sea Otter Game Refuge

Pacific Ocean

0 — 1 mi / 1.6 km — N

Back on Calif. 1, you'll soon reach the village of Big Sur, where commercial services are available.

About 26 miles south of Carmel you'll come to the **U.S. Forest Service Ranger Station,** where you can pick up maps and other information about the region. It's located ¹/₄ mile past the entrance to **Pfeiffer–Big Sur State Park** (☎ 408/667-2315), an 810-acre park that offers 218 camping sites along the Big Sur River, picnicking, fishing, and hiking. It's a scenic park of redwoods, conifers, oaks, and open meadows. For this reason it gets very crowded. The Lodge in the park has cabins with fireplaces and other facilities (see "Where to Stay" and "Camping in Big Sur," below). Sycamore Canyon Road (unmarked; it's the only paved road west of Calif. 1 between the Big Sur post office and the state park entrance) will take you 2 miles to sandy **Pfeiffer Beach,** which has an arch-shaped rock formation just offshore. It's open for day use only and is the only beach accessible by car. Admission to the park is $5, and it's open daily from dawn to dusk.

Back on Calif. 1, the road travels 11 miles past Sea Lion Cove to Julia Pfeiffer Burns State Park. High above the ocean is the famous **Nepenthe** restaurant (☎ 408/667-2574), the retreat bought by Orson Welles for Rita Hayworth in 1944. A few miles farther south is the **Coast Gallery,** the premier local art gallery, which shows lithographs of works by Henry Miller. Miller fans will also want to stop at the **Henry Miller Memorial Library,** on Calif. 1, 30 miles south of Carmel and ¹/₄ mile south of Nepenthe restaurant. The library displays and sells books and artwork by Miller and houses a permanent collection of first editions. It also serves as a community art center, hosting concerts, poetry readings, and art exhibitions. The rear gallery room is a video-viewing space where films about Henry Miller can be seen. There's a sculpture garden, plus tables on the adjacent lawn where visitors can rest and enjoy the surroundings. Admission is free, and it's open Tuesday to Sunday from 11am to 5pm.

Julia Pfeiffer Burns State Park (☎ 408/667-2315) encompasses some of Big Sur's most spectacular coastline. To get a closer look, take the trail from the parking area at McWay Canyon, which leads under the highway to a bluff overlooking an 80-foot-high waterfall dropping directly into the ocean. It's less crowded here than at Pfeiffer–Big Sur, and there are miles of trails to explore in the 3,580-acre park. Scuba divers can apply for permits to explore the 1,680-acre underwater reserve.

From here, the road skirts the Ventana Wilderness, passing Anderson and Marble Peaks and the **Esalen Institute,** before crossing the Big Creek Bridge to Lucia and several campgrounds farther south. **Kirk Creek Campground,** about 3 miles north of Pacific Valley, offers camping with ocean views and beach access. Beyond Pacific Valley, the ✪ **Sand Dollar Beach** picnic area is a good place to stop and enjoy the coastal view and take a stroll. A ¹⁄₂-mile trail leads down to the sheltered beach, from which there's a fine view of Cone Peak, one of the coast's highest mountains. Two miles south of Sand Dollar is **Jade Cove,** a popular spot for rock hounds. From here, it's about another 27 miles past the Piedras Blancas Light Station to San Simeon.

WHERE TO STAY

Few area accommodations offer the kind of pampering and luxury you'd expect in a fine urban hotel; even direct-dial phones and TVs (often considered philistine in these parts) are rare. Big Sur hotels are especially busy in summer, when advance reservations are required. There are more accommodations than those listed here, so if you're having trouble securing a room or a site, contact the Visitors Bureau for other options.

✪ **Big Sur Lodge.** In Pfeiffer–Big Sur State Park, Calif. 1 (P.O. Box 190), Big Sur, CA 93920. ☎ **800/424-4787** or 408/667-3100. Fax 408/667-3110. Website: www.bisurlodge.com. 61 cabins. $79–$139 cabin for two; $99–$159 cabin with kitchen or fireplace; $109–$179 cabin with kitchen and fireplace. Rates include park entrance fees. AE, MC, V. From Carmel, take Calif. 1 south 26 miles.

A family-friendly place, the Big Sur Lodge—sheltered by towering redwoods, sycamores, and broad-leafed maples—is situated in the enormous state park. The rustic accommodations are motel-style cabins, which are huge, with high peaked cedar- and redwood-beamed ceilings. They're clean and heated, and have private baths and reserved parking spaces. Some have fireplaces and/or kitchenettes (bring your own cooking utensils, though). All offer porches or decks with views of the redwoods or the Santa Lucia Range. Cabins 34 to 50 will put you in Siberia.

An advantage to staying here is that you're entitled to free use of all the facilities of the park, including hiking, barbecue pits, and picnic areas. In addition, the lodge has its own large, outdoor heated swimming pool, gift shop, grocery stores, and laundry facilities.

The lodge dining room is open for breakfast and dinner (and lunch in the summer), but it doesn't have the ambiance of other nearby options. Evening menus feature fresh seafood, steaks, and pasta dishes. Reservations are recommended and should be made far in advance during summer months.

Deetjen's Big Sur Inn. Calif. 1, Big Sur, CA 93920. ☎ **408/667-2377.** 20 rms, 15 with bath. Sun–Thurs from $70 double without bath, from $100 double with bath. Fri–Sat from $85 double without bath, from $115 double with bath. MC, V.

Camping in Big Sur

Big Sur is one of the most spectacular places in the state for camping. One of the most glorious settings can be found at **Pfeiffer–Big Sur State Park,** on Calif. 1, 26 miles south of Carmel (☎ **800/444-7275** or 408/667-2315; fax 408/667-2886). The 810-acre state park offers hundreds of secluded, woodsy sites, each tucked into the property's hundreds of acres of redwood forest. Hiking trails, streams, and the river are steps away from your sleeping bag, and the most modern amenities are the 25¢ showers (for 3 minutes). Water faucets are located between sites, and each spot has its own picnic table and fire pit. There are, however, no RV hookups or electricity. Riverfront sites are most coveted, but others promise more seclusion among the shaded hillsides of the park. Campfire programs and nature walks are also offered. At the entrance there's a store, gift shop, restaurant, and cafe. There are 218 sites in total (fees are $20 for regular sites, $23 for riverside sites). Rates include park entrance fees. Senior discounts are available, and dogs are permitted ($6 extra).

The entrance to the **Ventana Campground,** on Calif. 1, 28 miles south of Carmel and 4¼ miles south of the River Inn (☎ **408/667-2688**), is adjacent to the entrance to the resort of the same name, but the comparison stops there. This is pure rusticity. The 75 campsites, on 40 acres of a redwood canyon, are set along a hillside and spaced well apart for privacy. Each is shaded by towering trees, has a picnic table and fire ring, but offers no electricity, RV hookups, or river access. There are, however, three bathhouses with hot showers (25¢ fee), which are conveniently located. To reserve a space, send one night's deposit, the dates you'd like to stay, and a stamped, self-addressed envelope at least 2 weeks in advance (earlier during peak months). Rates are $25 for a site for two. An additional person is $5 extra, and it'll cost you $5 to bring Fido. Rates include entrance fee for your car. No credit cards.

Big Sur Campground and Cabins is on Calif. 1, 26 miles south of Carmel (½ mile south of the River Inn; ☎ **408/667-2322**). The sites are cramped, so the feel is more like a camping village than an intimate retreat. However, it's very well maintained and perfect for families, who love the playground, river swimming, and inner-tube rentals. Each campsite has its own wood-burning fire pit, picnic table, and freshwater faucet within 25 feet of the pitching area. There are also RV water and electric hookups available. Facilities include bathhouses with hot showers, laundry facilities, an aged volleyball/basketball court, and a grocery store. There are 81 tent sites (40 with electricity and water hookup), plus 17 cabins (all with shower). The all-wood cabins are absolutely adorable, with stylish country furnishings, wood-burning ovens, patios, and full kitchens. Rates are $24 for a tent site for two, $24 for an RV hookup (plus $3 extra for electricity and water), or $72–$144 for a cabin for two. Rates include entrance for your car. MC, V are accepted. Pet or extra person $10. Open year-round.

In the 1930s, before Calif. 1 was built, this homestead was an overnight stopping place on the coastal wagon road. It was begun by Norwegian homesteader Helmuth Deetjen, who over the years built several accommodations constructed out of hand-hewn logs and lumber. Folks either love or hate the rooms, which are set in a redwood canyon. They're rustic, cozy, and (we think) adorable with their old-fashioned furnishings and down-home feel. But those who want extensive creature comforts should go elsewhere. Single-wall construction means that the rooms are far from soundproof, so children under 12 are allowed only if families reserve both rooms of a two-room building. There's no insulation, so prepare to crank up the fire or wood-burning stove.

The restaurant is a local favorite and consists of four intimate, English country inn–style rooms lit by candlelight (See "Where to Dine" for complete details).

✪ **Post Ranch Inn.** Calif. 1 (P.O. Box 219), Big Sur, CA 93920. ☎ **800/527-2200** or 408/667-2200. Fax 408/667-2824. 30 rms, 1 suite. TEL. $285–$545 double; $375 suite. Rates include breakfast. AE, MC, V.

Okay, so the attitude here can be a little stuffy. But that, in conjunction with some of the most amazing accommodations on earth, adds to the exclusivity of the ultraelite Post Ranch Inn. Perched on 98 acres of pristine seaside ridges 1,200 feet above the Pacific, this resort opened in 1992 and was instantly declared one of the world's finest retreats. What's the big deal? The Post Ranch doesn't attempt to beat its stunning natural surroundings, but rather to join them. The wood-and-glass guest cottages are built around existing trees; some are elevated on stilts to avoid damaging native redwood root structures; and the ultra private Ocean and Coast cottages are so close to the edge of the earth, you get the impression that you've joined the clouds (imagine that from your private spa tub). Other cottages are equally impressive in design and face the woodlands. Each room contains a fireplace, terrace, massage table, cassette and CD player, and wet bar filled with complimentary goodies. The bathrooms, fashioned out of slate and granite, feature spa tubs. There's also a small workout room, two heated outdoor pools, and sundecks on the premises.

Dining: The Sierra Mar restaurant is open only to guests for continental breakfasts, and to the public nightly for dinner (when there's a four-course, fixed-price meal for $55). It, too, has floor-to-ceiling views of the ocean. The most acclaimed dish on the menu is the breast of duck with foie gras, quince, and walnuts.

Services: Room service, complimentary newspaper, concierge, complimentary valet, twice-daily maid. Among the services available are massage, yoga, spa services, guided hikes, tarot reading, aromatherapy, and facials.

Facilities: Library, fitness room, pool, Jacuzzi, nature trails.

✪ **Ventana Big Sur Country Inn Resort.** Calif. 1, Big Sur, CA 93920. ☎ **800/628-6500** or 408/667-2331. Fax 408/667-2419. 56 rms, 3 suites. A/C MINIBAR TV TEL. $215–$475 double; from $375 suite. Rates include continental breakfast and afternoon wine and cheese. AE, CB, DC, DISC, MC, V.

Luxuriously rustic and utterly romantic, Ventana has been a wildly popular wilderness outpost for more than 20 years, and with good reason. Located on 243 mountainous oceanfront acres, Ventana has an elegance that's atypical of the region, and has continually attracted famous guests such as Barbra Streisand, Goldie Hawn, and Francis Ford Coppola, since its opening in 1975.

The accommodations, in one- and two-story, natural-wood buildings along winding, wildflower-flanked paths, blend in with the magical Big Sur countryside. The extensive grounds are dotted with hammocks and hand-carved benches, which are strategically located under shady trees and vista points. The guest rooms are divinely decorated in warm, cozy luxury, with such amenities as a VCR, refrigerator, and private terrace or balcony overlooking the ocean or forest. Most rooms offer wood-burning fireplaces, and some have hot tubs and high cathedral ceilings. A small fitness center offers the basics—but you'll be more inspired to hike the grounds, where you'll not only find plenty of pastoral respite, but also a pool, a rustic library, and clothing-optional tanning decks and spa tubs. This, along with Post Ranch, is one of the best retreats in the region, if not the state. *Families take heed:* Children are permitted, but not exactly embraced.

Dining: The Ventana Restaurant is an incredibly romantic and first-rate dining experience; see "Where to Dine" for complete details.

Services: Concierge, massage, newspaper delivery, twice-daily maid service, free coffee.

Facilities: Two 90-foot heated outdoor swimming pools, bathhouse, Japanese hot bath, sauna, fitness room, gift store, art gallery.

WHERE TO DINE

Big Sur River Inn. On Calif. 1. Main courses $7.95–$12.25 lunch, $8.25–$15 dinner. AE, CB, DC, DISC, MC, V. Daily 8am–9pm. CALIFORNIA/AMERICAN.

Trying to seat a small army? No problem. Want to watch sports on TV at a local bar? Pull up a stool. Looking to snag a few rays from a deck right beside the Big Sur River? Break out the suntan lotion. Popular with everyone from families to bikers, The River Inn is an unpretentious, rustic, down-home restaurant that's got something for everyone. While in winter, the wooden dining room is the prime spot; on summer days some folks grab their patio chair and a cocktail and hang out literally midstream. Along with the local color, attractions include a full bar, good ol' American breakfast (steak and eggs, omelets, pancakes, etc., plus espresso with most dishes is around $6), lunch (an array of salads, sandwiches, and baby back ribs, or fish and chips) and dinner (which features a few selections: fresh catch, pasta, burger, or ribs).

Café Kevah. Calif. 1, 28 miles south of Carmel (5 miles south of the River Inn). ☎ **408/667-2344.** Main courses $5.75–$10.75. Daily 9am–3pm. AE, MC, V. SOUTHWEST/ CALIFORNIA.

Located one level below Nepenthe, Café Kevah offers the same celestial view at a fraction of the price, and in a more casual environment. Seating is entirely outdoors—a downside when the biting fog rolls in, but perfect on a clear day. You can order breakfast or lunch from the small shack of a kitchen, then grab an umbrella-shaded table, and enjoy the feast for your eyes and taste buds. Fare here is more eclectic than Nepenthe's, with such choices as homemade granola, pastries, baby greens with broiled salmon and papaya, chicken brochettes, omelets, and new potato hash. It ain't cheap; but quality, innovative cuisine, the view, and a surprisingly decent mocha make it a worthwhile stopover. Don't forget to bring a coat.

Deetjen's Restaurant. On Calif. 1. ☎ **408/667-2377.** Reservations recommended. Main courses $7–$9.50 breakfast, $14.50–$22.50 dinner. MC, V. Mon–Sat 8am–11:30am, Sun 8am–noon; daily 6–8:30pm. AMERICAN.

With the feel of an English farmhouse, this cozy, country setting is the perfect venue for the delicious comfort food and friendly service that you'll find here. Mornings start off with a jump after a cup of the delicious and strong coffee, and breakfast offers all the basics: omelets, eggs Benedict, pancakes, granola, etc., most of which come piled high with breakfast potatoes. Dinner is highly regarded by locals, and might include lamb with au jus and twice-baked potato; grilled chicken with mushrooms and a garlic marsala sauce; and roast duckling with brandy, peppercorn, and molasses sauce.

Glen Oaks Restaurant. Calif. 1, 26 miles south of Carmel. ☎ **408/667-2264.** Reservations recommended. Main courses $12–$18. MC, V. Wed–Mon 6–9pm. INTERNATIONAL.

Not much changes in this neck of the woods, but Glen Oaks is a recent exception. The down-home restaurant got a new owner and a new chef, and was redecorated in 1996. The atmosphere still complements the surroundings with beamed ceilings, a wood-burning copper-chimneyed fireplace, and plenty of plants and local art. Dinner specials change daily, but you can always count on a basket of homemade bread (baked daily) and such main dishes as grilled marinated chicken, lemon prawns, and mushroom Stroganoff. Desserts are prepared daily on the premises, and a small selection of California wines is available.

✪ **Nepenthe.** Calif. 1, 28 miles south of Carmel (5 miles south of the River Inn). ☎ **408/ 667-2345.** Reservations accepted only for parties of five or more. Main courses $9–$25. AE, MC, V. Daily 11:30am–10pm. AMERICAN.

We scoff at a $10 burger (without fries!) and a $4 draft beer even when we're in the finest of San Francisco restaurants. But we'd cough up the cash all over again for an encore lunch on the terrace at Nepenthe. Think of it as nominal admission to dine at heights only angels usually enjoy. Sitting 808 feet above sea level along the cliffs overlooking the ocean, Nepenthe's atmosphere is naturally celestial—especially when fog lingers above the water below.

Though most folk opt for the patio (weather permitting), the restaurant— constructed of redwood and adobe—offers a warm, wooden dining room that gets packed with locals and tourists on most nights. With its big wood-burning fireplace, redwood ceilings, large bayfront windows, and friendly staff, the atmosphere is something you can't find anywhere else. Unfortunately, that's not the case with the fare. Though adequate, it will not send you to gastronomic heaven. But if the sun is shining and you're sipping a chardonnay, who cares? Lunch is basic: burgers, sandwiches, and salads. Dinner main courses include steak, broiled chicken, and fresh fish prepared any number of ways.

✪ **Ventana Restaurant.** At Ventana Big Sur Country Inn Resort Restaurant, Hwy. 1, Big Sur. ☎ **408/667-2331.** Reservations recommended for dinner. Main courses $9.50–$15 lunch, $20–$25 dinner. AE, CB, DC, DISC, MC, V. Mon–Fri 11am–3pm, Sat–Sun noon–3pm; daily 6– 10pm. CALIFORNIA.

Like the resort, Ventana's restaurant is woodsy but extravagant and romantic. The airy cedar interior is divided into two spaces: the lounge, where a wooden bar and cocktail tables look onto a roaring fire and through picturesque windows; and the dining room, which overlooks the mountains and/or the ocean. But during summer it's the outdoor patio, with its views of the ocean expanse and 50 miles of Big Sur coast, that's the coveted lunch spot. Unlike some costly restaurants in the area, a meal here is as gratifying as the surroundings. Lunch offers sandwiches, burgers, and an array of gourmet salads, as well as main courses such as grilled Atlantic salmon. Dinner begins with stellar starters like a perfectly dressed Caesar salad and a well-balanced chanterelle mushroom risotto. Main courses, such as the Texas antelope spareribs with bacon, Swiss chard, chili reduction, roasted garlic, and fried onions, or the roasted duck breast with hazelnut risotto and sun-dried cherry sauce will send your taste buds sailing. And as you'd expect, desserts are equally heavenly.

8 Pinnacles National Monument

by Andrew Rice

Once a little-known outpost of the national park system, Pinnacles National Monument has become one of the most popular weekend climbing destinations in central California over the past decade. The mild winter climate and plentiful routes make this a perfect off-season training ground for climbers. It's also a popular haven for campers, hikers, and nature lovers. One of the unique chaparral ecosystems in the world supports a large community of plant and animal life here, including one of California's largest breeding population of raptors.

The Pinnacles themselves—hundreds of towering crags, spires, and hoodoos—are seemingly out of place in the voluptuously rolling hills of the coast range. And they *are,* in fact, out of place, part of the eroded remains of a volcano formed 23 million years ago 195 miles south in the middle of the Mojave Desert. It was carried here by the movement of the San Andreas Fault, which runs just east of the park. (The other half of the volcano remains in the Mojave.)

You could spend days here without getting bored, but it's possible to cover the most interesting features in a weekend. With a single hike you can go from the lush oak woodland around the Bear Gulch Visitor Center to the dry and desolate crags of the high peaks, then back down through a 1/2-mile-long cave complete with underground waterfalls.

JUST THE FACTS

ACCESS POINTS   Two entrances lead to the park. The **West Entrance** from Soledad and U.S. 101 is a dry, dusty, winding single-lane road (not suitable for trailers) with the best drive-up view of the park. It doesn't connect with the east side.

The alternative route is via the **East Entrance.** Unless you're coming from nearby, take the longer drive on Calif. 25 to enter through the east. Because most of the peaks of the Pinnacles face east and the watershed drains east, most of the interesting hikes and geologic features are on this side. No road crosses the park.

FEES   Park entrance fees, which are good for 7 days, are $2 per person or $5 per car. Note: Camping fees do not include park entrance fee.

VISITOR CENTER   The first place you should go upon entering the park from the east is the **Bear Gulch Visitor Center** (☎ **408/389-4485**). This small center is rich with exhibits about the park's history, wildlife, and geology, and also has a great selection of nature handbooks and climbing guides for the Pinnacles. Climbers should check with rangers about closures and other information before heading out: Many routes are closed during hawk and falcon nesting season, and rangers like to know how many climbers are in the park.

Adjacent to the visitor center, the Bear Gulch picnic ground is a great place to fuel up before setting out on a hike or, if you're not planning on leaving your car, one of the best places to gaze up at dramatic spires of the high peaks (the ultimate spot is from the west side).

REGULATIONS & WARNINGS   Beware of poison oak, particularly in Bear Gulch. Rattlesnakes are common throughout the park but rarely seen. Bikes and dogs are prohibited on all trails, and no backcountry camping is allowed anywhere in the park.

Hiking through this variety of landscapes demands versatility. Come prepared with a good pair of hiking shoes, snacks, lots of water, and a flashlight.

Daytime temperatures often exceed 100°F in summer, so the best times of year to visit are spring, when the wildflowers are blooming, followed by fall. Crowds are common during spring weekends.

HIKING/SEEING THE HIGHLIGHTS

To see most of the park in a single, moderately strenuous morning, take the **Condor Gulch Trail** from the visitor center. As you climb quickly out of the parking area, the Pinnacles' wind-sculpted spires seem to grow taller. In less than 2 miles you're among them, and Condor Gulch intersects with the **High Peaks Trail.** The view from the top spans miles: the Salinas Valley to your west, the Pinnacles below, and miles of coast to the east. After traversing the high peaks (including stretches of footholds carved in steep rock faces) for about a mile, the trail drops back toward the visitor center via a valley filled with eerie-looking hoodoos.

In another $1^{1}/_{2}$ miles, you'll reach the reservoir marking the top of **Bear Gulch Cave.** You'll need your flashlight and might get wet, but this .6-mile-long talus cave is a thrill. From the end of the cave you're just a short walk through the most popular climbing area of the park away from the visitor center. It's also possible to hike just Bear Gulch and the cave, then return via the **Moses Spring Trail.** It's about 2 miles round-trip, but you'll miss the view from the top.

If you're coming from the west entrance, the **Juniper Canyon Trail** is a short (1.2 miles), but very steep, blast to the top of the high peaks. You'll definitely earn the view. Otherwise, try the short **Balconies Trail** to the monument's other talus cave, **Balconies Cave.** Flashlights are required here, too.

CAMPING

The campground on the west side (☎ **408/389-4485**) is just an open field with a few pit toilets and picnic tables. To top things off, it's not open on spring weekends, prime visiting season. Rates are $10 per night.

The campground on the east side, privately run **Pinnacles Campground, Inc.** (☎ **408/389-4462;** $6 per person), is just outside the park (off Calif. 25, 32 miles south of Hollister), with lots of privacy and space between sites, showers, a store, and a pool. It's close enough so you can hike into the park from the campground, though it will add a few miles to your outing. Though private campgrounds often are over-developed, the management here saw the benefits of leaving the surroundings natural. Park rangers hold campfire programs here on weekends. Dogs are not recommended.

The Central Coast 12

by Erika Lenkert and Matthew R. Poole

California's Central Coast—a spectacular amalgam of beaches, lakes, and mountains—is the state's most diverse region. The narrow strip of coast that runs for more than 100 miles from San Simeon to Ventura spans several climate zones and is home to an eclectic mix of students, middle-class workers, retirees, farmers, computer techies, and fishermen. The ride along Calif. 1, which follows the ocean cliffs, is almost always packed with rental cars, RVs, and bicycles. Traffic may give your brakes a workout, but it also allows you to take longer looks at one of the most spectacular vistas in the world.

Whether you're driving up from Los Angeles or down from San Francisco, Calif. 1 is the most scenic and leisurely route (U.S. 101 gets you there faster, but is less picturesque). Most bicyclists pedal from north to south, the direction of the prevailing winds. Those in cars may prefer to drive south to north, so they can get a better look at the coastline as it unfolds toward the west. No matter which direction you drive, break out the camera—you're about to experience unparalleled beauty, California style.

1 San Simeon: Hearst Castle

Few places on earth compare to Hearst Castle. The 165-room estate of publishing magnate William Randolph Hearst, situated high above the coastal village of San Simeon, atop a hill he called La Cuesta Encantada ("the Enchanted Hill"), is an ego trip par excellence. One of the last great estates of America's Gilded Age, it's an astounding, completely over-the-top monument to wealth—and to the power that money brings.

Hearst Castle is a sprawling compound of structures, constructed over 28 years in a Mediterranean Revival architectural style, set in undeniably magical surroundings. The focal point of the estate is the you-have-to-see-it-to-believe-it **Casa Grande,** a 100-plus-room mansion brimming with priceless art and antiques. Hearst acquired most of his vast European collection via New York auction houses, where he bought entire rooms (including walls, ceilings, and floors) and shipped them here. The result is an Old-World castle done in a priceless mix-and-match style. You'll see fantastic 400-year-old Spanish and Italian ceilings, enormous 500-year-old fireplace mantels, 16th-century Florentine bedsteads, Renaissance paintings, Flemish tapestries, and innumerable other treasures.

Three opulent "west houses" also contain magnificent works of art. A lavish private movie theater was used to screen first-run films twice nightly—once for employees, and again for the guests and host.

And then there are the swimming pools. The Roman-inspired indoor pool has intricate mosaic work, Carrara marble replicas of Greek gods and goddesses, and alabaster globe lamps that create the illusion of moonlight. The breathtaking outdoor Greco-Roman Neptune pool, flanked by marble colonnades that frame the distant sea, is one of the mansion's most memorable features.

In 1957, in exchange for a massive tax write-off, the Hearst Corporation donated the estate to the State of California (while retaining ownership of approximately 80,000 acres); the California Department of Parks and Recreation now administers it as a State Historic Monument.

TOURING THE ESTATE

✪ **Hearst Castle** can be visited only by guided tour. Four distinct daytime tours are offered on a daily basis, each lasting almost 2 hours. Evening tours also available most Friday and Saturday evenings during spring and fall.

Wear comfortable shoes—you'll be walking about a 1/2 mile per tour, which includes between 150 and 400 steps to climb or descend. (Wheelchair tours are available by calling ☎ 805/927-2020 at least 10 days in advance.)

The latest addition to the estate is the giant-screen Hearst Castle Theatre, which shows "The Enchanted Castle," a movie about Hearst, his castle, and his dreams. The film shows hourly at half past the hour, and tickets cost $6 for adults and $4 for children 12 and under.

Tours are conducted daily beginning at 8:20am, except on New Year's Day, Thanksgiving Day, and Christmas Day. Two to six tours leave every hour, depending on the season. Allow 2 hours between starting times if you plan on taking more than one tour.

Reservations are recommended and can be made up to 8 weeks in advance. Tickets can be purchased by telephone through **Destinet** (☎ 800/444-4445). Daytime tours cost $14 for adults, $8 for children 6 to 12. The evening tour costs $25 for adults, $13 for children 6 to 12.

Hearst Castle is located directly on Calif. 1, about 42 miles north of San Luis Obispo and 94 miles south of Monterey. From San Francisco or Monterey, take U.S. 101 south to Paso Robles, then Calif. 46 west to Calif. 1, and Calif. 1 north to the castle. From Los Angeles, take U.S. 101 north to San Luis Obispo, then Calif. 1 north to the castle. Park in the visitor center parking lot; a tour bus will take you the 5 miles up the hill to the estate.

NEARBY TOWNS: CAMBRIA & SAN SIMEON

After driving for close to an hour without passing anything but lush green hills and nature at its most glorious (especially from Calif. 46 off U.S. 101), it's a remarkably quaint surprise to roll into the adorable coastal minitowns of Cambria and nearby San Simeon. Cambria, in particular, is so charming that the town itself is reason enough to make the drive. With little more than two streets' worth of charming shops, restaurants, and a handful of B&Bs, Cambria is the perfect place to escape the everyday, enjoy the endless expanses of pristine coastal terrain, and meander through little shops selling local artwork.

Gray whales pass through the area from late December to early February, and for the past few years hundreds of elephant seals have made the shore along Moonstone Beach Drive their year-round playground—much to the delight of locals and nature enthusiasts. (Don't approach the seals, but watch them from the bluffs. They're wild

Weekends at the Ranch: William Randolph Hearst & the Legacy of Hearst Castle

The lavish palace that William Randolph Hearst always referred to simply as "the ranch" took root in 1919. William Randolph ("W. R." to his friends) had inherited 275,000 acres from his father, mining baron George Hearst, and was well on his way to building a formidable media empire. He often escaped to a spot known as "Camp Hill" on his newly acquired lands in the Santa Lucia Mountains above the village of San Simeon, the site of boyhood family outings. Complaining that "I get tired of going up there and camping in tents," Hearst hired architect Julia Morgan to design the retreat that would become one of the most famous private homes in the world.

An art collector with indiscriminate taste and inexhaustible funds, Hearst overwhelmed Morgan with interiors and furnishings from the ancestral collections of Europe. Each week, railroad cars carrying fragments of Roman temples, lavish doors and carved ceilings from Italian monasteries, Flemish tapestries, hastily rolled paintings by the old masters, ancient Persian rugs, and antique French furniture arrived—5 tons at a time—in San Simeon. *Citizen Kane,* which depicts a Hearst-like mogul with a similarly excessive estate called Xanadu, has a memorable scene of hoarded priceless treasures warehoused in dusty piles, stretching as far as the eye can see. Like Kane, Hearst, once described as a man with an "edifice complex," purchased so much that only a fraction of what he bought was ever installed in the estate.

In 1925 Hearst separated from his wife and began to spend time in Los Angeles overseeing his movie company, Cosmopolitan Pictures. His principal starlet, Marion Davies, became W. R.'s constant companion and hostess at Hearst Castle; this would be her main role for the rest of his life. The ranch soon became a playground for the Hollywood crowd as well as dignitaries like Winston Churchill and playwright George Bernard Shaw, who is said to have wryly remarked of the estate that, "this is the way God would have done it if He had the money."

animals and will bite if molested.) The beaches and coves are wonderful places for humans to frolic as well—stone collectors will be especially enamored by the natural bounty of jade and moonstones mingled with the sand.

WHERE TO STAY

Best Western Cavalier Oceanfront Resort. 9415 Hearst Dr. (Calif. 1), San Simeon, CA 93452. ☎ **800/826-8168** or 805/927-4688. 90 rms. TV TEL. $69–$165 double. AE, CB, DC, DISC, MC, V.

"Oceanfront" and "budget" are generally a contradiction, but this family-friendly hotel offers the best of both. Aside from the basics, the rooms are all outfitted with VCRs (video rentals are available next door), refrigerators, computer jacks, and hair dryers; some even have fireplaces. Other bonuses include two outdoor heated pools, an exercise room, two restaurants, a launderette, a shopping center, and a video arcade.

Blue Dolphin Inn. 6470 Moonstone Beach Dr., Cambria, CA 93428. ☎ **805/927-3300.** Fax 805/927-7311. 18 rms. TV. $75–$225 double. Rates include continental breakfast. AE, DC, DISC, MC, V.

Voted one of the best moderately priced California accommodations by *Los Angeles Times* readers in 1996, the Blue Dolphin offers high-quality rooms along the Cambria

Despite its opulence, Hearst promoted "the ranch" as a casual weekend home. He regularly laid the massive refectory table in the dining room with paper napkins and bottled ketchup and pickles to invoke a rustic camplike atmosphere. In Hearst's beautiful library, his priceless collection of ancient Greek pottery—one of the greatest collections of its kind in the world—is arranged casually among the rare volumes, like knickknacks.

The Hollywood crowd would take Hearst's private railway car from Los Angeles to San Luis Obispo, where a fleet of limousines waited to transport them to San Simeon. Those who didn't come by train were treated to a flight on Hearst's private plane from the Burbank airport (MGM head Irving Thalberg and his wife, Norma Shearer, preferred this mode of transportation). Hearst, an avid aviator, had a sizable landing strip built; Charles Lindbergh used it when he flew up for a visit in the summer of 1928.

Oh, if the walls could talk. Atop one of the castle's looming towers are the hexagonal Celestial Suites. One was a favorite of Clark Gable and Carole Lombard, who would be startled out of their romantic slumber by the clamor of 18 carillon bells directly overhead. David Niven, a frequent guest, was one of the unknown number who defied teetotaler Hearst's edict against liquor in private rooms; Niven was called upon more than once to explain the several "empties" under the bed (which Cardinal Richelieu once owned and slept in) in his customary suite.

W. R. Hearst and Marion Davies hosted frequent costume parties at the ranch, which were as intricately planned as a movie production. The most legendary, the Circus Party, was held to celebrate W. R.'s 75th birthday on April 29, 1938. Much of Hollywood attended to honor the tycoon, including grande dame Bette Davis—dressed as a bearded lady.

—Stephanie Avnet

coastline. Designed in English country style, the guest rooms brim with frilly opulence and include gas fireplaces, refrigerators, hair dryers, and VCRs. Rooms 111, 112, and 114 have good ocean views from their private patios.

California Seacoast Lodge. 9215 Hearst Dr., San Simeon, CA 93452. ☎ **805/927-3878.** Fax 805/927-1781. 54 rms, 3 suites. June–Sept 15, $85–$95 double; from $185 suite. Sept 16–May, $50–$60 double; from $185 suite. Additional person $5 extra. Rates include continental breakfast. AE, MC, V.

You'll find clean, newly renovated accommodations at this hotel located 3 miles from the entrance to Hearst Castle. There are an array of options here; you can go budget with a basic room, kick in a few extra bucks for one of the most expensive doubles (which comes with a king-size bed and fireplace), or splurge on a minisuite that comes with a fireplace, Jacuzzi, canopied bed, and French furnishings. There's also a glass-enclosed pool on the premises.

✪ **Olallieberry Inn.** 2476 Main St., Cambria, CA 93428. ☎ **888/927-3222** or 805/927-3222. Fax 805/927-0202. 8 rms, 1 suite. $85–$150 double; $175 cottage suite. Rates include full breakfast and evening wine and hors d'oeuvres. MC, V.

The minute we walked into this 1873 Greek Revival house, we knew it was our kind of place. The grounds were perfectly manicured but whimsically blooming, the air smelled of baked brie and homemade bread (we'd come during the afternoon wine hour), and guests lounged on couches, cradling plates of delectables. The owners have a passion for cooking and gardening (the herb garden has been featured in *Sunset* magazine), but the decor doesn't fall by the wayside: Victorian floral-and-lace reigns, and the guest rooms are lovingly and individually appointed. Each has its own private bath, although some are across or down the hall. Follow the deck off the dining area to the backyard, and you'll find rooms in a newer building overlooking a creek; they're remarkably charming and have a fireplace and private deck. The delicious full breakfast—accompanied by olallieberry jam, of course—is gourmet all the way.

Ragged Point Inn. P.O. Box 110 (15 miles north of Hearst Castle), San Simeon, CA 93452. ☎ **805/927-4502.** Fax 805/927-8862. 20 rms. TV. $89–$150 double. Extra person $10. AE, DISC, MC, V.

There'd be little reason to stay here if it weren't for the surroundings: grassy, ocean-front grounds on a cliff at the base of Big Sur country. Rooms, though newish, are just a step above motel style. But if you get one with a view that looks directly onto the ocean, you probably won't care. A visit here promises more seclusion than staying in Cambria or San Simeon. The only establishments in the area are a restaurant, snack bar, gift ship, minimart, and gas station that belong to the hotel. As this book goes to press, the hotel is adding new cliff-front accommodations, which will most likely be a step up from existing rooms. *Tip:* Second-floor rooms generally have better views.

The Squibb House Bed & Breakfast. 4063 Burton Dr., Cambria, CA 93428. ☎ **800/ 927-9600** or 805/927-9600. Fax 805/927-9606. 5 rms. $95–$140 double. Rates include continental breakfast. MC, V.

If you don't mind small rooms and no TV or telephone, there may be no sweeter place to spend the night than at the Squibb House. Each room in this lovingly restored 1877 Victorian reflects its history, with beautiful wooden reproductions, wood-burning stoves, and attention to detail. Even the garden is worthy of perusal. Owner/ renovator Bruce Black makes sure everything is in the finest of taste and that a night here is a romantic step back in time.

WHERE TO DINE

✪ **Ian's.** 2150 Center St., Cambria. ☎ **805/927-8649.** Reservations highly recommended. Main courses $15–$27. AE, MC, V. Daily 5–9pm. CALIFORNIA.

Ask locals where they'd prefer to dine and they're likely to mention Ian's. Chef Mark Sahaydak's specials, which change daily, reflect his take on the local bounty. His individual artistry is apparent in dishes like porcini-mushroom ravioli with spicy Italian sausage, and sautéed scallops in a crème fraîche and chardonnay sauce flavored with sun-dried tomatoes. Ian's wine list reflects the very best of local and regional vineyards.

✪ **Ragged Point Restaurant & Resort.** Calif. 1, San Simeon (15 miles north of Hearst Castle). ☎ **805/927-5708.** Reservations recommended. Main courses $8–$12 lunch, $11–$23 dinner. AE, DISC, MC, V. Daily noon–4pm and 5–9pm. CALIFORNIA.

It's not the food that makes us like this place so much, although it was surprisingly good. What won us over was the atmosphere. On a sunny afternoon, there's no better place in the area to dine than at the base of the Big Sur foothills amidst Japanese-style landscaping overlooking a grassy expanse, nature trail, and the ocean beyond. The small dining room, with its classic California redwood architecture and partially enclosed, trellised redwood patio, serves up some darn good herb cheese–stuffed mushrooms, a perfectly dressed Pacific Salad (an Oriental chicken-style salad with greens, moist chicken, toasted cashews, and mandarin oranges), and respectable sandwiches. Heartier fare is available at both lunch and dinner (all entrees come with salad or soup, veggies, and bread at dinner). After your meal, stroll down to the lookout point for the ultimate coastal view. An adjoining snack bar offers basic fast-food grub—burgers, hot dogs, and sandwiches, all for under $5.

Robin's. 4095 Burton Dr., Cambria. ☎ **805/927-5007.** Reservations recommended. Main courses $9–$17. MC, V. Mon–Sat 11am–9pm, Sun 5–9pm. ECLECTIC.

It's surprising to find such an adventurous kitchen in a small town, but after hearing locals rave about the sophisticated food here, we had to check it out. Robin's is a restaurant with something for everyone, from exotic dishes from Mexico, Thailand, India, and beyond to more straightforward preparations like a tasty salad or juicy steak and an array of vegetarian dishes. Offerings include a salmon bisque appetizer; porcini raviolis with roasted-pepper/cream sauce, fresh spinach, basil, and Parmesan; and other flavorful combinations such as Thai prawns in green curry with basmati brown rice, fruit chutney, and chapati. Don't miss dessert—try the espresso-soaked cake with mascapone mousse and shaved chocolate or vanilla-custard bread pudding. Tempt your taste buds on-line at **www.cambria-online.com**.

The Sow's Ear Cafe. 2248 Main St., Cambria. ☎ **805/927-4865.** Reservations recommended. Main courses $14–$22; early-bird specials $10.25–$12.25. DISC, MC, V. Daily 5–8 or 9:30pm, depending on business. AMERICAN COUNTRY.

The name is anything but romantic; the dining room definitely is. It's a casually elegant spot, lit just enough to catch the warmth of its rustic wooden surroundings. You'll be inspired to lean over a bottle of California red and share travel fantasies with a companion while enjoying fresh-baked bread (served in cute flower pots!) and a hearty plate of beer-spiced shrimp, chicken and dumplings, or baby pork ribs. Early dinner specials might consist of grilled chicken, a fresh catch, and a vegetarian dish.

2 Morro Bay

Morro Bay is separated from the ocean by a long peninsula of towering sand dunes. It's best known for dramatic **Morro Rock,** an enormous egg-shaped monolith that juts out of the water just offshore. Part of a chain of long-extinct volcanoes, the huge domed rock is a winter and fall sanctuary for thousands of migrating birds, including cormorants, pelicans, sandpipers, and the rare peregrine falcon.

But other than gawking at the amazing "Gibraltar of the Pacific," there's little reason to visit the town itself. The motel strip and the horrific, gigantic, absurdly placed oceanfront electrical plant (directly blocking the view of the rock) mar the appeal. If you do stay for more than a quick stop to snap a few photos, you'll find a touristy and unimpressive bayfront strip of stores and a pathetic "aquarium" that makes you want to free the seals and fish jailed within it. The town's saving grace is its natural surroundings; the beaches and wildlife sanctuaries can be quite peaceful and wondrous.

ESSENTIALS

The **Morro Bay Chamber of Commerce,** 880 Main St., Morro Bay, CA 93442 (☎ **800/231-0592** or 805/772-4467), offers armfuls of area information. It's open Monday to Friday from 8am to 5pm and on Saturday from 10am to 3pm.

EXPLORING THE AREA

Most visitors come to Morro Bay to ogle **Morro Rock,** the much-photographed Central Coast icon. It's definitely worth a gander (you couldn't miss it even if you wanted to).

BEACHES   Popular **Atascadero State Beach,** just north of Morro Rock, has gentle waves and lovely views. Rest rooms, showers, and dressing rooms are available. Just north of Atascadero is **Morro Strand State Beach,** a long, sandy stretch with normally gentle surf. Rest rooms and picnic tables are available here. Morro Strand has its own campgrounds; for information, call ☎ **805/772-2560,** or reserve a spot through **Destinet** (☎ **800/444-7275**).

STATE PARKS   Cabrillo Peak, located in the lovely **Morro Bay State Park** (☎ **805/772-7434**), makes for a terrific day hike and offers fantastic 360° views from its summit. There's a faint zigzagging trail, but the best way to reach the top is by bushwhacking straight up the gentle slope—a hike that takes about 2 hours roundtrip. To reach the trailhead, take Calif. 1 south and turn left at the Morro Bay State Park/Montana de Oro State Park exit. Follow South Bay Boulevard for three-quarters of a mile, then take the left fork another half a mile to the Cabrillo Peak dirt parking lot, located on your left.

   Montana de Oro State Park ("Mountain of Gold") is fondly known as "petite Big Sur" because of its stony cliffs and rugged terrain. There's great swimming at Spooner's Cove and lots of easy hiking trails here, including a number that lead to spectacular coastal vistas or hidden forest streams. The Hazard Reef Trail will take you up on the Morro Bay Sandspit dunes. The park's campground is in the trees, across from the beach. For information, call the park rangers at ☎ **805/528-0513** or 805/772-7434, or reserve a spot through **Destinet** (☎ **800/444-7275**).

IN TOWN   In addition to soaking up the tourist vibe at the Embarcadero, you'll find the dilapidated **Morro Bay Aquarium** (☎ **805/772-7647**), whose only redeeming quality is that it takes injured and abandoned sea otters and seals and nurses them back to health, eventually releasing the recovered animals back into the sea. It's open daily from 9am to 6pm in summer and to 5pm in winter.

   You can escape landlock by renting a kayak or taking a minisubmarine tour through **Kayaks of Morro Bay** (☎ **805/772-1119**), which is located at the Embarcadero at the end of Pacific Street. Rentals range from $3 to $30 depending on the kind of boat you want and length of time you use it. Submarine tours run daily and cost $5.50 for children under 12 and $12.50 for folks 12 and above.

WHERE TO STAY

Baywood Bed & Breakfast Inn. 1370 2nd St., Baywood Park, CA 93042. ☎ **805/ 528-8888.** 5 rms, 10 suites. TV TEL. $80–$110 double; $110–$160 suite. Additional person $15 extra. Rates include breakfast. MC, V.

   Rarely will you find such affordable accommodations with so many extras. Each room at the 2-story bayfront inn, located in Baywood Park just south of Morro Bay, is decorated with a distinct (over-the-top) theme and grandma-style flair. Guests can cuddle in a floral and light-wood country cottage, stretch out in a 19th-century English affair, or saddle down in a Southwestern suite. Every room has a private entrance, gas fireplace, microwave, coffeemaker, and a refrigerator stocked with complimentary sodas and snacks; all but a few have ocean views. Breakfast is brought to your room, and wine and cheese are served each evening.

The Inn at Morro Bay. 60 State Park Rd., Morro Bay, CA 93442. ☎ **800/321-9566** or 805/ 772-5651. Fax 805/772-4779. 96 rms. TV TEL. $98–$265 double (highest rates on weekends). AE, MC, V.

   One of the most upscale hotels on the San Luis coast is strategically sandwiched along the shoreline between monumental Morro Bay and an 18-hole golf course. Two-story Cape Cod–style buildings house guests and have contemporary interiors tempered by blond-wood cabinetry, polished-brass fittings and beds, and reproduction 19th-century European furnishings. The best rooms enjoy unobstructed views of Morro Rock; those in back face the swimming pool and gardens.

WHERE TO DINE

Hoppe's at 901. 901 Embarcadero (at Pacific). ☎ **805/772-9012.** Reservations recommended. Main courses $12–$22. AE, DISC, MC, V. Mon, Wed, and Thurs 5–9pm, Fri–Sun 11am–2pm and 5–9pm. CALIFORNIA.

Ask locals where to go for a special meal in Morro Bay and they're likely to send you to Hoppe's. Here you get a stellar view of Morro Rock, as well as such dishes as potato-crusted free-range chicken with mushroom sauce, rack of lamb with white beans and homemade curry sausage, and a variety of fresh seafood. The service can be slow, but the atmosphere is surprisingly upscale, and the food respectable. Considering the neighboring options, Hoppe's is as good as it gets.

3 San Luis Obispo

Because the actual town of San Luis Obispo is not visible from U.S. 101, even many Californians don't know that it's more than a McDonald's-and-gasoline stopover on the way to Southern California. But its secret location is exactly what keeps it a quaint little Central Coast jewel.

San Luis Obispo is neatly tucked into the mountains about halfway between San Francisco and Los Angeles and is surrounded by green, pristine mountain ranges and filled with college kids and friendly locals. The atmosphere is small-town casual.

The town grew up around an 18th-century mission, and its dozens of historical landmarks, Victorian homes, shops, and restaurants are its primary attractions. Today it's still quaint, almost undiscovered, and best ventured on foot. It also makes a good base for an extensive exploration of the region as a whole. To the west of town, a short drive away, are some of the state's prettiest swimming beaches; turning east, you enter the Central Coast's wine country, home to dozens of respectable wineries.

ESSENTIALS

GETTING THERE   U.S. 101, one of the state's primary north-south roadways, runs right through San Luis Obispo; it's the fastest land route here from anywhere. If you're driving down along the coast, Calif. 1 is the way to go for its natural beauty and oceanfront cliffs. If you're entering the city from the east, take Calif. 46 or 41.

VISITOR INFORMATION   The **San Luis Obispo Visitors Center,** 1039 Chorro St., Suite E, San Luis Obispo, CA 93401 (☎ **805/781-2777;** fax 805/543-1255), is located downtown, between Monterey and Higuera streets. This helpful office is one of the best-run visitors bureaus we've ever come across. Drop in to ask questions and to pick up maps, a calendar of events, or specialized information on local sights. Ask for a "Path of History" map, which details many of the sights listed below. The visitors bureau can also make reservations and issue tickets for Hearst Castle at San Simeon. The center is open Tuesday to Friday from 8am to 5pm, and Saturday to Monday from 10am to 5pm.

ORIENTATION   San Luis Obispo is about 10 miles inland, at the junction of Calif. 1 and U.S. 101. The downtown is laid out in a grid, roughly centered around the historic mission and its Mission Plaza (see below). Most of the main tourist sights are around the mission, within the small triangle created by U.S. 101 and Santa Rosa and Marsh streets.

Area Code Change Notice

Please note that, effective June 13, 1998, portions of San Luis Obispo are scheduled to change to the **831** area code. You will be able to dial 408 until February 20, 1999, after which you will be required to use 831 for affected numbers.

EXPLORING THE TOWN

Definitely make a pit stop at the perpetually pink **Madonna Inn,** 100 Madonna Rd. (off U.S. 101; ☎ **805/543-3000**), if for no other reason than to use its unique public rest rooms (the men's has a waterfall urinal; the women's is a barrage of crimson and pink). Every over-the-top inch of this place is an exercise in excess, from the dining room, complete with pink leather booths, pink table linens, and colored sugar that's—you guessed it—piquantly pink, to the rock-walled, cavelike guest rooms.

Ah Louis Store. 800 Palm St. (at Chorro St.). ☎ **805/543-4332.** Usually Mon–Sat 2–5:30pm, but hours vary.

This establishment, practically unchanged since its opening in 1874, is still in the hands of the original Cantonese family owners. Entrepreneurial Mr. Ah Louis was lured to California by gold fever in 1856. Emerging from the mines empty-handed, he soon began a lucrative career as a labor contractor, hiring and organizing Chinese crews that would build the railroad. Later he opened this store. Ah Louis also founded one of the country's first brickyards, built county roads, ran a vegetable and flower-seed business, bred racehorses, and oversaw eight farms.

Today you can chat with Ah Louis's heir, Howard, while you browse through the clutter of Asian merchandise. Ask for a free brochure detailing the family's history. Hours are somewhat irregular, though, since Howard often just closes up and goes fishing.

✪ **Farmer's Market.** Higuera St. (between Osos and Nipomo sts.). Thurs 6:30–9pm.

If you're lucky enough to be in town on a Thursday, take an evening stroll down Higuera Street, when the state's largest weekly street fair fills 4 downtown city blocks. You'll find much more here than fresh-picked produce—there's an ever-changing array of street entertainment, open-pit barbecues, food stands, and market stalls selling fresh flowers, cider, and other seasonal goodies. Surrounding stores stay open until 9pm.

Mission San Luis Obispo de Tolosa. 782 Monterey St. ☎ **805/543-6850.** Free admission ($2 donation requested). Summer daily 9am–5pm (sometimes later); winter daily 9am–4pm.

Founded by Father Junípero Serra in 1772, California's fifth mission was built with adobe bricks by Native American Chumash people. It remains one of the prettiest and most interesting structures in the Franciscan chain.

Serra chose this valley for the site of his fifth mission based on tales told to him of friendly natives and bountiful food (including grizzly bears—yum!). Here the traditional red-tile roof was first used atop a California mission, after the original thatched tule roofs repeatedly fell to hostile Native Americans' burning arrows. The former padres' quarters are an excellent museum chronicling both Native American and missionary life through all eras of the mission's use. Allow about 30 to 45 minutes to tour the mission and its grounds.

Mission Plaza, a pretty garden with brick paths and park benches fronting a meandering creek, still functions as San Luis Obispo's town square. It's the focal point for local festivities and activities, from live concerts to poetry readings and dance and theater productions. Check at the visitors center (see "Essentials," above) to find out what's on when you're in town.

At Mission Plaza you'll also find the **San Luis Obispo Art Center** (☎ 805/543-8562), whose three galleries display and sell an array of California-made art. Admission is free, and hours are Tuesday to Sunday from 11am to 5pm.

San Luis Obispo Children's Museum. 1010 Nipomo St. (at Monterey St.) ☎ 805/544-KIDS. Admission $4 adults and children 2 and older, free for kids under 2. Mid-June to Aug, Thurs–Tues 10am–5pm; Sept to mid-June, Mon and Sat 10am–5pm and Thurs–Fri and Sun 1–5pm.

This terrific children's museum features a playhouse of interesting manipulatives for toddlers, an authentic reproduction of a Native American Chumash cave dwelling, a music room, a computer corner, a pint-sized bank and post office, and more. Special events like mask making, sing-alongs, and stage-makeup classes are scheduled regularly; call for a list of events.

San Luis Obispo County Historical Museum. Mission Plaza, 696 Monterey St. ☎ 805/543-0638. Free admission. Wed–Sun 10am–4pm.

This little museum, run by the San Luis Obispo County Historical Society in a Carnegie library, houses an extensive research library and historical photograph collection. The permanent exhibit includes artifacts from Native American Chumash and early European settlers.

SHOPPING

Don't expect Rodeo Drive here, but rather a few charming boutiques (among many uninteresting ones) scattered throughout town. The best place to exercise your credit cards is on the downtown streets surrounding the mission, specifically the 5 blocks of **Higuera Street** from Nipomo to Osos streets, as well as a short stretch of **Monterey Street** between Chorro and Osos streets.

On Higuera Street, check out **Hands Gallery,** 777 Higuera St. (☎ 805/543-1921), which has a playful, bright collection of local and international art. Trinkets range from glass candies to vases, jewelry, and ceramics and can be viewed or bought Monday to Wednesday from 10am to 6pm, Thursday to Saturday from 10am to 9pm, and Sunday from 11am to 5pm.

You might also want to check out **The Creamery,** 570 Higuera St., at Nipomo Street (☎ 805/541-0106), which was one of the state's most important dairies for more than 40 years. Restored, remodeled, and opened as a shopping and restaurant mall, the complex is centered around the creamery's old cooling tower. Antique freezer doors, overhead workhouse lights, and milk-can lamps pointedly remind visitors of the structure's original function.

Central Coast wineries produce some excellent vintages, some of which are available for tasting at the **Central Coast Wine Room,** 10 Old Creamery Rd., Harmony (☎ 805/927-7337). If you don't mind wading through the mediocre ones, you'll find some excellent selections from Paso Robles and the Edna Valley that compete favorably with those of Napa Valley. The tasting room is open daily from 11am to 5pm (closed Tuesday in winter); tastings are $2.

OUTSIDE OF TOWN

There are dozens of **wineries** in the area, which offer tastings and tours daily and make for a fun country diversion. See "Vintage Central Coast" later in this chapter for further details.

If you're into history and architecture, another worthy side trip is the **Mission San Miguel Arcangel,** 775 Mission St., in San Miguel (7 miles north of Paso Robles on U.S. 101). Found in 1824, this mission is less spoiled by restoration than many others in the state and is still run by the Franciscan order and inhabited by brown-robed friars. The modest exterior belies one of the most elaborate and best-preserved interiors of the entire central California chain. Painted and decorated by area Native Americans under the supervision of Spanish designer Estevan Munras, the walls and woodwork glow with luminous colors untouched since their original application. Behind the altar and its statue of San Miguel (St. Michael), is splendid tilework featuring a radiant Eye of God.

Mission San Miguel is open to the public daily from 9:30am to 4:30pm; the church remains open until 5pm. Admission is $1 per family, 50¢ per person; allow 30 minutes to see the sights. For further information, call ☎805/467-3256.

WHERE TO STAY

In addition to what's listed below, there's a pristine branch of **Holiday Inn Express** (☎ 800/465-4329 or 805/544-8600) and the reliable **Motel 6** (☎ 800/4-MOTEL-6 or 805/541-6992).

If you'd like free help making reservations in the area, contact the **Accommodations Reservation Service** (☎ 800/292-2222).

✪ **Adobe Inn.** 1473 Monterey St., San Luis Obispo, CA 93401. ☎ **800/676-1588** or 805/549-0321. Fax 805/549-0383. 15 rms, 8 with kitchenette but no stove. TV TEL. $55–$95 double. Additional person $6 extra in winter, $10 in summer. Rates include breakfast. Seasonal discounts available. AE, DISC, MC, V.

Okay, it's not *actually* adobe, or even remotely close for that matter, but Michael and Ann Dinshaw have taken this old motor inn and given it a creatively homey atmosphere at unbeatable prices. Each spotless room is named after a cactus, has a corresponding hand-painted sign on its door, and is individually decorated in southwestern style with quirky additions such as playfully painted cupboards or a windowside reading nook. Breakfast is served in a clean dining area that unfortunately faces the street, but coffee snobs will delight in the strong, locally roasted blend. Plants adorn the inn's exterior, and there's a minicactus garden and fountain beyond the parking lot. Either Michael or Ann is usually on-site, and they go out of their way to make guests happy and offer a slew of packages that explore the surrounding areas and attractions. A great bargain.

✪ **Apple Farm Inn.** 2015 Monterey St., San Luis Obispo, CA 93401. ☎ **800/255-2040** or 805/544-2040. Fax 805/546-9495. 69 rms. A/C TV TEL. $109–$200 double. AE, DISC, MC, V.

Ultrapopular, the Apple Farm Inn is a peaceful getaway in a Disney plantation kind of way. Every square inch of the immaculate Victorian-style farmhouse is cheek-pinchingly cute with floral wallpaper, fresh flowers, and sugar-sweet colorful touches. No two rooms are alike, although all have a gas fireplace, large well-equipped bathroom, pine antiques, lavish country decor, and either a canopy four-poster or brass bed. Some bedrooms open onto cozy turreted sitting areas with romantic window seats; others have bay windows and a view of San Luis Creek, where a working mill spins its huge wheel to power an apple press. There's an on-site restaurant.

Service here is outstanding and includes nightly turndown and a morning wake-up knock, delivered with complimentary coffee or tea and a newspaper. Other features include complimentary cribs and train and airport shuttle service. Cider is always on hand in the lobby. An outdoor heated swimming pool and Jacuzzi are open year-round.

Lamp Lighter Inn. 1604 Monterey St. (at Grove St.), San Luis Obispo, CA 93401. ☎ **800/ 547-7787** or 805/547-7777. Fax 805/547-7787. 29 rms, 11 suites. A/C TV TEL. $49–$80 double; from $69 suite. Rates include continental breakfast. AE, DISC, MC, V.

Even if you're not looking for a bargain, you'll be pleasantly surprised with the value you get at this motel. The rooms boast traditional motel style and colors, but look brand new, are squeaky clean, and have firm mattresses. Other bonuses are coffeemakers, refrigerators (except in three rooms), and a heated pool and whirlpool. Breakfast is served in the lobby by an amazingly enthusiastic staff.

✪ **Madonna Inn.** 100 Madonna Rd. (off U.S. 101), San Luis Obispo, CA 93405. ☎ **800/ 543-9666** or 805/543-3000. Website: www.madonnainn.com. Fax 805/543-1800. 109 rms, 25 suites. TV TEL. $97–$198 double; from $145 suite. MC, V.

You've got to see this one for yourself. The creative imaginations of owners Alex and Phyllis Madonna gave birth to the wildest—and most superfluously garish—fantasy world this side of Graceland. The only consistent element of the decor is the color scheme—perpetual pink. Beyond that, it's a free-for-all. Every nook and cranny has been built to delight—even the men's room has a rock-waterfall urinal and clam-shell sinks. Each room offers a different thematic fantasy. One unit features a trapezoidal bed—it's 5 feet long on one side and 6 feet long on the other. "Rock" rooms with zebra- or tiger-patterned bedspreads and stonelike showers and fireplaces resemble a Flintstones' Playboy palace. There are also blue rooms, red rooms, and over-the-top Spanish, Italian, Irish, Alps, Currier and Ives, Native American, Swiss, and hunting rooms. The coffee shop, dining room, and two cocktail lounges are also outlandishly ornate. Even if you don't stay here, stop by and check it out. *One major bummer:* There's no pool here, and there definitely should be.

WHERE TO DINE

Big Sky Cafe. 1121 Broad St. ☎ **805/545-5401.** Main courses $6–$11; salads and sandwiches $5–$6; breakfast $4–$6. MC, V. Mon–Sat 7am–10pm, Sun 8am–8pm. AMERICAN.

The folk-artsy fervor of San Luis really shines at this Southwestern mirage, where local art and a blue, star-studded ceiling surround diners who come for fresh, healthy food. Most everything on the menu, like shrimp tacos and herb-infused roasted chicken, is created with local ingredients. Lighter meals, such as black-bean vegetarian chili, charcoal-broiled eggplant sandwich, and white-bean and yellowtail tuna salad are equally inventive and tasty. Breakfasts include buttermilk pancakes, a jambalaya omelet, turkey hash, and black-bean huevos rancheros. Unfortunately, the last time we ate here the kitchen was slow and our food arrived cold, but one local assured us it was an unusual occurrence.

✪ **Buona Tavola.** 1037 Monterey St. ☎ **805/545-8000.** Reservations recommended. Main courses $8.25–$17. DC, DISC, MC, V. Mon–Fri 11:30am–2:30pm; Sun–Thurs 5:30–9:30pm, Fri–Sat 5:30–10:30pm. NORTHERN ITALIAN.

While most choices in town are burger-and-sandwich casual, Buona Tavola offers well-prepared Italian food in a more upscale setting. You can stroll in wearing jeans, but the dining room, with checkerboard floors and original artwork, is warmer and more intimate than other spots in town. There's also backyard-terrace seating where you can enjoy your meal surrounded by magnolias, ficus, and grapevines. The menu boasts a number of salads on the antipasti list. Favorite pastas include *agnolotti de scampi allo zafferand,* which is homemade, filled with scampi, and served in a cream-saffron sauce. The *spaghettini scoglio d'oro* comes with lobster, sea scallops, clams, mussels, shrimp, and diced tomatoes in a saffron sauce. Don't worry—once you've gotten past trying to pronounce your desired dish, the rest of the evening should be both relaxing and satisfying.

Mondéo Pronto. 893 Hugeura St., #D4. ☎ **805/544-2956.** Wraps and bentos $4.75–$5.75. MC, V. Sun–Wed 11am–9pm, Thurs–Sat 11am–10pm. ECLECTIC/WRAPS.

Wrap shops are the hottest new thing in fast food, providing patrons an affordable bite of international fillings in a burrito-type wrap. But Mondéo goes a step beyond by paying attention to detail with presentation and freshness. Choices range from Americana versions like the "mardi gras," which comes in a tomato tortilla packed with Cajun sausage, rock shrimp, creole veggies, and jambalaya sauce; to Mediterranean selections like "the Sicilian," with grilled Portobello mushrooms, herb polenta, veggies, goat cheese, olives, capers, and sun-dried tomato pesto. "Bentos" satisfy non-wrappers with such combinations as basil scampi, a lovely shrimp dish over bow-tie pasta with pesto, marinara, pine nuts, and herbs. Big bonuses: Everything on the kids' menu is under $2, and as the menu announces, "Substitutions and sides are no problem."

Mo's Smokehouse BBQ. 970 Higuera St. (at Oso St.). ☎ **805/544-6193.** Sun–Wed 11am–9pm, Thurs–Sat 11am–10pm. AE, MC, V. BARBECUE.

When friends of ours moved from San Francisco to San Luis Obispo, we asked them to keep tabs on the best places to eat in the area. They insisted we dine at Mo's, a local spot that satisfies residents' love for good barbecue. It's not fancy, but you name it, it's here—pork or baby back ribs, BBQ beef, tritip and chicken in either a mild or hot sauce, all accompanied by baked beans, bread, potato salad, coleslaw, and onion rings. To top off this delectable deal, practically everything on the menu is under $10.

SLO Brewing Company. 1119 Garden St. ☎ **805/543-1843.** Reservations accepted. Main courses $6–$9. DISC, MC, V. Mon–Wed 11:30am–10:30pm, Thurs–Sat 11:30am–12:30am, Sun noon–5pm. AMERICAN.

This brewpub's homemade beer has created such a buzz that it's now nationally distributed. Three distinct variations—Pale Ale, Amber Ale, and Porter—are brewed from all-natural ingredients and wash down the menu's burgers and fried food perfectly. Join the festive collegiate crowd at night, stop by for lunch, or check the place out on the web at www.slobrew.com.

Thai Classic. 1101 Higuera St. (at Oso St.). ☎ **805/541-2025.** Reservations recommended on weekends. Most dishes $6–$11. DISC, MC, V. Sun–Thurs 11am–10pm, Fri–Sat 11am–11pm. THAI.

It's not much to look at, but if you ignore the cheesy white booths and plain walls and focus on what's coming out of the kitchen, you won't be sorry you came. There's an extensive vegetarian selection and trademark Thai appetizers such as satay with peanut and cucumber sauces, phad Thai, and spring rolls. Locals favor the pineapple fried rice with shrimp, chicken, and cashews as well as the curry plates, all of which should be eaten family style. Lunch specials on weekdays are a real bargain at $3 to $4 for soup, salad, spring roll, fried wonton, steamed rice, and one of 21 main courses.

4 Pismo Beach

Just outside San Luis Obispo, on Pismo's 23-mile-stretch of prime beachfront, flip-flops are the shoes of choice and surfwear is the dominant fashion. It's all about beach life here, so bring your bathing suit, your board, and a good book.

If building sand castles or tanning isn't your idea of a tantalizing time, explore isolated dunes, cliff-sheltered tide pools, and old pirate coves. Bring your dog (Fido's welcome here) and play an endless game of fetch, or go fishing—it's permitted from

Pismo Beach Pier, which also offers arcade entertainment, bowling, and billiards. Pismo is also the only beach in the area that allows all-terrain vehicles on the dunes.

Unfortunately, the town itself consists of little more than tourist shops and surf-and-turf restaurants. San Luis Obispo is a far more charming place to stay in this area, but if you want a few days on a beautiful beach at half the price of an oceanfront room in Santa Barbara, Pismo is a perfect choice.

ESSENTIALS

The **Pismo Beach Chamber of Commerce and Visitors Bureau,** 581 Dolliver St., Pismo Beach, CA 93448 (☎ **800/443-7778** in California, or 805/773-4382), offers free brochures and information on local attractions, lodging, and dining. The office is open Monday to Saturday from 9am to 5pm and Sunday from 10am to 4pm. You can peruse their information on the Internet at **webmill.com/pismo**.

WHAT TO SEE & DO

Beaches in Pismo are exceptionally wide, making them some of the best in the state for sunning and playing. The beach north of Grand Avenue is popular with families and well suited to jogging and strolling. North of Wadsworth Street, the coast becomes dramatically rugged as it rambles northward to Shell Beach and Pirates Cove. Some areas of the beach are open to all-terrain vehicles and automobiles.

Pismo Beach was once one of the most famous places in America for **clamming,** but the clam population was depleted almost to extinction. Government intervention has saved the clams, and you're now permitted to pick them up in limited numbers directly from the sand. Clams must measure at least $4^1/_2$ inches in diameter, and catches are limited to 10. You'll need to dig down about a foot to find them. Clam forks can be rented at **Pismo Bob's True Value Hardware,** 930 Price St. (☎ **805/773-6245**), for $5 per day.

No license is required to **fish** from Pismo Beach Pier. Catches here are largely bottom fish like red snapper and ling cod. There's a bait-and-tackle shop on the pier.

Livery Stables, 1207 Silver Spur Place (☎ **805/489-8100**), in Oceano (about 5 minutes south of Pismo Beach), is one of the very few places in the state that rents horses for riding on the beach. These are not guided rides; you rent the horses for $15 per hour and go at your own pace.

You can hike along the **Guadalupe-Nipomo Dunes** year-round. This 18-mile strip of coastline 20 minutes south of Pismo has the highest beach dunes in the West. It's a great place for observing native plants and birds, including the California brown pelican, one of 200 species that migrates here each year.

From late November to February, tens of thousands of migrating **monarch butterflies** take up residence in the area's eucalyptus and Monterey pine tree groves. The colorful butterflies form dense clusters on the trees, each hanging with its wings over the one below it, providing warmth and shelter for the entire group. During the monarchs' stay, naturalists at **Pismo State Beach** conduct 45-minute narrative walks every Saturday and Sunday at 11am and 2pm (call ☎ **805/772-2694** for tour information). Most of the "butterfly trees" are located on Calif. 1, between Pismo Beach and Grover Beach, to the south.

WHERE TO STAY

The Clamdigger. 150 Hinds Ave., Pismo Beach, CA 93449. ☎ **805/773-2342.** 10 studio cabins, 4 motel suites, 1 one-bedroom cottage. TV. $50–$75 cabin; $60–$90 suite; from $110 cottage. 7th night free. AE, DISC, DC, MC, V.

Who cares about blow dryers, VCRs, and plush new furnishings? This adorable cluster of cabins just south of the pier offers a true old-style California beach vacation.

Little more than a one-room shack on the beach (it does have a bathroom), each cabin welcomes you with a stained-glass ship on the door, a queen-size bed, cable TV, a kitchenette with microwave, a coffeemaker (bring your own ground beans), and basic furniture. The cottage has a queen-size bed and a hide-a-bed, a private deck, and it sleeps up to four. The motel suites sleep up to six. The place has some history, too—Valentino stayed here when he filmed on location in the 1920s. *Note:* Bedding can be a bit scratchy, so you may want to bring your own sheets.

SeaVenture Resort. 100 Ocean View Ave., Pismo Beach, CA 93449. ☎ **800/662-5545** or 805/773-4994. Fax 805/773-0924. 50 rms. MINIBAR TV TEL. $99–$289 double. Rates include continental breakfast. AE, DC, DISC, MC, V. Take U.S. 101 to the Price St. exit and turn west onto Ocean View (at the beach).

If luxury accommodations overlooking the beach and an outdoor spa on your private deck sound like heaven to you, head for SeaVenture, a brand-new resort providing the most luxurious accommodations in Pismo. Once in your room, you need only drag your tired traveling feet through the thick forest-green carpeting, past the white country furnishings, and turn on your gas fireplace to begin what promises to be a relaxing stay. Then rent a movie from the video library, schedule a massage, or simply bathe your weary bones in your own outdoor hydrotherapy spa tub. With the beach right outside your door, there's not much more you could ask for—although there *is*, in fact, more provided: a wet bar, refrigerator, coffeemaker, continental breakfast delivered to your room, and a restaurant on the premises. Most rooms have ocean views and many have a private balcony overlooking the beach. Services include room service from 4 to 10pm, laundry, and massage, and there's a swimming pool on the premises.

Surf Motel. 250 Main St., Pismo Beach, CA 39449. ☎ **800/472-7873** or 805/773-2070. 33 rms. TV TEL. $65–$85 double (lower on off-season weekends). Rates include continental breakfast. MC, V.

Strategically located just half a block from the beach, the Surf Motel is a good bet if you want basic, clean accommodations. All rooms have refrigerators; some have fully stocked kitchenettes. The indoor swimming pool is open year-round. Unless you prefer modernity and new motel amenities, however, you'll get more of Pismo's true flavor at the rustic oceanfront cottages of the Clamdigger.

WHERE TO DINE

PierSide Seafood. In the Boardwalk Plaza Mall, 175 Pomeroy St. ☎ **805/773-4411.** Reservations recommended on weekends. Main courses $9–$20. Summer daily 10am–11pm; winter Sun–Thurs 11am–9pm, Fri–Sat 11am–10pm. AE, DISC, MC, V. AMERICAN.

If the food is simply decent and the menu offers surf and turf just like every other place in town, why are we sending you here? Well, first of all, this 2-story restaurant is practically on top of Pismo Beach Pier, which gives it unparalleled views. Second, the decor is fun: Mermaids and surfboards hang overhead, and an array of trinkets and an ocean mural keep the eye wandering and interested throughout the meal. Finally, on a sunny day there's no better place to kick back than at one of the outdoor umbrella-topped tables. The place is *tourist maximus*, but few places here aren't.

Rosa's Italian Restaurant. 491 Price St. ☎ **805/773-0551.** Reservations recommended on weekends. Main courses $8–$15. AE, DC, DISC, MC, V. Mon–Fri 11:30am–2pm and 4–9:30pm, Sat–Sun 4–10pm. ITALIAN.

Look beyond the boring decor and you'll find that Rosa's is the finest Italian-American restaurant in town. It ain't Italy, but fresh bread is made on the premises, as are the ravioli, canneloni, and other pastas. Veal Parmesan, chicken cacciatore, and the fresh seafood dishes are dependably tasty. There are a few tables on a small heated patio, and though there's no ocean view, it's a welcome change from the overly abundant local surf-and-turf fare.

Splash Cafe. 197 Pomeroy St. (near Pismo Beach Pier). ☎ **805/773-4653.** Most items $2.50–$5.75. No credit cards. Daily 10am–8pm. AMERICAN.

This beachy burger stand, with a short menu and just a few tables, gets high marks for its excellent clam chowder, served in a sourdough bread bowl. Fish-and-chips, burgers, hot dogs, and sandwiches are also available.

5 En Route to Santa Barbara: The Santa Ynez Valley

The compact and beautiful Santa Ynez Valley (surrounded by mountains of the same name) is located between San Luis Obispo and Santa Barbara. The valley is home to five small towns: Buellton, Santa Ynez, Los Olivos, Ballard, and **Solvang,** the region's top tourist draw.

SOLVANG

Founded in 1911 by Danish-Americans originally intent on preserving their heritage, the old-country town of Solvang ("sunny valley" in Danish) has prostituted its Scandinavian heritage and become a popular and tacky tourist trap. The "quaint" village now looks as if Disney did Denmark, with white-and-blue fringed buildings housing hokey import shops and numerous pancake and pastry restaurants. Solvang's immense popularity has cost the town its charm. A trip here wouldn't ordinarily be worth going out of your way for—except that Solvang's **bakeries** are still among California's very best. Accordingly, it's worth a detour for lunch.

To reach Solvang from U.S. 101 south, turn east (left) onto Calif. 246 at Buellton; it's a well-marked 20-minute drive along an extremely scenic two-lane road. From Santa Barbara, take U.S. 101 north to Calif. 154, a truly breathtaking 45-minute drive over San Marcos Pass.

There's no real reason to stay here, since there are so many great places just to the north and south, but if you've just got to wake up here to eat more pastries, try Solvang's comfortable **Royal Scandinavian Inn** (☎ **800/624-5572** or 805/688-8000) or the good-value **Motel 6** (☎ **800/4-MOTEL6** or 805/688-7797), just west of Solvang in Buellton.

Old Mission Santa Ines. 1760 Mission Dr., Solvang. ☎ **805/688-4815.** $3 donation requested, free for children under 16. Summer, Mon–Fri 9am–7pm, Sat 9am–4pm, Sun 1:30–5:30pm; winter, Mon–Fri 9am–5:30pm, Sat 9am–4pm, Sun 1:30–5:30pm. From downtown Solvang, take Calif. 246 1 mile east to Mission Dr.

Founded in 1804, this perfectly restored mission is by far the oldest structure in town. The main building contains early Native American artifacts and relics once belonging to the missionaries. Like many other missions, Santa Ines still maintains an active congregation. The church, chapel, museum, and surrounding grounds are open to the public.

CACHUMA LAKE: A BALD EAGLE HABITAT

On Calif. 154 between Solvang and Santa Barbara, the **Cachuma Lake Recreation Area** surrounds Cachuma Lake, which is both the primary town reservoir for Santa Barbara and a particularly beautiful habitat for the American bald eagle. In the winter months dozens of bald eagles migrate here from as far north as Alaska, where food is plentiful, and human development minimal. Over the last few years some have chosen to remain at Cachuma to raise their young. Perching on treetops and branches overlooking the water, the eagles hunt for trout and waterfowl. Other migratory birds, including loons, white pelicans, and Canada geese, also come in large numbers.

You can simply drive into the recreation area and go birding on your own, or you can board the *Osprey* (☎ **805/568-2460**), a 48-foot boat with viewing platforms at both bow and stern. Two-hour Eagle Cruises are offered November to February, Wednesday to Sunday at 10am; additional tours are offered Fridays and Saturdays at 2pm. Wildlife Cruises, from which you can view deer, bobcats, and mountain lions, are offered March to October on Friday at 3pm, on Saturday at 10am and 3pm, and on Sunday at 10am. All cruises cost $10 for adults and $5 for children 11 and under; reservations are recommended. Contact the **Santa Barbara County Parks Department,** Cachuma Lake HC-58, Santa Barbara, CA 93105 (☎ **805/686-5054**).

6 Santa Barbara

Between the Santa Ynez Mountains and the Pacific, charming, spoiled Santa Barbara is coddled by wooded mountains, caressed by baby breakers, and sheltered from tempestuous seas by rocky offshore islands. And it's just far enough from Los Angeles to make the big city seem at once remote and accessible. There are few employment opportunities and real estate is expensive here, so demographics favor college students and rich retirees (referred to by the locals as the "almost wed and almost dead").

Downtown Santa Barbara is distinctive for its Spanish-Mediterranean architecture; all the structures sport matching red-tile roofs. But it wasn't always this way. Santa Barbara had a thriving Native American Chumash population for hundreds, if not thousands, of years. The European era began in the late 18th century, around a presidio (fort) that's been reconstructed in its original spot. The earliest architectural hodgepodge was destroyed in 1925 by a powerful earthquake that leveled the business district. Out of the rubble rose the Spanish-Mediterranean town of today, a stylish planned community that continues to rigidly enforce its strict building codes.

ESSENTIALS

GETTING THERE   U.S. 101 runs right through Santa Barbara; it's the fastest and most direct route from north or south (2 hours from Los Angeles, 6 hours from San Francisco).

The **Santa Barbara Municipal Airport** (☎ **805/967-7111**) is located in Goleta, about 10 minutes north of downtown Santa Barbara. Airlines serving Santa Barbara include American Eagle (☎ **800/433-7300**), Skywest/Delta (☎ **800/453-9417**), **United** (☎ **800/241-6522**), and **US Air Express** (☎ **800/428-4322**). **Yellow Cab** (☎ **805/965-5111**) and other metered taxis line up outside the terminal; the fare is about $20 to downtown.

Amtrak (☎ **800/USA-RAIL**) offers daily service to Santa Barbara. Trains arrive and depart from the **Santa Barbara Rail Station,** 209 State St. (☎ **805/963-1015**). Fares can be as low as $21 from Los Angeles.

VISITOR INFORMATION   The **Santa Barbara Visitor Information Center,** 1 Santa Barbara St., Santa Barbara, CA 93101 (☎ **800/927-4688,** or 805/965-3021 to order a free destination guide), is on the ocean, at the corner of Cabrillo Street. The staff distribute maps, literature, an events calendar, and excellent advice. Ask for their handy guide to places of interest and public parking. The office is open Monday to Saturday from 9am to 5pm and on Sunday from 10am to 5pm. Be sure to pick up a free copy of *Things to See and Do* at one of the offices.

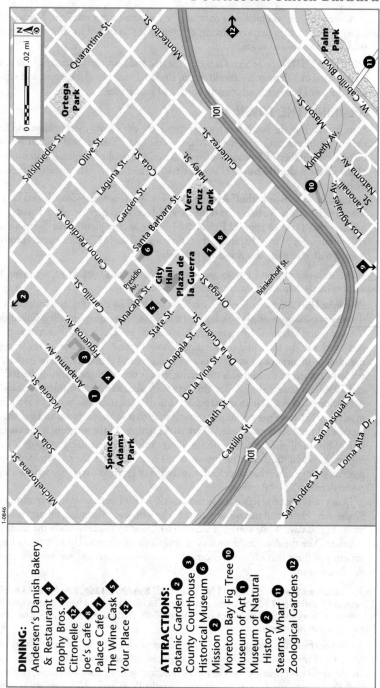

Downtown Santa Barbara

DINING:
Andersen's Danish Bakery & Restaurant 4
Brophy Bros. 9
Citronelle 12
Joe's Cafe 8
Palace Cafe 7
The Wine Cask 5
Your Place 12

ATTRACTIONS:
Botanic Garden 2
County Courthouse 3
Historical Museum 6
Mission 2
Moreton Bay Fig Tree 10
Museum of Art 1
Museum of Natural History 2
Stearns Wharf 11
Zoological Gardens 12

1-0846

385

Also make sure you pick up a copy of *The Independent,* an excellent, free weekly paper with a comprehensive listing of events. It's available in shops and from sidewalk racks around town.

ORIENTATION State Street is the geographic and commercial center of town. It ends at Stearns Wharf and Cabrillo Street; the latter runs along the ocean and separates the city's beaches from touristy hotels and restaurants.

EXPLORING THE TOWN

State Street from the beach to Victoria Street is the city's main thoroughfare and has the largest concentration of shops. Many specialize in T-shirts and postcards, but there are a number of boutiques as well. If you get tired of strolling, hop on one of the **electric shuttle buses** (25¢) that run up and down State Street at regular intervals.

Also check out **Brinkerhoff Avenue** (off Cota Street, between Chapala and De La Vina streets), Santa Barbara's "antique alley." Most shops here are open Tuesday to Sunday from 11am to 5pm. **El Paseo,** at 814 State St., is a picturesque shopping arcade reminiscent of an old Spanish street. Built around an 1827 adobe home, the mall is lined with charming shops and art galleries.

✪ **Santa Barbara Mission.** Laguna and Los Olivos sts. ☎ **805/682-4149.** Admission $3 adults, free for children 15 and under. Daily 9am–5pm.

Established in 1786 by Father Junípero Serra and built by the Chumash Indians, this is a very rare example of the blending of Indian and Hispanic spirituality. Called the "Queen of the Missions" for its twin bell towers and graceful beauty, this hilltop mission overlooks the town and the Channel Islands beyond. The design of the imposing church incorporates many Moorish and classical elements. Santa Barbara's residents embraced the church's distinctive look as the town grew during the 1920s and 1930s, utilizing red-roof tiles, thick stucco walls, arches, and outdoor arcades.

Brochures are available in six languages, and docent-guided tours can be arranged in advance ($1 extra per person). It's worthwhile to tour the museum and gift shop, established in the restored padres' quarters. A highlight of the museum is the collection of historical photographs of the buildings and the surrounding area, some dating from the 1850s, featuring brown-robed friars tending the old orchards and gardens. The gift shop has an extensive collection of crucifixes, religious statuary, and pottery crafted by local artisans.

Don't miss the cemetery outside the church, its yard populated with centuries of headstones, vaults, and mausoleums. Shaded by a majestic Australian fig tree, it's still in use to this day. While you're in the cemetery, take a minute to study the church's exterior. Over the door are three sets of skulls and crossbones. Upon careful observation, you'll see that only one is carved in stone—two sets are *real* bones embedded in the plaster.

Santa Barbara Museum of Art. 1130 State St. ☎ **805/963-4364.** Admission $4 adults, $3 seniors 65 and over, $1.50 students and children 6–16, free for children 5 and under, free for everyone Thurs and the first Sun of each month. Tues–Wed and Fri–Sat 11am–5pm, Thurs 11am–9pm, Sun noon–5pm.

A trip here feels like visiting the private galleries of a wealthy art collector. Works by Monet and other mid-quality oils by Dalí, Picasso, Matisse, Chagall, and Rousseau are displayed on a rotating basis in rooms that, for the most part, are ample, airy, and well lit. Quantitatively, the museum's strengths lie in early 20th-century western American paintings and 19th- and 20th-century Asian art. Qualitatively, the best are the antiquities and Chinese ceramics collections. Many pieces are often on loan to other museums, but good temporary exhibits show a high degree of reciprocity. Some awkward arrangements don't always make sense, and lighting could be improved on the placards. For the most part, though, Santa Barbara Museum of Art is a jewel of a museum. Free docent-led tours are given Tuesday to Sunday at 1pm. Focus tours are held on Wednesday and Saturday at noon. A new wing to be completed in 1998 is slated to include more galleries, a larger gift shop, and a cafe.

County Courthouse. 1100 Anacapa St. ☎ **805/962-6464.** Free admission. Mon–Fri 8am– 5pm, Sat–Sun and holidays 10am–4:45pm. Free guided tours Mon–Sat at 2pm, and Wed and Fri at 10:30am.

Even the accused are afforded exquisite surroundings in stunning Santa Barbara— the courthouse is the most flamboyant example of Spanish-Mediterranean architecture in the entire city. Built in 1929 to mimic a much older style, the ornate building is Santa Barbara's literal and figurative centerpiece. There are great views of the ocean, the mountains, and the city's terra-cotta–tile roofs from the observation deck atop the clock tower.

Moreton Bay Fig Tree. Chapala and Montecito sts.

Santa Barbara's best-known tree has a branch spread that would cover half a football field, and its roots run under more than an acre of ground. It is, hands down, the largest of its kind in the world. It's so broad, in fact, that an estimated 10,000 people could stand in its shade. Planted in 1877, it's a native of Moreton Bay in eastern Australia. The tree is related to both the fig and the rubber tree, but produces neither. Once in danger of being leveled for a proposed gas station and later threatened by excavation for nearby U.S. 101, the revered tree now shelters Santa Barbara's homeless.

Santa Barbara Botanic Garden. 1212 Mission Canyon Rd. ☎ **805/682-4726.** Admission $3 adults, $2 seniors 60 and over and children 13–19, $1 children 5–12, free for children 4 and under. Mon–Fri 9am–5pm, Sat–Sun 9am–6pm.

The gardens, about 1¹/₂ miles north of the mission, encompass 65 acres of native trees, shrubs, cacti, and wildflowers, and more than 5 miles of trails. They're at their aromatic peak just after spring showers. Docent tours are offered daily at 2pm, with additional tours on the weekend at 10:30am.

Santa Barbara Historical Museum. 136 E. De La Guerra St. ☎ **805/966-1601.** Free admission, but donations requested. Tues–Sat 10am–5pm, Sun noon–5pm.

Local-lore exhibits include late 19th-century paintings of the California missions by Edwin Deakin; a 16th-century carved Spanish coffer from Majorca, home of Junípero Serra; and objects from the Chinese community that once flourished here, including a magnificent carved shrine from the turn of the century. A knowledgeable docent leads an interesting free tour every Wednesday, Saturday, and Sunday at 1:30pm.

Santa Barbara Museum of Natural History. 2559 Puesta del Sol Rd. (2 blocks uphill from the mission). ☎ **805/682-4711.** Admission $5 adults, $4 seniors and teens, $3 children. Mon– Sat 9am–5pm, Sun and holidays 10am–5pm.

This museum focuses on the study and interpretation of Pacific Coast natural history, which includes mammals, birds, marine life, plants, and insects and displays ranging from fossil ferns to the complete skeleton of a blue whale. Native American history is emphasized in exhibits including basketry, textiles, and a full-size replica of a Chumash canoe. Recent additions include a replica of a pygmy mammoth skeleton and the "Lizard Lounge," featuring live reptiles and amphibians. An adjacent planetarium projects sky shows every Saturday and Sunday.

Santa Barbara Zoological Gardens. 500 Ninos Dr. ☎ **805/962-5339,** or 805/962-6310 for a recording. Admission $6 adults, $4 seniors and children 2–12, free for children under 2. Daily 10am–5pm (last admission is 1 hour before closing). Closed Thanksgiving Day and Christmas Day.

When you're driving around the bend on Cabrillo Beach Boulevard, look up—you might spot the head of a giraffe poking up through the palms. This is a thoroughly charming, pint-sized place, where all 700 animals can be seen in about 30 minutes. Most of the animals live in natural, open settings. The zoo has a children's Discovery Area, a miniature train ride, and a small carousel. The picnic areas (complete with barbecue pits) are underutilized and especially recommendable.

Stearns Wharf. At the end of State St.

In addition to a small collection of second-rate shops, attractions, and restaurants, the city's 1872-vintage pier offers terrific inland views and good drop-line fishing. The Dolphin Fountain at the foot of the wharf was created by local artist Bud Bottoms for the city's 1982 bicentennial.

BEACHES & OUTDOOR PURSUITS

BEACHES   Santa Barbara has an array of beaches perfect for stretching out on a towel, playing volleyball, or frolicking seaside. **Hendry's Beach,** at the end of Cliff Drive, is popular with families, boogie-boarders who come to ride the excellent beach breaks, and sunset strollers. ✪ **Cabrillo Beach** is a wide swath of clean white sand that hosts beach umbrellas, sand-castle builders, and spirited volleyball games. A grassy, parklike median keeps the noise of busy Cabrillo Boulevard away. On Sunday local artists set up shop beneath the palms.

Note: A tragic oil spill off the coast of Santa Barbara in 1969 left surfers and sea critters dodging gobs of floating tar for the next 20 years. Although the area has finally cleared up, the staining brown substance still finds its way onto clothes and skin from time to time even if you don't go in the water (that's why the Four Seasons Biltmore hotel includes "Tar Off" in its baskets of toiletry goodies).

BIKING   A relatively flat, palm-lined, 2-mile coastal pathway runs along the beach and is perfect for biking. More adventurous riders can pedal through town, up to the mission, or to Montecito, the next town over. The best mountain-bike trail begins at the end of Tunnel Road and climbs up along a paved fire road before turning into a dirt trail to the mountaintop.

Beach Rentals, 22 State St. (☎ **805/966-6733**), rents well-maintained one-speeds. They also have tandem bikes and surrey cycles that can hold as many as four adults and two children. Rates vary depending on equipment. Bring your driver's license or passport to expedite your rental. They're open daily from 8am to dusk.

GOLF   At the **Santa Barbara Golf Club,** 3500 McCaw Ave., at Las Positas Road (☎ 805/687-7087), there's a great 18-hole, 6,009-yard course and driving range. Unlike many municipal courses, the Santa Barbara Golf Course is well maintained and was designed to present a moderate challenge for the average golfer. Greens fees are $24 Monday to Friday and $28 on weekends ($17 for seniors). Optional carts rent for $20 for 18 holes, $10 for 9 holes.

The 18-hole, 7,000-yard **Sandpiper** course, at 7925 Hollister Ave. (☎ **805/ 968-1541**), a scenic oceanside course, has a pro shop and driving range, plus an enormous new clubhouse. Greens fees are $60 Monday to Thursday and $90 Friday to Sunday. Carts cost $24.

HIKING   The hills and mountains surrounding Santa Barbara have excellent hiking trails. One of our favorites begins at the end of Tunnel Road. Take Mission

Canyon Road past the mission, turn right onto Foothill Road, and take the first left onto Mission Canyon Drive. Bear left onto Tunnel Road and park at the end (where all the other cars are). You can buy a trail map at the Santa Barbara Visitor Information Center (see "Essentials," above).

HORSEBACK RIDING   Several area stables rent horses, including the **Circle Bar B Ranch,** 1800 Refugio Rd. (☎ **805/968-3901**), and **Rancho Oso,** Paradise Road, off Calif. 154 (☎ **805/964-8985**).

POWERBOATING & SAILING   The **Sailing Center of Santa Barbara,** at the Santa Barbara Breakwater (☎ **800/350-9090** or 805/962-2826), rents sailboats from 13 to 50 feet, as well as powerboats, kayaks, and jet skis. Both crewed and bare-boat charters are available by the day or hour. Sailing instruction for all levels of experience is also available. Coastal, island, whale-watching, dinner, and adventure tours are also available on the 50-foot sailing catamaran *Double Dolphin.*

SKATING   The paved beach path that runs along Santa Barbara's waterfront is perfect for skating. **Beach Rentals,** 22 State St. (☎ **805/966-6733**), located nearby, rents in-line skates. The $5-per-hour fee includes wrist and knee pads.

SPORTFISHING, DIVE CRUISES & WHALE WATCHING   **Sea Landing,** at the foot of Bath Street and Cabrillo Boulevard (☎ **805/963-3564**), makes regular sportfishing runs from specialized boats. It also offers a wide variety of other fishing and diving cruises. Food and drink are served on board, and rental rods and tackle are available. Rates vary according to excursion; call for reservations.

Whale-watching cruises are offered from February to April, when California gray whales make their migratory journey from Baja California, Mexico, to Alaska. Tours are $24 for adults and $14 for children; sightings of large marine mammals are guaranteed.

WHERE TO STAY

Before you even begin calling around for reservations, keep in mind that Santa Barbara's accommodations are expensive—especially in summer. Then decide whether you'd like to stay beachside (even more expensive) or downtown. The town is small, but not small enough to happily stroll between the two areas.

Hot Spots Accommodations, 36 State St., Santa Barbara, CA 93101 (☎ **800/793-7666** or 805/564-1637), a one-stop shop for hotel, motel, and B&B rooms, keeps an updated list of what's available in all price categories. There's no charge for their services. Significantly discounted rates are often available at the last minute, when hotels need to fill their rooms.

Another option is **Accommodations Reservations Service** (☎ **800/292-2222**), a company that books rooms along California's coast from Oxnard to Monterey. The service is free and has information on all price ranges.

VERY EXPENSIVE

✪ **Four Seasons Biltmore.** 1260 Channel Dr. (at the end of Olive Mill Rd.), Santa Barbara, CA 93108. ☎ **800/332-3442** or 805/969-2261. Fax 805/969-4682. 234 rms, 24 suites. MINIBAR TV TEL. $335–$475 double; from $675 suite. Additional person $30 extra. Special midweek and package rates available. AE, DC, MC, V.

If you've got the bucks, you can't do better than this. The now-divorced king and queen of tattoo-and-lace, Tommy Lee (Motley Crue) and Heather Locklear (*Melrose Place*), tied the knot with class at the beach club next door and later indulged in the hotel's infamously decadent Sunday brunch. They weren't the first to celebrate here— other Hollywood highbrows such as Greta Garbo, Errol Flynn, and Bing Crosby also knew that the Biltmore is one of the most beautiful hotels in the country. Although the hotel debuted in 1927, Four Seasons acquired the property in 1987 and brought its beauty to its full potential with a $20-million renovation.

Today the hotel still captivates guests with Spanish Revival architecture, hand-painted Mexican tiles, and 19 acres of incredibly landscaped oceanfront gardens. It has a light, warm aura, with flora and fauna almost everywhere you look. The guest rooms are less elaborate but come complete with comfortable beds, fluffy towels and robes, and bath soaps you can't help but pack in your luggage when you depart. They also boast striking views of the mountains or the ocean, and some have Spanish balconies and/or fireplaces, or private patios; all come with VCRs.

Dining/Entertainment: This is resort dining at its finest. The elegant La Marina offers surprisingly innovative specialties. The Patio is more casual, serving three meals daily and Santa Barbara's best Sunday brunch; it's a beautiful setting, with an oceanfront view, indoor and outdoor seating, and a retractable atrium roof. La Sala is a comfortable lounge serving afternoon tea and evening cocktails; there's live jazz on Wednesday and Friday nights.

Services: Concierge, room service (24 hours), laundry service, nightly turndown, twice-daily maid service, overnight shoe shine.

Facilities: Two outdoor heated pools, two health clubs, sundeck, three lighted tennis courts, shuffleboard and croquet courts, complimentary bicycle use, putting green, beachfront cabanas, special children's programs, beauty salon, gift shop.

✪ **San Ysidro Ranch.** 900 San Ysidro Lane (off U.S. 101), Montecito, CA 93108. ☎ **800/368-6788** or 805/969-5046. Fax 805/565-1995. 43 cottages, 15 suites. MINIBAR TV TEL. $240–$475 cottage for 2; from $575 suite. AE, MC, V.

For 100 years, folks (such as Vivien Leigh and Laurence Olivier, who were married here) have come here to replenish themselves, and for good reason: One night here, and you'll feel like you've vacationed a week—but you won't be ready to leave, by any means.

Imagine a summer camp for the wealthy: quaint winding trails overgrown with wildflowers and trees, peaceful rolling hills beyond, and 540 acres of lush countryside all around. San Ysidro Ranch is just that—a rustically indulgent retreat for those who are lucky enough to be able to afford it. This is the kind of place where the noisiest time of day is when the sun comes up and birds begin to celebrate their surroundings; a strenuous afternoon consists of leaning up from a poolside lounge chair to accept a bowl of complimentary berries from an accommodating pool hand.

Upon arrival, guests are escorted to their freestanding "cottages" (with their last name posted in rustic block letters next to the door), which were renovated in 1996 and are impeccably outfitted in country luxury, with a wood-burning stove or fireplace, outdoor terrace, goose-down comforter and Frette linens, VCR, and dozens of other amenities that'll pamper every aspect of your being. Each individually decorated accommodation feels more like a rich uncle's country home than a resort and boasts such personal touches as books and magazines, fresh flowers, and a stereo with CDs.

Facilities: The property has tennis courts, a fitness center and exercise course, spa treatments, and a renowned restaurant.

EXPENSIVE

El Encanto. 1900 Lasuen Rd., Santa Barbara, CA 93103. ☎ **800/346-7039** or 805/687-5000. Fax 805/687-3903. 84 rms. MINIBAR TV TEL. $180–$290 double; from $380 suite. AE, DC, MC, V.

On 10 acres of hillside overlooking Santa Barbara, El Encanto is a romantic retreat perched high enough above the city to afford incredible Pacific Ocean and town views, but low enough that it's still close to all the action. This vintage getaway was built in 1915 in a combination of craftsman cottage and Spanish colonial revival. Enchanting gardens with sitting nooks and lush landscaping surround the bungalow and cottage-style accommodations, which are tastefully decorated with wood furnishings, oriental carpets, and English-country prints. Many rooms have fireplaces, hardwood floors, and patios or balconies.

The romantic restaurant is highly regarded for both its view and its fare. Facilities include a pool, tennis court, and library.

Montecito Inn. 1295 Coast Village Rd., Santa Barbara, CA 93108. ☎ **800/843-2017** or 805/969-7854. Fax 805/969-0623. 50 rms, 10 suites. $150–$195 double; from $225 suite. Rates include continental breakfast. 2-night minimum stay on weekends. AE, DISC, MC, V. From U.S. 101, take the Olive Mill Rd. exit and turn west on Olive Mill Rd. to Coast Village.

This Mediterranean-style inn isn't at 95% capacity year-round just because Charlie Chaplin built it in 1928 to serve as Hollywood elite's romantic retreat. It's in demand because it's professional and charming. The guest rooms are not as impressive as some of the common areas adorned with Chaplin memorabilia, but are well appointed with French provincial–style furnishings, floral prints, and hand-painted tiles in the small bathrooms; some have VCRs and refrigerators. The new luxury suites are eye-poppingly lavish, with large living rooms and bedrooms and Italian marble bathrooms bigger than many hotel rooms we've seen; Jacuzzi tubs and fireplaces put them over the top. The only drawback is the lack of views.

Out back are a small heated pool, spa, and sauna. Athletic folks will enjoy the free touring bikes and exercise room.

The Upham. 1404 De La Vina St. (at Sola St.), Santa Barbara, CA 93101. ☎ **800/727-0876** or 805/962-0058. Fax 805/963-2825. 50 rms, 4 suites. TV TEL. $130–$195 double; from $260 suite. Rates include continental breakfast. AE, CB, DC, DISC, MC, V.

This upscale B&B right in the heart of town celebrated its 125th anniversary in 1996. What's kept it so popular for so long? It could be the great service, which keeps businesspeople happy. Or maybe the European atmosphere, which makes foreigners feel right at home. Or perhaps it's the accommodations themselves—they have private entrances and are distinctively outfitted with some truly impressive antiques, and brass or four-poster beds; many even have private porches and fireplaces. Combined with the complimentary continental breakfast and evening wine and cheese served in the lobby and garden (with a feisty cat that hangs out at the gazebo), the Upham is a charming alternative to other downtown hotels. Louie's at the Upham, a cozy restaurant, is open for lunch and dinner.

MODERATE

In addition to the listing below, there are moderately priced rooms at the **Best Western Encina Lodge and Suites** (☎ 800/526-2282 or 805/682-7277) and **Tropicana Inn and Suites** (☎ 800/468-1988 or 805/966-2219).

✪ **Bath Street Inn.** 1720 Bath St. (north of Valerio St.), Santa Barbara, CA 93101. ☎ **800/341-BATH,** 800/549-BATH in CA, or 805/682-9680. 12 rms. TV TEL. $100–$190 double. Rates include breakfast. Midweek rates up to 25% off. AE, MC, V.

This is one of the cutest, most meticulously cared for B&Bs we've ever seen. The minute we walked in, a gracious innkeeper guided us to the redwood patio to see an amazing wisteria canopy in bloom (lucky guests can have breakfast beneath it). We were then treated to fresh-baked cookies, which are served with tea and wine each afternoon. After our snack, we wandered from room to room, astonished by the exquisite details of each nook and cranny throughout the 3-story Victorian (two unique features include a semicircular "eyelid" balcony and a hipped roof). Each adorable (and immaculate) room is intimately and individually decorated with antiques, colorful wallpaper, and fresh flowers. Some include a Jacuzzi and/or a VCR. The common areas are equally attractive and include a third-floor reading nook with a VCR (there's a video library downstairs). No smoking.

INEXPENSIVE

All the best buys fill up fast in the summer months, so be sure to reserve your room well in advance—even if you're just planning to stay at the nice, reliable **Motel 6** (☎ **800/4-MOTEL6** or 805/564-1392) near the beach, or the good-value **Sandpiper Lodge** (☎ **805/687-5326**) just a little farther away.

✪ **Casa del Mar Inn at the Beach.** 18 Bath St., Santa Barbara, CA 93101. ☎ **800/433-3097** or 805/963-4418. Fax 805/966-4240. Website: www.casadelmar.com. 14 rms, 7 suites. TV TEL. $79–$169 double; from $114 suite. Rates include continental breakfast and wine-and-cheese social. Additional person $10 extra; $10 extra per pet. Midweek discounts available. AE, DISC, DC, MC, V. From northbound U.S. 101, exit at Cabrillo, turn left onto Cabrillo and head toward the beach; Bath is second street on right after the wharf. From southbound U.S. 101, take the Castillo exit, turn right on Castillo, left on Cabrillo, and left on Bath.

A half block from the beach (sorry, no views), Casa del Mar is an excellent-value motel with one- and two-room suites. The largish rooms have brand-new furnishings, with plenty of pastels. The flower-sprinkled grounds are well maintained, and the staff is eager to please. Many rooms have kitchenettes, fridges, and stoves. The Jacuzzi here stays open half an hour later than the neighboring Francisan's. Considering the prices of hotels in this town, Casa del Mar is a great bargain.

Franciscan Inn. 109 Bath St. (at Mason St.), Santa Barbara, CA 93101. ☎ **805/963-8845.** Fax 805/564-3295. 53 rms, 25 suites. TV TEL. $65–$99 double; from $85 suite. Rates include continental breakfast. Additional person $8 extra. AE, CB, DC, MC, V.

One of the best bargains beachside can be found a block from the shore at the Franciscan Inn. The exterior is motel-like. Inside, the rooms are a quirky combination of country pine furnishings and floral and plaid prints. In some cases the decor just doesn't work, but the immaculate, recently renovated rooms and the price more than make up for it. Several rooms have fully equipped kitchenettes and/or balconies, and most bathrooms come with a tub. All rooms have coffeemakers, computer jacks, and VCRs; hair dryers are available upon request. The suites come complete with a living room, a separate kitchen, and sleeping quarters for up to four adults; one has a fireplace. Breakfast, afternoon appetizers, and a complimentary newspaper are included in the price, as is the use of the heated outdoor pool, Jacuzzi, and coin-operated laundry. Reserve well in advance, especially for May to September.

Orange Tree Inn. 1920 State St., Santa Barbara, CA 93101. ☎ **800/LEM-ORNG** or 805/569-1521. 44 rms, 2 suites. A/C TV TEL. $65–$150 double; from $90 suite. AE, DISC, MC, V.

We'd personally prefer to stay by the beach, but if you want cheap downtown accommodations, you're safe with the Orange Tree. Don't get too excited, though—it's a motel. Still, the rooms are newly renovated and have new carpets and bedspreads. Most have a balcony or patio, and some have bathtubs. Guests also get free local calls and use of the pool.

WHERE TO DINE
EXPENSIVE

✪ **Citronelle.** At the Santa Barbara Inn, 901 Cabrillo Blvd. ☎ **805/966-2285.** Main courses $22–$24. AE, DISC, MC, V. Daily noon–9pm. CALIFORNIA/FRENCH.

Chef Felicien Cueff heads the kitchen at Michel Richard's (of L.A.'s ultrapopular Citrus) upscale but casual restaurant. The dining room is remarkably airy and lined with windows that allow panoramic views of the ocean and promenade across the street. The atmosphere is peaceful and the room pleasantly quiet, except for the buzz of nearby diners and, on some evenings, live guitar music. Request a windowside table, order a bottle from the fine selection of wines, and dine à la carte or from the four- or five-course tasting menu. Each dish is delicately prepared, and meats and fish are always cooked to perfection. Most plates come with an exotic sauce that can, on occasion, overpower the subtle flavor of the courses themselves, but a few dishes we've sampled here are as fine as they come. If the roasted Chilean sea bass with lime sauce and mashed potatoes is on the menu, don't pass it up. Finish the meal with a dessert we've fantasized about ever since finishing up the last crumbs: crème brûlée layered with caramelized phyllo dough.

El Encanto. 1900 Lasuen Rd. ☎ **805/687-5000.** Main courses $14–$24.50. AE, DC, MC, V. Daily 7:30–10:30am, 11am–2pm, and 6–9:30pm. AMERICAN/ITALIAN.

Clinging to the hillside above Santa Barbara is El Encanto, a hotel and restaurant known for its romantic ambiance and breathtaking ocean views. But the fare doesn't take a backseat here; anyone who flies his salmon in from Scotland and the wood from the south of England obviously takes his food seriously. Starters include a superb lobster bisque and the incredible mussels a la mariniere (white wine, onions, and parsley sauce). Main courses include a perfectly cooked, roasted breast of free-range pheasant with celery root puree, pinot noir sauce, and veggies; and a tender sautéed sea bass with tarragon crust and garlic mashed potatoes with tomato and basil coulis. Don't miss the fantastic napoleon of chocolate, a perfect, sinful treat. The restaurant also has an excellent wine selection.

✪ **The Palace Café.** 8 E. Cota St. (at State St.). ☎ **805/963-5000.** Reservations limited: Sun–Thurs, and Fri–Sat from 5:30–6pm only. Main courses $11.75–$25. AE, MC, V. Sun–Thurs 5:30–10pm, Fri–Sat 5:30–11pm. CAJUN/CREOLE/CARIBBEAN.

When a restaurant stays this popular for more than 10 years, you know it's onto something, and when we ate here, its lure was obvious. When there's a line out the door (always the case on weekends), The Palace makes the wait enjoyable by serving free appetizers and providing live entertainment (weekends only) by a local magician. Inside the divided dining room, amidst the jazz memorabilia, lively music, and high ceilings, the staff pampers you silly as they provide you with an overflow of Cajun, Creole, and Caribbean favorites. We tried a knockout rum punch, splendid oysters Rockefeller, an outstanding blackened filet mignon, an absolutely divine blackened salmon, and some crispy Louisiana soft-shelled crabs, which were wonderful. Portions are large, but we did manage to squeeze in a few bites of the key lime pie and bread pudding soufflé—both very tasty. But it's not just the food that's outstanding and festive here. The atmosphere follows suit, even offering a unique sing-along surprise. The experience as a whole is the stuff of vacation memories.

✪ **Pan e Vino.** 1482 E. Valley Rd., Montecito. ☎ **805/969-9274.** Reservations required. Pastas $8–$10; meat and fish dishes $11–$19. AE, MC, V. Mon–Sat 11:30am–9:30pm, Sun 5:30–9:30pm. ITALIAN.

The perfect Italian trattoria, Pan e Vino offers food as authentic as you'd find in Rome. The simplest dish, spaghetti topped with basil-tomato sauce, is so delicious it's hard to understand why diners would want to occupy their taste buds with more complicated concoctions. But this kitchen is capable of almost anything. A whole-artichoke appetizer, steamed, chilled, and filled with breading and marinated

Vintage Central Coast

Have a penchant for a pinot noir? Craving a sauvignon blanc? Central California's dewy green hillsides and sun-kissed valleys have the perfect climate for grape growing. Though this budding wine country can't boast of hundreds of wineries or as many awards as its Northern California neighbor, it's definitely coming into its own. And even if you don't know the difference between Ernest & Julio Gallo and Dom Perignon, this region is a wonderful place to spend a relaxing day.

Central California has three distinct wine regions. The Paso Robles and Edna Valley/Arroyo Grande Valley wine-country regions are close to Cambria and San Luis Obispo, and the Santa Barbara wine region stretches along Santa Ynez Valley's mountainous terrain.

There are more than 35 wineries in the Paso Robles area, and among them is **Arciero Winery,** 6 miles east of U.S. 101 on Calif. 46 (☎ **805/239-2562**), which is open daily from 10am to 5pm and offers a lovely picnic area off the tasting room. **Bonny Doon** is at Sycamore Farms, 3 miles west of U.S. 101 on Calif. 46 (☎ **805/239-5614**). It's open daily from 10:30am to 5:30pm. And **Wild Horse,** located at 1437 Wild Horse Winery Court in Templeton (☎ **805/434-2541**), is open daily from 11am to 5pm except most major holidays.

The 18 wineries in Edna Valley/Arroyo Grande are a quick jaunt from the town of San Luis Obispo. Some recommended stops include **Corbett Canyon,** 2195 Corbett Canyon Rd., San Luis Obispo (☎ **805/544-5800**), which offers tastings daily from 10am to 4:30pm; **Edna Valley Vineyard,** 2585 Biddle Ranch Rd., San Luis Obispo (☎ **805/544-9594**), which is open daily from 10am to 4pm; and **Maison Deutz,** 453 Deutz Dr., Arroyo Grande (☎ **805/481-1763**), which is open Wednesday to Monday from 11am to 5pm.

For information on wine events, wineries, accommodations, and a winery map, write or call the **Paso Robles Vintners and Growers Association,** P.O. Box 324,

tomatoes, is absolutely fantastic. Pasta puttenesca, with tomatoes, anchovies, black olives, and capers, is always tops. Pan e Vino gets high marks for its terrific food, attentive service, and casual atmosphere. Although many diners prefer to eat outside on the intimate patio, some of the best tables are in the charming, cluttered dining room.

Wine Cask. 813 Anacapa St. (in El Paseo Center). ☎ **805/966-9463.** Reservations recommended. Main courses $8–$12 at lunch, $17–$23 at dinner. AE, DC, MC, V. Mon–Fri 11:30am–3:30pm, Sat–Sun 10am–3pm; Sun–Thurs 5:30–9pm, Fri–Sat 5:30–10pm. ITALIAN.

Take a 15-year-old wine shop; a large dining room with a big stone fireplace; a few large, abstract paintings; a hand-stenciled, gold-leaf, 1920s historic-landmark ceiling; and outstanding Italian fare. Mix them with an attractive (albeit stuffy) staff and clientele, and you've got the Wine Cask—one of the most popular upscale dining spots in Santa Barbara. Whether you go for the dining room (request fireside for romance) or patio dining (yes, there are heat lamps), you'll be treated to such creations as lamb sirloin with wild-mushroom risotto, toasted pine nuts, and truffle-infused pinot noir sauce or grilled swordfish with saffron quinoa, sautéed snow peas, carrot and pea shoots, wasabi butter sauce, and mango coulis and ginger swirl (whew!). The wine list reads like a novel, with over 1,000 wines (ranging from $14 to $1,400) and has deservedly received the *Wine Spectator* award for excellence. There's also a happy hour at the beautiful maple bar from 4 to 6pm daily. For cigars and a cozy cocktail

Paso Robles, CA 93447 (☎ **805/239-VINE**) and the **Edna Valley Arroyo Grande Valley Vintners Association,** 2195 Corbett Canyon Rd., Arroyo Grande, CA 93420 (☎ **805/541-5868**). Also contact the **San Luis Obispo County Visitors & Conference Bureau,** 1037 Mill St., San Luis Obispo, CA 93401 (☎ **800/ 634-1414** or 805/541-8000), for a free "Bounty of the County" food and wine tour map.

The Santa Ynez Mountains combined with coastal fog and ocean breezes make Santa Barbara County another prime grape-growing spot. There are more than 10,000 acres of vineyards here and dozens of wineries, but the drive over the coastal hills alone makes it worth the trip. But once you hit the wine country, you'll find some well-respected wineries amid the gorgeous Central California mountain range.

You'll be best off picking up a wine-country touring map, which offers information on locations, hours of operation, and picnic and touring facilities. It's free at many hotels and shops around Santa Barbara, including the Wine Cask (see "Where to Dine" in the Santa Barbara section of this chapter above). You can also order it by mail from the **Santa Barbara County Vintners Association,** P.O. Box 1558, Santa Ynez, CA 93460 (☎ **800/218-0881** or 805/688-0881).

A few recommended stops include the **Fess Parker Winery,** located at 6200 Foxen Canyon Rd., Los Olivos (☎ **805/688-1545**), which is open daily from 10am to 5pm; the **Gainey Vineyard,** at 3950 E. Calif. 246, Santa Ynez (☎ **805/ 688-0558**), which is open daily from 10am to 5pm; **Firestone Vineyard,** at 5017 Zaca Station Rd., Los Olivos (☎ **805/688-3940**), which is open daily from 10am to 5pm; and **Sunstone Vineyards & Winery,** at 125 N. Refugio Rd., Santa Ynez (☎ **800/313-WINE** or 805/688-WINE), which is open daily from 10am to 4pm.

environment, check out the Wine Cask Intermezzo cafe, their latest addition, which offers coffee drinks, bistro-style dining, and a lovely selection of wines from 7am to 11pm daily.

MODERATE

Brophy Bros. Clam Bar & Restaurant. Yacht Basin and Marina (at Harbor Way). ☎ **805/ 966-4418.** Reservations not accepted. Main courses $9–$16. AE, MC, V. Daily 11am–10pm. SEAFOOD.

First-class seafood combined with an unbeatable view of the marina makes dining here a favorite of both tourists and locals. Dress is casual, service is excellent, portions are huge, and everything on the menu is good. Favorites include New England clam chowder, *cioppino,* and any one of an assortment of seafood salads. The scampi is consistently good, as is all the fresh fish, which come with soup or salad, coleslaw, and pilaf or French fries. A nice assortment of beers and wines is available. *Be forewarned:* The wait at this small place can be up to 2 hours on a weekend night.

Joe's Cafe. 536 State St. (at Cota St.). ☎ **805/966-4638.** Reservations recommended. Main courses $9–$19. AE, DISC, MC, V. Mon–Thurs 11am–11:30pm, Fri–Sat 11am–12:30am, Sun 4– 11pm. AMERICAN.

Joe's may not have the best kitchen in town, but it's an institution (around since 1928). The feel is hunting-lodge-cum-picnic, and the menu offers lots of old-school choices: plenty of red meat (five different steak options), Southern fried chicken, and a shrimp dish and garden burger thrown in for good measure. Meals come with a barrage of side dishes. On weekends, the full bar turns out plenty of strong cocktails and late-night dinners to partying students.

Montecito Cafe. 1295 Coast Village Rd. (off Olive Mill Rd.). ☎ **805/969-3392.** Reservations recommended. Main courses $7–$13. AE, MC, V. Daily 10:30am–2:30pm and 5:30–10pm. CALIFORNIA NOUVEAU.

Overlooking Montecito's shopping street, the light and airy Montecito Cafe provides diners a high-quality culinary experience at an affordable price (some say it's the best value in the area). Menu items include a watercress salad with sesame vinaigrette and broiled oysters; an emmenthal-cheese-filled pork chop with lemon-wine-herb sauce; and capellini with mushrooms, tomato, basil, olive oil, and wine. The petite dining room itself is pleasantly simple, with well-set tables, a wall of windows, plants, a small fountain, and original art—it's the perfect place to impress a date.

Your Place. 22-A N. Milpas St. (at Mason St.). ☎ **805/966-5151.** Reservations recommended. Main courses $7–$13. AE, DC, MC, V. Tues–Thurs and Sun 11am–10pm, Fri–Sat 11am–10pm. THAI.

There are lots of Thai restaurants in Santa Barbara, but when locals argue about which one is best, Your Place invariably ranks high on the list. Traditional dishes are prepared with the freshest ingredients and represent a wide cross section of Thai cuisine. It's best to begin with *tom kah kai,* a hot-and-sour chicken soup with coconut milk and mushrooms, ladled out of a hotpot tableside—enough for two or more. Siamese duckling, a top main dish, is prepared with sautéed vegetables, mushrooms, and ginger sauce. Like other dishes, it can be made mild, medium, hot, or very hot.

INEXPENSIVE

Andersen's Danish Bakery and Restaurant. 1106 State St. (near Figueroa St.). ☎ **805/962-5085.** Reservations recommended on weekends. Breakfast $4–$8; lunch $5–$8. No credit cards. Wed–Mon 8am–8pm. DANISH.

Grandma will feel at home here and kids won't have a problem finding something they like on the menu (especially when it comes to dessert). The Danish Ms. Andersen greets you herself (when she's not baking) and offers substantial (and cheap!) portions of New York steak, chicken or crab salad, and an array of other edibles (including an honest-to-goodness smörgåsbord). Seating provides great State Street people-watching from both in- and outdoor tables.

La Super-Rica Taquería. 622 N. Milpas St. (between Cota and Ortega sts.). ☎ **805/963-4940.** Reservations not accepted. Main courses $3–$6. No credit cards. Daily 11am–9pm. MEXICAN.

Following celebrity chef Julia Child's lead, aficionados have deemed this place the state's best Mexican restaurant. Excellent soft tacos are the restaurant's real forte. Unfortunately, portions can be quite small—you have to order two or three items in order to satisfy an average hunger. There's nothing grand about La Super-Rica except the food; you might want to get your order to go and take it to the beach.

SANTA BARBARA AFTER DARK

To find out what's going on while you're in town, check the free weekly *The Independent,* or call the following venues: the **Center Stage Theater,** upstairs at the Paseo Nuevo Shopping Center, Chapala and De La Guerra streets (☎ **805/963-0408**); the **Lobero Theater,** 33 E. Canon Perdido St. (☎ **805/963-0761**); the **Arlington Theater,** 1317 State St. (☎ **805/963-4408**); and the **Earl Warren Showgrounds,** at Las Positas Road and U.S. 101 (☎ **805/687-0766**).

A young crowd spills out of the bars on lower State Street, while an older clientele flocks to a number of quieter destinations in the area. Here are a couple of our favorites:

Madhouse Martini Lounge. 434 State St. ☎ **805/962-5516.** No cover.

Young singles pack into this cocktail lounge that's eclectically decorated with Oriental rugs and interesting trinkets hanging overhead. Order a drink from one of the attractive young bartenders or forge your way to the back room—a heated, covered patio that's jazzed up with colorful hanging lamps, pool table, and "decayed grandeur decor"—where there's another bar and a little extra elbow room. The "Liquid Therapy" happy hour runs from 5 to 8 nightly and features a number of drink specials, and Tuesday nights feature live music.

Mel's. In the Paseo Nuevo Mall, 6 W. De La Guerra St. ☎ **805/963-2211.** No cover.

The compact bar of this old drinking dive in the heart of downtown attracts a good cross section of regulars.

7 The Ojai Valley

by Stephanie Avnet

In a crescent-shaped valley between Santa Barbara and Ventura, surrounded by mountain peaks, lies Ojai (pronounced "*o*-hi"). It's a magical place, selected by Frank Capra as Shangri-La, the legendary utopia of his 1936 classic *Lost Horizon*. The spectacularly tranquil setting has made Ojai a mecca for artists and a particularly large population of New Age spiritualists, both drawn by the area's mystical beauty.

Life is low-key in the peaceful Ojai Valley. Perhaps the most excitement generated all year happens during the first week of June, when the **Ojai Music Festival** draws world-renowned contemporary jazz artists to perform in the Libbey Bowl amphitheater.

While in Ojai, you're bound to hear folks wax poetic about something called the "pink moment." It's a phenomenon first noticed by the earliest Native American valley dwellers, when the brilliant sunset over the nearby Pacific is reflected onto the mountainside, creating an eerie and beautiful pink glow.

ESSENTIALS

GETTING THERE   The 45-minute drive south from Santa Barbara to Ojai is along two-lane Calif. 150, a beautiful road that's as curvaceous as it is stunning. From Los Angeles, take U.S. 101 north to Calif. 33, which winds through eucalyptus groves to meet Calif. 150—the trip takes about 90 minutes. Calif. 150 is called Ojai Avenue in the town center and is the village's primary thoroughfare.

VISITOR INFORMATION   The **Ojai Valley Chamber of Commerce,** 150 W. Ojai Ave., Ojai, CA 93023 (☎ 805/646-8126), distributes free area maps, brochures, and a *Visitor's Guide to the Ojai Valley,* which lists galleries and current events It's open daily from 10am to 4pm. For information on the **Ojai Music Festival,** call ☎ 805/646-2094.

EXPLORING TOWN & VALLEY

Small Ojai is home to more than 35 artists working in a variety of media; most have home studios and are represented in one of several galleries in town. The best for jewelry and smaller pieces is **HumanArts,** 310 E. Ojai Ave. (☎ 805/646-1525). They also have a home-accessories annex, **HumanArts Home,** 246 E. Ojai Ave. (☎ 805/646-8245). Artisans band together each October for an organized **Artists' Studio Tour** (October 11 and 12 in 1997; for information call ☎ 805/646-8126). It's fun to drive from studio to studio at your own pace, meeting various artists and perhaps purchasing some of their work. Ojai's most famous resident is world-renowned **Beatrice Wood,** who celebrated her 104th birthday in 1997 while overseeing a traveling exhibition of her whimsical sculpture and luminous pottery.

Strolling the Spanish arcade shops downtown and the surrounding area will yield a treasure trove, including open-air **Bart's Books,** Matilija St. at Canada St. (☎ 805/ 646-3755), an Ojai fixture for many years. **Heart of Light,** 451 E. Ojai Ave. (☎ 805/646-3812), calls itself a "New Age Emporium," a place where people compare Ojai to Taos and Sedona while perusing books, music, and jewelry. In a town peppered with ladies' boutiques, designer **Barbara Bowman**'s two eponymous shops, at 125 and 133 E. Ojai Ave. (☎ 805/646-2670), stand out in a crowd. Antique hounds head for **The Antique Collection,** 236 W. Ojai Ave. (☎ 805/646-6688), an indoor antique mall packed to the rafters with treasures, trash, and everything in between.

Residents of the Ojai Valley *love* their equine companions—miles of bridle paths are painstakingly maintained, and horse-crossing signs are everywhere. If you'd like to explore the equestrian way, call the **Ojai Valley Inn's Ranch & Stables** (☎ 805/ 646-5511, ext. 456).

Ojai has long been a haven for several esoteric sects of metaphysical and philosophical beliefs. The **Krotona Institute and School of Theosophy,** Calif. 33 and Calif. 150 at Hermosa Road (☎ 805/646-2653), has been in the valley since moving from Hollywood in 1926, and visitors are welcome at their library and bookstore.

In the **Lake Casitas Recreation Area** (☎ 805/649-2233 for visitor information), the incredibly beautiful Lake Casitas boasts nearly 32 miles of shoreline and was the site of the 1984 Olympic canoeing and rowing events. You can rent rowboats and small powerboats year-round from the **boathouse** (☎ 805/649-2043) or enjoy picnicking and camping by the lakeside. Because the lake serves as a domestic water supply, swimming is not allowed. From Calif. 150, turn left onto Santa Ana Road, then follow the signs to the recreation area.

When Ronald Coleman saw Shangri-La in *Lost Horizon,* he was really admiring the Ojai Valley. To visit the breathtakingly beautiful spot where Coleman stood for his view of **Shangri-La,** drive east on Ojai Avenue, up the hill, and stop at the stone bench near the top; the view is spectacular.

✪ **Wheeler Hot Springs Spa & Restaurant.** 16825 Maricopa Hwy. (Calif. 33; 7 miles north of downtown). ☎ 800/9-WHEELER or 805/646-8131. Fax 805/646-9787. Spa package for two (hot tub, massage, and dinner) $139–$165. Full-day, weekend brunch, and other combinations available, as well as spa services à la carte. AE, MC, V.

Nestled in a canyon and shaded by rustling palms, Wheeler is the place to purge all your inner demons. You'll be so relaxed after their pampering treatments that the walk across the gravel driveway to their world-class restaurant will be all you can manage. We recommend that you enjoy their famed mineral baths *à deux* in private redwood-lined and skylighted chambers, each containing hot-bubbling and cold-plunge wooden tubs—after dunking back and forth, it's time for a soothing massage. You can also come up just to dine on contemporary European cuisine prepared with a light touch, while listening to live jazz entertainment on the weekends.

WHERE TO STAY

Ojai Manor Hotel Bed & Breakfast. 210 E. Matilija, Ojai, CA 93023. ☎ 805/646-0961. 6 rms, none with bath. $90–$100 double. Rates include breakfast and evening wine and spirits. MC, V. No children under 12.

Conveniently located a block off Ojai Avenue, this comfortable clapboard B&B was built as a schoolhouse in 1874 and is Ojai's oldest building. A cozy parlor and inviting wraparound porch help make up for the lack of private baths, and a cottage on the grounds houses a friendly beauty-and-massage salon. A typical guest room is simply furnished with throw rugs on the wooden floors and wrought-iron beds.

Ojai Rancho Motel. 615 W. Ojai Ave. (at Country Club Dr.), Ojai, CA 93023. ☎ **800/ 362-1434** or 805/646-1434. 12 rms. A/C TV TEL. $80–$135 double. AE, DISC, MC, V.

This classic ranch-style motel has been well maintained and presents an attractively rustic alternative to the pricey country club around the corner (but don't expect the same gracious service from their cranky front office). The rooms all come with microwave, refrigerator, and coffeemaker, and there's a heated outdoor pool, sauna, and Jacuzzi; two have a fireplace. The rooms in back look out on ranch land and tend to be quieter than the front rooms near the street.

Ojai Valley Inn. Country Club Dr. (off Calif. 33), Ojai, CA 93023. ☎ **800/422-OJAI** or 805/ 646-5511. Fax 805/646-7969. 207 rms, 15 suites. A/C MINIBAR TV TEL. $195–$260 double; from $345 suite. Packages available. AE, DC, MC, V.

In 1923, famous Hollywood architect Wallace Neff designed the clubhouse that's now the focal point of this quintessentially Californian, colonial Spanish-style resort. The inn has carefully kept a sprawling ranch ambiance while providing gracious, elegant service and amenities, along with a beautifully oak-studded Senior PGA Tour golf course. Many of the unusually spacious rooms have fireplaces; most have sofas, writing desks, and secluded terraces or balconies that open onto expansive views of the valley and the magnificent Sierra Madre. Added comforts include coffeemakers, plush terry robes, and hair dryers. The inn is worth a splurge (at press time they were even offering a midweek, AAA-member rate of $99).

Dining/Entertainment: There's the first-rate Vista Dining Room—a beautiful choice for a pleasant culinary adventure at breakfast, lunch, and dinner that also offers a terrific Sunday brunch spread. There's also a terrace grill overlooking the golf course and two lounges.

Services: Concierge, room service (24 hours), nightly turndown.

Facilities: Two outdoor heated pools (including a 60-foot lap pool); state-of-the-art fitness center with exercise room, Jacuzzi, sauna, steam room; jogging trails; complimentary bicycles; horseback riding. There are eight hard-surface tennis courts (four lit for night play); charges are $12 per hour. Golf on the championship 18-hole, 6,258-yard course costs $95 for guests; greens fees include the use of a cart. "Camp Ojai" offers special children's programs including a supervised play area and activities during peak holiday periods.

WHERE TO DINE
EXPENSIVE

L'Auberge. 314 El Paseo (at Rincon St.). ☎ **805/646-2288.** Reservations recommended. Main courses $15–$20. AE, MC, V. Sat–Sun 11am–2:30pm; daily 5:30–9pm. FRENCH/ BELGIAN.

Possibly the most romantic restaurant in the Ojai Valley, L'Auberge is located in a 1910 mansion with a fireplace, chandeliers, and a charming terrace with an excellent view of Ojai's famous sunset "pink moment." The dinner menu is traditional, featuring scampi, frog legs, poached sole, tournedos of beef, sweetbreads, and duckling à l'orange. The weekend brunch menu offers a selection of crepes. Service is expert and friendly, and this elegant house is an easy walk from downtown.

✪ **The Ranch House.** S. Lomita Ave. ☎ **805/646-2360.** Reservations recommended. Main courses $19–$25. AE, CB, DC, DISC, MC, V. Wed–Sat 6–8:30pm, Sun 11am–7:30pm. CALIFORNIA.

This restaurant has been placing emphasis on the freshest vegetables, fruits, and herbs in its cuisine since opening its doors in 1965, long before this practice became a national craze. Freshly snipped sprigs from the restaurant's lush herb garden will aromatically transform your simple meat, fish, or game dish into a work of art. From an appetizer of cognac-laced liver pâté served with their own chewy rye bread to leave-room-for desserts like fresh raspberries with sweet Chambord cream, the ingredients always shine through. And you'll dine in a magical setting, for The Ranch House offers alfresco dining year-round on the wooden porch facing the scenic valley, as well as in the romantic garden amid twinkling lights and stone fountains.

MODERATE

Lanna Thai. 849 E. Ojai Ave. ☎ **805/646-6771.** Reservations recommended on weekends. Main courses $8–$17. MC, V. Mon–Sat 11:30am–2:30pm and 4:30–9:30pm. THAI.

Chiedo Latawan Lopez, a transplant from northern Thailand, runs this cheerful, casual restaurant with a garden-style decor. His dishes contain little sugar and no MSG, but otherwise they're Thai traditionals. Fresh salmon poached in a spicy-and-sour broth, the house specialty, is terrific. Also worth trying is pla goong salad—grilled shrimp on spikes with julienne vegetables, lemongrass, mint, cilantro, and hot chiles. A children's menu is available.

Roger Keller's Restaurant. 331 E. Ojai Ave. ☎ **805/646-7266.** Reservations recommended on weekends. Main courses $8–$22. AE, CB, DC, DISC, MC, V. Daily 11:30am–10pm. AMERICAN/CONTINENTAL.

Installed in a former storefront in the center of downtown, Roger Keller's has a casual ambience with exposed brick walls, bare wooden tables, and works by local artists. The food is rich in both American and European-bistro tradition. Linguine tossed with pesto and sun-dried tomatoes, topped with rock shrimp and bay scallops, is fantastic. Or try the filet mignon encrusted in cracked peppercorns and flamed with brandy. The small but well-selected wine list includes several good buys, and live piano music enhances the mood each Friday and Saturday evening.

INEXPENSIVE

Boccali's. 3277 Ojai–Santa Paula Rd. ☎ **805/646-6116.** Reservations not accepted. Pizza $9–$19; pasta $6–$12. No credit cards. Mon–Tues 4–9pm, Wed–Sun noon–9pm. ITALIAN.

This small, wood-frame restaurant, set among citrus groves, is a pastoral pleasure spot where patrons eat outside at picnic tables under umbrellas and twisted oak trees, or inside at tables covered with red-and-white-checked oilcloths. Pizza is the main dish served here, topped California-style with the likes of crab, garlic, shrimp, and chicken. Fresh lemonade, squeezed from fruit plucked from local trees, is the usual drink of choice.

Tottenham Court. 242 E. Ojai Ave. (in the Downtown Shopping Arcade). ☎ **805/646-2339.** Reservations recommended for afternoon tea on weekends. Main courses $5–$10. AE, MC, V. Thurs–Mon 10am–6pm. ENGLISH TEAROOM.

Besides being purveyors of a variety of British imports, Tottenham Court is a delightful change of pace for breakfast or lunch, offering a menu of quiches, salads, sandwiches, and pastries in addition to a traditional afternoon English tea service. They have a selection of English beers, and the store itself sells food items, gifts, and housewares imported from the United Kingdom.

8 En Route to Los Angeles: Ventura

by Jim Moore, with Stephanie Avnet

Nestled between gently rolling foothills and the sparkling blue Pacific Ocean, Ventura may not have the cultural and gastronomic appeal of Los Angeles or even nearby Santa Barbara, but it does boast the picturesque setting and clean sea breezes typical of California coastal towns. Southland antique hounds know about Ventura's quirky collectible shops, and time-pressed vacationers zip up to charming bed-and-breakfast inns just an hour from Los Angeles. Ventura is also the headquarters and main point of embarkation for Channel Islands National Park (see below).

Most travelers don't bother exiting U.S. 101 for a closer look. But think about stopping to wile away a couple of hours around lunchtime; sleepy Ventura's charm might even convince you to spend a night.

ESSENTIALS

GETTING THERE If you're traveling northbound on U.S. 101, exit at California Street; southbound take the Main Street exit. If you are coming west on Calif. 33 from Ojai, there's also a convenient Main Street exit. By the way, don't let the directions throw you off; because of the curve of the coastline, the ocean is not always to the west, but often southward.

VISITOR INFORMATION For a visitor's guide and genial answers to any questions you might have, stop in at the **Ventura Visitors & Convention Bureau,** 89-C S. California St., Ventura, CA 93001 (☎ **800/333-2989** or 805/648-2075). Their web address is **www.ventura-usa.com**.

EXPLORING THE TOWN

Much of Ventura's recent development has taken place inland and to the south, so many folks overlook the charming seaside **Main Street,** the town's historic center, which grew outward from the Spanish Mission of San Buenaventura (see below). The best section for strolling is between the mission (to the north) and Fir Street (to the south). Both sides of the street are lined almost entirely with antique stores, used bookstores, and charity thrift stores, making it perfect for browsing.

Although Ventura stretches south to one of California's most picturesque little harbors (the jumping-off point for the Channel Islands; see below), the town has its own simple **pier** at the end of California Street. Exceptionally well maintained and favored by area fishers, the charming wooden pier is the longest of its kind in California.

Mission San Buenaventura. 225 East Main St. ☎ **805/643-4318.** Free admission but donations appreciated. Mon–Sat 10am–5pm, Sun 10am–4pm.

Founded in 1782 (current buildings date from 1815) and still in use for daily services, this whitewashed and red-tile church lent its style to the contemporary civic buildings across the street. Step back into time by touring the mission's inside garden, where you can examine the antique water pump and olive press once essential to daily life here. Good for a quick history fix, the mission is small and near the rest of Ventura's action. Pick up a self-guided tour brochure in the adjacent gift shop for the modest donation of $1 per adult, 50¢ per child.

San Buenaventura City Hall. 501 Poli St. ☎ **805/658-4726.** Guided tours $4 adults, $3 seniors, free for children 6 and under. One-hour tours given May–Sept, Sat 11am–1pm.

This majestic neoclassical building was built in 1912 to serve as the Ventura County Courthouse. It sits on the hillside, regally overlooking old downtown and the ocean.

To either side on Poli Street are some of Ventura's best-preserved and most ornate late 19th- and early 20th-century houses. Full of architectural detail (like the carved heads of Franciscan friars adorning the facade) inside and out, City Hall can be fully explored by escorted tour.

Ventura County Museum of History & Art. 100 East Main St. ☎ **805/653-0323.** Admission $3 adults, free for children 16 and under. Tues–Sun 10am–5pm.

This museum is worth visiting for its rich Native American Room, filled with Chumash treasures, and its Pioneer Room, which contains a collection of artifacts from the Mexican-American War (1846–48). The art gallery features revolving exhibits of local painters and photographers, and the museum has an enormous archive (20,000 and counting) of photos depicting Ventura County from its origin to the present. There is also a small archaeological museum across Main Street from the main building.

WHERE TO STAY

Bella Maggiore Inn. 67 S. California St. (^{1}/2 block south of Main St.), Ventura, CA 93001. ☎ **800/523-8479** or 805/652-0277. 24 rms and suites. TEL TV. $75–$150 double; $100–$130 suite. Extra adult $10, extra child (under 12) $5. Rates include full breakfast and afternoon refreshments and appetizers. Ask about midweek specials. AE, DISC, MC, V.

The Bella Maggiore is an intimate Italian-style inn whose simply furnished rooms (some with fireplaces, balconies, or bay window seats) overlook a romantic courtyard or roof garden. Complimentary breakfast is served each morning around the patio fountain, an intimate spot known to nonguests as Nona's Courtyard Cafe. Nona's also serves dinner on Friday and Saturday nights. A kind of European elegance pervades all but the reasonable rates here.

The Country Inn at Ventura by the Sea. 298 Chestnut St. (^{1}/2 block south of Thompson), Ventura, CA 93001. ☎ **800/44-RELAX** or 805/653-1434. 120 rms, 2 suites. $74–$99 double; $129–$199 suite. Extra adult $10, extra child (under 12) free. Rates include full breakfast and afternoon cocktails and appetizers. AE, DISC, MC, V.

Set within walking distance of the beach and Ventura pier, the Country Inn is a good choice for families. It blends the convenience of a chain hotel (the Country Inns are operated by the Comfort Inn chain) with the perks of a bed-and-breakfast. All rooms come with a microwave and refrigerator, and for an additional $10, you can add a canopy bed and fireplace. Try and get a room facing away from the highway—the traffic can get pretty loud.

La Mer European Bed & Breakfast. 411 Poli St. (west of City Hall), Ventura, CA 93001. ☎ **805/643-3600.** 5 rms, 4 with private entrance. $105–$155 double. Rates include full breakfast and complimentary wine in room. Packages available. MC, V. No children accepted.

Perfect for a romantic getaway, La Mer is an 1890 Cape Cod–style home with a spectacular view of the ocean from the parlor and two of the five guest rooms, each of which is furnished in a different international style. Whether you choose the "Madame Pompadour" French chamber with wood-burning stove, the "Vienna Woods" Austrian hideaway with sunken bathtub, or one of three other rooms, you'll love this cozy little cottage. It offers generous midweek packages for couples, which can include gourmet candlelit dinners, cruises to Anacapa Island, country carriage rides, therapeutic massages . . . or all of the above.

WHERE TO DINE

Andria's Seafood Restaurant and Market. In Venura Harbor Village, 1449 Spinnaker Dr. ☎ **805/654-0546.** Main courses $6–$30. No credit cards; ATM cards accepted. Sun–Thurs 11am–9pm, Fri–Sat 11am–10pm. SEAFOOD.

Set aside your hesitation upon seeing the fast-food decor of this place and proceed to the counter to place your order—Andria's has been voted Ventura County's best seafood restaurant for 11 years running. The place doubles as a fresh-seafood market and restaurant. The fish here basically goes from the ocean, into the deep-fat fryer (charbroiled selections are also available), and onto your plate, with only a short stint on the boat in between. The food isn't fancy but it's fresh, and the outdoor harborside seating is pleasant.

Rosarito Beach Cafe. 692 E. Main St. (at Fir St.). ☎ **805/653-7343.** Main courses $10–$19. AE, DISC, MC, V. Tues–Sat 11:30am–2pm; Tues–Thurs and Sun 5:30–9pm, Fri–Sat 5–10pm. MEXICAN.

The Rosarito Beach Cafe really packs them into this 1938 Aztec Revival Moderne building and its welcoming outdoor patio. Diners in-the-know bring their palates for superb Baja-style cuisine whose tangy elements are borrowed from the Caribbean, delicious handmade tortillas, and a culinary sophistication rare in modest Ventura.

The Sportsman. 53 California St. (^{1}/2 block south of Main). ☎ **805/643-2851.** Main courses $4–$14. AE, MC, V. Mon–Fri 11am–10pm; Sat–Sun 9am–2pm; Sat 5–10pm, Sun 4–10pm. AMERICAN.

You might walk right by the inconspicuous facade of Ventura's oldest (since 1950) restaurant. Like the intriguingly retro lettering on its awning, the interior hasn't changed a lick since then: plush leather booths, brass lamps, wood-paneled bar, giant trophy swordfish on the back wall, and light kept at dimness levels normally reserved for planetariums. The Sportsman looks fancy but is quite affordable (especially at breakfast and lunch), and they serve up fine hearty breakfasts, burgers, steaks, and other grilled items. Or you can wet your whistle with $2.50 well drinks from the bar.

Yolie's Fresh Mex Grill. 26 S. Garden St. (corner of Main, west of Mission). ☎ **805/652-0338.** Main courses $5–$13. AE, DISC, MC, V. Mon–Thurs 11am–9pm, Fri–Sat 11am–10pm, Sun 10am–9pm. MEXICAN.

This colorful cantina is better than its nondescript business-park exterior leads you to believe. Yolie's offers an impressive fresh salsa bar (authentic and delicious) as well as an admirable beer, margarita, and tequila menu. The patio and dining room are festooned with rainbow serapes and sombreros, and the kitchen quickly sends out traditional combination plates (as well as lighter and/or vegetarian adaptations). Yolie's all-day hours make it a good road-trip rest stop.

9 Channel Islands National Park

by Jim Moore, with Andrew Rice

There's nothing like a visit to the Channel Islands for discovering the sense of awe the explorers must have felt over 400 years ago. It's miraculous what 25 miles of ocean can do, for compared to the mainland, this is wild and empty land. Whether you approach the islands by sea or air, you'll be bowled over by how untrammeled they remain despite neighboring Southern California's teeming masses.

Channel Islands National Park encompasses the five northernmost islands of the eight-island chain: Santa Barbara, Anacapa, Santa Cruz, Santa Rosa, and San Miguel. Tiny Santa Barbara Island sits very much by itself, about 46 miles off the Southern California coast. The other four are clustered in a 40-mile-long chain that begins with tiny Anacapa; it continues with Santa Cruz, then Santa Rosa, and ends with wild and windy San Miguel. The park also protects the ocean 1 nautical mile offshore from each island, thereby prohibiting oil drilling, shipping, and other industrial uses.

The islands are the meeting point of two distinct marine ecosystems: The cold waters of Northern California and the warmer currents of Southern California swirl together here, creating an awesome array of marine life. On land, the relative isolation from mainland influences has allowed distinct species, like the island fox and the night lizard, to develop and survive here. The islands are also the most important seabird nesting area in California and home to the biggest seal and sea lion breeding colony in the United States.

JUST THE FACTS

GETTING THERE   Each of the five islands is relatively distinct and difficult to reach. Odds are you're only going to visit one island on a given trip, so it's a good idea to study your options before going.

Visit the **Channel Islands National Park Headquarters and Visitor Center,** 1901 Spinnaker Dr., Ventura, CA 93001 (☎ **805/658-5700**), to get acquainted with the various programs and individual personalities of the islands through maps and displays. Rangers run interpretive programs both on the islands and at the center year-round.

Island Packers, next door to the visitor center at 1867 Spinnaker Dr. (recorded information ☎ **805/642-7688,** reservations ☎ **805/642-1393**), is the park's concessionaire for boat transportation to and from the islands. They're another great source of information.

There are no park fees, but getting to the islands is expensive—anywhere from $32 to $120 per person—since you must go by boat or plane. Island Packers will take you on a range of regularly scheduled boat excursions, from $3^1/2$-hour nonlanding tours of the islands ($21 per person) or full-day tours of individual islands led by naturalists ($49 per person) to 2-day excursions to two islands ($245). Private yachts and commercial dive and tour boats from all over Southern California also visit the park on a regular basis.

If you want to get to Santa Rosa in a hurry, **Channel Islands Aviation,** 305 Durley Ave., Camarillo (☎ **805/987-1678),** will fly you there in one of their small, fixed-wing aircraft. If you just want a quick overflight and maybe a picnic stop with a short hike, **Heli-Tours, Inc.** at the Santa Barbara Airport (☎ **805/964-0684**), offers 3- to 4-hour flights to Santa Cruz Island.

THE WEATHER   While the climate is mild, with little variation in temperature year-round, the weather in the islands is always unpredictable. Thirty-mile-an-hour winds can blow for days, or sometimes a fog bank will settle in and smother the islands for weeks at a time. Winter rains can turn island trails into mud baths. In general, plan on wind, lots of sun (bring sunscreen), cool nights, and the possibility of hot days. Water temperatures are in the 50°s and 60°s year-round. If you're camping, bring a good tent—if you don't know the difference between a good and a bad tent, the island wind will gladly demonstrate it for you. Also be aware that inclement weather or sea conditions can cause Island Packers to cancel trips on the day of the excursion, so it's a good idea to have a plan B just in case.

CAMPING   Camping is permitted on all the park-owned islands, but is limited to 30 people per island per night. Camping is also allowed on Santa Cruz, through special arrangement with the private owners. Fires and pets are prohibited on all the islands. You must bring everything you'll need; there are no supplies on any of the islands. To reserve free camping permits for any of the islands, schedule your transportation, then call the visitor center (see "Getting There," above) no more than 90 days in advance (no more than 30 days in advance for San Miguel).

EXPLORING THE ISLANDS

SANTA BARBARA   As you come upon Santa Barbara Island after a typical 3-hour crossing, you'll think that someone took a single, medium-sized, grassy hill, ringed it with cliffs, and plunked it down in the middle of the ocean. When you drop anchor, you'll realize that your initial perception is basically on target. Landwise, there's just not a lot here. But the upside is that, of all the islands, Santa Barbara gives you the best sense of what it's like to be stranded on a desert isle. Being on Santa Barbara, far enough out to sea that the mainland is almost invisible, gives you an idea of just how immense the Pacific really is.

Other than the landing cove, there's no access to the water's edge. The snorkeling in the chilly cove is great. You can hike the entire 640-acre island in a few hours; then, it's time to stare out to sea. You won't be let down. The cliffs and rocks are home to elephant seals, sea lions, and swarms of seabirds such as you'll never see on the mainland. There's also a small campground, pit toilets, and a tiny museum chronicling island history. Camping is available year-round. Island Packers only schedules boats to Santa Barbara in summer and fall (see "Getting There," above).

ANACAPA   Most people who visit the park come to Anacapa. It's only 14^1/$_2$ nautical miles from Ventura, an easy half-day trip. At only 1.1 square miles, Anacapa—actually three small islets divided by narrow stretches of ocean—is only marginally larger than Santa Barbara and, consequently, not a place for those who need a lot of space to roam around. Only East Anacapa is open to visitors, as the other two islets are important brown-pelican breeding areas. Several trails on the island will take you to beautiful overlooks of clear-watered coves and wild ocean. **Arch Rock,** a natural land bridge, is visible from the landing cove, where you'll clamber up 154 stairs to the island's flat top.

Camping is allowed on East Anacapa year-round, but don't bring more than you can carry the half mile from the landing cove. Bring earplugs and steer clear of the foghorn, which can leave permanent hearing damage. Most of the waters around the island, including the landing cove, are protected as a National Marine Preserve, where divers can look but not take anything. Pack a good wet suit, mask, fins, and snorkel; you can dive right off the landing cove dock.

SANTA CRUZ   By far the biggest of the islands—nearly 100 square miles—Santa Cruz is also the most diverse. It has huge canyons, year-round streams, beaches, cliffs, the highest mountain in the Channel Islands (2,400 feet), now-defunct early cattle and sheep ranches, and Native American Chumash village sites—2,000 Chumash were probably living on the island when Cabrillo first visited in 1542. The island also hosts seemingly endless displays of flora and fauna, including 650 species of plants, nine of which are endemic; 140 land bird species; and a small group of other land animals, including the island fox.

Most of the island is still privately owned: The Nature Conservancy holds the western nine-tenths. On February 10, 1997, the park service took over the eastern end from the Gherini family who had owned a sheep ranch here. Most visitors come to Scorpion Ranch and Smuggler's Ranch on the park service's land. Unfortunately, the island's ranching heritage has left its mark on the land—the island has been badly overgrazed by feral sheep. Much of the most beautiful land is on the Nature Conservancy property, including Santa Cruz's lush Central Valley and the islands' highest peaks. It's more difficult, but not impossible, to get access to the Conservancy land; Island Packers runs occasional trips to Prisoner's Harbor. At one point, it was possible to arrange stays at Christy Ranch on the windswept west end of the island and visits to the Main Ranch in the Central Valley, but at press time the ranches were under restoration and access was restricted. Contact the **Nature Conservancy** (☎ 805/962-9111) for up-to-date information.

Valdez Cave (also known as Painted Cave for its colorful rock types, lichens, and algaes) is the largest and deepest known sea cave in the world. The huge cave stretches nearly a quarter-mile into the island and is nearly 100 feet wide. The entrance ceiling rises 160 feet, and in the spring, a waterfall tumbles over the opening. Located on the northwest end of the island, the cave can only be entered via dinghy or kayak. Contact Island Packers for the most current information on this as well as the entire, continually changing Santa Cruz access situation.

Island Packers (see "Getting There," above) runs day trips as well as overnights to Santa Cruz. Camping is allowed in the western park-owned portion of the island year-round; apply for a free permit at the visitor center.

SANTA ROSA   Windy Santa Rosa was California's only singly owned, private island until it was purchased by the park service for $30 million in the 1980s from the Vail and Vickers ranching company. As part of the purchase agreement, the Vails are allowed to ranch the island until 2011. Close to 6,500 cattle still call the 54,000-acre island home. You can camp in the old ranch compound on the island's northeast end, where you might be lucky enough to see the Vail and Vickers cowboys working the herd, just as they have for more than 100 years.

Santa Rosa is also home to a large concentration of endangered plant species, 34 of which occur only on the islands. And like Santa Cruz, Santa Rosa is home to the diminutive island fox, a tiny cousin of the gray fox that has become nearly fearless as it has evolved in the predator-free island environment. They'll walk right through your camp if you let them. Santa Rosa also has great beaches, a benefit somewhat outweighed by the nearly constant winds.

SAN MIGUEL   People often argue about what's the wildest place left in the lower 48 states. They bat around names like Montana, Colorado, and Idaho. Curiously, no one ever thinks to consider San Miguel. They should, for this 9,500-acre island is a wild, wild place. The wind blows constantly, and the island can be shrouded in fog for days at a time. Human presence is definitely not the status quo here.

Visitors land at Cuyler Harbor, a half-moon–shaped cove on the island's east end. Arriving here is like arriving on earth the day it was made: perfect water, perfect sand, outrageously blue water. Seals bask on the offshore rocks. The island's two most interesting features are the **Caliche Forest,** a sort of petrified forest left when the wind exposed sandstone casts of a forest that once stood on the island; and **Point Bennett,** the outrageous-sounding (and smelling) breeding ground of six separate species of seals and sea lions. During the winter, thousands carpet the beach; their barking is deafening.

The waters around San Miguel are the richest and most dangerous of all the islands. The island is exposed to wave action from all sides. Many ships have sunk here. A 3-foot-tall stone cross stands in memory of Juan Rodriguez Cabrillo, the Spanish explorer credited with discovering the Channel Islands in 1542. Although his grave has never been found, Cabrillo is believed to be buried on the island.

Island Packers' schedule to San Miguel is sporadic in summer and almost nonexistent in winter, so call ahead. Primitive camping is allowed near the ranger's residence, but no potable water is available, and fires are prohibited.

THE EXTRA MILE: EXPLORING THE COASTLINE AND WATERS OFF THE CHANNEL ISLANDS

DIVING   A good portion of Channel Islands National Park is underwater. In fact, twice as many visitors come annually to dive the waters than ever set foot on the islands. Scuba divers come here from all over the globe for the chance to explore stunning kelp forests, shipwrecks, and underwater caves, all with the best visibility in California. Everything from sea snails and urchins to orcas and great white sharks call these waters home. **Truth Aquatics** in Santa Barbara (☎ **805/962-1127**) is the best provider of single- and multiday dive trips to all the islands. **Ventura Dive & Sport** (☎ **805/650-6500**) also leads trips, including their "Discover Program," which allows novice and uncertified divers to explore the waters accompanied by an instructor. **Channel Islands Scuba** (☎ **805/644-3483**) and **Pacific Scuba** (☎ **805/ 984-2566**) also lead regular trips, as do boats from San Pedro and other Southern California ports.

SEA KAYAKING   One of the best ways to explore the fascinating coastline of the islands is by kayak. Warren Glaser of **OAARS** (Outdoor and Aquatic Recreation Specialist), based in Ventura (☎ **805/642-2912**), leads small-group tours by sea kayak to all five Channel Islands. The trips allow you to explore sea caves and rock gardens. Channel crossing by charter boat, brief lessons, and lunch are included. Fares generally run $125 per person. Three-day adventures to Santa Rosa, with meals, campsite, and guide included are offered for $295. **Aqua Sports** (☎ **805/968-7231**) and **Paddle Sports** (☎ **805/899-4925**) also lead similar trips, or trips can be arranged through Island Packers (recorded information ☎ **805/642-7688,** reservations ☎ **805/642-1393**).

13

Los Angeles

by Stephanie Avnet

The entire world knows what Los Angeles looks like. It's a real-life version of one of those souvenir postcard folders, which spills out images accordion-style: tall palm trees sweeping an azure sky; the gleaming white "Hollywood" sign; freeways flowing like concrete rivers; a lone surfer riding the day's last wave silhouetted against the sunset's glow. These seductive images are just a few of many that bring to mind the city that everyone loves to hate—and to experience, at least once in a lifetime.

Los Angelenos know their city will never have the sophisticated style of Paris or the historical riches of London—but we cheerfully lay claim to being the most fun city in the United States, maybe the world. Home to the planet's first amusement park, L. A. kind of feels like one, as the line between fantasy and reality is so often obscured. The colors of the city seem just a little bit brighter—and more surreal—than in other cities, the angles just a little sharper. Everything seems larger than life. Drive down Sunset Boulevard, and you'll see what I mean: The billboards are just a little bit taller, the wacky folks just a touch wackier.

Part of the spontaneity and excitement of L.A. comes from the fact that the city is constantly redefining itself. Just like the movies and TV shows that come to life here, the physical landscape, social doctrines, and popular pastimes of the city itself are fluid and unreliable. L.A. gleefully embraces individuality and weirdness and change. Collectively, the city is like a theatrical actor projecting to the very back row: We want everyone else to sit up and take notice—and we're constantly reinventing ourselves so they will. We'd never want our city to be Paris or London for all the Mona Lisas in the world.

1 Orientation

ARRIVING
BY PLANE

LOS ANGELES INTERNATIONAL AIRPORT (LAX)   Most visitors to the area fly into Los Angeles International Airport, better known as LAX (☎ **310/646-5252**). Situated oceanside just off I-405, between Santa Monica and Manhattan Beach, LAX is a convenient place to land; it's minutes away from all the city's beach communities, and about a half-hour drive from the Westside, Hollywood, or downtown.

Area Code Change Notice

Please note that, effective June 13, 1998, the region serviced by area code 213 is scheduled to be split, with all portions *excluding the downtown business district* changing to **323.** You will be able to dial 213 until January 16, 1999, after which you will be required to use 323 for affected numbers.

Transportation from LAX   You'll probably be **renting a car** from LAX; you'll need one (see "Getting Around," below). All the major car-rental firms provide shuttles from the terminals to their off-site branches. To reach Santa Monica and other northern beach communities, exit the airport, take Sepulveda Boulevard north, then follow the signs to Calif. 1 (Pacific Coast Highway, or PCH) north. To reach the southern beach communities, take Sepulveda Boulevard south, then follow the signs to Calif. 1 (PCH) south. To reach Beverly Hills or Hollywood, exit the airport via Century Boulevard, then take I-405 north to Santa Monica Boulevard east. To reach downtown, exit the airport, turn right onto Sepulveda Boulevard south, then take I-105 east to I-110 north. To reach Pasadena, drive through downtown (following the directions above), and continue north on Calif. 110 (the Pasadena Freeway).

Many city hotels provide free shuttles for their guests; ask about transportation when you make reservations. You can also catch a **taxi** from your terminal. Taxis line up outside each terminal, and rides are metered. Expect to pay about $30 to Hollywood and downtown, $25 to Beverly Hills, $20 to Santa Monica, and $45 to Pasadena, including a $2.50 service charge for rides originating at LAX.

The **Super Shuttle** (☎ **800/554-3146** from LAX, or 310/782-6600) offers regularly scheduled minivans from LAX to any location in the city. The set fare can range from about $10 to $50 per person, depending on your destination (you're unlikely to pay more than $35, which will get you as far as Burbank or Universal City). It's cheaper to cab it to most destinations if you're a group of three or more, but the vans are infinitely more comfortable; however, you might have to stop at other passengers' destinations before you reach your own.

When you arrive at LAX, you can call Super Shuttle from a pay phone in baggage claim at the toll-free number above or at the courtesy phones at the services information board. If you call during a very busy time, however, expect a wait. Reservations are strongly advised, even if you just make them the day before you arrive; call the 310 number above to book. When traveling to the airport for your trip home, reserve your shuttle at least a day in advance.

City **buses** also go between LAX and many parts of the city; phone **MTA Airport Information** (☎ 800/252-7433 or 213/626-4455) for schedules and fares.

OTHER AREA AIRPORTS   One of the area's smaller airports might be more convenient for you, landing you closer to your destination and allowing you to avoid the traffic and bustle of LAX. **Burbank–Glendale–Pasadena Airport** (☎ 818/840-8840) is the best place to land if you're locating in Hollywood or the Valleys. This small airport has especially good links to Las Vegas and other southwestern cities. **Long Beach Municipal Airport** (☎ 310/421-8293), south of LAX, is the best place to land if you're visiting Long Beach or northern Orange County, and want to avoid L.A. entirely. The **Orange County/John Wayne International Airport** in Anaheim (☎ 714/252-5200) is closest to Disneyland, Knott's Berry Farm, and other Anaheim-area attractions (see chapter 14 for details).

BY CAR

If you're driving in **from the north,** you have two choices: the quick route, along I-5 through the middle of the state; or the scenic route along the coast.

Heading south along I-5, you'll pass a small town called Grapevine. This marks the start of a mountain pass known as the Grapevine. Once you've reached the southern end of the mountain pass, you'll be in the San Fernando Valley, and you've arrived in Los Angeles County. To reach the beach communities and L.A.'s Westside, take I-405 south; to get to Hollywood, take Calif. 170 south to U.S. 101 south (this route is called the Hollywood Freeway the entire way); I-5 will take you through downtown and into Orange County.

If you're taking the scenic coastal route in from the north, take U.S. 101 to I-405 or I-5, or stay on U.S. 101, following the instructions as listed above to your final destination.

If you're approaching **from the east,** you'll be driving in on I-10. For Orange County, take Calif. 57 south. I-10 continues through downtown and terminates at the beach. If you're heading to Hollywood, take U.S. 101 north; if you're heading to the Westside, take I-405 north. To get to the beaches, take Calif. 1 (PCH) north or south, depending on your destination.

If you're coming in **from the south,** head north on I-5. At the southern end of Orange County, I-405 splits off to the west; take this road to the Westside and beach communities. Stay on I-5 to reach downtown.

BY TRAIN

Passengers arriving via **Amtrak** (☎ **800/USA-RAIL**) will disembark at Union Station, on downtown's northern edge. From the station, you can take one of the many taxis that line up outside the station.

BY BUS

The main Los Angeles bus station for arriving **Greyhound/Trailways** (☎ **800/231-2222**) buses is downtown at 1716 E. 7th St., east of Alameda. For additional area terminal locations, call the toll-free number above.

VISITOR INFORMATION

The **Los Angeles Convention and Visitors Bureau,** 633 W. 5th St., Suite 6000, Los Angeles, CA 90071 (☎ **213/624-7300**), is the city's main source for information. Call or write for a free visitor's kit. The bureau staffs a **Visitors Information Center** at 685 S. Figueroa St., between Wilshire Boulevard and 7th Street; it's open Monday to Friday from 8am to 5:30pm and Saturday from 8:30am to 5pm.

Many Los Angeles–area communities also have their own tourist offices: **Visitor Information Center Hollywood** (☎ 213/236-2331); **Beverly Hills Visitors Bureau** (☎ 800/345-2210 or 310/271-8174; fax 310/858-8032); **Marina del Rey Chamber of Commerce** (☎ 213/821-0555); **Pasadena Convention and Visitors Bureau** (☎ 626/795-9311); website: www.ci.pasadena.ca.us; **Redondo Beach Chamber of Commerce** (☎ 310/376-6911); **Santa Monica Convention and Visitors Bureau** (☎ 310/393-7593; website: www.ci.santa-monica.ca.us); **West Hollywood Convention & Visitors Bureau** (☎ 800/368-6020 or 310/289-2525). Call for information, hours, and locations.

OTHER INFORMATION SOURCES   Several city-oriented newspapers and magazines offer up-to-date information on current happenings. The *L.A. Weekly,* a free weekly listings magazine, is packed with information on current events around town. It's available from sidewalk news racks and in many stores and restaurants around the city. The *Los Angeles Times* "**Calendar**" section of the Sunday paper is an excellent guide to the world of entertainment in and around L.A., and includes listings of what's doing and where to do it. The *Times* also maintains an Internet "Guide to Tinseltown" at **www.latimes.com/home/ent/tinsel**. *Los Angeles* magazine and the even trendier upstart *Buzz* are city-based monthlies full of news, information, and previews of L.A.'s art, music, and food scenes. Both are available at newsstands around town.

CITY LAYOUT

Los Angeles is not a single compact city, but a sprawling suburbia comprising dozens of disparate communities. Most of the city's communities are located between mountains and ocean, on the flatlands of a huge basin. Even if you've never visited L.A. before, you'll recognize the names of many of these areas: Hollywood, Beverly Hills, Santa Monica, Malibu. Ocean breezes push the city's infamous smog inland, toward dozens of less well-known residential communities, and through mountain passes into the suburban sprawl of the San Fernando and San Gabriel valleys.

Downtown Los Angeles—which isn't where most tourists will stay—is in the center of the basin, about 12 miles east of the Pacific Ocean. Most visitors will spend the bulk of their time either on the coast or on the city's Westside. (See "The Neighborhoods in Brief," below, for details on all the city's sectors, as well as the map on pp. 412–413 for an overview of the Los Angeles area's neighborhoods and freeway system.)

Main Arteries & Streets

L.A.'s extensive freeway system connects the city's patchwork of communities; they work well together to get you where you need to be, although rush-hour traffic can sometimes be bumper-to-bumper. You might only drive on a couple of L.A's freeways, but here's an overview of the entire system:

U.S. 101, called the "Ventura Freeway" in the San Fernando Valley and the "Hollywood Freeway" in the city, runs across L.A. in a roughly northwest-southeast direction, from the San Fernando Valley to the center of downtown.

Calif. 134 continues as the Ventura Freeway after U.S. 101 turns into the city and becomes the Hollywood Freeway. The Calif. 134 branch of the Ventura Freeway continues directly east, through the valley towns of Burbank and Glendale, to **I-210** (the "Foothill Freeway"), which will take you through Pasadena and out toward the eastern edge of Los Angeles County.

I-5, otherwise known as the "Golden State Freeway" north of I-10 and the "Santa Ana Freeway" south of I-10, bisects downtown on its way from San Francisco to San Diego.

I-10, labeled the "Santa Monica Freeway" west of I-5 and the "San Bernardino Freeway" east of I-5, is the city's major east-west freeway, connecting the San Gabriel Valley to downtown and Santa Monica.

I-405, also known as the "San Diego Freeway," runs north-south through L.A's Westside, connecting the San Fernando Valley with LAX and the southern beach areas.

I-105, Los Angeles's newest freeway—called the "Century Freeway"—extends from LAX east to I-605.

I-110, commonly known as the "Harbor Freeway," starts in Pasadena as **Calif. 110** (the "Pasadena Freeway"); it turns into the Interstate in downtown Los Angeles and runs directly south, where it dead-ends in San Pedro. The section that's now the Pasadena Freeway is Los Angeles's historic first freeway, known as the Arroyo Seco when it opened in 1940.

The Los Angeles Area at a Glance

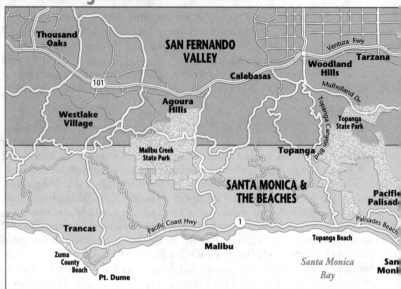

1. Lincoln Blvd.
   Sepulveda Blvd.
   Pacific Coast Hwy.

2. Santa Monica Blvd.
   Glendale Fwy.

5. Golden State Fwy.
   Santa Ana Fwy.

10. Santa Monica Fwy.
    San Bernardino Fwy.

22. Garden Grove Fwy.

27. Topanga Canyon Blvd.

39. Beach Blvd.
    San Gabriel Canyon Rd.

47. Terminal Fwy.
    Ocean Blvd.

55. Newport Fwy. and Blvd.

57. Orange Fwy.

60. Pomona Fwy.

90. Marina Fwy.

91. Artesia Blvd. & Fwy.
    Gardena Fwy.
    Riverside Fwy.

101. Ventura Fwy.
     Hollywood Fwy.

105. Century Fwy.

110. Pasadena Fwy.

110. Harbor Fwy.

134. Ventura Fwy.

170. Hollywood Fwy.

210. Foothill Fwy.

405. San Diego Fwy.

605. San Gabriel
     River Fwy.

710. Long Beach Fwy.

LEGEND

22. **State Highway**

101. **U.S. Highway**

210. **Interstate Highway**

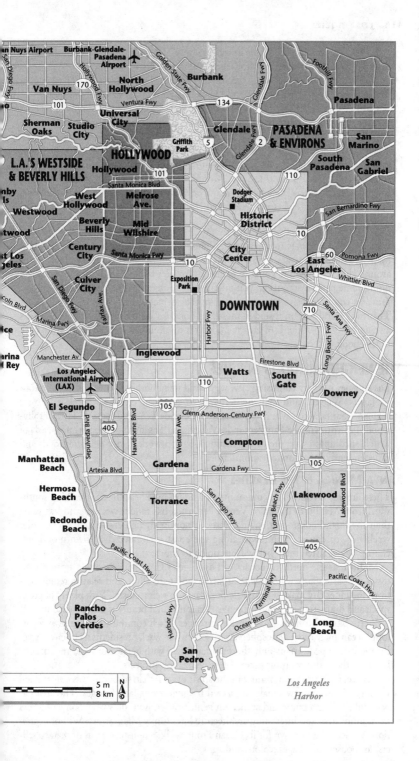

I-710, also called the "Long Beach Freeway," runs in a north-south direction through East Los Angeles and dead-ends at Long Beach.

I-605, the "San Gabriel River Freeway," runs roughly parallel to I-710 farther east, through the cities of Hawthorne and Lynwood and into the San Gabriel Valley.

Calif. 1—called "Highway 1," the "Pacific Coast Highway," or simply "PCH"— is really a highway (more like a surface thruway) rather than a freeway. It skirts the ocean, linking all of L.A.'s beach communities, from Malibu to the Orange Coast.

The freeways are complemented by a complex web of surface streets. The major east-west thoroughfares connecting downtown to the beaches (listed from north to south) are Sunset Boulevard, Santa Monica Boulevard, Wilshire Boulevard, and Olympic, Pico, and Venice boulevards. The section of Sunset Boulevard that runs between Crescent Heights Boulevard and Doheny Drive is the famed Sunset Strip.

STREET MAPS

Because Los Angeles is so spread out, a good map of the area is essential. Foldout maps are available at gas stations, hotels, book shops, and tourist-oriented shops around the city. If you're going to be in Los Angeles for a week or more, or plan on doing some extensive touring, you might want to invest in the all-inclusive *Thomas Guide,* a comprehensive book of city maps that depicts every single road in the city. The ring-bound edition is sold in most area bookstores and costs about $16. There's also an overview of the L.A. area included on the four-color sheet map in the back of this book.

THE NEIGHBORHOODS IN BRIEF

Los Angeles is a very confusing city, with fluid neighborhood lines and equally elastic labels. We've found that the best way to grasp the city is to break it into six regions—Santa Monica and the Beaches, Westside L.A. and Beverly Hills, Hollywood, Downtown, the San Fernando Valley, and Pasadena and environs—each of which encompasses a more-or-less distinctive patchwork of city neighborhoods and independently incorporated communities.

SANTA MONICA & THE BEACHES

These are our favorite L.A. communities. The 60-mile beachfront stretching southward from Malibu to the Palos Verdes Peninsula has milder weather and less smog than the inland communities, and traffic is nominally lighter—except on summer weekends, of course. The towns along the coast each have their own mood and charm. We've listed them below from north to south:

Malibu, at the northern border of Los Angeles County, is 25 miles from downtown. Its particularly wide beaches, sparsely populated hills, and relative remoteness from the inner city make it extremely popular with rich recluses. With plenty of green space and dramatic rocky outcroppings, Malibu's rural beauty is unsurpassed in L.A.

Pretty **Santa Monica,** Los Angeles's premier beach community, is known for its long ocean pier, artsy atmosphere, and somewhat wacky residents. The 3rd Street Promenade, a pedestrians-only thoroughfare lined with great shops and restaurants, is one of the country's most successful revitalization projects.

Venice, a planned community in the spirit of its Italian forebear, was constructed with a series of narrow canals connected by quaint one-lane bridges. The area has been infested with grime and crime, but gentrification is in full swing. Some of L.A.'s most innovative and interesting architecture lines funky Main Street. Without question, Venice is best known for its Ocean Front Walk, a nonstop circus of skaters, sellers, and posers of all ages, colors, and sizes.

Marina del Rey, just south of Venice, is a somewhat quieter, more upscale community best known for its small-craft harbor, one of the largest of its kind in the world.

Manhattan, Hermosa, and **Redondo beaches** are relatively sleepy residential neighborhoods with modest homes, mild weather, and easy parking. These communities have excellent beaches for volleyballers, surfers, and sun worshipers, but there's not much else about these South Bay suburbs for visitors to get very excited about—when it comes to good restaurants or cultural activities, pickings are slim.

L.A.'S WESTSIDE & BEVERLY HILLS

The Westside, an imprecise, misshapen L sandwiched between Hollywood and the city's coastal communities, includes some of the Los Angeles's most prestigious neighborhoods, all with names you're sure to recognize:

Beverly Hills is roughly bounded by Olympic Boulevard on the south, Robertson Boulevard on the east, and Westwood and Century City on the west; it extends into the hills to the north. Politically distinct from the rest of Los Angeles, this famous enclave is best known for its palm tree–lined streets of palatial homes and high-priced shops (does Rodeo Drive ring a bell?), but it's the healthy mix of the filthy rich, tourists, and wannabes that creates a unique—and sometimes bizarre—atmosphere.

West Hollywood is a key-shaped community (go ahead, look at your map) whose epicenter is the intersection of Santa Monica and La Cienega boulevards. It's bounded on the west by Doheny Drive and on the south roughly by Melrose Avenue; the tip of the key extends east for several blocks north and south of Santa Monica Boulevard as far as La Brea Avenue, but it's primarily located to the west of Fairfax Avenue. Nestled between Beverly Hills and Hollywood, this politically independent town can feel either tony or tawdry, depending on which end of it you're in. In addition to being home to the city's best restaurants, shops, and art galleries, West Hollywood is the center of L.A.'s gay community.

Bel Air and **Holmby Hills,** located in the hills north of Westwood and west of the Beverly Hills city limits, comprise a wealthy residential area and feature prominently on most maps to the stars' homes.

Brentwood, the world-famous backdrop for the O. J. Simpson melodrama, is really just a tiny, quiet, relatively upscale neighborhood with the typical L.A. mixture of homes, restaurants, and strip malls. It lies west of I-405 and north of Santa Monica and West Los Angeles.

Westwood, an urban village that the University of California, Los Angeles (UCLA) calls home, is bounded by I-405, Santa Monica Boulevard, Sunset Boulevard, and Beverly Hills. The village, which used to be a hot destination for a night on the town, has lost much of its appeal because of overcrowding, rudeness, and even street violence. There's still a high concentration of movie theaters, but we're all waiting for Westwood to regain the charm it once had.

Century City is a compact, busy, rather bland high-rise area sandwiched between West Los Angeles and Beverly Hills. Once the back lot of 20th Century Fox studios, Century City is home to the Shubert Theatre and the outdoor Century City Marketplace. Its three main thoroughfares are Century Park East, Avenue of the Stars, and Century Park West; it's bounded on the north by Santa Monica Boulevard and on the south by Pico Boulevard.

West Los Angeles is a label that basically applies to everything that isn't one of the other Westside neighborhoods. It's generally the area south of Santa Monica Boulevard, north of Venice Boulevard, east of the communities of Santa Monica and Venice, and west and south of Century City.

HOLLYWOOD

Yes, they still come. Young aspirants are attracted to this town like moths fluttering in the glare of neon lights. But Hollywood is now much more a state of mind than a glamour center. Many of the neighborhood's former movie studios have moved to less expensive, more spacious venues. Hollywood Boulevard is now one of the city's seediest strips. The area is now just a less-than-admirable part of the whole of Los Angeles, but the legend of the neighborhood as the movie capital of the world endures, and it's still home to several important attractions, such as the Walk of Fame and Mann's Chinese Theatre.

For our purposes, the label "Hollywood" extends beyond seedy Hollywood itself—centered around Hollywood and Sunset boulevards—to surrounding neighborhoods. It generally encompasses everything between Western Avenue to the east and Fairfax Avenue to the west and from the Hollywood Hills (with its dazzling homes and million-dollar views) south.

Melrose Avenue, a scruffy but fun neighborhood, is the city's funkiest shopping district.

The stretch of Wilshire Boulevard that runs through the southern part of Hollywood is known as the **Mid-Wilshire District,** or Miracle Mile. It's lined with contemporary apartment houses and office buildings; the stretch just east of Fairfax Avenue, now known as **Museum Row,** is home to almost a dozen museums, including the Los Angeles County Museum of Art, the La Brea Tar Pits, and that shrine to L.A. car culture, the Petersen Automotive Museum.

Griffith Park, up Western Avenue in the northernmost reaches of Hollywood, is one of the country's largest urban parks and home to the Los Angeles Zoo and the famous Griffith Observatory.

DOWNTOWN

Roughly bounded by the U.S. 101, I-110, I-10, and I-5 freeways, L.A.'s downtown is home to a tight cluster of high-rise offices, the El Pueblo de Los Angeles Historic District, and the neighborhoods of **Koreatown, Chinatown,** and **Little Tokyo.** For our purposes, the residential neighborhoods of **Los Feliz** and **Silverlake** (a grungy burgeoning artistic community that has been called the "West Coast Soho"), **Exposition Park** (home to Los Angeles Memorial Coliseum, the L.A. Sports Arena, and several downtown museums), and **East and South-Central L.A.,** the city's famous barrios, all fall under the downtown umbrella.

The construction of skyscrapers—facilitated by earthquake-proof technology—transformed downtown Los Angeles into the business center of the city. Despite the relatively recent construction of numerous cultural centers—including the Music Center and the Museum of Contemporary Art—and a few smart restaurants, downtown is not the hub it would be in most cities; the Westside, Hollywood, and the beach communities are all more popular.

THE SAN FERNANDO VALLEY

The San Fernando Valley, known locally as "The Valley," was nationally popularized in the 1980s by the notorious, mall-loving "Valley Girl" stereotype. Snuggled between the Santa Monica and the San Gabriel mountain ranges, most of the Valley is residential and commercial, and off the beaten tourist track. But there are some attractions bound to draw you over the hill: **Universal City,** located west of Griffith Park between U.S. 101 and Calif. 134, is home to Universal Studios and CityWalk, a vast shopping and entertainment complex. And you may make a trip to **Burbank,** just north of Universal City, to see one of your favorite TV shows being filmed at the NBC or Warner Bros. studios. There are also many good restaurants and shops along Ventura Boulevard in and around **Studio City.**

PASADENA & ENVIRONS

Best known to the world as the site of the Tournament of Roses Parade each New Year's Day, **Pasadena** was mercifully spared from the tear-down epidemic that swept L.A., so it has a refreshing old-time feel. Once upon a time, Pasadena was every Angeleno's best-kept secret—a quiet community whose slow and careful regentrification meant excellent, unique restaurants and boutique shopping without the crowds in a revitalized downtown respectful of its old brick and stone commercial buildings. Although the area's natural and architectural beauty still shines through— so much so that Pasadena remains Hollywood's favorite backyard location for countless movies and TV shows—Old Town has become a pedestrian mall similar to Santa Monica's Third Street Promenade, complete with huge crowds, predictable midrange chain eateries, and standard mall-issue stores. It still gets my vote as an scenic alternative to the congestion of central L.A., but it has lost much of its small-town charm.

Neighboring **Glendale** seems to be undergoing a similar renewal. Nestled between Pasadena, Burbank, and Griffith Park, Glendale's biggest visitor draw is Forest Lawn Memorial Park. The city used to be dead commercially, too, but Brand and Central avenues have been slowly sprucing themselves up, attracting high-profile tenants like Borders Books & Music and drawing denizens of nearby Silverlake and Los Feliz to its suburban comfort zone.

2 Getting Around

BY CAR

Despite its hassles, driving is the way to get around L.A. The golden rule is this: Always allow more time to get to your destination than you reasonably think it will take, especially during morning and evening rush hours.

RENTALS   Los Angeles is one of the cheapest places in America to rent a car. Among the national firms operating in L.A. are **Alamo** (☎ 800/327-9633), **Avis** (☎ 800/331-1212), **Budget** (☎ 800/527-0700), **Dollar** (☎ 800/800-4000), **Hertz** (☎ 800/654-3131), **National** (☎ 800/328-4567), and **Thrifty** (☎ 800/367-2277).

PARKING   Parking in L.A. is usually ample, but in some sections—most notably downtown and in Santa Monica, West Hollywood, and Hollywood—finding a space can be fraught with frustration. In most places, though, you'll be able to find metered street parking—be sure to carry plenty of quarters. When you can't, expect to valet or garage your car for somewhere between $4 and $10. Many restaurants and nightclubs, and even some shopping centers, offer valet parking; they usually charge about $3 to $5. Most of the hotels listed in this book offer off-street parking; it's often complimentary, but can cost as much as $20 per day in high-density areas.

DRIVING TIPS   On surface roads, you may turn right at a red light (unless otherwise indicated) after making a complete stop and yielding to traffic and pedestrians. Pedestrians always have the right-of-way at intersections and crosswalks.

Many Southern California freeways have designated carpool lanes, also known as High-Occupancy-Vehicle (HOV) lanes. Some require two passengers, others three. The minimum fine for an HOV violation is $246. Most on-ramps are metered to control the traffic flow; carpools are exempt and pass in their own lane.

When it comes to radio traffic reporter jargon, the names of L.A.'s freeways (as opposed to their numbers) are usually used. A "SigAlert" is the term used for an unplanned freeway crisis (a serious accident) that will affect the movement of traffic for 30 minutes or more. When you hear "a big rig is blocking the number one lane," you can determine the lane by counting out from the center divider.

BY PUBLIC TRANSPORTATION

We've heard rumors about visitors to Los Angeles who have toured the city entirely by public transportation, but they can't be more than that—rumors. It's hard to believe that visitors can comprehensively tour this Auto Land without a car of their own. Still, if you're in the city for only a short time, are on a very tight budget, or don't expect to be moving around a lot, public transport might be for you. The city's trains and buses are operated by the **Los Angeles County Metropolitan Transit Authority (MTA),** 425 S. Main St., Los Angeles, CA 90013 (☎ **213/626-4455**).

LOCAL SHUTTLES　Some of L.A.'s more popular (read: more congested) neighborhoods offer the opportunity to park once and take advantage of shuttle service. These include **downtown,** where Downtown Area Short Hop (**DASH**) buses run every 5 to 15 minutes and cost only 25¢. DASH also runs shuttles in **Hollywood** (along Sunset and Hollywood blvds.), and between **Fairfax Avenue** and the **Beverly Center** (via Melrose Avenue and 3rd Street). Call the MTA for schedules and route information.

In **Pasadena,** free **Arts Buses** run between Old Town and the Lake Avenue shopping district. Shuttles come every 20 minutes (12 minutes during lunchtime) between 11am and 8pm Monday to Saturday; stops are marked with ARTS BUS signs. The Visitors Center can provide additional information, including route maps.

FAST FACTS: Los Angeles

American Express　In addition to those at 327 N. Beverly Dr., Beverly Hills (☎ **310/274-8277**), and at 901 W. 7th St., downtown (☎ **213/627-4800**), offices are located throughout the city. To report lost or stolen cards, call ☎ **800/528-4800.** To report lost or stolen traveler's checks, call ☎ **800/221-7282.**

Area Codes　Within the past 20 years, L.A. has gone from having a single (213) area code to, by the end of 1998, a whopping six. Even residents can't keep up with the changes. As of press time, here's the basic layout: Those areas west of La Cienega Boulevard, including Beverly Hills and the city's beach communities, use the **310** area code. Portions of Los Angeles county east and south of the city, including Long Beach, are in the **562** area. The San Fernando Valley has the **818** area code, while points east—including parts of Burbank, Glendale, and Pasadena—use the newly created **626** code. What happened to 213, you ask? That code is scheduled to be split on June 13, 1998, after which only the downtown business area will still use **213.** All other numbers, including Griffith Park, Hollywood, and parts of West Hollywood (east of La Cienega Boulevard) will change to the new area code **323.** If it's all too much to remember, just call ☎ **411.**

Baby-sitters　If you're staying at one of the larger hotels, the concierge can usually recommend a reliable baby-sitter. If not, contact the **Baby-Sitters Guild** in Glendale (☎ **818/552-2229**) or **Sitters Unlimited** (☎ **800/328-1191**).

Dentists　For a recommendation in the area, call the **Dental Referral Service** (☎ **800/422-8338**).

Doctors　Contact the Uni-Health Information and Referral Hotline (☎ **800/922-0000**) for a free, confidential physician referral.

Emergencies   For police, fire, highway patrol, or in case of life-threatening medical emergencies, dial ☎ **911.**

Liquor Laws   Liquor and grocery stores can sell packaged alcoholic beverages between 6am and 2am. Most restaurants, nightclubs, and bars are licensed to serve alcoholic beverages during the same hours. The legal age for purchase and consumption is 21; proof of age is required.

Newspapers/Magazines   The *Los Angeles Times* is a plump high-quality daily with strong local and national coverage and meager international offerings. Its Sunday "Calendar" section is an excellent and interesting guide to the world of entertainment in and around L.A. The free events magazine *L.A. Weekly* is packed with news of events and a calendar of happenings around town; it's available from sidewalk news racks and in many stores and restaurants around the city. *Los Angeles* magazine and *Buzz* are hip monthlies with good listings and entertainment news.

Police   See "Emergencies," above. For nonemergency police matters, phone ☎ **213/485-2121,** or 213/550-4951 in Beverly Hills.

Post Office   Call ☎ **213/586-1467** to find the one closest to you.

Taxes   The combined Los Angeles County and California state sales taxes amount to 8.25%; hotel taxes range from 12% to 17%, depending on the municipality you're in.

Taxis   You can order a taxi in advance from **Checker Cab** (☎ **213/221-2355**), **L.A. Taxi** (☎ **213/627-7000**), or **United Independent Taxi** (☎ **213/483-7604**).

Time   For the correct time, call ☎ **853-1212** (good for all local area codes).

Weather   Call **Los Angeles Weather Information** (☎ **213/554-1212**) for the daily forecast. For beach conditions, call the **Zuma Beach Lifeguard** recorded information (☎ **310/457-9701**).

3 Accommodations

CHOOSING A LOCATION   In sprawling Los Angeles, location is everything. Choosing the right neighborhood as a base can make or break your vacation; if you plan to while away a few days at the beach but base yourself downtown, for example, you're going to lose a lot of valuable relaxation time on the freeway. For business travelers, choosing a location is easy: Pick a hotel near your work—don't commute if you don't have to. For vacationers, though, the decision about where to stay is a more difficult one. Take into consideration where you'll be wanting to spend your time before you commit yourself to a base. But wherever you stay, count on doing a good deal of driving—no hotel in Los Angeles is convenient to everything.

In general, downtown hotels are business oriented; they're sometimes popular with groups, but are largely ignored by independent tourists. The top hotels here are very good, but cheaper ones can be downright nasty. If you're on a budget, locate elsewhere.

Hollywood, which is centrally located between downtown and Beverly Hills and within easy reach of Santa Monica, makes a great base if you're planning to do a lot of touring—but there are fewer hotels here than you'd expect. The accommodations in Hollywood are usually moderately priced and generally well maintained, but otherwise unspectacular.

Most visitors stay on the city's Westside, a short drive from the beach and close to most of L.A.'s most colorful sights. The city's most elegant—and

Los Angeles Area Accommodations

The Argyle 38
Barnabey's Hotel 13
Best Western Hollywood Motor Hotel 47
Best Western Sunrise–
Redonda Beach Marina 12
Beverly Garland Holiday Inn 41
Beverly Hills Hotel & Bungalows 32
Beverly Hills Inn 31
Beverly House Hotel 30
Beverly Prescott Hotel 26
Carlyle Inn 27
Casa Malibu 1
Chateau Marmont 39
Century Plaza Hotel & Tower 17
Century Wilshire Hotel 20
Courtyard by Marriott 11
Doubletree Hotel Los Angeles/
Westwood 24
Gateway Hotel–Los Angeles Airport 14
Holiday Inn Hollywood 46
Hollywood Celebrity Hotel 44
Hollywood Roosevelt 45
Hotel Bel-Air 23
Hotel Del Capri 25
Hotel Inter-Continental Los Angeles 54
Hotel Nikko 28
Hotel Shangri-La 2
Hotel Oceana 3
Hyatt Regency Los Angeles 49
Hyatt West Hollywood 37
Kawada Hotel 55
Le Montrose Suite Hotel 34
Le Parc Hotel 35
Loews Santa Monica Beach Hotel 6
Los Angeles Airport Marriott 15
Los Angeles West Travelodge 18
Mansion Inn 8
Marina del Ray Hotel 10
Marina International 9
Mondrian 36
New Otani Hotel & Garden 53
Park Sunset Hotel 33
Radisson Huntley Hotel 4
Radisson Valley Center 22
Ramada Limited Hotel 21
Regal Biltmore 51
Regent Beverly Wilshire 29
Sheraton Grande 48
Sheraton Universal 42
Shutters on the Beach 5
Sportsmen's Lodge 40
Travelodge at LAX 16
Universal City Hilton & Towers 43
Venice Beach Historic House Inn 7
Westin Bonaventure 52
Westwood Marquis Hotel & Gardens 19
Wyndham Checkers Hotel 50

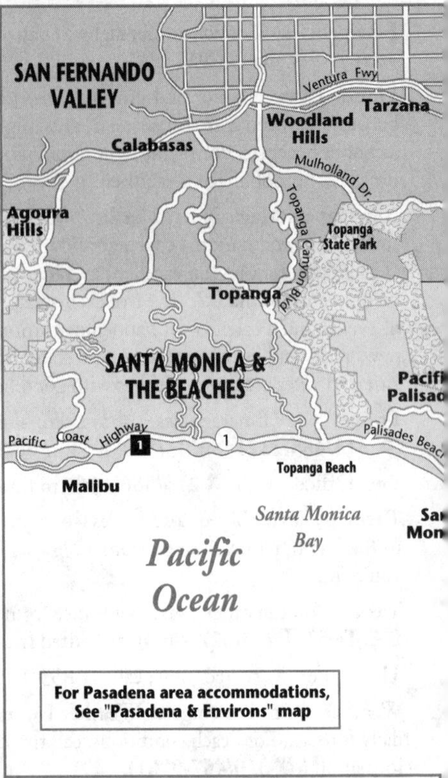

SAN FERNANDO VALLEY
Ventura Fwy
Tarzana
Woodland Hills
Calabasas
Mulholland Dr.
Agoura Hills
Topanga Canyon Blvd
Topanga State Park
Topanga
SANTA MONICA & THE BEACHES
Pacific Coast Highway
1
Palisades Beach
Topanga Beach
Malibu
Santa Monica Bay
Pacific Ocean
For Pasadena area accommodations, See "Pasadena & Environs" map

1	Lincoln Blvd. Sepulveda Blvd. Pacific Coast Hwy.	91	Artesia Blvd. & Fwy. Gardena Fwy. Riverside Fwy.
2	Santa Monica Blvd. Glendale Fwy.	101	Ventura Fwy. Hollywood Fwy.
5	Golden State Fwy. Santa Ana Fwy.	105	Century Fwy.
10	Santa Monica Fwy. San Bernardino Fwy.	110	Pasadena Fwy.
22	Garden Grove Fwy.	110	Harbor Fwy.
27	Topanga Canyon Blvd.	134	Ventura Fwy.
39	Beach Blvd. San Gabriel Canyon Rd.	170	Hollywood Fwy.
47	Terminal Fwy. Ocean Blvd.	210	Foothill Fwy.
55	Newport Fwy. and Blvd.	405	San Diego Fwy.
57	Orange Fwy.	605	San Gabriel River Fwy.
60	Pomona Fwy.	710	Long Beach Fwy.
90	Marina Fwy.		

LEGEND

22	**State Highway**
101	**U.S. Highway**
210	**Interstate Highway**

1-1316

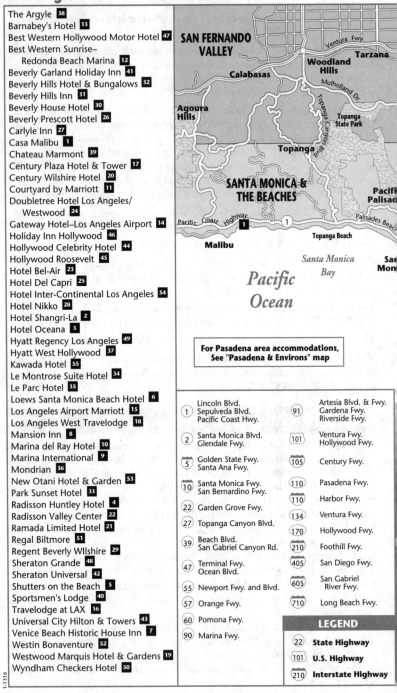

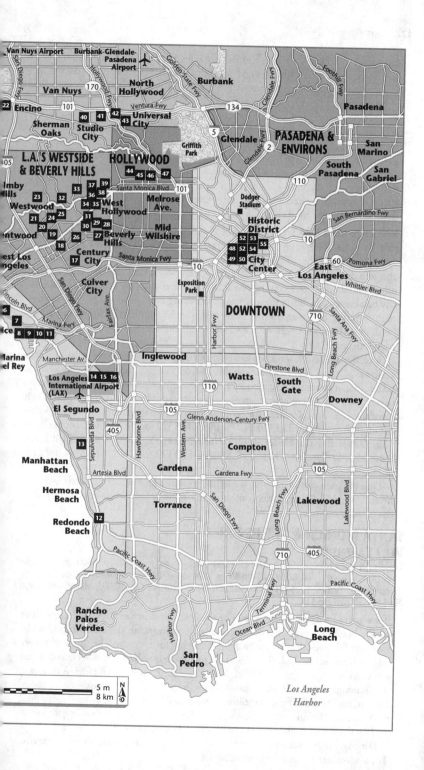

expensive—accommodations are in Beverly Hills and Bel Air. You'll find the city's best hotel values in West Hollywood, an exciting and convenient place to settle in.

Trendy, relatively smogless Santa Monica and its coastal neighbors are home to lots of hotels; book ahead because they fill up quickly in the summer, when everyone wants to be by the water. Santa Monica also enjoys convenient freeway access to the popular tourist sights inland. Malibu and the South Bay communities (Manhattan, Hermosa, and Redondo beaches) are more out of the way, and hence quieter.

Families might want to head to the San Fernando Valley to be near Universal Studios, or straight to Anaheim or Buena Park for easy access to Disneyland and Knott's Berry Farm (see chapter 14, "Side Trips from Los Angeles," for places to stay in the Anaheim area). Pasadena is a charming community with some unique accommodations, but it's not a good choice if you'll need to get back and forth across town.

RATES & RESERVATIONS   The hotels listed below are categorized first by area, then by price. Rates given are the rack rates for a standard room for two with private bath (unless otherwise noted); you can often do better. Ask about weekend packages and discounts, AAA or AARP discounts, corporate rates, family plans, and any other special rates that might be available. The prices given do not include state and city hotel taxes, which run from 12% to a whopping 17%, depending on which community you're in. Be aware that many hotels make additional charges for parking (with in-and-out privileges, except where noted) and some levy heavy surcharges for telephone use.

Several hotel reservations services offer one-stop shopping; they'll tell you what's available at many of L.A.'s hotels and book you into the one of your choice, all at no additional charge. These services are particularly helpful for last-minute reservations, when rooms are often scarce—or discounted. Here are two companies that serve the L.A. area: **Central Reservation Service,** 505 Maitland Ave., Suite 100, Altamonte Springs, FL 32701 (☎ **800/548-3311** or 417/339-4116; fax 407/ 339-4736); and the **Hotel Reservations Network,** 8140 Walnut Hill Lane, Suite 203, Dallas, TX 75231 (☎ **800/96-HOTEL** or 214/361-7311; fax 214/ 361-7299).

Due to space considerations, we've had to limit the number of hotels included here. If you'd like a larger selection, check out *Frommer's Los Angeles,* which has dozens of other options.

SANTA MONICA & THE BEACHES
VERY EXPENSIVE

Loews Santa Monica Beach Hotel. 1700 Ocean Ave. (south of Colorado Blvd.), Santa Monica, CA 90401. ☎ **800/223-0888** or 310/458-6700. Fax 310/458-6761. 349 rms, 22 suites. A/C TV TEL. $225–$315 double; from $450 suite. AE, CB, DC, EU, MC, V. Valet parking $15, self-parking $13.

If it weren't for Shutters, this would be the finest hotel in Santa Monica. Loews isn't exactly beachfront; it's on a hill less than a block away, but the unobstructed ocean views are fabulous. But realize that you're paying for location: The drone of the ice makers is audible in the hallways, and the plumbing is noisy at times—blemishes that you wouldn't expect from a hotel of this caliber. But it's still a great hotel. A dramatic, multistory glass and green-steel atrium lobby gives way to ample cookie-cutter rooms that are outfitted with the latest luxury amenities. This popular hotel doesn't need my recommendation to stir business; it has become something of a darling for industry functions, and it's booked to capacity in the summer months.

Dining/Entertainment: There are two restaurants and poolside snack service. There's live jazz in the lounge most nights.

Services: Concierge, room service (24 hours), nightly turndown, baby-sitting, valet parking, overnight shoe shine.

Facilities: VCRs on request, outdoor heated pool, fitness center with cardio machines, Jacuzzi, bike and roller-skate rental, summer children's program, business center.

✪ **Shutters on the Beach.** 1 Pico Blvd. (at the beach), Santa Monica, CA 90405. ☎ **800/ 334-9000** or 310/458-0030. Fax 310/458-4589. 186 rms, 12 suites. TV TEL. $290–$475 double; from $675 suite. AE, DC, DISC, EU, MC, V. Parking $16.

Light and luxurious Shutters enjoys one of the city's most prized locations: directly on the beach, a block from Santa Monica Pier. Guest rooms fall into two categories: cottagelike beachfront rooms, and those housed in a taller tower. Although the beach-cottage rooms are plainly more desirable, when it comes to rates the hotel doesn't distinguish between them. The views and sounds of the ocean are the most outstanding qualities of the rooms, some of which have fireplaces and Jacuzzis; all have floor-to-ceiling windows that open. Showers come with waterproof radios, biodegradable bath supplies, and toy duckies. Despite this welcome whimsy, there's a relaxed and elegant atmosphere throughout the contemporary art–filled hotel. The small swimming pool on an elevated deck and the sunny lobby lounge overlooking the sand are two great places for spotting the celebrities who swear by Shutters as an alternative hangout to smoggy Hollywood.

Dining/Entertainment: One Pico, the hotel's premier restaurant, is very well regarded. The best meals at the more casual Pedals are prepared on the wood-burning grill. The overdesigned Handle Bar offers good happy-hour specials.

Services: Concierge, room service (24 hours), overnight laundry, nightly turndown, in-room massage, valet parking.

Facilities: VCRs, outdoor heated pool, exercise room with cardio machines, Jacuzzi, sauna, sundeck, beach-equipment rental, bicycle rental.

EXPENSIVE

In addition to the Hotel Oceana, another Santa Monica option in this price category is the recently renovated, reliable **Radisson Huntley Hotel** at 1111 2nd St., north of Wilshire Boulevard (☎ **800/333-3333** or 310/394-5454).

Hotel Oceana. 849 Ocean Ave., Santa Monica, CA 90403. ☎ **800/777-0758** or 310/ 393-0486. Fax 310/458-1182. 63 suites. TV TEL. $200–$395 suite. AE, DC, DISC, MC, V. Rates include breakfast. Parking $13.50.

If you stayed in the former Oceana Suites Hotel, you won't even recognize the renovated and renamed Hotel Oceana. Excellently located in a residential neighborhood right on Ocean Avenue, this all-suite hotel is great for families. You'll immediately know you've arrived at the beach; light and airy and capped by an enormous skylight, the newly built lobby is completely covered with Jean Cocteau–inspired floor-to-ceiling murals. With the bright Matisse-inspired colors and cushy IKEA-ish furniture, the completely renovated suites appear to have been decorated by the set designer from *Friends.* Some suites have ocean views; VIP suites feature air-conditioning and two-person Jacuzzi tubs. In-room lunch and dinner service is provided by Wolfgang Puck's Cafe, but since all suites come with fully equipped kitchens, cooking for yourself is another option.

Services: Concierge, room service 11am to 10pm, continental breakfast in suite, dry cleaning/laundry service, newspaper delivery, massage, baby-sitting, valet parking.

Facilities: Kitchens, LodgeNet movie channels, outdoor heated pool, health club, sundeck, self-service Laundromat.

MODERATE

In addition to the hotels recommended below, another moderately priced option is **Courtyard by Marriott,** 13480 Maxella Ave., Marina del Rey (☎ **800/628-0908** or 310/822-8555), a resortlike hotel conveniently located only a few blocks from the marina and the Villa Marina Center.

✪ **Barnaby's Hotel.** 3501 Sepulveda Blvd. (at Rosecrans Blvd.), Manhattan Beach, CA 90266. ☎ **800/552-5285** or 310/545-8466. 123 rms. A/C. $155–$179 double. Rates include breakfast. AE, DC, DISC, EU, MC, V. Valet parking $6.

The most unusual hotel on the coast, Barnaby's sounds like a guest house, operates like a bed-and-breakfast, and feels like a quaint old hotel. The pink-stucco facade and trademark green awnings give way to European-style guest rooms; each is decorated with antique headboards, lace curtains, hardcover books, and 19th-century prints. Some rooms feature balconies, chandeliers, and attractive but nonfunctioning fireplaces. The best rooms are in back and overlook the courtyard. Romantic Barnaby's is an excellent place for couples and celebrants. Full English breakfasts are served buffet style. The hotel offers complimentary airport service as well as a glass-enclosed heated pool, Jacuzzi, and a sundeck.

✪ **Casa Malibu.** 22752 Pacific Coast Hwy. (about $1/4$-mile south of Malibu Pier), Malibu, CA 90265. ☎ **800/831-0858** or 310/456-2219. Fax 310/456-5418. 19 rms, 2 suites. TV TEL. $99–$135 double with garden view; $150 double with ocean view; $169 beachfront double; from $169 suite. Room with kitchen $10 extra. AE, EU, MC, V. Free parking.

I'm hesitant to crow too loudly about Casa Malibu—one of my favorite L.A. hotels—for fear that it'll be even harder to get a room here. The modest two-story motel wraps around a palm-studded inner courtyard with well-tended flower beds and cuppa d'oro vines climbing the facade. Just past the garden is the blue Pacific and a large swath of private Malibu beach for the exclusive use of hotel guests. The rooms are surprisingly contemporary and cheerful, with top-quality mattresses, bathrobes, coffeemakers, and refrigerators; some rooms have fireplaces and/or air-conditioning. The king-size-bedded oceanfront rooms have balconies directly over the sand—they're a great place to watch the pelicans dive for fish in the late afternoon. If you've got a room without a view, you can only see the ocean from the communal balcony; but since the sound of the waves will put you soundly to sleep in any of the rooms, that criticism seems like complaining that the caviar is too cold.

Hotel Shangri-La. 1301 Ocean Ave., Santa Monica, CA 90401. ☎ **800/345-STAY** or 310/394-2791. Fax 310/451-3351. 8 studios, 47 suites. A/C TV TEL. $120 studio; from $160 suite. Rates include continental breakfast. AE, CB, DC, DISC, EU, MC, V. Free parking.

Perched right on Ocean Avenue overlooking the Pacific and just 2 blocks from the Third Street Promenade, the Shangri-La has a great location. The small lobby opens to a large plant-filled courtyard (suprisingly lacking a pool) bordered on two sides by the hotel. The rooms—which are accessed motel style, from outside balconies overlooking the courtyard—are spacious, and almost all offer ocean views. The overall art deco feel of the hotel carries through into the rooms—the lamps and mirrors, even the faucets and doorknobs evoke the early part of the century. The large Formica-covered furniture, however, evokes the Starship Enterprise more than the Golden Age of Hollywood. There's a small oceanview exercise room.

Marina del Rey Hotel. 13534 Bali Way (west of Lincoln Blvd.), Marina del Rey, CA 90292. ☎ **800/882-4000** or 310/301-1000. Fax 310/301-8167. 154 rms, 6 suites. A/C TV TEL. $140–$170 double; from $300 suite. Packages available. AE, CB, EU, MC, V. Free parking.

This hotel, on a pier jutting into the harbor, is bounded on three sides by the world's largest manmade marina. The guest rooms are surprisingly well decorated, with fine contemporary furnishings and a few nautical nods. Most rooms have balconies or patios as well as harbor views; ask for one overlooking the main channel for the best day-long parade of boats. The hotel is peaceful and quiet—the only noise you'll hear is the soothing metallic clang of sailboat rigging. The on-site bar and grill overlooks the marina and serves California-style cuisine all day. Services and facilities include a concierge, room service, complimentary airport limousine, an outdoor heated waterside pool, sundeck, nearby tennis and golf, putting green, and car-rental service.

Marina International. 4200 Admiralty Way (west of Lincoln Blvd.), Marina del Rey, CA 90292. ☎ **800/529-2525** or 310/301-2000. Fax 310/301-6687. 110 rms, 25 bungalows. A/C TV TEL. $125–$300 double; from $150 bungalow. AE, CB, DC, EU, MC, V. Free parking.

This hotel's lovely rooms are bright, contemporary, and very, very private. Most rooms are decorated in a casual California style; all have balconies or patios. The bungalows are plush and absolutely huge—some are even split-level duplexes—with sitting areas and sofa beds. The Crystal Fountain serves continental fare indoors or out, and the hotel offers concierge, room service, and complimentary airport shuttle. There's an outdoor heated pool, whirlpool, sundeck, nearby golf and tennis, a business center, and a tour desk.

INEXPENSIVE

Best Western Sunrise–Redondo Beach Marina. 400 N. Harbor Dr., Redondo Beach, CA 90277. ☎ **800/334-7384** or 310/376-0746. Fax 310/376-7384. 111 rooms. A/C TEL TV. $79–$109 double. Extra person $10; children under 12 stay free. AE, CB, DC, DISC, MC, V. Free parking.

Across the street from the charming King Harbor marina, the Sunrise is clean and well-cared for, with pleasant and quiet interior hallways, a heated outdoor pool, and an extra-large whirlpool. Casual, beachy watercolors adorn the hallways and rooms, which have refrigerators and cable TV. Guests can rent bicycles on the premises to explore the marina and adjacent beaches; there's also a bike and skate rental hut directly across the street. The hotel's restaurant is a classy Northern Italian seafood place; if that doesn't interest you, there are a half-dozen restaurants in the surrounding 2 blocks.

The Mansion Inn. 327 Washington Blvd., Marina del Rey, CA 90291. ☎ **800/828-0688** or 310/821-2557. Fax 310/827-0289. 38 rooms, 5 suites. A/C TV. $79–$89 double; $125 suite. Extra person $10; children under 12 stay free. AE, CB, DC, DISC, EU, JCB, MC, V. No cash or checks accepted. Rates include breakfast. Free parking.

A charming, friendly, well-located inn with affordable rates that even include breakfast—it sounds too good to be true, but the Mansion Inn is all that and more. Each room has a small balcony and a refrigerator, and features such thoughtful touches as hair dryers, complimentary weekday newspapers, free movies, and separate vanity areas. Since the hotel is just 3 blocks from the ocean on the border between Venice and Marina del Rey, there's an endless parade out front of people exploring the Marina, the beach, or the nearby canals on foot, bike, or in-line skates (rentals are 2 blocks away; inquire at the front desk). Breakfast is served in a cobblestone outdoor courtyard shielded from the noisy boulevard. About the only thing missing is a swimming pool, but the staff will cheerfully lend you beach towels for an ocean dip. Suites, which have a high-ceilinged living room and spacious sleeping loft with queen-size bed, are the best deal here.

Venice Beach House Historic Inn. 15 30th Ave. (off Pacific Ave.), Venice, CA 90291. ☎ **310/823-1966.** Fax 310/823-1842. 9 rms, 5 with bath. TV TEL. $85–$165 double. Rates include continental breakfast. AE, EU, MC, V. Free parking.

This 1911 Victorian house is now a homey bed-and-breakfast on one of funky Venice's unique sidewalk streets, just one block from the beach. The interiors bear witness to years of family life: well-worn hardwood floors, faded Oriental rugs, and shelves of vintage hard-bound books. Ask innkeeper Elaine Alexander to recount the home's colorful history, including its many notable houseguests. My favorite room is the upstairs Pier Suite—light and airy, with a fireplace and sunny sitting room, this is as romantic as it gets. An expanded continental breakfast is served in the sunroom overlooking a splendid garden; afternoon tea or cool lemonade is served with fresh-baked cookies every day. The inn lends bicycles and can prepare picnic baskets for day excursions. *Beware:* The inn hums noisily with activity when there's a full house; seekers of absolute quiet and pristine appointments will not be comfortable here. Smoking is not permitted.

ACCOMMODATIONS NEAR LAX

If you have an early-morning flight and you need an airport hotel, here are two good, moderately priced choices: **Gateway Hotel–Los Angeles Airport,** 6101 W. Century Blvd., near Sepulveda Boulevard. (☎ **800/325-3535** or 310/642-1111), a comfortable, California-style hotel that literally overlooks the runway; and the **Los Angeles Airport Marriott,** Century Boulevard at Airport Boulevard (☎ **800/228-9290** or 310/641-5700), a reliable choice for travelers on the fly. If you're looking for an inexpensive option, try the **Travelodge at LAX,** 5547 W. Century Blvd. (☎ **800/ 421-3939** or 310/649-4000), an otherwise standard member of the reliable chain with a surprisingly beautiful tropical garden surrounding the pool area.

L.A.'S WESTSIDE & BEVERLY HILLS
VERY EXPENSIVE

✪ **The Argyle.** 8358 Sunset Blvd., West Hollywood, CA 90069. ☎ **800/225-2637** or 213/654-7100. Fax 213/654-9287. 19 rms, 48 suites. TV TEL. $225 double; from $325 suite. AE, CB, DC, EU, MC, V.

Completed in 1929, this landmark 15-story, Streamline Moderne-style hotel is one of the most pristine art deco buildings in the city. It's also terrifically located, at the base of the Hollywood Hills between Beverly Hills and Hollywood. As the Sunset Tower, it was home to Jean Harlow, Errol Flynn, and John Wayne (who kept a cow on his balcony so he could have fresh milk every day). More recently it made an appearance in *The Player.* The rooms are on the small side, but they're lovely, with art deco reproductions and specially commissioned, hand-crafted Italian furnishings, such as unique gondolalike beds. Corner rooms have marvelous rounded windows and spectacular city views. Though the hotel appears straight out of the 1920s, modern conveniences haven't been overlooked—all rooms come equipped with VCRs, CD players, fax machines, and space-age phones with display screens that do everything from tell the temperature to control the lighting.

Dining/Entertainment: Book a table at Fenix when you reserve your room (see "Dining," below). Ken Frank, one of the area's most respected restaurateurs, sold his celebrated French restaurant La Toque in order to cook here; it's one of the neighborhood's most prominent dining rooms.

Services: Concierge, room service (24 hours), laundry service, secretarial services.

Facilities: Heated outdoor pool, small exercise room with free weights and cardio machines, sundeck, car-rental desk.

✪ **Beverly Hills Hotel & Bungalows.** 9641 Sunset Blvd. (at Rodeo Dr.), Beverly Hills, CA 90210. ☎ **800/283-8885** or 310/276-2251. Fax 310/281-2905. 194 rms, 21 bungalows and garden suites. A/C TV TEL. $300–$350 double; from $300 bungalow; from $595 suite. AE, DC, EU, MC, V. Parking $15.

After a 4$^{1}/_{2}$-year, $100-million restoration, the Pink Palace is back. The famous stucco facade, impeccably landscaped grounds, and grand lobby have been restored to their former over-the-top glory, and then some: Despite declarations that the custom pink color has been painstakingly re-created, most everyone will tell you—myself included—that the hotel should now be known as the "Salmon Palace." Despite this controversy, the reborn hotel is glorious again. This is the kind of place where legends are made, and many were: This was center stage for deal- and star-making in Hollywood's golden days. Today, plenty of current stars and industry hotshots can be found lazing around the pool Katharine Hepburn once dove into fully clothed.

The hotel was reconfigured to compete in today's luxury market. There are fewer rooms, and each is more spacious and loaded with modern amenities. Gone are the sorry plumbing and tiny bathrooms of yesteryear; today's larger ones are outfitted with double Grecian marble sinks, TVs, and telephones for sinkside deal making. The best original touches have been retained as well, like a butler at your service with the touch of a button. The bungalows are more luxurious than ever—and who knows who you'll have as a neighbor?

Dining/Entertainment: The iconic Polo Lounge is back, with the original atmosphere and traditional comfort fare, like Dutch apple pancakes or its signature guacamole. The adjacent Polo Grill takes up the nouvelle torch, specializing in California cuisine. The famous Fountain Coffee Shop has also returned, while the Tea Lounge is a new addition.

Services: Concierge, room service (24 hours), dry cleaning, laundry service, nightly turndown, massage, valet parking, airport limo service.

Facilities: VCRs (video rentals delivered to the rooms), large outdoor heated pool, fitness room with cardio machines, Jacuzzi, sundeck, car-rental desk, beauty salon, boutiques.

✪ **Hotel Bel-Air.** 701 Stone Canyon Rd. (north of Sunset Blvd.), Bel Air, CA 90077. ☎ **800/648-4097** or 310/472-1211. Fax 310/476-5890. 52 rms, 40 suites. $325–$435 double; from $525 suite. AE, DC, MC, V. Parking $12.50.

The Hotel Bel-Air is your address if you want to impress. This Mission-style hotel is truly one of the finest—and most beautiful—hotels in Southern California. It regularly wins praise for its attentive service and luxurious rooms. The parklike grounds— lush with ancient trees, fragrant flowers, and a swan-dotted pond—are magical, and the welcoming, richly traditional public rooms are filled with fine antiques. The guest villas, decorated in Mediterranean style with compulsive attention to detail, dot the property. The rooms and garden suites are equally stunning; all have two phones, a VCR, and CD player. Some units have wood-burning fireplaces. The hotel is a natural for honeymooners and other celebrants, but families might be put off by the Bel-Air's relative formality, which is geared more to the jet set and business professionals.

Dining/Entertainment: It's worth having dinner at the restaurant. Even if you don't stay here, you might consider brunch or lunch on the hotel's outdoor woodsy terrace, or drinks at the cozy bar.

Services: Concierge, room service (24 hours), nightly turndown, valet parking, welcome tea upon arrival.

Facilities: VCRs, large outdoor heated pool, health club (with treadmills, Stair-Masters, Lifecycles), sundeck, nature trails.

Hotel Nikko. 465 S. La Cienega Blvd., Los Angeles, CA 90048. ☎ **800/645-5687** or 310/ 247-0400. Fax 310/247-0315. 300 rms and suites. A/C TV TEL. $295–$395 double; from $600 suite. AE, DC, DISC, JCB, MC, V. Valet parking $16.50; free self-parking.

Finally—a hotel designed for business travelers where the primary goal isn't mimicking every other business hotel. The Nikko refers to its interior decor as Pacific Rim (Organic Pacific Rim for the suites, which use all-organic textiles), but well-thought-out seems just as appropriate. Thanks to amenities such as in-room fax machines, three two-line phones, and large counter/desk space, the rooms function equally well as sleeping quarters and workspaces. And after a long day at work, the huge Japanese soaking tubs are perfect for unwinding. Shoji screens replace curtains, allowing light to filter through or block it out entirely.

Dining/Entertainment: Pangaea restaurant blends French and American dishes with Asian influences; it also offers a 14-piece, big-band brunch. There's also a cocktail lounge with nightly entertainment.

Services: Concierge, room service (24 hours), same-day dry cleaning and laundry, nightly turndown.

Facilities: Heated pool, exercise room, massage, sauna, business center.

✪ Regent Beverly Wilshire. 9500 Wilshire Blvd. (east of Santa Monica Blvd.), Beverly Hills, CA 90210. ☎ **800/421-4354** or 310/275-5200. Fax 310/274-2851. 206 rms, 69 suites. A/C TV TEL. $255–$405 double; from $425 suite. AE, CB, DC, DISC, EU, MC, V. Parking $15.

If the Beverly Hills Hotel is where new money exhibits itself, then this is the place for seasoned sophisticates. But that doesn't mean that it hasn't seen its share of color: Actor Warren Beatty earned his playboy reputation while living here, and parts of *Pretty Woman* were filmed in one of the palatial suites. You just can't beat the location, close to Rodeo Drive shops and an easy cruise down Wilshire to just about anywhere else. The rooms are refined, with a mix of period furniture, three phones, three TVs, and special double-glazed windows that ensure absolute quiet. Wilshire Wing rooms are unusually huge, but those on the Beverly side are prettier and include balconies overlooking the pool. The bathrooms have an extra-deep soaking tub and a glass-enclosed shower that's large enough for two. There's steward service on every floor, and butlers can be called from a bedside bell.

Dining/Entertainment: The elegant dining room offers fine dining and live dance music. The Lounge, a European-style salon, serves a terrific tea from 3 to 5pm, light menus, and cocktails; at night it's packed with media moguls and beautiful hangers-on.

Services: Concierge, room service (24 hours), nightly turndown, express checkout, valet parking, overnight shoe shine.

Facilities: Small outdoor heated pool, large health club with cardio and weight machines and free weights, hot tubs, sundeck, massage, business center, shops.

Westwood Marquis Hotel & Gardens. 930 Hilgard Ave., Los Angeles, CA 90024-3033. ☎ **800/421-2317** or 310/208-8765. Fax 310/824-0355. 257 suites. A/C TV TEL. From $235 suite; from $325 penthouse suite. AE, DC, DISC, JCB, MC, V.

This terrific all-suite hotel near UCLA, which attracts behind-the-scenes industry types, offers accommodations that are straightforward without being boring. Hidden behind a severe concrete exterior, each stylish room is unique and loaded with amenities. The 15-story hotel underwent a major renovation in 1995; each suite was outfitted with multiline speakerphones and fresh textiles. South-facing suites have the best city and ocean views. *Beware:* The hotel can be noisy during graduation and other large school events.

Dining/Entertainment: The Garden Terrace serves breakfast, lunch, and Sunday champagne brunch; dinner is served in the Dynasty Room. There are cocktails and afternoon tea in the lounge, and cocktails and casual fare at the outdoor cafe.

Services: Concierge, room service (24 hours), dry cleaning, laundry service, nightly turndown, valet parking.

Facilities: Two outdoor heated pools, small fitness center, Jacuzzi, sundeck, gift shop, flower shop.

EXPENSIVE

Beverly Prescott Hotel. 1224 S. Beverwil Dr. (north of Pico Blvd.; P.O. Box 3065), Beverly Hills, CA 90212. ☎ **800/421-3212** or 310/277-2800. Fax 310/203-9537. 128 rms, 12 suites. A/C TV TEL. $190–$275 double; from $250 suite. AE, DC, DISC, EU, MC, V. Parking $15.

This hotel opened its doors in 1993, after a multimillion-dollar renovation that rendered the former Beverly Hillcrest unrecognizable. Managed by the Kimpton Group, owners of about a dozen top-quality boutique hotels in San Francisco, the Prescott is knowledgeably run and joyfully decorated; its comfortable, colorful, funky furnishings were carefully chosen by a confidently quirky designer. Thus it was in perfect character for the hoteliers to commission the late legendary rock musician and neckwear designer Jerry Garcia to remodel one of the suites. The resulting Garcia Suite is surprisingly sedate, designed with fish themes, subtly psychedelic fabrics, a top-of-the-line sound system, and an eclectic art collection that includes a dozen pieces by Captain Trips himself. Each room has an oversize TV screen, cordless phones, and a private balcony with good city views.

Dining/Entertainment: The Chez serves up robustly flavored fusion cuisine in a bright, Caribbean-influenced interior.

Services: Concierge, room service (24 hours), overnight laundry/shoe shine, free morning newspaper, nightly turndown, massage and manicure services, complimentary shuttle service to nearby business centers and shopping.

Facilities: Large outdoor heated pool, fitness room with cardio machines, sundeck, business center.

Century Plaza Hotel & Tower. 2025 Ave. of the Stars (south of Santa Monica Blvd.), Century City, CA 90067. ☎ **800/228-3000** or 310/277-2000. Fax 310/551-3355. 996 rms, 76 suites. A/C TV TEL. $150–$220 double; from $250 suite. AE, CB, DC, EU, MC, V. Valet parking $19.50, self-parking $10.

Located on a former Twentieth Century Fox back lot, this Westin-managed property sits on 10 of L.A.'s most centrally located acres. It's so close to film and TV's Century City nerve center that it has become the de facto home-away-from-home for countless rank-and-file industry execs and creative types. Because it's so huge (the main building has 19 floors; the tower has 30), the hotel is also a natural for conventions and meetings; there's always something going on here. All this makes it the antithesis of warm and cozy, but the rooms are large, the freeways nearby, and your anonymity is assured. Rooms in the Tower building were renovated in 1995 and are considerably nicer—and pricier—than those in the main building. They feature large sitting areas, two sinks, and a separate tub and shower stall (some rooms in the main building have only a shower, no tub). Tower suites are head and shoulders above Hotel ones.

Dining/Entertainment: The hotel has two restaurants and two lounges, but dine in only if you have to.

Services: Concierge, room service (24 hours), same-day laundry service, nightly turndown, valet parking, complimentary car service to/from Beverly Hills.

Facilities: Two large outdoor heated pools, two exercise rooms, Jacuzzi, sundeck, business center, conference rooms, car-rental desk, airline desk, ticket agency, tour desk.

✪ **Chateau Marmont.** 8221 Sunset Blvd. (between La Cienega and Crescent Heights blvds.), West Hollywood, CA 90046. ☎ **800/242-8328** or 213/656-1010. Fax 213/655-5311. 63 rms, 53 suites, 4 bungalows. A/C TV TEL. $195 double; from $260 suite; from $600 bungalow. AE, CB, DC, EU, MC, V. Valet parking $15.

The Norman-style Chateau Marmont, perched in a curve of the Sunset Strip, is a landmark from 1920s-era Hollywood; step inside and you expect to find John Barrymore or Errol Flynn holding inebriated court in the baronial living room. Greta Garbo regularly checked in as "Harriet Brown"; Jim Morrison was only one of many to call this home in later years. This historical monument built its reputation on exclusivity and privacy, a posture that was shattered when John Belushi overdosed in Bungalow No. 2. Chateau Marmont is popular because it's close to the Hollywood action and a luxurious world away at the same time. The standard rooms have views of the city and the Hollywood Hills; some have kitchenettes. The suites are large, and most come with cloth-canopied balconies. The poolside Cape Cod bungalows—large, secluded, cozy, with full kitchens—are some of the most coveted in town.

Services: Concierge, room service (24 hours), laundry service, nightly turndown.
Facilities: Large outdoor heated pool, small fitness room, sundeck.

Hyatt West Hollywood. 8401 Sunset Blvd. (2 blocks east of La Cienega Blvd.), West Hollywood, CA 90069. ☎ **800/233-1234** or 213/656-1234. Fax 213/650-7024. 240 rms, 22 suites. A/C TV TEL. $185–$220 double; $235–$400 suite. Special weekend and AAA rates available. AE, CB, DC, DISC, EU, MC, V. Parking $10.

In 1997, this 13-story Sunset Strip hotel completed extensive renovations that erased any last remnants of its former debauched life as the rock 'n' roll "Riot Hyatt." It doesn't even look like other Hyatts, since the management eschewed the corporate standard decor and contracted locally; the end result is a stylish cross between the clean black-and-white geometrics of a 1930s movie set and a Scandinavian birch-and-ebony aesthetic. While not as haute couture as the Mondrian across the street, neither is it as haute attitude. Rooms all have beautiful city or hillside views (about half have balconies), but stay away from front-facing rooms on the lower floors—too close to noisy Sunset. The Hyatt woos both business and leisure travelers, providing secure access to guest floors and ergonomic desk chairs in each room; in-room minifridges are an extra $5 a day. *Auto club members take note:* Special AAA rates are as low as $139.

Dining/Entertainment: The casual Silver Screen Bistro is a notch above any good diner. There's also a sports bar and lobby coffee/pastry cart.
Services: Concierge, room service from 6am to midnight, same-day laundry service, secretarial services, valet parking.
Facilities: Serene rooftop heated pool with food and beverage service, tour desk, in-room movies, two-line phones with voice mail, business center.

✪ **Le Montrose Suite Hotel.** 900 Hammond St., West Hollywood, CA 90069. ☎ **800/776-0666** or 310/855-1115. Fax 310/657-9192. 128 suites. $185–$475 suite. Weekend and breakfast packages available. AE, CB, DC, EU, MC, V. Parking $14.

Nestled on a quiet residential street just 2 blocks from the bustling Strip, this all-suite hotel features large one-bedroom apartments that feel more like upscale condos than standard hotel rooms. Each has a large bedroom, kitchen, and bathroom, as well as a sizable sunken living room complete with gas fireplace, fax machine, and Nintendo games. You have to go up to the roof for anything resembling a view, but once you're up there, you can swim in the pool or play on the lighted tennis court. For location, quality, and price, this is one of L.A.'s best values, and it is already popular among music-industry clientele; let's hope that when this place catches on, prices will stay reasonable and reservations won't be hard to come by.

Dining/Entertainment: The Library Restaurant serves continental meals all day. Light bites are served poolside.

Services: Concierge, room service (24 hours), nightly turndown, voice-mail, currency exchange.

Facilities: VCRs, video library, outdoor heated pool, small exercise room, Jacuzzi, sauna, sundeck, one lighted tennis court, complimentary bicycles.

Le Parc Hotel. 733 N. West Knoll Dr., West Hollywood, CA 90069. ☎ **800/5-SUITES** or 310/855-8888. Fax 310/659-7812. 154 suites. A/C TV TEL. $200–$275 suite. AE, DC, EU, JCB, MC, V. Parking $12.

Situated on a quiet residential street, Le Parc is a high-quality, all-suite hotel with a pleasantly mixed clientele. Designers stay here because it's a few minutes' walk to the Pacific Design Center, patients and medical consultants check in because it's close to Cedars-Sinai, and tourists enjoy being near the Farmer's Market and Museum Row. The nicely furnished, apartmentlike units each have a kitchenette, dining area, living room with fireplace, and balcony. What this hotel lacks in cachet it more than makes up for in value. Although your L.A. friends may not have heard of this place, thanks to an overall renovation in 1996 they'll be impressed when you invite them up for drinks.

Dining/Entertainment: Cafe Le Parc is open from 6:30am to 11pm and features a fully licensed bar.

Services: Concierge, room service from 6:30am to 11pm, dry cleaning/laundry service, newspaper delivery, in-room massage, twice-daily maid service, baby-sitting, valet parking, courtesy car, bathrobes, ironing board and iron in room.

Facilities: Outdoor heated pool, basketball hoop, rooftop night-lit tennis court, kitchenettes, VCRs, video rentals, Spectravision movie channels, health club with sauna and whirlpool, business center, self-service Laundromat, car-rental desk.

Mondrian. 8440 Sunset Blvd., West Hollywood, CA 90069. ☎ **800/525-8029** or 213/650-8999. Fax 213/650-5215. 53 rooms with minibar, 182 suites with kitchenette. A/C TEL TV. $195–$215 double; $200–$430 suite. Weekend rates available. AE, CB, DC, EU, MC, V. Parking $18.

Theatrical, enchanted, sophisticated—this is the kind of place boutique hotelier Ian Schrager has created from a once-drab apartment building that he transformed in late 1996. Working with French designer Philippe Starck (as he successfully did at Manhattan's Royalton and Miami's Delano), Schrager used the Mondrian's already breathtaking views (from *every* room) as the starting point for his vision of a "hotel in the clouds." Starck created much of the hotel's whimsy by investing everyday objects with simplicity and humor; the contemporary Alice-in-Wonderland effect is also achieved through the manipulation of space, proportion, and natural and man-made light.

Because it's a seductive lure for the local scene, the Mondrian's public areas can be off-putting to outsiders, but guest quarters are sophisticated and welcoming. Purposely underlit hallways lead to bright, clean rooms done in shades of white, beige, and pale gray and outfitted with casually slip-covered furniture. No luxury is spared; amenities include down comforters and pillows, in-room entertainment centers (including CDs), and tons of the grooviest giveaway hotel notepads and pencils I've ever seen.

Dining/Entertainment: In addition to its pricey, ultra-hip Italian restaurant Coco Pazzo, the Mondrian serves light meals off the lobby at a quirky communal table. There's also Skybar, overlooking the pool and cityscape and usually filled with L.A.'s starlets *du jour.*

Services: 24-hour concierge, 24-hour room service, dry cleaning/laundry service, video library, in-room CD players, newspaper delivery, valet parking, twice-daily maid service, fresh flowers in room.

Facilities: Exercise room with sauna and whirlpool, outdoor heated pool, fully equipped kitchens, outdoor supervised children's play area, full-service business center, billiards area, sundry and gift shop.

MODERATE

Two good, moderately priced options near UCLA are the comfortable **Doubletree Hotel Los Angeles/Westwood,** 10740 Wilshire Blvd., at Selby Avenue (☎ **800/ 472-8556** or 310/475-8711); and the **Century Wilshire Hotel,** 10776 Wilshire Blvd., between Malcolm and Selby avenues (☎ **800/421-7223** outside California, or 310/474-4506), with large, somewhat-worn units that nevertheless offer great value in an expensive neighborhood.

If you're traveling with a group or as a family, be sure to consider the suite hotels listed under "Expensive" above; they can become quite a deal when you realize that you can accommodate four (or more) in a suite.

Beverly Hills Inn. 125 S. Spalding Dr., Beverly Hills, CA 90212. ☎ **800/463-4466** or 310/ 278-0303. Fax 310/278-1728. 45 rms, 4 suites. A/C TV TEL. $130–$145 double; from $180 suite. Rates include full breakfast, plus afternoon fruit and cheese. AE, DC, EU, MC, V. Free parking.

The secret to a Beverly Hills lifestyle is knowing how to put on a good appearance—any face-lifted, tummy-tucked socialite will tell you that. So go ahead and brag about your Beverly Hills address to your friends—they'll never know about the bargain you're really enjoying. You can honestly say you've got a quiet, newly decorated room outfitted with cable TV, refrigerator, and other thoughtful touches, like a bathrobe for strolling down to the small but lushly landscaped garden swimming pool. Popular with Asian business travelers, the hotel is impeccably furnished in a bland but vaguely tropical motif. Most rooms have a view of either the pool or quiet, tree-lined street out front. When you're ready to face the world, you'll find yourself ideally located just a block from Rodeo Drive shopping and dining, plus an easy walk from Century City. Breakfast is served in the aptly named Garden Hideaway Room (which does double-duty, serving afternoon snacks as well as a full bar). All in all, one of the best deals going in a high-rent neighborhood.

✪ **Carlyle Inn.** 1119 S. Robertson Blvd. (south of Wilshire Blvd.), Los Angeles, CA 90035. ☎ **800/322-7595** or 310/275-4445. Fax 310/859-0496. 24 rms, 8 suites. A/C TV TEL. $120 double; $190 suite. Rates include full breakfast. AE, DC, DISC, EU, MC, V. Parking $8.

Hidden on an uneventful stretch of Robertson Boulevard just south of Beverly Hills, this 4-story inn is one of the best-priced finds in L.A. An exceedingly clever design has transformed an ordinary square lot in a high-density district into an delightfully airy hotel. Despite its small size and unlikely location, architects have managed to create a multistory interior courtyard, which almost every room faces. Well-planned, contemporary interiors are fitted with recessed lighting, deco wall lamps, pine furnishings, and well-framed, classical architectural monoprints. Amenities include coffeemakers and VCRs. The hotel's primary drawback is that it lacks views; curtains must remain drawn at all times to maintain any sense of privacy. The suites are only slightly larger than standard rooms.

INEXPENSIVE

In addition to the hotels listed below, the **Los Angeles West Travelodge,** 10740 Santa Monica Blvd., at Overland Avenue (☎ **310/474-4576**), is a terrific option, offering pleasant, modern, recently renovated rooms and friendly service.

Beverly House Hotel. 140 S. Lasky Dr., Beverly Hills, CA 90212. ☎ **800/432-5444** or 310/271-2145. Fax 310/276-8431. 39 rooms. A/C TV TEL. $93–$99 double. Rates include continental breakfast. AE, CB, DC, JCB, MC, V. Free parking.

Tucked discreetly away on a quiet, tree-shaded residential street, this European-style, small hotel is just a half block from the well-heeled streets of Beverly Hills' "Golden Triangle" shopping district. Location and value are the hotel's main draws, but the smallish rooms are nicer than you'd expect: sparsely but comfortably furnished, with brand-new carpeting, upholstery, and wallpaper. Although there's no view to speak of, plenty of sunlight streams in. More than half of the little bathrooms have only a stall shower; if you prefer a tub/shower, specify when you reserve your room. A plush, spacious lobby is furnished with antiques plus a checkers and backgammon table; it's a nice place to enjoy your morning coffee. The hotel also provides complimentary morning newspapers, in-room minifridges, and free parking (an amenity virtually unheard of in these parts). *Tip:* Ask for one of the four front rooms—they're larger and have a lovely street view.

○ **Hotel Del Capri.** 10587 Wilshire Blvd. (at Westholme Ave.), Los Angeles, CA 90024. ☎ **800/444-6835** or 310/474-3511. Fax 310/470-9999. 36 rms, 43 suites. A/C TV TEL. $90–$110 double; from $115 suite. Rates include continental breakfast. AE, CB, DC, EU, MC, V. Free parking.

The Del Capri is one of the best values in trendy Westwood. This well-located and fairly priced hotel is popular with tourists, business travelers, and parents visiting their UCLA offspring. There are two parts to the property: a 4-story building on the boulevard and a quieter 2-story motel that surrounds a kidney-shaped swimming pool. Though the rooms are beginning to show wear and tear, all are of good quality and have electrically adjustable beds—a decidedly novel touch. The more expensive rooms are slightly larger and have whirlpool baths and an extra phone in the bathroom. Most of the suites have kitchenettes. The hotel provides free shuttle service to nearby shopping and attractions in Westwood, Beverly Hills, and Century City.

Park Sunset Hotel. 8462 Sunset Blvd., West Hollywood, CA 90069. ☎ **800/821-3660** or 213/654-6470. Fax 213/654-5918. 62 rms, 20 suites. A/C TV TEL. $75–$80 double; $150 suite. AE, CB, DC, DISC, EU, MC, V. Parking $5.

You'd think that the Park Sunset's location—right on the Strip—would make this one of the noisiest places to sleep in L.A. But all the guest rooms are in the back of the modest 3-story hotel, away from the cars and cacophony. The rooms are well kept and surprisingly well decorated, though the carpets are a bit worn and the bathroom color schemes are a tad dated. Some rooms have balconies and/or kitchens, and corner rooms have panoramic city views. There's a small heated pool in a lush courtyard and a continental restaurant on the lobby level.

Ramada Limited Hotel. 1052 Tiverton Ave. (near Glendon Ave.), Los Angeles, CA 90024. ☎ **800/631-0100** or 310/208-6677. Fax 310/824-3732. 27 rms, 9 suites. A/C TV TEL. $66–$76 double; from $75 suite. AE, CB, DC, DISC, EU, MC, V. Free parking.

This isn't a fancy place by any stretch of the imagination, but the rooms are comfortable and have recently been updated—they're in better condition than those in many hotels that cost more. Some have stoves, refrigerators, and stainless-steel countertops; others have microwave ovens. The bathrooms have marble vanities. Facilities include an exercise room, a lounge, and an activities desk.

👪 Family-Friendly Hotels

The highest concentration of family-friendly accommodations—those that make families with kids their primary concern—are found close to Disneyland (see chapter 14). That doesn't mean that families aren't welcome in L.A. hotels; in fact, a few welcome kids with open arms.

Century Plaza Hotel & Tower *(see p. 429)*   The Century Plaza offers spacious, family-size rooms and lots of facilities. Because it's a veritable city unto itself, older kids love to explore this labyrinthine hotel.

Hotel Oceana *(see p. 423)*   This is a spacious all-suite hotel overlooking the beach at Santa Monica. Kids will love the brightly colored walls and cushy furniture, and all suites come with Nintendo video games.

Le Parc Hotel *(see p. 431)* and **Le Montrose Suite Hotel** *(see p. 430)*   These fairly comparable all-suite hotels are centrally located in West Hollywood. Multiple rooms means privacy for parents, and kitchenettes can cut down on restaurant and room-service bills.

Loews Santa Monica Beach Hotel *(see p. 422)*   Offering comprehensive children's programs throughout the summer, and more like a resort than any other L.A. hotel, Loews boasts an unbeatable location—right by the beach and the boardwalk. What more could make the kids happy? It also offers baby-sitting services, so you can enjoy a kid-free evening on the town.

The Mansion Inn *(see p. 425)*   Location and value make this a great choice for ocean-loving families. The three-block walk to the beach is lined with snack bars, surf shops, and bike and skate rentals; the resident ducks of the Venice canals are equally close, as are the attractions of Marina del Rey. The under-12 set is welcomed free of charge, and everyone starts the day with complimentary breakfast.

Sheraton Universal Hotel *(see p. 438)*   This Sheraton enjoys a terrifically kid-friendly location, adjacent to Universal Studios and the enormously fun CityWalk mall. Baby-sitting services are available to give mom and dad a break, and there's a large games room on the premises.

HOLLYWOOD
MODERATE

Holiday Inn Hollywood. 1755 N. Highland Ave. (between Franklin and Hollywood blvds.), Hollywood, CA 90028. ☎ **800/465-4329** or 213/462-7181. Fax 213/466-9072. 448 rms, 22 suites. A/C TV TEL. $150 double; from $170 suite. AE, DC, DISC, EU, MC, V. Parking $6.50.

This 23-story hotel in the heart of Hollywood offers perfectly acceptable rooms that are both pleasant and comfortable—as long as you don't mind being on a busy thoroughfare and sharing the pavement with bikers, wannabe rockers, and the other colorful characters that make up the neighborhood melange. A major guest-room renovation was completed in 1995, so the hotel's standard furnishings are now stain-free. The suites, which include small kitchenettes, are particularly good buys. There's a swimming pool, a sundeck, and a revolving rooftop restaurant.

✪ **Hollywood Roosevelt.** 7000 Hollywood Blvd., Hollywood, CA 90028. ☎ **800/950-7667** or 213/466-7000, Fax 213/466-9376. 311 rms, 19 suites. $119–$149 double; from $300 suite. AE, CB, DC, DISC, EU, MC, V. Valet parking $9.50.

This 12-story movie-city landmark is located on a slightly seedy, very touristy part of Hollywood Boulevard, across from Mann's Chinese Theatre and just down the street from the Walk of Fame. The Roosevelt was one of the city's grandest hotels when it opened its doors in 1927, and was home to the first Academy Awards ceremony. The exquisitely restored 2-story lobby features a Hollywood minimuseum. The rooms, however, are typical of chain hotels, far less appealing—in both size and decor—than the public areas; but a few are charmed with their original 1920s-style bathrooms. The suites are named after stars who stayed in them during the glory days; some have grand verandas, while others are rumored to be haunted by the ghosts of Marilyn Monroe and Montgomery Clift. High floors have unbeatable skyline views. David Hockney decorated the famous Olympic-size pool. The Cinegrill supper club draws locals with a zany cabaret show and guest chanteuses from Eartha Kitt to Cybill Shepherd.

INEXPENSIVE

Best Western Hollywood Motor Hotel. 6141 Franklin Ave. (between Vine and Gower sts.), Hollywood, CA 90028. ☎ **800/287-1700** (in CA only) or 213/464-5181. Fax 213/962-0536. 82 rooms. $79–$89 double. Senior and auto club discounts available. DC, DISC, MC, V. Free parking.

Location is a big selling point for this chain representative, just off the U.S. 101 (Hollywood) freeway and within walking distance of the famed Hollywood and Vine intersection. They know it, too: The walls showcase images from the Golden Age of movies, and the front desk offers an endless variety of arranged tours, ranging from the Hollywood Walk of Fame to Six Flags Magic Mountain. Check out their package deals for extra value. Rooms are plain and clean, but lack much warmth—outer walls are painted cinder block, and closets are hidden behind institutional metal accordion doors. On the plus side, however, all come with a refrigerator and free movies and cable TV. The rooms in back have an attractive view of the neighboring hillside. There's a gleaming blue-tiled, heated outdoor pool, and one of the city's most trendy retro-eateries, the Hollywood Hills Coffee Shop (see "Dining," below) off the lobby.

Hollywood Celebrity Hotel. 1775 Orchid Ave. (north of Hollywood Blvd.), Hollywood, CA 90028. ☎ **800/222-7017,** 800/222-7090 (in CA), or 213/850-6464. Fax 213/850-7667. 32 rms, 6 suites. A/C TV TEL. $60–$70 double; from $75 suite. Rates include continental breakfast. AE, CB, DC, DISC, EU, JCB, MC, V. Free parking.

This small but centrally located hotel is one of the best budget buys in Hollywood. Located just a half block behind Mann's Chinese Theatre, it offers spacious and comfortable art deco–style units. Breakfast is delivered to your door along with the newspaper every morning. Small pets are allowed, but a $50 deposit is required.

DOWNTOWN
VERY EXPENSIVE

Regal Biltmore. 506 S. Grand Ave. (between 5th and 6th sts.), Los Angeles, CA 90071. ☎ **800/245-8673** or 213/624-1011. Fax 213/612-1545. 640 rms, 43 suites. A/C TV TEL. $225–$235 double; from $350 suite. AE, CB, DC, DISC, EU, MC, V. Parking $18.

Built in 1923, the historic and opulent Biltmore is considered the grande dame of L.A. hotels. During the 1930s and 1940s, the Academy Awards were held in the spectacular Crystal Ballroom—the first sketch of the Oscar statuette was scrawled on a linen napkin here—and the hotel was the top choice for presidents and the elite. You've seen the Biltmore in many movies, including *The Fabulous Baker Boys, Beverly Hills Cop,* and Barbra Streisand's *A Star Is Born;* the Crystal Ballroom appeared upside down in *The Poseidon Adventure.* The 11-story hotel sparkles with Italian marble and traditional French-reproduction furnishings, but the overall elegance has been compromised by an ugly office tower that was added in the mid-1980s. Still, the sense of refinement and graciousness endures, with a vaulted, hand-painted lobby ceiling, and attentively decorated—though small—rooms with marble baths.

Dining/Entertainment: Bernard's features high-quality continental cuisine. Smeraldi's serves homemade pastas and lighter California fare. Afternoon tea and evening cocktails are served in the lobby's stately Rendezvous Court; a full bar is also available in the Grand Avenue Sports Bar.

Services: Concierge, room service (24 hours), dry cleaning, laundry service, newspaper delivery, nightly turndown, express checkout, valet parking.

Facilities: Beautiful, original 1923 tile- and brass-inlaid swimming pool; state-of-the-art health club; Jacuzzi; sauna; business center.

Wyndham Checkers Hotel Los Angeles. 535 S. Grand Ave., Los Angeles, CA 90071. ☎ **800/996-3426** or 213/624-0000. Fax 213/626-9906. 173 rms, 15 suites. A/C TEL TV. $240 double; from $400 suite. AE, DC, DISC, EU, MC, V. Parking $18.

The atmosphere at the Wyndham Checkers, a boutique version of the Biltmore across the street, is as removed from "Hollywood" as a top L.A. hotel can get. Built in 1927, the hotel is protected by the City Cultural Heritage Commission as a Historic Cultural Monument. It has the feel of a grand old home, with cozy (and freshly upgraded) public areas such as a wood-paneled library. The top-of-the-line guest rooms are outfitted with oversize beds and coffeemakers.

Dining/Entertainment: Checkers Restaurant is one of downtown's finest dining rooms.

Services: Concierge, room service (24 hours), dry cleaning, laundry service, nightly turndown, express checkout, valet parking.

Facilities: Rooftop spa, heated lap pool, Jacuzzi, sundeck.

EXPENSIVE

In addition to the hotels listed below, downtown is home to local branches of the luxury chains, all of which are particularly suitable for business travelers, including the ultracontemporary **Hotel Inter-Continental Los Angeles,** 251 S. Olive St. (☎ **213/617-3300**), the best-managed property in the neighborhood; the functional but sterile **Hyatt Regency Los Angeles,** 711 S. Hope St., at 7th Street (☎ **800/233-1234** or 213/683-1234), whose most outstanding features are absolutely enormous windows that offer great views of downtown from every room; and the spacious, warm **Sheraton Grande,** 333 S. Figueroa St., between 3rd and 4th streets (☎ **800/325-3535** or 213/617-1133), attractively decorated and located right in the heart of the downtown hustle.

New Otani Hotel & Garden. 120 S. Los Angeles St. (at 1st St.), Los Angeles, CA 90012. ☎ **800/421-8795,** 800/273-2294 (in CA), or 213/629-1200. Fax 213/622-0980. 434 rms, 20 suites. A/C TV TEL. $180–$305 double; from $550 Japanese-style suite. Cultural packages available. AE, CB, DC, DISC, EU, MC, V. Parking $13.

Most of the plush rooms in this anonymous 21-story concrete tower are Western style and comparable to other top downtown hotels in quality (and price). The best reason to stay here is to experience the unique Japanese-style suites, outfitted with futons on tatami floors, Ofuro baths, and sliding rice-paper shoji screens. Hotel guests have exclusive use of the half-acre rooftop classical tea garden. The 1- and 2-night Japanese Experience cultural packages include suite accommodations, sake and Japanese appetizers served at check-in by a kimono-clad waitress, dinner in any of the hotel's restaurants, shiatsu massages, and a live bonsai tree to take home with you.

Dining/Entertainment: There are two Japanese restaurants, one California-style dining room, and a coffee shop (fresh-baked breads and pastries are a specialty). The beautiful Garden Grill, a Tokyo-style teriyaki grill, features rare Japanese Kobe beef (which is beer-fed and massaged daily!). Chefs prepare seafood and prime steaks.

Services: Concierge, room service (6am to 11pm), same-day laundry service, nightly turndown, valet parking, airport limousine service.

Facilities: Japanese-style health club (with saunas, baths, and shiatsu massages); golf and tennis are available at a nearby country club; car-rental desk; arcade with more than 30 shops.

Westin Bonaventure. 404 S. Figueroa St. (between 4th and 5th sts.), Los Angeles, CA 90071. ☎ **800/228-3000** or 213/624-1000. Fax 213/612-4800. 1,368 rms, 155 suites. A/C TV TEL. $175–$215 double; from $190 suite. AE, CB, DC, EU, MC, V. Parking $18.50.

The 35-story Bonaventure is the hotel that locals most love to hate. It's certainly architecturally unique: The hotel's five gleaming glass silos–like giant mirrored rolls of paper towels—constitute one of downtown's most distinctive landmarks. This is an enormous convention hotel, designed on the scale of a minicity. The 6-story skylit lobby houses splashing fountains, gardens, trees, and even a large lake. There's a tangle of concrete ramps and 12 glass-enclosed, high-speed elevators that appear to rise from the reflecting pools. The guest rooms begin on the 10th floor; each has a wall of windows offering good views, but they're smaller than similarly priced rooms in the neighborhood. One of the towers is a completely remodeled all-suite facility where rooms come with an additional parlor room and half bath.

Dining/Entertainment: The rooftop Top of Five features panoramic views along with adequate, but not distinctive, continental cuisine. Ask for an exterior table— they're the only ones with the view. The views from the Bona Vista cocktail lounge are worth the price of a drink. There's nightly entertainment—jazz combos, cocktail-hour dancing—at the Sidewalk Cafe, a California bistro, and the adjacent Lobby Court.

Services: Concierge, room service (24 hours), nightly turndown, express checkout, valet parking, Executive Club level with upgraded facilities and services.

Facilities: Large outdoor pool, sundeck, business center, conference rooms, car-rental desk, five levels of shops and boutiques.

INEXPENSIVE

Kawada Hotel. 200 S. Hill St. (at 2nd St.), Los Angeles, CA 90012. ☎ **800/752-9232** or 213/621-4455. Fax 213/687-4455. 115 rms, 1 suite. A/C TV TEL. $79–$119 double; $145 suite. AE, DC, DISC, EU, MC, V. Parking $6.60.

This pretty, well-kept, and efficiently managed hotel is a pleasant oasis in the otherwise gritty heart of downtown, conveniently located to the Civic Center, the Museum of Contemporary Art, and Union Station. Behind the clean 3-story, redbrick exterior are over a hundred pristine rooms, all with handy kitchenettes and simple furnishings. The rooms aren't large, but they're extremely functional, each outfitted with a VCR (movies are available free of charge) and two phones. Nonsmoking rooms are available. The hotel's lobby-level restaurant features an eclectic international menu all day.

THE SAN FERNANDO VALLEY

In addition to the hotels listed below, another comfortable option close to Universal Studios is the **Radisson Valley Center,** 15433 Ventura Blvd. (at the junction of I-405 and U.S. 101), Sherman Oaks (☎ **818/981-5400**).

VERY EXPENSIVE

Sheraton Universal. 333 Universal Terrace Pkwy., Universal City, CA 91608. ☎ **800/ 325-3535** or 818/980-1212. Fax 818/985-4980. 417 rms, 25 suites. A/C TEL TV. $250 double; from $325 suite. AE, CB, DC, DISC, EU, JCB, MC, V. Valet parking $14, self-parking $10.

This 21-story concrete rectangle, situated on the grounds of Universal Studios, is a good-quality, mixed-use hotel catering to tourists, businesspeople, and industry folks visiting the studios' production offices. A major 1994 renovation updated every room with contemporary fabrics and floor-to-ceiling windows that actually open; each is equipped with Nintendo games. The hotel is very close to the Hollywood Bowl, and you can practically roll out of bed and into the theme park.

Dining/Entertainment: The hotel's restaurant serves California cuisine, but the many restaurants and nightspots of Universal City and CityWalk are a quick tram ride away.

Services: Concierge, room service from 6am to 10:30pm, dry cleaning/laundry service, twice-daily maid service, express check-out, valet parking.

Facilities: LodgeNet movie channels, outdoor pool and whirlpool, health club, game rooms, gift shop.

EXPENSIVE

Universal City Hilton & Towers. 555 Universal Terrace Pkwy., Universal City, CA 91608. ☎ **800/HILTONS** or 818/506-2500. Fax 818/509-2031. 446 rms, 26 suites. A/C TV TEL. $155– $215 double; from $250 suite. AE, DC, DISC, EU, MC, V. Valet parking $13.

Though this 24-story hotel sits right outside the Universal Studios theme park, there's more of a conservative-business-traveler feel than the raucous family-with-young-children vibe you might expect here. The large lobby is built almost entirely of glass, giving it an openness that doesn't seem hollow or empty. The rooms are tastefully decorated in light earth tones with English-style furniture.

Dining/Entertainment: Cafe Sierra serves California cuisine all day, as well as Sunday brunch.

Services: Concierge, room service (24 hours), dry cleaning, laundry service, express checkout.

Facilities: Heated pool, privately run health club available for guest use at no extra charge, Jacuzzi.

MODERATE

Beverly Garland Holiday Inn. 4222 Vineland Ave., North Hollywood, CA 91602. ☎ **800/ BEVERLY** or 818/980-8000. Fax 818/766-5230. 258 rms, 12 suites. A/C TV TEL. $149–$159 double; from $199 suite. AE, DISC, DC, MC, V. Free parking.

Don't get confused by the name—this hotel is named for its owner, the actress Beverly Garland (of *My Three Sons* fame), not Beverly Hills. Grassy areas and greenery abound at this North Hollywood Holiday Inn, a virtual oasis in the concrete jungle that is most of L.A. The Southern California Mission-style buildings that make up the hotel are a bit dated, but if you grew up with *Brady Bunch* reruns, this only adds to the charm—it looks like something Mike Brady would have designed. Southwestern-themed fabrics complement the natural-pine furnishings in the recently renovated guest rooms; unfortunately, the painted cinder-block walls give off something of a college dorm feel. There are a pool, sauna, and two tennis courts, and all rooms feature balconies. The Paradise Restaurant serves Polynesian-influenced cuisine throughout the day. A complimentary shuttle to Universal is available.

Sportsmen's Lodge. 12825 Ventura Blvd. (west of Coldwater Canyon), Studio City, CA 91604. ☎ **800/821-8511** or 818/769-4700. Fax 213/877-3898. 178 rms, 13 suites. A/C TV TEL. $117–$156 double; from $180 suite. AE, DC, DISC, EU, MC, V. Free parking.

£113

It's been a long time since this part of Studio City was wilderness enough to justify the lodge's name. This sprawling motel has been enlarged and upgraded since those days, the most recent improvements—sprucing up the worn room furnishings—made within the last 3 years. Relaxing around the heated, Olympic-size swimming pool surrounded by a fleet of chaise lounges, you might take advantage of the new pool cabana bar and forget all about busy Ventura Boulevard beyond this garden setting. The guest rooms are large and comfortable but not luxurious; all have balconies or patios, and refrigerators are available. There's a well-equipped exercise room and a variety of shops and service desks, and both golf and bowling are nearby. A hunting-lodge motif bar and grill is on the property, adjoining a fine dining room that serves only weekend dinner and brunch in stunning glass-enclosed dining surroundings. Don't miss the beautiful black and white swans frolicking out back in the koi-filled ponds.

PASADENA & ENVIRONS

To locate these hotels, see map on p. 481.

EXPENSIVE

✪ **Ritz-Carlton Huntington Hotel.** 1401 S. Oak Knoll Ave. (west of Elliott), Pasadena, CA 91109. ☎ **800/241-3333** or 626/568-3900. Fax 626/568-3700. 355 rms, 22 suites, 6 cottages. A/C MINIBAR TV TEL. $145–$240 double; from $350 suite. AE, DC, MC, V. Parking $12.

Built in 1906 and still one of America's grandest hotels, the Spanish-Mediterranean Huntington gained popularity early on among celebrated writers, entertainers, political and business leaders, even royalty. Set on 23 meticulously landscaped acres, it seems a world apart from downtown Los Angeles, though it's only about 20 minutes away. Closed for 6 years after a particularly destructive earthquake, the hotel reopened in 1991 as a full replica of itself under the Ritz-Carlton banner. Each oversize guest room is dressed in conservatively elegant Ritz-Carlton style, with marble baths, thick carpets, terry robes, and the like. Behind the hotel is a bucolic Japanese garden that's great for strolling.

Dining/Entertainment: Locals seniors love to celebrate in the Georgian Room, where continental meals are prepared by a classically trained French chef. The less formal Grill serves traditional fare in a comfortable clublike setting. The Cafe serves all day, either indoors or out; it's best on Sunday for champagne brunch. High tea is served daily in the Lobby Lounge.

Services: Concierge, room service (24 hours), nightly turndown, baby-sitting.

Facilities: Olympic-size heated outdoor pool, small exercise room, outdoor Jacuzzi, sundeck, three lighted tennis courts, mountain-bike rental, pro shop, car-rental desk, full-service spa/salon, shopping promenade.

MODERATE

The Artists' Inn Bed-and-Breakfast. 1038 Magnolia St., South Pasadena, CA 91030. ☎ **888/799-5668** or 626/799-5668. Fax 626/799-3678. 5 rms. A/C. $105–$130 double. Rates include full breakfast. Additional person $20 extra. AE, MC, V.

This Victorian-style inn, an unpretentious yellow-shingled home pleasantly furnished with wicker throughout, was built in 1895 as a farmhouse. Each of the five rooms is decorated to reflect the style of a particular artist or period, including Impressionist, Fauve, and Van Gogh. The English Room, fitted with good-quality antique furnishings and cheerful rose-patterned wallpaper, is the best room in the house; it's also the only one with a king-size bed. The Italian Suite has a queen-size bed and an adjoining sunroom with twin beds, making it a perfect choice for families. The inn is on a quiet residential street 5 minutes from the heart of downtown.

Bissell House. 201 Orange Grove Ave. (at Columbia St.), South Pasadena, CA 91030. ☎ **626/441-3535.** Fax 626/441-3671. 4 rms. A/C. $100–$150 double. Rates include full breakfast on weekends, expanded continental breakfast weekdays, plus afternoon snacks and all-day beverages. AE, MC, V.

Hidden behind tall hedges that carefully isolate it from busy Orange Grove Avenue, this 1887 gingerbread Victorian is furnished with antiques and offers a delightful taste of life on what was once Pasadena's "Millionaire's Row." All rooms have private bath with both shower and tub (one an antique clawfoot, one a private whirlpool). There's a swimming pool and Jacuzzi on the beautifully landscaped grounds, and a downstairs library offers telephone and fax machine for guests' use.

INEXPENSIVE

Pasadena Hotel Bed & Breakfast. 76 N. Fair Oaks Ave. (between Union and Holly sts.), Pasadena, CA 91103. ☎ **800/653-8886** or 626/568-8172. Fax 626/793-6409. 12 rms, 1 with half-bath. A/C TV TEL. $65–$165 double. Rates include continental breakfast. AE, DISC, MC, V. Parking $5.

This old-style hostelry is definitely not for everyone. In true turn-of-the-century rooming-house style, the guest rooms all have washbasins, but all but one must share hallway bathrooms (three full, two half). Part of the attraction here is the well-restored National Historic Register building, and part is the hotel's flawless location: It's the only accommodation literally in the heart of Old Pasadena. The guest rooms are small but comfortable. The central sitting room/lounge is elegant and welcoming, and there's a lively coffeehouse in the courtyard behind the hotel where you can enjoy your breakfast and complimentary afternoon teas. Shuttle buses to the Rose Bowl depart 1 block away during major events.

Saga Motor Hotel. 1633 E. Colorado Blvd. (between Allen and Sierra Bonita aves.), Pasadena, CA 91106. ☎ **626/795-0431.** Fax 626/792-0559. 69 rms, 1 suite. A/C TV TEL. $62–$69 double; $75 suite. Rates include continental breakfast. AE, CB, DC, MC, V.

This 1950s relic of old Route 66 is a little bland by modern standards but has far more character than most others in its price range. The rooms are small, clean, and simply furnished with just the basics. The best rooms are in the front building surrounding the gated swimming pool, which is shielded from the street and inviting in warm weather. The grounds are attractive and surprisingly well kept, if you don't count the Astroturf "lawn" around the pool. The motel is about a mile from the Huntington Library and within 10 minutes of both the Rose Bowl and Old Pasadena.

4 Dining

Since the advent of California cuisine, now a staple across the country, trend-watchers have looked to L.A. restaurants for culinary fashion tips. These days, instead of the trattoria of the week, you'll find a wave of pan-Asian eateries fusing Thai, Vietnamese, Szechwan, or Indian elements with often inspired results. Also look for the return of traditional comfort foods, jazzed up with culinary twists and dubbed "New American."

The restaurants below are categorized first by geographic area, then by price. Keep in mind that many of the restaurants listed as "Expensive" are moderately priced at lunch. Reservations are recommended almost everywhere, particularly on weekends and during peak lunch (noon to 1:30pm) and dinner (7 to 8:30pm) times.

Our limited space forced us to make tough choices; for a greater selection of reviews, see *Frommer's Los Angeles.* If you're looking for L.A.'s theme restaurants, you'll find the **Hard Rock Cafe** at two locations: at the Beverly Center, 8600 Beverly

Blvd. (at San Vicente Boulevard), Los Angeles (☎ **310/276-7605**); and at Universal CityWalk, Universal Center Drive exit off U.S. 101 (☎ **818/622-7625**). **Planet Hollywood** is at 9560 Wilshire Blvd. (west of Rodeo Drive), Beverly Hills (☎ **310/275-7828**).

For additional late-night dining options see "Late-Night Bites" under "Los Angeles After Dark," below.

THE WOLFGANG PUCK EXPERIENCE   For perhaps the quintessential L.A. dining experience, be sure to try at least one of Wolfgang Puck's L.A. restaurants. Of, course, there's **Spago** (see p. 446). In May 1997, Puck opened a second **Spago** in the heart of Beverly Hills at 176 N. Canon Dr. (at Wilshire Boulevard; ☎ **310/385-0880**). This one is more spacious and formal, but disciple Lee Hefter was brought back from Granita to ensure the kitchen mimics the original. In addition to the Spago twins, Puck also has two terrific restaurants near the beach. **Chinois on Main,** 2709 Main St., Santa Monica (☎ **310/392-9025**), serves terrifically quirky East-meets-West Franco-Chinese cuisine. At **Granita,** 23725 W. Malibu Rd. (in the Malibu Colony Mall), Malibu (☎ **310/456-0488**), Puck applies his signature California style to seafood—very successfully, of course. His latest venture is **ObaChine,** 242 N. Beverly Dr. in Beverly Hills (☎ **310/274-4440**), a Pan-Asian bistro and satay bar interpreting exotic Asian for mainstream tastes.

SANTA MONICA & THE BEACHES
EXPENSIVE

Encounter at LAX. 209 World Way (Theme Building, Los Angeles International Airport). ☎ **310/215-5151.** Reservations recommended for dinner. Dinner, main courses $15–$29; lunch $7–$14. AE, CB, DC, DISC, MC, V. Daily 10:30am–10pm. CALIFORNIA.

There's always been a restaurant in the spacey, around-1961 Theme Building perched in LAX's midst, but these days it draws as many Angelenos as fly-by travelers (including John Travolta, who had his star-studded birthday party here). The reason? A recent makeover transforming the staid Continental dining room (whose best feature was a panoramic view over the runways) into a '60s *Star Trek* set gone Technicolor. Outer-space lounge music dominates the entire place, and waitresses endure silver satin minidress costumes complete with go-go boots. The menu features art-food, that L.A. specialty that combines too many ingredients and focuses more on creating sculptural arrangements on the plate than culinary delights for the taste buds; that said, the food is entertaining and adequately tasty. I suggest at least coming up and having a blue cocktail at the lava lamp–festooned bar, because quirky Encounter is worth an encounter.

JiRaffe. 502 Santa Monica Blvd. (corner of 5th St.), Santa Monica. ☎ **310/917-6671.** Reservations recommended. Main courses $14–$20. AE, CB, DC, MC, V. Tues–Thurs 12–2pm and 6–10pm, Fri 12–2pm and 6–11pm, Sat 5:30–11pm, Sun 5:30–9pm. CALIFORNIA/FRENCH.

"JiRaffe"—it isn't a quirky long-necked zoo creature, but a blending of names from the two chefs responsible for this overnight sensation. Always popular at West Hollywood's Jackson's, friends-since-cooking-school Josiah Citrin and Raphael Lunetta defected in late 1996 to open an instantly crowded, upscale bistro in restaurant-hungry Santa Monica. The deafening din of conversation here is usually praise for JiRaffe's artistic treatment of whitefish (spiced and served with sugar snap peas, glazed carrots, and ginger-carrot sauce), roasted rabbit, crispy salmon, or pork chop (grilled with wild rice, smoked bacon, apple chutney, and cider sauce). JiRaffe also wins culinary points for highlighting oft-ignored vegetables like salsify, Swiss chard, and fennel, as well as complex appetizers that are more like miniature main dishes.

Michael's. 1147 3rd St. (west of Wilshire Blvd.), Santa Monica. ☎ **310/451-0843.** Reservations required. Main courses $15–$25. AE, CB, DC, DISC, MC, V. Tues–Fri noon–3pm and 6–10:30pm, Sat 6–10:30pm. CALIFORNIA.

Chef-owner Michael McCarty, L.A.'s answer to Alice Waters, is considered by many to be the father of California cuisine. Since the opening of Michael's in 1979 (when McCarty was only 25), several top L.A. restaurants have caught up to it—most notably Wolfgang Puck's Spago, Joachim Splichal's Patina, and Michel Richard's Citrus—but this fetching Santa Monica restaurant remains one of the city's best. A recent price rollback has made dishes like Michael's simple grilled pork tenderloin with cream sauce and apples, as well as duck with Grand Marnier and oranges, even more appetizing. Spaghetti tossed in a creamy chardonnay sauce with large sea scallops, roasted sweet peppers, baby asparagus, and American golden caviar is just one example of the delicious, complex pastas here. Don't miss Michael's famous goat-cheese salad, served warm with walnuts and vinaigrette.

✪ **Röckenwagner.** 2435 Main St. (north of Ocean Park Blvd.), Santa Monica. ☎ **310/399-6504.** Reservations recommended. Dinner, main courses $18–$22; lunch, $8–$13. AE, CB, DC, MC, V. Mon 6–9:45pm, Tues–Fri 11:30am–2:30pm and 6–9:45pm, Sat–Sun 9am–2:30pm and 6–9:45pm. CALIFORNIA.

Set in Frank Gehry's starkly modern Edgemar complex (itself a work of art), chef Hans Röckenwagner's eponymous restaurant continues the motif by presenting edible sculpture amid gallerylike decor. Set in the midst of a popular shopping area, the space manages to be refreshingly quiet. Röckenwagner takes his art—and his food—very seriously, once orchestrating an entire menu around German white asparagus at the height of its short season. The delightfully unpretentious staff carries out deliciously pretentious dishes fusing Pacific Rim ingredients with traditional European preparations; a good example is the Langostine ravioli with mangoes in port-wine reduction and curry oil. The menu tastes as good as it reads, and desserts are to die for. Don't overlook the lunch bargains here, nor the unique European-style breakfast of bread and cheese.

✪ **Valentino.** 3115 Pico Blvd. (west of Bundy Dr.), Santa Monica. ☎ **310/829-4313.** Reservations required. Pasta $12–$16; meat and fish dishes $18–$25. AE, CB, DC, DISC, MC, V. Mon–Thurs 5:30–10:30pm, Fri 11:30am–2:30pm and 5:30–11pm, Sat 5:30–11pm. ITALIAN.

All of Los Angeles ached for charming owner Piero Selvaggio when he lost 20,000 bottles of wine in the 1994 earthquake. But elegant Valentino never lost its position as *Wine Spectator* magazine's top wine cellar, and *New York Times* food critic Ruth Reichl calls this the best Italian restaurant in America. The creations of Selvaggio and his brilliant young chef, Angelo Auriana, make dinners here lengthy multicourse affairs (often involving several bottles of wine). You might begin with a crisp pinot grigio paired with caviar-filled cannoli; or *crespelle*, thin little pancakes with fresh porcini mushrooms and a rich melt of fontina cheese. A rich barolo is the perfect accompaniment to rosemary-infused roasted rabbit; the fantastically fragrant risotto with white truffles is one of the most magnificent dishes we've ever had. Jackets are all but required in the elegant dining room. Valentino is a good choice if you're splurging on just one special dinner.

MODERATE

Alice's. 23000 Pacific Coast Hwy. (at the Malibu Pier), Malibu. ☎ **310/456-6646.** Reservations recommended. Dinner, main courses $9–$18; lunch $7–$15. MC, V. Mon–Fri 11:30am–10pm, Sat–Sun 11am–11pm. CALIFORNIA.

Alice's, situated on the Pacific Coast Highway on the pier above the beach, has a long history as a Malibu fixture. The dining room is glassed in on three sides and faces the ocean; rear tables sit on a raised platform so that everyone has a million-dollar view. It's a light and airy place, with a casual menu to match. Admittedly, most people are here for the one-of-a-kind atmosphere, but the food is a lot better than it needs to be. Seared yellowtail tuna is served simply, on a bed of spinach, with lemon and tarragon butter. Grilled chicken breast is marinated in garlic and soy and served with tomato-cilantro relish. Pastas and pizzas are also available, and there's a full bar.

Aunt Kizzy's Back Porch. 4325 Glencove Ave. (in the Villa Marina Shopping Center), Marina del Rey. ☎ 310/578-1005. Reservations not accepted. Main courses $8–$13. AE. Mon–Thurs 11am–11pm, Fri–Sat 11am–midnight, Sun 11am–3pm and 4–11pm. SOUTHERN.

This is a real southern restaurant, owned by genuine southerners from Texas and Oklahoma. Kizzy's chicken Créole, jambalaya, and smothered pork chops are just about as good as it gets in this city. Almost everything comes with vegetables, red beans and rice, and corn muffins. Fresh-squeezed lemonade is served by the mason jar. These are huge meals that, as corny as it sounds, are as delicious as they are filling. Sunday brunches are all-you-can-eat affairs, served buffet style. The biggest problem with Aunt Kizzy's is its location, hidden in a shopping center that has too few parking spaces to accommodate its customers. Look for the restaurant to the right of Vons supermarket.

Border Grill. 1445 Fourth St. (between Broadway and Santa Monica Blvd.), Santa Monica. ☎ 310/451-1655. Reservations recommended. Main courses $10–$20. AE, CB, DC, DISC, MC, V. Mon–Thurs 5–10pm, Fri–Sun 12–3pm and 4:30–11pm. MEXICAN.

Before Mary Sue Milliken and Susan Feniger spiced up cable TV as "Too Hot Tamales," they started this restaurant over in West Hollywood. Now Border Grill has moved too a boldly painted, cavernous (read: loud) space in Santa Monica, and the gals aren't in the kitchen here very much at all (though cookbooks and paraphernalia from their Food Network show are displayed prominently for sale). But their influence on the inspired menu is enough to maintain the cantina's enormous popularity with folks who swear by the authentic flavor of Yucatan fish tacos, rock shrimp with ancho chiles, and meaty *ropa vieja,* the traditional Latin stew. The menu earns my praise for including *chilaquiles,* a saucy tortilla casserole not often seen outside Mexico. Distracting desserts are displayed prominently near the entrance, so you may spend the meal fantasizing about the yummy coconut flan or key lime pie.

Camelions. 246 26th St. (south of San Vicente Blvd.), Santa Monica. ☎ 310/395-0746. Reservations required. Dinner, main courses $14–$22; lunch $10–$13. AE, CB, DC, MC, V. Tues–Sun 11:30am–2:30pm and 6–9:30pm. CALIFORNIA/FRENCH.

Either indoors or out, dining here is one of Los Angeles's most romantic dining experiences. Camelions' three 1920s stucco cottages, each with beamed ceiling and a crackling fireplace, are built around an ivy-trellised brick patio. Contrary to its Provençal setting, the tasty French-inspired cuisine is plenty California trendy. Red lentil crepes arrive garnished with smoked salmon and arugula salad, and roasted duck breast is sliced thin and fanned out over a plate of walnut-merlot sauce, accompanied by a risotto-and-berry timbale. There are traditional French dishes like sautéed rabbit stewed in a clay pot with sweet garlic. A large selection of sandwiches and salads (like spinach with warm new potatoes, bacon, and mustard vinaigrette) are available at lunch.

Joe's. 1023 Abbot Kinney Blvd., Venice. ☎ 310/399-5811. Reservations recommended. Main courses $8–$10 lunch; $15–$18 dinner. AE, MC, V. Tues–Fri 11:30am–2:30pm and 6–11pm, Sat–Sun 11am–3pm and 6–11pm. AMERICAN ECLECTIC.

This is one of West L.A.'s best dining bargains. Chef/owner Joe Miller excels in simple New American cuisine, particularly grilled fish and roasted meats accented with piquant herbs. Set in a tiny, quirky storefront, the humble room is a blank palette that belies Joe's popularity; the best tables are tucked away on the enclosed back patio. Lunch is a hidden treasure for those with a champagne palate but seltzer pocketbook: Topping out at $10, all include salad, one of Miller's exquisite soups, and especially prompt service. Beer and wine are served, except during weekday lunchtime (regulation, due to the elementary school across the street).

There's a nearly identical (but more spacious) sister restaurant in Sherman Oaks, called **Joe Joe's,** 13355 Ventura Blvd. (☎ **818/990-8280**).

Mobay. 1031 Abbot Kinney Blvd., Venice. ☎ **310/452-7472.** Reservations recommended for dinner. Main courses $9–$15; lunch/brunch $7–$9. AE, MC, V. Mon–Thurs 12–3pm and 6–10pm, Fri 12–3pm and 6–11:30pm, Sat 10am–3:30pm and 6–11:30pm, Sun 10am–3:30pm and 6–10pm. CARIBBEAN.

Not Montego Bay, but an amazing simulation! Within 5 minutes of entering Mobay's vibrant indoor/outdoor atmosphere, you'll think you're on a Caribbean vacation isle. Awash with color and the festive strains of steel drum music (live on weekends), the dining patio sits under a flower-laden trellis and canopy of trees. The short menu blends elements of Jamaican, Cuban, and Spanish cooking to create specialties like guava-glazed salmon, eggplant terrine with red pepper sauce, curried goat with rice and crispy sweet potatoes, and the old Jamaican standby, jerk chicken with plantain fritters. The full bar dispenses cool tropical concoctions. The restaurant is located in a funky, artist-infested Venice neighborhood that's perfect for a pre- or post-meal stroll.

INEXPENSIVE

Benny's Bar-B-Q. 4077 Lincoln Blvd. (south of Washington Blvd.), Marina del Rey. ☎ **310/821-6939.** Sandwiches $4–$6; dinner specials $7–$10. AE, MC, V. Mon–Fri 11am–10pm, Sat noon–10pm, Sun 4–10pm. BARBECUE.

It's mostly take-out at this cook-shack dive, but there are a few tables, where the city's luckiest diners gorge themselves on Los Angeles's best barbecued pork and beef ribs and hot-link sausages. Like almost everything on the menu, the barbecued chicken is bathed in a tangy hot sauce and served with baked beans and a choice of coleslaw, potato salad, fries, or corn on the cob. Beef, ham, and pork sandwiches are also available. To reach Benny's, find Lincoln Boulevard, then follow the heavy aroma.

Bread & Porridge. 2315 Wilshire Blvd. (3 blocks west of 26th St.), Santa Monica. ☎ **310/453-4941.** Main courses $4.50–$9. No credit cards. Tues–Sun 8am–8pm. INTERNATIONAL.

A dozen tables are all that comprise this neighborhood cafe, but a steady stream of locals mills outside, reading their newspapers and waiting for a vacant seat. Once inside, surrounded by the vintage fruit-crate labels adorning the walls and tabletops, you can sample the delicious breakfasts, fresh salads and sandwiches, and superaffordable entrees. There's a vaguely international twist to the menu, which leaps from breakfast quesadillas and omelets—all served with black beans and salsa—to the southern comfort of Cajun crab cakes and coleslaw to typical Italian pastas adorned with Roma tomatoes and plenty of garlic. All menu items are cheap—truck-stop cheap—but with an inventive elegance that truly makes this a best-kept secret. Get a short stack of one of five varieties of pancakes with any meal; they thoughtfully serve breakfast 'til 3pm.

Jody Maroni's Sausage Kingdom. 2011 Ocean Front Walk (north of Venice Blvd.), Venice. ☎ **310/822-JODY.** Sandwiches $4–$6. No credit cards. Daily 10am–sunset. SANDWICHES/SAUSAGES.

Your cardiologist might not approve, but Jody Maroni's all-natural, preservative-free "haut dogs" are some of the best wieners served anywhere. The grungy walk-up (or in-line skate-up) counter looks fairly foreboding—you wouldn't know there was gourmet fare behind that aging hot-dog-stand facade, from which at least 14 different grilled sausage sandwiches are served up. Bypass the traditional hot Italian and try the Toulouse garlic, Bombay curried lamb, all-chicken apple, or orange-garlic-cumin. Each is served on a freshly baked onion roll and smothered with onions and peppers. Burgers, BLTs, and rotisserie chicken are also served, but why bother?

Other locations include the Valley's **Universal CityWalk** (☎ 818/622-JODY), and inside LAX's Terminal 6, where you can pick up some last-minute vacuum-packed sausages for home.

✪ **Kay 'n Dave's Cantina.** 262 26th St. (south of San Vicente Blvd.), Santa Monica. ☎ **310/ 260-1355.** Main courses $5–$10. MC, V. Mon–Thurs 11am–9:30pm, Fri 11am–10pm, Sat 8:30am–10pm, Sun 8:30am–9:30pm. HEALTHY MEXICAN.

A beach community favorite for "really big portions of really good food at really low prices," Kay 'n Dave's cooks with no lard and has a vegetarian-friendly menu with plenty of meat items, too. Come early (and be prepared to wait) for breakfast, as local devotees line up for five kinds of fluffy pancakes, zesty omelets, or one of the best breakfast burritos in town. Grilled tuna Veracruz, spinach and chicken enchiladas in tomatillo salsa, seafood fajitas tostada, vegetable-filled corn tamales, and other Mexican specialties really are served in huge portions, making this mostly locals minichain a great choice to energize for (or re-energize after) an action-packed day of beach sightseeing. Bring the family—there's a kids' menu and crayons on every table.

L.A.'S WESTSIDE & BEVERLY HILLS
EXPENSIVE

Fenix at the Argyle. 8358 Sunset Blvd., W. Hollywood. ☎ **213/848-6677.** Reservations required. Dinner, main courses $23–$32; lunch $10–$22. AE, CB, DC, EU, MC, V. Daily 7am–10pm. FRENCH/CALIFORNIA.

Fenix is much more than the classy, art deco Argyle hotel's dining room. Chef Ken Frank built up quite a cult following cooking at legendary La Toque, and since coming to Fenix has continued blending haute and nouvelle touches to create pricey works of art for the palate. Well-coifed and -suited beautiful people gather for Frank's signature appetizer: perfect little potato pancakes topped with your choice of four varieties of caviar. To follow, choose from creations like Texas black antelope grilled with cabernet foie gras sauce or salmon broiled with zucchini scales on cannelini bean ragout. *Note:* Open all day, Fenix serves breakfast, lunch, and dinner for the benefit of the attached hotel, but only an abbreviated menu is available between 2:30 and 6pm Monday to Saturday; ditto Sunday after noon.

✪ **Four Oaks.** 2181 N. Beverly Glen Blvd., Los Angeles. ☎ **310/470-2265.** Reservations required. Main courses $22–$29. AE, MC, V. Mon 6–10pm, Tues–Sat 11:30am–2pm and 6–10pm, Sun 10:30am–2pm and 6–10pm. CALIFORNIA.

Just looking at the menu here makes me swoon. The country-cottage ambiance and chef Peter Roelant's superlative blend of fresh ingredients with luxurious continental flourishes make a meal at the Four Oaks one of my favorite luxuries. Dinner is served beneath trees festooned with twinkling lights. Appetizers like lavender-smoked salmon with crisp potatoes and horseradish crème fraîche complement mouthwatering dishes like roasted chicken with sage, Oregon forest mushrooms, artichoke hearts, and port-balsamic sauce. If you're looking for someplace special, head to this canyon hideaway—you won't be disappointed.

Lawry's The Prime Rib. 100 N. La Cienega Blvd. (north of Wilshire Blvd.), Beverly Hills. ☎ **310/652-2827.** Reservations required. Main courses $20–$30. AE, CB, DC, DISC, MC, V. Mon–Thurs 5–10pm, Fri 5–11pm, Sat 4:30–11pm, Sun 4–10pm. PRIME RIB/SEAFOOD.

Most Americans know Lawry's only as a brand of seasoned salt (it was invented at this family-run institution that dates back to 1938). Going to Lawry's is an Old-World event; the main menu offerings are four cuts of prime rib that vary in thickness from two fingers to an entire hand. Every standing rib roast is dry-aged for 2 to 3 weeks, sprinkled with Lawry's famous seasoning, then roasted on a bed of rock salt. A carver wheels the cooked beef tableside, then slices it properly, rare to well done. All dinners come with creamy whipped horseradish, Yorkshire pudding, and the Original Spinning Bowl Salad (drenched in Lawry's signature Sherry French dressing). Lawry's moved across the street from its original location a few years ago, but retained its throwback-to-the-30s clubroom atmosphere, complete with Persian-carpeted oak floors, high-backed chairs, and European oils.

Maple Drive. 345 N. Maple Dr. (at Alden Dr.), Beverly Hills. ☎ **310/274-9800.** Reservations recommended. Dinner, main courses $17–$29; lunch $10–$18. AE, CB, MC, V. Mon–Thurs 11:30am–2:30pm and 6–10pm, Fri 11:30am–2:30pm and 6–11pm, Sat 6–11pm. AMERICAN.

Opened by celebrities including producer/director Tony Bill, Maple Drive is one of the best traditional American restaurants in, well, America. Chef Leonard Schwartz cooks great meat loaf, terrific chili, and out-of-this-world veal chops (which regulars ask for Milanese style—lightly breaded and served with a squeeze of lemon). The restaurant attracts the biggest celebrities—Barbra, Elton, Arnold, and others who have enjoyed fame for so long they often seem tired of the attention; they enter through a second, more discrete, door and sit in relatively secluded booths in back of the multilevel dining room. That's a bonus for us nobodies; on warm nights, the best seats are out on the patio. Maple Drive is a classy place with great food, high prices, and live dinnertime jazz. Even if Clint isn't at the next table, it's worth lingering for the extraordinary desserts.

The same celebrity team also runs one of the beach's trendiest restaurants, **72 Market Street,** 72 Market St., just west of Pacific Avenue, Venice (☎ **310/392-8720**), where Franco-American staples draw loyal crowds, along with the requisite meat loaf and chili.

✪ **Matsuhisa.** 129 N. La Cienega Blvd. (north of Wilshire Blvd.), Beverly Hills. ☎ **310/659-9639.** Reservations required. Main courses $14–$22; full dinner $26–$29. AE, DC, MC, V. Mon–Fri 11:45am–2:15pm and 5:45–10:15pm, Sat–Sun 5:45–10:15pm. JAPANESE/PERUVIAN.

Japanese chef/owner Nobuyuki Matsuhisa arrived in Los Angeles via Peru and opened what may be the most creative restaurant in the entire city. A true master of fish cookery, Matsuhisa creates fantastic, unusual dishes by combining Japanese flavors with South American spices and salsas. Broiled sea bass with black truffles, sautéed squid with garlic and soy, and Dungeness crab tossed with chiles and cream are good examples of the masterfully prepared delicacies that are available in addition to thickly sliced nigiri and creative sushi rolls. Matsuhisa is perennially popular with celebrities and hard-core foodies, so reserve early for those hard-to-get tables. The small, crowded main dining room suffers from bad lighting and precious lack of privacy; many big names are ushered through to private dining rooms. There's lots of action behind the sushi bar, and a frenetic service staff keeps the restaurant humming at a fiery pace.

✪ **Spago.** 1114 Horn Ave. (at Sunset Blvd.), West Hollywood. ☎ **310/652-4025.** Reservations required. Main courses $18–$28. DC, DISC, MC, V. Tues–Fri 6–11pm, Sat 5:30–11pm, Sun 6–10pm. CALIFORNIA.

Wolfgang Puck is more than a great chef: He's also a masterful businessman and publicist who has made Spago one of the best-known restaurants in America. Despite all the hoopla—and more than 17 years of service—Spago remains one of L.A.'s top-rated restaurants. German-born Puck originally won fame serving imaginative "gourmet" pizzas. These individually sized thin-crust pies are baked in a wood-burning oven and topped with goodies like duck sausage, shiitake mushrooms, leeks, and artichokes, and other combinations once considered to be on the culinary edge. Of meat dishes, roast Sonoma lamb with braised shallots and grilled chicken with garlic and parsley are two perennial favorites. The celebrated (and far from secret) off-menu meal is Jewish pizza, a crispy pie topped with smoked salmon, crème fraîche, dill, red onion, and dollops of caviar.

MODERATE

Bombay Cafe. 12113 Santa Monica Blvd. (at Bundy Dr.). ☎ **310/820-2070.** Reservations not accepted. Main courses $9–$15. MC, V. Tues–Thurs 11:30am–10pm, Fri–Sat 11:30am–11pm, Sun 11:30am–4pm. INDIAN.

Bombay Cafe's unlikely generic interior and storefront location (on the second floor of a nondescript minimall) belie excellent curries and kurmas that are typical of South Indian street food. Once seated, immediately order *sev puri* for the table; these crispy little chips topped with chopped potatoes, onions, cilantro, and chutneys are the perfect accompaniment to what's sure to be an extended menu-reading session. Also recommended are the burritolike "frankies," juicy little bread rolls stuffed with lamb, chicken, or cauliflower. The best dishes come from the tandoor, and include spicy yogurt-marinated swordfish, lamb, and chicken. The food is served authentically spicy, unless you specify otherwise. The restaurant is phenomenally popular and gets its share of celebrities: Meg Ryan and Dennis Quaid hired the Bombay Cafe to cater an affair at their Montana ranch.

Cava. 8384 W. 3rd St. (at Orlando Ave., in the Beverly Plaza Hotel). ☎ **213/658-8898.** Reservations recommended on weekends. Main courses $8–$17; breakfast $3–$9; lunch $4–$14. AE, CB, DC, DISC, MC, V. Daily 6:30am–midnight. SPANISH.

Trendy types in the mood for some fun are attracted to Cava's great mambo atmosphere; the tapas bar is made festive with flamboyant colors, and the loud, lively flamenco really is live on weekends. The dining room is less raucous, with velvet drapes and tassels adorning the walls and comfortable booths. The cuisine is Spanish livened up with Caribbean touches, an influence reflected in dishes like black-bean tamales with tomatillo salsa and golden caviar; thick, dark tortilla soup; jerk chicken with sweet yams; and pan-seared shrimp in spicy peppercorn sauce. Spanish paella is stewed up three ways—with seafood, chicken and sausage, or all-vegetable—and is featured in Monday's all-you-can-eat "Paella Festival." If you have room for dessert, try the ruby-colored pears poached in port, the rice pudding, or the flan.

Kate Mantilini. 9101 Wilshire Blvd. (at Doheny Dr.), Beverly Hills. ☎ **310/278-3699.** Reservations recommended. Main courses $7–$16. AE, MC, V. Mon–Thurs 7:30am–1am, Fri 7:30am–3am, Sat noon–3am, Sun 10am–midnight. AMERICAN.

It's rare to find a restaurant that feels comfortably familiar yet cutting-edge trendy at the same time—and also happens to be one of L.A.'s few late-night eateries. Kate Mantilini fits the bill perfectly. One of the first to bring meat loaf back into fashion, Kate's offers a huge menu of upscale truck-stop favorites like "white" chili (made with chicken, white beans, and Jack cheese), grilled steaks and fish, a few token pastas, and just about anything you could crave. At 2am, nothing quite beats a steaming bowl of lentil-vegetable soup and some garlic-cheese toast, unless your taste runs to fresh oysters and a dry martini—Kate has it all. The huge mural of the Hagler-Hearns boxing match that dominates the stark, open interior provides the only clue to the namesake's identity: Mantilini was an early female boxing promoter, around 1947.

⭐ **Locanda Veneta.** 8638 W. 3rd St. (between San Vicente and Robertson blvds.). ☎ **310/274-1893.** Reservations required. Main courses $10–$22. AE, DC, DISC, MC, V. Mon–Thurs 11:30am–2:30pm and 5:30–10:30pm, Fri 11:30am–2:30pm and 5:30–11pm, Sat 5:30–11pm. VENETIAN.

Locanda Veneta's citywide renown belies its tiny size and unpretentious setting. Its location, across from the unsightly monolith that is Cedars-Sinai Hospital, is a far cry from Venice's Grand Canal, and the single, loud, tightly packed dining room can sometimes feel like Piazza San Marco at the height of tourist season. But the sensible prices reflect the restaurant's efficient decor. While the dining room is decidedly unfancy, the kitchen is dead serious, making this restaurant a kind of temple for knowledgeable foodies, who flock here to sample the latest creations of chef Massimo Ormani, a gifted artist and culinary technician who's building a national reputation. The soups are excellent, seafood dishes extraordinary, and pastas as good as they can get. Signature dishes include pasta-and-bean soup, veal chops, lobster ravioli, shrimp risotto, and perfectly grilled vegetables. Though the dessert menu is long and tempting, I always order the *crema de vaniglia,* a dense silky custard topped with caramel and chocolate sauces.

Replay Country Store Cafe. 8607 Melrose Ave. (between San Vicente and La Cienega blvds.), West Hollywood. ☎ **310/657-6404.** Reservations suggested on weekends. Main courses $6–$13. AE, DISC, MC, V. Mon–Fri 11am–11pm, Sat–Sun 11am–midnight. ITALIAN/CONTINENTAL.

The two things to remember at Replay are (1) don't buy the clothes, and (2) always order the soup. Most of the cafe's tables are on the wraparound wood porch of the overpriced boutique it's attached to. This faux country general store on trendy Melrose Avenue near the Pacific Design Center won't fool anyone into plunking down $150 for denim overalls, but the restaurant is one of West Hollywood's hidden treasures. Everything on the casual, vaguely Italian menu is outstanding, from gourmet pizzas and pasta with delicately puréed tomato-basil sauce to the warm chicken salad—a surprise combination of bleu cheese, walnuts, and mandarin orange wedges—and the exquisite pastries for dessert. Each day a different soup, always a simple purée allowing the fresh ingredients to shine through, is ladled into wide bowls at your table from heavy copper saucepans.

INEXPENSIVE

The Apple Pan. 10801 Pico Blvd. (east of Westwood Blvd.). ☎ **310/475-3585.** Main courses $6–$7. No credit cards. Tues–Thurs and Sun 11am–midnight, Fri–Sat 11am–1am. SANDWICHES/AMERICAN.

There are no tables, just a U-shaped counter, at this classic American burger shack and L.A. landmark. Open since 1947, the Apple Pan is a diner that looks—and acts—the part. It's famous for juicy burgers, bullet-speed service, and its authentic frills-free atmosphere. The hickory burger is best, though the tuna sandwich also has its huge share of fans. Ham, egg salad, and Swiss cheese sandwiches round out the menu. Definitely order fries and, if you're in the mood, the home-baked apple pie, too.

Cadillac Cafe. 359 N. La Cienega Blvd. (1 block north of Beverly Blvd.), Los Angeles. ☎ **310/657-6591.** Reservations recommended for dinner. Main courses $7–$11. AE, MC, V. Mon–Thurs 11am–11pm, Fri 11am–midnight, Sat 10am–midnight, Sun 10am–11pm. AMERICAN ECLECTIC.

The buzz around town is all about the Cadillac Cafe—at least this month. It's smaller and friendlier than you'd expect from an ultratrendy hipster hang less than a block from the Beverly Center. The attitude here says "coffeehouse." Vinyl booths and '50s-style dinette tables are offset by brightly colored geometrics and artwork as edgy as the new wave and punk soundtrack; the menu has a split-personality, too. New twists on comfort food basics, like a light Waldorf salad redux or the turkey "sundae" (my fave: turkey and mashed potatoes with gravy and cranberry toppings sprinkled with pecans) share space with stuffed grape leaves, Chinese chicken salad (another winner), and other ethnic surprises. *Helpful hint:* There's a free parking lot in back.

Dive! In the Century City Marketplace, 10250 Santa Monica Blvd. ☎ **310/788-3483.** Reservations accepted only for parties of 10 or more. Main courses $6–$15. AE, DC, MC, V. Sun–Thurs 11:30am–10pm, Fri–Sat 11:30am–11pm. SANDWICHES/AMERICAN.

"Prepare to dive!" the public address system cries without warning. Red lights flash, the room darkens, water bubbles through "portholes," video monitors go black . . . and a waitress casually delivers another Coke to an adjacent table. Created by Steven Spielberg and Jeffrey Katzenberg (two-thirds of the mega-company Dreamworks SKG) with kids specifically in mind, this perpetually packed restaurant-cum–theme park's insulated underwater ambiance is the ultimate in dining entertainment. Except for the fries and the thin-cut onion rings, however, the same cannot be said of the food, which is decent at best. The menu is mainly submarine sandwiches (get it?), along with salads and some wood-roasted dishes like salmon served with assorted dipping sauces, such as homemade ketchup and cheddar cheese sauce. Stick with the subs, and you'll be content while your kids have a blast.

✪ **Skewer.** 8939 Santa Monica Blvd. (between Robertson and San Vicente blvds.), West Hollywood. ☎ **310/271-0555.** Main courses $7–$9; salads and pitas $4–$7. AE, MC, V. Daily 11am–midnight. MIDDLE EASTERN.

Santa Monica Boulevard is the heart of West Hollywood's commercial strip, and Skewer's sidewalk tables are a great place to see all kinds of neighborhood activity (and audacity). Inside is a New York–like narrow space with changing artwork adorning bare brick walls. From the zesty marinated carrot sticks you get the moment you're seated to sweet, sticky squares of baklava for dessert, this Mediterranean grill is sure to please. The cuisine features baskets of warm pita bread for scooping up traditional salads like *baba ghanoush* (grilled eggplant with tahini and lemon) and *tabbouleh* (cracked wheat, parsley, and tomatoes). Try marinated chicken and lamb off the grill, or *dolmades* (rice- and meat-stuffed grape leaves) seared with a tangy tomato glaze.

Versailles. 1415 S. La Cienega Blvd. (south of Pico Blvd.). ☎ **310/289-0392.** Main courses $5–$11. AE, MC, V. Daily 11am–10pm. CUBAN.

Outfitted with formica tabletops and looking something like an ethnic IHOP, Versailles feels very much like any number of Miami restaurants that cater to the exiled Cuban community. The menu reads like a veritable survey of Havana-style cookery and includes specialties like "Moors and Christians" (flavorful black beans with white rice), *ropa vieja* (a stringy beef stew), *eastin lechón* (suckling pig with sliced onions), and fried whole fish (usually sea bass). Shredded roast pork is particularly recommendable, especially when tossed with the restaurant's trademark garlic-citrus sauce. But what everyone comes for is the chicken—succulent, slow roasted, smothered in onions and either the garlic-citrus sauce or barbecue sauce. Most everything is served with black beans and rice; wine and beer are also available. Because meals are good, bountiful, and cheap, there's often a wait.

Area Code Change Notice

Please note that, effective June 13, 1998, the region serviced by area code 213 is scheduled to be split, with all portions *excluding the downtown business district* changing to **323.** You will be able to dial 213 until January 16, 1999, after which you will be required to use 323 for affected numbers.

Another **Versailles** restaurant is located in Culver City at 10319 Venice Blvd. (☎ **310/558-3168**).

HOLLYWOOD
EXPENSIVE

Campanile. 624 S. La Brea Ave. (north of Wilshire Blvd.). ☎ **213/938-1447.** Reservations required. Main courses $18–$28. AE, MC, V. Mon–Thurs 7:30am–2:30pm and 6–10pm, Fri 7:30am–2:30pm and 5:30–11pm, Sat 8am–1:30pm and 5:30–11pm, Sun 8am–1:30pm. CALIFORNIA/MEDITERRANEAN.

Built as Charlie Chaplin's private offices in 1928, this lovely building has a multi-level layout with flower-bedecked interior balconies, a bubbling fountain, and a skylight through which diners can see the *campanile* (bell tower). The crisply contemporary dining rooms are successful amalgams of vintage and modern, making this one of the most attractive spaces in Los Angeles. The kitchen, headed by Spago alumnus chef/owner Mark Peel, gets a giant leg up from baker (and wife) Nancy Silverton, who runs the now-legendary La Brea Bakery next door. Meals here might begin with fried zucchini flowers drizzled with melted mozzarella or lamb carpaccio surrounded by artichoke leaves—a dish that arrives looking like one of van Gogh's sunflowers. Chef Peel is particularly known for his grills and roasts; try the grilled prime rib smeared with black-olive tapenade or papardelle with braised rabbit, roasted tomato, and collard greens. And don't skip dessert—the restaurant's many enthusiastic sweets fans have turned Nancy's dessert book into a best-seller.

✪ **Patina.** 5955 Melrose Ave. (west of Cahuenga Blvd.). ☎ **213/467-1108.** Reservations required. Main courses $18–$26. AE, DC, DISC, MC, V. Sun–Mon and Wed–Thurs 6–9:30pm, Tues 12–2pm and 6–9:30pm, Fri 6–10:30pm, Sat 5:30–10:30pm. CALIFORNIA/FRENCH.

Joachim Splichal, arguably L.A.'s very best chef, is also a genius at choosing and training top chefs to cook in his kitchens while he jets around the world. Patina routinely wins the highest praise from demanding gourmands, who are happy to empty their bank accounts for unbeatable meals that almost never miss their intended mark. The dining room is straightforwardly attractive, low key, well lit, and professional, without the slightest hint of stuffiness. The menu is equally disarming: "Mallard Duck with Portobello Mushrooms" gives little hint of the brilliant colors and flavors that appear on the plate. The seasonal menu features partridge, pheasant, venison, and other game in winter and spotlights exotic local vegetables in warmer months. Seafood is always available; if Maine lobster cannelloni or asparagus-wrapped John Dory is on the menu, order it. Patina is justifiably famous for its mashed potatoes and potato-truffle chips; be sure to include one (or both) with your meal.

MODERATE

Chianti Cucina. 7383 Melrose Ave. (between Fairfax and La Brea aves.). ☎ **213/653-8333.** Reservations recommended. Main courses $12–$20. AE, CB, DC, MC, V. Chianti Cucina, Mon–Thurs and Sun 11:30am–11:30pm, Fri–Sat 11:30am–midnight; Ristorante Chianti, Sun–Thurs 5:30–10:30pm, Fri–Sat 5:30–11pm. TUSCAN.

Innocent passersby, and locals in search of a secret hideaway, go to the dimly lit, crimson-colored Ristorante Chianti, where waiters whip out flashlights so customers can read the menu. Cognoscenti, on the other hand, bypass this 60-year-old standby and head straight for Chianti Cucina, the bright, bustling eat-in "kitchen" next door, which features excellent meals of its own at fair prices. The menu, which changes frequently, is always interesting and often exceptional. Hot and cold appetizers range from fresh handmade mozzarella and prosciutto to lamb carpaccio with asparagus and marinated grilled eggplant filled with goat cheese, arugula, and sun-dried tomatoes. As for main dishes, the homemade pasta is both superior and deliciously inventive. Try the black tortellini filled with fresh salmon, or the giant ravioli filled with spinach and ricotta.

Dar Maghreb. 7651 Sunset Blvd. (between Fairfax and La Brea aves.). ☎ **213/876-7651.** Reservations recommended. Fixed-price dinner $30. CB, DC, MC, V. Mon–Fri 6–11pm, Sat 6:30–11pm, Sun 5:30–10:30pm. MOROCCAN.

If you're a lone diner in search of a quick bite, this isn't the place for you. Dinner at Dar Maghreb is an entertaining dining experience that increases exponentially the larger your party and the longer you linger. Enter an exotic Arab world of genie waitresses who wash your hands with lemon water and belly dancers who shimmy around an exquisite fountain in the center of a Koranic patio. You'll feel like a guest in an ornately tiled palace as you dine at traditional tables on either low sofas or goatskin cushions.

Nothing is available à la carte here. The fixed-price meal is a multicourse feast, starting with bread and traditional Moroccan salads, followed by *b'stilla,* an appetizer of shredded chicken, eggs, almonds, and spices wrapped in a flaky pastry shell and topped with powdered sugar and cinnamon. The main courses, your choice of lamb, quail, chicken, and more, are each sublimely seasoned and delectable. Perhaps it's the exotic atmosphere that makes everyone eat more than they expected, but you'll be thankful that desert is a simple fruit-and-nut basket, accompanied by warm spice tea poured dramatically into traditional glasses. All is eaten with your hands—a slithery sensual experience that grows on you as the night progresses.

Georgia. 7250 Melrose Ave. (at Alta Vista Ave.). ☎ **213/933-8420.** Reservations recommended. Main courses $15–$22. AE, MC, V. Mon–Sat 6:30–11pm, Sun 5:30–10pm. SOUTHERN.

Soul food and power ties come together at this calorie-unconscious ode to southern cooking in the heart of Melrose's funky shopping district. Owned by a group of investors that includes Denzel Washington and Eddie Murphy, the restaurant is popular with Hollywood's African-American crowd and others who can afford L.A.'s highest-priced pork chops, fried chicken, and grits. It's great for people-watching. The antebellum-style dining room is built to resemble a fine southern house, complete with mahogany floors, Spanish moss, and wrought-iron gates; a bourbon bar continues the theme. The smoked baby back ribs are particularly good and, like many other dishes, are smothered in onion gravy or rémoulade, and sided with corn pudding, grits, string beans, or an excellent creamy garlic coleslaw. Other recommendations include turtle soup, grilled gulf shrimp, and a Créole-style catfish that's more delicately fried than it would traditionally be.

✪ Katsu. 1972 Hillhurst Ave., Los Angeles. ☎ **213/665-1891.** Reservations recommended. Main courses $10–$15, full dinner $15. AE, MC, V. Mon–Fri noon–2pm and 6–10pm, Sat 6–10pm. JAPANESE/SUSHI BAR.

Quietly operating behind discreet vertical blinds—and with no sign other than the street number—Katsu nevertheless consistently ranks among L.A.'s top three sushi bars, and it's definitely the most affordable. Japanese combination plates feature reliable standbys like yakitori, airy tempura, and grilled fish, but they're made memorable by tasty garnishes like sweet, creamy baked eggplant or crispy vegetable roll. Most devotees don't even know there are tables, as they sit in rapt attention at the minimalist black marble sushi bar, watching three artisans create sublimely perfect sushi and sashimi. If there's a live offering, such as giant scallop or live shrimp, order it if you're up to it—that's where the chefs truly shine. Vegetaians will delight in nearly a dozen nonfish sushis like plum roll, asparagus, or mushroom. Lighter dishes are served at lunch, including broth with soba or udon noodles, and a traditional bento box.

There is another location, called **Katsu 3rd,** 8636 W. 3rd St., Los Angeles (☎ 310/273-3605) near the Beverly Center. The atmosphere is less intimate, and although the menu is virtually the same, purists claim the kitchen (and sushi chefs) are less innovative.

Musso & Frank Grill. 6667 Hollywood Blvd. (at Cahuenga Blvd.). ☎ **213/467-7788.** Reservations recommended. Main courses $13–$28. AE, CB, DC, MC, V. Tues–Sat 11am–11pm. AMERICAN/CONTINENTAL.

A survey of Hollywood restaurants that leaves out Musso & Frank is like a study of Las Vegas showrooms that fails to mention Wayne Newton. As L.A.'s oldest eatery (since 1919), Musso & Frank is the paragon of Old Hollywood grill rooms, an almost kitschy glimpse into a meat-and-potatoes world that has remained the same for generations. This is where Faulkner and Hemingway drank during their screenwriting days, where Orson Welles used to hold court. The restaurant is still known for its bone-dry martinis and perfectly seasoned Bloody Marys. The setting is what you'd expect: oak-beamed ceilings, red-leather booths and banquettes, mahogany room dividers, chandeliers with tiny shades. The extensive menu is a veritable survey of American/continental cookery. Hearty dinners include veal scaloppine marsala, roast spring lamb with mint jelly, and broiled lobster. Grilled meats are the restaurant's specialties, as is the Thursday-only chicken pot pie. Regulars also flock in for Musso's trademark "flannel cakes," crepe-thin pancakes flipped to order.

INEXPENSIVE

Authentic Cafe. 7605 Beverly Blvd. (at Curson Ave.). ☎ **213/939-4626.** Main courses $8–$13. AE, MC, V. Mon–Thurs 11:30am–10pm, Fri–Sat 11:30am–midnight, Sun 10am–10pm. SOUTHWESTERN.

True to its name, this restaurant serves authentic southwestern food in a casual atmosphere. It's a winning combination that quickly made this place an L.A. favorite, although popularity has dropped off recently due to the decline in Southwestern cuisine and the rush for the next big thing. But Authentic Cafe still has a loyal following of locals who appreciate generous portions and lively flavor combinations. You'll sometimes find an Asian flair to chef Roger Hayot's dishes. Look for brie, papaya, and chile quesadillas; other worthwhile dishes are the chicken casserole with a corn bread crust, fresh corn and red peppers in chile-cream sauce, and meat loaf with caramelized onions.

✪ **El Cholo.** 1121 S. Western Ave. (south of Olympic Blvd.). ☎ **213/734-2773.** Reservations recommended. Main courses $7–$13. AE, DC, MC, V. Mon–Thurs 11am–10pm, Fri–Sat 11am–11pm, Sun 11am–9pm. MEXICAN.

There's *authentic* Mexican and then there's *traditional* Mexican—El Cholo is comfort food of the latter variety, south-of-the-border cuisine regularly craved by Angelenos. They've been serving it up in this pink adobe hacienda since 1927, even though the once-outlying mid-Wilshire neighborhood around them has turned into

Koreatown. El Cholo's expertly blended margaritas, invitingly messy nachos, and classic combination dinners don't break new culinary ground, but the kitchen has perfected these standards over 70 years. I wish they bottled their rich enchilada sauce! Other specialties include seasonally available green-corn tamales and creative sizzling vegetarian fajitas that go *way* beyond just eliminating the meat. The atmosphere is festive, as people from all parts of town dine happily in the many rambling rooms that comprise the restaurant. There's valet parking as well as a free self-park lot directly across the street.

Hollywood Hills Coffee Shop. 6145 Franklin Ave. (between Gower and Vine sts.). ☎ 213/467-7678. Most items less than $8. AE, DISC, MC, V. Tues–Sat 7am–10pm; Sun–Mon 7am–4pm. DINER.

Having for years served as the run-of-the-mill coffee shop for the attached freeway-side Best Western, this place took on a life of its own when chef Susan Fine commandeered the kitchen and spiked the menu with quirky Mexican and Asian touches. Hotel guests spill in from the lobby to rub noses with the actors, screenwriters, and other artistic types who converge from nearby canyons while awaiting that sitcom casting call or feature-film deal—a community immortalized in the 1996 film *Swingers,* which was filmed in the restaurant. Prices have gone up (to pay for the industrial-strength cappuccino-maker visible behind the counter?) and the dinner menu features surprisingly sophisticated entrees. But breakfast and lunch are still bargains, and the comfy Americana atmosphere is a nice break from the bright lights of nearby Hollywood Boulevard.

Pink's Hot Dogs. 709 N. La Brea Ave. (at Melrose Ave.) ☎ 213/931-4223. Hot dogs $2.10. Sun–Thurs 9:30am–2am, Fri–Sat 9:30am–3am. HOT DOGS.

Pink's isn't your usual guidebook recommendation, but then again, this crusty corner stand isn't your usual doggery either. The heartburn-inducing chili dogs are so decadent that otherwise-upstanding, health-conscious Angelenos crave them. Bruce Willis reportedly proposed to Demi Moore at the 59-year-old shack that grew around the late Paul Pink's 10¢ wiener cart. Pray the bulldozers stay away from this little nugget of a place.

Roscoe's House of Chicken 'n' Waffles. 1514 N. Gower St. (at Sunset Blvd.). ☎ 213/466-7453. Main courses $4–$11. No credit cards. Sun–Thurs 9am–midnight, Fri–Sat 9am–4am. AMERICAN.

It sounds like a bad joke: Only chicken and waffle dishes are served here, a rubric that also encompasses eggs and chicken livers. Its close proximity to CBS Television City has turned this simple restaurant into a kind of de facto commissary for the network. A chicken-and-cheese omelet isn't everyone's ideal way to begin the day, but it's de rigueur at Roscoe's. At lunch, few calorie-unconscious diners can resist the chicken smothered in gravy and onions—a house specialty that's served with waffles or grits and biscuits. Large chicken-salad bowls and chicken sandwiches also provide plenty of cluck for the buck. Homemade cornbread, sweet-potato pie, homemade potato salad, and corn on the cob are available as side orders, and wine and beer are sold.

Roscoe's can also be found at 4907 W. Washington Blvd., at La Brea Avenue (☎ 213/936-3730), and 5006 W. Pico Blvd. (☎ 213/934-4405).

Sofi Estiatorion. 8030³/₄ W. 3rd St. (between Fairfax Ave. and Crescent Heights Blvd.). ☎ 213/651-0346. Reservations recommended. Main courses $7–$14. AE, DC, MC, V. Mon–Thurs noon–2:30pm and 5:30–10:30pm, Fri–Sat noon–2:30pm and 5:30–11pm, Sun 5:30–10:30pm. GREEK.

Look for the simple black awning over the narrow passageway leading from the street to this hidden Aegean treasure. Be sure to ask for a table on the romantic patio amid twinkling lights, and immediately order a plate of their thick, satisfying *tzatziki* (yogurt-cucumber-garlic spread) accompanied by a basket of warm pitas for dipping. Other specialties (recipes courtesy of Sofi's Old-World grandmother) include herbed rack of lamb with rice, fried calamari salad, *saganaki* (kasseri cheese flamed with ouzo), and other hearty taverna favorites. Located near the Farmer's Market in a popular part of town, Sofi's odd, off-street setting has made it an insiders' secret.

Swingers. 8020 Beverly Blvd. (west of Fairfax Ave.). ☎ **213/653-5858.** Most items less than $8. AE, MC, V. Sun–Thurs 6am–2am; Fri–Sat 9am–4am. DINER/AMERICAN.

Resurrected from a motel coffee shop so dismal I can't even remember it, Swingers was transformed by a couple of L.A. hipster nightclub owners into a '90s version of comfy Americana. The interior seems like a slice of the '50s until you notice the plaid upholstery and Warhol-esque graphics, which contrast nicely with the retro red-white-and-blue "Swingers" logo adorning *everything*. Guests at the attached Beverly Laurel Motor Hotel chow down alongside body-pierced industry hounds from nearby Maverick Records (Madonna's company), while a soundtrack that runs the gamut from punk rock to *Schoolhouse Rock* plays in the background. It's not all attitude here, though—you'll enjoy a menu of high-quality diner favorites spiked with trendy crowd-pleasers: Steel-cut Irish oatmeal, challah French toast, grilled Jamaican jerk chicken, and a nice selection of tofu-enhanced vegetarian dishes are just a few of the eclectic offerings. Sometimes I just "swing" by (ha ha) for a malt or milkshake to go— theirs are among the best in town.

DOWNTOWN
EXPENSIVE

Pacific Dining Car. 1310 W. 6th St. (at Witmer St.). ☎ **213/483-6000.** Reservations recommended. Dinner, main courses $20–$42; lunch $14–$29; breakfast $11–$20. AE, CB, DC, MC, V. Daily 24 hours (breakfast 11pm–11am). STEAKS.

It's 4am and you're in the mood for a well-marbled, patiently aged New York steak. Well, even in these health-conscious times there are still enough nocturnal carnivores in Los Angeles to justify not one, but two all-night Pacific Dining Car steak houses. The flagship location, just a few short blocks from the epicenter of downtown, is dark and clubby, a vestige of an age when diners guiltlessly indulged in fist-sized medaillons of beef. The mesquite-charred steaks are terrific indeed, a cut above the restaurant's other hearty offerings, like lamb and chicken. There's a good wine selection. A separate breakfast menu features egg dishes, salads, and ministeaks.

A second restaurant is located in Santa Monica, at 2700 Wilshire Blvd., a block east of 26th Street (☎ 310/453-4000).

MODERATE

Cafe Pinot. In the L.A. Public Library, 700 W. 5th St. (between Grand and Flower sts.). ☎ 213/239-6500. Reservations recommended. Main courses $13–$22. AE, MC, V. Mon 11:15am–2:30pm and 5:30–9pm, Tues–Thurs 11:15am–2:30pm and 5:30–9:30pm, Fri 5:30–10pm, Sat 5–10pm, Sun 5–9pm. CALIFORNIA/FRENCH.

A member of superstar-chef Joachim Splichal's L.A. restaurant empire, Cafe Pinot is modeled after the top-ranked Patina, but designed to be less formal and lighter on the palate—and the pocketbook. Situated in the front garden of the L.A. Public Library, Cafe Pinot's tables are mostly on the patio, shaded by umbrellas and the well-landscaped library courtyard. The restaurant's location makes it a natural for downtown business folk; at night there's a free shuttle to the Music Center.

Splichal has installed a giant rotisserie in the kitchen, and the best meals come from it. The moist, tender mustard-crusted roast chicken is your best bet—unless it's Friday night when you can order the roast suckling pig with its crackling skin. Other recommendable dishes include duck leg confit, grilled calf's liver, and seared peppered tuna.

Cha Cha Cha. 656 N. Virgil Ave. (at Melrose Ave.), Silverlake. ☎ 213/664-7723. Reservations recommended. Main courses $8–$15. AE, DC, DISC, MC, V. Sun–Thurs 8am–10:30pm, Fri–Sat 8am–11:30pm. CARIBBEAN.

Cha Cha Cha serves the West Coast's best Caribbean food in a fun and funky space on the seedy fringe of downtown. The restaurant is a festival of flavors and colors that are both upbeat and offbeat. It's impossible to feel down when you're part of this eclectic hodgepodge of pulsating Caribbean music, wild decor, and kaleidoscopic clutter; still, the intimate dining rooms cater to lively romantics, not obnoxious frat boys. Claustrophobes should choose seats in the airy covered courtyard. The very spicy black-pepper jumbo shrimp gets top marks, as does the paella, a generous mixture of chicken, sausage, and seafood blended with saffron rice. Other Jamaican-, Haitian-, Cuban-, and Puerto Rican–inspired recommendations include jerk pork and *mambo gumbo*, a zesty soup of okra, shredded chicken, and spices. Hardcore Caribbeanites might visit for breakfast, when the fare ranges from plantain, yucca, onion, and herb omelets to scrambled eggs with fresh tomatillos served on hot grilled tortillas.

✪ La Serenata de Garibaldi. 1842 E. 1st St. (between Boyle and State sts.), Boyle Heights. ☎ 213/265-2887. Reservations recommended. Dinner, main courses $9–$19; lunch $6–$11. AE, DC, MC, V. Tues–Sun 11am–10pm. MEXICAN.

Once a humble neighborhood hangout indistinguishable from the many tiny thriving Latino businesses on this street, La Serenata grew to prominence as word of its superior cuisine spread to business lunchers in nearby downtown. Soon affluent patrons came from far and wide—menu prices are decidedly more Westside than East L.A.—including O. J.'s legal "dream team," who lunched here often during the Trial of the Century. Seafood is the focus of the hardworking kitchen. Trademark dishes include shrimp in cilantro sauce and Mexican sea bass fillets in a tangy chipotle sauce, plus a rich, simmered-all-day mole sauce served on giant shrimp or chicken. This brand of authentic Mexican cuisine, done so expertly, has made La Serenata a consistent draw despite its far-flung location in this earthy ethnic neighborhood. There's a secure rear parking lot, and the food is worth the drive.

A smaller-scale sister restaurant called **La Serenata Gourmet** recently opened near the Westside Pavilion at 10924 W. Pico Blvd., Los Angeles (☎ 310/441-9667).

INEXPENSIVE

The Original Pantry Cafe. 877 S. Figueroa St. (at 9th St.). ☎ 213/972-9279. Main courses $6–$11. No credit cards. Daily 24 hours. AMERICAN.

An L.A. institution if there ever was one, this place has been serving huge portions of comfort food around the clock for more than 60 years. In fact, they don't even have a key to the front door. Owned by L.A. Mayor Richard Riordan, the Pantry is especially popular with politicos, who come here for weekday lunches, and conference-goers en route to the nearby L.A. Convention Center. The well-worn restaurant is also a welcoming beacon to clubbers after hours, when downtown becomes a virtual ghost town. A bowl of celery stalks, carrot sticks, and whole radishes greets you at your Formica table, and creamy coleslaw and sourdough bread come free with every meal. Famous for quantity rather than quality, the Pantry serves huge T-bone steaks, densely packed meat loaf, macaroni and cheese, and other American favorites.

A typical breakfast (served all day) might consist of a huge stack of hotcakes, a big slab of sweet cured ham, homefries, and coffee.

✪ **Yorkshire Grill.** 610 W. 6th St. (between Flower and Hope sts.), Los Angeles. ☎ **213/629-3020.** Main courses $4–$8. AE, DC, DISC, MC, V. Mon–Fri 5am–4pm, Sat 6am–2pm. DELI.

High-rise office workers in the know flock to this cross between the traditional L.A. lunchroom and a New York delicatessen—far from the clubby, high-priced image suggested by its oddly misleading name. The menu has 1940s graphics and retro prices, too: Towering combination sandwiches with names like the "Brooklyn," the "Dodger," and the "Biltmore" never exceed $7, including potato salad or coleslaw. Compared to most of L.A.'s delis, you're stealing the food! There are hot lunches too, like Monte Cristo sandwiches, baked ham, or corned beef and cabbage; salads and fountain treats round out the menu. The Yorkshire caters to a business crowd and is closed at dinnertime, but if you're starting a day of sightseeing and museum-hopping, go for one of their well-priced hearty breakfasts, which begin making their way out of the kitchen before sunrise.

THE SAN FERNANDO VALLEY
EXPENSIVE

Pinot Bistro. 12969 Ventura Ave. (west of Coldwater Canyon Ave.), Studio City. ☎ **818/990-0500.** Reservations required. Dinner, main courses $16–$22; lunch $7–$13. AE, DC, DISC, MC, V. Mon–Thurs 11:30am–2:30pm and 6–10pm, Fri 11:30am–2:30pm and 6–10:30pm, Sat 5:30–10:30pm, Sun 5:30–9:30pm. CALIFORNIA/FRENCH.

When the Valley crowd doesn't want to make the drive to Patina, they pack into Pinot Bistro, one of Joachim Splichal's other hugely successful restaurants. The Valley's only great bistro is designed with dark woods, etched glass, and cream-colored walls that scream "trendy French" almost as loudly as the rich, straightforward cooking. The menu is a symphony of California and continental elements which includes a beautiful warm potato tart with smoked whitefish, and baby lobster tails with creamy polenta—both studies in culinary perfection. The most popular dish here is chef Octavio Becerra's Frenchified Tuscan bean soup, infused with oven-dried tomatoes and roasted garlic and served over crusty ciabatta bread. The generously portioned main dishes continue the gourmet theme: baby lobster risotto, braised oxtail with parsley gnocchi, and puff pastry stuffed with bay scallops, Manila clams, and roast duck. The service is good, attentive, and unobtrusive. Many regulars prefer Pinot Bistro at lunch, when a less expensive menu is served to a more easygoing crowd.

INEXPENSIVE

Casa Vega. 13371 Ventura Blvd. (at Fulton Ave.), Sherman Oaks. ☎ **818/788-4868.** Reservations recommended. Main courses $5–$11. AE, CB, DC, MC, V. Mon–Fri 11am–2am, Sat–Sun 4pm–2am. MEXICAN.

I believe that everyone loves a friendly dive, and Casa Vega is one of my local favorites. A faux-weathered adobe exterior conceals red Naugahyde booths lurking amongst fake potted plants and 1960s amateur oil paintings of dark-eyed Mexican children and red-cape-waving bullfighters. (The decor achieves critical mass at Christmas, when everything drips with tinsel.) Locals love it for its good, cheap margaritas (order on the rocks), bottomless baskets of hot and salty chips, and traditional combination dinners, which all come with Casa Vega's patented tostada-style dinner salad. Street parking is so plentiful here you should use the valet only as a last resort.

Du-par's Coffee Shop. 12036 Ventura Blvd. (1 block east of Laurel Canyon Blvd.), Studio City. ☎ **818/766-4437.** All items under $10. AE, MC, V. Sun–Thurs 6am–1am, Fri–Sat 6am–4am. AMERICAN/DINER.

It's been called a "culinary wax museum," the last of a dying breed, the kind of coffee shop Donna Reed took the family to for blue-plate specials. This isn't a trendy new theme place, it's the real deal—and that motherly waitress who calls everyone under 60 "hon" has probably been slinging hash here for 20 or 30 years. It's popular among old-timers who made it part of their daily routine decades ago, show-business denizens who eschew the industry watering holes, a new generation who appreciates a tasty, cheap meal . . . well, everyone, really. It's common knowledge that Du-par's makes the best buttermilk pancakes in town, though some prefer the eggy, perfect French toast (extra-crispy around the edges, please). Mouth-watering pies (blueberry cream cheese, coconut cream, etc.) line the front display case and can be had for a song.

There's another **Du-par's** in Los Angeles at the Farmer's Market, 6333 W. 3rd St. (☎ **213/933-8446**), but it doesn't stay open as late.

Jerry's Famous Deli. 12655 Ventura Ave. (just east of Coldwater Canyon Ave.), Studio City. ☎ **818/980-4245.** Dinner, main courses $9–$14; breakfast $2–$11; sandwiches and salads $4–$12. AE, MC, V. Daily 24 hours. DELI.

Here's a simple yet sizable deli where all the Valley's hipsters go to relieve their late-night munchies. This place probably has one of the largest menus in America—a tome that spans cultures and continents, from Central America to China to New York. From salads to sandwiches to steak-and-seafood platters, everything—including breakfast—is served all day. Jerry's is consistently good at lox and eggs, pastrami sandwiches, potato pancakes, and all the deli staples. It's also an integral part of L.A.'s cultural landscape and a favorite of the show-business types who populate the adjacent foothill neighborhoods. It also has a full bar.

Miceli's. 3655 Cahuenga Blvd. (east of Lankershim), Universal City. ☎ **818/508-1221.** Main courses $7–$12; pizza $9–$15. AE, DC, MC, V. Mon–Thurs 5pm–midnight, Fri 5pm–1am, Sat 4pm–1am, Sun 4pm–11pm. ITALIAN.

Mostaccioli marinara, lasagna, thin-crust pizza, and eggplant parmigiana are indicative of the Sicilian-style fare at this cavernous, stained-glass-windowed Italian restaurant whose waitstaff sings showtunes or opera favorites in between serving dinner (and sometimes instead of). Make sure you have enough Chianti to get into the spirit of it all. This is a great place for kids, but way too rollicking for romance.

PASADENA & ENVIRONS

During the past decade or so, Pasadena has grown into one of the premier dining destinations for Angelenos in the know. Now it's packed with restaurants ranging from elegant art-food dining to casual sidewalk cafes, and Pasadena isn't anybody's secret anymore.

EXPENSIVE

Parkway Grill. 510 S. Arroyo Pkwy. (at California Blvd.), Pasadena. ☎ **626/795-1001.** Reservations recommended. Main courses $8–$23. AE, CB, DC, MC, V. Mon–Thurs 11:30am–2:30pm and 5:30–11pm, Fri 11:30am–2:30pm and 5pm–midnight, Sat 5pm–midnight, Sun 10am–2pm and 5–11pm. CALIFORNIA ECLECTIC.

This vibrant, quintessentially Southern California restaurant has been one of the L.A. area's top-rated spots since it opened in 1985, quickly gaining a reputation for avant-garde flavor combinations and gourmet pizzas to rival Spago's. Although some critics find many of chef Hugo Molina's dishes too fussy, others thrill to appetizer innovations like lobster-stuffed cocoa crepes or Dungeness crab cakes with ginger cream and two salsas. The stars of the menu are meat and game from the iron mesquite grill, followed by richly sweet (and substantial) desserts. Located where the old Arroyo Seco

Parkway glides into an ordinary city street, the Parkway Grill is within a couple of minutes' drive from Old Pasadena and thoughtfully offers free valet parking.

Pinot at the Chronicle. 897 Granite Dr. (behind Lake Ave.), Pasadena. ☎ **626/792-1179.** Reservations recommended. Main courses $14–$20. AE, DC, DISC, MC, V. Mon–Fri 11:30am–2:30pm and 6–10pm, Sat–Sun 5:30–10:30pm. CALIFORNIA/FRENCH.

Superstar chef Joachim Splichal is everywhere, opening cousins to his acclaimed Patina in fanciful locations throughout the city. His latest replaces The Chronicle, the venerable Pasadena grande dame that, for decades, was synonymous with dining elegance. The decor is clubby and the crowd tends to the traditional, jacket-and-tie socialite set that's so common in conservative Pasadena, but the menu is the standard Splichal hybrid of California ingredients and French preparations. With the exception of the spa menu, dishes are rich and saucy, like chicken atop a parsnip-potato pancake with mushroom reduction sauce, or crispy whitefish on cod/garlic-mashed potatoes with buttery cream sauce. Pinot aficionados eagerly order the *profiteroles* dessert: three perfect cream puffs drenched in chocolate sauce.

Shiro. 1505 Mission St. (at Fair Oaks Ave.), Pasadena. ☎ **626/799-4774.** Reservations required. Main courses $15–$20. AE, MC, V. Tues–Sun 6pm–on. FRANCO-JAPANESE.

Ever since chef/owner Shiro defected from the late, great Cafe Jacoulet, his eponymous restaurant has been consistently ranked at the top of Zagat's lists. Although the menu changes nightly at this minimalist bento box, certain favorites are always among the half-dozen selections. Look first for the whole sizzling catfish in cilantro-tangy ponzu sauce; many devotees insist you should stop reading right there, but there's also Canadian scallops in saffron sauce, and often chicken or lamb charbroiled with inventive herb sauces. Shiro's careful attention to detail extends to desserts like fruit-filled won tons with ginger custard—the perfect sweet follow-up to the savory catfish.

✪ **Xiomara.** 69 N. Raymond Ave. (2 blocks north of Colorado Blvd.), Pasadena. ☎ **626/796-2520.** Reservations recommended. Main courses $14–$27; fixed-price menu $25. AE, DC, DISC, MC, V. Mon–Fri 11:30am–2:30pm and 5:30–10:30pm, Sat–Sun 5:30–10:30pm. COUNTRY FRENCH.

By any other name, Xiomara (pronounced "*see*-o-ma-ra") would still be one of the top restaurants in Los Angeles, despite the fact that it has never made Zagat's top 25 list. Chef Patrick Healy's best dishes are rustic country concoctions like sausage-laden cassoulet, and veal shanks braised so long the meat practically falls off the bone. Chicken is simmered for an eternity in a sealed cast-iron pot with artichokes and carrots. The nightly fixed-price meal, a three-course menu determined by the chef's mood and the fresh ingredients at hand, is a remarkably good value. A long list of obscure country wines complements the menu. The dining room, a sleek black bistro setting, is as pleasing as the food, fitted with comfortable armchairs and presided over by the enthusiastic Xiomara herself. An oyster and clam bar features oyster shooters, ceviche, and a large selection of raw oysters and clams on the half-shell.

Xiomara's back room is its alter-ego **Oye!** (☎ **626/796-3286**), where white linen and organza are a suitably blank palette for the zesty "Nuevo Latino" cuisine that filters traditional Cuban through chef Healy's European sensibilities. While the Caribbean cassoulet (featuring black beans, rabbit, smoked pork, and Cuban chorizo) is a treat for the palate, I was surprised to see prices right up there with the fancier front room.

MODERATE

Twin Palms. 101 W. Green St. (at Delacey Ave.), Pasadena. ☎ **626/577-2567.** Reservations recommended on weekends. Main courses $9–$17. AE, CB, DC, MC, V. Mon–Thurs 11:30am–midnight, Fri–Sat 11:30am–1:30am, Sun 10:30am–midnight. MEDITERRANEAN/FRENCH.

Twin Palms is able to seat nearly 400 at spacious tables shaded by the fronds of 100-year-old palm trees. It's busy, having become a hit with recession-weary Angelenos who come for some of the best-value meals in the entire L.A. area. The quasi-outdoor and tented space creates a festival atmosphere, augmented by two lively bars and a bandstand with entertainment every night except Monday. Or come on Sunday until 1:30pm for the Gospel Brunch, during which Twin Palms also offers alternative entertainment for children. Co-owner/chef Michael Roberts is well known for the French "comfort food" he created as a backlash against pricey haute cuisine. Everyone talks about the salt-cod mashed potato brandade, a delicious appetizer that's big enough to serve four—for only $5. The best main courses come off the crackling rotisserie and outdoor grill; they include juicy, roasted sage-infused pork and honey-glazed coriander-scented duck. Sautéed dishes and salads are not as successful. A number of exciting wines are priced well, under $20.

Yujean Kang's Gourmet Chinese Cuisine. 67 N. Raymond Ave. (between Walnut St. and Colorado Blvd.), Pasadena. ☎ **626/585-0855.** Reservations recommended. Main courses $14–$21. AE, MC, V. Daily 11:30am–2:30pm and 5–10pm. CONTEMPORARY CHINESE.

Many Chinese restaurants put the word "gourmet" in their name, but few really mean—or deserve—it. Not so at Yujean Kang's, where Chinese cuisine is taken to an entirely new level. A master of "fusion" cuisine, the eponymous chef/owner snatches bits of techniques and flavors from both China and the West, comingling them in an entirely fresh way. Can you resist such provocative dishes as "Ants on Tree" (beef sautéed with glass noodles in chili and black sesame seeds), or lobster with caviar and fava beans, or Chilean sea bass in passion fruit sauce? Kang is a wine aficionado and has assembled a magnificent cellar of California, French, and particularly German wines. Try pairing a German Spätlese with tea-smoked duck salad. The red-wrapped dining room is less subtle than the food, but just as elegant.

There's a second **Yujean Kang's** in West Hollywood, at 8826 Melrose Ave. (☎ **310/288-0806**). Even though Kang consulted with a *feng shui* master on the location and layout of the new space, some Angelenos grumble about the less adventurous menu and higher prices. Others are merely grateful they don't have to trek to Pasadena anymore.

INEXPENSIVE

Goldstein's Bagel Bakery. 86 W. Colorado Blvd. (at Delacey Ave.), Old Pasadena. ☎ **626/79-BAGEL.** Most items under $3. AE, MC, V. Sun–Thurs 6am–9pm, Fri–Sat 6am–10:30pm. BAKERY/DELI.

Join the locals who storm Goldstein's each morning for freshly baked (in the authentic New York style, they'll assure you) bagels—the reliable plain and onion are as good as exotic honey oat raisin or banana nut. In addition to six flavored cream cheeses, you can choose a bagel sandwich prepared with your choice of every deli ingredient under the sun. Centrally located in the heart of Old Pasadena, this is a good choice for snacks and light meals without interrupting the rhythm of your day.

Old Town Bakery & Restaurant. 166 W. Colorado Blvd. (at Pasadena Ave.), Pasadena. ☎ **626/792-7943.** Main courses $5–$11. DISC, MC, V. Sun–Thurs 7:30am–10pm, Fri–Sat 7:30am–midnight. CONTINENTAL.

Set back from the street in a quaint fountain courtyard, this cheery bakery is an especially popular place to read the morning paper over one of their tasty breakfasts like pumpkin pancakes or zesty omelets. The display counters are packed with cakes, muffins, scones, and other confections, all baked expressly for this shop. The rest of the menu is a mishmash of pastas, salads, and the like, borrowing heavily from Latin and Mediterranean cuisines. A great place to spy on local Pasadenans in their natural habitat.

Pasadena Baking Company/Mi Piace. 25–29 E. Colorado Blvd. (east of Fair Oaks Ave.), Old Pasadena. ☎ **626/796-9966** or 626/795-3131. Main courses $6–$15; bakery items under $3. AE, MC, V. Mon–Thurs 7am–11pm, Fri 7am–midnight, Sat 8am–midnight, Sun 8am–11pm. BAKERY/ITALIAN CAFE.

This little cafe holds just a handful of small tables, which spill out onto the sidewalk during nice weather (which is to say, 90% of the time). The large and sweet-smelling selection of fresh pastries, tarts, truffles, cakes, and candies are all proudly displayed. There's also an assortment of fresh breads and a fresh-fruit stand to accompany the breakfast and lunch menu.

Mi Piace is the adjoining casual trattoria, offering the usual pastas and Northern Italian dishes done unusually well. The Baking Company commandeers the sidewalk tables at breakfast, but starting around 11:30am it's not unusual to see Pasadena locals enjoying an espresso with their dogs tethered to a table leg.

5 The Top Attractions

SANTA MONICA & THE BEACHES

Venice Ocean Front Walk. On the beach, between Venice Blvd. and Rose Ave.

Venice is one of the world's most engaging bohemias. It's not an exaggeration to say that no visit to L.A. would be complete without a stroll along the famous beach path, an almost surreal assemblage of every L.A. stereotype—and then some. Among stalls and stands selling cheap sunglasses, Mexican blankets, and "herbal ecstasy" pills, swirls a carnival of humanity that includes bikini-clad roller skaters, tattooed bikers, muscle-bound pretty boys, panhandling vets, beautiful wannabes, and plenty of tourists and gawkers. On any given day you're bound to come across all kinds of performers: white-faced mimes, break-dancers, buskers, chainsaw jugglers, talking parrots, an occasional apocalyptic evangelist. Last time I was there, a man stood behind a table and railed against the evils of circumcision. "It's too late for us, guys, but we can save the next generation." But a chubby guy singing "Kokomo"—out of tune but with all his heart—cheered me up.

L.A.'S WESTSIDE & BEVERLY HILLS

Rancho La Brea Tar Pits/George C. Page Museum. 5801 Wilshire Blvd. (east of Fairfax Ave.), Los Angeles. ☎ **213/936-2230** or 213/857-6311. Admission $6 adults, $3.50 seniors 62 and older and students with ID, $2 children 5–12, free for kids 4 and under, free for everyone the second Tues of every month. Museum, Tues–Sun 10am–5pm; Paleontology Laboratory, Wed–Sun 10am–5pm; Tar Pits, Sat–Sun 10am–5pm.

An odorous, murky swamp of congealed oil continuously oozes to the earth's surface in the middle of Los Angeles. No, it's not a low-budget horror-movie set: It's the La Brea Tar Pits, an awesome, primal pool right on Museum Mile, where hot tar has been bubbling from the earth for over 40,000 years. The glistening pools, which look like murky water, have enticed thirsty animals throughout history. Thousands of mammals, birds, amphibians, and insects—many of which are now extinct—mistakenly crawled into the sticky sludge and stayed forever. In 1906 scientists began a systematic removal and classification of entombed specimens, including ground sloths, giant vultures, mastodons, camels, bears, lizards, even prehistoric relatives of today's beloved superrats. The best finds are on display in the adjacent George C. Page Museum of La Brea Discoveries, where an excellent 15-minute film documenting the recoveries is also shown. Archaeological work is ongoing; you can watch as scientists clean, identify, and catalog new finds in the Paleontology Laboratory.

The Tar Pits themselves are only open on weekends; guided tours are given on Saturday and Sunday at 1pm. Swimming is prohibited.

HOLLYWOOD

Hollywood Sign. At the top of Beachwood Dr., Hollywood.

These 50-foot-high, white sheet-metal letters have come to symbolize both the movie industry and the city itself. Erected in 1923 as an advertisement for a fledgling real estate development, the full text originally read Hollywoodland. The recent installation of motion detectors around the sign just made this graffiti tagger's coup a target even more worth boasting about. A thorny hiking trail leads to it from Durand Drive near Beachwood Drive, but the best view is from down below, at the corner of Sunset Boulevard and Bronson Avenue.

Hollywood Walk of Fame. Hollywood Blvd., between Gower St. and La Brea Ave.; and Vine St., between Yucca St. and Sunset Blvd. ☎ **213/469-8311.**

More than 2,500 celebrities are honored along the world's most famous sidewalk. Each bronze medallion, set into the center of a granite star, pays homage to a famous television, film, radio, theater, or recording personality. Although about a third of them are just about as obscure as Andromeda—their fame simply hasn't withstood the test of time—millions of visitors are thrilled by the sight of famous names like **James Dean** (1719 Vine St.), **John Lennon** (1750 Vine St.), **Marlon Brando** (1765 Vine St.), **Rudolph Valentino** (6164 Hollywood Blvd.), **Greta Garbo** (6901 Hollywood Blvd.), **Louis Armstrong** (7000 Hollywood Blvd.), and **Barbra Streisand** (6925 Hollywood Blvd).

The sight of bikers, metalheads, druggies, hookers, and hordes of disoriented tourists all treading on memorials to Hollywood's greats makes for quite a bizarre tribute indeed. But the Hollywood Chamber of Commerce has been doing a terrific job sprucing up the pedestrian experience with filmstrip crosswalks, swaying palms, and more. And at least 1 weekend a month a privately organized group of fans calling themselves Star Polishers busy themselves scrubbing tarnished medallions.

Recent subway digging under the boulevard has caused the street to sink several inches. When John Forsythe's star cracked, authorities removed many others to prevent further damage. In the next few years, up to 250 stars, including those of **Marilyn Monroe** (6744 Hollywood Blvd.) and **Elvis Presley** (6777 Hollywood Blvd.) will be temporarily removed as the subway project expands.

The legendary sidewalk is continually adding new names. The public is invited to attend dedication ceremonies; the honoree is usually in attendance. Contact the **Hollywood Chamber of Commerce,** 6255 Sunset Blvd., Suite 911, Hollywood, CA 90028 (☎ **213/469-8311**), for information on who's being honored this week.

Mann's Chinese Theatre. 6925 Hollywood Blvd. (3 blocks west of Highland Ave.). ☎ **213/ 464-8111** or 213/461-3331. Movie tickets $8. Call for show times.

This is one of the world's great movie palaces and one of Hollywood's finest landmarks. The Chinese Theatre was opened in 1927 by entertainment impresario Sid Grauman, a brilliant promoter who's credited with originating the idea of the paparazzi-packed movie "première." Outrageously conceived, with both authentic and simulated Chinese embellishments, gaudy Grauman's theater was designed to impress. Original Chinese heaven doves top the facade, and two of the theater's exterior columns once propped up a Ming Dynasty temple.

Hollywood Area Attractions

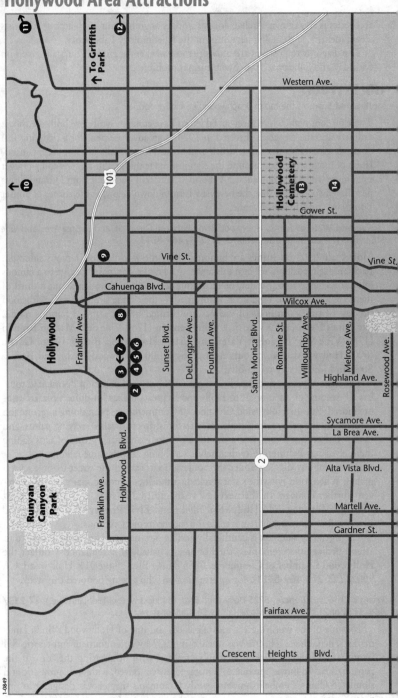

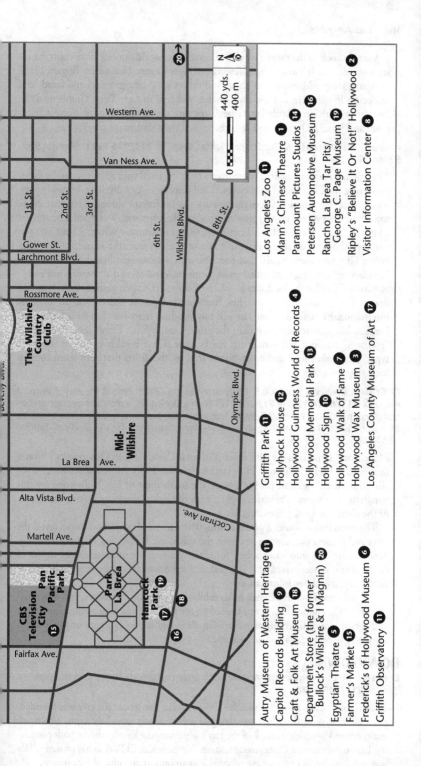

Western Ave.

Van Ness Ave.

1st St.

2nd St.

3rd St.

Gower St.
Larchmont Blvd.

Rossmore Ave.

6th St.

Wilshire Blvd.

8th St.

The Wilshire
Country
Club

Olympic Blvd.

La Brea Ave.

Mid-
Wilshire

Alta Vista Blvd.

Martell Ave.

Cochran Ave.

CBS
Television
City **15**

Pan
Pacific
Park

Park
La Brea

Hancock
Park

17

18

19

16

Fairfax Ave.

N

0   440 yds.
    400 m

20→

Autry Museum of Western Heritage **9**
Capitol Records Building **18**
Craft & Folk Art Museum **18**
Department Store (the former
  Bullock's Wilshire & I Magnin) **20**
Egyptian Theatre **5**
Farmer's Market **15**
Frederick's of Hollywood Museum **6**
Griffith Observatory **11**

Griffith Park **11**
Hollyhock House **12**
Hollywood Guinness World of Records **4**
Hollywood Memorial Park **13**
Hollywood Sign **10**
Hollywood Walk of Fame **7**
Hollywood Wax Museum **3**
Los Angeles County Museum of Art **17**

Los Angeles Zoo **1**
Mann's Chinese Theatre **11**
Paramount Pictures Studios **14**
Petersen Automotive Museum **16**
Rancho La Brea Tar Pits/
  George C. Page Museum **19**
Ripley's "Believe It Or Not!" Hollywood **2**
Visitor Information Center **8**

463

Visitors flock to the theater by the millions for its world-famous entry court, where stars like Elizabeth Taylor, Paul Newman, Ginger Rogers, Humphrey Bogart, Frank Sinatra, Marilyn Monroe, and about 160 others set their signatures and hand- and footprints in concrete. It's not always hands and feet, though: Betty Grable made an impression with her shapely leg, Gene Autry with the hoofprints of his horse, Champion, and Jimmy Durante and Bob Hope used their trademark noses.

Farmer's Market. 6333 W. 3rd St. (near Fairfax Ave.). ☎ **213/933-9211.** Mon–Sat 9am–6:30pm, Sun 10am–5pm.

The original market was little more than a field clustered with stands set up by farmers during the Depression so they could sell directly to city dwellers. It slowly grew into permanent buildings recognizable by the trademark shingled 10-story clock tower and has evolved into a sprawling food marketplace with a carnival atmosphere, a kind of "turf" version of San Francisco's surfy Fisherman's Wharf. About 100 restaurants, shops, and grocers cater to a mix of workers from the adjacent CBS Television City complex, locals, and tourists, who are brought here by the busload. Retailers sell greeting cards, kitchen implements, candles, and souvenirs; but everyone comes here for the food stands, which offer oysters, Cajun gumbo, fresh-squeezed orange juice, roast beef sandwiches, fresh-pressed peanut butter, and all kinds of international fast foods. You can still buy produce here—no longer a farm-fresh bargain, but a better selection than the grocery stores offer. Don't miss **Kokomo,** a "gourmet" outdoor coffeeshop that has become power breakfast spot for show-biz types. Red turkey hash and sweet-potato fries are the dishes that keep them coming back.

✪ **Griffith Observatory.** 2800 E. Observatory Rd. (in Griffith Park, at the end of Vermont Ave.). ☎ **213/664-1191,** or 213/663-8171 for the Sky Report, a recorded message on current planet positions and celestial events. Free admission; planetarium show tickets $4 adults, $3 seniors, $2 children. June–Aug, daily 12:30–10pm; Sept–May, Tues–Fri 2–10pm, Sat–Sun 12:30–10pm.

Made world famous in the film *Rebel Without a Cause,* Griffith Observatory's bronze domes have been Hollywood Hills landmarks since 1935. Most visitors never actually go inside; they come to this spot on the south slope of Mt. Hollywood for unparalleled city views. On warm nights, with the lights twinkling below, this is one of the most romantic places in L.A.

The main dome houses a **planetarium,** where narrated projection shows reveal the stars and planets that are hidden from the naked eye by the city's lights and smog. Mock excursions into space search for extraterrestrial life or examine the causes of earthquakes, moonquakes, and starquakes. Presentations last about an hour. Show times vary, so call for information.

The adjacent **Hall of Science** holds exhibits on galaxies, meteorites, and other cosmic objects, including a telescope trained on the sun, a Foucault pendulum, and earth and moon globes 6 feet in diameter. On clear nights you can gaze at the heavens through the powerful 12-inch telescope.

DOWNTOWN

El Pueblo de Los Angeles Historic District. Enter on Alameda St. across from Union Station. ☎ **213/628-1274.**

This historic district was built in the 1930s, on the site where the city was founded, as an alternative to the wholesale razing of a particularly unsightly slum. The result is a contrived nostalgic fantasy of the city's beginnings, a kitschy theme park portraying Latino culture in a Disneyesque fashion. Nevertheless, El Pueblo has proven wildly successful, as L.A.'s Latinos have adopted it as an important cultural monument.

El Pueblo is not entirely without authenticity. Some of L.A.'s oldest extant buildings are located here, and the area really does exude the ambiance of Old Mexico. At its core is a Mexican-style marketplace on old Olvera Street. The carnival of sights and sounds is heightened by mariachis, colorful piñatas, and more than occasional folkloric dancing. **Olvera Street,** the district's primary pedestrian thoroughfare, and adjacent Main Street are home to about two dozen 19th-century buildings; one houses an authentic Mexican restaurant, **La Golondrina.** Stop in at the **visitor center,** 622 N. Main St. (☎ 213/628-1274); open Monday to Saturday from 10am to 3pm). Don't miss the **Avila Adobe,** at E-10 Olvera St. (open Monday to Saturday from 10am to 5pm); built in 1818, it's the oldest building in the city.

THE SAN FERNANDO VALLEY

Universal Studios. Hollywood Hwy. (Lankershim Blvd. exit), Universal City. ☎ 818/508-9600. Admission $34 adults, $29 seniors 60 and older, $26 children 3–11, free for kids under 3. Parking $6. Summer, daily 7am–11pm; the rest of the year, daily 9am–7pm.

Believing that filmmaking itself was a bona fide attraction, Universal Studios began offering tours to the public in 1964. The concept worked. Today Universal is more than just one of the largest movie studios in the world—it's one of the biggest amusement parks.

The main attraction continues to be the **Studio Tour,** a 1-hour guided tram ride around the company's 420 acres. En route you pass stars' dressing rooms and production offices before visiting famous backlot sets that include an eerily familiar Old West town, a clean New York City street, and the famous town square from the *Back to the Future* films. Along the way the tram encounters several staged "disasters," which I won't divulge here lest I ruin the surprise.

Other attractions are more typical of high-tech theme park fare, but all have a film-oriented slant. On **Back to the Future—The Ride,** you're seated in a mock time-traveling DeLorean and thrust into a fantastic multimedia roller-coasting extravaganza—it's far and away Universal's best ride. The **Backdraft** ride surrounds visitors with brilliant balls of very real fire spewing from imitation ruptured fuel lines. Kids love it. A **Waterworld** live-action stunt show is thrilling to watch (and probably more successful than the film that inspired it), while the latest special effects showcase, **Jurassic Park—The Ride,** is short in duration but long on dinosaur illusions and computer magic lifted from the Universal blockbuster. In 1997, Universal plans to unveil a permanent interactive live show based on **Nickelodeon's** popular kids' programming—and yes, there will be a gazillion gallons of green slime.

Universal Studios is really a fun place. But just as in any theme park, lines can be long; the wait for a 5-minute ride can sometimes last more than an hour. In summer, the stifling Valley heat can dog you all day. To avoid the crowds, skip weekends, school vacations, and Japanese holidays.

PASADENA & ENVIRONS

✪ **Huntington Library, Art Collections, and Botanical Gardens.** 1151 Oxford Rd., San Marino. ☎ **626/405-2141.** Admission $7.50 adults, $6 seniors 65 and over, $4 students and children 12 and under. Tues–Fri noon–4:30pm, Sat–Sun 10:30am–4:30pm. Closed major holidays.

The Huntington Library is the jewel in Pasadena's crown. The 207-acre hilltop estate was once home to industrialist and railroad magnate Henry E. Huntington (1850–1927), who bought books on the same massive scale that he acquired businesses. The continually expanding collection includes dozens of Shakespeare's original works, Benjamin Franklin's handwritten autobiography, a Gutenberg Bible from the 1450s, and the earliest known manuscript of Chaucer's *Canterbury Tales.* Although some rarer works are only available to visiting scholars, the library has a regularly changing (and always excellent) exhibit showcasing different items in the collection.

If you prefer canvas to parchment, Huntington also put together a terrific 18th-century British and French art collection. His most celebrated paintings are Gainsborough's *The Blue Boy,* and *Pinkie,* a companion piece by Sir Thomas Lawrence depicting the youthful aunt of Elizabeth Barrett Browning. These and other works are displayed in the stately Italianate mansion on the crest of this hillside estate, so you can also get a glimpse of its splendid furnishings.

But it's the botanical gardens that draw most locals to the Huntington. The Japanese Garden is complete with a traditional open-air Japanese house, koi-filled stream, and serene Zen garden; the cactus garden is exotic, the jungle garden intriguing, the lily ponds soothing—and there are plentiful benches scattered about encouraging you to sit and enjoy.

Because the Huntington surprises many with its size and the wealth of activities to choose from, first-timers might want to start by attending one of the regularly scheduled 12-minute introductory slide shows; or take the more in-depth 1-hour garden tour, given each day at 1pm.

I also recommend that you tailor your visit to include the popular English high tea served Tuesday to Sunday from 1:30 to 3:30pm. The charming tearoom overlooks the Rose Garden (home to 1,000 varieties displayed in chronological order of their breeding), and since the finger sandwiches and desserts are served buffet style, it's a genteel bargain (even for hearty appetites) at $11 per person. Phone ☎ **626/ 683-8131** for reservations.

6 TV Tapings

Being part of the audience for the taping of a television show might be the quintessential L.A. experience. This is a great way to see Hollywood at work, to find out how your favorite sitcom or talk show is made, and to catch a glimpse of your favorite TV personalities. But you might end up with tickets to a show that may never make an appearance in *TV Guide* rather than for one of your favorites, like *Mad About You* or *Friends.* Tickets to top shows are in greater demand than others, and getting your hands on them usually takes advance planning—and possibly some time waiting in line.

Request tickets as far in advance as possible. Several episodes may be shot on a single day, so you may be required to remain in the theater for up to 4 hours (in addition to the recommended 1-hour early check-in). If you phone at the last moment, you may luck into tickets for your top choice. More likely, however, you'll be given a list of shows that are currently filming, and you won't recognize many of the titles; studios are always taping pilots, few of which end up on the air. But you never know who may be starring in them—look at all the famous faces that have launched new sitcoms in the past couple of years. Tickets are always free, usually limited to two per person, and are distributed on a first-come, first-served basis. Many shows don't admit children under the age of 10; in some cases no one under the age of 18 is admitted.

In addition to the suppliers listed below, tickets are sometimes given away to the public outside popular tourist sites like Mann's Chinese Theater in Hollywood and Universal Studios in the Valley; L.A.'s Visitor Information Centers in downtown and Hollywood often have tickets as well (see "Orientation," above). But if you're determined to see a particular show, contact the following sources:

Audiences Unlimited (☎ **818/506-0043** or 818/506-0067 for the ticket information hotline) distributes tickets for the top sitcoms, including *Saved By The Bell,*

Stargazing in L.A.: Top Spots About Town for Sighting Celebrities

Celebrities pop up everywhere in L.A. If you spend enough time here, you'll surely bump into a few of them. If you're only in the city for a short time, however, it's best to go on the offensive.

Restaurants are your surest bet. **Matsuhisa, Fenix, Locanda Veneta,** and **Maple Drive** can almost guarantee sightings any night of the week. If you're not up to committing yourself to dining at one of these pricey hot spots, walk in confidently at 9pm and tell the maître d' that you just want to take a look at the dining room. The trendiest clubs and bars—**House of Blues, Viper Room, Skybar at the Mondrian,** and **The Gate**—are second-best for star sighting, but cover charges can be astronomical and the velvet ropes oppressive. And it's not always Mick and Rod and Madonna; a recent night on the town only turned up Yanni, Ralph Macchio, and Dr. Ruth.

Often, the best places to see members of the A-list aren't as obvious as a back-alley stage door or the front room of Spago. Shops along Sunset Boulevard, like **Tower Records** and the **Virgin Megastore,** are often star-heavy. **Book Soup,** that browser's paradise across the street from Tower, is usually good for a star or two. You'll often find them casually browsing the international newsstand (if they're not there to sign their latest tell-all autobiography). You might even pop into **Sunset Strip Tattoo,** where Cher, Charlie Sheen, Lenny Kravitz, and members of Guns 'N' Roses all got inked. A mid-afternoon stroll along Melrose Avenue might also produce a familiar face; check out **Drake's Gift and Novelty Shop, Retail Slut,** and **Billy Martin's.**

Keep your eyes peeled for celebrities—everyone does in L.A.—and you'll more than likely be rewarded. And don't feel bad if you only see Bob Denver. What greater sighting than Gilligan himself?

Seinfeld, and *Frasier.* **Television Tickets** (☎ 213/467-4697) distributes tickets for the most popular talk and game shows. Their services are free, and you can reserve by phone. Or you can get tickets directly from the studios:

ABC, 4151 Prospect Ave., Hollywood, CA 90027 (☎ 310/557-7777). Taped messages on the hotline let you know what's currently going on. Order tickets for a taping either by writing 3 weeks in advance or by showing up the day of the taping. For tickets to *Politically Incorrect with Bill Maher,* call the show's ticket line at ☎ 213/852-2655 to make a reservation (taken on a first-come, first-served basis), or order them on-line at **www.abc.com/pi.**

CBS, 7800 Beverly Blvd., Los Angeles, CA 90036 (☎ **213/852-2345,** or 213/852-2458 for the ticket information hotline). Call to see what's being filmed while you're in town. Tickets for tapings are distributed on a first-come, first-served basis; you can write in advance to reserve them or pick them up directly at the studio up to an hour before taping.

NBC, 3000 W. Alameda Ave., Burbank, CA 91523 (☎ **818/840-4444** or 818/840-3537). Call to see what's on while you're in L.A. Tickets for NBC tapings, including *The Tonight Show with Jay Leno,* can be obtained in two ways: Pick them up at the NBC ticket counter on the day of the show you want to see (they're distributed on a first-come, first-served basis at the ticket counter off California Ave.); or at least 3 weeks before your visit, send a self-addressed, stamped envelope with your ticket request to the address above.

7 Exploring the City

ARCHITECTURAL HIGHLIGHTS

Los Angeles is a veritable Disneyland of architecture. The city is home to an amalgam of distinctive styles, from art deco to Spanish revival to coffee-shop kitsch to suburban ranch to postmodern—and much more. Cutting-edge, over-the-top styles that would be out of place in other cities, from the oversize hot dog that is Tail o' the Pup to the mansions lining the streets of Beverly Hills, are perfectly at home in movie city.

SANTA MONICA & THE BEACHES

When you're strolling the historic canals and streets of Venice, be sure to check out **Chiat/Day Headquarters** at 340 Main St. What would otherwise be an unspectacular contemporary office building is made fantastic by a 3-story pair of binoculars that frames the entrance to this advertising agency. The sculpture is modeled after a design created by Claes Oldenburg and Coosje van Bruggen.

When you're flying in or out of LAX, be sure to stop for a moment to admire the **Control Tower and Theme Building.** The spacey *Jetsons*-style "Theme Building," which has always loomed over LAX, has been joined by a brand-new silhouette. The main control tower, designed by local architect Kate Diamond to evoke a stylized palm tree, is tailored to present Southern California in its best light. You can go inside to enjoy the view from the Theme Building's observation deck, or have a space-age cocktail at the Technicolor bachelor-pad that is Encounter restaurant (see "Dining," above).

L.A.'S WESTSIDE & BEVERLY HILLS

In addition to the **Argyle** and the **Beverly Hills Hotel** (see "Accommodations," earlier in this chapter), be sure to wind your way through the streets of Beverly Hills off Sunset Boulevard, where you'll see everything the overactive, deep-pocketed imagination can conjure up, from faux Merry-Olde-England hunting lodges to turreted Sleeping Beauty castles.

The **Rudolph M. Schindler House,** 835 N. Kings Rd. (☎ **310/651-1510**) is distinguished by the intermingling of indoors and out, daring modern (1921–22) design, and technological innovations. A protégé of Frank Lloyd Wright and contemporary of Richard Neutra, the Austrian architect was very active in Los Angeles; little survives of his work, and his own home barely escaped the wrecking ball. But Austria's Museum of Applied Arts (MAK) now maintains the restored house as a mini-MAK, as well as offers guided tours on weekends.

Postmodern architecture lovers should check out the **Pacific Design Center** at 8687 Melrose Ave. Designed by Argentinean Cesar Pelli, the bold architecture and overwhelming scale of the center aroused plenty of controversy when it was erected in 1975. Sheathed in gently curving cobalt-blue glass, the 7-story building, housing over 750,000 square feet of wholesale interior-design showrooms, is known to locals as "the blue whale." Nearby on San Vicente Boulevard—on a totally different scale—is the iconic **Tail o' the Pup.** This is roadside art, and the wiener, at its best.

HOLLYWOOD

In addition to the **Griffith Observatory** and **Mann's Chinese Theatre** (see "The Top Attractions," above), and the **Hollywood Roosevelt Hotel** (see "Accommodations"), check out the old **Egyptian Theatre,** 6712 Hollywood Blvd. Conceived by grandiose Sid Grauman, it's just down the street from Grauman's better-known

Chinese Theatre, but remains less altered from its 1922 design based on the then-headline news discovery of hidden treasures in Pharaohs' tombs. It's undergoing a (hopefully) sensitive restoration by American Cinematheque, who plans to re-open by the end of 1998 for public screenings.

Farther east is the **Capitol Records Building.** This 12-story tower just north of the legendary intersection of Hollywood and Vine is one of the city's most recognizable buildings. Often, but incorrectly, rumored to have been made to resemble a stack of 45s on a turntable (it kinda does, really), this circular tower is nevertheless unmistakable. Nat "King" Cole, songwriter Johnny Mercer, and other 1950s Capitol artists populate a giant exterior mural.

Built between 1917 and 1920, **Hollyhock House** was the first Frank Lloyd Wright residence to be constructed in Los Angeles. The centerpiece of art-filled Barnsdall Park, the house, at 4800 Hollywood Blvd. (☎ **213/485-4581**), is now owned by the city and operates as a small gallery and house museum, although it's undergoing extensive repairs for structural damage from the 1994 earthquake.

Formerly Bullock's, then I. Magnin, the **department store** on Wilshire Boulevard at Vermont Avenue is a classy art deco gem featuring a stylish interior with mottled marble wall panels, cubist wall reliefs, and luxurious wood veneers. The main entrance faces the parking lot in the rear; the streetside facade was meant to be admired while flying past.

DOWNTOWN

Built in 1928, the 27-story **City Hall,** at 200 N. Spring St., remained the tallest building in the city for over 30 years. The structure's distinctive ziggurat roof was featured in the film *War of the Worlds,* but is probably best known as the headquarters of the *Daily Planet* in the *Superman* TV series. On a clear day the top-floor observation deck (open Monday to Friday from 10am to 4pm) offers views of Mount Wilson, 15 miles away.

On West 5th Street, between Flower Street and Grand Avenue, is one of L.A.'s early architectural achievements, the carefully restored **Central Library** (the majestic main entrance is actually on Flower Street). Working in the 1920s, architect Bertram G. Goodhue played on the Egyptian motifs and materials popularized by the discovery of King Tut's tomb, combining them with modern concrete block to great effect.

The 1893 **Bradbury Building,** at South Broadway and 3rd Street, is Los Angeles's oldest commercial building, and one of the city's most revered architectural landmarks. You've got to go inside to appreciate it. The glass-topped atrium is often used as a movie and TV set; you've seen it in *Chinatown* and *Blade Runner.*

Union Station, at Macy and Alameda streets, is one of the finest examples of California Mission–style architecture, built with the opulence and attention to detail that characterize 1930s W.P.A. projects. The cathedral-size, richly paneled ticket lobby and waiting area of this fantastic cream-colored structure stand sadly empty most of the time, but the MTA does use Union Station for Blue Line commuter trains.

For a taste of what downtown's Bunker Hill was like before the bulldozers tore through, visit the residential neighborhood of **Angelino Heights,** near Echo Park. Entire streets are still filled with stately gingerbread Victorian homes; most yet enjoy the splendid views which led early L.A.'s elite to build here. The 1300 block of Carroll Avenue is the best preserved. Don't be surprised if a film crew is scouting locations while you're there—these blocks appear often on the silver screen.

The **Watts Towers,** at 1765 E. 107th St. (☎ **213/847-4646**), are more than a bit off the beaten track, but they warrant a visit. The fantastically colorful,

Stargazing, Part II: The Less-Than-Lively Set

Almost everybody who visits L.A. hopes to see a celebrity—they are, after all, our most common export item. Celebrities usually don't cooperate, failing to gather in readily viewable herds. They occasionally tread predictable paths, frequenting certain watering holes, but on the whole, celeb-spotting is a chancy proposition.

There's a much, much better alternative. An absolutely guaranteed method of being within 6 feet of your favorite star: cemeteries. Cemeteries are *the* place for star (or at least headstone) gazing: The star is always available, and you're going to get a lot more up close and personal than you probably would to anyone who's actually alive. And L.A. is a big place, with a lot of cemeteries—and there are a lotta stars in them thar hills. What follows is a guide to the most fruitful cemeteries, listed in order (more or less) of their friendliness to stargazers:

Weathered Victorian and deco memorials add to the decaying charm of **Hollywood Memorial Park,** 6000 Santa Monica Blvd., Hollywood (☎ 213/469-1181). Fittingly, there's a terrific view of the Hollywood sign over the graves, as many of the founders of the community rest here. You'll see their names on the nearby street signs: the Gowers, the Wilcoxes, the Coles. The most notable tenant is Rudolph Valentino, who rests in an interior crypt. And there's silent director William Desmond Taylor (under his real name, William Deane Tanner), whose 1922 murder was an enormous scandal, ruining the careers of silent stars Mary Miles Minter and Mabel Normand, who were considered guilty by association. (Sidney Kirkpatrick's excellent *A Cast of Killers* delves into this decades-old mystery in great detail, even solving the crime at last.) Outside are Tyrone Power, Jr.; Douglas Fairbanks, Sr.; *Sheik* co-star Agnes Ayers; Cecil B. DeMille (facing Paramount, his old studio); Alfalfa from *The Little Rascals* (contrary to what you might think, the dog on his grave is not Petey); Hearst mistress Marion Davies; Charlie Chaplin's mother, Hannah, and son, Charlie, Jr.; John Huston; and a headstone for Jayne Mansfield (she's really buried in Pennsylvania with her family). In other mausoleums are the Talmadge sisters and "Bugsy" Siegel.

Catholic **Holy Cross Cemetery,** 5835 W. Slauson Ave., Culver City (☎ 310/670-7697), hands out maps to the stars' graves. Religion makes for strange gravefellows: In one area, within feet of each other, lie Bing Crosby, Bela Lugosi (buried in his Dracula cape), and Sharon Tate; not far away are Rita Hayworth and Jimmy Durante. Also here are "Tin Man" Jack Haley and "Scarecrow" Ray Bolger, Mary Astor, John Ford, Spike Jones, gossip queen Louella Parsons, Mack Sennett, Elizabeth Taylor's first husband Conrad "Nicky" Hilton, and Rosalind Russell, as well as Gloria Morgan Vanderbilt.

The front office at **Hillside Memorial Park,** 6001 Centinela Ave., Baldwin Hills (☎ 310/641-0707), can provide a guide to this Jewish cemetery, which has an L.A. landmark: the behemoth tomb of Al Jolson, another humble star. His rotunda, complete with a bronze reproduction of Jolson in his Mammy pose and cascading fountain, is visible from I-405. Also on hand are Georgie Jessel, Jack Benny, Eddie Cantor, Vic Morrow, comic Dick Shawn, and *Fugitive* David Janssen.

You just know developers get stomach aches looking at **Westwood Memorial Park,** 1218 Glendon Ave., Westwood (☎ 310/474-1579; the staff can direct you around), smack-dab in the middle of some of L.A.'s priciest real estate. But it's not going anywhere. Especially when you consider its most famous resident: Marilyn

Monroe. It's also got Truman Capote, John Cassavetes, Armand Hammer, Donna Reed, Edith Massey (John Waters's Egg Lady), Natalie Wood, *Playboy* playmate Dorothy Stratten (who was murdered by her husband; remember *Star 80* ?), Darryl Zanuck, and Will and Ariel Durant, the husband and wife historian/writer team (most notably, the 11-volume *Story of Civilization*), who died within days of each other after a nearly 70-year romance.

Forest Lawn Glendale, 1712 S. Glendale Ave. (☎ **213/254-3131**), likes to pretend it has no celebrities. The most prominent of L.A. cemeteries, it's also the most humorless, which is pretty silly when you realize they've done their darndest to turn their graveyard into an amusement park. What else would you call their regular "dramatic" (read: cheesy) unveilings (complete with music and narration) of such works of "art" as a reproduction of da Vinci's *Last Supper* in stained glass? The place is full of Bad Art, all part of the continuing vision of founder Hubert Eaton, bane of cemetery buffs everywhere. Eaton thought cemeteries—excuse me, *memorial parks*—should be happy places, uninterrupted by nasty thoughts of, ick, death. So he banished all those gloomy upright tombstones and monuments in favor of flat, pleasant, character-free, flush-to-the-ground slabs. Voilà! A rolling, parklike vista, easy on the eyes and easy to mow.

Contrary to what you've heard, Walt Disney was *not* frozen and placed under Cinderella's castle at Disneyland. He was cremated and resides in a little garden to the left of the Freedom Mausoleum. Turn around and just behind you are Errol Flynn (in the Garden of Everlasting Peace) and Spencer Tracy (to right of the George Washington statue). In the Freedom Mausoleum are Alan Ladd, Clara Bow, Nat "King" Cole, Chico Marx, Gummo Marx, Larry Fine (of *The Three Stooges*), and Gracie Allen—finally joined by George Burns. In a columbarium near the Mystery of Life is Humphrey Bogart. Keep moving to your left and you should find Mary Pickford. Unfortunately, some of the best celebs—such as Clark Gable and Carole Lombard, W. C. Fields, and Jean Harlow—are in the Great Mausoleum, which you often can't get into unless you're visiting a relative.

You'd think a place that encourages people just to visit for fun would understand what the real attraction is. But no—Forest Lawn Glendale won't tell you where any of their illustrious guests are, so don't even bother asking. And this place is immense—and, frankly, dull in comparison to the previous cemeteries, unless you appreciate the kitsch value of the Forest Lawn approach to art.

Forest Lawn Hollywood Hills, 6300 Forest Lawn Dr. (☎ **800/204-3131**), is slightly less anal than the Glendale branch, but the same basic attitude prevails. On the right lawn, beside the wall near the statue of George Washington, is Buster Keaton. Marty Feldman is in front of the next garden, over on the left. From Buster's grave, go up several flights of stairs to the last wall on the right—there's Stan Laurel. In the Courts of Remembrance are Lucille Ball, Charles Laughton, Freddie Prinze, George Raft, Forrest Tucker, and the not-quite-gaudy-enough tomb of Liberace. Outside, in a vault on the Ascension Road side, is Andy Gibb. Bette Davis's sarcophagus is in front of the wall, to the left of the entrance to the Courts. Also on the grounds are Ozzie Nelson, Ricky Nelson, Sammy Davis, Jr., Ernie Kovacs, Jack Webb, and John Travolta's mother, Helen.

—*Mary Susan Herczog*

99-foot-tall concrete-and-steel sculptures are ornamented with mosaics of bottles, sea shells, cups, plates, generic pottery, and ceramic tiles. They were completed in 1954 by folk artist Simon Rodia, an immigrant Italian tile setter who worked on them for 33 years. Call for a tour schedule.

THE SAN FERNANDO VALLEY

At first glance the **Walt Disney Corporate Office,** at 500 S. Buena Vista St. (at Alameda Avenue) in Burbank, is just another neoclassical building. But wait a minute: Those aren't Ionic columns holding up the building's pediment . . . they're the Seven Dwarfs—giant-size, of course.

PASADENA & ENVIRONS

For a quick but profound architectural fix, stroll past Pasadena's grandiose and baroque **City Hall,** 100 N. Garfield Ave., 2 blocks north of Colorado; closer inspection will reveal its classical colonnaded courtyard, formal gardens, and spectacular tiled dome.

Architects Charles and Henry Greene built prolifically in Pasadena's Arroyo Seco area (overlooking the Rose Bowl) in the early 1900s, their masterpiece being the **Gamble House,** 4 Westmoreland Place (off Orange Grove, north of the Ventura Freeway) Intricately crafted teakwood interiors, custom furnishings, and California-specific features like a sleeping porch make this a one-stop primer in Craftsman design. One-hour tours are given Thursday to Sunday afternoons; call ☎ **626/ 793-3334** for more information. Additional elegant Greene & Greene creations (still privately owned) abound 2 blocks away along **Arroyo Terrace,** including address nos. **368, 370, 400, 408, 424,** and **440;** the Gamble House book shop can give you a walking-tour map and conducts guided neighborhood tours by appointment.

While the Greenes were building retreats for the wealthy, scaled-down Craftsman bungalows were becoming the standard in affordable housing nearby. An exceptionally well-preserved neighborhood of around 900 pre-Depression homes is the Landmark District **Bungalow Heaven,** between Lake and Hill avenues north of Orange Grove Boulevard. The Bungalow Heaven Neighborhood Association (☎ **626/ 585-2172**) conducts a house tour each April, or they can give you information on taking a self-guided walking tour of this charming enclave.

BOTANICAL GARDENS

These Pasadena-area gardens are in addition to Pasadena's splendid Huntington Library and Botanical Gardens (see "The Top Attractions," above).

The Arboretum of Los Angeles County. 301 N. Baldwin Ave., Arcadia. ☎ **626/821-3222.** Admission $5 adults, $3 students and seniors 62 and over, $1 children 5–12, free for kids 4 and under. Daily 9am–5pm. Closed Christmas Day.

This horticultural and botanical center was formerly the estate of silver magnate "Lucky" Baldwin—the man responsible for bringing horse racing to Southern California—who lived until 1909 on these lushly planted 127 acres overlooking Santa Anita racetrack. You might recognize Baldwin's red-and-white Queen Anne cottage from the opening sequence of *Fantasy Island* ("de plane, de plane"); the gardens are also a favorite location for movie filming and local weddings. In addition to spectacular flora, the Arboretum boasts a bevy of resident peafowl who seem unafraid of humans—one of the best treats here is being up close when the peacocks, attempting to impress passing hens, unfold their brilliant rainbow plumage. Avid gardeners will want to visit the nurserylike gift shop on the way out.

Descanso Gardens. 1418 Descanso Dr., La Cañada. ☎ **818/952-4402** or 818/952-4401. Admission $5 adults, $3 students and seniors 62 and over, $1 children 5–12, free for kids 4 and under. Daily 9am–4:30pm.

Camellias—evergreen flowering shrubs from China and Japan—were the passion of amateur gardener E. Manchester Boddy, who began planting them here in 1941. Today his Descanso Gardens contain more than 100,000 camellias in over 600 varieties, blooming under a 30-acre canopy of California oak trees. The shrubs now share the limelight with a 5-acre Rose Garden, home to hundreds of varieties. This is really a magical place, with paths and streams that wind through the towering forest, bordering a lake and bird sanctuary. Each season features different plants: daffodils, azaleas, tulips, and lilacs in the spring; chrysanthemums in the fall; and so on. Monthly art exhibits are held in the garden's hospitality house.

There's also a beautifully landscaped Japanese-style teahouse that serves tea and cookies on Saturday and Sunday from 11am to 4pm. Free docent-guided walking tours are offered every Sunday at 1pm; guided tram tours, which cost $1.50, run Tuesday to Friday at 1, 2, and 3pm, and on Saturday and Sunday at 11am and 1, 2, and 3pm. Picnicking is allowed in specified areas.

MISSIONS

Two of the 21 missions built by Franciscan missionaries in the late 18th century along the California coast from San Diego to Sonoma are in the Los Angeles area. The valleys in which they're nestled eventually took their names.

THE SAN FERNANDO VALLEY

Mission San Fernando. 15151 San Fernando Mission Blvd., Mission Hills. ☎ **818/361-0186.** Admission $4 adults, $3 seniors and children 12 and under. Daily 9am–5pm. From I-5, exit at San Fernando Mission Blvd. east and drive 5 blocks to the mission.

Established in 1797, Mission San Fernando once controlled more than 1.5 million acres, employed 1,500 Native Americans, and boasted over 22,000 head of cattle and extensive orchards. The mission complex was destroyed several times, but was always faithfully rebuilt with low buildings surrounding grassy courtyards. The aging church was replaced in the 1940s, and again in the 1970s after a particularly destructive earthquake. The Convento, a 250-foot-long colonnaded structure dating from 1810, is the compound's oldest remaining part. Some of the mission's rooms, including the old library and the private salon of the first bishop of California, have been restored to their late-18th-century appearance. A half-dozen padres and many hundreds of Shoshone Indians are buried in the adjacent cemetery.

PASADENA & ENVIRONS

Mission San Gabriel Arcangel. 537 W. Mission Dr., San Gabriel. ☎ **626/457-3048.** Admission $4 adults, $1 children 6–12 years, free for kids 5 and under. Daily 9am–5pm. Closed Christmas Day, Good Friday, Easter, and Thanksgiving Day.

Founded in 1771, Mission San Gabriel Arcangel still retains its original facade, notable for its high oblong windows and large capped buttresses that are said to have been influenced by the cathedral in Cordova, Spain. The mission's self-contained compound encompasses an aqueduct, a cemetery, a tannery, and a working winery. In the church stands a copper font with the dubious distinction of being the first one used to baptize a native Californian. The most notable contents of the mission's museum are Native American paintings depicting the Stations of the Cross, painted on sailcloth, with colors made from crushed desert flower petals. The mission is about 15 minutes south of Pasadena.

MUSEUMS & GALLERIES
SANTA MONICA & THE BEACHES

Museum of Flying. Santa Monica Airport, 2772 Donald Douglas Loop North, Santa Monica. ☎ **310/392-8822.** Admission $7 adults, $5 seniors, $3 children. Wed–Sun 10am–5pm.

Once headquarters of the McDonald Douglas corporation, the Santa Monica Airport is the birthplace of the DC-3 and other pioneers of commercial aviation. The museum celebrates this bit of local history with 24 authentic aircraft displays and some interactive exhibits. In addition to antique Spitfires and Sopwith Camels, there's a new kid-oriented learning area, where hands-on exhibits detail airplane parts, pilot procedures, and the properties of air and aircraft design. The shop is full of scale models of World War II birds; the coffee-table book *The Best of the Past* beautifully illustrates 50 years of aviation history.

L.A.'s WESTSIDE & BEVERLY HILLS

J. Paul Getty Museum at the Getty Center. 1200 Getty Center Dr., Los Angeles. ☎ **310/440-7300.** Free admission. Open Tues–Sun, possible nighttime hours. Advance reservations required. Parking $5.

In 1997, the J. Paul Getty Museum in Malibu, known for a superb antiquities collection presented in a reproduction Roman villa, closed for 4 years of renovation and enlargement, after which it will reopen exclusively as a center for the display and study of Greek and Roman antiquities. Until then, a portion of the antiquities collection will be on display at the hulking Richard Meier–designed Getty Center overlooking Brentwood, along with the museum's other collections—important paintings by van Gogh, Cezanne, Rembrandt, and Manet; French decorative arts displayed in splendid, newly designed period rooms; and fine illuminated manuscripts from the Middle Ages to the Renaissance—but without the awesome ocean views. The new complex is primarily a research and study center, since the uber-wealthy Getty Trust is involved in a number of research, education, and conservation concerns. Visitors to the center park at the base of the hill and ascend via a cable-driven electric tram.

Museum of Tolerance. 9786 W. Pico Blvd. (at Roxbury Dr.). ☎ **310/553-8403.** Admission $8 adults, $6 seniors, $5 students, $3 children 3–12, free for children 2 and under. Advance purchase recommended. Mon–Thurs 10am–5pm, Fri 10am–3pm (to 1pm Nov–Mar), Sun 11am–5pm. Closed many Jewish and secular holidays; call for schedule.

The Museum of Tolerance is designed to expose prejudices and teach racial and cultural tolerance. It's located in the Simon Wiesenthal Center, an institute founded by the legendary Nazi-hunter. While the Holocaust figures prominently here, this is not just a Jewish museum—it's an academy that broadly campaigns for a live-and-let-live world. Tolerance is an abstract idea that's hard to display, so most of this $50-million museum's exhibits are high tech and conceptual in nature. Fast-paced interactive displays are designed to touch the heart as well as the mind, and engage both serious investigators and the MTV crowd. One of two major museums in America that deals with the Holocaust, the Museum of Tolerance is considered by some to be inferior to its Washington, D.C., counterpart, and visitors can be frustrated by the museum's policy of insisting that you follow a prescribed 2^1/$_2$-hour route through the exhibits.

Museum of Television and Radio. 465 N. Beverly Dr. (at Santa Monica Blvd.), Beverly Hills. ☎ **310/786-1000.** Website: www.mtr.org/camsm. Admission $6 adults, $4 students and seniors, $3 kids 12 and under. Wed and Fri–Sun noon–5pm, Thurs noon–9pm. Closed New Year's Day, July 4, Thanksgiving Day, and Christmas Day.

Want to see the Beatles on *The Ed Sullivan Show* (1964) or Edward R. Murrow's examination of Joseph McCarthy (1954), watch Arnold Palmer win the 1958

Masters Tournament, or listen to radio excerpts like FDR's first "Fireside Chat" (1933) and Orson Welles's famous *War of the Worlds* UFO hoax (1938)? All these, plus a gazillion episodes of *The Twilight Zone, I Love Lucy,* and other beloved series, can be viewed within the starkly white walls of architect Richard Meier's neutral, contemporary museum building. Like the ritzy Beverly Hills shopping district that surrounds it, the museum is more flash than substance. Once you gawk at the celebrity and industry-honcho names adorning every hall, room, and miscellaneous area, it becomes quickly apparent that "library" would be a more fitting name for this collection, since the main attractions are requested via sophisticated computer catalogs and viewed in private consoles. Although no one sets out to spend a vacation watching TV, it can be tempting once you start browsing the archives. The West Coast branch of the 20-year-old New York facility succeeds in treating our favorite pastime as a legitimate art form, with the respect history will prove it deserves.

UCLA at the Armand Hammer Museum of Art and Cultural Center. 10899 Wilshire Blvd. (at Westwood Blvd.). ☎ **310/443-7000.** Admission $4.50 adults, $3 students and seniors 55 and over, $1 kids 17 and under, free for everyone Thurs 6–9pm. Tues–Wed and Fri–Sat 11am–7pm, Thurs 11am–9pm, Sun 11am–5pm. Validated parking $2.75–$7.

Created in 1990 by the former chairman and CEO of Occidental Petroleum, the Armand Hammer Museum has had a hard time winning the respect of critics and the public alike. Barbs are usually aimed at both the museum's relatively flat collection and its patron's tremendous ego. Ensconced in a 2-story Carrara marble building attached to the oil company's offices, the Hammer is better known for its high-profile and often provocative visiting exhibits, such as the opulent pre-Revolution treasures of Russian ruler Catherine the Great or an exhibition entitled "Sexual Politics" assembled around avant-garde artist Judy Chicago's controversial 1970s feminist creation *The Dinner Party.* In conjunction with UCLA's Wight Gallery, a feisty gallery with a reputation for championing contemporary political and experimental art, the Hammer continues to present often daring and usually popular special exhibits, and it's most definitely worth calling ahead to find out what will be there during your visit to L.A. The permanent collection (Armand Hammer's personal collection) consists mostly of traditional Western European and Anglo-American art, and contains noteworthy paintings by Toulouse-Lautrec, Degas, and van Gogh.

HOLLYWOOD

✪ **Autry Museum of Western Heritage.** 4700 Western Heritage Way (in Griffith Park). ☎ 213/667-2000. Website: www.questorsys.com/autry-museum. Admission $7.50 adults, $5 seniors 60 and over and students 13–18, $3 children 2–12, free for kids under 2. Tues–Sun 10am–5pm.

If you're under the age of 45, you might not be familiar with Gene Autry, a Texas-born actor who starred in 82 westerns and became known as the "Singing Cowboy." Opened in 1988, Autry's museum is one of L.A.'s best—it's north of downtown in Griffith Park. This collection of art and artifacts of the European conquest of the West is remarkably comprehensive and intelligently displayed. Evocative exhibits illustrate the everyday lives of early pioneers, not only with antique firearms, tools, saddles, and the like, but with many hands-on exhibits that successfully stir the imagination and the heart. There's footage from Buffalo Bill's Wild West Show, movie clips from the silent days, contemporary films, the works of Wild West artists, and plenty of memorabilia from Autry's own film and TV projects. The "Hall of Merchandising" displays Roy Rogers bedspreads, Hopalong Cassidy radios, and other items from the collective consciousness—and material collections—of baby boomers.

Craft & Folk Art Museum. 5800 Wilshire Blvd. (at Curson Ave.). ☎ **213/937-5544.** Admission $4 adults, $2.50 seniors and students, free for children under 12. Tues–Sun 11am–5pm.

This gallery has grown into one of the city's largest, opening in a prominent Museum Mile building in 1995. "Craft and folk art" is quite a large rubric that encompasses everything from clothing, tools, religious artifacts, and other everyday objects to wood carvings, papier-mâché, weaving, and metalwork. The museum displays folk objects from around the world, but its strongest collection is masks from India, America, Mexico, Japan, and China. Special exhibitions in 1997 included a retrospective of California woodworker Sam Maloof (whose custom-made chairs grace many a celebrity home) and a collection examining parallels between Italy's rich textile heritage and traditional bread shapes and textures. The museum is well known for its annual International Festival of Masks, a colorful and ethnic celebration held each October in Hancock Park, across the street.

Frederick's of Hollywood Museum. 6608 Hollywood Blvd. ☎ **213/466-8506.** Free admission. Mon–Sat 10am–6pm, Sun noon–5pm.

God bless Frederick Mellinger, inventor of the push-up bra (originally known as the "Rising Star"). Frederick's of Hollywood opened this world-famous purple-and-pink art deco panty shop in 1947, and dutifully installed a small exhibition saluting all the stars of stage, screen, and television who glamorized lingerie. The collection now includes Madonna's pointy-breasted corset, a pair of Tony Curtis's skivvies, and a Cher-autographed underwire bra (size 32B). Some exhibits were lost during the 1992 L.A. riots, when looters ransacked the exhibit. Mercifully, the bra worn by Milton Berle on his 1950s TV show was saved.

☼ **Los Angeles County Museum of Art.** 5905 Wilshire Blvd. ☎ **213/857-6111,** or 213/857-6000 for a recording. Website: www.lacma.org. Admission $6 adults, $4 students and seniors 62 and over, $1 children 6–17, free for kids 5 and under; regular exhibitions free for everyone the second Wed of every month. Tues–Thurs 10am–5pm, Fri 10am–9pm, Sat–Sun 11am–6pm.

This is one of the finest art museums in the United States. The huge complex was designed by three very different architects over a span of 30 years. The architectural fusion can be migraine inducing, but this city landmark is well worth delving into.

The newest wing is the **Japanese Pavilion,** which has exterior walls made of Kalwall, a translucent material that, like shoji screens, permits the entry of soft natural light. Inside is a collection of Japanese Edo paintings that's rivaled only by the holdings of the emperor of Japan.

The **Anderson Building,** the museum's contemporary wing, is home to 20th-century painting and sculpture. Here you'll find works by Matisse, Magritte, and a good number of Dada artists.

The **Ahmanson Building** houses the rest of museum's permanent collections. Here you'll find everything from 2,000-year-old pre-Columbian Mexican ceramics to a unique glass collection spanning the centuries to 19th-century portraiture. There's also one of the nation's largest holdings of costumes and textiles, and an important Indian and Southeast Asian art collection.

The **Hammer Building** is primarily used for major special loan exhibitions. Free guided tours covering the museum's highlights depart on a regular basis from here.

☼ **Petersen Automotive Museum.** 6060 Wilshire Blvd. (at Fairfax Ave.). ☎ **213/930-2277.** Website: www.lam.mus.ca.us/petersen. Admission $7 adults, $5 seniors and students, $3 children 5–12, free for kids 4 and under. Tues–Sun 10am–6pm.

When the Petersen opened in 1994, many locals were surprised that it had taken this long for the City of Freeways to salute its most important shaper. Indeed, this museum says more about the city than probably any other one in L.A. Named for Robert Petersen, the publisher responsible for *Hot Rod* and *Motor Trend* magazines, the 4-story museum displays over 200 cars and motorcycles, from the historic to the futuristic. Cars on the first floor are depicted chronologically, in period settings. Other floors are devoted to frequently changing shows of race cars, early motorcycles, and famous movie vehicles. Recent exhibits have included the Flintstones' fiberglass-and-cotton movie car; a customized dune buggy, with seats made from surfboards, created for the Elvis Presley movie *Easy Come, Easy Go;* and a three-wheeled scooter that folds into a Samsonite briefcase, created in competition by a Mazda engineer.

DOWNTOWN

California Museum of Science and Industry. 700 State Dr., Exposition Park. ☎ 213/744-7400, or 213/744-2014 for the IMAX theater. Museum, free; IMAX theater, $6 adults, $4.75 youths 18–21, $4 seniors and children. Multishow discounts available. Daily 10am–5pm.

Celebrating Los Angeles's long-standing romance with the aerospace industry, this museum is best known for its collection of airplanes and other flying objects, including a Boeing DC-3 and a DC-8, and several rockets and satellites. Other industrial science exhibits include a working winery and a behind-the-scenes look at a functioning McDonald's restaurant. Exhibits on robotics and fiber optics thrill kids, as does the hatchery, where almost 200 chicks are born daily. Temporary exhibits are well planned and thoughtfully executed. The museum's IMAX theater shows up to three different films daily, from about 10am to 9pm. Most of the films are truly awesome exposés of events on earth and in space.

Japanese American National Museum. 369 E. 1st St. (at Central Ave.). ☎ 213/625-0414. Admission $4 adults, $3 seniors and children 6–17, $2 students. Tues–Thurs and Sat–Sun 10am–5pm, Fri 11am–8pm.

Located in a beautifully restored historic building in Little Tokyo, this museum is a private nonprofit institute created to document and celebrate the history of the Japanese in America. Its fantastic permanent exhibition chronicles Japanese life in America, while temporary exhibits highlight distinctive aspects of Japanese-American culture.

Los Angeles Children's Museum. 310 N. Main St. (at Los Angeles St.). ☎ 213/687-8800. Admission $5, free for kids under 2. Summer (late June–early Sept), Mon–Fri 11:30am–5pm, Sat–Sun 10am–5pm; the rest of the year, Sat–Sun 10am–5pm.

This thoroughly enchanting museum is a place where children learn by doing. Everyday experiences are demystified by interesting interactive exhibits displayed in a playlike atmosphere. In the Art Studio, kids are encouraged to make finger puppets from a variety of media and shiny rockets out of Mylar. Turn the corner and you're in the unrealistically clean and safe City Street, where kids can sit on a police officer's motorcycle or pretend to drive a bus or a fire truck. Kids (and adults) can see their shadows freeze in the Shadow Box and play with giant foam-filled, Velcro-edged building blocks in Sticky City. Because this is Hollywood, the museum wouldn't be complete without its own recording and TV studios, where kids can become "stars."

Museum of Contemporary Art/Geffen Contemporary at MOCA. 250 S. Grand Ave. and 152 N. Central Ave. ☎ 213/621-2766. Admission $6 adults, $4 seniors and students, free for children 11 and under. Tues–Wed and Fri–Sun 11am–5pm, Thurs 11am–8pm.

MOCA is Los Angeles's only institution exclusively devoted to art from 1940 to the present. Displaying works in a variety of media, it's particularly strong in works by Cy Twombly, Jasper Johns, and Mark Rothko, and shows are often superb. For many experts, MOCA's collections are too spotty to be considered world-class, and the

Downtown Area Attractions

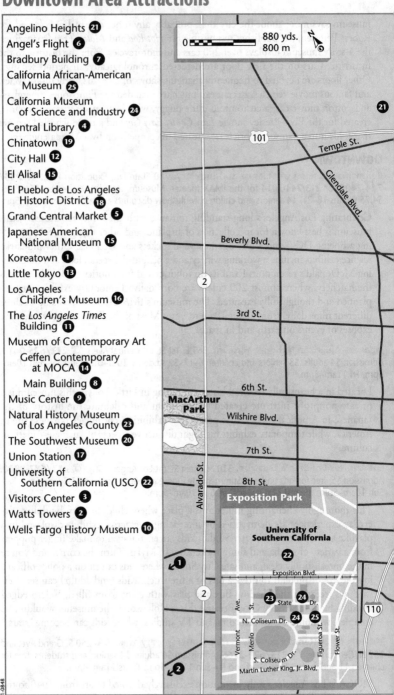

1-0848

Dodger Stadium ↗
🔟20 ↗

110

College St.

Sunset Blvd.

Pasadena Fwy.

N. Broadway

Hill St.

N. Main St.

Alpine St.
🔟19

cho ark

101

Cesar E. Chavez Ave.

Olvera St.

Arcadia St.

🔟17 Union Station
■
🔟18

101

Harbor Fwy.

Temple St.

🔟16

Civic Center
■

1st St.

🔟12

🔟10
🔟9

2nd St.

🔟11

🔟15 🔟14

🔟8

3rd St.

🔟13

San Pedro St.

Alameda Ave.

🔟6 🔟5 🔟7

4th St.

110

5th St.

🔟4

Pershing Square
■

6th St.

🔟3

Wilshire Blvd.

7th St.

Central Ave.

n St.

Figueroa St.

Flower St.

Hope St.

Grand Ave.

Olive St.

Hill St.

9th St.

Broadway

Spring St.

Main St.

Los Angeles St.

Maple Ave.

Wall St.

Olympic Blvd.

11th St.

12th St.

Pico Blvd.

conservative museum board blushes when offered controversial shows (they passed on a Whitney exhibit that included photographs by Robert Mapplethorpe). Nevertheless, we've seen some excellent exhibitions here.

MOCA is one museum housed in two buildings that are close to one another but not within walking distance. The Grand Avenue main building is a contemporary red sandstone structure by renowned Japanese architect Arata Isozaki. The museum restaurant, **Patinette** (☎ 213/626-1178), located here, is the casual dining creation of celebrity chef Joachim Splichal (see Patina in "Dining," above).

The museum's second space, on Central Avenue in Little Tokyo, was the "temporary" Contemporary while the Grand structure was being built, and now houses a superior permanent collection in a fittingly neutral warehouse-type space recently renamed for entertainment mogul and passionate art collector David Geffen. An added feature here is a detailed timeline corresponding to the progression of works. Unless there's a visiting exhibit of great interest at the main museum, we recommend that you start at the Geffen building—where it's also easier to park.

Natural History Museum of Los Angeles County. 900 Exposition Blvd., Exposition Park. ☎ **213/744-3466.** Website: www.lam.mus.ca.us/facmnh. Admission $6 adults; $3.50 children 12–17, seniors, and students with ID; $2 children 5–12; free for kids 4 and under; free for everyone the first Tues of every month. Tues–Sun 10am–5pm. Free docent-led tours offered daily at 1pm.

The "Fighting Dinosaurs"—they're not a high-school football team but the trademark symbol of this massive museum, *Tyrannosaurus rex* and triceratops skeletons poised in a stance so realistic that every kid feels inspired to imitate their *Jurassic Park* bellows. Opened in 1913 in a beautiful columned and domed Spanish Renaissance building, the museum is a 35-hall warehouse of the Earth's history, chronicling the planet and its inhabitants from 600 million years ago to the present day. There's a mind-numbing number of exhibits of prehistoric fossils, bird and marine life, rocks and minerals, and North American mammals. The best permanent displays include the world's rarest shark, a walk-through vault of priceless gems, and an Insect Zoo.

PASADENA & ENVIRONS

✪ **Norton Simon Museum of Art.** 411 W. Colorado Blvd., Pasadena. ☎ **626/449-6840.** Admission $4 adults, $2 students and seniors, free for children 12 and under. Museum, Thurs–Sun noon–6pm; book shop, Thurs–Sun noon–5:30pm.

Named for a food-packing king and financier who reorganized the failing Pasadena Museum of Modern Art, the Norton Simon Museum has become one of California's most important museums. Comprehensive collections of masterpieces by Degas, Picasso, Rembrandt, and Goya are augmented by sculptures by Henry Moore and Auguste Rodin, including *The Burghers of Calais,* which greets you at the gates. The "Blue Four" collection of works by Kandinsky, Jawlensky, Klee, and Feininger is particularly impressive, as is a superb collection of Southeast Asian sculpture. *Still Life with Lemons, Oranges, and a Rose* (1633), an oil by Francisco de Zurbarán, is one of the museum's most important holdings. One of the most popular pieces is Mexican artist Diego Rivera's *The Flower Vendor/Girl with Lilies.* Watch out for hard-hat areas as the museum enlists architect Frank Gehry's help in enhancing the galleries.

Pacific Asia Museum. 46 N. Los Robles Ave., Pasadena. ☎ **626/449-2742.** Admission $4, free for children under 12, free for everyone on the third Sat of each month. Wed–Sun 10am–5pm.

The most striking aspect of this museum is the building itself. Designed in the 1920s in Chinese Imperial Palace style, it's rivaled in flamboyance only by Mann's Chinese Theatre in Hollywood (see "The Top Attractions," above). Rotating exhibits of Asian

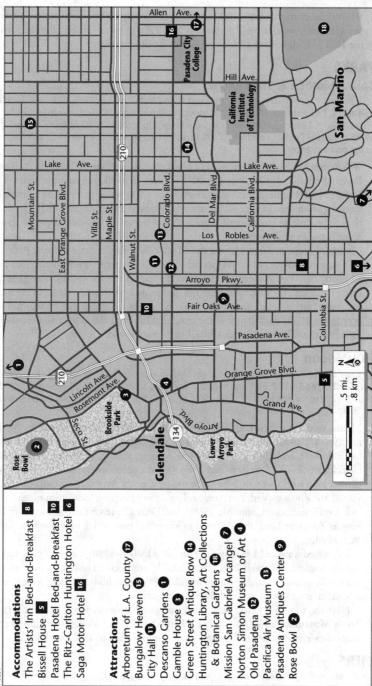

Pasadena & Environs

Allen Ave.
Pasadena City College
Hill Ave.
California Institute of Technology
San Marino
Lake Ave.
Mountain St.
East Orange Grove Blvd.
Villa St.
Maple St.
Walnut St.
Colorado Blvd.
Del Mar Blvd.
California Blvd.
Los Robles Ave.
Arroyo Pkwy.
Fair Oaks Ave.
Pasadena Ave.
Columbia St.
Orange Grove Blvd.
Lincoln Ave.
Rosemont Ave.
Brookside Park
Grand Ave.
Arroyo Blvd.
Lower Arroyo Park
Rose Bowl
Glendale
Arroyo Seco St.

N
0 .5 mi.
   .8 km

210
134

1-0851

Accommodations

The Artists' Inn Bed-and-Breakfast **8**
Bissell House **5**
Pasadena Hotel Bed-and-Breakfast **10**
The Ritz-Carlton Huntington Hotel **6**
Saga Motor Hotel **16**

Attractions

Arboretum of L.A. County **17**
Bungalow Heaven **15**
City Hall **11**
Descanso Gardens **1**
Gamble House **3**
Green Street Antique Row **14**
Huntington Library, Art Collections & Botanical Gardens **18**
Mission San Gabriel Arcangel **7**
Norton Simon Museum of Art **4**
Old Pasadena **12**
Pacifica Air Museum **13**
Pasadena Antiques Center **9**
Rose Bowl **2**

art span the centuries, from 100 B.C. to the current day. This manageably sized museum is usually worth a peek, particularly for 1998's showcase exhibit of artifacts from the 16th to 19th centuries Far East Galleon Trade.

PARKS
SANTA MONICA & THE BEACHES

Will Rogers State Historic Park. 1501 Will Rogers State Park Rd., Pacific Palisades. ☎ **310/454-8212.** Park entrance $6 per vehicle, including all passengers. Daily 8am–sunset. The house opens daily at 10am; guided tours can be arranged for groups of 10 or more. From Santa Monica, take the Pacific Coast Hwy. (Calif. 1) north, turn right onto Sunset Blvd., and continue to the park entrance.

Will Rogers (1879–1935) was born in Oklahoma and became a cowboy in the Texas Panhandle before drifting into a Wild West show as a folksy, humorous roper. The "cracker-barrel philosopher" performed lariat tricks while carrying on a deadpan monologue on current events. The showman moved to Los Angeles in 1919, where he become a movie actor as well as the author of numerous books detailing his down-home "cowboy philosophy."

Located between Santa Monica and Malibu, Will Rogers State Historic Park was once Rogers's private ranch and grounds. The 168-acre estate is now both a park and a historic site. You can explore the grounds, the former stables, and the 31-room house filled with the original furnishings, including a porch swing in the living room and many Native American rugs and baskets. Charles Lindbergh and his wife hid out here in the 1930s during part of the craze that followed the kidnap and murder of their first son. There are picnic tables, but no food is sold.

HOLLYWOOD

✪ **Griffith Park.** Entrances along Los Feliz Blvd. at Riverside Dr., Vermont Ave., and Western Ave. ☎ **213/665-5188.** Park and museum, free; zoo, $8.25 adults, $5.25 seniors, $3.25 children 2–12, free for kids under 2. Park, daily 24 hours; zoo, daily 10am–5pm; museum Mon–Fri 10am–4pm, Sat–Sun 10am–5pm.

Mining tycoon Griffith J. Griffith donated these 4,000 acres of parkland to the city in 1896. Today Griffith Park is one of the largest city parks in America. There's a lot to do here, including hiking, horseback riding, golfing, swimming, biking, and picnicking (see "Outdoor Activities," below). For a general overview, drive the mountainous loop road that winds from the top of Western Avenue, past Griffith Observatory, and down to Vermont Avenue. For a more extensive foray, turn north at the loop road's midsection, onto Mt. Hollywood Drive. To reach the golf courses or Los Angeles Zoo, take Los Feliz Boulevard to Riverside Drive, which runs along the park's western edge.

L.A.'s medium-sized **Los Angeles Zoo** (☎ 213/666-4090) is an easy place to tote the kids around. Animal habitats are divided by continent. The best features are the zoo's walk-in aviary and Adventure Island, an excellent children's zoo that re-creates mountain, meadow, desert, and shoreline habitats.

Near the zoo, in a particularly dusty corner of the park, you'll find the **Travel Town Museum,** 5200 Zoo Dr. (☎ 213/662-5874), a little-known outdoor museum with a small collection of vintage locomotives and old airplanes. Kids love it.

PIERS

Santa Monica Pier. Ocean Ave. at Colorado Ave., Santa Monica.

This famous pier is doing a pretty good job of recapturing the glory days of Southern California piers. Built in 1909 for passenger and cargo ships, the wooden wharf is now home to seafood restaurants and snack shacks, a touristy Mexican cantina at the far end, and a gaily colored turn-of-the-century indoor wooden carousel (which Paul Newman operated in *The Sting*). Summer evening concerts, which are free and range from Big Band to Miami-style Latin, draw huge crowds, as does the new fun-zone perched halfway down. Its name, Pacific Park, hearkens back to the granddaddy pier amusement park in California, Pacific Ocean Park; this new version has a roller coaster and other rides, plus a high-tech arcade shoot-out. But fishermen still head to the end to angle, and nostalgia buffs to view the photographic display of the pier's history. This is the last of the great pleasure piers, offering rides, romance, and perfect panoramic views of the bay and mountains.

The pier is about a mile up Ocean Front Walk from Venice; it's a great round-trip stroll. For information on twilight concerts (generally held Thursdays between mid-June and the end of August), call ☎ 310/393-7593.

THEME PARKS

You'll find L.A.'s most famous theme park, **Universal Studios,** under "The Top Attractions," above.

Six Flags California (Magic Mountain & Hurricane Harbor). Magic Mountain Pkwy. (off Golden State Fwy. [I-5] north), Valencia. ☎ **805/255-4100.** Magic Mountain $34 adults, $20 seniors 55 and older, $17 children age 2 to 48" height, under 2 free; Hurricane Harbor $18 adults, $11 seniors, $11 children; adult combo ticket $49. Magic Mountain open daily Mar–Oct, weekends and holidays only Nov–Feb. Hurricane Harbor open daily Memorial Day–Labor Day, weekends May and Sept, closed Oct–Apr. Both parks open 10am, closing hours vary from 6pm–midnight. Take the San Diego Fwy. (I-405) or the Hollywood Fwy. (U.S. 101/170) north; both will eventually merge with I-5; from I-5, take the Magic Mountain Pkwy. exit.

What started as a countrified little amusement park with a couple of relatively tame roller coasters in 1971 has since been transformed by Six Flags into a thrill-a-minute daredevil's paradise. Located about 20 to 30 minutes north of Universal Studios, **Magic Mountain** is the lesser known of the two attractions, but enormously popular with teenagers and young adults—height-based ride restrictions make the place a big bore for little kids who haven't yet sprouted over 48 inches tall. Likewise those without an iron constitution; rides with names like Ninja, Viper, Colossus, and Psyclone will have your cheeks flapping with the G-force, and queasy expressions are common at the exit. But where else can you experience zero-gravity weightlessness, careen down vertical tracks into relentless hairpin turns, or "race" another train on a side-by-side wooden roller coaster? Some rides are themed to action-film characters like *Superman—The Escape* and *Batman—The Ride;* others are loosely tied to their themed surroundings, like a Far East pagoda or Gold Rush mining town. Arcade games and summer-only entertainment (stunt shows, zany carnivals, and parades) round out the park's attractions.

Hurricane Harbor is Six Flags' over-the-top water park. While advertised as a companion to Magic Mountain, you really can't see both in one day—combo tickets allow you to return within a year's time. Bring your own swimsuit; the park has changing rooms with showers and lockers. Like Magic Mountain, areas have themes like a tropical lagoon or African river (complete with ancient temple ruins). The primary activities are swimming, water slides, rafting, volleyball, and lounging; many areas are designed especially for the "little buccaneer."

TOURIST TRAPS

You've heard of all of the following attractions, of course, but you should know exactly what you're in for before you part with your dollars.

Hollywood Guinness World of Records. 6746 Hollywood Blvd., Hollywood. ☎ **213/463-6433.** Admission $7.95 adults, $6.50 seniors, $4.95 children 6–11. Sun–Thurs 10am–midnight, Fri–Sat 10am–2am.

Scale models, photographs, and push-button displays of the world's fattest man, biggest plant, smallest woman, fastest animal, and other superlatives don't make for a superlative experience.

The Hollywood Wax Museum. 6767 Hollywood Blvd., Hollywood. ☎ **213/462-8860.** Admission $9 adults, $7.50 seniors, $7 children 6–12, free for kids 5 and under. Sun–Thurs 10am–midnight, Fri–Sat 10am–2am.

Cast in the Madame Tussaud mold, the Hollywood Wax Museum features dozens of lifelike figures of famous movie stars and events. The "museum" is not great, but it can be good for a cheeky laugh or two. A "Chamber of Horrors" exhibit includes the coffin used in *The Raven,* as well as a diorama from the Vincent Price classic *The House of Wax.* The "Movie Awards Theatre" exhibit is a short film highlighting Academy Award presentations from the last 4 decades.

Ripley's "Believe It Or Not!" Hollywood. 6780 Hollywood Blvd. ☎ **213/466-6335.** Admission $8.95 adults, $7.95 seniors, $5.95 children 5–11.

Believe it or not, this amazing and silly "museum" is still open. A bizarre collection of wax figures, photos, and models depicts unnatural oddities from Robert Leroy Ripley's infamous arsenal. My favorites include the skeleton of a two-headed baby, a statue of Marilyn Monroe sculpted with shredded money, and a portrait of John Wayne made from laundry lint.

8 Organized Tours

STUDIO TOURS

HOLLYWOOD

Paramount Pictures. 5555 Melrose Ave. ☎ **213/956-1777.** Tours $15 per person. Mon–Fri 9am–2pm.

Paramount's 2-hour walking tour around its Hollywood headquarters is both a historical ode to filmmaking and a real-life look at a working studio. Tours depart hourly; the itinerary varies, depending on what productions are in progress. Visits might include a walk through the sound stages of TV shows like *Entertainment Tonight* and *Frasier.* Cameras, recording equipment, and children under 10 are not allowed.

THE SAN FERNANDO VALLEY

NBC Studios. 3000 W. Alameda Ave., Burbank. ☎ **818/840-3537.** Tours $6 adults, $5.50 seniors, $3.75 children 6–12. Mon–Fri 9am–3pm.

According to a security guard, John Wayne and Redd Foxx once got into a fight here after Wayne refused to ride in the same limousine as Foxx, who called the movie star a "redneck." Well, your NBC tour will probably be a bit more docile than that. The guided 1-hour tour includes a behind-the-scenes look at *The Tonight Show with Jay Leno* set, wardrobe, makeup, and set-building departments, and several sound studios. The tour includes some cool video demonstrations of high-tech special effects.

✪ **Warner Brothers Studios.** Olive Ave. (at Hollywood Way), Burbank. ☎ **818/972-TOUR.** Admission $29 per person. Mon–Fri 9am–4pm, Sat (summer only) 10am–2pm.

This is the most comprehensive—and the least theme park–like—of the studio tours. The tour takes visitors on a 2-hour informational drive-and-walk jaunt around the studio's faux streets. After a brief introductory film, you'll pile into glorified golf carts and cruise past parking spaces marked *Clint Eastwood, Michael Douglas,* and *Sharon Stone,* then walk through active film and television sets. Whether it's an orchestra scoring a film or a TV show being taped or edited, you'll get a glimpse of how it's done. Stops may include the wardrobe department or the mills where sets are made. Whenever possible, guests visit working sets to watch actors filming actual productions. Reservations are required; children under 10 not admitted.

SIGHTSEEING TOURS

Oskar J's Tours (☎ 818/501-2217) operates regularly scheduled, panoramic motor-coach tours of the city. Buses (or plush minivans) pick up passengers from major hotels for morning or afternoon tours of Sunset Strip, the movie studios, Farmer's Market, Hollywood, homes of the stars, and other attractions. Tours vary in length from 2 to 5 hours and cost $25 to $50. Call for details and to make reservations.

Next Stage Tour Company offers a unique Insomniacs' Tour of L.A. (☎ 213/939-2688), a 3am tour of the predawn city that usually includes trips to the *Los Angeles Times;* the flower, produce, and fish markets; and the top of a skyscraper to watch the sun rise over the city. The fact-filled tour lasts about $6^1/_2$ hours and includes breakfast. Tours depart twice monthly and cost $47 per person. Phone for information and reservations.

Grave Line Tours (☎ 213/469-4149) is a terrific journey through Hollywood's darker side. You're picked up in a renovated hearse and taken to the murder sites and final residences of the stars. You'll see the Hollywood Boulevard hotel where female impersonator/actor Divine died, the liquor store where John Belushi threw a temper tantrum shortly before his overdose, and the telephone pole that Montgomery Clift crashed his car into. Tours are $40 per person and last about $2^1/_2$ hours. They depart at 9:30am daily from the corner of Orchid Street and Hollywood Boulevard, by Mann's Chinese Theatre. Reservations are required.

The **L.A. Conservancy** (☎ 213/623-2489) conducts a dozen fascinating, information-packed walking tours of historic downtown L.A., seed of today's sprawling metropolis. The most popular is "Broadway Theaters," a loving look at movie palaces. Other intriguing ones include "Marble Masterpieces," "Art Deco," "Mecca for Merchants," "Terra-Cotta," and tours of the landmark Biltmore Hotel and City Hall. They're usually held on Saturday mornings and cost $5. Call Monday to Friday between 9am and 5pm for exact schedule and information.

In Pasadena, various tours spotlighting architecture or neighborhoods are lots of fun, given this area's history of wealthy estates and ardent preservation. Call **Pasadena Heritage** (☎ 626/793-0617) for a schedule of guided tours, or pick up "Ten Tours of Pasadena," self-guided walking or driving maps available at the **Pasadena Convention and Visitors Bureau,** 171 S. Los Robles Ave. (☎ 626/795-9311).

Heli USA Helicopter Adventures, 6033 W. Century Blvd. Suite 950, Los Angeles (☎ 800/443-5487), cruises the Paramount, Universal, Burbank, and Disney studios; hovers over the mega-estates of the stars in Beverly Hills and Bel Air; then winds up over Hollywood's Mann's Chinese Theatre, Sunset Strip, and the Hollywood sign. The cost of this helicopter "flightseeing" tour, including lunch or dinner, ranges from $99 to $149, depending on the itinerary.

9 Beaches

Los Angeles County's 72-mile coastline sports over 30 miles of beaches, most of which are operated by the **Department of Beaches & Harbors,** 13837 Fiji Way, Marina del Rey (☎ 310/305-9503). County-run beaches usually charge for parking ($4 to $8). Alcohol, bonfires, and pets are prohibited, so you'll have to leave Fido

Beaches & Coastal Attractions

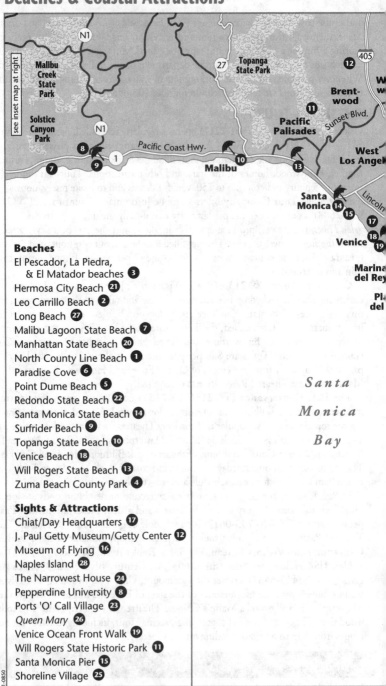

Beaches

El Pescador, La Piedra,
  & El Matador beaches **3**
Hermosa City Beach **21**
Leo Carrillo Beach **2**
Long Beach **27**
Malibu Lagoon State Beach **7**
Manhattan State Beach **20**
North County Line Beach **1**
Paradise Cove **6**
Point Dume Beach **5**
Redondo State Beach **22**
Santa Monica State Beach **14**
Surfrider Beach **9**
Topanga State Beach **10**
Venice Beach **18**
Will Rogers State Beach **13**
Zuma Beach County Park **4**

Sights & Attractions

Chiat/Day Headquarters **17**
J. Paul Getty Museum/Getty Center **12**
Museum of Flying **16**
Naples Island **28**
The Narrowest House **24**
Pepperdine University **8**
Ports 'O' Call Village **23**
Queen Mary **26**
Venice Ocean Front Walk **19**
Will Rogers State Historic Park **11**
Santa Monica Pier **15**
Shoreline Village **25**

1-0850

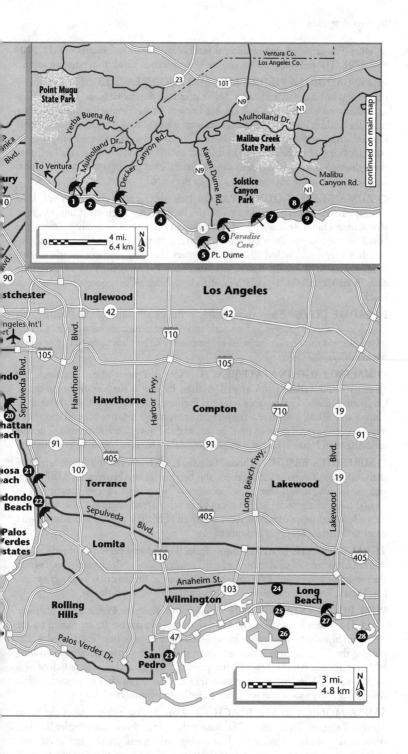

continued on main map

Ventura Co.
Los Angeles Co.

**Point Mugu
State Park**

Yerba Buena Rd.

Mulholland Dr.

To Ventura

Decker Canyon Rd.

Mulholland Dr.

23

101

N9

N1

Mulholland Dr.

**Malibu Creek
State Park**

Kanan Dume Rd.

N9

**Solstice
Canyon
Park**

Malibu
Canyon Rd.

N1

1

2

3

4

1

6 *Paradise
Cove*

7

8

9

5 Pt. Dume

0 ____ 4 mi.
6.4 km

N

stchester

Inglewood

Los Angeles

42

42

ngeles Int'l
ort

1

105

Sepulveda Blvd.

Hawthorne

Blvd.

Hawthorne

Harbor Fwy.

110

105

Compton

710

19

91

ndo Blvd.

20

hattan
each

91

405

107

Torrance

Sepulveda

Blvd.

91

405

Long Beach Fwy.

Lakewood

19

Lakewood

Blvd.

91

19

405

osa
each

21

dondo
Beach

22

**Palos
Verdes
states**

Lomita

110

Anaheim St.

103

24

**Long
Beach**

**Rolling
Hills**

Palos Verdes Dr.

47

Wilmington

25

26

27

28

San
Pedro

23

0 ____ 3 mi.
4.8 km

N

at home. For recorded surf conditions (and coastal weather forecast) call ☎ **310/ 457-9701.** The following are the county's best beaches, listed from north to south:

EL PESCADOR, LA PIEDRA & EL MATADOR BEACHES   These relatively rugged and isolated beaches front a 2-mile stretch of the Pacific Coast Highway (Calif. 1) between Broad Beach and Decker Canyon roads, about 10 minutes' driving from the Malibu Pier. Picturesque coves with unusual rock formations, are perfect for sunbathing and picnicking, but swim with caution as there are no lifeguards or other facilities. These beaches can be difficult to find, marked only by small signs on the highway. Visitors are limited by the small number of parking spots atop the bluffs. Descend to the beach via stairs that cling to the cliffs.

✪ ZUMA BEACH COUNTY PARK   Jam-packed on warm weekends, L.A. County's largest beach park is located off the Pacific Coast Highway (Calif. 1) a mile past Kanan Dume Road. While it can't claim to be the most lovely beach in the Southland, Zuma has the most comprehensive facilities: plenty of rest rooms, lifeguards, playgrounds, volleyball courts, and snack bars. The southern stretch, toward Point Dume, is Westward Beach, separated from the noisy highway by sandstone cliffs. A trail leads over the point's headlands to Pirate's Cove, once a popular nude beach.

PARADISE COVE   This private beach in the 28000 block of the Pacific Coast Highway (Calif. 1) charges $15 to park and $5 per person if you walk in. Changing rooms and showers are included in the price. The beach is often full by noon on weekends.

✪ MALIBU LAGOON STATE BEACH   Not just a pretty white-sand beach, but an estuary and wetlands area as well, Malibu Lagoon is the historic home of the Chumash Indians. The entrance is on the Pacific Coast Highway (Calif. 1) south of Cross Creek Road, and there's a small admission charge. Marine life and shorebirds teem where the creek empties into the sea, and the waves are always mild. The historic Adamson House is here, a showplace of Malibu tile now operating as a museum.

✪ SURFRIDER BEACH   Without a doubt, L.A.'s best waves roll ashore here. One of the city's most popular surfing spots, this beach is located between the Malibu Pier and the lagoon. In surf lingo, few "locals only" wave wars are ever fought here— surfing is not as territorial here as it can be in other areas, where out-of-towners can be made to feel unwelcome. Surrounded by all of Malibu's hustle and bustle, don't come to Surfrider for peace and quiet.

TOPANGA STATE BEACH   Noise from the highway prevents solitude at this short, narrow strip of sand located where Topanga Canyon Boulevard emerges from the mountains. Why go? Ask the surfers who wait in line to catch Topanga's excellent breaks. There are rest rooms and lifeguard services, but little else.

WILL ROGERS STATE BEACH   Three miles along the Pacific Coast Highway (Calif. 1) between Sunset Boulevard and the Santa Monica border are named for the American humorist whose ranch-turned-state-historic-park (see "Parks" under "Exploring the City," above) is nestled above the palisades that provide the striking backdrop for this popular beach. A pay parking lot extends the entire length of Will Rogers, and facilities include rest rooms, lifeguards, and a snack hut in season. While the surfing is only so-so, the waves are friendly for swimmers of all ages.

SANTA MONICA STATE BEACH   The beaches on either side of the Santa Monica Pier (see "Piers" under "Exploring the City," above) are popular for their white sands and easy accessibility. There are big parking lots, eateries, and lots of well-maintained bathrooms. A paved beach path runs along here, allowing you to walk, bike, or skate to Venice and points south. Colorado Boulevard leads to the pier; turn north on the Pacific Coast Highway (Calif. 1) below the coastline's striking bluffs, or south along Ocean Avenue; you'll find parking in both directions.

✪ VENICE BEACH   Moving south from the city of Santa Monica, the paved pedestrian Promenade becomes Ocean Front Walk and gets progressively weirder until it reaches an apex at Washington Boulevard and the Venice fishing pier. Although there are people who swim and sunbathe, Venice Beach's character is defined by the sea of humanity that gathers here, plus the bevy of boardwalk vendors and old-fashioned "walk-streets" a block away (see "The Top Attractions," earlier in this chapter). Park on the side streets or in the plentiful lots west of Pacific Avenue.

MANHATTAN STATE BEACH   The Beach Boys used to hang out (and surf, of course) at this wide, friendly beach backed by beautiful oceanview homes. Plenty of parking on 36 blocks of side streets (between Rosecrans Avenue and the Hermosa Beach border) draw weekend crowds from the L.A. area. Manhattan has some of the best surfing around, along with rest rooms, lifeguards, and volleyball courts. Manhattan Beach Boulevard leads west to the fishing pier and adjacent seafood restaurants.

✪ HERMOSA CITY BEACH   A very, very wide white-sand beach with tons to recommend it, Hermosa extends to either side of the pier and includes "The Strand," a pedestrian lane that runs its entire length. Main access is at the foot of Pier Avenue, which itself is lined with interesting shops. There's plenty of street parking, rest rooms, lifeguards, volleyball courts, a fishing pier, playgrounds, and good surfing.

REDONDO STATE BEACH   Popular with surfers, bicyclists, and joggers, Redondo's white sand and ice plant–carpeted dunes are just south of tiny King Harbor, along "The Esplanade" (South Esplanade Drive). Get there via the Pacific Coast Highway (Calif. 1) or Torrance Boulevard. Facilities include rest rooms, lifeguards, and volleyball courts.

10 Outdoor Activities

ATTENDING A DODGER GAME   The **Los Angeles Dodgers** (☎ 213/224-1500) play at Dodger Stadium, 1000 Elysian Park, near Sunset Boulevard. If you're lucky, you just may get to see Hideo Nomo, the Dodgers' Japanese sensation, pitch before a hometown crowd (Hideo was actually the second Japanese player to play in the big leagues, but the first to reach star status). If you go to a game, don't be surprised by the apparent apathy of the crowd; traffic is so bad getting to and from Dodger Stadium that the fans usually arrive late, around the second or third inning, and leave early—the stands empty out during the seventh inning. Dodgers' fans are an odd bunch.

BIKING   L.A. is great for biking. If you're into distance pedaling, you can do no better than the flat 22-mile paved **Ocean Front Walk** that runs along the sand from Pacific Palisades in the north to Torrance in the south. The path attracts all levels of riders, so it gets pretty busy on weekends. For information on this and other city bike routes, phone the **Metropolitan Transportation Authority** (☎ 213/244-6539).

The best place to mountain bike is along the trails of **Malibu Creek State Park** (☎ 800/533-7275 or 818/880-0350), in the Santa Monica Mountains between Malibu and the San Fernando Valley. Fifteen miles of trails rise to a maximum of 3,000 feet and are appropriate for intermediate to advanced bikers. Pick up a trail map at the park entrance, 4 miles south of U.S. 101 off Las Virgenes Road, just north of Mulholland Highway. Park admission is $5 per car.

Sea Mist Rental, 1619 Ocean Front Walk, Santa Monica (☎ **310/395-7076**), rents 10-speed cruisers for $5 per hour and $14 a day; 15-speed mountain bikes rent for $6 per hour and $20 a day.

DAY HIKES   The Santa Monica Mountains, a small range that runs only 50 miles from Griffith Park to Point Mugu, on the coast north of Malibu, makes Los Angeles a great place for hiking. The mountains peak at 3,111 feet and are part of the **Santa Monica Mountains National Recreation Area,** a contiguous conglomeration of 350 public parks and 65,000 acres. Many animals make their homes in this area, including deer, coyote, rabbit, skunk, rattlesnake, fox, hawk, and quail. The hills are also home to almost 1,000 drought-resistant plant species, including live oak and coastal sage.

Hiking is best after spring rains, when the hills are green, flowers are in bloom, and the air is clear. Summers can be very hot; hikers should always carry fresh water. Beware of poison oak, a hearty shrub that's common on the West Coast. Usually found among oak trees, poison oak has leaves in groups of three, with waxed surfaces and prominent veins. If you come into contact with this itch-producing plant, bathe yourself in calamine lotion, or the ocean.

Santa Ynez Canyon, in Pacific Palisades, is a long and difficult climb that rises steadily for about 3 miles. At the top, hikers are rewarded with fantastic views over the Pacific. Also at the top is Trippet Ranch, a public facility providing water, rest rooms, and picnic tables. From Santa Monica, take the Pacific Coast Highway (Calif. 1) north. Turn right onto Sunset Boulevard, then left onto Palisades Drive. Continue for 2¹/₂ miles, turn left onto Verenda de la Montura, and park at the cul-de-sac at the end of the street, where you'll find the trailhead.

Temescal Canyon, in Pacific Palisades, is far easier than the Santa Ynez Trail and, predictably, far more popular with locals. It's one of the quickest routes into the wilderness. Hikes here are anywhere from 1 to 5 miles. From Santa Monica, take the Pacific Coast Highway (Calif. 1) north; turn right onto Temescal Canyon Road and follow it to the end. Sign in with the gatekeeper, who can also answer your questions.

Will Rogers State Historic Park, Pacific Palisades, is also a terrific place for hiking. An intermediate-level hike from the park's entrance ends at Inspiration Point, a plateau from which you can see a good portion of L.A.'s Westside. See "Parks" in "Exploring the City," above, for complete information.

Griffith Park (also discussed in "Parks," above) is an urban hiker's paradise. This 100-year-old park used to have dozens of paved roads popular for weekend motorists, but cuts in funding over the years have forced the park to stop maintenance and close them to auto traffic. The good news is that they make great hiking routes—safe, easy to follow, and leading to some of the most spectacular city vistas in L.A. The park also has dozens of dirt trails at every endurance level; you can get a map of both paved roads and hiking trails at the ranger center 1 mile inside the Riverside Drive main entrance. Ask them for directions to Dante's View or Amir's Garden, two privately tended (for public enjoyment) groves inside the park.

FISHING   **Marina del Rey Sports Fishing,** 13759 Fiji Way (☎ **310/822-3625**), known locally as "Captain Frenchy's," has four deep-sea boats departing daily on half- and full-day ocean fishing trips. Of course, it depends on what's running when you're out, but bass, barracuda, halibut, and yellowtail tuna are the most common catches on these party boats. Excursions cost $20 to $25, including bait and tackle. Phone for reservations.

No permit is required to cast from shore or to drop a line from a pier. Local anglers will hate us for giving away their secret spot, but the best saltwater fishing spot in all of L.A. is at the foot of Torrance Boulevard in Redondo Beach. Centuries of tides and currents have created a deep underwater canyon here that's known among local fisherman as a glory hole.

GOLF   Most of the city's public courses are administered by the Department of Recreation and Parks, which follows a complicated registration/reservation system for tee times. While visitors cannot reserve start times in advance, you're welcome to play any of the courses by showing up and getting on the call sheet. Expect to wait for the most popular tee times, but try to use your flexible vacationer status to your advantage by avoiding the early morning rush.

Of the city's seven 18-hole and three 9-hole courses, you can't get more central than the **Rancho Park Golf Course,** 10460 W. Pico Blvd. (☎ 310/838-7373), located smack-dab in the middle of L.A.'s Westside. The par-71 course has lots of tall trees, but not enough to blot out the towering Century City buildings next door. Rancho also has a 9-hole, par-3 course.

For a genuinely woodsy experience, try one of the three courses inside **Griffith Park,** northeast of Hollywood (see "Parks," above; ☎ 213/664-1191). All named for presidents, the courses are extremely well maintained, challenging without being frustrating, and (despite some holes alongside I-5) a great way to leave the city behind. Bucolic pleasures abound, particularly on 9-hole **Roosevelt,** on Vermont Avenue across from the Greek Theatre; early morning wildlife often includes deer, rabbits, skunks, and raccoons (fore!). **Wilson** and **Harding** are each 18 holes and start from the main clubhouse off Riverside Drive, the park's main entrance.

Greens fees on all city courses are $17 Monday to Friday, and $22 on weekends and holidays; 9-hole courses charge $8.50 weekdays, $11.50 on weekends and holidays. For details on other city courses, or to contact the starter directly by phone, call the **Department of Recreation and Parks** at ☎ 213/485-5566.

The **Industry Hills Golf Club,** 1 Industry Hills Pkwy., City of Industry (☎ 818/810-4455), has two 18-hole courses designed by William Bell. Together they encompass 8 lakes, 160 bunkers, and long fairways. The Eisenhower Course, which consistently ranks among *Golf Digest*'s top 25 public courses, has extra-large, undulating greens and the challenge of thick kikuyu rough. An adjacent driving range is lit for night use. Greens fees are $45 weekdays and $60 on weekends, including cart.

American Golf Corp., 1633 26th St., Santa Monica (☎ 800/468-7952 or 310/829-4653; fax 310/829-4990), guarantees reserved tee times at more than 16 top area courses. They can also arrange lessons and provide information on local tournaments.

HORSEBACK RIDING   The **Los Angeles Equestrian Center,** 480 Riverside Dr., Burbank (☎ 818/840-9066), rents horses by the hour for western or English riding through Griffith Park's hills. There's a 200-pound weight limit, and children under 12 are not permitted to ride. Horse rental costs $13 per hour, and there's a 2-hour rental maximum. The stables are open Monday to Friday from 8am to 7pm and on Saturday and Sunday from 8am to 4pm.

Sunrise Downs Equestrian Center, 11900 Big Tujunga Canyon Rd., Tujunga (☎ 818/353-9410), offers 2-, 3-, and 4-hour guided day or evening horseback tours through the San Gabriel Mountains and the scenic San Fernando Valley. They charge $25 per hour per person, and there's a two-person minimum.

SKATING   The 22-mile-long **Ocean Front Walk** that runs from Pacific Palisades to Torrance is one of the premier skating spots in the country. In-line skating is especially popular, but conventionals are often seen here, too. Roller skating is allowed just about everywhere bicycling is, but be aware that cyclists have the right-of-way. **Spokes 'n Stuff,** 4175 Admiralty Way, Marina del Rey (☎ **310/ 306-3332**), is just one of many places to rent wheels near the Venice portion of Ocean Front Walk. Skates cost $5 per hour; kneepads and wrist guards come with every rental.

SURFING   Shops near all top surfing beaches in the L.A. area rent boards, including **Zuma Jay Surfboards,** 22775 Pacific Coast Hwy., Malibu (☎ **310/456-8044**). You'll find the shop about a quarter-mile south of the Malibu Pier. Rentals are $20 per day, plus $8 to $10 for wet suits in winter.

TENNIS   You'll find mostly hard-surface courts in California. If your hotel doesn't have a court, try the well-maintained, well-lit **Griffith Park Tennis Courts,** on Commonwealth Road just east of Vermont Avenue. Or call the **City of Los Angeles Department of Recreation and Parks** (☎ **213/485-5555**) to make a reservation at a municipal court near you.

11 Shopping

Here's a rundown of the primary shopping areas, along with descriptions of a few of their best stores. For a more complete guide to shopping in Los Angeles, see *Frommer's Los Angeles.*

The **sales tax** in Los Angeles is 8¹/₄%, but savvy shoppers know to have more expensive items shipped directly home and save the tax.

SANTA MONICA & THE BEACHES

3rd Street Promenade (3rd Street, from Broadway to the Wilshire Boulevard, Santa Monica)

Packed with chain stores and boutiques as well as dozens of restaurants and a large movie theater, Santa Monica's pedestrians-only section of 3rd Street is one of the most popular shopping areas in the city. The Promenade bustles on into the evening with a seemingly endless assortment of street performers, and an endless parade of souls. Stores stay open late (often till 1 or 2am on the weekends) for the movie-going crowds. There's plenty of metered parking in structures on the adjacent streets, so bring lots of quarters!

Hennessey & Ingalls. 1254 3rd Street Promenade. ☎ **310/458-9074.**

This bookstore is devoted to art and architecture, from magnificent coffee-table photography books to graphic-arts titles and obscure biographies of artists and art movements.

Mayhem. 1411 3rd Street Promenade. ☎ **310/451-7600.**

This shop sells autographed guitars and other memorabilia from U2, Nirvana, Springsteen, Bon Jovi, Pearl Jam, and other rockers to collectors, including the owners of the Hard Rock cafes.

Midnight Special Bookstore. 1318 3rd Street Promenade. ☎ **310/393-2923.**

This medium-size general book shop is known for its good small-press selection and regular poetry readings.

Na Na. 1228 3rd Street Promenade. ☎ **310/394-9690.**

This is what punk looks like in the 1990s: clunky shoes, knit hats, narrow-striped shirts, and baggy streetwear.

Puzzle Zoo. 1413 3rd Street Promenade. ☎ **310/393-9201.**

Puzzles have proved so popular here that the Zoo recently expanded to better accommodate a selection chosen "Best in L.A." by *Los Angeles* magazine. You'll find the double-sided World's Most Difficult Puzzle, the Puzzle in a Bottle, and collector's serial-numbered Ravensburger series, among others.

Pyramid Music. 1340 3rd Street Promenade. ☎ **310/393-5877.**

Seemingly endless bins of used compact discs and cassette tapes line the walls of this long, narrow shop on the Promenade. LPs, posters, cards, buttons, and accessories are also available.

Main Street in Santa Monica & Venice (between Pico Boulevard & Rose Avenue)

Another good strip for strolling, Main Street boasts a healthy combination of mall standards as well as upscale, left-of-center individual boutiques. You'll also find plenty of casually hip cafes and restaurants. The primary strip connecting Santa Monica and Venice, Main Street has a relaxed, beach-community vibe that sets it apart from similar strips. The stores here straddle the fashion fence between upscale trendy and beach-bum edgy.

C.P. Shades. 2925 Main St., Santa Monica. ☎ **310/392-0949.**

Fans of C.P. Shades, a San Francisco ladies' clothier whose line is carried by many department stores and boutiques, will love this boutique devoted solely to their loose, casual cotton and linen separates. Their trademark monochromatic neutrals are meticulously arranged in an airy, well-lit store.

Horizons West. 2011 Main St. (south of Pico Blvd.), Santa Monica. ☎ **310/392-1122.**

Brand-name surfboards, wet suits, leashes, magazines, waxes, lotions, and everything else you need to catch the perfect wave are found here. Stop in and say "hi" to Randy, and pick up a free tide table.

Pepper's Eyeware. 2904 Main St. (between Ashland and Pier sts.). ☎ **310/392-0633.**

If you're looking for some truly sophisticated, finely crafted eyeware, this friendly shop is for you. Ask for frames by cutting-edge L.A. designers Bada and Koh Sakai. If you're lucky enough to have perfect vision, consider some stylish shades.

Bergamot Station (2525 Michigan Ave., Santa Monica)

Once a station for the Red Car trolley line, the industrial space of Bergamot Station (☎ 310/829-5854) is now home to the Santa Monica Museum of Art plus two dozen art galleries, a cafe, a bookstore, and offices. Most of the galleries are closed Monday; the train yard is located at the terminus of Michigan Avenue west of Cloverfield Boulevard.

Exhibits change often and vary widely, ranging from a Julius Shulman black-and-white photo retrospective of L.A.'s Case Study Houses, to a provocative exhibit of Vietnam War propaganda posters from the U.S. and Vietnam, to whimsical furniture constructed entirely of corrugated cardboard. A sampling of offerings includes the **Gallery of Functional Art** (☎ **310/829-6990**), featuring one-of-a-kind and limited-edition furniture, lighting, bathroom fixtures, and other functional art pieces, as well as smaller items like jewelry, flatware, ceramics, and glass. The **Rosamund Felson Gallery** (☎ **310/828-8488**) is well known for showcasing L.A.–based contemporary artists; this is a good place to get a taste of current trends. **Track 16 Gallery** (☎ **310/264-4678**) has exhibitions that range from pop art to avant-garde inventiveness—try to see what's going on here.

L.A.'S WESTSIDE & BEVERLY HILLS

West 3rd Street (between Fairfax Avenue & Robertson Boulevard)

You can shop till you drop on this trendy strip, anchored on the east end by the Farmer's Market (see "The Top Attractions," above). Many of Melrose Avenue's shops have relocated here, alongside some terrific up-and-comers, several cafes, and the much-lauded restaurant Locanda Veneta (see "Dining," above). "Fun" is more the catchword here than "funky," and the shops (including the vintage clothing stores) tend a bit more to the refined than do those along Melrose; you'd never find upscale book shops dedicated to travel tomes and cookbooks in that neck of the woods—but you will here.

✪ **Chado Tea Room.** 8422 W. 3rd St. ☎ **213/655-2056.**

A temple for tea lovers, Chado is designed with a nod to Paris's renowned Mariage Frères tea purveyor. One wall is lined with nooks whose recognizable brown tins are filled with over 250 different varieties of tea from around the world. Among the choices are 15 kinds of Darjeeling, Indian teas blended with rose petals, and ceremonial Chinese and Japanese blends. They also serve tea meals here, featuring delightful sandwiches and individual pots of any loose tea in the store.

The Cook's Library. 8373 W. 3rd St. ☎ **213/655-3141.**

There's a specialty book shop for everyone in L.A.; this is where the city's top chefs find both classic and deliciously offbeat cookbooks and other food-oriented tomes. Browsing is welcomed, even encouraged, with tea, tasty treats, and rocking chairs.

GOAT Cadeaux. 306 S. Edinburgh (at 3rd St. east of Crescent Heights). ☎ **213/651-3133.**

Cadeaux means "gifts" in French, and this is the kind of shop where you can always find just the right present. From unusual candles to antique bookends to carved wooden boxes to art deco picture frames, GOAT carries a intriguing variety.

Memory Lane. 8387 W. 3rd St. (at Orlando). ☎ **213/655-4571.**

This narrow trove of '40s, '50s, and '60s collectibles features such treasures as Formica dinner sets, bakelite radios, cocktail shakers and sets, unusual lamps, and a few well-chosen coats, dresses, and accessories.

Polkadots & Moonbeams. 8367 and 8381 W. 3rd St. ☎ **213/651-1746.**

This is actually two stores several doors apart, one carrying (slightly overpriced) hip young fashions for women, and a vintage store with clothing, accessories, and fabrics from the 1920s to the 1960s, all in remarkable condition.

Traveler's Bookcase. 8375 W. 3rd St. ☎ **213/655-0575.**

This store, one of the best travel book shops in the West, stocks a huge selection of guidebooks and travel literature, as well as maps and travel accessories. A quarterly newsletter chronicles the travel adventures of the genial owners, who know firsthand the most helpful items to carry.

Sunset Strip (between La Cienega Boulevard & Doheny Drive, West Hollywood)

The monster-size billboards advertising the latest rock god make it clear that this is rock 'n' roll territory. The "Strip" is lined with trendy restaurants, industry-oriented hotels, and dozens of shops offering outrageous fashions and chunky stage accessories. One anomaly is Sunset Plaza, an upscale cluster of Georgian-style shops resembling Beverly Hills at its snootiest.

Billy Martin's. 8605 Sunset Blvd., West Hollywood. ☎ **310/289-5000.**

Founded by the legendary Yankee manager in 1978, this chic men's western shop—complete with fireplace and leather sofa—stocks hand-forged silver and gold belt buckles, Lucchese and Liberty boots, and stable staples like flannel shirts.

✪ **Book Soup.** 8800 Sunset Blvd., West Hollywood. ☎ **310/657-1072.**

This has long been one of L.A.'s most celebrated book shops, selling both mainstream and small-press books and hosting regular book signings and author nights. A great browsing shop, it has a large selection of show-biz books and an extensive outdoor news and magazine stand on one side. The Book Soup Bistro has an appealing bar, a charming outdoor patio, and an extensive traditional bistro menu catering to hungry intellectuals.

Tower Records. 8811 W. Sunset Blvd., Hollywood. ☎ **310/657-7300.**

Tower insists that it has L.A.'s largest selection of compact discs—over 125,000 titles—despite the Virgin Megastore's contrary claim. Even if Virgin has more, Tower's collection tends to be more interesting and browser friendly. And the shop's enormous blues, jazz, and classical selections are definitely greater than the competition's. Open 365 days a year.

Virgin Megastore. 8000 Sunset Blvd., Hollywood. ☎ **213/650-8666.**

Some 100 CD "listening posts" and an in-store "radio station" make this megastore a music lover's paradise. Virgin claims to stock 150,000 titles, including an extensive collection of hard-to-find artists.

La Brea Avenue (north of Wilshire Boulevard)

This is L.A.'s artsiest shopping strip. Anchored by the giant **American Rag, Cie.** alterna-complex, La Brea is home to lots of great urban antiques stores dealing in deco, arts and crafts, 1950s modern, and the like. You'll also find vintage clothiers, furniture galleries, and other warehouse-size stores, as well as some of the city's hippest restaurants, such as Campanile (see "Dining," above).

Dishes a la Carte. 5650 W. 3rd St. (at LaBrea Ave.), Los Angeles. ☎ **213/938-6223.**

Modeled after New York's Fish's Eddie, this little ceramics shop carries factory seconds and obsolete patterns of well- and little-known brands alike. You'll find Fiestaware next to locally hand-painted pieces and durable restaurant dishes.

✪ **Drea Kadilak.** 463 S. LaBrea Ave. (at 6th St.), Los Angeles. ☎ **213/931-2051.**

The art of millinery often seems to have gone the way of white afternoon gloves for ladies, but inventive Drea Kadilak charms you with her tiny hat shop. Designing in straw, cotton duck, wool felt, and a number of more unusual fabrics, she does her own blocking, will cheerfully take measurements for custom ladies' headware, is reasonably priced, and gives away signature hatboxes with your purchase.

Liz's Antique Hardware. 453 S. LaBrea Ave., Los Angeles. ☎ **213/939-4403.**

Stuffed to the rafters with hardware and fixtures of the last 100 years, Liz's thoughtfully keeps a canister of wet-wipes at the register—believe us, you'll need one after sifting through bags and crates of doorknobs, latches, finials, and any other home hardware you can imagine needing. Perfect sets of Bakelite drawer pulls and antique ceramic bathroom fixtures are some of the more intriguing items. Be prepared to browse for hours, whether you're redecorating or not!

The Swell Store. 126 N. La Brea Ave., Los Angeles. ☎ **213/937-2096.**

Styles come and styles go—and Hush Puppies are back with such a vengeance it takes this *entire* store to showcase every configuration and shade of these suede retro loafers.

Rodeo Drive & Beverly Hills' Golden Triangle
(Santa Monica Boulevard, Wilshire Boulevard & Crescent Drive)

Everyone knows about **Rodeo Drive,** the city's most famous shopping street. Couture shops from high fashion's Old Guard are located along these 3 hallowed blocks, along with plenty of newer high-end labels. And there are two examples of the Beverly Hills version of minimalls, albeit more insular and attractive—the **Rodeo Collection,** 421 N. Rodeo Dr., and **Two Rodeo,** at Wilshire Boulevard. The 16-square-block area surrounding Rodeo Drive is known as the "Golden Triangle." Shops off Rodeo are generally not as name-conscious as those on the strip (you might actually be able to buy something!), but they're nevertheless plenty upscale. **Little Santa Monica Boulevard** has a particularly colorful line of specialty stores, and **Brighton Way** is as young and hip as relatively staid Beverly Hills gets.

The big names to look for here are **Giorgio Beverly Hills,** 327 N. Rodeo Dr. (☎ 800/GIORGIO or 310/274-0200); **Gucci,** 347 N. Rodeo Dr. (☎ 310/278-3451); **Hermès,** 343 N. Rodeo Dr. (☎ 310/278-6440); **Louis Vuitton,** 307 N. Rodeo Dr. (☎ 310/859-0457); **Polo/Ralph Lauren,** 444 N. Rodeo Dr. (☎ 310/281-7200); and **Tiffany & Co.,** 210 N. Rodeo Dr. (☎ 310/273-8880).

Barney's New York. 9570 Wilshire Blvd., Beverly Hills. ☎ **310/276-4400.**

The celebrated New York clothier opened this Beverly Hills satellite shop in 1994, and L.A. is already looking better. Saxophonist and former bandleader for *The Tonight Show with Jay Leno* Branford Marsalis gets his Gaultiers here. Barney Greengrass, New York's "sturgeon king," has opened a restaurant on the top floor.

PaceWildenstein. 9540 Wilshire Blvd., Beverly Hills. ☎ **310/205-5522.**

A stark, modern art gallery ideal for showcasing the oversize contemporary pieces that draw art-minded members of L.A.'s entertainment elite like Steve Martin and David Geffen.

The Wine Merchant. 9701 Santa Monica Blvd. (at Roxbury), Beverly Hills. ☎ **310/278-7322.**

"The Wine Merchant to the Stars" is more like it. Linger while looking for the right bottle or exploring the cigar humidor, and you may run into a famous local. After-dark entertainment turns this place into a cigar bar/nightclub.

Beverly Boulevard (from Robertson Boulevard to LaBrea Avenue)

Every Picture Tells a Story. 7525 Beverly Blvd. (between Fairfax and LaBrea aves.), Los Angeles. ☎ **213/932-6070.**

This gallery, devoted to the art of children's literature, displays antique children's books as well as the works of over 100 illustrators, including lithos of *Curious George, Eloise,* and *Charlotte's Web.* Whether you're indulging your inner child or introducing your kids to their first "art gallery," you'll also enjoy the story readings and interactive workshops.

Mysterious Bookshop. 8763 Beverly Blvd., West Hollywood. ☎ **310/659-2959.**

Over 20,000 used, rare, and out-of-print titles make this the area's best mystery, espionage, detective, and thriller book shop. Author appearances and other special events are regularly hosted.

Opera Shop of Los Angeles. 8384 Beverly Blvd. (3 blocks east of La Cienega Blvd.), Los Angeles. ☎ **213/658-5811.**

If you can name more than three tenors, this pleasantly cluttered little gift shop is for you. Everything imaginable is available with an opera theme: musical motif jewelry, stationery, T-shirts, opera glasses (of course!), and tapes, videos, and CDs of your favorite productions.

Re-Mix. 7605¹/₂ Beverly Blvd. (between Fairfax and LaBrea aves.), Los Angeles. ☎ **213/936-6210.**

If you complain that they just don't make 'em like they used to . . . well, they do at Re-Mix. Selling only vintage (1940s to 1970s) but brand-new (as in unworn) shoes for men and women, it's more like a shoe-store museum featuring wingtips, Hush Puppies, Joan Crawford pumps, and 1970s platforms. A rackful of unworn vintage socks all display their original tags and stickers, and the prices downright reasonable. Celebrity hipsters and hep cats from Madonna to Roseanne are often spotted here.

Second Time Around Watch Co. 8840 Beverly Blvd. (west of Robertson Blvd.), Los Angeles. ☎ **310/271-6615.**

The city's best selection of collectible timepieces includes dozens of classic Tiffanys, Cartiers, Piagets, and Rolexes, plus rare pocket watches. Priced for collectors, but a fascinating browse for the Swatch crowd too.

HOLLYWOOD

Melrose Avenue (between Fairfax & La Brea avenues)

It's showing some wear—some stretches have become downright ugly—but this is still one of the most exciting shopping streets in the country for cutting-edge fashions—and some eye-popping people-watching to boot. There are scores of shops selling the latest in clothes, gifts, jewelry, and accessories. Melrose is a playful stroll, dotted with plenty of hip restaurants and funky shops that are sure to shock. Where else could you find green patent-leather cowboy boots, a working 19th-century pocket watch, an inflatable girlfriend, and glow-in-the-dark condoms in the same shopping spree?

Aardvark's Odd Ark. 7579 Melrose Ave. ☎ **213/655-6769.**

This large storefront near the Venice Beach Walk is crammed with racks of antique and used clothes from the 1960s, 1970s, and 1980s. They stock vintage everything, from suits and dresses to neckties, hats, handbags, and jewelry. And they manage to anticipate some of the hottest new street fashions. There's another Aardvark's at 1516 Pacific Ave., Venice (☎ **310/392-2996**).

Betsey Johnson Boutique. 7311 Melrose Ave., Los Angeles. ☎ **213/931-4490.**

The New York–based designer has brought her brand of fashion—trendy, cutesy, body-conscious womenswear in colorful prints and faddish fabrics—to L.A. Also in Santa Monica at 2929 Main St. (☎ **310/452-7911**).

Boy London. 7519 Melrose Ave., Los Angeles. ☎ **213/655-0302.**

Once on the cutting edge of London's King's Road, Boy has toned down a bit, now selling shirts and other clothes emblazoned with its own logo. It's still cool, though.

Condomania. 7306 Melrose Ave., Los Angeles. ☎ **213/933-7865.**

A vast selection of condoms, lubricants, and kits creatively encourage safe sex. Curious? Check out their Internet website at www.condomania.com.

Retail Slut. 7308 Melrose Ave., Los Angeles. ☎ **213/934-1339.**

You'll find new clothing and accessories for men and women at this famous rock 'n' roll shop. The unique designs are for a select crowd (the name says it all), so don't expect to find anything for your next PTA meeting here.

Wasteland. 7428 Melrose Ave., Los Angeles. ☎ **213/653-3028.**

An enormous steel-sculpted facade fronts this L.A. branch of the Berkeley/Haight-Ashbury hipster hangout that sells vintage and contemporary clothes for men and women. There's a lot of leather, denim, and some classic vintage—but mostly funky 1970s garb. This ultratrendy store is a packed with the flamboyantly colorful polyester halters and bell-bottoms from the decade some of us would rather forget.

Hollywood Boulevard (between Gower Street & La Brea Avenue)

One of Los Angeles's most famous streets is, for the most part, a sleazy strip. But along the Walk of Fame, between the T-shirt shops and greasy pizza parlors, you'll find some excellent poster shops, souvenir stores, and Hollywood-memorabilia dealers that are worth getting out of your car for—especially if there's a chance of getting your hands on that long-sought-after Ethel Merman autograph or *200 Motels* poster.

Book City Collectibles. 6631 Hollywood Blvd., Hollywood. ☎ **213/466-0120.**

More than 70,000 color prints of past and present stars are available, along with a good selection of autographs from the likes of Lucille Ball ($175), Anthony Hopkins ($35), and Grace Kelly ($750).

Frederick's of Hollywood. 6606 Hollywood Blvd., Hollywood. ☎ **213/466-8506.**

Behind the garish pink-and-purple facade lies one of the most famous panty shops in the world. Everything from Spandex suits to bikini bras and sophisticated nighties is here. Even if you're not buying, stop in and pick up one of their famous catalogs.

Hollywood Book and Poster Company. 6349 Hollywood Blvd., Hollywood. ☎ **213/465-8764.**

Owner Eric Caidin's excellent collection of movie posters (from about $15 each) is particularly strong in horror and exploitation flicks. Photocopies of about 5,000 movie and television scripts are also sold for $10 to $15 each, and the store also carries music posters and photos.

The Last Moving Picture Company. 6307 Hollywood Blvd. (near Vine St.), Hollywood. ☎ **213/467-0838.**

Movie-related merchandise of all kinds is sold here, including stills from 1950s movies and authentic production notes from a variety of films.

DOWNTOWN

Since the late, lamented grande dame department store Bullock's closed in 1993 (its deco masterpiece salons were rescued to house the Southwestern Law School's library), downtown has become even less of a shopping destination than ever. Savvy Angelenos still go for bargains in the garment and fabric districts, florists and bargain hunters arrive at the vast Flower Mart before dawn for the city's best selection of fresh blooms, and families of all ethnicities stroll the Grand Central Market. Although many of the once-splendid streets are lined with cut-rate luggage and cheap electronics storefronts, shopping downtown can be a rewarding if gritty experience for the adventuresome.

Cooper Building. 860 S. Los Angeles St., downtown. ☎ **213/622-1139.**

The centerpiece of downtown's Garment District, the Cooper Building and surrounding blocks are full of shops selling name-brand clothes for men, women, and children at significantly discounted prices.

Golf Exchange. 830 S. Olive St. (between 8th and 9th sts.), downtown. ☎ **213/622-0403.**

L.A.'s golf megastore fills 10 rooms with clubs and accessories: An entire room is devoted to golf shoes, another to bags, another to used clubs, and so on. There's also an indoor driving range so you can try before you buy.

✪ **Grand Central Market.** 317 S. Broadway (between 3rd and 4th sts.), downtown. ☎ **213/624-2378.**

Opened in 1917, this bustling market has watched the face of downtown L.A. change while changing little itself. Today it serves Latino families, enterprising restaurateurs, and home cooks in search of unusual ingredients and bargain-priced fruits and vegetables. On weekends you'll be greeted by a lively mariachi band at the Hill Street entrance, near our favorite market feature—the fruit juice counter, which dispenses 20 fresh varieties from wall spigots and blends up the tastiest, healthiest "shakes" in town. Farther into the market you'll find produce sellers and prepared-food counters, plus spice vendors who seem straight out of a Turkish alley, and a grain and bean seller who'll scoop out dozens of exotic rices and dried legumes.

La Plata Cigars. 1026 S. Grand Ave. (between 11th St. and Olympic Blvd.). ☎ **213/747-8561.**

Los Angeles's only cigar factory, family-run La Plata has been hand-rolling stogies since 1947. The public is welcome to visit the downtown factory and watch how Cuban artisans create these premium prizes. Afterward enter the shop's huge humidor to choose from thousands of fresh cigars in all sizes—for about half what the fancy places charge.

THE SAN FERNANDO VALLEY

Studio City (Ventura Boulevard between Laurel Canyon & Fulton Avenue)

Long beloved by Valley residents, Studio City is conveniently located freeway- and canyon-close to Hollywood and the Westside. Ventura Boulevard has a distinct personality in each of the several Valley communities it passes through, but Studio City is where you'll find small boutiques and antiques stores, quirky little businesses, and less congested branches of popular chains like The Gap.

The Cranberry House (Studio City Antique Mall). 12318 Ventura Blvd. (2 blocks east of Whitsett), Studio City. ☎ **818/506-8945.**

Under a berry-colored awning, several storefront windows hint at the treasures within this antiques and collectibles store featuring over 100 different sellers. Be sure to haggle—even front-desk staff are often authorized by the individual dealers to strike a bargain.

Samuel French Book Store. 11963 Ventura Blvd., Studio City. ☎ **818/762-0535.**

This is L.A.'s biggest theater and movie bookstore. Plays, screenplays, and film books are all sold here, as well as scripts for Broadway and Hollywood blockbusters. Also in Hollywood at 7623 Sunset Blvd., between Fairfax and LaBrea avenues (☎ **213/876-0570**).

Studio City Camera Exchange. 12174 Ventura Blvd. (1 block west of Laurel Canyon), Studio City. ☎ **818/762-4749.**

Where to Find Hollywood's Hand-Me-Downs

Admit it: Like everyone else, you've dreamed of being a glamorous movie or TV star. Well, you shouldn't expect to be "discovered" during your L.A. vacation, but you can live out your fantasy by dressing the part. Costumes from famous movies, TV show wardrobes, castoffs from celebrity closets—they're easier to find (and more affordable to own) than you might think.

A good place to start is **Star Wares,** 2817 Main St., Santa Monica (☎ **310/ 399-0224**). This deceptively small shop regularly has leftovers from Cher's closet as well as celebrity-worn apparel from the likes of Winona Ryder, Tom Cruise, and Sarah Jessica Parker. They also stock movie production wardrobes and genuine collector's items. If the $5,000 *Star Trek* uniform or *Independence Day* flight suit you covet is out of your price range, don't worry: You can still pick up some threads from *Pulp Fiction* or *Jurassic Park,* dresses from the closets of Lucille Ball and Greer Garson, or E.T.'s bathrobe, all of which are surprisingly affordable. Many pieces have accompanying photos or movie stills, so you'll know exactly who donned your piece before you.

That isn't the case, however, at **The Place & Co.,** 8820 S. Sepulveda Blvd., Westchester (☎ **310/645-1539**), where the anonymity of their well-heeled clientele (sellers and buyers) is strictly honored. Here you'll find men's and women's haute couture—always the latest fashions and gently worn—at a fraction of the Rodeo Drive prices. All the designers are here—Bill Blass, Krizia, Donna Karan, Hugo Boss. You may even have seen that Armani suit or Sonia Rykiel gown you find in the racks on an Academy Awards attendee last year!

For sheer volume, you can't beat **It's A Wrap,** 3315 W. Magnolia Blvd., Burbank (☎ **818/567-7366**). Every item here is marked with its place of origin, and the list is staggering: *Melrose Place, Seinfeld, Baywatch, All My Children, Forrest Gump, The Brady Bunch Movie,* and so on. Many of these wardrobes (which

---

There's comfort in the 1940s architecture of this corner photography store—like an old friend, Studio City Camera is there if you need supplies, film, processing, batteries, frames, albums, used cameras (some quite collectible), or just to talk shop with fellow shutterbugs behind the counter.

Universal CityWalk (Universal Center Drive, Universal City)

Technically an outdoor mall rather than a shopping area, Universal CityWalk (☎ **818/622-4455**) gets mention here because it's so utterly unique. A pedestrian promenade next door to Universal Studios, CityWalk is dominated by brightly colored, outrageously surreal, oversize storefronts. The heavily touristed faux street is home to an inordinate number of restaurants, including B. B. King's Blues Club, the newest Hard Rock Cafe, and a branch of the Hollywood Athletic Club featuring a restaurant and pool hall. This is consumer culture gone haywire, an egotistical eyesore not worth a special visit, unless you have the kids in tow—they'll love it.

PASADENA & ENVIRONS

Compared to L.A.'s behemoth shopping malls, the streets of pretty, compact Pasadena are a true pleasure to stroll. As a general rule, stores are open daily from about 10am, and while some close at the standard 5 or 6pm, many stay open till 8 or 9pm to accommodate the before- and after-dinner/movie crowd.

include shoes and accessories) aren't outstanding but for their Hollywood origins: Jerry Seinfeld's trademark polo shirts, for instance, are standard mall-issue. Some collectible pieces, like Sylvester Stallone's *Rocky* stars-and-stripes boxers, are framed and on display.

When you're done at It's A Wrap, stop in across the street at **Junk For Joy,** 3314 W. Magnolia Blvd., Burbank (☎ **818/569-4903**). A Hollywood wardrobe coordinator or two will probably be hunting through this wacky little store right beside you. The emphasis here is on funky items more suitable as costumes than everyday wear (the store is mobbed each year around Halloween). Always strong in '70s polyester shirts and tacky slacks, it's not surprising costumers from the Brady Bunch movies and *The People vs. Larry Flynt* came here first.

The grande dame of all wardrobe and costume outlets is **Western Costume,** 11041 Vanowen St., North Hollywood (☎ **818/760-0900**). In business since 1912, it still designs and executes entire wardrobes for major motion pictures; when filming is finished, the garments are added to their staggering rental inventory. This place is perhaps best known for outfitting Vivien Leigh in *Gone with the Wind;* several of Scarlett O'Hara's memorable gowns were even available for rent until they were auctioned off at a charity event. Western maintains an "outlet store" on the premises, where damaged garments are sold at rock-bottom (nothing over $15) prices. If you're willing to do some rescue work, there are definitely some hidden treasures here.

Finally, don't miss **Golyester,** 136 S. LaBrea Ave. (☎ **213/931-1339**). This shop is almost a museum of finely preserved (but reasonably priced) vintage clothing and fabrics. The staff will gladly flip through stacks of *Vogue* magazines from the 1930s, '40s, and '50s with you, pointing out the star-studded original advertisements for various outfits in their stock.

Old Pasadena (centered around the intersection of Colorado Boulevard & Fair Oaks Avenue)

In my opinion, Old Pasadena is some of the best shopping in L.A., but I hope they retain more of the mom-and-pop businesses currently being pushed out by the likes of Banana Republic and Crate & Barrel. As you move eastward, the mix begins to include more eclectic shops and galleries comingling with dusty, pre-yuppie relics.

Del Mano. 33 E. Colorado Blvd. ☎ **626/793-6648.**

Stepping into this gallery of contemporary crafts, it's a whole lot of fun to see the creations—some whimsical, some exquisite—of American artists working with glass, wood, ceramics, or jewelry.

Distant Lands Bookstore and Outfitters. 54 and 62 S. Raymond Ave. ☎ **626/449-3220.**

Travelers always seem to find something they need at this duo of related stores. The bookstore has a terrific selection of maps, guides, and travel-related literature, while the recently opened outfitters two doors away offers everything from luggage and pith helmets to space-saving and convenient travel accessories.

Penny Lane. 12 W. Colorado Blvd. ☎ **626/564-0161.**

Carrying new and used CDs, Penny Lane also has a great selection of music magazines and kitschy postcards. The selection is less picked-over here than at many record stores in Hollywood.

Rebecca's Dream. 16 S. Fair Oaks Ave. ☎ **626/796-1200.**

Men and women can both find vintage clothing treasures in this small and meticulously organized (by color scheme) store. Be sure to look up; vintage hats adorn the walls.

Tournament Souvenirs. 88 E. Colorado Blvd. ☎ **818/395-7066.**

It's exactly what it sounds like: Rose Parade and Rose Bowl clothing, hats, pennants, glassware, and sports sippers for anyone visiting during the 51 *other* weeks of the year.

Other Pasadena Shopping

In addition to Old Town Pasadena, there are numerous good hunting grounds in the surrounding area. Antique hounds might want to head to the **Green Street Antique Row,** 985–1005 E. Green St., east of Lake Avenue; or the **Pasadena Antique Center,** on South Fair Oaks Boulevard south of Del Mar. Each has a rich concentration of collectibles that can captivate for hours.

You never know what you'll find at the **Rose Bowl Flea Market,** at the Rose Bowl, 991 Rosemont Ave., Pasadena (☎ **626/577-3100**). Built in 1922, the horseshoe-shaped Rose Bowl is one of the world's most famous stadiums, home to UCLA's football Bruins, the annual Rose Bowl Game, and an occasional Super Bowl. California's largest monthly swap meet, on the second Sunday of every month from 9am to 3pm, is a favorite of Los Angeles antique hounds (who know to arrive as early as 6am for the best finds). Antique furnishings, clothing, jewelry, and other collectibles are assembled in the parking area to the left of the entrance, while the rest of the flea market surrounds the exterior of the Bowl. Expect everything from used surfboards and car stereos to one-of-a-kind lawn statuary and bargain athletic shoes. Admission is $5 after 9am (early bird admission $10 to $15).

STORES WORTH SEEKING OUT ELSEWHERE IN THE CITY

California Map and Travel Center. 3312 Pico Blvd., Santa Monica. ☎ **310/396-6277.**

As the name says, this store carries a good selection of domestic and international maps and travel accessories, including guides for hiking, biking, and touring. Globes and atlases are also sold. Visit their website at www.mapper.com.

✪ **Rhino Records.** 1720 Westwood Blvd., Westwood. ☎ **310/474-3786.**

This is L.A.'s premier alternative shop, specializing in new artists and independent-label releases. In addition to new releases, there's a terrific used selection; this is where record industry types come to trade in the records they don't want for the records they do, so you'll be able to find never-played promotional copies of brand-new releases at half the retail price. You'll also find the definitive collection of records on the Rhino label here.

Trashy Lingerie. 402 N. La Cienega Blvd., Hollywood. ☎ **310/652-4543.**

This shop will tailor-fit their house-designed clothes—everything from patent-leather bondage wear to elegant bridal underthings—for you. There's a $2 "membership" fee to enter the store, but, even for browsers, it's worth it.

12 Los Angeles After Dark

The *L.A. Weekly,* a free weekly paper available at sidewalk stands, shops, and restaurants, is the best place to find out what's going on about town, especially for club happenings. The "Calendar" section of the Sunday *Los Angeles Times* is also a good place to find out what's going on after dark. *Buzz* magazine has unabashedly opinionated listings of clubs, bars, live venues, restaurant hot spots and much more, including art galleries. *Los Angeles* magazine has performance listings as well, but sticks to more highbrow happenings.

For weekly updates on music, art, dance, theater, special events, and festivals, call the **Cultural Affairs Hotline** (☎ **213/688-ARTS**), a 24-hour directory listing a wide variety of events, most of which are free.

Ticketmaster (☎ **213/480-3232**) and **Telecharge** (☎ **800/447-7400**) are the major charge-by-phone ticket agencies in the city, selling tickets to concerts, sporting events, plays, and special events.

THEATER

Tickets for most plays usually cost $10 to $30. **Theater L.A.,** an association of live theaters and theatrical producers in the greater Los Angeles area (and the organization which puts on the L.A. version of Broadway's Tony Awards each year), has plans to operate a half-price ticket booth in late 1997. Using New York City's highly successful TKTS as a model, they expect to open a centrally located booth for same-day, walk-up sales only; it should be in place by the time you hold this book. For updated information, call them at ☎ **213/614-0556.**

MAJOR THEATERS & COMPANIES

The Ahmanson Theater and Mark Taper Forum, the city's top two playhouses, are both part of the all-purpose **Music Center,** 135 N. Grand Ave., downtown. The **Ahmanson** (☎ 213/972-7401) is active year-round, either with shows produced by the in-house Center Theater Group or with traveling Broadway productions. Each season has a guaranteed handful of high-profile shows, ranging from Andrew Lloyd Webber's *Phantom of the Opera* to the Pulitzer and Tony award-winning *Rent.* A recent highlight was the Olivier award-winning (and slightly controversial) Matthew Bourne's production of *Swan Lake,* which featured contemporary settings and *male* swans. The Ahmanson is so huge that you'll want seats in the front third or half of the theater.

The **Mark Taper Forum** (☎ 213/972-0700) is a more intimate, circular theater staging contemporary works by international and local playwrights. Kenneth Branagh's Renaissance Theatre Company staged its only American productions of *King Lear* and *A Midsummer Night's Dream* at the Mark Taper, to give you an idea of the quality of the shows here; I also saw a respectable production of Tom Stoppard's complex and highbrow comedy *Arcadia.* Productions are usually excellent, run with plenty of spirit and no shortage of controversy.

Ticket prices vary depending on the performance. Discounted tickets are usually available on the day of performance for students and seniors.

Big-time traveling troupes and Broadway-bound musicals that don't go to the Ahmanson head instead for the **Shubert Theater,** in the ABC Entertainment Center, 2020 Ave. of the Stars, Century City (☎ 800/233-3123). This plush playhouse presents major musicals on the scale of *Cats, Sunset Boulevard,* and *Les Misérables;* 1997 saw the debut of a musical adaptation of E. L. Doctorow's *Ragtime.*

Top-quality Broadway-caliber productions are also staged at the **UCLA James A. Doolittle Theater,** 1615 N. Vine St., Hollywood (☎ **213/462-6666** or 213/972-0700).

SMALLER PLAYHOUSES

Like New York's Off Broadway or London's fringe, L.A.'s small-scale theaters often outdo the slick, high-budget shows. Because this is Tinseltown, movie and TV stars sometimes headline, but more often than not the talent is up-and-coming. Who knows—the unknown on stage today might be the next David Duchovny tomorrow.

There are about 100 other stages of varying quality throughout the city. Good bets are the **Colony Studio Theater,** 1944 Riverside Dr., Silverlake (☎ 213/665-3011), which has an excellent resident company that has played in this air-conditioned, 99-seat, converted silent-movie house for over 20 years; the **Actors Circle Theater,** 7313 Santa Monica Blvd., West Hollywood (☎ 213/882-8043), a 47-seater that's as acclaimed as it is tiny; and the **Los Angeles Theater,** 615 S. Broadway (☎ 213/ 629-2939), a grand movie palace recently converted to live theater.

One of the most highly acclaimed professional theaters in L.A., the **Pasadena Playhouse**, 35 S. El Molino Ave. (near Colorado Blvd.), Pasadena (☎ 626/356-7529), is a registered historic landmark and has served as the training ground for many theatrical, film, and TV stars, including William Holden and Gene Hackman. Productions are staged both on the main theater's elaborate Spanish Colonial Revival stage and in a smaller theater on the second floor.

CLASSICAL MUSIC & OPERA

Beyond the pop realms, music in Los Angeles generally falls short of that found in other cities. For the most part, Angelenos rely on visiting orchestras and companies to fulfill their classical music appetites; scan the papers to find out who's playing and dancing while you're in the city.

The **Los Angeles Philharmonic** (☎ 213/850-2000) isn't just the city's top symphony; it's the only major classical music company in Los Angeles. Finnish-born music director Esa-Pekka Salonen concentrates on contemporary compositions; despite complaints from traditionalists, he does an excellent job attracting younger audiences. Tickets can be hard to come by when celebrity players like Itzak Perlman, Issac Stern, Emanuel Ax, and Yo-Yo Ma are in town. In addition to regular performances at the Music Center's Dorothy Chandler Pavilion, 135 N. Grand Ave., downtown, the Philharmonic also plays a popular summer season at the Hollywood Bowl (see "Concerts Under the Stars," below).

Slowly but surely, the **L.A. Opera** (☎ 213/972-8001) is gaining both respect and popularity with inventive stagings of classic operas, usually with guest divas. The Opera also calls the Music Center home.

CONCERTS UNDER THE STARS

✪ **Hollywood Bowl.** 2301 N. Highland Ave. (at Odin St.), Hollywood. ☎ **213/850-2000.**

Built in the early 1920s, the Hollywood Bowl is an elegant Greek-style natural outdoor amphitheater cradled in a small mountain canyon. This is the summer home of the Los Angeles Philharmonic Orchestra; internationally known conductors and soloists often sit in on Tuesday and Thursday nights. Friday and Saturday concerts often feature orchestral swing or pops concerts. The summer season also includes a jazz series; past performers have included Natalie Cole, Mel Torme, Dionne Warwick, and Chick Corea. Other events, from Tom Petty concerts to an annual Mariachi Festival, are often on the season's schedule.

For many concert-goers, a visit to the Bowl is an excuse for an accompanied picnic under the stars. Gourmet picnics at the Bowl—complete with a bottle or two of wine—are one of L.A.'s grandest traditions. You can prepare your own or order a picnic basket with a choice of hot and cold dishes and a selection of wines and desserts from the theater's catering department. A la carte baskets run $16.95 to $25.95 per person; appetizers and drinks are extra. Call ☎ 213/851-3588 the day before you go.

THE CLUB & MUSIC SCENE

by Steve Hochman and Heidi Siegmund Cuda; updated by Stephanie Avnet

The L.A. club and music scene is truly something-for-everybody territory, from blues fanatics to leather freaks. *But be forewarned:* You're not in Kansas anymore. Or for that matter, San Francisco. Friendlier cities greet out-of-towners with arms extended and advice at hand. Travel to the City by the Bay, and a waiter might tip you off to the best restaurant or the hottest dance club for that moment in time. Sit in a Los Angeles cafe, however, and be grateful if you're acknowledged. It's nothing personal—it's more a matter of Social Darwinism. This is a town where only the strongest—and the most resourceful—survive, and too many folks are angling to get out of the cattle line, past the velvet rope, and into clubland's hot zones.

The competition is compounded by L.A.'s short attention span. What might have been the hip ticket last week could be belly up by the time you find the door. That said, don't lose all hope. A smart visitor has ammo: This guide, along with a current *L.A. Weekly* (which can be found for free around town), offers a plethora of dance and music club information for the adventurous at heart.

Note: Unless otherwise noted, to enter the clubs listed below you must be at least 21—with ID to prove it.

LIVE MUSIC

It's a good bet that someone of interest will be in town during any one stay. The best way to see what's on is by checking the *L.A. Weekly* or the "Calendar" in Sunday's *Los Angeles Times*.

Mid-Size Concerts

B.B. King's Blues Club. CityWalk, Universal City. ☎ **818/622-5464.**

B.B. King's is a bit more "real" than the House of Blues. Its three-floor seating area, resembling an old southern club, is tastefully decorated, the music stays closer to authentic blues, and the ribs are terrific.

House of Blues. 8430 Sunset Blvd., West Hollywood. ☎ **213/848-5100.**

Despite its Disneyland-ish decor, this club—co-owned by some really strange bedfellows, including Hard Rock founder Issac Tigrett, Jim Belushi, Dan Ackroyd, Aerosmith, and Harvard University—does earnestly honor its namesake music with informative displays and a wealth of colorful folk art. Still, it's permeated with industry types more interested in being seen than hearing the music. Even so, there's enough top-notch music here to keep many who routinely bad-mouth the place coming back, and the food in the upstairs restaurant can be superb (reservations are a must).

John Anson Ford Theatre. 2580 Cahuenga Blvd. West Hollywood. ☎ **213/464-2826.**

Once, during a late-1980s Ramones concert at this lovely alfresco facility, the punk sounds carried across U.S. 101 and into the ears of people who were trying to hear the L.A. Symphony play Beethoven at the Hollywood Bowl. They were not amused, and rock was virtually banned from the Ford for some time. But lately it's been back, and a night with a rising star under the stars (Alanis Morissette played there on her way to superstardom) can be wonderful. Parking, though, is nightmarish—prepare for a long walk uphill.

The Palace. 1735 N. Vine St., Hollywood. ☎ **213/461-3504.**

A classic vaudeville house, this 1,200-capacity theater, just across Vine from the famed Capitol Records tower, has been the site of numerous significant alternative rock shows in the 1990s, including key appearances by Nirvana and Smashing Pumpkins. But its dominance has been challenged of late by several other venues of similar size.

✪ **Wiltern Theatre.** 3790 Wilshire Blvd. ☎ **213/380-5005.**

Saved from the wrecking ball in the mid-1980s, this WPA-era art deco showcase is perhaps the most beautiful theater in town. You could have an entertaining evening just sitting and staring at the ornate ceiling—but usually you don't have to. Countless national and international acts have played here, from Jerry Garcia to Joan Osborne, with such nonpop music events as Penn & Teller and top ballet troupes complementing the schedule.

Club Shows

Alligator Lounge. 3321 Pico Blvd., Santa Monica. ☎ **213/453-8477.**

An unassuming dive with a neighborhood feel, the Alligator has become one of the top sites for emerging roots and alternative music. It has been home to weekly New Music Mondays hosted by avant-garde guitarist Nels Cline with challenging music that crosses rock, jazz, and classical forms performed by Cline and his band, as well as guests drawn from the cream of category-busting musicians.

Ash Grove. On the Santa Monica Pier (Colorado Ave.), Santa Monica. ☎ **310/656-8500.** All ages. Ticket prices vary.

Named for the swing-era dance hall that used to grace the pier, the recently resurrected Ash Grove features eclectic performers ranging from The Magnificent Seven (featuring R.E.M.'s Peter Buck) to Cuban salsa combos to a special engagement of Pete Seeger. There's a full restaurant and bar.

Bar Deluxe. 1710 N. Las Palmas Ave., Hollywood. ☎ **213/469-1991.** Generally no cover.

This is the club to go to when you're looking for a hassle-free, no-lines affair. This dimly lit, black-and-red, voodoo-meets-hoodoo haven specializes in surf, blues, and rockabilly bands and is as comfortable as an old pair of Doc Martens.

Billboard Live. 9039 Sunset Blvd., West Hollywood. ☎ **310/786-1712.** Cover varies.

With a gala opening in August 1996 that closed down the Sunset Strip for the first time in history, this mammoth club has breathed some life into the legendary Strip. Among its state-of-the-art distinctions: two gigantic exterior "Jumbotrons," which reveal the on-stage performances to passersby and, during the day, feature continuous music programming; a unique "industrial plush" interior design (think corrugated metal draped in velvet); and numerous monthly performances selected from *Billboard*'s "Heatseekers" charts, so you can be the first to see the Next Big Thing. Ultimately, the 400-capacity club is an excellent live music showcase.

Doug Weston's Troubadour. 9081 Santa Monica Blvd., West Hollywood. ☎ **310/276-6168.** All ages, cover varies.

The Troubadour has worked long and hard to shed its creepy 1980s Spandex-'n'-big-hair image, and it has emerged vibrant and vigorous once again. Turning 40 in 1997, the club counts the Byrds and the Eagles among the bands that virtually formed here, and even in the metal years saw Motley Crue and others rise to the big time. Today the Troub can be counted on for excellent sound and a wide array of up-and-coming break-out bands and already-made-its. A fine, fine venue.

Jack's Sugar Shack. 1707 Vine St., Hollywood. ☎ **213/466-7005.**

Jack doesn't mess around. The *Gilligan's Island* meets *The Love Boat* decor combined with a select booking policy makes this nightclub a tasty treat. Less interested in trends than in quality music, Jack's books national and local blues, country and western, and alternative music, and is the current host to Ronnie Mack's Barndance, a free Tuesday-night affair of alternative country music.

Lava Lounge. 1533 La Brea Ave., Hollywood. ☎ **213/876-6612.** Cover varies.

Described by its lovely owner, a former set decorator, as a "Vegas in hell" motif, the interior of this small bar and performance space located in a très-ugly strip mall is very inventive. Think tiki-tacky coupled with big-city chic. Live music includes jazz and surfabilly, and live regulars include Quentin Tarantino.

LunaPark. 665 N. Robertson Blvd., West Hollywood. ☎ **310/652-0611.** Cover none–$15.

Proprietor Jean-Pierre Boccarra has turned this bilevel restaurant/performance space into one of the most unpredictable yet reliable venues in the area—not just for music, which ranges from up-and-coming sensations (Ani DiFranco played her first L.A. show here) to global music stars (Cape Verde's "barefoot diva" Cesaria Evora), but for performance art, cabaret, and comedy, too. Insiders know to come hungry, because LunaPark's kitchen rivals the hottest restaurants in West Hollywood.

McCabe's. 3101 Pico Blvd., Santa Monica. ☎ **213/828-4497.**

Since the early 1970s the back room of this earthy guitar shop has been the leading folk club in L.A., and possibly west of the Mississippi. Bonnie Raitt, Jackson Browne, and Linda Ronstadt are among those who played here early in their careers, and top-flight folk, country, and even rock musicians still return regularly to perform in an unbeatable, low-key, almost living room–esque setting.

The Roxy. 9009 Sunset Blvd. West Hollywood. ☎ **213/276-2222.**

Veteran record producer/executive Lou Adler opened this Sunset Strip club in the mid-1970s with concerts by Neil Young and a lengthy run of the pre-movie *Rocky Horror Show.* Since then it has remained among the top showcase venues in Hollywood—though it lost its unchallenged preeminence among cozy clubs to increased competition from the revitalized Troubadour and such new entries as the House of Blues.

Spaceland at Dreams. 1717 Silverlake Blvd., Silverlake. ☎ **213/413-4442.** Cover varies.

In less than a year promoter Mitchell Frank took over a spacious, dowdy bar on the eastern edge of Hollywood and turned it into one of the most happening nightspots in Los Angeles. With his eclectic bookings (everyone from the Foo Fighters and the Beasties to hometown faves Extra Fancy), Frank built a scene from scratch; Spaceland now rivals such Hollywood fixtures as the Whisky and Roxy as a place to see and be seen.

✪ **Viper Room.** 8852 Sunset Blvd., West Hollywood. ☎ **310/358-1880.** Cover varies.

This place is so delightfully hot that you might get singed on the way out. It's definitely a club to witness firsthand before exiting town—despite what you might have heard: Yes, Johnny Depp owns it (with partner Sal Jenco), and yes, River Phoenix overdosed here, and the combo either attracts or repulses club-goers. But, hands down, the Viper Room has the most varied and exciting live music bookings in town. From Johnny Cash to Iggy Pop, the small, bilevel venue doesn't disappoint. The expensive sound system is a delight to true music fans, and there are enough stars on hand nightly to keep gazers excited.

The Whisky. 8901 Sunset Blvd., West Hollywood. ☎ **310/535-0579.** All ages, cover varies.

If you don't go to any other club in L.A., you must a go-go to the Whisky. The bilevel venue personifies L.A. rock 'n' roll, from Jim Morrison to X to Guns 'N' Roses. Every trend has passed through this club, and it continues to be the most vital venue of its kind. Recently an in-house booker was hired to bring more local music to the club, which already offers one of the best local showcases in town: Bianca's Hole on Monday nights, an always-free night of mostly L.A. bands.

DANCE CLUBS & BARS

To give outsiders an idea of the lightning speed with which dance clubs come and go in this town, the Roxbury doesn't even register on the map anymore. It's still there, but folks aren't lining up like they used to, so I can't recommend it this time out. But no worries: There are plenty of sonic offerings to take its place, but best to move quickly and precisely. Take great pains to follow the recommended nights closely— you'll be glad you did.

You'll hear an eclectic mix of electronic, acid jazz, and other interesting musical treats at **Bossa Nova,** Thursdays at the **Pink,** 2810 Main St., Santa Monica (☎ **310/ 392-1077**), a happening club featuring guest DJs (including Tricky).

Deejay Mike Messex keeps the dance floor packed all evening at **Cherry,** Fridays at the **Love Lounge,** 657 N. Robertson Blvd., West Hollywood (☎ **310/659-0472**). In addition to '80s glam rock, New Wave, and disco, the club keeps the energy level high with selective live performances—often with a homoerotic edge—as well as theme nights.

Placate the inner swinger in you at **The Derby,** 4500 Los Feliz Blvd., Los Angeles (☎ **213/663-8979**), a classy East Hollywood club with a heavy 1940s edge. Come decked out in garb from that era to swing the night away to such musical acts as Big Bad Voodoo Daddy and the Royal Crown Revue (whose popularity soared after weekly bookings at the club).

Despite its modest strip-lot locale, **El Floridita,** 1253 N. Vine St., Hollywood (☎ **213/871-8612**) is hot, hot, hot. The tiny Cuban restaurant-cum-salsa joint attracts the likes of Jennifer Lopez, Sandra Bullock, Jimmy Smits, and Jack Nicholson; the hippest nights are Monday and Thursday, when Johnny Polanco and his swinging New York–flavored salsa band get the dance floor jumpin'.

The Garage, 4519 Santa Monica Blvd., Silverlake (☎ **213/683-3447**) is a key Silverlake club firmly planted in the underground. The sparkling erstwhile Garage attracts a comfortable gay/straight clientele with such events as Sucker, a Sunday beer bust hosted by drag diva Miss Vaginal Creme Davis; and Hai Karate, a dazzling Friday-night funky fest.

The Gate, 643 N. La Cienega Blvd., West Hollywood (☎ **310/289-8808**) is one despicable club, but folks seem to migrate here anyway. Most famous for its repeated mentions in Faye Resnick's ode to Nicole Brown Simpson, the Gate attracts chemically altered, surgically enhanced Eurotrash bimbos and himbos, who enjoy its elaborate decor and gargoyles a-plenty. Dancing is scheduled Wednesday to Saturday—and don't wear shorts if you want to get in.

Saturday Night Fever (☎ **213/848-9300** for location) has been the biggest Saturday-night dance bash in Hollywood for 5 years running. Although it has moved numerous times since its inception, it continues to outgrow each venue. Wherever it lands, it's sure to be the bomb: With popular L.A. DJ Mike Messex behind the main console, the temperature's always sizzling.

COCKTAIL LOUNGES

Dresden Room. 1760 N. Vermont Ave. (south of Franklin Ave.), Hollywood. ☎ **213/ 665-4294.** No cover.

A ski resort–like lounge unchanged since the '60s, the Dresden is home to the unexplainably popular duo Marty & Elayne, who cover everything from Jack Jones to the Beatles on piano and (I use the term loosely) vocals. Although weekend crowds soared after the bar was featured in the slacker flick *Swingers,* it's still a great hang-out during the week.

Four Seasons Hotel Los Angeles. 300 S. Doheny Dr. (at Burton Way), Los Angeles. ☎ **310/ 273-2222.** No cover.

The sprawling lobby bar of this slightly pretentious but always eventful hotel serves as both celebrity magnet and unofficial parlor for monied regulars who virtually live in the high-rise. The bar is actually comprised of several sitting rooms and an out-door patio, through which waft the sounds of the house pianist tinkling the ivories. The bartenders here have seen it all—no request is too outrageous, from a platter of oysters courtesy of the hotel's restaurant to a bowl of water for a canine companion (dogs served on patio only). The current cigar trend has found a home here: You may select from the bar's expansive humidor, but stay away if the smoke will offend you (or your dry cleaner).

Good Luck Bar. 1514 Hillhurst Ave. (between Hollywood and Sunset blvds.), Los Angeles. ☎ **213/666-3524.** No cover.

Until they installed a flashing sign—which simply reads "GOOD LUCK"—only locals and hipsters knew about this Kung Fu–themed room in the Los Feliz/Silverlake area. The dark red windowless interior boasts Oriental ceiling tiles, fringed Chinese paper lanterns, sweet-but-deadly drinks like the "Yee Mee Loo" (translated as "blue drink"), and a jukebox with selections from Thelonius Monk to Cher's "Half Breed." The spacious sitting room, furnished with mismatched sofas, armchairs, and ban-quettes, provides a great atmosphere for conversation or romance. Arrive early to avoid the throngs of L.A. scenesters.

Lounge 217. 217 Broadway (between 2nd and 3rd sts.), Santa Monica. ☎ **310/281-6692.** Cover varies.

A lounge in the true sense of the word, these plush art deco surroundings just scream "martini"—and the bartenders stand ready to shake or stir up your favorite. Com-fortable seating lends itself well to intimate socializing, or enjoying Monday's classi-cal guitarist; Thursday night brings a torch singer and cigar bar. Come early on the weekends, when Lounge 217 hosts a more raucous late-night crowd.

Windows On Hollywood. 1755 N. Highland Ave. (in the Holiday Inn), Hollywood. ☎ **213/ 462-7181.** No cover.

There's nothing like a revolving bar/restaurant to enjoy a panoramic view of the city; this one is 23 floors above the heart of Hollywood. While it scores low on the hipness scale, we're glad trendy bar-hoppers have taken their scene elsewhere, freeing up the prime window tables for you and me. The slowly revolving outer circle will show you downtown's skyline, the lights of Hollywood, and the hills to the north; the noncirculating center offers entertainment and dancing. If you're lucky, there'll be some young Sinatra wannabe providing a schmaltzy soundtrack for your cocktail hour.

COMEDY & CABARET

Except for the Cinegrill, which is in its own league, each of the following venues claims—and justly so—to have launched the careers of the comics who are now household names. The funniest up-and-comers are playing all the clubs (except for the Groundlings, which is an improvisation group), so you're probably best off choos-ing a club for its location. Call ahead for show times and reservations.

In addition to the venues listed below, see what's on at **Luna Park** (see "The Club and Music Scene" above), whose three stages allow for an amazing diversity of performers—a solo diva might have 'em weeping into their martinis while upstairs some grungy kids spew jangly guitar pop.

The Cinegrill. 7000 Hollywood Blvd. (in the Hollywood Roosevelt Hotel), Hollywood. ☎ **213/ 466-7000.** Cover $10–$15, 2-drink minimum.

There's something going on every night of the week here at one of L.A.'s most historic hotels. Some of the country's best cabaret singers pop up here regularly. The Cinegrill draws locals with a zany cabaret show and guest chanteuses from Eartha Kitt to Cybill Shepherd.

Comedy Store. 8433 Sunset Blvd., West Hollywood. ☎ **213/656-6225.** Cover varies, 2-drink minimum.

You can't go wrong here: New comics develop their material, and established ones work out the kinks from theirs, at owner Mitzi Shore's (Pauly's mom) landmark venue. The talent here is always first-rate, and includes comics who regularly appear on *The Tonight Show* and other shows.

✪ **Groundling Theater.** 7307 Melrose Ave., Los Angeles. ☎ **213/934-9700.** Tickets $7–$18.

L.A.'s answer to Second City has been around for over 20 years, yet remains the most innovative and funniest group in town. Their collection of skits changes every year or so, but they take new improvisational twists every night, and the satire is often savage. The Groundlings were the springboard to fame for Pee-Wee Herman, *Friend's* Lisa Kudrow, and former *Saturday Night Live* stars Jon Lovitz, Phil Hartman, and Julia "It's Pat" Sweeney. Trust me—you haven't laughed this hard in ages.

The Ice House. 24 N. Mentor Ave. ☎ **626/577-1894,** or 626/577-9133 for the Annex. Cover $8–$12, 2-drink minimum.

Pasadena's best-known comedy and music club claims to have launched the careers of Robin Williams, Steve Martin, David Letterman, and Lily Tomlin, among others. There are usually three acts nightly, with two shows on Friday and three shows on Saturday. The Ice House Annex presents blues, improvisational theater, and intimate performance art.

The Improvisation. 8162 Melrose Ave., West Hollywood. ☎ **213/651-2583.** Cover $8–$11, 2-drink minimum.

A showcase for top stand-ups since 1975, the Improv offers something different each night. Owner Bud Freedman's buddies—like Jay Leno, Billy Crystal, and Robin Williams—hone their skills here more often than you'd expect. But even if the comedians on the bill the night you go are all unknowns, they won't be for long.

THE OTHER BAR SCENE: L.A.'S TOP COFFEEHOUSES

by Steve Hochman; updated by Stephanie Avnet

Los Angeles's romance with '90s coffee culture is hardly unique; every major urban city in America is similarly enthralled. But a few of L.A.'s coffeehouses are distinctly Angeleno in their funky characters, which basically range from seedy funky to arty funky. They're definitely worth checking out if you're craving a half-caf cap nonfat with a twist—and maybe some music or poetry to go with it.

The Abbey. 692 N. Robertson Blvd., West Hollywood. ☎ **310/289-8410.**

This coffeehouse in the heart of West Hollywood is really a cafe, offering full meals. But it's also perhaps the best casual hangout in the heavily gay neighborhood, with desserts galore. Lingering over an iced mocha on the patio with a few friends makes for a perfect evening time-waster.

Bourgeois Pig. 5931 Franklin Ave., Hollywood. ☎ **213/962-6366.**

With a bit more of a bar atmosphere than the usual coffeehouse, this veteran, on a hot business strip at the Hollywood/Los Feliz border, is a youth and show-biz drone favorite. An added draw is the terrific newsstand next door.

Equator. 22 Mills Place, Pasadena. ☎ **626/564-8656.**

Airy and comfy, this brick room on a busy alleyway in the heart of resurgent Old Town Pasadena has withstood the challenge of a Starbucks that moved in a block away. The menu—with smoothies, soup, and desserts in addition to a wide variety of coffee drinks—and the friendly service keep people coming back. Even the post-Haring art on the walls gives the room a distinctive character, which has been used for scenes in such films and TV shows as *Beverly Hills, 90210* and *A Very Brady Sequel.*

Espresso Bar. 1039 E. Green St. (near Catalina), Pasadena. ☎ **626/577-9113.**

This simply named coffeehouse has been around so long that it almost seems as though Pasadena grew up around it. It was formerly hidden down a hard-to-find alleyway, but its new location is on Green Street's Antique Row—outside Old Town but close to Pasadena City College. Open-mike nights are popular with beat poets and singers, and bands play on Friday and Saturday nights to an eclectic crowd lounging on the hodgepodge of dingy furniture typical of Espresso Bar's Greenwich Village ambience. There's a spacious upstairs loft and a beverage menu with some exotic entries like steamed milk with molasses.

Highland Grounds. 742 N. Highland Ave., Hollywood. ☎ **213/466-1507.**

Predating the coffeehouse explosion, this comfortable, relatively unpretentious place set the L.A. standard with a vast assortment of food and drink—not just coffee—and often first-rate live music, ranging from nationally known locals, such as Victoria Williams, to open-mike Wednesdays for all-comers.

LATE-NIGHT BITES

L.A. is no 24-hour town. Surprisingly, the city has only a couple dozen bona fide restaurants that are open after hours; even fewer serve all night.

If you want a serious meal after 2am, head for one of the following places, all of which are open 24 hours: **Pacific Dining Car,** 1310 W. 6th St., at Witmer Street, downtown (☎ **213/483-6000**), is the place for a well-marbled, patiently aged New York steak any time of day or night. For Westsiders, there's a Santa Monica location at 2700 Wilshire Blvd., a block east of 26th Street (☎ **310/453-4000**); but they're only open till 2am. **The Original Pantry Cafe,** 877 S. Figueroa St., at 9th Street downtown (☎ **213/972-9279**), has been serving huge portions of comfort food around the clock for more than 60 years; in fact, they don't even have a key to the front door.

How good can you look at 3am? See how skimpily dressed model-types (and celebrity hangers-on like Mick Jagger) answer that question at trendy **Caffe Luna,** 7463 Melrose Ave., Los Angeles (☎ **213/655-8647**), which serves rustic Italian until 5am Friday and Saturday, 3am other nights. **Operetta,** 8223 W. 3rd St. (near Harper Street), Los Angeles (☎ **213/852-7000**), is unremarkable except for being a rare round-the-clock bakery/cafe—you can get salads, sandwiches, omelets and French pastries any time. **Kate Mantilini,** 9101 Wilshire Blvd., at Doheny Drive, Beverly

Hills (☎ **310/278-3699**), serves up stylish fare until 1am most weeknights, and to 3am on weekends. Dine into the wee hours in the authentic Spanish style at **Cava,** 8384 W. 3rd St. (at Orlando St.), Los Angeles (☎ **213/658-8898**). They'll keep the pot of paella warm until 1am Friday and Saturday, midnight other days.

There's not the usual line for those coveted stools at **The Apple Pan,** 10801 W. Pico Blvd. (east of Westwood Boulevard), West L.A. (☎ **310/475-3585**), but the late-night burgers are just as tasty; they're open till 1am Friday and Saturday, midnight the rest of the week. You can catch the Beverly Hills set grabbing a bite at the Beverly Hills Hotel's tony **Polo Lounge,** 9641 Sunset Blvd. (☎ **276-2251**), where oysters, caviar, sandwiches, and more are served until 1:30am nightly.

Another late-night option is **Canter's Fairfax Restaurant, Delicatessen & Bakery,** 419 N. Fairfax Ave. (☎ **213/651-2030**), a Jewish deli that's been a hit with late-nighters since it opened more than 65 years ago. If you show up after the clubs close, you're sure to spot a bleary-eyed celebrity or two alongside the rest of the after-hours crowd, chowing down on a giant pastrami sandwich, matzo-ball soup, potato pancakes, or another deli favorite.

Jerry's Famous Deli, 12655 Ventura Blvd., at Coldwater Canyon Avenue, Studio City (☎ **818/980-4245**), is where Valley hipsters go to relieve their late-night munchies. Another Valley favorite is **Du-par's Coffee Shop,** 12036 Ventura Blvd., a block east of Laurel Canyon, Studio City (☎ **818/766-4437**), which only serves its blue-plate specials till 1am on weeknights; however, come the weekend, they're slingin' hash until 4am.

Side Trips from Los Angeles

14

by Stephanie Avnet

The area within a 100-mile radius of Los Angeles is one of the most diverse regions in the world: There are arid deserts, rugged mountains, industrial cities, historic towns, alpine lakes, rolling hillsides, and sophisticated seaside resorts. You'll also find an offshore island that's been transformed into the ultimate city-dweller's hideaway, not to mention the Happiest Place on Earth.

1 Long Beach & the *Queen Mary*

21 Miles S of downtown Los Angeles

The fifth-largest incorporated city in California, Long Beach consists mostly of business and industrial areas interspersed with unremarkable neighborhoods. The city is best known as the permanent home of the former cruise liner *Queen Mary* and for the annual Long Beach Grand Prix in mid-April, whose star-studded warm-up race sends the likes of young hipster Jason Priestly (*Beverly Hills, 90210*) and perennial racer Paul Newman burning rubber through the streets of the city. Although Long Beach is too far away to be considered part of Los Angeles as a tourist destination, and it's not as attractive as most of the smaller coastal communities to either the north or south, the *Queen Mary* makes a trip here worthwhile.

ESSENTIALS

GETTING THERE   From Los Angeles, take either I-5 or I-405, to I-710 south; it follows the Los Angeles River on its path to the ocean and leads directly to both downtown Long Beach and the *Queen Mary* Seaport.

ORIENTATION   Most of seaside Long Beach is in vast San Pedro Harbor, L.A.'s busy industrial port. Terminal Island sits right in the middle. To the west across the pretty Vincent Thomas Bridge is the city of San Pedro, home to the nautical and touristy Ports O' Call Village. The *Queen Mary* is docked near the eastern end of Long Beach, looking out over the actual "long beach" extending along peaceful, affluent Belmont Shore to tiny Long Beach Marina, home to charming Naples Island (see "The *Queen Mary* & Other Port Attractions," below).

VISITOR INFORMATION   Contact the **Long Beach Area Convention & Visitors Bureau,** One World Trade Center, Suite 300

(☎ **800/4LB-STAY** or 562/436-3645). There's a city-run website at www.ci.
long-beach.ca.us, which offers a section with tourism listings. For further information on the **Long Beach Grand Prix,** call ☎ **562/981-2600** or check out
www.longbeachgp.com.

THE *QUEEN MARY* & OTHER PORT ATTRACTIONS

Queen Mary. Pier J (at the end of I-710), Long Beach. ☎ **562/435-3511.** Admission $11
adults, $9 seniors 55 and over and military, $6 children 4–11, free for kids 3 and under. Daily
10am–6pm (last entry at 5:30pm), with extended summer hours. Charge for parking.

It's easy to dismiss the *Queen Mary* as a barnacle-laden tourist trap, but it *is* the only
surviving example of this particular kind of 20th-century elegance and excess. From
the staterooms paneled lavishly in now-extinct tropical hardwoods to the miles of
hallway handrails made of once-pedestrian Bakelite and the perfectly preserved crew
quarters, wonders never cease aboard this deco luxury liner. Stroll the teakwood decks
with just a bit of imagination and you're back in 1936 on the maiden voyage from
Southampton, England. Kiosk displays of photographs and memorabilia are everywhere, and the ship has been virtually unaltered since its heyday. Especially evocative is the first-class observation lounge, a Streamline Moderne masterpiece you might
recognize from *Barton Fink; Beverly Hills, 90210;* and other shows. Regular admission includes a self-guided tour. For an additional $6 for adults or $3 for kids, you
can take a behind-the-scenes guided tour of the ship, peppered with worthwhile anecdotes and details.

Gondola Getaway. Naples Island, Long Beach. ☎ **562/433-9595.** 1-hour cruise $55 for 2.
Daily 11am–11pm.

Since 1982 these authentic Venetian gondolas have been snaking around the
man-made canals of Naples Island, under gracefully arched bridges and past the
gardens of resort cottages. Feel free to bring your beverage of choice, for they send
you out with a nice basket of bread, cheese, and salami plus wine glasses and a full
ice bucket. Perhaps your traditionally clad oarsman will sing an Italian aria or relate
the many tales of marriage proposals by romance-minded passengers (some not so
successful!).

Shoreline Village. 407 Shoreline Dr. (at Pine Ave. across the channel from the *Queen Mary*).
☎ **562/435-2668,** or 562/432-3053 for information. Daily 10am–9pm (later in summer and
on holidays).

If you've seen the real thing in New England you won't be overly impressed, but
Long Beach likes to promote this cluster of shops, restaurants, and waterside cafes
as a replica 19th-century seaport village. Our favorite surprise was an ornate merry-
go-round hand-carved in 1906 by Charles Looff, master carousel maker who helped
build The Pike, an old-fashioned seaside amusement park that stood on this spot
in the 1930s. The 62 wooden carousel animals include not only horses but leaping camels, giraffes, and rams, all illuminated by glittering Austrian crystal; rides
are $1.

The Tall Ship *Californian.* ☎ **800/432-2201** for reservations.

The flagship of the Nautical Heritage Society, the *Californian,* sails from Long Beach
between late August and mid-April (it's based in Northern California in summer).
At 145 feet long, this two-masted wooden cutter-class vessel offers barefooters the
opportunity to help raise and lower eight sails, steer by compass, and generally experience the "romance of the high seas." Landlubbers will want to choose the 4-hour
day sail for $75 ($113 for two), including lunch, while old salts can take 2-, 3-, or

4-day cruises out to Catalina or the Channel Islands at $140 per person per day. Overnight sails should be booked well in advance.

WHERE TO STAY

❁ **Hotel *Queen Mary*.** 1126 Queen's Hwy. (end of I-710), Long Beach, CA 90802-6390. ☎ **800/437-2934,** 562/435-3511, or 562/432-6964. Fax 562/437-4531. 365 rms, 17 suites. A/C TV TEL. $75–$160 double; from $350 suite. AE, DC, EU, MC, V. Charge for parking.

Although the *Queen Mary* is considered the most luxurious ocean liner ever to sail the Atlantic, with the largest rooms ever built aboard a ship, the quarters aren't exceptional when compared to those on terra firma today, nor are the amenities. The idea is to enjoy the novelty and charm of features like the original bathtub watercocks ("cold salt," "cold fresh," "hot salt," "hot fresh"). The beautifully carved interior is a feast for the eye and fun to explore, and the weekday rates are hard to beat. Three on-board restaurants are overpriced but convenient, and the shopping arcade has a decidedly British feel (one shop sells great *Queen Mary* souvenirs). An elegant Sunday champagne brunch—complete with ice sculpture and harpist—is served in the ship's Grand Salon, and it's always worth having a cocktail in the art deco Observation Bar. If you're too young or too poor to have traveled on the old luxury liners, this is the perfect opportunity to experience the romance of an Atlantic crossing— and with no seasickness, cabin fever, or week of formal dinners.

WHERE TO DINE

Belmont Brewing Company. 25 39th Place (at the Belmont Pier), Long Beach. ☎ **562/ 433-3891.** Main courses $6–$16. AE, CB, DC, MC, V. Mon–Fri 11:30am–10pm, Sat–Sun 10:30am–10pm. (Bar, daily till midnight.) BREWPUB/AMERICAN.

This brewed-on-premises beer restaurant's outdoor patio has a million-dollar harbor view of the *Queen Mary,* fiery sunsets, and the pier's unusual chameleon street lamps. The five fine house brews include "Top Sail" (amber) and "Long Beach Crude" (porter). The menu consists of salads, sandwiches, pizzas, pasta, and happy-hour appetizer favorites, including a deep-fried whole onion "flower" served with sweet-spicy dipping sauce.

Papadakis Taverna. 301 W. 6th St. (at Centre St.), San Pedro. ☎ **310/548-1186.** Reservations recommended. Main courses $12–$25. CB, DC, MC, V. Sun–Thurs 5–9pm, Fri–Sat 5–10pm. GREEK.

The food here rates higher than the ambiance—even genial host John Papadakis's hand-kissing greeting doesn't soften the blunt lines and bright lights of this banquet room–like space decorated with equal parts Aegean murals and football art (in deference to Papadakis's glory days as a University of Southern California football legend). The waiters dance and sing loudly when they're not bringing plates of *spanikopita* (spinach-filled phyllo pastries) or thick, satisfying *tsatziki* (garlic-laced cucumber-and-yogurt spread) to your table. Servings are very generous, and the wine list has something for everyone.

Parker's Lighthouse. 435 Shoreline Village Dr., Long Beach. ☎ **562/432-6500.** Reservations recommended on weekends. Lunch $6–$15; dinner $9–$27. AE, DC, DISC, MC, V. Mon–Thurs 11am–10pm, Fri 11am–11pm, Sat 3–11pm, Sun 3:30–9:30pm. SEAFOOD GRILL.

Built to look like a giant Cape Cod lighthouse, Parker's fits right into the Shoreline Village motif. It's actually kind of fun to wind upstairs to one of three dining levels, including the circular bar on the top floor, which looks out over the harbor and the behemoth *Queen Mary.* The main dining room specializes in mesquite-fired fresh seafood, but also offers steaks and chicken.

2 Santa Catalina Island

22 miles W of mainland Los Angeles

Santa Catalina—which everyone calls simply Catalina—is a small, cove-fringed island famous for its laid-back inns, largely unspoiled landscape, and crystal-clear waters. Many devotees consider it Southern California's alternative to Capri or Malta. Because of its relative isolation, out-of-state tourists tend to ignore it; but those who do show up have plenty of elbow room to boat, fish, swim, scuba, and snorkel. There are miles of hiking and biking trails, plus golf, tennis, and horseback riding.

Catalina is so different from the mainland that it almost seems like a different country, remote and unspoiled. In 1915 the island was purchased by William Wrigley, Jr., the chewing-gum manufacturer, in order to develop a fashionable pleasure resort. To publicize the new vacation land, Wrigley brought big-name bands to the Avalon Ballroom and moved the Chicago Cubs, which he owned, to the island for spring training. His marketing efforts succeeded, and this charming and tranquil retreat became—and still is—a favorite vacation resort for mainlanders.

Today about 86% of the island remains undeveloped, owned and preserved by the Santa Catalina Island Conservancy. Some of the spectacular outlying areas can only be reached by arranged tour (see "Exploring the Island," below).

ESSENTIALS

GETTING THERE   The most common way to get to and from the island is via the **Catalina Express** (☎ 562/519-1212), which operates up to 20 daily departures year-round from San Pedro and Long Beach. The trip takes about an hour. One-way fares from San Pedro are $17.75 for adults, $16 for seniors, $13 for children 2 to 11, and $1 for infants. Long Beach fares are about $2 higher for all except infants, who are still charged $1. The trip is an additional $1.80 if you travel to Two Harbors. The Catalina Express departs from the Sea/Air Terminal at Berth 95, Port of L.A. in San Pedro; from the Catalina Express port at the *Queen Mary* in Long Beach; and from the Catalina Express port at 161 N. Harbor Dr. in Redondo Beach. Call ahead for reservations. *Note:* Luggage is limited to 50 pounds per person; reservations are necessary for bicycles, surfboards, and dive tanks; and there are restrictions on transporting pets.

Catalina Cruises (☎ 800/CATALINA) also ferries passengers from Long Beach to Avalon Harbor. It has the best rates going (about $5 cheaper than above) because it runs monstrous 700-passenger boats, which take longer to make the crossing (about 1 hour and 50 minutes). But it does offer twice-daily sailings during the high season, plus frequent runs to Twin Harbors. If you want to save money, particularly if you're staying overnight and don't have to maximize your island time, Catalina Cruises is the choice for you.

Island Express Helicopter Service, 900 Queens Way Dr., Long Beach (☎ 310/510-2525; fax 310/510-9671), flies from Long Beach or San Pedro to Catalina in about 15 minutes. They fly on demand between 8am and sunset year-round, charging $66 each way. If you just want an airborne tour of Catalina, they'll spend 10 to 30 minutes showing you island sights. There's a four-passenger minimum and the cost is $50 to $90 per person.

VISITOR INFORMATION   The **Catalina Island Chamber of Commerce and Visitor's Bureau,** (P.O. Box 217), Avalon, CA 90704 (☎ 310/510-1520; fax 310/510-7606), located on the Green Pleasure Pier, distributes brochures and information on island activities, hotels, and boat and helicopter transport. Call for a free 100-page visitor's guide.

The Santa Catalina Island Company–run **Visitor's Information Center,** just across from the Chamber of Commerce on Crescent Avenue (☎ **310/510-2000**), handles hotel reservations, sightseeing tours, and other island activities.

There's also a colorful Internet site at **www.catalina.com** that offers current news from the *Catalina Islander* newspaper in addition to updated activities, events, and general information.

ORIENTATION   The picturesque town of **Avalon** is the island's only city and the port of entry for the island. From the ferry dock you can wander along Crescent Avenue, the main road along the beachfront, and easily explore adjacent side streets.

Northwest of Avalon is the village of **Two Harbors,** accessible only by boat or the most intrepid of hikers. Its twin bays are favored by pleasure yachts from L.A.'s various marinas, so there's more camaraderie and a less touristy ambiance overall.

GETTING AROUND   Visitors are not allowed to drive cars on the island. There are only a limited number of autos permitted; most residents motor around in golf carts (many of the homes only have golf cart–size driveways). But don't worry—you'll be able to get everywhere you want to go by renting a cart yourself or just hoofing it, which is what most visitors do.

If you want to explore the area around Avalon beyond where your feet can comfortably carry you, try renting a mountain bike or tandem from **Brown's Bikes,** 107 Pebbly Beach Rd., Avalon (☎ **310/510-0986**), or even a gas-powered golf cart from **Cartopia,** 615 Crescent Ave., Avalon (☎ **310/510-2493**), where rates are $30 per hour.

EXPLORING THE ISLAND

ORGANIZED TOURS   The Santa Catalina Island Company's **Discovery Tours,** Avalon Harbor Pier (☎ **800/626-7489** or 310/510-TOUR), operates several motorcoach excursions that depart from the tour plaza in the center of town on Sumner Avenue. The **Skyline Drive Tour** basically follows the perimeter of the island and takes about 1³/₄ hours. Trips leave several times a day from 11am to 3pm and cost $18 for adults, $16 for seniors, and $10 for children 3 to 11.

The **Inland Motor Tour** is more comprehensive; it includes some of the 66 square miles of preserve owned by the Santa Catalina Island Conservancy. You'll see El Rancho Escondido and probably have a chance to view buffalo, deer, goats, and boars. Tours, which take about 3³/₄ hours, leave at 9am; from June to October, they leave at other times as well. Tours are $29 for adults, $26 for seniors, $16 for children 3 to 11, and free for children 2 and under.

Other excursions offered by the company include the 40-minute **Casino Tour,** which explores Catalina's most famous landmark; the 50-minute **Avalon Scenic Tour,** a 9-mile introductory tour of the town; and the 1-hour **Flying Fish Boat Trip,** during which an occasional flying fish lands right on the boat. Call for additional tour offerings, as well as for information on multiple excursion packages.

VISITING TWO HARBORS   If you want to get a better look at the rugged natural beauty of Catalina and escape the throngs of beachgoers, head over to Two Harbors, the quarter-mile "neck" at the island's northwest end that gets its name from the "twin harbors" on each side, known as the Isthmus and Cat Harbor. An excellent starting point for campers and hikers, Two Harbors also offers just enough civilization for the less intrepid traveler:

The **Banning House Lodge** (☎ **310/510-7265**) is an 11-room bed-and-breakfast overlooking the Isthmus. The clapboard house was built in 1910 for Catalina's pre-Wrigley owners and has seen duty as a girls' camp, army barracks, and on-location lodging for movie stars like Errol Flynn and Dorothy Lamour. The innkeepers are gracious, the atmosphere peaceful and isolated. Call from the pier and they'll even drive you up to the lodge.

Everyone eats at **Doug's Harbor Reef** (☎ 310/510-7265), down on the beach. This nautical/South Seas–themed saloon/restaurant serves breakfast, lunch, and dinner, the latter being hearty steaks, ribs, swordfish, chicken teriyaki, and buffalo burgers in the summer. The house drink is sweet "buffalo milk," a potent concoction of vodka, crème de cacao, banana liqueur, milk, and whipped cream.

Avalon Casino and Catalina Island Museum. At the end of Crescent Ave. ☎ 310/510-2414. Museum admission $1.50 adults, $1 seniors, 50¢ children 6–11, free for children 5 and under. Daily 10:30am–4pm.

This is the most famous structure on the island, and one of its oldest. It was built in 1929 to house a ballroom and theater, but its massive circular rotunda topped with a red-tile roof is its most notable feature. The Casino is widely known for its beautiful art deco ballroom, which once hosted the Tommy Dorsey and Glenn Miller orchestras and other top bands. You can see the inside of the building by attending a ballroom event or watching a film (the Casino is Avalon's primary movie theater). Otherwise, admission is by guided tour only, operated daily by the Santa Catalina Island Company (see "Organized Tours," above).

The **Catalina Island Museum,** on the ground floor, features exhibits on island history, archaeology, and natural history—it also has a contour relief map of the island that can be helpful to anyone planning to venture into the interior.

SNORKELING, DIVING & KAYAKING

Snorkeling, scuba diving, and sea kayaking are among the main reasons mainlanders head to Catalina. Purists will prefer the less-spoiled waters of Two Harbors, but Avalon's many coves have plenty to offer as well. **Banana Boat Riders,** 107 Pebbly Beach Rd., Avalon (☎ 800/708-2262 or 310/510-1774), offers snorkel gear and sea kayak rentals, as well as half- and full-day excursions to Two Harbors and other island coves. **Catalina Divers Supply** (☎ 800/353-0330 or 310/510-0330) offers guided snorkel and scuba tours with certified instructors, in addition to gear rental, at three Avalon locations. **Descanso Beach Ocean Sports** (☎ 310/510-1226) offers sea kayak and snorkel rentals with instruction, plus specialty expeditions and kids' programs.

At Two Harbors, sit-on-top beginner kayaks as well as advanced touring types can be rented at **Two Harbors Kayak Center** (☎ 310/510-7265). They offer instruction and guided tours of the secluded coves on the northern end of the island.

WHERE TO STAY

If you plan to stay overnight, be sure to reserve a room in advance, since most places fill up pretty quickly during the summer and holiday seasons. **Catalina Island Accommodations** (☎ 310/510-3000) might be able to help you out in a pinch; it's a reservations service with updated information on the whole island. Below are three of the most noteworthy places to stay in Avalon. If you'd like to stay on the less-visited side of the island, see "Visiting Two Harbors" under "Exploring the Island," above.

Catalina Island Inn. 125 Metropole (P.O. Box 467), Avalon, CA 90704. ☎ 800/246-8134 or 310/510-1623. Fax 310/510-7218. 35 rms, 1 minisuite. TV TEL. May–Sept, and holidays and weekends year-round, $89–$179 double; $189 minisuite. Oct–Apr weekdays, $45–$99 double; $155 minisuite. Rates include continental breakfast. AE, DISC, MC, V. Closed December 24 and 25.

Innkeepers Martin and Bernadine Curtin provide clean, comfortable rooms simply furnished with a vaguely tropical motif. Many rooms have balconies with views of the harbor, and you can't beat the location right in the center of bustling Avalon.

✪ **The Inn on Mt. Ada.** 398 Wrigley Rd. (P.O. Box 2560), Avalon, CA 90704. ☎ **800/ 608-7669** or 310/510-2030. Fax 310/510-2237. 6 rms, 2 suites. Nov–May Mon–Thurs, $250–$390 double; $390–$495 suite. June–Oct, and Fri–Sun year-round, $340–$515 double; $515–$620 suite. Rates include three meals. MC, V.

When William Wrigley, Jr. purchased Catalina Island in 1921, he built this ornate Georgian Colonial mansion as his summer vacation home; it's now one of the finest small hotels in California. The opulent inn has several ground-floor salons, a fireplaced club room, a deep-seated formal library, and a wickered sunroom where tea, cookies, and fruit are always available. The best guest room is the Grand Suite, fitted with a fireplace and a large private patio. Amenities include bathrobes. TVs are available on request, but there are no telephones in the rooms. A hearty full breakfast, a light deli-style lunch, and a beautiful multicourse dinner complemented by a limited wine selection are included in the tariff.

Zane Grey Pueblo Hotel. Off Chimes Tower Rd. (north of Hill St.; P.O. Box 216), Avalon, CA 90704. ☎ **800/378-3256** or 310/510-0966. 17 rms. Apr–Oct, $75–$125 double; Nov–Mar, $59 double. Rates include continental breakfast. AE, MC, V.

You'll have the most superb views on the island from this Shangri-la mountain retreat, the former home of novelist Zane Grey, who spent his last 20 years in Avalon. He wrote many books here, including *Tales of Swordfish and Tuna,* which tells of his fishing adventures off Catalina Island. The hotel has teak beams that the novelist brought from Tahiti on one of his fishing trips. Most of the rooms also have large windows and ocean or mountain views. They have all been renovated in the last few years with new furniture, carpeting, and ceiling fans. An outdoor patio has an excellent view. The original living room has a grand piano, a fireplace, and a TV. The hotel also has a pool and sundeck, with chairs overlooking Avalon and the ocean. Coffee is served all day, and there's a courtesy bus to town.

WHERE TO DINE

On the Two Harbors side of the island, **Doug's Harbor Reef** is the place to eat; see "Exploring the Island," above.

The Busy Bee. 306 Crescent Ave. (north of the Pleasure Pier). ☎ **310/510-1983.** Reservations not accepted. Main courses $7–$15. AE, CB, DC, DISC, MC, V. Summer, daily 8am–10pm; winter, daily 10am–8pm. AMERICAN.

The Busy Bee, an Avalon institution since 1923, is located right on the beach. The fare is light-deli style. The extensive menu offers breakfast, lunch, and dinner at all times. The restaurant grinds its own beef, cuts its own potatoes for French fries, and makes its own salad dressings. Even if you're not hungry, come here for a drink—it's Avalon's only waterfront bar.

El Galleon. 411 Crescent Ave. ☎ **310/510-1188.** Reservations recommended on weekends. Main courses $11–$37 at dinner. AE, DISC, MC, V. Daily 11am–2:30pm and 5–10pm. (Bar, daily 10am–1:30am.) AMERICAN.

El Galleon is large, warm, and woody, complete with portholes, rigging, anchors, wrought-iron chandeliers, oversize leather booths, and tables with red-leather captain's chairs. There's additional balcony seating, plus outdoor cafe tables overlooking the ocean harbor. Lunch and dinner feature seafood. Favorite dinner dishes include fresh swordfish steak and broiled Catalina lobster tails in drawn butter. "Turf" main dishes range from country-fried chicken to broiled rack of lamb with mint jelly.

Sand Trap. Avalon Canyon Rd. (north of Tremont St.). ☎ **310/510-1349.** Reservations not accepted. Main courses $6–$12. No credit cards. Daily 7:30am–3:30pm. CALIFORNIA/ MEXICAN.

This local favorite is a great place to escape from the bayfront crowds. Enjoy breakfast, lunch, or snacks while overlooking the golf course. Specialties of the house include delectable omelets served until noon and soft tacos served all day. Either can be made with any number of fillings. Burgers, sandwiches, salads, and chili are also served. Beer and wine are available.

3 Big Bear Lake & Lake Arrowhead

100 miles NE of Los Angeles

These two deep blue lakes lie close to one another in the San Bernardino Mountains, and have long been a favorite year-round alpine playground for city-weary Angelenos.

Big Bear Lake has always been popular with skiers as well as avid boaters (it's much larger than Arrowhead, and equipment rentals abound). In the past decade the area has been given a much-needed face-lift. Big Bear Boulevard was substantially widened to handle high-season traffic, and downtown Big Bear Lake (the "Village") was spiffed up without losing its woodsy charm. In addition to two excellent ski slopes less than 5 minutes from town (see "Winter Fun," below), you can enjoy the comforts of a real supermarket (there's even a Kmart now) and several video-rental shops, all especially convenient when staying in a cabin! Most people choose Big Bear over Arrowhead because there's so much more to do, from boating, fishing, and hiking to snow sports, mountain biking, and horseback riding. The weather is nearly always perfect at this 7,000-foot-plus elevation; If you want proof, ask Caltech, which operates a solar observatory here to take advantage of nearly 300 days of sunshine per year.

Lake Arrowhead has always been privately owned, as is immediately apparent from the affluence of the surrounding homes, many of which are gated estates rather than rustic mountain cabins. The lake and the private docks lining its shores are reserved for the exclusive use of homeowners, but visitors can enjoy Lake Arrowhead by boat tour (see "Organized Tours," below) or use of the summer-season beach clubs, a privilege included in nearly all private home rentals (see "Where to Stay at Lake Arrowhead," below). Reasons to choose a vacation at Lake Arrowhead? The roads up are less grueling than the winding ascent to Big Bear Lake and, being at a lower elevation, Arrowhead gets little snow (you can forget those pesky tire chains). It's very easy and cost-effective to rent a luxurious house from which to enjoy the spectacular scenery, crisp mountain air, and relaxed resort atmosphere—and if you do ski, the slopes are only a half hour away.

ESSENTIALS

GETTING THERE   Lake Arrowhead is reached by taking Calif. 18 from San Bernardino. The last segment of this route takes you along the aptly named ✪ **Rim of the World Highway,** offering a breathtaking panoramic view out over the valley below on clear days. Calif. 18 then continues east to Big Bear Lake, but to get to Big Bear Lake it's quicker to bypass Arrowhead by taking Calif. 330 from Redlands, which meets Calif. 18 in Running Springs. During heavy-traffic periods it can be worthwhile to take scenic Calif. 38, which winds up from Redlands through mountain passes and valleys to approach Big Bear from the other side.

Big Bear Lake & Lake Arrowhead

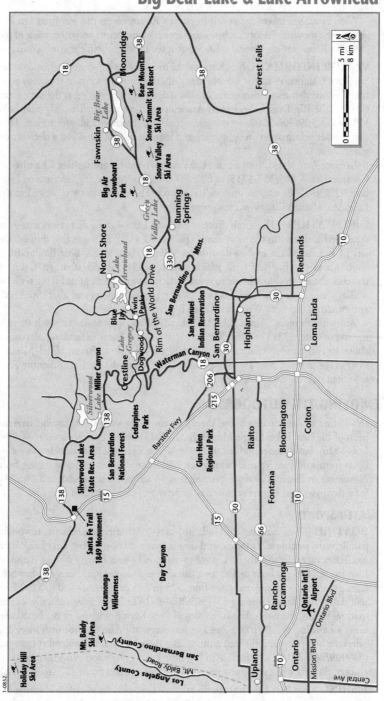

1-0852

Note: Nostalgia lovers can revisit legendary **Route 66** on the way from Los Angeles to the mountain resorts, substituting scenic motor courts and other relics of the "Mother Road" for impersonal I-10. See chapter 15 for a complete driving tour.

VISITOR INFORMATION   National ski tours, mountain-bike races, and one of Southern California's largest Oktoberfest gatherings are just some of the many year-round events that may either entice or discourage you from visiting at the same time. Contact the **Big Bear Lake Resort Association,** 630 Bartlett Rd., Big Bear Lake Village (☎ **909/866-7000;** www.bigbear.com), for schedules and information. They also provide information on sightseeing and lodging and will send you a free visitors' guide.

In Lake Arrowhead, contact the **Lake Arrowhead Communities Chamber of Commerce** (☎ 909/337-3715, or 800/337-3716 for the Lodging Information Line; fax 909/336-1548; www.apsm.com/lakearrow). The visitor center is located in the Lake Arrowhead Village lower shopping center.

ORIENTATION   The south shore of Big Bear Lake was the first resort area to be developed and remains the most densely populated. Calif. 18 passes first through the city of Big Bear Lake and its downtown Village; then, as Big Bear Boulevard, it continues east to Big Bear City, which is more residential and suburban. Calif. 38 traverses the north shore, home to pristine national forest and great hiking trails, as well as a couple of small marinas (see "Water Sports," below) and a lakefront bed-and-breakfast inn (see "Where to Stay in Big Bear Lake," below).

Arrowhead's main town is Lake Arrowhead Village, located on the south shore at the end of Calif. 173. The village's commercial center is home to factory-outlet stores, about 40 chain and specialty shops, and the Lake Arrowhead Resort Hotel. Minutes away is the town of Blue Jay (along Calif. 189), where the Ice Castle Skating Rink is located (see "Winter Fun," below).

ENJOYING THE OUTDOORS

In addition to the activities below, there's a great recreation spot for families near the heart of Big Bear Lake: **Magic Mountain,** on Calif. 18/Big Bear Boulevard (☎ **909/866-4626**), has a year-round bobsled-style Alpine Slide, a splashy double water slide open from mid-June to mid-September, and bunny slopes for snow tubing from November to Easter. The dry Alpine Slide is $3 a ride, the water slide is $1 (or $10 for a day pass), and snowplay costs $10 per day including tube and rope tow.

WATER SPORTS

BOATING   You can rent all kinds of boats—including speedboats, rowboats, paddleboats, pontoons, sailboats, and canoes—at a number of Big Bear Lake marinas. Rates vary only slightly from place to place: A 14-foot dinghy with an outboard runs around $10 per hour or $30 for a half day; pontoon (patio) boats that can hold large groups range in size and price from $25 to $45 per hour or $80 to $150 for a half day. **Pine Knot Landing** (☎ **909/866-BOAT**) is the most centrally located marina, behind the post office at the foot of Pine Knot Boulevard in Big Bear Lake. **Gray's Landing** (☎ **909/866-2443**) is just across the dam on the north shore and offers the best prices and the least attitude. **Big Bear Marina,** Paine Road at Lakeview (☎ **909/866-3218**), is also close to Big Bear Lake Village and provides take-along chicken dinners when you rent a pontoon boat for a sunset cruise ($75 for 3 hours).

FISHING   Big Bear Lake brims with rainbow trout, bass, and catfish in spring and summer, the best fishing seasons. Phone ☎ **310/590-5020** for recorded stocking information. A fishing license is required and costs $8.95 per day, $24.95 per year.

Pine Knot Landing, Gray's Landing, and **Big Bear Marina** (see "Boating," above) all rent fishing boats and have bait and tackle shops that sell licenses.

JET SKIING   Personal Water Craft (PWCs) are available for rent at **Big Bear Marina** (see "Boating," above) and **Pleasure Point Landing,** 603 Landlock Landing Rd. (☎ **909/866-2455**), where you can rent a single-rider SeaDoo (easier than the stand-up JetSki) for $35 an hour, or opt for a two-seat Waverunner ($55 per hour). **North Shore Landing,** on Calif. 38, 2 miles west of Fawnskin (☎ **909/868-4386**), rents JetSkis and two- and three-person Waverunners ranging from $55 to $65 per hour. Call ahead to reserve your craft and check age and deposit requirements.

WATERSKIING   At Big Bear Lake, **Pine Knot Landing, North Shore Landing,** and **Big Bear Marina** (see "Boating," above) all offer water-ski lessons and speedboat rentals. Lake Arrowhead is home to the **McKenzie Water Ski School,** dockside in Lake Arrowhead Village (☎ **909/337-3814**), famous for teaching Kirk Douglas, George Hamilton, and other Hollywood stars to ski. It's open from Memorial Day to the end of September and offers group lessons for $115 per hour, short refresher lessons for $35, and boat rental (including driver) for $95 an hour.

OTHER WARM-WEATHER ACTIVITIES

GOLF   The **Bear Mountain Golf Course,** Goldmine Drive, Big Bear Lake (☎ **909/585-8002**), is a nine-hole, par-35, links-style course that winds through a gently sloping meadow at the base of the Bear Mountain Ski Resort. The course is open daily from April to November. Greens fees are $17 and $23 for 9 and 18 holes, respectively. Both riding carts and pull carts are available. Phone for tee times.

HIKING   Hikers will love the San Bernardino National Forest. The gray squirrel is a popular native; you may see them scurrying around gathering acorns or material for their nest. You can sometimes spot deer, coyotes, and American bald eagles, which come here with their young during winter months. The black-crowned stellar jay and the talkative red, white, and black acorn woodpecker are the most common of the great variety of birds in this pine forest.

Stop in at the **Big Bear Ranger Station** on Calif. 38, 3 miles east of Fawnskin on Big Bear Lake's north shore (☎ **909/866-3437**). There you can pick up free trail maps, as well as other information on the area's plants, animals, and geology. The best trail for a short mountain hike is the **Woodland Trail,** which begins near the ranger station. The best long hike is the **Pacific Crest Trail,** which travels 39 miles through the mountains above Big Bear and Arrowhead lakes. The most convenient trailhead is located at Cougar Crest, half a mile west of the Big Bear Ranger Station.

The best place to begin a hike in Lake Arrowhead is at the **Arrowhead Ranger Station,** located in the town of Skyforest on Calif. 18 (☎ **909/337-2444**), a quarter-mile east of the Lake Arrowhead turnoff (Calif. 173). The staff will provide you with maps and information on the best area trails, which range from easy to difficult. The **Enchanted Loop Trail,** near the town of Blue Jay, is an easy half-hour hike. The **Heaps Peak Arboretum Trail** winds through a grove of redwoods; the trailhead is on the north side of Calif. 18, half a mile east of Santa's Village.

The area is home to a **National Children's Forest,** a 20-acre area developed so that children, the wheelchair-bound, and the visually impaired could enjoy nature. To get to the Children's Forest from Lake Arrowhead, take Calif. 330 to Calif. 18 east, past Deer Lick Station; when you reach a road marked IN96 (only open in the summer season), turn right and go 3 miles.

HORSEBACK RIDING   Horses are permitted on all the mountain trails through the national forest. **Bear Mountain Stables,** at Bear Mountain Ski Resort, City of

Big Bear Lake (☎ **909/878-HORSE**), offers 1- and 2-hour guided rides for $20 per hour, and sunset hay rides for $45. The stables are open daily from May to December; phone for reservations. **Baldwin Lake Stables,** southeast of Big Bear City (☎ **909/585-6482**), also conducts hourly, lunch, and sunset rides in addition to offering lessons.

MOUNTAIN BIKING   Big Bear Lake has become a mountain-bicycling center, with most of the action around the **Snow Summit Ski Area** (see "Winter Fun," below), where a $7 lift ticket will take you and your bike to a scenic web of trails, fire roads, and meadows at about 8,000 feet. Call its **Summer Activities Hotline** at ☎ **909/866-4621.** The lake's north shore is also a popular biking destination; the Forest Service Ranger Stations (see "Hiking," above) have maps to the historic Gold Rush–era Holcomb Valley and the 2-mile Alpine Pedal Path (an easy lakeside ride).

Big Bear Bikes, 41810 Big Bear Blvd. (☎ **909/866-4565**), rents mountain bikes for $6 an hour or $21 for 4 hours. **Bear Valley Bikes,** 40298 Big Bear Blvd. (☎ **909/866-8000**), rents bikes and offers free lessons on Sunday. **Team Big Bear** is located at the base of Snow Summit (☎ **909/866-4565**); it rents bicycles and provides detailed maps and guides for all Big Bear–area trails.

At Lake Arrowhead, bikes are permitted on all hiking trails and backroads except the Pacific Crest Trail. See the local ranger station for an area map. Gear can be rented from **Above & Beyond Sports,** 32877 Calif. 18, Running Springs (☎ **909/867-5517**).

WINTER FUN

SKIING & SNOWBOARDING   When the L.A. basin gets wintertime rain, skiers everywhere rejoice, for they know snow is falling up in the mountains. The last few seasons have seen abundant natural snowfall at Big Bear, augmented by sophisticated snowmaking equipment, which also compensates during drier years. While the slopes can't compare with those in Utah or Colorado, they do offer diversity, difficulty, and convenience.

Snow Summit at Big Bear Lake (☎ **909/866-5766;** www.bigbear.com/summit) is the skier's choice, especially since they installed their second high-speed quad express from the 7,000-foot base to the 8,200-foot summit. Another nice feature is green (easy) runs *even* from the summit, so beginners can also enjoy the Summit Haus lodge and breathtaking lake views from the top. Advanced risk-takers will appreciate three *double*-black-diamond runs. Lift tickets range from $30 to $42. The resort offers midweek, beginner, half-day, night, and family specials, as well as ski and snowboard instruction. Hey, you can even ski free on your birthday here! Other helpful Snow Summit phone numbers include **advance lift ticket sales** (☎ **909/866-5841**), the **ski school** (☎ **909/866-4546**), and a **snow report** (☎ **310/390-1498** in L.A. County).

The **Bear Mountain Ski Resort** at Big Bear Lake (☎ **909/585-2519,** or 213/683-8100 in L.A. for a snow report) is smaller than the other two, but experts flock to the double-black-diamond "Geronimo" run from the 8,805-foot Bear Peak. Natural terrain skiers and snowboarders will enjoy legal access to off-trail canyons, but the limited beginner slopes and kids' areas get pretty crowded in season. One high-speed quad express rises from the 7,140-foot base to 8,440-foot Goldmine Mountain; most runs from there are intermediate. Bear Mountain has a ski school, abundant dining facilities, and a well-stocked ski shop.

The **Snow Valley Ski Resort** in Arrowbear, midway between Arrowhead and Big Bear (☎ **800/680-SNOW** or 909/867-2751; www.aminews.com/snowvalley), has improved its snowmaking and facilities to be competitive with the other two major ski areas, and is the primary choice of skiers staying at Arrowhead. From a base elevation of 6,800 feet, Snow Valley's 13 chair lifts (including 5 triples) can take you from the beginner runs all the way up to black-diamond challenges at the 7,898-foot peak. Lift tickets cost $35 to $40 for adults; children's programs, night skiing, and lesson packages are available.

The **Big Air Snowboard Park** in Green Valley (☎ **909/867-2338**)—take Green Valley Lake Road from Arrowbear—is the answer to a snowboarder's dream. No skiers are allowed on Big Air's 50 rideable acres full of hits, bonks, spines, and more. Use the rope tow or take the high-speed chair to untouched forest full of natural hits. It offers equipment rentals, lessons, and package deals. All-day passes are $24 for adults, $18 for kids 12 and under; half-day passes are $20 and $14, respectively.

ICE-SKATING   The **Blue Jay Ice Castle,** at North Bay Road and Calif. 189 (☎ **909/33-SKATE**), near Lake Arrowhead Village, is a training site for world champion Michelle Kwan and boasts Olympic gold medalist Robin Cousins on its staff. Several public sessions each day—as well as hockey, broomball, group lessons, and book-in-advance private parties—give nonpros a chance to enjoy this impeccably groomed "outdoor" rink (it's open on three sides to the scenery and fresh air).

ORGANIZED TOURS

LAKE TOURS   The *Big Bear Queen* (☎ **909/866-3218**), a midget Mississippi-style paddlewheeler, cruises Big Bear Lake on 90-minute tours daily from late April to November. The boat departs from Big Bear Marina (at the end of Paine Avenue). Tours are $9.50 for adults, $8 for seniors 65 and older, and $5 for children 3 to 12. Call for reservations and information on the special Sunday brunch, champagne sunset, and dinner cruises. Fifty-minute tours of Lake Arrowhead are offered year-round on the *Arrowhead Queen* (☎ **909/336-6992**), a sister ship that departs hourly each day between 10am and 6pm from Lake Arrowhead Village. Tours are $9.50 for adults, $8.50 for seniors, and $6.50 for children 2 to 12. This is about the only way to really see this alpine jewel, unless you know a resident with a boat.

FOREST TOURS   **Big Bear Jeep Tours** (☎ **909/878-JEEP**) journeys into Big Bear Lake's backcountry, including historic Holcomb Valley, relic of the Gold Rush, plus the panoramic viewpoint Butler Peak. These off-road adventures range in length from 2 to 4¹/₂ hours, and cost from $38 to $80 per person. Bring your own snack though because although the guide carries ample water, the longer excursions have short but appetite-building hikes scheduled into the itinerary. Phone for reservations, particularly on weekends and holidays.

WHERE TO STAY
BIG BEAR LAKE

Vacation rentals are plentiful in the area, from cabins to condos to private homes. Some can accommodate up to 20 people and can be rented on a weekly or monthly basis. The oldest realtor, with seven area offices and a wide range of rental properties, is **Spencer Real Estate** (☎ **800/237-3725** or 909/866-7591). The **Village Reservation Service** (☎ **909/866-8583** or 909/585-5850) can arrange for everything from Jacuzzi condos to lakefront homes, or call the **Big Bear Lake Resort Association** (☎ **909/866-7000**) for information and referrals on all types of lodging.

Grey Squirrel Resort. 39372 Big Bear Blvd., Big Bear Lake, CA 92315. ☎ **909/866-4335.** Fax 909/866-6271. 18 cabins. TV TEL. $75–$95 1-bedroom cabin; $99–$125 2-bedroom cabin; $125–$275 3-bedroom cabin. Value rates available; higher rates on holidays. AE, DISC, MC, V.

This is the most attractive of the many cabin cluster–type motels near the city of Big Bear Lake, offering a wide range of rustic cabins, most with fireplace and kitchen. They're adequately, if not attractively, furnished—the appeal here is the flexibility and privacy it gives long-term or large parties. A heated pool is enclosed in winter, and there is an indoor spa, a fire pit and barbecues, volleyball and basketball courts, laundry facilities, and completely equipped kitchens. Pets are welcome for a $5 daily surcharge.

Janet Kay's Bed & Breakfast. 695 Paine Rd., Big Bear Lake, CA 92315. ☎ **800/243-7031** or 909/866-6800. 19 rms and suites. TV TEL. $59–$175 double or suite. Rates include full breakfast and afternoon tea with snacks. Winter ski and summer fun packages available. AE, DISC, MC, V.

This large, colonial-style inn within walking distance of Big Bear Lake Village is more comfortable than the standard hotel but less personal than most true B&Bs. Still, it offers a centrally located alternative and spacious, comfortable rooms each decorated to a theme (Victorian, jungle, garden, and so on). All have Jacuzzis; some have terraces and/or fireplaces.

Windy Point Inn. 39015 North Shore Dr., Fawnskin, CA 92333. ☎ **909/866-2746.** Fax 909/866-1593. 2 rms, 3 suites. $125–$225 double. Rates include full breakfast and afternoon hors d'oeuvres. AE, DISC, MC, V.

A contemporary home on the scenic north shore, the Windy Point is the only shorefront B&B in Big Bear, and two rooms have a spectacular view of the sunrise over the lake. Hosts Val and Kent Kessler's attention to detail is impeccable—if you're tired of knotty pine and Victorian frills, here's a grown-up place for you. There's an outdoor Jacuzzi, a romantic master suite, private whirlpools in two rooms, fireplaces in all units, a casual sunken living room with floor-to-ceiling windows overlooking the lake, and a custom gourmet breakfast served on the deck in summertime. The city of Big Bear Lake is only a 10-minute drive across the dam.

LAKE ARROWHEAD

There are far more private homes than tourist accommodations in Arrowhead, but rental properties abound, from cozy cottages to palatial mansions; and many can be surprisingly economical for families or other groups. Two of the largest agencies are **Arrowhead Cabin Rentals** (☎ **800/244-5138** or 909/337-2403) and **Arrowhead Mountain Resorts Rentals** (☎ **800/743-0865** or 909/337-4413). **The Forrester Homes of Lake Arrowhead** (☎ **800/587-5576** or 909/845-1004) is worth a call; they represent only six private homes but have a warm, personal touch.

Overnight guests enjoy some resident lake privileges—be sure to ask when you reserve.

Chateau du Lac. 911 Hospital Rd. (near Calif. 173), Lake Arrowhead, CA 92352. ☎ **909/337-6488.** 5 rms. TV TEL. $135–$240 double. Rates include full breakfast and afternoon tea. AE, DISC, MC, V.

The Chateau du Lac is one of the newest inns in the area. It enjoys an enviable location, directly on Lake Arrowhead about 3 miles from the village. The 6,000-square-foot clapboard, stone, and brick chateau has more than 100 windows that provide spectacular views. The best—and most expensive—room is aptly named Lake View; it features a private balcony overlooking the lake, a fireplace, beamed ceilings, and a large bathroom with a Jacuzzi and double sinks.

Lake Arrowhead Resort. 27984 Calif. 189, Lake Arrowhead, CA 92352. ☎ **800/800-6792** or 909/336-1511. Fax 909/336-1378. 177 rms and suites. A/C MINIBAR TV TEL. $119–$229 double; $299–$399 suite. Inquire about auto club discounts. AE, CB, DC, DISC, MC, V.

This sprawling resort has been upgraded somewhat since it was part of the Hilton chain, but location is still its most outstanding feature, coupled with unparalleled service and facilities. Situated on the lakeshore adjacent to Lake Arrowhead Village, the hotel has its own beach, plus docks that are ideal for fishing. The rooms are fitted with good-quality, bulk-purchased contemporary furnishings, and most have balconies, king-size beds, and fireplaces. The suites, some in private cottages, are equipped with full kitchens and whirlpool tubs.

The hotel offers a casual restaurant serving all meals (and room service), plus the elegant Seasons, which serves dinner but has only limited days off-season. Facilities include a fully equipped health club, a heated outdoor pool and whirlpool, racquetball courts, massage, and a video arcade. A full program of supervised children's activities, ranging from nature hikes to T-shirt painting, is offered on weekends year-round.

Pine Rose Cabins. 25994 Calif. 189, Twin Peaks, CA 92391. ☎ **800/429-PINE** or 909/337-2341. Fax 909/337-0258. 15 cabins. $69–$159 cabin for up to 4 people; $350 5-bedroom lodge. Ski packages offered in season. AE, DISC, MC, V.

The only place of its kind in Lake Arrowhead, Pine Rose Cabins is a good choice for families. Situated on 5 forested acres about 3 miles from the lake, the wonderful, free-standing cabins offer lots of privacy. Innkeepers Tricia and David Dufour have 15 cabins, ranging in size from romantic studios to a large five-bedroom lodge, each decorated in a different theme: The Indian cabin has a tepeelike bed; the bed in Wild Bill's cabin is covered like a wagon. One- and two-bedroom units have a fully stocked kitchen and a separate living area. There's a large heated swimming pool on the premises, plus swing sets, croquet, tetherball, and Ping-Pong.

WHERE TO DINE
BIG BEAR LAKE

Blue Whale Lakeside. 350 Alden Rd. (2 blocks east of Pine Knot Blvd.), Big Bear Lake. ☎ **909/866-5771.** Reservations recommended. Main courses $10–$22. AE, MC, V. Daily 4–9pm. SEAFOOD/STEAK.

This nautically themed restaurant has great views of Big Bear Lake from every table. Fresh fish and lobsters are delivered three times a week, and the broiled steaks and roasted poultry are imaginatively prepared. A guitar/piano combo entertains while you dine. The adjoining lounge and oyster bar serves lunch Thursday to Sunday from 11am and has its own dancing and entertainment, clambakes, and beach parties in the summer.

The Captain's Anchorage. Moonridge Way at Big Bear Blvd., Big Bear Lake. ☎ **909/866-3997.** Reservations recommended. Full dinners $10–$23. AE, MC, V. Sun–Thurs 4:30–9pm, Fri–Sat 4:30–10pm. STEAK/SEAFOOD.

Historic and rustic, this knotty-pine restaurant has been serving fine steaks, prime rib, seafood, and lobster since 1947. Inside, the dark, nautical decor and fire-warmed bar will hit the spot on blustery winter nights. It's got one of those mile-long soup-and-salad bars, plus some great early-bird and weeknight specials.

Madlon's. 829 W. Big Bear Blvd., Big Bear City. ☎ **909/585-3762.** Reservations required. Main courses $8–$16. AE, MC, V. Mon and Wed–Fri 8am–3pm and 5–9pm, Sat–Sun 8am–3pm. Winter hours may vary. AMERICAN/CONTINENTAL.

One of the few nonretro-fare dining rooms at the mountain resorts, Madlon's brings a bit of European flair to this fairy-tale cottage. A variety of creative croissant sandwiches at lunch are complemented by dinner selections like black-pepper filet mignon with mushroom-and-brandy sauce, and lemon-pepper–marinated chicken breast over pasta, all of which are prepared with a sophisticated touch.

Old Country Inn. 41126 Big Bear Blvd., Big Bear Lake. ☎ **909/866-5600.** Main courses $5–$14. AE, CB, DC, DISC, MC, V. Sun–Thurs 7am–9pm, Fri–Sat 7am–10pm. DINER/GERMAN.

The Old Country Inn has long been a favorite for hearty pre-ski breakfasts and stick-to-your-ribs Old-World dinners. The restaurant is casual and welcoming; the adjacent cocktail lounge, raucous on weekends. At breakfast enjoy German apple pancakes or colossal omelets, while salads, sandwiches, and burgers are lunch choices. At lunch or dinner feast on Wiener schnitzel, sauerbraten, and other gravy-topped German standards, along with grilled steaks and chicken.

Paoli's Italian Country Kitchen. At Pine Knot Blvd. and Village Dr., Big Bear Lake. ☎ **909/866-2020.** Pizzas $11–$17; pastas and entrees $7–$15. MC, V. Mon–Thurs 10:30am–10pm, Fri 10:30am–midnight, Sat 8am–midnight, Sun 8am–10pm. ITALIAN.

You can't beat Paoli's for authentic thin-crust pizzas, tangy antipasto, and saucy lasagnas. They've augmented their traditional menu with a few trendy touches, like pesto, primavera, and the absence of politically incorrect veal, but Paoli's will always be a checked-tablecloth/woven-Chianti-bottle kind of place. As such, it's perfect.

LAKE ARROWHEAD

Surprisingly for an affluent residential community, there aren't many dining options around Lake Arrowhead. But not surprisingly, what there is tends to run to pricey elegance—elegant for a rustic mountain resort, that is. Although there is both a California/Continental restaurant and a casual family eatery in the Lake Arrowhead Resort (see "Where to Stay," above), you might want to venture out to some of the locals' choices. These include the **Chef's Inn & Tavern,** 29020 Oak Terrace, Cedar Glen (☎ 909/336-4488), a moderate to expensive continental restaurant in a turn-of-the-century former bordello; the **Antler's Inn,** 26125 Calif. 189, Twin Peaks (☎ 909/337-4020), serving prime rib, seafood, and buffalo in a historic log lodge; the **Royal Oak,** 27187 Calif. 189, Blue Jay Village (☎ **909/337-6018**), an expensive American/Continental steak house with a pub; and **Belgian Waffle Works,** dockside at Lake Arrowhead Village (☎ **909/337-5222**), an inexpensive coffee shop with Victorian decor, known for its generous, crispy waffles with tasty toppings.

4 Disneyland & Other Anaheim Area Attractions

27 miles SE of downtown Los Angeles

The sleepy Orange County town of Anaheim grew up around Disneyland, the West's most famous theme park. Now, even beyond this Happiest Place on Earth, the city and its neighboring communities are kid-central: Otherwise unspectacular, sprawling suburbs have become a playground of family-oriented hotels, restaurants, and unabashedly tourist-oriented attractions. Among the nearby draws are Knott's Berry Farm, another family-oriented theme park, in nearby Buena Park. At the other end of the scale is the Richard Nixon Library and Birthplace, a surprisingly compelling presidential library and museum, just 7 miles northeast of Disneyland in Yorba Linda.

ESSENTIALS

GETTING THERE   **Los Angeles International Airport (LAX)** is located about 30 minutes from Anaheim via I-5 south (see section 1 in chapter 13). If you're heading directly to Anaheim and want to avoid L.A. altogether, try to land at the **John Wayne International Airport** in Irvine (☎ 714/252-5200), Orange County's largest airport. It's about 15 miles from Disneyland. The airport is served by **Alaska, American, Continental, Delta, Northwest, TWA,** and **United** airlines. Check to see if your hotel has a free shuttle to and from either airport, or call one of the following commercial shuttle services (fares are generally $10 one-way from John Wayne): **L.A. Xpress** (☎ **800/I-ARRIVE**); **Prime Time** (☎ **800/262-7433**); or **SuperShuttle** (☎ **714/517-6600**). Car-rental agencies located at the John Wayne Airport include **Budget** (☎ **800/221-1203**) and **Hertz** (☎ **800/654-3131**).

VISITOR INFORMATION The **Anaheim/Orange County Visitor and Convention Bureau,** at 800 W. Katella Ave. (P.O. Box 4270), Anaheim, CA 92803 (☎ **714/999-8999**), can fill you in on area activities and shopping shuttles. It's located just inside the Convention Center (across the street from Disneyland), next to the dramatic cantilevered arena, and welcomes visitors Monday to Friday from 8:30am to 5:30pm. The **Buena Park Convention and Visitors Office,** 6280 Manchester Blvd., Suite 103 (☎ **800/541-3953** or 714/562-3560), will provide specialized information on its area, including Knott's Berry Farm.

DISNEYLAND

Disney was the originator of the mega-theme park. Opened in 1955, Disneyland remains unsurpassed. Despite constant threats from pretenders to the crown, Disneyland and its sibling park, Walt Disney World outside Orlando, Florida, remain the kings of the theme parks. At no other park is fantasy elevated to an art form. Nowhere else is as fresh and fantastic every time you walk through the gates, whether you're 6 or 60—and no matter how many times you've done it before. There's nothing like Disney Magic.

NEW & NOTEWORTHY The park stays on the cutting edge by continually updating and expanding, while still maintaining the hallmarks that make it the world's top amusement park (a term coined by Walt Disney himself). Look for the most recent Disney additions during your visit—1995's **Indiana Jones Adventure** is a high-tech thrill that's not to be missed, no matter how long the wait. It was lights out in 1996 for the beloved Main Street Electrical Parade's 24-year run; **Light Magic,** a new nighttime spectacular featuring enchanted pixies and larger-than-life fiber-optic and video light displays, premiered in its place in 1997. Also look for live-action musical extravaganzas based on Disney's most recent animated features, *Pocahontas, The Hunchback of Notre Dame,* and *Hercules.*

And keep your eyes open as Disney prepares to round the century mark—work has already begun on a new, separate sister park and great big hotel/resort that will debut in 2001 adjacent to Disneyland. Until then, related construction obstructions are likely to add time and frustration to your park experience, so be prepared.

ESSENTIALS

GETTING THERE Disneyland is located at 1313 Harbor Blvd. in Anaheim. It's about an hour's drive from downtown Los Angeles. Take I-5 south to the well-marked Harbor Boulevard exit.

ADMISSION, HOURS & INFORMATION Admission to the park, including unlimited rides and all festivities and entertainment, is $36 for adults and children 12 and over, $32 for seniors 60 and over, and $26 for children 3 to 11; children under 3 enter free. Parking is $6. Also, 2- and 3-day passes are available; in addition, some area accommodations offer lodging packages that include 1 or more days' park admission.

Disneyland is open every day of the year, but operating hours vary, so we recommend that you call for information that applies to the specific day(s) of your visit

Disneyland

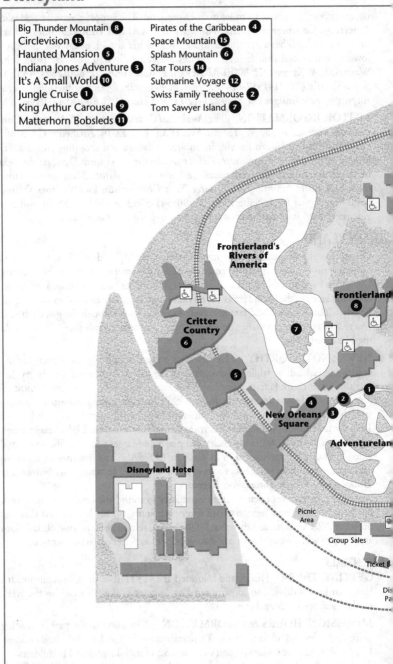

Frontierland's
Rivers of
America

Frontierland
8

Critter
Country
6

7

5

4

New Orleans
Square

3

2

1

Adventureland

Disneyland Hotel

Picnic
Area

Group Sales

Ticket B

Dis
Pa

1-0853

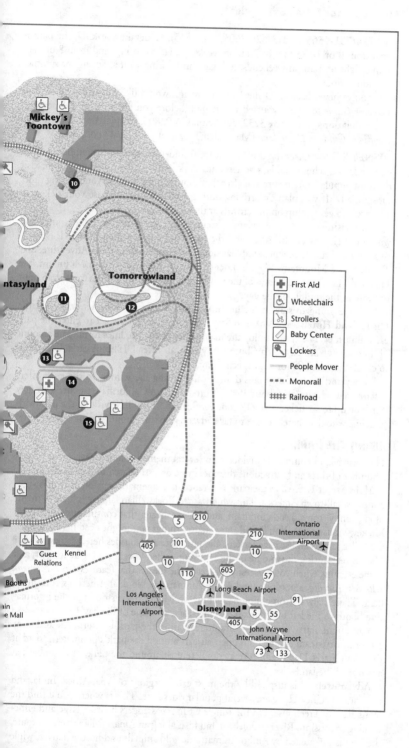

Mickey's Toontown

10

Tomorrowland

...ntasyland

11

12

13

14

15

Guest Relations   Kennel

...Booths

...ain ...e Mall

	First Aid
	Wheelchairs
	Strollers
	Baby Center
	Lockers
	People Mover
	Monorail
	Railroad

5   210

405   101   210

210   10   Ontario International Airport

1   10   605   57

110   710   Long Beach Airport

Los Angeles International Airport   91

Disneyland   5   55

405   John Wayne International Airport

73   133

(☎ **714/781-4565** or 213/626-8605, ext. 4565). Generally speaking, the park is open from 9 or 10am to 6 or 7pm on weekdays, fall to spring; and from 8 or 9am to midnight or 1am on weekends, holidays, and during winter, spring, or summer vacation periods.

If you've never been to Disneyland before and would like to get a copy of their *Souvenir Guide* to orient yourself to the park before you go, write to **Disneyland Guest Relations,** P.O. Box 3232, Anaheim, CA 92803. Or pick up a copy of *The Unofficial Guide to Disneyland* (Macmillan Travel) at your local bookstore.

DISNEY TIPS Disneyland is busiest from mid-June to mid-September, and on weekends and school holidays year-round. Peak hours are from noon to 5pm; visit the most popular rides before and after these hours, and you'll cut your waiting times substantially. If you plan on arriving during a busy time, purchase your tickets in advance and get a jump on the crowds at the ticket counters.

Many visitors tackle Disneyland systematically, beginning at the entrance and working their way clockwise around the park. But a better **plan of attack** is to arrive early and run to the most popular rides first—the Indiana Jones Adventure, Star Tours, Space Mountain, Big Thunder Mountain Railroad, Splash Mountain, the Haunted Mansion, and Pirates of the Caribbean. Lines for these rides can last an hour or more in the middle of the day.

If you're going to stay in Anaheim, you might want to consider staying at the **Disneyland Hotel;** see "Where to Stay," below. Hotel guests get to enter the park early almost every day and enjoy the major rides before the lines form. The amount of time varies from day to day, but usually you can enter 1 1/2 hours early. Call ahead to check the schedule for your specific day.

Disneyland's attendance falls dramatically during the winter, so the park offers **discounted admission** (about 25% off) to Southern California residents who may purchase up to six tickets per ZIP code verification. If you'll be visiting the park with someone who lives here, be sure to take advantage of this money-saving opportunity.

TOURING THE PARK

The Disneyland complex is divided into several themed "lands," each of which has a number of rides and attractions that are, more or less, related to that land's theme.

Main Street U.S.A., at the park's entrance, is a cinematic version of turn-of-the-century small-town America. This whitewashed Rockwellian fantasy is lined with gift shops, candy stores, a soda fountain, and a silent theater that continuously runs early Mickey Mouse films. You'll find the practical things you might need here too, such as stroller rentals and storage lockers. Because there are no rides here, it's best to tour Main Street during the middle of the afternoon, when lines for rides are longest, and in the evening, when you can rest your feet in the theater that features *Great Moments with Mr. Lincoln,* a patriotic (and Audio-Animatronic) look at America's 16th president. There's always something happening on Main Street; stop in at the information booth to the left of the main entrance for a schedule of the day's events.

You might start your day by circumnavigating the park by train. An authentic 19th-century steam engine pulls open-air cars around the park's perimeter. Board at the Main Street Depot and take a complete turn around the park, or disembark at any one of the lands.

Adventureland is inspired by the most exotic regions of Asia, Africa, India, and the South Pacific. There are several popular rides here. This is where you'll find the Swiss Family Treehouse. On the Jungle Cruise, passengers board a large authentic-looking Mississippi River paddleboat and float along an Amazon-like river. En route, the boat is threatened by Audio-Animatronic wild animals and hostile natives, while

Disney Dossier

Believe it or not, the Happiest Place on Earth keeps more than a few skeletons—as well as some just plain interesting facts—in its closet. Did you know that:

• Disneyland was carved out of orange groves, and the original plans called for carefully chosen individual trees to be left standing and included in the park's landscaping. On groundbreaking day, July 21, 1954, each tree in the orchard was marked with a ribbon—red to be cut and green to be spared. But the bulldozer operator went through and mowed down *every* tree indiscriminately . . . no one had foreseen his color-blindness.

• Disneyland designers utilized forced perspective in the construction of many of the park's structures to give the illusion of height and dramatic proportions while keeping the park a manageable size. The buildings on **Main Street U.S.A.,** for example, are actually 90% scale on the first floor, 80% on the second, and so forth. The stones on Sleeping Beauty Castle are carved in diminishing scale from the bottom to the top, giving it the illusion of towering height.

• The faces of the **Pirates of the Caribbean** were modeled after some of the early staff of Walt Disney Imagineering, who also lent their names to the second-floor "businesses" along Main Street U.S.A.

• Walt Disney maintained two apartments inside Disneyland. His private apartment above the **Town Square Fire Station** has been kept just as it was when he lived there.

• The elaborately carved horses on Fantasyland's **King Arthur Carousel** are between 100 and 120 years old; Walt Disney found them lying neglected in storage at Coney Island in New York and brought them home to be carefully cleaned and restored.

• **It's a Small World** was touted at its opening as "mingling the waters of the oceans and seas around the world with Small World's Seven Seaways." This was more than a publicity hoax—records from that time show such charges as $21.86 for a shipment of sea water from the Caribbean.

• The peaceful demeanor of Disneyland was broken during the summer of 1970 by a group of radical Vietnam protesters who invaded the park. They seized **Tom Sawyer Island** and raised the Viet Cong flag over the fort before being expelled by riot specialists.

• **Indiana Jones: Temple of the Forbidden Eye,** Disneyland's newest thrill ride, won't be experienced the same way by any two groups of riders. Like a sophisticated computer game, the course is programmed with so many variables in the action there are 160,000 possible combinations of events.

• After the 24-year run of the enormously popular **Main Street Electrical Parade** ended in 1996, 700,000 of the floats' light bulbs were sold, at $10 a piece, with the benefits going to several local charities.

a tour guide entertains with a running patter. A spear's throw away is the Enchanted Tiki Room, one of the most sedate attractions in Adventureland. Inside, you can sit down and watch a 20-minute musical comedy featuring electronically animated tropical birds, flowers, and "tiki gods."

The Indiana Jones Adventure is Adventureland's newest ride. Based on the Steven Spielberg series of films, this ride takes adventurers into the Temple of the Forbidden Eye, in joltingly realistic all-terrain vehicles. Riders follow Indy and experience the perils of bubbling lava pits, whizzing arrows, fire-breathing serpents, collapsing bridges, and the familiar cinematic tumbling boulder (this effect is *very* realistic in the front seats!). Disney "imagineers" reached new heights with the design of this ride's line which—take my word for it—has so much detail throughout its twisting path that a half-hour or more simply flies by.

New Orleans Square, a large, grassy, gas lamp–dotted green, is home to the Haunted Mansion, the most high-tech ghost house we've ever seen. The spookiness has been toned down so kids won't get nightmares anymore, so the events inside are as funny as they are scary. Even more fanciful is Pirates of the Caribbean, one of Disneyland's most popular rides. Here, visitors float on boats through mock underground caves, entering an enchanting world of swashbuckling, rum-running, and buried treasure. Even in the middle of the afternoon you can dine by the cool moonlight and to the sound of crickets in the Blue Bayou Restaurant, the best eatery in the land.

Critter Country is supposed to be an ode to the backwoods—a sort of Frontierland without those pesky settlers. Little kids like to sing along with the Audio-Animatronic critters in the musical Country Bear Jamboree show. Older kids and grown-ups head straight for Splash Mountain, one of the largest water flume rides in the world. Loosely based on the Disney movie *Song of the South,* the ride is lined with about 100 characters who won't stop singing "Zip-A-Dee-Doo-Dah." Be prepared to get wet, especially if someone sizable is in the front seat of your log-shaped boat.

Frontierland gets its inspiration from 19th-century America. It's full of dense "forests" and broad "rivers" inhabited by hearty-looking (but, luckily, not-smelling) "pioneers." You can take a raft to Tom Sawyer's Island, a do-it-yourself play island with balancing rocks, caves, and a rope bridge, and board the Big Thunder Mountain Railroad, a runaway roller coaster that races through a deserted 1870s gold mine. You'll also find a petting zoo and an Abe Lincoln–style log cabin here; both are great for exploring with the little ones.

On Saturdays, Sundays, holidays, and vacation periods, head to Frontierland's Rivers of America after dark to see the FANTASMIC! show—a mix of magic, music, live performers, and sensational special effects. Just as he did in *The Sorcerer's Apprentice,* Mickey Mouse appears and uses his magical powers to create giant water fountains, enormous flowers, and fantasy creatures. There's plenty of pyrotechnics, lasers, and fog, as well as a 45-foot-tall dragon that breathes fire and sets the water of the Rivers of America aflame. Cool!

Mickey's Toontown is a colorful, wacky, whimsical world inspired by the *Roger Rabbit* films. This is a gag-filled land populated by toons. There are several rides here, including Roger Rabbit's CarToonSpin, but these take a backseat to Toontown itself—a trippy smile-inducing world without a straight line or right angle in sight. This is a great place to talk with Mickey, Minnie, Goofy, Roger Rabbit, and the rest of your favorite toons. You can even visit their "houses" here. Mickey's red-shingled house and movie barn is filled with props from some of his greatest cartoons.

Fantasyland has a storybook theme and is the catch-all "land" for all the stuff that doesn't quite seem to fit anywhere else. Most of the rides here are geared to the under-6 set, including the King Arthur Carousel, Dumbo the Flying Elephant ride, and the Casey Jr. Circus Train, but some, like Mr. Toad's Wild Ride and Peter Pan's Flight, grown-ups have an irrational attachment to as well. You'll also find Alice in Wonderland, Snow White's Scary Adventures, Pinocchio's Daring Journey, and more in Fantasyland. The most lauded attraction is It's a Small World, a slow-moving indoor river ride through a saccharine nightmare of all the world's children singing the song everybody loves to hate. For a different kind of thrill, try the Matterhorn Bobsleds, a zippy roller coaster through chilled caverns and drifting fog banks. It's one of the park's most popular rides.

Tomorrowland, conceived as an optimistic look at the future, has always had a hard time keeping a jump on real advances. 1955's "Rocket to the Moon" became "Mission to Mars" in 1975, only to be a dated laughingstock by the early '80s. In 1997, Disney architects are redesigning Tomorrowland with a vengeance, employing an angular, metallic look popularized by futurists like Jules Verne. During the transformation, scheduled to be completed in Spring 1998, two of Disneyland's most popular attractions in Tomorrowland will remain up and running; Space Mountain, a pitch-black indoor roller coaster which assaults your equilibrium and ears, is a modern cousin to the classic coaster experience. Star Tours, the original Disney/George Lucas joint venture, is a 40-passenger StarSpeeder that encounters a spaceload of misadventures on the way to the Moon of Endor, achieved with wired seats and video effects (not for the queasy); the line can last an hour or more, but it's worth the wait. New attractions in the works include a 3-D adventure called "Honey, I Shrunk the Audience," which promises, using a variety of theatrical effects, to impart the sensation that you've shrunk to thumbnail size; and an interactive pavilion of near-future technology called "Innoventions"—this one sounds much closer to what old Walt originally envisioned for Tomorrowland, when he created exhibits like the "House of the Future" and "Bathroom of Tomorrow" that showcased imaginative technology of the day.

The "lands" themselves are only half the adventure. Other joys include roaming Disney characters, penny arcades, restaurants and snack bars galore, summer fireworks, mariachi and ragtime bands, parades, shops, marching bands, and much more. Oh, yeah—there's also the storybook Sleeping Beauty Castle . . . can you spot the evil witch peering from one of the top windows?

KNOTT'S BERRY FARM

Cynics say that Knott's Berry Farm is for people who aren't smart enough to find Disneyland. Well, there's no doubt that visitors should tour Disney first, but it's worth staying in a hotel nearby so you can play at Knott's during your stay.

Like Disneyland, Knott's Berry Farm is not without its historical merit. Rudolph Boysen crossed a loganberry with a raspberry, calling the resulting hybrid the "boysenberry." In 1933 Buena Park farmer Walter Knott planted the boysenberry, thus launching Knott's berry farm on 10 acres of leased land. When things got tough during the Great Depression, Mrs. Knott set up a roadside stand, selling pies, preserves, and home-cooked chicken dinners. Within a year she was selling 90 meals a day. Lines became so long that Walter decided to create an Old West Ghost Town as a diversion for waiting customers.

The Knott family now owns the farm that surrounds the world-famous Chicken Dinner Restaurant, an eatery serving over a million fried meals a year. And Knott's Berry Farm is the nation's third-most-attended family entertainment complex (after the two Disney parks, of course).

During the last half of October locals flock to Knott's Berry Farm. Why? Because the entire park is revamped as "Knott's *Scary* Farm"—the ordinary attractions are made spooky and haunted, every grassy area is transformed into a graveyard or gallows, and even the already-scary rides get special surprise extras, like costumed ghouls who grab your arm in the middle of a roller-coaster ride!

ESSENTIALS

GETTING THERE   Knott's Berry Farm is located at 8039 Beach Blvd. in Buena Park. It's about a 5-minute ride north on I-5 from Disneyland. From I-5 or Calif. 91, exit south onto Beach Boulevard. The park is located about half a mile south of Calif. 91.

ADMISSION, HOURS & INFORMATION   Admission to the park, including unlimited access to all rides, shows, and attractions, is $29 for adults and children 12 and over, $19 for seniors 60 and over and children 3 to 11, and free for children under 3. Admission is $14 for everyone after 4pm. Like Disneyland, Knott's offers discounted admission during off-season for Southern California residents, so if you're bringing local friends or family members along, be sure to take advantage of the bargain. Also like Disneyland, Knott's Berry Farm's hours vary from week to week, so you should call about the day you plan to visit. Generally speaking, the park is open during the summer every day from 9am to midnight. The rest of the year, it opens at 10am and closes at 6 or 8pm, except Saturday when it stays open till 10pm. Knott's is closed Christmas Day. Special hours and prices are in effect during Knott's Scary Farm in late October. For recorded information, call ☎ 714/220-5200.

TOURING THE PARK

Knott's Berry Farm still maintains its original Old West motif. It's divided into five "Old Time Adventures" areas:

Old West Ghost Town, the original attraction, is a collection of refurbished 19th-century buildings that have been relocated from actual deserted Old West towns. Here, you can pan for gold, ride aboard an authentic stagecoach, ride rickety train cars through the Calico Mine, get held up aboard the Denver and Rio Grande Calico Railroad, and hiss at the villain during a melodrama in the Birdcage Theater.

Fiesta Village has a south-of-the-border theme that means festive markets, strolling mariachis, and wild rides like Montezooma's Revenge and Jaguar!, a roller coaster that includes two heart-in-the-mouth drops and a loop that turns you upside down.

The Roaring '20s Amusement Area contains Sky Tower, a parachute jump/drop with a 20-story free-fall. Other white-knuckle rides include XK-1, an excellent flight simulator "piloted" by the riders; and Boomerang, a state-of-the-art roller coaster that turns riders upside down six times in less than a minute. Kingdom of the Dinosaurs features extremely realistic *Jurassic Park*–like creatures. It's quite a thrill, but it may scare the little kids.

Wild Water Wilderness is a $10-million, 3½-acre attraction styled like a turn-of-the-century California wilderness park. The top ride here is a white-water adventure called Bigfoot Rapids, featuring a long stretch of artificial rapids; it's the longest ride of its kind in the world.

Camp Snoopy will probably be the youngsters' favorite area. It's meant to re-create a wilderness camp in the picturesque High Sierra. Its 6 rustic acres are the playgrounds of Charles Schulz's beloved beagle and his pals, Charlie Brown and Lucy, who greet guests and pose for pictures. The rides here, including Beary Tales Playhouse, are tailor-made for the 6-and-under set.

Thunder Falls contains Mystery Lodge, a truly amazing high-tech, trick-of-the-eye attraction based on the legends of local Native Americans. Don't miss this wonderful theater piece.

The Boardwalk is Knott's newest themed area, presented as a salute to Southern California's beach culture—it's main attraction is Windjammer, a wind-whipping dual roller coaster originally intended to evoke the flips and glides of windsurfing, but often advertised as a twister tornado.

Stage shows and special activities are scheduled throughout the day. Pick up a schedule at the ticket booth.

ATTRACTIONS BEYOND THE THEME PARKS

To locate these attractions, see the map on p. 543.

Crystal Cathedral. 12141 Lewis St., Garden Grove. ☎ **714/971-4000.**

This angular, mirror-sheathed church (think the movie Superman's Fortress of Solitude), otherwise known as the Garden Grove Community Church, is a shocking architectural oddity, with nine-story-high doors and a vast, open interior that's shaped like a four-pointed star. Opened in 1980, it's the pulpit for televangelist Robert Schuller, who broadcasts sermons and hymns of praise on radio and TV to an international audience of millions. Each Sunday an overflow crowd listens to the service blaring from loudspeakers into the parking lot. Annual Christmas and Easter pageants feature live animals, floating "angels," and other theatrics. A $5-million stainless-steel carillon, which began ringing in 1991, has prompted some of the cathedral's neighbors to complain that they want less joyful noise and more peace on earth.

Medieval Times Dinner and Tournament. 7662 Beach Blvd., Buena Park. ☎ **800/ 899-6600** or 714/521-4740. Admission $34–$36 adults, $23 children 12 and under. Shows Mon–Thurs at 7pm, Fri at 6:30 and 8:45pm, Sat at 6 and 8:15pm, Sun at 5 and 7:15pm. Call for reservations (be sure to inquire about auto-club discounts).

Guests crowd around long wooden tables and enjoy a four-course banquet of roast chicken, ribs, herbed potatoes, and pastries—all eaten with your hands in medieval fashion, of course, just like Jim Carrey and Matthew Broderick in *The Cable Guy.* More than 1,100 people can fit into the castle, where sword fights, jousting tournaments, and various feats of skill are performed by colorfully costumed actors, including fake knights on real horses. It's kind of ridiculous, but kids of all ages love it. *A word of warning:* The horses (and horseplay) kick up lots of dirt, so if you have any allergies to dust or animal dander, keep an eye on the nearest exit.

Movieland Wax Museum. 7711 Beach Blvd. (Calif. 39), Buena Park. ☎ **714/522-1155.** Admission $12.95 adults, $10.55 seniors, $6.95 children 4–11, free for children 3 and under. Daily 9am–7pm. Discount combination admission includes Ripley's Believe It Or Not! Museum (across the street).

At this goofy museum, located 1 block north of Knott's Berry Farm in Buena Park, you can see wax-molded figures of all your favorite film stars, from Marilyn Monroe in *Gentlemen Prefer Blondes* to Leslie Nielsen in the *Naked Gun* movies. "America's Sweetheart," Mary Pickford, dedicated the museum on May 4, 1962; it has risen steadily in popularity ever since, with new stars added yearly, taking their place next to the time-tested favorites. The museum was created by film addict Allen Parkinson, who saw to it that some of the most memorable scenes in motion pictures were re-created in exacting detail in wax. In the seemingly unrelated Chamber of Horrors, you almost expect the torture victims to scream "tourist trap!"

Richard Nixon Library and Birthplace. 18001 Yorba Linda Blvd., Yorba Linda. ☎ **714/ 993-5075.** Fax 714/993-3393. Admission $5.95 adults, $3.95 seniors, $2 children 8–11, free for children 7 and under. Mon–Sat 10am–5pm, Sun 11am–5pm.

Although he was the most vilified U.S. President in modern history, there has always been a warm place in the hearts of Orange County locals for Richard Nixon. This presidential library, located in Nixon's boyhood town, celebrates the roots, life, and legacy of America's 37th President. The 9-acre site contains the modest farmhouse where Nixon was born, manicured flower gardens, a modern museum containing presidential archives, and the final resting place of both Nixon and his wife, Pat.

Displays include videos of the famous Nixon-Kennedy TV debates, an impressive life-size statuary summit of world leaders, gifts of state (including a gun from Elvis), and exhibits on China and Russia. There's also an exhibit of Pat Nixon's sparkling First Lady gowns and a 12-foot-high graffiti-covered chunk of the Berlin Wall, symbolizing the defeat of Communism, but hardly a mention of Nixon's leading role in the anti-Communist witch hunts of the 1950s. There are exhibits on Vietnam, yet no mention of Nixon's illegal expansion of that war into neighboring Cambodia. Only the Watergate Gallery is relatively forthright, where visitors can listen to actual White House tapes and view a montage of the president's last day in the White House.

WHERE TO STAY

EXPENSIVE

✪ Disneyland Hotel. 1150 W. Cerritos Ave. (west of the Disneyland parking lot), Anaheim, CA 92802. ☎ **714/778-6600.** Fax 714/965-6597. 1,136 rms, 62 suites. A/C MINIBAR TV TEL. $175–$270 double; from $425 suite. AE, MC, V. Parking $10.

The "Official Hotel of the Magic Kingdom," attached to Disneyland via a monorail system that runs right to the hotel, is the perfect place to stay if you're doing the park. You'll be able to return to your room anytime you need to during the day, whether it's to take a much-needed nap or to change your soaked shorts after your Splash Mountain Adventure. Best of all, hotel guests get to enter the park early almost every day and enjoy the major rides before the lines form. The amount of time varies from day to day, but usually you can enter 1 1/2 hours early. Call ahead to check the schedule for your specific day.

The theme hotel is a wild attraction unto itself. The rooms aren't fancy, but they're comfortably and attractively furnished like a good-quality business hotel. Many rooms feature framed reproductions of rare Disney conceptual art, and the Disney Channel is free on TV, naturally. The beautifully landscaped hotel is an all-inclusive resort, offering six restaurants, five cocktail lounges, every kind of service desk imaginable, a "wharfside" bazaar, a walk-under waterfall, and even an artificial white-sand beach. The complex also includes the adjoining Pacific Hotel, which offers a Disney version of Asian tranquility (including a fine and pricey Japanese restaurant.)

When you're planning your trip, inquire about multiday packages that allow you to take on the park at your own pace and usually include free parking for the duration of your stay.

Dining/Entertainment: The best restaurant is Stromboli's, an Italian/American eatery that serves all the pasta staples. Kids love Goofy's Kitchen, where the family can enjoy breakfast and dinner with the Disney characters.

Services: Concierge, room service, laundry, nightly turndown, baby-sitting, express checkout, shoe shine.

Facilities: Three large heated outdoor pools, complete health club, sundeck, shuffleboard and croquet courts, putting green, special children's programs, beauty salon, 20 shops.

Sheraton Anaheim Hotel. 1015 W. Ball Rd. (at I-5), Anaheim, CA 92802. ☎ **800/325-3535** or 714/778-1700. Fax 714/535-3889. 500 rms, 26 suites. A/C MINIBAR TV TEL. $170–$190 double; $290–$360 suite. AE, CB, DC, MC, V. Free parking; shuttle to Disneyland.

This hotel rises to the festive theme-park occasion with its fanciful English Tudor architecture, a castle that lures business conventions, Disney-bound families, and area high-school proms equally successfully. The public areas are quiet and elegant, and you'll find intimate gardens with fountains and koi ponds—a pleasing touch after a frantic day at the amusement park. The rooms are modern and unusually spacious, but otherwise not distinctive; a large swimming pool is located in the center of the complex, surrounded by attractive landscaping. Don't be put off by the high rack rates; rooms more commonly go for $100 to $130, even on busy summer weekends.

Dining/Entertainment: The Garden Court Bistro offers indoor and outdoor ambiance, while the California Deli is open from 6am to midnight and serves standard delicatessen fare. There's also a wood and tapestry cocktail lounge.

Services: Concierge, room service, laundry service, nightly turndown, overnight shoe shine.

Facilities: Heated outdoor pool, sundeck, gift shop.

MODERATE

Anaheim Plaza Hotel. 1700 S. Harbor Blvd., Anaheim, CA 92802. ☎ **800/228-1357** or 714/772-5900. Fax 714/772-8386. 300 rms and suites. A/C TV TEL. $79–$119 double; from $175 suite. AE, DC, DISC, MC, V. Free parking; shuttle to Disneyland.

You can easily cross the street to Disneyland's main gate, or you can take advantage of the Anaheim Plaza's free shuttle to the park. Once you return, you'll appreciate the way this 30-year-old hotel's clever design shuts out the noisy world. In fact, the seven 2-story garden buildings remind me of 1960s Waikiki more than busy Anaheim. The Olympic-size heated outdoor pool and whirlpool are unfortunately surrounded by Astroturf, but the new management was halfway through a total room renovation in 1997, so there's always hope. They won't change a thing about the light-filled modern lobby, nor the friendly rates, which can often drop as low as $49. There's room service from the casual cafe in the lobby, plus valet service and coin-operated laundry.

Buena Park Hotel. 7675 Crescent Ave. (at Grand), Buena Park, CA 90620. ☎ **800/422-4444** or 714/995-1111. Fax 714/828-8590. 350 rms and suites. A/C TV TEL. $99–$109 double; $175–$250 suite. AE, DC, DISC, MC, V. Free parking; shuttle to Disneyland.

Within easy walking distance of Knott's Berry Farm, the Buena Park Hotel also offers a free shuttle to Disneyland just 7 miles away. The pristine lobby has the look of a business-oriented hotel, and that it is. But vacationers can also benefit from the elevated level of service designed for the business traveler. Be sure to inquire about Executive Club rates as well as Knott's or Disneyland package deals. The rooms in the 9-story tower are tastefully decorated, and facilities and services include room service, a charming heated outdoor pool and spa, two restaurants and a 1950s-1960s dance club, and rental-car desk.

Candy Cane Inn. 1747 S. Harbor Blvd., Anaheim, CA 92802. ☎ **800/345-7057** or 714/774-5284. Fax 714/772-5462. 173 rms. A/C TV TEL. $74–$95 double. Rates include expanded continental breakfast. AE, DC, DISC, MC, V. Free parking; shuttle to Disneyland.

Take your standard U-shaped motel court with outdoor corridors, spruce it up with cobblestone drive- and walkways, old-time street lamps, and flowering vines engulfing the balconies of attractively painted rooms, and you have the Candy Cane. The face-lift worked, making this motel near Disneyland's main gate a real treat for the stylish bargain hunter. The guest rooms are decorated in bright floral motifs with comfortable furnishings, including queen beds and a separate dressing and vanity area. Complimentary breakfast is served in the courtyard, where you can also splash around in a heated pool, spa, or kids' wading pool.

Howard Johnson Hotel. 1380 S. Harbor Blvd., Anaheim, CA 92802. ☎ **800/422-4228** or 714/776-6120. Fax 714/533-3578. 320 rms. A/C TV TEL. $74–$94 double. AE, CB, DC, DISC, MC, V. Free parking.

This hotel occupies an enviable location, directly opposite Disneyland, and a cute San Francisco trolley car runs to and from the park every 30 minutes. The rooms are divided among several low-profile buildings, all with balconies opening onto a central garden with two heated pools for adults and one for children. Garden paths lead under eucalyptus and olive trees to a splashing circular fountain. During the summer you can see the nightly fireworks display at Disneyland from the upper balconies of the parkside rooms. Try to avoid the rooms in the back buildings, for they get some freeway noise. Services and facilities include in-room movies and cable, room service from the attached Coco's Restaurant, gift shop, games room, laundry service plus coin-laundry room, airport shuttle, and family lodging/Disney admission packages. We think it's pretty classy for a HoJo's.

Jolly Roger Hotel. 640 W. Katella Ave. (west of Harbor Blvd.), Anaheim, CA 92802. ☎ **800/446-1555** or 714/772-7621. Fax 714/772-2308. 225 rms, 11 suites. A/C TV TEL. $75–$118 double; $98–$200 suite. AE, DC, DISC, MC, V. Free parking; shuttle to Disneyland.

The only thing still sporting a buccaneer theme here is the adjoining Jolly Roger Restaurant, and that's just fine. The comfortable but blandly furnished rooms are in either an older, 2-story L-shaped motel or two newer 5-story annexes. We prefer the older units for their quiet and also for the palm-shaded heated pool in the center of it all. Across the driveway is the swashbuckling restaurant where dinner will set you back a few doubloons. The all-day coffee shop is more reasonable, and there's nightly entertainment and dancing in the lounge. Conveniently located across the street from Disneyland, the Jolly Roger also has meeting and banquet rooms, plus a second pool, a spa, beauty salon, and gift shop.

WestCoast Anaheim Hotel. 1855 S. Harbor Blvd. (south of Katella Ave.), Anaheim, CA 92802. ☎ **800/421-6662** or 714/750-1811. Fax 714/971-3626. 500 rms. A/C TV TEL. $150 double. AE, DC, DISC, MC, V. Parking $8; free shuttle to Disneyland.

Although the inn is in the Anaheim Convention Center Complex (across the street from Disneyland) and draws primarily a business crowd, there's much to appeal to the leisure traveler. The contemporary and comfortable rooms in the 12-story tower all have balconies overlooking either Disneyland or the hotel's luxurious pool area, which includes a large heated pool, deluxe spa, attractive sundeck, and snack/cocktail-bar gazebo. The hotel offers guest laundry and valet, an activities desk, room service, and a gift shop, plus an Old West frontier-themed restaurant serving up steak and seafood plus a few colorful game selections.

INEXPENSIVE

Best Western Anaheim Stardust. 1057 W. Ball Rd., Anaheim, CA 92802. ☎ **800/222-3639** or 714/774-7600. Fax 714/535-6953. 103 rms, 18 suites. A/C TV TEL. $70–$85 double; $105 family room. Rates include full breakfast. AE, DC, DISC, MC, V. Free parking.

Located on the back side of Disneyland, this modest hotel will appeal to the budget-conscious traveler who isn't willing to sacrifice everything. All rooms have a refrigerator and microwave, breakfast is served in a refurbished train dining car, and you can relax by the large outdoor heated pool and spa while doing wash in the laundry room. The extra-large family rooms will accommodate virtually any brood, and shuttles run regularly to the park.

Colony Inn. 7800 Crescent Ave. (west of Beach Blvd.), Buena Park, CA 90620. ☎ **800/98-COLONY** or 714/527-2201. Fax 714/826-3826. 130 rms and suites. A/C TV TEL. $49–$98 double or suite. AE, MC, V. Free parking.

Although it's composed of two modest U-shaped motels, the recently refurbished Colony Inn has a lot to offer. It's the closest lodging to Knott's Berry Farm's south entrance and is just 10 minutes away from Disneyland. They cheerfully offer discount coupons for Knott's and other nearby attractions, as well as complimentary coffee and doughnuts to jump-start your morning. The rooms are spacious (doubles sleep up to four people, and suites sleep up to eight) and comfortably outfitted with conservatively styled furnishings. There are two pools, two wading pools for kids, two saunas, and a coin-operated laundry on the premises.

WHERE TO DINE

Inland Orange County isn't known for its restaurants, most of which are branches of reliable California or national chains. We've listed a few intriguing options, but if you're visiting the area just for the day, you'll probably eat inside the theme parks; there are plenty of restaurants to choose from at both Disneyland and Knott's Berry Farm. At Disneyland, in the Créole-themed **Blue Bayou,** you can sit under the stars inside the Pirates of the Caribbean ride—no matter what time of day it is. At Knott's, try the fried chicken dinners and boysenberry pies at Mrs. Knott's historic **Chicken Dinner Restaurant.** For the most unusual dinner you've ever had, go to **Medieval Times** (see "Attractions Beyond the Theme Parks," above).

EXPENSIVE

Chanteclair. 18912 MacArthur Blvd. (opposite John Wayne Airport), Irvine. ☎ **714/752-8001.** Reservations required. Main courses $15–$24. AE, CB, DC, MC, V. Mon–Fri 11am–3pm and 6–11pm, Sat 6–11pm. CONTINENTAL/FRENCH.

Chanteclair is expensive and a little difficult to reach, but it's worth seeking out. Designed in the style of a provincial French inn, the rambling stucco structure houses several dining and drinking areas, each with its own unique ambiance. The antique-furnished restaurant has five fireplaces. At lunch you might order grilled lamb chops with herb-and-garlic sauce, chicken-and-mushroom crepes, or Cajun charred ahi. Dinner is a worthwhile splurge that might begin with a lobster bisque with brandy or Beluga caviar with blinis. For a main dish, we recommend the rack of lamb with thyme sauce and roasted garlic.

Mr. Stox. 1105 E. Katella Ave. (east of Harbor Blvd.), Anaheim. ☎ **714/634-2994.** Reservations recommended on weekends. Main courses $12–$23. AE, CB, DC, DISC, DC, MC, V. Mon–Fri 11am–2:30pm and 5:30–10pm, Sat 5:30–10pm, Sun 5–9pm. AMERICAN.

Hearty steaks and fresh seafood are served in an early California manor-house setting here at Mr. Stox. Specialties include roast prime rib and mesquite-broiled fish, veal, and lamb. Chef Scott Raczek particularly excels at reduction sauces and innovative herbal preparations. Sandwiches and salads are also available. The homemade breads and desserts, such as chocolate-mousse cake, are unexpectedly good. Mr. Stox has an enormous and renowned wine cellar, and there's live entertainment every night.

MODERATE

Felix Continental Cafe. 36 Plaza Sq. (at Chapman and Glassell), Orange. ☎ **714/633-5842.** Reservations recommended for dinner. Main courses $6–$14. AE, DC, MC, V. Mon–Thurs 7am–9pm, Fri 7am–10pm, Sat 8am–10pm, Sun 8am–9pm. CUBAN/SPANISH.

If you like the re-created Main Street in the Magic Kingdom, then you'll love the historic 1886 town square in the city of Orange, on view from the cozy sidewalk tables outside this cafe. Dining on traditional Cuban specialties and watching traffic spin around the magnificent fountain and rosebushes of the plaza evokes old Havana or Madrid rather than the cookie-cutter Orange County communities just blocks away. The food receives glowing praise from reviewers and locals alike.

Peppers Restaurant and Nightclub. 12361 Chapman Ave. (west of Harbor Blvd.), Garden Grove. ☎ **714/740-1333.** Reservations recommended on weekends. Main courses $9–$14. AE, CB, DC, DISC, MC, V. Mon–Thurs 11am–10pm, Fri–Sat 11am–11pm, Sun 10am–10pm. CALIFORNIA/MEXICAN.

This colorful California/Mexican–themed restaurant just south of Disneyland looks like a partying kind of place, and it doesn't disappoint. The varied menu features mesquite-broiled dishes and fresh seafood daily. Mexican specialties include lots of variations of tacos and burritos, but the grilled meats and fish are best, especially Pepper's signature King Fajitas with crab legs or lobster tails. Dancing is available nightly to Top 40 hits starting at 9pm, and Monday nights a Mexican group plays live music. There's a free shuttle to and from six area hotels between 6pm and the nightclub closing time of 2am.

Renata's Caffè Italiano. 227 E. Chapman Ave. (at Grand), Orange. ☎ **714/771-4740.** Reservations recommended for dinner. Main courses $8–$15. AE, DISC, MC, V. Mon–Thurs 11am–9pm, Fri 11am–10pm, Sat 4–10pm. ITALIAN.

Near Felix Cafe in the historic plaza district, owner Renata Cerchiari draws a steady stream of regulars with good if not great contemporary Italian specialties. We found the charming patio dining in this small-town atmosphere a welcome change from Orange County's frantic pace (particularly if you're staying by the amusement parks) and the wide selection of appetizers and pasta dishes more authentic and reasonably priced than anywhere else, although the creamy Caesar salad wins higher marks than the disappointing cannolli.

INEXPENSIVE

Belisle's Restaurant. 12001 Harbor Blvd. (at Chapman), Garden Grove. ☎ **714/750-6560.** Main courses $3–$23. MC, V. Sun–Thurs 7am–midnight, Fri–Sat 7am–2am. AMERICAN.

Harvey Belisle's modest pink cottage has been doling out "Texas-size" portions of diner-style food since before Disneyland opened in 1955. This is the place to bring a ravenous football team or just your hollow-legged teenage boys. Portions are enormous; we can't say that enough, from the four-egg omelets accompanied by mountains of hash browns to the 12-ounce chicken-fried steak to a chocolate eclair the size of a log—we think Paul Bunyan would feel right at home. Just say, "fill 'er up!"

5 The Orange Coast

Whatever you do, don't say "Orange County." The mere name evokes images of smoggy industrial parks, cookie-cutter housing developments, and the staunch Republicanism that prevails behind the so-called orange curtain. We're talking instead about the Orange Coast, one of Southern California's best-kept secrets, a string of seaside jewels that have been compared with the French Riviera or the Costa del Sol. Here, 42 miles of beaches offer pristine stretches of sand, tide pools teeming with marine life, ecological preserves, charming secluded coves, quaint pleasure-boat harbors, and legendary surfers atop breaking waves. Whether your bare feet want to stroll a funky wooden boardwalk or your gold card gravitates toward a yacht club, you've come to the right place.

ESSENTIALS

GETTING THERE   See section 1 of chapter 13 for airport and airline information. By car from Los Angeles, take I-5 or I-495 south. The scenic, shore-hugging Pacific Coast Highway (Calif. 1, or just PCH to the locals) links the Orange Coast communities from Seal Beach in the north to Capistrano Beach just south of Dana Point, where it merges with I-5. To reach the beach communities directly, take the following freeway exits: **Seal Beach,** Seal Beach Boulevard from I-405; **Huntington Beach,** Beach Boulevard/Calif. 39 from either I-405 or I-5; **Newport Beach,** Calif. 55 from either I-405 or I-5; **Laguna Beach,** Calif. 133 from I-5; **San Juan**

Anaheim Area & Orange Coast Attractions

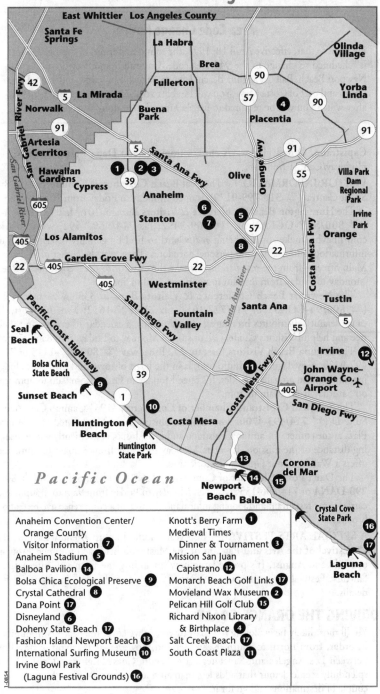

Anaheim Convention Center/
Orange County
  Visitor Information **7**
Anaheim Stadium **5**
Balboa Pavilion **14**
Bolsa Chica Ecological Preserve **9**
Crystal Cathedral **8**
Disneyland **6**
Doheny State Beach **17**
Fashion Island Newport Beach **13**
International Surfing Museum **10**
Irvine Bowl Park
  (Laguna Festival Grounds) **16**

Knott's Berry Farm **1**
Medieval Times
  Dinner & Tournament **3**
Mission San Juan
  Capistrano **12**
Monarch Beach Golf Links **17**
Movieland Wax Museum **2**
Pelican Hill Golf Club **15**
Richard Nixon Library
  & Birthplace **4**
Salt Creek Beach **17**
South Coast Plaza **11**

Area Code Change Notice

Please note that, effective April 18, 1998, the southern portion of Orange County is scheduled to change to the **949** area code. Communities affected will include Newport Beach, Balboa, Laguna Beach, Laguna Niguel, San Juan Capistrano, Dana Point, and part of Costa Mesa. You will be able to dial 714 until October 17, 1998, after which you will be required to use 949 for affected numbers.

Capistrano, Ortega Highway/Calif. 74 from I-5; and **Dana Point,** Pacific Coast Highway/Calif. 1 from I-5.

VISITOR INFORMATION   The **Seal Beach Chamber of Commerce,** 201 8th St., at Central (☎ **310/799-0179**), is open Monday to Friday from 10am to 2pm.

The **Huntington Beach Conference & Visitors Bureau,** 101 Main St., Suite A-2 (☎ **800/SAY-OCEAN** or 714/969-3492; fax 714/969-5592; www.imark. com/hbcvb), makes up for being *really* hard to find by genially offering tons of information, enthusiasm, and personal anecdotes. They're at the corner of PCH and Main Street—from the rear parking lot take the elevator to the second floor. Open Monday to Friday from 8:30am to noon and 1:30 to 5pm.

The **Newport Beach Conference & Visitors Bureau,** 3300 W. Coast Hwy. (☎ **800/94-COAST** or 714/722-1611; fax 714/722-1612; www.newport.lib. ca.us/default), distributes brochures, sample menus, a calendar of events, and their free and helpful Visitor's Guide. Call or stop in Monday to Friday from 8am to 5pm.

The **Laguna Beach Visitors Bureau,** 252 Broadway (☎ **800/877-1115** or 714/ 497-9229; www.lagunabeachinfo.org), is in the heart of town and distributes lodging, dining, and art gallery guides. It's open Monday to Friday from 9am to 5pm and on Saturday from 10am to 4pm.

The **San Juan Capistrano Chamber of Commerce,** 31931 Camino Capistrano, Suite D (☎ **714/493-4700;** www.sanjuancapistrano.com), is located in El Adobe Plaza at the corner of Camino Capistrano and Del Abispo, conveniently within walking distance of the mission. It's open Monday to Friday from 8:30am to 4pm, and offers a Walking Tour Guide to historic sites.

The **Dana Point Chamber of Commerce,** 24681 La Plaza, Suite 120 (☎ **800/ 290-DANA** or 714/496-1555), is open Monday to Friday from 9am to 4:30pm and carries some restaurant and lodging information as well as a comprehensive recreation brochure.

A SPECIAL ARTS FESTIVAL   A 60-year tradition in arts-friendly Laguna, the ✪ **Festival of the Arts and Pageant of the Masters** is held each summer throughout July and August. It's pretty large now, including the formerly "alternative" Sawdust Festival across the street. See the "Calendar of Events" in chapter 2 for details.

DRIVING THE ORANGE COAST

You'll most likely be exploring the coast by car, so we cover the beach communities in order, from north to south. Keep in mind, however, that if you're traveling between Los Angeles and San Diego, the Pacific Coast Highway (Calif. 1) is a splendidly scenic detour that adds less than an hour to the commute. So pick out a couple of destinations and go for it.

Seal Beach, on the border between Los Angeles and Orange Counties and neighbor to Long Beach's Naples harbor, is geographically isolated both by the adjacent

U.S. Naval Weapons Station and the self-contained Leisure World retirement community. As a result, the charming beach town appears untouched by modern development—Orange County's answer to small-town America. Taking a stroll down Main Street is a walk back in time which culminates in the Seal Beach Pier. Although there are no longer clusters of the sunbathing, squalking seals that gave the town its name, old-timers fish hopefully, lovers stroll swooningly, and families cavort by the seaside, perhaps capping off the afternoon with an old-fashioned double dip from **Main Street Ice Cream & Yogurt,** at the corner of Main Street and Ocean Avenue, where the walls are decorated with sepia-toned photographs of Seal Beach's yesteryear.

Huntington Beach is probably the largest Orange Coast city; it stretches quite a ways inland and has seen the most urbanization. To some extent this has changed the old boardwalk and pier to a modern outdoor mall where cliques of gang kids co-exist with families and the surfers who continue to flock here, for Huntington is legendary in surf lore. Hawaiian surfer Duke Kahanamoka brought the sport here in the 1920s, and some say the breaks around the pier and Bolsa Chica are the best in California. The world's top wave-riders flock to Huntington each August for the rowdy but professional **U.S. Open of Surfing** (call ☎ **310/286-3700** for information). If you'll be around during Christmastime, try to see the gaily decorated marina homes and boats in Huntington Harbour by taking the **Cruise of Lights,** a 45-minute narrated sail through and around the harbor islands. The festivities generally last from mid-December until Christmas; call ☎ **714/840-7542** for schedules and ticket information.

The name **Newport Beach** conjures comparisons to Rhode Island's Newport, where the well-to-do enjoy seaside living with all the creature comforts. That's the way it is here too, but on a less grandiose scale. From the million-dollar Cape Cod–style cottages on sunny Balboa Island in the bay, to elegant shopping complexes like Fashion Island and South Coast Plaza (an *über*-mall with valet parking, car detailing, limo service, and concierge), this is where fashionable socialites, right-wing celebrities, and business mavens can all be found. Alternatively, you could explore **Balboa** peninsula's historic Pavilion and old-fashioned pier or board a passenger ferry to Catalina Island.

Laguna Beach, whose breathtaking geography is marked by bold elevated headlands, coastal bluffs, and pocket coves, is known as an artists' enclave, but the truth is that Laguna has became so *in* (read: expensive) that it drove most of the true bohemians *out*. Their legacy remains with the annual **Festival of the Arts and Pageant of the Masters** (see "A Special Art Festival," above), as well as a proliferation of art galleries intermingling with high-priced boutiques along the town's cozy streets. In warm weather Laguna Beach has an overwhelming Mediterranean-island ambiance, which makes *everyone* feel beautifully, idly rich.

San Juan Capistrano, nestled in the verdant headlands just inland of Dana Point, is defined by Spanish missions and its loyal flock of swallows. The Mission architecture is authentic, and history abounds. Consider San Juan Capistrano a compact, life-size diorama illustrating the evolution of a small western town from Spanish-mission era to secular rancho period, into statehood and the 20th century. Ironically, Mission San Juan Capistrano (see "Seeing the Sights," below) is once again the center of the community, just as the founding friars intended 200 years ago.

Dana Point, the last town south, has been called a "marina development in search of a soul." Overlooking the harbor stands a monument to 19th-century author Richard Henry Dana, who gave his name to the area and described it in *Two Years Before the Mast*. Activities generally center around yachting and Dana Point's jewel of a harbor. Nautical themes are everywhere; particularly charming are the series of streets named for old-fashioned shipboard lights, a rainbow that includes "Street of the Amber Lantern," ". . . the Violet Lantern," ". . . the Golden Lantern," and so on. Bordering the harbor is Doheny State Beach (see "Beaches & Nature Preserves," below), which wrote the book on seaside park and camping facilities.

ENJOYING THE OUTDOORS

BEACHES & NATURE PRESERVES   The **Bolsa Chica Ecological Reserve,** in Huntington Beach (☎ 714/897-7003), is a 300-acre restored urban salt marsh that's a haven to more than 200 bird species, as well as a wide variety of protected plants and animals. Naturalists come to spot herons and egrets as well as California horn snails, jackknife clams, sea sponges, common jellyfish, and shore crabs. An easy 1½-mile loop trail begins from a parking lot on the Pacific Coast Highway (Calif. 1) a mile south of Warner Boulevard; docents lead a narrated walk the first Saturday of every month. The trail heads inland, over Inner Bolsa Bay and up Bolsa Chica bluffs. It then loops back toward the ocean over a dike that separates the Inner and Outer Bolsa bays and traverses a coastal sand dune system. This beautiful hike is a terrific afternoon adventure. The Bolsa Chica Conservancy has been working since 1978 on reclaiming the wetlands from oil companies that began drilling here 70 years ago. It's an ongoing process, and you can still see those "seesaw" drills dotting the outer areas of the reserve. Although Bolsa Chica State Beach across the road has superb facilities, fantastic surfing, and well-equipped campsites, you might find that the hulking offshore oil rigs spoil the view.

Huntington City Beach, adjacent to Huntington Pier, is a haven for volleyball players and surfers; dense crowds abound, but at least so do amenities like outdoor showers, beach rentals, and rest rooms. Just south of the city beach is 3-mile-long **Huntington State Beach.** Both popular beaches have lifeguards and concession stands seasonally. The state beach also has rest rooms, showers, barbecue pits, and a waterfront bike path. The main entrance is on Beach Boulevard, and there are access points all along the Pacific Coast Highway (Calif. 1).

Newport Beach runs for about 5 miles and includes both Newport and Balboa piers. There are outdoor showers, rest rooms, volleyball nets, and a vintage boardwalk that just may make you feel as though you've stepped 50 years back in time. **Balboa Bike and Beach Stuff** (☎ 714/723-1516), at the corner of Balboa and Palm near the pier, can rent you a variety of items, from pier fishing poles to bikes, beach umbrellas, and bodyboards. The **Southwind Kayak Center,** 2801 W. Pacific Coast Hwy. (☎ 800/768-8494 or 714/261-0200), rents sea kayaks for use in the bay or open ocean at rates of $8 to $12 per hour; instructional classes are available on weekends, with some midweek classes in summer. They also conduct bird-watching kayak expeditions into the Upper Newport Bay Ecological Reserve at rates of $40 to $65.

Crystal Cove State Park, which covers 3 miles of coastline between Corona del Mar and Laguna Beach and then extends up into the hills around El Moro Canyon, is a good alternative to the more popular beaches for you seekers of solitude. There are, however, lifeguards and rest rooms. The beach is a winding sandy strip, backed with grassy terraces; high tide sometimes sections it into coves. The entire area offshore is an underwater nature preserve. There are four entrances, including Pelican Point and El Moro Canyon. For more information, call ☎ 714/494-3539 or 714/848-1566.

Salt Creek Beach Park lies below the palatial Ritz-Carlton Laguna Niguel; guests who tire of the pristine swimming pool venture down the staircase on Ritz Carlton Drive to wiggle their toes in the sand. The setting is marvelous, with wide white-sand beaches looking out toward Catalina Island (why do you think the Ritz-Carlton built here?). There are lifeguards, rest rooms, a snack bar, and convenient parking near the hotel.

Doheny State Beach in Dana Point has long been known as a premier surfing spot and camping site. Just south of lovely Dana Point Marina (enter off Del Abispo St.), Doheny has the friendly vibe of beach parties in days gone by: Tree-shaded lawns give way to wide beaches, and picnicking and beach camping are encouraged. There are 121 sites for both tents and RVs, plus a state-run visitors center featuring several small aquariums of sea and tide-pool life. For more information and camping availability, call ☎ 714/492-0802.

BIKING Bicycling is the most popular beach activity up and down the coast. A slower-paced alternative to driving, it allows you to enjoy the clean, fresh air and notice smaller details of these laid-back beach towns and harbors. Bikes and equipment can be rented at **Zack's Too,** Pacific Coast Highway at Beach Boulevard, Huntington Beach (☎ 714/536-2696); **Balboa Bike & Beach Stuff,** 601 Balboa Blvd., Newport Beach (☎ 714/723-1516); **Laguna Beach Cyclery,** 240 Thalia St. (☎ 714/494-1522); and **Dana Point Bicycle,** 34155 Pacific Coast Hwy. (☎ 714/661-8356).

GOLF Many golf-course architects have used the geography of the Orange Coast to its full advantage, molding challenging and scenic courses from the rolling bluffs. Two beautiful courses open to the public are the **Monarch Beach Golf Links,** 23841 Stonehill Dr., Dana Point (☎ 714/240-8247), and the **Pelican Hill Golf Club,** 22651 Pelican Hill Rd. South, Newport Beach (☎ 714/760-0707). Both offer holes with breathtaking views of the ocean (remember, the break is always toward the water!)

SEEING THE SIGHTS

International Surfing Museum. 411 Olive Ave., Huntington Beach. ☎ **714/960-3483.** Admission $2 adults, $1 students, free for kids 5 and under. Mid-June–late Sept, daily noon–5pm; the rest of year, Wed–Sun noon–5pm.

Nostalgic Gidgets and Moondoggies shouldn't miss this monument to this laid-back sport that has become synonymous with California beaches. There are gargantuan longboards from the sport's early days, memorabilia of Duke Kahanamoka and the other surfing greats represented on the "Walk of Fame" near Huntington Pier, and a gift shop where a copy of the "Surfin'ary" can help you bone up on your surfer slang even if you can't hang ten.

Balboa Pavilion. 400 Main St., Balboa, Newport Beach. ☎ **714/673-5245.** From Calif. 1, turn south onto Newport Blvd. (which becomes Balboa Blvd. on the peninsula); turn left at Main St.

This historic cupola-topped structure, a California Historical Landmark, was built in 1905 as a bathhouse for swimmers in ankle-length bathing costumes. Later during the Big Band era, dancers rocked the Pavilion doing the "Balboa Hop." Now it serves as the terminal for Catalina Island passenger service, harbor and whale-watching cruises, and fishing charters. The surrounding boardwalk is the Balboa Fun Zone, a collection of carnival rides, game arcades, and vendors of hot dogs and cotton candy. For **Newport Harbor or Catalina cruise information,** call ☎ 714/673-5245; for **sportfishing and whale watching,** call ☎ 714/673-1434.

Balboa Island

The charm of this pretty little neighborhood isn't diminished by knowing that the island was man-made—and it certainly hasn't affected the price of real estate. Tiny clapboard cottages in the island's center and modern houses with 2-story windows and private docks along the perimeter make a colorful and romantic picture. You can drive onto the island on Jamboree Road to the north or take the three-car ferry from Balboa Peninsula (about $1 per vehicle). It's generally more fun to park and take the ferry as a pedestrian, since the tiny alleys they call streets are more suitable for strolling, there are usually crowds, and parking spaces are scarce. **Marine Avenue,** the main commercial street, is lined with small shops and cafes that evoke a New England fishing village. Refreshing shaved ices sold by sidewalk vendors will relieve the heat of summer.

Mission San Juan Capistrano. Ortega Hwy. (Calif. 74), San Juan Capistrano. ☎ **714/ 248-2048.** Admission $5 adults, $4 children and seniors. Daily 8:30am–5pm.

The seventh of the 21 California coastal missions, Mission San Juan Capistrano is continually being restored. The mix of old ruins and working buildings is home to small museum collections and various adobe rooms that are as quaint as they are interesting. The intimate mission chapel with its ornate baroque altar is still regularly used for religious services, and the mission complex is the center of the community, hosting performing arts, children's programs, and other cultural events year-round.

This mission is best known for its swallows, which are said to return to nest each year at their favorite sanctuary. According to legend, the birds wing their way back to the mission annually on March 19, St. Joseph's Day, arriving here at dawn; they are said to take flight again on October 23, after bidding the mission farewell. In reality, however, you can probably see the well-fed birds here any day of the week, winter or summer.

SHOPPING

Just as the communities along the coast range from casually barefoot summer playgrounds to meticulously groomed yacht-clubby enclaves, so does the shopping scene stretch to both ends of the spectrum. **Seal Beach,** indifferent to tourists, has charming low-tech shops designed to service the year-round residents, while **Huntington Beach** offers a plethora of surf and water-sport shops, reflecting its sporty nature. Both Huntington and Balboa have more than their share of T-shirt and souvenir stands, while tony **Newport Beach** has been called "Beverly Hills south" because of the many European designer boutiques and high-priced shops there. **Corona del Mar,** immediately south of Newport Beach on Calif. 1, is more like "Pasadena south," with branches of stylish but affordable L.A. boutiques sharing several fun blocks with local boutiques and services. **Laguna Beach** is art-gallery intensive; there are too many to list, but most are along the Pacific Coast Highway or Ocean, Forest, and Park avenues. Reflecting a wide range of artistic media, their wares can also come from all over the country—try to purchase the work of local artists unavailable elsewhere. There's little shopping in **Dana Point** and mostly mission-themed souvenirs in **San Juan Capistrano.**

Shoppers from all over the Southland flock to the two excellent malls listed below. If that isn't to your taste, a drive along the Pacific Coast Highway will yield many other opportunities for browsing and souvenir purchases.

Fashion Island Newport Beach. 401 Newport Center Dr., Newport Beach. ☎ **714/ 721-2000.**

Not an island at all, this shopping center is located next to the harbor and is designed to resemble an open-air Mediterranean village. A pretty upscale village, that is, with tiled streets and plazas dotted with strolling pull-cart vendors and lined with upscale stores and boutiques, including Neiman-Marcus and Macy's department stores as well as Baywatch (they sell timepieces) and other specialty shops.

✪ **South Coast Plaza.** 3333 Bristol St. (at I-405), Costa Mesa. ☎ **800/782-8888** or 714/435-2000.

South Coast Plaza is one of the most upscale shopping complexes in the world, and it's so big that it's a day's adventure unto itself. This beautifully designed center is home to some of fashion's most prominent boutiques, including Emporio Armani, Chanel, Alfred Dunhill, and Coach; beautiful branches of the nation's top department stores such as Saks Fifth Avenue and Nordstrom; and outposts of the best high-end specialty shops like Williams Sonoma, L.A. Eyeworks, and Rizzoli Booksellers.

The mall is home to many impressive works of art, including a 1.6-acre environmental sculpture by Isamu Noguchi. In between shoe-store browsing or sale-rack pillaging, you can stroll along the sculpture garden path, climb its hill, listen to its rushing water, cross its bubbling stream, and wonder at the sculpture's striking geometric forms from the garden benches. Not the usual rest in the food court, is it?

Speaking of food, you won't find Hot-Dog-on-a-Stick among the 40 or so restaurants scattered throughout. Wolfgang Puck Cafe, Morton's of Chicago, Ghiradelli Soda Fountain, Planet Hollywood, and Scott's Seafood Grill lure the hungry away from Del Taco and McDonald's.

WHERE TO STAY
VERY EXPENSIVE

Four Seasons Hotel Newport Beach. 690 Newport Center Dr., Newport Beach, CA 92660. ☎ **800/332-3442** or 714/759-0808. Fax 714/760-8073. 221 rms, 64 suites. A/C MINIBAR TV TEL. $260–$300 double; from $350 suite. AE, DC, MC, V. Valet parking $13.50.

This polished member of the world-class Four Seasons group gets the highest marks for its comprehensive facilities and impeccable service. The guest rooms, conservatively designed in inoffensive beiges, have lovely touches like terry robes, oversize closets, and marble baths. Most have small balconies, even though the Newport skyline is nothing special to look at. Butlers are on call around the clock. Because of their larger size, rooms with two double beds are the hotel's best value. Guests are encouraged to bring their pets; doggie biscuits and food are always available.

Dining: The Pavilion Restaurant, serving California/French cuisine, is popular with locals at lunch. The poolside Cabana Cafe enjoys a nice garden setting. Afternoon tea and evening cocktails are served in the Gardens Cafe and Lounge.

Services: Concierge, room service (24 hours), overnight laundry and shoe shine, nightly turndown, complimentary transportation to/from the John Wayne Airport.

Facilities: Large heated outdoor pool, small fitness club, Jacuzzi, sundeck, two outdoor lighted tennis courts, business center, gift shop.

✪ **Ritz-Carlton Laguna Niguel.** 1 Ritz-Carlton Dr., Dana Point, CA 92629. ☎ **800/241-3333** or 714/240-2000. Fax 714/240-0829. 393 rms and suites. A/C MINIBAR TV TEL. $260–$495 double; suites from $600. Children 17 and under stay free in parents' room. Midweek and special packages available. AE, CB, DC, DISC, MC, V. Parking $20.

The Old World meets the Pacific Rim at this glorious hotel, majestically set among terraces and fountained gardens on a 150-foot-high bluff above a 2-mile-long beach. There's a beautiful limestone fireplace in the elegant, silk-lined lobby, and lush foliage abounds throughout the interior. A ravishingly arched lounge is perfect for watching the sun set over the Pacific. The service, in Ritz-Carlton style, is unassuming and impeccable. Some guests, however, might find the hotel's palatial airs out of keeping with the beachy location.

The spacious rooms are outfitted with sumptuous furnishings and fabrics; despite their generous size, some are overfurnished to the point of being cramped. All come with a terrace; an Italian marble bath equipped with double vanity, hair dryer, and bathrobes; three phones (with voice-mail); and a refrigerator; a shoe polisher; and a safe. Some rooms even have fireplaces.

Dining/Entertainment: The Dining Room is the most elegant of the hotel's four restaurants, offering Continental/French cuisine served by a knowledgeable staff. Dine by the numbers, choosing from two- to seven-course prix-fixe dinners with matching wines from the formidable cellar. There's also a clubby lounge for nightcaps and five bars (two with nightly entertainment).

Service: Room service (on Rosenthal china, no less), twice-daily maid service (they'll even stick a bookmark in the appropriate page of your *TV Guide*), masseur, baby-sitting, children's programs, regular shuttle to/from the beach and the golf course; the two staffers for every room are generally alert in responding to requests.

Facilities: Beach with lifeguard, games room, lawn games, sauna, steam room, whirlpool, beauty salon, day-care center, 24-hour business center, car-rental desk; first-rate sports facilities include a smart fitness center with unisex steam rooms and a public golf course designed by Robert Trent Jones, Jr.

EXPENSIVE

Surf and Sand Hotel. 1555 S. Coast Hwy. (south of Laguna Canyon Rd.), Laguna Beach, CA 92651. ☎ **800/524-8621** or 714/497-4477. Fax 714/494-2897. 156 rms, 12 suites. MINIBAR TV TEL. Apr–Oct, $200–$275 double; from $375 suite. Nov–Mar, $190–$240 double; from $300 suite. AE, CB, DC, DISC, MC.

The fanciest hotel in Laguna Beach has come a long way since it started life in 1937 as a modest little place with just 13 units. Still occupying the same fantastic oceanside location, it now features dozens of top-of-the-line luxurious rooms that, despite their standard size, feel enormously decadent. Done entirely in white, they're very bright and beachy, and every one has a private balcony with an ocean view, a marble bath, and plush robes; some have whirlpool tubs. Try to get a deluxe corner room.

Dining: Splashes Restaurant (see "Where to Dine," below) serves three meals daily in a beautiful oceanfront setting. Towers offers contemporary northern Italian cuisine for dinner. Because the windows don't open, a sound system was installed to pipe in the sounds of the surf below.

Services: Concierge, room service, dry cleaning, overnight laundry, complimentary morning newspaper, nightly turndown.

Facilities: Heated outdoor pool, salon, boutique, gift shop.

MODERATE

Blue Lantern Inn. 34343 St. of the Blue Lantern, Dana Point, CA 92629. ☎ **800/950-1236** or 714/661-1304. Fax 714/496-1483. 29 rms. A/C TV TEL. $135–$350 double. Rates include full breakfast. AE, DC, MC, V.

A newly constructed 3-story New England–style gray clapboard inn, the Blue Lantern is a pleasant cross between romantic B&B and sophisticated small hotel. Almost all the rooms, which are decorated with reproduction traditional furniture and plush bedding, have a balcony or deck overlooking the harbor. All have a fireplace and Jacuzzi tub. Have your breakfast here in private (clad perhaps in the fluffy robe provided), or choose to go downstairs to the sunny dining room that also serves complimentary afternoon tea. There's an exercise room and a cozy lounge with menus for many area restaurants. The friendly staff welcomes you with home-baked cookies at the front desk.

Doryman's Inn Bed & Breakfast. 2102 W. Ocean Front, Newport Beach, CA 92663. ☎ **800/634-3303** or 714/675-7300. 8 rms, 2 suites. A/C TV TEL. $135–$230 double; from $185 suite. Rates include breakfast. AE, MC, V.

The Doryman's rooms are both luxurious and romantic, making this one of the nicest B&Bs to be found anywhere. The rooms are outfitted with French and American antiques, floral textiles, beveled mirrors, and cozy furnishings. Every room has a working fireplace and a sunken marble tub (some have Jacuzzi jets). King- or queen-size beds, lots of plants, and good ocean views round out the decor. The location, directly on the Newport Beach Pier Promenade, is also enviable, though some may find it a bit too close to the action. Breakfast includes fresh pastries and fruit, brown eggs, yogurt, cheeses, and international coffees and teas.

Vacation Village. 647 S. Coast Hwy., Laguna Beach, CA 92651. ☎ **800/843-6895** or 714/494-8566. Fax 714/494-1386. 100 rms, 38 suites and apts. TV. $80–$155 double; from $175 suite. AE, CB, DC, DISC, MC, V.

Vacation Village has something for everyone. This cluster of seven oceanfront and near-the-ocean motels offers rooms, studios, suites, and apartments. Most of the accommodations are standard motel fare: bed, TV, table, basic bath. The best rooms are oceanfront in a 4-story structure overlooking the Village's private beach. Umbrellas and backrests for beachgoers are available in summer. There's a restaurant on the premises, and facilities include a private beach, two pools, and a whirlpool.

WHERE TO DINE
EXPENSIVE

Splashes Restaurant and Bar in the Surf and Sand Hotel, 1555 S. Coast Hwy., Laguna Beach. ☎ **714/497-4477.** Reservations recommended. Main courses $16–$26. AE, CB, DC, DISC, MC, V. Mon–Fri 7am–10pm, Sat–Sun 7am–11pm. MEDITERRANEAN.

Splashes is truly stunning. Almost directly on the surf, this light and bright restaurant basks in sunlight and the calming crash of the waves. At dinner, a basket of fresh-baked crusty bread prefaces a long list of appetizers that might include wild-mushroom ravioli with lobster sauce or sautéed Louisiana shrimp with red chiles and lemon. Gourmet pizzas also make great starters; they come topped with interesting combinations like grilled lamb, roasted fennel, artichokes, mushrooms, and feta cheese. Main courses change daily and might offer baked striped bass and braised duck in a cabernet.

MODERATE

Five Feet. 328 Glenneyre, Laguna Beach. ☎ **714/497-4955.** Reservations recommended on weekends. Main courses $14–$24. AE, MC, V. Sun–Thurs 5–10pm, Fri 11:30am–2:30pm and 5–11pm, Sat 5–11pm. CALIFORNIA/ASIAN.

Chef/proprietor Michael Kang has created one of the area's most innovative and interesting restaurants, combining the best in Californian cuisine with Asian technique and ingredients. If the atmosphere were as good as the food, Five Feet would be one of the best restaurants in California. Main courses run the gamut from tea-smoked filet mignon topped with Roquefort cheese and candied walnuts to a hot Thai-style mixed grill of veal, beef, lamb, and chicken stir-fried with sweet peppers, onions, and mushrooms in curry-mint sauce. Unfortunately, the dining room's gray-concrete walls aren't much to look at, and the exposed vents on an airplane hangar–scale wooden ceiling just look unfinished, not trendy industrial. Fortunately, this unspectacular decor is brightened by an exceedingly friendly staff and unparalleled food.

Harbor Grill. 34499 St. of the Golden Lantern, Dana Point. ☎ **714/240-1416.** Reservations suggested on weekends. Main courses $8–$18. AE, CB, DC, DC, MC, V. Mon–Sat 11:30am–10pm, Sun 9am–10pm. SEAFOOD.

In a business/commercial mall right in the center of the pretty Dana Point Marina, the Harbor Grill is enthusiastically recommended by locals for mesquite-broiled, ocean-fresh seafood. Hawaiian mahimahi with a mango-chutney baste is on the menu, along with Pacific swordfish, crab cakes, and beef steaks.

Las Brisas. 361 Cliff Dr. (off the PCH north of Laguna Canyon), Laguna Beach. ☎ **714/ 497-5434.** Reservations recommended. Main courses $8–$17. AE, MC, V. Mon–Sat 8am– 10:30pm, Sun 9am–10:30pm. MEXICAN.

Boasting a breathtaking view of the Pacific, Las Brisas is popular for sunset drinks and alfresco appetizers—so much so that it can get pretty crowded during the summer months. Affordable during lunch but pricey at dinner, the menu consists mostly of seafood recipes from the Mexican Riviera. Even the standard enchiladas and tacos get a zesty update with crab or lobster meat and fresh herbs. Calamari steak is sautéed with bell peppers, capers, and herbs in a garlic-butter sauce, and king salmon is mesquite broiled and served with a creamy lime sauce. Although a bit on the touristy side, Las Brisas can be a fun part of the Laguna Beach experience.

Twin Palms. 630 Newport Center Dr., Newport Beach. ☎ **714/721-8288.** Reservations suggested. Main courses $9–$17. AE, CB, DC, MC, V. Sun–Wed 11:30am–10pm, Thurs–Sat 11:30am–1am. MEDITERRANEAN/FRENCH.

Opened in late 1995, this sibling restaurant to one of Pasadena's most popular eateries seems to be leading the Newport Beach pack as well. From the famous original started by, among others, movie star Kevin Costner, comes the high-tented, palm-accented, huge circuslike space that is Twin Palms's trademark. Amid this festival atmosphere you can enjoy the French "comfort food" original chef Michael Roberts created as a backlash against pricey haute cuisine. Favorites include juicy, roasted sage-infused pork and honey-glazed coriander-scented duck from the rotisserie grill, as well as the popular salt cod mashed potato brandade appetizer. Sautéed dishes and salads are not as successful, but Twin Palms has brought its traditional Sunday "Gospel Brunch" to the new location.

INEXPENSIVE

El Adobe de Capistrano. 31891 Camino Capistrano (near the mission), San Juan Capistrano. ☎ **714/493-1163** or 714/830-8620. Dinner $8–$15; lunch $5–$10. AE, DISC, MC, V. Mon– Thurs 11:30am–10pm, Fri–Sat 11:30am–11pm, Sun 10:30am–2:30pm and 4–10pm. CLASSIC MEXICAN.

This restaurant is housed in a historic landmark 1778 Spanish adobe near San Juan Capistrano's main attraction, the mission. It's understandably touristy, but there's some interesting history inside, like the enclosed lobby that was originally a dirt pathway between two buildings. A former dungeon jail cell makes a fine wine cellar, and El Adobe proudly offers a menu combination named "the President's Choice" after Richard Nixon, who visited often from his Summer White House at the shore nearby. Hot plates overflow with cheesy combinations featuring chiles rellenos, tamales, and enchiladas topped with rich, red sauce. Dinner selections also include steak and seafood.

Ruby's. 1 Balboa Pier, Balboa. ☎ **714/675-7829.** Most items under $5. AE, MC, V. Sun–Thurs 7am–10pm, Fri–Sat 7am–11pm. AMERICAN DINER.

With their trademark red-and-white hamburger-stand decor sprouting up all over the Southland, Ruby's is fast becoming a local institution. Housed in a former baithouse, the Balboa Pier Ruby's is the original. Ruby's sells nostalgia and food in equal measure. The hamburgers, fries, milkshakes, and flavored sodas are reasonably priced, and the fun, kid-friendly atmosphere really suits the surroundings.

The Southern California Desert

by Stephanie Avnet

To the casual observer, Southern California's desert seems desolate—nothing but vast landscapes baking under a relentless sun. Its splendor is subtle, and you have to discover its beauty in your own time. For some travelers it will be the surprising lushness of trees, flowering cacti, fragrant shrubs, and other plants—many of them unique to the region—that have adapted ingeniously to the harsh climate. The unique Joshua tree, which some deem majestic and others call ugly, thrives in the upper Mojave Desert. Each spring the ground throughout the Lancaster area is carpeted with brilliant golds and oranges of the poppy, California's state flower. Like the autumn leaves in New England, the poppies along Calif. 14 draw seasonal tourists in droves.

If it looks as if nothing except insects could survive here, look again: You're bound to see a speedy roadrunner or a tiny gecko dart across your path. Close your eyes and listen for the cry of a hawk or an owl. Check the ground for coyote or bobcat tracks. Notice the sparkle of fish in the streams running through flourishing palm oases. Road signs warn of desert tortoise crossings. The tortoise is just one of the many endangered species found only here; fortunately, most of the Southern California desert's flora and fauna is protected by the federal government in a wildlife sanctuary.

Or perhaps the beauty you seek is that of personal renewal in the spectacular desert landscape. Whether it's in the shadow of purple-tinged mountains, amid otherworldly rock formations, or beside a sparkling swimming pool, you'll find as much or as little to occupy your time as you desire. Destinations range from gloriously untouched national parks to ultra-luxurious resorts—and it's a rare day when the sun doesn't shine out here.

1 En Route to the Palm Springs Resorts

If you're making the drive from Los Angeles via I-10, your first hour or so will be spent just, well, getting out of the L.A. metropolitan sprawl. Soon you'll leave the Inland Empire auto plazas behind, sail past the last of the bedroom-community shopping malls, and edge ever closer to the snow-capped (if you're lucky) San Bernardino and San Jacinto mountain ranges. (Coming from San Diego via I-15, the areas discussed below are east of the junction with I-10.)

Antiquing is a very popular pastime in Southern California (I'm not talking Louis XIV here; mostly late 19th- and 20th-century stuff), and there will be some great opportunities to stop and poke around. What used to be a ramshackle string of junk shops along the I-10 service road in **Yucaipa** is now a respectable "antique row" worth exiting the freeway for. Farther along I-10 lies **Beaumont,** touting itself as "City of Antiques," for it holds almost a dozen (at last count) mall-style antiques and collectibles emporiums.

If all this sifting through tchotchkes makes you hungry, how about some kitschy roadside dining? Although their fare is coffee-shop standard, don't tell the enthusiastic gingham- and overall-clad service staff at **The Farm House** in **Banning** (signs will direct you off the freeway). From the giant rooster and rusty agricultural tools out front to the proudly framed photos of Banning's heyday as "Stagecoach Town U.S.A.," this is just the kind of place where you'd expect the rural Kiwanis Club to meet each week, and it's a far sight more interesting than the Denny's next door.

Or, as the horse- and silo-dotted fields give way to pale, dry desert, keep your eyes peeled for the **dinosaurs** that stand guard over the Wheel Inn Restaurant in **Cabazon.** That's right, a four-story-tall *Brontosaurus* and his *Tyrannosaurus rex* pal. They were built in the 1960s by Claude K. Bell, a sketch artist and sculptor at Knott's Berry Farm with a way-before-his-time dream of an entire dinosaur amusement park. These two behemoths were all he completed. You can stop and climb up into the belly of the larger one, where you'll find a remarkably spacious gift shop selling dinosaur toys, books, and souvenirs.

Cabazon is also the home of **Hadley's Orchards,** a fixture on this stretch of road since 1931. They're always packed with folks shopping for dates, dried fruits, nuts, honey, preserves, and other regional products. A snack bar serves the date shake so beloved in this region, and gift packs of tasty treats to carry home (for more about the date mystique, see "Exploring the Area" in section 3, later in this chapter). Nearby, you'll either love or hate the **Desert Hills Factory Stores.** Southern California's largest outlet mall contains more than 100 stores, the most intriguing of which is Barney's New York, presenting a nice opportunity to pick up designer threads at a fraction of the cost.

Soon after leaving Cabazon you'll enter the **San Gorgonio Pass.** Be prepared for an awesome and otherworldly sight—never-ending windmill fields that harness the powerful force of the wind gusting through this passage, converting it to electricity for air conditioners throughout the Coachella Valley. The Calif. 111 turnoff leads you past the Albert Frey–designed "hyperbolic paraboloid" **gas station** at Tramway Road, which for 30 years has served as the unofficial gateway to Palm Springs—and a symbol that you've arrived!

2 Get Your Kicks—On Historic Route 66

There's a way for nostalgia buffs to take a detour down memory lane on their way to desert destinations—by eschewing the fast-paced, faceless I-10 for a very special interstate highway, Route 66.

It's been immortalized in film, song, literature, memory, and in the popular imagination . . . but is anything really left of this great snaking highway, a dependable, comforting spirit John Steinbeck called "the Mother Road"? What of the path to adventure traveled by Tod and Buz in their trademark red Corvette on the namesake 1960s TV series? Well, it's still there, if you're willing to look for it.

Until the final triumph of the multilane superslab in the early 1960s, Route 66 was the *only* automobile route between the windy Chicago shores of Lake Michigan and L.A.'s golden Pacific beaches. "America's Main Street" rambled through eight states; today in each one there are enthusiastic organizations dedicated to preserving its remnants. California is fortunate to have a lengthy stretch of the original highway, many miles of which still proudly wear the designation "California State Highway 66." It's not just weed-split abandoned blacktop. These are active streets, often the main commercial drag of the community. Many stretches have become clusters of new home developments, stucco shopping centers, and fast-food chains. Pretty mundane—until you round a curve and unexpectedly see a vintage wood-frame house, perhaps from a pre-Depression ranch. It tells the poignant story of being set way back from the road, amidst a shady grove, until highway workers buried the front yard under asphalt.

Other picturesque relics of that bygone era—single-story motels, friendly two-pump gas stations—exist beside their modern neighbors, inviting nostalgia for a slower, simpler time—a time when the vacation began the moment you backed out of the driveway.

ESSENTIALS

THE ROUTE   Our drive begins in Pasadena and ends in downtown San Bernardino, 56 miles west of Palm Springs. In San Bernardino, I-215 intersects Route 66; take it 4 miles south to rejoin I-10 and continue east.

Note: This detour works equally well if your destination is Lake Arrowhead or Big Bear Lake; take I-215 north 3 miles to Calif. 30 and continue into the mountains (see chapter 14). The drive will add anywhere from 30 minutes to 3 hours to your trip, depending on how many relics and photo opportunities you stop to enjoy. I've included some suitably retro meal suggestions in case you want to incorporate lunch into your drive.

INFORMATION   For more information, contact the **California Historic Route 66 Association** (☎ **310/997-9817**). There's also a quarterly *Route 66 Magazine,* 326 W. Route 66, Williams, AZ 86046 (☎ **520/635-4322**).

LET'S HIT THE ROAD!

Although Route 66 *officially* ended at the picturesque Pacific, there are very few remainders left in the heart of L.A. Besides, I assume you've already seen the city, so Pasadena is the best point to begin your time-warp experience.

One of my favorite places is the **Fair Oaks Pharmacy,** Fair Oaks Avenue and Mission Street, 1.6 miles south of Colorado Boulevard (☎ **818/799-1414;** open Monday to Saturday from 9am, Sunday from 11am), a fixture on this street corner since 1915. If you're in the mood for a treat, try an authentic ice-cream soda, a sparkling phosphate, a "Route 66" sundae, or an old-fashioned malt (complete with the frosty mixing can), all served by today's fresh-faced soda jerks from behind the marble counter. They also serve soup, sandwiches, and other snacks. The Fair Oaks is still a dispensing pharmacy, and offers a variety of charming gifts, including an abundance of Route 66–themed items.

Perhaps you'd like some appropriate driving music, or a souvenir to help you reminisce about your Route 66 experience later. There's no better place than **Canterbury Records,** 805 E. Colorado Blvd., a block west of Lake Avenue (☎ **818/792-7184;** open Monday to Saturday from 9am, Sunday from 10am). They have L.A.'s finest selection of Big-Band and pop vocalists on CD and cassette; perhaps you'll choose one of the many renditions of Bobby Troup's homage, "(Get Your Kicks on) Route 66."

As you continue east on Colorado Boulevard, keep your eyes peeled for motels like the **Saga Motor Hotel, Swiss Lodge, Siesta Inn, Astro** (fabulous *Jetsons*-style

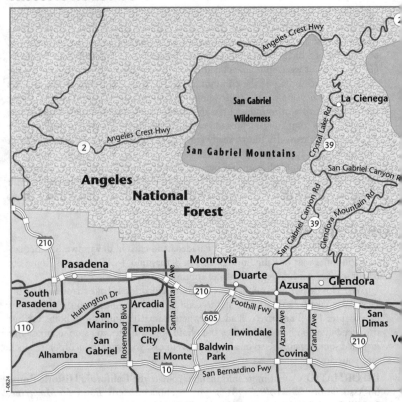

architecture), and **Hi-Way Host.** In fact, lodgings have proven the hardiest post-66 survivors, and you'll be seeing many unique frozen-in-time motor courts along the way.

Turn left on Rosemead Boulevard, passing under the freeway (boo, hiss) to Foothill Boulevard. Turning right, you'll soon be among the tree-lined residential streets of **Arcadia,** home to the **Santa Anita Racetrack** and the **Los Angeles Arboretum,** the picturesque former estate of "Lucky" Baldwin, whose Queen Anne cottage has been the setting for many movies and TV shows (see chapter 14 for details). Passing into **Monrovia,** look for the life-size plastic cow on the southeast corner of Mayflower. It marks the drive-thru called **Mike's Dairy**—a splendid example of this auto-age phenomenon. If you're observant, you'll see many drive-thru dairies along our route (mostly Alta-Dena brand). Mike's has all the typical features, including the refrigerated island display case still bearing a vintage "Driftwood Dairy Products" price sign.

Next, look for Magnolia Avenue and the outrageous **Aztec Hotel** on the northwest corner. Opened in 1925, the Aztec was a local showplace, awing guests with its overscale, dark Native American–themed lobby, garish Mayan murals, and exotic Brass Elephant bar. An arcade of shops once held the city's most prominent barbershop, beauty salon, and pharmacy. Little has changed about the interior, and a glance behind the front desk will reveal the original cord-and-plug telephone switchboard still in use. If you care to wet your whistle, stop into the bar before continuing on.

Leaving the Aztec, you'll pass some splendid Craftsman bungalows and other historic homes. The street dead-ends at Mountain Avenue; turn right to catch up with

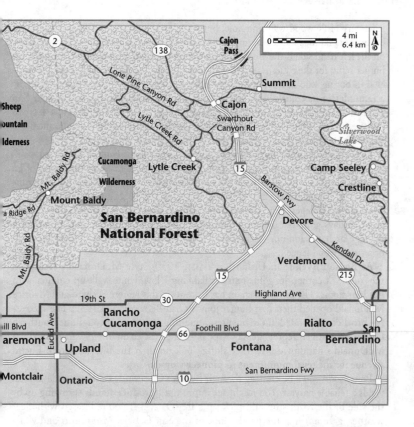

the 1930s alignment of Route 66. Make a left turn on Huntington Drive, and look out for **The Trails,** a prime example of the "wagon wheel/Wild West" theme restaurants. Its super-tall DINING sign will let you know when you're getting close. Now you're in **Duarte,** where Huntington Drive is lit by graceful and ornate **double street lamps** on the center median. This stretch also has many fabulous old motor courts; see if you can spot the **Filly, Ranch Inn, Evergreen,** and the **Capri.**

Crossing over the wide but nearly dry **San Gabriel River,** glance right from the bridge to see cars streaming along the Interstate that supplanted Route 66. In **Irwindale**—which smells just like the industrial area it is, with manufacturing plants ranging from a Miller brewery to Health Valley Foods—the street resumes the Foothill Boulevard name, and you'll pass into **Azusa.** Look for the elegant 1932 Azusa City Hall and Auditorium, whose vintage lampposts and Moorish fountain enhance a charming courtyard.

Our route swerves right onto Alosta Avenue at the **Foothill Drive-In Theater,** Southern California's last single-screen drive-in. As you cruise by, think of the days when our cars were an extension of our living rooms (with the great snacks Mom wouldn't allow at home), and the outdoor theaters were filled every summer evening by dusk.

Continuing on Alosta, you'll enter **Glendora,** named in 1887 by founder George Whitcomb for his wife, Ledora. Look for the **Palm Tropics,** one of the best-maintained old motels along the route. On the northeast corner of Grand Avenue stands the "world famous" **Derby East** restaurant. It's not affiliated with the legendary Hollywood watering hole, but was clearly built in the 1940s to capitalize on both its famous namesake and the nearby Santa Anita Racetrack. Farther along on the left-hand side is the **Golden Spur,** which began 70 years ago as a ride-up hamburger stand for the equestrian crowd. Unfortunately, the restaurant has been remodeled in boring stucco, leaving only the original sign, with its neon cowboy boot, as a reminder of its colorful past. In a block or two, you'll pass briefly through **San Dimas,** a ranchlike community where you must pay attention to the HORSE crossing street signs. At the corner of Cataract Avenue, a covered wagon announces the **Pinnacle Peak** restaurant, guarded by a giant steer atop the roof.

Don't blink because almost immediately the street rejoins Foothill Boulevard, passing underneath the ramps to I-210 (boo, hiss); now you're in **La Verne,** home of **La Paloma** Mexican cafe, a fixture on the route for many years. Continue on to the community of **Claremont,** known these days for the highly respected group of **Claremont Colleges.** You'll pass several of them along this eucalyptus-lined boulevard. In days gone by, drivers would cruise along this route for mile upon mile, through orchards and open fields, the scenery punctuated only by ambling livestock or a rustic wood fence.

At Benson Avenue in **Upland,** a classic 1950s-style **McDonald's** stands on the southeast corner, its golden arches flanking a low, white walk-up counter with outdoor stools. The fast-food chain has its roots in this region: Richard and Maurice McDonald opened their first burger joint in San Bernardino in 1939. The successful brothers expanded their business, opening locations throughout Southern California, until entrepreneur Ray Kroc purchased the chain in 1955 and franchised McDonald's nationwide. Farther along, look north at the intersection of Euclid Avenue for the regal **monument to pioneer women.**

Pretty soon you'll be cruising through **Rancho Cucamonga,** whose fertile soil still yields a reliable harvest. You might see impromptu **produce stands** springing up by the side of the road; stop and pick up a fresh snack. If you're blessed with clear weather, gaze north at the gentle slope of the **San Gabriel Mountains** and you'll understand how Foothill Boulevard got its name. The construction codes in this community are among the most stringent in California, designed to respect the region's heritage and restrict runaway development. All new buildings are Spanish/Mediterranean in style and amply landscaped. At the corner of San Bernardino Road, the playful architectural bones of a wonderful old service station can't be obscured by the flashy car-stereo/cellular-phone store which inhabits it now. Across the street is the **Sycamore Inn,** nestled in a grove of trees and looking very much like an oldstyle stagecoach stop. This reddish-brown wooden house, dating from 1848, has been a private home and gracious inn; today it serves the community of Cucamonga as a restaurant and civic hall.

Rancho Cucamonga has earnestly preserved two historic wineries. First you'll see the **Thomas Vineyards,** at the northeast corner of Vineyard Avenue, established in 1839. Legend holds that the first owner mysteriously disappeared, leaving hidden treasure still undiscovered on the property. The winery's preserved structures now hold two eateries (including the Roadhouse Cafe, below), a country crafts store, and a bookstore housed in the former brandy still.

☕ **TAKE A BREAK** If all this driving has made you hungry, consider the **Magic Lamp Inn,** 8189 Foothill Blvd. (☎ **909/981-8659;** open for lunch and dinner Tuesday to Friday, dinner only on Saturday and Sunday). Built in 1957, the Magic Lamp offers excellent continental cuisine (nothing *nouvelle* about Route 66!) in a setting that's part manor house and part "Aladdin" theme park. Dark, stately dining rooms lurk behind a funky banquette cocktail lounge punctuated by a psychedelic fountain/ fire pit and a panoramic view. The genie bottle theme is everywhere, from the restaurant's dinnerware to the plush carpeting, which would be right at home in a Las Vegas casino. Lovers of kitsch and hearty retro fare shouldn't pass this one up.

The aging room at Thomas Winery is now the **Roadhouse Cafe** (☎ **909/ 941-8793;** open for lunch and dinner daily), offering hearty steaks, ribs, fish, and chicken in addition to salads and lighter lunches. Share one of their batter-dipped, deep-fried whole onions, served with a zesty dipping sauce. Even if you don't stop to eat, be sure to stop in the shopping mall behind the Thomas Winery to tour the **Route 66 Territory Museum and Visitor's Bureau,** a minimuseum and gift shop. They have lovingly tended exhibits of old gas pumps, road signs, and other relics. You'll also find an array of books, maps, glassware, garments, jewelry, and other souvenirs. Many items bear the original black-on-white Route 66 shield, the ubiquitous highway marker purged from the old route by state transportation officials in 1984. The brown markers you see today were subsequently placed by the historical associations.

Continuing on to Hellman Avenue, look for the **New Kansan Motel** (on the northeast corner). With that name, it must have seemed welcoming to Dust Bowl refugees. Near the northwest corner of Archibald Avenue you'll find lonely remnants of a **1920s-era gas station.** Empty now, those service bays have seen many a Ford, Studebaker, or Packard in need of a helping hand. Next you'll pass the **Virginia Dare Winery,** at the northwest corner of Haven Avenue, whose structures now house part of a large business park/shopping mall, but retain the flourish of the original (1830s) winery logo.

Soon you'll pass the I-15 junction and be driving through **Fontana,** whose name in Italian means "fountain city." There isn't too much worth stopping for along this stretch, but definitely slow down to have a look at the **motor-court hotels** lining both sides of the road. They're of various vintages, all built to cater to the once-vigorous stream of travelers passing through. Although today they're dingy, the melody of their names once again conjures up those glory days: **Ken-Tuck-U-Inn, Rose Motel, Moana, Dragon, Sand & Sage, Sunset, 40 Winks, Redwing.**

After entering **Rialto,** be on the lookout for Meriden Avenue, site of the fanciful **Wigwam Motel.** Built in the 1950s (along with an identical twin motor court in Holbrook, Arizona), these stucco teepees lured many a road-weary traveler in for the night with their whimsy. Their catchy slogan, "Sleep in a wigwam, get more for your wampum," has been supplanted today by the more to-the-point "Do it in a teepee." But as with many of the motor courts we'll pass on this drive, you need only picture a few large, shiny Buicks, T-bird convertibles, and "woodie" station wagons pulling in for the night and your imagination will drift back to days gone by.

Soon Foothill Boulevard will become 5th Street, a sign that you're nearing **San Bernardino,** which must've been a welcome sight for hot and weary west-bound travelers emerging from the Mojave desert. Route 66 wriggled through the steep Cajon Pass into a land fragrant with orange groves, where agricultural prosperity had quickly earned this region a lasting sobriquet, "the Inland Empire."

The year 1928 saw the grand opening of an elegant movie palace, the **California Theater,** at 562 W. 4th St., only 1 block from Route 66. From 5th Street east, turn right at E Street, then make a right on 4th Street, where you can pull over to view the theater. Lovingly restored and still popular for nostalgic live entertainment and the rich tones of its original Wurlitzer pipe organ, the California was a frequent site of Hollywood "sneak previews." Here humorist Will Rogers made his last public appearance, in 1935. (Following his death, the highway was renamed the "Will Rogers Memorial Highway" in his honor, but it remained popularly known as Route 66.) Notice the intricate relief of the theater's stone facade, and peek into the lobby to see the red velvet draperies, rich carpeting, and gold banistered double staircase leading up to the balcony.

The theater is the last stop on your time-warp driving tour. Continue west on 4th Street to the superslab highway only 2¹/₂ blocks away—that's I-215, your entry back into the '90s (see "Essentials," above).

3 The Palm Springs Desert Resorts

Palm Springs had been known for years as a golf course–studded retirement mecca annually invaded by raucous hordes of libidinous college kids at spring break. Well, the city of Palm Springs has been quietly changing its image and attracting a whole new crowd. Former mayor (now U.S. Congressman) Sonny Bono's revolutionary "anti-thong" ordinance in 1991 put a lightning-quick halt to the spring break migration by eliminating public display of the bare co-ed derrière, and the upscale fairway-condo crowd has decided to congregate in the tony outlying resort cities of **Rancho Mirage, Palm Desert, Indian Wells,** and **La Quinta.**

These days, there are no billboards allowed in Palm Springs itself, all the palm trees in the center of town are appealingly backlit at night, and you won't see the word "motel" on any establishment. Senior citizens are everywhere, dressed to the nines in brightly colored leisure suits and keeping alive the retro-kitsch establishments from the days when Elvis, Liberace, and Sinatra made the balmy desert a swingin' place. But they're not alone: Baby boomers and yuppies nostalgic for the kidney-shaped swimming pools and backyard luaus of the Eisenhower/Kennedy glory years are buying ranch-style vacation homes and restoring them to their 1950s splendor. Hollywood's young glitterati are returning, too. Today the city fancies itself a European-style resort with a dash of good ol' American small town thrown in for good measure—think *Jetsons* architecture and the crushed-velvet vibe of piano bars with the colors and attitude of a laid-back Aegean island village. One thing hasn't changed: Swimming, sunbathing, golfing, and playing tennis are still the primary pastimes in this convenient little oasis.

Another important presence in Palm Springs has little to do with socialites and Americana. The Agua Caliente band of Cahuilla Indians settled in this area 1,000 years before the first golf ball was ever teed up. Recognizing the beauty and spirituality of this wide-open space, they lived a simple life around the natural mineral springs on the desert floor, migrating into the cool canyons during the hot summer months. Under a treaty with the railroad companies and the U.S. government, the tribe owns half the land on which Palm Springs is built and actively works to preserve Native American heritage. It's easy to learn about the American Indians during your visit, and it will definitely add to your appreciation of this part of California.

ESSENTIALS

GETTING THERE   Several airlines service the **Palm Springs Regional Airport,** 3400 E. Tahquitz Canyon Way (☎ 760/323-8161), including **Alaska Airlines** (☎ 800/426-0333), **America West** (☎ 800/235-9292), **American** (☎ 800/433-7300), **Delta/Skywest** (☎ 800/453-9417), **United** (☎ 800/241-6522), and **US Airways** (☎ 800/428-4322). Flights from Los Angeles International Airport (see section 1 in chapter 13) take about 40 minutes.

If you're driving from Los Angeles, take I-10 to the Calif. 111 turnoff to Palm Springs. You'll breeze into town on North Palm Canyon Drive, the main

The Palm Springs Desert Resorts

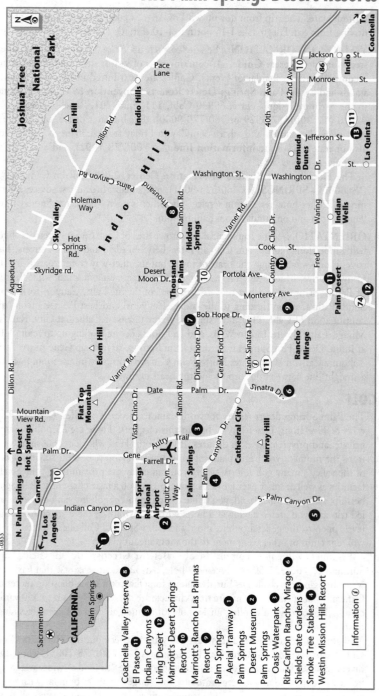

To Coachella

Joshua Tree National Park

Fan Hill
Pace Lane
Indio Hills
Indio Hills

Dillon Rd.
Palms Canyon Rd.

Jackson St.
Monroe St.
Indio
42nd Ave.
40th Ave.

La Quinta
Jefferson St.
St.

Sky Valley
Holeman Way
Hot Springs Rd.
Skyridge rd.

Washington St.
Thousand
Ramon Rd.
Hidden Springs

Bermuda Dunes
Washington
Dr.
Waring

Aqueduct Rd.

Desert Moon Dr.
Thousand Palms

Varner Rd.
Portola Ave.

Indian Wells
Club Dr.
Cook St.

Edom Hill

Bob Hope Dr.
Dinah Shore Dr.
Gerald Ford Dr.
Frank Sinatra Dr.

Monterey Ave.
Country Club St.
Fred

Palm Desert

Dillon Rd.
Varner Rd.

Flat Top Mountain
Date
Palm Dr.
Ramon Rd.

Rancho Mirage
Sinatra Dr.

Mountain View Rd.
Palm Dr.
Gene
Vista Chino Dr.
Autry Trail
Farrell Dr.

Palm
Dr.
Canyon Dr.
Cathedral City
Murray Hill

N. Palm Springs
To Desert Hot Springs
Garnet

Palm Springs Regional Airport
Taquitz Cyn. Way
E. Palm Canyon Dr.

Indian Canyon Dr.
To Los Angeles

S. Palm Canyon Dr.

1-0855

Coachella Valley Preserve 8
El Paseo 11
Living Desert 12
Marriott's Desert Springs Resort 10
Marriott's Rancho Las Palmas Resort 9
Palm Springs Aerial Tramway 1
Palm Springs Desert Museum 2
Palm Springs Oasis Waterpark 3
Ritz-Carlton Rancho Mirage 6
Shields Date Gardens 13
Smoke Tree Stables 4
Westin Mission Hills Resort 7

CALIFORNIA
Sacramento
Palm Springs

Information ℹ

561

thoroughfare. The trip from downtown Los Angeles takes about 2 hours. If you're driving from San Diego, take I-15 north to I-10 east; it's 135 miles.

VISITOR INFORMATION Be sure to pick up *Palm Springs Life* magazine's free monthly "**Desert Guide.**" It contains tons of visitor information including a comprehensive calendar of events. Copies are distributed in hotels and news-stands and by the **Palm Springs Desert Resorts Convention & Visitors Bureau,** in the Atrium Design Centre, 69930 Calif. 111, Suite 201, Rancho Mirage, CA 92270 (☎ 800/417-3529 or 760/770-9000). The bureau's office staff can help with maps, brochures, and advice Monday to Friday from 8:30am to 5pm. They also operate a **24-hour information line** (☎ 760/770-1992), and a website at www.desert-resorts.com.

The **Palm Springs Visitors Information Center,** 2781 N. Palm Canyon Dr. (☎ 800/34-SPRINGS; fax 760/323-3021), offers maps, brochures, advice, souve-nirs, and a free hotel reservation service. The office is open Monday to Sunday from 9am to 5pm and on Sunday from 8am to 4pm.

ORIENTATION The commercial downtown area of Palm Springs stretches about half a mile along North Palm Canyon Drive between Alejo and Ramon streets. The street is one-way through the heart of town, but its other-way counterpart is Indian Canyon Drive, 1 block east. The mountains lie directly west and south, while the rest of Palm Springs is laid out in a grid to the southeast. Palm Canyon forks into South Palm Canyon (leading to the Indian Canyons) and East Palm Canyon (the continuation of Calif. 111) traversing the resort towns of Cathedral City, Rancho Mirage, Palm Desert, Indian Wells, and La Quinta before looping up to rejoin I-10 at Indio. Desert Hot Springs is north of Palm Springs, straight up Gene Autry Trail. Tahquitz Canyon Way creates North Palm Canyon's primary intersection, tracking a straight line between the airport and the heart of town.

GOLF

The Palm Springs desert resorts are world-famous meccas for golfers (see the "Fair-ways & Five-Irons, Desert Style" box in this chapter). There are 85 public, semi-private, and private courses in the area. If you're the kind who starts polishing your irons the moment you begin planning your vacation, you're best off staying at one of the valley's many golf resorts, where you can enjoy the proximity of your hotel's facilities as well as smart package deals that can give you a taste of country club mem-bership. If, on the other hand, you'd like to fit a round of golf into an otherwise var-ied trip and you aren't staying at a hotel with its own links, there are courses at all levels open to the general public, mostly in Palm Springs. Call ahead to see which will rent clubs or other equipment to the spontaneous player.

Beginners will enjoy **Tommy Jacobs' Bel-Air Greens,** 1001 El Cielo, Palm Springs (☎ 760/322-6062), a scenic 9-hole, par-32 executive course that has some water and sandtrap challenges but also allows for a few confidence-boosting successes. Generally flat fairways and mature trees characterize the relatively short (3,350 yards) course. The complex also offers an 18-hole miniature golf course. Greens fees range from $23 to $27.

Slightly more intermediate amateurs will want to check out the **Tahquitz Creek Golf Resort,** 1885 Golf Club Dr., Palm Springs (☎ 760/328-1005), whose two diverse courses both appeal to mid-handicappers. The "Legend's" wide, water-free holes will appeal to anyone frustrated by the "target" courses popular with many architects, while the new Ted Robinson–designed "Resort" course offers all those accuracy-testing bells and whistles more common to lavish private clubs. Greens fees range from $35 to $85, depending on day and cart rental.

Fairways & Five-Irons, Desert Style

Two hours outside of Los Angeles in the Coachella Valley, strung like ripe dates from I-10, lie the resort cities of Palm Springs, Rancho Mirage, Palm Desert, Indian Wells, and La Quinta. This all-season golfer's paradise boasts more than 80 courses, their lush fairways and velvety greens incongruously carved from the arid desert scruff. Both public and resort/semiprivate courses range in difficulty to accommodate low-handicappers and weekend duffers alike, and every imaginable service is available nearby.

If you'd like to sharpen your game, all the principal clubs have resident pros, and there are several schools and clinics, including the **Indian Wells Golf School** at Indian Wells Resort (☎ 800/241-5782 or 760/346-4653), the **Golf Center at Palm Desert** (☎ 760/779-1877), and the **Leadbetter Golf Academy** at PGA West in La Quinta (☎ 800/424-3542 or 760/564-0777). If you're looking to pick up new equipment or some stylish attire, try **Nevada Bob's Discount Golf** in Palm Springs (☎ 760/324-0196) and Indian Wells (☎ 760/346-6166), the **Roger Dunn Golf Shop** in Palm Desert (☎ 760/345-3133) and Cathedral City (☎ 760/324-1160), and **Lady Golf** in Rancho Mirage (☎ 760/773-4949).

Many fine resorts offer generous golf packages, among them **Marriott's Desert Springs Resort** in Palm Desert (☎ 760/341-2211), **Marriott's Rancho Las Palmas** in Rancho Mirage (☎ 760/568-2727), the **Hyatt Grand Champions** in Indian Wells (☎ 760/341-1000), **La Quinta Resort & Club** in La Quinta (☎ 760/346-2904), and the **Estrella Inn** (☎ 800/237-3687 or 760/320-4417).

Tee times at many courses cannot be booked more than a few days in advance for nonguests, but several companies are able to make arrangements several months earlier and even construct a custom package for you with accommodations, golf, meals, and other extras. Among them are **Golf a la Carte** (☎ 760/324-5012; fax 760/321-1242; e-mail glfalacart@aol.com) and **Palm Springs Golf and Tours** (☎ 800/PS-GOLF-1 or 760/346-3331; fax 760/346-4473).

For the nonplaying spectator (or anyone longing to see the pros make it look *so* easy) there are dozens of golf tournaments year-round, including many celebrity and pro-am events in addition to regular PGA, LPGA, and Senior Tour stops. February brings the PGA Tour **Bob Hope Chrysler Classic** at the Bermuda Dunes Country Club and the **Frank Sinatra Celebrity Invitational** at Marriott's Desert Springs Resort & Spa. In March, catch the LPGA Tour **Nabisco Dinah Shore** at the Mission Hills Country Club, then in April the Senior PGA **Liberty Mutual Legends of Golf** comes to PGA West. November brings two of the desert's longest-running charity events, the **22nd Annual Frostig Center/Chris Korman Celebrity Tournament** at the Westin Mission Hills, and the 24-year-old **Billy Barty/7Up Celebrity Golf Classic** at the Mesquite Country Club in Palm Springs. Also in November, check out the wacky **Palm Desert Golf Cart Parade** along El Paseo.

For more information you can call the **Palm Springs Desert Resorts Convention and Visitors Bureau** (☎ 800/41-RELAX or 760/770-9000). The bureau also maintains an **Activities Hotline** (☎ 760/770-1992).

The **Palm Springs Country Club,** 2500 Whitewater Club Dr. ☎ **760/323-8625**), is the oldest public-access golf course within the city of Palm Springs, and is especially popular with budget-conscious golfers, as greens fees are only $40 to $50, including the required cart. The challenge of bunkers and rough can be amplified by the oft-blowing wind along the 5,885 yards of this unusually laid-out course.

The ✪ **Westin Mission Hills Resort Course,** Dinah Shore and Bob Hope drives, Rancho Mirage (☎ **760/328-3198**), is somewhat more forgiving than most of legendary architect Pete Dye's courses, but don't play the back tees unless you've got a consistent 220-yard drive and won't be fazed by the Dye-trademark giant sand bunkers and elevated greens. Water only comes into play on four holes, and the scenery is an exquisite reward for low-handicappers. Nonguest greens fees are $120 to $130, including cart.

One of our favorite desert courses is the ✪ **PGA West TPC Stadium Course,** La Qunita Resort & Club, 49499 Eisenhowser Dr., La Quinta (☎ **760/564-4111**), which received Golf Magazine's 1994 Gold Medal Award for the total golf resort experience. The par-3 17th has a picturesque island green where Lee Trevino made Skins Game history with a spectacualr hole-in-one. The rest of Pete Dye's 7,261-yard design is flat with huge bunkers, lots of water, and severe mounding throughout. Also open for semiprivate play is the **Mountain Course at La Quinta,** another Dye design that regularly appears on U.S. top-100 lists. It's set dramatically against the rocky mountains, which thrust into fairways to create tricky doglegs, and its small Bermuda greens are well guarded by boulders and deep bunkers. Greens fees for non–resort guests are $185 at both La Quinta courses.

A complete golfer's guide is available from the Palm Springs Desert Resorts Convention & Visitors Bureau (see "Essentials," above).

MORE OUTDOOR FUN

The Coachella Valley desert is truly a playground, and what follows is but a sampling of the opportunities to enjoy the abundant sunshine during your vacation here. But the strong sun and dry air that are so appealing can also sneak up on you in the form of sunburn and heat exhaustion. Especially during the summer, but even in milder times, always carry and drink plenty of water.

A FAMILY WATER PARK **Palm Springs Oasis Waterpark,** off I-10 south on Gene Autry Trail between Ramon Road and East Palm Canyon Drive (☎ **760/325-7873**), is a water playground with 13 water slides, body- and boardsurfing, an inner-tube ride, beach volleyball, and more. Dressing rooms, lockers, and private beach cabanas (with food service) are available. Admission is $16.95 for visitors over 60 inches tall, $11.50 for 40 to 60 inches, and free for kids under 40 inches ($9.95 for seniors). The park is open mid-March to Labor Day, daily from 11am to 6pm, plus weekends through all of October.

BALLOONING This is perhaps the most memorable way to see the desert: floating above the landscape in a colorful hot-air balloon. Choose from specialty themes like sunrise, sunset, or romantic champagne flights. Rides are offered by **American Balloon Charters** (☎ **800/FLY-OVER** or 760/327-8544), **Dream Flights** (☎ **800/933-5628** or 760/321-5154), and **Fantasy Balloon Flights** (☎ **800/GO-ABOVE** or 760/568-0997).

BIKING The clean, dry air here just cries out to be enjoyed—what could be better than to pedal your way around town or into the desert? **Adventure Bike Tours** (☎ **760/328-2089**) will outfit you with bike, helmet, souvenir water bottle, and a certified guide. If you're just looking to rent some wheels and a helmet, **Mac's Bicycle Rental** (☎ **760/321-9444**) offers hourly, daily, and weekly rates on bikes, including children's and mountain models. **The Bike Man** (☎ **760/771-3619**) sweetens his deals by including water bottles, locks, maps, and free delivery. The

Bighorn Bicycle Rental & Tour Company (☎ 760/325-3367) has hourly and daily rental rates in addition to guided bike treks.

GUIDED JEEP & WAGON EXCURSIONS **Desert Adventures** (☎ 760/864-6530) offers four-wheel-drive eco-tours led by experienced naturalist guides. Your off-road adventure may explore the lush palm oases of the ancestral Indian Canyons, the rugged Santa Rosa Mountain roads overlooking the Coachella Valley and the Bighorn Sheep Preserve, or picturesque ravines on the way to the San Andreas Fault. Tours range in duration from 2 to 4 hours and in price from $60 to $99. Advance reservations are required. The company's trademark red Jeeps depart from the Desert Adventures Ranch on South Palm Canyon near the entrance to the Indian Canyons, but most of the longer excursions include hotel pickup and return.

Covered Wagon Tours (☎ 760/347-2161) embraces the pioneer spirit with a 2-hour ride through the Coachella Valley Nature Preserve followed by a good, old-fashioned barbecue cookout and live country music. They operate 7 days a week from October to mid-May, and the price is $55 for adults, $27.50 for children 7 to 16, and free for kids 6 and under. Without the "grub," the tour is $40 per adult and $20 per child. Advance reservations are required.

HIKING The most popular spot for hiking is the nearby **Indian Canyons** (☎ 760/325-5673 for information). The Agua Caliente tribe made their home here centuries ago, and remnants of their simple lifestyle can be seen among the streams, waterfalls, and astounding palm groves in Andreas, Murray, and Palm canyons. Striking rock formations and herds of bighorn sheep and wild ponies will probably be more appealing than the "Trading Post" in Palm Canyon, but it does sell detailed trail maps. This is Indian land, and the Tribal Council charges admission of $6 per adult, with discounts for seniors, children, students, and military. The canyons are closed to visitors from late June to early September.

Ten miles east of Palm Springs is the 13,000-acre **Coachella Valley Preserve** (☎ 760/343-1234), which is open daily from sunrise to sunset. There are springs, mesas, both hiking and riding trails, the Thousand Palms Oasis, a visitor center, and picnic areas.

If you're heading up to Joshua Tree National Park (see section 4 of this chapter), consider stopping at the **Big Morongo Canyon Preserve** (☎ 760/363-7190), which was once an Indian village and later a cattle ranch. It's open for visitors Wednesday to Sunday from 7:30am. The park's high water table makes it a magnet for birds and other wildlife; the lush springs and streams are an unexpected desert treat.

HORSEBACK RIDING Equestrians from novice to advanced can experience the natural solitude and quiet of the desert on horseback at **Smoke Tree Stables** (☎ 760/327-1372). Located south of downtown and ideal for exploring the nearby Indian Canyon trails, Smoke Tree offers guided rides for $25 per hour. But don't expect your posse leader to be primed with facts on the nature you'll encounter—this is strictly a do-it-yourself experience.

SKYDIVING **Parachutes over Palm Springs** (☎ 800/535-5867 or 760/345-8321)—the name says it all! Their tandem skydiving system allows even the most timid beginner the opportunity to experience the exhilaration of a 30-second freefall followed by the serenity of a parachute descent while enjoying the panoramic beauty of the desert. You're harnessed to your instructor for the entire jump, and you can even take home a videotaped record of your bravery. The single-jump rate is $169; ask about group rates for two or more. The company operates from the Bermuda Dunes Airport 7 days a week November to April. Advance reservations are required.

TENNIS　Virtually all the larger hotels and resorts have tennis courts, but if you're staying at a B&B, you might want to play at the **Tennis Center,** 1300 Baristo Rd., Palm Springs (☎ **760/320-0020**), which has nine courts and offers day and evening clinics for adults, juniors, and seniors, as well as ball machines for solo practice. USPTA pros are on hand.

If you'd like to play for free, the night-lighted courts at **Palm Springs High School,** 2248 E. Ramon Rd., are open to the public on weekends, holidays, and during the summer. There are also eight free night-lighted courts in beautiful **Ruth Hardy Park** at Tamarisk and Caballero streets.

EXPLORING THE AREA

Haven't seen any celebrities wandering the streets? You may want to hook up with **Celebrity Tours,** located on East Palm Canyon Drive at Gene Autry Trail (☎ **760/770-2700**). Advance reservations are required for their 1- and 2¹/₂-hour tours of Palm Springs, which include some history and lore but mostly the opportunity to gawk at the homes of movie stars and celebrities. The longer tours take in the estates of surrounding Rancho Mirage and Palm Desert, "playground of the international elite."

Palm Springs Desert Museum. 101 Museum Dr. (just west of the Palm Canyon/Tahquitz intersection), Palm Springs. ☎ **760/325-0189.** Admission $6 adults, $5 military and seniors 62 and over, $3 children 6–17, free for children under 6, free for everyone the first Fri of every month. Tues–Thurs and Sat–Sun 10am–5pm, Fri 10am–8pm.

This well-endowed museum combines world-class Western and Native American art collections, the natural history of the desert, and an outstanding anthropology department, primarily representing the local Cahuilla tribe. Traditional Indian life as it was lived for centuries before the white presence is illustrated by tools, baskets, and other relics. Check local schedules to find out about (usually excellent) visiting exhibits; plays, lectures, and other events are presented in the museum's Annenberg Theater.

The Living Desert Wildlife and Botanical Park. 47900 Portola Ave., Palm Desert. ☎ **760/346-5694.** Admission $7.50 adults, $6.50 seniors 62 and over, $3.50 children 3–12, free for kids under 2. Daily 9am–5pm (last admission 4:30pm); call for summer schedule. Closed Aug and Christmas Day.

This 1,200-acre desert reserve, museum, zoo, and educational center is designed to acquaint visitors with the unique habitats that make up the Southern California deserts. You can walk or take a tram tour through sectors that re-create life in several distinctive desert zones. See and learn about a dizzying variety of plants, insects, and wildlife, including bighorn sheep, mountain lions, rattlesnakes, lizards, owls, golden eagles, and the ubiquitous roadrunner.

Palm Springs Aerial Tramway. Tramway Rd. off Calif. 111, Palm Springs. ☎ **760/325-1391.** Tickets $18 adults, $15 seniors, $11 children 5–12, free for kids 4 and under; Ride 'n' Dine combination (available after 2:30pm, dinner served after 4pm), $21 adults, $14 children. Mon–Fri 10am–8pm, Sat–Sun 8am–8pm (closes 1 hour later Memorial Day thru Labor Day). Free parking.

To gain a bird's-eye perspective on the Coachella Valley, take this 14-minute ascent up 2¹/₂ miles to the top of Mt. San Jacinto. The whole experience has a fabulous 1960s feel, from the original Swiss funicular equipment to the scratchy recording broadcast during the trip up (often drowned out by the periodic squeals of white-knuckled passengers). There's a whole other world once you arrive: alpine scenery, a ski lodge–flavored restaurant and gift shop, and temperatures typically 40° cooler than the desert floor. The most dramatic contrast is during the winter when the mountaintop is a snowy wonderland, irresistible to hikers and bundled-up kids with saucers. The excursion might not be worth the expense during the rest of the year. Guided mule rides and cross-country ski equipment are available at the top.

✪ **Shields Date Gardens.** 80225 Calif. 111, Indio. ☎ **760/347-0996.** Free admission. Daily 8am–6pm.

In a splendid display of wishful thinking and clever engineering, the Coachella Valley has grown into a rich agricultural region, known internationally for grapefruit, figs, and grapes—but mostly for dates. The fascination of 1920s entrepreneurs with Arabian lore, fueled by the Sahara-like conditions of the desert around Indio, led to the planting of date palm groves. Started with just a few parent trees imported from the Middle East, the groves now produce 95% of the world's date crop. The trees are hand-pollinated by farmers, a process detailed in *The Romance and Sex Life of the Date,* a film running continuously (its racy title is the best part). Also housed in the splendid 1930s Moderne building is a lunch counter (date shake anyone?) and store selling an endless variety of dates and related goodies.

SHOPPING

Downtown Palm Springs revolves around **North Palm Canyon Drive;** many art galleries, souvenir shops, and restaurants are located here, along with a couple of large-scale hotels and shopping centers. This wide, one-way boulevard is designed for pedestrians, with many businesses set back from the street itself—don't be shy about poking around the little courtyards you'll encounter. On Thursday night from 6 to 10pm the blocks between Amado and Baristo roads are transformed into **VillageFest,** a street fair tradition celebrating its fifth anniversary. Handmade-crafts vendors and aromatic food booths compete for your attention with wacky street performers and even-wackier locals shopping at the mouth-watering fresh produce stalls.

The northern section of Palm Canyon is becoming known for vintage collectibles and is being touted as the "**Antique and Heritage Gallery District.**" The plain truth is that, as the older residents of Palm Springs say good-bye to this life, consignment and estate-sale companies are becoming better stocked than ever before. Check out **John's Resale Furnishings,** in the Village Attic, 849 N. Palm Canyon Dr. (☎ **760/320-6165**), if you're interested in reliving the '50s in all their fabulous glory; it's one of the best places to see well-preserved relics from Palm Springs' heyday of development.

Down in Palm Desert lies the delicious excess of **El Paseo** (the name of the avenue), a glitzy cornucopia of high-rent boutiques, salons, and upscale eateries reminiscent of Rodeo Drive in Beverly Hills, along with a dozen or more major shopping malls just like back home.

Factory outlet shopping is 20 minutes away in Cabazon (see section 1, "En Route to the Palm Springs Resorts," earlier in this chapter).

One of my favorite local spots is **Bloomsbury Books,** 555 S. Sunrise Way No. 105 (at Ramon Road; ☎ **760/325-3862**), which is great for browsing. Proprietor Brad Confer is hard at work compiling an impressive array of out-of-print books and signed and rare editions, all reasonably priced and in great condition. Bloomsbury is especially strong in gay-lesbian literature (including rare early magazines and foreign publications) that's meticulously organized by topic. Every section is cleverly decorated with related memorabilia and noteworthy selections. Located in an ugly strip mall several blocks from the center of town, this treasure is well worth the detour. Open Monday to Saturday from 11am to 9pm.

If it's Palm Springs history or literature you seek, visit the appealingly cluttered **Celebrity Bookstore,** 170 E. Tahquitz Canyon (half a block east of Palm Canyon

Dr.; ☎ **800/320-6575** or 760/320-6575). Owner Darrell Meeks is the resident expert on local publications, and he also sets up tables for VillageFest each week. Open Monday to Saturday from 9am to 8pm and on Sunday from 9am to 4pm.

Looking for a simply fabulous sequined evening frock, some blindingly tacky golf pants, gabardine leisure suits, or other retro-garb? **Patsy's,** 4121 E. Palm Canyon Drive. (☎ **760/324-8825**), is a consignment shop filled with entire wardrobes (some are from the local rich and famous) and frequented by young hipsters and cabaret costumers. She's open Wednesday to Saturday from 10am to 4:30pm and on Sunday from noon to 4:30pm.

GAY LIFE IN PALM SPRINGS

Don't think the local chamber of commerce doesn't recognize that the Palm Springs area is one of the current top three American destinations for gay travelers. After just a short while in town it's easy to tell how the gay tourism dollar is courted as aggressively as straight spending. Real estate agents cater to gay shoppers for vacation properties, and entire condo communities are marketed toward the gay resident. Advertisements for these and scores of other proudly gay-owned businesses can be found in *The Bottom Line,* the desert's free biweekly magazine of articles, events, and community guides for the gay reader, is available at hotels, newsstands, and select merchants.

Throughout the year events are held that transcend the gay community to include everyone. In March the **Desert AIDS Walk** benefits the Desert AIDS Project, while the world's largest organized gathering of lesbians coincides with the **Nabisco Dinah Shore Golf Tournament.**

Be sure to visit **Between the Pages Bookstore,** on Arenas Road east of Indian Canyon (☎ **760/320-7158**). Besides offering an extensive selection of gay- and lesbian-oriented books and videos, you'll find a wealth of free brochures and guides in the adjacent espresso bar, which also serves as the lobby for the **Between the Pages Playhouse.** This short block of Arenas is home to a score of gay establishments, including **Streetbar** (☎ **760/320-1266**), a neighborhood gathering spot for tourists and locals alike.

Just a few blocks away is a cozy neighborhood of modest homes and small hotels, concentrated on Warm Sands Drive south of Ramon. Known simply as "**Warm Sands,**" this area holds the very nicest "private resorts"—mostly discreet and gated B&B–style inns. Locals recommend the co-ed **El Mirasol Villas** (☎ **800/327-2985** or 760/326-5913) and the all-male **Warm Sands Villas** (☎ **760/323-3006**). Near the center of town lies the historic **Harlow Club Hotel,** 175 E. El Alameda (☎ **800/223-4073** or 760/320-4333), where men enjoy luxury haciendas amid lush gardens. The **Bee Charmer Inn,** 1600 E. Palm Canyon (☎ **760/778-5883**), caters to a female clientele, as does the party-atmosphere **Delilah's Enclave,** 641 San Lorenzo Rd. (☎ **800/621-6973** or 760/325-5269).

Gay nightlife is everywhere in the Valley, and especially raucous on holiday weekends. Pick up *The Bottom Line* for the latest restaurant, nightclub, theater, and special events listings.

WHERE TO STAY

The city of Palm Springs offers a wide range of accommodations—I particularly like the inns that have opened as new owners renovate the many fabulous 40- to 60-year-old cottage complexes in the wind-shielded "Tennis Club" area west of Palm Canyon Drive. The other desert resort cities offer mostly sprawling resort complexes, many boasting world-class golf, tennis, or spa facilities and multiple on-site restaurants. Most are destinations in and of themselves, offering activities for the whole family (including a whole lot of relaxing and being pampered). So if you're looking for a good base from which to shop or sightsee, Palm Springs is your best bet.

Regardless of your choice, remember that the rates given below are for high season (winter, generally October to May). During the hotter summer months, it's common to find $300 rooms going for $89 or less as part of off-season packages. Even in season, midweek and golf packages are common, so always ask when making your reservation.

PALM SPRINGS
Expensive

Ingleside Inn. 200 W. Ramon Rd. (at Belardo Rd.), Palm Springs, CA 92264. ☎ **800/ 772-6655** or 760/325-0046. Fax 760/325-0710. 29 rms, 16 suites. A/C MINIBAR TV TEL. $75–$235 double; $205–$285 minisuite; $135–$265 villa; from $295 full suite. Rates include continental breakfast. AE, DISC, MC, V. Free valet parking.

Once the 1920s estate of the Humphrey Birge family, manufacturers of the Pierce Arrow automobile, this hideaway offers some of the most charming rooms in town. Each guest room and suite is uniquely decorated with antiques—perhaps a canopied bed or a 15th-century vestment chest. Many rooms have wood-burning fireplaces; all have in-room whirlpools and steam baths.

There's an Old-World charm here that's matched by fine service. The Ingleside is hardly low-key, however, for the management is quick to mention in brochures, on wall plaques, and other places that celebrities such as Elizabeth Taylor, Howard Hughes, John Wayne, Bette Davis, Salvador Dalí, John Travolta, and Goldie Hawn have stayed here (the celebrity watching is still first-rate). They also like to boast of the inn's *two* appearances on *Lifestyles of the Rich & Famous.*

Dining/Entertainment: Melvyn's is the expensive continental dining room, and the adjacent piano bar and lounge attract a fancy, old-money crowd. Frank and Barbara Sinatra hosted a dinner here on the eve of their wedding.

Services: Concierge, room service, in-room massage, complimentary limousine service.

Facilities: Large heated outdoor pool, Jacuzzi, sundeck, croquet, shuffleboard, business center, car-rental desk, tour desk, boutiques.

La Mancha Villas, Spa & Court Club. 444 Avenida Caballeros, Palm Springs, CA 92262. ☎ **800/64-PRIVACY** or 760/323-1773. 66 suites and villas. A/C TV TEL. $130–$225 suite for 2; $145–$595 villa. AE, DC, DISC, MC, V. Free parking.

The security-gated entry makes La Mancha look like a private community, and it was designed that way. Once inside, though, a warmly respectful staff will pamper you, just the way they've coddled the countless celebs who've lent their names to the brochure. The quiet elegance and service distinguish La Mancha from the other resorts, not its modern but unoriginal furnishings. Fruit baskets welcome guests to the quarters, most of them suites with TVs and phones in every room, and VCRs (they'll even provide Nintendo for the kids). Many guests opt for the countless pleasures of the villas, which have private pools, fireplaces, and wet bars. Scores of bicycles and a private fleet of rental cars stand ready should you want to venture the half mile into town, and there's a spa and fitness center—how about a massage on your personal patio?

Dining/Entertainment: In keeping with the La Mancha theme, the aptly named Don Quixote Dining Room is open for breakfast, lunch, and dinner.

Services: Concierge, room service (limited), laundry (for units without their own washer/dryer), morning newspaper, nightly turndown, valet, courtesy airport limo.

Facilities: Video rental, heated outdoor pool with Jacuzzi, spa and fitness center (fee for massage, fitness classes, personal trainer, or salon services), seven tennis courts (four lighted for night play), two paddle tennis courts (one lighted), three croquet lawns (one lighted), two practice greens, gift shop, conference rooms.

Moderate

Estrella Inn. 415 S. Belardo Rd. (south of Tahquitz Way), Palm Springs, CA 92262. ☎ **760/ 320-4117.** Fax 760/323-3303. 37 rms, 25 cottages. A/C TV TEL. $120–$150 double; $160– $250 1-bedroom cottage; $200–$350 2-bedroom cottage. Rates include continental breakfast. Monthly rates available. AE, CB, DC, MC, V. Free parking.

One of the best moderately priced choices, the Estrella Inn is located on a quiet, secluded street that seems to be miles from everywhere, even though it's just a block from the center of town. Clark Gable and Carole Lombard often trysted at this 1930s property, which was recently restored to its early Hollywood charm. The rooms vary widely in size from very small quarters to cottages with decks, wet bars, full kitchens, and fireplaces. There are two swimming pools and a children's pool, two Jacuzzis, an outdoor barbecue, and a lawn and court games area. Ask about attractive golf packages that include play at one of several nearby courses.

✪ **Korakia Pensione.** 257 S. Patencio Rd., Palm Springs, CA 92262. ☎ **760/864-6411.** 20 rms and suites. $79–$239 double or suite. Rates include breakfast. No credit cards. Free parking.

If you can work within the Korakia's rigid deposit-cancellation policy, you're in for a special stay at this Greek/Moroccan oasis just a few blocks from Palm Canyon Drive. The simply furnished rooms and unbelievably spacious suites are peaceful and private, surrounded by flagstone courtyards and flowering gardens. Rooms are divided between the main house, a second restored villa across the street, and surrounding guest bungalows. Most have kitchens, while many sport fireplaces. This former artist's villa from the 1920s draws a hip international crowd of artists, writers, and musicians. All beds are blessed with thick feather duvets, while the windows are shaded by flowing white canvas draperies in the Mediterranean style. Add a sumptuous breakfast served in your room or poolside (*korakia* is Greek for "crow," and a tile mosaic example graces the pool bottom). This unusual B&B shapes up as a good buy.

Spa Hotel & Casino. 100 N. Indian Canyon Dr., Palm Springs, CA 92263. ☎ **800/854-1279** or 760/325-1461. Fax 760/325-3344. 230 rms, 20 suites. A/C MINIBAR TV TEL. $129–$194 double. Rates include continental breakfast. AE, CB, DC, MC, V. Free parking.

Located on the Indian-owned parcel of land containing the original mineral springs for which Palm Springs was named, this is one of the more unusual choices in town. The Cahuilla claimed that the springs had magical powers to cure illness, and today's travelers still come here to pamper both body and soul by "taking the waters." There are three pools on the premises. One is a conventional outdoor swimming pool; the other two are filled from the underground natural springs brimming with revitalizing minerals. Inside the hotel's extensive spa are private sunken marble swirlpools fed by the springs, and after your bath, you can avail yourself of the many other pampering treatments offered. The spa recently opened the adjoining Vegas-style Casino, featuring the familiar hush of card gaming tables and clanging of video poker and slot machines. Other hotel facilities include a fitness center, steam room, concierge, car-rental desk, two restaurants, and two bars.

Villa Royale. 1620 Indian Trail (off East Palm Canyon), Palm Springs, CA 92264. ☎ **800/ 245-2314** or 760/327-2314. Fax 760/322-3794. 31 rms and suites. A/C TV TEL. $75–$165 double; $150–$225 suite. Rates include breakfast. Additional person $25 extra. AE, MC, V. Free parking.

Located 5 minutes from the hustle and bustle of downtown Palm Springs, this B&B evokes a European cluster of villas, complete with climbing bougainvillea and rooms filled with international antiques and artwork. The main building was once home to Olympic and silver-screen ice skater Sonya Henie. The present owner, Bob Lee, later commandeered and combined two adjacent apartment buildings. The guest rooms vary widely in quality, so you might find that the trade-off for quiet seclusion is a small, dark room in back. Some rooms and suites, on the other hand, are spacious and have fireplaces and/or private patios with spas.

Continental breakfast is served in an intimate garden setting surrounding the main pool. At lunch and dinner this patio becomes the Europa Restaurant, serving slightly pricey but inventive continental fare. Europa is heavily advertised as a "romantic" dining spot, but the service can sometimes be frustratingly leisurely.

Inexpensive

Casa Cody. 175 S. Cahuilla Rd. (between Tahquitz Way and Arenas Rd.), Palm Springs, CA 92262. ☎ **760/320-9346.** Fax 760/325-8610. 23 rms, studios, and suites. A/C TV TEL. $69–$79 double; $89–$129 studio; $129–$159 1-bedroom suite; $189–$199 2-bedroom suite. Rates include continental breakfast. Midweek and summer rates available. AE, CB, DC, DISC, MC, V.

Once owned by "Wild" Bill Cody's niece, this 1920s *casa* with a double courtyard (each with swimming pool) has been restored to fine condition, sporting a vaguely southwestern decor and peaceful grounds marked by large lawns and mature, blossoming fruit trees. You'll feel more like a house guest than a hotel client at the Casa Cody. It's located in the primarily residential "Tennis Club" area of town, a couple of easy blocks from Palm Canyon Drive. Many units here have fireplaces and full-size kitchens. Breakfast is served poolside, as is complimentary wine and cheese on Saturday afternoon.

Orchid Tree Inn. 261 S. Belardo Rd. (at Baristo Rd.), Palm Springs, CA 92262. ☎ **800/733-3435** or 760/325-2791. Fax 760/325-3855. 40 rms and suites, 1 two-bedroom bungalow. A/C TV TEL. $95–$110 double; $100–$155 suite; $290 bungalow. AE, MC, V.

Although it's billed as a "1930s desert garden retreat," the Orchid Tree bears many marks of a 1970s remodeling (like contemporary sliding glass doors). If you're not too picky about authenticity, however, the Orchid Tree's beautifully landscaped, sprawling grounds and three swimming pools, complemented by two outdoor whirlpools, make this a good choice in the genuinely historic "Tennis Club" area near the heart of town. Flowering shrubs, mature citrus trees, and other foliage surrounding the red-tile-roofed 1- and 2-story buildings make for pleasant and private accommodations, 30 of which have kitchens. An added treat are the multitudes of twittering hummingbirds, sparrows, and quail drawn by the bird feeders and baths on the grounds.

RANCHO MIRAGE

Marriott's Rancho Las Palmas Resort & Country Club. 41000 Bob Hope Dr., Rancho Mirage, CA 92270. ☎ **800/I-LUV-SUN** or 760/568-2727. Fax 760/568-5845. 450 rms, 22 suites. A/C MINIBAR TV TEL. $175–$250 double; $250–$280 suite. AE, MC, V.

The early California charm of this relaxing Spanish hacienda makes Rancho Las Palmas one of the less pretentious luxury resorts in the desert. Dedicated golfers come to play on the adjoining country club's 27 holes of golf, and tennis buffs flock to the 25 hotel courts (3 of them red clay). The rooms are arranged in a complex of low-rise, tile-roofed structures, and the public areas have an easygoing elegance, filled with flower-laden stone fountains, smooth terra-cotta–tile floors, and rough-hewn wood trim. All rooms have a balcony or patio.

Dining/Entertainment: The Marriott's four restaurants range from casual patio dining to dressy dinner fare, and Miguel's Lounge offers cocktails, snacks, and music in a cantina setting.

Services: Room service, laundry service, baby-sitting.

Facilities: Two swimming pools with adjacent whirlpools, fully equipped free fitness center, 25 tennis courts, golf and tennis pro shops.

Ritz-Carlton Rancho Mirage. 68900 Frank Sinatra Dr., Rancho Mirage, CA 92270. ☎ **800/ 241-3333** or 760/321-8282. Fax 760/321-6928. 240 rms and suites. A/C MINIBAR TV TEL. $260–$395 double; from $650 suite. Additional person $25 extra; children 9 and under stay free in parents' room. AE, MC, V. Indoor valet parking $12.

This desert resort is situated on a spectacular mountain bluff, which provides a breath-taking setting but can make you feel isolated from the community below. It's a bit too clubby and formal, and the service is a little stuffy for this relaxed desert location. The accommodations themselves, all with terraces, sport the tasteful elegance that's the hallmark of Ritz-Carlton hotels, and feature the usual Ritz touches like hair dry-ers, movie channels, refrigerators, and bathrobes. If you have a taste for posh luxury and want to get away from it all, this might be the place for you.

Dining/Entertainment: There are three restaurants, including the Club Grill, which serves regional American fare in a sophisticated ambiance created by crystal chandeliers, fine china, and piano music playing softly in the background. Jackets are required for men. There's also a bar with live entertainment.

Services: Concierge, room service, dry cleaning/laundry, masseur, twice-daily maid service, baby-sitting.

Facilities: Swimming pool (the only chilled pool in Palm Springs), compact but well-equipped fitness center, whirlpool, spa, sauna, 10 tennis courts, games room, volleyball, basketball, car-rental desk, children's program, business center.

Westin Mission Hills Resort. Dinah Shore Dr. and Bob Hope Dr., Rancho Mirage, CA 92270. ☎ **800/WESTIN-1** or 760/328-5955. Fax 760/321-2955. 512 rms and suites. A/C MINIBAR TV TEL. $239–$299 double; from $390 suite. Additional person $25 extra. Children 17 and under stay free in parents' room. AE, MC, V. Free valet and self-parking.

Designed to resemble a Moroccan palace surrounded by pools, waterfalls, and lush gardens, this self-contained resort stands on 360 acres. It's an excellent choice for families and for travelers who take their golf game seriously.

The rooms are a bit bland when compared to the spectacular exterior of the hotel, but they do have views of the mountains and golf course. They all have terraces and come with coffeemakers, hair dryers, movie channels, voice mail, and bathrobes. Pets are accepted.

Dining/Entertainment: The dining options include Bella Vista, an atrium dining room serving California cuisine. There are also three bars, two of which offer live entertainment.

Services: Concierge, room service, dry cleaning, laundry, masseur, twice-daily maid service, baby-sitting.

Facilities: Three swimming pools, fitness center, spa, steam room, whirlpool, seven tennis courts, running track, bikes and bike trails, renowned championship golf course, games room, lawn games, car-rental desk, business center, beauty salon. The fully staffed activities center for children offers educational instruction about the flora, fauna, and history of the desert.

PALM DESERT

Marriott's Desert Springs Spa & Resort. 74885 Country Club Dr., Palm Desert, CA 92260. ☎ 800/331-3112 or 760/341-2211. Fax 760/341-1872. 833 rms, 51 suites. A/C MINIBAR TV TEL. $210–$395 double; from $575 suite. Children 17 and under stay free in parents' room. AE, CB, DC, DISC, MC, V.

A tourist attraction in its own right, Marriott's Desert Springs Resort is worth a peek even if you're not lucky enough to stay here. Most of the guests are attracted by the excellent golf and tennis facilities. The huge, luxurious, full-service spa is an added perk, offering massages, facials, aerobics classes, and supervised weight training. Visitors enter this artificial desert oasis via a sweeping palm tree–lined road wending its way past a small pond that's home to a gaggle of pink flamingos. Once inside, guests are greeted by a shaded marble lobby "rain forest" replete with interior moat and the squawk of tropical birds. Canopied water taxis congregate here, ready to float guests to their rooms.

While the rooms here are not as fancy as the lobby would lead you to believe, they're exceedingly comfortable, decorated with muted pastels and contemporary furnishings. All have terraces with views of the golf course and the San Jacinto Mountains. Most units have large baths and are outfitted with hair dryers, ironing boards and irons, and separate tubs. The suites have large sitting/dining areas furnished with Murphy beds.

Dining/Entertainment: There are six restaurants, four snack bars, and two lounges, one of which features live entertainment. The poolside snacks are remarkably tasty.

Services: Concierge, room service, overnight laundry, masseur, twice-daily maid service, baby-sitting.

Facilities: Four heated outdoor pools, sunbathing "beach" with volleyball court, full-service spa and health club with aerobic classes, 3 outdoor Jacuzzis, sundecks, 20 tennis courts (hard, clay, and grass; seven lighted), jogging trail, 2 18-hole golf courses, putting green, driving range, special children's programs, games room, car-rental desk, tour desk, José Eber beauty salon.

LA QUINTA

❍ **La Quinta Resort & Club.** 49499 Eisenhower Dr., La Quinta, CA 92253. ☎ 800/854-1271, 800/472-4316 in CA, or 760/564-4111. Fax 760/564-5758. 640 rms and suites. A/C MINIBAR TV TEL. $200–$255 double; from $650 suite. Additional person $15 extra; children 17 and under stay free in parents' room. AE, MC, V.

A luxury resort set amid citrus trees, towering palms, cacti, and desert flowers at the base of the rocky Santa Rosa Mountains, La Quinta is *the* place to be if you're serious about your golf or tennis game. All rooms are in comfortable single-story, Spanish-style casitas scattered throughout the grounds. Each has a private patio and access to one of two dozen small pools, enhancing the feeling of privacy at this re-treat. All accommodations come with two phones, movie channels, and refrigerators; some have fireplaces or their own Jacuzzis. Pets are accepted.

Dining/Entertainment: The tranquil lounge/library in the unaltered original hacienda hearkens back to the early days of the resort, when Clark Gable, Greta Garbo, Frank Capra, and other luminaries chose La Quinta as their hideaway. There are three restaurants, including Montanas with outstanding Mediterranean fare, and three bars (two with entertainment).

Services: Concierge, room service, dry cleaning, laundry, masseur, twice-daily maid service, baby-sitting.

Facilities: The resort is renowned for its 5 championship golf courses—including one of California's best, Pete Dye's PGA West TPC Stadium Course—and 30 tennis courts. There's a large main swimming pool, plus 24 smaller pools and dozens of whirlpools, a fitness center, bicycles, children's program, car-rental desk, a business center, and a beauty salon.

DESERT HOT SPRINGS

✪ **Two Bunch Palms.** 67425 Two Bunch Palms Trail, Desert Hot Springs, CA 92240. ☎ **800/ 472-4334** or 760/329-8791. Fax 760/329-1317. 40 rms, suites, and efficiencies; 4 cottages and villas. A/C TV TEL. $135–$260 double; $235–$395 suite or efficiency; $252–$570 cottage or villa. Rates include breakfast. AE, MC, V. Closed Aug.

Posh yet intimate, this spiritual sanctuary in Desert Hot Springs has been drawing weary city dwellers with its healing mineral springs since Chicago mobster Al Capone hid out here in the 1930s. Two Bunch Palms later became a playground for the movie community, but today it's a friendly and informal haven offering renowned spa services, quiet bungalows nestled on lush grounds, and trademark pools of steaming mineral water. All accommodations have terraces and such thoughtful extras as coffeemakers, hair dryers, and refrigerators, and some units have fireplaces or their own Jacuzzis. The staff offers discreet, excellent service.

Dining/Entertainment: Surrounding Desert Hot Springs offers little incentive to leave this sybaritic paradise; you'll probably eat your meals at the unremarkable but health-conscious Casino Dining Room.

Facilities: Legions of return guests will attest that the outstanding spa treatments (nine varieties of massage, mud baths, body wraps, facials, salt glo, and more) and therapeutic waters are what make the luxury of Two Bunch Palms worth the price. Other amenities include a swimming pool, bicycles, two tennis courts, a fitness center, and private sunning bins.

WHERE TO DINE

PALM SPRINGS

You can get rid of the caffeine shakes in Palm Springs at **Lalajava,** 300 N. Palm Canyon Dr., at the corner of Amado (☎ **760/325-3494**). The cheerful staff will help you navigate their extensive menu of coffee items, which run the gamut from steaming hot cappuccinos to blended ice mochas, including flavored lattes, mochas, and cocoas. Nibble on a fresh muffin or a bagel spread with plain or honey-walnut cream cheese, and you'll be well prepared for your day.

Expensive

✪ **Palmie.** 276 N. Palm Canyon Dr. (across from the Hyatt). ☎ **760/320-3375.** Reservations recommended. Main courses $15–$22. AE, DC, MC, V. Mon–Sat 5:30–9:30pm. CLASSIC FRENCH.

You can't see Palmie from the street, and once you're seated inside its softly lit, lattice-enclosed dining patio, you won't see the bustle outside anymore, either. Art deco posters of French seaside resorts abound, transporting you to the cozy bistro of owners Martine and Alain Clerc. Chef Alain sends out dishes of traditional French masterpieces such as bubbling cheese soufflé, green lentil salad dotted with pancetta, steak au poivre rich with cognac sauce, and lobster raviolis garnished with caviar; in fact, every carefully garnished plate is a work of art. To the charming background strains of French chanteuses, hostess/manager Martine circulates between tables, determined that visitors should enjoy their meals as much as the loyal regulars she greets by name. Forget your cardiologist for one night and don't leave without sampling dessert: My favorite is the trio of petite crème brûlées, flavored with ginger, vanilla, and Kahlúa.

Moderate

La Provence. 254 N. Palm Canyon Dr. (upstairs from an arcade). ☎ **760/416-4418.** Reservations recommended. Main courses $10–$21. AE, DC, DISC, MC, V. Thurs–Tues 5:30–10:30pm. COUNTRY FRENCH.

A favorite of locals and recommended by knowledgeable innkeepers, the casually elegant La Provence eschews heavy traditional French cream sauces in favor of carefully married herbs and spices. The second-story terrace filled with tables sets a lovely mood on balmy desert evenings, whether or not it "subtly infuses the diner with an elevated sense of tranquillity" as the restaurant gushingly promises. The menu offers some expected items (escargots in mushroom caps, bouillabaisse, steak au poivre) as well as inventive pastas like wild-mushroom raviolis in a sun-dried tomato and sweet-onion sauce. Like Palmie, La Provence is run by French expatriates who've brought their culinary expertise to the desert.

Las Casuelas Terraza. 222 S. Palm Canyon Dr. ☎ **760/325-2794.** Reservations recommended on weekends. Main courses $7–$13. AE, CB, DC, DISC, MC, V. Mon–Thurs 11am–10pm, Fri–Sat 11am–11pm, Sun 10am–10pm. CLASSIC MEXICAN.

The original Las Casuelas is still open, a tiny storefront several blocks from this popular *terraza* (terrace) offspring, but the bougainvillea-draped front patio here is a much better place to people-watch over Mexican standards like quesadillas, enchiladas, and mountainous nachos washed down with equally super-size margaritas. Inside, the action heats up with live music and raucous happy-hour crowds. During hot weather, the patio and even sidewalk passersby are cooled by the restaurant's well-placed misters, making this a perfect late-afternoon or early-evening choice.

Livreri's. 350 Indian Canyon Dr. (between Tahquitz Way and Ramon Rd.). ☎ **760/327-1419.** Reservations recommended. Pizza, pasta, and main courses $8–$24. AE, MC, V. Wed–Mon 5–10pm. CLASSIC ITALIAN.

The Livreri family came to the desert from Long Island, New York, in the mid-1970s and began preparing traditional Italian cuisine served in generous portions: steaming pastas, cheesy pizzas, and garlicky seafood specialties. It's not the glamorous, old-money Sinatra spot (for that, try Dominick's or Alberto's in Rancho Mirage), but it's conveniently located and satisfying. Separate rooms hold a long, leather-upholstered bar and the "Celebrity Room," where a retirement-age crowd gathers to enjoy dinner-theater performances of Broadway showtunes.

Inexpensive

✪ **Edgardo's Café Veracruz.** 494 N. Palm Canyon (at W. Alejo Rd.). ☎ **760/360-3558.** Reservations recommended. Main courses $3.50–$15. DISC, MC, V. Mon–Fri 11am–3pm and 5:30–9:30pm, Sat–Sun 8am–10pm (sometimes later). REGIONAL CENTRAL MEXICAN.

The pleasant but humble ambiance at Edgardo's is a welcome change from touristy Palm Springs, and is the perfect backdrop for its expert menu of authentic Mayan, Huasteco, and Aztec cuisine. The dark interior boasts an array of colorful masks and artwork from Central and South America, but the postage-stamp–sized front patio with a trickling fountain is the best place to sample Edgardo's tangy quesadillas, desert cactus salad, and traditional poblano chiles rellenos—perhaps even a oyster/tequila shooter from the oyster bar!

Lincoln View Café. 278 N. Palm Canyon (in back of the courtyard). ☎ **760/327-6365.** Breakfast $2–$7; salads and sandwiches $4–$6; coffee drinks $1.25–$3.75. AE, DC, DISC, MC, V. Daily 7:30am–5:30pm. CAFE/BAKERY.

Tucked into the same quiet courtyard as Palmie (see above), this tasteful purveyor of coffee specialties, baked treats, and light meals is named for the unlikely "historic" view of Abraham Lincoln. Okay, it's not quite Mt. Rushmore, but the city makes the most of it. Use the purple scope outside the cafe's entrance to help fix your gaze on Lincoln's profile, formed in the scraggy hillside beyond the skyline. Enjoy live jazz here on the weekends.

Louise's Pantry. 124 S. Palm Canyon ☎ **760/325-5124.** Reservations not accepted. Most items under $10. DISC, MC, V. Daily 7am–8:30pm. AMERICAN.

A real old-fashioned diner, Louise's has been a fixture in Palm Springs since it opened as a drugstore lunch counter in 1945. Locals line up for the very few booths (expect a wait during mealtimes) to enjoy premium-quality comfort foods such as Cobb salad, Reuben and French dip sandwiches, chicken and dumplings, hearty breakfasts with biscuits and gravy, and tasty fresh-baked pies. There's another branch in Palm Desert in the Town Center Plaza, Fred Waring Drive and Town Center Way (☎ **760/346-1315**).

Mykonos. 139 Andreas (just off Palm Canyon). ☎ **760/322-0223.** Reservations not accepted. Most items under $10. MC, V. Wed–Mon 11am–10pm. GREEK.

Sit at the simple, candlelit tables in this off-street brick courtyard with locals who've been enjoying authentic Greek specialties at this family-run spot for 9 years. Mykonos is super-casual (vinyl tablecloths and so forth) and decorated in white and blue like its Aegean namesake, but it's a pleasant treat in a town of mostly mediocre retro-diner fare. Traditional lamb shanks over rice, *dolmades* (stuffed grape leaves), salad tangy with crumbled feta cheese, and sweet, sticky baklava are among their best items.

RANCHO MIRAGE

The Chart House. 69934 Calif. 111 (between Country Club and Frank Sinatra drives). ☎ **760/324-5613.** Reservations not accepted. Full dinners $13–$25. AE, CB, DC, DISC, MC, V. Mon–Fri 5–10pm, Sat 5–10:30pm, Sun 5–10pm. STEAKS/SEAFOOD.

Looking like a giant alien crustacean partially embedded in the earth, this traditional steak house is a treasure of wild 1960s architecture. You've seen this menu before— fine steaks, prime rib and seafood, endless salad bar, oversize baked potatoes— but the Chart House prepares each meal superbly, and the surreal setting makes it worth the expenditure.

LA QUINTA

La Quinta Cliffhouse. 78250 Calif. 111. ☎ **760/360-5991.** Reservations recommended. Main courses $14–$27. AE, DC, MC, V. Mon 5:30–9:30pm, Tues–Fri noon–2pm and 5:30–9:30pm, Sat 5:30–9:30pm, Sun (in fall only) 10am–2pm, closed for lunch in summer. REGIONAL AMERICAN.

King of its own little hill on the east side of Calif. 111, La Quinta Cliffhouse successfully combines high-quality cuisine with a lovely setting. The stairs leading to the restaurant's entrance wind through a rocky waterfall. Try to get a table on the outdoor terrace or near a window to enjoy the Cliffhouse's best-known non-culinary draw: breathtaking sunsets virtually every night of the year. The entirely à la carte menu ensures that you'll pay handsomely for your dinner, but plenty of regulars attest to its worth. A large steamed artichoke served with drawn butter is a popular appetizer pick, perhaps followed by fresh mahimahi prepared with soy and ginger and topped with razor-thin stir-fried vegetables. Aged filet mignon, pork ribs, and several chicken selections keep the grill busy. The bar offers a great early-bird dinner.

PALM DESERT

Max's Opera Cafe. 73030 El Paseo (Monterey at Calif. 111). ☎ **760/776-6635.** Reservations not accepted. Salads and sandwiches $9–$11; main courses $12–$19 at dinner.

AE, DC, DISC, MC, V. Mon–Thurs 11:30am–10pm, Fri 11:30am–11pm, Sat 11am–11pm, Sun 11am–10pm. DELI.

There's plenty of schmaltz at this upscale deli in the Beverly Hills of the desert, from the "secret recipe" of the "Matzo Ball Queen" to cute menu Sinatra-isms like "Luck Be a Latke Tonight." The robust overstuffed pastrami sandwich falls just shy of New York–deli authenticity, but after 7pm nightly the place swings to opera and showtunes performed by the service staff!

THE DESERT RESORTS AFTER DARK

Every month a different club or disco is the hot spot in the Springs, and the best way to tap into the trend is by consulting *The Desert Guide, The Bottom Line* (see "Gay Life in Palm Springs," above), or one of the many other free newsletters available from area hotels and merchants. **VillageFest** (see "Shopping," above) turns Palm Canyon Drive into an outdoor party each Thursday night. Below I've described a few more of the enduring arts and entertainment attractions around the desert resorts.

Billing itself as "the Coachella Valley's Country Music Nightclub," the **Cactus Corral,** 67501 Calif. 111, Cathedral City (☎ 760/321-8558), has stood the test of time with billiards, a sports bar, and live country bands, plus firewater and good, greasy grub. Early in the evening they offer western-style dance lessons. Open 6pm to 2am; call ahead for exact days, which vary by season.

One of the desert's in spots for the old-money/celebrity set, **Touché Restaurant & Nightclub,** 42250 Bob Hope Dr., Rancho Mirage (☎ 760/773-1111), offers dining and dancing in the old style. Hip devotees of the "cocktail nation" movement can be seen swinging alongside perfectly coifed retirees. Open Wednesday to Sunday from 6:30pm.

The **Fabulous Palm Springs Follies,** at the Plaza Theatre, 128 S. Palm Canyon Dr., Palm Springs (☎ 760/327-0225), a vaudeville-style show filled with lively production numbers, is celebrating its fifth year of running in the historic Plaza Theatre in the heart of Palm Springs. With a cast of energetic retired showgirls, singers, dancers, and comedians, the revue has been enormously popular around town. Call for show schedule; tickets range from $28 to $59.

The **McCallum Theatre for the Performing Arts,** 73000 Fred Waring Dr., Palm Desert (☎ 760/340-ARTS), offers the only cultural high road around. Frequent symphony performances with visiting virtuosos such as conductor Seiji Ozawa or violinist Itzhak Perlman, musicals like Tommy Tune's *Grease* or a *Chorus Line* revival, and pop performers like the Captain and Tennille or the Ink Spots are among the theater's recent offerings. Call for upcoming event information.

4 Joshua Tree National Park

The trees themselves are merely a jumping-off point for exploring this seemingly barren desert. Viewed from the roadside, the dry land only hints at hidden vitality, but upon closer examination reveals a giant mosaic of intense beauty and complexity. From lush oases teeming with life to rusted-out relics of man's attempts to tame the wilderness, from low plains of tufted cactus to mountains of exposed, twisted rock, the park is much more than a tableau of the curious tree for which it is named.

The Joshua tree is said to have been given its name by early Mormon settlers traveling west, for its upraised limbs and bearded appearance reminded them of the prophet Joshua leading them to the promised land.

Other observers were not so kind. Explorer John C. Frémont called it "the most repulsive tree in the vegetable kingdom." Nature writer Charles Francis Saunders opined: "The trees themselves were as grotesque as the creations of a bad dream; the shaggy trunks and limbs were twisted and seemed writhing as though in pain, and dagger-pointed leaves were clenched in bristling fists of inhospitality."

Harsh criticism for this hardy desert dweller, which is really not a tree, but a variety of yucca, member of the lily family. The relationship is apparent when pale yellow, lilylike flowers festoon the limbs of the Joshuas when they bloom (depending on rainfall) in March, April, or May. When Mother Nature cooperates, the park also puts on quite a wildflower display, and you can get an updated report on prime viewing sites by calling the park ranger (see below).

Joshua Tree National Park's name is fitting, for here the peculiar tree reaches the southernmost boundary of its range. The park straddles two desert environments; there's the mountainous, Joshua tree–studded Mojave Desert forming the northwestern part of the park. Hotter, drier, lower, and characterized by a wide variety of desert flora including cacti, cottonwood, and native California fan palms, the Colorado Desert comprises the southern and eastern sections of the park. Between them runs the "transition zone," displaying characteristics of each.

The area's geological timeline is fascinating, stretching back 8 million years to a time when the Mojave landscape was one of rolling hills and flourishing grasslands; horses, camels, and mastadons abounded, preying upon by sabre-tooth tigers and wild dogs. Displays at the Oasis Visitor Center show how resulting climatic, volcanic, and tectonic activity have created the park's signature cliffs and boulders and turned Joshua Tree into the arid desert you see today.

Human presence has been traced back nearly 10,000 years with the discovery of Pinto Man, and evidence of more recent habitation can be seen in the form of Native American pictographs carved into rock faces throughout the park. Miners and ranchers began coming in the 1860s, but the boom went bust by the turn of the century. Then a Pasadena doctor, treating World War I veterans suffering from respiratory and heart ailments caused by mustard gas, prescribed the desert's clean, dry air—and modern Twentynine Palms was (re)born.

During the 1920s a worldwide fascination with the desert emerged, and cactus gardens were very much in vogue. Entrepreneurs hauled truckloads of desert plants into Los Angeles for quick sale or export, and souvenir hunters removed archaeological treasures. Incensed that the beautiful Mojave was in danger of being picked clean, Los Angeles socialite Minerva Hoyt organized a desert conservation movement and successfully lobbied for the establishment of Joshua Tree National Monument in 1936.

In 1994, under provisions of the federal California Desert Protection Act, Joshua Tree was "upgraded" to national park status and expanded to nearly 800,000 acres.

JUST THE FACTS

No restaurants, lodging, gas stations, or stores are found within Joshua Tree National Park. In fact, water is only available at four park locations: Cottonwood Springs, the Black Rock Canyon Campground, the Indian Cove Ranger Station, and the Oasis Visitor Center. Twentynine Palms and Yucca Valley have lots of restaurants, markets, motels, and B&Bs.

Admission to the park is $5 per car (good for 7 days).

ACCESS POINTS   From metropolitan Los Angeles, the usual route to the Oasis Visitor Center in Joshua Tree National Park is via I-10 to its intersection with Calif. 62 (some 92 miles east of downtown). Calif. 62 (the Twentynine Palms Highway) leads northeast for about 43 miles to the town of Twentynine Palms. Total driving time is around 2¹/₂ hours. In town, follow the signs at National Park Drive or Utah Trail to the visitor center and ranger station.

VISITOR CENTERS & INFORMATION   In addition to the main **Oasis Visitor Center** at the Twentynine Palms entrance, there is **Cottonwood Visitor Center** at the south entrance, and the privately operated **Park Center,** located in the town of Joshua Tree.

The Oasis Visitor Center is open daily (except Christmas) from 8am to 4:30pm. Check here for a detailed map of park roads, plus schedules of ranger-guided walks and interpretive programs. Ask about the weekend tours of the Desert Queen Ranch, once a working homestead and now part of the park.

For information, contact the **Park Superintendent's Office,** 74485 National Park Dr., Twentynine Palms, CA 92277 (☎ **760/367-7511**). A terrific Internet website on the park and surrounding communities is www.desertgold.com.

SEEING THE HIGHLIGHTS

An excellent first stop, outside the park's north entrance, is the main **Oasis Visitor Center,** located alongside the Oasis of Mara, also known as the Twentynine Palms Oasis. For many generations the native Serrano tribe lived at this "place of little springs and much grass." Get maps, books, and the latest in road, trail, and weather conditions before beginning your tour.

Two paved roads explore the heart of the park. The first loops through the high northwest section, visiting Queen and Lost Horse valleys, as well as the awesome boulder piles at Jumbo Rocks and Wonderland of Rocks. The second angles north-south across the park and crosses both the Mojave Desert Joshua tree woodland and the cactus gardens of the Colorado Desert before ending up at Cottonwood, the park's southern entrance.

From the Oasis Visitor Center, drive south to **Jumbo Rocks,** which captures the complete essence of the park: a vast array of rock formations, a Joshua tree forest, the yucca-dotted desert open and wide. Check out Skull Rock (one of the many rocks in the area that appears to resemble humans, dinosaurs, monsters, cathedrals, and castles) via a 1¹/₂-mile-long nature trail that provides an introduction to the park's flora, wildlife, and geology.

At Cap Rock Junction, the main park road swings north toward the **Wonderland of Rocks,** 12 square miles of massive jumbled granite. This curious maze of stone hides groves of Joshua trees, trackless washes, and several small pools of water.

From Cap Rock Junction south, Keys View Road dead-ends at mile-high **Keys View.** From the crest of the Little San Bernardino Mountains, enjoy grand desert views that encompass both the highest (Mt. San Gorgonio) and lowest (Salton Sea) points in Southern California.

Pinto Basin Road tours the Colorado Desert side of the park. You'll pass both the **Cholla Cactus Garden** and spindly **Ocotillo Patch** on your way to vast, flat Pinto Basin, a barren lowland surrounded by austere mountains and punctuated by trackless sand dunes. The dunes are an easy hike (2 miles round-trip) from the backcountry camping board, or you might want to continue to **Cottonwood Springs,** near the southern park entrance. Besides a small ranger station and well-developed campground, Cottonwood has a cool, palm-shaded oasis that is the trailhead for a tough hike to Lost Palms Oasis.

ACTIVITIES WITHIN THE PARK

HIKING & NATURE WALKS   The national park holds a variety of nature trails ranging in difficulty from strenuous challenges to kid- (and wimp-) friendly interpretive walks—two of these (**Oasis of Mara** and **Cap Rock**) are even paved and wheelchair accessible. My favorite of the 11 short interpretive trails is **Cholla**

This Is Our Life: The Roy Rogers & Dale Evans Museum

Passing through Victorville, it's tough to miss a log fort visible from I-15, with the words "Roy Rogers and Dale Evans Museum" emblazoned on the side, Las Vegas style—larger than life, brightly lit, embellished with stars.

Fans of cowboy lore, western movies, or country music can all tell you the museum is legendary for being the final resting place of Roy's faithful horse Trigger, which he had stuffed and mounted. For company, Trigger has Buttermilk (Dale's golden horse), Bullet (their canine companion), and a veritable Noah's Ark of taxidermy—Roy's trophies from safaris in every corner of the globe.

These are among the many surprises awaiting visitors to the museum, a glorified attic containing the relics and souvenirs of two lifetimes. The displays are folksy, accented by tags saying "my first cowboy boots" (bronzed, of course), "the 1923 Dodge I came to California in, in 1930," and other personal remarks. But because of Roy and Dale's wealth, years of travel, varied interests, and an apparent inability to throw anything away, this museum truly has something for everyone. Some of the highlights are:

- Beautifully arranged cases commemorating each of Roy and Dale's three children who died in childhood. On display are photos, toys, letters, and report cards, as well as the inspirational books written in tribute by Dale Evans Rogers after each of their deaths. Their many living children and grandchildren are also well represented; in fact, by the end of your visit you might feel as if you know the whole family personally!

- Gifts from the couple's fans all over the world, including a pair of stitched samplers framed near the entrance, containing poetic tributes both epic and homespun.

- Every piece of Roy Rogers and/or Dale Evans merchandise from over the years: comic books, breakfast cereal boxes, fan club items, war effort promotions, and more. See the 1950s-era "den/playroom" filled with vintage furniture and littered with dozens of Roy and Dale toys, storybooks, dolls, model horses, and board games.

- Roy's personal collection of western memorabilia from his role models—real-life and movie cowboys—includes Tom Mix's director's chair, Buck Jones's saddle, Hoot Gibson's piano, and last but not least, an autographed picture of Lee Majors (remember him in *The Big Valley?*).

The museum is open daily from 9am to 5pm except Thanksgiving and Christmas Day. For more information, call ☎ **760/243-4547.**

Cactus Garden, smack-dab in the middle of the park, where you stroll through dense clusters of the deceptively fluffy-looking "teddy bear cactus."

For the more adventurous, **Barker Dam** is an easy 1.1-mile loop accessible by a graded dirt road east of Hidden Valley. A small, man-made lake is framed by the majestic Wonderland of Rocks. In addition to scrambling atop the old dam, it's fun to search out Native American petroglyphs carved into the base of cliffs lining your return to the trailhead.

The moderately challenging **Lost Horse Mine** trail near Keys View leads through rolling hills to the ruins of a successful gold-mining operation; once there, a short, steep hike leads uphill behind the ruins for a fine view into the heart of the park.

When you're ready for a strenuous hike, try the **Fortynine Palms Oasis** trail, accessible from Canyon Road in Twentynine Palms. After a steep, harsh ascent to a cactus-fringed ridge, the rocky canyon trail leads to a spectacular oasis, complete with palm-shaded pools of green water and abundant birds and other wildlife. Allow 2 to 3 hours for the 3-mile (round-trip) hike.

Another lush oasis lies at the end of **Lost Palms Oasis** trail at Cottonwood Springs. The first section of the 7.5-mile trail is moderately difficult, climbing slowly to the oasis overlook; from there a treacherous path continues to the canyon bottom, a remote spot attractive to the elusive bighorn sheep.

ROCK CLIMBING   From Hidden Valley to the Wonderland of Rocks, the park has emerged as one of the world's premier rock-climbing destinations. The park offers some 4,000 climbing routes, ranging from the easiest of bouldering to some of the sport's most difficult technical climbs. November to May is the prime season to watch these lizardlike humans scale sheer rock faces with impossible grace. Even beginners can get into the act: At **First Ascent** (☎ 800/325-5462), certified guides start the day with detailed instruction, then stay with you providing guidance as you learn the ropes. All equipment is provided, and prices start at $75.

MOUNTAIN BIKING   Much of the park is designated wilderness, meaning that bicycles are limited to roads; they'll damage the fragile ecosystem if you venture off the beaten track. None of the paved roads have bike lanes, but rugged mountain bikes are a great tool to explore the park via unpaved roads where distraction from autos is light.

Try the 18-mile **Geology Tour Road,** which begins west of Jumbo Rocks; dry lake beds contrast with towering boulders along this sandy downhill road—you'll also encounter abandoned mines.

A shorter but still rewarding ride begins at the **Covington Flats** picnic area; a steep 4-mile road climbs through Joshua trees, junipers, and pinion pines to Eureka Peak, where you'll be rewarded by a panoramic view.

For other bike-friendly unpaved and four-wheel-drive roads, consult the official park map.

ACCOMMODATIONS & CAMPING

If you're staying in the Palm Springs area, it's entirely possible to make a day trip to the national park. But if you'd like to stay close by and spend more time here, Twentynine Palms, just outside the north boundary of the national park on Calif. 62, offers budget to moderate lodging.

Near the Visitor Center in the Oasis of Mara is the rustic **29 Palms Inn** (☎ 760/367-3505; fax 760/367-4425), a cluster of adobe cottages and old cabins dating from the 1920s; their garden-fresh restaurant is the best in town.

There's also the 100-room **Best Western Gardens Motel** (☎ 760/367-9141; fax 760/367-2584), a comfortable base from which to maximize your outdoor time.

For a complete listing of Twentynine Palms lodging, contact the **29 Palms Chamber of Commerce,** 5672 Historic Plaza, Twentynine Palms, CA 92277 (☎ 760/367-3445; fax 760/367-3366). Nine **campgrounds** scattered throughout the park offer pleasant though often Spartan accommodations, with just picnic tables and pit toilets for the most part. Only two (**Black Rock Canyon** and **Cottonwood Springs**) have potable water and flush toilets—plus a $10 overnight fee.

5 Mojave National Preserve

Two decades of park politicking finally ended in 1994 when President Clinton signed into law the California Desert Protection Act, which created the new Mojave National Preserve. Thus far the Mojave's elevated status has not attracted hordes of sightseers, and devoted visitors are happy to keep it that way. Unlike a fully protected National Park, the National Preserve designation allows certain commercial land uses, and the continued grazing and mining within the preserve's boundaries are a sore spot for ardent environmentalists.

To most Americans, the East Mojave is that vast, bleak, interminable stretch of desert to be crossed as quickly as possible while leaving California via I-15 or I-40. Few realize that these highways are the boundaries of what desert rats have long considered the crown jewel of the California desert.

This land is a hard one to get to know—unlike more developed desert parks, it has no lodgings or concessions, few campgrounds, and only a handful of roads suitable for the average passenger vehicle. But hidden within this natural fortress are some true gems—the preserve's 1.4 million acres include the world's largest Joshua tree forest; abundant wildlife, spectacular canyons, caverns, and volcanic formations; nationally honored scenic backroads and footpaths to historic mining sites; tabletop mesas; and a dozen mountain ranges.

JUST THE FACTS

GETTING THERE   I-15, the major route taken between the Southern California metropolis and the state line by Las Vegas–bound travelers, extends along the northern boundary of Mojave National Preserve. I-40 is the southern access route to the East Mojave.

WHEN TO GO   Spring is a splendid time (autumn is another) to visit this desert. From March to May the temperatures are mild, the Joshua trees are in bloom, and the lower Kelso Dunes are bedecked with yellow and white desert primrose and pink sand verbena.

VISITOR CENTERS & INFORMATION   The best source for up-to-date weather conditions and a free topographical map is the **Mojave Desert Information Center,** 72157 Baker Blvd. (under the "World's Tallest Thermometer"), Baker, CA 92309 (☎ 760/733-4040), which is open daily and also has a superior selection of books for sale.

There's the **California Desert Information Center,** 831 Barstow Rd., Barstow, CA 92311 (☎ 760/255-8760), which has a minimuseum and educational displays on the history and characteristics of the desert. It's open daily 9am to 5pm.

Additional information and maps are available inside the preserve at the **Hole-in-the-Wall Campground's Visitor Center,** which is open seasonally (as staffing allows).

SEEING THE HIGHLIGHTS

One of the preserve's spectacular sights is the **Kelso Dunes,** the most extensive dune field in the West. The 45-square-mile formation of magnificently sculpted sand is famous for its "booming": Visitors' footsteps cause mini-avalanches and the dunes to go "sha-boom-sha-boom-sha-boom." Geologists speculate that the extreme dryness of the East Mojave Desert, combined with the wind-polished, rounded nature of the individual sand grains, has something to do with their musicality. Sometimes the low rumbling sound resembles a Tibetan gong; other times it sounds like a 1950s doo-wop musical group.

A 10-mile drive from the Kelso Dunes is **Kelso Depot,** built by the Union Pacific in 1924. The Spanish Revival–style structure was designed with a red-tile roof, graceful arches, and a brick platform. The depot continued to be open for freight-train crew use through the mid-1980s, although it ceased to be a railroad stop for passengers after World War II. The National Park Service is considering refurbishing the building for use as the preserve's visitor center.

On and around Cima Dome, a rare geological anomaly, grows the world's largest and densest **Joshua tree forest.** Botanists say Cima's Joshuas are more symmetrical than their cousins elsewhere in the Mojave. The dramatic colors of the sky at sunset provide a breathtaking backdrop for Cima's Joshua trees, some more than 25 feet tall and several hundred years old.

Tucked into the Providence Mountains, in the southern portion of the preserve, is a treat everyone should try to see. The **Mitchell Caverns,** contained in a State Recreation Area *within* the National Preserve, are a geological oddity exploited for tourism but still quite fascinating. Regular tours are conducted of these cool rock "rooms"; in addition to showcasing marvelous stalactites, stalagmites, and other limestone formations, the caves have proven to be rich in Native American archaeological finds.

Hole-in-the-Wall and Mid Hills are the centerpieces of Mojave National Preserve. Both locales offer diverse desert scenery, fine campgrounds, and the feeling of being in the middle of nowhere, though in fact they're located right in the middle of the preserve.

Linking the two sites is the preserve's best drive. In 1989 **Wildhorse Canyon Road,** which loops from Mid Hills Campground to Hole-in-the-Wall Campground, was declared the nation's first official "Back Country Byway," an honor federal agencies bestow upon America's most scenic backroads. The 11-mile, horseshoe-shaped road crosses wide-open country dotted with cholla and, in season, delicate purple, yellow, and red wildflowers. Dramatic volcanic slopes and flattop mesas tower over the low desert.

Mile-high **Mid Hills,** so named because of its location halfway between the Providence and New York mountains, recalls the Great Basin Desert topography of Nevada and Utah. Mid Hills Campground offers a grand observation point from which to gaze out at the coffee-with-cream-colored Pinto Mountains to the north and the rolling Kelso Dunes shining on the western horizon.

Hole-in-the-Wall is the kind of place Butch Cassidy and the Sundance Kid would have chosen as a hideout. This twisted maze of rocks called rhyolite is a form of crystallized red lava rock. A series of iron rings aids descent into Hole-in-the-Wall; they're not particularly difficult for those who are reasonably agile and take their time.

Kelso Dunes, Mitchell Caverns, Cima Dome, Hole-in-the-Wall—these highlights of the preserve can be viewed in a weekend. But you'll need a week just to see all the major sights, and maybe a lifetime to really get to know the East Mojave. And right now, without much in the way of services, the traveler to this desert must be well prepared and self-reliant. For many, this is what makes a trip to the East Mojave an adventure.

If Mojave National Preserve attracts you, you'll want to return again and again to see the wonders of this desert, including **Caruthers Canyon,** a "botanical island" of pinion pine and juniper woodland, and **Ivanpah Valley,** which supports the largest desert tortoise population in the California Desert.

HIKING & MOUNTAIN BIKING

HIKING The free-form ambling climb to the top of the **Kelso Dunes** is 3 miles round-trip. A cool, inviting pinion pine/juniper woodland is explored by the

Caruthers Canyon Trail (3 miles round-trip). The longest pathway is the 8-mile (one-way) **Mid Hills to Hole-in-the-Wall Trail,** a grand tour of basin and range tabletop mesas, large pinion trees, and colorful cactus.

If you're not up for a long day hike, the 1-mile trip from **Hole-in-the-Wall Campground** to **Banshee Canyon** and the 5-mile jaunt to **Wildhorse Canyon** offer some easier alternatives.

Be sure to pick up trail maps at one of the visitor centers.

MOUNTAIN BIKING   Opportunities are as extensive as the preserve's hundreds of miles of lonesome dirt roads. The 140-mile-long historic **Mojave Road,** a rough four-wheel-drive route, visits many of the most scenic areas in the East Mojave; sections of this road make excellent bike tours. Prepare well—the Mojave Road and other dirt roads are rugged routes through desert wilderness.

CAMPING

The **Mid Hills Campground** is located in a pinion pine/juniper woodland and offers outstanding views. This mile-high camp is the coolest in the East Mojave. Nearby **Hole-in-the-Wall Campground** is perched above two dramatic canyons. *Warning:* The washboard dirt road between the two might be too jarring for many two-wheel-drive passenger cars.

There are also some sites at **Providence Mountain State Recreation Area** (Mitchell Caverns, see "Seeing the Highlights," above).

One of the highlights of the East Mojave Desert is camping in the open desert all by your lonesome, but certain rules apply. Call the Mojave Desert Information Center for suggestions.

NEARBY TOWNS WITH TOURIST SERVICES

BARSTOW   This sizable town has a great many restaurants and motels, and is roughly a 1¹/₂-hour drive from the center of the preserve. Call the **Barstow Chamber of Commerce** (☎ **760/256-8617**) for suggestions.

BAKER   Accommodations and food are available in this small desert town, a good point to fill up your gas tank and purchase supplies before entering Mojave National Preserve.

The **Bun Boy Coffee Shop** is open 24 hours. For a tasty surprise, stop at the **Mad Greek Restaurant.** Order a Greek salad, a souvlaki, or baklava, and marvel at your good fortune—imagine finding such tasty food and pleasant surroundings in the middle of nowhere.

Inexpensive lodging can be secured at a couple of motels, including the **Bun Boy Motel** (☎ **760/733-4363**).

NIPTON   This tiny, charming town boasts a "trading post" that stocks snacks, maps, ice, and Native jewelry; and the **Hotel Nipton** (☎ **760/856-2335**), a B&B with a sitting room, two bathrooms down the hall, and four guest rooms, each going for $50 a night. Jerry Freeman, a former hard-rock miner who purchased the entire town in 1984, says hotel occupancy is up 80% since the East Mojave became a national preserve. He and his wife, Roxanne, moved from the famous sands of Malibu to the abandoned ghost town and have gradually brought it back to life. Nipton is located on Nipton Road, a few miles from I-15 near the Nevada state line.

STATELINE   The aptly named town on the California-Nevada border features three hotel/casinos, each as large and garish as an amusement park. **Whiskey Pete's, Buffalo Bill's, and Primadonna** are managed by the same company—rooms here are pretty nice, really cheap, and (if you have a twisted sense of humor) an ironic counterpoint to the wilderness you came for. With a dozen restaurants, including those low-cost Vegas-style buffets, Stateline might also be your best dining bet. For reservations call ☎ **800/FUN-STOP.**

6 Death Valley National Park

Park? Death Valley National Park? The Forty-niners, whose suffering gave the valley its name, would have howled at the notion. "Death Valley National Park" seems a contradiction in terms, an oxymoron of the great outdoors. To them, other four-letter words would have been more appropriate: gold, mine, heat, lost, dead. And the four-letter words shouted by teamsters who drove the 20-mule-team borax wagons need not be repeated.

Americans looking for gold in California's mountains in 1849 were forced to cross the burning sands to avoid severe snowstorms in the nearby Sierra Nevada. Some perished along the way, and the land became known as Death Valley.

Mountains stand naked, unadorned. The bitter waters of saline lakes evaporate into bizarre, razor-sharp crystal formations. Jagged canyons jab deep into the earth. Ovenlike heat, frigid cold, and the driest air imaginable combine to make this one of the most inhospitable locations in the world.

But, human nature being what it is, it's not surprising that people have long been drawn to challenge the power of Mother Nature, even in this, her home court. Man's first foray into tourism began in 1925, a scant 76 years after the "Forty-niners" harrowing experiences (which would discourage most sane folks from ever returning!). It probably would've begun sooner, but the valley had been consumed with lucrative borax mining since the late 1880s.

Death Valley is raw, bare earth, the way it must have looked before life began. Here forces of the earth are exposed to view with dramatic clarity; just looking out on the landscape, it's impossible to know what year—what century—it is. It's no coincidence that many of Death Valley's topographical features are associated with hellish images—the Funeral Mountains, Furnace Creek, Dante's View, Coffin Peak, and the Devil's Golf Course. But it can be a place of serenity.

In one of his last official acts, President Herbert Hoover signed a proclamation designating Death Valley as a national monument on February 11, 1933. With the stroke of a pen he not only authorized the protection of a vast and wondrous land, but helped to transform one of the earth's least hospitable spots into a popular tourist destination.

The naming of Death Valley National Monument came at a time when Americans began to discover the romance of the desert. Land that had previously been considered hideously devoid of life was now celebrated for its spare beauty; places that had once been feared for their harshness were now admired for their uniqueness.

In 1994, when President Clinton signed the California Desert Protection Act, Death Valley National Park became the largest national park outside Alaska, with over 3.3 million acres. Though remote, it's one of the most heavily visited, and you're likely to hear less English spoken than German, French, and Japanese.

Today's visitor to Death Valley drives in air-conditioned comfort, stays in comfortable hotel rooms or well-maintained campgrounds, orders meals and provisions at park concessions, even quaffs a cold beer at the local saloon. You can take a swim in the Olympic-size pool, tour a Moorish castle, shop for souvenirs, and enjoy the desert landscape while hiking along a nature trail with a park ranger.

JUST THE FACTS

ACCESS POINTS There are several routes into the park—all involve crossing one of the steep mountain ranges that isolate Death Valley from, well, everything. Perhaps the most scenic entry to the park is via Calif. 190, east of Calif. 178 from Ridgecrest. Another scenic drive to the park is by way of Calif. 127 and Calif. 190 from Baker. You'll be required to pay a $10 per car entrance fee, valid for 7 days' stay.

VISITOR CENTER & INFORMATION The **Death Valley Visitor Center** at Furnace Creek, 15 miles inside the eastern park boundary on Calif. 190 (☎ 760/786-2331), offers well-done interpretive exhibits and an hourly slide program. Ask at the information desk for ranger-led nature walks and evening naturalist programs. Visitor center hours are daily 8am to 7pm in the winter, daily 8am to 5pm in the summer. For information before you go, contact the **Superintendent,** Death Valley National Park, Death Valley, CA 92328 (☎ **760/786-2331**).

SEEING THE HIGHLIGHTS

A good first stop after checking in at the main park visitor center in Furnace Creek is the **Harmony Borax Works**—a rock-salt landscape as tortured as you'll ever find. Death Valley prospectors called borax "white gold," and though it wasn't exactly a glamorous substance, it was a profitable one. From 1883 to 1888 more than 20 million pounds of borax were transported from the Harmony Borax Works, and borax mining continued in Death Valley until 1928. A short trail with interpretive signs leads past the ruins of the old borax refinery and some outlying buildings.

Transport of the borax was the stuff of legends, too. The famous 20-mule teams hauled the huge loaded wagons 165 miles to the rail station at Mojave. (To learn more about this colorful era, visit the Borax Museum at Furnace Creek Ranch and the park visitor center, also located in Furnace Creek.)

At **Racetrack Playa,** a dry lake bed, visitors puzzle over rocks that weigh as much as a quarter of a ton and yet move mysteriously across the mud floor, leaving trails as a record of their movement. Research suggests that a combination of powerful winds and rain may skid the rocks over slick clay.

Badwater, at 282 feet below sea level, the lowest point in the western hemisphere, is also one of the hottest places in the world, with regularly recorded summer temperatures of 120°.

Salt Creek is the home of the **Salt Creek pupfish,** found nowhere else on earth. This little fish, which has made some amazing adaptations to survive in this arid land, can be glimpsed from a wooden boardwalk nature trail. In spring a million pupfish might be wriggling in the creek; but by summer's end only a few thousand remain.

Before sunrise, photographers set up their tripods at **Zabriskie Point** and aim their cameras down at the pale mudstone hills of Golden Canyon and the great valley beyond. This panoramic view is magnificent; another grand park vista is seen at **Dante's View,** a 5,475-foot viewpoint looking out over the shimmering Death Valley floor backed by the high Panamint Mountains.

Just south of Furnace Creek is the 9-mile loop **Artist Drive,** an easy must-see for visitors (except those in RVs, which can't negotiate the sharp, rock-bordered curves in the road). From the highway, you can't see the splendid palette of colors splashed on the rocks behind the foothills; once inside, though, stop and climb a low hill that offers an overhead view, then continue through to aptly named **Artists Palette,** where an interpretive sign explains the source of nature's rainbow.

Scotty's Castle, the Mediterranean-to-the-max mega-hacienda in the northern part of the park, is unabashedly Death Valley's premier tourist attraction. Visitors are wowed by the elaborate Spanish tiles, well-crafted furnishings, and innovative construction that included solar water heating. Even more compelling is the colorful history of this villa in remote Grapevine Canyon, brought to life by park rangers dressed in 1930s period clothing. Don't be surprised if the castle cook or a friend of Scotty's gives you a special insight into castle life.

Construction of the "castle"—more officially, Death Valley Ranch—began in 1924. It was to be a winter retreat for eccentric Chicago millionaire Albert Johnson. The insurance tycoon's unlikely friendship with prospector/cowboy/spinner-of-tall-tales Walter Scott put the $2.3-million structure on the map and captured the public's imagination. Scotty greeted visitors and told them fanciful stories from the early hard-rock-mining days of Death Valley.

The 1-hour walking tour of Scotty's Castle is excellent, both for its inside look at the mansion and for what it reveals about the eccentricities of Johnson and Scotty. Tours fill up quickly; arrive early for the first available spots (there's an $8 fee). A snack bar and gift shop make the wait more comfortable. To learn more about the castle grounds, pick up the pamphlet, "A Walking Tour of Scotty's Castle," which leads you on an exploration from stable to swimming pool, from bunkhouse to powerhouse.

Near Scotty's Castle is **Ubehebe Crater.** It's known as an explosion crater—one look and you'll know why. When hot magma rose from the depths of the earth to meet the ground water, the resultant steam blasted out a crater and scattered cinders.

HIKING & MOUNTAIN BIKING

HIKING   The trails in Death Valley range from the half-mile **Salt Creek Nature Trail,** an easy boardwalk path suitable for everyone in the family, to the grueling **Telescope Peak Trail** (14 miles round-trip), an all-day challenge. Telescope Peak is a strenuous, 3,000-foot climb to the 11,049-foot summit, where you'll be rewarded by the view described by one pioneer: "You can see so far, it's just like looking through a telescope." Snow-covered during the winter, the peak is best climbed from May to November.

But there are lots of levels in between. I like the trail into **Mosaic Canyon,** near Stovepipe Wells, where water has polished the marble rock into white, gray, and black mosaics. It's a relatively easy 2^1/$_2$-mile scramble through long, narrow walls that seem quite "gallery"-like—and provide welcome shade at every turn.

Romping among the **Sand Dunes** on the way to Stovepipe Wells is also fun, particularly for kids. It's a free-form adventure, and the dunes aren't particularly high—but the sun can be merciless. The sand in the dunes is actually tiny pieces of rock, most of them quartz fragments. As with all desert activities, your water supply is crucial.

Near the park's eastern border, two trails lead from the **Keane Wonder Mill,** site of a successful gold mine. The first is a steep and strenuous 2-mile challenge leading to the mine itself, passing along the way the solid, efficient wooden tramway that carried ore out of the mountain.

If that's beyond your fitness level, try the **Keane Wonder Spring Trail,** leading in another direction. This 2-mile walk is much easier, and the spring which supplied water for the Keane Wonder operation will announce itself with a sulfur smell and piping birdcalls.

If you're visiting **Ubehebe Crater,** there's a steep but plain trail leading from the parking area up to the crater's lip and around some of the contours. Fierce winds can hamper your progress, but you'll get the exhilarating feeling you're truly on another planet.

Park rangers can provide topographical maps and detailed directions to these and a dozen other hiking trails within the National Park.

MOUNTAIN BIKING   Because most (94%) of the park is federally designated wilderness, cycling is allowed only on roads used by automobiles. Cycling is not allowed on hiking trails.

Good routes for bikers include Racetrack (28 miles, mainly level), Greenwater Valley (30 miles, mostly level), Cottonwood Canyon (20 miles), and West Side Road (40 miles, fairly level with some washboard sections). Artists Drive is 8 miles long, paved, with some steep uphills. A favorite is Titus Canyon (28 miles on a hilly road—it's highly recommended that you make this a one-way descent).

CAMPING & ACCOMMODATIONS

The park's nine campgrounds are located at elevations ranging from below sea level to 8,000 feet. In Furnace Creek, **Sunset** offers 1,000 spaces with water and flush toilets. **Furnace Creek Campground** has 200 similarly appointed spaces. **Stovepipe Wells** has 200 spaces with water and flush toilets.

The **Furnace Creek Ranch** (☎ 760/786-2345) has 224 no-frills cottage units with air-conditioning and showers. The swimming pool is a popular hangout for tired lodgers. Nearby are a coffee shop, saloon, steak house, and general store.

The **Furnace Creek Inn** (☎ 760/786-2345), an elegant resort, boasts 66 deluxe rooms with a formal dining room, heated pool, golf, and tennis courts.

Stove Pipe Wells Village (☎ 760/786-2387) has 74 modest rooms with air-conditioning and showers, plus a casual dining room which closes between meals.

The only lodging within the park not operated by the official concessionaire is the **Panamint Springs Resort** (☎ 702/482-7680), a truly charming rustic motel, cafe, and snack shop about an hour east of Furnace Creek.

Because accommodations in Death Valley are both limited and expensive, you might consider the money-saving (but inconvenient) option of spending a night at one of the two gateway towns: **Lone Pine** on the west side of the park or **Baker** on the south. **Beatty, Nevada,** which has inexpensive lodging, is an hour's drive from the park's center. The restored **Amargosa Hotel** (☎ 760/852-4441) in Death Valley Junction offers 14 rooms in a historic, out-of-the-way place, 40 minutes from Furnace Creek.

Helpful hint: Meals and groceries are exceptionally costly due to the remoteness of the location. If possible, consider bringing a cooler with some snacks, sandwiches, and beverages to last the duration of your visit. Ice is easily obtainable, and you'll also be able to keep water chilled.

16

San Diego & Environs

by Elizabeth Hansen

San Diego is best known for its benign climate and fabulous beaches—but it offers much more than sunny skies, offshore breezes, and miles of clean sand. The city is home to top-notch attractions, including three world-famous animal parks, a wide variety of great dining, and some of the country's best regional theater. But what's most striking about San Diego is its refreshing small-town ambiance, which it has managed to preserve despite its status as the sixth-largest city in the United States. Welcome! I think you're going to have a great time.

1 Orientation

ARRIVING
BY PLANE

San Diego International Airport, 3707 N. Harbor Dr. (☎ **619/231-7361**), locally known as Lindbergh Field, is just 3 miles from downtown. Most of the major domestic carriers fly here. Lindbergh Field consists of two adjacent airport terminals, no. 1 (formerly "East Terminal") and no. 2 (formerly "West Terminal"), and the Commuter Terminal, which is a half-mile away. The "red bus" provides free service from the main airport to the Commuter Terminal.

TRANSPORTATION FROM THE AIRPORT   Several major rental-car companies operate at the airport, including **Avis** (☎ 800/331-1212), **Budget** (☎ 800/527-0700), **Dollar** (☎ 800/800-4000), **Hertz** (☎ 800/654-3131), and **National** (☎ 800/CAR-RENT). If you're driving into the city from the airport, take Harbor Drive south to Broadway, the main east-west thoroughfare, and turn left.

   San Diego Transit's bus no. 2 stops at the center traffic aisle of the East Terminal and the intersection of Harbor Island and Winship Lane near the Commuter Terminal. The no. 2 bus runs weekdays every 15 minutes from 5:30am to midnight (every 30 minutes on weekends); the fare is $2. The bus connects the airport with downtown, stopping at Broadway and Fourth Avenue. At Broadway and First Avenue is the **Transit Store** (☎ 619/233-3004), where the staff can answer your transit questions and provide free route maps to help you get where you're going.

   Several **shuttles** run regularly from the airport to downtown hotels. They charge about $5 per person, and you'll see designated

The San Diego Area at a Glance

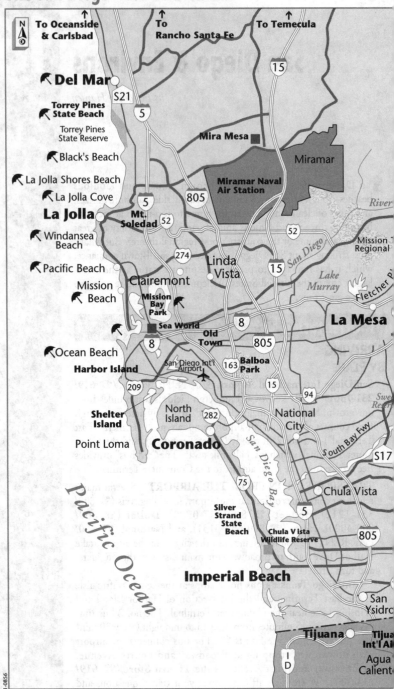

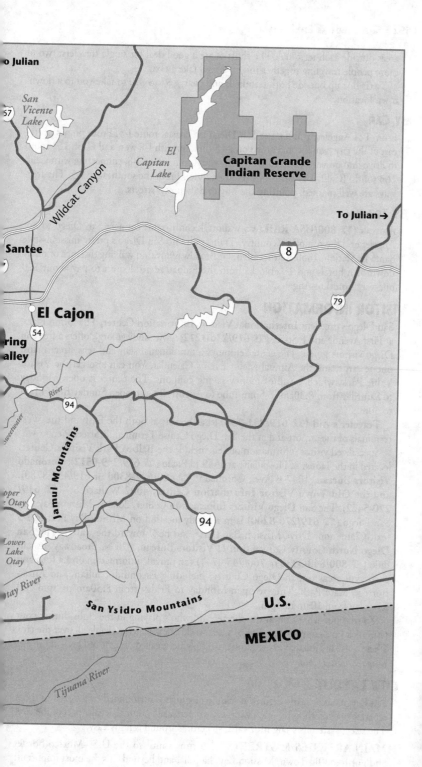

areas outside each terminal. The shuttles are a good deal for single travelers; two or more people traveling together might as well take a taxi.

   Taxis line up outside both terminals and charge $7 to $10 to take you to a downtown location.

BY CAR

From Los Angeles, you'll enter San Diego via coastal route I-5. From points northeast of the city, you'll come down on I-15 (link up with I-8 west and Calif. 163 south to drive into downtown). From the east, you'll come in on I-8, connecting with Calif. 163 south. (Calif. 163 turns into 10th Avenue). From the south, take I-5. The freeways are well marked, pointing the way to downtown streets.

BY TRAIN

Amtrak (☎ 800/USA-RAIL; www.amtrak.com) trains connect San Diego to Los Angeles and the rest of the country. Trains pull into San Diego's pretty mission-style Santa Fe Station, 1850 Kettner Blvd. (at Broadway), within walking distance of many downtown hotels and 1^1/$_2$ blocks from the Embarcadero. Expect to pay about $20 one-way from Los Angeles.

VISITOR INFORMATION

San Diego's excellent **International Visitors Information Center,** 11 Horton Plaza, at First Avenue and F Street (☎ 619/236-1212; www.sandiego.org), offers a free San Diego visitors guide. The center employs a multilingual staff and sells street maps, phone cards, and the Annual Major Events Calendar. You can also get the Visitor Value Pack, which is full of money-saving coupons. The center is open Monday to Saturday from 8:30am to 5pm; June to August, it's also open Sunday from 11am to 5pm.

   Traveler's Aid (☎ 619/231-7361) has booths at both the East and the West terminals of the airport and at the San Diego Cruise Terminal, B Street Pier.

   Specialized visitor information outlets include the **Balboa Park Visitors Center,** located in the House of Hospitality at 1549 El Prado (☎ 619/239-0512); **Coronado Visitors Bureau,** 1047 B Ave., Coronado (☎ 800/622-8300 or 619/437-8788); and the **Old Town Visitor Information Center,** 4002 Wallace St. (☎ 619/220-5422). The **San Diego Visitors Information Center,** 2688 E. Mission Bay Dr., San Diego (☎ 619/276-8200) is in a handy location on Mission Bay next to I-5 (exit Clairemont Drive/Mission Bay Drive and head toward the water). The **San Diego North County Convention & Visitors Bureau,** 720 N. Broadway, Escondido (☎ 800/848-3336 or 760/745-4741) can provide information on La Jolla and excursion areas in San Diego County, including Escondido, Julian, and Anza–Borrego State Park. They're open Monday to Friday from 8:30am to 5pm and Saturday from 10am to 4pm.

   To find out what's on at the theater and who's playing in the clubs during your visit, pick up a copy of *The Reader,* a free weekly newspaper available all over the city. There's also a Thursday entertainment supplement called "Night & Day" in the *San Diego Union-Tribune.*

CITY LAYOUT

San Diego has a clearly defined downtown, which is surrounded by a dozen or more separate neighborhoods—each with its own personality, but all legally part of the city. The street system is straightforward, so getting around is fairly easy.

MAIN ARTERIES & STREETS   I-5 runs south to the U.S.–Mexico border and north to Old Town, Mission Bay, La Jolla, and beyond. It's the most important thoroughfare in San Diego, connecting the city's divergent parts with one another and the entire region with the rest of the state. Access to the Coronado Bay Bridge is via I-5. Balboa Park is most easily accessible via Twelfth Avenue, which becomes Park Boulevard.

Downtown, Broadway is the main street; in the heart of the central business district it's intersected by Fourth and Fifth avenues (running south and north respectively). Harbor Drive, hugging the waterfront (Embarcadero), connects downtown with the airport to the northwest and the Convention Center to the south.

FINDING AN ADDRESS   It's easy to find an address when you're downtown. Avenues run north-south and are numbered from 1 to 12. Streets run east-west and most of them are lettered A to L (in order they are A, B, C, Broadway, E, F, G, Market Street, Island Street, J, K, and L). If the address is 411 Market St., for example, you'll find it between Fourth and Fifth avenues on Market Street. Most downtown streets are one-way.

Outside the city center, street names get a little more complex, but most are laid out in a grid.

NEIGHBORHOODS IN BRIEF

Downtown   Business travelers will most likely want to stay in this area, which encompasses Horton Plaza, the Gaslamp Quarter, the Embarcadero, Seaport Village, and the Convention Center. San Diego's dining and entertainment heart is the **Gaslamp Quarter,** a 16-square-block Victorian-style National Historic District, bordered by Fourth and Fifth avenues between Broadway and Market Street. **Horton Plaza,** immediately north of the Gaslamp Quarter, is a colorful multilevel 6-block shopping mall that's a major attraction in itself. **Seaport Village,** a themed shopping/dining area just south of the Embarcadero, is sandwiched between a waterfront walkway and Harbor Drive. **Harbor Island** and **Shelter Island,** both just minutes from the airport and downtown, are two man-made peninsulas with excellent views.

Old Town   Northwest of downtown, San Diego's first commercial center was designated a state historic park in 1968 and now operates primarily as a tourist attraction. The region encompasses the Old Town State Historic Park, Presidio Park, Heritage Park, a couple of museums, and restaurants which are popular with visitors seeking Mexican food and huge margaritas. Not far from Old Town, **Mission Valley/Hotel Circle** offers midprice and budget accommodations options on either side of I-8.

Hillcrest/Uptown   These two adjacent neighborhoods offer a slightly funky dining and nightlife scene. Hillcrest is the center of San Diego's gay community and site of the San Diego Gay Pride Parade held in July. Hillcrest and Uptown lie northwest and west of **Balboa Park,** which comprises more than 1,400 acres northeast of downtown and contains the San Diego Zoo and numerous museums. The park is the city's cultural center and a recreational focal point.

Mission Bay/Pacific Beach   A playground for swimmers, boaters, and sun-seekers, this is one of your options for hitting the beach. It's also home to Sea World, one of San Diego's top attractions. Pacific Beach is one of the city's most colorful regions, known for its nightlife and hip, casual dining. The boardwalk runs from South Mission Beach through "P.B." (Pacific Beach) and is popular for in-line skating, biking, and sunset watching.

La Jolla   About 12 miles north of downtown San Diego, La Jolla is one of the prettiest parcels of San Diego County. For over half a century, wealthy seniors and successful professionals have chosen to live in La Jolla because of its rugged coastline, lush landscaping, good restaurants, beautiful homes, great beaches, and proximity to the city. La Jolla still retains its "old-money" image despite its openness to adventurous Yuppies, emigrants from various countries, and retirees from the Midwest. The University of California San Diego and the Museum of Contemporary Art are here.

Coronado   Coronado is actually an incorporated city in its own right, but it's included as a neighborhood for our purposes because it's so easily reached from downtown San Diego. It's a lovely, upscale community, full of retired naval officers; here you'll find a terrific beach, several good restaurants, and the famed Hotel del Coronado.

2 Getting Around

BY CAR

Traffic has been getting heavier in recent years, but in general, the city is pretty easy to negotiate.

Many streets run one-way, which may hamper you until you learn the lay of the land. The map available from the International Visitor Information Center (see "Visitor Information," above) is extremely helpful, since arrows indicate which way each street runs. For local highway conditions, call ☎ **800/427-7623.**

You can turn right on a red light unless an intersection is otherwise posted.

RENTALS   All the large, national car-rental firms have rental outlets at the airport (see "Arriving," above), in the major hotels, and at other locations around the city.

Several car rental companies including **Avis** (☎ **800/331-1212** or 619/231-7171) and **Courtesy Auto Rentals** (☎ **800/252-9756** or 619/497-4800) allow their cars into Mexico. The vehicles may be driven as far as Ensenada, several hours south, providing that you stop before crossing the border and buy Mexican auto insurance. You would also be wise to buy insurance if you drive your own car south of the border.

PARKING   For the most part, you'll find plenty of metered parking on San Diego streets. Things tighten up downtown, where you'll probably have to put your car in an enclosed garage. The garage at Horton Plaza, G Street, and Fourth Avenue is free to shoppers for the first 3 hours, then costs $1 for each additional hour; it's free daily after 5pm. The parking lot at G Street and Sixth Avenue charges $3.25 for the day and $3 at night and on weekends and holidays.

BY PUBLIC TRANSPORTATION

Both city buses and the **San Diego Trolley** (☎ **619/685-4900**), which runs to the Mexican border, Old Town, and East County, are operated by the San Diego Metropolitan Transit System (MTS). The system's **Transit Store,** 102 Broadway, at First Avenue (☎ **619/234-1060**), is a complete public-transportation information center, supplying travelers with passes, tokens, timetables, maps, and brochures. It's open Monday to Friday from 8:30am to 5:30pm, Saturday and Sunday from noon to 4pm. Request a copy of the useful brochure, "Your Open Door to San Diego," detailing the city's most popular tourist attractions and the buses that take you to them. For **bus route information,** you can also call ☎ **619/233-3004** daily from 5:30am to 8:30pm.

The $5 **Day-Tripper pass** allows for one day of unlimited rides on the public transit system; you can also get a 4-day pass for $15. Passes are available from the Transit Store.

BY BUS   Bus stops are marked by rectangular blue signs, every other block or so on local routes. More than 20 bus routes traverse downtown, including nos. 2, 7, 9,

29, 34, and 35. Most fares range from \$1.75 to \$2.25, depending on the distance and type of service (local or express). Express buses charge fares that range from \$1.75 to \$3. Exact change is required (\$1 bills are accepted). Most buses run every half hour. Transfers are available at no extra charge as long as you continue your journey on a bus or trolley with an equal or lower fare (if it's higher, you simply pay the difference). Transfers must be used within two hours and should be obtained from the driver when boarding.

The **Coronado Shuttle,** route no. 904, runs between Le Meridien Hotel and the Old Ferry Landing along Orange Avenue to the Hotel del Coronado, Glorietta Bay, Loews Coronado Bay Resort, and back again. It costs only 50¢ per person. Route no. 901 goes to Coronado from downtown San Diego; the fare is \$1.75 for adults, 75¢ for seniors and children. Call ☎ **619/233-3004** for information.

BY TROLLEY   The San Diego Trolley system runs south to the Mexican border (a 40-minute trip), north to Old Town, and east to the city of Santee. Downtown, trolleys run along C Street and stop at the Santa Fe Station, Third Avenue (Civic Center), Fifth Avenue, Twelfth Avenue (City College), Seaport Village, and the Convention Center. Trolley travel within the downtown area costs only \$1; the fare to the Mexican border is \$2. Children under 5 ride free; seniors and riders with disabilities pay only 75¢. For **recorded trolley information,** call ☎ **619/685-4900.** To talk to a live body, you can call ☎ **619/233-3004** daily from 5:30am to 8:30pm.

Trolleys operate on a self-service fare-collection system; riders purchase tickets from machines in stations before boarding. The machines list fares for each destination and dispense change. Tickets are valid for 2 hours from the time of purchase in one direction only. Fare inspectors board trains at random to check tickets. The bright-red trains run every 15 minutes during the day (every half hour at night) and stop for only 30 seconds at each stop. To board, push the lighted green button beside the doors; to exit the car, push the lighted white button.

Trolleys generally operate daily from 5am to about 12:30am, although the Blue Line, which goes to the border, runs around the clock on Saturday.

BY TRAIN   Within the San Diego area, **Amtrak** (☎ **800/USA-RAIL**) stops downtown, in Solana Beach, and in Oceanside. A ticket from downtown San Diego to Solana Beach costs \$5 one way; it's \$7.50 to Oceanside. You can also get to San Juan Capistrano and Disneyland in Anaheim (see chapter 14, "Side Trips from Los Angeles") via the train; call for details.

San Diego's expressrail commuter service, **The Coaster** (☎ **800/COASTER**), travels between downtown and Oceanside with stops en route at Old Town, Sorrento Valley, Solana Beach, Encinitas, and Carlsbad.

BY FERRY & WATER TAXI   There's regularly scheduled **ferry service** (☎ **619/ 234-4111**) between San Diego and Coronado. Ferries leave from the Broadway Pier on the hour from 9am to 9pm Sunday to Thursday and from 9am to 10pm Friday and Saturday, and return from the Old Ferry Landing in Coronado to the Broadway Pier every hour on the 42-minute mark from 9:42am to 9:42pm Sunday to Thursday and from 9:42am to 10:42pm Friday and Saturday. Ferries also run from the Fifth Avenue Landing near the Convention Center to the Old Ferry Landing every hour on the half-hour from 9:30am to 9:30pm Sunday to Thursday and from 9:30am to 10:30pm Friday and Saturday. The trip from Coronado to the Fifth Avenue Landing is every hour at the 18-minute mark from 9:18am to 9:18pm Sunday to Thursday and from 9:18am to 10:18pm Friday and Saturday. The fare is \$2 for each leg of the journey (50¢ extra if you bring your bike). Purchase tickets in advance at the Harbor Excursion kiosk on Broadway Pier, the Fifth Avenue Landing in San Diego, or at the Old Ferry Landing in Coronado.

Water taxis (☎ 619/235-TAXI) will take you around most of San Diego Bay for $5. If you want to go to the southern part of the bay (to Loews Coronado Bay Resort, for example), you'll be charged a flat fee of $25.

BY TAXI

Cab companies don't have standardized rates, except from the airport into town, which costs $1.80 per mile. Taxis may be hailed in the street, but you'll be lucky if you can find one; phone for a guaranteed pick-up. Companies include **Orange Cab** (☎ 619/291-3333), **San Diego Cab** (☎ 619/226-TAXI), and **Yellow Cab** (☎ 619/234-6161). The **Coronado Cab Company** (☎ 619/435-6211) serves Coronado. In La Jolla, use **La Jolla Cab** (☎ 619/453-4222).

BY ORGANIZED TOUR

The **Old Town Trolley** (☎ 619/298-8687) isn't a trolley at all; rather, it's a privately operated open-air tour bus that travels in a continuous loop around the city, stopping at sightseeing highlights. It stops at more than a dozen places around the city, and you can hop on and off as many times as you please during one entire loop (but once you've completed the circuit, you can't go around again). A nonstop tour takes 90 minutes and is accompanied by a fast-moving live commentary on city history and sights. Major stops include Old Town, Presidio Park, Bazaar del Mundo, Balboa Park, the San Diego Zoo, the Embarcadero, Seaport Village, and the Gaslamp Quarter. Tours operate daily from 9am to 5pm in summer, to 4pm the rest of the year; they cost $20 for adults and $8 for children ages 4 to 12; under 4 ride free.

Gray Line Tours (☎ 619/491-0011) offers a 4-hour escorted bus tour of San Diego that costs $24 for adults (half-price for children). **San Diego Mini Tours** (☎ 619/477-8687) also offers excursions throughout the area.

BY BICYCLE

San Diego is great for bikers; it's relatively flat and many roads have designated bike lanes. If you didn't bring your own wheels, you can rent from **Pennyfarthing's,** 314 G St. in the Gaslamp Quarter (☎ 619/233-7696), or **Hamel's Action Sports Center,** 704 Ventura Place, off Mission Boulevard at the roller coaster in North Mission Beach (☎ 619/488-5050). In Coronado, there's **Bikes & Beyond** at the Old Ferry Landing (☎ 619/435-7180).

If a bus stop has a bike-route sign attached (not all of them do), you can place your bike on the bus's bike rack for free while you ride. The San Diego Trolley also allows bikes on board for free. You just need a bike permit, which is available for $4 from the **Transit Store,** 102 Broadway at First Avenue (☎ 619/234-1060). Bikes can also be brought aboard the San Diego–Coronado ferry.

FAST FACTS: San Diego

American Express   A convenient downtown office is at 258 Broadway (at Third Avenue; ☎ 619/234-4455); it's open Monday to Friday from 9am to 5pm.

Dentists/Doctors   For dental referrals, contact the **San Diego County Dental Society** at ☎ 800/201-0244 or 800/DENTIST. **Hotel Docs** (☎ 800/468-3537 or 619/275-2663) is a 24-hour network of physicians, dentists, and chiropractors who claim they'll come to your hotel room within 35 minutes of your call. They accept credit cards, and their services are covered by most insurance policies.

Emergencies   For police, fire, highway patrol, or life-threatening medical emergencies, dial ☎ 911 from any phone. No coins are required.

Hospitals   **UCSD Medical Center-Hillcrest,** 200 W. Arbor Dr. (☎ **619/ 543-6400**), has the best-located emergency room. **Coronado Hospital,** 250 Prospect Place (☎ **619/435-6251**), is a good pick in Coronado. In La Jolla, head to **Scripps Memorial,** 9888 Genesee Ave. (☎ **619/457-4123**).

Liquor Laws   Liquor shops, grocery stores, and most supermarkets sell packaged alcoholic beverages between 6am and 2am. Most restaurants, nightclubs, and bars are licensed to serve alcoholic beverages during the same hours. The legal age for purchase and consumption is 21, and proof of age is strictly enforced.

Newspapers/Magazines   *The San Diego Union-Tribune* is published daily, and its informative entertainment section, "Night & Day," is in the Thursday edition. *The Reader,* published weekly (on Thursday), is an alternative source of dining and entertainment information. *San Diego Magazine* is also filled with extensive entertainment and dining listings. The free *San Diego This Week* has restaurant listings and information about shopping, attractions, nightlife, and the latest goings-on about town.

Police   See "Emergencies," above. For nonemergency matters, contact the downtown precinct, 1401 Broadway (☎ **619/531-2000**).

Post Office   The main post office, 2535 Midway Dr., San Diego, CA 92110 (☎ **800/275-8777**), is between Barnett Avenue and Rosecrans Street. Counter service is offered 8am to 5pm Monday to Saturday, but full service is also available at a window in the box area until 1am Monday to Friday. A convenient downtown branch is at 815 E St. (open Monday to Friday from 8:30am to 5pm and Saturday from 8:30am–noon).

Safety   As cities go, San Diego is pretty safe. But use particular caution on beaches after dark, and stay on designated walkways and away from secluded areas in Balboa Park—night or day. In the Gaslamp Quarter, stay west of Fifth Avenue. Take particular care to lock your car and park in well-lit areas; San Diego's proximity to the border contributes to its high rate of auto theft.

Taxes   A 7.75% sales tax is added on at the register for all goods and services purchased in San Diego. The city hotel tax is $10^{1}/_{2}$%.

Time   For the correct time, call ☎ **619/853-1212.**

Weather   For local weather and surf reports call ☎ **619/289-1212.**

3 Accommodations

Remember to factor in the city's 10.5% hotel tax. Rates tend to be higher in summer (especially true of beach hotels) and when there's a big convention in town. Most San Diego hotels offer nonsmoking rooms, so request one if it matters to you.

Mission Valley/Hotel Circle, north of Balboa Park and east of Mission Bay, consists of cheek-to-jowl motels on either side of I-8. As awful as this sounds, the area is a good bet for budget-minded visitors. Harbor Island and Shelter Island—minutes from the airport and downtown—are two man-made peninsulas that command excellent views. Coronado is a bit out of the way from everything else, but that's part of the charm of staying on this "island." La Jolla offers some lovely lodging alternatives, as do the beach areas of Mission Bay and Pacific Beach.

For good prices in all accommodation categories, contact **San Diego Hotel Reservations** (☎ **800/SAVE-CASH** or 619/627-9300; www.savecash.com). For information on 30 bed-and-breakfasts in the San Diego area, send $3.95 for a 20-page directory to **B&B Resources,** P.O. Box 3292, San Diego, CA 92163 (☎ **800/ 619-7666** or 619/297-3130).

San Diego Area Accommodations

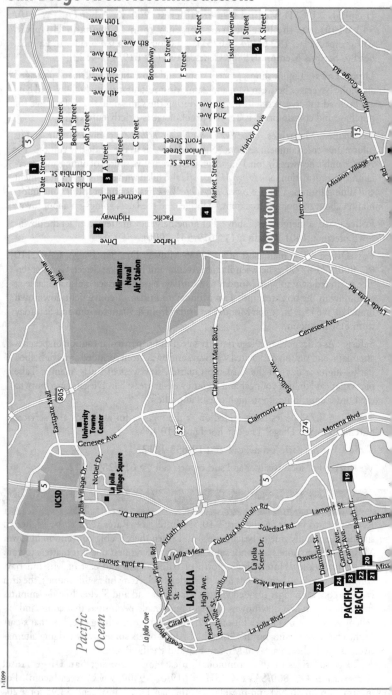

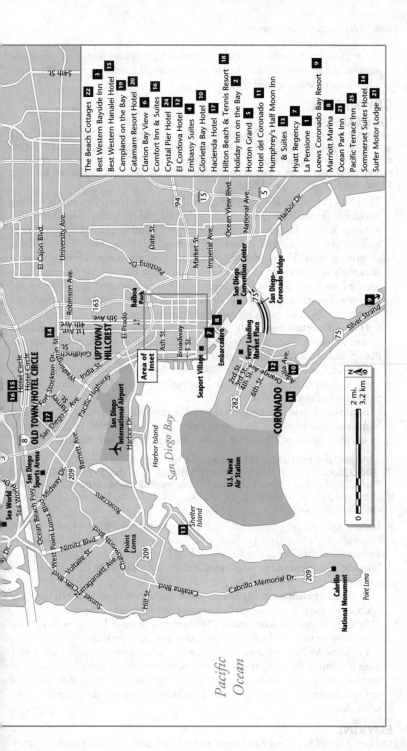

The Beach Cottages 22
Best Western Bayside Inn 3
Best Western Hanalei Hotel 15
Campland on the Bay 19
Catamaran Resort Hotel 20
Clarion Bay View 6
Comfort Inn & Suites 16
Crystal Pier Hotel 24
El Cordova Hotel 12
Embassy Suites 4
Glorietta Bay Hotel 10
Hacienda Hotel 17
Hilton Beach & Tennis Resort 18
Holiday Inn on the Bay 2
Horton Grand 5
Hotel del Coronado 11
Humphrey's Half Moon Inn & Suites 13
Hyatt Regency 7
La Pensione 1
Loews Coronado Bay Resort 9
Marriott Marina 8
Ocean Park Inn 23
Pacific Terrace Inn 14
Sommerset Suites Hotel 25
Surfer Motor Lodge 21

599

For more accommodations options, check out *Frommer's San Diego*. Note that some of the properties listed below also provide information on-line at www.infopost.com/sandiego/hotels/index.

DOWNTOWN
VERY EXPENSIVE

Hyatt Regency San Diego. 1 Market Place, San Diego, CA 92101. ☎ **800/233-1234** or 619/232-1234. Fax 619/239-5678. 819 rms, 56 suites. A/C MINIBAR TV TEL. $235–$280 double; from $400 suite. Extra person $25. Children under 12 stay free in parents' room. Packages and much lower weekend rates available. AE, DC, DISC, MC, V. Parking $13 valet, $9 self. Bus: 1. Trolley: Seaport Village.

The Hyatt Regency enjoys a convenient position on San Diego Bay, within walking distance of the Gaslamp Quarter, Seaport Village, and the Convention Center, and its rooms have terrific views. The impressive high-rise features a contemporary 3-story lobby of green marble and Italian limestone topped by an additional three floors of meeting space. The rooms are pretty much what you'd expect from a Hyatt—attractively done in a kind of an updated 18th-century English-style decor and high-standard amenities. Spacious two-bedroom suites are located on the top floors and feature walk-in closets, whirlpool tubs, and minikitchens. There's a club floor, and more than 80% of all rooms are designated nonsmoking.

Dining/Entertainment: Sally's, a rather formal seafood restaurant, attracts locals as well as guests. There are two other less formal spots (all three offer alfresco dining) and two bars, including one with a spectacular 40th-floor view.

Services: Concierge, room service (24 hours), dry cleaning, laundry, newspaper delivery, in-room massage, twice-daily maid service, baby-sitting, express checkout, valet parking, courtesy car, shoe shine.

Facilities: Movie channels, video rental, heated outdoor pool, state-of-the-art health club/spa, whirlpool, four tennis courts, water-sports rental, boat and bicycle rental, business center, conference rooms, car-rental desk, beauty salon, gift shop.

San Diego Marriott Marina. 333 W. Harbor Dr. (at Front St.), San Diego, CA 92101-7700. ☎ **800/228-9290** or 619/234-1500. Fax 619/234-8678. 1,355 rms, 50 suites. A/C MINIBAR TV TEL. $225–$245 double; from $375 suite. Children under 18 stay free in parents' room. AARP discounts and packages available. AE, CB, DC, DISC, MC, V. Parking $13 valet, $9 self. Bus: 1. Trolley: Convention Center.

Located right on the waterfront, this striking modern hotel has a 446-slip marina, lush grounds, and a great location, just a short walk from Seaport Village, the Embarcadero, the Convention Center, and the Gaslamp Quarter. Many rooms have balconies with breathtaking water views, and when you tire of the view, you can rent videos from the on-site library.

Dining/Entertainment: My favorite of the several on-site restaurants is the Yacht Club, a popular place for informal dining and dancing on the waterfront.

Services: Concierge, room service (24 hours), dry cleaning, laundry service, newspaper delivery, secretarial services, express checkout, valet parking.

Facilities: VCR, pay-per-view movies, two outdoor pools (including one with a waterfall), fitness center, daily aerobics classes, two whirlpools, sauna, spa, six lighted tennis courts, bicycle and boat rentals, game room, business center with secretarial services, conference rooms, self-service laundromat, car-rental desk, tour desk, hair salon, shops.

EXPENSIVE

✪ **Clarion Hotel Bay View San Diego.** 660 K St. (at Sixth Ave.), San Diego, CA 92101. ☎ **800/766-0234** or 619/696-0234. Fax 619/231-8199. 312 rms and suites. A/C TV TEL.

$109–$139 double; $149–$169 suite. Children under 18 stay free in parents' room. Extra person $10. AE, CB, DC, DISC, MC, V. Parking $8. Bus: 1. Trolley: Gaslamp/Convention Center.

This newish entry on the San Diego hotel scene provides an economical alternative for those attending meetings at the Convention Center—it's nearly as close as the Marriott and the Hyatt, but considerably less expensive. It's also close to the Gaslamp Quarter, which makes it an excellent choice for those who plan to enjoy nightlife and want to avoid walking far late at night. All quarters are spacious, bright, and modern, and more than half offer views of San Diego Bay and the Coronado Bridge. All rooms have sliding-glass doors that provide ample fresh air, and many have minibars. In-room safes are standard; 80% of the rooms are reserved for nonsmokers.

Dining/Entertainment: The Gallery Cafe serves breakfast, lunch, and dinner daily. There's a big-screen TV in the bar, and the hotel's dinner theater is popular on Friday and Saturday nights.

Services: Concierge, room service (6am to 10pm), dry cleaning, laundry service, express checkout.

Facilities: Pay-per-view movies; in-room touch-screen TVs that can be used for express checkout, ordering breakfast, and retrieving voice mail; conference rooms; coin-operated washer and dryer. The rooftop sundeck offers a great view as well as a workout room, Jacuzzi, sauna, and video arcade.

Horton Grand. 311 Island Ave. (at Fourth Ave.), San Diego, CA 92101. ☎ **800/542-1886** or 619/544-1886. Fax 619/544-0058. 108 rms, 24 minisuites. TV TEL. $109–$149 double; $129–$189 suite. Weekend and special packages available. Children under 12 stay free in parents' room. AE, CB, DC, MC, V. Valet parking $8. Bus: 1. Trolley: Convention Center.

A cross between an elegant hotel and a charming B&B, the Horton Grand combines two hotels dating from 1886, both of which were saved from demolition, moved to this spot, and connected by an airy atrium lobby filled with white wicker. Each room is uniquely furnished, but all have antiques, a gas fireplace (on a timer so you can fall asleep in front of it), and a comfortable queen-size bed; even the baths, complete with pedestal sink, are genteel. Rooms overlook either the city or the fig tree–filled courtyard. Each suite has a microwave, a minibar, two TVs and telephones, a sofa bed, and computer modem hookup. This is an old hotel, and sounds carry more than they might in a modern one, so if you're a light sleeper request a room with no neighbors above or adjacent.

Dining/Entertainment: Ida Bailey's restaurant, named for the well-loved madam whose establishment used to stand on this spot, opens onto the hotel's courtyard, which is used for Sunday brunch on warm days. Breakfast, lunch, and dinner are available daily, and afternoon tea is served Tuesday to Saturday from 2:30 to 5pm; live entertainment is featured Friday and Saturday evenings.

Service: Room service (7am–10pm), dry cleaning/laundry, express checkout, valet parking, courtesy car, free coffee in lobby 5am to 7am daily.

Facilities: Access to nearby pool and weight room, conference rooms.

MODERATE

In addition to the properties described below, there's also an **Embassy Suites** at 601 Pacific Hwy. (☎ **800/EMBASSY** or 619/239-2400), and the **Holiday Inn on the Bay,** 1355 N. Harbor Dr. (☎ **800/HOLIDAY** or 619/232-3861).

Best Western Bayside Inn. 555 W. Ash St. (at Columbia St.), San Diego, CA 92101. ☎ **800/341-1818** or 619/233-7500. Fax 619/239-8060. 122 rms. A/C TV TEL. $85–$105 double. Harbor view $10 extra. Children under 12 stay free in parents' room. All rates include continental breakfast. Weekend rates (except in summer) and packages available. AE, CB, DC, DISC, ER, MC, V. Free covered parking. Bus: 5 or 105. Trolley: C St. and Kettner.

The friendly, accommodating staff and stunning city and harbor views of this quiet, unassuming hotel may very well please you. It's an easy walk to the Embarcadero (it should be called Bayview rather than Bayside), a bit farther to Horton Plaza, 4 blocks to the trolley stop, and 5 blocks to the train station. The comfortable rooms are decorated in restful colors, with king- or queen-size beds as well as balconies overlooking the bay or downtown. The hotel's bar and grill serves breakfast, lunch, and dinner; the bar has a 50-inch TV. Good restaurants and bars are nearby, and meals are also available from room service. Complimentary airport transport is provided as are cable TV, in-room movies, outdoor pool, and Jacuzzi.

INEXPENSIVE

✪ **La Pensione Hotel.** 606 W. Date St. (at India St.), San Diego, CA 92101. ☎ **800/ 232-4683** or 619/236-8000. Fax 619/236-8088. 80 rms. TV TEL. $44–$64 double. Packages available. AE, CB, DC, MC, V. Free daily parking, or $10 per week. Bus: 5 or 105. Trolley: County Center/Little Italy.

This place has a lot going for it: modernity, cleanliness, a friendly staff, a quiet location—in San Diego's Little Italy that's within walking distance of restaurants (mostly Italian) and nightspots as well as the central business district—and parking, which is a premium for small hotels in San Diego. Built around a courtyard, La Pensione feels like a small European hotel. The lobby is small but inviting; the rooms, while not overly large, make the most of their space and leave you with area to move around. Each offers a ceiling fan, wet bar, microwave, and small fridge. Quarters are cleaned once a week for weekly guests, daily for those who stay a shorter period.

Caffé Italia offers sandwiches and salads as well as Sunday brunch and jazz on Friday and Saturday. The fourth floor is reserved for nonsmokers. One reader complained about noise filtering up to his room from the ground-level restaurants; several other readers have raved about this property. All in all, a remarkable value.

HILLCREST/UPTOWN

✪ **Sommerset Suites Hotel.** 606 Washington St. (at Fifth Ave.), San Diego, CA 92103. ☎ **800/962-9665,** 800/356-1787 in CA, or 619/692-5200. Fax 619/299-6065. 80 suites. A/C TV TEL. $95 studio suite; $170 1-bedroom suite; $200 executive suite. Children under 12 stay free in parents' room. Rates include large continental breakfast. AE, CB, DC, DISC, MC, V. Free covered parking. Bus: 16 or 25. Take Washington St. exit off I-5.

This terrific bargain is a good choice for those who find traditional hotels too impersonal. The staff is friendly and helpful, and in the late afternoon they serve complimentary snacks, soda, beer, and wine in the cozy guest lounge. The poolside patio, set up for barbecues, encourages impromptu gatherings and picnics among guests. Your options here include studio, one-bedroom, and executive suites; all are tastefully furnished and have in-room safes and fully equipped, modern kitchens (including dishwashers in the executive suites), large closets, and balconies. Even the studios are spacious.

Services include a concierge; laundry and dry cleaning; baby-sitting; courtesy van service (7am to 9pm) to the airport, Sea World, the zoo, and other attractions within a 5-mile radius; video rentals; and two-line phones and voice mail. Rollaway beds and cribs are available. Facilities include a small heated pool, a Jacuzzi, a rooftop sundeck, gas barbecue grills, a snack room, and coin-operated laundry.

SHELTER ISLAND

Humphrey's Half Moon Inn & Suites. 2303 Shelter Island Dr., San Diego, CA 92106. ☎ **800/345-9995** or 619/224-3411. Fax 619/224-3478. 182 rms and suites. A/C TV TEL. $115–$169 double; from $189 suite. Children under 18 stay free in parents' room. AE, CB, DC, DISC, MC, V. Free parking.

This is a favorite choice for families. The grounds are lovely, with palm trees, tropical flowers, and a pond; and the rooms, done in Hawaiian style with bamboo and rattan furnishings, are very attractive. Included are free in-room coffee, refrigerator, a movie channel, free newspaper delivery, and free transportation to the airport or the Amtrak station. There are heated pools for adults and children, a whirlpool, table tennis, laundry facilities, bicycles, and room for lawn games.

IN & AROUND OLD TOWN

In addition to the places described below, you might also be interested in the **Best Western Hanalei Hotel,** 2270 Hotel Circle N. (☎ **800/882-0858** or 619/297-1101).

Comfort Inn & Suites. 2485 Hotel Circle Place, San Diego, CA 92108. ☎ **800/647-1903** or 619/291-7700. Fax 619/297-6179. 200 rms. A/C TV TEL. $69–$99 double. Additional person $10. Children under 18 stay free in parents' room. Rates include continental breakfast. AE, CB, DC, DISC, MC, V. Free parking.

This well-priced modern motel at the western end of Hotel Circle is a high-rise, complete with box balconies and a small free-form pool. It underwent a complete refurbishment in 1996, and all rooms are large and comfortably furnished with king- or queen-size beds, plus baths with separate dressing areas. Higher-priced rooms have whirlpool baths, refrigerators, and terraces. There's a heated outdoor pool and Jacuzzi, a car-rental desk, a game room, and a washer/dryer. Tennis courts are across the street, as is an 11-hole golf course (yes, *11* holes).

Hacienda Hotel Old Town. 4041 Harney St. (just east of San Diego Ave.), San Diego, CA 92110. ☎ **800/888-1991** or 619/298-4707. Fax 619/298-4771. 150 suites. A/C TV TEL. $115 double. Children under 16 stay free in parents' room. AE, CB, DC, DISC, ER, MC, V. Free underground parking. Bus: 4, 5, or 105. From I-5, exit at Old Town Ave.; turn left onto San Diego Ave. and right onto Harney St.

Perched above Old Town, this brightly lit Best Western all-suite hotel creates an impressive sight at night and affords excellent views of Old Town from its outdoor pool and patio. The comfortable suites have 20-foot-high ceilings, ceiling fans, refrigerators, microwave ovens, coffeemakers, VCRs, and furnishings right out of the American Southwest. The one-room units are done in desert colors and have either one or two queen-size beds. Walkways thread through courtyards filled with bubbling fountains, swaying palms, and bougainvillea-trimmed balconies. A Mexican restaurant serves breakfast, lunch, and dinner daily from its perch atop the hotel; guests also have signing privileges at several nearby restaurants. Amenities include weekday concierge service, room service (6:30am to 2pm and 4 to 10pm), hosted manager's social Monday to Thursday, complimentary airport/train transportation, movie rentals with complimentary bag of microwave popcorn, pool, Jacuzzi, spa, fitness center, con-ference suites, meeting rooms, and coin-operated laundry.

MISSION BAY/PACIFIC BEACH
Very Expensive

Hilton Beach & Tennis Resort. 1775 E. Mission Bay Dr., San Diego, CA 92109. ☎ **800/962-6307** in CA, AZ, and NV; 800/445-8667 elsewhere; or 619/276-4010. Fax 619/275-7991. 357 rms, 8 suites. A/C MINIBAR TV TEL. $175–$230 double; from $325 suite. Extra person $20. Children under 18 stay free in parents' room. Lower off-season rates. AE, CB, DC, DISC, MC, V. Free parking. Take I-5 to Sea World Dr. exit, and turn north on E. Mission Bay Dr.

Completely renovated in 1995, this handsome resort occupies 18 acres on the east side of Mission Bay and is a handy quarter-mile from the Visitor Information Center. This Mediterranean-style resort offers pleasant rooms in sand and sea-green tones; all come with ceiling fans, a balcony or terrace, a king-size bed or two queens, an elegant bath, a refrigerator, a coffeemaker, an iron and ironing board, a hair dryer, and a makeup mirror. Even the standard rooms are spacious, and many are interconnecting. The staff is friendly and helpful here, and the shops are fun for browsing in between lolling by the pool, biking along the bay, and taking tennis lessons. Sea World is just across the bay, and the ocean is 5 miles to the west.

Dining/Entertainment: There's a casual cafe open all day, an Italian restaurant serving dinner nightly, and a bayfront restaurant and bar as well as lobby and poolside bars.

Services: Concierge, room service (7am–11pm), dry cleaning, laundry service, baby-sitting, supervision for children on weekends and in summer.

Facilities: Pay-per-view movies, Olympic-size pool, children's wading pool, weight-training room, massage, four Jacuzzis, sauna, full-service spa, five lighted tennis courts, pro shop, water sports, scuba diving, bike and jogging trails, bike and boat rental, yacht charters, putting green, arcade, arts and crafts for kids, children's playground, 24-hour business center, meeting rooms, laundromat, salon, shops, in-room dataports.

EXPENSIVE

✪ **Catamaran Resort Hotel.** 3999 Mission Blvd. (4 blocks south of Grand Ave.), San Diego, CA 92109. ☎ **800/288-0770,** 800/233-8172 in Canada, or 619/488-1081. Fax 619/488-1387. 160 rms, 100 studios, 50 suites. A/C TV TEL. $160–$205 double; from $265 suite. Children under 18 stay free in parents' room. AE, DISC, MC, V. Self-parking $5, valet $7. Take Grand/Garnet exit off I-5 and go west on Grand Ave., then south on Mission Blvd.

The Catamaran is beautifully situated on Mission Bay, with its own beach, lots of watersports facilities, and lovely grounds. The Polynesian-style decor includes a 15-foot interior waterfall, lush foliage, squawking parrots, and plenty of island artifacts, like a full-size dugout canoe in the lobby. The guest rooms are divided between a 13-story tower and six 2-story bungalows; each continues the tropical theme and opens onto a balcony or patio. Tower rooms have memorable views of the bay, the skyline, La Jolla, and Point Loma, but the bungalows are far more intimate. Pets are allowed.

Dining/Entertainment: There's a restaurant offering indoor and alfresco dining, a lively bar showcasing live bands and videos, and an intimate, crowded piano bar.

Services: Concierge, room service (until 11pm), dry cleaning, laundry service, nightly turndown, baby-sitting, secretarial services, express checkout, valet parking.

Facilities: Kitchenettes, movie channels, outdoor heated pool, beach, health club, whirlpool spa, sundeck, water-sports concessions, jogging track, stroller joggers, bike rental, children's program during the summer, business center, conference rooms, car-rental desk, tour desk, gift shop.

Crystal Pier Hotel. 4500 Ocean Blvd., San Diego, CA 92109. ☎ **800/748-5894** or 619/483-6983 (call between 8am–8pm). 26 cottages. TV. Cottages for up to 4 people, $145–$250 mid-June to mid-Sept; $95–$200 rest of the year. 3-day minimum in summer; weekly and monthly rates available. DISC, MC, V. Free parking. Take I-5 to Grand/Garnet exit; follow Garnet to the pier.

This historic property, which dates from 1927, offers a unique opportunity to sleep *over* the water. Built on a private pier jutting into the ocean in the center of Pacific Beach, the hotel has 20 older cottages dating from 1936 and six more built in 1992. The management recently did a great job of remodeling 12 of the older cottages, but try not to get one of the untouched units. All quarters have a living room, bedroom, kitchenette, and private deck. The quietest units are farthest out on the pier, away from the noise of the boardwalk. Boogie boards, fishing poles, beach chairs, and umbrellas are available.

👪 Family-Friendly Hotels

The Beach Cottages *(see p. 605)*   Kids enjoy the informality and the terrific location near the beach.

Hilton Beach & Tennis Resort *(see p. 603)*   This bayfront hotel has myriad sports and recreation facilities, and plenty of space for active offspring. The tranquil water of the bay is more inviting for small children than the sometimes-intimidating waves at the ocean.

Hotel del Coronado *(see p. 608)*   In addition to a beautiful beach, this historic hotel offers special supervised children's programs led by experienced counselors.

Humphrey's Half Moon Inn *(see p. 602)*   A great value, with lovely tropical grounds and a lighthearted Hawaiian theme that kids love. A washer/dryer is an added convenience for parents.

Loews Coronado Bay Resort *(see p. 609)*   The Commodore Kids Club, for children ages 4 to 12, is a terrific supervised program with arts and crafts projects, nature hikes, beach games, and evening events.

✪ **Pacific Terrace Inn.** 610 Diamond St., San Diego, CA 92109. ☎ **800/344-3370** or 619/ 581-3500. Fax 619/274-3341. 65 rms, 8 suites. A/C MINIBAR TV TEL. $185–$225 double; $195– $225 double with kitchenette; from $285 suite. Extra person $10. AE, CB, DC, DISC, MC, V. Rates include continental breakfast. Free security parking. Bus: 34 or 34A. Take I-5 to Grand/ Garnet exit and follow either Grand or Garnet west to Mission Blvd., turn right (north), then left (west) onto Diamond; it's at end of the street on right.

This is a wonderful choice along the Pacific Beach boardwalk. It's attractive and up-scale, and it's quieter than the other nearby beachfront properties. Rooms are large and comfortable, and have balconies or terraces, refrigerators, wall safes, hair dryers, cotton robes, vanities with separate sinks, and voice mail; 40 rooms have kitchens. Third-story rooms have particularly nice views, and the suites have large baths with Jacuzzis. There's popcorn, coffee, and lemonade set out for guests in the Caribbean Room.

Services: Valet dry cleaning, laundry service, complimentary copy of *USA Today* delivered daily.

Facilities: Kitchenettes, outdoor heated pool facing the ocean, beach, Jacuzzi, conference rooms, coin-operated laundry.

MODERATE

The Beach Cottages. 4255 Ocean Blvd. (a block south of Grand Ave.), San Diego, CA 92109. ☎ **619/483-7440** (call between 9am–9pm). Fax 619/273-9365. 28 rms, 12 studios, 18 apts, 17 cottages, 3 suites. TV TEL. Summer, $95–$115 double; $125 studio for up to 4; $145–$180 cottage for up to 6; $145–$190 apt for up to 6; $220–$240 2-bedroom suite for up to 6. Lower rates rest of year. Weekly rates available (except in summer). AE, CB, DC, DISC, MC, V. Free parking. Take I-5 to Grand/Garnet exit; go west on Grand Ave. and left on Mission Blvd.

The Beach Cottages are particularly suited for young couples and families who want to stay right on the beach. The property is within walking distance of shops and restaurants, and features barbecue grills, shuffleboard courts, table tennis, and a laundry. In addition to regular motel rooms, the hotel offers cottages, apartments, studios, and suites; all accommodations except the motel rooms have fully equipped kitchens. The rustic cottages, which are literally sandside, contain either one or two bedrooms and sleep up to six; each has a private patio with tables, chairs, and recliners. The other units are outfitted with more contemporary interiors, but they're farther from the waves. Guests gather in a lovely patio courtyard with plant-filled trellises, or head straight for the beach.

Ocean Park Inn. 710 Grand Ave., San Diego, CA 92109. ☎ **800/231-7735** or 619/ 483-5858. Fax 619/274-0823. 73 rms, 4 suites. A/C TV TEL. Summer, $104–$154 double; $179–$189 suite. Lower rates rest of the year. Rates include continental breakfast. AE, DC, DISC, MC, V. Free indoor parking. Take Grand/Garnet exit off I-5, and follow Grand Ave. to the ocean.

This 3-story standout right on Pacific Beach's lively beach path is visually appealing both inside and out. Behind the modern Spanish/Mediterranean facade is a sharply designed marble lobby that gives way to the less splendid but completely comfortable guest rooms. The rooms are contemporary but bland; all have terraces and refrigerators. The most expensive ones have oceanfront balconies but can be a bit noisy. King suites are extra-large and have Roman tubs; some also have kitchenettes. Facilities include a sundeck, a heated pool, an outdoor Jacuzzi, and coin-operated laundry.

INEXPENSIVE

Surfer Motor Lodge. 711 Pacific Beach Dr. (at Mission Blvd.), San Diego, CA 92109. ☎ **800/ 787-3373** or 619/483-7070. Fax 619/274-1670. 52 rms. TV TEL. Summer, $89–$122 double; winter, $69–$90. Weekly rates offered in winter. AE, DC, MC, V. Free parking.

This 5-story motel isn't remarkable, but it does offer acceptable low-cost accommodations right on the beach. Almost all the rooms have balconies and ocean views and are cooled by ocean breezes; fans are also available. In addition to standard doubles, there are kitchenette units, one-bedroom units that can sleep as many as four, and family units that can sleep up to six. In addition to a heated outdoor pool, there are self-serve laundry facilities on the premises. The hotel can arrange fishing and golf outings as well as city tours.

CAMPING

Campland on the Bay. 2211 Pacific Beach Dr., San Diego, CA 92109-5699. ☎ **800/ 4BAYFUN**, 619/581-4200, or 619/581-4212 (24 hours). 600 hookup sites. Summer, $26–$52 for up to 4 people; off-season, $19–$37 for up to 4 people. Lowest-priced sites do not have hookups. Senior rates available. MC, V. Take I-5 to Grand/Garnet exit, and follow Grand to Olney and turn left; turn left again onto Pacific Beach Dr.

This family-oriented bayside campground draws RVs, campers (with or without vans), and boaters. Conveniently located nearby are parks, a beach, bird sanctuary, and dog walk. Other facilities include pools, a Jacuzzi, catamaran and windsurfer rentals and lessons, bike and boat rentals, a game room, a cafe, a market, and a laundry. Sea World is 5 minutes away.

LA JOLLA
VERY EXPENSIVE

La Valencia Hotel. 1132 Prospect St. (at Herschel Ave.), La Jolla, CA 92037. ☎ **800/ 451-0772** or 619/454-0771. Fax 619/456-3921. 90 rms, 13 suites. A/C MINIBAR TV TEL. $190– $230 standard double; $385–$400 full oceanview double; from $500 suite. Children under 12 stay free in parents' room. AE, DC, DISC, MC, V. Valet parking $8. Take Ardath Rd. exit off I-5 north, or the La Jolla Village Dr. west exit off I-5 south; take Torrey Pines Rd. to Prospect Place and turn right; Prospect Place becomes Prospect St.

This gracious Spanish-colonial hotel overlooking the ocean delights the senses at every turn. From the colonnaded entrance with vine-covered trellis to the lush gardens surrounding the large pool to the exquisite mosaic tile-work within, it's a beauty. Old World charm, outstanding personal service, and an impressive location have made this a haven for celebrities since the early days of Hollywood. The guest rooms are outfitted with European antique reproductions and fine-quality linens; other luxury amenities include terry robes, oversize towels, and bathroom phones. The ocean-view rooms have fantastic vistas. At the back of the hotel, garden terraces open toward the ocean.

Dining/Entertainment: The elegant rooftop Sky Room offers French cuisine in an intimate setting; the Mediterranean Room serves California cuisine either indoors or out. Once upon a time, Ginger Rogers and Charlton Heston hung out in the legendary Whaling Bar & Grill and its adjoining cafe. There's piano music in the lobby lounge Monday to Saturday evenings; refreshments are served on the adjoining oceanview terrace on request.

Services: Concierge, room service (24 hours), dry cleaning, laundry service, morning newspaper, nightly turndown, in-room massage, daily maid service, baby-sitting, secretarial services, express checkout, valet parking.

Facilities: Kitchenettes; VCRs; video rental; free-form heated pool is edged with a lawn, flowering trees, shrubs, and a flagstone sundeck. There's also a minihealth club, Jacuzzi, sauna, massage room, shuffleboard, access to tennis courts, and three conference rooms.

EXPENSIVE

Also consider the spectacularly sited **Sheraton Grande Torrey Pines,** 10950 N. Torrey Pines Rd., La Jolla, CA 92037 (☎ **800/762-6160** or 619/558-1500), perched on a bluff above the Pacific and adjacent to the renowned Torrey Pines Golf Course.

✪ **Colonial Inn.** 910 Prospect St., La Jolla, CA 92037. ☎ **800/826-1278** or 619/454-2181. Fax 619/454-5679. 64 rms, 11 suites. TV TEL. $165 double with village view; $185–$210 double with ocean view; from $230 suite. Lower off-season rates. Children under 18 stay free in parents' room. AE, CB, DC, MC, V. Valet parking $5. Take Ardath Rd. exit off I-5 north, or the La Jolla Village Dr. west exit off I-5 south; follow Torrey Pines Rd. to Prospect Place and turn right; Prospect Place becomes Prospect St.

This outstanding choice offers Old World atmosphere, tasteful decor, and spacious rooms enhanced by traditional furnishings and elegant fabrics. The property, which was built in 1913, stands 1 block from the ocean and just down the street from the more expensive La Valencia. Guests who choose to stay here instead of at "La V" will sacrifice air-conditioning for a ceiling fan in each room, but will gain elbow room— and save money. Originally an apartment hotel, the inn has oversize closets and feels more homey. Refrigerators and terry robes are available on request.

Dining/Entertainment: The bar in Putnam's (see "Where to Dine," below) was once a drugstore soda-fountain; today it's a popular watering hole. A large spray of fresh flowers is the focal point in the lounge, where guests gather in front of the fireplace for drinks. The restaurant serves excellent California cuisine.

Services: Room service, dry cleaning, laundry service, nightly turndown on request, baby-sitting, valet parking, complimentary shoe shine. Walking tours of La Jolla depart from the hotel at 11am Thursday to Saturday or other times by appointment. Airport transportation is available for $11 one-way.

Facilities: An outdoor heated pool set in a landscaped garden, outdoor terrace, conference rooms.

Sea Lodge. 8110 Camino del Oro (at Avenida de la Playa), La Jolla, CA 92037. ☎ **800/ 237-5211** or 619/459-8271. Fax 619/456-9346. 128 rms, 8 suites. TV TEL. $175–$379 double; $409 suite. Children under 12 stay free in parents' room. Lower off-season rates. AE, CB, DC, DISC, MC, V. Free covered parking. Take Ardath Rd. exit off I-5 north, or the La Jolla Village Dr. west exit off I-5 south; take La Jolla Shores Dr.; turn west onto Avenida de la Playa, then north (right) on Camino del Oro.

This 3-story sunset-colored hotel is sited right on mile-long La Jolla Shores Beach. The large rooms are in a long, low stucco building that's highlighted by fountains, attractive landscaping, open-air walkways, ceramic tile, graceful arches, and Mexican antiques like the 200-year-old cathedral doors leading into the main dining room. Third-floor rooms—my favorites—have high, sloped barnwood ceilings. Almost all rooms have ocean views; every one has a balcony or patio, and some have kitchens.

Dining/Entertainment: The Shores, open all day, features indoor and patio seating, with ocean views from every table; seafood is the specialty.

Services: Concierge, room service.

Facilities: Outdoor heated pool, children's pool, sauna, tennis and volleyball courts, tour desk, complimentary underground parking.

MODERATE

There's also the **Radisson Hotel La Jolla,** 3299 Holiday Court, La Jolla, CA 92037 (☎ **800/333-3333** or 619/453-5500), the **Residence Inn by Marriott,** 8901 Gilman Dr., La Jolla, CA 92037 (☎ **800/331-3131** or 619/587-1770), and the **Bed & Breakfast Inn at La Jolla,** 7753 Draper Ave., La Jolla, CA 92037 (☎ **619/ 456-2066;** fax 619/456-0510). The Bed & Breakfast Inn is adorable, but the quality of management has varied quite a bit over the last couple of years.

✪ **Empress Hotel of La Jolla.** 7766 Fay Ave. (at Silverado), La Jolla, CA 92037. ☎ **888/ 369-9900** or 619/454-3001. Fax 619/454-6387. 73 rms and suites. A/C TV TEL. $109–$135 double; $300 Jacuzzi suite. Extra person $10. Children under 18 stay free in parents' room. Lower off-season and long-stay rates. Rates include continental breakfast. AE, CB, DC, DISC, MC, V. Valet parking $5. Take Ardath Rd. exit off I-5 north, or the La Jolla Village Dr. west exit off I-5 south; follow Torrey Pines Rd. to Girard and turn right, then left on Silverado to Fay.

This hotel offers spacious, traditionally furnished quarters with just a block or 2 away from La Jolla's main drag. It's definitely quieter here than at the Colonial Inn or the Prospect Park Inn. All rooms come equipped with hair dryers, coffeemakers, and terry robes. The top two floors in this 5-story building have partial ocean views. I like the European ambiance, marble bathrooms with large mirrors, and tasteful decor. Room service comes from the award-winning Manhattan Restaurant located on the ground floor.

INEXPENSIVE

La Jolla Cove Travelodge. 1141 Silverado St. (at Herchel), La Jolla, CA 92037. ☎ **800/ 578-7878** or 619/454-0791. Fax 619/459-8534. 30 rms. A/C TV TEL. $59–$89 double. AE, DC, MC, V. Rates are seasonal and subject to availability. Free parking.

This 3-story motel offers good value in a good location, close to shops, nightlife, and restaurants. The rooms are clean and basic, and come with coffeemakers, free HBO, and a queen-size, a king-size, or two double beds. There isn't a pool, but there's a modest sundeck on the third floor with a view to the ocean, which is about ³/₄-mile away.

CORONADO
VERY EXPENSIVE

✪ **Hotel del Coronado.** 1500 Orange Ave., San Diego, CA 92118. ☎ **800/468-3533** or 619/522-8000. Fax 619/522-8238. 700 rms. A/C MINIBAR TV TEL. From $195 standard; from $235 deluxe; from $295 ocean view; from $385 oceanfront; from $600 suite. Packages available. Children under 18 stay free in parents' room. AE, CB, DC, DISC, MC, V. Parking $10. From I-5 take the Coronado Bridge; turn left onto Orange Ave.

Opened in 1888 and designated a National Historic Landmark in 1977, the "Hotel Del," as it's affectionately known, is the last of California's grand old seaside hotels. Here the Duke of Windsor met his duchess, and Marilyn Monroe frolicked in *Some Like It Hot.* This monument to Victorian grandeur boasts tall cupolas, red turrets, gingerbread trim, all spread out on 33 acres. Rooms run the gamut from compact to extravagant, and all are packed with antique charm. Most have custom-made furnishings. The best rooms have balconies fronting the ocean and large windows that take in one of the city's finest white-sand beaches.

Dining/Entertainment: Each of the Del's nine restaurants and lounges has its own special charm. My favorite is the alfresco Ocean Terrace, the only outside restaurant in Coronado with a beach view. The newly renovated Prince of Wales Grill has garnered rave reviews for both cuisine and atmosphere. The Garden Patio serves afternoon tea on Sundays. Traditionalists still flock to the Crown Room (see "The Club & Music Scene," below), where the magnificent architecture remains unchanged since the turn of the century, but the menu features up-to-date interpretations of classic cuisine; it also serves one of the city's finest Sunday brunches. There's music and dancing nightly in the Ocean Terrace Lounge, and piano music in the Palm Court Bar.

Services: Concierge, room service (24 hours), dry cleaning, laundry service, nightly turndown, in-room massage, baby-sitting, secretarial services, express checkout, valet parking, guided tours of the hotel ($10).

Facilities: Movie channels, two outdoor pools, beach, state-of-the-art health spa, Jacuzzi, sauna, sundeck, six night-lit championship tennis courts, water-sports equipment rentals, bicycle rentals, 18-hole golf course nearby, game room, children's center, business center, conference rooms, car-rental desk, tour desk, beauty salon, shopping arcade.

✪ **Loews Coronado Bay Resort.** 4000 Coronado Bay Rd., Coronado, CA 92118. ☎ **800/ 81-LOEWS** or 619/424-4000. Fax 619/424-4400. 400 rms, 37 suites. A/C MINIBAR TV TEL. $195–$245 double; $395–$595 executive suite; $595–$1,500 bayside villa. Additional person $20. Children under 18 stay free in parents' room. Romance packages available. AE, CB, DC, DISC, MC, V. Self-parking (under cover) $10; valet parking $13. Take I-5 to the Coronado Bridge; go left onto Orange Ave.; continue 6$^{1}/_{2}$ miles down Silver Strand Hwy., then make a left at Coronado Bay Rd., the entrance to the resort.

This lovely hideaway occupies a secluded 15-acre peninsula, 20 minutes from the airport and 4$^{1}/_{2}$ miles from downtown Coronado. Your room will overlook the resort's private 80-slip marina (boat rentals and sailing lessons available) or San Diego Bay. Each room is very well appointed with elegant furnishings and large marble baths; extras include terry-cloth robes and in-room safes. A private pedestrian underpass leads to nearby Silver Strand State Beach.

Dining/Entertainment: Azzura Point serves up California cuisine and a memorable view, while the more casual RRR's American Cafe has both indoor and outdoor seating. There's also a lounge, a poolside bar and grill, and a specialty food market.

Services: Concierge, room service (24 hours), laundry/valet, newspaper delivery, nightly turndown; in-room massage, twice-daily maid service, baby-sitting, secretarial services, express checkout, valet parking.

Facilities: VCRs; video rentals; three outdoor swimming pools; fitness center with equipment, saunas, steam room, and whirlpools; massage; large sundeck; hydro spas; five night-lit tennis courts and pro shop; water sports; bicycle, in-line skate, and water-sports rentals; marina; business center; faxes in suites; meeting space; washer and dryer; car-rental desk; beauty salon; boutiques. The Commodore Kids Club, for children 4 to 12, offers supervised half-day, full-day, and evening programs with meals.

EXPENSIVE

Glorietta Bay Inn. 1630 Glorietta Blvd. (near Orange Ave.), Coronado, CA 92118. ☎ **800/ 283-9383** or 619/435-3101. Fax 619/435-6182. E-mail rooms@gloriettabayinn.com. Website: www.gloriettabayinn.com. 81 rms, 17 suites. A/C TV TEL. Annex, $115–$155 double; suites from $189. Mansion, $145–$155 double; $165–$200 suite; $300 penthouse. AE, DC, DISC, MC, V. Free parking. Take I-5 to the Coronado Bridge and turn left on Orange Ave.; after 2 miles, turn left onto Glorietta Blvd.; the inn is across the street from the Hotel del Coronado.

Once the summer mansion of 19th-century multimillionaire sugar-baron John Spreckels, former owner of the Hotel del Coronado, the Glorietta Bay Inn is a beautifully restored 1908 house surrounded by lush gardens, with intricate moldings and a fine brass-and-marble staircase leading to well-appointed rooms. The rooms in the original mansion have a nice Victorian style; those in the less charming annex are contemporary, with bright furnishings and large windows overlooking Glorietta Bay. The hotel is within walking distance (1 block) of the beach. There's a heated pool, spa pool, bike rentals, and guest laundry; free morning coffee is offered, and continental breakfast is available for a charge.

INEXPENSIVE

✪ **El Cordova Hotel.** 1351 Orange Ave. (at Adella St.), Coronado, CA 92118. ☎ **800/ 229-2032** or 619/435-4131. Fax 619/435-0632. 14 rms, 26 suites. TV TEL. $85–$95 double; $105–$115 studio with kitchen; $130–$145 1-bedroom suite; $155–$175 2-bedroom suite. Weekly and monthly rates available off-season. Children under 12 stay free in parents' room. AE, DC, DISC, MC, V. Take I-5 to the Coronado Bridge and turn left onto Orange Ave. No off-street parking.

Entering the El Cordova, with its colorful little shops and an atmospheric Mexican restaurant, is like stepping into a village south of the border. Built as a mansion in 1902, the Spanish-style low-rise is across a busy street from the beachfront Hotel del Coronado. The lobby has a quarry-tile floor and hacienda-style furnishings, and the theme is carried out in the comfortable rooms and suites. Each one is slightly different from the next, and about half are air conditioned. The best accommodations are the suites, with oak floors and bay windows; several come with kitchenettes that, like that baths and stairways, are accented with hand-crafted Mexican designs.

This is a good family choice; you're welcome to bring the kids, and even the dog. All the family activity does increase the noise level at times, however, so if you're looking for a quiet retreat, the El Cordova probably isn't for you. If you do decide to give it a try, reserve well in advance. In addition to Miguel's Cocina, there's a heated pool, a barbecue area with a picnic table, and a coin-operated laundry.

4 Dining

What follows is only a sampling of San Diego's dining scene. For a greater selection of reviews, see *Frommer's San Diego*.

Smokers should note that many local restaurants don't even allow you to light up in their outdoor areas, so call ahead to inquire if it matters to you.

DOWNTOWN

In addition to the restaurants listed below, you'll find San Diego's branch of **Planet Hollywood** at 197 Horton Plaza (☎ **619/702-STAR**), which is open daily from 11am to 2am.

EXPENSIVE

Dobson's. 956 Broadway Circle (between Broadway and Horton Plaza). ☎ **619/231-6771.** Fax 619/696-0861. Reservations recommended. Main courses $15–$24. AE, CB, DC, MC, V.

Mon–Wed 11:30am–10pm, Thurs–Fri 11:30am–11pm, Sat 5:30–11pm. Valet parking $3 after 5pm. CONTINENTAL.

This place has long attracted the city's political movers and shakers. Owner Paul Dobson or his wife, Carol, often greet diners personally at the door. The menu changes twice daily and includes popular dishes such as mussel bisque; confit of Muscovy duck leg with horseradish cream; risotto with rock shrimp, calamari, prawn, sun-dried tomatoes, and asparagus; and for lunch, Dobson's famous 8-ounce. "Bar Room Burger" or Cobb salad. There's a good wine list, including a nice selection of wines by the glass. Downstairs there's a handsome wooden bar adorned with the brass nameplates of frequent customers; the bar stays open 'til midnight.

The Fish Market/Top of the Market. 750 N. Harbor Dr. ☎ **619/232-FISH** (Fish Market) or 619/234-4TOP (Top of the Market). Reservations not accepted at Fish Market; reservations recommended for Top of the Market. Main courses $8.65–$25 at Fish Market; $15–$31.50 at Top of the Market. AE, CB, DC, MC, V. Daily 11am–10pm. Bus: 7 or 7B. Trolley: Seaport Village. SEAFOOD.

The red building perched on the end of the G Street Pier at the Embarcadero houses two of San Diego's most popular seafood establishments: The Fish Market and its pricier cousin, The Top of the Market. Both offer superb fresh seafood and menus that change daily. The chalkboard out front tells you what's right off the boats, be it catfish from Mississippi, lobster from Maine, salmon from Canada, or yellowtail from Mexico.

The ground-level Fish Market, a casual market/restaurant, has oyster and sushi bars and a cocktail lounge. Upstairs, the elegant, more expensive Top of the Market looks like a private club, with teakwood accents, mounted fish trophies, and a panoramic view that encompasses the bay, the Coronado Bay Bridge, and—sometimes—aircraft carriers (the restaurant thoughtfully provides binoculars). In addition to seafood there's homemade pasta and a wine list that's as extensive as the menu. This lofty place inspires many to dress up and make a reservation, but you're also welcome to drop by just for a drink and to enjoy the view.

MODERATE

✪ **Croce's Restaurant and Jazz Bar.** 802 Fifth Ave. (at F St.). ☎ **619/233-4355.** Fax 619/232-9836. Reservations recommended. Main courses $13.50–$22.95. AE, DC, DISC, MC, V. Daily 7:30am–3pm and 4–11pm. Valet parking $6 with validation. AMERICAN.

This very popular jazz restaurant/bar is named after the late musician Jim Croce and is owned by his wife, Ingrid. You might think the food would be an afterthought to the scene here, but that's not the case. The menu runs the gamut from casual breakfast and lunch fare to salmon baked in puff pastry and served with wild-spinach hollandaise (one of my favorite dishes in San Diego), and grilled breast of chicken with figs and goat cheese accompanied by a peach and caramelized-onion chutney.

In addition to the main restaurant, there's Ingrid's Cantina & Sidewalk Cafe next door for southwestern cuisine, and Upstairs at Croce's for cocktails, coffee, and desserts. Two adjacent nightspots, The Jazz Bar and The Top Hat, serve up jazz and R&B; if you have dinner in the restaurants, you won't have to pay the cover charge to get in (see "San Diego After Dark," below, for more information).

Dakota Grill & Spirits. 901 Fifth Ave. (at E St.). ☎ **619/234-5554.** Reservations required. Main courses $9–$18. AE, DC, DISC, MC, V. Mon–Fri 11:30am–2:30pm; Mon–Thurs 5–10pm, Fri–Sat 5–11pm, Sun 5–9pm. Valet parking $5, self-parking $7 after 5pm. AMERICAN/SOUTHWEST.

This pretty glass-wrapped Gaslamp Quarter restaurant is San Diego's most upscale Southwest restaurant. Its succulent mesquite-grilled chicken, meats, and seafood are consistently excellent and very fairly priced, and the portions are large. My vote goes

Views to Dine For

Visitors to San Diego often want much more from a restaurant than a tasty meal. They also want a panoramic view of the city's beautiful coastline—and lots of local restaurants are more than happy to comply.

Downtown, the **Fish Market** and its pricier cousin, **Top of the Market,** overlook San Diego Bay (see p. 611); the management provides guests with binoculars for an even better view. Across the harbor in Coronado, the **Bay Beach Cafe** (see p. 617) offers a panoramic view of the San Diego skyline. In Pacific Beach, **The Green Flash** (see p. 615) is just steps from the sand, and the **Firehouse Beach Cafe's** lofty dining deck (see p. 614) provides another view of the same scene. Nearby, **The Atoll** in the Catamaran Resort Hotel (see p. 614) faces tranquil Mission Bay. In La Jolla, **George's at the Cove** and **Top O' the Cove** (see p. 615) are near the water, but **Brockton Villa** (see p. 616) actually offers the most postcard-perfect La Jolla Cove view.

to the shrimp tasso, sautéed with Tasso Cajun ham and sweet peas in an ancho chile cream. The atmosphere is casual but polished, and the service is unpolished but attentive. For good value, award-winning Dakota is definitely worth a letter home.

INEXPENSIVE

Filippi's Pizza Grotto. 1747 India St. (between Date and Fir sts. in Little Italy). ☎ **619/ 232-5095.** Fax 619/695-8591. Main courses $4.75–$12.50. AE, DC, DISC, MC, V. Mon–Sat 11am–11pm, Sun 11am–10pm. Free parking. Trolley: America Plaza. ITALIAN.

This is one of those down-home Italian places, right down to the Chianti bottles lining the dining areas. It's been around since the 1950s and has given birth to a dozen spin-off locations throughout the city. You enter through an Italian deli that will stir your hunger pangs with a selection of cheeses, pastas, wines, and salamis. Choose from 15 pizzas and the requisite pasta dishes. Kids will feel right at home here.

Galaxy Grill. Horton Plaza (top level). ☎ **619/234-7211.** Main courses $3.50–$6.50. AE, DISC, MC, V. Mon–Thurs 11am–9pm, Fri–Sat 11am–10pm, Sun 11am–8pm. 3 hours free parking with validation. Trolley: America Plaza. AMERICAN/DINER.

A wait staff straight out of the '50s serves up good old-fashioned burgers, shakes, tuna melts, cherry Cokes, and the like. Can you remember the last time you had a cherry Coke, or got two tunes on the jukebox for a quarter?

Kansas City Barbecue. 610 W. Market St. ☎ **619/231-9680.** Reservations taken only for large parties. Main courses $8.75–$10.50. MC, V. Daily 11am–1am. Trolley: Seaport Village. AMERICAN.

Scenes from *Top Gun* were filmed at this old-fashioned honky-tonk barbecue joint. The barbecue is done right—slow-cooked over an open fire and served with sliced white bread and your choice of beans, fries, slaw, extra-large and flaky onion rings, potato salad, or corn on the cob.

✪ **Mandarin House.** 2604 Fifth Ave.(at Maple). ☎ **619/232-1101.** Most main courses $6.50–$10. AE, DC, MC, V. Mon–Thurs 11am–10pm, Fri 11am–11pm, Sat noon–11pm, Sun 2–10pm. CHINESE.

This multiple award-winner is the most popular Chinese restaurant in San Diego. My favorite dish is the kung pao chicken, which comes hot and spicy and laced with peanuts, in traditional Szechuan style. If you expect the usual Chinese-red decor, you'll be surprised by the pleasant sea-foam-and-peach color scheme. Mandarin House also has locations in La Jolla and Pacific Beach.

✪ **Old Spaghetti Factory.** Fifth Ave. and K St. ☎ **619/233-4323.** Main courses $4.25–$8. DISC, MC, V. Mon–Thurs 11:30am–10pm, Fri 11:30am–10pm, Sat–Sun noon–10pm. Trolley: Gaslamp Quarter. ITALIAN.

This Victorian-themed family restaurant allows you and your kids to dine in a trolley car that's been converted into a dining room. Main courses—mostly old standbys such as lasagna and spaghetti—come with lots of extras, such as salad, sourdough bread, ice cream, and coffee or tea with refills. The word is out about what a great deal this place offers, so there's always a wait. There's a small play area for kids.

HILLCREST/UPTOWN

Celadon. 3628 Fifth Ave. (between Brooks and Pennsylvania). ☎ **619/295-8800.** Reservations recommended on weekends. Main courses $8.50–$14. AE, MC, V. Mon–Fri 11:30am–2pm and 5–10pm, Sat 5–10pm. THAI.

With its pink stucco exterior, Celadon is easy to spot. Inside you'll discover a very pretty interior done in pinks and greens, with Thai artifacts lining the walls. The lemongrass beef is outstanding, as are the sautéed scallops in "burnt" sauce with a touch of garlic and onions.

Liaison. 2202 Fourth Ave. (at Ivy). ☎ **619/234-5540.** Reservations recommended. Main courses $9.50–$18.75. AE, CB, DC, DISC, MC, V. Tues–Sun 5–10:30pm. FRENCH.

This cozy little cafe, with its stone walls, candlelit tables, and copper pots and pans, would be right at home in the French countryside. The lunch menu features salads, pastas (such as homemade crab ravioli in lobster sauce), and three fresh fish dishes daily; at dinner, your main course might be roast duck à l'orange or coquilles St-Jacques. Favorite desserts include Grand Marnier chocolate or Amaretto soufflé for two, at $5 per person.

The Vegetarian Zone. 2949 Fifth Ave. (between Palm and Quince). ☎ **619/298-7302** or 619/298-9232 for deli/takeout. Reservations not accepted. Main courses $6.50–$9.50. Mon–Thurs 11:30am–9pm, Fri 11:30am–10pm, Sat 8:30am–10pm, Sun 8:30am–9pm. DISC, MC, V. VEGETARIAN.

San Diego's best-known vegetarian restaurant offers an extensive menu created from natural ingredients—no meat products, no bleached flours, no sugar, and lots of low-fat choices. But that doesn't mean the food is boring or bland. The menu includes Greek spinach pie, tofu-vegetable enchiladas, lentil-walnut loaf, and garden burgers. There is indoor and outdoor seating, and soothing music sets the scene. Beer and wine are served.

OLD TOWN
EXPENSIVE

Cafe Pacifica. 2414 San Diego Ave. ☎ **619/291-6666.** Reservations recommended. Main courses $13.40–$21.30. AE, DC, DISC, MC, V. Tues–Fri 11:30am–2pm, daily 5:30–10pm. Valet parking free at lunch, $4 at dinner (5–9:30pm). CALIFORNIA.

Excellent fresh fish, grilled over mesquite, keeps visitors happy and locals returning. The setting is charming and slightly formal, with tiny twinkling lights overhead and soft candlelight below. On my last visit, I started with the Dungeness crab salad, an intriguing combination of flavors that included papaya, avocado, and endive, then moved onto the Hawaiian ahi with shiitake mushrooms and ginger butter, which was equally as good. The menu changes daily but always offers excellent dishes like pan-fried catfish, shrimp tacos, and perfect crab cakes—crunchy outside, moist inside.

Casa de Bandini. Opposite Old Town Plaza, Old Town. ☎ **619/297-8211.** Main courses $6.50–$14. AE, DC, MC, V. Mon–Thurs 11am–9pm, Fri–Sat 11am–9:30pm, Sun 10am–9pm. Bus: 4, 5, or 105. MEXICAN.

As much an Old Town tradition as the mariachi music that's played here on weekends, this lively restaurant—with its appealing balcony and courtyard—fills the nooks and crannies of an adobe hacienda built in 1823 for Juan Bandini, once a merchant and politician in these parts. Today it's the scene of many a happy repast over dishes like crab enchiladas, chicken-and-avocado salad, crab brochette with mild green chiles, and jumbo cod filet with sautéed vegetables. Some of the dishes are gourmet Mexican, others simple south-of-the-border fare; you'll never run short of refried beans, guacamole, or jumbo margaritas. It's the house itself that makes this restaurant extra-special.

INEXPENSIVE

La Piñata. 2836 Juan St. ☎ **619/297-1631.** Reservations recommended on weekends. Main courses $5–$11. MC, V. Sun–Thurs 11am–9pm, Fri–Sat 11am–9:30pm. Free parking. MEXICAN.

The brightly colored Mexican toys that give this restaurant its name hang from the ceiling in this cozy, friendly spot. La Piñata is an all-around winner: It's attractive, the food is always good, the prices are moderate, and the service is pleasant and prompt. It's slightly out of the way, but a pleasant alternative to the larger, noisier tourist emporiums, and it has a small outdoor patio for alfresco dining. Familiar Mexican dishes like fajitas, tacos, and tostadas are well prepared and usually preceded by a complimentary cheese quesadilla. Good margaritas are served in glasses the size of a small bird bath.

Old Town Mexican Cafe. 2489 San Diego Ave. ☎ **619/297-4330.** Reservations accepted for parties of 10 or more. Main courses $7.50–$11.50. AE, DISC, MC, V. Sun–Thurs 7am–11pm, Fri–Sat 7am–midnight. MEXICAN.

A fun margarita bar and homemade tortillas are the primary draws of this boisterous Mexican restaurant that's popular with both families and couples (expect a wait). It's nothing fancy; the food speaks for itself. All the south-of-the-border standards—tacos, burritos, fajitas, and the like—are served with excellent salsa. Upon arrival, you'll see the staff in the window, making each day's fresh tortillas by hand. Check out the Mexican-style rotisserie pork ribs.

MISSION BAY/PACIFIC BEACH

✪ **The Atoll.** 3999 Mission Blvd. (in the Catamaran Resort Hotel), ☎ **619/539-8635.** Reservations recommended for Sunday brunch. Main courses $8–$20. AE, CB, DC, DISC, MC, V. Sun–Thurs 6:30am–10pm, Fri–Sat 6:30am–11pm. Valet parking $7, free self-parking with validation. CALIFORNIA.

You can dine at a wrought-iron table on the waterfront patio overlooking Mission Bay or in the elegant dining room outfitted with rattan chairs, crisp tablecloths, and Villeroy and Boch china. I'd start with the spicy crab cakes with lime and ginger-butter sauce, then move onto the broiled lamb chops. If you're looking for something light and simple, there are selections like club sandwiches to keep you happy. The service is friendly and polished.

Firehouse Beach Cafe. 722 Grand Ave. ☎ **619/272-1999.** Reservations recommended on weekends. Main courses $8–$12. AE, CB, DC, DISC, MC, V. Sun–Thurs 7am–9pm, Fri–Sat 7am–10pm. Free parking. AMERICAN.

This casual place is always packed, though not oppressively so; if you're lucky, you can get an umbrella table on the upstairs deck with an ocean view. Locals love eating breakfast here—the omelets are especially popular. The kitchen turns out one of the best burgers in San Diego, in addition to perennial favorites like taco salad, fish-and-chips, and lasagna. An oceanview patio bar, new in 1996, is a nice addition.

The Green Flash. 701 Thomas Ave. (at Mission Blvd.). ☎ **619/270-7715.** Reservations recommended. Main courses $10–$25. AE, DC, DISC, MC, V. Mon–Thurs 8am–9:30pm, Fri 8am–10pm, Sat 7:30am–10pm, Sun 7:30am–9:30pm. Bus: 34 or 34A. SEAFOOD/INTERNATIONAL.

You can spend as much or as little as you choose in this oceanfront place, which has a menu to match a variety of budgets and hankerings. It's known for its fresh fish, but you may also order steaks and prime rib, surf 'n' turf combos, chicken dishes, or burgers. Or simply make a meal of appetizers: fresh oysters, steamed clams, shrimp cocktail, and ceviche. Salads and sandwiches are available at lunch, and there are sunset dinner specials Sunday to Thursday from 5 to 7pm for $9.95. The outdoor tables here are prime real estate, especially when the sky begins to blush. The ambiance couldn't be livelier. Ask your waitperson to explain how the restaurant got its name.

Ichiban. 1441 Garnet Ave. ☎ **619/270-5755.** Sushi $4–$9. No credit cards. Mon–Sat 11am–2:30pm, daily 5–9:30pm. JAPANESE.

Trendy 20-somethings have claimed this budget sushi shop as their own, and for good reason. The fish is morning fresh, the service is excellent, and the crowd is always lively. While the dining room is decidedly downscale, the unstudied casual atmosphere is one of the main attractions. Diners order at the counter and are then served at a table. In addition to sushi, there's chicken teriyaki, ginger chicken, mixed fried seafood, vegetable sukiyaki, and fried salmon. Japanese beer and sake are served.

LA JOLLA

Most of La Jolla's top restaurants are clustered along Prospect Street and Pearl Street in the village.

VERY EXPENSIVE

If you're trying to decide between George's and the Top o' the Cove, George's is trendier and better for entertaining business clients, while Top o' the Cove is traditional, cozy, and perfect for a private tête-à-tête.

George's at the Cove. 1250 Prospect St. ☎ **619/454-4244.** Reservations recommended. Main courses $17–$39. AE, DC, DISC, MC, V. Mon–Thurs 11:30am–10pm, Fri–Sat 11:30am–11pm, Sun 11am–10pm. Valet parking $3 in daytime, $4 at night. CALIFORNIA.

This popular local restaurant gets raves for its fresh seafood, creative pastas, ocean view, and great summer sunsets. For lunch, you can go light with a soup and salad or have one of the many seafood choices. Owner George Hauer, whom you might meet Tuesday to Saturday, started out as a waiter in Pacific Beach and became a legend in San Diego's restaurant scene. For dinner, start with the house specialty smoked-chicken soup and proceed to the rack of lamb; sautéed venison chops with yam cakes; steak; or mixed grill of shrimp, king salmon, and swordfish with three sauces. On a recent visit, though, I was disappointed with the chocolate soufflé-cake dessert—chocoholics might do better getting a fix across the street at the Rocky Mountain Chocolate Factory.

Upstairs, the more casual Café Bar and George's Ocean Terrace have indoor and outdoor seating overlooking La Jolla Cove and offer light fare of sandwiches, soups, salads, and pastas, as well as lower prices.

Top o' the Cove. 1216 Prospect St. ☎ **619/454-7779.** Fax 619/454-3783. Reservations recommended on weekends. Jackets suggested for men at dinner. Main courses $26–$32; Sun brunch $18.50. AE, DC, MC, V. Daily 11:30am–10:30pm. Valet parking $5. CONTINENTAL.

This restaurant, in a historic cottage with fig trees out front, has fireplaces glowing on chilly evenings, an intimate piano bar, and a gazebo and patio for dining on balmy days—perfect for Sunday brunch with champagne, fruit, pastries, one of 10 main dishes, and coffee or tea. Lunch is on the light side—creative salads, fettuccine dishes, or a tenderloin burger on a sourdough bun. Dinner is romantic and more lavish, with fish, duck, veal, lamb, and venison prepared and served elegantly. A computerized wine list keeps track of the 10,000-plus bottles in the cellar. Proprietor and community dynamo Ron Zappardino heads a stellar staff.

The less expensive upstairs bar/bistro is open daily 11:30am to 10pm; meals in this oceanview area run $6 to $16.

EXPENSIVE

✪ **Putnam's Restaurant & Bar.** 910 Prospect St. (in the Colonial Inn), ☎ **619/454-2181.** Reservations recommended. Main courses $18–$23; early-bird special $12.95 (daily 5–8pm). AE, DC, MC, V. Mon–Fri 7–10am and 11am–2:30pm, Sat–Sun 7am–2:30pm; Sun–Thurs 5–10pm, Fri–Sat 5–11pm. Free valet parking. NEW AMERICAN/CALIFORNIA.

When the Colonial Inn was completed in 1928, it housed a drugstore named Putnam's, known in La Jolla as "Putty's." Gregory Peck's father was the pharmacist, and locals flocked there to buy their sundries and enjoy a soda. Today, that corner of the hotel is the site of Putnam's Restaurant, which retains an elegant, Old World atmosphere, complete with polished terrazzo floors, gleaming woodwork, brass fixtures, crisp white tablecloths, and fresh flowers. The dinner menu changes seasonally and offers items such as grilled farm-raised chicken with honey-onion marmalade, grilled marinated duck breast with golden tomato-curry sauce, grilled Atlantic salmon filet, and roasted rack of lamb with mustard-herb crust. I love the lamb shanks here, but the salmon with hot mustard was a recent disappointment. *Insider tip:* Unlike at some dining spots, the early-bird specials offered here are full-size portions and represent a really good value.

MODERATE

✪ **The Cottage.** 7702 Fay Ave. (at Kline). ☎ **619/454-8409.** Reservations accepted for dinner only. Breakfast and lunch $5–$7; dinner main courses $7–$12. MC, V. Aug–June, daily 7:30am–3pm; July, daily 7:30am–3pm and 4–9pm. LIGHT FARE.

This turn-of-the-century cottage, on a sunny corner in downtown La Jolla, is light and airy inside; outside, there's a welcoming white fence, trellis, and large brick patio. You can start the day with farm-fresh eggs prepared most any style, granola and fresh fruit, oatmeal pancakes, Belgian waffles, or a vegetable frittata. The dinner menu (summer only) features California bistro cuisine. The Cottage bakery makes wonderful desserts, pastries, and bread (with the exception of foccacia—we've had better).

INEXPENSIVE

✪ **Brockton Villa.** 1235 Coast Blvd. (across from La Jolla Cove). ☎ **619/454-7393.** Reservations accepted (call by Thurs for Sun brunch). Breakfast $4–$7.25; dinner, main courses $8–$18. AE, DISC, MC, V. Mon–Wed 8am–5pm, Thurs–Sun 8am–9pm (later in summer). Validated parking in Coast Walk Shopping Center. CALIFORNIA.

Located in a beach cottage dating from 1894, Brockton Villa offers good food, a great view of the La Jolla Cove, and charming historic surroundings. The blue-and-white bungalow has a wooden floor that's appropriately worn and perhaps not entirely level. Diners can sit inside, outside on the patio, or on a semienclosed porch. My favorite dinner here is the basil ravioli with saffron-shrimp sauce; at lunch, I regularly go for Shari's turkey meat loaf sandwich on toasted sourdough bread with spicy tomato-mint chutney. For breakfast, it's a toss-up between the homemade granola, "coast toast" (French toast that resembles a soufflé), and Greek steamers (three eggs steam-scrambled using the espresso machine and mixed with feta, tomato, and basil). Note that there's no access for people with disabilities.

✪ **D'Lish.** 7514 Girard Ave. (at Pearl St.), La Jolla, CA 92037. ☎ **619/459-8118.** Reservations accepted. Main courses $6–$9. AE, DC, DISC, MC, V. Sun–Thurs 11:30am–10pm, Fri–Sat 11:30am–11pm. CONTEMPORARY ITALIAN.

This is the place for Spago-style wood-fired pizzas with designer toppings you wouldn't have imagined a decade or so ago. My favorite is the Greek grilled chicken, but I also like the one with shrimp, mozzarella, Roma tomatoes, Kalamata olives, sun-dried tomatoes, pesto sauce, and pine nuts. Their salads make it painless to feel virtuous when ordering. There are also good pasta dishes, especially the shrimp-scallop angel hair, one of many heart-healthy choices. Singing servers add to the fun of it all. *Insider tip:* Don't sit upstairs when the weather's warm.

CORONADO

Bay Beach Cafe. 1201 1st St. (in the Ferry Landing Marketplace), ☎ **619/435-4900.** Reservations recommended for dinner on weekends. Main courses $9–$17. AE, DISC, MC, V. Mon–Fri 7–10:30am, 11am–4pm, and 5–10:30pm; Sat–Sun 7–11:30am, noon–4pm, and 5–10:30pm. AMERICAN/SEAFOOD.

Whether you dine indoors or out, you can't beat the skyline views across the water from this place. Choose from items such as daily fresh-fish specials, vegetarian pasta, and roasted free-range chicken with wild mushroom sauce. There's also a bar menu featuring sandwiches and burgers.

✪ **Mandarin Cafe.** 1330 Orange Ave. (in Coronado Plaza, second floor). ☎ **619/435-2771.** Reservations not accepted. Main courses $5.75–$12.50. AE, MC, V. Mon–Thurs 11:30am–10pm, Fri 11:30am–11pm, Sat 3–11pm, Sun 1–10pm. Free parking with validation. MANDARIN/SZECHUAN.

This local favorite just steps from the beach is a reliable standby for those times when nothing but Chinese food will satisfy the munchies. House favorites are the honey shrimp and the sizzling seafood noodles. The kitchen will hold the MSG, sugar, and salt on request.

✪ **Primavera.** 932 Orange Ave. ☎ **619/435-0454.** Reservations recommended. Main courses $11–$20. AE, DC, DISC, MC, V. Daily 11am–2:30pm and 5–10:30pm. Free parking. NORTHERN ITALIAN.

This dining room is a lovely setting for delicious, creatively prepared Italian dishes. One of the most popular appetizers is *bagna caoda primavera:* grilled eggplant, roasted red peppers, sun-dried tomatoes, Montrachet and Parmesan cheeses, with bagna caoda sauce—fantastic. Main courses include angel-hair pasta with mushrooms, garlic, prosciutto, capers, anchovies, and herbs; osso buco; and chicken breast with eggplant, mozzarella cheese, mushrooms, and wine sauce. For dessert, I can't resist the homemade tiramisu. This is the best restaurant in Coronado, but the last time I dined here the service felt slightly robotic.

5 The Main Attractions: The Zoo, the Wild Animal Park & Sea World

✪ **San Diego Zoo.** Park Blvd. and Zoo Place, Balboa Park. ☎ **619/234-3153**; TDD 619/233-9639. Website: www.sandiegozoo.org. Admission $15 adult, $6 children 3–11, military in uniform free. Deluxe package (including admission, guided bus tour, and round-trip skyfari aerial tram): $21 adults, $18.90 seniors 60 and over, $11 children. Combination Zoo/Wild Animal Park package (including deluxe package at zoo and admission to Wild Animal Park and is valid for

Pandamonium

Two giant pandas from China, Shi Shi (a 13-year-old male) and Bai Yun (a 3-year-old female), finally arrived at the San Diego Zoo in late 1996 after three years of intense negotiation between the U.S. Department of the Interior, the Wolong Giant Panda Conservation Centre, and the Chinese government. These two are the only pair of giant pandas in the United States (a single male is housed at the National Zoo in Washington, D.C.). In total, only about 15 giant pandas live in zoos outside of China and North Korea.

Because giant pandas are endangered and protected under the Convention on International Trade in Endangered Species (CITES), a federal permit was required for their importation. The Zoo's previous requests had been denied, but this time the powers-that-be were convinced that this project would make a significant contribution to the effort to save wild pandas.

Giant pandas live in dense bamboo and coniferous forests at altitudes of 5,000 to 10,000 feet and are among the rarest mammals in the world—fewer than 1,000 remain in the wild. Their numbers have dwindled due to destruction of their habitat and poaching—still a problem despite the fact that the Chinese government has imposed life sentences for those convicted of this crime. As part of the agreement to get the pandas here, the San Diego Zoo agreed to contribute $1 million each year to wild panda habitat protection projects in China, where the government hopes to double the number of existing panda preserves and establish protected wildlife corridors connecting these areas.

You needn't worry that Shi Shi and Bai Yun will be gone before you get here: The loan is for a period of 12 years. During that time, scientific study of their breeding and behavior patterns will take place. (Any baby pandas born at the Zoo will belong to the People's Republic of China.)

Shi Shi, who weighs 230 pounds, was born in the wild but was taken to the Wolong Giant Panda Conservation Centre after he was found critically wounded, probably from a fight with another male panda. Bai Yun was born at this center on September 7, 1991, and was raised by her mother, Dong Dong.

Giant pandas are related to both bears and raccoons. They are bearlike in shape, with striking black-and-white markings, and they have unique front paws that enable them to grasp stalks of bamboo. This plant makes up about 95% of their diet, and they eat 20 to 40 pounds of food every day. This takes them 10 to 16 hours, so there's a pretty good chance that while you're watching them they'll be munching away. Please don't be offended—they're just doing what it takes to survive.

Because of the enormous popularity of this exhibit, the Zoo provides a panda-viewing hotline (☎ **888/MY PANDA**).

5 days from date of purchase): $31.95 adult, $18.35 children. DISC, MC, V. Daily 9am–4pm (grounds close at 5pm); extended summer hours. Free parking. Bus: 7 or 7B.

More than 4,000 animals reside at this world-famous zoo, founded in 1916 with a handful of animals originally brought here for the 1915–16 Panama-California International Exposition. The zoo's founder was Dr. Harry Wegeforth, a local physician and lifelong animal lover who once braved the fury of an injured tiger in order to toss needed medicine into its mouth while it was roaring. In the early days of the zoo, "Dr. Harry" would take native southwestern animals like rattlesnakes and sea lions to trade around the world for more exotic species; this tradition is carried on today—the loan of two giant pandas from the People's Republic of China is a perfect example (see box below).

Today, the giant pandas are the big attention-getters, but the zoo has many other rare and exotic species: cuddly koalas from Australia, long-billed kiwis from New Zealand, wild Przewalski's horses from Mongolia, lowland gorillas from Africa, and giant tortoises from the Galapagos. The usual lions, elephants, giraffes, and tigers are present, too, not to mention a great number of tropical birds. Most of the animals are housed in barless, moated enclosures with names like Polar Bear Plunge, Gorilla Tropics (my personal favorite), and Hippo Beach that resemble their natural habitats. The zoo is also an accredited botanical garden, representing over 6,000 species of flora from many climate zones, all installed to help simulate native environments for the animals who live here.

The **Children's Zoo** is scaled to a youngster's viewpoint. There's a nursery with baby animals and a petting area where kids can cuddle up to sheep, goats, and the like. The resident wombat is a special favorite here.

The zoo offers two types of **bus tours;** both provide a narrated overview and show you about 75% of the park. You can choose the 35-minute guided bus tour, which completes a circuit around the zoo; the cost is $4 for adults and $3 for kids 3 to 11 (there's a daily tour in Spanish at noon). Or you might opt to take the Kangaroo Bus, which for $8 for adults and $5 for children provides unlimited use; you can get on and off the bus as many times as you desire at any of the eight stops and even complete the circuit more than once. Alternatively, you can get an aerial perspective via the **Skyfari,** which costs $1 per person each way. Packages are available which include zoo admission, bus tour, and Skyfari Tramway.

The Zoo offers wheelchair and stroller rentals and numerous food outlets, including a delightful restaurant called Albert's. *Insider tip:* If you're planning on going to the Zoo and Wild Animal Park, you might want to consider buying a Zoological Society Membership, which costs $68 a year for two adults living in the same household. The adult/couple membership gives each cardholder unlimited entrance to the Zoo and Wild Animal Park, plus two adult admission passes, six discounted admission passes, and four two-fer bus tickets, plus a subscription to *Zoo News* magazine. A Koala Club membership for a child costs $15 and provides unlimited entry for a year.

✪ **Wild Animal Park.** 15500 San Pasqual Valley Rd., Escondido. ☎ **760/747-8702;** TDD 760/738-5067. Website: www.sandiegozoo.org. Admission $18.95 adults, $17.05 seniors 60 and over, $11.95 children 3–11, free for children 2 and under and military in uniform. Combination Zoo/Wild Animal Park package (including deluxe package at zoo and admission to WAP and is valid for 5 days from date of purchase): $31.95 adult, $18.35 children. DISC, MC, V. Daily 9am–4pm (grounds close at 5pm); extended hours during the summer and the Festival of Lights in Dec. Parking $3. See "Insider tip" under San Diego Zoo above for details on zoo membership, including reduced admission. Take I-15 to Via Rancho Pkwy.; follow signs from here for about 3 miles.

Many zoos could learn a lesson from the Wild Animal Park: More than 3,000 animals, many of them endangered species, roam freely over 1,800 acres—it's the humans who are enclosed. This living arrangement encourages breeding colonies, so it's not surprising that more than 75 white rhinoceroses have been born here. Several other species that had vanished from the wilds have been reintroduced to their natural habitats from stocks bred here. The park is also is a botanical preserve with more than 2 million plants, including 300 species and subspecies.

The best way to see the animals is by riding the 5-mile **Wgasa Bush Line monorail** (included in the price of admission); for the best views, sit on the right side.

San Diego Attractions

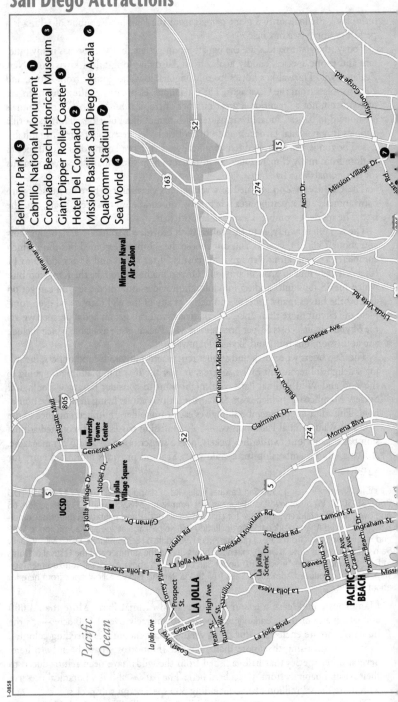

Belmont Park **5**
Cabrillo National Monument **1**
Coronado Beach Historical Museum **3**
Giant Dipper Roller Coaster **5**
Hotel Del Coronado **2**
Mission Basilica San Diego de Acala **6**
Qualcomm Stadium **7**
Sea World **4**

Miramar Naval Air Staion

Pacific Ocean

UCSD

University Towne Center

Eastgate Mall

Genesee Ave.

La Jolla Village Square

Nobel Dr.

La Jolla Village Dr.

Gilman Dr.

Ardath Rd

Torrey Pines Rd.

La Jolla Shores

LA JOLLA

La Jolla Mesa

La Jolla Scenic Dr.

Soledad Mountain Rd.

Soledad Rd.

La Jolla Mesa

Prospect St.

High Ave.

Nautilus

Pearl St.

Rushville St.

Girard

Coast Blvd

La Jolla Cove

La Jolla Blvd.

Lamont St.

Dawes St.

Diamond St.

Garnet Ave.

Grand Ave.

Ingraham St.

Pacific Beach

PACIFIC BEACH

Mission

Genesee Ave.

Claremont Mesa Blvd.

Balboa Ave.

Clairmont Dr.

Morena Blvd

Aero Dr.

Linda Vista Rd.

Mission Village Dr.

Mission Gorge Rd

1-0858

620

Pacific
Ocean

San Diego Bay

54th St.

805

5

15

94

163

El Cajon Blvd.

University Ave.

Robinson Ave.

Date St.

Pershing Dr.

Ocean View Blvd.

National Ave.

Harbor Dr.

Market St.

Imperial Ave.

UPTOWN/
HILLCREST

Balboa
Park

El Prado

5th Ave.

4th Ave.

1st Ave.

DOWNTOWN

SAN DIEGO

Ash St.

Broadway

F St.   E St.

San Diego
Convention
Center

Seaport
Village

Embarcadero

Ferry Landing
Market Place

Silver Strand

75

San Diego–
Coronado Bridge

75

2

3

Adella Ave.

Orange Ave.

6th St.

4th St.

3rd St.

2nd St.

282

CORONADO

U.S. Air
Naval Station

Washington St.

Goldfinch St.

India St.

Pacific Highway

Harbor Dr.

San Diego
International Airport

Harbor Island

Shelter
Island

Fort Stockton Dr.

Hotel Circle
Hotel Circle

OLD
TOWN/
HOTEL
CIRCLE

8

San Diego Ave.

Barnett Ave.

Rosecrans

Point
Loma

209

Nimitz Blvd.

Chatsworth Blvd.

Voltaire St.

Narragansett Ave.

Sunset
Cliffs Blvd.

West Point Loma Blvd.

Ocean Beach Fwy.

Midway Dr.

Sea World Dr.

Sea World

San Diego
Sports Arena

Catalina Blvd.

Hill St.

209

Cabrillo Memorial Dr.

209

1

Cabrillo
National Monument

Point Loma

N

0   2 mi.
          3.2 km

During the 50-minute ride, as you pass through areas resembling Africa and Asia, you'll learn interesting tidbits (did you know that rhinos are susceptible to sunburn and mosquito bites?). Trains leave every 20 minutes; you can watch informative videos while you wait in the stations.

On the 1³/₄-mile **Kilimanjaro Safari Walk,** you'll see tigers, elephants, and cheetahs close up, as well as the Australian rain forest and views of East Africa. There are three animal shows a day, and you also won't want to miss the **petting kraal, Lorikeet Landing, Mombasa Lagoon,** and the WAP's newest exhibit, **Heart of Africa.**

Photo Caravans take place May to September on Wednesday, Thursday, Saturday, and Sunday, costing $60 or $85 (depending on the tour).

Stroller and wheelchair rentals are available. Take a jacket along; it can get cold in the open-air monorail. Local public transportation will get you here, but it takes three buses and 3¹/₂ hours. **Gray Line** offers a 7-hour tour for $40 for adults and $24 for kids, including admission and transportation; for more information, call ☎ **619/ 491-0011.**

Sea World. 1720 S. Shores Rd., Mission Bay. ☎ **619/226-3901,** or 714/939-6212 in L.A.; TDD 619/226-3907. Admission $32.95 adults, $29.65 seniors 55 and older, $24.95 children 3–11, children 2 and under free. DISC, JCB, MC, V. Parking $5 per car, $2 per motorcycle, and $7 per RV. June–Aug, daily 9am–10pm; rest of the year, daily 10am–5pm. Ticket sales stop 1¹/₂ hours before closing. Bus: 9 or 81. By car, exit I-5 west onto Sea World Dr.; from I-8, take W. Mission Bay Dr. to Sea World Dr. E..

Sea World is one of the best-promoted attractions in California. The 150-acre, multimillion-dollar aquatic playground is a zoo and showplace for marine mammals, made politically correct with a nominally "educational" atmosphere. At its heart, Sea World is a family entertainment center where the performers are dolphins, otters, sea lions, walruses, and seals. Several successive 4-ton black-and-white killer whales have functioned as the park's mascot, all named Shamu. Shows are presented continuously throughout the day, while visitors rotate to various theaters to watch the performances.

The 2-acre hands-on area called **Shamu's Happy Harbor** encourages kids to handle everything, including a pretend pirate ship, with plenty of netted towers, tube crawls, slides, and chances to get wet. Other attractions include **Baywatch at Sea World,** a water-ski show named for the popular TV show; and **Shamu Backstage,** which makes it possible for visitors to get up close and personal with killer whales. **Wild Arctic,** a virtual reality trip to the frozen north, opened in mid-1997.

The **Dolphin Interaction Program** creates an opportunity for people to interact with bottlenose dolphins. Although this program doesn't allow swimming with the dolphins, it does give you the opportunity to wade waist-deep into the water and plenty of time to stroke the mammals and give commands like the trainers. This 2-hour program (1 hour of education and instruction, 15 minutes of wet suit fitting, and 45 minutes of interaction in the water with the dolphins) costs $125 per person ($95 per person for SeaWorld members). Space is limited to eight people per day, so advance reservations are required. Participants must be 13 years old or older.

Although Sea World is best known as Shamu's home, the facility also plays an important role in rescuing and rehabilitating animals found beached along the San Diego coast—more than 300 seals, sea lions, marine birds, and dolphins in a recent year; they've even rescued a baby whale. Sea World also helps out with injured marine species in other parts of the world, such as the oil-soaked victims of the *Exxon Valdez* disaster in Alaska. You might like to take a guided tour of the park and get an insider's view for $6 per adult and $5 per child.

6 Beaches

San Diego County is blessed with 70 miles of sandy coastline and more than 30 beaches that attract surfers, snorkelers, swimmers, and sunbathers. In summer, the beaches teem with locals and visitors alike. The rest of the year they're less crowded but still popular places to walk and jog, and surfers don wet suits to pursue their passion.

The following are some of San Diego's most accessible beaches, each with its own personality and devotees. If you're interested in others, *The California Coastal Access Handbook,* published by the California Coastal Commission, is helpful. All California beaches are public to the mean high-tide line. If you plan to poke around in tide pools, get a tide chart, available free or for a nominal charge from many surf and diving shops, including **Emerald City Surf Shop,** at 118 Orange Ave., Coronado (☎ 619/435-6677), and **San Diego Divers Supply,** at 5701 La Jolla Blvd., La Jolla (☎ 619/459-2691).

BLACK'S BEACH The area's unofficial (and illegal) nude beach lies between La Jolla Shores Beach and Torrey Pines State Beach. Set below some steep cliffs, it's out of the way and not easy to reach. To get here, take North Torrey Pines Road, park at the Glider Port, and walk from there. *Note:* Though the water is shallow and pleasant for wading, this area is known for its rip currents, so beware.

BONITA COVE, MARINER'S POINT & MISSION POINT Facing Mission Bay in South Mission Beach, these spots are perfect for families, with calm waters, grassy areas for picnicking, and playground equipment.

CORONADO BEACH Lovely, wide, and sparkling white, this romantic beach fronting Ocean Boulevard is conducive to strolling and lingering, especially in late afternoon. It's especially pretty in front of the Hotel del Coronado. The islands visible from here, but 18 miles away, are named Los Coronados, and they belong to Mexico.

DEL MAR After a visit to the famous fairgrounds that host the Del Mar Thoroughbred Club, you may want to make tracks for this beach about 15 miles from downtown San Diego, a long stretch of sand backed by grassy cliffs and a playground area.

IMPERIAL BEACH A half-hour south of San Diego by car or trolley and only a few minutes from the Mexican border lies Imperial Beach. Besides being popular with surfers, it hosts the annual U.S. Open Sandcastle Competition in July, where competitors build world-class sand creations ranging from sea scenes to dragons and dinosaurs.

✪ LA JOLLA COVE The protected, calm waters here—praised as the clearest along the California coast—attract swimmers, snorkelers, scuba divers, and families on outings. There's a small sandy beach and, on the cliffs above, Ellen Browning Scripps Park. The Cove's "look but don't touch" policy protects the colorful Garibaldi, California's state fish, plus other marine life, including abalone, octopus, and lobster. The unique Underwater Park stretches from here to the northern end of Torrey Pines State Reserve and incorporates kelp forests, artificial reefs, two deep submarine canyons, and tidal pools.

LA JOLLA SHORES BEACH This mile-long flat stretch of beach is popular for joggers, swimmers, and beginning body and board surfers. Families often come here, as lifeguards are on duty year-round.

San Diego & North County Beaches

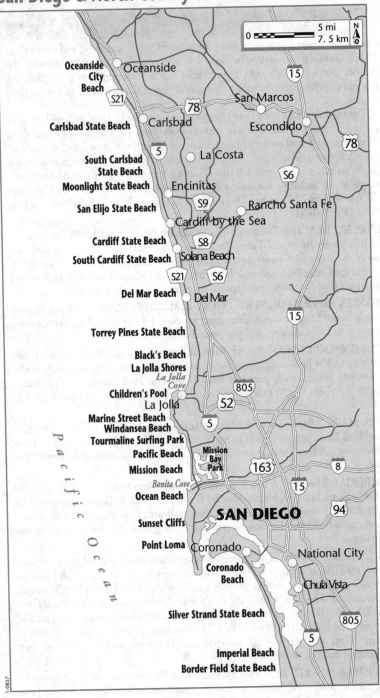

0857

624

MISSION BAY PARK In this 4,600-acre aquatic playground you'll discover 27 miles of bayfront, 17 miles of oceanfront beaches, picnic areas, children's playgrounds, and paths for biking, roller-skating, and jogging. The bay lends itself to windsurfing, sailing, jet skiing, waterskiing, and fishing. There are dozens of access points; one of the most popular is off I-5 at Clairemont Drive, where there's a visitor information center.

MISSION BEACH Surfing is popular year-round here. The long beach and boardwalk extend from Pacific Beach Drive south to Belmont Park and beyond to the jetty.

NORTHERN SAN DIEGO COUNTY BEACHES Those inclined to venture even farther north in San Diego County won't be disappointed. Pacific Coast Highway (Calif. 1) leads to some inviting beaches, such as these in Encinitas: peaceful **Boneyards Beach, Swami's Beach** for surfing, and **Moonlight Beach,** which is popular with families and volleyball buffs. Farthest north in this beach-blessed county is **Oceanside,** which has one of the West Coast's longest wooden piers and several popular surfing areas.

OCEAN BEACH Near the pier off I-8 and Sunset Cliffs Boulevard is this surfers' and sunset-lovers' heaven; it's the stuff Beach Boys songs are made of. Not far away are **Dog Beach,** where four-legged beach lovers roam unleashed, and **Garbage Beach,** another surfing spot (don't worry—it doesn't live up to its name).

PACIFIC BEACH Here you'll find a popular beach and boardwalk for meeting friends, grabbing a bite to eat, jogging, biking, or in-line skating. It runs along Ocean Boulevard (just west of Mission Boulevard), north of Pacific Beach Drive.

WINDANSEA One of California's finest surfing beaches, this area along Neptune Street in La Jolla achieved cult status in 1968, when the serious surfers who rode its waves were the subject of Tom Wolfe's book *The Pumphouse Gang.* Hang around for the usually memorable sunset.

7 Exploring the Area

BALBOA PARK

Balboa Park is one of the nation's largest, loveliest, and most important municipal greenbelts. This is no simple city park; it boasts walkways, gardens, historical buildings, a couple of restaurants, an ornate pavilion with one of the world's largest outdoor organs, and the world-famous San Diego Zoo (see above). Stroll along **El Prado,** the park's main street, and admire the distinctive Spanish/Mediterranean buildings, which house an amazing array of museums. *Insider tip:* If you want to hang out with the locals, this is where they congregate on weekends. It's not unusual for buskers and musicians to entertain along El Prado while families picnic around the lily pond in front of the Botanical Building.

Entry to the park is free, but most of its museums have admission charges and varying open hours. A free tram will transport you around the park. Get details from the **Balboa Park Visitor Center,** located in the House of Hospitality (☎ **619/ 239-0512**). Below are the highlights:

✪ **Aerospace Museum & International Aerospace Hall of Fame,** 2001 Pan American Plaza (☎ **619/234-8291**): Great achievers and achievements in the history of aviation and aerospace are celebrated by this superb collection of historical aircraft and related artifacts, including art, models, dioramas, and films.

Museum of Art, 1450 El Prado (☎ **619/232-7931**): The impressive painting and sculpture collections here include outstanding Italian Renaissance and Dutch and Spanish baroque art. Exhibits in the Grant-Munger Gallery include works by Monet,

Toulouse-Lautrec, Renoir, Pissarro, and van Gogh; in the Fitch Gallery is El Greco's *Penitent St. Peter,* and in the Gluck Gallery hangs Modigliani's *Boy with Blue Eyes* and Braque's *Coquelicots.* June 28 to August 30, 1998, the Museum will present a special exhibit of the late paintings of Claude Monet at Giverny from the Musee Marmottan.

✪ **Museum of Photographic Arts,** 1649 El Prado, in Casa de Balboa (☎ 619/ 239-5262): One of the finest museums in the city occupies an imitation Spanish baroque building that served as part of Charles Foster Kane's Xanadu in the film *Citizen Kane.* It displays a wide range of historic and contemporary work and has made a commitment to issue-oriented photography.

Natural History Museum, 1788 El Prado (☎ 619/232-3821): The best exhibits display the plants, animals, and minerals of the San Diego and Baja California region. There's also a Foucault pendulum, a seismograph, and a life-size *Allosaurus* skeleton. The Hall of Desert Ecology features a discovery lab, with living desert denizens.

Reuben H. Fleet Space Theater and Science Center, 1875 El Prado (☎ 619/ 238-1233, or 619/232-6866 for advance ticket sales): Easily the park's busiest museum, this large complex contains a Science Center with 65 hands-on exhibits, a laser light show, and an OMNIMAX movie theater with a 76-foot screen. In the theater, sophisticated effects give simulated journeys an incredible feeling of reality. The giant dome is also the setting for thrilling travelogues and voyages under the sea and inside a volcano. *Insider tip:* Call to charge tickets in advance; you may save yourself a long wait in line.

Museum of Man, 1350 El Prado (☎ **619/239-2001**): This museum is devoted to the sociology and anthropology of the peoples of North and South America, and includes life-size replicas of a dozen varieties of *Homo sapiens.* The annual Indian Fair, held in June, features American Indians from all over the Southwest demonstrating tribal dances and selling ethnic food, art, and crafts.

The San Diego Automotive Museum, 2080 Pan American Plaza (☎ **619/ 231-2886**): Check out that classic Bentley and the rare 1948 Tucker, among other gems that appear in a changing array of shows featuring classic, antique, and exotic cars.

Botanical Building (☎ **619/235-1100** for information): More than a thousand varieties of tropical and flowering plants are sheltered within this structure, and the lily pond out front attracts the occasional street performer.

Hall of Champions, 1649 El Prado, in Casa de Balboa (☎ **619/234-2544**): Sports fans will want to check out this museum, which highlights dozens of different professional and amateur sports and athletes.

Japanese Friendship Garden, 2216 Pan America Rd. (☎ **619/232-2780**): Stop in the garden's information center to see a scale model of the garden, which is still under development. For now you can see a *sekitei,* the most ancient kind of garden, made only of sand and stone.

Marston House Museum, 3525 7th Ave. at Upas St., in the northwest corner of the park (☎ **619/232-6203**): Designed by local architect Irving Gill, this fine example of Craftsman-style architecture exhibits fine antique and reproduction period furniture.

Model Railroad Museum, 1649 El Prado, in Casa de Balboa (☎ **619/ 696-0199**): Four scale-model railroads depict Southern California's transportation history and terrain. There's a terrific gift shop, plus multimedia exhibits and hands-on Lionel trains for kids.

Balboa Park

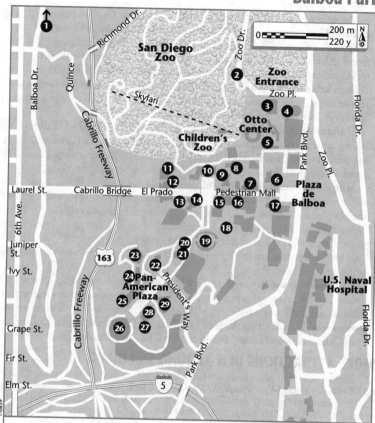

1-0859

Museum of San Diego History, 1649 El Prado, in Casa de Balboa (☎ 619/232-6203): Photographs and other changing exhibits tell the city's story.

Spanish Village, 1770 Village Place (☎ 619/233-9050): This is a working space for 50 artisans and craftspeople who sell their handiwork. Tenants include the Sculptors Guild of San Diego in Studio 36 and the Photographic Arts Building.

Spreckels Organ Pavilion (☎ 619/226-0819): The ornate pavilion houses a fantastic organ with more than 4,000 individual pipes. Free concerts are given Sunday at 2pm year-round and on summer evenings.

Timken Museum of Art, 1500 El Prado (☎ 619/239-5548): On display here is the Putnam Foundation's collection of American and European paintings, including works by Boucher, Rembrandt, and Brueghel. The private gallery also exhibits a rare collection of Russian icons and 19th-century American paintings.

Mingei International Museum of World Folk Art, 1439 El Prado, in the House of Charm (☎ 619/239-0003): Its name is pronounced min-*gay* (meaning "art of the people" in Japanese), and it offers changing exhibitions celebrating human creativity around the world as it is manifested in textiles, costumes, jewelry, toys, pottery, paintings, and sculpture, all created using natural materials. This is one of only two major museums in the United States devoted to crafts on a worldwide scale (the other is in Santa Fe).

Christmas on the Prado takes place in Balboa Park from 5 to 9pm on the first Friday and Saturday nights in December. This popular event features free entry to all museums, carol singing in the Spreckels Organ Pavilion, holiday decorations, and various food booths. (If you'll be in San Diego in December, be sure to check out the "Christmas in San Diego" box in chapter 2 for other area events).

MORE ATTRACTIONS IN & AROUND SAN DIEGO

✪ **Cabrillo National Monument.** 1800 Cabrillo Memorial Dr., Point Loma. ☎ 619/557-5450. Admission $4 per vehicle, $2 for walk-ins; ages 62 and over (with a National Parks Service Golden Age Passport) and 16 and younger free. Daily 9am–5:15pm. Follow I-5 or I-8 to Rosecrans St. (Calif. 209), which leads to Point Loma and the monument via Catalina Blvd.

Enjoy stunning views while you learn about California history at this monument commemorating Juan Rodríguez Cabrillo, the European discoverer of America's West Coast. At the restored Old Point Loma Lighthouse, you'll be treated to a sweeping vista of the ocean, bays, islands, mountains, valleys, and plains that make up San Diego. From mid-December to February, the lighthouse is a good vantage point for watching the migration of the Pacific gray whales. National Park rangers offer free 30-minute films about the monument daily from 10am to 4pm, and there are tide pools that beg for exploration. A free film about the whale migration is shown during winter.

Children's Museum of San Diego. 200 W. Island Ave. ☎ 619/233-8792. Admission $5 for adults and children over 2, $3 for seniors; children under 2 free. Tues–Sun 10am–5pm, closed most Mondays. Trolley: Convention Center stop; the museum is a block away.

This interactive museum encourages hands-on participation and provides ongoing supervised activities, as well as a special celebration and changing exhibits every month. A big draw for kids ages 2 to 10 is the indoor and outdoor art studio. There's also a theater with costumes for budding actors to don.

Maritime Museum. 1306 N. Harbor Dr. ☎ 619/234-9153. Admission (to all 3 ships) $5 adults, $4 seniors and children 13–17, $2 children 6–12. DISC, MC, V. Daily 9am–8pm. Bus: 4, 9, 29, 34, 34A, 35.

This nautical museum consists of three restored historic vessels docked downtown at the Embarcadero. *The Berkeley,* a propeller-driven ferry launched in 1898, participated in the evacuation of San Francisco after the Great Earthquake and fire of 1906. *The Medea*, a steam yacht built in Scotland in 1904, was used in both World Wars. *The Star of India*, launched in 1863, is the oldest square-rigged merchant vessel still afloat. Each vessel can be boarded and explored. April to October you can even watch movies on the deck of the *Star of India* (see "Movies, San Diego Style," in "San Diego After Dark," below).

Museum of Contemporary Art, Downtown (MCA). 1001 Kettner Blvd. (at Broadway). ☎ **619/234-1001.** Admission $4 adults; $2 students, military with ID, and seniors; children 12 and under free; free on first Tues of the month. Tues–Sat 10:30am–5pm, Fri 10:30am–8pm, Sun noon–5pm. Parking $2 with validation at America Plaza Complex. Trolley: America Plaza.

Two large galleries and two smaller ones present changing exhibitions of distinguished contemporary artists. Lectures and tours for adults and children are offered. Another branch of the museum is located in La Jolla.

Villa Montezuma. 1925 K St. (at 20th Ave.). ☎ **619/239-2211.** Admission $3 adults, $5 in combination with Marston House, free for children 12 and under. MC, V. Sat–Sun noon–4:30pm; Dec, Thurs–Sun noon–4:30pm. Bus: 3, 3A, 4, 5, 16, or 105 to Market and Imperial sts.

Just east of downtown, this stunning mansion was built in 1887 for then internationally acclaimed musician and author Jesse Shepard. Lush with Victoriana, it features stained-glass windows depicting Mozart, Beethoven, Sappho, Rubens, St. Cecilia (patron saint of musicians), and other notables. The San Diego Historical Society painstakingly restored the house, which is on the National Register of Historic Places, and furnished it with period pieces. Unfortunately, the neighborhood is not as fashionable as the house, but it's safe to park your car here in the daytime. If you love Victorian houses, don't miss this one for its quirkiness.

OLD TOWN AND BEYOND: A LOOK AT CALIFORNIA'S BEGINNINGS

The birthplace of San Diego—indeed, of California—Old Town brings back to life Mexican California, which existed here until the mid-1800s. You can get to Old Town on the trolley or Coaster (see "Getting Around," above). Free walking tours leave daily at 2pm from the **Old Town State Historic Park's** visitor center (☎ 619/220-5422), located at the head of the pedestrian walkway that is the continuation of San Diego Avenue. Admission to the center, open daily from 10am to 5pm, is free. The following are area highlights:

Heritage Park. 2455 Heritage Park Row (corner of Juan and Harney sts.), Old Town. For information, call the Parks Department at ☎ **619/694-3049.** Admission free. Daily 9:30am–3pm. Bus: 4, 5, or 105.

This small 7.8-acre park is filled with seven original 19th-century houses moved here from other places and given new uses, among them a B&B, a doll shop, and a gift shop. Take a tour and have tea for $10 Tuesday through Sunday from 2:30 to 5pm.

Junípero Serra Museum. 2727 Presidio Dr., Presidio Park, Old Town. ☎ **619/297-3258.** Admission $3 adults, free for children 12 and under. Tues–Sat 10am–4:30pm, Sun noon–4:30pm. Take I-8 to Taylor St. exit; turn right on Taylor, then left on Presidio Dr. Or take a bus to the intersection of Taylor and Juan sts. and walk uphill.

Perched on a hill above Old Town, the stately mission-style building overlooks the spot where California began: It was here in 1769 that the first mission and first non-native settlement on the West Coast of the U.S.–Canadian landmass was founded. Inside, the museum's exhibits introduce you to California's origins and to the Native American, Spanish, and Mexican peoples who first called this place home. On display are their belongings, from cannons to cookware. The mission remained San Diego's only settlement until the 1820s, when families began to move down the hill into what is now known as Old Town. Watch an ongoing archaeological dig uncover more of the items used by early settlers.

The museum is located in **Presidio Park,** called the "Plymouth Rock of the Pacific." The large cross in the park was made from floor tile from the Presidio ruins. Sculptor Arthur Puntnam made the statues of Father Serra (founder of the missions in California) and the Native American. Climb up to Inspiration Point for a sweeping view of the area.

Mission Basilica San Diego de Alcala. 10818 San Diego Mission Rd., Mission Valley. ☎ **619/281-8449.** Admission $2 adults, $1 seniors and students, 50¢ children 12 and under. Daily 9am–5pm; mass, daily 7am and 5:30pm. Bus: 6, 16, 25, 43, or 81. Take I-8 to Mission Gorge Rd. to Twain Ave.

Established in 1769, this was the first link in the chain of 21 missions founded in California by Spanish missionary Junípero Serra. In 1774, the mission was moved to its present site for agricultural reasons and to separate Native American converts from a fortress that included the original building. A few bricks belonging to the original mission can be seen in Presidio Park in Old Town. Mass is held regularly in this still-active Catholic parish.

Whaley House. 2482 San Diego Ave. ☎ **619/298-2482.** Admission $4 adults, $3 seniors 65 and over, $2 children 5–18. Daily 10am–5pm (until 4:30pm in winter).

In 1856, this striking 2-story house (the first one in these parts) just outside Old Town State Historic Park was built for Thomas Whaley and his family. Whaley was a New Yorker who arrived here via San Francisco, where he had been lured by the Gold Rush. The house is one of only two authenticated haunted houses in California, and 10,000 schoolchildren come here each year to see for themselves. Exhibits include a life mask of Abraham Lincoln, one of only six made; the spinet piano used in the movie *Gone with the Wind;* and the concert piano that accompanied Swedish soprano Jenny Lind on her final U.S. tour in 1852. Director June Reading will make you feel at home, in spite of the ghost.

MISSION BAY/PACIFIC BEACH

This area is great for walking, jogging, in-line skating, biking, and boating; for details, see "Outdoor Activities," below.

Giant Dipper Roller Coaster. 3146 Mission Blvd. ☎ **619/488-1549.** Summer, Sun, Mon, and Thurs 11am–8pm, Tues–Wed 11am–9pm, Fri–Sat 11am–10pm; closes earlier rest of the year. Admission to park is free; ride on Giant Dipper is $3. Take I-5 to the Sea World exit, and follow W. Mission Bay Dr. to Belmont Park.

A local landmark for 70 years, the Giant Dipper is one of two surviving fixtures from the original Belmont Amusement Park (the other is The Plunge indoor swimming pool). After sitting dormant for 15 years, this vintage wooden roller coaster, with over 2,600 feet of track and 13 hills, underwent an extensive restoration and reopened in 1991.

You can also ride on the Giant Dipper's neighbor, the Liberty Carousel ($1), or the newer rides: Tilt-a-Whirl, Crazy Sub, Thunder Boats, and Baja Buggies. You might like to participate in the **Dive-In Movies** shown at **The Plunge** (☎ **619/ 488-3110**), in which viewers float on rafts in 91°F water and watch water-related movies projected onto the wall. *Jaws* is a perennial favorite. (See "Movies, San Diego Style" in "San Diego After Dark," below.)

LA JOLLA

Some folks just enjoy driving around La Jolla, taking in the sea views and the 360° vista from the top of **Mount Soledad.** However, La Jolla also offers other attractions,

La Jolla

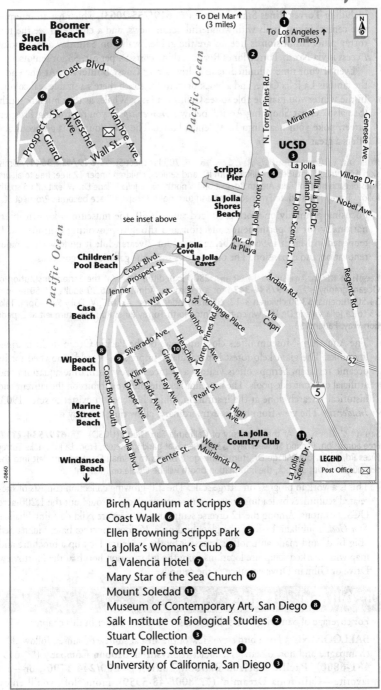

Boomer Beach
Shell Beach
Coast Blvd.
Prospect St.
Girard
Herschel Ave.
Wall St.
Ivanhoe Ave.
⑤
⑥
⑦

To Del Mar ↑
(3 miles)
To Los Angeles ↑
(110 miles)
①
②
N

Pacific Ocean

N. Torrey Pines Rd.
Miramar
UCSD
③
La Jolla
Villa La Jolla Dr.
Gilman Dr.
La Jolla Scenic Dr. N.
Genesee Ave.
Village Dr.
Nobel Ave.

Scripps Pier
④
La Jolla Shores Beach
La Jolla Shores Dr.
Av. de la Playa
Regents Rd.

see inset above

Pacific Ocean

Children's Pool Beach
La Jolla Cove
La Jolla Caves
Coast Blvd.
Prospect St.
Jenner
Wall St.
Cave St.
Exchange Place
Ivanhoe Ave.
Ardath Rd.
Via Capri

Casa Beach

Wipeout Beach
⑧
Silverado Ave.
⑨
⑩
Herschel Ave.
Torrey Pines Rd.
Girard Ave.
Kline St.
Eads Ave.
Fay Ave.
Pearl St.
52

Coast Blvd. South
Draper Ave.
High Ave.
5

Marine Street Beach

La Jolla Blvd.
Center St.
West Muirlands Dr.
La Jolla Country Club
⑪
La Jolla Scenic Dr. S.

Windansea Beach ↓

LEGEND
Post Office ✉

1-0860

Birch Aquarium at Scripps ④
Coast Walk ⑥
Ellen Browning Scripps Park ⑤
La Jolla's Woman's Club ⑨
La Valencia Hotel ⑦
Mary Star of the Sea Church ⑩
Mount Soledad ⑪
Museum of Contemporary Art, San Diego ⑧
Salk Institute of Biological Studies ②
Stuart Collection ③
Torrey Pines State Reserve ①
University of California, San Diego ③

including **Torrey Pines State Reserve** (☎ 619/755-2063), which has an interpretive center, hiking trails with wonderful ocean views, and a chance to see the rare torrey pine. Admission is free, as are the guided walks on Saturday and Sunday. Access is via North Torrey Pines Road; parking costs $4 per car, $3 for seniors.

Even if your time is limited, take a drive along **Coast Boulevard.** At one end is the famous La Jolla Cove, and a block or so to the south there's a sizable seal colony. In the winter you may be able to see California Gray Whales as they migrate south. (See also "Great Shopping Areas," below.) *Insider tip:* If you're strolling Prospect Street, poke your head into La Valencia Hotel. The *sala* (lounge) is gorgeous and offers a great view.

Museum of Contemporary Art, San Diego. 700 Prospect St. ☎ **619/454-3541.** Admission $4 adults; $2 students, military with ID, and seniors; children under 12 free; free to all first Tues of each month. Take Ardath Rd. exit off I-5 north, or La Jolla Village Dr. W. exit off I-5 south; follow Torrey Pines Rd. to Prospect Place and turn right; Prospect Place becomes Prospect St.

Focusing primarily on work produced since 1950, the museum is known internationally for its permanent collection and thought-provoking exhibitions. It reopened in March 1996 after being closed for 2 years while it underwent a major renovation and expansion. The ocean views from the galleries are gorgeous.

Stephen Birch Aquarium-Museum. 2300 Expedition Way (at the Scripps Institution of Oceanography). ☎ **619/534-3474** for a recording. Admission $6.50 adults, $5.50 seniors, $4.50 students, $3.50 children 3–12, children under 3 free. AE, MC, V. Daily 9am–5pm. Take I-5 to La Jolla Village Dr. W., which turns into North Torrey Pines Rd., then turn left at Expedition Way. Parking $3.

The Aquarium-Museum offers close-up views of the Pacific Ocean in 33 marine-life tanks. The giant kelp forest is particularly impressive. World renowned for its oceanic research, Scripps offers visitors a chance to view its marine aquarium and artificial outdoor tide pools. The museum has interpretive exhibits on the current and historical research done at the institution, which has been in existence since 1903. *Insider tip:* The view from here is extraordinary; allow time to enjoy it.

Stuart Collection. At the University of California San Diego (UCSD). ☎ **619/534-2117.** Free admission. Parking $6 weekdays, $3 weekends at parking meters. From La Jolla, take Torrey Pines Rd. to La Jolla Village Dr., turn right, go 2 blocks to Gilman Dr., and turn left into the campus; in about a block, the information booth will be visible on the right.

This is a work in progress on a large scale. The still-growing collection consists of site-related sculptures by leading contemporary artists placed throughout the 1,200-acre UCSD campus. Among the 12 diverse sculptures on view are Niki de Saint-Phalle's *Sun God,* a jubilant 14-foot fiberglass bird on a 15-foot concrete base, nicknamed "Big Bird" and made an unofficial mascot by the students. Pick up a brochure and map with marked sculpture locations from the information booth at the Northview Drive or Gilman Drive entrance to the campus.

8 Outdoor Activities

For coverage of San Diego's best beaches, see section 6 earlier in this chapter.

BALLOONING For a bird's-eye view of the area at sunrise or sunset, followed by champagne and hors d'oeuvres, contact **A Skysurfer Balloon Company** (☎ 619/481-6800), **Pacific Horizon Balloon Tours** (☎ 800/244-1790), or—my favorite—**California Dreamin'** (☎ 800/748-5959). From aloft, you'll enjoy sweeping views of the entire Southern California coast.

BIKING & MOUNTAIN BIKING Mission Bay and Coronado are especially good for leisurely bike rides. The boardwalks in Pacific Beach and Mission Beach can get very crowded, especially on weekends. Most major thoroughfares offer a bike lane. Just remember to wear a helmet; it's the law. For information on bike rentals, see "Getting Around," earlier in this chapter.

For a downhill thrill of a lifetime, take the **Palomar Plunge.** From the top of Palomar Mountain to its base, you'll experience, courtesy of gravity, a 5,000-foot vertical drop stretched out over 16 miles. Or try the **Desert Descent,** a 12-mile, 3,700-foot descent down the Montezuma Valley Grade to the desert floor, followed by a tour of the Visitor Center and a delicious lunch. **Gravity Activated Sports** (☎ 800/985-4427 or 760/742-2294) supplies the mountain bike, helmet, gloves, and souvenir photo and T-shirt.

Adventure Bike Tours, based at the Hyatt (☎ 619/234-1500, ext. 6514) offers a "Bay to Breakers" bike ride that starts in downtown San Diego and includes Coronado. The cost of $39 covers bikes, helmets, the ferry, and guiding.

BOATING **Club Nautico,** at the San Diego Marriott Marina, 333 W. Harbor Dr. (☎ 619/233-9311; fax 619/689-2363), provides you with an exhilarating way to see the bay by the hour, half day, or full day in 20- to 27-foot offshore powerboats. Rentals start at $89 per hour. They also rent wave runners and allow their boats to be taken into the ocean, and provide diving, waterskiing, and fishing packages.

Seaforth Boat Rental, 1641 Quivira Rd., Mission Bay (☎ 619/223-1681), has a wide variety of fishing boats for bay and ocean, powerboats for $50 to $90 per hour, and 14- to 27-foot sailboats for $20 to $45 per hour; with half-day and full-day rates. Canoes, pedal boats, kayaks, and rowboats are available for those who prefer a slower pace. They also rent bicycles and equipment with which you could fish off the Municipal Pier (see "Fishing," below). **Downtown Boat Rental,** at the Marriott Marina, 333 W. Harbour Dr., (☎ 619/239-2628), has sailboats and kayaks for rent. They also offer lessons and guided tours.

Coronado Boat Rental, 1715 Strand Way, in Coronado (☎ 619/437-1514), has powerboats renting from $65 to $90 per hour, with half- and full-day rates; 14- to 30-foot sailboats from $25 to $40 per hour; and jet skis, ski boats, canoes, pedal boats, kayaks, fishing skiffs, and charter boats.

Sail USA (☎ 619/298-6822) offers custom-tailored skippered cruises on a 34-foot Catalina sloop. A half-day bay cruise costs $275 for up to six passengers.

FISHING Public fishing piers are at Shelter Island (where there's a statue dedicated to anglers), Ocean Beach, and Imperial Beach. Anglers of any age can fish free of charge without a license off any municipal pier in California. Lake Murray is a great place for freshwater fishing (Wednesday, Saturday, and Sunday only). Call the **City Fish Line** at ☎ 619/465-3474 for information on fishing on city lakes.

For **sportfishing,** you can go out on a large boat for about $25 for half a day or $40 to $100 for three-quarters to a full day. To charter a boat for up to six people, the rates run about $550 for half a day and $1,000 for an entire day, more in summer; call around and compare prices. Summer and fall are excellent times for excursions. Locally, the waters around Point Loma are filled with bass, bonita, and barracuda; the Coronado Islands, which belong to Mexico but are only about 18 miles from San Diego, are popular for abalone, yellowtail, yellow fin, and big-eyed tuna. Some outfitters will take you farther into Baja California waters.

Fishing charters depart from Harbor and Shelter islands, Point Loma, the Imperial Beach pier, and Quivira Basin in Mission Bay (near the Hyatt Islandia

Hotel). The following outfitters offer short or extended outings with daily departures: **H&M Landing** (☎ 619/222-1144), **Islandia Sportfishing** (☎ 619/222-1164), **Lee Palm Sportfishers** (☎ 619/224-3857), **Point Loma Sportfishing** (☎ 619/223-1627), and **Seaforth Boat Rentals** (☎ 619/223-1681). Participants over the age of 16 need a California fishing license.

GOLF   With nearly 80 courses, 50 of them open to the public, San Diego County has much to offer the golf enthusiast. Courses are diverse, some with vistas of the Pacific, others with views of country hillsides or of desert. **Par-Tee Golf** (☎ 800/PAR-TEE-1) and **M&M Tee Times** (☎ 619/456-8366) can arrange tee times for you at most golf courses. **Greenlink** (☎ 619/456-8346) is also a valuable source of information about golf courses, schools, and equipment.

And where else but San Diego can you practice your golf swing in the middle of the central business district? The **Harborside Golf Center,** on Broadway at Pacific Highway (☎ 619/239-GOLF), is open from 7am to 10pm daily. Here you'll find 80 tees, a USGA putting and chipping area, a pro shop, and golf school. It's lit for after-dark play. Club rental is available at $1 each; a large bucket of balls costs $6; a small bucket, $3.

Space constraints prevent us from listing all of the San Diego area's fine courses; for a more extensive listing, see *Frommer's San Diego.*

✪ **Torrey Pines Golf Course,** 11480 Torrey Pines Rd., La Jolla (☎ 619/552-1784 for information, 619/570-1234 for tee times, or 619/452-3226 for the pro shop), is actually two gorgeous 18-hole championship courses located on the coast between La Jolla and Del Mar, only 15 minutes from downtown San Diego. Home of the Buick Invitational Tournament, these municipal courses are very popular. Both overlook the ocean; the north course is more picturesque, the south course more challenging. Tee times are taken by computer starting at 5am up to 7 days in advance by telephone only. Confirmation numbers are issued, and you must have the number and photo identification with you when you check in with the starter 15 minutes ahead of time. If you're late, your time may be forfeited. *Insider tip:* Single golfers stand a good chance of getting on the course if they just turn up and wait for a threesome. Likewise, the locals also sometimes circumvent the reservation system by spending the night in a camper in the parking lot. The starter lets these die-hards on before the reservations made by the computer go into effect at 7:30am. Golf professionals are available for lessons, and the pro shop rents clubs if you left yours at home. Greens fees for out-of-towners are $47 during the week and $52 Saturday and Sunday for 18 holes, and $27 for nine holes; city residents pay $18, $20, and $10; county residents pay $26, $29, and $13, respectively.

Coronado Municipal Golf Course, 2000 Visalia Row, Coronado (☎ 619/435-3121), is the first sight that welcomes you as you cross the Coronado Bay Bridge (the course is off to the left). It is an 18-hole, par-72 course overlooking Glorietta Bay, and there's a coffee shop, pro shop, and driving range. Two-day prior reservations are strongly recommended; call anytime after 7am. Greens fees are $20 to walk and $32 to ride for 18 holes; $10 to walk and $17 to ride after 4pm. Club rental is $15, and pull-cart rental is $4.

San Diego hosts some of the country's most important golf tournaments, including the **Mercedes Championships,** held at La Costa Resort in Carlsbad in early January (☎ 800/918-4653 for tickets and information). Another popular event is the **Buick Invitational of California,** held every February at Torrey Pines Golf Course in La Jolla (☎ 800/888-BUICK or 619/281-4653). The **HGH Pro-Am Golf Classic** is held at Carlton Oaks Country Club every September (☎ 619/448-8500).

HEADING TO THE TRACK   Live thoroughbred racing takes place at the **Del Mar Racetrack** from late July to mid-September every year. Bing Crosby and Pat O'Brien founded the track in 1937, and it has been frequented by stars ever since. Del Mar's 1993 season marked the opening of a new $80-million grandstand, built in the Spanish-mission style of the original structure; the new grandstand features more seats, better race viewing, and a centrally located scenic paddock. Post time is 2pm for the nine-race program; there's no racing on Tuesdays. Reserved seating in both the clubhouse and grandstand costs $4 per person, in addition to admission charges of $6 for the clubhouse and $3 for the grandstand. Seating is also available in the members-only Turf Club (if you are or know a member). For information, call ☎ **619/755-1141;** the ticket office is at ☎ 619/792-4242.

HIKING/WALKING   The **Sierra Club** sponsors regular hikes in the San Diego area, and nonmembers are welcome to participate. There's always a Wednesday mountain hike, usually in the Cuyamaca Mountains, though sometimes in the Lagunas; there are evening and day hikes as well. Most are free. For a recorded message of **upcoming hikes,** call ☎ **619/299-1744,** box no. 4000, or call the office at ☎ 619/ 299-1743 Monday to Friday from noon to 5pm and on Saturday from 10am to 4pm.

The Bayside Trail near **Cabrillo National Monument** is popular because it affords great views. Drive to the Monument and follow signs to the trail. Parking costs $4 per car. ✪ **Mission Trails Regional Park,** 8 miles northeast of downtown, offers a glimpse of what San Diego looked like before development. Located between Calif. 52 and I-8 and east of I-15, its rugged hills, valleys, and open areas provide a quick escape from urban hustle-bustle. A visitor and interpretive center (☎ **619/668-3275**) is open daily from 9am to 5pm. Access is via Mission Gorge Road from either Calif. 52 or I-8.

There's also a wonderful walkway around **Lake Murray;** take the Lake Murray Blvd. exit off I-8 and follow the signs. **Torrey Pines State Park** in La Jolla is another great spot for hiking; docents lead guided nature walks on weekends. (See also "La Jolla," above.)

The best beaches for walking are La Jolla Shores, Mission Beach, and Coronado. You can also walk around **Mission Bay** on a series of connected foot paths. If a four-legged friend is your walking companion, head for **Dog Beach** in Ocean Beach or **Fiesta Island** in Mission Bay, two of the few areas where dogs can legally go unleashed. *Insider tip:* While droves of folks stroll the sidewalks adjacent to the San Diego–La Jolla Underwater Park and La Jolla Cove, only a few know about **Coast Walk,** which starts near the **La Jolla Cave & Shell Shop,** 1325 Coast Blvd. (☎ **619/ 454-6080**), and affords a fabulous view of beach and beyond.

HORSEBACK RIDING   Hosts Earl and Liz Hammond at **Holidays on Horseback** (☎ **619/445-3997**), located 40 miles east of San Diego in Descanso, offer half- and full-day outings, as well as overnight camping trips, through Cuyamaca Rancho State Park. Riders pass through beautiful scenery that includes native chaparral, live oak, and manzanita. A 4-hour ride with a picnic lunch on the trail costs $60, and a 1^1/2-hour ride is $25.

IN-LINE SKATING   Gliding around San Diego, especially the Mission Bay area, on in-line skates is as much a Southern California experience as sailing or surfing. In Mission Beach, rent a pair of regular or in-line skates from **Mike's Bikes & Skates,** 756A Ventura Place (☎ **619/488-1444**), or **Hamel's Action Sports Center,** 704 Ventura Place, off Mission Boulevard at the roller coaster (☎ **619/488-5050**); and in Pacific Beach at **Pacific Beach Sun & Sea,** 4539 Ocean Blvd. (☎ **619/ 483-6613**). In Coronado, go to **Bikes & Beyond,** 1201 1st St. and at the Ferry Landing (☎ **619/435-7180**).

SANDCASTLE COMPETITIONS   Sandcastle enthusiasts will want to attend the 2-day **Annual U.S. Open Sandcastle Competition** at the pier in Imperial Beach in July. There's a parade and children's castle contest Saturday at 2pm, but Sunday is the main event. For information, call ☎ 619/424-6663. A similar event, the **Ocean Beach Sandcastle Event and Family Fun Carnival,** is held in October; for information, call ☎ 619/226-8613.

SCUBA DIVING & SNORKELING   The San Diego–La Jolla Underwater Park, especially the La Jolla Cove, is the best spot for scuba and snorkeling. For more information see section 6, "Beaches," earlier in this chapter.

SURFING   Get where-to-go info from "Beaches" above, and rent a board (if you didn't BYO) from **La Jolla Surf Systems,** 2132 Avenida de la Playa, La Jolla Shores (☎ 619/456-2777); or **South Coast Windansea,** 740 Felspar St., Pacific Beach (☎ 619/483-7660; www.southcoast.com/browse/scwindan).

TENNIS   There are 1,200 public and private tennis courts in San Diego. Public courts are located throughout the city, including the **La Jolla Recreation Center** (☎ 619/459-9950) and **Morley Field** (☎ 619/295-9278) in Balboa Park.

9 Great Shopping Areas

Shops in San Diego tend to stay open late. Expect to find the welcome mat out until 9pm on weeknights, 8pm on Saturdays, and 6pm and sometimes 8pm on Sundays. In addition to the specific shopping clusters listed below, you might like to check out the local malls: **Fashion Valley,** 352 Fashion Valley Rd. (☎ 619/297-3381); **Mission Valley,** 1640 Camino del Rio N. (☎ 619/296-6375); and **University Towne Center,** 4545 La Jolla Village Dr. ☎ 619/546-8858.

A 7.75% sales tax is added on at the register for all goods purchased in San Diego.

Bazaar del Mundo. 2754 Calhoun St., Old Town State Historic Park. ☎ **619/296-3161.** Bus: 4, 5, or 105. Trolley: Old Town.

Always festive, the central courtyard here vibrates with folkloric music, mariachis, and a splashing fountain. Shops are pricey, but feature one-of-a-kind folk art, home furnishings, clothing, and textiles from Mexico and South America. You'll find a top-notch bookstore called **Libros,** with a large kids' selection. If you're pooped, collapse at **Casa de Pico** and enjoy one of their bathtub-sized margaritas.

The Ferry Landing Market Place. 1201 1st St. (at B Ave.), Coronado. ☎ **619/435-8895.** Take I-5 to Coronado Bay Bridge to B Ave., and turn right. Bus: 901. Ferry: From Broadway Pier.

The entrance is impressive—turreted red rooftops with jaunty blue flags that draw closer as the ferry to Coronado pulls into the slip. Once you stroll up the pier, you're in the midst of shops filled with gifts, imported and designer fashions, jewelry, and crafts. You can get a quick bite to eat or have a leisurely dinner with a view, wander along landscaped walkways, or laze on a friendly beach or grassy bank.

Horton Plaza. 324 Horton Plaza. ☎ **619/238-1596.** Bus: 2, 7, 9, 29, 34, or 35. Trolley: City Center.

The Disneyland of shopping malls, Horton Plaza is almost as much a San Diego attraction as Sea World or the zoo, partly for its eclectic designs and colors. It's right in the heart of San Diego; in fact, bounded by Broadway, First and Fourth avenues, and G Street, it *is* the heart of the revitalized city center. Covering 6¹/₂ city blocks, this multilevel shopping center has 140 specialty shops, including art galleries, clothing and shoe stores, several fun shops for kids, bookstores, a seven-screen cinema, three major department stores, and a variety of restaurants and short-order eateries.

The plaza is purposefully designed for meandering, so expect to take some wrong turns and make some delightful discoveries. Among the favorite shops here are **Horton Toy & Doll,** for inexpensive toys for kids and great gag gifts for adults. Horton Plaza usually has free entertainment daily from noon to 2pm. Parking is free the first 3 hours with validation, $1 per half hour thereafter; parking levels are confusing, and temporarily losing your car is part of the Horton Plaza experience.

La Jolla. Prospect St. and Girard Ave. Bus: 34 or 34A.

"The village," as it's still referred to by longtime locals, has become a cross between Rodeo Drive and a shopping mall. A few of the old-time stores remain, including **Warwick's** for books and stationery, **Burns Drugs, John Cole's Book Shop,** and **Meanley Hardware,** but these are outnumbered by the glossy newcomers like **Armani Exchange, Banana Republic, Georgiou, Talbots** (a personal favorite of mine), and **Tina's Boutique.** You can park on the street, but watch your time; the local parking enforcement officers are slightly overzealous.

The Paladion. 777 Front St. (opposite Horton Plaza, between 1st Ave. and G St.). ☎ **619/232-1627.** Bus: 2, 7, 9, 29, 34, or 35. Trolley: Civic Center.

The posh Paladion brought world-class shopping to downtown San Diego when it opened early in 1992, with tony tenants like Cartier, Tiffany & Co., H. Stern, Bernini, Gianni Versace, and Hemingway's Fine Cigars. Sadly, the timing couldn't have been worse from the developer's point of view. The combined devaluation of the Mexican peso and economic downturn of San Diego caused many of the original businesses in this center to close for lack of customers. As we go to press, the fate of the Paladion is uncertain; discussions include the addition of theaters and mid-priced shops. The **Ivy Court,** on the ground level, is a lovely spot for coffee, a light lunch, or cocktails, all with piano music as a backdrop. There's also a rooftop French/Caribbean restaurant called **Alizé,** and free valet parking and concierge service.

Seaport Village. 849 W. Harbor Dr. (at Kettner Blvd.). ☎ **619/235-4014** or 619/235-4013 for events information. 2 hours free parking with validation; $2 per half hour thereafter. Bus: 7. Trolley: Seaport Village.

This 14-acre ersatz village snuggled alongside San Diego Bay was built to resemble a small Cape Cod community, but the 75 shops are very much of the Southern California cutesy variety. Favorites include the **Tile Shop,** the **Seasick Giraffe** for resort wear, and the **Upstart Crow** book shop/coffeehouse with the **Crow's Nest** children's bookstore inside. Be sure to see the 1890 carousel imported from Coney Island. *Insider tip:* Seaport Village is a great place to hang out, even if you aren't in the mood to shop. The view of San Diego Bay is terrific, and there's a walkway along the water.

FARMERS' MARKETS

Farmers' Markets throughout San Diego County sell fresh local fruits, vegetables, and flowers, as well as specialty items such as raw apple cider (in the fall), macadamia nuts, and rhubarb pies.

Sunday: In El Cajon at "The Boulevard" at Marlborough (3 blocks east of 40th Street) from 10am to 2pm.

Tuesday: In Coronado at the Old Ferry Landing, corner of First and B streets, from 2:30 to 6pm; and in Escondido at Grand Avenue and Broadway from 3 to 7pm.

Wednesday: North County Market in Escondido, 3660 Sunset Dr. (across from North County Fair), 9am to noon. In Ocean Beach, in the 4900 block of Newport Avenue (west of Sunset Cliffs Boulevard) from 4 to 8pm. In Carlsbad at Roosevelt Street, between Grand Avenue and Carlsbad Village Drive, from 3 to 6pm.

Thursday: In downtown Oceanside at the corner of N. Hill and third Street from 9am to 12:30pm. In Mission Valley at Hazard Center, Friars Road at Calif. 163, 3 to 6:30pm. In Chula Vista at Third Avenue and E Street from 3 to 6pm.

Friday: In Rancho Bernardo at Bernardo Winery, 13330 Paseo del Verano Norte, from 9am to noon. In La Mesa at 8500 Allison St. (east of Spring Street) from 3 to 6pm.

Saturday: In Pacific Beach at Promenade Mall, Mission Boulevard between Reed and Pacific Beach Drive, 8am to noon. In Vista, in the City Hall parking lot at the corner of Eucalyptus and Escondido avenues from 8 to 11am. In Poway at Old Poway Park, corner of Midland and Temple, from 8 to 11am. In Del Mar at the City Hall parking lot, corner of El Camino Del Mar and 10th Street, from 1 to 4pm. In Carlsbad in the parking lot north of Andersen's Pea Soup, 2 to 5pm.

10 San Diego After Dark

San Diego is hardly the wild 'n' crazy nightlife capital of America, but pockets of lively after-dark entertainment *do* exist around the city. On the more sedate side of things, the city offers wonderful and varied live theater experiences—both the Old Globe and La Jolla Playhouse have won Tony awards for Best Regional Theater.

For a rundown of the latest performances, gallery openings, and other events in the city, check the listings in "Night and Day," the Thursday entertainment section of the *San Diego Union-Tribune,* or *The Reader,* San Diego's free alternative newspaper, published every Thursday. For what's happening in the gay scene, get the weekly *San Diego Gay & Lesbian Times.* The *San Diego Performing Arts Guide,* produced every 2 months by the San Diego Theatre Foundation, is also very helpful; you can pick one up at the Times Art Tix booth.

THE PERFORMING ARTS

Half-price tickets to theater, music, and dance events are available at the **Times Arts Tix** booth, in Horton Plaza Park, at Broadway and Third Avenue (park in the Horton Plaza parking garage and have your parking validated or pause at the curb nearby). The kiosk is open Tuesday to Saturday from 10am to 7pm. Half-price tickets for Sunday performances are sold on Saturday. Only cash payments are accepted. For a daily listing of half-price offerings, call ☎ **619/497-5000.** Full-price advance tickets are also sold; the kiosk doubles as a Ticketmaster outlet, selling tickets to concerts throughout California.

THEATER

The **Gaslamp Quarter Theatre Company,** at 444 Fourth Ave. (☎ **619/232-9608** or 619/234-9583), stages contemporary productions in the 250-seat Hahn Cosmopolitan Theatre.

The **San Diego Repertory Theatre** offers professional, culturally diverse productions of contemporary and classic dramas, comedies, and musicals at the Lyceum Theatre, 79 Horton Plaza (☎ **619/235-8025** or 619/231-3586; fax 619/235-0939). Its annual *A Christmas Carol* is a perennial favorite.

Founded in 1948, the **San Diego Junior Theatre,** at Balboa Park's Casa del Prado Theatre (☎ **619/239-8355;** fax 619/239-5048), is the country's oldest continuously producing children's theater, providing training and performance opportunities for children and teenagers 4 to 18. Students act and technically crew five main stage shows each year.

In Coronado, **Lamb's Players Theatre,** at 1142 Orange Ave. (☎ **619/437-0600;** fax 619/437-6053), is a professional repertory company whose season runs from

February to December. Shows are staged in their 340-seat theater in Coronado's historic Spreckels building, where no seat is more than seven rows from the stage.

⭕ **Old Globe Theatre.** Balboa Park. ☎ **619/239-2255** or 619/23-GLOBE for 24-hour hotline. Website: www.oldglobe.org. Tickets $28.50–$39 (previews $22); seniors and students $25 matinees, $29 weeknights. Bus: 7 or 25.

Near the entrance to Balboa Park and just behind the Museum of Man is this Tony Award–winning theater, fashioned after Shakespeare's, which has produced the revival of *Damn Yankees* and has billed such notable performers as John Goodman, Marsha Mason, Cliff Robertson, Jon Voight, and Christopher Walken.

The 581-seat Old Globe is part of the **Simon Edison Centre for the Performing Arts,** which also includes the 245-seat Cassius Carter Centre Stage and the 620-seat open-air Lowell Davies Festival Theatre, and mounts a dozen plays a year on the three stages between January and October. Tours are offered Saturday and Sunday at 11am and cost $3 ($1 students, seniors, and military). The box office is open Tuesday to Sunday from noon to 8:30pm.

La Jolla Playhouse. La Jolla Village Dr. and Torrey Pines Rd., La Jolla. ☎ **619/550-1010.** Website: www.lajollaplayhouse.com.

Winner of the 1993 Tony Award for outstanding American regional theater, the La Jolla Playhouse stages six productions each year in its 500-seat Mandell Weiss Theater and 400-seat Mandell Weiss Forum on the campus of UCSD. Performances are held May to November. Playhouse audiences cheered *The Who's Tommy* and Matthew Broderick in *How to Succeed in Business Without Really Trying* before they went on to Broadway fame and fortune. The box office is open Monday from noon to 6pm, and Tuesday to Sunday from noon to 8pm. Each show designates one Saturday matinee as a "pay-what-you-can performance." Reduced-price "Public Rush" tickets are available 10 minutes before curtain, subject to availability. Tickets run $19 to $39. Self-parking is $3.

OPERA & CLASSICAL MUSIC

The **San Diego Opera** performs at the Civic Theater, 202 C St. (☎ **619/232-7636**), and often showcases international stars. The 1998 season will run January to May; call for schedule. The box office is located across the plaza from the theater and is open Monday to Friday from 9am to 5pm. Tickets run from $25 to $100. Student and senior discounts and $17 standing-room tickets are available an hour before the performance.

The future of the **San Diego Symphony,** whose home is Copley Symphony Hall, 750 B St., is up in the air. In early 1996, it was announced that the symphony would play no more due to financial problems. Now it appears a civic-minded angel may rescue them. Should the symphony play again, they will probably be lead by Israeli-born conductor Yoav Talmi.

MOVIES, SAN DIEGO STYLE

In addition to the usual multiplex theaters, San Diegans like to watch movies in some unusual settings. **Movies Before the Mast** are shown on a special "screensail" April to October aboard the *Star of India* (see entry for the Maritime Museum under "Exploring the Area," above). All the films shown are nautical in genre, such as *Black Beard the Pirate* and *Hook.* Call ☎ **619/234-9153** for the schedule.

In August, you can view a mix of classic and current films free of charge from a blanket or chair on the beach during the **Sunset Cinema Film Festival.** Films are projected on screens mounted on a floating barges from San Diego to Imperial Beach. Call ☎ **619/454-7373** for details.

Dive-In Movies are shown at The Plunge (☎ **619/488-3110**), an indoor swimming pool in Mission Beach. Viewers float on rafts in 91° water and watch water-related movies projected onto the wall. *Jaws* is a perennial favorite.

THE CLUB & MUSIC SCENE

Clubs come and go, so your best bet for finding the latest hotspot is to stroll through the Gaslamp Quarter. The current favorites are **Johnny Loves,** 664 Fifth Ave. (☎ **619/595-0123**), which endears itself to an over-30 crowd; **Club 66,** at 901 Fifth Ave. (☎ **619/234-4166**), which has a Route 66 motif and caters to those aged 25 to 45; **E Street Alley,** on the north side of E Street between Fourth and Fifth avenues (☎ **619/231-9200**), which is a dressier club; **Blue Tattoo,** 751 Fifth Ave. (☎ **619/557-0146**), the destination of choice for Europhiles; **Dick's Last Resort,** 345 Fourth Ave., with entrances on both Fourth and Fifth avenues (☎ **619/231-9100**), popular with the college crowd; and **Buffalo Joe's,** 600 Fifth Ave. (☎ **619/236-1616**). Cover charges vary from nil to $10, depending on who's playing and what night of the week it is.

Fans of alternative music might enjoy the **Casbah,** 2501 Kettner Blvd. (☎ **619/232-4355**), where breakthrough bands are the norm.

If you're under 21, **SOMA Live,** 5305 Metro St., Mission Bay (☎ **619/239-SOMA**), is the place for you. This concert venue in a warehouselike building has hosted Courtney Love and her band Hole, Social Distortion, and Faith No More.

From May to October a series of contemporary concerts take place outdoors at **Humphrey's,** 2241 Shelter Island Dr., San Diego (☎ **619/523-1010;** www.user.aol.com/humconcert). During a recent season Ray Charles, Willie Nelson, and Wayne Newton were just three of the popular performers who appeared here. For the 1998 schedule, call or check their website.

Videos and live bands—sometimes local, sometimes nationally known—take center stage in the **Cannibal Bar,** in the Catamaran Hotel, 3999 Mission Blvd. (☎ **619/539-8650**). Open Wednesday to Sunday till about 2am; weekend cover charges range from $3 to $15.

The nautical theme and waterfront location, with a curving window wall looking onto the marina, make **The Yacht Club,** in the San Diego Marriott Marina, 333 W. Harbor Dr. (☎ **619/234-1500**), a comfortable spot. There's live dance music nightly, with appetizers and light fare available until 11pm, along with a dinner menu served from 5 to 11pm. A band plays 5 nights a week, a DJ 2 nights at 9pm. No cover, no drink minimum.

COMEDY

Top L.A. comics regularly visit the **Comedy Store,** 916 Pearl St., La Jolla (☎ **619/454-9176**). Monday and Tuesday are amateur nights; the acts improve as the week progresses. Showtime is 8pm Sunday to Thursday, 8 and 10:30pm Friday and Saturday. The cover is $8 to $10, with a two-drink minimum.

JAZZ & BLUES

Croce's. 802 Fifth Ave. (at F St.). ☎ **619/233-4355.** No cover at Croce's Jazz Bar or Croce's Top Hat if you have dinner at Croce's Restaurant or Ingrid's Cantina. Cover $3–$7 for regional bands, $10–$18 for national acts. Minimum at both bars $5.

There's traditional jazz every night in Croce's Jazz Bar and rhythm and blues at Croce's Top Hat, both named after the late musician Jim Croce and owned by his wife, Ingrid. Jim Croce's son, A. J., an accomplished musician in his own right, sometimes performs. Jazz holds sway in the Jazz Bar and drifts easily into the adjoining restaurant (see "Where to Dine," above); it opens nightly at 5pm, and the music starts at 8:30pm. Next door, in Croce's Top Hat, balcony seating overlooks the stage; it's open daily, with music starting at 9pm.

SWING

Hotel del Coronado. 1500 Orange Ave., Coronado. ☎ **619/435-6611.** Cover $16.95 without dinner.

The West Coast's most glorious Victorian hotel kicks up its heels on Sunday nights, when it's swing time in the Crown Room. Besides the music and dancing, the architecturally memorable room makes the trip here worthwhile. Prices are $26.95 with buffet dinner.

GAY & LESBIAN CLUBS

The Flame. 3780 Park Blvd. ☎ **619/295-4163.** Cover Sun–Fri $2, Sat $3.

The Flame has a large dance floor and two bars, including a video bar open Tuesday to Saturday. A different style of music is played every night of the week: Tuesday is "progressive music night"; Wednesday is "trash disco"; on Saturday Top-40s dance music is played; Sunday night there's Latin music. Open daily from 5pm till 2am.

Rich's. 1051 University Ave. (between 10th and 11th aves.). ☎ **619/497-4588** for upcoming events. Thurs–Sat $4–$5; Sun, no cover before 9pm, $3 after.

This popular club/dance space welcomes primarily gay men 21 and older. Sunday is popular for Tea and Me, when there's no cover between 7 and 9pm, and Thursday for Club Hedonism, with techno tunes and more. On Friday night, go-go dancers and high-energy music set the tone for the night, Saturday it's dance music and erotic dancers. Always check the events hotline, since the schedules can change. Open Thursday to Sunday 'til 2am.

THE BAR & COFFEEHOUSE SCENE

The **Top o' The Cove,** 1216 Prospect St., La Jolla (☎ **619/454-7779**), is an intimate setting, where the pianist plays old favorites, and leans heavily toward Gershwin. Nab the corner table next to the piano. On nice evenings, the music is piped to the patio, another idyllic spot to sit and sip. Valet parking is $5.

BREWPUBS

Karl Strauss' Old Columbia Brewery, at 1157 Columbia St. (☎ **619/234-BREW**), opened several years ago and started something of a microbrewery trend in San Diego. Strauss named his brews after local attractions—Gaslamp Gold Ale, Red Trolley Ale, Black's Beach Extra Dark, Star of India Pale Ale—but he brought the recipes from the Old World. Want to try them all and still be able to walk? You can order a Taster Series, 4 ounces. of eight different brews for only $5.95. Old Columbia also serves up hearty American fare in addition to great beer. Hours are 11:30am to 10pm Sunday to Thursday and 11:30am to midnight Friday and Saturday. The newest Karl Strauss brewpub is located at 1044 Wall St., La Jolla (☎ **619/551-BREW**).

The **La Jolla Brewing Company,** 7536 Fay Ave., La Jolla (☎ **619/456-BREW**), feels more like a neighborhood pub. The wood floor is appropriately worn, and pool and darts are played in the back room. Brewmaster John Atwater makes his handcrafted beers from his own recipes and names them after local spots. John offers TVs for sports fans and serves meals such as Baja fish tacos, brewhouse pasta, and a "cheeseburger in paradise."

COFFEEHOUSES

Pannikin Hillcrest, 523 University Ave., Hillcrest (☎ **619/295-1600**), is a laid-back place to enjoy your latte or espresso. The desserts are rich, and the art on the wall is the work of local artists. Open Sunday to Thursday from 6am to 11pm, Friday and Saturday from 6am to midnight.

Upstart Crow, on the central plaza at Seaport Village (☎ **619/232-4855**), is a coffeehouse/bookstore where tables and chairs fill cozy spaces surrounded by books. The selection of books, coffees, and desserts are scrumptious. And coffee refills are only 25¢. Open Sunday to Thursday from 9am to 10pm (until 11pm in summer), Friday and Saturday from 9am to 11pm.

Centrally located in the Gaslamp Quarter and particularly popular with students, **Cafe Lulu,** 419 F St. near Fourth Avenue (☎ **619/238-0114**), is open weeknights till 2am, until 4am on Friday and Saturday. Light fare at this sparsely decorated coffeehouse runs the gamut from brie or pizza baguettes to bagels to croissants to quiche to lasagna. Drinkwise, the emphasis is on coffees, but you can also get teas, natural sodas, Aqua Libra, sarsaparilla, and beer or wine by the glass or bottle.

In La Jolla, try the **Wall Street Cafe,** at 1044 Wall St., between Girard and Herschel avenues (☎ **619/551-1044**), which was once a bank (the old vault now houses the rest rooms). Live entertainment, such as light jazz or a mellow guitar, makes this a particularly popular place on Friday and Saturday nights.

11 North County Beach Towns

Picturesque beach towns, each poised over a stretch of sand, dot the coast of San Diego County from Del Mar to Oceanside. These make great day-trip destinations for sun worshipers and surfers.

ESSENTIALS

Getting there is easy: Del Mar is only 18 miles north of downtown San Diego, Carlsbad about 33, and Oceanside approximately 36. If you're driving, follow I-5 north: You'll find freeway exits for Del Mar, Solana Beach, Cardiff by the Sea, Encinitas, Leucadia, Carlsbad, and Oceanside. The farthest point, Oceanside, will take you about 45 minutes. The other choice by car is to wander up the coast road—known variously along the way as Camino del Mar, Pacific Coast Highway, Old U.S. 101, and County Highway S-21.

Amtrak and **The Coaster** provide service to Carlsbad and Oceanside, and Amtrak also stops in Solana Beach, a few minutes north of Del Mar. Check with Amtrak (☎ **800/USA-RAIL**), The Coaster (☎ **800/COASTER**), or the local tourist information offices about schedules.

The **San Diego North County Convention & Visitors Bureau** (☎ **800/ 848-3336**) is also a good information source.

DEL MAR

Less than 20 miles up the coast from San Diego lies Del Mar, a community with just over 5,000 inhabitants in a 2-square-mile municipality. The town has adamantly maintained its independence, eschewing incorporation into the city of San Diego. Sometimes known as "the people's republic of Del Mar," this community was one of the nation's first to ban smoking. The upscale folks who live here grin and bear it during the summer racing season when the Del Mar Thoroughbred Club attracts droves of out-of-towners.

Del Mar Beach connects with **Torrey Pines Beach,** providing miles of sand for walking; swimmers congregate north of Jake's seaside restaurant; surfers go south. On

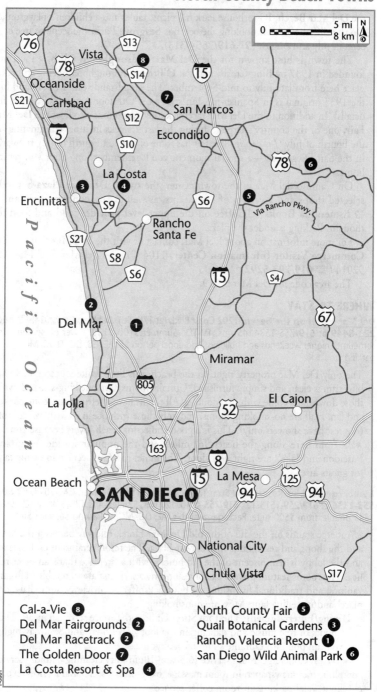

North County Beach Towns

0 ▭▭▭▭ 5 mi	N
0 ▭▭▭▭ 8 km	

Pacific Ocean

76
78
Vista
S13
S14 ❽
Oceanside
S21
Carlsbad
❼
5
S12
San Marcos
S10
Escondido
La Costa ❹
❸
78 ❻
Encinitas
S9
S6
❺
Via Rancho Pkwy.
S21
Rancho Santa Fe
S8
15
S4
S6
❷
Del Mar
67
❶
Miramar
La Jolla
5 805
52
El Cajon
163
8
Ocean Beach
15 La Mesa 125
SAN DIEGO
94 94
National City
Chula Vista S17

Cal-a-Vie ❽
Del Mar Fairgrounds ❷
Del Mar Racetrack ❷
The Golden Door ❼
La Costa Resort & Spa ❹

North County Fair ❺
Quail Botanical Gardens ❸
Rancho Valencia Resort ❶
San Diego Wild Animal Park ❻

1-0861

643

the **Del Mar Beach,** Powerhouse Park has picnic tables and a children's playground. On the cliff above it overlooking the ocean is **Seagrove Park,** the scene of free concerts in July and August (☎ **619/755-9313**).

The town is best known for the **Del Mar Thoroughbred Club,** a racetrack founded in 1937 by Bing Crosby and Pat O'Brien. Thoroughbred racing still takes place here from late July to mid-September. The grandstand seats 14,300, and like the 1937 original is in Spanish-mission style (see "Outdoor Activities," above, for details). In addition to the Del Mar racetrack, the fairgrounds also host the **Del Mar Fair,** one of the country's largest, during the last 2 weeks in June, culminating on the Fourth of July. *Insider tip:* The fair has some of the best Fourth of July fireworks in the San Diego area—a special moment you'll remember long after you return home.

On Camino del Mar in the town center, the stylish **Del Mar Plaza** has well-selected shops and a variety of restaurants, as well as jazz concerts in summer. ✪ **Esmeralda Books & Coffee** on the upper level provides food and food for thought. Parking is under the plaza.

For more information about Del Mar, contact or visit the **Del Mar Chamber of Commerce Visitor Information Center,** 1104 Camino del Mar, Del Mar, CA 92014 (☎ **619/793-5292**).

The area code for Del Mar is **619.**

WHERE TO STAY

Del Mar Motel on the Beach. 1702 Coast Blvd. (at 17th St.), Del Mar, CA 92014. ☎ **800/ 223-8449** or 619/755-1534. 45 rms. TV TEL. Summer $100–$130; lower off-season rates; sometimes higher weekends and holidays. Additional person $5. AE, CB, DC, DISC, MC, V. Free parking.

The only Del Mar property right on the beach, this little white-stucco motel with blue trim is clean and simply furnished. Upstairs rooms have one king-size bed, while those downstairs come with two doubles. All rooms have a refrigerator, coffeemaker, and fan. Half are no-smoking rooms, and only those with ocean views have bathtubs (the rest have showers only). This is a good choice for beach lovers because you can walk from here along the beach for miles, and the popular seaside restaurants Poseidon and Jake's are right next door. The motel has a barbecue and picnic table for guests' use.

L'Auberge Del Mar Resort and Spa. 1540 Camino del Mar, Del Mar, CA 92014. ☎ **800/ 553-1336** or 619/259-1515. Fax 619/755-4940. 120 rms, 8 suites. A/C MINIBAR TV TEL. $189– $349 double; from $500 suite. Packages available. AE, DC, MC, V. Parking $6, valet $8.

L'Auberge stands on the site of the old Del Mar Hotel, midway between the beach and the shops and restaurants in Del Mar Plaza. The resort retains an exclusive air, and the lobby is reminiscent of the old hotel's, with a fireplace that's an exact replica. The rooms feature private balconies or terraces, sitting areas, marble baths and vanities, and traditional furnishings. About half offer ocean views; some have fireplaces and/or ceiling fans. Most are nonsmoking.

Dining/Entertainment: The 15th Street Grille and Terrace serves all meals. There are 3 hours of free music and dancing in the lobby on Friday and Saturday nights, and you can pop into Durante's Pub most anytime.

Services: Concierge, room service (6:30am–10pm), dry cleaning, laundry service, complimentary newspaper, in-room massage, baby-sitting, secretarial services, express checkout, valet parking, in-room coffee service.

Facilities: In-room movies, pool, lap pool, health club, Jacuzzi, full European-style spa (massage, hydrotherapy, herbal wraps, steam room, sauna, spa cuisine, yoga on nearby beach), two tennis courts, jogging track, bicycle rental, nearby golf, nature trails, VIK (Very Important Kids) program during summer months and holidays, business center, conference rooms, salon, gift shops.

✪ **Wave Crest.** 1400 Ocean Ave., Del Mar, CA 92014. ☎ **619/755-0100.** Fax 619/793-8232. 31 condos. TV TEL. Mid-June to mid-Sept $1,195–$1,370 studio for 2 for a week; $1,420–$1,630 1-bedroom for 2 for a week; $1,975 2-bedroom for 4 for a week. MC, V. Free parking.

On a bluff over the Pacific, these gray-shingled time-share condominiums are beautifully maintained and offer a high standard of self-contained living. All the modern units surround a landscaped courtyard and have a queen-size bed and sofa beds, artwork by local artists, TVs in living rooms and bedrooms, VCRs, stereos, full baths with great showers, and fully equipped kitchens. The studios can sleep one or two, the one-bedroom units up to four, and the two-bedrooms up to six. Guests share a communal lounge with a fireplace, wetbar, and TV, plus a really nice pool and bubbling Jacuzzi overlooking the ocean and the attractive grounds. A clifftop walking path and Seagrove Park are adjacent. It's only 5 minutes to the beach, and shopping and dining spots are only a few blocks away. There's an extra fee for maid service. Laundry facilities are on-site.

WHERE TO DINE

Head to the upper level of the centrally located **Del Mar Plaza,** at Camino del Mar and 15th Street (☎ **619/792-1555**), and consider **Il Fornaio Cucina Italiana** for excellent Italian cuisine; **Epazote** for Mexican, Tex-Mex, and southwestern fare; or **Pacifica Del Mar** for outstanding seafood. Kids like to eat at **Johnny Rockets,** an old-fashioned diner on the lower level. Down on the beach, ✪ **Jake's** and **Poseidon** are both good for California cuisine and sunset views. The racetrack crowd congregates at **Bully's,** 1404 Camino del Mar (☎ **619/755-1660**), for Bully Burgers, prime rib, and crab legs.

CARLSBAD

Fifteen miles north of Del Mar and 33 miles from downtown San Diego (about a 45-minute drive), the pretty beach community of Carlsbad provides many reasons to linger: good swimming and surfing beaches (with a mile-long two-tiered beach walk that's accessible for travelers with disabilities); three lagoons perfect for walks or bird-watching; landscaped streets; memorable restaurants; and an abundance of antique and gift shops. There's a small-town atmosphere—the population is 63,000, but Carlsbad actually feels smaller than Del Mar. You won't see any highrise buildings. The town extends a warm welcome to travelers in the recycled train depot (1887) that's now home to the **Visitors Information Center** (☎ **760/434-6093**).

Carlsbad was named for Karlsbad, Bohemia because of the similar mineral (some say curative) waters they both produced, but the town's once-famous artesian well has long been plugged up. You can picnic in small **Florence Magee Park;** while there, peek into tiny **St. Michael's by the Sea** Episcopal Church (1894); the original organ is to the right.

In spring, visit the 200 acres of cultivated flower fields that transform the hills south of town into a startling rainbow from March to May; in winter, witness a profusion of poinsettias here. The latest **Flower Fields** info is available at ☎ **760/431-0352.** You can also see 3,000 varieties of flowers, plants, and trees year-round at the serene, 30-acre **Quail Botanical Garden** in nearby Encinitas (☎ **760/436-3036**), open daily from 9am to 5pm.

The area code for Carlsbad is **760.**

WHERE TO STAY

Beach Terrace Inn. 2775 Ocean St., Carlsbad, CA 92003. ☎ **800/622-3224** in CA, 800/433-5415 elsewhere, or 760/729-5951. Fax 760/729-1078. 41 rms, 5 suites. A/C TV TEL. Summer $110–$220 double, from $140 suite; winter $100–$180 double, from $120 suite. Extra person $10. Rates include continental breakfast. AE, CB, DC, DISC, ER, MC, V. Free parking.

Carlsbad's only beachside hotel (others are across the road or a little farther away), this Best Western property has a helpful staff, a living room–like lobby, and rooms and an outdoor pool with ocean views. Though not elegant, the rooms are extra large, and some have balconies, fireplaces, and kitchenettes; suites have separate living rooms and bedrooms. VCRs and tapes are available at the front desk. This place is good for families. You can walk everywhere from here.

La Costa Resort and Spa. Costa del Mar Rd., Carlsbad, CA 92009. ☎ **800/854-5000** or 760/438-9111. Fax 760/931-7585. 478 rms and suites. A/C TV TEL. $245–$440 double; from $500 suite. Golf, spa, and tennis packages available. AE, CB, DC, DISC, MC, V. Valet parking $10, self-parking free.

La Costa Resort boasts two championship 18-hole golf courses (home of the annual Mercedes Championships); a 21-court racquet club comprising 2 grass, 4 clay, and 15 composite courts (home of the WTA Toshiba Tennis Classic); resident tennis pro Pancho Segura (who has coached Jimmy Connors and Andre Agassi); an extensive spa with a multitude of treatments available; and five restaurants. These amenities are spread over 450 landscaped acres. Attractive accommodations offer all the bells and whistles you'd expect at this price level. The big advantage is that travel partners can do their own things during the day—golf, tennis, or the spa—and still rendezvous for dinner. However, this resort—built in the mid-1960s—isn't looking as fresh as it once did.

✪**Pelican Cove Inn.** 320 Walnut Ave., Carlsbad, CA 92008. ☎ **760/434-5995.** 8 rms. $85–$175 double. Extra person $15. Rates include full breakfast. AE, MC, V. Free parking.

This Cape Cod–style hideaway near the beach combines romance with luxury—down to the bed covers, which resemble clouds more than comforters. All rooms have fireplaces and private entrances; two have spa tubs. You can lounge or have breakfast in the garden with a gazebo and a sundeck. Hosts Kris and Nancy Nayudu can provide beach towels and chairs or prepare a wonderful picnic basket (with 24-hour notice) you can enjoy on the lovely local beaches or parks. All rooms are nonsmoking. Extras include complimentary transfer from Oceanside train station or Palomar Airport.

Tamarack Beach Resort. 3200 Carlsbad Blvd., Carlsbad, CA 92008. ☎ **800/334-2199** or 760/729-3500. Fax 760/434-5942. 23 rms, 54 condos. A/C TV TEL. $150 double; $200–$260 condos. Weekly rates available. Children under 12 stay free in parents' room. AE, MC, V. Free secured parking.

This resort's rooms, across the street from the beach, are restfully decorated in tropical colors and outfitted with wicker furniture, small refrigerators, coffeemakers, and VCRs (movies are complimentary). The fully equipped condos (including washer/dryer) are available on a daily or weekly basis. The pretty Tamarack also has a pleasant lobby, a heated pool in a sunny courtyard, two Jacuzzis, exercise facilities, valet services, barbecue grills, and a good restaurant, Dini's by the Sea, which is popular with locals.

WHERE TO DINE

Local favorites include **Branci's Caldo Pomodoro,** 2907 State St. (☎ 760/720-9998); **Neiman's,** 2978 Carlsbad Blvd. (☎ 760/729-4131); and **Tip Top Meats,** 6118 Paseo del Norte (☎ 760/438-2620).

OCEANSIDE

The most northerly town in San Diego County (actually it's a city of 100,000) and 36 miles from San Diego, Oceanside claims almost 4 miles of beaches and one of the West Coast's longest wooden piers (a tram does nothing but transport people 1,600 feet from the street to the end and back for 25¢ one-way; the restaurant at the end of the pier is a great place for lunch over the ocean). The beach, the pier, and a well-tended recreational area with playground equipment and an outdoor amphitheater are within easy walking distance of the train station. The small **California Surf Museum,** across from the pier, at 308 Pacific St. (☎ 760/721-6876), is open Monday, Thursday, and Friday from 10am to 4pm, Saturday and Sunday from 10am to 4pm.

Try not to miss **Mission San Luis Rey** (☎ 760/757-3651), a few miles inland from I-5 on Mission Road. Founded in 1798, it's the largest of California's 21 missions. There's a small charge to tour the impressive church, exhibits, grounds, and cemetery. You might recognize it as the backdrop for several Zorro movies.

For an information packet about the area and its attractions, send a check for $3 to the **Oceanside Chamber of Commerce,** 928 North Coast Hwy., Oceanside, CA 92051 (☎ 760/722-1534).

The area code for Oceanside is **760.**

A SIDE TRIP INLAND

The coastal and inland sections of North San Diego County are as different as night and day. Beaches and laid-back villages where work seems to be the curse of the surfing class characterize the coast, while inland you'll find beautiful barren hills, citrus groves, and conservative communities where agriculture plays an important role.

Rancho Santa Fe is located about 27 miles north of downtown San Diego; from there, the Del Dios Highway (Calif. 6) leads to **Escondido,** almost 32 miles from the city. **San Marcos, Vista,** and **Fallbrook** are even farther north. Nearly 70 miles away is **Palomar Mountain** in the Cleveland National Forest, which spills over the border into Riverside County. The **San Diego North County Convention & Visitors Bureau** (☎ 800/848-3336) can answer all your questions.

RANCHO SANTA FE

Certainly one of the county's loveliest communities, exclusive Rancho Santa Fe was once the property of the Santa Fe Railroad, and the eucalyptus trees they grew there create a stately atmosphere. The Del Dios Highway (Calif. 6) is the scenic route to Escondido and the Wild Animal Park. This road affords views of Lake Hodges, as well as glimpses of expansive estates, some of the most expensive in the country.

✪ **Rancho Valencia Resort.** 5921 Valencia Circle (P.O. Box 9126), Rancho Santa Fe, CA 92067. ☎ **800/548-3664** or 619/756-1123. Fax 619/756-0165. 43 suites in 21 casitas. MINIBAR TV TEL. $360–$900 suite. Tennis, golf, and romance packages available. AE, CB, DC, MC, V. Free valet and self-parking.

If you need pampering and relaxation or a romantic getaway, head to this member of Relais et Châteaux and Preferred Hotels, a sun-baked Spanish- and Mediterranean-style resort on 40 rolling acres. Small and intimate, the resort is far removed from the fast-paced world, even though it's only a short drive from I-5 and only 6 miles inland from Del Mar. Imagine having your own terra-cotta–tiled and Berber-carpeted casita with cathedral ceilings, wood-burning fireplace, ceiling fans, oversize bath, walk-in closet, patio, and private terrace. Fresh-squeezed juice and a newspaper are left outside your door in the morning; you can even have a full range of spa treatments without leaving your room. Those who actually do venture outside will discover grounds filled with 2,000 citrus trees, bougainvillea, and air sweetened by flowers and birdsong.

There are multiple pools, three Jacuzzis, a fitness room, and 18 tennis courts and tennis clinics with a 4-to-1 student/teacher ratio. You also might check out the championship croquet lawn, or play a round of golf at nearby private courses. Bikes for both adults and kids are available at no extra charge, and there are plenty of hiking trails to enjoy. I highly recommend this place; I don't think you'll be disappointed.

Dining/Entertainment: The pretty dining room serves three Mediterranean/California meals a day, accompanied by a cellist or guitarist on Friday and Saturday nights; there's dancing under the stars on Thursday nights in July and August. The Clintons dined here while they were in town. Tea and cocktails are served in La Sala, from which there is a great view of the hot-air balloons at sunset.

Services: Concierge, room service (24 hours), dry cleaning, laundry service, complimentary morning paper and fresh orange juice, nightly turndown, in-room massage, twice-daily maid service, baby-sitting, secretarial services, valet parking, airport transportation from San Diego's Lindbergh Field.

Facilities: Two cable TVs and VCRs in each suite; video rentals; in-room safes; two pools; fitness room; massage rooms; three Jacuzzis; unlimited use of 18 hard-turf tennis courts, tennis clinics, and match arranging; regulation croquet court; bicycles; golf privileges at 4 nearby private golf courses.

12 Julian: Apples, Pies & a Slice of Small-Town California

A trip 60 miles northeast of San Diego to Julian (pop. 1,500) is a trip back in time. The old gold mining town, now best known for its apples, has some good restaurants and a handful of cute B&Bs that offer city-weary folks a chance to get away from it all. However, when it's sunny in San Diego it may be snowing in Julian, since it's perched 4,235 feet above sea level.

Before you leave, try Julian's apple pies. Whether the best pies come from Mom's Pies, Mrs. Glad's Bakery, or the Julian Pie Company is a toss-up; it's fun to sample all of them and decide for yourself.

ESSENTIALS

The area code in Julian is **760.**

GETTING THERE The 90-minute drive from San Diego can be made via Calif. 78 or I-8 to Calif. 79. I suggest taking one route going and the other coming back, since Calif. 79 winds through scenic Rancho Cuyamaca State Park, while Calif. 78 traverses open country and farmland.

Side Trip: If you come by Calif. 78, you'll pass the mission church of **Santa Ysabel** (1812), where there's a tiny museum and a large Native American cemetery on your right, as well as **Dudley's Bakery,** off to the left at the junction with Calif. 79 and just 7 miles from Julian. The bakery, here since 1963, is known for its breads, from raisin date nut to jalapeño, and on weekends 5,000 to 6,000 loaves come out of the ovens. Dudley's is open 8am to 5pm Wednesday to Sunday.

VISITOR INFORMATION Town maps and flyers for accommodations are available from the Town Hall on Main Street at Washington Street. The town has a **24-hour hotline** (☎ 760/765-0707) that provides information on lodging, dining, shopping, activities, upcoming events, weather, and road conditions. For a brochure on what to see and do, contact the **Julian Chamber of Commerce** (☎ 760/

765-1857). The **Julian Arts Guild** (☎ 760/765-0560) can answer questions about the Spring Fine Arts Show (see below).

SPECIAL EVENTS   Special events here have special appeal, especially Julian's popular **fall apple harvest** starting in mid-September and continuing for an entire month. The annual **wildflower show** lasts for a week in early May; there's also a **Spring Fine Arts Show** in May. And the **annual weed show,** a tradition since 1961, is usually held the last few weeks in August or the beginning of September. Contact the Julian Chamber of Commerce (see above) for details on all of these events.

EXPLORING THE TOWN

It's fun to learn about the town and surrounding area by visiting the **Julian Cider Mill.** The father-and-son team of Turk and Fred Slaughter run the mill, where you can see cider being made. Homemade peanut butter is ground on the premises too, and in the spring a glass-enclosed beehive bustles with activity. Because the town is relatively near to both desert and sea (both are within 1 1/2 hours' drive), Julian honey is particularly good. It's hard not to feel like a kid in this store filled with jawbreakers, preserves, nuts, trail mix, and easy conversation around a potbellied stove.

On the right as you come into town is the **Julian Pioneer Museum** (☎ 760/765-0227), at 4th and Washington streets, housed in an old brewery and open Tuesday to Sunday from 10am to 4pm April to November, weekends and holidays December to March. Here you can learn about some of the old-timers buried up the hill in the **Haven of Rest Cemetery.**

The **Eagle & High Peak Mines** (☎ 760/765-0036), 6 blocks from Main Street via C Street, operate daily from 9am to 4pm but only for educational reasons, since the gold is long gone.

It's fun to dart in and out of the little shops in Julian. My favorites are the **Julian Farms Antiques Shop,** 2818 Washington St. (☎ 760/765-0250), for gifts and patio accessories, and **Warm Hearth,** 2125 Main St. (☎ 760/765-1022), for gifts, cassettes, and wood-burning stoves if you're in the market for one. **Applewood,** next to Julian Farms Antiques, is also very good.

Country Carriages (☎ 760/765-1471) will show you the sights and give you a spin down a country lane in a horse-drawn wagon for $20 per couple, or around the town for $5 per adult, $2 per child. Hop on in front of or catty-corner to the drugstore; the ride lasts a half-hour.

JULIAN AFTER DARK   You can mix culture with barbecue at the **Pine Hills Dinner Theater** on Friday and Saturday nights at Pine Hills Lodge, a few miles from Julian off Pine Hills Road (☎ 760/765-1100). The rustic lodge opened its doors on July 4, 1912; in 1980, Dave and Donna Goodman bought it and opened the 96-seat dinner theater, which has staged almost 70 productions, among them *I'm Not Rappaport* and *Last of the Red-Hot Lovers.* The dinner buffet of delicious baby-back pork ribs or barbecue chicken starts promptly at 7pm (give them 24-hour notice and you can get a vegetarian plate). Showtime is 8pm, and the price for the dinner and the theater is $28.50; for the show alone, it's $14.50.

EXPLORING THE COUNTRYSIDE

If there's something about being in the country that makes you want to hop in the car and drive down one rural road after another, Julian is an ideal starting point. You'll pass rolling hills, country stores, rambling houses, and fruit stands and come upon towns with names like Ramona, Ballena, and Wynola.

One of my favorite short drives is along the road leading to the **Menghini Winery,** owned and run by Toni and Michael Menghini; it's 2 miles out on Farmer's

Road (follow it west out of town until you see the winery sign, then bear to the left down the hill). The winery is usually open Monday, Friday, Saturday, and Sunday from 10am to 4pm, daily in October and December, or call for an appointment (☎ **760/765-2072**). The grapes come from Ramona and Temecula, and the local favorite wine is Julian Blossom. The tanks are right in the tasting room, and the wines are sold only locally, for $7 to $10 per bottle. You may enjoy your purchase right away in the picnic area in the apple orchard.

If you don't make it to the desert this trip, at least take a moment to gaze out at it and the Salton Sea from **Inspiration Point**, just 1¹/₂ miles south of Julian on Calif. 79, opposite Pinecroft Park. **Lake Cuyamaca** (pronounced *kwee-yah-mack-ah*), 10 miles south on Calif. 79, offers boating, fishing (bass, trout, and crappie), and recreational vehicle camping on a first-come, first-served basis. Its facilities are open from sunrise to sunset daily (☎ **760/765-0515** or 619/447-8123). There are motorboat and rowboat rentals, a 3¹/₂-mile hiking trail around the lake, and a charge for fishing ($4.75 for adults, $2.50 for children 8 to 15). A restaurant with a deck and adjoining store overlook the lake.

For a different way to tour, try **Llama Trek**, P.O. Box 2363, Julian, CA 92036 (☎ **800/LAMAPAK** or 760/765-1890; fax 760/765-1512). Trips include rural neighborhoods, a historic gold mine, mountain and lake views, and apple orchards. They even conduct a trek to the local winery. Rates for the 4- to 5-hour trips vary from $65 to $85 per person and include lunch (the winery trek also includes wine tasting).

WHERE TO STAY

For a list and a description of a dozen interesting B&Bs, contact the **Julian Bed & Breakfast Guild**, P.O. Box 1711, Julian, CA 92036 (☎ **760/765-1555** daily from 9am to 9pm). All members are within a few miles of the town center. My favorites are the **Julian White House** (☎ **800/WHT-HOUS** or 760/765-1764) and the **Artists' Loft** (☎ **760/765-0765**).

✪ **Julian Farms Lodging.** 2818 Washington St. (just down the hill from Main St.), Julian, CA 92036. ☎ **760/765-0250.** 4 attached cottages, 1 cabin. TV. $69 double; $99 cabin. Extra person $5. AE, MC, V.

Driving into town, you'll find it easy to pass right by this little place on the left. That would be a shame because the yellow cottages with blue shutters and a grape arbor in front make the perfect secret hideaway. Three of the cottages have a double bed and a daybed in a single room; one, with two double beds in two rooms, is perfect for families. All have small private baths with showers, hot pots, country antiques, goose-down comforters, and a split of Julian Blossom wine. A nearby cabin has a queen-size bed and a sitting area. You can pick all the grapes you want and eat them in the vine-covered gazebo. Reserve 3 to 4 months ahead for weekends. Smoking is permitted outside only.

Julian Hotel. Main and B sts. (P.O. Box 1856), Julian, CA 92036. ☎ **760/765-0201.** 15 rms, 2 cottages. $72–$110 double; $125–$160 cottage. Rates include full breakfast. AE, MC, V.

The Julian Hotel has been putting a roof over travelers' heads since the days when the Butterfield stagecoach stopped across the street. A potbellied stove still sits in the parlor, along with an upright piano that arrived from Philadelphia via Cape Horn. The hotel's original owners, Albert and Margaret Robinson, were former slaves; their photograph hangs on the parlor wall. There are a dozen rooms in the original part of the house, and each room is decorated in a variation of a Victorian theme. Another three rooms were added off the front porch in 1920. One of the cottages, the

Honeymoon House, features a Franklin (freestanding) fireplace and an old-fashioned tub. The cottages book up 2 months in advance. The hotel's generous breakfast menu includes apple-filled pancakes and omelets. Coffee, tea, cakes, and cookies are served in the parlor at 5pm.

○ **Orchard Hill Country Inn.** 2502 Washington St. (at 2nd St.), (P.O. Box 425), Julian, CA 92036-0425. ☎ **760/765-1700.** Fax 760/765-0290. 22 suites and rooms. A/C MINIBAR TV TEL. $140–$195 double. Extra person $25. 2-night minimum stay if including Fri or Sat. Deposit required. Midweek discounts available. Rates include full breakfast and afternoon hors d'oeuvres. AE, MC, V. Limited free parking.

Darrell and Pat Straube offer the most upscale lodging in Julian: a 2-story lodge and four 1928 California Craftsman-style cottages on a hill with a panoramic view that includes the historic townsite. Ten guest rooms, a guests-only dining room, and a "great room" with a massive stone fireplace are in the lodge; 12 suites are in cottages over 3 acres of grounds. All quarters feature attractive furnishings including plantation shutters. Suite amenities include fireplaces, whirlpool tubs, wetbars, VCRs, books, videos, games, and wraparound porches. Breakfast can be delivered to the suites.

CAMPING

Cuyamaca Rancho State Park (☎ 760/765-0755) is 11 miles from Julian, and a new camp store and interpretive center are located a mile from the entrance. It's another 2 miles to a little museum and park headquarters where you can stock up on maps, information, and even books to help you identify local flora and fauna. The park has more than 100 miles of trails, and you can see Mexico from Cuyamaca Peak (6,512 feet).

Campsites are set amid trees and scrubs; each one has a table and fire ring. Reserve a spot in **Paso Picacho** or **Green Valley Campground,** both of which have about 80 sites (☎ 800/444-PARK for reservations). The camping fee is $15 to $16 in summer, $12 off-season, or $5 for day use only. They book up fast on weekends from Easter to Thanksgiving, so plan ahead. Park headquarters is open Monday to Friday from 8am to 5pm.

WHERE TO DINE

Julian Cafe. Main St. ☎ 760/765-2712. Menu items $2.50–$9. MC, V. Mon–Fri 8am–7:30pm, Sat–Sun 7am–8:30pm. AMERICAN.

A tasty, filling chicken pie is the specialty here; buy it at lunch for $6.95, or pay $8.95 for the full dinner. Mashed potatoes come the old-fashioned way, smothered in country gravy. Other home-cooked offerings include fried chicken, liver and onions, meat loaf dinner, and a hot vegetable plate. This is a good place to bring kids; the waitresses are friendly and service is quick, even when it's packed.

13 Anza-Borrego Desert State Park

The vast, striking landscapes of Anza-Borrego comprise the largest state park in the lower 48 states. Most visitors come during the spring **wildflower season,** when a colorful carpet of flowers blankets the desert floor and climbs into the surrounding hills and mountains.

ESSENTIALS

Anza-Borrego Desert State Park (☎ 760/767-4205 or 760/767-5311) is open from October to May daily from 9am to 5pm; June to September, it's only open

Saturdays, Sundays, and holidays from 9am to 5pm. The park lies about 90 miles northeast of San Diego or 150 miles southwest of Los Angeles between I-10 and I-8. It's reached by Calif. 78 and Calif. 79 from the east and by I-8 from the south.

Information on the park is available from the **Borrego Springs Chamber of Commerce** (☎ 760/767-5555); the **California Desert Tourism Association** (☎ 760/328-9256); and the **Julian Chamber of Commerce** (☎ 760/765-1857). Call the **Wildflower Hotline** at ☎ 619/767-4684 to find out what's blooming during your trip.

EXPLORING THE PARK

At the **Visitor Center,** you're introduced to the park and desert with a 15-minute slide show and exhibits that cover the local ecosystem and the history of the Native Americans who once lived here. Hiking maps are on sale here as well.

Hikers can choose from more than 100 miles of designated trails. About 35 miles are part of the **Pacific Crest Trail** that goes from Mexico to Canada. Register at the Visitor Center before setting out. If you don't want to attempt a serious hike, there are a number of shorter **nature trails.** The **Borrego Palm Canyon Trail** starts at the main campground and will take you to a grove of California fan palms, the largest palm species in North America, and a year-round stream, one of the 25 oases in the park. Brochures are available at the Visitor Center for a number of these nature trails.

A few hundred rare bighorn sheep live in the park's rough, rocky terrain, and other animal residents include rabbits, desert mice, the chuckwalla (the largest lizard in the park), coyotes, mule deer, and bobcats.

Horseback trails surround the park's Vernon Whitaker horse camp. One trail ascends 12 miles to the top of the mountains for a spectacular vista. Riders may use all the dirt roads in the park, but not the nature or hiking trails.

CAMPING

There are two developed campgrounds in the park. **Borrego Palm Canyon Campground** has 52 full hookup sites (fees are $16 to $22) and 65 multi-use sites without hookups ($10 to $16). Another 27 multi-use nonhookup sites are situated at **Tamarisk Grove** ($10 to $16). All of the park's nonhookup sites have shade ramadas.

You and your horse can stay at the park's **Vernon Whitaker horse camp.** All of the 10 campsites can hold up to eight people and have corrals for four horses. Reservations for the campgrounds and horse camp are made through **Destinet** (☎ 800/444-PARK). Payment can be made with MasterCard, Visa, or personal check. The horse camp is the hub of many miles of riding trails.

Bow Willow is a primitive camping site off Calif. 2 with picnic tables and portable toilet facilities. Once you're out of the developed areas of the park, you can camp just about anywhere along its 500 miles of primitive roads. Only two restrictions apply: First, you must keep your vehicle within one car length of the road so as not to damage the fragile plant life; second, you can't camp near a watering hole or spring, as it scares away the wildlife.

WHERE TO STAY NEARBY IN BORREGO SPRINGS

The nearby town of Borrego Springs, just down the road from the Visitor Center, offers restaurants, shops, and motels, plus one very special accommodation.

✪ **La Casa del Zorro.** 3845 Yaqui Pass Rd., Borrego Springs, CA 92004. ☎ **800/824-1884** or 760/767-5323. Fax 760/767-5963. 79 rms and suites, 19 cottages/villas. A/C TV TEL.

$85–$100 double; from $125 suite; from $150 cottage/villa. Lower summer and midweek rates. Children under 12 stay free in parents' room. Special packages available. AE, DC, DISC, MC, V.

This is a beautiful 38-acre oasis in the desert, surrounded by more than 500,000 acres of the unforgettable scenery of Anza-Borrego State Park. Each room is accented with pieces that reflect the early California heritage of Borrego Springs and comes with thoughtful touches such as bathrobes, hair dryers, and coffeemakers. Some units have terraces, fireplaces, or Jacuzzis. Facilities include three swimming pools, bicycles, six tennis courts, a fitness center, a whirlpool, and a beauty salon; there's also a restaurant on the premises as well as a bar offering live entertainment.

14 The Temecula Wine Country

Located in Riverside County, 60 miles north of San Diego, Temecula is known for its wineries and the excellent vintages they produce. The name of the town is pronounced te-*mec*-u-la, a Native American word meaning "where the sun shines through the mist." It's the only town on California's coast that still goes by its aboriginal name, and if you gaze out over the vineyards early in the morning or in the middle of the afternoon, the name still holds true. The region was used as the setting for Helen Hunt Jackson's novel *Ramona,* first published in 1884.

Temecula has a couple of unique claims to fame. Granite from its quarries (most of which closed down in 1915, when reinforced concrete became popular) constitutes most of the street curbs in San Francisco. The last person sentenced to death by hanging in California was Temecula's blacksmith, John McNeil, who killed his wife in 1936.

When you turn onto Rancho California Road, all you'll see at first is new construction, but soon the vineyards come into view and the countryside turns natural again—a relief after the onslaught of progress, something relatively new to this area. Back in 1968, one vintner recalls, "if you heard a car come down Rancho California Road, you'd go to the window to see who could possibly be lost way out here."

Temecula's microclimate allows grapes to flourish due to a notch in the coastal mountains called Rainbow Gap, which lets breezes blow through from the ocean, 22 miles away. They result both in temperatures that are 8° to 10°F cooler than on the coast, giving Temecula a longer growing season that lets grapes ripen more slowly. Most vineyards here are more than 1,400 feet above sea level.

ESSENTIALS

The area code in this region is **909.**

GETTING THERE   From San Diego, take I-15 for 50 miles; when the Temecula Valley comes into view, it'll take your breath away. To reach the vineyards (they're well marked), head east on Rancho California Road.

VISITOR INFORMATION   For information on accommodations and maps and brochures on Old Town Temecula and the vineyards, contact the **Temecula Valley Chamber of Commerce,** 27450 Ynez Rd., Suite 104, Temecula, CA 92591 (☎ **909/676-5090;** www.temecula.org). The **Temecula Valley Vintners Association,** P.O. Box 1601, Temecula, CA 92593-1601 (☎ **909/699-3626**), is another good source, especially on the vineyards.

A SPECIAL EVENT   This area is especially popular in April during the annual **Temecula Valley Balloon and Wine Festival** (☎ **909/676-4713**), which features food, entertainment, wine tasting, a western village, and balloon launches.

WHAT TO SEE & DO
VISITING THE WINERIES

Temecula isn't as well known for its wines as Napa or Sonoma because those wine-producing regions have been at it a hundred years longer. Franciscan missionaries planted the first grapevines here in the early 1800s, but the land ended up being used primarily for cattle raising on the 87,000-acre Vail Ranch from 1904 until 1964, when the ranch was sold. Grapevines began to take root in the receptive soil again in 1968, and the first Temecula wines were produced in 1971.

Today there are 14 wineries in the region, most of them strung side by side for a couple of miles along Rancho California Road, producing white, red, and rosé wines. Most of them are not sold outside of California or the West, although some have made it as far as the White House.

Since the wineries in Temecula are smaller than their counterparts in Northern California and are mostly family-owned and -operated, you're more likely to meet and talk with the vintners when you come to their property. You're not likely to be there alone, however; it can get pretty crowded on the weekends.

Harvest time is usually mid-August through September; visitors are welcome then and all year-round to tour, taste, and stock up. Most wineries in the area are closed New Year's Day, Easter, Thanksgiving Day, and Christmas Day. In addition to wine tasting, area activities include hot-air balloon rides over the vineyards, an unforgettable sight. One company that has been around for about 20 years is **Sunrise Balloons** (☎ **800/548-9912**); proprietor Dan Glick also offers horse-drawn carriage rides through the vineyards.

As you drive along Rancho California Road, you'll first come to **Thornton Winery** (☎ **909/699-0099**), housed in a striking stone building with a waterfall and sloping lawn in front and an herb garden in back. Today Thornton produces Culbertson sparkling wine, à la méthode champenoise, as well as Brindiamo premium varietals. You can pay $6 to taste two champagnes and two still wines (and keep the glass). Tastings are offered Monday to Friday from 11am to 5pm and Saturday and Sunday from 11am to 4pm. There are free tours on Saturday and Sunday from 11am to 4pm, every hour on the hour. Café Champagne, the vineyard's award-winning restaurant, is open for lunch and dinner and serves California cuisine (see "Where to Dine," below). The winery hosts jazz concerts from April to October.

Across the road from Thornton is **Callaway** (☎ **909/676-4001**), in a long, low white building with brown trim and set amid grounds lush with 2,500 rose bushes and orange trees. Producing wine here since 1974—13 labels in all, mostly whites—it offers the most in-depth tour. There's a $4 charge to sample four different wines; you get to keep the glass. A vine-covered picnic area overlooks the vineyards (if you didn't come prepared to dine alfresco, there's a market 4 miles down the road). Open daily from 10:30am to 5pm (tasting until 4:45pm), with free tours Monday to Friday at 11am, 1pm, and 3pm; on the hour from 11am to 4pm weekends. Callaway's Vineyard Terrace bistro is open weekends and holidays from 11:30am to 5pm.

Turn off the main road and follow the blacktop up and over the hill to **Mount Palomar Winery** (☎ **909/676-5047**), where tastings of four wines of your choice cost $3, including the souvenir glass. Outside, 60 tables are available for picnicking, some on a spot overlooking the property belonging to the vineyard. From the winery, you can gaze out at Mount San Jacinto and, behind it, Mount San Gorgonio, the highest mountain in Southern California. Deli snacks are always available, and a full-service deli operates Friday to Sunday. Open daily from 10am to 5pm. Free tours are Monday to Friday at 1:30 and 3:30pm; Saturday and Sunday at 11:30am,

1:30pm, and 3:30pm. Try to come before 1pm on weekends, when people may stand five deep for tastings, so popular are Mount Palomar's Reisling and chardonnay, along with their port and cream sherry.

Turn off on Calle Contento to **Cilurzo Vineyard & Winery** (☎ **909/676-5250**), whose owner, Vince Cilurzo, may be better known in some circles in Los Angeles as the man who has lighted the TV game show *Jeopardy!* for many years (he still does so a couple of days a week). Out here, he's known as a vintner who established this 52-acre vineyard in 1968 and started producing wines in 1978. One of the most popular Cilurzo labels is the Petite Sirah, which, Vince claims, can be served with anything from tomato sauce to curry. Unlike many other Temecula wineries, this one has no bar for tastings; instead, visitors sit in chairs and are served by personable staff members. A tasting of at least five or six wines costs $1, refundable with a purchase. A picnic area overlooks the pond. Open daily from 9:30am to 4:45pm.

Lastly on Rancho California Road, we come to **Maurice Carrie** (☎ **909/ 676-1711**), in a large two-story pseudo-Southern building with veranda and gazebo—a "Victorian farmhouse," owner Maurice Van Roekel likes to call it. She and her husband, Budd, came here to retire, but soon were producing red and white wines instead. Four of their wines are named after their grandchildren. The property has a wine boutique and a lovely oak bar trimmed with black and white tiles that draws a good afternoon crowd. A deli section carries juice, crackers, and cold wine. Complimentary tastings available. Open daily 10am to 5pm.

A WALKING TOUR OF OLD TOWN TEMECULA

A wonderful, eccentric counterpoint to the vineyards is the old part of the city of Temecula, preserved as it was in the 1890s—Western storefronts and all. It lies 4 miles west of the vineyards off Rancho California Road, stretches along 6 short blocks, and has a reputation as an antique hunter's haven.

Park at the south end of town near the Swing Inn Café or Butterfield Plaza and walk north along Main Street to Sixth Street and back, going up one side of the street and back on the other. Take time to read the plaques on the old buildings along the way. Be forewarned that Temecula has become a traffic-clogged town—you'll hear the drone of cars most everywhere, even on the golf course.

One of my favorite spots in town, partly for the name, is the **Swing Inn Café,** at 28676 Front St. (☎ **909/676-2321**), where a sign claims that the cafe's been in existence since 1927. I asked my waitress if that was true. "Look around," she said. "Some of our customers have been here that long."

At Front and Sixth streets, turn right and walk a short block to **Sam Hicks Park,** home to the "They Passed This Way" Monument and the Old St. Catherine's Church, which dates from the early 1920s and is now part of the **Temecula Valley Museum** (☎ **909/676-0021**). The museum houses Native American artifacts from the area that are more than 1,000 years old, along with memorabilia from 1846 to the 1940s, and a model of the town from 1914. It's open Wednesday to Sunday from 11am to 4pm and by appointment.

Cross Front Street and walk back down the west side of the street. At Front and Sixth streets is the **Chaparral Antique Mall** (☎ **909/676-0070**), which houses more than 70 dealers under one roof. Down at Front and Main streets stands the **First National Bank,** which was built in 1912 and managed to stay open during the Great Depression, gaining it the nickname the "Pawn Shop." The bank finally closed in 1941, and the building now houses a Mexican restaurant. For many years, its second floor was the town's community center and dance hall.

Nearby are two plunderable antiques malls: **Morgan's Antiques,** 42049 Main St. (☎ **909/676-2722**), in a brick building dating from 1891 that for 60 years was

Burnham's Store, the mainstay of local ranchers; next door is the **Temecula Trading Post,** 42081 Main St. (☎ **909/676-5759**). Across the street stands the **Old Welty/Temecula Hotel,** built in 1882, the year the railroad came to Temecula; it burned and was rebuilt in 1891 and now is a private residence. Check out the store beside it, **Country Seller and Friends,** 42050 Main St. (☎ **909/676-2322**), which sells furniture and antiques.

At the southwest corner of Main and Front streets, the **Welty Building,** which dates from the 1880s, now houses a deli, but it used to be a gym where Jack Dempsey worked out.

A NEARBY NATURE PRESERVE

For an outing in more than 7,000 acres of unspoiled terrain, take I-15 north to Clinton Keith Road and drive west on it for about 5 miles to get to the **Santa Rosa Plateau Ecological Reserve,** 22115 Tenaja Rd., Murrieta, owned and maintained by the Nature Conservancy (☎ **909/677-6951** or 909/699-1856), where walking trails, coyotes, hawks, migrating birds, and maybe even an eagle or two await you.

WHERE TO STAY

Butterfield Inn Motel. 28718 Front St., Temecula, CA 92390. ☎ **909/676-4833.** Fax 909/676-2019. 39 rms. A/C TV TEL. $45–$89 double weekdays; $55–$94 double weekends. Extra person $5. AE, DISC, MC, V. Take I-15 north to Rancho California Rd. W. to Front St.

Within walking distance of Old Town Temecula shops, this motel (it's not really an inn) has an Old West facade; rooms with double or king-size beds; a small, unheated outdoor pool; and a Jacuzzi. It's easy to imagine the Butterfield stagecoach pulling up any moment. Complimentary coffee awaits you in the lobby each morning.

Loma Vista. 33350 La Serena Way, Temecula, CA 92591. ☎ **909/676-7047.** Fax 909/676-0077. 6 rms. A/C. $95–$135 double; $75–$115 midweek. Rates include full champagne breakfast. DISC, MC, V. Take I-15 to Rancho California Rd. E.; inn is on left just beyond Callaway vineyard.

Montana natives Betty and Dick Ryan came here from Los Angeles in 1987 and designed and built this tiled-roof, Mission-style house for their B&B. Perfectly named, it sits on a hill (*loma* in Spanish) with the best vista around: From the living room, you can look out at the Callaway vineyard and the Santa Ana Mountains. All of the guest rooms have full private bath and a queen- or king-size bed. Four have private balconies; of these, my favorites are Sauvignon Blanc, with white-pine Southwestern furnishings and a four-poster queen-size bed; and Fumé Blanc, done in California garden style with white wicker. In addition to complimentary fruit and a decanter of sherry in each room, free wine and cheese are served by the fire at 6pm. A spa bubbles away on the back patio, while the front patio, a great place just to wile away the hours, has a fire pit. The property is a real oasis, with 85 rosebushes, daisies, Australian tea bushes, and 325 grapefruit trees. The resident dog is a Dalmatian named Casey. Old Town Temecula is 5 miles away.

✪ **Temecula Creek Inn.** 44501 Rainbow Canyon Rd., Temecula, CA 92592. ☎ **800/962-7335** or 909/694-1000. Fax 714/676-3422. 70 rms, 10 junior suites. A/C MINIBAR TV TEL. Sun–Thurs $115–$130 double; $145–$150 junior suite. Fri–Sat $135–$130 double; $165–$170 junior suite. Golf and wine-country packages available. AE, DC, DISC, MC, V. From San Diego, take I-15 north to exit 79 (Indio); turn right off the exit ramp and proceed to Pala Rd.; turn right, go over a little bridge, then take an immediate right onto Rainbow Canyon Rd. for ¹/2 mile.

This is a great spot for golfers, and a convenient location for visiting the wineries. Mag-nolia trees line the walkway from the resort's lobby to the restaurant. The pleasant lobby includes adobe walls, leather couch, Native American artifacts, and fireplace. Rooms in five 2-story buildings all have restful views and Native American–inspired decor that creatively combines art, muted colors, and textures. Most of the furnishings were custom designed or selected especially for the rooms from local antiques shops to evoke the region's Native American, Spanish, and Western heritage. Junior suites are oversize corner rooms with two queen-size beds or a king-size bed, sitting areas, in-room safes, two balconies, and floor-to-ceiling windows. If you're not allergic to feathers, you'll enjoy the down pillows. There are no porters, but you can drive up close to many of the rooms.

Dining/Entertainment: The Temet Grill (see "Where to Dine," below) is outstanding all around, from the service to the California wine-country cuisine to the view beyond the dramatic window wall. There's live music nightly in the lounge adjoining the restaurant. Food and cocktail service is available poolside.

Services: Dry cleaning, laundry service, complimentary newspaper in lobby.

Facilities: Hairdryer and magnifying mirror in baths, coffee and tea in room (including beans and a grinder), in-room safe, cribs. Outdoor pool, spa, barbecue under live oaks, 2 tennis courts, volleyball, croquet, 27 holes of golf, driving range, golf and tennis pro shop, meeting rooms.

WHERE TO DINE

Baily Wine Country Cafe. 27644 Ynez Rd. (in the Albertson's shopping center, at Rancho California Rd.). ☎ **909/676-9567.** Reservations recommended, especially on weekends. Lunch, main courses $8–$11; dinner, main courses $13–$22. AE, CB, DC, MC, V. Mon–Thurs 11am–2:30pm and 5–9pm, Fri 11am–2:30pm and 5–9:30pm, Sat 11am–9:30pm, Sunday 11am–9pm. The restaurant is to your right and up the hill after you enter the shopping center. CALIFORNIA/CONTINENTAL.

If you aren't interested in winery tours and tastings, just come here. Baily's has the largest selection of Temecula Valley wines anywhere, including those from the Baily family's own winery. To show them off to best advantage, the chef has concocted a mouth-watering menu, which changes every few months. At lunch, try the penne with roasted garlic, fresh vegetables, and tomato sauce made chunky with Italian sausage; or better yet, the southwestern-style grilled cheese sandwich with cilantro (a regional prize winner). At night, consider such appetizers as crab cakes with roasted red bell–pepper sauce and mixed greens. For a main course, choose from the likes of southwestern pork tenderloin with garlic mashed potatoes, salmon Wellington with cucumber and papaya relish and fresh vegetables, or chicken ravioli in a basil pesto. Finish off the meal with the white chocolate cheesecake, a top choice with local diners.

✪ **Cafe Champagne.** 32575 Rancho California Rd. (at Thornton Winery) ☎ **909/699-0088.** Reservations recommended up to a week ahead. Lunch, main courses $11–$21; dinner, main courses $18–$25. AE, DC, MC, V. Tues–Sun 11am–9pm, Mon 11am–4pm. CALIFORNIA.

The toast of the Temecula wine country, this bistro and cafe features tasty dishes specially created to be served with nine Thornton champagnes. The wine list also features other Temecula and California labels. Featuring California cuisine at its best, the lunch and dinner menus offer appetizers like warm brie en crûte with honey-walnut sauce, crab-and-shrimp strudel, and smoked salmon carpaccio. Among the entrees are angel-hair pasta primavera with seafood, mesquite-grilled tuna, and baked pecan chicken. The list of mesquite-grilled entrees expands at dinner. The setting, overlooking the vineyard, is sublime. If you have a high regard for top-notch cuisine, you'll be very happy here.

Temet Grill. 44501 Rainbow Canyon Rd. (in the Temecula Creek Inn) ☎ **909/676-5631.** Reservations recommended. Lunch, main courses $8–$14; dinner, main courses $15–$20. AE, MC, V. Mon–Sat 6:30am–2:30pm and 5–10pm, Sun 6:30am–2pm and 5–10pm. An abbreviated lunch menu is available in the lounge Mon–Sat 2:30–5pm and Sunday 11am–5pm. CALIFORNIA/SOUTHWESTERN.

The very attractive dining room has five striking chandeliers, Native American artifacts in glass cases, and floor-to-ceiling picture windows overlooking the golf course. The menu changes frequently, but you might find such specialties of the house as grilled tortilla pizza or grilled chiles rellenos with chipotle salsa. Creatively presented main courses might include roasted sea bass in a five-spice crust, sautéed or grilled chicken breast with beer mustard and chipotle hollandaise, or grilled swordfish or steak. The wine list emphasizes California vintages, along with some from Oregon and Washington and a few French champagnes. Sunday brunch (10am to 2pm) is very popular.

TEMECULA AFTER DARK

The **Old Town Temecula Entertainment Center,** located in the heart of Old Town Temecula (☎ **909/695-7711**), is due to open mid-1988. This western-style theater complex will include a 6,000-seat Wild West arena, a 2,200-seat opera house, two theaters with 1,750 and 350 seats respectively, a virtual reality theater, a giant-screen theater, as well as several dining and shopping options.

For a fun evening out in Old Town Temecula, indulge in a little bit of country-western dancing at **The Temecula Stampede,** 28721 Front St., opposite the Butterfield Inn (☎ **909/695-1760**). This may be California's biggest saloon/dance hall, with 4,000 square feet incorporating dance areas for two-steppers, swing dancers, and line dancers. There's even room left for eight pool tables, tables and chairs, and two impressive bars. Devotees range in age from the minimum of 21 to 80-plus, most decked out in western garb; weekends are crowded. Open Thursday to Saturday from 6pm; the cover, which starts at 7pm, is $5 on Thursday, $7 Friday and Saturday. The entrance is around back.

On a spring or fall afternoon, head over to the **Thornton Winery** to hear jazz (see "Visiting the Wineries," above). There's an admission charge.

Appendix: Useful Toll-Free Numbers & Websites

Airlines

Air Canada
☎ 800/776-3000
www.aircanada.ca

Alaska Airlines
☎ 800/426-0333
www.alaskaair.com

America West Airlines
☎ 800/235-9292
www.americawest.com

American Airlines
☎ 800/433-7300
www.americanair.com

British Airways
☎ 800/247-9297
☎ 0345/222-111 in Britain
www.british-airways.com

Canadian Airlines International
☎ 800/426-7000
www.cdair.ca

Carnival Airlines
☎ 800/824-7386
www.carnivalair.com

Continental Airlines
☎ 800/525-0280
www.flycontinental.com

Delta Air Lines
☎ 800/221-1212
www.delta-air.com

Hawaiian Airlines
☎ 800/367-5320
www.hawaiianair.com

Kiwi International Air Lines
☎ 800/538-5494
www.jetkiwi.com

Midway Airlines
☎ 800/446-4392

Northwest Airlines
☎ 800/225-2525
www.nwa.com

Southwest Airlines
☎ 800/435-9792
iflyswa.com

Tower Air
☎ 800/34-TOWER (800/348-6937) outside New York
(☎ 718/553-8500 in New York)
www.towerair.com

Trans World Airlines (TWA)
☎ 800/221-2000
www2.twa.com

United Airlines
☎ 800/241-6522
www.ual.com

US Airways
☎ 800/428-4322
www.usair.com

Virgin Atlantic Airways
☎ 800/862-8621 in Continental U.S.
☎ 0293/747-747 in Britain
www.fly.virgin.com

Car Rental Agencies

Advantage
☎ 800/777-5500
www.arac.com

Alamo
☎ 800/327-9633
www.goalamo.com

Avis
☎ 800/331-1212 in the Continental U.S.
☎ 800/TRY-AVIS in Canada
www.avis.com

Budget
☎ 800/527-0700
www.budgetrentacar.com

Dollar
☎ 800/800-4000

Enterprise
☎ 800/325-8007

Hertz
☎ 800/654-3131
www.hertz.com

National
☎ 800/CAR-RENT
www.nationalcar.com

Payless
☎ 800/PAYLESS
www.paylesscar.com

Rent-A-Wreck
☎ 800/535-1391
rent-a-wreck.com

Thrifty
☎ 800/367-2277
www.thrifty.com

Value
☎ 800/327-2501
www.go-value.com

Major Hotel & Motel Chains

Best Western International
☎ 800/528-1234
www.bestwestern.com

Clarion Hotels
☎ 800/CLARION
www.hotelchoice.com/cgi-bin/res/webres?clarion.html

Comfort Inns
☎ 800/228-5150
www.hotelchoice.com/cgi-bin/res/webres?comfort.html

Courtyard by Marriott
☎ 800/321-2211
www.courtyard.com

Days Inn
☎ 800/325-2525
www.daysinn.com

Doubletree Hotels
☎ 800/222-TREE
www.doubletreehotels.com

Econo Lodges
☎ 800/55-ECONO
www.hotelchoice.com/cgi-bin/res/webres?econo.html

Fairfield Inn by Marriott
☎ 800/228-2800
www.fairfieldinn.com

Hampton Inn
☎ 800/HAMPTON
www.hampton-inn.com

Hilton Hotels
☎ 800/HILTONS
www.hilton.com

Holiday Inn
☎ 800/HOLIDAY
www.holiday-inn.com

Howard Johnson
☎ 800/654-2000
www.hojo.com/hojo.html

Hyatt Hotels & Resorts
☎ 800/228-9000
www.hyatt.com

ITT Sheraton
☎ 800/325-3535
www.sheraton.com

La Quinta Motor Inns
☎ 800/531-5900
www.laquinta.com

Marriott Hotels
800/228-9290
www.marriott.com

Motel 6
☎ 800/4-MOTEL6 (800/466-8536)

Quality Inns
☎ 800/228-5151
www.hotelchoice.com/cgi-bin/res/webres?quality.html

Radisson Hotels International
☎ 800/333-3333
www.radisson.com

Ramada Inns
☎ 800/2-RAMADA
www.ramada.com

Red Carpet Inns
☎ 800/251-1962

Red Lion Hotels & Inns
☎ 800/547-8010
www.travelweb.com

Red Roof Inns
☎ 800/843-7663
www.redroof.com

Residence Inn by Marriott
☎ 800/331-3131
www.residenceinn.com

Rodeway Inns
☎ 800/228-2000
www.hotelchoice.com/cgi-bin/res/webres?rodeway.html

Super 8 Motels
☎ 800/800-8000
www.super8motels.com

Travelodge
☎ 800/255-3050

Vagabond Hotels
☎ 800/255-3050
www.vagabondinns.com

Index

WHEREVER YOU TRAVEL, *H*ELP IS NEVER FAR AWAY.

From planning your trip to

providing travel assistance along

the way, American Express®

Travel Service Offices are always

there to help you do more.

For the office nearest you in California, call
1-800-AXP-3429.

http://www.americanexpress.com/travel